HUMAN SEXUALITY

Garland Reference Library of Social Science
(Vol. 685)

HUMAN SEXUALITY

An Encyclopedia

EDITED BY

Vern L. Bullough

and

Bonnie Bullough

GARLAND PUBLISHING, INC.

New York & London

1994

Library of Congress Cataloging-in-Publication Data

Human sexuality : an encyclopedia /edited by Vern L. Bullough and
Bonnie Bullough.
     p. cm. — (Garland reference library of social science ; vol.
685)
    ISBN 0–8240–7972–8 (alk. paper)
    1. Sex—Dictionaries.   I. Bullough, Vern L. II. Bullough,
Bonnie. III. Title: Human sexuality. IV. Series: Garland reference
library of social science ; v. 685.
HQ9.H846   1994
306.7'03—dc20   93–32686
                                        CIP

Printed on acid-free, 250-year-life paper
Manufactured in the United States of America

*To Our Contributors and Colleagues
in the Field of Human Sexuality*

Contents

Introduction

The purpose of an encyclopedia is to gather in one place information that otherwise would be difficult to find. By its very nature, however, an encyclopedia can never be complete because information keeps changing and new interpretations emerge. We did, however, try to make the encyclopedia as comprehensive as possible, and we have gathered together approximately 100 contributors, who have collectively turned out over 200 articles. We tried to select the individuals who were experts in their field, and all the contributors met the scholarly and scientific standards we tried to set. In some cases, we deliberately sought out younger scholars to diversify the points of view represented.

We believe the articles are authoritative and reflect a variety of viewpoints. This is natural, since the contributors come from a wide range of disciplines—from nursing to medicine, from biology to history—and include sociologists, psychologists, anthropologists, political scientists, literary specialists, academics and nonacademics, clinicians and teachers, researchers and generalists. Our task was made somewhat easier than we originally anticipated because after our work on this encyclopedia started, *A Descriptive Dictionary and Atlas of Sexology* (1991) was published. Editors Robert T. Francoeur, Timothy Perper, and Norman A. Scherzer took as their task brief definitions of many of the sexual phenomena on which we had originally planned articles. Their book allowed us to concentrate on longer articles and major issues (which include many of the sexual phenomena), and it should be regarded as an additional reference work in this field.

This is not the first set of volumes to claim the title of encyclopedia of human sexuality. Only two claimants to the title, however, would meet our definition of encyclopedia. The first is the one-volume *Encyclopedia Sexualis* (1936), edited by Victor Robinson, and the second is the two-volume *Encyclopedia of Sexual Behavior* (1961), edited by Albert Ellis and Albert Abarbanel. Robinson was a pioneer sexologist in the United States, while Ellis and Abarbanel were major figures in sexology in the 1960s. Though most of the contributors to the Ellis and Abarbanel volumes are dead, a handful are still active, and some of them—such as John Money and Ira Reiss—contributed to this work. We are proud to follow in the footsteps of Robinson, Ellis, and Abarbanel.

This current work includes articles on many of the same topics found in the two earlier encyclopedias, but a surprising number of topics included here were not listed by them because new research has broadened our knowledge. Those interested in the history of sex and the changing nature of sex research can judge the pace of developments in understanding human sexuality by comparing what was said 60 years ago in the Robinson encyclopedia or 30 years ago in the Ellis and Abarbanel volumes with what is said now. Albert Ellis was one of the founders of the then newly formed Society for the Scientific Study of Sex (SSSS), and its early members contributed significantly to his volume, as current members of the SSSS and other sex groups such as SIECUS and AASECT contributed to this encyclopedia.

Since the 1960s, the study and teaching of human sexuality have grown. Most college campuses now offer courses in human sexuality, and some courses have been extended down to the high-school level. There are a number of first-class college textbooks in the field, and some are now beginning to be made available to high schools. Courses in human sexuality are either required or recommended for many of the professional help givers, and a few universities even offer doctorates in some field of human sexuality. There are a number of specialized refereed journals dealing with various aspects of human sexuality, and there are a growing number of sexuality professionals. There is also a public appetite for more accurate sex information, which this encyclopedia is designed to meet.

There is also a growing shelf of specialized reference books on various aspects of sexuality. One such reference work, the *Encyclopedia of Homosexuality*, edited by Wayne F. Dynes (New York: Garland Publishing, 1990), was important in the genesis of this one, since Gary Kuris of Garland, encouraged by the success Dyne's work, commissioned this one. Much to our own surprise, there is very little overlap between the two works.

As in any encyclopedia, various subtopics are often included under a general topic, and to help the reader find them we have prepared a comprehensive index of subjects and individuals. If you do not find an article with the heading in which you are interested, please turn to the index, and, we hope, it will be found there. Almost all articles include a list of references where the interested reader can find additional information. Brief biographies of some of the more important sex researchers, educators, and therapists have been included, but only those of individuals who are deceased or are elder statespersons in the field. There is also an appendix of sources of sex information.

In the end, however, the strength of an encyclopedia depends on its contributors and we think few reference works in any field can match the collective expertise of the contributors to this volume. Perhaps because they recognized the importance of an encyclopedia in their field, they were also dedicated, and this project was completed much faster than we had anticipated. The contributors' names and affiliations are listed elsewhere in this book, as are the names of our contributing and advisory editors (often the same people); the name of the author appears at the end of each article.

Works such as this, however, require more than a set of editors and expert advisers and contributors; they require expert help in putting all the manuscripts into computer-readable form, help in keeping track of the various contributors, and a crew of dedicated professionals at Garland. Special thanks are due not only to Gary Kuris, Phyllis Korper and Eunice Petrini, but also to Alice Stein, who oversaw much of the first phase of the manuscript in her capacity as managing editor and prepared the final index. Thanks to all.

Authors

A.R. ALLGEIER, PH.D.
Department of Psychology
Bowling Green State University
Bowling Green, Ohio

ELIZABETH RICE ALLGEIER, PH.D.
Department of Psychology
Bowling Green State University
Bowling Green, Ohio

TARA ANTHONY
Syracuse, New York

HOPE E. ASHBY, M.A.
Department of Health Studies
New York University
New York, New York

REBECCA BALES
History Department
Arizona State University
Tempe, Arizona

GERALDINE E. BARD, PH.D.
Associate Professor of English
State University of New York College at Buffalo
Buffalo, New York

JOHN A. BATES, PH.D.
Associate Professor of Psychology
Alaska Pacific University
Anchorage, Alaska

R. BRUCE BAUM, ED.D.
Associate Professor, Exceptional Education Department
State University of New York College at Buffalo
Buffalo, New York

JOANI BLANK
Open Enterprises Inc.
San Francisco, California

ANNE BOLIN, PH.D.
Department of Sociology
Elon College
Burlington, North Carolina

SUSAN B. BOND, PH.D.
Bond-Mosher Psychological Associates
Tolland, Connecticut

JAMES A. BRUNDAGE, PH.D.
Ahmanson-Murphy Distinguished Professor of History,
*   History Department and School of Law*
University of Kansas
Lawrence, Kansas

BONNIE BULLOUGH, R.N., PH.D.
Dean Emeritus, School of Nursing
State University of New York at Buffalo
Buffalo, New York

VERN L. BULLOUGH, R.N., PH.D.
SUNY Distinguished Professor, Emeritus
State University of New York College at Buffalo
Buffalo, New York

Authors

JOHN C. BURNHAM, PH.D.
Department of History
Ohio State University
Columbus, Ohio

CAROL CASSELL, PH.D.
Institute for Sexuality Education and Equity
Albuquerque, New Mexico

ELI COLEMAN, PH.D.
Director, Program in Human Sexuality
Department of Family Practice
School of Medicine
University of Minnesota
Minneapolis, Minnesota

MARY COOK
Stormgart Books
San Francisco, California

A. ROBERT CORBIN, PH.D.
Criminal Justice Department
Boise State University
Boise, Idaho

MARTHA CORNOG, M.A., M.S.
Manager: Membership Services
American College of Physicians
Philadelphia, Pennsylvania

CLIVE M. DAVIS, PH.D.
Department of Psychology
Syracuse University
Syracuse, New York

SANDRA L. DAVIS
Syracuse, New York

DWIGHT DIXON, J.D., PH.D
Basic Research Service
San Diego, California

JOAN K. DIXON, PH.D.
Basic Research Service
San Diego, California

MOHAMED EL-BEHAIRY, PH.D.
Political Science Department
State University of New York College at Buffalo
Buffalo, New York

VERONICA DIEHL ELIAS, PH.D.
Professor of Sociology, The Center for Sex Research
California State University, Northridge
Northridge, California

ROBERT A. EMBREE, PH.D.
Professor of Psychology
Teikyo Westmar University
Lemars, Iowa

JAY R. FEIERMAN, M.D.
Department of Psychiatry, School of Medicine
University of New Mexico
Albuquerque, New Mexico

MARIANNE FERGUSON, F.M.D.C., PH.D.
State University of New York College at Buffalo
Buffalo, New York

MARILYN A. FITHIAN, PH.D.
Center for Marital and Sexual Studies
Long Beach, California

ROBERT T. FRANCOEUR, PH.D.
Professor of Biological and Allied Health Sciences
Fairleigh Dickinson University
Madison, New Jersey

SUZANNE G. FRAYSER, PH.D.
Cultural Anthropologist
Conifer, Colorado

SARAH B. FREEMAN, PH.D.
Assistant Professor, Nell Hodson Woodruff
  School of Nursing
Emory University
Atlanta, Georgia

RICHARD A. FRIEND, PH.D.
Human Sexuality Education Program
University of Pennsylvania
Philadelphia, Pennsylvania

JANICE FULTON, F.N.P., M.S.
Northern Michigan Health Services
Houghton Lake, Minnesota

LIESL L. GAMBOLD, M.A.
Department of Anthropology
California State University, Los Angeles
Los Angeles, California

MARIANNE GLASEL, R.N., M.S., M.A.
Director, Oncology Program
School of Nursing
Columbia University
New York, New York

STEPHEN L. GOETTSCH, PH.D.
Hamilton, Ohio

DEBRA W. HAFFNER
Executive Director
Sex Information and Education Council of the United
States (SIECUS)
New York, New York

MARGARET H. HARTER, M.L.S.
Head, Information Services
Kinsey Institute
Bloomington, Indiana

WILLIAM E. HARTMAN, PH.D.
Center for Marital and Sexual Studies
Long Beach, California

ROBERT W. HATFIELD, PH.D.
Department of Psychology
University of Cincinnati
Cincinnati, Ohio

JAMES D. HAYNES, PH.D.
Professor of Physiology
State University of New York College at Buffalo
Buffalo, New York

MICHEL HAYWORTH
Los Angeles, California

ARNO KARLEN
Researcher, Psychotherapist, Writer
New York, New York

NANCY KEITH, B.S.
Albuquerque, New Mexico

DONALD KUTSCHALL
Associate Professor, Performing Arts
State University of New York College at Buffalo
Buffalo, New York

DOROTHY I. LANSING, M.D.
Private Practice
Paoli, Pennsylvania

HANS LEHFELDT, M.D.
New York, New York

GREGORY K. LEHNE, PH.D., P.A.
Assistant Professor, Medical Psychology
School of Medicine
Johns Hopkins University
Baltimore, Maryland

HANNY LIGHTFOOT-KLEIN
Tucson, Arizona

SARI LOCKER, M.S.
New York, New York

JOSEPH LoPICCOLO, PH.D.
Professor, Department of Psychology
University of Missouri
Columbia, Missouri

ILSA LOTTES, PH.D.
Department of Sociology and Anthropology
University of Maryland
Baltimore, Maryland

DONNA R. MACRIS
Fresno, California

FLOYD M. MARTINSON, PH.D.
Research Professor of Sociology
Gustavus Adolphus College
St. Peter, Minnesota

THOMAS MAZUR, PSY.D.
Psychologist; Director, Psychoendocrinology
Children's Hospital of Buffalo
Buffalo, New York

NAOMI B. McCORMICK, PH.D.
Professor, Department of Psychology
State University of New York College at Plattsburgh
Plattsburgh, New York

TED McILVENNA, PH.D.
Institute for the Advanced Study of Human Sexuality
San Francisco, California

MARILYN FAYRE MILOS
Executive Director, National Organization
of Circumcision Information Resource Centers
San Anselmo, California

LISA MONAGLE, C.N.M., PH.D.
Department of Social and Preventive Medicine
State University of New York at Buffalo
Buffalo, New York

JOHN MONEY, PH.D.
Professor Emeritus, Medical Psychology and Pediatrics
School of Medicine
Johns Hopkins University and Hospital
Baltimore, Maryland

DIANE MORRISSETTE, PH.D.
Palo Alto, California

DONALD L. MOSHER, PH.D.
Department of Psychology
University of Connecticut
Storrs, Connecticut

Authors

CHARLES C. MURDOCK
History Department
Arizona State University
Tempe, Arizona

MYRON HOWARD NADEL
Professor Performing Arts
State University of New York College at Buffalo
Buffalo, New York

SUZANNE L. OSMAN
Syracuse, New York

ANDREA PARROT, PH.D.
Assistant Professor, Department of Human Service
   Studies
Cornell University
Ithaca, New York
Assistant Professor of Psychiatry
State University of New York
Syracuse, New York

IRA B. PAULY, M.D.
Professor and Chairman, Department of Psychiatry and
   Behavioral Sciences
University of Nevada
Reno, Nevada

W. ROBERT PENMAN, M.D.
Assistant Clinical Professor, Obstetrics and Gynecology
Jefferson Medical College
Philadelphia, Pennsylvania

ROGER E. PEO, PH.D.
Private Practice
Poughkeepsie, New York

WILLIAM A. PERCY
History Department
University of Massachusetts
Boston, Massachusetts

TIMOTHY PERPER, PH.D.
Private Practice
Philadelphia, Pennsylvania

ALLEN HOWARD PODET, PH.D.
Department of Philosophy and Religious Studies
State University of New York College at Buffalo
Buffalo, New York

WILLIAM E. PRENDERGAST, PH.D.
Diplomate Certified Sex Therapist
Edison, New Jersey

JUNE MACHOVER REINISCH, PH.D.
Director Emeritus
Kinsey Research Institute
Bloomington, Indiana

IRA L. REISS, PH.D.
Department of Sociology
University of Minnesota
Minneapolis, Minnesota

STELLA RESNICK, PH.D.
Los Angeles, California

FANG-FU RUAN, M.D., PH.D.
Burlingame, California

HERBERT SAMUELS, PH.D.
Assistant Professor
La Guardia College of the City University of New York
New York, New York

LEAH CAHAN SCHAEFER, ED.D.
Private Practice
New York, New York

ANN SEIDL, R.N., PH.D.
Assistant Professor, School of Nursing
State University of New York at Buffalo
Buffalo, New York

SARAH SLAVIN, PH.D.
Department of Political Science
State University of New York College at Buffalo
Buffalo, New York

JULIAN W. SLOWINSKI, PSY.D.
Clinical Assistant Professor, Department of Psychiatry
University of Pennsylvania
School of Medicine
Philadelphia, Pennsylvania

WILLIAM R. STAYTON, TH.D.
Wayne, Pennsylvania

ALICE P. STEIN, M.A., M.S.
Alice P. Stein Editorial Services
Tonawanda, New York

CARRIE M. STEINDORFF
Women's Health Services
Rockland County Health Department
Pomona, New York

HILARY STERNBERG
Assistant Librarian
State University of New York College at Buffalo
Buffalo, New York

IVAN STORMGART
Stormgart Books
San Francisco, California

LOUIS H. SWARTZ, R.N., LL.M., PH.D.
School of Law
State University of New York at Buffalo
Buffalo, New York

RUSSELL C. VANNOY, PH.D
Philosophy Department
State University of New York College at Buffalo
Buffalo, New York

ANTHONY WALSH, PH.D.
Department of Sociology, Anthropology, and Criminal Justice
Boise State University
Boise, Idaho

TINA WEIL
History Department
Arizona State University
Tempe, Arizona

THOMAS S. WEINBERG, PH.D.
Professor of Sociology
State University of New York College at Buffalo
Buffalo, New York

JAMES D. WEINRICH, PH.D.
Assistant Adjunct Professor, Department of Psychiatry
Senior Investigator, Sexology Project
University of California
San Diego, California

CONNIE CHRISTINE WHEELER, PH.D.
New York, New York

BEVERLY WHIPPLE, R.N., PH.D., F.A.A.N.
Associate Professor, College of Nursing
Rutgers, The State University of New Jersey
Newark, New Jersey

MICHAEL W. WIEDERMAN
Department of Psychology
Bowling Green State University
Bowling Green, Ohio

WALTER L. WILLIAMS, PH.D.
Professor of Anthropology, Program for the Study of Men and Women in Society
University of Southern California
Los Angeles, California

JAMES HARVEY YOUNG, PH.D.
Professor of History
Emory University
Atlanta, Georgia

the encyclopedia

a

ABORTION

Abortion is the termination of a pregnancy before the fetus reaches viability. Traditionally, a fetus was considered viable between the 20th and 28th week of pregnancy. Abortions can be classified as spontaneous or induced. Spontaneous abortions are usually caused by faulty development of the embryo, abnormalities of the placenta, endocrine disturbances, acute infections, severe trauma, or shock. Spontaneous abortions are often called "miscarriages" to differentiate them from abortions that are induced.

Abortions in Ancient Times

Inducing abortions was widely practiced in the ancient world as a method of controlling family size. A Chinese document dated 3000 B.C.E. mentions abortions, and an Egyptian medical papyrus of 1550 B.C.E. describes an abortion technique. Plato advised that any pregnant woman over age 40 be aborted, and Aristotle argued that abortion should be used to control population growth, particularly for persons who felt an aversion to exposing unwanted offspring to the elements.

The Greeks, Romans and Egyptians all developed an extensive literature on abortive techniques. These techniques included inserting papyrus into the cervix, irritating the uterus with laurel and peppers, and using drugs believed to stimulate uterine contractions. The second-century B.C.E. Greek physician Soranus of Ephesus discussed indications for abortions, such as a contracted pelvis, and described methods of abortion, mentioning purging, carrying heavy weights, injecting olive oil into the vagina, and using drugs such as wallflower, cardamom, and brimstone. Although the document describing these methods was written by a physician, abortions in ancient times were ordinarily the work of midwives or they were induced by the pregnant woman herself. Throughout most of history, physicians were seldom involved in gynecological procedures; the female reproductive system was considered the domain of women.

Some ancient abortifacients have survived until modern times as folk remedies. Modern Egyptian nurses indicate that village women use mullohaya, a stiff grass used in making soup, to cause abortions—which is not unlike the ancient practice of using papyrus. Ergot, a fungus that grows on rye, was widely used in ancient times as an abortifacient wherever rye was grown. Ergot can cause severe poisoning, even death, so using it to induce abortion was not without danger. Ergotamine, a modern drug used to stimulate uterine contractions, is an alkaloid of ergot.

The women of Thailand use a deep massage technique that dates back to ancient times.

Anti-Abortion Laws

Ancient Roman law and customs supported abortion, since the fetus was not considered a human being. Christianity, however, opposed both birth control and abortion and declared that abortion was murder. The early Christian writers were against abortion, although they were divided in their perception as to when the soul enters the fetus. Most did not consider abortion a sin until after quickening (i.e., the point at which the woman first feels the fetus moving), but many medieval theologians allowed abortion only for the first 40 days after conception. For example, St. Thomas Aquinas differentiated between the male fetus and the female fetus, arguing that the soul is infused into the male embryo at about 40 days after conception but it does not enter the female embryo until the 80th day. In 1869, Pope Pius IX eliminated the distinction between the early nonviable fetus and the later viable fetus by declaring that abortion at any point after conception would be considered murder for Catholics.

There were also other moves against abortion in the 19th century. English common law, which had accepted abortions as legal until quickening, was changed in 1803 when a law was passed outlawing abortion by poisoning. Later revisions strengthened the law by outlawing surgical procedures and dropping the distinction between abortions before and after quickening. In the United States, abortions were caught up in the struggle between physicians and midwives that occurred as physicians moved into the field of obstetrics and gynecology. The physicians—who argued that midwives were unsavory characters who performed abortions, so midwives and their skills should be eliminated to save the lives of women—prevailed. Laws were passed in the late 19th and early 20th centuries outlawing midwives in most states. Laws were also passed against abortions, with the first such statute enacted in Connecticut in 1821 outlawing abortions after quickening. A revision in 1860 made all abortions illegal. Other states followed; by the beginning of the 20th century abortion had been outlawed in all of the states, although there was some state-to-state variation in what was prohibited. Most states allowed an exception to the law, recognizing the right of physicians to perform allowed therapeutic abortions if it was essential to save the woman's life.

Problems Caused by the Laws

The U.S. anti-abortion statutes were written in an era in which there was an expanding labor market fueled by industrial expansion. In spite of the nation's need for a large work force, however, the pay for laborers was meager and the number of children who could be fed with a worker's salary was limited, so the working-class family was trapped in an irremediable situation. The options for limiting births were relatively few, with coitus interruptus, celibacy, anal intercourse, vaginal sponges, and condoms being the available choices. Since only the wealthy could afford condoms before the 1920s, unwanted pregnancies were common, and desperate women turned to illegal practitioners. Even if these practitioners were skilled, they were cut off from hospitals and physicians who could help them manage such complications as hemorrhages and infections. When antibiotics became available in the 1940s, the illegal abortionists had difficulty obtaining them for their patients because they were obtainable only with a physician's prescription. In the early 1960s, it was estimated that 8,000 therapeutic abortions were performed in the United States each year, but there were 400,000 to 800,000 illegal abortions each year with a high maternal mortality rate associated with them. This situation helped create a movement in the 20th century to reform abortion laws.

In addition to concern for the women involved, there was also a growing concern about untrammeled population growth. Thomas Malthus had published an essay on population growth in 1798, arguing that while population growth occurs in geometric steps, doubling every generation, food supply tends to grow only in numeric steps, so without major catastrophes, such as war or plagues, famine is inevitable. Although his theory often proved true on local levels, such as the famine in Ireland in the 19th century, the worldwide implications of his theory became apparent only in the 20th century as advances in sanitation and health allowed many people to live longer and the real dimensions of the population problem started to emerge. From 1650 to 1850, the number of people worldwide approximately doubled, from about 500 million to just over one billion, but the population doubled again in only one hundred years—from 1850 to 1950—when it reached two billion. Since 1950, the world's population has been increasing at an even faster rate, so it will soon reach the four billion mark. Most of the world's people are now hungry, and famines have become common in many parts of the world.

Changing Policies

The first country to legalize abortion in modern times was the Soviet Union, which, in 1920, made abortions legal as a part of its revolution. Abortions quickly became the major method of birth control. In 1936, Joseph Stalin banned abortions and the prohibition remained until his death. They were legalized again in 1955, and most of the countries then in the Soviet bloc legalized them. Poland, now free of domination from the former Union of Soviet Socialist Republics, has again instituted prohibitions against abortions. Most of the other former members of the U.S.S.R. have, however, retained legal abortions as public policy.

In 1938, Sweden passed a law allowing pregnancies to be interrupted if the woman was ill, if she had been impregnated under illegal circumstances, or if there was the possibility of a hereditary disease being transmitted to the fetus. The law was amended in 1946 to allow abortions if it could be assumed that the woman's physical or mental strength would be seriously impaired by the birth and care of the child.

Japan, in 1948, became the first country to legalize abortions for the purpose of regulating population growth. The original law legalized abortion only for women whose health might be impaired from a physical or economic standpoint, but within a few years it was broadened to allow abortion on request. The birthrate quickly dropped from 34.3 per thousand in 1947 to 16.0 per thousand by 1961. In recent years, the number of abortions has dropped somewhat with the improvements in contraceptive technology and the growing wealth of the country, but abortions are still available and selected by many women as the method of choice for controlling pregnancies. The birthrate in Japan remains low, with a virtually stable level of population growth.

The leaders of the Chinese revolution in 1949 opposed all birth control measures, but within a few years it became apparent that the rapidly increasing population was wiping out all efforts to improve the standard of living. Various measures were tried, with little success, given the degree of political upheaval at the time. By 1981, the population had reached approximately one billion people, and the People's Republic of China embarked on a comprehensive and deliberate effort to cut population growth to the zero level by the year 2000. This effort included a campaign to limit family size to one child. To accomplish this goal, contraceptives and abortions were not only offered freely, a variety of positive and negative sanctions were instituted to enforce the policy. While the "one-child" goal proved impossible to achieve and the population is not yet stable, significant strides have been made in curbing the rapid growth of the Chinese population.

U.S. policy toward abortion started changing in the 1960s. Relatively insulated from concerns about world population growth because of limitations on immigration, Americans were primarily influenced by the growing women's movement. Improved methods of contraception, including oral contraceptives, had begun to give women a sense of control over their biological destiny and as they experienced this power over the reproductive cycle they wanted more. Betty Friedan's 1963 book, *The Feminine Mystique*, raised the consciousness of many women and made the concept of choice over whether to reproduce respected, but to turn concept into reality required changes in the state laws.

The Model Penal Code adopted by the American Law Institute proposed that state laws be amended to allow termination of pregnancy when the physical or mental health of the woman was greatly impaired; when the infant might be born with a grave physical or mental defect; or when the pregnancy resulted form rape, incest, or other felonious intercourse, including illicit intercourse with a girl under age 16. Little action on this proposal was taken until the publicity related to Mrs. Sherri Finkbine, a Phoenix, Arizona, mother of four, illustrated the problems created by the restrictive state abortion laws. Mrs. Finkbine had taken the drug thalidomide during the first few months of her fifth pregnancy. Although the drug had not been approved by the U.S. Food and Drug Administration, and was therefore not marketed in the United States, Mr. Finkbine had obtained a bottle of thalidomide pills in Europe. Two months after Mrs. Finkbine had taken the pills, news of the deformities the pill was causing in European children was made public. Mrs. Finkbine's physician estimated that the chance her infant would be deformed was at least 50 percent, and he arranged to admit her to the hospital for a therapeutic abortion. Because Mrs. Finkbine's story reached the media, the hospital was fearful of further publicity and canceled the abortion. The Finkbines flew to Los Angeles, planning to travel to Japan for the abortion, but the Japanese counsel, also afraid of negative publicity, refused to issue them a visa. The couple then flew to Sweden, where Mrs. Finkbine had the abortion. The fetus was deformed.

This incident brought the discussion of antiabortion laws and practices out in the open and helped to crystalize a movement for abortion law reform. An influential book by Lawrence Lader, entitled *Abortion*, was published in 1966. It argued that abortion was a right of privacy. Also in 1966, the National Organization for Women was established, with reproductive rights as one of its major concerns. At the same time groups of clergymen, physicians, and civil liberties advocates organized local groups, including the California Committee for Therapeutic Abortion and a similar group in New York. The National Association for the Repeal of Abortion Laws was established in 1968. These groups worked through state legislatures and the courts. As a result of their efforts, 18 states had liberalized their abortion laws by 1972, and court decisions had changed abortion privileges in three jurisdictions. In 1973, the U.S. Supreme Court heard *Roe v. Wade*, and struck down state prohibitions against first trimester abortions. The Court ruled that during the first three months of pregnancy the decision to abort could be made by the woman and her physician. During the second trimester the states could regulate abortion to ensure reasonable standards of care. Only in the last trimester could abortions be outlawed, but not if they were necessary to preserve the life of the woman. This decision made more restrictive state legislation illegal.

The Right to Life and Pro-Choice Movements

The Supreme Court's decision in *Roe v. Wade* brought strong reactions from those who opposed abortions on moral and religious grounds, including the leaders of the Catholic church, many fundamental Protestant churchmen, as well as individuals who felt moral repugnance to the idea of abortion. A strong backlash movement followed. Some anti-abortion activity was sponsored directly by churches, but most was coordinated by several different organizations that used the title "Right to Life." The radical fringe of these groups bombed abortion clinics or formed picket lines to block entrance to the doors of clinics. The more mainstream members of the groups worked through the political process. On the legislative front, efforts were made to weaken the right to abortion by passing restrictive state laws. Some of these laws required husband's consent; others added parental consent for minors; made public funding illegal; or added procedural requirements, such as waiting periods. Until 1986, the courts generally supported the rights of women to make decisions, but approved some of the restrictions. The situation changed in 1986, primarily because of the efforts of the Reagan administration.

President Ronald Reagan (who served as president from 1980 to 1988) made an anti-abortion stance the most important selection criterion for federal judges and Supreme Court justices. By 1986, his policy could be felt in the judicial decision-making process because there had been enough turnover of justices to affect the decisions on this matter. President George Bush followed the same policy, making an anti-abortion stance the litmus test for judge selection. The Supreme Court has already allowed states to limit abortions and additional limitations are anticipated in some, but not all of the states.

A countermovement, using the slogan "free choice," has grown up with the National Abortion Rights Action League (NARAL) furnishing leadership. Its major focus is on abortion as a right of privacy for women. NARAL focuses its efforts primarily on the political arena.

Abortion Procedures

Abortion procedures vary by the stage of fetal development. They can be separated into early abortion procedures, first trimester methods, and second trimester methods.

Early abortion procedures are carried out before the fertilized ovum reaches the uterus and attaches to its wall. They are sometimes called postcoital methods, or menstrual regulation. These procedures occur before the pregnancy tests are performed, and they are often used for rape victims. Various hormones have been used for this purpose, including diethylstilbestrol and oral contraceptives that contain estrogen and progesterone combinations. The doses of these hormones when used for early abortions are large enough to cause unpleasant side effects, such as nausea and vomiting, so their use should always be medically supervised. Oral contraceptives have not been approved for this purpose by the U.S. Food and Drug Administration, so federally funded clinics are not allowed to used this method, although it is commonly used in other countries.

The compound RU–486 is also used as a postcoital or abortifacient drug in France. It is one of a family of antiprogestins that can prevent implantation of the egg in the uterus or cause an abortion during the first nine weeks of pregnancy. It has been approved for testing by the Food and Drug Administration in the United States but is not yet available for general use.

Postcoital insertion of a copper intrauterine device (IUD) has also proven effective in regulating menses by preventing implantation of the fertilized ovum in the uterus. The IUD is inserted one to seven days following unprotected intercourse and can be left in place to prevent future pregnancies.

The third postcoital method is menstrual extraction. A canula is inserted into the uterus and a syringe or suction machine is used to extract the uterine lining. The procedure is similar to that used for a suction abortion, but has the advantage of being carried out before the pregnancy is diagnosed, which for some women causes a moral problem. Casual use of the technique is not recommended because there is risk of hemorrhage or infection.

First trimester abortions usually utilize a suction procedure that was developed in Asia, used in the U.S.S.R., and began to be used in the United States in the 1960s. It is the most common abortion procedure, although U.S. physicians combine it with curettage to make sure the uterine lining is completely removed. A dilatation and curettage is used if the pregnancy is late in the first trimester or if the physician feels there is some problem requiring the procedure. The cervix is dilated and a curette is used to scrape the uterine walls. Various techniques can be used to facilitate the dilatation of the cervix, including the insertion of laminaria (i.e., cervical tampons that swell to three or five times their original diameter when placed in a moist environment).

Second trimester abortions usually involve the insertion of a hypertonic saline solution into the amniotic sac. Prostaglandin, which stimulates uterine contractions, is sometimes used in addition to the hypertonic saline solution.

Dilatation and curettage is used for most second trimester abortions, along with the hypertonic saline solutions and prostaglandins, although sometimes a hysterotomy is done. Many second trimester abortions are done because of fetal abnormalities discovered through amniocentesis. Recently, improvements in the technique of amniocentesis make it possible to do the procedure as early as ten weeks, so there will probably be fewer second trimester abortions.

Ethical and Political Issues

The ethical issue marking the abortion debate focuses on the rights of the fetus. Conservatives argue that the minute the sperm enters the ovum, the ovum has exactly the same moral status as a person and its rights should not be terminated by abortion. Some adherents to this argument hold that this is true even if the fetus is grossly deformed or if several eggs have been removed

from the woman for purposes of in vitro fertilization. In this case, all of the fertilized eggs should be saved and as soon as possible be reintroduced into the woman for development. Since the procedure involves the use of fertility drugs that produce multiple eggs and an unlimited number of births can threaten the viability of all of the fetuses, judging how many to reintroduce is difficult.

A liberal view of abortion claims that fetuses are not human beings and have no rights. Liberals argue that abortion on request should be legal and without punishment by moral sanctions. The moderate view holds that fetuses may have some rights after they reach viability, but moderates do not worry about the rights of fertilized eggs. Moderates would allow abortions for a variety of reasons, including anything that would harm the fetus if it becomes a child, as well as for rape, incest, teenage pregnancy, and poor maternal health. Most moderates in the United States do not accept economic deprivation as a criterion for abortion although it is probably the major reason for both legal and illegal abortions in most of the Third World where food is scarce.

This broad spectrum of views can also be identified in the national surveys of public opinion. Gallup polls on abortion repeatedly indicate that the overwhelming majority of Americans favor abortion under certain circumstances, including rape, incest, unmarried minor children, genetic or intrauterine problems, or illness of the woman, but they do not favor granting women the right to abortion under all circumstances. A small group favors outlawing abortions altogether and a small group at the other end of the spectrum favors a free choice for women. Although earlier polls showed Catholics significantly more opposed to abortion, the differences between Protestants and Catholics on the issue have narrowed.

References

Baird, R.M., and S.E. Rosenbaum. *The Ethics of Abortion.* Buffalo, N.Y.: Prometheus Books, 1989.

Bayles, M.D. *Reproductive Ethics.* Englewood Cliffs, N.J.: Prentice-Hall, 1984.

Bullough, V.L., and B. Bullough. *Contraception: A Guide to Birth Control Methods.* Buffalo, N.Y.: Prometheus Books, 1990.

Calderone, M.S. *Abortion in the United States.* New York: Hoeber-Harper, 1958.

Franke, L.B. *The Ambivalence of Abortion.* New York: Random House, 1978.

Lader, L. *Abortion.* Boston: Beacon Press, 1966; Also Indianapolis: Bobbs-Merrill, 1966.

McCormick, R.A. *How Brave a New World: Dilemmas in Bioethics*. Garden City, N.Y.: Doubleday, 1981.

Reiterman, C. *Abortion and the Unwanted Child; The California Committee on Therapeutic Abortion*. New York: Springer, 1971.

Rodman, H., B. Sarvis, and J.W. Bonar. *The Abortion Question*. New York: Columbia Univ. Press, 1987.

Bonnie Bullough

ADDICTION: SEX ADDICTION

Sex addiction refers to excessive, obsessive, or compulsive sexual behavior. The term was popularized by Carnes, who describes sex addiction as an obsessional illness that transforms sex into the primary basis for a relationship or need, for which all else may be sacrificed, including family, friends, values, health, safety, and work. Support for this concept has come from many others, including Money, who feels it appropriate to classify the rituals of the paraphilias among the addictions.

According to Carnes, "sex addicts" exhibit a constellation of preferred sexual behaviors, arranged in a definite ritualized order, which are acted out in an obsessional scenario. He describes sex addicts as experiencing little or no pleasure, often feeling despair even in the midst of sex. Carnes views "sexual compulsion" as one component of an addictive cycle, which includes preoccupation (obsessions), ritualization, shame, and despair. He maintains that the addiction concept describes the phenomenon of compulsive sexual behavior because of the distinct similarity of the symptoms or behaviors to alcohol or drug addiction. The term has also been widely used in a number of publications.

Carnes posits three levels of sexual addiction. Level one is socially acceptable, tolerable, or controversial (e.g., masturbation, heterosexual relationships, pornography, strip shows, prostitution, and homosexual relationships). Level two is unacceptable (e.g., exhibitionism, voyeurism, indecent telephone calls, and indecent liberties). Level three is very unacceptable, illegal behavior (e.g., child molesting, incest, and rape).

The genesis of this concept can be traced back to the growth of Alcoholics Anonymous (AA)—a self-help group of individuals who identify themselves as alcoholics. This social movement led to recognition of alcoholism as a separate disease entity, a lifetime disease that can be controlled through treatment but not cured. Medical treatment for alcoholism embraces the 12-step model and traditions of AA. Treatment focuses on helping alcoholics both recognize that they are powerless to overcome their alcoholism

and adopt a spiritual program of recovery which involves adhering to AA principles. Many of those who criticize this method of treatment endorse alternative treatment models. However, the success of AA-style treatment, based on the 12 steps and traditions, led to speculation it would also work for other "addictions."

In the 1970s, a looser definition of "addiction" developed, and it became a popular metaphor for other behaviors including those that, in excess, resembled alcohol and other drug addictions. Overeaters Anonymous (modeled after AA) was formed to help compulsive overeaters. Other groups followed, such as Narcotics Anonymous, Smokers Anonymous, Gamblers Anonymous, Spenders Anonymous, Parents Anonymous (for child-abusing parents)—and then Sex Addicts Anonymous, Sexaholics Anonymous, Sex Abusers Anonymous, and Sex and Love Anonymous.

For many sexologists and other scientists, however, the term "sex addiction" is an unfortunate misnomer because people do not become addicted to sex in the same way they become addicted to alcohol or to other drugs. In addition the term obfuscates the complex interplay of biological, social and psychological factors which causes compulsive or excessive sexual behavior. (See also Sexual Compulsion.)

REFERENCES

Carnes, P. *Out of the Shadows: Understanding Sexual Addiction*. Minneapolis: CompCare Publishers, 1983.

——. *Don't Call It Love: Recovery From Sexual Addiction*. Minneapolis: Bantam, 1991.

Coleman, E. Compulsive Sexual Behavior: New Concepts and Treatments. In E. Coleman, ed., *John Money: A Tribute*. New York: Haworth Press, 1991.

Money, J. *Lovemaps: Clinical Concepts of Sexual/Erotic Health and Pathology, Paraphilia, and Gender Transpositions in Childhood, Adolescence, and Maturity*. New York: Irvington Publishers, 1986.

Eli Coleman

ADULTERY

In legal, religious, and moral terminology, adultery is technically defined as sexual intercourse between a married person and a partner other than the spouse. In modern usage, adultery is a sexual activity of a married person with a nonspouse when that activity is unacceptable to the spouse. This usage distinguishes adultery as an unacceptable extramarital activity, or "cheating" behavior, from consensual extramarital sexual activities that are acknowledged and accepted by both spouses.

Historical Concepts of Adultery

Civil laws in the Western world have long prohibited adultery, for example, the Code of Hammurabi, in Babylonia (c. 1790 B.C.E.); Draco, in ancient Greece (c. 620 B.C.E.); and Solon, in ancient Rome (c. 590 B.C.E.). The condemnation of adultery is even more specific in the religious traditions of the Torah, on which much of our current civil legislation is based (Exodus 20:17; Deuteronomy 5:21, 22:22–29; Leviticus 20:10). However, these ancient laws applied only to women, requiring them to limit their sexual activity to one man. Since a woman was viewed as property attached to a particular man, laws against adultery (and fornication—sexual intercourse between an unmarried man and woman) were meant to protect the property rights of husbands and fathers. However, the laws against fornication and adultery generally did not apply to married or single men and their liaisons with unattached women, such as widows, concubines, or servants.

As societal views of women and marriage have changed, so have the concept and dimensions of adultery. The idea of marriage based on romantic love is relatively new. For centuries, marriage was an economic arrangement between families. In ancient Greece, true love could exist only between two men; women were believed to be incapable of truly intense love. Although women were available for men's sexual pleasure, the Stoic tradition frowned on passion and physical love which distracted men from their higher intellectual endeavors.

Christianity rejected homosexual love but adopted the Stoic suppression of physical love. It glorified spiritual celibate love, viewing sexual love as second-rate, tolerated only because it could produce more souls for the Kingdom of Heaven.

The emergence of the concept of courtly love in southern France during the early Middle Ages set the stage for a radical change in the concept of adultery, the extension of adultery to men, and development of the idea of romantic and emotional marital fidelity. Courtly love had four roots: (1) the lusty male-dominated Teutonic values of the Franks, who viewed women as playthings for men's enjoyment; (2) a certain hedonism introduced by Eleanor of Aquitaine; (3) a new interest in and misinterpretation of Ovid's classic Roman poem *The Art of Love*; and (4) the growing veneration of the Virgin Mary. Medieval knights vied for the honor of their ladies in jousting tournaments and sang of their love. But these ladies were unattainable, the wives of a noble or a king. In addition, sex—the expression of physical love—was considered the mortal enemy of true, noble love. True love was not then linked with sex or with marriage, which was arranged by the family and based on property and power motives or simple practicalities.

During the Renaissance, romantic courtly love began to be imbued with sexual passion. By the 14th century, the extramarital affair was recognizable as it is known today: an illicit sexual and emotional relationship outside marriage. Prior to this, affairs were expressions of male lust without emotional involvement or interest.

The Protestant Reformation (c. 1500 C.E.) produced two social models of the affair and two views of adultery that have dominated in Western societies ever since: a pagan courtly love model and a bourgeois-puritan model.

In the Mediterranean countries and much of France, the traditional economic basis of marriage, the Catholic condemnation of divorce, and the courtly love code combined in a social pattern in which marriage remains primarily an institution designed for social benefit and to create progeny. The exuberance of sex, passion, and emotion is expressed in the extramarital relationship. This tradition has subtle customs and often-unspoken rules that regulate the relationships of married persons and their lovers or mistresses. In Latino cultures today, this tradition implies that a true man, "*un hombre completo,*" is expected to have a wife and children, and one or more mistresses in "*la casa chica*" (his little homes). By implication, although it is seldom discussed among the men, Latino women are also allowed discreet extramarital relationships. In northern Europe, the aristocracy and royalty adopted this pagan-courtly love tradition. In the United States, it is found among the rich and upper class society.

In northern Europe, the early Protestants fused romantic love with marriage. They rejected the medieval Catholic ascetic view of marriage as an inferior way of life and restored the Jewish view of the importance of sexual love and family as the center of religious life and nurturance. The emerging middle-class families of northern Protestant Europe incorporated the virtues of courtly love into marriage and championed the value of conjugal love and passion, even while leaving intact traditional patriarchal values and attitudes. As the Protestants came to accept divorce, adultery and the extramarital affair became the mortal enemy of marriage and society because they were often the prelude to and cause of divorce. This bourgeois-Puritan tradition flourished through the 19th century and down to the present in American society.

Family historians believe that a major step in the evolution of love and the extramarital affair occurred during the Victorian period in America around 1880. They offer no explanation for the burst of popular literature, novels, poetry, and advice manuals that glorified romantic, marital love, and the expectation that a man or a woman should satisfy all of the partner's needs.

In the 20th century, important social changes have affected the character and incidence of adultery. Women have moved closer to the level of sexual freedom men have enjoyed for centuries as their financial independence, presence in the work force, education, legal rights, control over reproduction, mobility, socioeconomic options, and personal expectations have increased. Increasing life expectancy and the reduced proportion of time wives spend in the mother and housewife roles have also strained the traditional values of sexual exclusivity.

Modern Concepts and Patterns of Adultery

The current concept of marital fidelity that has evolved over three thousand years of Western Judaeo-Christian culture is clearly expressed in the marriage ritual's phrase "forsaking all others until death do us part." Today, this concept includes sexual and emotional exclusivity for both spouses. However, the radical social changes mentioned above have created a growing tension in these values.

Traditionally, men have been more active extramaritally than women, but recent surveys indicate some changes. In the 1940s, Alfred Kinsey projected that at least half of all married men would some time experience extramarital sex. One in four married women under age 40 reported having had an extramarital experience. In 1970, a survey of *Psychology Today* readers showed that 40 percent of the husbands and 36 percent of the wives polled had had affairs. Married men and currently divorced males under age 45 in Hunt's 1974 nationwide survey reported a 47 percent rate of infidelity. A year later, married women age 40 and older, in a Tavris and Sadd survey for *Redbook*, reported a 39 percent frequency. In Linda Wolfe's *Sexual Profile of That Cosmopolitan Girl*, 69.2 percent of the married women over age 35 reported having had an extramarital experience. Both the 1975 *Redbook* and the 1980 *Cosmopolitan* surveys were of more educated, upper-class women rather than random samples. Such nonrandom surveys are hardly representative of American women in general. It may be that the increasing sexual experience of women in college, especially in college dormitories where parental control is re-

duced and peer pressures often prevail, predisposes more educated women to view multiple and nonexclusive relationships in a more positive framework than in the past when extramarital sex was considered a male prerogative tolerated by women. Also, many single women prefer having affairs with married men because they want a male who can provide emotional and sexual fulfillment without the pressure to take on the commitment of marriage and family.

Since most surveys of marital infidelity were done before heterosexuals became concerned about AIDS, little can be said about the incidence of adultery in recent years. However, of the persons reporting having had extramarital sex in the recent surveys that have been done, 40 to 50 percent had only one outside partner, 40 to 45 percent had two to five partners, 5 to 11 percent had between six and ten partners, and 3 to 5 percent had more than ten extramarital partners. In some respects, women now seem to be equaling or surpassing the men in extramarital relations. In one study of 200 couples in marital therapy, the affairs of husbands lasted an average of 29 months, compared with 21 months for the affairs of wives. While many studies indicate that an overwhelming majority of Americans consider adultery wrong, some psychotherapists and marital therapists see women's increasing access to sexual choices as potentially positive because it equalizes power within the marriage.

Despite our cultural values and the obvious trauma caused by adultery, marital therapists now rank adultery behind eight other factors in the breakup of marriages, such as poor communications, unrealistic expectations, and power struggles.

In 1982, Atwater found that about 25 percent of the women in her sample had discussed the possibility of having an extramarital affair with their husbands before doing so. But as long as the primary relationship is successful and for the most part satisfying, many tend to ignore that their partner is emotionally or sexually involved with another person.

Swinging

As Americans become increasingly concerned about the personal and financial costs of divorce and remarriage, various adjustments to sexual exclusivity have become more visible and perhaps more commonly accepted. One form of consensual adultery based on the "togetherness" value of traditional romantic monogamy is "swinging." Swinging is recreational social-sexual sharing among consenting adults. In swinging, two or more couples mutually agree to engage in sex with each other's partners. The extent of swinging is not well documented, but surveys indicate that between two and five percent of American adults have at sometime participated in swinging.

Many couples feel that swinging is a catalyst for positive growth, a sharing activity that promotes understanding, communication, and intimacy in their relationships. They report that it helps free their relationship of routine, sex-role playing, and socially imposed inhibitions. Other writers, principally those involved in marriage counseling, report that swinging was a negative factor in the lives of those they investigated.

The North American Swing Club Association listed over 100 active, organized American swing clubs in its 1991 directory, as well as dozens of publications catering to the swing community. Annual lifestyles conventions in the South, Midwest, and West draw several thousand swingers each year.

Swinging, according to participants, involves much more than sexual activities, with the couples sharing business, emotional, and social interests. Yet, in 1971, Bartell reported that the swingers he interviewed typically limited their swinging with another couple to one or two exchanges and were thus constantly looking for new partners. Several researchers have reported that swingers are generally *not* liberal or highly educated. They are predominantly conservative or moderate in their politics, and far from permissive on a wide range of social and political issues. Most of the women are housewives, with few outside interests. Swingers also tend to be church-goers. Swingers, however, are not a homogeneous group but come rather from several distinct and very different subcultures.

Open Marriage

A second form of consensual adultery, which emerged in the 1960s, reflects contemporary values of equality of the sexes within the pagan-courtly love model. The open marriage described by anthropologists Nena and George O'Neill is based on "an equal partnership between two friends" who respect each other as persons. Open marriages are flexible and allow each partner privacy and room to grow and develop, even in unexpected directions. Within a trusting relationship, the concept of an open marriage accepts the possibility of both spouses having emotionally and sexually intimate friendships within the context of a healthy primary relationship. Blumstein and Schwartz's 1983 study of American couples found that 15 percent of married

couples and nearly 30 percent of the cohabiting couples reported they had sexually open relationships. Among the terms used by researchers for consensual extramarital sex based on the sexually open marriage model are intimate friendship, co-marital, or satellite relationships.

In the 1990s, as increasing numbers of married and cohabiting couples become more open about their healthy patterns of sexually open, nonexclusive relationships, some mainstream churches have established special task forces to reexamine traditional sexual values in the context of current lifestyles. Several of these task forces, particularly those of the United Presbyterian Church of the United States and the Episcopal Church, have called for reinterpretation of the traditional sexual values that uphold sexually exclusive monogamy as the sole morally acceptable lifestyle for sexually active adults and condemn all forms of premarital and extramarital sexual relations. Such reinterpretations are based on a redefinition of sexual morality and fidelity in broader terms than sexual exclusivity and heterosexual monogamy. Fidelity, in this new context, means a commitment to the covenant or contract agreed upon. Adultery, which etymologically means "polluting the relationship," is then viewed as any action or behavior that violates the couple's commitment to each other. Where couples have agreed to have a sexually open marriage, the terms "extramarital" and "adultery" are not applicable to relationships that are incorporated within the dynamics of the primary relationship.

If accepted, such reinterpretations would recognize the right of couples to redefine marital fidelity and adultery by creating their own covenant of commitment and fidelity within a liberal context. These efforts, however, are vehemently denounced and strongly opposed by the majority of church members and leaders.

In civil law, a charge of adultery was, until the 1960s, a common and widely accepted ground for granting a divorce in the United States. In some states, adultery was the only legal ground for a divorce, so that couples often concocted evidence of this felony. In 1961, Illinois adopted a consenting adult law that abolished criminal penalties for adultery and fornication. At present, few states still have laws prohibiting adultery between consenting adults, and those that do seldom, if ever, arrest or prosecute offenders.

References

Atwater, L. *The Extramarital Connection: Sex, Intimacy, and Identity.* New York: Irvington, 1982.

Bartell, G. *Group Sex*. New York: Wyden, 1971.

Blumstein, P., and P. Schwartz. *American Couples: Money, Work and Sex*. New York: Pocket Books, 1983.

Hunt, M. *The Natural History of Love*. New York: Minerva Press, 1967.

———. *The Affair: A Portrait of Extramarital Love in Contemporary America*. New York: New American Library, 1973.

Lampe, P.E. *Adultery in the United States: Close Encounters of the Sixth (or Seventh) Kind*. Buffalo, N.Y.: Prometheus Press, 1987.

Lawrence, R. J. *The Poisoning of Eros: Sexual Values in Conflict*. New York & Roanoke, Va.: Augustine Moore Press, 1989.

O'Neill, N., and G. O'Neill. *Open Marriage: A New Lifestyle for Couples*. New York: Evans, 1972.

Ramey, J. *Intimate Relationships*. Englewood Cliffs, N.J.: Prentice-Hall, 1976.

Singer, I. *The Nature of Love*. Vols. 1–3. Chicago: Univ. of Chicago Press, 1984a, 1984b, 1987.

Robert T. Francoeur

AGING AND SEXUALITY

Since the 1960s, whenever the media have focused on changing sexuality in Western societies, adolescents and young adults have usually been spoken of. However, there has been just as much change, in attitudes and perhaps in behavior, in the sexuality of the mature—men and women in middle age (40–60) and late life (over 60). Over the past few decades, the normal life span has increased almost 20 years; in most economically advanced nations, it is now 80 or more. Thus age 40 has changed from the threshold of decline to the midpoint of life. At the same time knowledge about mature sexuality has increased enormously.

Furthermore, more people in middle and late life are now fit, active, youthful-looking, and able to avoid or control debilitating diseases. More of them are likely to think of themselves as romantic and sexual participants in life. They are also conscious of becoming a larger and more influential segment of society. When the much discussed baby boom that followed World War II has entered middle age, at the turn of the 21st century, the United States will have as many mature people as youngsters.

As the duration and quality of life increase, public and private attitudes toward mature sexuality will doubtless continue to change. In fact, it has already become difficult to imagine just how taboo the subject of later-life sexuality was when the sexual revolution of the 1960s got under way. The mass media never discussed it. No serious book on the subject appeared for general readers until the middle 1960s, and information remained sparse until the next decade. In television and films, when mature sexuality was treated at all it was treated as an aberration or a joke. Even sex researchers were slow to shed light on sex and aging. Reliable baseline data on sexual aging did not appear until the landmark work of Masters and Johnson was published, in 1966.

If one believed public discourse, one would have thought that sometime between the ages of 40 and 50 most people became asexual. It was not true, of course, but the pretense was widespread, and many people viewed the exceptions as comic or repulsive. What was considered virile or seductive at 25 was called lecherous or repulsive at 55. Many young people did not—and still do not—accept the reality that people the age of their parents and grandparents still feel sexual desire, passion, and pleasure. Even many middle-aged and old people, who knew better, felt ashamed of what today would be called normal mature sexuality.

Aging is not a unitary and consistent process. It differs from person to person, and within each individual it varies from one organ system to another. The skin, circulatory system, bones and joints, kidneys, eyes, ears, and brain may each age relatively early or late, quickly or slowly. Furthermore, environmental and nutritional factors, general fitness, and health care may all minimize or exaggerate various aging processes.

But eventually all people and organ systems do age; the reproductive and sexual systems are not exceptions. The changes are similar in many ways in women and men, but there are also significant differences. Because the male system has fewer reproductive functions to perform and is therefore less complex, its aging process is more simply defined and measured. Moreover, since the majority of men usually experience orgasm with predictable regularity from puberty until middle age, frequency of orgasm is one of several good indicators of male sexual aging.

In terms of physical capacity for erection and orgasm, most males reach the height of their sexual functioning in their late teens. A gradual decline in male steroid hormones becomes measurable by age 30 and continues throughout life. As these hormones decrease, so does the frequency of arousal and orgasm. There is also an increase in the refractory period, the interval from orgasm until erection is possible again. These changes remain slight, even imperceptible, in most men for a decade or so.

As men reach age 40, they are almost sure to have noticed some decrease in sexual function; it is rarely great or dramatic. By 50, changes are unmistakable. Although there is great individual variation, a man of 50 is likely to be about half as active sexually as he was at 20. For instance, if he normally had orgasmic sex four times a week at age 20, he probably does so about twice a week at 50.

Through the 50s and after, erection and orgasm require more time than in the past. Ejaculation becomes less forceful, and the refractory period lengthens. However, there is no subjective decline in pleasure. For the great majority of men, sex remains an important and gratifying part of life.

Sexual desire and response continue to slow with the continuing decline in hormone levels in the 70s and 80s, but in the majority of men they never disappear. The urgency of desire declines, and erection and orgasm require more stimulation but the capacity for sexual activity and pleasure remains. Although they may produce fewer sperm, some men remain fertile and capable of fathering children into advanced old age.

Most women's sexual frequency is more variable than men's; it tends to lack an independent, long-term regularity. It depends less on hormonal regulation and more on personality, social learning, and the quality of sexual relationships. The capacities for desire, arousal, and orgasm do not, as in men, peak in late adolescence or early in young adulthood. In fact, many women's sexual expression does not peak until their 30s or even later. However, a decline in female hormones does begin to affect women's ability to conceive and carry a healthy fetus to term. There is individual variation, but some changes in reproductive potential are usually evident by age 40.

A dramatic and important event in female sexual aging is the menopause, usually between the ages of 45 and 55 (or earlier as a result of radical hysterectomy or other pelvic surgery). A fall in relative estrogen levels brings an end to ovulation, menstruation, and fertility. In the past, some people assumed that menopause meant the end not only of fertility but also of desire and pleasure, and the discomforts of this "change of life" were viewed virtually as an illness.

A minority of women do experience severe discomfort at menopause; often it can be reduced medically. For the majority, the discomforts are transient and not debilitating, and menopause does not affect sexual interest or pleasure. Some women actually find that it brings heightened or renewed eroticism, perhaps because of freedom from worry over unwanted pregnancies.

In women, as in men, hormonal decline does make some sexual tissues and responses less vigorous. The vaginal wall starts becoming thinner and less elastic after menopause. From the 50s on, arousal and orgasm may take longer than in the past. Vaginal lubrication, which signals arousal, becomes scantier. Prolonged or unaccustomed genital stimulation may irritate the vagina and clitoris, especially in women whose sex activity is infrequent. However, these changes need not interfere with a pleasurable sex life; for many women, systemic or local hormone therapy combats aging changes.

Other aging processes come to both men and women—changes in skin tone, body contours, body image, and overall strength and endurance. They can directly or indirectly reduce sexual frequency or pleasure. However, a list of aging changes can suggest a less satisfying picture than exists in reality.

In recent years, studies have shown just how tenacious a force sex is in middle and late life. The great majority of people over 50 are still sexually active, mostly through coitus, oral-genital intercourse, and masturbation. Although sex is less frequent and eventually less intense than in youth, it may become more tender, more satisfying, and less inhibited.

A large-scale study by Brecher found that most happily married older people still find sex an important part of their relationships; two-thirds of the unmarried over age 70 are sexually active. A smaller, more recent study of people from 80 to 102 years of age found that half of them said sex was at least as interesting and important to them as in the past.

For the sexually active mature person, sex may not only reflect health but promote health. The sexual system, like other organ systems, stays more fit if it is used. Masters and Johnson found that postmenopausal women who remain regularly active (through coitus, masturbation, or otherwise) show less vaginal thinning and more vaginal lubrication than the sexually inactive. They are less likely to feel discomfort when they engage in sex than are the infrequently active. In short, in sex as in most physical and mental activities, one tends to "use it or lose it."

Other health issues are important in sexual aging. From midlife on, major and minor illnesses can take a sexual toll; so can many widely used medications. Decreased mobility or endurance can be a hindrance. However, Brecher's survey found that even severe health problems affect many people's sex lives only modestly. Greater awareness of this by older people and their health-care providers could further reduce the impact of sexual aging.

It is true that some people retreat from sex in middle or late life. Some were never very interested. Some always associated sex with shame, guilt, fear, or inner conflict. Menopause, slower arousal, or illness in themselves or their partners gives them a welcome excuse to bow out. Some people retreat from sex because they feel wounded or humiliated by aging or by a partner's lack of sexual interest. Entrenched relationship conflicts, power struggles, or sexual habituation makes some couples drift into a pattern of mutual avoidance that assumes a stubborn life of its own. Such problems may yield to skillful counseling at any age.

Some of these people say they are content with a life lacking sexual pleasure or a sexual relationship. There is no arguing with personal choice or with individual definitions of happiness. But most people—old or young, male or female, straight or gay—find that an important part of health and happiness is a lasting, loving sexual relationship.

Other people actually blossom sexually in midlife or even later. With child rearing and the peak of work and financial pressures behind them, they have more time for their relationships. Emotional maturity may have taught them more healthy self-assertion along with more empathy and flexibility toward others. The tendency toward sexual adversary relationships, so common in adolescence and early adulthood, often dwindles. It may not matter that the urgency of desire has declined; from late middle age on, some people are satisfied with pleasurable sex even if it does not always culminate in orgasm. Greater self-acceptance and acceptance of others can reduce the need to give a performance, in others' eyes or one's own.

It is no surprise, then, that many mature people say their sex lives are warmer and more rewarding than before. Some women lose the sexual inhibitions and conflicts of youth; some men learn a less demanding, more empathic appreciation of their partners, evoking a warmer response. The fading of old emotional power struggles can allow greater trust, affection, and relaxed pleasure.

Even habituation, eventually a major or minor problem in many or most mateships, need not interfere seriously with sex. When psychiatrist Olga Knopf was in her 80s, she wrote that people who have spent a lifetime together "see each other not only as they are but also retain an image of how the other looked in the early days, like a double exposure that hides to a large extent the telltale signs of the passage of time."

Some of time's worst effects on mature sexuality come from depression, loneliness, and isolation. This is a growing problem as life is extended and patterns of marriage and divorce change. More and more people find themselves single in middle or late life. This is a more difficult problem for women, because they live longer than men; with the passage of years, their chances of finding new partners decline more rapidly than men's. Moreover, for older people of both sexes, lack of a regular partner tends to reduce erotic desire and activity. Finding a new partner often restores lost sexual interest.

Unfortunately, many mature people were raised to see their own sexuality as unseemly or repellent. Even if they were not, they may meet strong emotional resistance to their sexuality in the reactions of friends, children, grandchildren, health-care workers, and sometimes potential partners. Many people still believe that sexuality, and sexuality education, are for kids. They do not see sex as a healthy and healthful part of the entire life cycle.

Therefore, it remains necessary to remind people that we never outgrow the need for emotional intimacy and physical pleasure, the desire to touch and be touched. For people of any age, sexuality can be a tonic, a personal affirmation, a tie to other people and to life. It can bring heightened confidence and a strengthened sense of competence. As more people live longer, old and young will both benefit from appreciating how great an antidote sexuality is for the forces that can rob later life of health, joy, and meaning.

REFERENCES

Brecher, E.M. *Love, Sex and Aging*. Boston: Little, Brown, 1984.

Bretschneider, J.G., and N.L. McCoy. Sexual Interest and Behavior in Healthy 80- to 102-Year-Olds. *Journal of Sex Research,* Vol. 17 (1988), pp. 109-29.

Butler, R., and M. Lewis. *Midlife Love Life*. New York: Harper & Row, 1988.

Doress, P.D., and D.L. Siegal. *Ourselves, Growing Older*. New York: Simon & Schuster, 1987.

Knopf, O. *Successful Aging*. New York: Knopf, 1975.

Masters, W.H., and V.E. Johnson. *Human Sexual Response*. Boston: Little, Brown, 1966.

Weinstein, E., and E. Rosen. *Sexuality Counseling: Issues and Implications*. Pacific Grove, Calif.: Brooks/Cole, 1988.

Winn, R.L., and N. Newton. Sexuality in Aging: A Study of 106 Cultures. *Archives of Sexual Behavior,* Vol. 11 (1982), pp. 283-98.

Zeiss, A.M. Expectations for the Effects of Aging on Sexuality in Parents and Average Married Couples. *Journal of Sex Research*, Vol. 18 (1982), pp. 47-57.

Arno Karlen

AIDS AND HIV INFECTION

AIDS (acquired immune deficiency syndrome) is caused by infection with the human immuno-deficiency virus, commonly called HIV. HIV enters the body in two main ways: (1) through bodily fluids (e.g., blood or semen) in anal or vaginal intercourse, or through oral genital contact; or (2) through sharing drug needles with infected persons. It can also be transmitted to infants either in utero or during birth. Occasionally, it has been transmitted through breast milk. One may also become infected by receiving HIV-infected blood or certain blood products, as do surgical patients, accident victims, and hemophiliacs. In rare instances, transmission has occurred through receiving bone grafts or organ transplants from HIV-infected donors.

AIDS is a progressive destruction of the immune system leading to opportunistic infections that would not be successful in attacking those with healthy immune systems. HIV infection is an "equal opportunity" disorder, striking young or old; male or female; homosexual, bisexual, or heterosexual; rich or poor; Anglo or person of color. Former Surgeon General of the United States C. Everett Koop stressed this in his 1988 report *Understanding AIDS*: "[W]ho you are has nothing to do with whether you are in danger of being infected. . . . What matters is what you do." But Koop also stated that AIDS is *not* transmitted by donating blood, from everyday casual contact, from insect bites (including those of mosquitos), nor from tears, saliva, sweat, nonbloody urine or feces, nor from kissing.

AIDS was first identified in the United States in 1981, among homosexual and bisexual men. Since then it has spread to virtually all segments of the population. The various infected groups represent shifting percentages of known AIDS cases and of those infected with HIV. HIV infection ordinarily leads to AIDS and to its resultant opportunistic and life-threatening infections (e.g., Kaposi's sarcoma and pneumocystis carinii). Also included are central nervous system effects of HIV infection, primarily in individuals already symptomatic.

Prevalence

By 1991, the Centers for Disease Control stated that nearly 196,000 cases of AIDS had been reported in the United States and that 65 percent of those diagnosed had died of AIDS-related diseases. The percentages of cases were divided among groups as follows: 58.6 percent homosexual or bisexual males; 22.4 percent heterosexual intravenous drug users; 6.5 percent male homosexual and bisexual intravenous drug users; 5.7 percent heterosexuals; 3.7 percent "undetermined"; 2.2 percent recipients of transfusions; and .8 percent hemophiliacs. At least 40 cases of infection of health care workers contracted by blood from infected patients were reported, with more such cases suspected. Apparently, only one case of transmission had occurred by 1992 from caretaker to patients. In that case, a Florida dentist was reported to have infected five of his patients while engaging in procedures such as tooth extraction. It is *absolutely crucial* to recognize that these percentages have varied over time and will no doubt shift again. For example, a sharp escalation has occurred in the number of heterosexual cases, including those among women, since the Centers for Disease Control first began keeping statistics on AIDS incidence and fatalities. Undoubtedly also, many cases have gone unrecognized or unreported for various reasons. A compelling example is that many physicians fail to think of, or to test for, HIV infection in women with such symptoms as recurrent yeast infections and pelvic inflammatory disease, sometimes indicative of AIDS. Already there is evidence of increased infection through heterosexual transmission, including teenagers, a group of great concern because of its complacent "it can't happen to me" attitude. Heartening perhaps, a *Los Angeles Times* poll, taken shortly after a major sports figure, Earvin "Magic" Johnson, announced he had tested positive for HIV in the fall of 1991, sampled 1,709 adult Americans nationwide. It found that 23 percent of those polled responded that they had changed their sexual behavior after hearing this news. On a more pessimistic note, however, Eleanor Singer, a senior research scholar at Columbia University and a polling specialist, observed that "when you compare [actual] behavior and response . . . the likelihood is . . . that very little change has taken place."

At about the same time, the Geneva-based World Health Organization reported that at least eight million cases of HIV infection were *officially* reported worldwide.

Testing

Among those who should consider being tested for exposure to HIV, some experts say, are people who have multiple sex partners and those whose partner's HIV status is not known; those who have unprotected sex outside of a stable monogamous relationship extending back perhaps, at least 15 years; all others who have unprotected sex with partners; and finally, all intravenous (IV) drug users who share needles. It might be more accurate and inclusive to say anyone who could possibly be at risk should be tested.

To determine HIV status, the most widely used test as of 1992 was the ELISA (enzyme-linked immunoabsorbent assay). While there are some false negatives or positives, the ELISA test was incorrect in less than one percent of samples. To be doubly sure, a further test, called the Western blot test, can be used after the ELISA. While even this two-step testing process is not perfect, it is more accurate than most medical screening procedures.

HIV infection is believed by some to have originated in Central Africa. A widely accepted theory is that it was transmitted from monkeys infected with a different strain of virus to humans (a not unusual cross-species occurrence for viral transmission). The African green monkeys that test positive for the presence of the similar strain, unlike humans, do not show evidence of compromised immune systems, so far as can now be determined. Put simply, in humans the virus attacks, among other cells, the T cells that play a dominant role in helping the body ward off infections. A compelling reason for the especial virulence of HIV infection is that it invades the core of the cell, where it becomes part of the cell's genetic structure.

As the body attempts to fight other infections, the immune system eventually weakens until it becomes vulnerable to assorted "opportunistic" infections that it cannot overcome. HIV infection may proceed rapidly to a diagnosis of AIDS, but more typically it has a markedly long latency in which infected persons may feel quite healthy. At present, the median latency appears to be about ten years. With the passage of time since the recognition of HIV, and with the invention of increasingly effective treatments, this latency may be far longer, perhaps even as long as one's (otherwise usual) life span.

Research and Treatment

By 1992, the most commonly used drug to combat AIDS was the antiviral drug zidovudine, commonly known as AZT. There has been considerable disagreement over when, in the course of HIV infection, treatment should begin. Increasingly, physicians and medical researchers lean toward earlier treatment with AZT, as well as with other drugs that enhance the immune system's performance. While AZT may produce adverse side effects, including anemia, more serious side effects are experienced primarily by those in more advanced stages of AIDS. In October 1991, federal health officials announced that they had approved use of another AIDS antiviral drug, DDI (i.e., dideoxyinosine and didanosine). This drug provides alternative treatment for persons with AIDS for whom the adverse effects of AZT are too devastating. In addition, it may be used by those for whom AZT has been (or has become) ineffective. It is not unusual for AZT to lose effectiveness after two or three years of treatment, so the development of alternative drug therapies remains a top priority.

Such antiviral drugs are of special importance because they directly attack the HIV infection rather than the resultant opportunistic infections and cancers that attack the body because of immune system damage. As with AZT, DDI suppresses HIV infection in previously uninfected "helper" cells. An advantage of DDI over AZT is that it apparently increases the number of these T4 helper cells. While it was not yet known whether DDI prolongs survival, or whether it might make possible still longer latency before opportunistic infections develop, its approval by the U.S. Food and Drug Administration was a landmark in that it signaled a willingness (under heavy lobbying from interested citizens and from health professionals) to be more proactive and timely in responding to those who urgently need immediate treatment.

Meanwhile, research and testing of possible effective vaccines against HIV continues, with the prediction by some of the possible discovery of an effective vaccine by the year 2000. In addition to the scientific challenges presented by the complexities of this viral infection, other constraints placed on research are due to outright hostility toward certain target groups leading "disapproved" lifestyles. Reactionaries both inside the government and among the public are not only judgmental, but also carry the misperception that only "they" get AIDS, and when they do, "they deserve it" (a position hard to maintain as people from all groups get AIDS). Also, it is difficult to compete for research funding in a mismanaged and overstressed economy, no matter what the need. It is a tribute to the organization and activism of the gay community especially, that AIDS has received the attention it has. There is always the danger of public apathy stopping the momentum for funding of AIDS research and treatment if such activists do not remain energized or if the burden of pressing for action is not taken up by many others who are likewise increasingly at risk.

Psychosocial Aspects of AIDS

Medical aspects of AIDS have understandably received considerable attention in the scientific community. Since HIV was first identified, there has been a growing awareness of the need for psychosocial research to assist in understanding and treating HIV infection. This includes research into the psychosocial factors affecting whether an individual seeks testing or treatment in the first place. It also includes finding better means of helping individuals and their loved ones deal with the emotional, physical, and economic consequences of AIDS, as well as counseling the "worried well." Also, research must deal with optimally assisting health care providers and the public to cope with the consequences of HIV infection, which touches all members of the community, whether directly or indirectly.

A 1991 survey by the American Medical Association (AMA) found that nearly a third of primary care physicians surveyed do not assume they have a responsibility to treat persons with AIDS. These 2,000 internists and general and family practitioners show an attitude that is decidedly contrary to medical ethics. To some degree, this was related in self-reports to disapproval of homosexuals and of IV drug users. Those who conducted the study attributed the doctors' positions to bias against the groups thus far hardest hit by the epidemic. One physician commented that homosexuals are "a threat to many of our basic social institutions." Respondents specifically evidenced homophobia and discomfort with IV drug users. Half of these physicians said they would not work with AIDS patients if they had a choice. In an accompanying editorial, AMA officials stated: "[P]ractitioners are not free to ignore [their ethical duties] simply because it entails a small degree of personal risk" or because they do not like their patients. "Nor can physicians expect less medically sophisticated members of the public or government officials to react to health care crisis with reason and compassion when they themselves do not demonstrate these characteristics."

As to what role the psychological profession might play in dealing with the AIDS epidemic (in a 1984 interview, a few years after the first AIDS-related opportunistic infections were recorded), San Francisco Director of Health Mervyn Silverman was quoted as reflecting a far more enlightened view than the majority of physicians in the above 1991 AMA survey:

> I think because AIDS has impacts far beyond the medical issues, it is most important for individuals who are going to be working with people with AIDS . . . to first of all understand the disease and try to have an understanding of what mental processes are associated with it. The mental health concerns include not only fear of death, but also [of] ostracism, a whole number of reactions from peers, and the reaction of the general community. We need very understanding people in the mental health field, very understanding [psychotherapists] who comprehend the political and social ramifications and who understand the disease [syndrome].

Loved ones too, are affected by the medical, economic, and mental health challenges accompanying AIDS. They also experience anxiety and distress and can benefit greatly from support, both from members of the medical community and from other health care professionals.

Another category of people requiring support and assistance is the health care professionals who work intensively with AIDS patients and those who are HIV positive. These AIDS "experts" are at considerable risk of "burnout" and stress-related illnesses, both physical and psychological. Growing close to patients and to their loved ones while watching their diseases slide in what seems an inevitable downhill progression can be extremely debilitating for overworked professionals. This is especially so because many of their peers avoid participating in AIDS-related care. The workers need a periodic "time off" and the opportunity to participate in group sessions so that they can share events and feelings about their work and personal experiences as caregivers.

The "worried well" may also require support and empathy from others. Numerous individuals, even those not objectively at risk, are anxious or even phobic about AIDS. When well-meaning experts, politicians, or members of the media conjure up images of the war against the "plague" of AIDS, they evoke counterproductive feelings of pessimism and distress, even among optimistic persons. These themes have persisted throughout the course of the "AIDS experience."

Treatment Groups

Although all persons with AIDS are vulnerable to serious infections, some face unique challenges as well.

The term "pediatric AIDS" is an unfortunate choice. It can be misused by some, who are homophobic or otherwise judgmental, to distinguish HIV-infected infants and children from other HIV-positive persons. This makes possible a (false) distinction between "the innocent," deserving of care and public concern, and "the guilty," whose HIV status is the result of purported sinful behavior, thus of little concern to the self-righteous. Having said this, it is true that infants with AIDS have their own needs as to treatment modalities.

For older children with AIDS or HIV-positive status, the Centers for Disease Control guidelines recommend that the children lead normal lives insofar as possible. It is convinced that the psychosocial and educational benefits of the classroom experience outweigh the risk of infection from other children.

In general, AIDS has gone hand-in-hand with negative community reactions to persons known or presumed to be HIV infected. This has included cases of stigmatization in the school environment, where HIV infected children are ostracized at a time when interaction with peers is crucial for their social and emotional development. This is especially distressing in light of the (typically) relatively long period in which hemophiliacs (which includes most of these children) are asymptomatic. While such behavior is not only cruel and irrational but also illegal, some families have found that stigmatization and ostracism are so painful that it is preferable to undergo the emotional upheaval and expense of relocating.

Not surprisingly, research to date indicates that adolescents as a group are not only often ill-informed about cautionary guidelines that may prevent HIV infection, but also frequently feel "immune from AIDS." Although adolescence is, historically, a life stage in which teenagers usually feel immortal, they are prone to many high-risk behaviors, including drug use and sexual experimentation in a country where influential church leaders and political right-wing minorities vigorously oppose the availability of sex information or condom distribution to young people. Just as the United States generally experiences the highest rate of unplanned teen pregnancy, abortion, and teenage sexually transmitted diseases (STDs) in the Western world, so too it can expect a sharp escalation in HIV infection among teens in the future, unless the "just say no" position is abandoned. The Centers for Disease Control reports that the number of adolescent AIDS cases has been rising steadily since 1985. Physicians and educators are especially alarmed because studies indicate that this age group is becoming sexually active at ever-younger ages. National data indicate that the highest rates of syphilis and chlamydia, as well as of gonorrhea ("markers" for estimating future HIV infection), show that females ages 10 to 14, and 15 to 19 have the highest rates of STDs compared with older age groups. For minority adolescents, the incidence is even higher. Given the typically long latency from HIV infection to a diagnosis of AIDS, there is indeed cause for alarm.

For heterosexual men and women, it may be projected that HIV transmissions will continue to rise as more individuals are infected by partners who have engaged in high-risk sexual behaviors in the past. Thus far, the government and public health agencies have been especially negligent in addressing the issue of women and AIDS. Shortsightedness and the misperception that AIDS is a disease associated only with prostitution and intravenous drug use among women have unfortunately provided a rationale for neglect of women among judgmental political conservatives. Future educational and other AIDS-related programs must recognize that AIDS is a health issue for all and certainly not an issue that should be approached from a morally judgmental position. Further, vigorous outreach to racial and ethnic groups, whose culture or religion usurps women's reproductive rights, must be accompanied with sensitivity to cultural differences.

Homosexual and bisexual males are particularly burdened in coping with AIDS because of frequent homophobia, even among physicians. In too many cases, these men must cope not only with the debilitating physical and psychological effects of AIDS, but also with the isolation imposed by unsympathetic relatives and acquaintances and with the stresses of trying to conceal their sexual orientation from others. Given mistreatment of companions by some families of deceased persons with AIDS, it is imperative that persons with HIV-related infections legally set forth their wishes to prevent such injustices in an uncertain future. Men living alone are especially likely to find themselves totally isolated, depending exclusively on health care professionals for human contact.

Intravenous drug users are a singular population in that they are involved in the spread of HIV infection not only through sharing needles and syringes, but also through sexual transmission, and transmission from mother to child. Drug users are also a frequently stigmatized group, often poor, without shelter or support, and dependent on an overloaded public health system whose representatives may be both disapproving, uncaring, or both. In this highly individualistic society, there is little compassion for those who are not self-sufficient and certainly none for those who engage in a disapproved lifestyle.

The reluctance of policy makers (based on the belief that it will encourage drug abuse) to endorse the distribution of free bleach, alcohol, and clean needles and syringes compounds the escalation of IV-related infection. "Street-wise" outreach programs are required to teach IV drug users how to sterilize their equipment and to provide basic AIDS information. It is laudable that such outreach programs exist in San Francisco and in New York City, though most other major cities have shown considerable reluctance to initiate them. The challenge of reaching out to those in the drug community is exacerbated by the fact that death occurs frequently for IV drug users, and did so long before the emergence of AIDS.

The problems of minorities, such as African-Americans and Latinos, are compounded by their overrepresentation among inner-city IV drug users; by lack of access to social services for the poorer segments of these populations; by high levels of unemployment and discrimination; and by cultural or religious pressures discouraging contraceptive use. Additionally, African-American and Latino children are overrepresented in the public school systems, which are not known generally for vigorously promoting sex education or for making available to students contraceptive information and/or condoms. Early onset of sexual activity and the absence of adequate sex information contribute greatly to the high rates of STDs in general among inner-city youths. Unless the situation improves, undoubtedly these groups will continue to acquire HIV infection disproportionate to their representation in the total population. A serious threat is posed by the spread of crack cocaine use among drug users, including inner-city teens as well as adults. (Crack is a relatively inexpensive and readily available street drug, which is often smoked as an accompaniment to sexual activity.)

Finally, both the disabled and the severely mentally ill are often overlooked by the medical and health care communities, by the educational system, and to some extent, by AIDS-related researchers. Both economic and moral constraints operate within these groups. Health care professionals and families of the disabled or mentally ill are strongly inclined to treat those thus afflicted as asexual. Indeed many are repulsed when confronted with the sexuality of these people.

For the transient or homeless, who include some of the two groups just mentioned, it has been difficult to assess, much less to help curb, the spread of HIV infection they are experiencing. There has long been an urgent need to find the best ways to educate and assist these individuals to stop behaviors that increase their risk of becoming HIV infected. Many of them are, sometimes understandably, suspicious of those who attempt to help them. They avoid others because they do not want to be stigmatized or because they wish for privacy.

Other Issues of Economics and of Public Policy

Policy makers at the federal, state and local levels have been justly criticized for concentrating on *prevention* of infection to the detriment of already infected persons who either need care immediately or will in the future. The gay community, perhaps because of insufficient or untimely official response, stands as a model of coordinated volunteer effort for all citizens.

When the government does act, too often it is with counterproductive and sometimes unconstitutional efforts to control infected individuals (as through talk of quarantine of HIV-infected persons). AIDS may be used as an excuse to push a conservative agenda over such issues as availability of contraceptive information to teenagers, legalization of drug use, and women's reproductive rights. A conservative political climate at the time that HIV infection was discovered until the present has allowed the federal government to refuse to make AIDS a top priority. This has extended from reluctance to fully fund research to the refusal to fund education and public health care programs directed at persons with AIDS. It has extended also to neglect of their caretakers and their loved ones. Assorted economic, legal, and moral issues have also been neglected. These issues include drug dissemination and testing, health insurance needs, confidentiality for those who are HIV infected, and the rights of infected people in the work place and as U.S. citizens.

The need for improved health care benefits and for related services is acutely felt among virtually all citizens today, but even more so among persons with AIDS. As a result of the vacuum left by the lack of specific government programs to deal with AIDS, much of the responsibility has been left to reluctant and sometimes negligent private health care insurers, to city budgets, to state Medicaid programs, and, perhaps most regrettably, to infected individuals and their loved ones, friends, and volunteers.

Perhaps the most successful response at the local level has been that of San Francisco, with a diversity of both funded and organized volunteer efforts directed to meeting the needs of persons with AIDS and organized services directed at general community outreach.

The need for public education to have a more active roll in dissemination not only of AIDS information, but also of contraceptive and overall sex education, was addressed earlier. In addition, the efforts of public schools to provide facilities for HIV testing and for condom distribution in a confidential setting have been woefully inadequate, where they exist at all.

Training in cultural sensitivity and in factual information about AIDS must be addressed for public officials and others who may have contact with HIV-infected individuals in their daily work. Law enforcement personnel particularly must be prohibited from behaving prejudicially toward persons with AIDS or toward those who are suspected to be HIV-infected.

Despite all that has been learned about HIV infection and its transmission, and about AIDS-related diseases, each time a medical professional visibly overreacts to the threat of infection by, as in one case, resigning from surgical practice, a powerful and destructive message is sent to the general public and to others who look to such professionals as role models. Policies addressing health care professionals especially require an assumption of some risk in dealing with most infectious diseases, as has been the case through much of medical history until the recent discovery of antibiotics and vaccines. Some physicians have not yet acknowledged the historically accepted commitment of medicine to the acceptance of risk, however remote, in the course of patient care. These groups, as are all service providers, are rightly held to a standard of service even under difficult circumstances. It is both unethical and unprofessional for well-compensated workers to refuse to deal with HIV-positive individuals. This is especially true for those on the "front lines," as are members of the health professions.

Addressing the regulation of health care insurers, both federal and state governments have been for the most part overprotective of the insurance industry, especially since the pro-big-business decade of the 1980s. Richard Mohr, in *Gay Community News*, wrote eloquently in 1986 of the plight of persons with AIDS when faced with an intransigent insurance industry. Little has occurred since that time to negate his observation: "Insurance companies come to the AIDS crisis with dirty hands. . . . They make their money from the statistical norm, and so they suppose that is also the moral norm. They mistakenly think they are promoting something normal, something American, when they have discriminated against gays." This statement might be applied more broadly to all who share positive HIV status, and even to those who live in Zip Code areas reflecting heavy concentrations of groups significantly affected by AIDS in the past.

Turning to AIDS in the work place, a 1988 *Wall Street Journal* article reported that to that date only five percent of U.S. employers had developed an AIDS policy. This was attributed to concerns about image, client relationships, or the appearance of endorsing homosexuality or IV drug use. More companies have taken positive action since then, notably IBM, which mailed copies of a Centers for Disease Control AIDS brochure to all of its U.S. employees. The mailing included a letter from IBM's medical director, who wrote, "IBMers affected by AIDS will be encouraged to work as long as they are able, and their privacy will be respected." The issue of AIDS in the work place was still not uniformly resolved by the end of 1992. AIDS-related income losses in the work place have wide implications that extend to the nation's economy, including possible social security deficits and bankruptcy of some pension plans.

AIDS and Politics

AIDS emerged as a public health issue at a time of conservative national government. President Ronald Reagan established an agenda based on diminished federal responsibility in addressing social needs. A pro-business, elitist philosophy created much uncertainty regarding the health needs and other social requirements of those who are vulnerable. While the government has strengthened national leadership since that time, it continues to stop short of much public support of those who are HIV infected. So long as religious and political conservatives maintain a disproportionate hold on the national agenda, there is reason for serious concern. In an attempt to move toward a comprehensive national strategy for addressing AIDS, the Presidential Commission that issued *The Human Immunodeficiency Virus Epidemic Report* in 1988 recommended:

1. replacement of the obsolete term "AIDS" (Acquired Immunodeficiency Syndrome) with the term "HIV infection"
2. early diagnosis of HIV infection
3. increased testing to facilitate understanding of the incidence and prevalence of HIV infection

4. treatment of HIV infection as a disability under federal and state law[s]
5. stronger legal protection of the privacy of HIV-infected persons
6. immediate implementation of preventive measures, such as confidential partner notification
7. prevention and treatment of intravenous drug abuse
8. implementation of drug and alcohol abuse education programs
9. establishment of federal and state scholarship and loan programs to encourage nurses to serve in areas of high HIV impact
10. extension and expansion of the National Health Service Corps
11. aggressive biomedical research
12. more equitable and cost-effective financing of care for HIV-infected persons
13. addressing the concerns of health care workers
14. federal assurance of the safety of the blood supply
15. undertaking all reasonable efforts to avoid transfusion of another person's blood
16. development and implementation of education programs
17. addressing the problem of HIV-infected "boarder babies" (i.e., those left in the hospital nursery)
18. addressing the problem of high-risk adolescents
19. addressing ethical issues raised by the HIV epidemic
20. support and encouragement of international efforts to combat the spread of HIV infection.

In its report, the Commission blamed societal and governmental apathy for the failure to develop a national strategy and estimated that fatalities from HIV-related diseases would grow to 350,000 early in the 1990s. The report stated, "Our nation's leaders have not done well." The White House "has rarely broken its silence" on AIDS and Congress "has often failed to provide adequate funding for AIDS programs" [despite developing some important AIDS legislation]. As of 1992, a number of these recommendations had not been formally addressed by the federal government.

Legal and Ethical Issues

Mandatory testing for AIDS is not recommended by the Centers for Disease Control. It is questionable on several legal grounds as well. It constitutes a physical intrusion that challenges the Fourth Amendment, especially for an infection not easily communicable compared with other infectious diseases. Further, there is the question whether the government or other agencies should have access to personal information gathered during mandatory testing. Instead, the Centers for Disease Control stresses that testing be offered anonymously insofar as possible. Enforcement of confidentiality contributes greatly to encouraging participation in voluntary testing. Current public health practice is to protect the privacy of the HIV-infected individual and to maintain the strict confidentiality of health records. The issue of confidential testing becomes even more compelling as new life-prolonging drugs are discovered. The threat to civil rights and the abuses that might occur among insurers, in the work place and elsewhere, make mandatory testing a very questionable policy. In addition, given the length of time that may pass before HIV antibodies appear in blood samples after infection, initial false negative results may cause tremendous harm to the well-being of the individual and of possible partners. Also, testing is no guarantee for the safety of caretakers, who may be falsely assured about HIV status during the early stages of infection.

Addressing research involving HIV-positive persons, such studies are subject to the Department of Health and Human Services Regulations for Protection of Human Subjects. In addition, the Department sets forth three ethical considerations that must be observed in conducting AIDS-related research:

1. There must be fairness in the distribution of both risks and benefits of research.
2. Possible benefits of the research must be maximized and possible harms minimized.
3. The rights of research subjects to make choices based on informed judgments must be respected.

Issues of personal ethics and AIDS include the question of trust between partners. A study by Susan Cochran and Vicki Mays, published in 1990 in *The New England Journal of Medicine*, cautions that significant percentages of both males and females lie, or would lie, about past sexual experience and HIV status to prospective partners. From these results, one may conclude that condom use in sexual activity is a wise choice, barring a decision to remain abstinent.

A Cross-Cultural View

As noted above, the World Health Organization reported in late 1991 that at least eight million adults worldwide had been reported as HIV positive. Some estimates of all HIV infections, reported and unreported, may extend to more than ten million worldwide, including six million in Africa alone, and one million in the Caribbean and South America, added to one to one and one-half million in the United States, with the remainder in Asia and Europe.

In Africa, heterosexual transmission is quite prevalent. Several studies characterize African persons with AIDS as having had multiple partners, as among the better-educated, as urban dwellers, having sexual contacts while traveling a good deal, and as typically having a history of other STDs.

In Haiti and the Dominican Republic, HIV infection is prevalent among heterosexuals. There is also significant evidence of infection among infants and children.

In Japan, it was not until mid-1986 that the government mandated screening of all donated blood for HIV antibodies. Japan has had to overcome a long-standing policy of not informing patients with life-threatening diseases of their health status. This policy is now fast-changing in light of the advent of AIDS.

HIV in Latin America has received less worldwide attention than has the infection in either the United States or Africa. While AIDS appeared relatively later in Latin America, the rate of infection is growing alarmingly in such countries as Mexico and Brazil. Cases are in the thousands in these two countries. While homosexual transmission predominated early on, it seems likely that the social pressure to lead an apparently heterosexual life style will lead to further increases in heterosexual transmission as time goes on.

AIDS and the Future

The World Health Organization predicted in late 1991 that 40 million people would be HIV infected by the 21st century. While research on, and the development of, new drugs continue, many experts doubt there will ever be a cure.

Of considerable concern is a 1990 finding by the American Civil Liberties Union (ACLU) that AIDS-related discrimination was rising in the United States and that it was directed not only at those who are infected but at their families and caregivers as well. One expert concluded: "This report suggests that we are far less reasonable and compassionate than we . . . care to believe." Discrimination also extended to employment, housing, insurance, delivery of government benefits, and access to health care from private dentists and other providers. The ACLU recommended further efforts to educate health care

workers about their legal and ethical responsibilities, expanded legal services, and increased training of lawyers in legal issues relating to AIDS. It also recommended more vigorous enforcement of antidiscrimination laws and greater regulation of the insurance industry so as to "create a system in which all Americans are assured access to health care."

REFERENCES

Bayer, R. *Private Acts, Social Consequences.* New York: Free Press, 1989.

Bullough, V.L. AIDS: Avoiding Witch Hunts. *SIECUS Report*, Vol. 14 (Jan. 1986), pp. 1–3.

Cohen, P.T., M.A. Sande, and P.A. Volberding, eds. *The AIDS Knowledge Base.* Waltham, Mass.: The Medical Publishing Group, 1990.

Corless, I.B., and M. Pittman-Lindeman, eds. *AIDS: Principles, Practices, and Politics.* New York: Hemisphere Publishing, 1989.

Grossman, M. Pediatric AIDS. In I.B. Corless and M. Pittman-Lindeman, eds., *AIDS: Principles, Practices, and Politics, op. cit.*

McKenzie, M.F., ed. *The AIDS Reader: Social, Political, Ethical Issues.* New York: Meridian, 1991.

Masters, W., V. Johnson, and R. Kolodny. *Crisis: Heterosexual Behavior in the Age of AIDS.* New York: Grove Press, 1988.

Pierce, C., and D. VanDeVeer, eds. *AIDS: Ethics and Public Policy.* Belmont, Calif.: Wadsworth Publishing, 1988.

Scott, J., and S. Harris. The *Times Poll*: Johnson Case Raises AIDS Concerns If Not Caution. *Los Angeles Times* (Nov. 28, 1991), pp. 1, 32, 42.

Shilts, R. *And The Band Played On: Politics, People, and the AIDS Epidemic.* New York: St. Martin's Press, 1987.

Sontag, S. *AIDS and Its Metaphors.* New York: Farrar, Straus & Giroux, 1988.

Sprecher, Susan. The Impact of the Threat of AIDS on Heterosexual Dating Relationships. *Journal of Psychology and Human Sexuality*, Vol. 3 (1990), pp. 3–23.

Veronica Diehl Elias

AIDS, RELIGION, AND SEXUAL ORIENTATION

Historically, organized religion has responded to societal crises according to the teachings and tradition of the particular faith. When faced with matters of the general health of the community, religious institutions have characteristically responded with compassion and pastoral concern. On the one hand, the AIDS (acquired immune deficiency syndrome) crisis presents an occasion for supportive concern by religious groups; on the other hand, it raises questions and challenges organized religion to examine teachings about illness and morality. Since AIDS can be sexually transmitted, religious institutions have been required to examine their attitudes and teachings about sexual morality, sexual orientation, and sexual behavior. The AIDS crisis also has required church groups to reexamine their teachings on homosexuality.

This entry examines how organized religion in the Judaeo-Christian tradition interfaces with the religious response to AIDS and the issue of sexual orientation. This discussion explores traditional religious attitudes toward homosexuality and current interpretations and responses by church groups to gay AIDS victims.

The plight of the gay AIDS patient (who, for purposes of this discussion, has acquired the virus through sexual contact) has called attention to the impact that a religious belief system has on a person suffering with a disease. Persons afflicted with AIDS, a life-threatening illness, can respond only within the psychological and spiritual frameworks of their total life experience. That religious system impacts on the person's sense of self-worth and feelings of well-being. Most gay persons are usually aware that many, if not most, organized mainstream religions share a negative and often condemnatory stance on homosexuality. It is the internalization of the negative aspects of religious teachings about homosexuality that makes the spiritual dilemma of the AIDS victim at times so acute. Some of those teachings and traditions are examined below.

A number of organized religious groups confronted their traditional attitudes about homosexuality in the late 1980s and early 1990s as part of their general conventions and official proclamations. Most of them were negative in content. The Methodist Church reaffirmed its position that homosexual behavior is "incompatible with Christian teaching." The Southern Baptist Convention saw homosexuality as "an abomination in the eyes of God." The General Convention of the Episcopal Church was unable to reach a consensus on many sexual issues, including homosexuality, and remained "non-judgmental."

Since at least 1975, the Roman Catholic Church has opposed homosexual behavior as "intrinsically disordered and in no case to be approved of." In a 1986 letter to the bishops of the Catholic church, the Vatican Congregation for the Doctrine of the Faith reminded Catholic bishops of the traditional teaching against homosexual behavior. Despite a pastoral call for compassion, little change is expected in church teaching. In the letter, Biblical interpretations that Scripture "has nothing to say on the subject of homosexuality" are viewed as "gravely erroneous." In fact, the document states that it "is likewise essential to recognize that the Scriptures are not properly understood when they are interpreted in a way which contradicts the Church's living tradition. To be correct, the interpretation of Scripture must be in substantial accord with that tradition."

This is the same Vatican document that directs Catholic bishops to exclude proactive gay groups from using church facilities for their meetings or worship, since "no authentic pastoral program will include organizations in which homosexual persons associate with each other without clearly stating that homosexual activity is immoral." Such a stance is the church's right to proclaim, and it has placed a burden on sexually active Catholic gay men and women by excluding them from the use of church facilities. They often have moved their place of worship to more supportive non-Catholic churches.

Catholic theologians, including feminist reformers, are also criticizing traditional Church views on homosexuality. In a book commissioned by the Catholic Theological Society (however, not officially approved) Father Anthony Kosnick and his colleagues reassessed Catholic sexual ethics that focus on procreation, natural law, and specific sexual acts: "Wholesome human sexuality is that which fosters a creative growth towards integration. Destructive sexuality results in personal frustration and interpersonal alienation." This view allows for a holistic approach to human sexuality that is more relationship-oriented than arts-centered.

It is within the mainstream Protestant churches that some range of opinion on sexual issues exists and some balance is noticed. For example, the *New York Times* reported in 1988 that the United Church of Canada had voted to admit gay men and women in the clergy in its statement that "all persons regardless of their sexual orientation, who profess faith in Jesus Christ and obedience to him, are welcome to become members of the United Church. All members of the Church are eligible to be considered for the ministry."

Another example of acceptance of gay sexual orientation is reflected in a statement by the English Quakers: "[O]ne should no more deplore 'homosexuality' than left-handedness. . . . Homosexual affection can be as selfless as heterosexual affection and therefore we cannot see that it is in some way morally worse."

Judaism has long affirmed sexuality as a good gift from God and does not emphasize the body-soul dualism that underlies Christian tradition.

In brief, Orthodox Judaism opposes homosexuality, while Conservative and Reformed Jews are more questioning of traditional condemnation of homosexuality. Gay synagogues have existed in the United States since the 1970s.

Ethicist James Nelson, who has written eloquently on sexuality and homosexuality, summarizes the views of different churches on homosexuality into four major categories: (1) rejecting and punitive, (2) rejecting and nonpunitive, (3) qualified acceptance, and (4) full acceptance. Nelson asserts that only full acceptance of homosexual orientation can lead to the view that same-sexed relationships can express a divine humanizing intention. He feels that any lesser view places the gay person in a bind that accepts the person but condemns the behavior. Accepting the person but condemning the behavior is what the Catholic Church and many Protestant denominations have been doing.

Scripture and Tradition

The review of denominational teachings on homosexuality is a reflection of the way Judaeo-Christian tradition has interpreted and understood homosexuality for generations. It is the primarily condemnatory view of homosexual behavior that has made the AIDS issue so prominent a task for church groups to face. A great part of church tradition rests on the accepted interpretation of biblical references to homosexuality. It is here that more literal interpretation of the words of Scripture can be cited to condemn homosexual behavior. Over the generations, both gay and nongay people have shared a more literal interpretation of biblical reference to homosexuality along with the consequent prejudices that attain to it.

Modern biblical scholarship has allowed a wider interpretation and understanding of Scripture relating to homosexuality. These modern approaches are not without critics, and there is genuine disagreement about the meaning of scriptural texts. However, by departing from the literalist interpretation, the Scriptures can be viewed in terms of what was being said within the context of biblical times. For example, some modern authors agree that homosexuality as a sexual orientation is not addressed in the Bible. One view is that biblical injunctions cannot be made into eternal truths independent of historical and cultural contexts. Therefore, it is essential to first understand the meaning as seen by the writers in their own concrete situation.

For scriptural references to have meaning today, some feel that the biblical statement must be consonant with the larger, major theological and ethical judgments that lie at the heart not only of Scripture but of the historical church. In addition, the context today must be reasonably similar to the context of the statement at the time it was written. Following this line of reasoning, for example, even if St. Paul's judgments in his epistles are eternally valid, they remain valid only against what he opposed. Biblical references, then, cannot be generalized without risk of violating the integrity of the text. Thus, the question for some scholars is not whether the Bible is authoritative but whether it addresses the issue involved (i.e., current understanding of homosexual orientation and behavior).

These principles can be applied to understanding the basic biblical texts, which are relatively few, that have been used as examples to condemn homosexuality. The Old Testament has three references traditionally linked with homosexuality: the Sodom and Gomorrah passage in Genesis 19 and the two denunciations in Leviticus (18:23, 20:13). Principal New Testament references are St. Paul's letters: Romans 1:24–27, I Corinthians 6:9–10; and Timothy 1:8–11. The New Testament provides no words of Jesus on homosexuality.

No reference to, or understanding of, homosexuality as a sexual orientation is mentioned in biblical passages. Rather, specific same-sex acts are at issue. The Scriptures were written at a time when heterosexual nature was considered "natural" and the need for procreation in a male-dominated society was paramount.

A closer look at traditional biblical passages illustrates the point. A more modern interpretation of the destruction of Sodom and Gomorrah (Genesis 19) is that of a punishment for the violation of standards of social justice and hospitality. The prospects of violent gang rape or intercourse with a divine messenger—rather than a prohibition of homosexual orientation or consenting behavior between adults—can be seen as being condemned. The two references in Leviticus are part of the Holiness Code which includes many other prohibitions on diet and behavior, many of which are ignored in common observance today. Taken as a whole, the purpose of the Code, as seen by some scholars today, was to keep the Jews pure and separate from the practices of pagan influences and practices.

As for St. Paul's comments about same-sex behavior, current scholarship suggests that he may have been reacting against same-sex acts expressing idolatry and undertaken in lust. Pederasty was common among the Romans in St. Paul's time and often involved young male prostitutes. When this is considered, his words appear to address the unnaturalness of an adult heterosexual male engaging in homosexual acts.

As mentioned before, the concept of sexual orientation was foreign in biblical times. Loving, caring, and committed same-sex relationships are not dealt with in Scripture, although there are examples of strongly bonded same-sex relationships. Placed within the context of the times, both the Old and New Testaments were written in cultures battling foreign influences that threatened a religious way of life. Procreation was for the Jews essential for survival; exclusive homosexuality was nonprocreative. Pagan cult practices threatened Jewish purity. ·New Testament writers were influenced by Greek philosophy and avoided contamination by sexual excesses ascribed to Greek and Roman practices.

In the following early Christian centuries, the foundation of Greek dualism eventually became a part of Christian theology in the development of the conflict between the body and the spirit. The writings of Sts. Augustine and Jerome, and their negative view of man's sexual nature, had great influence even then (and still does today). Later, St. Thomas Aquinas's arguments based on Natural Law became the foundation for traditional Catholic teachings on sexual matters. As mentioned, literalist interpretation of Scripture also serves as the foundation for current negative views on homosexual orientation and behavior by many church groups. Such are the seeds of the current and traditional attitudes about homosexuality which, when linked causatively with the development of AIDS, have inflicted so much pain on both victims of AIDS and their religious denominations.

Whatever present or future pronouncements contain about the attitude toward homosexuality and AIDS, few gay AIDS victims and certainly not all clergy or committed believers are aware of both the history of the religious teachings on homosexuality and the more recent scriptural and theological research. What remains is that an important part of the struggle and spiritual dilemma of the gay AIDS victim may be neglected. The religious response of the AIDS patient is important in the overall response to the illness. It provides both an opportunity and a challenge to face and understand long-standing conflicts regarding sexual orientation and behavior. If accepted, this opportunity and challenge can lead to greater personal comfort in religious support, on the one hand. On the other hand, it can result in a feeling of even deeper alienation not only because the denomination

condemns the behavior that perhaps led to fatal illness, but also because those with AIDS may feel personally condemned because of their nature.

The initial religious response of a person who contracts AIDS through homosexual activity is usually a recognition that they must confront their homosexuality in the context of their earlier religious experiences. This response frequently means that the AIDS victim has rationalized his sexual identity, lived with the cognitive and spiritual dissonance, and far too often has accepted the role of a social outcast. The frequent result is that the gay AIDS patient experiences a resurgence of his or her own homophobia. While this is understandable, the situation calls for pastoral sensitivity by church groups, family, and friends.

The term "spiritual" is important here, since it suggests a difference between the formulation of earlier church-related experiences of organized religion and a more universal experience of mankind that is not necessarily associated with a particular denomination or doctrinal system. The dilemma of the AIDS victim is indeed spiritual, even if the person professes no formal religious orientation. The person faces a journey that goes beyond religion to roots that give a sense of meaning and belonging. This sense of achieving a feeling of grounding is even more important for the gay AIDS patient who feels particularly alienated from organized religion. The journey must still be undertaken.

Terms such as "sinner" and "unnatural" can over the years result in feelings of guilt and even social withdrawal. What is important for spiritual healing is embracing a positive attitude toward the body and sexuality. The holistic approach emphasized by Nelson can help a person integrate his or her sexuality and spirituality in a satisfying way; he contends that too much time has been spent defending and justifying sexual orientation.

Today, some denominations are providing support to their gay members within a religious context: Integrity (Episcopalian), Dignity (Catholic), Reformation (Lutheran), Affirmation (Mormon). The Fellowship of Metropolitan Community Churches was founded by a gay minister to serve the gay community.

The pastoral support by various religious denominations for AIDS victims has been compassionate, merciful, and consistent with religious teachings of the responsibility toward the sick and needy. It is the emotionally laden issue of sexual orientation and sexual behavior as they relate to the incidence of AIDS that remains a challenge for all and a cause for further study and dialogue.

REFERENCES

Congregation for the Doctrine of the Faith. Letter to the Bishops of the Catholic Church on the Pastoral Care of Homosexual Persons. In J. Gramick and P. Furey, eds. *The Vatican and Homosexuality*. New York: Crossroad, 1988.

Fortuanato, J. *AIDS, The Spiritual Dilemma*. San Francisco: Harper & Row, 1987.

Gramick, J., and P. Furey, eds. *The Vatican and Homosexuality*, op. cit.

Kosnick, A., et al. *Human Sexuality: New Directions in American Catholic Thought*. New York: Paulist Press, 1977.

Nelson, J. *Embodiment: An Approach to Sexuality and Christian Theology*. Minneapolis: Augsburg Publishing House, 1978.

———. Religious and Moral Issues in Working With Homosexual Clients. In J. Gonsiorek, ed., *Homosexuality and Psychotherapy*. New York: Haworth Press, 1982.

———. Sexuality Issues in American Religious Groups: An Update. *Marriage and Family Review* (1983), Vol. 6:3/4, pp. 35–46.

Scroggs, R. *The New Testament and Homosexuality*. Philadelphia: Fortress Press, 1983.

Julian W. Slowinski

AMBISEXUALITY

The term "ambisexuality" was first published by Masters and Johnson in 1979 to describe men and women who had frequent sexual interaction with members of both sexes but who reported absolutely no preference for the gender of the partner. Sexual interaction was viewed as simply a matter of sexual release. They defined the term as "a man or woman who unreservedly enjoys, solicits, or responds to overt sexual opportunity with equal ease and interest regardless of the sex of the partners, and who, as a sexually mature individual, has never evidenced interest in a continuing relationship."

The terms ambisexual and bisexual are used to describe the relationship between heterosexuality and homosexuality. Alfred Kinsey produced a scale that classifies human psychosexual and behavioral response into seven categories ranging from exclusively heterosexual (the Kinsey 0) to exclusively homosexual (the Kinsey 6). The numbers 1 through 5 represent a ratio between homosexual and heterosexual behavior.

The criteria established by Masters and Johnson for the identification of an ambisexual are "(1) that the individual express no preference in terms of sexual partner selection either through personal history or by subjective description, (2) that he or she [is] currently living an uncommitted ambisexual lifestyle and [has] never as an adult evidenced any interest in a continuing relationship, and (3) that the man or woman could be rated close to Kinsey 3 in sexual preference" (this would be the midpoint on the scale). Fantasy patterns were not considered a part of the definition.

After a national search of about eight months in 1968, only six men and six women were found who fit the criteria. They said that their sexual preference was "that of the partner of the moment." These numbers are too small to allow generalizations about ambisexuality.

The term "ambisexuality" is often equated with the term "bisexuality," a designation that has been used in many ways that have very little precise meaning. The true bisexual is equally attracted to both sexes (i.e., a Kinsey 3). This definition incorporates the criteria for ambisexuality. However, in widely accepted use of the term, those classified as Kinsey 1 through 5 could also be identified (or identify themselves) as bisexual with a preference for homosexual behavior (Kinsey 4 and 5) or for heterosexual behavior (Kinsey 1 and 2).

The original Kinsey scale was established using sexual behavior as the sole criterion. Complicating factors (e.g., love, sexual attraction, fantasy, and self-identification) have only recently been used to enhance it. Using the old scale, it seems easy to determine the exclusive heterosexual (Kinsey 0) or the exclusive homosexual (Kinsey 6); however, when the fantasies of these persons are considered, their orientation may not be so exclusive. The categories between the two extremes represent a continuum, especially when the additional elements are considered, and they have received little research attention. It does seem, however, that when all of the factors are considered, an individual's rating may change over time. That is, the individual may be a Kinsey 2 at one time and a Kinsey 5 at another; the rating should not be viewed as being fixed, describing all behaviors, or predicting future behavior.

Given the ambiguities of the Kinsey 1 through 5 definitions, perhaps ambisexuality rather than bisexuality is the better term to use. Ambisexuality would recognize the continuum and be defined as "the ability for a person to eroticise both genders under some circumstances," since equal attraction to males and females is virtually nonexistent. The term "bisexuality" could then be used to describe the Kinsey 3s.

REFERENCES

Blumstein, P., and P. Schwartz. Bisexuality in Men. Urban Life, Vol. 5, No. 3 (1976), pp. 339–358.

————. Bisexuality: Some Social Psychological Issues. *Journal of Social Issues*, Vol. 33, No. 2 (1977), pp. 30–45.

Masters, W.H., and Virginia E. Johnson. *Homosexuality in Perspective*. Boston: Little, Brown, 1979.

Masters, W.H., Virginia E. Johnson, and R.C. Kolodny. *Human Sexuality* (3rd ed.). Glenview, Ill.: Scott, Foresman, 1988.

Reinisch, J.M. *The Kinsey Institute New Report on Sex.* New York: St. Martin's Press, 1990.

James D. Haynes

ANAL SEX

The anus is the opening to the lower end of the digestive tract and is surrounded by two sets of muscles called the anal sphincters. A person can learn to control the contractions of the outer sphincter. The anal opening leads into the short anal canal and the larger rectum. Perineal muscles support the area around the anus and are in close contact with the bulb of the penis in the male and the outer portion of the vagina in the female. All of these tissues are well supplied with blood vessels and nerves. The inner third of the anal canal is less sensitive to touch than the outer two-thirds, but is more sensitive to pressure. The rectum is a curved tube about eight or nine inches long and has the capacity, like the anus, to expand.

One form of anal intercourse involves the insertion of an object into the anus. The object may be a finger, penis, dildo, or other objects. Some people engage in "fisting," which is the insertion of the hand and sometimes part of the forearm into the anus and rectum. The pleasure derived from penetration of the anus is both physical and psychological. Psychological satisfaction may be derived by the feelings of dominance and submission produced in the participants. Fantasy is often an important factor in achieving satisfaction. The stimulation of the nerve endings in the tissues and muscles, the bulb of the penis, and connections to the vagina; the feeling of fullness in the rectum; and the rubbing against the prostate gland in the male create physical pleasure in many people. Various objects may be used to stimulate the anus during masturbation. This may be done by one person using the object (often a dildo), or by mutual masturbation during group sex in which a partner inserts the object. One person may also insert a finger or fingers into the anus while rubbing the penis or clitoris. Some people insert "butt plugs" into their anus and wear them during the day to prolong a feeling of sexual pleasure. A butt plug is similar to a dildo, but may be shorter and thicker in diameter. It is usually composed of flexible rubber and may be molded into various shapes. It is held in place with straps that attach to other clothing or wrap around the waist.

The anus is also used sexually in ways that do not involve penetration. The rubbing of the external sphincter and the flexing of the muscle during masturbation are common. Anilingus (i.e., the kissing, licking, sucking, and insertion of the tongue into the anus) is not uncommon.

Contrary to popular belief, anal sex is not an activity exclusive to the male homosexual, nor is it the activity most often practiced by him. Although statistics on this subject are suspect, some investigators report that 47 percent of predominantly heterosexual men and 61 percent of the women have tried anal intercourse. Thirteen percent of married couples reported having anal intercourse at least once a month. Approximately 37 percent of both men and women have practiced oral-anal contact. A study of homosexual men revealed that only 20 percent had experience as insertor and 18 percent as insertee.

Anal sex has been known since records of human sexual activity have been kept. Depending on the culture, or even on the time of the evolution of the culture, the practice has been tolerated, accepted, expected, or condemned. Definite roles were sometimes assigned to the participants. For example, it was common in many cultures for the insertor to be an older man teaching the insertee, a young man. In other cultures, the participants were of equal status and alternated roles. It was considered unusual by the people in those cultures if such relationships did not exist. Anal intercourse was sometimes used as an act of dominance over a conquered enemy or to exert superiority over women. It has also been used as a means of birth control and as an alternative to vaginal intercourse during menstruation. In some instances, partners in a heterosexual relationship engage in anal penetration because they find it more satisfying. Women have also used dildos and other objects to penetrate their male and/or female partners. In some societies, men assumed the roles of women (the berdache) and held honored places within the society.

In some cultures, men would insert fingers during certain rituals, or wear butt plugs while meditating. Anal sex has often had mystical significance. The berdache was often thought to have magical powers. In China, anal intercourse with a wife was permitted because it was thought that by doing so the husband could get the essence of yin. Even gods of ancient Egypt, Seth and Horus, practiced anal sex as a means of establishing dominance.

Anal sex was often punished by hanging, burning, decapitation, and mutilation in societies where it was not accepted. Participants were sometimes banished or publicly disgraced. The Judaeo-Christian ethic began to exert a very negative influence on the acceptance of anal sex. Words such as "buggery" or "sodomy" became strongly pejorative. The fear of being considered homosexual lent a strong negative connotation to anal sex, although the insertor could retain his masculinity more easily than the insertee. The idea that the anus was somehow dirty or disgusting led to further denial of anal sex.

Certain precautions must be followed if practicing anal sex, but it is not as dangerous as often thought. Penetration should be done slowly and carefully by a penis or a soft rubber object that has no sharp edges or points. Anything inserted into the anus should be well covered by a water-based lubricant. The pain of insertion can be overcome by the insertee by practicing relaxation techniques, and, if done properly, there should be no tearing of the soft anal tissues. Positioning of the inserted object is important because of the curve of the rectum. Fisting is an activity that should be practiced, if at all, with great care. Few people are capable of relaxing enough to accommodate something as big as a fist in their anus, and there is real danger of damage to the delicate rectal tissues.

Disease-causing organisms can be transmitted during anal sex. These include syphilis, gonorrhea, nongonococcal urethritis, herpes, anal warts, hepatitis, and various organisms that cause intestinal infections. They can also be transmitted from anus to mouth or to vagina if a penis or dildo is not thoroughly cleaned before it is inserted into those openings. Since about 1979, AIDS has produced a new danger for those who practice anal sex. The causative organism, HIV, is most often transmitted sexually through anal intercourse. Because the disease is so deadly, special consideration must be given to anal penetration by a penis. The penis should be covered by a condom that contains a spermicide and should be well lubricated with a water-based lubricant. Great care should be taken that there be no tears in the anal tissue or in the penis or condom. Precautions should be taken to ensure that blood-to-blood or semen-to-blood mixing not take place. Anilingus (rimming) is another activity that presents an avenue for transmission of disease-causing organisms. At least one study reports that there is an association between the frequency of anal intercourse and the occurrence of certain kinds of cancer of the rectum.

REFERENCES

Bullough, V.L. *Sexual Variance in Society and History.* New York:Wiley-Interscience, 1976.

Morin, Jack. *Anal Pleasure and Health* (2nd ed.). Burlingame: Down There Press, 1986.

James D. Haynes

ANATOMY AND PHYSIOLOGY

Male Anatomy and Physiology

In simple terms, the male reproductive system consists of a pair of testes that produce sperm and hormones, a network of ducts designed to transport the sperm from the testes to other points on their journey, a variety of glands that produce semen, and the penis. The testes are egg-shaped structures located in the scrotum, a sacklike structure that hangs outside the male body at the base of the penis. Physiologically, the testes are located in the scrotum because it is cooler than the abdominal cavity, where the higher temperature would (as it does in the undescended testicles) destroy the sperm.

The average testicle measures one to one and a half inches in length, and each manufactures and secretes the hormone testosterone as well as small amounts of estrogen, the female hormone, and androsterone, another male hormone. Within the scrotum, each testis (or testicle) is suspended at the end of what is called the spermatic cord. The cord contains blood vessels, nerves, a sperm duct called the vas deferens, and a thin muscle called the cremaster muscle, which encircles each testicle and raises it closer to the body in response to fear, cold, anger, and sexual arousal. Each testicle contains hundreds of structures called seminiferous tubules where sperm is produced. If these tightly coiled tubules were stretched out, they would extend one to three feet in length. At the back portion of each testis is the epididymis, a storage and excretory unit for sperm. Its smooth walls contract when ejaculation takes place, moving the sperm out into the connecting tube or vas deferens. The two vas deferens (both of which are severed when a male is sterilized) run along the testicle, up into the abdominal cavity, and around the bladder before emptying into the ejaculatory ducts, which enter the prostate gland. It is here that sperm from each testicle is combined with fluid from the prostate gland to produce the semen that enters the urethra. The urethra in the male serves double duty, functioning as a carrier not only of the semen but also of urine.

The sexual process starts with arousal, which causes the penis to change from its flaccid resting state to an erect condition called tumescence. This is possible because the penis includes two cylinders, corpora cavernosa, made up of spongy tissue. Cells in this tissue have spaces between them, and arousal causes the space to fill with blood. With further stimulation of the tumescent penis from intercourse or other sexual activity, ejaculation occurs and the semen is expelled from the urethra.

The ejaculate of the average male contains from 200 million to 400 million sperm, but the sperm account for only about 1 percent of the total volume of the semen. In addition to fluid from the epididymis, the seminal vesicles, and the prostate gland, semen also contains secretions from the Cowper's glands. These glands flank the urethra and empty into it through tiny ducts. It is believed that the secretion of the glands helps neutralize the acidity of the urine in the urethra, thus making possible the survival and mobility of the sperm. Cowper's glands also contain a small number of sperm (proportionately smaller, though the number is still in the millions), and this preejaculatory fluid can impregnate a woman even if the man withdraws before ejaculation takes place. (See illustrations of the male reproductive system.)

Female Anatomy

The female reproductive system is not as visible as that of the male. It consists of a pair of ovaries, two Fallopian tubes, a uterus, cervix, vagina, and vulva. The ovaries are almond-shaped organs located in the pelvic cavity, nestled in the curve of the Fallopian tubes. Ovaries are the female counterparts of testes and develop from similar tissue during the fetal differentiation between male and female, a process that takes place early in the development of the fetus. Both ovaries and testes produce reproductive cells (eggs in the case of ovaries) and both secrete hormones. The ovaries primarily produce estrogen and progesterone, although they also secrete small amounts of masculinizing hormones, including testosterone. At birth, the ovaries contain between 230,000 and 400,000 ovarian follicles, clusters of nutrient- and hormone-secreting cells with an immature egg in the center. Only 400 to 500 of these eggs, or ova, will be released from their follicles, usually one each month, from puberty to menopause.

Each Fallopian tube, which is connected to the uterus, is about four inches long. The end of the Fallopian tube nearest the ovary is not connected to it directly. Instead, it has a funnel-like opening tube with fingerlike edges (called fimbria) that help the ovum enter the tube through a process not yet fully understood. Inside the tube are hairlike structures known as cilia that sway in the direction of the uterus and guide the ovum. The tube also contracts to help push the ovum along. Fertilization, if it takes place, occurs in the Fallopian tubes near the entrance closest to the ovaries.

The uterus resembles an upside-down pear and is held suspended in the pelvic cavity by a series of ligaments. It is located between the bladder and the rectum. It shifts and contracts in response to pregnancy, the filling or emptying of the bladder or rectum, and sexual intercourse. The walls are partially composed of smooth muscles; it is the contraction of these muscles that occurs during orgasm, childbirth, and menstruation. The contractions during menstruation are more pronounced (and painful) in some women than in others.

At the lower end of the uterus is the cervix, which extends into the vagina. It has an opening or mouth (referred to as the os) through which sperm can enter the uterus and travel up to the Fallopian tubes. It is also the opening through which childbirth takes place. The cervix has glands that excrete varying amounts of mucus. This mucus plugs the entrance to the cervix and forms a barrier against the entry of sperm during most of the menstrual cycle. During ovulation, the mucus is thinner and more permeable.

The vagina is a thin-walled muscular tube that extends from the uterus to the external opening, the introitus. The walls contain many blood vessels that become engorged with blood during sexual excitement and during childbirth. Under congestion or pressure from the blood, small amounts of fluid are squeezed through the cell walls. This fluid acts as a lubricant during sexual intercourse and delivery. The process is very similar to that which leads to arousal in the male.

"Vulva" is the term usually given to the external genitalia of the female, including the mons pubis, the outer and inner lips (labia), the clitoris, the introitus or vaginal opening, and the urinary opening (entrance to the urethra). The mons pubis is a cushion of fatty tissue covering the pubic bone. It is covered with pubic hair and has a large number of touch receptors. The labia majora (outer lips) cover the external genitalia; they merge with the rest of the body skin at the back at the perineum, the area between the anus and the labia, and in the front they come together a small distance above the clitoris. The

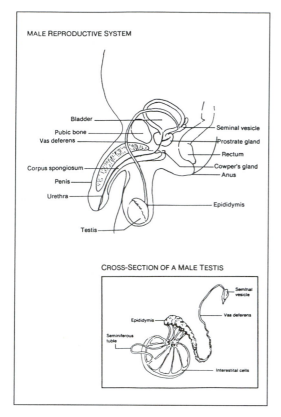

Male Reproductive System

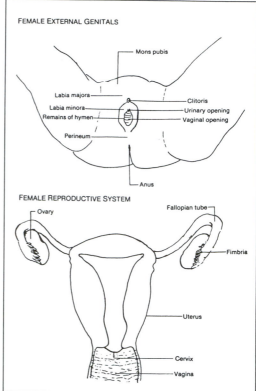

Female Reproductive System

labia majora are similar to the scrotum in the male (in male-to-female transsexual operations, the scrotum is used to form the labia) and have fewer touch and pressure receptors than the mons. The labia minora (inner lips) are the inner covering of the entrance to the vagina. They are thinner than the outer labia and have no hair on them. They enclose both the vaginal and the urethral openings as well as the ducts of the Bartholin glands, which produce a small amount of mucus. The clitoris is composed of two small erectile, cavernous bodies enclosed in a fibrous membrane and ending in a glans, an exposed head homologous to the penile glans. It is one of the most erotically sensitive parts of the female body and is permeated with both pressure and sensory receptors.

The female reproductive system undergoes two physiological processes, menstruation and childbirth, which are exclusive to the female. All other physiological processes are shared in common between the sexes. Unlike male fertility, which is relatively constant during the reproductive years, female fertility is cyclical and involved with the menstrual cycle. (See illustrations for details of female reproductive anatomy.) For physiological changes during menstruation,

childbirth, and orgasm see the discussions elsewhere in this encyclopedia..

Vern L. Bullough

ANORGASMIA

Introduction

Anorgasmia, or the inability to obtain orgasm during a sexual encounter, affects about ten percent of women. Generally defined as resulting from not having learned how to achieve an orgasm, this condition is classified as either preorgasmia or primary anorgasmia. Secondary anorgasmia is the loss of ability to have an orgasm. Situational and random anorgasmia are types of secondary anorgasmia. Figure 1 shows a range of orgasmic activity.

Orgasmic Response

Physiologically, orgasm results from the release of vasocongestion and myotonia. During the orgasmic phase, there is a release of myotonia through contractions of muscles of the pelvic floor that surround the lower third of the vagina. Between five to 12 contractions occur at about one-second intervals. Vasocongestion is relieved as the vaginal muscles contract against the engorged vessels forcing out the trapped blood. Contractions of the uterus begin at the fundus and progress to the lower segment. Orgasmic pleasure is related to both the intervals and the intensity of the contractions.

Extragenital orgasmic responses are seen in several other body systems. Seventy-five percent of women have a sexual flush. The intensity of the flush appears to parallel the intensity of the orgasm. Both respiratory and heart rates increase, with respiration going as high as 30 to 40 breaths per minute while the pulse rate ranges from 110 to 180 beats per minute. There is also an elevation in blood pressure of between 30 to 80 mm/Hg systolic to 20 to 40 mm/Hg diastolic. The rectal sphincter also experiences muscle contractions similar to those of the vagina.

Preorgasmia or Primary Anorgasmia

Preorgasmia is a term used to describe a person who has never achieved an orgasm through any type of sexual encounter. The inability to achieve orgasm can be complicated by a culture that is sexually inhibiting. For example, expectations that a female lover be compliant and self-sacrificing are still common. This passive sexual role for women can be repressive and lead them to deny sexual desires and experience inhibition of their sexual response cycle.

Most sexual therapists believe a woman can learn to be orgasmic. While learning to achieve orgasm may be relatively easy, learning to do so in every desired situation is more difficult.

Women with preorgasmia usually experience some sexual excitement. They may feel that intercourse is pleasant, but most of their pleasure comes from touching, holding, kissing, and caressing. They feel rewarded by the attention and approval they receive. If the level of sexual arousal is high, women may find the experience frustrating. High levels of muscle tension and pelvic engorgement without orgasmic release can lead to emotional irritability, restlessness, and pelvic pain.

Several factors appear to be related to preorgasmia. Sociocultural inhibitions that interfere with normal masturbation experimentation may prevent a woman from understanding what sexually excites her. Since orgasm is a learned response that contains both sensory and motor components, self-sexual exploration is an excellent way to learn this response. Providing a safe, secure, and supporting environment in which to explore their sexuality can enhance the chances that women can learn to have an orgasm.

Misinformation or a lack of factual information about sex and sexuality can also interfere with normal sexual development. Much success in treating preorgasmia has been obtained by using both educational and behavioral learning strategies. The first step in treating preorgasmia may be an educational program that teaches facts and corrects misconceptions. Understanding the normal sexual response cycle is important in learning to achieve orgasm. In addition, the presence of a sensuous, sexually knowledgeable woman as a role model (instead of one who is self-sacrificing and compliant) can contribute to the ability to achieve orgasm.

Partners with their own sexual problems (e.g., erectile difficulties and/or ejaculatory problems) can also be a factor in the orgasmic difficulties of women.

A woman can learn to become orgasmic alone or with a partner. For some, practicing self-stimulation may greatly enhance the learning process. An environment that maximizes stimulation while minimizing inhibition provides the greatest opportunity to learn. However, a woman who has never masturbated may need specific instruction on self-pleasuring. Self-stimulation can be performed manually or by using such devices as a vibrator or a pulsating steam of water. In some cases, counseling may be needed to help the woman become comfortable with her sensuous and sexual being.

After the woman has achieved orgasm through self-stimulation, the next step is for her to teach her partner what types of stimulation lead her to orgasm. Used with coital thrusting, a success rate of 83.49 percent in treating women with preorgasmia has been reported with this method.

Secondary Anorgasmia

Secondary anorgasmia is the loss of ability to achieve orgasm. Its occurrence usually coincides with a "causal event." The causal event may be related to: alcoholism or drug addiction, depression, grief, medications, chronic or acute illness, or estrogen deprivation. Violation of sexual values, and loss of self-esteem are also factors that could be related to the causal event.

To regain the ability to achieve orgasm, both the biophysical and psychosocial needs of the woman must be met. Once these needs are recognized and fulfilled, orgasmic function generally returns. Treatment of secondary anorgasmia involves helping identify the unmet needs and formulating a plan to fulfill those needs. Needs may be as simple as a comfortable, warm, and private place in which to engage in sexual activities or as complex as confirming the trust and respect of the woman's partner.

Situational Anorgasmia

Situational anorgasmia describes the condition of a woman who is orgasmic in some but not all sexual situations. Situational anorgasmia can take several forms. One form is the ability to reach orgasm through one type of sexual activity but not another (e.g., achieving orgasm through manual stimulation rather than the penis in vagina intercourse). A second form is the ability to achieve orgasm with one partner but not another. The ability to achieve orgasm in only one place or after a specific type or amount of foreplay is another form. These variations in orgasmic function may fall within the normal range of sexual expression and are usually not considered pathological. But a woman who experiences situational anorgasmia and wishes to extend or to change her current sexual patterns may find this condition problematic.

To learn to manage situational anorgasmia, the woman should first examine situations in which she achieves orgasm. If she can identify the factors that promote orgasm, she may be able to transfer them to her nonorgasmic encounters. The opposite is also helpful. A woman should explore her nonorgasmic situation and try to identify certain factors (e.g., fatigue, anxiety, or stress) that interfere with her sexual pleasure. In general she should try to improve communication, avoid performance anxiety, focus on sensation not cerebration, and use voluntary muscle contractions.

The woman must learn to bridge the difference between orgasmic and nonorgasmic situations. Bridging is the use of a successful sexual stimulation technique with the desired sexual technique so that the body learns to associate orgasm with the desired technique. An example is to perform manual stimulation of the clitoris simultaneously with penile thrusting so that the body begins to associate thrusting as well as manual stimulation with excitement and orgasm.

Random Anorgasmia

When a woman is dissatisfied with the number of sexual encounters in which orgasms occur, she is said to have random anorgasmia. Because there is no fixed number of encounters in which orgasm should be achieved, random anorgasmia is present only if the woman is unsatisfied with her orgasmic response. For many women, a sexual encounter can be gratifying and enjoyable even when no orgasm occurs, so the fact that each encounter is not orgasmic is not a problem for them.

When random anorgasmia occurs, it may be followed by performance anxiety. By focusing on whether she will have an orgasm, a woman can become tense and unresponsive; she must learn to focus on sensation rather than cerebration. Some women with random anorgasmia find it difficult to give up control of their sexual feelings and allow sensation to take over. Their treatment should include helping them give up the need to control their sexual feelings.

Summary

Achieving orgasm involves both physical and psychosocial factors. To be orgasmic, a woman's needs must be met within her sexual value system. While most women can learn to be orgasmic, transferring that ability to every sexual situation may be more difficult. Treatment includes behavioral therapy, education, and psychotherapy. Orgasm, however, is only one part of a gratifying sexual encounter.

REFERENCES

Annon, J.S. *The Behavioral Treatment of Sexual Problems.* Vol. 1. Honolulu: Mercantile Printing, 1974.

Barbach, L. *For Yourself: The Fulfillment of Female Sexuality.* Garden City, N.Y.: Anchor Press, 1976.

Heiman, J., L. LoPiccolo, and J. LoPiccolo. *Becoming Orgasmic.* New York: Prentice-Hall, 1976.

Hite, S. *The Hite Report.* New York: Macmillan: 1976.

Masters, W., and V. Johnson. Principles of the New Sex Therapy. *American Journal of Psychiatry,* Vol. 133 (May 1976), pp. 554–84.

Weisberg, M. Physiology of Female Sexual Function. *Clinical Obstetrics and Gynecology,* Vol. 27 (1984), pp. 697–705.

Sarah B. Freeman

Figure 1: Range of Orgasmic Responses

Total anorgasm	Orgasm with masturbation	Orgasm with some sexual activity	Orgasm with a portion of sexual encounters	100% Orgasmic
Can be primary		Situational	Random	Absolute

ANTHROPOLOGY: INFLUENCE OF CULTURE ON SEX

Central to the definition of anthropology as a discipline is the concept of culture. This concept pervades the diverse directions of research in the subfields of anthropology: physical anthropology, archaeology, linguistics, social–cultural anthropology, and psychological anthropology. The culture that underlies anthropology guides the questions it asks or does not ask, the concepts it employs, the content areas on which it focuses, the methods it uses, and the interpretation of information it collects. More specifically, it has guided the unique way in which anthropologists have investigated and analyzed human sexuality.

The first part of this discussion defines culture, establishes its importance to anthropology's paradigm as a discipline, and indicates the ways this paradigm has influenced anthropologists' approaches to human sexuality. The second part considers the ways in which the anthropological paradigm has shaped the research methods and the interpretation of findings about human sexuality.

The Culture of Anthropology: Its Paradigm

Tylor, the founder of social anthropology, proposed culture as the central concern of anthropology in 1871, defining it as "that complex whole which includes knowledge, belief, art, law, morals, custom, and any other capabilities and habits acquired by man as a member of society." Fundamental to this definition are the attributes of holism, sharing in a social context, and tradition. Since then, definitions of the term have proliferated so much that the distinguished anthropologists Kroeber and Kluckhohn devoted their 1953 book *Culture* to a critical review of concepts and definitions. Their concluding definition is this:

> Culture consists of patterns, explicit and implicit, of and for behavior acquired and transmitted by symbols, constituting the distinctive achievement of human groups, including their embodiments in artifacts; the essential core of culture consists of traditional (i.e., historically derived and selected) ideas and especially their attached values; culture systems may, on the one hand, be considered as products of action, on the other as conditioning elements of further action.

In other words, the defining attributes of culture are that it is (1) patterned; (2) a basis for interpreting behavior and experience; (3) symbolic, containing many layers of meaning; (4) traditional, passed down from one generation to the next through learning; and (5) shared by members of a group. These core attributes of culture still define its domain. While art, music, and literature express and are a part of culture, the concept reaches beyond these domains to include ideas and beliefs that shape and interpret any behavior. Therefore, culture is different from society, which refers to shared patterns of behaving and interacting in a group. Culture relates to the meaning of behavior; society relates to the patterns of behavior. Clearly, the two overlap, but it is essential that they not be confused. Patterns of behavior can be observed, but the meaning is not apparent, although meaning can be inferred, analyzed, or derived from asking the participants to interpret their behavior.

Culture centers on knowledge, beliefs, and interpretation of behavior. The distinction between cultural and social factors is even more crucial to interpreting behavior because people's behavior (social aspect) and people's beliefs, ideas, and knowledge (cultural aspect) are not necessarily consistent with each other. The lack of consistency between them is just as interesting to research as their conformity with each other. To mesh them together is to lose an understanding of how culture functions in human societies. For example, a couple may *know* (a cultural factor) that they should use condoms during intercourse to lower the chances of contracting a sexually transmitted disease. However, they *do not use* a condom (a social factor). In this case, knowledge does not translate to behavior. Why? Judgment may be impaired because of drug use (a biological factor); a woman may not suggest condom use because of a *belief* that women are not supposed to be knowledgeable about sexual matters (a cultural factor); or a woman's partner may *refuse* to wear a condom because he says intercourse would be more pleasurable if he did not use one (a social factor).

A specific example of culture is Kuhn's concept of the paradigm, which he introduces in *The Structure of Scientific Revolutions* to describe ideas in the scientific community that define acceptable ways of conducting research and developing theories. What is acceptable depends on the assumptions of the era that underlie the methods, concepts, and interpretation of behavior, that is, the culture. Therefore, the way a discipline like anthropology applies a concept like culture to a topic like human sexuality is partly a product of its own culture—its traditions, its beliefs, and its symbols. A full understanding of the ways in which anthropologists interpret the link between culture and human sexuality depends on an appreciation of the ways in which the anthropological paradigm shapes its research methods and analyses. This helps to explain why some questions are focused on and others are not considered, and how human sexuality is conceptualized and interpreted.

Anthropology developed during the 19th century, a period of tremendous social and cultural change in the West: expansion of the British empire, the movement of settlers west in the United States, industrialization, and the impact of Darwin's theory of evolution. Explorers, government officials, missionaries, travelers, and intellectuals had been exposed to the social, cultural, and physical diversity of human beings. Questions revolved around how to order and interpret this diversity. Darwin's *On the Origin of Species* (1859) suggested an explanation for the diversity of life forms that he observed and became a basis for academic and popular interpretations of other kinds of diversity. His theory turned the guiding assumptions of 19th century Western culture on their head, shifting their bedrock from a spiritual to a natural view. Darwin asserted that all species are subject to natural laws; just as physical scientists had established physical laws of nature, Darwin was suggesting that biological life was governed by underlying natural laws that could be investigated and discovered.

The idea challenged traditional coventions that humans are special creations of God. In effect, it introduced a new worldview into the culture, postulating that there is a pattern underlying the physical, behavioral, and mental life of living things. This led to the development of new disciplines, including anthropology. Physical anthropologists began to investigate the evidence for human evolution, analyzing fossil remains and comparing the anatomy and physiology of humans with those of other animals. Archaeologists complemented the work of physical anthropologists by unearthing and analyzing artifacts (material remains of culture) of prehistoric humans. Because Darwin's evolutionary theory relied on natural selection rather than creation by God to explain the emergence of humans, science rather than God was positioned at the helm of the Western world's philosophical ship. Theorists of social evolution applied the principles of biological evolution to social and cultural groups; they eased the transition from a model of special creation to one of natural laws, because they hypothesized that there was a progression from primitive to civilized societies, a type of social evolution that gradually separated humans from other animals and resulted in the pinnacle of civilization: Western society, characterized by a monogamous nuclear family, superiority of males over females, belief in one God, and technological sophistication.

The initial anthropological framework for interpreting sexual behavior and customs was derived from the more general culture of the late 19th century: an emphasis on science and naturalistic explanations, evolutionary theory, ideas that would maintain social order in the face of a changed worldview, and explanation for diversity. The core tenets of anthropology fit in with that culture, as did anthropological approaches to sex.

Early anthropologists interpreted sex in evolutionary terms, primarily as a way to distinguish primitive from civilized societies. If humans were subject to natural laws, like other animals, it was more comforting to assume that some humans were less connected to animals than others. Social evolution provided a convenient buffer zone for "civilized" humans. Nineteenth-century theorists like Morgan used sexual behavior to define different stages of social evolution. Documented variations in customs in different societies could be incorporated into this view; societies with fewer restraints on sexual behavior were more primitive, closer to other animals, while those with more restraints and containment of sexuality in a monogamous marriage and family context were more civilized. The study of primitive societies gave clues to the origins of, and to the earlier forms of, human society. In a sense, these theories provided new creation myths based on natural social processes. Degree of control of sexuality was an essential aspect of these theories and overshadowed the study of sexual behavior itself.

A search for the origins of Western institutions, thought to be the height of civilized human existence, guided the theory and research at the time. Tylor's classic 1889 article "On a Method of Investigating the Development of Institutions" sought to explain the shift from matrilineality to patrilineality. Westermark's *History of Human Marriage* (1891) delved into the origins of human marriage by looking at the behavior of "lower" animals and "primitive" peoples, documenting how marriage evolved into the human family. Unwin's 1934 cross-cultural study, *Sex and Culture*, suggested that limitations on opportunities to gratify sexual desires are accompanied by a rise in "cultural condition." The emphasis on the institutional containment and regulation of sexuality has persisted in anthropology.

A general cultural commitment to maintaining order in the face of social and cultural changes encouraged a reinforcement of stable sex roles and a denial of sexual variations that could disrupt the social order. Darwin's theory of evolution supported current sexual biases by focusing on sexual selection as a process in which males actively competed for and initiated sex with females, who passively responded to advances. As a natural order replaced a spiritual one, it was women's place to remain subservient to men; reproductive functions sapped women of intellectual parity with men. Nevertheless, Birkin points out in *Consuming Desire* (1988) that Darwin may have been the first sexologist, because he did acknowledge the importance of female desire and choice, especially in shaping male secondary sexual characteristics (e.g., larger size, body hair, musculature); however, Tanner notes in her book *On Becoming Human* (1981) that when Darwin applied this principle to humans "male choice is now assumed, and it is female beauty that is seen as attracting the male" because, according to Darwin, "man is more powerful in body and mind than woman." Furthermore, although the middle-class, public version of sexual decorum was sexual restraint, the private world of sexual behavior teemed with prostitution, homosexuality, and nonmarital sex. In other words, the cultural proscriptions and the social behavior were at odds with each other. Why, then, was there such an effort to suppress acknowledgment of nonreproductive sexual behavior?

Denial of nonreproductive sex was consistent with the Christian tradition that was part of the social fabric of Europe and the United States. An ideal of sex within a context of heterosexual, monogamous marriage, bound by rules against premarital and extramarital sex, prevailed. To acknowledge some of these spiritual views would soften the transition to a more natural way of looking at the world. An emphasis on the danger and fear of sex has lingered, not only in anthropology but also in the educational system. Foucault's *The History of Sexuality* suggests that the avoidance of discourse about sex invested it with power over the imagination. In addition, fear and danger of sex could derive from its apparent ability to burst the confines of institutions, in a primal show of strength, and thus challenge the stability and order that theorists of the time were striving so valiantly to compose.

Finally, an emphasis on scientific investigation diverted direct attention from the erotic. Guided by principles of observation and objectivity, scientifically committed anthropologists would find it difficult to study what Western societies regarded as a private, subjective realm.

In sum, there is a clear relationship between the culture of the 19th century and the anthropological paradigm that has guided sex research. Concepts of culture, holism, and variety recur. Culture could explain varieties of belief and behavior, whether incorporated into an evolutionary theory or not. Holism could address concerns about the link among biological, social, cultural, and psychological aspects of human existence. Together, culture and holism could suggest an orderly way to interpret different kinds of variety. Sex was embedded in this theoretical context, transformed from sexual acts, desires, and attitudes into respectable theories, rules, and institutions.

Methods, Findings, and Interpretations

According to Pelto and Pelto's *Anthropological Research* (1978), methodology is "the structure of procedures and transformational rules whereby the scientist shifts information up and down the ladder of abstraction in order to produce and organize increased knowledge." In other words, methodology defines the steps between the "real world" and general theory; the rules, procedures, and models provide a firm basis for believing that conclusions are sound. Methods derive from beliefs (i.e., cultural factors) about adequate evidence for thinking that something is true. This means that culture not only affects the paradigms of so-called objective scientists but also influences the type of methodology that is used to implement the goals of the discipline. In sociocultural anthropology, the central concepts of the discipline have guided the types of methods that anthropologists have used to acquire knowledge. The advantages and constraints of these methods affect the kinds of information that anthropologists acquire for analysis. they have particularly affected whether and how anthropologists have gathered information on human sexuality.

The foundation of anthropological methodology was formed with its central concepts, culture and holism, and designed to explain the focus of anthropological research, an explanation for variety, whether it is physical, social, cultural, or psychological. One major method overshadows all others in cultural anthropology—participant observation. Important, but given much less attention in the discipline, is the cross-cultural method. The following discussion considers each of these methods, their application to research on human sexuality, and the types of analyses based on them.

Participant Observation: Method

Cultural anthropologists strive to understand shared meanings as they relate to physical events, individuals, and groups. Therefore, they enter the "field" (i.e., the social context or site of research) for a specific purpose—to observe, document, describe, and interpret the culture of the people in the field. Individual anthropologists endure physical hardship, psychological disorientation, and cognitive challenges in their attempts to glean meaning out of their new context, just as people in the 19th century tried to construct meaning in the face of social and cultural changes. Anthropologists in the field become explorers of shared meanings, as well as social and cultural detectives who articulate and construct the worldview and social organization of a group. Usually, the results of this method appear as an ethnography (i.e., a specific description of a culture and its social organization) or as a study emphasizing a particular aspect of a group's existence. The primary task of the anthropologist is to be a participant observer—to straddle the line between objectivity and subjectivity by becoming involved enough to be a participant in the group yet distant and objective enough to describe the ideas and behaviors of the group. Consequently, anthropologists try to enter the field without many preconceived ideas of what they will find so that they will be open to the new beliefs and behaviors that they want to describe and interpret. The seeming lack of guidelines for a field experience is a deliberate attempt to counter bias and explore meaning.

The tenets of participant observation limit the investigation of sex even further. Canons of science encourage observation and objective description, but much of sexual behavior is private and not easily observed. Therefore, the anthropologist is likely to focus on more observable manifestations of sexual behaviors and attitudes, in economic life (e.g., the division of labor), in religion (e.g., rituals, gods and goddesses), in marriage and the family, in kinship categories, and in public sex roles. In addition, obtaining information about sex could require more time in the field to secure the trust of those providing such information. Also, the values of the anthropologist could deter him or her from obtaining information by engaging in sex with the people being studied. To have sex with an informant could be immoral and bias interpretations according to subjective experience. Finally, the gender of the anthropologist could affect the domains of experience in which she or he could participate. For example, men rarely observe childbirth, and women are not privy to aspects of men's initiation ceremonies. Therefore, beyond the constraints of the method, the field context could significantly limit the exploration of sexuality. The physical anthropologists Jane Goodall and Dian Fossey conducted research in a different kind of field: the primate habitat of chimpanzees and gorillas, respectively. Their research examines the similarities and differences between some of our closest primate relatives and human beings. Sexual behavior and a range of social interaction are more readily observed in this context than among humans.

Holism is another anthropological theme that has affected methodology. First, its influence emerges in the types of groups that anthropologists study. Usually, anthropologists study small communities or segments of larger societies so they can analyze the role that culture plays in the entire social context. This is advantageous in studying sexuality, because it enables the anthropologist to investigate nuances of meaning that a large-scale study would not permit. It also accentuates the diversity of contexts within which sexuality functions. Second, holism means that anthropologists are supposed to balance their descriptions of cultures by including a variety of information. Consequently, descriptions of sexual behavior and customs are likely to be integrated into an overall characterization of culture and not given central attention. However, they are likely to reveal connections to other aspects of social life that more specialized investigations are not likely to uncover.

Participant Observation:
Findings and Interpretations

Detailed descriptions of one or a few cultures and their social organization provide valuable information on the ways that sex is integrated into the culture and society. They also establish the variety of behaviors, customs, and nuances of meaning associated with sex. Finally, they allow anthropologists to prove in detail the ways in which order is established within one context. The interpretations and uses of this information vary according to the scope of the investigation, the goals of the researcher, and the reception of others.

Detailed Ethnographies and Case Studies. Malinowski, the father of fieldwork, established the tone for later studies in the field. He advocated meticulous investigation of the culture and the social organization, particularly how each aspect contributed to the functioning of the group. He viewed sex as more than a physical connection between bodies; it is a "sociological and cultural force" that cannot be studied apart from its cultural context. Beyond description, Malinowski had a theoretical agenda to confirm, that is, that culture and social organization function to fulfill human needs. Despite its sensational title, *The Sexual Life of Savages* (1929) deals more with institutions like marriage and the family than with descriptions of sexual behavior, all of which are interpreted as contributing to the coherence of the group's functioning.

Gregor's *Anxious Pleasures* (1985) is another illustration of the fruits of participant observation. Gregor did not intend to focus on sexuality when he went to Brazil to study the Mehinaku. However, his openness to meaning in the culture gave him no choice but to study sexuality, because it was "an organizing metaphor" for their lives; to describe their sexuality was to describe their culture. Suggs had a similar experience when he described the degree of sexual freedom and variety among the Marquesans in *Marquesan Sexual Behavior* (1966).

Some anthropologists provide insight into a culture by focusing on the life of an individual. Shostake does this in *Nisa* (1981), the biography of a !Kung Bushman woman whose life is enriched and exciting as she shifts from one man—husband or lover—to another just as other !Kung enjoy sex throughout the life cycle.

Other anthropologists focus their field research on a specific type of behavior or cultural category that they want to understand. For example, Mead focused on the nature of adolescence in *Coming of Age in Samoa* (1928). Spiro concentrated on the way culture modifies biology through acculturation in his monographs on the Israeli kibbutz—for example, *Children of the Kibbutz* (1958) and *Gender and Culture* (1979). Herdt studied why Sambian culture in highland New Guinea seems to encourage homosexual behavior before marriage in *Guardians of the Flutes* (1981) and continued his inquiry by focusing on the development of masculinity in *Rituals of Manhood* (1982); *The Sambia: Ritual and Gender in New Guinea* (1987) contextualizes the descriptions of the previous studies. Martin probes the symbolic significance of reproduction in *The Woman in the Body* (1987). Bolin studies the transition of transsexual males into women in *In Search of Eve* (1987). In *The Zuni Man-Woman* (1991) Roscoe explores the meaning of gender categories, as does Nanda's study of the hijras of India, *Neither Man Nor Woman* (1990). The linguist Tannen investigates the communication styles of men and women in U.S. society as part of their gendered subcultures in *You Just Don't Understand* (1990).

Comparative Studies. Some anthropologists conduct field research or use the case studies and ethnographies of others to establish the variety of customs, categories, and beliefs that relate to a specific domain of culture. Comparison with other groups is informal. For example, Mead compared sex roles among three New Guinea groups (Arapesh, Mundugumor, Tchambuli) in *Sex and Temperament in Three Primitive Societies* (1963) to demonstrate that sex roles and attitudes are not inborn but are a product of learning. In *Women and Men* (1975) Friedl explores how technological levels of society constrain sex roles. Marshall and Suggs's edited volume of case studies, *Human Sexual Behavior* (1971), is intended to derive comparative similarities and differences and then develop generalizations about influences on sexual behavior.

Often, collections and monographs concentrate on comparing cultures in terms of specific topics. For example, Gilmore's *Manhood in the Making* (1990) concentrates on cultural concepts of masculinity worldwide; Williams investigates the berdache and similar phenomena in *The Spirit and the Flesh* (1986); Kerns and Brown's edited volume, *In Her Prime* (1992), deals with women in midlife; and Buckley and Gottlieb's edited work, *Blood Magic* (1988) explores the meaning of menstruation. Feldman's edited book, *Culture and AIDS* (1990) as well as Herdt and Lindenbaum's *The Time of AIDS* (1992) emphasizes the relevance of culture to understanding AIDS (acquired immune deficiency syndrome). All these works illustrate the variety of meanings that apply to different aspects of sexuality.

Some anthropologists use fieldwork and ethnographic data to establish consistency of meaning across cultures rather than to illustrate variety. For example, the physical anthropologist Symons draws on primate and comparative data in *The Evolution of Human Sexuality* (1979) to confirm his hypothesis that natural selection has produced marked sex differences in sexuality, extending to behavior, attitudes, and feelings. He thinks that selective pressures have produced consistent human patterns (e.g., male sexual jealousy, intense intrasexual competition among males, males' desire for a variety of sexual partners, females' tendency to be more conservative and selective about sexual partners). In contrast, the physical anthropologist Hrdy draws on her field data and other primate studies in *The Woman That Never Evolved* (1981) to demonstrate that sexually passive, noncompetitive, all-nurturing females are not a part of our primate heritage; competitive, sexually assertive, independent females were probably the norm. Fisher's *The Sex Contract* (1983) focuses on the evolutionary basis for male-female bonding, and cultural anthropologist Fox's *The Red Lamp of Incest* (1980) explains the widespread occurrence of the incest taboo as a human adaptation. All these studies address the link between biology and culture, primarily within a framework of sociobiology, where selective pressures guide the development of specific sexual behavior (e.g., mating patterns) as well as cultural and social forms (e.g., marriage, divorce, incest taboos). These perspectives are sometimes referred to as "essentialist" because they posit invariant aspects of human sexual behavior, attitudes, and feelings.

Cases as Examples. Ethnographic data often become part of a catalog of information on human sexuality, designed to illustrate its malleability and variety. Mantegazza's early *Anthropological Studies on Sexual Relations of Mankind* (1932), as well as Gregersen's more recent *Sexual Practices* (1983), illustrate this approach.

Cross-Cultural Research: Method

Ethnographies and case studies are extremely valuable bases for establishing the way in which culture is patterned and organized in a specific society, for highlighting the intricacies of meaning that culture entails, and for establishing the variety of sexual beliefs and behavior. However, they are not sufficient by themselves to generate valid generalizations about sexual behavior. They may be suggestive and compelling cases but are indicative rather than conclusive statements about general trends in human sexuality. A less popular but relevant method for dealing with patterns of human sexuality is the cross-cultural method. Ideally, it complements participant observation by using ethnographic data to establish which behavior and ideas are specific to a cultural context and which span across cultural contexts. However, anthropologists who have participated in fieldwork often argue that the cross-cultural method strips behavior and ideas of their meaning, while those who use the cross-cultural method say that case studies are not a sound basis for generalization about social and cultural life.

The cross-cultural method began with Tylor's classic article, "On a Method of Investigating the Development of Institutions" (1889) in which he classified, tabulated, and statistically analyzed data on 300–400 peoples to test his hypothesis about the development of marriage and rules of descent; Murdock's *Social Structure* (1949) was a major articulation of the main principles of the method and its usefulness in testing hypotheses about culture and social organization, particu-

larly as they apply to the link between marriage, family, and sexual behavior. The elements of the method included (1) a classification of information to be compared, (2) a sample of societies, and (3) a statistical analysis. By examining variables in different combinations in a large and representative sample of societies drawn from different historical periods and geographical regions, cross-culturalists try to determine whether patterns of ideas and behavior can be substantiated statistically.

The steps of the method reveal important dimensions of the meaning of cultural categories and the aspects of human sexuality that have been investigated on a large scale. First, comparative categories have to be defined. This means that concepts often taken for granted by the investigator have to be articulated and defined in such a way that they can be identified in a wide range of contexts. For example, marriage does not always include a ceremony, a change in residence, or rights to children born of the union. Frayser found that a useful definition of marriage was a relationship in which having children is approved and encouraged; other attributes of marriage had to be investigated, not assumed. In this sense, this method is a corrective to investigators' ethnocentrism; cross-culturalists confront their biases with a range of cultures, while fieldworkers confront it in their personal experience with one culture. Second, the researcher selects a sample of societies worldwide (at least 30) from which to obtain information. This ensures that different types of cultures are examined. Finally, appropriate statistical analyses are used to establish confidence in the patterns elucidated by this method. Trying to factor out what is consistent or variable across groups provides information about the dimensions of meaning attributed to a concept. Systematic cross-cultural research also has the benefit of identifying areas of human sexuality that have been neglected by field researchers—and many have, including homosexuality, forms of sexual stimulation, kinds of sexual interaction, the meaning of erotica, and interpretations of the body. Many of these gaps in the literature can be explained by the sexual paradigm of anthropologists that derives from a Western tradition steeped in beliefs about the fear and danger of sex.

Cross-Cultural Research:
Findings and Interpretations

Overviews. Unwin's *Sex and Culture* (1934) looked for grand patterns of sexual behavior in "uncivilized" cultures, while Murdock's *Social Structure* (1949) examined sexual behavior in relation to the development of patterns of descent, marriage, and the family. Ford and Beach's *Patterns of Sexual Behavior* (1951) combines a cross-cultural perspective with findings in biology to establish varieties of sexual life worldwide; the variables examined include sexual technique, homosexuality, and sexual partnerships. Frayser's *Varieties of Sexual Experience* (1985) goes beyond a description of sexual patterns to establish a model of human sexuality as a system in and of itself, related to but not incorporated by institutions like marriage, the family, and the economy. She establishes patterns of beliefs and behaviors that cluster together and apply across a range of societies, attempting to explain how social and cultural aspects of reproductive and nonreproductive sexuality relate to each other and to biological aspects. Naroll's *The Moral Order* (1983) summarizes findings from a variety of cross-cultural studies on sexual behavior, the family, and child abuse. *Specialized Topics.* Most cross-cultural studies of human sexuality are much less inclusive than the ones previously mentioned and concentrate on specific topics. For example, Schlegel looks at the configuration of power and authority between men and women in *Male Dominance and Female Autonomy* (1972), and Sanday examines the fundamental question of why cultures select different styles of interaction between the sexes in *Female Power and Male Dominance* (1981). In *Female of the Species* (1975), Martin and Voorhies use cross-cultural data to demonstrate the ways in which sex differences relate to subsistence type and to illustrate that culture rather than biology is a more crucial determinant of sexual differentiation. Schlegel and Barry's *Adolescence* (1991) studies variations and consistencies in adolescence as a socially demarcated stage of life. Frayser and Whitby's *Studies in Human Sexuality* (1985) provides informative abstracts of monographs in a variety of fields that indicate the ways in which the concept of culture has been influential in the study of sexuality.

Contemporary Perspectives and Concerns About Anthropology, Sex, and Culture

The original themes that guided anthropological research on human sexuality have not changed. Holism, the use of the concept of culture to establish the meaning of unfamiliar customs and beliefs, and an emphasis on documenting and explaining diversity are still with us. However, the conceptualization of human sexuality has changed over the last 100 years as the life, social, and behavioral sciences have contributed more research and data on the topic. Human sexuality does not refer to anatomy and physiology but to a complex whole of psychological, social, cultural, and biological attributes. Reproductive and nonreproductive aspects of sexuality are being studied as well as the way in which scientists have conceptualized sexual categories and behavior. Therefore, contemporary anthropological research on human sexuality is marked by a great deal of reflection and analysis focused on some familiar themes: (1) the impact of the biology of sex on the social, cultural, and psychological aspects of sex; (2) the social construction of concepts relating to sexuality, particularly ideas about gender, and the methods used to explore them, especially scientific ones; and (3) the meaning of consistent patterns of sexual behavior and beliefs worldwide (i.e., how to reconcile general trends with particular cultural contexts).

Feminist and gay anthropologists have been particularly productive and creative in their approaches to sexuality. For example, since the mid-1970s feminist anthropologists have examined the construction of sexuality itself, but have differed in what they think is constructed (e.g., acts identity, object choice, community). Rosaldo and Lamphere's *Woman, Culture, and Society* (1974); Ortner and Whitehead's *Sexual Meanings* (1981); Snitow, Stansell, and Thompson's *Powers of Desire* (1983); Vance's *Pleasure and Danger* (1984); and Ginsburg and Tsing's *Uncertain Terms* (1990) are notable collections of feminist discussions of sexuality as a social construction. Herdt and Stoller's *Intimate Communications* (1990) suggests a new method, clinical ethnography, as a way to study erotic aspects of life, and Bolton has recommended new uses of semantic-domain analysis and participant observation in the study of gay sexuality.

Nevertheless, as Vance says in her recent article "Anthropology Rediscovers Sexuality: A Theoretical Comment," "Anthropology as a field has been far from courageous or even adequate in its investigation of sexuality." The discipline still bears the burden of Western culture's ambivalence about sex and "appears to share the prevailing cultural view that sexuality is not an entirely legitimate area of study." Until this ambivalence is resolved on a wider level, anthropologists who study human sexuality will remain on the margins of the discipline.

REFERENCES

Birkin, L. *Consuming Desire: Sexual Science and the Emergence of a Culture of Abundance, 1871–1914.* Ithaca, N.Y.: Cornell Univ. Press, 1988.

Bolin, A. *In Search of Eve: Transsexual Rites of Passage.* South Hadley, Mass.: Bergin & Garvey, 1987.

Buckley, R., and A. Gottlieb, eds. *Blood Magic: An Anthropology of Menstruation*. Berkeley: Univ. of California Press, 1988.

Darwin, C. *On the Origin of Species by Means of Natural Selection, or, The Preservation of Favoured Races in the Struggle for Life*. London: Watts, 1859.

Feldman, D.A., ed. *Culture and AIDS*. New York: Praeger, 1990.

Fisher, H.E. *The Sex Contract: The Evolution of Human Behavior*. New York: Quill, 1983.

Ford, C.S., and F.A. Beach. *Patterns of Sexual Behavior*. New York: Harper & Row, 1951.

Foucault, M. *The History of Sexuality*. Vol. 1, *An Introduction*. New York: Vintage, 1990.

Fox, R. *The Red Lamp of Incest*. New York: Dutton, 1980.

Frayser, S.G. *Varieties of Sexual Experience: An Anthropological Perspective on Human Sexuality*. New Haven, Conn.: Human Relations Area Files Press, 1985.

Freidl, E. *Women and Men: An Anthropologist's View*. New York: Holt, Rinehart & Winston, 1975.

Gilmore, D.D. *Manhood in the Making: Cultural Concepts of Masculinity*. New Haven, Conn.: Yale Univ. Press, 1990.

Ginsberg, F., and A.L. Tsing, eds. *Uncertain Terms: Negotiating Gender in American Culture*. Boston: Beacon Press, 1990.

Gregersen, E. *Sexual Practices: The Story of Human Sexuality*. New York: Franklin Watts, 1983.

Gregor, T. *Anxious Pleasures: The Sexual Lives of an Amazonian People*. Chicago: Univ. of Chicago Press, 1985.

Herdt, G. *Guardians of the Flutes: Idioms of Masculinity*. New York: McGraw-Hill, 1981.

———. *The Sambia: Ritual and Gender in New Guinea*. New York: Holt, Rinehart & Winston, 1987.

———, ed. *Rituals of Manhood: Male Initiation in Papua, New Guinea*. Berkeley: Univ. of California Press, 1982.

Herdt, G., and S. Lindenbaum. *The Time of AIDS: Social Analysis, Theory, and Method*. Newbury Park, Calif.: Sage, 1992.

Hrdy, S.B. *The Woman That Never Evolved*. Cambridge, Mass.: Harvard Univ. Press, 1981.

Kerns, V., and J.K. Brown. *In Her Prime: New Views of Middle-Aged Women*. Urbana: Univ. of Illinois Press, 1992.

Kroeber, A.L., and C. Kluckhohn. *Culture: A Critical Review of Concepts and Definitions*. New York: Vintage, 1953.

Kuhn, T.S. *The Structure of Scientific Revolutions*. Chicago: Univ. of Chicago Press, 1962.

Malinowski, B. *The Sexual Life of Savages of North-Western Melanesia: An Ethnographic Account of Courtship, Marriage, and Family Life Among the Natives of the Trobriand Islands, British New Guinea*. London: Routledge & Sons, 1929.

Mantegazza, P. *Anthropological Studies of Sexual Relations of Mankind*. New York: Anthropological Press, 1932.

Marshall, D.S., and R.C. Suggs, eds. *Human Sexual Behavior: Variations in the Ethnographic Spectrum*. Englewood Cliffs, N.J.: Prentice-Hall, 1971.

Martin, M.K., and B. Voorhies. *Female of the Species*. New York: Columbia Univ. Press, 1975.

Mead, M. *Coming of Age in Samoa*. New York: William Morrow, 1928.

———. *Sex and Temperament in Three Primitive Societies*. New York: William Morrow, 1963.

Morgan, L.H. *Ancient Society*. 1877. Reprint. Cambridge, Mass.: Belknap, 1964.

Murdock, G.P. *Social Structure*. New York: Macmillan, 1949.

Nanda, S. *Neither Man Nor Woman: The Hijras of India*. Belmont, Calif.: Wadsworth, 1990.

Naroll, R. *The Moral Order: An Introduction to the Human Situation*. Beverly Hills, Calif.: Sage, 1983.

Ortner, S.B., and H. Whitehead. *Sexual Meanings: The Cultural Construction of Gender and Sexuality*. Cambridge: Cambridge Univ. Press, 1981.

Rosaldo, M.Z., and L. Lamphere, eds. *Woman, Culture and Society*. Stanford, Calif.: Stanford Univ. Press, 1974.

Roscoe, W. *The Zuni Man-Woman*. Albuquerque: Univ. of New Mexico Press, 1991.

Sanday, P.R. *Female Power and Male Dominance: On the Origins of Sexual Inequality*. Cambridge: Cambridge Univ. Press, 1981.

Schlegel, A. *Male Dominance and Female Autonomy: Domestic Authority in Matrilineal Societies*. New Haven, Conn.: Human Relations Area Files Press, 1972.

Shostake, M. *Nisa: The Life and Words of a !Kung Woman*. Cambridge, Mass.: Harvard Univ. Press, 1981.

Snitow, A., C. Stansell, and S. Thompson, eds. *Powers of Desire: The Politics of Sexuality*. New York: Monthly Review, 1983.

Spiro, M.E. *Children of the Kibbutz*. Cambridge, Mass.: Harvard Univ. Press, 1958.

———. *Gender and Culture: Kibbutz Women Revisited*. Durham, N.C.: Duke Univ. Press, 1979.

Suggs, R.C. *Marquesan Sexual Behavior*. New York: Harcourt, Brace & World, 1966.

Symons, D. *The Evolution of Human Sexuality*. New York: Oxford Univ. Press, 1979.

Tannen, D. *You Just Don't Understand: Women and Men in Conversation*. New York: William Morrow, 1990.

Tanner, N.M. *On Becoming Human*. Cambridge: Cambridge Univ. Press, 1981.

Tylor, E.B. On a Method of Investigating the Development of Institutions: Applied to Laws of Marriage and Descent. *Journal of the Royal Anthropological Institute*, Vol. 18 (1989), pp. 245–69.

———. *Primitive Culture*. Boston: 1871.

Unwin, J.D. *Sex and Culture*. London: Oxford Univ. Press, 1934.

Vance, C. Anthropology Rediscovers Sexuality: A Theoretical Comment. *Social Science and Medicine*, Vol. 33 (1991), pp. 875–884.

Vance, C.S., ed. *Pleasure and Danger: Exploring Female Sexuality.* Boston: Routledge & Kegan Paul, 1984.

Westermark, E. *History of Human Marriage.* New York: Macmillan, 1981.

Williams, W. *The Spirit and the Flesh: Sexual Diversity in American Indian Culture.* Boston: Beacon Press, 1986.

Suzanne G. Frayser

APHRODISIACS AND ANAPHRODISIACS

Aphrodisiacs

The word "aphrodisiac" derives from "Aphrodite," the name of the mythical Greek goddess of love and beauty. The Greeks considered her the personification of the sexual urge. The definition, and therefore the scope, of the word aphrodisiac varies among authors. In a limited sense, an aphrodisiac is a substance that either produces penile erections or, without other sexual stimulation, increases sexual desire. This definition differs from more expansive concepts of the word both in what is considered to cause the desired effect and in the effects desired. In its broadest sense, aphrodisiacs may be divided into two main categories:

1. Aphrodisiacs that are thought to have primarily a direct biochemical effect. This includes material that is ingested (e.g., certain foods, drugs, medicines, fluids), injected or inhaled into the body (e.g., certain drugs, fragrances, medicines), or applied onto a surface of the body (e.g., certain ointments, lotions).
2. Aphrodisiacs that are thought to have primarily a psychophysiological effect. This includes material that is seen or heard (e.g., erotic art, erotic dance, certain emotional music) or stimuli that are otherwise experienced (e.g., certain moving religious experiences, erotic fantasies, magic practices, high-risk adventures).

Under the broad definition of an aphrodisiac, the desired or supposed effect may arouse sexual feelings by stimulating genitals, increase sexual awareness, relax inhibitions, augment physical energy, strengthen the gonads or other glands involved with sexual activity, improve sexual health, increase the production of semen, overcome or delay sexual exhaustion, prevent premature ejaculation, prolong sexual life, recapture lost virility, reduce ejaculatory failure, increase pleasure during sexual activities, enhance sexual attractiveness, produce orgasms, or attain sexual mastery over someone.

Throughout recorded human history people at various times and in various cultures have used a wide variety of things to attempt to enhance aspects of their own sexual vigor or sexual desire or sexual desirability, or to enhance one or more of those factors in a desired other person. Early on, people became acutely aware of the importance of the continual renewal of the life forces they depended on: their crop and game food, the seasons, and their family, tribe, and eventually, their larger community. Failure to continually renew any of these threatened disaster to the individual and to the larger group. It was only natural for ancient peoples to seek some means of gaining some control over the inevitable renewal failures that could and did occur in all of those life forms.

Having little or no understanding of the actual physical and biological mechanisms involved in replenishing life forms, individuals and groups developed systems of belief about what was going on and why. And they began developing beliefs about what they could do to ensure their continued sexual successes and reproductive functioning. Early in human history, people who felt the need for such help sought the assistance of what they perceived to be superior powers: they worshiped naturalistic gods, invoked magic, and experimented with natural substances.

Stretching over such a long time and involving such diverse cultures, the list of items that have been tried and promoted as aphrodisiacs is immense. They range from the simple and the innocuous to the odious, the esoteric, and the harmful.

Among the earliest known aphrodisiacs were certain edible foods thought to resemble human sex organs (e.g., clams, oysters, cucumbers, asparagus, bananas, rhinoceros horns). Ingesting these foods, a practice that has not entirely abated even today, was based on the belief that God put a mark on all food to indicate its purpose. It was thought that the appearance, color, shape, or smell of a plant or other substance indicated its link to, and usefulness regarding, a particular ailment or body part. The logic being, why else are they thus? A 16th-century scholar dubbed that concept the "Doctrine of Signatures."

When families and clans evolved into larger groups, the interest of group survival became so important that something so vital as the reproductive success of the group could no longer be left to the inconsistent intellectual abilities of its individual members. Also, as is true even today, the power of knowledge and of control over the sexual and reproductive functions of a group directly translates into social and political power.

Control of that power became important to group leaders.

Those are some reasons why, as established groups grew and evolved into civilizations, the accumulated group knowledge of aphrodisiac "cures" and "remedies" devolved to and became part of the province of the members of the priesthoods that had also developed by then. With that transition came more complex "recipes." Magic (or "divine" intervention) often became important in many aphrodisiac mixtures, both in their preparation and in their administration. Often the rules governing the preparation of the concoctions were a study in complexity steeped in mysticism. For example, one potion consisted of a compound of the brains of a cat and of a lizard, the menstrual blood of a whore, human semen, the womb of a bitch in heat that had been denied the companionship of dogs, the entrails of a hyena, and the left skull bone of a toad.

A concept that appealed to ancient minds, as it still does to some modern minds, is the idea that there is curative, generative, or strengthening power in the genitals of animals. Two other themes that appear throughout much of the recorded history of aphrodisiacs are the persistent use of the waste products and the blood and semen of both humans and animals. The writings of Paulinus, which were popular during medieval times, are useful examples of these customs. They recognized the supposed efficacy of various animal genitals (e.g., testes of the hare and of the stag, and the donkey penis), of various animal waste products (e.g., bull urine, poultry excrement, vaginal discharges from sows), and of sparrow blood and the semen of various animals.

Many concoctions have been designed to be applied to the surface of the sexual organs. Through supposed magical powers, through chemical action, or through both, the potions applied were thought to increase the recipient's sexual desire or sexual organ functioning, or cause a desired increase in fecundity or other sexual power. The chemical action of some of the compounds causes irritation and increased blood flow to the application area, and some cause mild or serious injuries.

All forms of nourishing and not-so-nourishing foods have been recommended at times as aids to sexual vigor and interest. Long before the chemistry of food and the nutritional needs of humans were understood, it took only simple observational skills to recognize that the intake of certain foods would normally give one an energy boost and enhance one's overall sense of well-being, especially for someone whose regular nutritional intake was poor. It is therefore not surprising that two of the most common foods used for their perceived aphrodisiac effects are honey and milk.

The early authorities who extolled the aphrodisiac virtues of what are known today to be nourishing foods of various kinds were recognizing the health-enhancing benefits of adequate nutrition. In the process, at one time or another, items purported to have aphrodisiac qualities include many, if not most, of the known fruits, grains, vegetables, meats, edible herbs, and nutritional fluids.

In public libraries today one can find books on how to grow a whole garden of purported aphrodisiac herbs or aphrodisiac vegetables. Books also exist that describe how to cook meals said to turn on or turn up the libido, or to strengthen one's sexual capacities.

One striking fact emerging from the literature on aphrodisiacs is the dearth of reported studies on proclaimed aphrodisiacs that have used accepted scientific methodology. Hence, the efficacy of all but a very few purported aphrodisiacs is obscured in a cloud of unproven legends, magic rituals, folktales, and individual anecdotes; a placebo effect being apparent in some of them.

A person's response to an experience—such as an intake of food or a drug, or an emotional event—may be affected by many things. These include the individual's expectations; the accompanying environment; the strength, amount, and duration of the substance or event; one's preexisting conditions; and the interaction of other substances or events that are being or have been experienced. The methodology used by the researcher to measure and evaluate results may also affect the validity of conclusions. Seldom have all of these been adequately controlled in studies of a supposed aphrodisiac.

Recent reports in scientific literature concerning some substances indicate that they appeared to have an aphrodisiac effect in some individuals. Libido has been reportedly augmented by oral administration of L-dopa, of nomifensine, of chlomipramine, and of a compound made from extracts of avena sativa (oats) and urtica (nettles), and by intracerebral injection of acetylcholine. Fenfluramine (used to treat bulimia) and trazodone (used as an antidepressant) have reportedly caused an increased libido effect in some females. Three aliphatic nitrites—amyl, butyl, and isobutyl—have been shown to subjectively increase the pleasure of orgasm and to enhance sexual performance in some persons who inhale the substance during sexual activity.

Some reports hold that the intake of cocaine acts as an aphrodisiac in some cases, but that too appears to be dose-related and individual specific.

It is now well established that some compounds when injected into the penis will in all but rare cases cause an erection. Such substances include papaverine (sometimes combined with phentolamine) and prostaglandin E 1.

The U.S. Food and Drug Administration (FDA) issued a ruling in 1989 stating that any aphrodisiac drug product for over-the-counter human use is not generally recognized as safe and effective and is misbranded. The FDA warned of the serious health risks of some alleged aphrodisiacs, such as cantharides (Spanish fly), and ruled that the safety and effectiveness of ginseng, golden seal, gotu kola, nux vomica, Pega Palo, yohimbine, and strychnine as aphrodisiacs are unproven. The FDA stated: "Individuals suffering from decreased libido and impaired sexual performance should seek professional medical care or counseling."

Anaphrodisiac

Broadly defined an anaphrodisiac is any substance or experience that decreases sexual desire, sexual desirability, general sexual health, or sexual functioning. More narrowly defined, the word means any substance that decreases sexual desire or sexual functioning. Other terms sometimes used are antaphrodisiac, antiaphrodisiac, and refrigerant (Roman).

As they did with aphrodisiacs, the ancients also had a cornucopia of anaphrodisiacs. People have used as anaphrodisiacs a multiplicity of foods, plants, secretions and parts of humans and animals, chemical compounds, and magic. Ranging from the benign (e.g., cold baths) to the unpleasant (e.g., a drink made from pounded willow leaves) to the harmful (e.g., hemlock tea), many of the old remedies no doubt reduced sexual ardor by making the recipient uncomfortable, ill, or worse.

Ethyl alcohol has long been recognized as sometimes being a disinhibiting aphrodisiac when consumed in small doses but producing many anaphrodisiac effects when consumed in increasing volume.

In modern times, chemists have devised many compounds for humans to consume in their search for better health or recreation or mental escape. Some seem to have an anaphrodisiac effect, if only in certain doses or in certain people.

Amphetamines are drugs used for a variety of purposes, including mood elevation, depression control, alertness, and appetite suppression. Dose-related anaphrodisiac effects have been reported in some cases. There have been similar reports about other types of antidepressants (e.g., such as amitriptyline hydrochloride, imipramine, tranylcypromine, and mianserin).

Barbiturates are sedative or hypnotic drugs used to reduce tension or to induce sleep. In the few studies of their effects on sexual desire or functioning, there are some reports of an anaphrodisiac effect in some people from continued use.

Drugs used to treat various blood-related disorders, such as high blood pressure, may in some individuals cause diminished sexual functioning (e.g., reduced penile or vulval engorgement).

Medroxyprogesterone acetate (Depo-Provera) and flutamide combined with an LHRH agonist are two chemical treatments sometimes purposely administered to a male in order to alter his criminal or antisocial sexual behavior by reducing the level of his naturally produced androgen hormones or by blocking some of the effects on his body of those hormones. The results of an effective treatment may range from a general lowering of libido and no alteration of erectile ability to a near or total loss of libido and erectile ability.

REFERENCES

Sabatier, R., trans. *Magica Sexualis*. New York: Falstaff Press, 1934.

Taberner, P.V. *Aphrodisiacs: The Science and the Myth*. London: Croom Helm, 1985.

Walton, A.H. *Aphrodisiacs: From Legend to Prescription*. Westport, Conn.: Associated Booksellers, 1958.

Wedeck, H.E. *Dictionary of Aphrodisiacs*. New York: Philosophical Library, 1961.

Joan K. Dixon
Dwight Dixon

ART: PAINTING, SCULPTURE, AND OTHER VISUAL ART

It is a truism that people have always tended to humanize and sexualize their universe. Among paleolithic people, this was often done through giving sexual meaning to natural objects. An interesting example is found at Le Portel, one of a series of caves in southern France and northern Spain, where a protuberance on a cave wall is used as a phallus for a figure crudely outlined in red. There is also more deliberative art, exemplified by the so-called Paleolithic Venuses, female figurines with enormous breasts hanging heavily above a swelling belly and with enormous hips, buttocks, and thighs. One of the more famous of these figures is the Venus of Willendorf, found in Austria and dating from about 30,000 B.C.E.

As civilization developed, more sophisticated representations appeared. Egyptian tomb paintings, statues, and papyrus drawings often include scenes of sexual intercourse. Min, a god with bull-man attributes, is portrayed as clasping his phallus in various statues. The flooding of the Nile was identified with the semen of Osiris, and his phallus dominated some of the ceremonies associated with this annual event. Throughout the ancient world, amulets for love, magic, and fertility often included the cowrie shell, a vulva symbol.

In the Tigris-Euphrates valley, another center of early civilization, there are numerous terracotta reliefs depicting copulation from behind, although it often is not clear whether vaginal or anal intercourse is depicted. Surviving from ancient India are many representations of the lingam (penis) combined with the yoni (vulva), the most common being a round-topped cylinder standing in a shallow circular basin with a spout to one side. Indian temples are full of sculptures of women in a variety of sexual postures. A variety of positions of sexual intercourse are also depicted. Much of ancient Chinese art and literature is based on the coming together of the yin and the yang, the female and male principles, a union which is best achieved through sexual intercourse.

In ancient Peru, the early Mochica civilization, a predecessor to the Incas, was extremely prolific in its ceramic reproduction of sexual scenes. About 1 percent of the surviving cups and bowls are molded to form couples or individuals in various sexual poses. Aztec codices from Mexico include numerous sexual scenes. In fact, wherever one turns either in ancient civilizations or among contemporary primitives, sex seems to form a dominant feature of the art, and the miracle of procreation seems to be a dominant theme in the legends and religions of all peoples.

The theme of sex continued among the founders of Western culture, in the civilizations of Greece and Rome. Popular mythology recounting the love stories of the gods served as both erotic inspiration and symbolic representation of fertility in nature. The story of Leda and her swan lover is often portrayed in marble relief, and nude images of goddesses such as Aphrodite are common. However, the major sources of sex scenes in the Greek world are vase paintings which have survived in great quantity and include representations of almost every aspect of sexual activity from masturbation to ho-

mosexuality to bestiality. There is also widespread distribution of small, often crude erotic figurines of the gods, and many of the male gods have a massive phallus. In Rome, the cult of the phallus was part of the Roman religion, and penises are depicted literally everywhere—in floor mosaics, tombs, and amulets that have survived in great numbers. Lamps were formed in the shape of a phallus, and there were even phallic shrines. Initiation into various mystery religions involved the concept of rebirth, and various representations of female genitals were an essential part of such rituals. Often explicit sexual scenes were also part of the temple art, particularly that devoted to the god Dionysus, some of which survives in the Temple of Mysteries at Pompeii. Here the scenes vary: the god gently caresses the goddess Ariadne; a figure of a woman brandishes a whip, while another dances in the nude; they are what one author chose to label as portrayals of "sexual abandon." Also surviving from Pompeii are brothel scenes and various amulets depicting sexual intercourse in a variety of positions.

Western Christian Tradition

With the triumph of Christianity, the nature of sexual representation in art in the West changed. Whereas sexuality had played a major part in pre-Christian religions and sexuality was very much an element of the religious ceremony, sexuality tended to be something to be avoided and repressed in early Christian thinking. The nude, which had been the prime erotic figure, no longer appeared except in almost asexual representations of Jesus on the cross. When sexual and erotic art begins to appear again, it is equated more with humiliation and shame, at least on the official level. Undoubtedly, ordinary people kept alive some of the more erotic and sexual ideas, but little of this has survived. In fact, much information about sexuality known to earlier peoples seems to have been repressed or passed on only through oral rather than written traditions. Still, some sexual artifacts have survived, mainly articles of value owned by the rich. Jewelry, decorated furniture, and illustrated manuscripts with erotic scenes are examples. A set of silver plates in the Hermitage Museum, a 9th-century ivory casket from Italy in the Victoria and Albert Museum, and a 13th century gilt mirror in Frankfurt's Städelinstitut are all decorated with scenes of lovemaking. The manuscripts, usually from a later period, depict allegories such as the fountain of youth, the garden of love, and the garden of earthly delights, all themes that allowed the artist to include illustrations of sexual activity. Examples of such manuscripts are the *Douce Manuscript* in the Bodleian Library, Oxford, and the *Trés Riches Heures du Duc de Berry,* which has been reprinted in modern copies.

Since the church was the main patron of the artists, there were restrictions on what could be portrayed. Two different forms of sexual themes did appear, however, the more public one seen by all, and the more secretive or less public one known to a few. Among the more visible are the religious carvings found in the public parts of buildings, such as those surrounding doorways and facades. Many of the depictions of sexuality in these areas center around the story of Adam and Eve, the sin of unchastity, and the representation of the Last Judgment. Such portrayals are most evident in the new-style Gothic cathedrals of the 12th and later centuries.

Since the purpose of such art was to educate, inevitably it is not the sins of unchastity that are shown, for example, but the punishments that result from them—the breasts and vulva of the women being penetrated and eaten away by serpents and toads. Similarly, the Last Judgment emphasizes the sins of sexual intercourse taking place in hell, and portrayals of Adam and Eve show them covering their nudity.

There are, however, less public parts of the building, such as the rooftop gargoyles or the undersides of the seats in the choir stalls (misericord), where medieval artists could give freer expression to their erotic and scatological impulses. Among gargoyle representations that have survived are drainpipes that channel water through the anus of various figures or create the illusion that a female figure is urinating.

Many churches also include representations of what are called Shelah-na-Gig fertility figures, that is, figures of nude women exposing their vulvas. They are believed to be artifacts, or even a medieval continuation, of pre-Christian religious beliefs and were preserved as a sort of transition to the new religion of Christianity, part of a church policy not to destroy the idols of the heathen but to incorporate them into the Christian tradition. In some churches in Spain, couples are even shown engaged in intercourse.

The depictions of sexuality on the underside of the seats in churches are generally light-hearted—for example, showing dancing women whose garments are flying and exposing parts of their bodies. One favorite kind of carving is of devil figures with enlarged phalluses. Such carvings were usually seen only by the clergy, and knowledge of them was restricted.

Gradually, toward the end of the Middle Ages, the nudes became more realistic and erotic, particularly in northern Europe, where they were shown with pubic hair and, in the case of women, sometimes with a vulva as well. Some major artists, such as Hieronymus Bosch (1450–1516), Pieter Bruegel (1525–1569), and Albrecht Dürer (1471–1528), frequently used erotic themes in their drawings, woodcuts, and engravings. Particularly daring was the Swiss goldsmith Urs Graf (1485–1527/8), who is noteworthy for his lively and uninhibited drawings of prostitutes.

Climaxing this growing northern European tradition of eroticism were Lucas Cranach (1472–1553) and Hans Baldung (also called Grien; 1484–1545). Cranach's eroticism is most evident in his mythological panels of Venus, the Graces, the Judgment of Paris, and others, where his nudes are clothed in necklaces, transparent veils, and often large picture hats. Baldung, in contrast, has a penchant for the gruesome and macabre and often links sexuality and death. In his paintings, drawings and engravings, woman is the personification of lust and Death is her most frequent companion.

In Italy, the 15th and 16th centuries saw a return to the ideals of classical Greece and Rome in a period usually known as the Renaissance. Here the nude does not have the perverse element present in the north, but rather a kind of sensual eroticism. A number of Venetian painters were particularly important, including Giovanni Bellini (1430/40–1516), whose painting *The Feast of the Gods* emphasizes the increasing stress on eroticism. Two of his pupils, Giorgione (1475–1510) and Titian (1487–1576), carried on the tradition. Giorgione's *Fête Champêtre* is the prototype of the erotic pastoral idyll in European art, while his *Venus* and Titian's *Venus of Urbino* are the first in a long line of calmly erotic nudes.

In Florence, Donatello (1386–1466), the sculptor whose David is the first freestanding bronze sculpture cast since antiquity, portrays an erotic celebration of the adolescent body. Many of the Florentine artists had erotic and even pornographic themes in their work. Michelangelo (1475–1564), for example, included a man wearing a phallus on his bonnet in a drawing in the Vatican collection, and in an engraving, *The Dream of Human Life,* there is a mysterious giant hand grasping a huge phallus as well as a disembodied phallus floating in the sky. Botticelli (1445–1510) emphasized erotic nudeness in his group of the *Three Graces,* while Leonardo da Vinci (1452–1519), in a painting now lost, recreated the erotic myth of Leda and the swan, the first re-creation since antiquity. Leonardo's sketches, however, survive. Raphael (1483–1520), in *La Fornarina* portrayed his mistress with her breasts bared, marking a new type of painting, the erotic portrait. Raphael also designed the erotic frescoes of Venus and Cupid, Cupid and Psyche, and Vulcan and Pallas for the bathroom of Cardinal Bibbiena in the Vatican, although the actual painting was done by Raphael's pupils. Few, however, have seen the paintings, since permission, until recently, was rarely given, and some of the frescoes were later whitewashed.

This new sensuality did not go unchallenged. One result of the new morality associated with the Protestant and Catholic reformations was the so-called breeches makers, individuals who put clothing or fig leaves on nude representations in public places. When pants seemed unsuitable, fig leaves were painted on or attached to sculptures, and in Spain the nude itself was more or less perpetually banned. Even Michelangelo's frescoes on the ceiling of the Sistine Chapel were called obscene; Pope Paul IV, in 1555, was so concerned about this accusation that he ordered them removed from the chapel, an action which would in effect have meant destroying them. When his decision became public, such a storm of protest arose that he retracted his order and instead directed that clothes be put on the heavenly hosts in *The Last Judgment,* and on the Virgin Mary and the angels surrounding her. Michelangelo's picture of Leda and the Swan, on the same theme as the one by Leonardo, was burned by the French.

Artists became more daring in spite of reaction, and a few painted or sculpted specifically sexual scenes. The market for these works grew as the first mass market for art developed from the possibility of making copies of originals through engraving. Giulio Romano (1499–1546), a pupil and later assistant to Raphael, undertook to portray 16 different postures of coitus in a series called *Posizione* to illustrate some verses by Pietro Aretino (1492–1556). When Romano completed them in 1524, he turned to the new technique of engraving to have copies made on a wide scale. When these engravings came to the attention of Pope Clement VII, he expressed shock that such pictures could not only be published in Rome but be painted by an artist often employed by the Church. Ultimately, Romano, his engraver Marcantonio Raimondi, and the poet Aretino had to flee Rome. The original pictures were destroyed, but the engravings survived.

Engraving, in fact, opened up greater opportunities for more sexually explicit art, since it allowed the artist to circulate his work more or less underground. One artist who took advantage of this was Agostino Carrachi (1557–1602), who did a series of paintings on the theme of Love in the Golden Age, that shows various nude couples making love in a variety of different and detailed landscapes. His most famous erotic work is a series of engravings known as *Lascivie,* of which a dozen or so prints have survived. Until recently, they were kept in the locked collections of various museums. One print, owned by the British Museum, shows a satyr having intercourse with a nymph against a tree trunk. Most of the prints depict nymphs and satyrs and show, among other things, a masturbating satyr and a satyr whipping a nude nymph. They also include biblical subjects such as Lot committing incest with his daughters, a religious theme that lent itself to explicit sexuality.

Usually, however, it was safer to use classical themes rather than biblical ones since the artist could claim to be simply representing pagan customs. Francesco Mazzola Parmigiano (1503–1540), for example, did a series on Loves of the Gods, some of which (e.g., Mars having intercourse with Venus) has survived in the collections of the British Museum. Witches were also a favorite subject of erotic engravings, since they were seen to have particular sexual powers, and it was these sexual powers that made them such a threat to true believers. One engraving of Parmigianino, also in the British Museum and entitled *Witches Sabbath,* shows a witch riding a giant phallus.

Growth of Erotic Art

Generally, artists were reluctant until the end of the 16th century to anger the church publicly by using forbidden sexual themes, since the church was a major patron of the arts. As more secular buyers appeared, however, erotic themes became less disguised and more open. Major artists often sketched figures engaged in sexual activities either for their private customers or for their own edification, even if in their more public works they avoided sexual scenes. Rembrandt (1606–1669), for example, did several such sketches, including *Monk in a Cornfield* in which the monk is having intercourse; *Sleeping Shepherd,* in which a couple is engaging in sexual intercourse while the shepherd sleeps; and *Ledakant,* in which a couple is having intercourse on a large bed. *Ledakant* is believed to represent the artist and his mistress-model, Hendrickje Stoffels. Peter Paul Rubens (1577–1640) was the first artist who dared to paint an erotic portrayal of the woman he loved, *Helen Fourment in a Fur Cloak,* without concealing it behind a biblical or mythological story. Rubens had a powerful sensual technique, which played to advantage in such erotic scenes as *The Rape of the Daughters of Leukippos,* again a classical legend used to justify a sexually explicit work. In the painting, a crowd of nude girls is being attacked by sexually excited men.

Caravaggio (1573–1610), who had many of his religious commissions rejected on the ground of indecorum, also made many paintings of nude male saints that, in spite of their strong suggestions of homoeroticism, somehow passed the censors. In Spain, censorship was carried out by the court, upon which increasing numbers of artists depended for support; however, eroticism and sexuality still managed to make an appearance, though often subterfuges were used to disguise them. For example, Velazquez (1599–1660), a court painter, painted a nude Venus, known as the Rokeby Venus, but from the rear rather than the front, supposedly to circumvent sexual prohibitions. Still, the eroticism somehow manages to express itself in the buttocks, and some have regarded the Rokeby Venus as a particularly sensuous and erotic portrait. Francisco Goya (1746–1828) adopted another alternative in his nude painting of the *Naked Maja,* a courtesan in a full frontal position. It was painted to be enjoyed in private because it was hidden behind another painting of the woman in the same position but clothed (*Clothed Maja*). Goya also made sexually oriented etchings, many with sadistic and masochistic themes, which could be circulated privately.

Royal or noble mistresses often served as models for some of the more erotic paintings, a genre encouraged by various French royal patrons. Usually, the mistresses were used to illustrate various classical legends, which allowed them to appear nude or in various erotic positions without raising religious objections. Among the more erotic of the French court painters was François Boucher (1703–1770) who in the terms of one scholar was "passionately devoted" to the beauties of the female figure and made thousands of nude sketches. One of his favorite themes was Loves of the Gods, the same theme so widely used in the 16th century to escape censorship. He also painted the nude Venus in many different sexual poses, usually selecting a different mistress from among the many he had as a model for each. Madame de Pompadour, mistress of Louis XV, commissioned him to paint the highly erotic four Loves of Venus in 1754, in the hope of arousing the king, whose affections were beginning to stray. Boucher's erotic pictures were openly sexual, and many have not survived in their original form; the most famous of his erotic works, six rustic scenes that were destroyed by fire in 1871, survive only in photographic copies made shortly before the fire. The scenes include two of nude couples copulating on a bed, a girl buying a winged phallus from a man and playing with her vulva, a man having sex with a nude woman from behind, a man about to have intercourse with a partly unclothed woman whose breasts and genitals are exposed, and a girl with her hand on a boy's erect penis.

Another court painter was Jean Honoré Fragonard (1732–1806), who is today chiefly remembered for his erotic canvases such as *The Swing,* where a woman clothed in yards of pink and blue silk has kicked up her legs and revealed her satin stockings to an excited young man lying among the roses in the foreground. Fragonard, however, specialized in bedroom scenes, many of which were destroyed in the 19th century because they were regarded as indecent; sketches and prints remain of some of them.

In England in the 18th century, William Hogarth (1697–1764) made vice his specialty. He got away with much of his eroticism because in his engravings he presented what he called moral topics. In a series such as *The Harlot's Progress,* he attempted to tell the story of a young girl who takes up prostitution and dies within the year. Though his eroticism led to the cancellation of a royal commission, his popularity with the masses was great. One of his drawings, *Boys Peeping at Nature,* perhaps reflects his own feelings about the false "delicacy" of English taste, since he portrays a boy looking under the skirt that has been put around a statue of a nude woman.

Much more deliberately erotic was Thomas Rowlandson (1767–1827), who abandoned oils for watercolors and etching. He had a taste for the bawdy, and most of his works were apparently commissioned by the Prince of Wales before he became King George IV. Rowlandson's work falls into two main categories, one celebrating the sexual pleasures of ordinary people from all walks of life, with such scenes as soldiers whoring or a wife making time with her lover while her husband is absent. The second category is devoted to the upper classes. Included in this latter group of erotic works is a portrayal of a couple having intercourse on horseback, while another picture shows a couple having intercourse in a carriage. Both were part of a series published posthumously for the artist's friends and accompanied by a descriptive poem entitled "Pretty Little Games for Young Ladies and Gentlemen." Many of his prints, paintings, and drawings convey an almost voyeuristic element.

Also active at this period was Henry Fuseli (1741–1825), a Swiss artist, who spent much of his life in London. He produced hundreds of erotic drawings, many of them rather obscene and probably done for his own edification. This makes them more personal than most erotic art and they reveal his own obsession with lascivious, haughty, and dominating women. He explored various forms of sexuality, and among his drawings is one illustrating a young lesbian couple that represents a breakthrough into new topical areas.

By the 19th century, with the ability of artists to sell to a larger variety of patrons and customers, erotic art became more plentiful than ever before. Sexuality, or rather repressed sexuality, was a strong undercurrent in the Victorian period, and with it came the artist to satisfy the need for sexual arousal. Many prominent artists painted erotic and sexual scenes either for their own edification or for select customers. J.M.W. Turner (1775–1851), for example, famous for his sea pictures and landscapes, was a major producer of erotica, much of which was destroyed by his executor, John Ruskin, because it was considered objectionable. Still, many works survived, most of them still unpublished but found in his sketchbooks in the British Museum. They show very explicit erotic scenes. Numerous men with an erection are shown copulating with women or fondling them, and women are shown performing fellatio on men; other pictures are more detailed showing a penis entering a woman's vagina or a man kissing a woman while manipulating her vulva with his fingers.

The number of artists who dealt with erotic themes increased so much that only a few can be mentioned. They range from Jean Ingres (1780–1867), to Ferdinand-Victor Delacroix (1798–1863) and F. Rops (1833–1898). Rops, in fact, concentrated his whole vision on human sexual behavior as it existed in the world of prostitutes, cabarets, and cafés. Rops might be considered a minor artist, but covering the same theme and with more artistic effectiveness was Degas (1834–1917), although many of his sketchbooks were destroyed at his death. Better known for his paintings of the race course and the ballet, Degas executed about one hundred monotypes of brothel scenes. He referred to some of his art as "keyhole" art, and its eroticism is clearly evident.

Henri de Toulouse Lautrec (1864–1901) had much the same fascination with prostitutes as Rops and Degas, although he was more intrigued by the physical appearance of the brothels. Among his illustrations are the luxurious rooms in the better known brothels, as well as the torture rooms, which give another insight into brothel prostitution. Toulouse Lautrec was also fascinated with lesbianism and illustrates it with some of his studies such as the *Kiss,* or *Two Friends.* Much of his brothel art was not formally exhibited in his lifetime but was kept in back rooms for special purchasers—a fate that awaited many artists who turned to sexually explicit subjects.

Some examples of the art of this period are more titillating and erotic than others. The nudes of Renoir (1841–1919) seem to be more celebrations of female beauty than exploitations of women as sex objects for men. Similarly, the nudes and bathing scenes of Paul Gauguin (1848–1903) are not particularly erotic. Even when Renoir or Cezanne (1839–1906) use such classical themes as Leda and the swan, they are much less erotic than some of their predecessors. Vincent Van Gogh (1853–1890) produced three paintings of a nude girl sitting on her bed as well as three paintings of a nude girl reclining on her bed, none of which are particularly erotic. It seems that as nudity came to be more accepted as a fact of existence, what had once become eroticized became much less so. Instead, sexuality became more explicit, and several artists produced what might be called titillating work as a sideline to their major commissions. One such artist was Peter Fendi (1796–1842), the Austrian court painter, whose watercolors show intercourse taking place in almost every position possible. Mihaly Zichy, who held a similar position in the court of Tsar Alexander II of Russia, produced a set of 40 prints entitled *Love,* tracing the sexual life of the artist from infancy to fatherhood. These pictures are much more delicate than those of Fendi, whose illustrations by comparison are almost crude.

Photography became an art form during the last part of the 19th century and the photographer often turned both to explicit sexual scenes and to sexual topics. E.J. Bellocq, a New Orleans photographer of the first part of the 20th century, spent much of his spare time documenting the life of the prostitute in the Storyville district of New Orleans. New art forms such as lithography also opened up new potentials for eroticism. One was the erotic picture postcard or souvenir card, many of them not suitable for mailing, issued by various commercial enterprises. The cards, whether engravings or touched-up photographic representations, came in the American idiom to be known as French postcards. The pre-20th century examples were what might be called innocently erotic, but the longer they remained on the market, the more explicit they became. By the 1930s, even overtly lesbian cards were on sale, although no cards depicted male homosexuality, since in the English common-law countries such representations were considered both illegal and obscene.

Even art forms that had remained less overtly sexual than others—such as sculpture, perhaps because it was usually done for wide public viewing—became more sexually oriented in the 20th century. Auguste Rodin (1840–1917), best known for his sculpture, at first turned to lithographs to illustrate both heterosexual and homosexual couples in intercourse. His eroticism, however, spilled over into his sculpture, particularly his own belief that women were violent and demanding creatures who wanted to possess the male. His viewpoint is most evident in his sculpture of *Christ and the Magdalen,* in which he depicted the nude figure of Mary Magdalene pressed against the nude Christ crucified on the cross in a clearly sexual embrace. Much of his later life was taken up with his project *The Gates of Hell,* which comprised individually sculpted figures demonstrating Rodin's vision of the terrors of physical passion.

Increasingly in the 20th century, artists were less likely to hide their erotic and sexual productions but rather to openly display and publicize them. Each generation of artists seemed to find a new way of expressing themselves. Thus, a number of 20th-century figures such as Pablo Picasso (1881–1973) and Henry Moore (1898–1986), two giants of 20th-century art, did explicit sexual work. Picasso felt that art and eroticism were the same. Depending on the progress of his love life, Picasso's productions varied from a lyrical, tender eroticism to a view of women as brutal, menacing, and destructive. In some of his engravings from the 1960s, Picasso appears as an old man watching a young couple engaged in sexual intercourse, a representation of the fantasies of an old man perhaps recalling his youth. Whereas Picasso was open in his eroticism, Henry Moore remained more traditional. He once told an interviewer, Peter Webb, that he had never set out deliberately to create an erotic work of art, but recognized that his subconscious was probably engaged in making many of his works erotic. He indicated he did not like to examine this aspect of his art and was content to regard his sculpture as an intuitive process. Much less reticent was the Norwegian painter and sculptor Edvard Munch (1863–1944), who spent much of the later part of his life sculpting the behavior of the human family in a parklike setting in Oslo.

Much of it is explicitly sexual, although not particularly erotic.

Reticence about sex has not generally been a characteristic of most 20th-century artists, even if forthrightness got them into difficulties with the law or the public. Some seemed to be preoccupied with the erotic, such as Gustav Klimt (1862–1918) and Egon Schiele (1890–1918) were. Klimt was fascinated by the association of sexuality and death, as was Schiele. Both ran into difficulty over their avowed eroticism. The most heavily condemned of all Klimt's works were his ceiling decorations for Vienna University, which were commissioned and rejected by the university and destroyed by the Germans in 1945. The three huge oil paintings depicting philosophy, medicine, and jurisprudence portrayed a procession of starkly nude figures symbolizing varieties of human love and despair. Klimt also made a series of erotic drawings, as did Schiele, who was strongly influenced by him. In fact, Schiele's reputation as a pornographer resulted in his arrest and imprisonment for a time in 1912. He continued his work after his release and is generally recognized as the first major artist of the 20th century to produce a large body of frankly erotic art.

Sometimes sexual themes were used for shock purposes, at other times they were included simply because they were part of life. In the first quarter of the 20th century, for example, Dada was the fashion, and Marcel Duchamp (1887–1968) became famous when Anthony Comstock denounced his *Nude Descending a Staircase.* Comstock's attack was based more on the title than on the visible content, since Duchamp's picture combined cubism with a kind of iconoclasm known as futurism and was a different type of nude than that produced by Renoir. Dadaism, literally "nonsense," argued that no art could create anything as nonsensical as what went on in the world each day. The movement was short-lived, and its pieces were picked up and reconstituted by the surrealists, who added some of the Freudian ideas of the unconscious to their art. The surrealists set out to describe the aberrations and fantasies of mankind; because these elements were believed, following Freud, to be rooted in unconscious sexuality, most surrealist paintings were deliberately erotic. This was especially true in the works of André Masson (1896–1987), Salvador Dali (1904–1989), Max Ernst (1891–1976), and André Breton (1896–1966). Surrealism was in turn followed by pop art, represented in the United States by Larry Rivers (1923–), Tom Wesselman, and Andy Warhol (1927?–1987). Many pop artists viewed sexuality as a form of commercial exploitation. Movements, however, did not last long and often there were several. Also important in the 20th century was New Realism, the purpose of which was to achieve realism beyond that possible by photography by giving slices of absolute reality, specifically the erotic.

Art not only has mirrored the beliefs and assumptions of the time in which it was created, but it has often anticipated trends and developments. Because the artist is human, sexuality, whether conscious or unconscious, has always been an important element. In times of repression, this sexuality seems to be repressed, although it keeps breaking through into art. In the 20th century, as the importance of sexuality in the human personality has become a focus of major interest, artists themselves have become more openly sexual. This openness has often put the artist in conflict with society, not only in the past but also in recent years. In the early 1990s, the National Endowment for the Arts came under heavy criticism for supporting an exhibition by Robert Mapplethorpe that included photographs of homosexual activities, and even for indirectly supporting the performance artists Annie Sprinkle and Karen Finley, who appeared in the nude or engaged in explicit sexual activities on stage. The result of such criticism was presidential intervention and the firing of the director of the endowment. In spite of such setbacks, however, the artist in society has proven to be an accurate reflection not only of actual society but also of the hidden and secretive aspects of society, as well as an anticipator of trends and developments. One of the roles of the artist is to help us face up to ourselves, including our own sexuality.

REFERENCES

Anand, M.R. *Kama Kala: Some Notes on the Philosophical Basis of Hindu Erotic Sculpture*. Geneva: Nagel, 1962.

Bellocq, E.J. *Storyville Portraits*. Edited by John Szarkowski and reproduced from prints made by Lee Friedlander. New York: Museum of Modern Art, 1970.

Clark, K. *The Nude*. Bollingen Series. Princeton, N.J.: Princeton Univ. Press, 1956.

Étiemble, *Yuh Yu: An Essay on Eroticism and Love in Ancient China*. Geneva: Nagel, 1970.

Fendi, P. *Forty Erotic Watercolors*. New York: Arlington, 1984.

Grosbois, C. *Shuhga: Essays on Erotic Elements in Japanese Art*. Geneva: Nagel, 1964.

Hammond, P. *French Undressing: Naughty Postcards from 1900 to 1920*. London: Jupiter, 1976.

Hoyle, R.L. *Checan: Essay on Erotic Elements in Peruvian Art*. Geneva: Nagel, 1965.

Kronhausen, P., and E. Kronhausen. *Erotic Art: A Survey of Erotic Fact and Fancy in the Fine Arts*. New York: Bell, 1968.

Marcadé, J. *Eros Kalos: Essay on Erotic Elements in Greek Art*. Geneva: Nagel, 1965.

————. *Roma Amor: Essay on Erotic Elements in Etruscan and Roman Art*. Geneva: Nagel, 1965.

Melville, R. *Erotic Art of the West*. New York: G.P. Putnam's Sons, 1973.

Oullete, W., and B. Jones. *Erotic Postcards*. New York: Excalibur, 1977.

Smith, B. *Erotic Art of the Masters: The Eighteenth, Nineteenth & Twentieth Centuries*. New York: Lyle Smith, 1976.

————. *Twentieth Century Masters of Erotic Art*. New York: Crown, 1980.

Surieu, R. *Sarva é Naz: An Essay on Love and the Representation of Erotic Themes in Ancient Iran*. Geneva: Nagel, 1967.

Tucci, G. *Rati-Lilà: An Interpretation of the Tantric Imagery of the Temples of Nepal*. Geneva: Nagel, 1969.

Webb, P. *The Erotic Arts*. Boston: Little, Brown, 1976.

Vern L. Bullough

THE ARTS AND SEXUALITY

Sexuality is a powerful, pervasive force in life, and so it is in the arts. Images of nude bodies, sex organs, and erotic acts appeared in the Neolithic cave art of Africa and Australia. Carved phalli and images of fertility goddesses were part of public religious life in ancient Europe, Egypt, and the Near East. China, Japan, and India have long traditions of elaborately detailed erotic paintings and prints. Mochica pottery from ancient Peru shows coitus, fellatio, and anal intercourse. From ancient Rome to medieval India to modern America, poetry and fiction have described every aspect of erotic behavior and sexual relationship.

It would be possible to create a vast museum and library dedicated entirely to artistic renderings of sexuality. There are, in fact, library collections of art and literature and published anthologies of such works from around the world. Readers may find pleasure and enlightenment in consulting them (see References). Here we will limit ourselves mostly to Western culture and to how the arts can enlarge one's understanding of sexuality.

Unfortunately, sexuality textbooks so frequently misuse the arts that it is necessary to begin by saying what not to look for in them. Texts often state something like, "Painters and poets have always been brilliant observers," but fail to point out what artists have revealed that others have not. At most the textbooks proceed to use art merely as illustrations of social history or scientific findings. Actually, the arts are only partial, indirect sources of social history; the knowledge they do offer is unique and goes far beyond observations awaiting scientists' proofs.

Those who use the arts as social history may show such works as a Neolithic female figure, a Greek vase painted with erotic scenes, and an extract from the 18th-century erotic novel *Fanny Hill*. From these they blithely draw inferences about everyday sexual behavior and beliefs in the ancient Near East, ancient Greece, and 18th-century England. To see the flaw in this, one need only imagine an archaeologist excavating the ruins of, say, Indianapolis in the year 3000. He or she unearths three books—Hawthorne's *The Scarlet Letter*, Henry Miller's novel *Sexus*, and a conservative religious tract on "sexual hygiene." One can imagine the grotesque picture the archaeologist would draw of daily sex life in "ancient" America. Of course, the "ancient" Americans would not be there to laugh at it.

As this example suggests, most art does not reproduce common experience directly; usually it does not aim to. It selects details, is rich in fantasy and invention, and presents experience in condensed, symbolic ways. Even so-called realist art is a mixture of things observed and imagined, patterned in ways that make daily life seem chaotic and inconclusive by comparison. The arts may reveal something about sexuality in other times and cultures, but only when studied with caution and along with many other sources.

Artists' observations do sometimes presage scientific research. For instance, in the 1960s, Masters and Johnson discovered that during orgasm many or most people experience carpopedal spasm, a clutching or flaring of the fingers and toes. Centuries earlier, Japanese woodblock artists routinely included this detail in scenes of sexual pleasure.

One could cite other examples, but such details are not what make art convincing, let alone moving, insightful, and instructive. To emphasize them is to suggest that art is "soft" knowledge, a naive precursor of science waiting to be verified by "hard" data. To the contrary, good art is as precise as good science, and it contains unique, irreplaceable knowledge of a different sort. Some people fail to see this because they confuse accuracy with quantification and mistake art for vague emotion. Art, as the poet Ezra Pound said, is "news that stays news." It remains fresh and powerful because it captures people's inner reality with remarkable precision. It cannot be improved or superseded; new discoveries make it no less true. That cannot be said for most science. In fact, if permanence is the test, much art is "harder" than most science.

This does not trouble scientists. They know that most of their work is provisional; a new idea or a new measuring instrument can suddenly make today's accepted facts and theories obsolete. This is progress they welcome. They also know that science works by breaking reality into conceptual fragments that can be tested by replication and prediction. Like all approaches to knowledge, this one has its advantages and limits.

For instance, when science tries to understand so important a part of life as passionate attraction, it breaks reality into testable pieces. Its various branches would have to talk about visual cues, hormones, neurotransmitters, evolutionary trends, personality development, social scripts, communication, and mate selection. The results may be valuable, yet if these pieces are put together, they miss some important part of the original global experience. Compare with such findings what was written about passionate attraction by Sappho more than 2,500 years ago and by William Butler Yeats early in the 20th century.

> . . . as I look at you my voice fails,
> my tongue is broken and thin fire
> runs like a thief through my body.
> My eyes are dead to light, my ears
> pound, and sweat pours down over me.
> I shudder, I am paler than grass,
> and I am intimate with dying—but
> I must suffer everything, being poor.
> Sappho (Seventh century, B.C.E.)
> Translated by Willis Barnstone

> "A Last Confession"
> What lively lad most pleasured me
> Of all that with me lay?
> I answered that I gave my soul
> And loved in misery,
> But had great pleasure with a lad
> That I loved bodily.
>
> Flinging from his arms I laughed
> To think his passion such
> He fancied that I gave a soul
> Did but our bodies touch,
> And laughed upon his breast to think
> Beast gave beast as much.
>
> I gave what other women gave
> That stepped out of their clothes,
> But when this soul, its body off,

Naked to naked goes,
He it has found shall find therein
What none other knows.

And give his own and take his own
And rule in his own right;
And though it loved in misery
Close and cling so tight,
There's not a bird of day that dare
Extinguish that delight.

W.B. Yeats

The poems will still be fresh, moving, and true to experience when the terms "neurotransmitter," "social learning," and "mate selection" have been replaced by more useful ones and are known only to historians of science. Unlike such efforts of science, poetry seizes and illuminates human experience in its rich complexity. As a result, people can find through the poems a keener sense of their own and others' lives, a crystallization of what they had vaguely sensed and perhaps tried in vain to express.

The knowledge in these poems cannot be translated into science or even into other arts. If it could be expressed by data or in visual imagery or music, it would have been. For that reason, the experience of seeing Rodin's *The Kiss,* Michelangelo's *David,* or the erotic sculpture of medieval Indian temples must remain a visual event, beyond words. An essay such as this one can deal best with art in words, the arts of poetry and fiction.

Literature, fortunately, is rich in understanding of sexuality. It speaks with exquisite precision and detail about the entire range of erotic feelings, events, and relationships. Here are only some of the better known works in Western literature that should be seen as primary sources of knowledge about sexuality in all its expressions:

- Obsessive romantic love, with all its contradictions, has never been described more vividly than by the Greek poetess Sappho and the Roman poet Catullus. No one has captured better the kind of frenzied yearning that grows when it is frustrated or denied.

- No scientific or literary study of prostitution has captured whores, their trade, and their clients as well as the Roman poet Juvenal, in his *Satires,* and the Russian writer Aleksandr Kuprin, in his novel *Yama.* Their portraits are unjudging yet unsparing, and remain as lively and immediate as when they were written.

- Chaucer, in *Troilus and Cressida,* subtly depicts the unintentional betrayal of love. Shakespeare's *Othello* contains literature's greatest portrayal of the twin passions, envy and jealousy.

- Leo Tolstoi's long, ironically titled story *A Happy Marriage* is a harrowing account of the pain two people can inflict on each other from need and fear.

- In *Pride and Prejudice,* Jane Austen explores the power of social convention to shape love and courtship. In *Madame Bovary,* Gustav Flaubert shows how romantic fantasy can cripple marriage and destroy lives.

- Benjamin Constant's novel *Adolphe* and Ivan Turgenev's novella *First Love* are moving accounts of the clash of adolescent passion with adult realities.

- Henry James's novel *The Bostonians* recounts in subtle detail the struggle between a militant feminist and a traditional man for a pliant young woman. It remains a classic picture of the psychological and social claims on a woman's commitment.

- Vladimir Nabokov's novel *Lolita,* whose protagonist is drawn irresistibly and exclusively to pubescent girls, tells as much about sexual obsession as any clinical study, and more.

- James Baldwin's novel *Another Country* captures the nexus in our society of conflicts over race and sex—between white and black, man and woman, heterosexual and homosexual.

Any such list is bound to be partial and somewhat arbitrary. Even a limited library of major writers who have distinctly enriched our knowledge of the sexual experience would also include the poets of *The Greek Anthology,* Anton Chekhov, Collette, e.e. cummings, John Donne, James Joyce, D.H. Lawrence, Martial, Henry Miller, Marcel Proust, Theodore Roethke, Stendhal, Arthur Schnitzler, Junichiro Tanizaki, and many poets of ancient China and medieval India.

Clearly, literature, the visual arts, and cinema are not merely adornments of the study of sexuality; they are primary sources of knowledge. They provide discovery and illumination not found anywhere else. They clarify some of the experiences that most powerfully shape our lives—of being male or female, in or out of love, ecstatic or repelled or indifferent. They do so best about matters science is still struggling to apprehend.

REFERENCES

Cole, W. *Erotic Poetry.* New York: Random House, 1963.

Evans, T., and M. Evans. *Shunga: The Art of Love in Japan*. New York: Paddington/Gosset & Dunlap, 1975.

Fouchet, M. *The Erotic Sculpture of India*. New York: Criterion, 1959.

Lucie-Smith, E. *Sexuality in Western Art*. New York: Thames & Hudson, 1991.

Marcadé, J. *Eros Kalos*. Geneva: Nagel, 1962.

Merwin, W., and J. Masson. *Sanskrit Love Poetry*. New York: Columbia Univ. Press, 1977.

Packard, W. *Desire: Erotic Poetry Through the Ages*. New York: St. Martin's Press, 1980.

Rawson, P. *Erotic Art of the East*. New York: Putnam's, 1968.

Reynolds, M. *Erotica: An Anthology of Women's Writing*. London: Pandora, 1990.

Arno Karlen

ASEXUAL REPRODUCTION

Asexual reproduction is the ability of an organism to produce offspring without the union of sex cells (i.e., gametes). There are many methods to accomplish this. Asexual reproduction probably occurred before sexual reproduction in the evolutionary history of the earth. Sexual reproduction is the union of two gametes, which may be from the same or from different parents. It need not involve the use of specialized organs.

Some plants and animals, such as many algae and protozoans, produce their offspring by simply splitting into two (fission). Many algae and almost all fungi produce huge numbers of specialized asexual spore that reproduces large populations of the organism. Others, such as yeasts and hydra, may produce unicellular or multicellular buds from the parent cell or adult organism. Individual tiny plantlets may be produced on the leaves of some plants (e.g., kalanchoe), and others may produce new individuals vegetatively from a plant part, such as a leaf or a stem (e.g., African violets), that has reached the proper environmental conditions necessary for growth. Multicellular invertebrates may produce offspring from parts that have been broken off of the parent body (e.g., the arm of a starfish). Grafting is a method to attach a part (the scion) of a desirable plant to a more robust root system (the stock). This method is often used to propagate desirable apples and other fruits. Some organisms produce offspring from unfertilized eggs. In animals, this is called parthenogenesis and occurs in aphids, among others. The process is called agamospermy in plants; the most common example is the dandelion. Cloning is the process in which the parts of a desirable organism are used to asexually reproduce a large population of that organism. All of these methods of asexual reproduction produce offspring identical in those characteristics that are genetically inherited.

The selective evolutionary advantage of asexual reproduction is that huge populations of genetically identical organisms can be produced quickly and without a mate. Thus, an organism can quickly spread throughout a favorable environment. A major disadvantage is that there is no recombination of genetic material, such as occurs in sexual reproduction, and thus there are fewer inherited characteristics upon which the environment can act.

In humans, the only occurrence that could be defined as asexual reproduction is when the zygote splits and produces identical (monozygotic) twins. The zygote results from the union of an egg and a sperm; when it splits, it produces two individuals who are usually genetically identical. This fact has been used by science fiction writers, notably George Orwell in his book *1984*. All other forms of human reproduction are sexual. Various methods of getting the egg and sperm together (e.g., in vitro fertilization) have been developed, but the union of egg and sperm, the definition of sexual reproduction, remains constant.

REFERENCES

Arms, K., and P. Camp. *Biology*. Third Ed. Philadelphia: Saunders, 1987.

Curtis, Helena. *Biology*. Second Ed. New York: Worth, 1975.

James D. Haynes

AUTOEROTICISM

Near the end of the 19th century, the pioneering sexologist Havelock Ellis popularized the word "autoeroticism" and defined it as "the phenomena of spontaneous sexual emotion generated in the absence of an external stimulus proceeding, directly or indirectly, from another person." Ellis's definition excludes sexual arousal that occurs in the presence of a beloved person, any sexuality involving someone of one's own sex, and any involving erotic fetishism of any kind. Other authors had previously used such terms as autoerastia, geistige Onanie, onania psychica, monosexual idiosyncrasy, autophilia, self-abuse, and Onanism. Ellis proposed his new word after concluding that all of those in previous use were either erroneous in concept or inadequate in covering all activities he thought should be included in the category for its proper understanding.

Ellis's purpose in making those distinctions was to cast a clearer light on a category of sexual responses that were little understood but that had much in common. To more fully satisfy that purpose, sexologists today generally take a broader approach than did Ellis and define autoeroticism to include erotic responses that occur in an individual in the absence of tactile stimulation emanating from physical contact by or with another person or other animate body. Some authorities say it simply means sexual responses emanating from one's own organism.

The most discussed form of autoeroticism is masturbation. As such, some people tend to consider autoeroticism and masturbation one and the same. Yet, there are many autoerotic manifestations that are not properly described as masturbation.

The human body is capable of experiencing erotic arousal from birth to death. Indeed, some authorities say they have observed fetuses in utero engaging in activities they conclude produce erotic responses in the fetuses. In addition to there being no age for erotic responses to occur in humans, it also appears that the stimuli that elicit an erotic response in one or another person may come from a variety of sources. Many of those stimuli may be self-induced or may occur spontaneously—thus the importance of conceptualizing this category of erotic responses.

When such a self-induced or spontaneous stimulus event occurs to a person who is physically, and perhaps, though not necessarily, psychologically, susceptible to its erotic potential, an autoerotic response is likely to occur. Besides masturbation, one of the most common of autoerotic responses is that which occurs during sleep. That phenomenon has been the subject of much study, contemplation, and consternation throughout history.

Biblical pronouncements indicate that the ancient Jews considered the expulsion of semen during sleep an impurity, and the impure one was commanded to wash his clothes and body and consider himself unclean until the evening. But even earlier, the ancient Egyptians and Babylonians had also wrestled with the occurrence. The Egyptians felt that semen was a life force that when wasted (i.e., used for any purpose but procreation), was not only a drain on the offender's system, but also a pollution of the universe.

The Babylonians explained orgasms during sleep as being the work of a "maid of the night" who visited men during sleep and of a corresponding "little night man" who visited women during their sleep. The Egyptian/Jewish notion

of "pollution" carried over to Christians who treated it only slightly less alarmingly than they did voluntary masturbation; in the Middle Ages, they blamed it on the devil, who sent a succubus to lie under men and an incubus to lie upon women.

It is now known that orgasms during sleep are normal, harmless occurrences (as is the perhaps more common phenomenon of erotic dreams that do not necessarily lead to orgasm). In females, the result of such an event is often vulval vasocongestion and vaginal lubrication, and at times orgasm. In the male, the result is often erection of the penis, and at times ejaculation. This is known to most often occur during periods of the sleep cycle known as the rapid eye movement (REM) phase, which normally occurs about every 90 minutes during sleep.

Another form of autoerotic activity similar to erotic dreams during sleep is erotic daydreams (i.e., conscious erotic thoughts and fantasies occurring while awake). These may or may not lead to orgasm, which may occur in some people without any direct physical stimulation of their body.

A variation of erotic daydream is the occurrence of erotic responses in some people that result from visual, psychic, tactile, or auditory stimuli of a nature that is not perceived by the person (nor perhaps by others) as erotic. Examples of this type of autoeroticism are the experiencing of a heightened state of erotic arousal, and perhaps but not necessarily an orgasm, while listening to certain music, while contemplating a pleasing landscape or artwork, while involved in a dangerous or even life-threatening situation, or while engaged in religious reverie. There are many other possible experiences that may precipitate or accompany such a response in a person so inclined.

In contrast to the other forms of autoerotic activities, masturbation is by definition the erotic stimulation of one's own body (usually of the genital organs), commonly resulting in orgasm, achieved by manual or other bodily contact (exclusive of sexual intercourse) and/or by instrumental manipulation.

The word "masturbate" entered the English language around 1785. It was borrowed from the Latin *masturbari*, meaning to rub or to agitate by hand; the negative connotation ascribed is "defiling by hand." It joined and gradually superseded, at least in most of the developed world, other terms for the activity; most meaning some form of self-abuse or self-gratification, and all having quite negative implications.

Ancient Egyptian, Greek, and Roman civilizations were either mildly negative or almost indifferent about male masturbation. In each of those ancient cultures, there appears to have been little or no concern about female masturbation. In fact, masturbatory aids for females in the form of what are today called dildoes (i.e., objects resembling the male penis) were in quite common use.

Knowledgeable sexologists today have given clear and unambiguous evidence that masturbation, whether or not resulting in orgasm, when performed in a way that is not intentionally or inadvertently designed to injure the body is not harmful to the body in any way and that the act, by itself, causes no mental pathology. However, there remains in Western cultures a strong and pervasive residual of fear and ignorance concerning the supposed harmful effects to the individual who masturbates. The traditional Judaeo-Christian abhorrence of masturbation springs from the biblical prohibition against men "wasting" their seed. Strong strains of that negativity are still pervasive in modern Western society.

Prior to the 18th century, Western cultures saw masturbation as primarily a matter to be handled by religious dogma. However, the Christian, and particularly the Protestant, churches of those times were not inclined to give it much notice. As a result, in areas of the world controlled by the Christian churches, the practice of masturbation was practically a nonissue.

Then, in 1760, a Swiss physician named Tissot published the book *Onanism, or a Treatise Upon the Disorders Produced by Masturbation*. In one fell swoop it convinced much of the world that not only was masturbation a sin and a crime, it caused an enormous number of diseases and illnesses in those who practiced it.

Quickly, the medical profession became the loudest champions of the antimasturbation crusade. Physicians in increasing numbers began attesting in books, journals, and monographs as to the myriad mental and physical disorders that were, without question, caused by masturbating. The list of maladies grew until there was hardly a serious affliction of mind or body, including insanity and death, that some medical authority had not ascribed absolutely to the "solitary vice."

Remedies prescribed for offending children and adults ranged from special diets, loose clothes, and various forms of bondage, to surgery on the genitals and commitment to insane asylums.

The sound and fury reached its zenith during the Victorian years. In the latter part of the 19th century, medical authorities began to apply reason and to understand that masturbation, per se, is a benign, even at times beneficial, normal, and natural activity. That opinion is also now shared by many Christian religious denominations.

The percentage of people in a given culture or subculture who masturbate varies. However, researchers believe that in many Western societies only a small percentage of males and females have never masturbated and in general agree that more females than males have never done so.

Although masturbation, per se, in no way harms the person who engages in it, there is the possibility that the *way* in which it is performed may cause adverse physical consequences.

The almost infinite variety of methods that can be used in attempts at erotic self-stimulation inevitably include some that may harm the body of the person using them. These may involve injuries to the tissue of the genital area by excessive or too forceful rubbing or thrusting; injuries caused by inserting objects into the urethra or anus; the misuse of electrostimulation; and the ingestion, injection, or inhalation of harmful compounds thought to enhance one's response to self-stimulation. Autoerotic fatalities have resulted from accidental autoasphyxia while intentionally constricting the carotid vessels in one's own neck, from suffocation while wrapped in plastic or blankets, from the inhalation of various gases, from electrocution, from exposure, and from poisoning. It is estimated that in the United States and Canada, there are between 500 to 1,000 accidental autoerotic deaths a year.

References

Ellis, H. *Studies in the Psychology of Sex*. New York: Random House, 1936.

Haeberle, E.J. *The Sex Atlas*. New York: Seabury, 1978.

Masters, R.E.L., ed. *Sexual Self-Stimulation*. Los Angeles: Sherbourne, 1967.

Dwight Dixon
Joan K. Dixon

b

BENJAMIN, HARRY

Harry Benjamin (1885–1987) made significant contributions both to gerontology and to sexology. Born and educated in Berlin, he came to the United States in 1913 and soon joined the Neurological Institute of Columbia University, headed by Joseph Frankel. There he became interested in understanding internal secretions, an area of study that later came to be known as endocrinology. Encouraging his interest was his friendship with Eugen Steinach, of Vienna, who had claimed to have found a restorative effect in vasoligation of older men. Steinach had also masculinized castrated female guinea pigs by implanting testicles and feminized castrated males through ovarian implants.

Benjamin's understanding of the newly breaking developments in endocrinology led him to try these hormones to deal with the problems of aging and to coin the term "gerontotherapy." He is best known in the sexological field, however, for his work with transvestites, transsexuals, and what is often called gender dysphoria. In 1948, Alfred Kinsey referred to him a patient who would later be called a transsexual, and Benjamin's interest was aroused in the whole issue. He emerged quickly as the American leader in the field and published a seminal work on transsexualism. Over his career, he treated more than 1500 gender-dysphoric people, and he was known for the kindness and understanding he extended to all his patients. He emphasized that "our emotions are the very essence of life, and they are indeed the source of all that makes life worth living." In 1978, many of the professionals in the field organized the Harry Benjamin International Gender Dysphoria Association, which is still active. One of the major contributions of this organization was creating standards of care for the treatment of gender-dysphoric patients. Benjamin was also a founder and charter member of the Society for the Scientific Study of Sex. He died August 24, 1986, at 101 years of age.

REFERENCES

Benjamin, H. *The Transsexual Phenomenon*. New York: Julian Press, 1966.

Connie Christine Wheeler

BERDACHE AND AMAZON ROLES AMONG AMERICAN INDIANS

American Indian aboriginal cultures often saw sex as a gift from the spirit world to humans and animals to be enjoyed freely from youth to old age. Adults were more likely to view children's sexual play with amusement than alarm. In general, native religions highly valued the freedom of individuals to follow their own inclinations, as evidence of guidance from their personal spirit guardian, and to share generously what they had with others. This focus on freedom was exemplified by their attitudes toward sexual desires, including the inclinations of certain individuals toward same-sex eroticism.

The dual system of marriage (promoting close relationships between different genders) and friendship (promoting close same-gender relationships) functioned to keep band and tribal societies unified. Since extremely close relationships between two male "blood brothers," or between two female friends were emphasized, this context allowed private homosexual behavior to occur without attracting attention. Because this role of sex in promoting bonds of friendship was so accepted, there is relatively little information about this kind of casual same-sex activity. It demonstrates that the role of sex in promoting close interpersonal ties is often just as important for a society as the role of sex as a means of reproduction. While Christian ideology asserts that the only purpose of sex is reproduction, that is clearly not the view of many Native American (and other) religions.

Beyond its role in same-sex friendships, homosexual behavior among many aboriginal tribes was also recognized in the form of same-sex marriages. However, the purpose of marriage was to promote close ties between persons of different genders, so that one spouse could focus on "masculine" labor (mainly hunting and warfare) while the other on "feminine" labor (mainly plant-gathering and farming). This division of labor by gender was not absolute, since food preparation, domestic work, child care duties, and craft work varied by culture and even by individual preference. Such activities were often shared by both spouses. Nevertheless, a major purpose of marriage was to provide both meat and plant foods for the survival of the family and for child rearing.

With marriage partners complementing each other's labor roles, it is not surprising that marriage between two masculine men, or two feminine women, was frowned upon. Nevertheless, rather than prohibit same-sex marriages altogether, many Native American cultures recognized homosexual marriages when one partner took on an alternative gender role. Thus, an androgynous or feminine male was expected to marry a masculine man, while a masculine female most likely took a woman as a wife. By this

pairing, the mixed-gender aspect of marriage could be preserved, while still allowing those with same-sex inclinations to fulfill their erotic desires.

In many tribes, the feminine male had a special role as a "berdache," while the masculine female took on an "amazon" role. These androgynous roles were seen by society as being different and distinct from the regular roles of men and women. Some scholars suggest that this pattern is "gender-mixing," others as a form of a unique "alternative gender." Current researchers reject the older notion that berdaches and amazons were hermaphrodites, transsexuals, transvestites, or gender-crossers because American Indian cultures allotted more than two gender options.

In the concepts of spirituality in many Native American religions, the person who was seen as different by the "average" tribal member was thought to have been created that way by the spirit world. Berdaches and amazons were respected; their "spirit" (i.e., what Westerners refer to as their basic character) was more important than their biological sex in determining their social identity. In fact, they were considered exceptional not abnormal.

Berdache

The French term *berdache* derives from the Persian word *bardaj*, referring to a male courtesan. Early French explorers who observed androgynous male Indians used the word, and it has been adopted by modern anthropologists to describe this alternative gender role. The Europeans were amazed to discover that the Indian tribes often respected berdaches as spiritually gifted. Since women had high status in most Native American cultures, and the spirit of women was as highly regarded as the spirit of men, a person who combined the spirits of both was seen as having an extraordinary spirituality. Such sacred people were often honored with special ceremonial roles in religious ceremonies, and they were often known as healers and shamans. They had the advantage of seeing from both the masculine and the feminine perspectives, and so were respected as seers and prophets. Berdaches were known as creative persons who worked hard to help their extended family and their community. They often served as teachers of the young, healers, artists, and performers.

While the word berdache is usually applied only to American Indians, considering its derivations, it can be applied to other areas of the world. Similar traditions of an alternative gender role, with a homosexual component as part of its acceptance, exist in the Siberian Arctic, Polynesia, India, Southeast Asia, and areas of East Asia, Africa, and the Middle East. Some interpretations suggest close parallels with the "queen" concept in Western thought, although that role is not institutionalized as a distinct gender as much as it is in other cultures.

The berdache role represents one of the world's most common forms of socially recognized homosexual male relationships. In contrast, societies that accept male-male eroticism tend to emphasize intergenerational relationships between men and boys. These cultures tend to be super-masculine warrior societies in which women's status is low (e.g., Melanesia, medieval Japan, and ancient Greece). The berdache role is more common in societies with high status for women, allowing a man to take on a woman-like role without lowering his status.

Amazon

Early references to female Indians who took on masculine roles referred to them as "amazons" after the ancient Greek legend of women warriors. Although the Native American females did not live separately in an all-female society, Portuguese explorers named the Amazon River after female warriors of the Tupinamba tribe of northeastern Brazil. The extent to which this gender role was socially accepted in aboriginal American cultures is unclear, since women were not discussed in the male-written documents of the early European explorers. It is also unclear to what extent these females were "gender-crossers" who were accepted as men, or as "gender mixers" who combined elements of masculinity and femininity with other unique traits to become an alternative gender. There was likely variation among tribes and individuals.

Amazons were noted for their masculine interests from early childhood, and as adults they often became famous for their bravery as warriors and skill as hunters. In some cultures, parents with no son selected a daughter to raise as a hunter, and she grew up to fill all the male roles, including taking a woman as a wife. Since Amazons were not socially defined as women, they gained their status through hunting and military abilities rather than through motherhood and women's craft work. For example, a famous amazon named Woman Chief was a leader of the Crow Indians in the mid-19th century; she was the third-highest ranked warrior in the tribe and had four wives.

The amazon's avoidance of sex with a man protected her from pregnancy, and thus ensured her continued activity as a hunter or warrior. (The Kaska Indians of the Canadian subarctic believed if such a female had sex with a man, her luck in finding game would be destroyed. Her sexual affairs and marriage with a woman were the accepted norm.) Some tribes, like the Mohave, held that the true father of a child was the last person to have had sex with the mother before the baby's birth. This meant that an amazon could easily claim paternity of her wife's child after this wife had been impregnated by a man. Therefore, not only was marriage between an amazon and a woman socially recognized, so were their children as part of the family.

Same-Sex Marriage

The wife of an amazon was not defined as a lesbian, but rather as a "normal" woman because she did women's labor roles. Likewise, the husband of a berdache was not defined as a berdache merely because he had sex with a male. The community defined him based on his gender role as a "man" (i.e., a hunter and/or warrior) rather than on his sexual behavior. This gender-defined role did not categorize people as "heterosexual" versus "homosexual," but rather left a certain fluidity for individuals to follow their sexual tastes as they were attracted to specific individuals of whichever sex. In tribes that accepted marriage for the berdache or the amazon, the clan membership of one's intended spouse was much more important than one's sex.

While a berdache could not marry another berdache (since they occupied the same gender, and thus would not complement each other's differences), the fluidity of gender roles meant that a person who married a berdache or an amazon was not stigmatized as different and could later marry heterosexually. In fact, many tribes that accepted same-sex marriages did considerable kidding to the husband of the berdache and the wife of the amazon. This joking likely helped to break up these marriages after a time, so that the person would be heterosexually married at some point in his or her life. Conversely, some tribes allowed people to marry a person of the same sex only after they had produced children, while others viewed adopting orphaned children to be the prime duty of same-sex couples. By these various practices, social pressures ensured that most people would either beget or adopt children. After a person had done so, the sex of their lover did not much matter to society; what was important was that their gender role differed from that of their spouse.

European Impact

This view changed drastically after the arrival of the Europeans. Bringing with them their homophobic Christian religion, Spanish conquerors in Latin America used the Indians' acceptance of "sodomy" as a major justification for their conquest and plunder of the New World. Likewise, the English settlers brought a similar condemnation, and the early U.S. and Canadian governments followed a policy of suppressing Native Americans' sexuality as well as their native religions. The berdache and amazon traditions went underground, and the sex associated with them became a secret matter, since it was persecuted by reservation officials and Christian missionaries.

In the 20th century, while Christian condemnation of homosexuality has influenced many modern American Indians, those who have retained their traditions continue to respect berdaches and amazons. This attitude had a significant impact on the white founders of the homophile and gay liberation movements in the United States and Canada. In turn, younger gay and lesbian Indians have been influenced by gay liberation ideology to stand up openly in their urban or reservation Indian community. With a recent renaissance in American Indian culture, appreciation for the strength and the magic of human diversity has helped to revive respect for berdaches and amazons among contemporary Native Americans. Rather than expecting everyone to conform, traditionalist Indians respect the different gifts that gays and lesbians can provide as a benefit for society. With this social support, gay and lesbian Indians are assuming leadership roles and making many important contributions to their communities.

REFERENCES

Allen, P.G. *The Sacred Hoop: Recovering the Feminine in American Indian Traditions*. Boston: Beacon Press, 1986.

Blackwood, E. Sexuality and Gender in Certain Native American Tribes: The Case of Cross-Gender Females. *Signs*, Vol. 10, No. 4 (1984), pp. 27–42.

Roscoe, W. *The Zuni Man-Woman*. Albuquerque: Univ. of New Mexico Press, 1991.

Williams, W.L. *The Spirit and the Flesh: Sexual Diversity in American Indian Culture*. Boston: Beacon Press, 1986.

Walter L. Williams

BESTIALITY

Among the terms used for physical contact with an animal that facilitates human sexual arousal or orgasm have been *zoophilia* (stroking or petting an animal as an erotic stimulus), *bestiality* (contact involving human or animal genitals that is not pathological but rather due to "low morality" and great sexual desire with no opportunity for natural indulgence), *zooerasty* (direct sexual contact as in bestiality but with a decidedly pathological component), and *mixoscopic zoophilia* (sexual pleasure experienced while watching copulating animals). To confuse matters further, *sodomy* and *buggery* have also been used to include sexual contact with animals, particularly in legal writings. It was perhaps to bypass this terminological thicket that Kinsey adopted the neutral phrase "animal contacts." This entry uses the term *bestiality* because it is the one most commonly used in sexological and other writings, dating back to the late 17th century.

Folklore, Literature, and Humor

Folklore about bestiality is ancient, widespread, and enduring. Greek mythology tells of the god Zeus becoming a swan to seduce Leda, a bull to abduct Europa, and an eagle to carry off the beautiful youth Ganymede, with whom Zeus had fallen in love. Many other cultures have myths of men and particularly women mating with animals. According to the explorer Rasmussen, the Copper Eskimos said that the first white men were offspring of an Eskimo woman and a dog. A modern myth attributes the death of the Russian empress Catherine the Great to a mishap while attempting coitus with a bull (or horse).

Literary references are also widespread, from the fairy tales *Beauty and the Beast* and *The Frog Prince* to such erotic stories as the tale of the ape-as-lover in *The Book of the Thousand Nights and One Night*, to the ballet *Swan Lake* and the character of Bottom in Shakespeare's *A Midsummer-Night's Dream*, to Balzac's novelette *A Passion in the Desert* about a love affair between a soldier and a female panther. In this category belongs the giant ape King Kong's cinematic infatuation with a human heroine. Currently, Piers Anthony's immensely popular Xanth fantasy novels portray numerous interspecies couplings, resulting in such hybrids as flying centaurs (i.e., offspring of a centaur and a hippogriff, which are, respectively, offspring of a human and a horse, and a horse and a griffin, which itself is hybrid offspring of a lion and an eagle).

Most of these narratives involve a symbolically hyperpotent male animal mating with a human female, often with curious progeny. When it comes to humor, the plot changes. Legman provides numerous jokes about human males copulating with many kinds of animals (most typically sheep and pigs) or males raped by animals (typically apes, bulls, or dogs). The late comedian Lenny Bruce recited, "Psychopathia sexualis/I'm in love with a horse that comes from Dallas . . . ," and told a parable about a man and a chicken to illustrate the indiscriminate libido of the male sex. In *Everything You Always Wanted to Know About Sex*, Woody Allen's movie psychiatrist falls in love with a winsome sheep named Daisy, but the discovery of the affair drives him to the gutter, to drink Woolite in despair. "The Sheep Dip" by contemporary songwriter Roger Dietz addresses the same theme. Limericks, however, take a more catholic coverage of seduced females, males copulating with every conceivable sort of animal, and male rape, plus other scenarios such as the sexually omnivorous woman and ludicrous creature infants.

Behavior

Real-life sexual contacts between humans and beasts have also been reported across ages and cultures. Herodotus, Pindar, and Plutarch wrote of sacred congress with goats in ancient Egypt, and one may conjecture that the Hebrews and their neighbors practiced bestiality because the Bible explicitly forbids it. African and American Indian tribes and the Chinese are all reported to have tolerated some bestiality in the past, mostly by men.

During the Middle Ages, thousands of female witches were accused of having sex with the devil in animal form, although such accusations do not prove fact. The court records available in Europe and the United States, dating back to the 14th century and continuing into the 20th century, nearly always show males, rather than females, as the human parties. The animals have typically been mares, pigs, and sheep, and occasionally other domesticated farm animals, such as goats, rabbits, and chickens.

The first data on frequency of bestiality were collected by Kinsey. He found that about eight percent of males (mostly of rural background) had sexual contact with animals, and 3.6 percent of females. The males' partners were generally farm animals, while the females' partners were mostly pet dogs and cats. Hunt's data from 1974 show similar animal categories but a decrease over 20 years to 4.9 percent for males and 1.9 percent for females, attributed to a declining ru-

ral environment in the United States, plus greater opportunity and less inhibition for sex with other humans since the 1960s and the "sexual revolution." Both studies show actual incidents were infrequent for most subjects and rare after adolescence.

Kinsey found vaginal or anal copulation the most frequent form of contact for males, followed by masturbating the male or female animal. Contacts also included fellation by the animal of the male, and masturbation by friction against the animal's body. Kinsey's females showed a different pattern, usually general body contact or masturbation of the animal. Only a small minority experienced cunnilingus from the animal, or coitus. Hunt's sample showed higher percentages of oral contacts, especially among females, with no actual female–animal coitus. Other sources report occasional sexual contact by males with dead animals and masturbation with animal tissue.

Live sex shows have sometimes involved bestiality, reportedly dating back to ancient Rome. These performances follow the folklore paradigm of women copulating with symbolically stud-like animals: pony, donkey, large dog. (This may be the origin of the phrase "dog and pony show," a carefully prepared and elaborate presentation or performance.)

Some studies of sexual fantasy have shown that a small percentage of both sexes, but more men than women, fantasize about sex with animals.

The helping professions disagree whether bestiality is mostly harmless or usually pathological. Some researchers distinguish between cases resulting from lack of other partners coupled with high desire and lack of fastidiousness about animals, and cases showing sadism, obsessive-compulsive traits, or other neurotic symptoms. A few Freudian psychotherapists suggest that more cases than previously imagined might involve personality disturbances. Physical harm has been occasionally reported, such as injury to the genitals or allergic reactions.

Law

Bestiality has been almost universally proscribed in religious and civil laws in western Europe and in the United States from a tradition dating back to the Roman Empire of the fourth century A.D. and earlier to biblical injunctions in Exodus 22:19 and Leviticus 20:15–16. For many centuries, punishments were Draconian, usually death for both parties, as specified in Leviticus and merging with the medieval practice of subjecting animals to prosecution and punishment for the same crimes as their human cohorts.

In the United States, state statutes have included bestiality, variously named sodomy, buggery, crime against nature, and deviate sexual intercourse (among others). These laws proscribed any penile penetration into orifices other than the vagina of one's wife, which was formerly punishable at common law by death. Because the offense is defined in terms of penetration into a bodily orifice by the human or animal penis (ejaculation not being necessary), it does not include all forms of human-animal sexuality.

Currently, bestiality laws vary widely from state to state. Pennsylvania, for example, includes it in the offense of "voluntary deviate sexual intercourse," while Texas considers it an offense under the "public lewdness" category and only if it is committed in a public place or if the individual "is reckless about whether another is present who will be offended or alarmed by his act." States also vary as to whether particular types of animals, such as birds, are named in the law. "Beast" and "animal," however, are usually interpreted by the courts to mean any nonhuman living creature, regardless of zoological taxonomy.

The Imaginary and the Real

Real and imagined incidences of human-animal sexual contact differ sharply. In folklore and literature, bestiality is most often romanticized seduction and coitus by a large, virile beast of an ultimately not unwilling human female. However, as researchers have shown, few females have sexual contact with animals, even fewer have actual coitus, and far fewer still with large animals.

It seems that most sexual acts with animals involve human males, but such acts take up comparatively little space in the totality of fictional situations devoted to bestiality themes. Sex between animals and males seems to be regarded more as a subject for the most slapstick humor rather than as grist for a serious tale. Perhaps male bestiality is regarded as totally "beyond the fringe" and somehow more abnormal than female bestiality. In the very few serious fictional situations about men being sexually attracted to animals, the animal is usually identified as "really human" early on, or is unusually heroic or beautiful. Balzac's female panther is not an animal with which a real human male would have coitus—any more than a real human female would willingly have congress with a large ape—but is a literary symbol of female power.

With the increase in women-written erotica, a women's folklore of bestiality may be emerging. With the apparent lesser interest of women, however, such efforts are likely to be relatively rare.

Given the infrequency of actual human-animal sexual contacts, what can be said of the folklore and mythology about such forms of sexuality? Psychologically, one can speculate that tales of animal sex may be wish-fulfillment fantasies, centering on breaking taboos and motivated by yearnings for the exotic. From a literary viewpoint, animals can represent nature, and copulation with an animal may exhibit a yearning to become "natural" oneself. In addition, the animal may represent the power of free, "uncivilized" sexuality, as that is perceived by the tale-teller. Finally, in mythology, sexuality animal-style is the prerogative and province of the gods or of semi-deities like satyrs and fauns. In their copulation as beasts and with humans, the gods transcend human rules and link human with animal. Thus, many psychological, literary, and mythological processes interact in tales of human-animal sexual behavior.

But given how common farm animals were in the past and how common household pets have been for centuries, why are actual human-animal sexual contacts relatively rare? And why are these contacts almost always considered "fringey" in some way—if not grossly illegal and immoral, then the province of gods and the sacred, or an experience with enchantment, or a last-ditch desperate need for sex by the immature, the desperately lonely, or the mentally ill? Humans have exploited animals ruthlessly and systematically for food and labor; why not for sex? Like Sherlock Holmes's remark about the dog that did not bark in the night, one sometimes does not notice what is not there. But there are no animal brothels or markets to sell live animals for sex. The mere thought causes nervous tittering. Nor do children seem to "play veterinarian" routinely with the household Schnauzer. Even rebellious students and artists, perpetrators of outrageous acts, do not embrace animals (so to speak) as symbols of radicalism.

It is not quite true that there are no animal brothels because there is little interest. Hunt's 4.9 percent of males translates into millions of men in the United States, probably as many or more than the transvestites who seek large-size female clothing. Such clothing is not hard to find if one is alert, and mail-order catalogs for them are advertised discreetly in many places. Yet there is no "underground network" of animal aficionados or beastly pornography as there is for pedophilia. Also unlike transvestites, pedophiles, and other "sexual minorities," people involved in sex with animals do not seem to become involved in mutual support, advocacy, or even self-help. And it is not because bestiality is illegal. Pedophilia, prostitution, and homosexuality are all more or less illegal in the United States, and scores of groups exist to discuss, normalize, or treat these practices. Presuming the presently dominant view in modern sexology that sexual preferences are fundamentally learned and therefore free of "innate" biological mechanisms, it might be expected, say, that modern urban singles would turn to pets for sexual release when the bar scene flags. Why then have they not learned to do so?

Without denying that much sexual behavior is learned, we conjecture that bestiality confronts a genuinely biological species-specific limitation on human sexuality. All animals, in fact, preferentially mate with their own species. When they do not, it is usually within the artificial environment of captivity. The social scientist may argue that the (infrequent) occurrence of human-animal sex completely destroys the biological argument. However, this reflects a misconception of biology, for its mechanisms do not work with one hundred percent efficiency (in fact nothing in nature or in culture works all the time); from the viewpoint of evolutionary biology, it is sufficient that a mechanism work with high efficiency most of the time.

It is likely that such a biological mechanism for species-specific mating would not work independent of learning and culture, but rather upon learning: we learn easily and directly to prefer other humans as sex partners to Schnauzers, sheep, dogs, or chickens. No biological processes or mechanisms are presently known to achieve this "ethological isolation" in humans; however, few sexologists have looked for them. More research, by open-minded yet skeptical individuals, could shed light on this aspect of human sexuality. Judging from the absence of normative human-animal sexuality in the cross-cultural record, these biological mechanisms are extremely widespread. In short, human-animal sexuality is rare, but we do not know why.

REFERENCES

Corpus juris secundum. St. Paul: West, 1977.

Dubois-Desaulle, G. *Bestiality: An Historical, Medical, Legal and Literary Study.* New York: Panurge Press, 1933.

Ellis, H. Erotic Symbolism. In *Studies in the Psychology of Sex.* Vol. 2. New York: Random House, 1936.

Ford, C.S., and F.A. Beach. *Patterns of Sexual Behavior.* New York: Harper, 1951.

Holden, T.E., and D.M. Sherline. Bestiality, With Sensitization and Anaphylactic Reaction. *Journal of Obstetrics and Gynecology*, Vol. 42, No. 1 (1973), pp. 138–40.

Hunt, M. *Sexual Behavior in the 1970s.* Chicago: Playboy Press, 1974.

Kinsey, A.C., W.B. Pomeroy, and C.E. Martin. *Sexual Behavior in the Human Male.* Philadelphia: Saunders, 1948.

Kinsey, A.C., W.B. Pomeroy, C.E. Martin, and P.H. Gebhard. *Sexual Behavior in the Human Female.* Philadelphia: Saunders, 1953.

Knafo, D., and Y. Jaffe. Sexual Fantasizing in Males and Females. *Journal of Research in Personality*, Vol. 18 (1984), pp. 451–62.

Krafft-Ebing, R. von. *Psychopathia Sexualis.* New York: Scarborough Books, 1965.

Leach, E. Anthropological Aspects of Language: Animal Categories and Verbal Abuse. In E.H. Lenneberg, ed., *New Directions in the Study of Language.* Cambridge, Mass.: M.I.T. Press, 1964.

Legman, G. *The Limerick.* Paris: Les Hautes Etudes, 1953.

———. *Rationale of the Dirty Joke.* First Series. New York: Castle Books, 1968.

———. *Rationale of the Dirty Joke.* Second Series. New York: Breaking Point, 1975. [Cover title: *No Laughing Matter.*]

———, ed. *The New Limerick.* New York: Crown, 1977.

Mantegazza, P. *The Sexual Relations of Mankind.* Samuel Putnam, trans. New York: Eugenics Publishing Co., 1935.

Menninger, K.A. *Totemic Aspects of Contemporary Attitudes Towards Animals.* In G.B. Wilbur and W. Muensterberger, eds., *Psychoanalysis and Culture.* New York: International Universities Press, 1951.

Money, J. *Lovemaps.* New York: Irvington, 1986.

Price, J.H., and P.A. Miller. Sexual Fantasies of Black and White College Students. *Psychological Reports*, Vol. 54 (1984), pp. 1007–14.

Randall, M.B., R.P. Vance, and T.H. McCalmont. Xenolingual Autoeroticism. *American Journal of Forensic Medical Pathology*, Vol. 11, No. 1 (1990), pp. 89–92.

Sellers, N. Criminal Prosecution of Animals. *The Shingle*, Vol. 35 (1972), pp. 179–83.

———. Criminal Prosecution of Animals. *The Shingle*, Vol. 36 (1973), pp. 18–22.

Shenken, L.I. Some Clinical and Psychopathological Aspects of Bestiality. *Journal of Nervous and Mental Disorders*, Vol. 139, No. 2 (1964), pp. 137–42.

Simons, G.L. *Simons' Book of World Sexual Records.* New York: Bell, 1975.

The Tale of Wardan the Butcher and the Wazir's Daughter. In *The Book of the Thousand Nights and One Night.* Vol. 2. P. Mathers, trans. (from French translation of J.C. Mardrus). New York: St. Martin, 1972.

Martha Cornog
Timothy Perper

BISEXUALITY

Bisexuals are persons sexually attracted to people of either sex. They may or may not have had overt sexual activity with either or both sexes. Bisexuality can also mean possessing the characteristics of both sexes, although this definition is not widely held by scholars or researchers today.

There is no commonly agreed upon theory or understanding of bisexuality. Freud believed that everyone has the potential for bisexuality. Kinsey was the first researcher to describe sexual orientation on a continuum. (See also Ambisexuality.) He developed a seven-point rating scale (0–6) from exclusive heterosexuality to exclusive homosexuality to measure sexual experiences. A bisexual experience placed a person on the scale between a Kinsey 1 and 5. Klein, a psychiatrist from San Diego, describes bisexuality as a "complex state of sexual relatedness characterized by sexual intimacy with both sexes." He describes 21 different factors that make up a person's sexual orientation. Coleman, a researcher from the University of Minnesota, measures bisexuality in several dimensions (e.g., behavior, sex fantasy content, and emotional attachments). There are many other definitions and descriptions of bisexuality.

Individuals may experience bisexuality in various ways. A child or an adolescent, for example, may have a same-sex genital experience. Many of Kinsey's subjects who had homosexual experiences during early or middle adolescent sexual experimentation later identified themselves as heterosexuals, while others named themselves later as homosexual; few identified themselves as bisexual.

Others experience bisexuality as a situational or transitory experience. This often occurs when one sex is isolated from the other sex (e.g., in the armed services, in a sex-segregated school or college, or in prison). If heterosexual, these people generally return to that orientation when they can do so.

Bisexuality may also be a transitional or sequential process whereby the person is changing from one orientation to another. Most often, people experiencing this process have repressed or fought their real orientation for years, then experimented, and finally embraced their real orientation; for example, a man who married, had children, and later found his emotional or sexual desires could not be fulfilled in marriage. Such a person may fantasize or experience a same-sex lover, then eventually move to a same-sex relationship.

Bisexuality can also be experienced when a self-identified heterosexual seeks occasional impersonal homosexual contacts. An example is the "tearoom trade" practice (i.e., anonymous sex in a public restroom). This kind of sexual experience is similar to prostitution: the sex is impersonal, and performed to release sexual tension. One study found that tearoom trade participants were conservative, middle-class businessmen who were highly respected in their community. These people often deny their homosexual preference, hiding it through marriage and impersonal sexual contacts.

Finally, there are those who self-identify as bisexual. In the 1990s, this is not a popular identification in American culture for several reasons. First, Americans tend to be bipolar thinkers and classify sexual orientation as either heterosexual or homosexual. In this type of thinking, it is difficult to recognize true bisexuals. Second, Americans value monogamy, even though the majority do not practice it. Bisexuality implies that a person needs to be sexually involved with both sexes to be fulfilled. Finally, in this age of AIDS, many believe that bisexuals, along with intravenous-drug users, are primarily responsible for the transmissions of AIDS to the heterosexual population.

Historically, however, bisexuality is probably as old as life on this planet, or as Goethe wrote, as old as the human race. Ford and Beach, in their cross-cultural work *Patterns of Sexual Behavior*, found that 64 percent of the societies they studied considered bisexuality normal and natural. These societies expected, approved, and even prescribed bisexual experiences, especially for males.

Not much is known about past female sexuality; only in recent history are women providing historical records of themselves. It is known that lesbian experiences, while hidden, have existed since early times. (The word "lesbian" comes from Sappho, an ancient Greek poetess, who lived on an island, Lesbos, with a community of women.) Plato, in his *Symposium*, recognized female bisexuality, as did Plutarch when he remarked that "at Sparta love was held in such honor that even the most respectable women became infatuated with girls."

Bisexuality is not exclusive to humans; it is found in species throughout the phylogenetic order and thus is a constant variable in life. Evidence indicates that humans are born with at least a bisexual potential, although even bisexualism has been seen as limiting to human sexual experience (see Eroticism). Humans, unlike other species, are born with a panerotic orientation potential; bisexuality is that part of the orientation involving other humans: a person can also feel erotically oriented to oneself, to the animate and inanimate world, and to the transcendent dimension of life.

REFERENCES

Crooks, R., and K. Baur. *Our Sexuality*. Fourth Ed. Redwood City, Calif.: Benjamin/Cummings Publishing Co., Inc., 1990.

Duberman, M. The Bisexual Debate. In J.H. Gagnon, ed., *Human Sexuality in Today's World*. Boston: Little, Brown, 1977.

Ford, C.S., and F.A. Beach. *Patterns of Sexual Behavior*. New York: Harper Colophon Books, 1951.

Gramick, J. Homosexuality and Bisexuality Are as Natural and Normal as Heterosexuality. In R.T. Francoeur, ed., *Taking Sides: Clashing Views on Controversial Issues in Human Sexuality*. Second Ed., Guilford, Conn.: Dushkin Publishing Group, Inc., 1989.

Stayton, W.R. A Theory of Sexual Orientation: The Universe as a Turn On. *Topics in Clinical Nursing*. Vol.1, No. 4 (Jan. 1980), pp. 1–7.

Weinrich, J.D. *Sexual Landscapes: Why We Are What We Are, Why We Love Whom We Love*. New York: Charles Scribner's Sons, 1987.

Wolman, B.B., and J. Money. *Handbook of Human Sexuality*. Englewood Cliffs, N.J.: Prentice-Hall, Inc., 1980.

William R. Stayton

BLOCH, IWAN

Iwan Bloch (1872–1922), a German physician, might best be described as the intellectual founder of modern sexology. Bloch emphasized in his writings that sex could not be understood from the point of view of any one discipline or profession but that it required an interdisciplinary effort and the cooperation of various professions. One of the central figures in the German sexological movement, he probably was the mostly widely read in all fields and is said to have possessed a personal library of 80,000 volumes. His concept of the importance of historical, literary, sociological, ethnographic, and biological evidence as the basis of *Sexual wissenschaft* (sexual science) was carried out in his own research.

He concentrated on sexually transmitted diseases, since he felt that once these were overcome, humanity could look forward to a bright future. As part of this effort he also felt it was essential for society to come to terms with prostitution. Though originally he held that homosexuality was a sign of degeneration, through his research and Hirschfeld's influence he came to believe that homosexuality was not morbid but spontaneous and occurred in individuals who were able to function as well as other members

of society. He distinguished homosexuality per se from pedophilia, pederasty, hermaphroditism, misogyny, and "pseudo-homosexuality."

He was a prolific and insightful writer, but his citations are often somewhat careless, and he has been badly served by translators in those few works that did get translated into English, with the exception of the translation by M. Eden Paul. Bloch sometimes wrote under pseudonyms, including Eugen Dühren.

REFERENCES

Bloch, I. *Die Prostitution*. 2 vols. Berlin: L. Marcus, 1912–25.

———. *Der Ursprung der Syphilis*. 2 vols. Jena: G. Fischer, 1901–11.

———. *Sexual Life of Our Time*. Translated by M. Eden Paul. London: Heinemann, 1908.

Bloch, I. [Eugen Dühren, pseud.]. *Das Geschlechtsleben in England*. 3 vols. Berlin: Barsdorf, 1901–03. (The English translation of this work is inaccurate and misleading.)

Vern L. Bullough

BODY IMAGERY AND GUIDED IMAGERY

Many cultures have a preoccupation with the physical and aesthetic aspects of the human body. Chinese foot binding took on an erotic connotation and went from being originally a sign of wealth and status to being a sign of eroticism and sexual arousal of the male with respect to the deformed foot. In the past, teeth in various cultures have been knocked out, drilled, colored, chipped, filed, and decorated to denote beauty and sexual attractiveness. Even recently in America, a diamond has been noted in the tooth of a young man.

Decorating the skin by tattooing, painting, burning, or scarring in some way have been means of attracting others. Tattooing in America has been seen more often in men in the past but has taken on a new sexual meaning for women, who are having tattoos placed on the buttocks and near and on the genital areas.

Rings have been placed in nipples and labia for sexual purposes in the American female. In fact the genitalia in various societies, and among some groups in our own, have been altered in various ways by shaving, hacking, piercing, and cutting and by insertion of various objects into them.

This was true in the past as well. There is evidence, for example, that the Hellenistic ideal for the male gymnastic competitors who performed nude was to have a foreskin of a certain length. Even today, clients in body-imagery work may complain about the length of the foreskin or lack thereof.

The gay liberation movement, which saw the foreskin as a visual and tactile erotic organ, has decried its loss. Where this concept is internalized, the subject who is circumcised often feels mutilated. Where there is some disfigurement, as the person sees it, this part of the body often becomes a focus that can become obsessional. Even a small, almost invisible scar, or a toe that is considered to be too small or too big, can be a problem for some people.

American concerns about the body are manifest in obsession with height, weight, breasts, and penis size. Other matters of concern involving physical characteristics relate to the shape or description of various parts of the body. The centerfold of *Playboy*, in many cases, tends to be the measure of female self-acceptance and the definition of what many men see as an ideal sex partner.

In one way or another, we implant, reduce, or alter body parts to suit our concept of the body beautiful. How we feel about ourselves as persons is often reflected in how we see ourselves physically. We want to be "somebody." We want to feel like "somebody." Nobody wants to be a "nobody."

Where there is self-acceptance, we like who we are as a person. We may recognize that we should lose weight for reasons of better health, or that it would be nice if our breasts were larger or smaller but it is OK that they are the way they are. In many cases, we know that the breasts, for example, could be changed, but it is not important to our self-concept to do so. People who are self-accepting also tend to be able to feel confident and comfortable in asking for and going out on a date or having sex with a partner.

Body Imagery at the Center for Marital and Sexual Studies

In the process of conducting research with sexually dysfunctional individuals and couples at the Center for Marital and Sexual Studies, in Long Beach, it was observed that a poor body image and a poor self-concept often went together. Treatment modalities were developed to change this.

Following a sexological examination, clients are asked to remove their robe and stand nude facing a three-way tailor's mirror while a male and female therapy team is present. Clients are asked to place their hands on their head and to give tactile, visual, and emotional feedback on every part of their body. They examine themselves from the top of the head to the bottom of the feet. They express how they feel about each part of their body on all levels.

In evaluating their body, it is important that they look at it, since self-concept often is carried over from remarks and comments received in childhood from significant others. In working with clients, we found that a slim, trim, attractive male or female would often see himself or herself as that chubby youngster who was teased about being fat. The kid that everyone called ugly is now a good-looking young man or woman. Sometimes they saw themselves as inadequate sexually due to the size of the penis or the breasts whereas these features have little to do with sexual functioning.

During the examination, clients are asked to point out their best and worst physical features and to rate their overall body image on a scale of 0–100, 0 being the least worthwhile and 100 the most positive. Following a rating of 75, for example, they would be asked to justify the 25 missing points. Where do they lose the points in terms of what they see, and how do they feel about what they observe in the mirror?

Often their negative feelings stem from one or two minor imperfections. These seem out of proportion to the overall positive feelings they have felt for the rest of their body. A small scar can be seen as a major imperfection; although the therapists may see it as insignificant, it is important to be aware that the significance of a scar often goes beyond the scar itself to a view of any kind of disfigurement as being less than perfect.

Once the body imagery is completed, the wings of the mirror are closed around the person so he or she is alone and unseen in a world of mirrors. Are there any new views never seen before? Do new views raise or lower previous ratings? How many images of self are seen by turning the head without moving the feet? The number seen ranges from three to infinity, depending on the broadness of the vision of the subject.

This process can also be carried out at home. In doing it alone with a full-length mirror, it is suggested that the person write a response to each part of the body. While not as effective as ongoing dialogue with a dual-sex therapy team, this technique has been judged effective by most participants in university sexuality classes.

Some people have never looked at themselves in a mirror nude, let alone let anyone else see them nude. It forces one to become more comfortable with the self. Once a person becomes comfortable with his or her own body, feeling comfortable in the presence of others is easier. If a person is unable to accept his or her own body how can that person accept the body of a partner?

Another way of helping clients is through the guided-imagery procedure, which at the Center follows the body-imagery work. Guided imagery is usually done by having a person either lie supine or sit in a chair with the eyes closed while he or she is guided through a series of experiences. This may include music of some kind played softly in the background. It can be viewed as a form of hypnosis in which the client is led by the person talking them through a series of experiences. It usually starts with some focus on relaxation before the client is led through the series of steps to resolve the problem.

The dual sex therapy team directs the client to close their eyes and enter their body in fantasy. They may enter through any opening or directly through the skin or skull by osmosis. They are led from wherever they entered up or down in the body until the brain, heart, lungs, genitalia, seat of emotions, sexuality, masculinity, or femininity are explored. What do you see? What color is it? How do you feel about the function you are observing? Does it function well? Are you satisfied with it? If not, what do you see the problem to be? Blocks to sexual function are examined in detail (i.e., neural pathways from the brain to the penis or vagina). Removing the blocks is the client's responsibility. Most choose to remove them with the therapists' help, if requested.

Clients then are free to examine anything they wish, and through fantasy, to visualize the inside of the body. Therapists accompany them and dialogue enroute. Can they see out their closed eyes, penis, vagina, nipples? What do they see? Fantastic variations! Sexual problems may be resolved through fantasy—usually fantasy of coitus.

Finally, a rating is requested on the inside of the body. Where and why are points lost? Exit anyway you wish, and when you are out tell how you came out. Open your eyes; tell how you felt about the fantasy trip inside the body.

Where self-concept evaluations are unrealistically low, there is an attempt made to bring the evaluations into a more realistic perspective by therapy.

In those cases where clients are so fearful of either penetration or orgasm that they become severely disturbed at the point where either of these situations occurs, guided imagery can be extremely important in having them become relaxed enough to visualize penetration of the genitals. The therapist cautiously suggests to them what they will feel and helps them become comfortable with those sensations and feelings. In cases of vaginismus, visualization can facilitate relaxation. As the visualization proceeds, the partner inserts a finger to help stretch the vaginal introitus to make penetration without muscle spasms possible. When a woman equates orgasm with dying, guided imagery can talk her through the experience of orgasm so that she knows and understands what to expect. Fear of any of these situations can be factors in the inability to function sexually. The relaxation achieved in guided imagery helps the client work through fears and anxiety so that sexual function is possible.

In summary, research findings suggest that self-concept and body image are important aspects of one's sexual persona. Sex educators and counselors should stress the importance of positive self-concept and body imagery for developing a good sexual relationship.

REFERENCES

Anderson, B.L., and J. LeGrand. Body Image for Women: Conceptualization, Assessment, and a Test of its Importance to Sexual Dysfunction and Medical Illness. *Journal of Sex Research*. Vol. 28 (Aug. 1991), pp. 457–78.

Eilberg-Schwartz, H. People of the Body for the People of the Book. *Journal of the History of Sexuality*. Vol. 2 (July 1991), pp. 1–24.

Gregersen, E. *Sexual Practices: The Story of Human Sexuality*. New York: Franklin Watts, 1983.

Harrell, T., and R. Stolp. Effects of Erotic Guided Imagery on Female Sexual Arousal and Emotional Response. *Journal of Sex Research*. Vol. 21 (Aug. 1985), pp. 292–304.

Hartman, W.E., and M.A. Fithian. *Treatment of Sexual Dysfunction: A Bio-Psycho-Social Approach*. Long Beach, Calif.: Center for Marital and Sexual Studies, 1972.

Hartman, W.E., M.A. Fithian, and D. Johnson. *Nudist Society*. New York: Crown, 1970. Updated and edited by I. Bancroft. Los Angeles: Elysium Growth Press, 1992.

Hill, J. *Women Talking—Explorations in Being Female*. Secaucus, N.J.: Lyle Stuart, 1976.

Kirkendall, L.A., and L.G. McBride. Preadolescent and Adolescent Imagery and Sexual Fantasies: Beliefs and Experiences. In *Childhood and Adolescent Sexology*. Vol. 7 of *Handbook of Sexology*, edited by M.E. Perry. New York: Elsevier, 1990.

Smith, D., and R. Over. Enhancement of Fantasy-induced Sexual Arousal in Men Through Training in Sexual Imagery. *Archives of Sexual Behavior*, Vol. 19 (Oct. 1991), pp. 477–89.

William E. Hartman
Marilyn A. Fithian

BONDAGE

Bondage refers to restraining, binding, or otherwise immobilizing a person within a sadomasochistic scene. Bondage can range from the simple binding of an individual's hands to more elaborate methods. Bondage devotees use a wide variety of implements, including ropes, straps, and chains; gags, masks, and blinders; wrist, arm, ankle cuffs, and handcuffs; thumb cuffs, "butt plugs," and corsets; racks, stocks, and suspension and inversion devices.

Often seen as an end in itself, bondage may be separated from other sadomasochistic practices. Practitioners emphasize that it is consensual and planned.

Bondage is a common preference among sadomasochists. Spengler, for example, found that 60 percent of his sample were interested in it, and 67 percent of the males and 88 percent of the females studied by Breslow preferred it. In his analysis of letters published in a sexually oriented magazine, Baumeister also found that bondage was prevalent among the majority of correspondents.

Bondage and discipline (B & D) is used to describe the combination of restraint and control with punishment or humiliation.

References

Baumeister, R.F. Gender Differences in Masochistic Scripts. *The Journal of Sex Research*, Vol. 25 (November 1988), pp. 478–99.

Breslow, N., L. Evans, and J. Langley. "On the Prevalence and Roles of Females in the Sadomasochistic Subculture: Report on an Empirical Study. *Archives of Sexual Behavior*, Vol. 14 (1985), pp. 303–17.

Spengler, A. Manifest Sadomasochism of Males: Results of an Empirical Study. *Archives of Sexual Behavior*, Vol. 6 (1977), pp. 441–56.

Thomas S. Weinberg

BOOKSELLING IN THE FIELD OF SEXOLOGY

There are, broadly speaking, two methods of retail bookselling in the field of sexology: through a bookstore and by mail order, which in some cases includes "by appointment" arrangements. This entry discusses mainly the mail-order method.

For several reasons, the bookstore environment is not ideally suited for a bookseller who specializes in the field of human sexuality. First, the individuals most in need of materials of this sort—"the young, the shy, the misfits, the impotent, the maladjusted," as Peter Fryer describes them in *Private Case-Public Scandal*—are likely to be intimidated in such places. Second, scholars and professionals who need the materials for research or counseling often do not have the time to visit bookstores. Finally, casual browsers often damage inventory; this is a major problem, not only in bookstores but also in libraries, for books dealing with sexuality.

The mail-order business conveniently avoids all these drawbacks. It allows the sexually inexperienced to obtain what they want to enrich their fantasies or lives without embarrassment; the busy scholars can have their secretaries do their ordering for them; the casual smut hound, amusingly, finds himself in a position similar to that of the embarrassed misfit in the bookstore. Success in the mail-order (or customer-by-appointment) business has four basic ingredients: the customer, the mailing list and catalogs, the want list, and the inventory.

Customers for sexological books break down into five broad groups: (1) collectors; (2) researchers; (3) information seekers; (4) institutions, libraries, and other booksellers; and (5) individuals who want to find out more about their particular sexual needs; the latter might also fit into any one of the four preceding groups. Each of the groups is somewhat different from the others.

The collectors, and specifically those who collect paperbacks, are primarily interested in two things: publishers and the artists who do the cover illustrations. Weekend-long conventions are devoted to these subjects, and there are several fan publications, which contain articles and checklists displaying the most arcane knowledge of the paperback publishing business, including that part of it dedicated to erotica. Publishers such as Brandon House and Essex House (subsidiaries of the Parliament News empire of Milton Luros), Greenleaf Classics, Holloway House, and other paperback purveyors of erotica from about 1967–1974 all have their collectors.

Essex House is almost unique among them in that it required authors to use their real names rather than pseudonyms, common in so much of the field. Among the authors of the 50 titles issued by the house are Charles Bukowski, Philip José Farmer, and Michael Perkins. Their books command premium prices when found. Greenleaf Classics, ostensibly a publisher of conventional paperback pornography, was responsible for some amazingly stylish gay erotica by authors such as C.J. Bradbury Robinson (not a pseudonym) and the late Richard Amory, a San José schoolteacher whose real name was Richard Love. At the same time, Greenleaf was also guilty of piracy by illegally issuing the first American editions of Henry Miller's *Rosy Crucifixion* trilogy.

Some collectors specialize in books that are of a curious shape, have unusual bindings, or are in some other way uncommon. Pop-up editions of the *Kama Sutra* are an example of such books but there are others published in more limited editions. Among the rarer examples is a book on circumcision printed in fewer than 100 copies, each of which is tall and narrow in shape and cannot be opened without the removal of a prepuce-shaped paper cap.

Some books are given special value by their collector. One collector of gay books tried to put bindings on them to match the content, theme, or title. Included in his collection was Casimir Dukahz's *The Asbestos Diary*, bound in nontoxic asbestos with the title blocked in silver on the front cover. To be successful in selling such unique books, the bookseller has to have a customer in mind when he or she purchases them.

There are some important ground rules to follow in selling sex books successfully. Knowledge of the customer is important. Nonspecific inquiries from a stranger should elicit a reply in appropriately generalized terms. Such inquiries are too time-consuming and other sources are available, including libraries and bookstores. More welcome are specific enquiries, since they indicate a serious interest in the subject and quite possibly will lead to a profitable working relationship for both the bookseller and the customer. Again, a catalog should be sent, but in the event that the bookseller has several available on different aspects of the particular request, the catalog most closely approximating the request should be sent since catalogs cost money. Personal visits from customers are not ruled out in the mail-order business, but prudence dictates that visitors should be long-standing customers or referrals from such customers.

An important part of successful bookselling of erotica is a search service, the willingness and ability to locate scarce and hard-to-find titles. Searches can be done successfully only through an extensive network of contacts, both among collectors and among other booksellers. Many finds are due simply to serendipity. For example, a customer saw in Tokyo a copy of an important German work on erotic theater at a price he was unable to pay. He mentioned it to one of the authors of this entry in passing, and by chance shortly afterwards, while scouting for books in Europe, another and cheaper copy was located and purchased for the customer.

The lifeblood of the mail-order bookseller is the mailing list and catalogs. They ultimately are the most effective advertising that the bookseller has, particularly if they are attractively presented and if the entries are annotated in a professional manner. Care also should be taken to match specialties to the appropriate individuals on the mailing list.

The mailing list is compiled from various sources. Certain institutions or individuals working in the area of eroticism or related subjects should be included on the list. Referrals of customers from other booksellers add to the list, as do collectors who somehow hear about the bookseller. Advertising in specialized scholarly publications aimed at sex researchers is also important. Each catalog should have a cover sheet incorporating a "list of lists" to give customers the opportunity to see the scope of the business (and to order from back catalogs).

Catalogs themselves are not inexpensive to produce. They must be compiled, and in some instances the compiler must be paid; to this must be added printing and postage. The mail-order bookseller can stay in business only by keeping down costs, and this means sending catalogs to those primarily interested in buying. Many charge for catalogs while others limit the number of catalogs they send before purging from the mailing list those customers who have not responded. We believe that after sending three of our catalogs—whether they are general catalogue or specialized—we should have received a positive response of some sort, preferably firm orders. This also implies that the bookseller needs to know something of the customer's needs in order to send the catalogs from which the customer is most likely to order merchandise.

One customer who collects the publications of New York's Olympia Press provided the bookseller with a useful checklist of the titles he needed to complete his library. This serves to alert the bookseller of a potential customer whenever a book on the list appears on the market. The bookseller can also put such titles on the want list, which is sent out to other book dealers.

Back orders from old catalogs can pose a complicated economic situation, since prices change. Pricing used books is always a bit of a tightrope act. Skill and experience, combined with supply and demand, are the basic ingredients for pricing an item. In addition, the strangely inverted values found in the secondhand-erotica market only complicate the issue. This is because the collector of a well-known and collected modern author (e.g., James Joyce or D.H. Lawrence) who has unlimited financial resources can complete his or her library easily by a telephone call to one of the big specialist New York dealers. In contrast, a paperback pornography collector, no matter how well financed, is hard put to locate easily and on short notice some of the more exotic paperback pornography. Joyce and Lawrence are respectable; paperback erotica is not so well regarded. It is more subject to censorship and is less likely to survive and enter the used-book market. Even many of the original classics in sexology are in short supply, as are the sexological works published in Germany from 1900 to 1932. One reason for this scarcity is that Magnus Hirschfeld, X. Bloch, and many of the other scholars researching human sexuality were Jews, socialists, or homosexuals and were not "politically correct" in Nazi Germany. Not only Nazi Germany destroyed such books; even in the United States there has been periodic destruction of what many regard as smut.

The scarcity of a book and the demand for it are closely correlated with price. Prices change. A book priced at $20 in 1984 can be worth more or less than that at a later time, depending on the current market. This is often difficult for the customer to understand and is well illustrated by an incident that occurred in a Boston used-book store. A customer who very much wanted a book that had been autographed by Ernest Hemingway refused to pay the $300 requested by the bookstore owners because the intact dust jacket indicated it had cost only $3.95 when new.

One of the difficulties in being a bookseller who specializes in erotica and sexological works is that one rarely can purchase the general collections that come on the market. Going through such collections to find one or two titles does not justify the time or money spent on acquisition and cataloging. Though occasionally specialized collections of sex books and erotica do come on the market, the specialist in this area mostly has to rely on other secondhand retail outlets for stock. This is difficult when the bookseller is just starting in business but as one becomes better known, other booksellers become increasingly likely to make contact when they have books available in the sex or erotic area. Some books sell better than others in the used market, and there are some that end up in a stagnant inventory which does not move at all.

In conclusion, the business of buying and selling books in the field of sexology presents considerably more challenges than conventional bookselling. Starting out, the newcomer has few if any guidelines available to him or her. *Book Auction Records* and similar publications seldom include any yardsticks on which to base prices, and there is no reliable guide to collecting in the field to enable booksellers to distinguish the good material from the bad when they see it. Eroticism and sexology are not easy subjects for booksellers to specialize in, but they can be rewarding both in financial terms and in terms of friendship. Speaking personally, we have met many interesting people and dealt with institutions we might otherwise never have encountered.

Ivan Stormgart
Mary Cook

REFERENCE

Fryer, P. *Private Case-Public Scandal*. London: Secker and Warburg, 1966.

BUDDHISM AND SEX

Buddhism, one of the major religions of the world, was founded by Siddhartha Gautama, the Buddha, who lived in northern India from 560 B.C. to 480 B.C. His followers seek to emulate his example of perfect morality, wisdom, and compassion, culminating in a transformation of consciousness known as enlightenment. Buddhism teaches that greed, hatred, and delusion separate the individual from the true perception of the nature of things, namely that the apparent substantiality of all objects, including the self, is illusion; everything mundane is impermanent and ultimately unsatisfying. The central beliefs of Buddhism are based on the Buddha's Four Noble Truths, the last of which is the Eightfold Path by which enlightenment may be attained and the individual self-annihilated in nirvana.

It is common to divide Buddhism into two main branches. The Theravada (Way of the Elders) is the more conservative of the two; it is dominant in Sri Lanka, Burma, and Thailand. The Mahayana (Great Vehicle) is more diverse and liberal; it is found mainly in China, Korea, and Japan, and among Tibetan peoples, where it is distinguished by its emphasis on the Buddhist Tantras.

Most Buddhist schools de-emphasized sexual desire, and traditionally Buddhist monks have been celibate. But this is not so of the school of Mi-tsung (Mantrayana, mantra means secret, Tantrayana, or Tantrism), the True Word school (Chen-yen Tsung), or the Esoteric school of Buddhism. The term Tantrism, or Tantra, refers to a pan-Indian religious movement that arose in about the sixth century A.D. within both Buddhism and Hinduism and to the texts (either Buddhist or Hindu) setting forth its practices and beliefs. The main emphasis of Tantrism is on the development of the devotee's dormant psycho-physical powers by means of special meditations and ritual techniques. These are essentially esoteric and must be passed on personally from master to initiate. Stressing the coordination of the body, speech, and mind, they include the use of symbolic gestures (mudras); the uttering of potent formulas (mantras); the entering (through meditation) of sacred diagrams (mandalas) and yantras; the meditator's creative visualization of and identification with specific divine forms; and the physical, iconographic, or mental use of sexual forces and symbols. Although the particulars of practice vary between the Buddhist and Hindu Tantras and within each of these traditions form one text or lineage to another, they all stress the realization, within the body, of the union of polar opposites, whether these be conceived of as devotee and goddess, the masculine principle (Shiva) and the feminine (Shakti), reason and compassion, or samsara and nirvana. Tantrism is traditionally practiced in Tibet, Nepal, Bhutan, and other countries where Tibetan Buddhism is followed, as well as in India.

Sex was the major subject of Mi-tsung. Mi-tung was very similar to some sects of Taoism, and stressed the sexual union. Even Mi-tung said, "Buddheity is in the female generative organs." In China, the Tibetan Esoteric Sect (Tsang Mi-tsung, or Tibetan Mi-tsung) flourished in Yuan Dynasty, especially from the time of Kubilai Khan (1216–94 A.D.). Even the Chinese standard history *Yuan Shi* [The History of the Yuan Dynasty] recorded some kind of sexual Tantrism as follows:

> He [Ha-ma, prime minister] also presented to the emperor [Hui-tsung, 1333–67 A.D.] the Tibetan monk Ka-lin-chen, who was an expert in the secret [Tantric] ritual. The monk said to the emperor: "Your Majesty rules over all in the empire and owns all riches within the four seas. But Your Majesty should not think of this life only. Man's life is brief, therefore this secret method of the Supreme Joy [which ensures longevity] should be practiced." The emperor thereupon practiced this method, which is called "Discipline in Pairs." It is also called "yen-t'ieh-erh," and "secret." All these practices refer to the art of the bedchamber. The emperor then summoned Indian monks to direct those ceremonies, and conferred upon a Tibetan monk the title of Ta-yuan-kuo-shih [Master of the Great Yuan Empire]. They all took girls of good families, some four, some three, for these disciplines and called that "to sacrifice" (kung-yang). Then the emperor daily engaged in these practices,

assembling for the purpose great numbers of women and girls, and found his joy only in this dissolute pleasure. He also selected a number from among his concubines and made them perform the dance of the 16 Dakini (Shih-liu-t'ien-mo, the 16 Heavenly Devils) and the Eight Males (pa-lang) [the 16 may represent Tantric she-devils, who had intercourse with men representing their male companions, one pair of women with one man]. The brothers of the emperor and those men called "companions" all engaged in front of the emperor in these lewd embraces, men and women being naked. The hall where these things took place was called Chieh-chi-wu-kai ("Everything without obstacle"). Ruler and statesmen thus displayed their lewdness, and the crowd of monks went in and out the palace, and were allowed to do anything they liked. [Translated by R.H. van Gulik.]

REFERENCES

Needham, J. *Science and Civilisation in China*. Vol. 2, Sect. 8–18. Cambridge, U.K.: At the University Press, 1956.

Ruan, F.F. *Sex in China: Studies in Sexology in Chinese Culture*. New York: Plenum Press, 1991.

Van Gulik, R.H. *Sexual Life in Ancient China: A Preliminary Survey of Chinese Sex and Society From ca. 1500 B.C. till 1644 A.D.* Leiden: E.J. Brill, 1961.

Fang-fu Ruan

BUTCH AND FEMME, TOP AND BOTTOM, IN A GAY WORLD

It is a common misperception that all homosexual relationships are characterized by one partner playing the man's role in sex while the other plays the woman's role. Because this misperception is so widespread and so irritating to the homosexual community, most accounts of this phenomenon aimed at heterosexual readers concentrate on debunking the stereotype. (See also Homosexuality.) This entry discusses how various sex roles are enacted within the gay community. However, the patterns described are extremely fluid and cannot be viewed as simply corresponding to the polarities of "masculine" or "butch" and "feminine" or "femme."

The terms "butch" and "femme" (or "fem") refer to several different phenomena. Primarily, they refer to mannerisms: (e.g., how a person walks). Especially in the lesbian community, they also refer to particular aspects of personality with masculine or feminine connotations, including how those personalities express themselves during sex. For example, in bed, the butch's role is to make sure that the femme has an orgasm, but many butches refuse to let the femme return the favor (which illustrates, by the way, that homosexuals do not merely assume heterosexual roles).

The terms "top" and "bottom" were originally used by gay men to describe particular sexual preferences for, respectively, insertive and receptive sexual intercourse, especially anal intercourse. They are now used by both lesbians and gay men in sadomasochistic and bondage contexts as synonyms for the terms "S" (sadist) and "M" (masochist), respectively, especially when it is B & D (bondage and discipline) and not S & M that is at issue. The precise meaning is determined by the context: in a leather bar, the secondary meanings would probably be understood; in other bars, the primary meanings would be.

Butch and Femme in the Lesbian Community

The phenomenon of butch and femme has historically undergone remarkable transformations among lesbians. Allegedly, butch and femme was an extremely important phenomenon in working-class lesbian social circles in the 1950s. As one lesbian who served in the armed services in Korea put it, the femme washed the dishes, then handed them to the butch to be dried—and every other aspect of home life and sex life was dictated by similar circumscribed role playing.

In the 1960s and 1970s, such roles supposedly were abandoned except in the most politically incorrect circles. But the late 1980s and 1990s brought a renaissance of discussion about them in most lesbian circles, even those that continue to insist that they are outdated. JoAnne Loulan and Susie Bright are lesbian sexologists who have written extensively about this dimension.

Butch and Fem, Top and Bottom, Among Gay Men

Few gay men in modern Western societies can be characterized as taking only a masculine or a feminine role in sex, although in the United States men who prefer anal intercourse often indicate a preference for the top (inserting) role by wearing keys or a bandana handkerchief on the left side, and for the bottom (insertee) role by wearing such items on the right. (For a short time, such preferences could also be signalled by the side on which a man wore an earring. However, fashion has now overtaken communication, and the side on which an earring is worn has no significance.) Although these preferences are real, they can quickly change, as they could, for example, for a young man wearing a bandana on his right who, upon seeing a handsome fel-

low also wearing a handkerchief on the right, switches his to the left before the other fellow has seen him. These preferences also seem to be far more prominent among devotees of anal intercourse; those who prefer oral-genital contacts are apparently far less likely to have a preference for insertor or insertee. Those preferring anal intercourse do tend to engage in oral-genital sex too, but arguably they do so more as foreplay than as the main event.

Often in the United States today, gay men are typically expected to be versatile, not only in top versus bottom roles but also in the choice of particular acts (e.g., oral, anal, masturbatory). This is less true in other countries, especially those with macho cultures. But even in countries (such as Mexico) where anal intercourse is the rule and one is supposed to declare one's insertor/insertee preference (insertor is considered better) in every possible way (e.g., stance, mannerisms, voice), there is far more flexibility than observation of the outward cultural signs suggests. For example, in Mexico it is not so much that some men are insertors and others are insertees, but rather that in a particular pairing one man is thought to be more macho than the other and so always is the insertor; but in pairing of the same two men with others each might possibly play the reverse role.

Gay men who display a specific top or bottom preference do not necessarily display this preference through masculine or feminine characteristics in personality, mannerisms, or demeanor. Some gay men with stereotypical masculine interests and mannerisms are enthusiastic bottoms, while feminine-acting individuals who prefer the top role (although apparently much less common) also exist.

Nor can one assume that the top, while apparently in control of the sexual interaction, is also controlling it in a more general sense. It is a common expectation of many patrons of the leather-bar scene, for example, that the top is supposed to do to the bottom only what the bottom has already asked the top to do, and that the top should let the bottom control the pace and duration of the activities—even though part of the "scene" may involve the simulation of the bottom's lack of control.

Conclusions

Some, but far from all, members of the gay male and lesbian communities have specific preferences for specific genitoerotic roles; that is, there are particular scenarios involving certain sexual acts and not others which they find particularly arousing. Many of these roles have dominance/submission, masculine/feminine, or insertor/insertee aspects, which do not merely copy the superficially similar erotic practices of some heterosexual couples. In fact, many lesbians and gay men have little interest in such matters. At a typical young-crowd gay disco, for example, one sees few if any exposed key rings or bandanna handkerchiefs. Much of the variability in gay men's sexual expression is along the dimension of anal intercourse, with those preferring this mode of expression being more likely to make top and bottom distinctions than those preferring other outlets of sexual expression.

James D. Weinrich

C

CALDERONE, MARY S.

Mary Calderone, born on July 1, 1904, is the daughter of the renowned photographer Edward Steichen and one of the pioneers of sexuality education. She received her M.D. from the University of Rochester in 1939 and her M.P.H. from Columbia University in 1942. From 1953 to 1964, Calderone was medical director of Planned Parenthood-World Population, during which time she wrote *Abortion in the U.S.* and *The Manual of Family Planning and Contraceptive Practice*.

In 1964, Calderone and Lester Kirkendall co-founded the Sex Information and Education Council of the United States (SIECUS) to enhance the study and understanding of human sexuality. Through her leadership in SIECUS, Calderone demonstrated her dedication to promoting sexuality education, and as its executive director (1964–75), she developed the organization's public image. From 1975 to 1982, Calderone was both president of SIECUS and chairperson of its board of directors. She retired in 1982.

A strong proponent of sex education for children, Calderone co-authored both *Family Book About Sexuality* and *Talking With Your Child About Sex*. She was also editor of *Sexuality and Human Values*.

Calderone has received many distinguished awards, including the Society for the Scientific Study of Sex Award for Distinguished Scientific Achievement and the 1992 Award for Outstanding Contributions to the Field of Human Sexuality. She was named one of America's 75 Most Important Women by *Ladies Home Journal* in 1971 and one of the 50 Most Influential Women by the U.S. Newspaper Enterprises Association in 1975. She has received more than six honorary degrees and is an honorary life-member of the Society for the Scientific Study of Sex, of the American Association of Marriage and Family Counselors, and of the American Medical Association.

REFERENCES

Calderone, M.S. *The Manual of Family Planning and Contraceptive Practice*. 1970.

———, ed. *Abortion in the U.S.* New York: Paul B. Hoeber, Inc., 1958.

———, ed. *Sexuality and Human Values*. New York: Association Press, 1974.

Calderone, M.S., and E. Johnson. *Family Book About Sexuality*. New York: Harper & Row, 1981.

Calderone, M.S., and J.W. Ramey. *Talking With Your Child About Sex*. New York: Random House, 1982.

Leah Cahan Schaefer

CANCER AND SEXUALITY

The Catholic Theological Society defines sexuality as "one's being in and relating to the world as male or female." Clearly, it has both psychological and physiological functions. Within this broad context, this entry examines the effects of cancer therapy on reproductive and sexual functioning, as well as the related alterations in body image and self-esteem.

Treatment for cancer often involves radical surgery, chemotherapy, and/or radiation therapy. Many times these therapies can adversely affect the functioning of the reproductive or genital organs and the sexual response cycle. The person with cancer may also experience altered sexual identity or decreased self-esteem as a result of real or imagined bodily changes resulting from disease or therapy. How the person feels about and deals with the disease and an altered body image or lowered self-esteem can cause sexual problems.

Until the early 1980s, the sexuality of the person with cancer was largely ignored by health care professionals and researchers of human sexuality. However, earlier diagnosis and more effective treatments have lengthened survival, so sexuality issues have emerged for these people. These issues are part of what is commonly called "quality of life" and demand the attention of health professionals and scientists. Patients now question members of their health care team about the effects, short- and long-term, of their cancer therapy on their ability to have children and to engage in sexual activities. Informed consumers of health care now expect more information related to their treatment, and cancer patients, specifically, have become more aware of their right to sexual information.

Effects of Cancer Treatment on Male Sexuality

Radical treatment for cancer can affect the male's ability to engage in sexual acts and to reproduce. Certain therapies interfere with penile erection, ejaculation, or emission and decrease sexual desire. Sperm production may also be affected, resulting in temporary or permanent infertility or sterility.

Body image changes may also occur related to the loss, or alteration in function, of a body part, with accompanying feelings of decreased self-worth and loss of masculinity. Other related psychological problems that can affect sexuality include depression, fear of (or actual) pain; fear of rejection or abandonment by family, friends, and significant others; and fear of transmission of disease or even the effects of treatment.

Prostate Cancer

Radical prostatectomy (i.e., the removal of the prostate gland and surrounding area) often results in erectile dysfunction, which is the inability to achieve or to maintain a penile erection sufficient for sexual penetration with a partner. Loss of erectile function or ejaculation does not usually affect penile sensation or the ability to reach orgasm, however. Orgasm is basically a function of the brain and can be experienced even by men who are almost completely paralyzed (although this function may need to be relearned). For a large percentage of males erectile function does not return; but if a nerve-sparing surgical approach is utilized, many may regain the ability to achieve adequate erections. Recovery of this function, however, may take up to two years.

Since ejaculation and emission are not possible after prostatectomy, the operation always produces a "dry" (and sometimes weaker) orgasm. In addition, the male is functionally sterile. This may not be a concern for a man age 60 or older, but such an assumption is dubious without more evidence than advancing age.

In cases of advanced or recurrent prostate cancer with metastasis, castration may be performed to halt the production of testosterone to slow the progression of disease. The surgical method of castration involves removal of both testicles, which may be replaced with silicone prostheses for cosmetic reasons. This procedure produces profound body image changes for many males and for this reason chemical castration by drugs may be preferable. The effects of hormone therapy are outlined in Table 1.

Testicular Cancer

Testicular cancer, although rare, is the most common cancer in males ages 15 to 34. The initial treatment is orchiectomy (i.e., removal of the testicle). This is usually a unilateral procedure, since cancer is almost always found in only one testicle. A prosthesis can replace a surgically removed testicle to help maintain body image and appearance.

Fertility is not compromised by the removal of one testicle; however, men with testicular cancer often have a decreased sperm count upon diagnosis, probably related to the disease. If fertility is affected by therapy, it usually results from additional surgery to remove lymph nodes from the abdomen (i.e., retroperitoneal lymph node dissection, or RLND). This procedure may cause a reduction in the amount of semen ejaculated or, more often, loss of the ability to ejaculate, either temporarily or permanently, resulting in sterility. Erectile function should not be affected, but orgasmic pleasure may be mildly reduced. Recovery of ejaculation may occur over time, in months to years. A modified approach to the RLND usually preserves the function of ejaculation. In addition, some testicular cancer patients may receive radiation therapy that can also cause loss or reduction of ejaculation, as well as erectile dysfunction and infertility.

Bladder Cancer

Extensive surgical removal of the urinary bladder and surrounding structures (radical cystectomy) produces many of the same results as radical prostatectomy. There is a high incidence of erectile dysfunction (unless nerve-sparing surgery is utilized), and ejaculation and emission are lost. Bladder cancer mainly affects older males, but advancing age does not preclude sexual desire and activity. Therefore, the impact of loss of penile erections on the sexuality of these men and the options for sexual rehabilitation (e.g., penile implants for achieving a mechanically assisted erection) must be considered.

The patient with bladder cancer may also receive a urinary ostomy, which necessitates wearing a bag on the abdomen to collect urine. An ostomy may profoundly affect body image and sexual identity. Some men even react to it as if it were castration or demasculinization. Fortunately, surgeons are exploring alternatives to urinary ostomies that do not involve wearing a collection device.

Colon Rectal Cancer

Surgical removal of the upper portion of the rectum and the adjacent tissue, by a procedure known as an abdominal perineal resection (APR), can result in sexual dysfunction for some men. It may not be possible for the surgeon to spare the nerves that control erection during this procedure, but sometimes these nerves are only slightly affected and erectile function can return in six months or longer. Recovery of erectile function is greater in males under age 60 and in men who had full erections before surgery.

The ability to ejaculate may also be lost after an APR, resulting in functional sterility. This loss of reproductive capacity may be significant to the male with rectal cancer even at older ages.

Cancer of the colon or of the lower rectum may be surgically treated by a less radical procedure called a low anterior resection, which often preserves erectile function.

Some surgical procedures for colon rectal cancer may result in a colostomy. The psychological impact of this ostomy, whether permanent or temporary, on the quality of the patient's life must be considered. Fortunately, recent advances in surgical techniques have eliminated permanent colostomies for the majority of patients.

Penile Cancer

Early, noninvasive cancer of the penis can be treated with topical chemotherapy or radiation implants. More commonly, partial or total amputation of the penis is required.

A partial penectomy (resection of some of the penis) rarely affects the male's ability to achieve and maintain an erection, and ejaculation and orgasmic sensation remain normal. Penile reconstruction may be an option for some of these patients for cosmetic and functional reasons.

Total amputation of the penis precludes sexual intercourse; however, the ability to be a sexually functioning male is not lost. Stimulation of the remaining genital tissue can be pleasurable and can lead to ejaculation (through the new urinary passage) and to orgasm.

Chemotherapy and Radiation Therapy

The effects of cancer chemotherapeutic agents on sexuality vary depending on the drug(s), total dose, duration of treatment, age of the patient, and time since therapy was completed. Often, the effects of cancer chemotherapy on sexual and reproductive functions are not known. Some losses in fertility may be temporary, although lasting for years; others may be permanent. When several drugs are used in combination, the effect on sperm production is greater and more prolonged than with a single drug.

Disruptions of sexual functioning due to chemotherapy are less common; however, there are a few drugs that may cause erectile dysfunction or disturbances in ejaculation. Side effects of therapy, such as fatigue, can decrease sexual desire temporarily. Chemotherapy does not affect the production of testosterone.

Cancer chemotherapy may also affect self-concept and body image because of loss of hair, nausea and vomiting, skin changes, weight gain or loss, and other effects.

Sperm production and erectile function are adversely affected by radiation therapy to the pelvis or testicles, with greater effects resulting from direct radiation than from indirect or scatter radiation. If the testicles are shielded, fewer reproductive effects result. Radiation therapy is seldom used alone; most often it is combined with chemotherapy to treat certain cancers. The combination of chemotherapy and radiation has a multiplying effect, reducing sperm production more than the sum of the effects of each therapy.

Effects of Cancer Treatment on Female Sexuality

Radical surgery, chemotherapy, and/or radiation therapy for cancer can affect the female's ability to reproduce, to engage in, and to enjoy sexual activities. Loss of the ovaries or their function may cause sterility and side effects (e.g., hot flushes, night sweats, irritability, depression, decreased vaginal lubrication, decreased sexual desire, and pain on vaginal penetration).

Women can experience body image changes related to loss of a body part or its function, lowered self-concept, and feelings of loss of femininity as a result of cancer therapy. They may also experience fear of abandonment and rejection. In addition, disease-related depression often causes loss of sexual desire.

Gynecologic Cancers

A common procedure in the treatment of female reproductive cancers is the radical hysterectomy. The surgical removal of the uterus, ovaries, and Fallopian tubes and surrounding structures produces sterility. The vagina is shortened by as much as one-third by this procedure, which may cause pain on vaginal penetration. Pain on vaginal penetration always has the potential to adversely affect the sexual response cycle: desire, arousal, and orgasm. Surgical removal of the ovaries also causes abrupt premature menopause, often accompanied by severe symptoms related to decreased estrogen. Reduced estrogen usually causes loss of vaginal lubrication and elasticity over time, resulting in pain on vaginal penetration. If testosterone levels are also reduced, as they may be in some women, decreased sexual desire may occur. Moreover, some females report less pleasurable orgasms due to the loss of the uterus.

Any gynecologic cancer therapy—such as radical surgery, chemotherapy, or radiation therapy—may produce menopausal symptoms or premature menopause, infertility or sterility, and sexual dysfunction. (See Table 2.)

Cancer of the cervix is often treated locally with radiation. This therapy can cause loss of vaginal elasticity, fragile vaginal tissue, lack of vaginal lubrication, pain or tenderness on vaginal penetration, and sexual dysfunction.

Vulvar cancer, if advanced, is usually treated with radical surgery. In this surgery, the vulva (outer and inner lips surrounding the vagina), the clitoris, and part of the vagina are removed. Even with these losses, it is often possible for women to experience sexual pleasure and orgasm. If vulvar cancer is treated at an early stage, it does not require such radical surgery and sexual functioning is not usually affected. Although vulvar cancer is generally found in older women in their sixties and seventies, many of these women may be sexually functioning individuals.

Bladder Cancer

A radical cystectomy in the female is almost always accompanied by a radical hysterectomy with the above-mentioned side effects. Because this surgical procedure produces a much narrower or shallower vagina, the vagina often needs to be reconstructed. The anterior vaginal wall may be an erotic zone for some women, and its loss can result in sexual dysfunction. Even with reconstruction, some women may experience pain on vaginal penetration. If pain is not a problem, the female's orgasmic potential remains the same.

An ostomy and an external urinary collection device may alter body image and self-concept and interfere with sexual activities and relationships.

Colon Rectal Cancer

Extensive surgery for colon or rectal cancer in the female also often includes a radical hysterectomy. In addition to the sterility, menopausal symptoms, and sexual problems related to the hysterectomy, some women experience genital numbness after the abdominal perineal resection procedure.

If a colostomy is required, women often have difficulty coping with this alteration in body image, but many of them adjust over time. Intimate relationships can suffer during this adjustment period.

Breast Cancer

Surgery for breast cancer is usually performed by one of two procedures. A modified radical mastectomy is removal of the breast, minor chest muscle, and underarm lymph nodes. The limited resection, or "lumpectomy," involves removal of only the tumor and the surrounding tissue, and the lymph nodes, followed by radiation therapy to the chest. Neither of these procedures should affect sexual functioning, but because of the sometimes profound effects on body image and self-esteem, a woman may avoid intimate physical encounters. However, many report no decrease in feelings of femininity or in sexual identity.

Some women are treated with anti-estrogen therapy after breast cancer. This therapy appears to prevent the growth of undetected breast cancer cells and subsequent spread of disease. Currently, tamoxifen is the sole drug used for this purpose. Administration of this preparation to the premenopausal female results in premature menopause with its related side effects. In the postmenopausal woman, hot flushes may be exacerbated. The advantages of this treatment, however, usually outweigh any side effects.

Chemotherapy and Radiation Therapy
The female gonads (the ovaries) are more sensitive to chemotherapy and radiation than are the male testicles. Cancer chemotherapeutic effects for the female depend on the type of drug(s), dose, length of administration, time of therapy and, to a great degree, the age of the patient. Ovarian function may be temporarily or permanently affected by chemotherapy. The closer a woman is to menopause, the greater the effect. Females between ages 35 and 40 years are more likely to experience premature menopause. Sometimes in slightly younger women, menstrual periods cease but resume in time. In other cases, the ovaries may fail after pregnancy.

Some cancers are treated with radiation therapy and chemotherapy. Combined therapy produces greater effects on gonadal function in the female than in the male, often resulting in infertility or sterility, and menopausal symptoms or early menopause.

External radiation therapy directly to the pelvis produces loss of vaginal elasticity, fragile vaginal tissue, lack of vaginal lubrication, and pain or tenderness on vaginal penetration, plus some degree of ovarian dysfunction. Even if an attempt is made to shield the ovaries during radiation therapy, there may be some disruption in menstrual periods and fertility. Scatter radiation to the ovaries from treatment to nearby areas can also suppress ovarian function, temporarily or permanently.

Chemotherapy and/or radiation therapy can affect body image and self-concept if nausea and vomiting, hair loss, weight loss/gain, or skin changes are experienced. Sexual dysfunction may also result from these effects. In addition, infertility may cause sexual dysfunction because of psychological reasons. If lowered testosterone levels result from ovarian failure, loss of sexual desire may also occur.

Conclusion
Cancer therapy can affect many aspects of human sexuality: sexual function, gonadal function, fertility, body image, self-esteem, sexual identity, and sex roles. In addition, relationships may be disrupted. These are important issues for patients as they recover from and become survivors of cancer. As one former cancer patient said, "We are all survivors, no matter how long we live." The assessment of the quality of life for people with cancer should include sexuality. If problems arise, these men and women should know where to go for help. Fortunately, many cancer health care professionals see the need to address the sexuality of their patients. They possess the comfort, knowledge and skills to intervene appropriately and assist clients with cancer-related alterations in sexuality. Furthermore, important and much-needed research is being carried out by physicians, nurses, and mental health professionals to identify alterations in sexual and reproductive function and appropriate interventions.

If health professionals fail to address sexuality, patients may seek out information from other sources. Organizations such as the American Cancer Society, the National Cancer Institute, the Cancer Information Service, and the Sex Information and Education Council of the United States, among others, may be useful in helping patients find answers to their questions. (See Appendix.)

Table 1. Effects of Cancer Treatment on Male Sexuality

Cancer Treatment	Sexual Function	Reproduction
Radical prostatectomy	loss of emission & ejaculation, erectile dysfunction	sterility
Unilateral orchiectomy	none, usually	none
Retroperitoneal lymph node dissection	reduced, absent or retrograde ejaculation (into bladder), possible decreased orgasm	sterility with loss of ejaculation

Table 1. *Effects of Cancer Treatment on Male Sexuality (cont.)*

Cancer Treatment	Sexual Function	Reproduction
Bilateral orchiectomy	loss of desire, decreased semen volume, erectile dysfunction	sterility
Hormone therapy for prostate cancer	loss of desire, reduced semen volume, erectile dysfunction, penile atrophy	sterility
Radical cystectomy	loss of emission & ejaculation, erectile dysfunction	sterility
Abdominal perineal resection	sometimes loss of ejaculation &/or erectile function (temporary or permanent)	sterility with loss of ejaculation
Partial penectomy	none, usually	none
Total penectomy	absence of penis does not affect desire, arousal, ejaculation, or orgasm	none
Pelvic radiation therapy	loss of emission or ejaculation or reduced semen volume, erectile dysfunction (temporary or permanent)	infertility or sterility (temporary or permanent)
Chemotherapy	none, usually	infertility or sterility with some agents (temporary or permanent)

Table 2. *Effects of Cancer Treatment on Female Sexuality*

Reproductive/Cancer Treatment	Sexual Function	Gonadal Function
Radical hysterectomy	decreased vaginal lubrication, reduced vaginal size, sometimes decreased desire & change in orgasmic sensation	sterility, premature menopause
Abdominoperineal resection	sometimes decreased desire; decreased vaginal lubrication; sometimes reduced vaginal size, genital numbness &/or pain on vaginal penetration	sterility & premature menopause with removal of ovaries
Radical vulvectomy	reduced vaginal size, sometimes difficulty reaching orgasm	none

Table 2. Effects of Cancer Treatment on Female Sexuality (cont.)

Reproductive/Cancer Treatment	Sexual Function	Gonadal Function
Radical cystectomy	sometimes decreased desire, decreased vaginal lubrication, reduced vaginal size	sterility & premature menopause with removal of ovaries
Pelvic radiation therapy	sometimes decreased desire, decreased vaginal lubrication, reduced vaginal elasticity & size, pain &/or bleeding on vaginal penetration	infertility or sterility (temporary or permanent), menopausal symptoms
Mastectomy/ Lumpectomy	none, usually	none
Anti-estrogen therapy	sometimes decreased desire & decreased vaginal lubrication	infertility or sterility & menopausal symptoms
Chemotherapy	sometimes decreased desire & decreased vaginal lubrication (if ovarian function is affected)	infertility or sterility (temporary or permanent), menopausal symptoms/ premature menopause with some agents

APPENDIX
Resources for People with Cancer

American Cancer Society
1599 Clifton Road, NE
Atlanta, GA 30329
(Or a local division of the American Cancer Society)

National Cancer Institute
Office of Cancer Communications
Building 13, Room 10A-24
Bethesda, MD 20892

Cancer Information Service
1–800–4–CANCER

Sex Information and Education Council of the U.S. (SIECUS)
130 West 42nd Street, Suite 2500
New York, NY 10036
212–819–9770

American Association of Sex Educators, Counselors, and Therapists (AASECT)
11 Dupont Circle, NW, Suite 220
Washington, DC 20036

Society for the Scientific Study of Sex
P.O. Box 208
Mount Vernon, IA 52314
319–895–8407

REFERENCES

Schover, L.R. *Sexuality and Cancer. For the Woman Who Has Cancer, and Her Partner.* New York: American Cancer Society, 1988.

———. *Sexuality and Cancer. For the Man Who Has Cancer, and His Partner.* New York: American Cancer Society, 1988.

Marianne Glasel

CANON LAW AND SEX

Canon law, the legal system of the Christian church, dates back to the beginning of the second century of the Common Era. Since then, the Christian church, through its canons and the mechanisms used to enforce them, has played a key role in enunciating and defining the norms of sexual behavior within Christian communities, particularly among members of the Catholic, Orthodox, Lutheran, and Anglican branches of Christianity.

Canonical rules from the beginning were markedly concerned with the moral and disciplinary problems arising from sexual attractions and desires. Christians, like pagan Romans, were expected to be monogamous; unlike their pagan contemporaries, however, married Christians were also expected to remain sexually faithful to their mates, to refrain from divorce (save perhaps on the grounds of the spouse's adultery), and generally to observe restraint in their sexual behavior within marriage, while avoiding entirely any sexual intimacy outside of it.

Christian writers soon began to justify their canonical rules and other teachings about sex by arguing that these rules were grounded either in divine revelation or in human reason, or (when all else failed) in "nature" or "natural law." They felt compelled to do this in order to respond to criticisms of their way of life put forward not only by pagan and Jewish critics outside the Christian fold, but also by unorthodox critics within their ranks, whom mainstream Christians denounced as heretics.

St. Augustine's Influence

In the Western church, by far the most influential early writer on Christian sexual ethics was St. Augustine of Hippo (354–430). St. Augustine vigorously disapproved of any sexual laxity; more important, he gradually developed an elaborate rationale for the basic tenets of Christian sexual morality that seemed to him—and even today seem to many Christians—both reasonable and persuasive. Human sexuality, according to St. Augustine's theory, departs in many important ways from the original intentions of the divine Creator. In paradise, before Adam and Eve (the progenitors of the entire human race) had committed the first sin, sexual feelings and sexual relations were radically different from those that we now know. Intercourse in paradise brought none of the intense pleasure now associated with orgasm; the human sex drive was entirely subordinate to reason, and Adam and Eve knew nothing of the insistent urges and passions their descendants have experienced ever since the Fall from grace and the consequent expulsion of Adam, Eve, and all their descendants from the bliss of paradise. Sex, therefore is (like its sister, death) a consequence of sin, an aspect of humankind's continuing rebellion against God's wishes. It is a part of the punishment all must bear for being descendants of the first sinners and a depraved craving that must be repressed and overcome to merit salvation and the friendship of God in the world to come.

It seems to follow from these premises, as later Christians have often concluded, that sexual behavior presents a key moral issue, a benchmark by which virtue may be measured. Canonical rules about sexual conduct, therefore, aimed to encourage everyone who could do so

to reject sexual pleasure entirely and to embrace instead a life of perpetual virginity, unblemished by sexual experience. Those unable to renounce sex completely were sternly admonished to confine their obscene gropings to the marriage bed and under no circumstance allow themselves to experience sexual pleasure outside of marriage. Even within marriage, they were to engage in intercourse only when they intended to beget a child and never for carnal gratification and pleasure.

The Penitentials

General exhortations along these lines became specific guidelines for acceptable sexual behavior in the penitentials, or handbooks for confessors, that Christian spiritual authorities produced in considerable numbers beginning in the sixth century. The authors of penitentials agreed, for example, that married couples must abstain entirely from sexual relations during Lent, Pentecost, and Advent. In addition, it was grievously sinful for married persons to have intercourse on Wednesdays, Fridays, and Saturdays throughout the year, during the wife's menstrual period, during pregnancy, and after pregnancy so long as the child nursed at the mother's breast. Penitentials further warned couples that they sinned if they engaged in sexual relations during daylight, while they were naked, or in positions other than the one now described as the missionary position (i.e., with the wife supine and the husband on top of her). Nonmarital sex—whether social or solitary, heterosexual or homosexual, sleeping or waking, voluntary or involuntary—was likewise sinful according to these authorities, who often advised confessors in considerable detail about possible infractions of these prohibitions that repentant sinners might disclose to them in confession and prescribed penances they deemed appropriate for each situation.

During the second half of the 11th century, high-ranking church authorities began to require all clerics (or at least those in the upper ranks of the church's hierarchy) to renounce marriage and sex absolutely as a condition of ordination. While earlier spiritual writers and some church authorities had long praised clerical celibacy and encouraged all clergymen to embrace it, celibacy had previously been required only of monks and nuns who lived in religious communities. Now a vow of celibacy was required for ordination. This new asceticism created innumerable personal crises, not only for priests and other clerics, but also for their wives, children, families, and parishioners.

Gratian's Influence

Canon law first developed into a systematic intellectual discipline during the 12th century. With the appearance of the *Decretum* of Gratian in about 1140, canonists were provided with a reasoned, analytical textbook, which remained the basis for the teaching of canon law in the universities and schools throughout the Middle Ages; indeed the *Decretum* continued in use among Roman Catholics until the beginning of the 20th century. Medieval and modern canonistic treatments of sexual behavior were thus grounded largely on positions and ideas that canonists found in Gratian's work.

Gratian viewed sexual pleasure as a disturbing influence in human life, a temptation that distracted Christians from the goal of salvation, and an instrument that the devil regularly used to entice souls into hell. The clear message of Gratian's *Decretum*, therefore, was that sexual activity must be confined within stringent limits. Sex was lawful only between husband and wife and even then it must be carefully limited and controlled. A married person could properly engage in intercourse only under one of three conditions: to beget a child, to avert temptations to marital infidelity, or to accommodate the insistent (and probably sinful) demands of the spouse.

All other sexual activity, within marriage or outside of it, as well as any sexual desire or arousal other than that permitted for lawful purposes between husband and wife, was sinful and under many circumstances might be subject to criminal prosecution as well. Thus, even within marriage, one had to be careful. The husband who loved his wife too passionately, according to St. Jerome (c. 331–419/20), was an adulterer, and canonists strove to prescribe strict operational limits on legitimate marital intimacy. Among other things, for example, they focused on positions couples adopted during sexual relations. Medieval canonists and theologians were prepared to condone as "natural" only marital intercourse conducted in the missionary position. Intercourse in any position in which the woman lay or sat atop the man seemed to canonists "unnatural," since they believed that such a posture reversed the proper order of relationship between the sexes by making the female superior to the male. Canonists and theologians likewise condemned intercourse "from behind" (retro), that is, in which the husband entered his wife from the rear, since they considered intercourse in

such a posture "beastly" and hence entirely inappropriate for humans. Church authorities vehemently rejected all anal or oral sexual practices, which Gratian's book described as "extraordinary sensual pleasures" and "whorish embraces," both because such practices were clearly nonprocreative and because sexual pleasure seemed to be their sole objective. Writers on theology and canon law frequently branded any departure from heterosexual relations in the missionary position as "sodomy," on the theory that the biblical story of God's destruction of the city of Sodom (Genesis: 18–19) definitively demonstrated divine disapproval of activities, heterosexual or homosexual, that aimed primarily at enhancing sexual pleasure.

Gratian classed adultery as a heinous crime, much more serious than fornication, although not quite as grave a lapse as incest or sodomy. Both incest and sodomy (by which he apparently meant any sexual encounter between persons of the same gender or extra-vaginal intercourse between persons of different genders) deserved in his eyes to rank with such atrocious crimes as murder, forgery, arson, sacrilege, and heresy. While simple fornication between two unmarried persons was, to be sure, both a serious sin and a canonical crime, Gratian and other canonists tended to treat it as a routine offense, which called for fines and a humiliating penance that might discourage others from such unacceptable behavior. Most canonists followed Gratian in treating masturbation as a minor peccadillo, although a few later writers, particularly Jean Gerson (1363–1429), considered solitary sex so serious an offense that only a bishop might pardon the offender and prescribe suitable punishment.

The canonists in principle proscribed every sort of sexual experimentation or deviation from the approved version of marital intercourse, and even more stringently barred all types of nonmatrimonial sexual activity. In practice, even the most devout occasionally strayed from the strict paths authority prescribed, and sexual offenses, together with marriage problems, accounted for most of the business that came before local ecclesiastical courts almost everywhere.

Sexual Sins and Offenses

Numerous sex offenses, however, rarely found their way into the courts, but rather were usually dealt with privately in the so-called internal forum of confession. This was understandably true of solitary offenses, such as masturbation, as well as private deviations from the prescriptions for marital conduct—engaging in intercourse unclothed, for example, or during daylight, at forbidden times, or in unconventional postures. Pastoral manuals and handbooks for confessors often dealt at such great length and in such detail with sexual sins that one could conclude these behaviors must have flourished among medieval people; they certainly fascinated the celibate clergymen who constituted the intended audience for these works. Confessors' manuals also routinely cautioned priests to inquire diligently into the sexual habits of the penitents who came to them, but at the same time warned the confessor to take care that his questioning not supply penitents with fresh ideas for disapproved sexual behavior that had not already occurred to them. The dividing line was exceedingly fine, and many a confessor must have found it difficult to be sure he had not crossed it.

Punishment of sex offenses by canonical courts might, in theory, be extremely severe; in practice, the more common sex crimes, such as fornication, often brought little more than a casual fine, occasionally accompanied by ritual public humiliation to impress upon the rest of the community the seriousness of the offense. Even so, ample evidence suggests that many medieval people found it difficult to accept the theological opinion that something so common and natural as fornication could be a sin, much less that it was so grave an offense that it would doom its perpetrators to eternal torment in hell.

Adultery was far more serious, often punishable by both canonical tribunals and secular judges, not only because the act violated marital vows and threatened the stability of marriage, but also because children conceived in an adulterous relationship created formidable problems in the law of inheritance. Incest was likewise a troublesome problem in medieval society, and the courts tended to treat convicted offenders very harshly. The most serious sexual crime, most authorities agreed, was sodomy, by which they meant both sexual relations between persons of the same gender and also all sexual relations between a man and a woman other than vaginal intercourse—thus heterosexual fellatio, cunnilingus, or anal intercourse, for example, might be classified as sodomy and subject participants in these activities to severe penalties. Many authorities were inclined to class sexual contacts between humans and other animals as another type of sodomy, although some writers distinguished between these offenses and treated bestiality as a separate class of sex crime, slightly less serious than homosexual sodomy.

Despite their moral condemnation of all extramarital sex, most canonical writers, oddly enough, were prepared to tolerate prostitution in practice and even in principle. The reigning theory, enunciated by St. Augustine, argued that if prostitutes were not available to slake male lust, men would inevitably solicit sexual favors from respectable matrons and other "honest women." That, St. Augustine held, would dislocate the peaceful order of society. It was better, according to this line of reasoning, to allow prostitutes to continue their sinful and unsavory trade rather than to risk the social disorder that would accompany successful prohibition of commercial sex. Some medieval writers went so far as to argue that, although it was morally wrong for both the prostitute and her client to engage in relations, prostitution was necessary for the public good. One authoritative commentator compounded this paradox by explaining that sex with a prostitute was doubly evil, for it was a wrongful use of an evil thing, as opposed to marital sex, which was a rightful use of an evil thing. Nonetheless, just as God tolerated the evil of marital sex because of the good effects that it might produce (e.g., children and the mutual support and companionship of married couples), so Christian society must tolerate prostitution to secure the benefits of social harmony and domestic peace.

Prostitution, then, was not only tolerated in many medieval communities, but was sometimes treated as a public utility. When towns began to build and operate municipal brothels to regulate the sex trade, they realized a profit from it at the same time. Moral ambiguity concerning the prostitution industry long persisted and still remains a controversial topic.

Both lawyers and lawmakers typically sought to contain prostitution by restricting harlots and their trade to specially designated regions within towns. Municipal statutes, following a suggestion of the Fourth Lateran Council (1215), also required prostitutes in many towns to wear distinctive colors and clothing so as to spare respectable women from the sexual importuning of randy men, and incidentally to preserve civic peace and harmony at the same time.

Church leaders and civic authorities alike, moreover, were concerned to provide women who wished to abandon the life of shame with realistic opportunities to do so. Thus, for example, Pope Innocent III (1198–1216) early in the 13th century reversed a long-standing policy that had prohibited good Christian men from marrying prostitutes and instead promised spiritual favors for those who would do so, provided they kept close watch over their wives to make sure that they remained sexually faithful and did not return to their wanton ways. The prospect of marrying a reformed prostitute was especially alluring, no doubt, to financially disadvantaged men, since successful strumpets sometimes managed to accumulate substantial dowries from the profits of their trade.

The 13th century similarly witnessed the creation of convents and religious orders of women, which provided a haven and some security and chaste companionship for reformed daughters of joy. The most successful of these religious institutes, the Order of St. Mary Magdalene (whose members were informally known as the White Ladies), established houses in many major European cities, and in a surprising number of minor ones as well. Such institutions constituted a social security system of sorts for prostitutes who wished to retire from their occupation, but required both social and economic support to do so.

The moral ambivalence that canonists and other legal experts showed toward prostitution was emblematic of the difficulties medieval societies experienced in confronting the realities of human sexuality. Committed in principle to restricting sexual activity as much as possible, the canonists nonetheless had to take account professionally of the fact that systematic enforcement of the limits they wished to impose was difficult, if not impossible. For private deviations from the sexual norms, periodic confession of sins provided both some surveillance and the opportunity to counsel offenders to avoid future infringements of the rules. For offenses that became publicly known, lawmakers and administrators of the medieval church had to create a law enforcement system to detect suspected offenders and courts to try and punish them, in the hope that this would deter others from imitating their bad examples. The church's enforcement and court systems in the early Middle Ages were neither efficient nor effective. During the late 12th century, however, church leaders began to devise more elaborate and successful mechanisms to repress beliefs and behaviors they considered undesirable. By the end of the 13th century, popes and bishops had put in place a complex system of courts, spanning every level of Christian society, from the courts of the archdeacons at the local level through the consistory courts of the bishops and the regional courts of the archbishops to the central courts of the Roman Curia. Sexual misconduct and marital irregularities furnished all of these courts, especially those at the lower levels of the hierarchy, with most of their business. Offenders against canonistic sexual norms not only made this complex judicial structure necessary, but also supported it financially through the fees and fines the courts generated.

The sexual standards of medieval canon law have persisted with striking tenacity in modern European and American law. In the United States, for example, fornication, adultery, and sodomy remain crimes in many states and occasionally, under unusual circumstances, offenders may be prosecuted for them. The so-called spousal exception, which permits defendants in rape or sexual abuse cases to escape punishment if they can prove they were married to the victim when the alleged offense occurred, remains today the standard rule in many North American jurisdictions and constitutes a further example of the continuing presence of canonical legal doctrine in 20th-century civil law.

REFERENCES

Boswell, J. *Christianity, Social Tolerance, and Homosexuality: Gay People in Western Europe From the Beginning of the Christian Era to the Fourteenth Century.* Chicago: Univ. of Chicago Press, 1980.

Brooke, C.N.L. *The Medieval Idea of Marriage.* Oxford: Oxford Univ. Press, 1989.

Brundage, J.A. *Law, Sex, and Christian Society in Medieval Europe.* Chicago: Univ. of Chicago Press, 1887.

Bullough, V.L., and J.A. Brundage, eds. *Sexual Practices and the Medieval Church.* Buffalo: Prometheus Books, 1982.

Kelly, H.A. *Love and Marriage in the Age of Chaucer.* Ithaca, N.Y.: Cornell Univ. Press, 1975.

Levin, E. *Sex and Society in the World of the Orthodox Slavs. 900–1700.* Ithaca, N.Y.: Cornell Univ. Press, 1989.

Noonan, J.T. *Contraception: A History of Its Treatment by the Catholic Theologians and Canonists.* Cambridge, Mass.: Belknap Press, 1965.

Payer, P.J. *Sex and the Penitentials: The Development of a Sexual Code, 550–1150.* Toronto: Univ. of Toronto Press, 1984.

Salisbury, J.E. *Medieval Sexuality: A Research Guide.* New York: Garland, 1990.

———, ed. *Sex in the Middle Ages.* New York: Garland, 1991.

Sheehan, M.M., and J. Murray, comp. *Domestic Society in Medieval Europe: A Select Bibliography.* Toronto: Pontifical Institute of Medieval Studies, 1990.

James A. Brundage

CASANOVA; CASANOVISM

Giovanni Jacopo Casanova de Seingalt (1725–98) was a Venetian adventurer whose name exemplifies the hypersexual male. Casanova falsely appropriated the aristocratic "de Seingalt" as an aid to seducing women and impressing men; it apparently did both. Almost all of what is known about this libertine comes from his multivolume *Memoirs*. Written in his old age—a time when memory fades and imagination runs wild—his *Memoirs* portrays him as a man of engaging wit, charm, and intelligence with a distinguished, if not handsome, face. He both earned a law degree and bedded his first wench—"a pretty girl of thirteen"—at the age of 16, met and enlightened all the best minds of the age, fought and defeated the finest swordsmen, and broke all the casinos and half of the hymens in Italy and France.

Although perhaps a braggadocio, Casanova was indeed a man with an extraordinary sexual appetite; his descriptions and the naming of at least 116 of his conquests give credence to many of his claims. He made love without prejudice of age or social standing; females ranging from ages nine to 70 and of all classes fell to his allure. Nor did the incest taboo cool his ardor; he was sexually involved with at least one of his illegitimate daughters. All, he states, were eternally grateful for his services.

The syndrome to which Casanova lends his name, "Casanovism," is known also as "Don Juanism" (named after Don Juan, a fictional character), satyriasis, hyperphilia, and hypersexuality. Men afflicted with this syndrome view love as a compulsive game played with many partners in order to minimize commitment; women are play objects and notches on the bedpost. Practice has made them charming and attentive, but they lose interest in a woman almost immediately after making their conquest, as Casanova invariably did. Hypersexuality has been linked to manic-depression, psychopathy, and a defect in pair-bonding and childhood attachment. It has also been chemically linked to low levels of a major metabolizer of some major neurotransmitters called monoamine oxydase (MAO), which has been implicated in many psychopathic-like behaviors.

Casanova's life offers much case-study evidence for these claims. He was born (probably illegitimately) to two actors who abandoned him when he was one year old. Given the great importance of early bonding to the healthy formation of later relationships, it is easy to see why he was never able to form lasting attachments. His lack of commitment to, or concern for, his conquests; his many other deviant exploits; and his oft-stated lack of remorse or regret are certainly characteristic of a psychopathic personality. His gay abandon and boundless energy, coupled with the "black sorrow" (depression) he admitted suffering, are indicative of the manic-depression syndrome. All these syndromes have been linked to low MAO.

Casanova spent his last 14 years as the librarian of Count von Waldstein in the Castle of Dux in Bohemia, where he composed his *Memoirs*. He died in timely piety in 1798 ("I have lived a philosopher, and I die a Christian."), thus having had the best of both worlds.

REFERENCES

Bullough, V. *Sexual Variance in Society and History.* Chicago: Univ. of Chicago Press, 1976.

Casonova, J. *The Memoirs of Jacques Casanova de Seingelt.* A. Machen, trans. New York: A. & C. Bon, 1932.

Durant, W., and A. Durant. *Rousseau and Revolution: The Story of Civilization.* Vol. 10, New York: Simon & Schuster, 1967.

Frost, L., and L. Chapman. Polymorphous sexuality as an indicator of psychosis proneness." *Journal of Abnormal Psychology,* Vol. 96 (1987), pp. 299–304.

Liebowitz, M. *The Chemistry of Love.* New York: Berkeley, 1983.

Money, J. *Love and Lovesickness: The Science of Sex, Gender Difference and Pair Bonding.* Baltimore: Johns Hopkins Univ. Press, 1980.

Walsh, A. *The Science of Love: Understanding Love and Its Effects on Mind and Body.* New York: Prometheus, 1991.

Anthony Walsh

CASTRATION

Castration—the removal of the male testes and sometimes the penis—was practiced in many cultures until quite recently. The emperor of China employed 3,000 eunuchs (Greek for "guardian of the bed") as late as 1896, and castration disappeared from the Ottoman Empire only when the empire itself disappeared in 1923. Although valued primarily for their loyal service as guards and bureaucrats, eunuchs were also prized, by those so inclined, for their sexual services. Some believed eunuchs developed highly eroticized mouths and anuses if they lost both penis and testicles. Some young males in China became eunuchs by choice and were emasculated by professional "eunuch makers." Such a sacrifice might provide them with secure employment at the Imperial Palace as guards, secretaries, and many other governmental posts; several rose to become virtual dictators.

The position of eunuchs in the Byzantine Empire was even more exalted than in China—so much so that many ambitious young men voluntarily submitted to the knife. Eunuchs appointed to many prominent posts were loyal and reliable servants. Their privileged position in the paranoid world of Byzantium lay in the knowledge that they served as a foil to the hereditary nobility and, being unable to sire children, could not aspire to hereditary offices.

The Christian church, probably because of the undertones of homosexuality and transsexuality of castration, denounced the practice. Deuteronomy 23:1 warns: "He that is wounded in the stones, or hath his privy member cut off, shall not enter into the congregation of the lord." Nevertheless, aware that the seat of human lust lies in the "stones," Origen, an early church father in Rome, emasculated himself in an overly literal interpretation of Matthew 19:12. The testicle issue was so important to the church at one time that it required new popes to submit to the inspection of the papal privates by its cardinals. Having ascertained the presence of the holy scrotum, the examiners solemnly proclaimed in Latin: "He has testicles and they hang well."

The Catholic church prohibited women in church choirs, so it employed eunuchs to give voice to the higher notes in its musical repertoire while maintaining its opposition to castration. With the rising popularity of opera in Italy at the end of the 15th century, eunuchs were in high demand; many aspiring young opera stars submitted to the cruel operation hoping their fame would compensate them for their loss. These Italian eunuchs were the famed castrati. To maintain their high boyish voices, their testes had to be removed before their larynx enlarged under the influence of male hormones at puberty. (Castration after puberty has very little influence on voice pitch.) The pure tonal quality of these opera stars inspired their fans to cry "Long live the knife!"

No one studied how long the *castrati* lived, but it is known that cutting off the testes eliminates the primary source of testosterone, and that testosterone is the "villain" in many diseases afflicting primarily males. It is also known that neutered tomcats live longer than their intact brothers (spaying females does not lengthen their life span). A study of 297 "surgically docilized" (castrated) men in a Kansas institution for the mentally retarded found they outlived a matched group of noncastrated inmates by almost 14 years; they also outlived a group of female inmates.

Therapeutic castration of sex criminals has often been advised, but it is not particularly effective in adults, since testosterone and other androgens are also produced by the adrenal glands. Castration does not entirely eliminate the male sex drive; some eunuchs who retained their pe-

nises were sexually active, although, obviously, sterile. Castration after puberty often results in a penis of normal adult size that is capable of erection. More effective in the treatment of sex offenders is chemical "castration" through administration of anti-androgen drugs, such as medroxyprogesterone (Depo-Provera).

REFERENCES

Bradford, J. The Antiandrogen and Hormonal Treatment of Sex Offenders. In W. Marshall, D. Laws, and H. Barbaree, eds. *Handbook of Sexual Assault: Issues Theories, and Treatment of the Offender.* New York: Plenum Press, 1990.

Bullough, V. *Sexual Variance in Society and History.* Chicago: Univ. of Chicago Press, 1976.

Morris, D. *Bodywatching.* New York: Crown, 1985.

Runciman, S. *The Emperor Romanus Lecapenus and His Reign.* Cambridge: Cambridge Univ. Press, 1963.

Anthony Walsh

CATHOLIC ATTITUDES TOWARD SEXUALITY

A change in the attitude of the Roman Catholic Church toward sexuality has become apparent in contemporary times. Previously, the meaning and purposes of human sexual expression were defined primarily in terms of the natural law, with its emphasis on procreation. With the contemporary emphasis on personal development, the church has become aware of the psychological, social, affective, and religious elements as well as the biological aspects of human sexuality. Because sexuality is an essential factor in human development, it is also an integrating element in the Christian mission to extend God's love for all people. Since humans are by nature sexual beings, a factor that enables them to become lovers, the expression of sexuality must be kept within the context of love.

Love is experienced within a relationship that involves concern, care, and a willingness to assume responsibility for the other. A mutually shared life commitment in the form of marriage provides the best atmosphere for the complete loving gift of self in the act of sexual intercourse. It is in the sacrament of marriage publicly proclaimed that love, both human and divine, is best spread among God's people.

Sexuality in Marriage

The permanence of marriage continues to be a vital element in Catholic teachings on the sanctity of the intimate partnership. The continued existence of the sacred bond is necessary for the good of the spouses, children, and society.

Sexual fidelity contributes to the permanence of the union. Therefore, adultery continues to be prohibited because the couple in the marriage covenant of conjugal love "are no longer two, but one flesh" (Mt 19:6). The partners render mutual help and service to each other through this intimate union of their persons. Children need the stability of this oneness, which imposes total fidelity on the spouses.

The mutual love of the marriage partners is uniquely expressed and perfected through the marital act, the purpose of which is the procreation of children. Historical events, such as the rise in knowledge of techniques of birth control, appeared to frustrate the purpose of marriage. Confessors were looking for guidelines to advise penitents who were using coitus interruptus as well as technical instruments to prevent the birth of children from sexual intercourse. In reaction to the changing attitudes toward contraception, Pope Pius XI, in 1930, issued the encyclical *Casti Connubii* (On Chaste Marriage). He defined the primary purpose of the conjugal act as the begetting of children, with the secondary purposes of mutual aid of the spouses, the cultivating of mutual love, and the quieting of concupiscence. He went on to say that any time a couple engages in sexual intercourse "in such a way that the act is deliberately frustrated in its natural power to generate life . . . those who indulge in such are branded with the guilt of grave sin."

Pope Pius XII, in 1951, in an address to the Italian Catholic Society of Midwives, softened the stance toward birth control for serious reasons such as medical, eugenic, or social and economic considerations. Pius XII made the distinction between artificial birth control and the use of periodic abstinence or continence, whereby married couples refrain from sexual intercourse during the woman's fertile period. It follows from this viewpoint that once periodic abstinence or the use of rhythm, or natural family planning, is acknowledged as permissible, the primary purpose of marriage as the procreation and education of children appears to be altered.

Vatican II, in 1965, refused to designate primary or secondary purposes of marriage in the *Pastoral Constitution on the Church in the Modern World*. Marital acts of love "signify and promote that mutual self-giving by which spouses enrich each other with a joyful and thankful will." Marriage and conjugal love "are ordained for the procreation and education of children, and find in them their ultimate crown." Although both purposes are mentioned, there was no attempt to prioritize them. The concept of responsible parenthood was introduced in which

married couples, when planning their families, should "thoughtfully take into account both their own welfare and that of their children, those already born and those which may be foreseen." The Council Fathers encouraged spouses to practice conjugal chastity, which counseled married couples to avoid artificial means of birth control in their regulation of births.

The results of a papal commission appointed by Pope Paul VI to study the issue of contraception gave two divergent views. In 1966, the minority opinion, signed by four theologians, maintained the prohibition against all forms of contraception. The majority report, signed by the remaining members of the commission, recommended a change in the Church's official teaching on methods of contraception. Pope Paul's response came in 1968, when he issued his encyclical letter *Humanae Vitae* (Of Human Life), which declared that there could be no change in the Church's opposition to the use of artificial contraceptives. He did affirm the use of the "natural rhythm" of fecundity to regulate births. He based his argument on the two purposes of sexual intercourse, unitive (mutual support of the spouses) and procreative (the birth of children), which should not be separated.

In promulgating the encyclical, Pope Paul refrained from mentioning infallibility, and his spokesman, Monsignor Lambruschini, stated that it was "not irreformable." Many dissenting opinions arose against the idea that the procreative and unitive dimensions of human sexuality must be joined in every act of sexual intercourse. Women's recurring infertile periods indicate that a natural infecundity occurs, in which the unitive and procreative functions of sexual intercourse are separated. *Humanae Vitae* stressed that "every marriage act must remain open to the transmission of life." Dissenting theologians point out that conception cannot always follow intercourse; therefore, responsible parenthood calls for decision making between parents to regulate births.

The dissenters also point out that periodic abstinence places additional emotional or psychological strain on the spouses, especially women, who are more sexually responsive during their fertile periods. Many Catholic theologians maintain that, assuming spouses are responsibly motivated, the use of artificial contraception does not constitute a moral evil or sin and is not an objective moral wrong.

Premarital Sex

The most recent Vatican document (1975) on sexual ethics continues the basic teaching that genital sexual activity finds its truest meaning in marriage. Sexual union is only legitimate if a definitive community of life (i.e., marriage) has been established between the man and the woman. The problems associated with premarital sexual activity are that in the demand for responsible parenthood the act must be contraceptive. Since the intercourse is occurring outside a sacramental love union, it is not a love relationship publicly proclaimed, nor does it reflect God's love for us.

Premarital sexual actions violate the act of mutual self-giving by means of which two people express their willingness to assume unconditional responsibility for each other in a permanent manner. Couples engaging in premarital sex must be more socially sensitive to the view of marriage as the institution that intends to enhance personal relationships by helping each partner to overcome selfishness, immaturity, and dishonesty. Genital expression should reflect the level of personal commitment present between two persons following the example of God's love for humanity as being both creative and eternally faithful.

Some theologians see engaged couples as fulfilling the condition for marital sex because of their intent to provide for the mutual support of each other and to care for children.

Abortion

The Declaration on Abortion issued by the Sacred Congregation for the Doctrine of the Faith in 1974 reiterated the statement of Pius XI and Pius XII that condemned abortion, which is an end in itself or a means to an end. John XXIII asserted the sacredness of human life, which from its "very inception . . . reveals the creative hand of God." The Second Vatican Council condemned abortion by stating that "abortion and infanticide are abominable crimes." Paul VI said that this teaching of the church is unchanged and immutable on this subject .

The declaration based its premise on the principle that the right to life is the primordial right of human persons. Thus, every human life must be respected from the moment the process of generation begins. The declaration placed the beginning of life at fertilization of the egg, because a new genetic package develops, which they call an individual human being, with its characteristic traits already fixed. They base their arguments on the premise that "he who will be a human being is already a human being." Neither divine law nor human reason admit any right of directly killing an innocent person. Theo-

logians have sought to clarify, refine, and explain these principles to better understand their particular applications. Moral theologians say that abortion must not be called murder, because abortion is a physical act of expelling, or causing the expulsion of a presently living fetus from the womb prior to its viability. Murder is a moral act that means malicious, unwarranted, or unjust killing, or taking of human life with evil intent. To equate abortion with murder, two presuppositions must have already been reached: that in aborting a fetus a human life has been taken, and that this human life has been taken unjustly.

The questions that must be addressed regard the beginning of human life and on what occasions fetal life is taken unjustly. Although the Roman Catholic Church acknowledges the impossibility of deciding the moment at which life begins, it acts in practice as though human life were present from the moment of fertilization. This reasoning is based on the doubt of fact; since we are not sure when life begins, we must follow the safer course and regard human life as beginning at fertilization.

Some theologians have tried to answer the question about the time when life begins. For those who maintain that life begins at fertilization, they point out the fact that simply because the just-fertilized ovum is a genetically human organism, it does not mean that a human person exists from conception. Although the zygote has the potential for development into a human person, it is not a human person, because as each cell divides, it, too, would be a human person.

The theory of segmentation says that human life can be present only when that point of cellular division and multiplication has been reached so that twinning, tripleting, and so forth are no longer possible. If every person is an individual, one cannot be divided from oneself. The newly fertilized ovum can divide for a period of 14 to 21 days to become two or more beings; therefore, the fecundated ovum can be neither a person nor fully human. This theory is supported by scientists who say that one-third to one-half of the fertilized ova are never implanted in the uterus but rather are expelled during the woman's next menstrual cycle. Scientists support the theory that personal life begins at the establishment of individuality with the information that up to the time of implantation of the fertilized ovum, only the RNA (ribonucleic acid) of the mother is present. The sperm does not begin to play any part until implantation in the uterus, when the genetic capital of the new organism is activated and the conceptus begins to be directed by its own RNA. The transfer to the RNA of the conceptus occurs within 14 to 21 days after fertilization, at the same time that individuality is thought to be established.

The ramifications of these two theories are especially crucial to treatment of victims of rape or incest. Traditionally, the Catholic Church allowed the time limit of 10 to 12 hours for a D&C (dilation and curettage) or vaginal douche for victims of rape to prevent fertilization. Given the rapid entry of the sperm into the Fallopian tubes, this method would be most ineffective. Rather, the use of hormonal agents such as DES (diethylstilbestrol) to act in a contraceptive manner, within the longer period, would be permissible. These hormonal agents and morning-after pills can also act as abortifacients, which causes Catholic theologians to give cautious support to their use, because they also prevent implantation. The extended period of 14 to 21 days before the individuality and the personhood of the fetus are established allows more leniency toward their use for victims of rape and incest.

The Church says that there should be no direct or intended abortions, but does allow indirect abortions under certain conditions. A pregnant woman's cancerous uterus or Fallopian tubes containing an ectopic pregnancy may be removed for the preservation of the woman's life. Such abortions are called therapeutic because they remedy a pathological condition. Diseased organs are removed and the death of the fetus is not intended, but the result of the indirect abortion is to save the mother's life.

Homosexuality

The Congregation for the Doctrine of the Faith issued a letter to the bishops of the Catholic Church on the *Pastoral Care of Homosexual Persons,* signed by Pope John Paul II in 1986. It elaborated and reiterated many of the principles of the 1975 document on sexual ethics, in which homosexual genital activity was labeled as "intrinsically disordered" because it is deprived of its "essential and indispensable finality."

Both Scripture and tradition were cited as a basis for rejecting homosexual acts as immoral. The bishops, clergy, and religious were praised for their care of homosexual persons and encouraging the homosexual person to live a chaste life. Although the church recognizes homosexuals living in loving relationships that strive for permanence, the couple must aim at the elimination of all genital behavior from their lives.

The official Catholic teaching that homogenital acts must be judged as objectively immoral, regardless of circumstances, has resulted in various reactions on the pastoral level. Moral theologians have tried to find applications of this teaching that would include sensitivity and compassion toward homosexual persons. Some revisionist theologians suggest that in the light of mutual support, love, and enhancement of human growth that accompanies stable relationships that desire permanency, the genital activity occurring within these unions may be viewed as premoral, not objectively morally wrong.

The Roman Catholic Church of Baltimore, in 1981, announced a formal and public ministry to the homosexual community that promised sensitivity and regard to the person rather than emphasis on impersonal law. The Washington State Conference of Bishops as well as the San Francisco Senate of Priests recognized the distinction between objective homosexual acts and subjective culpability in the face of pressures and loneliness, which homosexual persons experience.

All pastoral approaches that try to understand and minister to homosexual persons admit there are elements in the homosexual subculture that are irreconcilable with Christian living. They exclude all violent or coercive, anonymous, impersonal, promiscuous sex or seduction of the young and innocent from acceptable behavior. The American Bishops advise confessors and pastors to avoid both harshness and permissiveness when counseling sexually active homosexuals in order that they may grow to be fuller, happier, and more spiritual Christians.

REFERENCES

Genovese, V. *In Pursuit of Love: Catholic Morality and Human Sexuality*. Wilmington, Del.: Glazier Press, 1987.

Gramick, J., and P. Furey, eds. *The Vatican and Homosexuality*. New York: Crossroad, 1988.

Keane, P. *Sexual Morality: A Catholic Perspective*. New York: Paulist Press, 1977.

Kosnick, A. *Human Sexuality: Catholic Theological Society of America Study*. New York: Paulist Press, 1977.

Lauber, R., OFM, J. Boyle, and W. May. *Catholic Sexual Ethics*. Huntington, Ind.: Sunday Visitor, 1985.

Liebard, O. *Official Catholic Teaching on Love and Sexuality*. Wilmington, N.C.: McGrath, 1978.

Noonan, J., Jr. *Contraception: A History of Its Treatment by Catholic Theologians and Canonists*. Cambridge, Mass.: Harvard Univ. Press, 1986.

Marianne Ferguson

CENSORSHIP AND SEX

Censorship has been defined as: "the active suppression of books, journals, newspapers, theater pieces, lectures, discussions, radio and television programs, films, art works, etc.—either partially or in their entirety—that are deemed objectionable on moral, political, military, or other grounds." More succinct than Hauptman's definition, but quite as telling, is the definition of *censor* found in the *Oxford English Dictionary*: "One who exercises official or officious supervision over morals or conduct." (Officious can mean either "informal" or "meddlesome.")

Censor and censorship derive from the title established in Rome under the Lex Canuela of 443 B.C.E. for certain magistrates who drew up the register or "census" of citizens, and also had under their jurisdiction the supervision of public morals regarding, for example, obligations of marriage, behavior towards family and slaves, and conduct of business, agriculture, and religion (Green, 1990, p 47). The practice is even older than the word, however. The Assyrian librarian Ashurbanipal of the 7th century B.C.E. is said to have amassed a collection of over 30,000 clay tablets, which he censored by removing from the collection whatever the king found disagreeable.

Censorship can be applied to any type of information or message, and may take many forms: the author or creator may suppress certain ideas or forms of expression (self-censorship); a publisher, producer, recording company, or other facilitator can refuse to allow the work to achieve its final form or mandate editorial changes; a bookstore, library, theater chain, radio station, or other disseminator can refuse to make the work available; an individual or group can demand, petition, or picket that the work, once available, be withdrawn, stopped, or destroyed; and a legally empowered agent can attempt to block the process at any stage.

The following history and discussion focuses upon United States censorship practice and its antecedents in England. Information about censorship in other countries appears in Green's *The Encyclopedia of Censorship*.

The Narrated and Written Word

Historically, censorship for moral reasons of speech and writing about sexuality was usually linked with and subordinate to the more primary objective of suppressing material deemed threatening to the status quo in religion or politics and was not considered a separate issue until well into the 18th and 19th centuries. In the 4th century B.C., Plato advocated extensive censorship for the young of tales about the gods so that Greek youth might not be exposed to bad examples. He was most concerned about greed, cowardice, lying, disrespect for religion, and wicked deeds such as rape and murder—all seen from the viewpoint of being detrimental to the character of a loyal (male) citizen of the state and good soldier. It was as a relatively minor point that he also added, "Nor will self-control among our youths be strengthened if they hear the same theme [of unbridled sexual passion] recounted in the story of Hephaestus fastening together the bodies of Ares and Aphrodite [when caught in the act of adultery]."*

In Rome shortly after the birth of Christ, the poet Ovid was exiled reportedly for his "immoral" work *The Art of Love*—perhaps the earliest known handbook on "how to pick up girls"—although the charge may have been a pretext to cover a political reason for his banishment. In the days before the printing press, censorship could take the form of imprisonment, banishment, or execution of the offending party, who was thus neatly prohibited from writing or speaking publicly.

In general, however, the classical world was rather permissive by modern standards about sexual expression, judging from the Pompeiian artifacts and the writings of Aristophanes, Ovid, Petronius, and Catullus. In particular, sexual and scatological obscenities were linked to comedy, satire, and polemic, and considered quite appropriate in these contexts.

The medieval world continued in this vein for some centuries, as exemplified by Boccaccio's *Decameron* (c. 1349–51) and several of Chaucer's *Canterbury Tales* (c. 1386–1400). Certainly the Catholic church was rising as a censorship power, taking its cue from St. Paul's report of the Ephesians' burning their books on "curious arts" (Acts 19:19); its banning of books began in 150 A.D. with, ironically, an unauthorized biography of St. Paul and continued sporadically until systematized under the pope in 1559 into what was officially termed the *Index Librorum Prohibitorum* in 1564. However, the early ecclesiastical efforts were nearly all directed toward works deemed religious heresy, including early scientific writings. The sexy *Decameron* seems to have survived unscathed for 150 years, until the Italian monk and reformer Savonarola burned copies in his

*Ironically, this and other "illustrations from Homer of the self-indulgences of heroes and gods and disrespect for rulers" are omitted (censored?) from the 1941 Oxford University Press edition of *The Republic*. See page 79.

"bonfire of vanities" in 1498. Finally, the Index picked up Boccaccio's classic in 1559.

But with the invention of moveable type in the mid-1400s, the entire nature of information and its dissemination changed irrevocably. In censorship, wrote Kendrick, "futility . . . was already guaranteed five hundred years ago. Once printed, a writer's words acquired a life independent of his and much larger; only neglect can kill a printed book." In a veritable literary dam exploding, some 20 million books were reported produced in England and Europe between 1450 and 1500. Shortly after in 1524, the Western world saw its first recorded purely "dirty" book, that is, prurience unmixed with satire, heresy, or insult: the so-called *Aretino's Postures*, a series of sonnets illustrated by drawings of a couple in various copulatory positions. Aretino's name became a byword for sexually arousing material for several centuries, and his works were duly condemned by the church.

Censorship of the Press in England and America

Sixteenth and Seventeenth Centuries

Not only the church, but also civil authorities were beginning to systematize their approaches to censorship, focusing, like the church, on heresy, both political and religious—and sometimes social. Book burning was a favorite technique, supplemented by Draconian punishments and sometimes execution of authors and publishers. In 1534, Henry VIII broke with the Catholic church to establish his own authority over state, church, and heretics with the Act of Supremacy. Henceforth civil censorship in England ran parallel with the ecclesiastical. In 1557, a sort of printers' guild called the Stationers' Company was chartered and empowered to control the English press. Subsequent decrees strengthened its powers, until 1640 when the Long Parliament abolished the entire censorship apparatus of the Stuart monarchs.

For the first few years of the Commonwealth, there were no statutory restrictions on the press, resulting in a massive and undisciplined flow of books, tracts, and pamphlets exhorting many undesirable points of view. To curb this flow, the Puritans soon reestablished full censorship in the Licensing Act of 1643. Despite protests, including Milton's famous pamphlet "Areopagitica," censorship continued into Cromwell's government. The Restoration continued in the same vein with the Licensing Act of 1662, which ultimately remained in effect until 1695.

While the civil authorities in the 17th century continued to focus on challenges to accepted political (and sometimes religious and social) doctrines, the church was slowly beginning to take note of sex in literature, particularly literature from France. The vigorously scatological *Gargantua* (1635) and *Pantagruel* (1633) of Rabelais were translated into English by 1660. In 1668, Pepys' *Diary* immortalized *L'escholle de Filles*, a "bawdy, lewd book" that led Pepys to masturbate, "and after I had done it, I burned it, that it might not be among my books to my shame." Among English authors, Shakespeare's art had arisen to full flower, including many bawdy references and puns, but apparently falling short of anything that would trigger notice from either the church or the state.

More problematic were the openly licentious writings of John Wilmot, second Earl of Rochester, who continued in the Roman tradition of using sex as a vehicle for comedy, satire, and invective. His poems and play (*Sodom: Or, the Quintessence of Debauchery*), written for private circulation but published after his death, were regularly prosecuted under the Licensing Act of 1662, probably as much for the anti-establishment satire as for the sexual components. Neither was sex unknown in books published during this period in the American colonies. The first recorded incident of censorship involving erotica was the seizure in 1668 of Neville's *The Isle of Pines*—a Robinson Crusoe-type tale involving a man and three women shipwrecked on an island—among other unlicensed material.

Eighteenth Century

With the 18th century began several trends that gradually coalesced into a specific consciousness of the sexually obscene and a concomitant desire to suppress it. Sexual explicitness in literature continued to flourish modestly. The year 1708 saw the first publication from the "father of English pornographic publishing," Edmund Curll, a quasi-medical guide on venereal disease later enhanced by certain "bawdy additions." Until his death in 1747, his publishing house specialized in translations from French and Latin of various exposés of alleged clerical concupiscence and treatises on such exotica as eunuchs and flogging. As was consistent with the earlier censorship practices, Curll ran afoul of British law only for his insinuations about the clergy and for a volume of "scandalous and seditious political recollections." Cleland's classic *Memoirs of a Woman of Pleasure* (1748–49)—usually called *Fanny Hill* and probably the most prosecuted literary work in history—was also a product of this century. Meanwhile, France produced the Marquis de Sade, whose literary work encompassed total political and religious rebellion as well as sexual anarchy and who served much time in prison from antisocial acts more than from his writing, most of which was not published or translated until much later.

In the colonies, Benjamin Franklin—sometimes credited with having been the first prominent American with a lusty sense of humor—produced "Advice to a Young Man in the Choice of a Mistress" (1745) and other whimsical but spicy pieces. However, most colonial erotica, like Neville's work, appears to have been imported from England or France, native colonial writers still being largely steeped in Puritan morality.

The 18th century also saw a new consciousness of the negative social and medical aspects of sex. The first publications on the "dangers" of masturbation were, in England, *Onania, or the Heinous Sin of Self-Pollution* (1710) and in France, Tissot's *L'Onanism, Dissertation sûr les Maladies produites par la Masturbation* (1758). The first significant work on prostitution appeared in 1769, Restif de la Bretonne's *Le Pornographe*, which outlined—albeit with questionable "levity"—a recommended program for state-run brothels.

The behavior of the small but growing reading public (especially women) was also coming under notice when a writer for the *Athenian Mercury* warned against "the softening of the Mind by Love" (i.e., romance novels), while an English evangelical journal warned, "Novels generally speaking are instruments of abomination and ruin."

A new consciousness of a more explicitly sexual past also emerged, with the excavations of Pompeii begun in the first half of the 17th century and continuing into the next. Simultaneously, the British Museum and the Louvre were founded, to serve as repositories for artifacts and scholarship. As a result, it became less likely that public law or private caprice (such as Pepys' burning of *L'escholle des Filles*) would result in the permanent or final destruction of works, even if openly erotic or even seditious or heretical.

On the censorship front, British law remained rather lax from 1695 until George III issued a proclamation in 1787 urging suppression of "all loose and licentious Prints, Books, and Publications, dispensing Poison to the Minds of the Young and Unwary, and to punish the Publishers and Vendors thereof." Still, enforcement was carried out by private agencies and tended to be small-scale efforts with small effect until the mid-18th century. However, private efforts at censorship led to the publication of expurgated (later, "bowdlerized") works, which would become widespread, particularly for Shakespeare and the Bible in both England and the United States. In the United States, the first censorship law appeared in 1711 when the Massachusetts Bay Colony prohibited the "Composing, Writing, Printing or Publishing, of any Filthy, Obscene or Prophane Song, Pamphlet, Libel or Mock-Sermon, in Imitation or in Mimicry of Preaching, or any other part of Divine Worship," making no distinctions between obscenity and anti-religious sentiment as was typical of the period. Other colonies adopted similar laws and carried them on into statehood after 1776.

The Nineteenth Century

Before the 19th century, literature, including bawdy materials, had remained limited in circulation because relatively few people could read, or, if they could, had sufficient leisure time to read for pleasure or enough money to pay for books, often imported from France. Thus, ecclesiastical and civil authorities perceived with some justification far greater dangers to the status quo from heresies and political freethinking than from sexual prurience. This began to change because of the growing middle class with its increased education, leisure, and income.

Consciousness of a need for social reform was also increasing, partly as a result of this newly educated middle class—which began to study itself, as it were, and what it saw it found wanting. The great social reforming censors were all products of the 19th century: notably Thomas Bowdler in England, whose expurgated *Family Shakespeare* in part gave English a new word *to bowdlerize*, and Anthony Comstock in the United States, the Carrie Nation of pornography, who claimed single-handedly to have "convicted persons enough to fill a passenger train of sixty-one coaches . . . [and] have destroyed 160 tons of obscene literature"—and to have caused at least 15 suicides. (See Comstock, Anthony; Comstockery.) Even Noah Webster, founder of America's great dictionary dynasty, abhorred "invective, ribaldry, or immorality" and opposed freedom of the press on the grounds that it would be abused, as was evident to him at the time "by the publication of salacious stories and scandalous libels." Webster's first dictionary of 1829 admitted few "naughty" words, not even "bundling," jocularly requested by one of his critics. Indeed, no Merriam-Webster dictionary was to define any of the four-letter words until the 1970s. Webster capped his career with an expurgated version of the Bible in 1833. Many social-reforming censorship organizations were also founded in the 1800s: the Society for the Suppression of Vice in England (1801) and in the United States (1873), the National Vigilance Association in England (1886), and the Public Morality Council in England (1890)—the last two enduring well into the 20th century.

Simultaneously, social reform consciousness led to the expansion of sex research from its "pornographic" beginnings by Restif de la Bretonne. The years 1830–60 saw additional studies of prostitution, both French and English. Other countries were advancing in this sphere also, with the publication of *Psychopathia Sexualis* by the Russian physician Heinrich Kaan in 1843 and a work of similar scope and title by the Austrian Krafft-Ebing in 1896. The most controversial in England was probably Havelock Ellis's *Sexual Inversion* (1892), an early study of homosexuality, whose publisher was prosecuted successfully for obscenity in 1899. Perhaps inevitably, these works were often seen as tarred with the same brush as the other pornography: "[Y]et, to the sensual, the vicious, the young and inexperienced, these scientific books thus popularized are too liable to be converted into mere guidebooks to vice."

Also increasingly under fire from worried social reformers was fiction: the novel became more respectable after Sir Walter Scott, and more novels were being read by many more people. Could there be antisocial effects, especially from the new "sensational" school of popular fiction? A court case in 1859 cited a young woman who connected reading romance novels to her crime of homicide.

As to what was available for reading by these "susceptible" folk in the 19th century, the new "realist" school of French writers was certainly causing some of the raised eyebrows, even in France. Flaubert's *Madame Bovary* was tried and acquitted of obscenity at home in 1857, but Baudelaire's *Les Fleurs du Mal* fared less well— six of its poems remained banned in France until 1949. The artists and writers on their part began to strike back at censorship: the image of the disaffected artistic genius at odds with mainstream society dates from this period. In a lighter vein but no less serious was Charles Dickens' benighted and censorious Mr. Podsnap, a caricature of Victorian prurience and prudery inhabiting *Our Mutual Friend* (1864–65). Meanwhile,

some much older English works were coming under fire: a bowdlerized Chaucer appeared in 1831, while Massachusetts discovered *Fanny Hill*, published for the first time in the United States in 1821, and promptly banned it. Erotica proliferated to the extent that bibliographers and bibliophiles also turned their attention to this genre— the first published bibliography of erotica appeared in 1860, the same date that the British Museum established its "Private Case" collection of obscene and other banned works.

Indigenous American literature about sex remained sparse by comparison, but noteworthy. Hawthorne's *Scarlet Letter* (1850) portrayed adultery realistically, Whitman's poems *Leaves of Grass* celebrated the frankly physical and the earthy, and Mark Twain's "1601" (1880) plus other short and largely unknown pieces continued in the long tradition of bawdy humor.

The classics—Greek and Roman literature— had begun to fall out of pedagogical fashion, especially in the United States; thus the hidden erotic treasures reserved for classics scholars in Ovid and Catullus appeared likely to remain even more hidden. However, toward the end of the century, the full ruins of Pompeii had finally come to light, inspiring numerous primitive attempts at the equivalent of airbrushing in the museum catalogues.

During the 19th century, laws against obscenity and pornography per se emerged in full flower. The first U.S. federal statute to mention obscenity was the Customs Act of 1842, which forbid imports of "indecent" and "obscene" books and pictures. Another federal statute of 1865 prohibited the shipment of obscenity through the mails; this was strengthened in 1857 and completely revamped in 1873 into the "Comstock Law," which was much more specific and wide-ranging than its predecessors. In England, the Obscene Publications Act of 1857, also known as Lord Campbell's Act, authorized seizure and destruction of obscene books.

The legal event in the 19th century with perhaps the most impact on censorship was the English trial *Regina v. Hicklin* in 1868, the first case tried under Lord Campbell's Act. Lord Chief Justice Alexander Cockburn, ruling against a sensationalist and voyeuristic narrative purporting to expose erotic practices during Catholic confession, proposed a definition for what had previously remained undefined: "The test for obscenity is this, whether the tendency of the matter charged as obscenity is to deprave and corrupt those whose minds are open to such immoral influences, and into whose hands a publication of this sort may fall." The "*Hicklin* test" assumed that an obscene work necessarily resulted from an obscene intent, and that the most susceptible individuals must constitute the yardstick for the definition. This test became the basis for anti-obscenity legislation in Britain and the United States until *Roth v. Alberts* in 1957.

Twentieth Century

The players all being arranged on stage, the 20th-century narrative of censorship has been largely a playing out of the conflict among them. There are the increased and stubborn interests of artists and authors in depicting frank portrayals of life, sex and all; a large and potentially "vulnerable" reading public, incorporating a growing intelligentsia but also incorporating even more vulnerable subgroups—traditionally, women, children, the poor, and the mentally nonnormal; a consciousness of social harm, perhaps stemming originally from Christian morality but long since encompassing consideration of social welfare and criminal behavior; and independent and liberal traditions of intellectual responsibility in England, plus a sister tradition of First Amendment–inspired intellectual freedom in the United States. The heart of the clash has lain within the movement for social welfare, specifically between those who hold that sexual materials reduce social welfare and those who hold that such materials are innocuous, or even necessary to the social welfare.

The opening salvo was the battle between two giants in their respective forces: Anthony Comstock, for whom all sex reeked social evil, and Margaret Sanger, crusader for birth control and sex education. Comstock, in his waning years, got Sanger indicted and managed to secure the imprisonment of her husband, but Margaret fled the country, and her case was ultimately dismissed in 1916 after Comstock's death. Yet neither side actually "won," for birth control information remained actionable in the United States for decades.

But the major censorship wars of the 20th century have been mostly fought in U.S. courtrooms. Long neglected until *Hicklin*, the major point of dispute was the definition of obscenity or pornography. The questions in contest have been thus:

- Is "art" different from obscenity?
- Does the intent of the creator enter into the definition?
- Should the most purportedly "vulnerable" audiences be taken as the standard?
- Should social, scientific, or other value of a work under dispute be considered?
- Should an obscene part of a work lead to proscription of the whole?
- What is the nature of the "social harm" deemed to result from obscenity or pornography?
- Is the sexual arousal potential of a work ("prurience") an index of harm per se?

The *Hicklin* test of 1868 rendered intent irrelevant, assumed evil effects of obscenity, took as a standard the most vulnerable audience, and judged the entire work by one passage. These elements remained relatively inviolate through a number of cases in both England and the United States for a half century. By 1913, however, U.S. Supreme Court Justice Learned Hand remarked in reference to *United States v. Kennerley* that it was perhaps inappropriate to "reduce our treatment of sex to the standards of a child's library in the interests of a salacious few."

The next step occurred in 1922 when the New York State Court of Appeals vindicated *Mademoiselle de Maupin* in *Halsey v. New York Society for the Suppression of Vice*. The judge declared that while certain passages may be vulgar, the book must be considered as a whole. Another milestone came 11 years later in the famous *Ulysses* case (*United States v. One Book Entitled Ulysses*), when Judge John M. Woolsey invoked the good intentions of the creator as well as suggesting that great art can, in fact, deal frankly with sex.

Of lesser future importance but also quite interesting were two state court cases: *Roth v. Goldman* in New York (1948) and *Commonwealth v. Gordon* in Pennsylvania (1949). The first resulted in a conviction for mailing a translation of Balzac's *Droll Stories*, but one of the judges questioned whether the arousal of normal sexual desires was socially dangerous. The second trial vindicated nine American novels, including Faulkner's *Sanctuary*, with Judge Curtis Bok proposing that obscenity statutes should incorporate a test for "clear and present danger"—not merely a presumptive tendency to corrupt.

With *Roth v. United States* (1957), the *Hicklin* test was finally superseded. In upholding a conviction for mailing erotic magazines and books, Justice William Brennan declared that: "Obscene material is material which deals with sex in a manner appealing to prurient interest, and the test of obscenity is whether to the average person, applying contemporary community standards, the dominant theme of the material appeals to prurient interest." Brennan also stated, "[I]mplicit in the history of the First Amendment is the rejection of obscenity as utterly without redeeming social importance." The *Roth* test set the standard for subsequent legal discussions of obscenity, and no doubt influenced England in establishing a new Obscene Publications Act in 1959, in which the concepts of "value" and "work as a whole" were incorporated. The United States had already liberalized its import laws somewhat with the Smoot-Hawley Tariff Act of 1930, which exempted classics and books of merit from prosecution when imported for noncommercial purposes.

In the wake of *Roth*, publication of erotic materials, including many pornographic classics, expanded greatly in both the United States and Britain, since it was not difficult to prove some "value" for most works. This was exemplified in the 1966 *Memoirs v. Massachusetts* decision, in which the Supreme Court ruled in favor of the redeeming social value of the notorious *Fanny Hill*. The value—a change from "importance"—lay in its historical details.

It was probably this sudden outpouring of sexual publications that inspired the 1967 creation by President Lyndon B. Johnson of the Commission on Obscenity and Pornography. The Commission was charged with analyzing current U.S. law on obscenity, traffic in pornographic materials, and the effects of such material on readers, including minors, and instructed to recommend future regulation. After three years and $20 million, the final report was released, stating the opinion of the majority of the Commission that pornography was basically harmless and proposing the repeal of all 114 existing state and federal laws regulating adult use of pornography because such laws are ineffective, are not supported by public opinion, and conflict with individual rights. The Commission did propose laws restricting minors' exposure to pornography and called for a wide-ranging program of sex education. Perhaps not surprisingly, the then President Richard M. Nixon condemned the report as morally bankrupt, and the Senate repudiated its findings.

In 1973, the *Roth* test was modified somewhat by *Miller v. California* to produce the standard still used as of 1992:

> The basic guidelines must be: (a) whether the average person, applying contemporary community standards, would find that the work, taken as a whole, appeals to prurient interest; (b) whether the work depicts or describes, in a patently offensive way, sexual conduct specifically defined by the applicable state law; and (c) whether the work, taken as a whole, lacks serious literary, artistic, political or scientific value.

The major modifications to *Roth* include the mention of applicable state law and the replacement of "utterly without redeeming social importance" with the somewhat more strict "lacks serious literary, artistic, political or scientific value." The effect was to turn the definition of obscenity in some measure back to individual communities and states, a development that was no doubt prefigured by the reaction of Congress to the 1970 President's Commission Report and certainly welcomed by the pro-censorship organizations.

For although the Victorian groups such as the Society for the Suppression of Vice had long since ceased functioning, new and vocal contemporary groups sprung up to replace them. The best known perhaps has been the Moral Majority, like many (but not all) such groups based in the U.S. fundamentalist Protestant community. The 1992 *Encyclopedia of Associations* lists dozens of additional groups working to suppress the sexual and the erotic in its various forms. On the opposing side, other groups fight against censorship, including People for the American Way, the Freedom to Read Foundation, and the American Civil Liberties Union. In the last decade, these organizations have been locked in a passionate battle, often in hand-to-hand combat at the local level over textbooks in public schools and books in public libraries.

The increasing influence of these pro-censorship and anti-obscenity groups led to the establishment in 1985 of another commission, the Attorney-General's Commission on Pornography (the Meese Commission), whose final report a year later presented conclusions different from those of the first commission: that certain kinds of pornography lead to sexual violence, notably against women and children, and that enforcement of existing laws should focus on child pornography and violent pornography. Books and the written word alone, however, were deemed "least harmful" and should be virtually exempt from censure, visual media being considered far more pernicious. The report also included a call to citizens to take grass-roots action against objectionable materials in their own communities—invoking item (a) in the *Miller* standard.

Meanwhile, a new approach to censorial legislation was under proposal, growing out of feminist antipornography efforts, particularly of the groups Women Against Pornography and Women Against Violence Against Women. The initial law was drafted by author Andrea Dworkin and attorney Catharine McKinnon for the city of Minneapolis in 1983; similar ordinances were subsequently drawn up in Indianapolis and other cities. This new approach defined pornography as a form of discrimination against women and as grounds for civil complaint: any woman could file a complaint either in court or with the local equal opportunity commission charging discrimination via production, sale, exhibition, or distribution of pornography; coercion into pornographic performance; forcing pornography on a person; or assault following the assailant's reading or viewing of pornography. The model ordinance defined pornography at some length according to nine criteria.

In Minneapolis, the bill was passed but vetoed by the mayor. Similar legislation in other cities also failed to be implemented, either through veto or through challenge and reversal in the courts. The judgment against the Indianapolis ordinance was summarily affirmed by the Supreme Court in *Hudnut v. American Booksellers Association* (1986).

However, the principle behind this type of law has been resurrected in the Pornography Victims Compensation Act, under congressional consideration as of 1992. If this bill becomes law, crime victims could sue the publishers, producers, and distributors of books, films, music, or art that they claim inspired the criminals to commit their crime. (Similar legislation was recently passed in Canada.) As worded in the bill, the "crime" need not be proved or even reported for a suit to be accepted. This development has been seen as inspired by the Meese Commission, as has also a governmental unit called the National Obscenity Enforcement Unit, which spearheaded prosecution of many distributors of recreational sexual material in 1990–91. While few of these cases have been won in court, the attacks are mounted so as to cripple the target financially, whether or not prosecution is successful. Another tactic is to charge the distributors with violating racketeering laws, which command greater penalties.

The federal government has been responsible for another, quite unusual form of censorship of the word in the past few years. Federal regulations termed the "Gag Rule," upheld by the Supreme Court in *Rust v. Sullivan* (1991), forbid any health care facility receiving Title X funds for family planning services from the Department of Health and Human Services to give a client any verbal or written information about abortion, even if requested and even if medically recommended.

Ironically, censorship of the word has also been promulgated by the educated, liberal establishment under the rubric of a sentiment some-times called "PC" for "politically correct." In a crystallization of the ideal, socially responsible individual, the perfect politically correct person completely eschews all racist, homophobic, sexist, ageist, or "ablelist" (biased against disabled people) language. In cartoonist parodies of PC talk, juvenile females are called baby women or pre-women—never girls. The university community has been something of an incubator for PC, and many students have been censured for such offenses as yelling derogatory remarks at other students, posting jocular but insulting signs in their rooms, or telling ethnic jokes. Antisexist PC in particular is showing signs of spreading throughout the workplace in the wake of Anita Hill's unsuccessful but well-publicized challenge in 1991 of Clarence Thomas's bid for the U.S. Supreme Court on the grounds of her claim that he sexually harassed her years before. In "workplace PC," telling dirty jokes is taboo and handing out compliments on appearance to the opposite sex can be suspect.

Through PC, the battle of censorship of the sexual word in the 20th century has come full circle, with one side ignoring sexism and damning sex, and the other side censoring much sex also—but entirely under the stated guise of fighting sexism. The locus of social harm changes with the perspective, but speech and writing about sexuality somehow end up in the focus, no matter which lens one looks through.

Theater and Performance

England has had a long tradition of state oversight of the theater, dating back to Henry VIII's Act of Supremacy in 1534, after which the Lord High Chamberlain gradually took over the function of theater censor. The Lord Chamberlain's de facto powers were finally given statutory authority in the Stage Licensing Act of 1737, which continued for over two centuries. The 1968 Theatres Act finally abolished the Lord Chamberlain's role and brought the stage under the general aegis of the 1959 Obscene Publications Act.

The United States does not seem to have had a similar tradition of central regulation of performance through any federal laws. However, individual performances have been ruled obscene or censored based on particular state laws, with the First Amendment being invoked as support about equally with its circumvention on various grounds. In 1932, a New York court ruled in *People v. Wendling* that the play *Frankie and Johnnie* could not be suppressed as "obscene" just because the plot was "tawdry" and the characters were vulgar and led lives of vice.

In perhaps a similar vein, the late black humor comic Lenny Bruce was ultimately acquitted by the Illinois Supreme Court in *People v. Bruce* (1964). The court ruled that because some of the topics commented on were of social importance, his monologue could not be judged obscene. And with an identical result although different legal precedent, the Supreme Court ruled in 1972 that an exhibition permit for the musical *Hair* must be issued in Chattanooga, Tennessee, because not to do so would constitute unlawful prior restraint and thus violate the First Amendment.

Much less clear have been many cases over recent decades concerned with burlesque and "exotic" dancing, with considerable local variation. In *Adams Theatre Co. v. Keenan* (1953), the New Jersey Supreme Court ruled (as with *Hair*) that a license could not be withheld from a production labeled a "burlesque show" because to do so before the performance would be unlawful prior restraint. With an opposite effect, ten years later a district court in Missouri ruled that a particular burlesque stripper violated a local indecent behavior ordinance.

In 1972, a case that generated some precedent was *California v. LaRue* in which the U.S. Supreme Court upheld the authority of the state of California to ban sexually explicit live entertainment and films in bars within the context of controlling the circumstances involving service of liquor. A similar case in 1981 was *New York State Liquor Authority v. Dennis Bellanca*. However, because censorship was interpreted as strictly limited to establishments selling liquor, the Supreme Court ruled in *Doran v. Salem Inn* (1975) that a New Hempstead, New York, ordinance prohibiting any public topless dancing was overbroad because it covered activity outside bars.

In a different approach to the problem, the U.S. Supreme Court ruled in *Schad v. Borough of Mt. Ephraim* (1981) that a zoning ordinance against performances could not be selectively applied to exclude nude dancing and that the ordinance violated the First Amendment. More recently, the Supreme Court affirmed in *Barnes v. Glen Theatre* (1991) the validity of Indiana's public indecency law as applied to prohibit nude dancing as entertainment. This decision—which ruled that regulation of nude dancing (in bars or not) could be justified despite the view of the Court that nude dancing was protected by the First Amendment—did not result from a unanimous opinion but from a bare majority of five justices for and four against upholding the Indiana local law.

Art

As with censorship of the word, early art censorship was oriented almost exclusively toward political and religious heresy. The first reported nude statue of Aphrodite around 360 B.C. in Greece was subject to religious disapproval—not for moral reasons, but "because the beauty of her body might seem an inducement to heresy." Christian artists of the Renaissance painted the nude or semi-nude in appropriate biblical contexts: the infant Christ, Adam and Eve, the Crucifixion, etc., with uncertain but usually tacit approval from the church—which disapproved of provocative images. In the 16th century, Pope Clement suppressed not only the notorious sonnets of Aretino, but the explicit illustrations: author, artist, and engraver all had to leave Rome.

One of the most censured works in the history of art has been Michaelangelo's magnificent ceiling for the Sistine Chapel, heavily populated with enormous nude figures. From the 16th to the 20th centuries, at least three popes ordered draperies painted over offending body parts. Even in 1933, U.S. Customs confiscated (but later released) a set of prints based on the ceiling nudes before any of the draperies were applied. After the 16th century, nudity was finally designated by the church as officially unacceptable in Christian art, although tolerated with heroic and mythological subjects.

This pattern continued on the continent for centuries, although there were some exceptions. During the 17th century, the Spanish Inquisition censored all potentially erotic art—including specifying that hairdressers should remove or make decent the wax busts in their windows used to display hairstyles.

The New World started out as much more conservative artistically, but from Puritan rather than Catholic moral influence. The first nude statue exhibited in America, a plaster cast of the Venus de Medici imported from Paris in 1784, raised such an uproar that the owner showed it only privately to friends. This pattern continued for many years: nude statues displayed in U.S. public buildings were often draped or shown only to single-sex groups of adults—even as late as 1937.

The first U.S. national censorship statute, the tariff law of 1842, barred import of obscene art. This was interpreted later in the century that nudes were acceptable in museums but not in photographs or prints that might be sold to anyone. Comstock operated on this principle, and he boasted in 1874 that he had seized 194,000 obscene pictures and photographs, some based on museum works.

Around the turn of the century, nudity became more accepted in the United States as legitimate in artistic contexts, although acceptance varied by locality. Massachusetts, in particular, remained conservative up to 1950, banning issues of *Life* magazine that showed photographs of museum nudes. Photographs of nude or erotically posed individuals were still grounds for government prosecution, however, and in 1949 Eastman Kodak set up a private system of censoring materials sent in for photo processing. But in 1957, the infamous painting "September Morn"—which had drawn Comstock's ire and had made its owner rich from the ensuing publicity—was sedately deposited in New York's Metropolitan Museum of Art, and the following year, the Justice Department dropped its seven-year battle to keep imported erotic art out of the Kinsey Institute.

In the 1960s and 1970s, the United States actually became more permissive than some European countries. Several displays of erotic art were tried for obscenity and acquitted, while an exhibit of Beatle John Lennon's lithographs of "intimate bedroom scenes" was banned in London but shown in California.

In the 1980s, two new forces for art censorship began to grow in the United States. The first was a popular and congressional backlash, led largely by conservatives and religious groups, against the use of public money to fund art considered indecent or obscene, particularly grant money distributed by the National Endowment for the Arts (NEA). Two NEA-funded artists in particular were subject to censure: Andres Serrano, whose "Piss Christ" (1988) was a photograph of a crucifix suspended in a vat of the artist's urine, and Robert Mapplethorpe, whose subjects included homoerotic and sadomasochistically posed nudes as well as conventional portraits and nature studies. In a test case, director Dennis Barrie of the Cincinnati Contemporary Art Center was indicted on obscenity for hosting a Mapplethorpe show in 1989; however, the case was decided in favor of the museum.

Meanwhile, in 1990, Congress imposed a "decency requirement" on artists applying for NEA grants, and the NEA initiated a pledge to be signed by grantees stating that they would not use funds to create obscene art. In 1991, the pledge was found by a federal judge to be in violation of freedom of speech, while a group of artists filed suit over the statutory decency requirement. As of 1992, the outcome of this suit was still pending.

The second movement resulting in censorship of both art and film has been directed at child pornography and specifically visual depictions of minors (under age 18) that may be considered erotic. Federal statutes originally aimed at producers and dealers in "kiddie porn" were broadened throughout the 1980s to criminalize possession, advertisement, and receipt of such materials through the mail. A 1988 law requires producers of erotic images to maintain records of the ages of models depicted.

The new laws have been interpreted to cover simple nudity of minors as well as erotic poses, and have resulted in arrest of a number of artists. In addition, some state laws have criminalized mere viewing of erotic or nude photographs of minors. While Dennis Barrie was acquitted of obscenity even though the Mapplethorpe photographs included some nude youths, it is still unclear to what extent museums and libraries may be subject to prosecutions under these laws for materials in their collections.

Music

Songs about sex have a long history. Bawdy folksong collections were published freely in the 16th and 17th centuries; and during the English Restoration, both bawdy songs and erotic lovers' songs were quite popular. In the 1700s, however, collectors and publishers began to edit, expurgate, and omit most of the sexual material. This censorship of music publication continued well into the 20th century, although without having much effect on singers—neither "folksingers" nor the performers who made the English music hall a particular haven for bawdry, nor the men who sang "dirty songs" in bars and drinking clubs, nor the students and soldiers who did the same.

Collections of unexpurgated bawdy songs began, sporadically, to be published again in the United States starting in the 1920s. In the 1960s, folksinger Oscar Brand popularized a number of classic ballads of this genre, but unfortunately with his own quasi-expurgations to make the obscenities more palatable. At about the same period, certain "party" bands, like The Hot Nuts, became notorious on college campuses for their *double-entendre* lyrics. These bands, as well as nightclub singers performing in a similar vein, sometimes made records that could be bought at performances or discreetly through the mail.

Sexual lyrics came much more into the open—and were subject to public censorship—with the popularization of rock music from the late 1960s on. No radio station would play the Rolling Stones' "Let's Spend the Night Together" (1967), and some had reservations about "Why Don't We Do It in the Road?" from the Beatles (1968). At that time, however, few rock groups were even that explicit about insinuating sex, with the exception of a few fringe groups like The Fugs who sang, "Do you like boobs a lot?" and "I'm a dirty old man."

In the 1970s, much mainstream rock caught up to the fringe, with the Stones singing, "Black girls just want to fuck all night, and I ain't got the jam." Radio stations did not play it, but the records sold. Shock value of lyrics began to assume equal importance to the erotica, as also indicated in the name of some of the bands (e.g., Sex Pistols, and Cycle Sluts From Hell).

With the advent of rap music in the 1980s, sexual lyrics became easy to understand (after all, who could discern the words with all those loud guitars?). In 1985, a group called Parents Music Resource Center began a campaign to convince the record industry to label voluntarily those recordings with lyrics about sex, drugs, and other taboo topics. The Recording Industry Association of America reluctantly agreed to endorse labeling among its member companies, although compliance was minimal up to 1990 and still sporadic thereafter. Simultaneously, a number of state legislatures considered mandatory record labeling bills; as of 1992, none had been implemented.

In the early 1990s, several rock groups and performers were arrested for obscene performances, and a scattering of music store clerks for selling obscene recordings. Convictions were few; however, reportedly some store chains stopped carrying records with warning labels. Yet other reports indicate that labeled records were selling much better than their nonlabeled "G-rated" counterparts.

Several current federal laws explicitly include recordings within matter that may be declared obscene: Sections 1462, 1465, and 1466 of Title 47 of the U.S. Code. However, rock music is protected by the First Amendment, as ruled by four different U.S. courts of appeals in the 1980s.

Film

Censorship of film in the United States dates back to 1907, when Chicago passed an ordinance requiring that the chief of police approve all films to be shown. A film could be banned for a number of reasons, including "immorality" or "obscenity." In 1909, New York State established the Board for the Censorship of Motion Pictures to review films, prohibiting obscenity and vulgarity among other types of depictions. In 1915, this Board changed its name to the National Board of Review of Motion Pictures (NBRMP), claiming to offer "selection not censorship."

The NBRMP filled the role of a national censor until other states established their own boards. The first federal attempt at control came in 1915 when legislation was proposed in Congress to create the Federal Motion Picture Commission. Wishing to avoid any form of external censorship, the film industry established the National Association of the Motion Picture Industry in 1916, which produced its own standards. However, this was unsuccessful in stemming the rise in state censorship boards. Finally, the industry reorganized in 1922 and established the Motion Picture Producers and Distributors Association (MPPDA), hiring former U.S. Postmaster General Will H. Hays to run the new organization, which became known as "the Hays office."

From 1922 to 1945, Hays involved a number of public groups in setting and implementing a stringent and detailed list of "Don'ts and Be Carefuls," including virtually anything involving sex. In 1931, the Motion Picture Production Code was adopted, largely backed by the Catholic-composed Legion of Decency. Producers were supposed to submit scripts in advance for review; approved films received a seal of approval. Pope Pius XI lent support to this effort with a 1936 encyclical "Vigilanti Cura," advising Catholic censorship of film and noting the role of films as "instruments in seduction."

The MPPDA was renamed the Motion Picture Association of America (MPAA) when Hays was replaced as head in 1945. A major break came ten years later, when United Artists refused to follow the code's dictates about censoring drug-related lines and scenes from *The Man With the Golden Arm*. The code was subsequently liberalized in 1956 and 1966, responding to several Supreme Court cases: *Superior Films v. Department of Education of Ohio, Division of Film Censorship* (1953) in which the film *M* (and by extension, all films) was ruled to be covered by the First Amendment; *Kingsley International Pictures Corp. v. Regents of the University of the State of New York* (1959), which ruled that local censorship on the basis of content (the adultery presented in the film *Lady Chatterley's Lover*) was unconstitutional; and *Jacobellis v. Ohio* (1964), which ruled that the film *Les Amants* was not obscene because the *Roth* standard incorporating redeeming "social importance" applied to film as well as to print.

In the late 1960s, the MPAA moved to a classification system for film rather than giving seals of approval, and created the Code and Ratings Administration with an accompanying Code and Ratings Appeal Board. The current classification is:

G   general audiences

PG–13   parental guidance suggested for those under age 13

R   restricted: no admission to those under age 17 unless accompanied by a parent or adult guardian

NC–17   no children under age 17 admitted

The previously used "X" (persons under age 17 not admitted) can still be assigned by the film's producer.

The U.S. video market operates in part under a parallel rating system. In 1988, the Independent Video Programmers Association set up a classification system for videos produced outside with MPAA. The rating system, revised in 1990, has the following categories:

C   children, age 7 and younger

F   family, some violence and fight scenes

M   mature, some sex scenes

VM   very mature, extreme language and nudity

EM   extremely mature, extreme language, sex/nudity, extreme violence, and substance abuse

AO   adults only, ages 18 and over, frontal nudity/erotica

Three sections of federal laws specifically include film as matter that may be declared obscene: Sections1462, 1465, and 1466 of Title 18 of the U.S. Code.

Radio

Regulation of radio in the United States began in 1910; the first formal regulatory body was the Federal Radio Commission (FRC), established by the Radio Act of 1927. The Commission established a broad but indirect form of censorship, generally in the form of selectively awarding frequencies to stations that met the FRC's standards for public interest, convenience, necessity, and—although not admitted—quality of the programs. Radio also established a self-regulation system. The National Association of Broadcasters was organized in 1923 and in 1929 issued a "Code of Ethics" and "Standards of Community Practices," which were apparently subscribed

to by less than half of commercial radio stations. The Code of Ethics declared that stations should prevent broadcasts of offensive or obscene matter.

The Communications Act of 1934 created the Federal Communications Commission (FCC), superseding the Federal Radio Commission and continuing today. The FCC, which controls radio, television, wire, cable, and satellite transmissions, is explicitly prohibited from censoring the airwaves by Section 326 of Title 47 of the U.S. Code. This is interpreted as preventing prior restraint. However, Section 1464 of Title 18 of the U.S. Code forbids "any obscene, indecent, or profane language by means of radio communication," and the FCC is charged with promulgating this regulation through fines and warnings about license revocations. Several such sanctions were applied to stations airing material about sex in the 1960s and early 1970s.

This was put to test in 1973, when WBAI in New York City broadcast George Carlin's "Filthy Words" monologue in midafternoon. The FCC characterized the broadcast as "indecent" and issued a warning to WBAI. The radio station appealed on the grounds that while "obscenity" is not protected by the First Amendment, "indecency" is. The case went to the Supreme Court as *Federal Communications Commission v. Pacifica Foundation* (1978), and the Court ruled that even though the broadcast was not obscene, the FCC under its statutory requirements had the right to make a note in WBAI's file. The Court noted that broadcast speech required special treatment because of possible exposure of children and unconsenting adults to "indecency." As a result of *Pacifica*, the FCC banned "indecent" speech—at that time, generally restricted to Carlin's "seven dirty words"—between 6:00 A.M. and 8:00 P.M.

In 1987, partly in reaction to so-called shockjock radio, the FCC broadened its definition of indecency to include "material that describes sexual or excretory activities or organs in terms that are patently offensive under contemporary community standards" as well as lengthened the restricted period to midnight. The following year, a court ruled that the lengthened evening ban violated the First Amendment, but simultaneously Congress passed an overriding 24–hour ban on indecency that the FCC did not enforce, pending court review.

In 1989, a court of appeals issued a temporary stay on the ban, and in 1991 struck it down completely as unconstitutional. The case, *Federal Communications Commission v. Action for Children's Television* went to the Supreme Court, which declined to hear the case in 1992, de facto upholding the earlier ruling on the ban. The FCC has been charged with establishing a "safe-harbor" period for broadcasters, and as of 1992 enforced a ban on indecency only from 6:00 A.M. to 8:00 P.M.

Television

When television emerged commercially in the 1940s, it was assimilated to the same oversight mechanisms as radio: in government, the FCC, and within the industry, the National Association of Broadcasters (NAB). The NAB Code of Good Practice for TV was first written in 1951, although abandoned in the early 1980s.

Sex on television seems to have been a relatively minor problem until the 1960s. The NAB Code, although not universally heeded, did prohibit nudity and obscenity. Enforcement was lax; yet apparently "ribald copy" was not common, probably because of the more proper social climate and because advertisers tended to support programs that were noncontroversial in all dimensions. Occasionally an exception occurred, as in 1959 when 19 television stations lost their NAB seal of good practice for airing advertisements for hemorrhoidal treatment. However, for nearly 30 years, the controversies surrounding television focused on the overabundance of commercials, lack of diversity, network corruption and dishonesty as revealed in the 1959 quiz show scandal, and the growing number of violent episodes and programs.

In the late 1960s, the most popular shows were "Laugh-In" and "The Smothers Brothers Comedy Hour." Peppy, topical, iconoclastic, and sometimes risqué, these programs attracted notice, including an effort from Rhode Island senator John Pastore to reduce both sex and violence on television by exerting pressure on the networks to honor the NAB Code. Nothing substantial resulted from the senator's efforts.

In 1971, "All in the Family" was the first, most famous, and possibly the best of a score of socially relevant comedy-dramas of the 1970s, many produced by Norman Lear and all making frequent use of formerly taboo themes: racial prejudice, the unglorious side of war, intergenerational conflict—and sexual topics like abortion, adultery, pregnancy, impotence, and rape. Concurrently, action and violence-oriented shows, notably police dramas, became more frequent. While both kinds of shows were extremely popular, a number of individuals and groups protested—both within the industry and among the viewers. An episode of "Maude" dealing with abortion was reported to have triggered 24,000 protest letters from right-to-life groups.

In 1975, the three major networks responded by jointly establishing the "Family Hour" under strong pressure from the FCC, which was itself under considerable pressure from Congress. The Family Hour was actually two hours (7:00 to 9:00 P.M.) when only shows "appropriate for family viewing" (i.e., children) were supposed to be aired. Within a year, a suit was filed on First Amendment grounds against the FCC, the NAB, and the three networks by the Writers Guild, the Directors Guild, the Screen Actors Guild, plus Norman Lear and many other independent producers as well as some of the television syndicators. The basis of the suit was that the networks and the NAB had instigated the Family Hour under coercion from the FCC—which, however, was explicitly forbidden from engaging in censorship under Section 326 of Title 47 of the U.S. Code. The case was heard by a federal district court in California, which found for the plaintiffs. The Family Hour concept was effectively finished, even after a U.S. court of appeals later overturned the ruling on the grounds that the FCC should have heard the case.

In the late 1970s, violence on television continued to increase, and shows with sexual themes became more common, although without much of the social relevance earlier in the decade. Opposition to both trends continued, this time with a new leverage mechanism: consumer boycotts against sponsors of shows judged too violent or too sexy. However, sex on television remained stable with even some increases, from 1975 to 1978 and to 1987, particularly in soap operas. The major censorship during this period seems to have been the FCC's attempt to crack down on indecency in broadcasting, as it did with radio, and in 1988 the agency fined a television station for airing an R-rated film at 8:00 P.M.

In the 1980s, some state laws attempted to regulate indecency in cable television, but were overturned by the courts on the grounds that only obscenity, not indecency, may be banned. It remains to be seen what the effects of *FCC v. Children's Television* will have on television programming.

Telephone

Obscene telephone calls as harassment are illegal under Section 223 of Title 47 of the U.S. Code and may be prosecuted directly by the courts.

The FCC also has jurisdiction over the telephone. Recent efforts of the Commission, as directed by Congress, have been aimed at regulating the so-called dial-a-porn industry, which began in the early 1980s. These services initially consisted of offering sexually explicit recorded messages for a fee, and have expanded to offer in addition live dialogue and party-line conversations.

In 1983, legislation was passed to prohibit both obscene and indecent commercial telephone services to anyone under age 18. Enforcement was deferred, however, until the FCC promulgated regulations that specified how dial-a-porn providers could effectively screen out minors. Over the next five years, the FCC struggled unsuccessfully to produce regulations that would not be overturned in court on various grounds. The final regulations, specifying several screening techniques, including prepayment by credit card, were deemed acceptable; but the court of appeals in *Carlin Communications v. Federal Communications Commission* (1988), held that the statute was invalid in that it applied to constitutionally protected indecent communications.

Congress tried a second time to produce a dial-a-porn law, with two separate pieces of legislation in 1988. The first completely prohibited all obscene and indecent commercial telephone services to anyone, regardless of age; the second split the text into two parts, the first applying to obscenity and the second to indecency, each with different penalties. In 1989, however, the section of the law applying to indecency was declared unconstitutional by the U.S. Supreme Court in *Sable Communications v. Federal Communications Commission.*

That same year, Congress tried a third time to amend the U.S. Code as it applies to dial-a-porn. This law prohibits all obscene commercial telephone services, while restricting indecent commercial telephone services to persons age 18 and older. The FCC subsequently promulgated regulations for screening out minors, but before these went into effect, a group of dial-a-porn providers filed for an injunction enjoining enforcement on the grounds that the statute was vague, that it constituted prior restraint, and that the "least restrictive means" had not been applied in the regulations. A New York district court granted the injunction in *American Information Enterprises v. Thornburgh,* which was later overturned by a court of appeals in *Dial Information Services v. Thornburgh* (1991).

Thus, the 1989 law remained in effect as of 1992, with dial-a-porn providers required to use one of the screening methods specified in the FCC regulations. A quick glance at some of the newspaper advertisements for these services suggests that a good many providers are requiring prepayment by credit card.

Conclusion

Over the centuries, censorship of sexuality messages has gradually increased along with the consciousness of social responsibility and social reform. Yet as higher incomes together with increased leisure and education allowed a greater diversification of attitudes and "cultures" within U.S. society, the consciousness of social responsibility is no longer unified. We no longer agree (if we ever did) on what constitutes social reform—which sexual messages (if any) are necessary for health, well-being, and happiness and which (if any) are or might be harmful.

The result, especially in the last few decades, has been a sometimes frantic, sometimes grimly dogged *pas de deux* between the pro-sex people and the pro-censorship people, who change partners disconcertingly as the issues shift. The educator fighting for an improved sexuality textbook may also protest sexist speech in the workplace or support a new zoning law that limits the location of X-rated video stores. Someone in favor of the Pornography Victims Compensation Act may be against the Gag Rule.

With this "fractalization" of social opinion, it becomes less likely that the extremes of either censorship or free expression of sex will be easily implemented. Rather, the tug of war will continue in small and large battles for some decades, with regulations being passed and repealed, and cases first won, then overturned—and perhaps overturned again.

Yet educational and informational messages about sexuality, the Gag Rule notwithstanding, may be finally breaking free of censorship, as sex-related social issues, new birth and birth control technologies, and especially AIDS have increased the demand and need for sex information for perhaps even a majority within the diversified U.S. cultures. Simultaneously, improved research may also help us target more specifically the origins of social harm—those elements that may lie in sexual messages or may lie elsewhere. The next century will doubtless shed much heat—but hopefully some light—on the matter.

The impulse toward censorship has itself puzzled historians, social commentators, and those who see themselves victimized by censorship. The censors' own view—that they are motivated by the highest ideals of morality, patriotism, and responsibility—covertly implies that others lack these virtues, and that some materials deserve obliteration. However, that "explanation" leaves much unanswered. If it is true that producers of material deserving obliteration are immoral, unpatriotic, or irresponsible, how comes their placental loyalty to such evils? On reflection, we see that the answer must lie in a moral framework external to acts of—or rationalization for—censorship. Thus, censors necessarily must feel themselves generically of superior moral, political, and socially responsible substance than those whose works are deemed fit only for destruction.

An apparent exception may suggest some additional truth for this formulation. At time of war, few deny the need for censoring information of potential use to the enemy. Indeed, wartime censorship, even widespread, of all media—radio, television, print, and "loose talk"—is perceived as a tolerable evil, yet warranted only by the extraordinary circumstances of warfare. Now, modern censors often describe their activities as representing a "war" against immorality, but the war they envision surely differs from the armed combat, espionage, and agent provocateurship of military action. Indeed, one might wonder in what sort of war a man like Comstock envisioned himself immersed. Because it cannot be war in the literal sense, only figurative meanings remain, strengthening the conclusion that censors act not from narrowly founded dislikes of sexual imagery, say, but from a broader worldview in which transcendent immorality wages war against the Good, and must be subdued.

As for censorship of sexual messages, an additional image of war arises—the battle of the sexes. Not a war in the military sense, yet conflicts between men and woman about sexual morality, purity, and expression seem to wax and wane according to a thermometer calibrated in intensity of censorship. Thus, in today's America, a curious conflation exists between urgent calls for restructuring sexual communication and more or less virulent debate about the role of women in society. The observation suggests that the history of censorship is, in part, the history of reaction on the part of moralists to changes in women's status, role, and prerogative. All sides of today's censorship battles hoist the banner of protecting womanhood to rally round the forces they see as threatening, in their enthusiasm for or against censorship. Strong symbols indeed are evoked in this history.

Obviously, few would argue that the battle of the sexes has the gut-bloodied horror of modern combat, or that sexuality messages have the same valence as defense-related information. Again, it seems that issues beyond mere sexuality inform the censoring mind: sexuality is perhaps best described as a symbol of something else when evoked by censors. Women's lives—and rules created so often by men for how women should live—are part of the larger something to which censorship is connected; yet images of masculine sexuality are equally taboo. Thus, the object of censorship appears to be rule-breaking sexual behavior, seen by the censor as a deliberate or inadvertent model for more global anarchistic behavior among the youth, and seen ultimately not so much as simple lust but as heresy and rebellion—a point Plato made long ago in the first defense of censorship. If so, the impulse to censor emerges when rebellion is close to the surface, and it seems probable to the censor that society is about to tear loose from traditional moral and political moorings. So an anarchy of sexuality has come to stand for the anarchy of social and religious heresy against which censorship was first and foremost directed.

It may be that less than we might think has changed since Plato's day. Still preeminent in the censor's mind and fears is the spectre of social dislocation, rebellion, heresy, and revolution, which, from time to time—as in today's America—seems to wear the paradoxical disguise of nudity, as if baring the skin and coupling in morally illicit postures augured both revelations of social evil, and revolutions directed against their perceived causes and patrons. Only time and history will determine if this view of sex prevails or if sexuality ultimately becomes no more radical or revolutionary than an embodied pleasure, a reproductive necessity, and a socially valued activity in reality and in image.

REFERENCES

Baughman, J.L. *Television's Guardians: The FCC and the Politics of Programming, 1958–1967.* Knoxville, Tenn.: Univ. of Tennessee Press, 1985.

Busha, C.H. Censorship and Intellectual Freedom. In *ALA World Encyclopedia of Library and Information Science.* Chicago: American Library Association, 1986.

Cornog, M., ed. *Libraries, Erotica, and Pornography.* Phoenix: Oryx, 1991.

Cowan, G. *See No Evil: The Backstage Battle Over Sex and Violence on Television.* New York: Simon & Schuster, 1979.

Diffily, A. The Wry Wit Behind "Politically Correct Person." *Brown Alumni Monthly* (Feb. 1991), pp. 28–30.

Franklin, B. *Fart Proudly: Writings of Benjamin Franklin You Never Read in School.* (C. Japikse, comp. and ed.), Columbus: Enthea, 1990.

Green, J. *The Encyclopedia of Censorship.* New York: Facts on File, 1990.

Haeberle, E.J. The Birth of Sexology: A Brief History in Documents. Catalog for exhibit shown at the 6th World Congress of Sexology, May 22–27, 1983, Washington, D.C., sponsored by the World

Association for Sexology and organized by the United States Consortium for Sexology.

Hauptman, R. *Ethical Challenges in Librarianship*. Phoenix: Oryx, 1988.

Hurwitz, L. *Historical Dictionary of Censorship in the United States*. Westport, Conn.: Greenwood, 1985.

Hyde, H.M. *A History of Pornography*. New York: Dell, 1965.

Jay, T. *Cursing in America*. Philadelphia: John Benjamins, 1991.

Kahn, F.J., ed. *Documents of American Broadcasting*. Third Ed. Englewood Cliffs, N.J.: Prentice-Hall, 1978.

Keating, W.S. Preface. In Ovid, *The Art of Love*. New York: Stravon, 1949.

Kendrick, W. *The Secret Museum: Pornography in Western Culture*. New York: Viking, 1987.

Legman, G. The Bawdy Song—In Fact and in Print. In *The Hornbook: Studies in Erotic Folklore and Bibliography*. New Hyde Park, N.Y.: University Books, 1964.

Lewis, F.F. *Literature, Obscenity, and the Law*. Carbondale, Ill.: South Illinois Univ. Press, 1976.

Lowry, D.T., and D.E. Towles. Soap Opera Portrayals of Sex, Contraception, and Sexually Transmitted Diseases. *Journal of Communication*, Vol. 39, No. 2 (1989), pp. 76–83.

Pembar, D.R. *Mass Media Law*. Fifth Ed. Dubuque, Iowa: William C. Brown, 1990.

Plato. *The Republic*. R.W. Sterling and W.C. Scott, trans. New York: Norton, 1985.

Rosen, P.T. *The Modern Stentors: Radio Broadcasting and the Federal Government, 1920–1934*. Westport, Conn.: Greenwood, 1980.

Salmons, J., and M. Macauley. Offensive Rock Band Names. Maledicta, Vol. 10 (1988–89), pp. 81–99.

Warfel, H.R. *Noah Webster: Schoolmaster to America*. New York: Octagon Books, 1966.

Martha Cornog
Timothy Perper

CENTER FOR MARITAL AND SEXUAL STUDIES

The Center for Marital and Sexual Studies in Long Beach, California, was one of the early centers for the treatment of sexual problems. It was founded by William E. Hartman and Marilyn A. Fithian. Hartman was born February 17, 1919, in Meadville, Pennsylvania, the first of four children of Hartley J. and Janet Ellis Hartman. Both his father and maternal grandfather were Methodist ministers. He was educated at New York University and Centenary College and served in the U.S. Army Air Force during World War II for four and a half years. In 1944, he married Iva Decker, and they had seven children and more than two dozen grandchildren. They were divorced in 1980.

After the war, Hartman went on to study at the University of Southern California, from which he received M.A. and Ph.D. degrees. He then joined the faculty of California State University at Long Beach, where he taught sociology for some 30 years before retiring in 1980. He is a past president of the Society for the Scientific Study of Sex.

Marilyn A. Fithian, the cofounder of the Center, was born in 1921 in Wasco, Oregon. She is the mother of four and grandmother of eight. After her children were born she went back to school and received a B.A. degree from California State University at Long Beach; she did graduate work at California State University at Los Angeles. She has an honorary doctorate from the Institute for Advanced Studies in Human Sexuality. She worked for a time in the Counseling Center at California State-Long Beach and eventually became a licensed marriage, family, and child counselor.

In the early 1960s, Hartman was a professor of sociology and chairman of the Department of Sociology and Social Welfare at California State University at Long Beach. He admired and respected the research in human sexuality done by Dr. William H. Masters in St. Louis. He felt that a similar research and therapy facility should be established in California and asked Fithian to join him as a member of a dual-sex research-therapy team.

In 1966, a group of professional people were asked to be an advisory board for the new center, the main purposes of which were to be research and treatment of sexual problems. The board comprised physicians, lawyers, therapists, educators, ministers, and one politician. It was designed to obtain feedback and support not only from professionals but also from the Long Beach community about the need and desire to have a treatment and research center in human sexuality.

Following consultation and advice, the Center opened in 1968 as a California nonprofit organization, and from the first it included a clinic for those with limited income. In 1972, Hartman and Fithian published a book, *Treatment of Sexual Dysfunction*, dealing with their 34-step treatment process. With publication came numerous requests for training, and eventually 54 dual-sex teams were trained. During the years immediately following, several teams at a time were going through training. Since each team often worked not only with Hartman or Fithian but also with other team members, a number of people were working at the Center at any one time. Training involved an intensive six-week,

360–400 hour, seven-day-a-week program. The time differential was due to required hours as opposed to the extra time most of the trainees spent in nonrequired activities, such as the ongoing physiological research being conducted at the Center.

There was also a demand for shorter training from therapists who wanted more than one- or two-day seminars but not the six-week program. The result was a week-long training program held several times a year for many years, with attendance ranging from 10 to 20 therapists. There were almost always a number of student interns working as well.

Initially, the Center developed audiovisual materials for its own use, but as other professionals saw them they wanted copies. The result was the production of some 35 films, which were made available to others.

In 1970, some rudimentary physiological research began. In 1972, the late Berry Campbell, a research physiologist from the University of California Medical School at Irvine, joined the Center quarter-time as part of his teaching load. Campbell initially used borrowed equipment, but the Center itself eventually purchased a Beckman R411 Dynograph eight-channel recorder.

To support the research, Hartman and Fithian offered short-term seminars on sexual therapy in most of the major cities in the United States. The first seminar was held for about 20 people, but the numbers built up to as many as 600 in such major centers as New York City. Short-term seminars continued to be held until 1982, and in some years more than two dozen such seminars were held. The money earned from them not only allowed the continuation of the research but also the upgrading and purchase of more and newer research equipment, some made specifically for the Center.

Hartman and Fithian not only used the laboratory for their own research, but they allowed a number of other professionals access to it as well. Though the cofounders were usually present, the researchers published the results under their own name. All the research subjects at the Center were volunteers, and none were paid. Those who volunteered to be in films, however, were given a modest amount to enable the Center to have a contract with them.

For the physiological research sample, Hartman and Fithian gathered records on 751 individuals (282 males and 469 females). To date, this is the largest number of subjects ever studied in human sexual response research. Some were monitored as many as 20 times. It is estimated that approximately 10,000 research hours were

spent on monitoring and evaluating this body of work, with many more uncalculated hours spent on ongoing study. The first multiply-orgasmic men were monitored in the laboratory in 1972; multiply-orgasmic women were also studied, as was penile sensitivity and many other topics.

The major purpose of the center was therapy, however. The basic therapy program was a 34-step two-week intensive residential treatment program, although there were slight variations to suit the needs of the client. The main therapy focus was on sexual problems, although traditional talk therapy was also provided where indicated.

Almost all the work was with couples, although some singles were also treated, some with the help of surrogates. Hartman and Fithian were the first to treat female singles with surrogates. During the height of the Center's activities in the 1980s, more single females were treated than males. A large proportion of both male and female singles were virgins or had extremely limited sexual experience. To be treated by surrogates clients must have had tests for human immunodeficiency virus (HIV) and sexually transmitted disease and have used safe sex; the treatment was aimed at heterosexual, not homosexual, men or women.

Hartman and Fithian were primarily interested in relationships, and this was just as true for singles as for married couples. Fear of intimacy is a major problem, and helping individuals learn to be warm, caring people has always been an important part of their therapy. Since 1985, Hartman and Fithian have seen fewer clients and have been most interested in analyzing their research data and writing. Some of the more innovative aspects of their work include sexological examination and body imagery.

In the 1970s and 1980s, when their practice was at its height, they conducted sex therapy in groups on a three- and five-day basis, with excellent follow-up results. This is probably the most economical way to do sex therapy for clients, but many people are not comfortable working in a group. Still, some long-standing sexual problems, such as impotency, were often resolved in this format.

At the conclusion of therapy, each client was asked to rate statistically the extent to which his or her goal in entering therapy had been accomplished. The overall ratings in such cases averaged 92 percent satisfaction. Since 1985, Hartman and Fithian have focused on research and writing. *Any Man Can*, a book on male multiply-orgasmic research subjects, was published in 1984. Further books are in process.

REFERENCES

Hartman, W.E. *Any Man Can.* New York: St. Martin's Press, 1984.

Hartman, W.E., and M.A. Fithian. *Treatment of Sexual Dysfunction.* Long Beach, Calif.: Center for Marital and Sexual Studies, 1972; New York: Jason Aaronson, 1974.

William E. Hartman
Marilyn A. Fithian

CERVICAL CAP

This method of contraception, not in broad use today, was widely used in contraceptive clinics in Great Britain in the 1920s and 1930s and for a brief time in the United States, until it was replaced by the diaphragm and spermicidal jelly. It was developed by Friedrich Adolph Wilde, a German gynecologist in 1838, out of the unvulcanized rubber in use at that time. It was also made with many different materials—gold, platinum, silver, stainless steel, copper, and later plastics. Only one type of cervical cap, the Prentif rubber cap has been approved by the U.S. Food and Drug Administration.

Rubber caps, though more difficult to fit and insert than the diaphragm, can be worn for 48 hours and need not be inserted at the last moment. The cap has about equal contraceptive effectiveness as the diaphragm if made of plastic and can be inserted from the last menstrual period to the onset of the new one. While the diaphragm is equally protective whether it is inserted "dome up" or "dome down," the cap has to sit on the cervix like a thimble on the fingers; to master the technique takes at least two sessions in the physician's office, and for many users somewhat more. Many sexologists, such as Hans Lehfeldt, were strong advocates of the cap and remain so because of the prolonged protection and the separation between contraception and coitus.

REFERENCES

Lehfeldt, H., and I. Sivin. Use Effectiveness of the Prentif Cervical Cap in Private Practice. *Contraception,* Vol. 30 (Oct. 1984), pp. 331–38.

Tietze, C., H. Lehfeldt, and H.C. Liebmann. "The Effectiveness of the Cervical Cap as a Contraceptive Method. *American Journal of Obstetrics and Gynecology,* Vol. 66 (1953), pp. 904–08.

Wheeler, C.C., and H. Lehfeldt. Sexual Satisfaction: Diaphragm versus Cervical Cap. In W. Eicher and G. Kockott, eds., *Sexology.* Berlin: Springer, 1988.

Hans Lehfeldt
Connie Christine Wheeler

CHASTITY GIRDLES

Technically, a chastity girdle is a device for ensuring female chastity. It usually consists of a jointed metal part that passes between the legs and hooks both to the back and to the front of a padded hip band. The jointed metal plates are furnished with openings, one over the urethra and one over the anus, which allow urination and evacuation but are not large enough to allow the insertion of a finger.

The earliest known reference to the chastity girdle is in 1405, in a Göttingen manuscript of Kyeser of Eichstadt's *Bellifortis,* a kind of military encyclopedia that also contains a number of drawings. There are, however, many more or less legendary references both before and after that time. They are often mentioned in fiction, such as *Lives of Fair and Gallant Ladies,* by Pierre de Bourdeilles, Signeur de Brantôme (1535–1614). He reports that jealous husbands bought them and proceeded to fit them to their wives but were thwarted when locksmiths were commissioned by them to make false keys.

How widespread chastity girdles were is debatable, and the issue is complicated by the fact that they are often confused with antimasturbatory devices, which were widely sold in the 19th century. Many of these were designed on the same principle. Still, it seems likely, in classes and times when female chastity was highly desirable, that chastity belts were regarded as a preventive measure. Several 20th-century legal cases reached the courts in Paris, usually involving husbands who required their wives to wear such items.

Though chastity belts per se are not said to have been designed for men, many of the antimasturbatory devices were. They consisted of sheaths to be worn over the penis, with prickly points on the inside. Any erection would therefore be extremely painful. Most of the devices that turn up in antique shops were developed to prevent masturbation.

REFERENCES

Bullough, Vern L. Technology for the Prevention of "Les Maladies Produite par la Masturbation." *Technology and Culture,* Vol. 28 (Oct. 1987), pp. 828-32.

Dinwall, Eric John. *The Girdle of Chastity.* London: Routledge & Sons, 1931.

Vern L. Bullough

CHILDREN AND SEX

The topic of sex and children is broad, complex, and, for many adults, full of fear and ambivalence. It is broad because it covers a wide range of behaviors. Sexual behavior includes such nongenital activity as touching, cuddling, and fondling. It also includes genital activities, such as masturbation, oral stimulation, and sexual contact with another person or persons. The topic is complex because human sexuality is not complete at birth. Completion of an infant's psychosexual makeup awaits the interaction of many environmental factors with those established before birth. Consequently, an infant's sexuality is in the making for years after birth. The topic is fearful for many adults because their sexual development as children and adolescents—complete with their questions, doubts, and confusion—was often addressed with silence, punishment, and overreaction. Consequently, while parents may wish to have their children grow up differently than they did, their own fears and confusion surface. Often they recreate, without meaning to, an environment similar to the one they had as children. Add to this today's fear of AIDS and the awareness of child sexual abuse and it is clear why the topic of children and sex can create strong, sometimes panicky, reactions. Such reactions could result in throwing out the baby (infant and childhood sexuality) with the bath water (the problems of AIDS, sexually transmitted diseases, teenage pregnancy, and sexual abuse). To not accept childhood sexuality and children's need to develop an early solid sexual foundation creates a vacuum where little accurate information exists for the child. The child will fill this vacuum, often with misinformation.

Repression or punishment of childhood sexuality, in its broadest definition, can result in serious sexual and relationship problems in adulthood. By not accepting infants and children as sexual, parents rob themselves of the opportunity to help nurture and guide this most basic dimension of humans.

The Infant's Developing Sexuality

Development of the internal and external sex organs in both males and females occurs during the first trimester of pregnancy. This process is complex and includes the presence or absence of hormones. The brain, which is also involved in sexual function, is developing at this time and continues to do so even after birth. Evidence of male penile erections in utero now exists. Such erections also occur shortly after birth and several times every night during REM sleep for the rest of a male's life. Erections have also been noted to happen during breast feeding and at other times of social interaction, such as a diaper changing or bathing. Those erections during in-

teractions with another human, usually the mother or the father, point to the importance of the parent-child bond in the development of the child's sexual system. Furthermore, some mothers have reported having sexual feelings during breast feeding, and some have discontinued breast feeding because they feel uncomfortable having these feelings. There is no evidence that such feelings are bad, wrong, or pathological; they appear to be a natural response some women have to this intimate situation.

There is currently no evidence of clitoral erection or vaginal lubrication of females in utero. However, female infants have been known to lubricate shortly after birth, so it would not be surprising if this does occur.

It is also during situations of intimacy and caring by the mother (such as bathing or diapering) that male infants discover their genitals. This usually occurs between six and eight months of age, approximately three months before baby girls discover their vulvas. For both infants, male and female, this exploration for the first year consists of casual touching of the external sex organs. Toward the beginning of the second year, boys' genital touching appears to be more focused. They intentionally reach for their penis, and they can self-stimulate, which is accompanied by what appears to be some sort of pleasure as evidenced by cooing, grunting, and smiling. This degree of genital sensitivity has been noted to increase during the latter half of the second year. Both boys and girls explore their external sex organs by touch and visual inspection. They also repetitiously stimulate themselves manually or by rocking, straddling objects, or positioning themselves so as to put pressure on their thighs. For boys, the testicles are often included; girls rub, squeeze, or push their labia and some insert their finger into their vaginal opening. Both girl and boy infants make affectionate gestures and touch their mother's body during or after genital self-stimulation. This behavior toward the mother is soon replaced by almost total self-absorption, suggesting true masturbation (i.e., genital stimulation accompanied by a fantasy or intense feeling state). During this time, girls sometimes use their toys for masturbation and start examining their dolls' crotch area.

Toddlers are also interested in not only their own defecation and urinary functions, but in those of others as well (e.g., peers, adults, and animals). They want to observe their parents, touch their genitals (the father's penis or mother's breasts and vulva), and even touch, by hand or by mouth, their father's urinary stream.

Children are also curious about each other, and it is not unheard of to find them playing the "show me" game. Flirtation and romance can usually be seen within the family, focused on the opposite sexual parent.

From diapering to the emergence of flirtation, the presence of parents or parent substitutes is important to aid the infant's developing sexuality.

Primates other than humans (i.e., monkeys) also engage in sexual exploration, stimulation, and play in their juvenile years in a manner similar to that of human children. In fact, it has been the study and observation of sexual rehearsal play in subhuman primates that suggest the importance of such juvenile behavior for adolescent and adult sexual functioning. Rhesus monkeys growing up in isolation and consequently deprived of juvenile sex rehearsal play (e.g., not touching others or being able to practice sexual positioning) grow up unable to copulate and, thereby, reproduce. If they are allowed a period of play with other juvenile monkeys, some can learn the proper sexual positioning. However, they learn this approximately nine months later than monkeys allowed to grow up in colonies where sex play and exploration are common, and their birth rates are lower as adults. Sanctions against human childhood sex play are typically very negative and, in some cases, cruel and abusive. It is not unreasonable to believe that the result of such negative sanctions might be a range of sexual and erotic problems in adolescence and adulthood.

Later Childhood Sexual Development

Overt heterosexual behavior is not uncommon in children as young as age three or four given the opportunity. Children have been observed running nude and playing with their own and other children's genitals. In some cases, simulated intercourse has been observed. In these situations, the children change roles, one being the male, the other being the female, and vice versa. This mutual exchange of sexual positioning and the pretend-like nature of intercourse point to the role of learning in sexual development and differentiation of human sexuality.

As children get older they continue to show interest in sexuality. They show this by overt behavior and in their increasing knowledge and willingness to discuss this knowledge. For example, children as young as age five are interested in sex differences and where babies come from. They use a range of words to describe various sexual body parts. This interest, revealed in many studies, debunks the concept of sexual latency—that sexual interest declines or is absent between ages seven and 12. For children between these ages interest in sex continues and may even increase.

Overt heterosexual play continues in the preteenage years as does masturbation. At each stage of preadolescence, boys report more sexual activity of every kind than do girls. Various explanations have been given: biological differences, male subculture's emphasis on sexual activity for the male, and the increased restraints placed on girls by their parents as they approach puberty. Friendship, romance, and sexual fantasies (e.g., attachments and crushes) begin to form at this time, if not earlier. How the feelings of love toward another person are expressed depends on many factors: the child's age and level of sexual and social maturity; and the attitudes toward sex and sexual expressions of adults, especially parents. Often these relationships start as close boy-girl friendships and progress to involve such behavior as handholding, kissing, fondling, caressing, and intercourse. Not all intense friendships between boys and girls include all these behaviors. Some may involve intense friendship with talking only. Others include various sexual behaviors. Regardless of the friendship, it appears these heterosexual relationships provide a context within which to learn the skills of sexual interaction, the success or failure of which may have consequences for later adult psychosocial and psychosexual functioning between the sexes.

It would be a mistake to conclude that sexual behavior between children and adolescents takes place only in heterosexual relationships and that if it occurs between the same sex (two boys or two girls) something is wrong. It is also a mistake to automatically believe a problem is present if sex play appears between siblings (same or opposite sex). Even in situations where the children are not the same ages, many factors must be considered. For example, stigmatized children or those who are slow learners can be excluded from social peer groups. Consequently, sexual learning opportunities are excluded too. Hence, the only opportunity may be at home with a sibling, younger or older, or with an adult. Sexual play can occur between siblings who are, for a time, best friends, confidantes, and playmates.

For older children and teenagers, sexual relationships sometimes develop between best friends of the same sex. While it would be correct to describe their sexual behavior as homosexual, it would be wrong to absolutely label them as homosexuals. Homosexuality refers to a person's status; that is, a person's general state of being. A homosexual is sexually orientated, aroused, and capable of falling in love with a person with the same external sex organs. Some children and teenagers are homosexual and their sexual contact with a same sex peer may well be a way of confirming their status. Sometimes fear of sexual contact with their peers means they seek affirmation with older homosexuals. Most adolescents do not have a homosexual status and stop their homosexual acts when they start to date girls or start heterosexual activity. Others continue to have homosexual activity along with their heterosexual activity. Such relationships can last into adulthood.

Pediatric and Adolescent Sexual Problems

Because children's and teenagers' sexuality is continuously unfolding, they can experience difficulties and problems. A developing discipline called pediatric sexology addresses the sexual problems, broadly defined, of children and teenagers. Little is known about sexual problems of the pediatric group because of negative attitudes toward sex in general, but most of all because of a resistance to acknowledge sexuality as an integral part of the developmental process of childhood. Still, some problems do come to the attention of parents, schoolteachers, and others who work with children.

Hypermasturbation (i.e., frequent masturbation which disrupts daily functioning) is one of the problems most typically found. It has been shown in some cases to be associated with an inability to achieve orgasm in children who have previously experienced or nearly experienced orgasm. In other cases, hypermasturbation is a symptom of a stressful environment. In most cases, it is brought to the attention of a professional by an adult who has observed the child, boy or girl, showing the behavior in a public place, such as the classroom.

Gender disorders in childhood exist and are now recognized by professionals. It is not uncommon to observe a boy or a girl change roles at a very early age, and even make statements suggesting that they are not settled as to whether they are male or female. However, children with genuine gender disorders persistently and intensely reject their sexual organs (penis for boys, breasts for girls) and say that they wish to have the sexual organs of the opposite sex. Furthermore, they reject the sex-stereotype play and toys for their sex in favor of the toys and play of the opposite sex. They also prefer the clothes of the opposite sex and often play "dress up" with their parents' or siblings' clothes, or use towels as pretend clothes if real clothes are not available.

Such children and their parents need professional help.

Teenagers can experience various sex problems. Boys especially can have their sexual arousal and ejaculation associated with female apparel to such a degree that they must always be dressed partially or totally in female clothes, or they must fantasize such, to function sexually. Such teenagers have the condition of either transvestism or a transvestic fetish. Some teenagers have the more severe gender disorder of transsexualism, where they wish to live, work, and play completely in the role of the opposite sex.

Some teenagers are confused about whether they are heterosexual, homosexual, or bisexual. Perhaps they had a homosexual experience or have homosexual thoughts or fantasies. They and their parents need the guidance of a person specially educated in the psychosexual development of children.

Some teenagers worry about sexual thoughts and feel any sexual thoughts are bad. These adolescents need to be reassured that their sexual thoughts are normal, a sign of healthy development.

Some teenagers have sexual thoughts and fantasies and/or engage in sexual activities that are constant and interfere with their ability to relate in a healthy way to others. Examples are fantasies of sex connected to violence, sex with much younger children, or masturbating with the use of drugs or some device (e.g., a rope) to cut off oxygen to the brain, thereby heightening sexual arousal and orgasm. These adolescents need to be evaluated professionally to assess what type of treatment of those available would be most helpful.

Most important, parents and teachers need to create an atmosphere of open communication on all topics of sex. They should resist the temptation to overreact when adolescents bring their questions or comments to them. Adults should be supportive and help the adolescents seek professional help.

Sexual Abuse of Children

Historically, the 1960s and 1970s might be remembered as a period of sexual revolution when people in Western industrialized countries were more vocal and expressive of their sexuality. The 1980s might be remembered for the advent of AIDS and the recognition of child sexual abuse. Because sexuality is part of being human, which includes childhood and adolescence, everyone must be concerned with AIDS, sexually transmitted diseases, teenage pregnancy, and sexual abuse of children. All of these exist. Sexual abuse of children, however, is not without controversy.

The controversy stems in part from the definition of "child sexual abuse," which is used by both professionals and lay people. It is assumed to have the same meaning for everyone; it does not. Even among professionals—as reviews of the professional literature show—there is no agreement on its meaning. For some, all sexual activity between an adult and a child is abuse. Furthermore, the term sometimes incorporates physical abuse of children. This lack of a clear definition not only reinforces the hysteria over this issue, but also runs the risk of creating problems where none exist (e.g., accusing a father of sexual abuse for applying prescribed medicine on his infant daughter's vagina) and missing actual abuse (e.g., the incident where Milwaukee police returned a teenage boy to a man with severe sexual problems who later killed him).

In addition to the lack of clarity about what constitutes sexual abuse, the term does not distinguish among legal, moral, and psychological issues. The term assumes a violation of a legal standard, that such a violation also violates a moral standard, and that such violation, without question, results in harm to the child as a consequence of the sexual activity. Such assumptions are not always true. Someone might engage in sexual behavior that is neither harmful nor illegal but that may be repugnant to another on moral grounds (e.g., homosexual behavior, sex before marriage, childhood sex rehearsal play). There are also sexual behaviors that are illegal but that are neither repugnant nor harmful to the individuals involved (e.g., heterosexual or homosexual anal sex, which is illegal in some states). On the other hand, there are behaviors that are legal but potentially harmful to the individuals involved (e.g., unprotected teenage sexual intercourse). A man and a 14–year-old boy masturbating each other are breaking the law in the United States. For most people, their behavior is repugnant and immoral; whether it is abusive (i.e., having short- or long-term negative effects) is debated by professionals. Some suggest that once sexual activity between children, between children and adolescents, between adolescents, or between children or adolescents and adults becomes known, the actual trauma the child or adolescent experiences results not from the behavior but from the response of the parents and various professionals within the system. There is no doubt that children are sexually abused and misused. However, given that children are sexual and the possibility that trauma can occur from the system when in fact no trauma

may have occurred, it is important for parents and professionals to be appropriately concerned, not to overreact, and to seek guidance and advice. In this way, children can be assured of being protected and at the same time nurtured to develop their sexual potential to its fullest.

REFERENCES

Constantine, L.M., and F. Martinson, eds. *Children and Sex: New Findings, New Perspectives.* Boston: Little, Brown, 1981.

Goldman, J.G.D. Children's Sexual Thinking: A Research Basis for Sex Education in Schools. In M.E. Perry, ed. *Handbook of Sexology. Vol. 7: Childhood and Adolescent Sexology.* New York: Elsevier, 1990.

Haugaard, J.J., and N.D. Reppucci. *The Sexual Abuse of Children: A Comprehensive Guide to Current Knowledge and Intervention Strategies.* San Francisco: Jossey-Bass, 1980.

Kilpatrick, A.C. Childhood Sexual Experiences: Problems and Issues of Studying Long-Range Effects. *Journal of Sex Research,* Vol. 23 (1987), pp. 173–96.

———. Some Correlates of Women's Childhood Sexual Experiences: A Retrospective Study. *Journal of Sex Research,* Vol. 22 (1986), pp. 221–42.

Nelson, J.A. Incest: Self-Report Findings From a Nonclinical Sample. *Journal of Sex Research,* Vol. 22 (1986), pp. 463–77.

Okami, P. Sociopolitical Biases in the Contemporary Scientific Literature on Adult Human Sexual Behavior With Children and Adolescents. In J.J. Feierman, ed. *Pedophilia: Biosocial Dimensions.* New York: Springer-Verlag, 1990.

Sandford, T. *Boys on Their Contacts with Men: A Study of Sexually Expressed Friendships.* Elmhurst, N.Y.: Global Academic Publishers.

SIECUS. *Guidelines for Comprehensive Sexuality Education: Kindergarten Through Twelfth Grade.* New York: Siecus, 1991.

Thomas Mazur

CHILDREN AND SEX, PART II: CHILDHOOD SEXUALITY

Humans are born prosocial. During the first minutes, hours, and days after birth, the neonate is in a state of readiness, ready to develop its first intimate relationship with a person. One of the states of consciousness of a healthy neonate is a recurring, quiet, alert stage during which eyes are wide open and the neonate is able to respond to the faces of others, especially their eyes, through eye-to-eye *en face* interaction. Such interaction captivates the newborn as it watches and responds to the movements and facial expressions of others. A high degree of eye-to-eye contact between mother and infant has been observed to lead to an immediate cessation of crying, for instance, and to the development of a strong bond with the mother. The neonate's motor behavior becomes entrained by and synchronized with the facial and speech behavior of its mother. Their communication becomes a sort of "mating dance" as their responses become synchronized. One researcher characterized the dyad as the true locus of intimacy. An infant-mother relationship at its best is such a dyad as the two interact with a high degree of emotional access to each other. In a healthy relationship, the two develop pronounced feelings for each other as they jointly engage in more and more facial and verbal activity. The interaction is very sensual because of the physical dependency of the neonate and its inability to interact at a distal or symbolic level.

Although the neonate is totally dependent, it is not merely passive and receptive. Those who observe newborns are struck by the initiative they display in the development of attachments. The infant-mother physical interaction is intense, involving physical care, nursing, fondling, kissing, vocalizing, cuddling, and prolonged gazing. Infants who have been held tenderly and carefully early on tend later to respond positively to close bodily contact as well. Intimate, or sensate dyadic, relationships can become so intense, concentrated, and consuming as to appear almost hypnotic. Ecstasy is another word used by interactionists to characterize intense and perhaps erotic activity, such as occurs when a baby nurses at its mother's breast.

Breast feeding is the most physiologically charged relationship of infant and mother. The two organisms mutually excite each other. This ecstatic intimacy for both infant and mother can on occasion be orgasmic for both. The suckling experience gives the infant oral sensate pleasure; penile erections for the boy (and perhaps clitoral erections for the girl) can occur in connection with breast feeding. But attributing erections to stimulations resulting from the pleasant sensual aspects of the sucking experience must be done with caution. Based on observations of sucking infants, one researcher's inclination was to interpret the erections as often related to abdominal pressure, for when thwarting was introduced (e.g., removing a nipple or giving the infant a difficult nipple), the resulting movements were conspicuously characterized by severe contractions of the abdominal wall. Pleasure, pain, and frustration can all result in erections when infants interact with adults.

In American society, mothers are assured that interaction with a baby that is intimate and sensual is appropriate. There is no quarrel with the prescription that the proper socialization of infants calls for intimate, tender, loving care. Child care experts and the society in general approve of it. Developmental studies suggest that infants' emotional maturation depends on such stimulation. On the other hand, clinical studies credit deficient physical contact between infant and parent as the cause of later inability to form attachments. It happens that it is this same intimate socialization that leads to development of the sexual potential of infants, for infants who are given optimum intimate attention are much more likely to masturbate than are children who are raised in an indifferent or inattentive way. Spitz reported that when the relationship between mother and infant was optimal, (i.e., there was tender, loving care of the infant), genital play was present in all infants in his study. In fact, autoerotic activity on the part of an infant in the first 18 months of life may be a reliable indicator of the adequacy of parenting according to Spitz. The highly emotional and physiologically charged interaction of parents and infants is an important phase in a child's sexual development.

Self-Exploration and Autoerotic Activity

During the first year of life, there is progression in an infant's discovery of its body and its exploration of parts of the body, including the genitals. The fingering or simple pleasurable handling of the genitals is referred to as genital play. Infants in their first year are generally not capable of the direct, volitional, rhythmic movement that characterizes masturbation, while genital play requires little coordination and begins as early as the second half of the first year of life. The greater autoerotic satisfaction climaxing in orgasm depends largely on rhythmic, repetitive movement. Rhythmic manipulation of the genitals involving use of the hands does not generally begin until the child is approximately two and one-half or three years old, probably because small muscle control is not well enough developed earlier, yet Kinsey reported on one seven-month-old infant and five infants under age one who were observed masturbating.

Large muscle control involving muscles used in rocking or in rubbing against persons or objects is well enough coordinated by six months of age to make such masturbatory activity possible. Many infants form a pattern of rocking that is more rhythmic and repeated than is possible in manual genital play. Once the infant is able to sit up, many types of rocking may be observed which appear to bring satisfaction. Some infants sit and sway rhythmically, some lift the trunk and pelvis and bounce up and down off the surface on which they are sitting. Elevating to hands and knees and rocking forward and backward appears to be most frequent and is not uncommon as early as six to twelve months. Rocking infants are not as easily distracted from what they are doing as are infants engaged in genital play.

From their observations of 66 infants, and from interviews with their mothers, Roiphe and Galenson hypothesized that there is an endogenously routed early genital phase in children, a sexual current that normally emerges early in the second year that is different from genital play that might occur in the first year of life. They contend that the genital zone emerges as a distinct and differentiated source of pleasure, exerting a new influence on the sense of sexual identity, relation to objects and persons, basic moods, and other aspects of functioning characterized by psychological awareness of the genitals. The height of genital sensitivity begins to serve as a source of focused pleasure with repetitive intense genital self-stimulation and thigh pressure. The accompanying erotic arousal includes facial expressions of excitement and pleasure, flushing, rapid respiration, and perspiration. In both sexes, open affectionate behavior toward the mother begins to disappear as an accompaniment to the new genital self-stimulation and is replaced by an inward gaze and a self-absorbed look more characteristic of a masturbatory state.

At age three, most boys masturbate manually, but many still lie on their stomachs and writhe while engaging in other activities, such as watching television, and a few use other means of stimulation. Girls at this age use many masturbatory techniques, including placing a soft toy or blanket between their legs in the region of the genitals and wriggling the body, manually titillating the clitoris, and, less frequently, inserting fingers or other objects into the vagina. Masturbation appears to be a common experience in the development of normal infants and children, and most parents believe that children do it.

To determine the capacity of infants to respond to sexual stimulation, it is necessary to distinguish between self-stimulation and stimulation by others. It does appear that many more infants are capable of a sexual response, at the reflexive level, than stimulate themselves to such response. One researcher reported that if the edge of an infant's foreskin was tickled with a feather, the penis would swell and become erect and the infant would grasp at it with his hand. Kinsey, reporting on stimulation to orgasm in nine male infants under age one, found that the response involved a series of gradual physiological changes, the development of rhythmic body movements with distinct penis throbs and pelvic thrusts, tension of muscles, and a sudden convulsive release followed by disappearance of all symptoms. This was followed by a quick loss of erection and calm that impressed the observer as typical following orgasm in adults. Further, Kinsey reported that 32 percent of boys two to 12 months old were able to reach climax. One boy of 11 months had ten climaxes in an hour and another of the same age had 14 climaxes in 38 minutes.

Sexual Fantasy

Whether sexual activity engaged in by young children is purely reflexive or whether it is sometimes accompanied or preceded by erotic or sexual fantasy, as it is apt to be in adolescents or adults, has not been determined. It is reasonable to assume that children in societies that are inclined to repress what sexual activity children see, hear about, or do have little sexual content in their fantasy lives and that if they do, they do not readily reveal it to adults. In analyzing stories told by American children ages two to five, researchers found many references to violence in the stories of both boys and girls, even among those as young as age two. Although one researcher did not find kind or friendly stories common at this or at any age, one research team, in its sample of children ages two to five, found that girls did refer to love, courtship, and marriage.

That activities involving bodily functions, including sexual intercourse, are present in the consciousness of the children even in repressive societies is apparent in children's riddles, songs, verses, and games dealing with forbidden topics. Younger children refer mainly to bodily activity related to the anus, (e.g., excrement, flatulence, and enemas), while children ages six and seven have what Borneman refers to as an inordinate number of verses about brother-sister incest and some verses about parental intercourse. A rich sexual fantasy life would depend on more observation and sexual knowledge than children in sexually repressive societies usually have.

Encounters With Peers

Children as young as age two are mobile and prosocial in their sensual and sexual lives, as well as being autoerotic. Healthy children show strong affection toward parents, and kissing, cuddling, and hugging parents and other children and adults are common. On the other hand, abused toddlers are more likely to avoid eye contact with adults and to respond negatively or to ignore friendly overtures and adult caring approaches.

If children are left unsupervised and find nothing to interest them more, their play together can be sexual. In other words, the interest in sex play is not a dominant interest of children; it tends to ebb and flow. In an Israeli *kevutza* wherein children with a mean age of two slept in the same room, showered together, sat on toilets together, and often ran around the room nude before dressing or after undressing, Spiro found that intimate heterosexual play included a simple embrace as its most common expression, followed in frequency by stroking and caressing, kissing, and touching the genitals.

Based on observation of a large number of peer relationships of children, one researcher reported that love relationships were apparent and that the emotion of love between the sexes during the ages three to eight was characterized by hugging, kissing, lifting each other, scuffling, sitting close to each other, confessing to each other, grieving at being separated, giving gifts, extending courtesies to each other, and making sacrifices for each other. These intimacies have been characterized as social, while intimacies of pairs from age eight and older were characterized as more sexual in nature.

How sexual relationships become after around age eight depends on how much sexual activity the children have observed and how permissive the society is. There are records of societies wherein children engage freely in a variety of sexual practices and where few children are said to be virgins beyond the age ten or eleven.

Inhibiting Sexual Experiences of Infants and Young Children

Children depend on adults, therefore how they are expected to behave sexually depends on the values and norms guiding the thoughts and actions of their parents and others. The sexual socialization of infants and young children in the United States has been largely the responsibility of their mothers throughout the 20th century. Generally, her task has been to discourage sexual self-stimulation, inhibit sexual impulses toward family members, supervise and thus frustrate attempts at sexual play with peers, and teach children to be wary of strangers. Her task, generally with the full support of her husband, includes information control. The family attempts to govern how, when, and how many of the "facts of life" the child learns. As part of the conspiracy of silence, parents maintain a secrecy and privacy concerning their own sexual activity. Sears indi-

cates a number of methods used as aids to sexual control in the home (e.g., closed bedroom doors, separate sleeping arrangements for each child, separate bathing, and early modesty training). Such methods have an implicit goal of keeping dormant the young child's pervasive curiosity and imitativeness, postponing the onset of sexual self-gratification, and limiting sexual activity.

Many families refrain from giving proper names or give no names to the genital organs and genital activity as a way of controlling information. Another form of mislabeling is to unwittingly, or wittingly, characterize a child's sexual activity in a nonsexual way, by suggesting that a child playing with its genitals needs to go to the bathroom, for instance. Controlling sexual observation and experience and nonlabeling or mislabeling have the effect of keeping sexual thoughts and fantasy unfocused, imprecise, and incorrect. As far as Sears and associates could judge, no mother in their study labeled genital activity as sexual activity or encouraged it. Twenty years later, Yates still found no one reenforcing children's sexuality, nor were parents transmitting enthusiasm, providing direction, or aiding in the development of a firm erotic base for their children's sexual lives.

Some change toward greater openness is occurring, however. For example, at least seven books published in the United States during the 1980s instructed parents how to educate their children about sexuality and how to deal with their children's sexuality. In general, the authors recognize that children are sexual and that sexual development and sexual expression are normal characteristics of childhood.

Child Sexuality as Society Sees It

Society's blueprint for child socialization and child-parent interaction is less clear and unequivocal than that for infancy. The child-parent relationship is to be loving and nurturant it is true, but the loving way to treat children in the United States is not necessarily intimate and permissive. Child-parent intimate interaction is restrained and proscribed; the parent represents a more demanding, authoritative, normative structure for the child than for the infant. In defense, it is argued that prolonged infant-parent attachment produces habits of dependency that are to be left behind. The "loving way" to treat a child is to make demands, to apply close supervision, and to use firm disciplinary measures that sometimes include physical punishment. In many homes and elementary schools, the "rod" is used so that the child not be "spoiled." So the ego, already as a young child, enters the stage of socially proscribed sensory and sexual intimacy that begins early in childhood and lasts at least until adolescence, until the getting-together and dating stages that young people enter—and for which they appear to be ill-prepared as witnessed by the number of unplanned, unwanted pregnancies during adolescence.

It has been the American practice to move offspring as rapidly as possible from a proximal, analogic mode of touching, holding, and caressing to a distal and digital mode in which interaction can be performed at a distance: looking at, smiling, and vocalizing. Children are socialized away from body contact with self as well as with others. According to one researcher, the American child-rearing climate is one of weaning before age two, consistent positive reinforcement of self-reliance and achievement, the encouragement of male physical aggression, lower status for the female child, the use of supernatural forces to elicit moral behavior, and culturally sanctioned physical violence in disciplining children.

Children begin early to consciously sense that touching patterns as part of their tactile communications system with their parents are nonreciprocative. In a study of intimacy of four-year-olds, Blackman has shown that at least by that age permission to touch parents has been proscribed. There was not much child-parent touching at all, and what there was, was not interactive. The blocked response was the essence of their emotional experience. Many children still, as young adults, remember their mother's restricted expressiveness—asexual, sexually repressive, or even sexually punitive. Mother's own sexuality is hardly perceived at all. According to Finkelhor, mothers were perceived by the children as holding a greater number of sexually repressive attitudes than their fathers and were over twice as likely as fathers to punish their daughters for masturbating, playing sex games, or asking sex questions.

"Too much" touching, especially for boys, causes discomfort for many parents. The male macho image and the fear of homosexuality appear to inhibit sons in many families from openly shared affection, especially with their fathers. Sons, imitating their fathers, express noticeably less physical affection than do daughters for friends and relatives as well. Appropriate behavior for men in showing affection toward one another is by a handshake, a punch on the arm, or a pat on the back. Some parents report that they would like their sons to be able to experience and express a fuller range of feelings, including affec-

tion, intimacy, and vulnerability. Their commitment to this espoused value appears to be tenuous and ambiguous, however. The majority of fathers are not modeling the kind of behavior they say they would like their sons to be able to exhibit. And parents refuse to model intimacy and affection for their children. American parents are more likely to be seen as associates than as lovers by their children; comrades rather than a couple. For American children, the adult is not a sexual, but rather a social, ideal. They experience conflict over how to find a balance between what they believe and what they want their children to believe about intimacy and affection. Equivocal social messages and parental uncertainty, or lack of clarity about their own beliefs, contribute to communication problems. In the Roberts' study, in talking about the most important reasons for educating a child about sexuality, only about ten percent of the parents replied that it is to help the child "enjoy his or her sexuality" when grown up. Two thirds of the mothers and about one half of the fathers said their child was the one who usually took the initiative in raising sexual issues for discussion. Hence, the level of sophistication of conversation about sexuality appears to depend in such homes on the level of the child's sophistication and how inquisitive the child is.

That infants and small children have the physiological capacity for sexual response, that they are curious about their bodies and the bodies of others, that they are attracted to intimate interaction with others have all been established. With a permissive environment, modeling, encouragement, and stimulation, there appears to be no cessation of sensual and sexual activity from first discovery and on through life. The question for any society is: Is there such a thing as age-appropriate sexual behavior for children? There is no agreement on the answer to that question in American society. There is one universal norm of child sexuality that is accepted by all responsible adults; namely, that children should not be sexually abused. Beginning in 1962 with the report on a study on battered children, it came to be recognized that there are parents who abuse their own children, including sexual abuse, and that measures must be taken to protect the child and prevent the abuse. That universal norm does not take one very far in understanding age-appropriate sexual behavior, however. In fact, rational discussion of age-appropriate sexual behavior and research on human sexual development have scarcely begun.

REFERENCES

Blackman, N. Pleasure and Touching: Their Significance in the Development of the Preschool Child—An Exploratory Study. In J.M. Sampson, ed., *Childhood and Sexuality*. Montreal: Editions Etudes Vivantes, 1980.

Borneman, E. Progress in Empirical Research on Children's Sexuality, *SIECUS Report*, Vol. 12 (1963), pp. 1–6.

Calderone, M.S. Fetal Erection and Its Message to Us. *SIECUS Report*, Vol. 11 (1983), pp. 9–10.

Constantine, L.L., and F.M. Martinson. *Children and Sex: New Findings, New Perspectives*. Boston: Little, Brown, 1981.

Finkelhor, D. Sexual Socialization in America: High Risk for Sexual Abuse. In J.M. Samson, ed., *Childhood and Sexuality, op. cit.*

Ford, C.S., and F.A. Beach. *Patterns of Sexual Behavior*. New York: Harper, 1951.

Galenson, E., and H. Roiphe. The Emergence of Genital Awareness During the Second Year of Life. In R.C. Friedman, ed., *Sex Differences in Behavior*. New York: Wiley, 1974.

Honig, A.S. Infant-Mother Communication. *Young Children*, Vol. 37 (1982), pp. 52–62.

Ilg, F.L., and L.B. Ames. *Child Behavior*. New York: Dell, 1950.

Kinsey, A.C., W.B. Pomeroy, and C.E. Martin. *Sexual Behavior in the Human Male*. Philadelphia: W.B. Saunders, 1948.

Kinsey, A.C., W.B. Pomeroy, C.E. Martin, and P.H. Gebhard. *Sexual Behavior in the Human Female*. Philadelphia: W.B. Saunders, 1953.

Klaus, H.M., and J.H. Kennell. *Maternal-Infant Bonding*. St. Louis: C.V. Mosby, 1976.

Levine, M. I. Pediatric Observations on Masturbation in Children. *Psychoanalytic Study of the Child*, Vol. 6 (1957), pp. 117–124.

Martinson, F M. *Infant and Child Sexuality: A Sociological Perspective*. St. Peter, Minn.: The Book Mark, 1973.

Mead, M., and N. Wolfenstein. *Childhood in Contemporary Cultures*. Chicago: Univ. of Chicago Press, 1955.

Moll, A. *The Sexual Life of the Child*. New York: Macmillan, 1913. (Originally published in German, 1909.)

Roberts, E. J., D. Kline, and J. Gagnon. *Family Life and Sexual Learning: A Study of the Role of Parents in the Sexual Learning of Children*. Cambridge, Mass.: Population Education, Inc., 1978.

Roiphe, H., and E. Galenson. *Infantile Origins of Sexual Identity*. International Universities Press, 1981.

Sampson, J.M. *Childhood and Sexuality*. Montreal: Editions Etudes Vivantes, 1980.

Sears, R.R., E.E. Maccoby, and H. Levin. *Patterns of Child Rearing*. Evanston, Ill.: Row, Peterson, 1957.

Spiro, M. *Children of the Kevutza*. Cambridge, Mass.: 1958.

Spitz, R.A. Autoerotism: Some Empirical Findings and Hypothesis on Three of Its Manifestations in the First Year of Life. *Psychoanalytic Study of the Child*, Vol. 3/4 (1949), pp. 85–120.

Spitz, R.A., and K.N. Wolf. Analytic Depression. *Psychoanalytic Study of the Child*, Vol. 2 (1946), pp. 313–342.

Wolff, P.H. Observations on Newborn Infants. *Psychosomatic Medicine*, Vol. 21 (1959), pp. 110–118.

Yates, A. *Sex Without Shame: Encouraging the Child's Healthy Sexual Development*. New York: William Morrow, 1978.

Floyd M. Martinson

CHINA AND SEX

Among the oldest of the surviving Chinese manuscripts are those dealing with sex. The two oldest extant texts, dating from 168 B.C.E., were discovered in 1973 in Chang-sa, Hunan Province, at Tomb No. 3. The interment included 14 medical texts, three of them sexological works: *Shi-wan* (Ten Questions and Answers), *He-yin-yang-fang* (Methods of Intercourse between Yin and Yang), and *Tian-xia-zhi-tao-tan* (Lectures on the Super Tao in the Universe).

Key to Chinese sexology is the concept of yin and yang. According to the yin-yang philosophy, all objects and events are the products of two elements, forces, or principles: yin, which is negative, passive, weak, female, and destructive; and yang, which is positive, active, strong, male, and constructive. It is quite possible that the two sexes—whether conceived of in terms of female and male essences, the different social roles of women and men, or the structural differences between female and male sex organs—are not only the most obvious results of the workings of yin and yang forces, but major sources from which the ancient Chinese derived these concepts. Certainly, it was very natural for yin-yang doctrine to become the basis of Chinese sexual philosophy.

The Chinese have used the words Yin and Yang to refer to sexual organs and sexual behavior for several thousand years. Thus, *yin fu* (the door of yin) means vulva, *yin dao* (the passageway of yin) means vagina, and *yang ju* (the organ of yang) means penis. The combination of these words into the phrases *huo yin yang, he yin yang,* or *yin yang huo he* (the union or combination of yin and yang) describes the act of sexual intercourse. These words were also used in constructing more abstract sexual terminology. According to *Han Shu* (History of the Former Han Dynasty) the earliest terms referring to classical Chinese sexology were *yin dao* (or *yin tao*) meaning "the way of yin," and *yang yang fang*, meaning "the method for maintaining yang in good condition."

Because the yin-yang theory holds that the harmonious interaction of male and female principles is vital, it is the basis of an essentially open and positive attitude toward sexuality. The following passage from the classic *I Ching* (Book of Changes), which is one of the earliest and most important Chinese classics equally cherished in both the Confucian and the Taoist traditions is representative of the traditional sex-positive viewpoint: "The constant intermingling of Heaven and Earth gives shape to all things. The sexual union of man and woman gives life to all things." Thus, any time a man and woman join in sexual intercourse, they are engaging in an activity that reflects and maintains the order of nature.

Pan Ku (Ban Gu, 32–92 A.D.), one of China's greatest historians, included in his *Han Shu* (The History of the Former Han Dynasty) a special heading for *fang zhong* (literally "inside the bedchamber," and usually translated as "the art of the bedchamber," "the art of the bedroom," or sometimes as "the sexual techniques"), immediately after his medical works. Pan Ku concluded his list of *fang zhong* with a commentary which is the earliest extant essay on Chinese sexology:

> The Art of the Bedchamber constitutes the climax of human emotions, it encompasses the Super Tao. Therefore the Saint Kings of antiquity regulated man's outer pleasures in order to restrain his inner passions and made detailed rules for sexual intercourse. A familiar quotation says: "The ancient Kings created sexual pleasure thereby to regulate all human affairs." If one regulates his sexual pleasure he will feel at peace and attain a high age. If, on the other hand, one abandons himself to its pleasure, disregarding the rules set forth in the above-mentioned treatises, one will fall ill and harm one's very life. [Translated by R.H. van Gulik.]

Pan Ku's work demonstrates that more than 2,000 years ago, sexology was not only a well-developed academic field, but a respected subject of inquiry. Unfortunately, the books Pan Ku listed were all lost in the many wars and repeated book-burnings which mar China's history.

In different periods from the Han dynasty (206 B.C.E. to 220 M.E.) until the end of the Tang dynasty (618–907 M.E.), more than 20 sex handbooks were produced and circulated. Some of them are still available including:

- *Su Nu Ching* (Canon of the Immaculate Girl)
- *Su Nu Fang* (Prescriptions of the Immaculate Girl)
- *Yu Fang Chih Yao* (Important Matters of the Jade Chamber)
- *Yu Fang Pi Chueh* (Secret Instructions concerning the Jade Chamber)
- *Tung Hsuan Tzu* (Book of the Mystery-Penetrating Master)

These manuals offer detailed advice on the selection of sexual partners, flirting, and every aspect of coitus, including foreplay, orgasm, and resolution.

Hundreds of erotic fictional works were written in the Ming (1368–1644) and Ch'ing (1644–1911) dynasties. Ruan has examined numerous classic Chinese stories and scored them on an eroticism Scale of 1–4 as follows:

Score of 1: Fully erotic fiction—Works receiving this score consist primarily or entirely of explicit sexual descriptions. An example is *Jou Pu Tuan* (The Prayer Mat of Flesh).

Score of 2: Partially erotic fiction—Works receiving this score include a considerable amount of explicit sexual description. An example is *Chin P'ing Mei* (The Golden Lotus).

Score of 3: Incidentally erotic fiction—Works receiving this score contain only a small amount of explicit sexual description, which is incidental to the overall character of the novel. Examples are the famous *Hung Lou Meng* (Dream of the Red Chamber), and *120 Hui Shiu Hu Chuan* (The Water Margin of 120 Chapters).

Score of 4: Nonerotic fiction—Works receiving this score contain no explicit sexual description. Examples are *Hsi Yu Chi* (Journey to the West, also known as Monkey), and *San Kuo Yen Yi* (The Romance of the Three Kingdoms).

Although the suppression of erotic fiction and other erotica began to occur in the 12th and 13th centuries and gradually became more oppressive, censorship became more extreme with the founding of the People's Republic of China in 1949, when a strict ban on erotic fiction and pornography of any kind was imposed nationwide. In the 1950s and 1960s, the policy of banning erotica was very effective. In the whole country, almost no erotic material was to be found. There were few difficulties implementing this policy until the mid-1970s. Then, the legalization and wide availability of pornography in several Western countries during the late 1960s and early 1970s, coupled with China's increasing openness to the outside world, increased the supply of such material available for underground circulation. In recent years, the suppression of

117

pornography has caused both political and legislative concerns. The number of arrests and the severity of sentences on people involved in pornography have increased in the attempt to suppress it entirely. In 1987, the deputy director of the National Publication Bureau announced that during the preceding three years 217 illegal publishers had been arrested. Perhaps the most massive arrests of 1987 occurred in Nanchang, the capital of Jiangxi province, where by October, 44 dealers in pornography had been arrested, and 80,000 erotic books and magazines confiscated. It was reported that an underground publishing house with 600 salesmen had been circulating erotic materials in 23 of China's 28 provinces, making a profit of one million yuan (in that period about U.S. $300,000) in two years. In Shanghai, a railway station employee named Qin-xiang Liang was sentenced to death. Liang and four other persons organized sex-parties on nine different occasions showing pornographic videotapes and engaging in sexual activity with female viewers. The other organizers were sentenced to prison, some for life. The climax of this wave of repression seemed to occur on January 21, 1988, when the 24th session of the Standing Committee of the sixth National People's Congress adopted supplemental regulations imposing stiffer penalties on dealers in pornography. Under these regulations, if the total value of the pornographic materials is between 150,000 yuan and 500,000 yuan, the dealer shall be sentenced to life imprisonment. However, Deng Xiaoping, China's top leader, went further by declaring that some publishers of erotica deserved the death penalty. In a later nationwide strike against pornography, beginning on the thirty-seventh day after the Tienanmen Square massacre, on July 11, 1989, 65,000 policemen and other bureaucrats were mobilized to investigate publishing houses, distributors, and booksellers. By August 21, more than 11 million books and magazines had been confiscated, and about 2,000 publishing and distributing centers, and 100 private booksellers were forced out of business.

Like other common sexual behaviors, homosexuality was probably a familiar feature of Chinese life in prehistoric times. The earliest record of homosexuality dates from the Shang (or Yin) dynasty (approximately the 16th–11th centuries B.C.E.). Some authors seemingly glorified homosexuality. The best example was *The Mirror of Theatrical Life*, the most representative Chinese classic novel of homosexuality. The author, Chen Sen, eloquently praises the charms of catamites (young male homosexuals).

In China today, however, the general policy has been to deny the existence of homosexuality. When public figures do speak out on homosexuality, it is usually to condemn it. One of the most famous attorneys of the 1980s, Dun Li, when asked to express his opinion concerning homosexuality, said:

> Homosexuality, though it exists in different societies and cultures, with some minor exceptions is considered abnormal and disdained. It disrupts social order, invades personal privacy and rights, and leads to criminal behavior. As a result, homosexuals are more likely to be penalized administratively and criminally.

This official attitude of denial or condemnation began to break down in the 1990s. In 1991, officials in Shanghai, the largest city in China, reported that there were about 10,000 homosexuals in the city. Changzheng Hospital in Tianjin, the third largest city in China, reported that of its 366 cases of sexually transmitted diseases, at least 61 cases of syphilis were acquired through male sexual contacts; 80 percent of them involved anal sex, 10 percent oral sex, and 10 percent anal and oral sex. Most of the incidents that were linked to infection (80 percent) were anonymous contacts in public toilets. The age of the victims ranged from 16 to 60: two thirds were between 20 and 30. Most were workers, some were cadres and teachers.

Lesbians in China are even more closeted than gay males. Some of the women who are willing to discuss their homosexuality have already been imprisoned and have little to lose. Still, two journalists were more successful in contacting lesbians than gay males in their 1989 survey of homosexuality in China, many of them through the criminal court system. Unfortunately, since so many investigations of female homosexuality have been based on interviews with prisoners, it has been all too easy for Chinese people to develop a stereotype of lesbians as immoral, frustrated people. It is clear that many lesbians do live painful lives. Given the general lack of sex information in China, and the repressive attitudes of the leadership, it will be a long time before Chinese homosexuals can hope to live normal, fulfilling lives.

Cross-dressing is a theme in ancient Chinese literature, and transvestism and transsexualism exist today. The first case of transsexual surgery, a male to female, took place in 1983.

Changing Attitudes Toward Sex in China Today

For much of China's history, the government was generally lax in enforcing laws pertaining to sexual behavior. Not until the 12th century, in the Sung dynasty, did the government begin to develop a consistent policy of exercising control over the sexual life of the people, and official constraints on sexual expression developed into a pervasive cultural conservatism. By the beginning of the Ming dynasty, repressive institutions and policies were firmly in place, and continued to be in force throughout the Ming and Ching dynasties. Thus, for example, writing about and publicly discussing sex were forbidden. Strict censorship and other controls persisted after the establishment of the Republic of China in 1912.

Despite the Chinese Communist Party's declared support of women's liberation, little changed after the establishment of Communist rule in 1949. In fact, the prevailing atmosphere, perhaps the most repressive period in all Chinese history, is maintained not only by informal social sanctions, but as a matter of government policy.

The only sexual behavior acknowledged to be legally and morally permissible is heterosexual intercourse within monogamous marriage. Every imaginable variation is explicitly proscribed: prostitution, polygamy, premarital and extramarital intercourse (including cohabitation arrangements), homosexuality, and variant sexual behavior are all illegal. Because sexual expression is viewed with contempt as the least important activity of life, not only are pornography and nudity banned, but any social activity with sexual implications—such as dancing—may be subject to restrictions. Even marriage is given little consideration. Thus, China's official prudishness and restrictiveness are unrelieved by any appreciation of individual happiness or romantic love.

But, beginning in the late 1970s, the increased tolerance of nonmarital cohabitation in the West began to influence China's younger generation. College students and young intellectuals in particular were attracted to this lifestyle. Some of the younger or more open-minded sociologists also asserted the necessity of overcoming the disadvantages of traditional marriage. Actually practicing cohabitation was an act of courage. Unlike Americans dealing with such impediments as reluctant landlords or restrictive zoning ordinances, these young Chinese risked arrest.

These policies are at odds with recent changes of attitude among the Chinese people. In a survey of 23,000 people in 15 provinces conducted by the Shanghai Sex Sociology Research Center in 1989–90, 86 percent of the respondents said they approved of premarital sex. In short, in spite of the official attitude of repression, China is changing.

REFERENCES

Chan, W., trans. and comp. *A Source Book in Chinese Philosophy.* Princeton, N.J.: Princeton Univ. Press, 1963.

Chou, E. *The Dragon and the Phoenix.* New York: Arbor House, 1971.

Humana, C., and W. Wu. *The Chinese Way of Love.* Hong Kong: CFW Publications, 1982.

Levy, H.S., and A. Ishihara, trans. *The Tao of Sex: The Essence of Medical Prescriptions (Ishimpo).* Third Rev. Ed. Lower Lake, Calif.: Integral Publishing, 1989.

Needham, J. *Science and Civilisation in China.* Vol. 2, Sect. 8–18. Cambridge, U.K.: At the University Press, 1956. Vol. 5, Part V: Sexuality and the Role of Theories of Generation, Cambridge, U.K.: At the University Press, 1983.

Ruan, F.F. *Sex in China: Studies in Sexology in Chinese Culture.* New York: Plenum Press, 1991.

van Gulik, R.H. *Sexual Life in Ancient China: A Preliminary Survey of Chinese Sex and Society From ca. 1500 B.C. till 1644 A.D.* Leiden: E.J. Brill, 1961.

Fang-fu Ruan

CIRCUMCISION: MALE—EFFECTS UPON HUMAN SEXUALITY

Circumcision, once accepted as the norm in the United States, has become controversial. Technically, circumcision is the surgical removal of the skin that normally covers and protects the head, or *glans,* of the penis. At birth, the penis is covered with a continuous layer of skin extending from the pubis to the tip of the penis where the foreskin (prepuce) folds inward upon itself, creating a double protective layer of skin over the glans penis. The inner lining of the prepuce is mucous membrane and serves to keep the surface of the glans penis (also mucous membrane) soft, moist, and sensitive. The prepuce is often erroneously referred to as "redundant" tissue, which allows the medical community and society-at-large to consider the foreskin an optional part of the male sex organ and, therefore, to condone its routine removal in a variety of procedures collectively known as "circumcision."

Circumcision, however, was also a part of religious ritual, including Judaism and Islam as well as others. However, 85 percent of the world's male population is not circumcised. Circumcision in 1992 was still the most commonly performed surgical procedure in America, where 59 percent of newborn males underwent this operation. Circumcision reached its peak of 85 to

90 percent during the 1960s and 1970s. The surgery, usually performed on baby boys within the first few days of life, is often considered "routine." The most popular methods, the Gomco clamp and the Plastibell procedures, differ somewhat in technique and instrumentation but the effects on the penis and the baby are basically the same. Most of the American circumcisions are not done for religious reasons, but rather, for hygienic ones.

Medical Procedure

Usually, the procedure for circumcision in America involves the baby being strapped spread-eagle to a plastic board, with his arms and legs immobilized by Velcro straps. A nurse scrubs his genitals with an antiseptic solution and places a surgical drape—with a hole in it to expose his penis—across his body. The doctor grasps the tip of the foreskin with one hemostat and inserts another hemostat between the foreskin and the glans. (In 96 percent of newborns, these two structures are attached to one another by a continuous layer of epithelium, which protects the sensitive glans from urine and feces in infancy and childhood.) The foreskin is then torn from the glans. The hemostat is used to crush an area of the foreskin lengthwise, which prevents bleeding when the doctor cuts through the tissue to enlarge the foreskin opening. This allows insertion of the circumcision instrument. The foreskin is crushed against this device circumferentially and amputated.

Anesthesia was not used to alleviate infant suffering until recently because it was believed that babies do not feel pain. Additionally, it was recognized that anesthesia was risky for the newborn, thus contributing to the medical reluctance to use it for painful procedures on infants, such as circumcision. Currently, some doctors use a dorsal penile nerve block to numb the penis during infant circumcision. While not always effective, this anesthesia may afford some pain relief during the surgery, although it offers no pain relief during the recovery period (which can last up to 14 days) when the baby urinates and defecates into the raw wound.

Function of the Foreskin

To understand the function of the prepuce, it is necessary to understand the function of the penis. While it is commonly recognized that the penis has two functions—urination and procreation—in reality, it is essential only for procreation, since it is not required for urination.

For procreation to occur, the normally flaccid penis must become erect. As it changes from flaccidity to rigidity, the penis increases in length about 50 percent. As it elongates, the double fold of skin (foreskin) provides the skin necessary for full expansion of the penile shaft. But microscopic examination reveals that the foreskin is more than just penile skin necessary for a natural erection; it is specialized tissue, richly supplied with blood vessels, highly innervated, and uniquely endowed with stretch receptors. These attributes of the foreskin contribute significantly to the sexual response of the intact male. The complex tissue of the foreskin responds to stimulation during sexual activity. Stretching of the foreskin over the glans penis activates preputial nerve endings, enhances sexual excitability, and contributes to the male ejaculatory reflex. Besides the neurological role of the preputial tissue, the mucosal surface of the inner lining of the foreskin has a specific function during masturbation or sexual relations.

During masturbation, the mucosal surface of the foreskin rolls back and forth across the mucosal surface of the glans penis, providing nontraumatic sexual stimulation. During heterosexual activity, the mucosal surfaces of the glans penis and foreskin move back and forth across the mucosal surfaces of the labia and vagina, providing nontraumatic sexual stimulation of both male and female. This mucous-membrane-to-mucous-membrane contact provides the natural lubrication necessary for sexual relations and prevents both the dryness responsible for painful intercourse and the chafing and abrasions which allow entry of sexually transmitted diseases, both viral and bacterial.

When normal, sexually functioning tissue is removed, sexual functioning is also altered. Changes of the penis that occur with circumcision have been documented. These may vary according to the procedure used and the age at which the circumcision was performed, nevertheless penile changes will inevitably occur following circumcision.

Circumcision performed in the newborn period traumatically interrupts the natural separation of the foreskin from the glans that normally occurs somewhere between birth and age 18. The raw, exposed glans penis heals in a process that measurably thickens the surface of the glans and results in desensitization of the head of the penis.

When circumcision is performed after the normal separation of the foreskin from the glans, the damage done by forcible separation of these two parts of the penis is avoided, but the glans must still thicken in order to protect itself from constant chafing and abrasion by clothing.

The thickened, drier tissue covering the glans of the circumcised penis may necessitate the use of synthetic lubricants to facilitate nontraumatic sexual intercourse. Often, it is erroneously considered the woman's lack of lubrication that makes intercourse painful rather than the lack of natural male lubrication, which is more likely the cause. During masturbation, the circumcised male must use his hands for direct stimulation of the glans, and this may require synthetic lubrication as well.

In addition to the predictable physical changes that occur with circumcision, there are inherent risks and potential complications from the surgery. These include, but are not limited to, hemorrhage, infection, surgical damage and, while rare, death. Surgical damage and healing complications can result in extensive scarring, skin bridging, curvature of the penis, and deformities of the glans penis and urethral meatus (urinary opening). Extreme mutilations have resulted from inappropriate electrocautery use in circumcision, causing loss of the entire penis. Sex-change operations have been used as a "remedy" for this iatrogenic condition.

While circumcision has potential risks and alters normal, sexual functioning of the penis, proponents of the practice consider it to confer many "prophylactic" benefits on the recipient. This rationale was initiated in the English-speaking countries during the 19th century when the etiology of diseases was unknown. At that time, circumcision evolved from a religious ritual or puberty rite into routine surgery for "health" reasons.

Within the miasma of myth and ignorance, a theory emerged that masturbation caused many and varied ills, so some physicians thought it logical to perform genital surgery on both sexes to stop masturbation. In 1891, P.C. Remondino advocated circumcision to prevent or to cure alcoholism, epilepsy, asthma, hernia, gout, rheumatism, curvature of the spine, and headaches. As scientific research uncovered legitimate pathological etiology for diseases previously thought to be prevented or cured by circumcision, new rationales were postulated to validate the practice. Prophylactic circumcision of females fell out of vogue in English-speaking countries, but the incidence of male circumcision steadily rose. In the early 20th century, circumcision was advocated as a hygienic measure. Though criticism of the practice mounted, it was not until 1975 that the American Academy of Pediatrics came out in opposition, arguing that good personal hygiene would offer all the advantages of routine circumcision without the attendant surgical risk. The advent of antibiotics negated the rationale that circumcision was needed to prevent venereal disease.

As a religious ritual, circumcision is practiced by Jews and Moslems in accordance with the biblical account of Abraham's covenant with God. Even so, the "purpose" of the Jewish ritual of circumcision has been argued by Jews throughout history. Noted Rabbi Moses Maimonides, in the *Guide of the Perplexed,* explains a rationale for circumcision that merits attention when circumcision is considered relative to human sexuality.

> As regards circumcision . . . [s]ome people believe that circumcision is to remove a defect in man's formation; but every one can easily reply: How can products of nature be deficient so as to require external completion, especially as the use of the foreskin to that organ is evident. This commandment has not been enjoined as a complement to a deficient physical creation, but as a means for perfecting man's moral shortcomings. The bodily injury caused to that organ is exactly that which is desired; it does not interrupt any vital function, nor does it destroy the power of generation. Circumcision simply counteracts excessive lust; for there is no doubt that circumcision weakens the power of sexual excitement, and sometimes lessens the natural enjoyment; the organ necessarily becomes weak when it loses blood and is deprived of its covering from the beginning.

The Moslems, who also circumcise in accordance with the biblical covenant between Abraham and God, traditionally circumcised their males at age 13. More recently, however, Moslem boys are circumcised at varying ages from birth to puberty.

In the United States, the religious rights of parents are being questioned in regard to the constitutional rights of infants and children. Freedom of religion became a legal issue when it was introduced in a circumcision lawsuit claiming a male had been denied *his* right to freedom of religion when his body was marked by circumcision in accordance with *his parents'* religion.

The inalienable body ownership rights of infants and children continue to be addressed within the U.S. legal system in lawsuits asserting that the only person who can legally consent to a circumcision is a person making this personal decision for himself. The reports of dissatisfaction with parental circumcision decisions by circumcised men help to illustrate this point. Performed on their penises without their consent, thousands are now undergoing foreskin restoration, either medical or surgical, to reconstruct what they consider was violently taken from their bodies early in their lives. The Declaration of the First International Symposium on Circumcision acknowledges the unrecognized victims of circumcision and, in support of genital ownership rights of infants and children, states: "We recognize the inherent right of every human being to an intact body. Without religious or racial prejudice, we affirm this basic human right." Due to the lifelong consequences of the permanent surgical alteration of children's genitals, it becomes imperative that children have the right to own their own reproductive organs and to preserve their natural sexual function.

> These, then, are the human genitals. Considering their great delicacy, complexity and sensitivity, one might imagine that an intelligent species like man would leave them alone. Sadly, this has never been the case. For thousands of years, in many different cultures, the genitals have fallen victim to an amazing variety of mutilations and restrictions. For organs that are capable of giving us an immense amount of pleasure, they have been given an inordinate amount of pain. (Morris, 1985)

REFERENCES

American Academy of Pediatrics. Care of the Uncircumcised Penis. Evanston, Ill.: American Academy of Pediatrics, 1984.

American Academy of Pediatrics' Task Force on Circumcision. Report of the Task Force on Circumcision. Elk Grove Village, Ill.: 1989.

Morris, D. *Body Watching*. New York: Crown, 1985.

Remondino, P.C. *History of Circumcision From the Earliest Times to the Present*. Philadelphia: F.A. Davis Co., 1892. Republished New York: AMS Press, 1974.

Wallerstein, E. *Circumcision: An American Health Fallacy*. New York: Springer Publishing Co., 1980.

Marilyn Fayre Milos
Donna R. Macris

CLIMACTERIC

In females, climacteric refers to the period of gradual decline in ovarian function in the years before menopause and at the time of menopause. In some women, it may be associated with depression, physiological symptoms including hot flashes, and concern about femininity. In males, the climacteric is a parallel physical or psychological phenomenon experienced by some men after about age 50. It may relate to the gradual reduction in sex-steroid hormones, but is more likely to be associated with a conscious-

ness of the aging process. Symptoms in men include weakness, fatigue, poor appetite, decreased sexual drive, reduction or loss of erectile capacity, irritability, and impaired ability to concentrate. In both sexes, it occasionally leads to desperate attempts to prove sexual capacity.

Vern L. Bullough

CLINICAL INTERVENTION WITH TRANSGENDERED CLIENTS AND THEIR PARTNERS

This entry discusses basic information about situations in which the client expresses a need to emulate the other gender. Such behaviors are called cross-gender, or transgendered, behaviors. Clinicians estimate that less than one percent of the population experiences such feelings, and few of these people are so uncomfortable with the gender roles socially prescribed by their sexual anatomy that they seek out a therapist. Although this entry includes insight into clinical interventions that can be useful with such clients, the information presented is not sufficient to make an unequivocal diagnosis. Some of the sources listed in the references can be useful in reaching such diagnoses.

Terminology

There are several basic terms used in defining cross-gender behaviors. *Gender identity* is a person's inner sense of himself or herself as either a man or a woman. *Gender role* is a person's outward behaviors that define her or him to society as a woman or a man; these actions are often socially defined for each gender. A person's gender identity and gender role usually match. *Sexual partner choice* is a person's selection of a partner for sexual interactions. There are four subcategories: heterosexual, homosexual, bisexual, and asexual. Gender identity and sexual partner choice are independent. Having some form of transgendered behavior does not automatically mean this person will make a particular sexual partner choice. Any combination of the two is possible. The three major categories of cross-gender behavior that the clinician may encounter are (1) transvestism (or cross-dressing); (2) transsexualism, and (3) transgenderism. This entry uses a differential diagnosis approach to describe the etiology and behaviors because this is more helpful in clinical assessment.

Transvestism literally means cross-dressing and is primarily a male phenomenon, although there have been scattered reports of women who cross-dress for similar reasons. Clinically, the term often describes any behavior in which a male becomes sexually aroused by wearing clothing that is socially reserved for women. It may describe any behavior from wearing a single article of women's clothing to completely dressing as a woman. More broadly the term includes the use of other gender clothing for nonerotic sensuality and psychological escape from the gender role in which the person normally lives. The term does not cover theatrical or political activities.

Transsexualism literally means cross-sex and, while it may share some behaviors with transvestism, there are significant differences. It appears that there are about equal numbers of male-to-female and female-to-male transsexuals, although the overall incidence is much lower than transvestism.

Transgenderism, a term recently coined by the transgender community, has been embraced by some clinicians. It describes a person who shares many characteristics of the transsexual. Transgenderists often live full time in the gender role of the other sex but do not desire genital surgery.

Clinical Intervention

Therapy involving transgender clients may be complicated by the clinician's acceptance of the assumption that sexual anatomy and the internal perception of being masculine or feminine should be integrated. A transgendered client presents behaviors and feelings (which are intense and highly subjective), that conflict with traditional social expectations. Also, the average transgendered person has often researched the behavior. Clients often attempt to "steer" the therapist toward an outcome that may not be in the client's best long-term interests. The clinician's objectivity is a crucial asset in this situation. It is imperative that the clinician take thorough sex and medical histories, looking for specific factors (e.g., alcohol or drug abuse, or that the client is a child of alcoholics or a victim of child abuse). Regardless of the data gathered from this history taking, it is important that the clinician not make an early diagnosis of transvestism or transsexualism. Equally important, the clinician should make his or her own diagnosis rather than accept the client's self-diagnosis at face value. Any intervention should probably always proceed as if the client is a cross-dresser even when transsexualism is suspected. Such an approach is safer for the client because diagnosing transsexualism too early can become a self-fulfilling prophecy.

Cross-dressing is so solidly fixed in a man's personality that it is usually neither possible nor desirable to eliminate it; in fact, many forms of therapy have failed to eliminate the desire to cross-dress. Cross-dressing creates problems for the individual, and those with whom he is intimately involved, because it does not conform to socially established behaviors for men and women. One misperception is that if the cross-dresser uses "enough willpower," he can stop cross-dressing. Under pressure to stop, he may temporarily do so, but the behavior will eventually reemerge. The most common feelings surrounding this behavior are low self-esteem, guilt, and shame. The best approach is to help these clients understand how they benefit from cross-dressing and assist them in finding ways to integrate cross-dressing into their lives without damaging other aspects of it. Any techniques that allow dynamic interaction with the client are useful; hypnosis or guided imagery, dream interpretation, working with artist's media (e.g., paints, crayons, and markers), gestalt techniques, videotaping and playback, and psychodrama have all proven useful.

It may be valuable to determine how the client would handle his cross-dressing if there were no constraints on his behavior or appearance. It can also be worthwhile to have the client investigate the woman's role in society because the average cross-dresser often has only a minimal grasp of this gender role.

Sometimes the client has an intense desire to go out in public dressed as a woman. While some men may carry this off quite convincingly, most cannot. The therapist should discourage this behavior because the risks generally outweigh any perceived advantages. The clinician can suggest alternatives, such as joining a transvestite club that sponsors safe social environments.

Issues of homosexuality may arise. Often the cross-dresser is quite homophobic, which is not inconsistent with the desire to emulate a woman because gender identity issues are not immutably linked to other sexual beliefs. Also, the man may be uncomfortable with the social expectations of the masculine gender role. He may be shy but cover it up with a macho image. He may also be socially immature and uncomfortable in many social situations.

The early counseling sessions are best done without the client being cross-dressed. This has the advantage of allowing the clinician to see the man in his usual state and provides a baseline from which to measure the influences of cross-dressing on the client. In later sessions, it may be appropriate for the client to cross-dress, but this should usually be done at the clinician's office rather than having the client arrive and leave cross-dressed.

Women Partners of Transvestites

Since most cross-dressers are heterosexual, they are often in an intimate relationship with a woman. These women, contrary to strong misunderstandings, are not unique; what is remarkable is that they are so unremarkable. They are neither self-destructive nor do they have "lesbian tendencies." Whether they knew about their partner's cross-dressing before entering the relationship or found out later, they seem to have a common characteristic—they love their partner and often put his needs ahead of their own. They are concerned, however, about themselves, the relationship, and societal issues.

In counseling these women, the clinicians should give immediate attention to supporting their self-image. Although often the woman's sexuality is threatened, and she may feel like a lesbian because she loves a man who sometimes emulates a woman, especially in sexual situations, some women find his sexual arousal from cross-dressing new and exciting. Later, such a woman may discover that he is aroused only by the clothing, not by her. She then has to cope with his sexual arousal, when it is no longer arousing for her.

This woman also needs information. Prey to society's misconceptions about cross-dressing—the most typical being that she is at fault for his cross-dressing—can lead to deep-seated feelings of guilt. She needs to know she is not to blame for her partner's cross-dressing; it began long before she knew him and is an immutable part of his personality. She may have fears generated by information her partner has given her. Much cross-dressing literature contains writing on such subjects as forced cross-dressing and living full time as a woman. Even if fantasy is not present, "helpful" literature may contain biased viewpoints that can leave her feeling confused or inadequate.

Probably the most difficult for her to accept is that he will never be "cured" of this need. It is important for her to understand that his behavior will probably not lead to genital reassignment surgery, although at times it may seem that he wants to spend all his time cross-dressed. So, if she decides to stay in the relationship, she has to accommodate his behavior in some way.

After trying to accommodate his cross-dressing, she may find that she cannot cope with the situations or emotions involved. Because she cannot predict how she may feel, she needs the therapist's support in withdrawing or modifying given situations or agreements. She may experience difficulty talking to her partner about her feelings because she is afraid he will be neither understanding nor supportive. Also, he may view her comments as criticism of his behavior, which can drive them further apart. She has to learn how to negotiate with her partner on issues such as when he can cross-dress and telling family members about his behavior. One of her greatest concerns is for their children, if there are any, and how to balance his needs and theirs.

Because cross-dressing is socially unacceptable, she is often hesitant to discuss her partner's behavior with her close friends, which leads to further isolation. As an adjunct to formal counseling, there are national and local transgender support groups that have groups for wives and partners of transgendered persons. In such groups, she may find support by talking to women who have experienced situations similar to hers.

Clinical Treatment of the Couple

The therapeutic environment should not be used to force the woman to accept her partner's cross-dressing any more than it should be used to force the man to stop cross-dressing. The therapist also has to be careful not to focus on cross-dressing issues and ignore the woman's needs. While her needs may seem simple compared with his, they are equally important. In fact, several typical relationship issues exist. He may want freedom to cross-dress whenever he wants while the woman may be willing to accommodate his cross-dressing so long as it does not dominate their relationship. He may want to cross-dress before lovemaking, during lovemaking, or both, while this may eliminate any sexual desire for the woman. He may be borrowing her clothes; because these are an intimate part of her being, she may feel violated if he wears them.

One pivotal issue is trust. If the husband has kept his cross-dressing a secret from his wife and then disclosed it, she may feel betrayed and can lose her trust in him. She may also wonder what other secrets he is still keeping from her. Rebuilding her trust in him is difficult. It takes a lot of time and sensitivity on the man's part to achieve this. While loss of trust is probably not an issue if the woman learns of his cross-dressing before marriage, it is doubtful that either of them truly realized the extent to which that behavior would influence and permeate their relationship over time. When working with the couple, the most important contribution the clinician can make is helping them establish clear communication within the relationship. By providing a safe environment, the therapist can support each person in stating his or her needs without threatening the other partner. Once these needs have been described, the clinician can assist the couple in finding appropriate solutions.

Clinical Treatment of the Transsexual

It takes several months of intensive work to determine that a person is transsexual. Critical to this determination is the clinician's assessment of the client's gender identity, especially whether or not gender identity is stable yet noncongruent with anatomy. It is also difficult to determine any erotic components or feelings because most people are hesitant to discuss this intimate behavior. Of some use are reliable reports of age at onset—the younger the person the more likely that a diagnosis of transsexualism can be made.

Next, it is crucial to assess how the client would function in the other gender role. Factors such as social environment, vocation, and relationships need to be considered. The clinician should not proceed if there is any doubt about any of these aspects. In some respects, clinical intervention is more straightforward when working with the transsexual. Much of this approach can be found in the Harry Benjamin International Gender Dysphoria Association's Standards of Care. There are several stages in this process. The first should not occur until the diagnosis of transsexualism is made, some three to six months after the initial contact. Before a diagnosis, the male client can begin electrolysis for beard removal if this seems appropriate. Once a firm diagnosis of transsexualism is made, hormone therapy can begin. The male-to-female transsexual (M-to-F) will take various female hormones under the supervision of an endocrinologist who is familiar with such intervention. Both physical and psychological effects are anticipated. Physically, there will be some breast growth. Some muscle strength will be lost and there will be a redistribution of fatty tissue in a more feminine pattern. Sex drive may lessen. Eventually, testicular function will cease and the testicles will atrophy. These latter effects are irreversible. Male pattern balding will not reverse, nor will the male's voice assume a feminine pitch or the beard stop growing.

For the female-to-male transsexual (F-to-M) hormone therapy involves taking male hormones. Irreversible effects begin almost immediately. These include deepening of the voice, cessation of menses, increase of muscle mass, and beard growth. Some acne may also occur.

For both the M-to-F and F-to-M transsexual, there can be a variety of psychological effects. It is here that the clinician must provide support and guidance. The M-to-F may experience more mood swings than experienced as a male. The F-to-M will experience increased sex drive and become more assertive. For both, there will be pleasure as their body image changes to fit their gender identity. During this period, the clinician should be laying the foundation for "real life test."

The second stage requires the transsexual client to begin living full time in the gender role of choice—socially, vocationally, and legally. This is the most critical phase because the client is disclosing his or her situation to family members and perhaps in the work environment. Rejection is not uncommon, resulting in isolation and perhaps loss of employment. While there is a sense of relief in being able to present to the world in the desired gender role, the practical problems can be overwhelming. There are groups nationwide that support transsexuals. If the client is not a member, this should be suggested. This stage should last a minimum of one year and usually longer, depending on the clinician's assessment of the client's adaptation to the new role. (A word of caution: the clinician should not force the client to meet the clinician's definition of how a man or woman should act, for there are many variants on gender roles.)

The primary therapist has to make the recommendation to proceed to the final stage—genital surgery. This recommendation should be confirmed by a second opinion. For the M-to-F, this involves the removal of penis and testicles and the construction of the vagina and labia. For the F-to-M, it involves a mastectomy and hysterectomy/oophorectomy. Unfortunately, the construction of a fully functional phallus is beyond today's surgical capability. Often the F-to-M elects not to take this step because of the severe scarring and doubtful outcome. In neither case does the surgery make the person a reproductively functioning member of the other sex. It is less common to have to deal with a significant other when working with a transsexual client; either the relationship has foundered on the complications or the client never chose to get into an intimate relationship due to the gender discomfort. Where a relationship still exists, the approaches and observations outlined above are appropriate.

Conclusion

Transgender feelings and the behaviors it causes influence more aspects of the cross-gendered person's life than almost any other behavior. Such a pervasive influence is difficult to deal with.

The clinician can do much to support each individual and the persons with whom they are in relationship. Yet the outcome is, at best, problematical, especially for cross-dressers. Often the most a clinician can do is to provide support and accurate information while assisting the person or couple find solutions to their unique situation.

REFERENCES

American Psychiatric Association, *Diagnostic and Statistical Manual of Mental Disorders*. Third Ed. Rev. Washington, D.C.: American Psychiatric Association, 1987.

Benjamin, H. *The Transsexual Phenomenon*. New York: Warner Books, 1966.

Brierly, H. *Transvestism: A Handbook of Case Studies for Psychologists, Psychiatrists and Counsellors*. Elmsford, N.Y.: Pergamon Press, 1979.

Docter, R.F. *Transvestites and Transsexuals*. New York: Plenum Press, 1988.

Feinbloom, D.H. *Transvestites and Transsexuals*. New York: Dell, 1976.

Green, R., and J. Money. *Transsexualism and Sex Reassignment*. Baltimore: Johns Hopkins Press, 1969.

Money, J. *Sex Errors of the Body*. Baltimore: Johns Hopkins Press, 1968.

Stoller, R.J. *Presentations of Gender*. New Haven: Yale Univ. Press, 1985.

Roger E. Peo

COERCION: SEXUAL COERCION

Sexual coercion is a term that characterizes phenomena as diverse as rape, child sexual abuse, sexual harassment, and prostitution. Each type of sexual coercion has been heavily researched and has its own associated literature. Since the 1980s, sexual coercion has also been construed more narrowly, focusing on coercive behavior in social, courtship, and dating interactions of adolescents and young adults. This new area of sexual coercion—which is the focus of this entry—developed from survey research demonstrating the high prevalence of unwanted sexual interactions resulting from coercive behaviors. (See also Date Rape.)

Sexual coercion occurs when someone is pressured or forced to engage in a sexual act against his or her will. Definitions and measures of coercion vary from study to study and these variations have led to different estimates of its incidence and prevalence. For example, the coercion may be physical where the aggressor holds a victim down, twists a victim's arm, or uses a weapon such as a knife or a gun. The coercion may involve threats of physical harm to the victim or to someone the victim knows. The coercion may also be psychological or manipulative where the aggressor gives someone alcohol or drugs, makes false commitments and promises of love, overwhelms a partner with continual arguments, threatens to end a relationship or leave someone stranded, uses his or her position of authority or status over a subordinate to pressure another into compliance, or makes another feel obligated or inadequate. In some studies of coercive sexual behavior, more subtle factors contributing to unwanted sexual interactions have been examined, such as peer pressure, self-pressure to be desirable, and the inability to say no. Most legal definitions of rape involve physical force rather than psychological or motivational factors that influence someone to engage in an unwanted sex act.

Most of the incidence and prevalence data on coercive sex have been gathered from studies of college students. In the most comprehensive study done in 1978 by Mary Koss and her colleagues involving over 3,000 women at 32 colleges, the following results were obtained for women who had unwanted intercourse: 25 percent because they were pressured by a man's continual arguments, 8 percent because a man had given them alcohol or drugs, and 9 percent because a man had used physical force. Of the almost 3,000 men in the Koss study, the following results were obtained for men reporting the use of coercive strategies that allowed them to have intercourse with an unwilling woman: 10 percent by pressuring with continual arguments, 4 percent by giving the woman alcohol or drugs, and 1 percent by using physical force. In two other studies of college males in the late 1980s, 42 percent had used verbal coercion in order to have intercourse with an unwilling woman and more than half had initiated some type of coercive sexual interaction. The rates of women who report being coerced have been consistently more than the rates of men who report doing the coercing.

Although most of the studies have focused on men as aggressors and women as victims, some have investigated coercion in homosexual relationships as well as coercive strategies used by women with men. In one study of gay and lesbian relationships, 12 percent of the gay men and 31 percent of the lesbians reported their partner had forced them to have sex against their will. Men report low rates of women using extreme physical force involving infliction of injury and weapons in order to engage in sex acts. More common coercive strategies used by women are psychological tactics, such as cajolery, blackmail, making their partner feel inadequate, and aggressive removal of the man's clothing followed by intense genital stimulation without the man's consent. A recent study of forced sex experienced by men found that 16 percent had had at least one forced sex experience in their lifetime and 9 percent had had forced sex experiences in college. Men also report having unwanted sexual intercourse because they were too drunk to give knowledgeable consent. One study investigating motivational factors contributing to unwanted sexual intercourse found that rates of such intercourse were higher for men than for women. Common reasons cited by men were peer pressure, inexperience, desire to be popular, and enticement.

Women report a series of both short- and long-term negative psychological and behavioral difficulties as a result of being subjected to sexual coercion. These include self-blame, relationship difficulties, and decreased self-esteem. The impact on men who have been raped by another man has also been shown to produce serious harmful effects on the survivors. The short- and long-term effects of nonphysical coercion exerted by women on men is less well known. One study found that few men experienced negative effects and that the most common after-effect mentioned was avoidance of sexually aggressive women.

Traditional socialization and the double standard of sexuality—a permissive standard for men and a restrictive one for women—have often been cited as contributing to high rates of coercive sexual behavior by men. This socialization has encouraged opposite roles and goals for men and women in dating and courtship and may lead to game playing, dishonesty, and adversarial interactions. Men have been socialized to enjoy their sexuality and pursue sexual encounters with numerous partners. For men, sexual conquest is one measure of status, self-esteem, and masculinity. To achieve their sexual goals, men have been taught they must initiate sexual activity and often overcome a woman's resistance to get sex. In contrast, traditional socialization has encouraged women not to make sexual advances, not to respond too eagerly to a man's sexual advances, and not to engage in sexual relationships outside of long-term or love relationships. In addition, women have been socialized to be submissive, kind, passive and accepting, and not to develop skills that would allow them to communicate their feelings assertively to men. Several studies support this view of traditional socialization. One found that 29 percent of women had unwanted intercourse due to altruism, another

found that 78 percent of women had engaged in some type of unwanted sexual behavior because of the inability to say no, and a third found that 64 percent of women did nothing to prevent a male from having unwanted sex with them when they were confronted with persuasion.

Social scientists also point out that women's roles have undergone substantial changes in the last 30 years, and there is evidence that the sexual experience of men and women has become more similar in that women typically have several nonmarital sexual relationships. In this view, although women still have not achieved equality with men in political and economic areas, they have made progress toward achieving equality in sexual relationships. Studies investigating traditional roles in dating, such as asking for dates and paying date expenses as well as initiating a first sexual involvement, do show that women are beginning to assume roles once thought to be appropriate only for men. However, although sharing date expenses is common, the role of initiating sex still is much more likely to be the male's. Thus, despite the current popularity of the more permissive norms allowing women to engage in nonmarital sexual relationships, they still appear to be at high risk of experiencing sexual coercion from men.

The solution to any large-scale problem such as sexual coercion is complex. Prevention programs almost always include sex education courses and university workshops that encourage discussions among groups of adolescents and young adults. This could lead to increased knowledge of both gender's feelings, socialization experiences, expectations, and desires regarding intimate relationships. In addition, both genders need to become active agents and assume responsibility for promoting consensus and mutuality in sexual relationships. Men need to know that a "no" response to their sexual advances means no and to proceed further after such a response puts them at risk for a rape charge. Several social scientists have emphasized that more assertiveness and improved communication on the woman's part could make a crucial difference. One study found that when women clearly stated early in the dating stage what they wanted to do sexually, men were less likely to use coercive sexual strategies with them. Another study found that if women gave stronger verbal or physical responses, men's coercive strategies were thwarted in about three fourths of the cases. Although such responses would not stop all coercion, especially attacks involving physical force or threats of force, they would likely reduce the incidence of some forms of coercion. Social scientists also stress that restructuring the male gender role would make a difference. Qualities such as warmth, equality, supportiveness, and sensitivity need to be encouraged and valued instead of sexual competitiveness, dominance, toughness, and violence.

Two other points are often made regarding the sexual coercion problem. The first is that societies with high rates of nonsexual violence and societies in which men have more power than women in the major institutions—especially political and economic institutions—usually have high rates of sexual coercion. So on a broad societal level, it appears what happens with respect to general levels of violence and the status of women directly affects the rates of sexual coercion. The second is that many social scientists, alarmed by the present high rates of coercion, believe that during this time of changing roles and power for men and women, more men will feel threatened and develop more hostile attitudes toward women and perhaps engage in coercive sexual behavior. One general solution to the current situation recommended by social scientists who have studied sexual coercion is widespread sex education courses in schools and colleges. Such courses should cover issues related to the continuum of sexual relationships— from mutual sex to unwanted sex to rape—so that adolescents and young adults can understand and develop skills to avoid sexual coercion.

REFERENCES

Craig, M. Coercive Sexuality in Dating Relationships: A Situational Model. *Clinical Psychological Review*, Vol. 10 (1990), pp. 395–423.

Grauerholz, E., and M. Koralewski, Eds. *Sexual Coercion, A Sourcebook on Its Nature, Causes and Prevention.* Lexington, Mass.: Lexington Books, D.C. Heath & Co., 1991.

Koss, M., C. Gidycz and N. Wisniewski. The Scope of Rape Incidence and Prevalence of Sexual Aggression and Victimization in a National Sample of Higher Education Students. *Journal of Higher Education and Clinical Psychology*, 55 (1987), pp. 102–170.

Lottes, I. The Relationship Between Nontraditional Gender Roles and Sexual Coercion. *Journal of Psychology and Human Sexuality*, Vol. 4 (1991), pp. 89–109.

Poppen, P., and N. Segal. The Influence of Sex and Sex Role Orientation on Sexual Coercion. *Sex Roles*, Vol. 19 (1988), pp. 689–701.

Ilsa Lottes

COITAL POSITIONS

"Coitus" is a derivative from the Latin *coire,* which means "to go together." It is the only word that means insertion of the penis into the vagina. Coital positions, therefore, are those that involve the penis in the vagina.

The earliest depictions of coital positions date from about 3500 B.C.E. in Ur in Mesopotamia. Early Greek, Chinese, Indian, Japanese, Roman, and Peruvian art also depicts coital positions. Depictions are not necessarily of the positions commonly used but they acknowledge their existence.

Acceptable coital positions in a society tend to be based on early religious beliefs. If there was a sky mother and an earth father, the female-superior position tended to be the acceptable position in earlier cultures. Where the earth mother was predominant in a culture and there was a sky father, then the male-superior position was the acceptable position. As humankind moved away from early religious beliefs, the concept of acceptable coital positions tended to stay with the culture, and variations from such positions often were viewed as deviant.

Early Christianity, based on Paulian theology, was a sex-negative religion. Sex was seen to be for procreation only, and a woman was not supposed to enjoy it. The woman did her wifely duty to satisfy her husband's so-called "lustful nature." The acceptable position was the man on top and the passive woman on the bottom. This attitude is still prevalent today and seen in many sex-therapy cases.

The coital position itself may not be as important as where it is or what it is on. The Kagaba Indians of Colombia, South America, for instance, believe semen penetrating the earth will result in sickness and "possibly destroy the world." Therefore, special magical stones must be placed beneath the sex organs to catch any seminal flow. Coitus must also maintain a specific rhythm, otherwise it will cause harm to the man's children, his partner, or himself.

Several cultures, such as those of India, Persia, and Japan, have books on coital positions, often called "pillow books." The *Kama Sutra* claims it contains 529 possible coital positions. Such a large number is derived by minutely detailing the exact positioning of fingers, arms, and legs as well as bodies. Each change is seen as another position. Even the traditional Christian position of the man on top has many possibilities, depending on where the hands, arms, legs, and trunk are positioned. The verbalizations during a position may be an important part of identifying the position. For example, the rear-entry position may be carried out in tandem with not only "acting like the animal but emitting sounds like a dog, goat, etc."

Books that describe sexual positions were often available only to a certain upper class. Proclivities toward a variety of coital positions were often looked on by the lower classes as "perverted." Anthropologists have found marked differences between the upper classes and the ordinary people in their sexual behavior, including positions. It has been suggested that the preferred coital position in a culture may be related to the woman's status in that culture.

In the last 50 years, as there was more intermingling of cultures and less religious fervor, there has been a greater acceptance of a wider variety of coital positions. Still, the male-superior position tends to be seen as the one most generally used by Western cultures, although it is not found to be the best position for effective sexual functioning.

As sexuality moved from the procreative emphasis to the pleasurable aspect of human relationships more creativity and spontaneity in lovemaking meant more acceptance of coital positions and greater experience of different ones. Early sculpture or writings encouraged wide variation in coital positioning in some cultures, especially among the elite.

In working with couples contemporarily, several things become apparent regarding coital positions. A 250-pound man lying on top of a 125-pound woman does not work very well. The same is also true of the reverse position where the woman is heavy. Differences in height also sometimes pose a problem for coital positioning. The positions used sometimes take the size of the couple into consideration.

A position that is comfortable to both partners is one in which they lie on their backs beside each other. The female is on the left of the male, and she lifts her legs up; the male turns on his left side and moves his pelvis up against her buttocks; then her right leg goes over his right leg and her left leg over his left leg so that the legs are entwined. This is an excellent position when there is a weight differential. It also allows both partners to move in intercourse and to use the hands to caress their bodies and stimulate the clitoris. Both can be involved in the touching and moving so that it is not something someone is doing to someone else. This is a physically comfortable position even after intercourse is over. The partners can lie still and relax with the flaccid penis remaining in the vagina. It is a particularly good position for older people for whom either one's being on top is too fa-

tiguing. Often older, and sometimes younger, people quit having intercourse because of the strenuous nature of the activity or because of discomfort or difficulty in getting into a coital position. It is not only the coital position that is important, but also what is done in that position. Thrusting rapidly for any length of time is fatiguing. To be maintained for some period from ten minutes to several hours, the position needs to be comfortable and the thrusting slow.

Variety of sexual positions among Americans is probably the greatest variant in their sexual behavior. Male above and female below is the main position, used even by those who employ a variety of positions in their lovemaking. In the past, the male on top represented, to many, male dominance. It was only with the advent of women's liberation that people in therapy would consider changing from male-above positions in lovemaking activity.

The degree of latitude in the sexual positions practiced depends on the flexibility of both partners. How one feels about a specific position has a lot to do with whether it is engaged in or not. Positions other than male superior tend to need the cooperation of the female, either to be on top, to roll over for rear entry, or to move to accommodate a specific position. Social class and education also have something to do with accepted coital positions, and in general, research data indicate that the more educated the couple is, the wider the variety of positions that become acceptable.

A Chinese sex manual that identifies 30 basic positions and utilizes names for each without describing the position (e.g., "gamboling wild horses," "hovering butterflies," "winding dragon") leaves the position to the imagination. The manual does mention that some positions are not for pleasure but to cure "various infirmities," especially if a specific number of thrusts occurs.

There are only a few basic positions, and all others are a variation or combination of these basic ones. These are male superior, female superior, rear entry, side by side, face to face, standing, sitting, kneeling, and squatting. The emotional tone of the sexual encounter may allow for behavior that includes coital positions that are seen as deviant in one situation, acceptable in another.

Male Superior

In Western society, the male on top is the most common position, although many other positions are reported to be used. Seventy percent of the males reported having intercourse only with the male on top in the Kinsey study on American sexual behavior published in 1948. His female sample reported that almost all their coital encounters involved the male-superior position.

Male on top has also been found to be the most common position reported from other cultures. It is found in such diverse cultures as those of Japan, Tibet, China, Europe, some tribes in Africa, and American Indians, as well as in some South American and South Pacific groups. However, in some societies, such as the Bororo Indians of southern Brazil, the members feel that such a position is an insult to whoever is underneath.

The advantage of the male-superior position is for pregnancy because the sperm does not easily seep out, as the vagina is lower in the back than at the opening. The penis is also less likely to slip out. It is generally less satisfying to the woman than other positions, although if the man is on his hands and knees while thrusting and her buttocks are on a pillow, she has more movement and less pressure and confinement from weight. The male superior is often dysfunctional since it is conducive to premature ejaculation.

In China, the male-superior face to face was also considered the normal position, although numerous other positions were used. This position is based on the belief that the male is born face down and the female face up.

Augmentation may, as in India, sometimes be part of the position. Biting, scratching, and making the sounds of various birds, as well as striking the partner on various parts of the body, may be a part of the position itself.

Female Superior

A position that is often helpful to non-orgasmic women is the female-superior position. This gives the woman some control, by her own body movements, over where the penis goes in her vagina. Also, if the man's penis is unusually large and full penetration is painful, she can regulate the depth of penetration. This position also allows for positioning the body for clitoral stimulation. If the woman is sitting on the penis, the man is able to do the squeeze technique if he comes close to ejaculation. He does this by using his index finger or several fingers to squeeze and hold at the base of the penis for 15 seconds before the point of ejaculatory inevitability.

Though in some cultures the female on top is the preferred or main position used, female superior is a position a woman can use during pregnancy, where with her knees under her she can freely move without the weight of her partner's body on her. It is often a good position if the male ejaculates rapidly since he is not as actively thrusting and is able to maintain his erection longer. Some men have difficulty ejaculating from this position and will only ejaculate when they move on top. Although this is an excellent position to try, it is difficult to do if the woman has an expectation of the male being on top and thrusting rapidly.

Other Positions

The rear-entry position cross-culturally is less evident in anthropological studies. However, some of the earliest depictions of coital positions have included rear entry. Some cultures see rear entry as "animalistic" behavior. This is most evident where it is labeled with an animal name, such as "doggie style." It is an excellent position for a pregnant woman and can easily be done with her on the floor and her arms and upper torso on the bed for support, especially when she is very large during the last stages of pregnancy. The side position with rear entry or the woman on top can also be used effectively at this time.

It has been suggested that in more primitive cultures rear entry allows a man to make a quick getaway in an illicit relationship or when a number of people share a dwelling or a camp fire, so that the couple can perform coitus on their side with rear entry without the behavior being obvious.

The side position is the preferred or only one utilized in a number of societies, especially in Africa. The Loango Negroes use the side position, and it is believed this is preferable due to the reportedly unusually large penis of the males. If this is true, the side position would produce shallower penetration.

In Western cultures, for example, intercourse while standing is thought to prevent conception. This belief, as well as the belief that withdrawal or failure to have orgasm will prevent conception, is not true.

Some positions are used for specific sexual activities; for instance, the standing position among the Fijians is only used for extramarital or premarital sex. A variation on the standing position allows the woman to wrap her legs around the male's waist, and using the bones of the hips as a fulcrum, the woman can move up and down on the man's penis as he holds her to keep her from falling. He may steady himself by leaning his back against a wall.

Both males and females can use a squatting position with their partner. A woman may squat onto the penis of the man, or in the squatting position the man can have the female sit on his penis. A male may kneel and pull his partner's pelvis up onto his penis or she may squat down on it.

The male sitting in a chair facing his partner is a position said to have been preferred by the ancient Chinese. It is not a strenuous position and the female is able to move freely. Males sometimes have difficulty ejaculating in this position—in fact any position that is new to them. Rear entry can be performed in this way with the woman sitting on the male's penis with her back to his head.

Coitus is often enhanced by where it takes place. Location may be an extension of or may determine the coital position itself. When coitus occurs in the shower, jacuzzi, or swimming pool, water plays an important part in the sexual act. The buoyancy of the water makes the pool an interesting place to experiment with different positions.

Other positions, such as "hanging from the chandelier," tend to be more fantasy than reality. Copulating standing up in a hammock, although difficult, is not impossible. The use of a swing for coitus is depicted in erotic art. There are swings made specifically for sexual activity, in which the male stands and the woman, sitting in the swing, swings against the male's erect penis. These behaviors tend to be for the adventurous few individuals who want to try it all. No one has ever mentioned such behavior occurring with any regularity or frequency. Once is enough seems to be the theme.

Coitus often includes patterned vocalization as well as patterned behavior. Repeated observations of the same couple over many years have shown them to utilize their own pattern of behavior—for example, the same vocalizations, body movements, perfume, and time factors, to name a few of the patterned behaviors that were consistently used in their coital activities. Some sex manuals have long descriptions of various vocalizations.

A couple has to determine through trial and error what coital positions are best for them. Many people avoid trying new positions because they feel awkward, unsure, or afraid they will look foolish due to lack of knowledge or experience. Sex can be fun, and it is all right to fall off the bed trying a new position. Laugh and go on. Variety of positions can make the sexual encounter more interesting for a couple. Trying various coital positions without a thought or concern about orgasm can help a person become more comfortable with more and new ways of having coitus. Factors such as size differential—

tall, short, fat, thin—are important in determining a position to use. Also, if there is a handicap, a variety of positions may be needed to be tried to find the best one.

REFERENCES

Crowley, E. *The Mystic Rose*. London: Spring Books, 1902–1921.

Gagnon, J.H., and W. Simon. *Sexual Conduct*. Chicago: Aldine, 1973.

Gregersen, E. *Sexual Practices: The Story of Human Sexuality*. New York: Franklin Watts, 1983.

Haeberle, E.J. *The Sex Atlas: A New Illustrated Guide*. New York: The Seabury Press, 1978.

Highwater, J. *Myth and Sexuality*. New York: Meridian, 1990.

Kirkendall, L.A., and L.G. McBride. Preadolescent and Adolescent Imagery and Sexual Fantasies: Beliefs and Experiences. In *Childhood and Adolescent Sexology*. Vol. 7 of *Handbook of Sexology*, edited by M.E. Perry. New York: Elsevier, 1990.

Mantegazza, P. *The Sexual Relations of Mankind*. New York: Eugenics, 1935.

Tannahill, R. *Sex in History*. New York: Stein & Day, 1980.

William E. Hartman
Marilyn A. Fithian

COMMUNICATION AND SEXUALITY

Communication is necessary for survival. However, there is virtually no other topic about which people have as much difficulty discussing than sexuality. Although there is no universally accepted definition of sexuality, in this entry it means those aspects of being human that relate specifically to being female or male, both socially and biologically, and to human experiences of erotic arousal.

Discussing sexuality could involve talking about reproduction or the chromosomal makeup of females and males. It may mean expressing ideas and feelings about gender roles, such as how we experience being female or male. It may also involve discussing what is erotic, romantic relationships, sexual fantasies and how to enjoy sex, or how to reduce risks of unwanted pregnancy and sexually transmitted disease. Talking about the mechanics of intercourse and sexual function are also topics of sexuality.

Conversations about sexual topics may take place informally between friends and family or more formally between teachers and students or doctors and patients. Discussing sexuality can be a way for people to sort out complex knowledge and experiences or to enhance intimacy. In any case, the words used, the way a message is delivered, and the feelings generated by discussing sexual topics all influence the nature of communication about sexuality.

Learning to Communicate

Earliest lessons in communication begin as infants. The way an infant is held and cared for expresses to the child his or her acceptance into the human family. In return, the infant communicates with adults through body movement and vocal sounds. Only after sufficient maturity does the child learn to communicate through speech and deliberate body expression.

As children develop language skills, they discover a powerful tool that will play a vital role in the way they define reality. Greater capacity for communication will widen their social contacts and possibilities for self-expression. Children eventually learn that the way in which they use words affects their message. Language maintains and creates an understanding of their world and affects lasting patterns of behavior.

As children develop, they learn to ask questions about their bodies, about other people's bodies, and about life's mysteries. Many answers are forthcoming, but not all of their questions and behaviors are met with calm, comprehensible, or meaningful responses. For many children, genitals and their functions, for example, become mystified. In fact, this mystification often lingers well into adulthood and is passed on to the next generation. Often, bound up in the responses from adults about the sexual concerns of children are the limitations and biases language lends to communication about sexuality. (See also Children and Sex; Children: Sexuality of Children.)

Messages are conveyed in three ways: verbally, through words; vocally, through pitch, volume, rate of delivery, and overall quality of the voice; and nonverbally, through body posture and facial expression. All three influence what is communicated. When the three modes deliver a consistent message, the communication is clear; that is, the words spoken are accompanied by a vocal quality and body language that match the intent of the speaker. When the three modes are communicating different messages, a mixed message is delivered.

Language Styles Used to Discuss Sexuality

There are four basic language styles used to discuss sexuality: the child, street, euphemistic, and medical or scientific language styles. Each is used in a different context and provokes a variety of responses from the listener. Many people find a language with which they are most comfortable and use it in most situations. While this makes it easier for them to express their sexual concerns and ideas, the listener may not be comfortable with the speaker's choice of words. The listener may be unfamiliar or uncomfortable with the sexual language style used and this may lead, at a minimum, to confusion and misunderstanding. Since there is no universal sexual language that suits all situations, awkward interactions between people are not uncommon.

In child language, parents and other adults use various names for the genitals and their functions that are generally reserved for use only with children. Adults use this child language to express affection for children while helping them perform necessary bodily functions. Labels such as "weenie," "pee-pee," "down there," and "privates" are given to genitals, while "number 1," "number 2," "grunt," and "poo-poo" name their functions. Many children carry these early words into adulthood, often with lingering confusion about sexual, elimination, and reproductive functions.

Street language, on the other hand, does not derive from the coddling of loving parents, but rather from the "in" group of peers. Street language empowers differently than early language. It is more adult-like and demonstrates a knowledge about sex that may or may not exist. The suggestive words of the street (e.g., ass, screw, hitting a home run) often create adult disapproval but buy membership in exclusive clusters of admired friends. Many people are offended by the graphic expressiveness of street language so it is generally used with discretion, at times to anger others or to get along with them.

Euphemistic sexual language predominates the adult world. Creative use of language allows sex to be discussed comfortably while disguising the explicit nature of the behaviors being described. Terms like "make love," "sleep with," "that time of the month" are obvious references to sex and menstruation, but they sound sophisticated without being offensive or too clinical.

Medical or scientific language uses time-honored Latin-based words to describe body parts, functions, and behaviors (i.e., penis, clitoris, urinate, coitus). This language style is often viewed as the "correct" one because it is used in text books and by physicians and teachers. Scientific words are perceived to be value-free and more universal, although this may not necessarily be true.

Cashman observes that each verbal style has a typical vocal quality. Child language has a distinctly higher pitch and volume; street language, a rougher, sharper sound; and euphemistic and medical or scientific styles, a more even, blander vocal quality.

Despite the variety of sexual languages, there is no one standard sexual vocabulary that communicates accurate messages to everyone. Difficulty people have in communicating openly about sexuality in their personal and professional lives, in part, stems from not having a universal language. Instead, people tend to use the language with which they are most comfortable regardless of the situation or the person with whom they are talking.

Nonverbal Sexual Communication

Cultural and individual differences create many variables affecting nonverbal communication. It is difficult to describe nonverbal sexual communication in ways that can be applied universally, but researchers have observed its pervasive use. From courtship to sexually intimate behavior, nonverbal expression characterizes every step of the process and plays a significant role in what is communicated sexually.

Despite the communicative nature of body language, it can be misread as easily as verbal language. Brown and Auerback found that in the initiation of sex between spouses, nonverbal cues were frequently misunderstood. They found the receiver's role as important as the sender's because much of what was heard was perceived through a filter of past experiences and expectations.

Factors Affecting Sexual Communication

One factor affecting sexual communications is gender. When communicating verbally, males and females use significantly different sexual vocabularies. For example, men and women use different words when referring to their own and their partner's genitals and to sexual intercourse: women most often say "penis" in any given context while men prefer to say "dick" or "cock." Terms for sexual intercourse are similar between the sexes but males use a wider variety of words where females prefer "make love." Heterosexual males reported rarely saying "make love" in any context other than with their spouse or lover. Despite word choice differences, men and women tend to use their gender-specific vocabularies when having intimate conversations with one another.

Not only do males and females use different words to communicate about sex, they also interpret them differently. Language evokes different meanings for women and men. This may have practical importance not only for sexual partners but for educators, counselors, and therapists.

The differences in gender-specific sexual vocabularies may be attributed to early childhood experiences. For example, parents are generally more permissive with boys in their use of slang terms and sexual language than they are with girls. The sexually repressive or permissive messages received in childhood influence sexual expression and intimate relationships in adulthood.

Gender is not the only factor influencing language choices. The erotic communication of heterosexual and homosexual females and males presents differences in erotic language use. Wells found both gender and sexual orientation as variables that significantly affect the perception and use of erotic vocabulary.

Gay males and lesbians communicate more about sex with their partners and make greater use of slang vocabulary as a way to increase eroticism in their sexual play. They are also more likely than heterosexuals to agree on what is erotic and to use such vocabulary with a mate. On the contrary, heterosexuals more often than homosexuals use sexual language with their partners they do not consider erotic.

In studies investigating communication patterns between college students in intimate relationships, researchers identified several topics most often avoided by couples. The topics that leave partners most vulnerable to hurt and violation of trust are the ones most often avoided. Bowen and Michal-Johnson found the following topics taboo for college students:

1. State of the relationship
2. Extra-relationship activity
3. Relationship norms
4. Prior relationships with people of the opposite sex
5. Conflict-inducing topics
6. Self-disclosures that could be judged negatively

The Bowen and Michal-Johnson study investigated how college students are confronting the threat of AIDS in their intimate relationships. Many students reported avoiding topics where their trust might be violated. Topics that were "too serious" or too high in intensity were also avoided, as were topics that could potentially "ruin the relationship." The researchers found students aware that talking about AIDS would change their relationships, so it was rarely discussed on a personal level.

Resistance to revealing personal information and deep feelings is an aspect of communication not just among college students. In his work with maturing homosexual couples, Lee observed, "[O]ur society does not encourage high levels of self-disclosure. We are reluctant to hand other people weapons and show them where to stab, by allowing them to know our sensitivities, deepfelt but hidden needs and vulnerabilities."

Feeling apprehensive about communicating sexual feelings, thoughts, and experiences may well be a product of fear of betrayal or loss. To many, challenging one's relationship or oneself may present too great a risk and as a result, one's sexual communication remains undeveloped and the potential for sexual fulfillment limited. This, however, does not have to be the case. Sexual communication can be improved.

Improving Sexual Communication

Communication about sexual topics requires practice and sensitivity. This applies to parent-child, teacher-student, and therapist-client relationships as well as to sexually intimate and romantic ones. The risks and benefits in such discussions are very similar in all relationships. For a child, the risk of punishment for bringing up a sexual topic with a parent is similar to the risk of rejection an adult may fear in initiating a similar topic with a lover. The feeling of relief and the bonding that can take place between the individuals involved is a benefit each may feel when sexual discussions are handled without judgment and with sincerity.

To communicate about sex, some skill is involved. One must develop a vocabulary, vocal style, and body language that can convey a message the listener can understand. Otherwise, barriers to communication are produced when the language styles are offensive or mixed. If, for example, an individual is most comfortable with child language and is confronted with medical or scientific language, or vice versa, the communication may well be blocked by reactions to the actual words used. In this case, communication would be further hampered by expressions of anger or displeasure concerning the words spoken.

Communication difficulties arise when partners have different goals for their communication. One may want to express his or her feelings and to feel understood while the other may want to help solve apparent problems. As each feels misunderstood and frustrated, communication breaks down.

Common communication problems that stifle potentially enriching conversations include blaming the other person. This often results in angry exchanges and limited cooperation. Making the other person feel guilty or shameful can undermine a person's confidence and lead to a deepening silence on the topic. Making threats or giving ultimatums too often results in anger and fear ultimately reducing the likelihood of open talks in the future. Presuming to read one's partner's mind may cause resentment and ultimately limit the possibilities of new discoveries and growth. Saying "always" or "never" leaves open numerous possibilities for argument which can effectively sidetrack the discussion. Interrupting may also result in frustration and truncated communication.

While it is important to express thoughts and feelings clearly, it is equally important to listen carefully. This involves focusing one's attention on the other person while he or she is speaking and not interrupting. Interjecting opinions or advice jeopardizes effective listening. To be an effective listener, one must listen to what the other person is saying and be able to repeat what was said. This is one way to verify that what was heard was what was meant.

Communication is a learned skill that can be enhanced. When discussing sexual topics, Baucom and Hoffman recommend that the following techniques be practiced to improve the quality of the discussion:

1. Do not overreact to the sexual language used and negotiate a mutually acceptable choice if necessary.
2. Keep a sense of humor; humor can relieve embarrassment and tension.
3. Discuss a problem when neither party is greatly upset and when it can be discussed free of distractions.
4. Clarify the goal. Is it to share feelings and be understood or is it to solve a problem?
5. Express acceptance of one another through empathy. Empathy is conveyed through eye contact, warm tone of voice, open body posture and facial expression, and verbal feedback that demonstrates understanding of how the other person feels and thinks. Empathy demonstrates acceptance of another person's feelings and thoughts without necessarily agreeing with them.

To express their thoughts and feelings, people need to have a language. Much of the difficulty people have in discussing sexual topics stems from not knowing the words to use or not feeling comfortable using them. The lack of a universal sexual language, gender differences, early childhood experiences, and sexual orientation all influence sexual communication. Indeed, there may be limitless variables affecting the sexual messages conveyed. From this mosaic of possibilities, however, patterns in human communication can be discerned and even consciously altered. By learning techniques that improve the interpersonal aspects of communication and by increasing comfort and familiarity with sexual language, sexual communication between individuals can be enriched.

Communication is essential for individuals and communities and is vital to the human experience. As sexual beings, from infancy to old age, humans communicate through and about their bodies as a way to connect with others. In this life-long challenge, the satisfaction one achieves in communicating about sexuality can be one's greatest frustration or greatest joy.

REFERENCES

Baucom, D., and J.A. Hoffman. Common Mistakes Spouses Make in Communicating. *Medical Aspects of Human Sexuality*, Vol. 17, No. 11 (1983), pp. 206–19.

Brown, M., and A. Auerback. Communication Patterns in Initiation of Marital Sex. *Medical Aspects of Human Sexuality*, Vol. 15, No. 4 (1981), pp. 101, 104, 112, 113, 117.

Cashman, P. Learning to Talk About Sex. *SIECUS Report*, Vol. 9, No. 1 (1980), pp. 3–5.

Hott, L.R., and J.R. Hott. Sexual Misunderstandings. *Medical Aspects of Human Sexuality*, Vol. 14, No. 1 (1980), pp. 13, 19, 23, 27, 31.

Lee, J.A. Can We Talk? Can We Really Talk? Communication as a Key Factor in the Maturing Homosexual Couple. *Journal of Homosexuality*, Vol. 20, No. 3/4 (1991), pp. 143–168.

McDermott, R.J., J.C. Drolet, and J.V. Fetro. Connotative Meanings of Sexuality-Related Terms: Implications for Educators and Other Practitioners. *Journal of Sex Education & Therapy*, Vol. 15, No. 2 (1989), pp. 103–113.

Reiss, I.L. *Journey into Sexuality an Exploratory Voyage.* Englewood Cliffs, N.J.: Prentice-Hall, 1986.

Sanders, J.S. Male and Female Vocabularies for Communicating with a Sexual Partner. *Journal of Sex Education and Therapy*, Vol. 4, No. 2 (1978), pp. 15–18.

Simkins, L., and C. Rinck. Male and Female Sexual Vocabulary in Different Interpersonal Contexts. *Journal of Sex Research*, Vol. 18, No. 20 (1982), pp. 160–72.

Valentich, M. Talking Sex: Implications for Practice in the 1990s. *SIECCAN Journal*, Vol. 5, No. 4 (1990), pp. 3–11.

Wells, J.W. The Sexual Vocabularies of Heterosexual and Homosexual Males and Females for Communicating Erotically With a Sexual Partner. *Archives of Sexual Behavior*, Vol. 19, No. 2 (1990), pp. 139–147.

Carrie M. Steindorff

COMPULSION: SEXUAL COMPULSION

Compulsive sexual behavior (CSB) has been called hypersexuality, hyperphilia, hypereroticism, hyperlibido, hyperaesthesia, erotomania, perversion, nymphomania, satyriasis, promiscuity, Don Juanism, Don Juanita-ism, Casanova type, and, more recently, sex addiction and sexual compulsion. These labels suggest that CSB is an exotic or rare phenomenon, but in fact, many men and women experience periods of intense involvement in sexual activity. Some of these may be short-lived or may reflect normal developmental processes. When sexual behavior becomes part of an obsessive-compulsive drive, the behavior is driven by anxiety-reduction mechanisms rather than by sexual desire. The obsessive thoughts and compulsive behaviors reduce anxiety and distress, but they create a self-perpetuating cycle. The sexual activity provides temporary relief, but it is followed by further distress. An individual engaging in CSB puts himself or herself and others at risk for STDs (sexually transmitted diseases), illnesses, and injuries; often experiences moral, social, and legal sanctions; and endures great emotional suffering.

There are many manifestations of CSB, which can be subsumed under two basic types: paraphilic and nonparaphilic CSB. Paraphilic behaviors are unconventional sexual behaviors that are compulsive and, consequently, devoid of love and intimacy. Money has defined nearly 50 paraphilias. The most common paraphilias are pedophilia, exhibitionism, voyeurism, sexual masochism, sexual sadism, transvestic fetishism, fetishism, and frotteurism.

Nonparaphilic CSB involves conventional and normative sexual behavior taken to a compulsive extreme. There are five subtypes: compulsive cruising and multiple partners, compulsive fixation on an unattainable partner, compulsive autoeroticism, compulsive multiple love relationships, and compulsive sexuality in a relationship.

There are no good national statistics to estimate how many people suffer from CSB. Estimates are complicated by simultaneous under- and overreporting. The best estimate is that the problem occurs in approximately 5 percent of the population.

More men than women have identified themselves with CSB, but this may be due to our restrictive definition of sexuality—or to the fact that we tend to define sexuality from a masculine perspective. Since males are socialized to be more sexually aggressive, visually focused, and experimental, it is not surprising that more males are identified with this problem.

Women are socialized to define their sexuality in terms of relationships and romance. It is not surprising, then, that women are more susceptible to certain types of CSB, such as compulsive multiple sexual relationships or compulsive sexuality in a relationship rather than compulsive cruising and multiple partners. This is not to say that women do not develop paraphilias or the other types of nonparaphilic CSB.

It is dangerous to define compulsive sexual behavior as simply behavior that does not fit normative standards. Individuals have problems related to compulsive sexual behavior to varying degrees. It is difficult to draw a line between someone who has some problems that can be easily corrected through education or brief counseling and someone who needs intensive treatment. It is common to experience periods in which sexuality is expressed in obsessive and compulsive ways. This may be part of a normal developmental process. In other cases, it may be problematic. During adolescence, it is quite normative to become "obsessed" with sex for long periods. However, some adolescents begin to use sexual expression to deal with the stress of adolescence, loneliness, or feelings of inadequacy. Compulsive sexuality can be a coping mechanism similar to alcohol and drug abuse. This pattern of sexual behavior can be problematic.

During adulthood, it is not uncommon for individuals to go through periods when sexual behavior may take on obsessive and compulsive characteristics. Relationships outside committed relationships or frantic searches to fill loneliness following dissolution of a relationship are common. For some, these common behaviors become problematic. When individuals recognize that their behavior is not solving problems but creating them, they can often alter their pattern of behavior on their own or after brief counseling.

Some individuals, however, lack the ability to alter problematic sexual behavior. Their behavior is "hard wired" in the erotosexual pathways in their brain, and the repetitive nature of the self-defeating behavior can be explained by neurotransmitter dysfunction. Compulsive sexual behavior is, at this point, pathological, because

brain pathology is causing anxiety and the pattern of sexual behavior is acting as a short-lived anxiolytic (similar to other obsessive and compulsive behaviors). In its obsessive and compulsive form, the sexual behavior is senseless, dysphoric, and harmful. The CSB often has damaging consequences, including arrest, injury, or loss of jobs or relationships.

CSB has been strongly linked to early childhood trauma or abuse, highly restricted environments regarding sexuality, dysfunctional attitudes about sex and intimacy, or low self-esteem, anxiety, and depression. It is speculated that these traumatic experiences create or amplify an underlying or evolving anxiety disorder. Dysthymia is often experienced secondary to this primary anxiety disorder. CSB is seen as a symptomatic response and disorder to this anxiety, and depression. In addition, many individuals with CSB experience acute and chronic anxiety or depression in response to their compulsive sexual behavior. They may describe a sexual act as a "fix" to their anxiety or depression. This relief is short-lived, however, and they experience further anxiety. Some become depressed and even suicidal. They attempt to resist further obsessive thoughts or compulsive behaviors, but these efforts are frustrating, and the individual usually ends up engaging in the behavior.

New developments in the understanding of obsessive-compulsive disorder (OCD) have suggested that most paraphilic and nonparaphilic CSB may be best understood as a variant of OCD. In other cases, the behavior may be caused by other psychiatric or neurological disorders, which explain the compulsive nature of the sexual expression. In most cases, contrary to common beliefs, individuals with CSB are not oversexed (in the sense of having high sexual desire or hormonal imbalances). Their hypersexuality is in response to anxiety caused by neuropsychiatric problems.

Overcoming CSB does not involve eradicating all sexual behavior. Sexual expression is an important ingredient of sexual health. Individuals need to set limits or boundaries around certain patterns of sexual expression. They set these boundaries by clearly identifying their obsessive and compulsive sexual behavior. For example, a man who has been involved in compulsive autoeroticism does not stop masturbating. He identifies the behaviors and patterns of obsessive and compulsive masturbation and eliminates these behaviors. At the same time, he needs to learn new ways and patterns of masturbation that are self-nurturing and pleasuring. At the same time that sexual behavior is being restricted, individuals should be given permission to be sexual human beings.

In conclusion, compulsive sexual behavior is a serious psychosexual disorder that needs to be identified and appropriately treated. CSB does not always involve strange and unusual sexual practices. Many conventional sexual behaviors become the focus of the individual's sexual obsessions and compulsions. Advances in the understanding and treatment of OCD have given us a new direction and hope for better treatment of individuals with CSB. New pharmacotherapies combined with traditional psychotherapies have been shown to be effective in treating the various types of CSB.

REFERENCES

Coleman, E. Compulsive Sexual Behavior: New Concepts and Treatments. In E. Coleman, ed., *John Money: A Tribute*. New York: Haworth Press, 1991.

———. Sexual Compulsivity: Definition, Etiology and Treatment Considerations. In E. Coleman, ed., *Chemical Dependency and Intimacy Dysfunction*. New York: Haworth Press, 1987.

Kafka, M. Successful Antidepressant Treatment of Nonparaphilic Sexual Addictions and Paraphilias in Males. *Journal of Clinical Psychiatry*, Vol. 52 (1991), pp. 60–65.

Kafka, M., and E. Coleman. Serotonin and Paraphilias: The Convergence of Mood, Impulse and Compulsive Disorders. *Journal of Clinical Psychopharmacology*, Vol. 11 (1991), pp. 223–24.

Money, J. *Lovemaps: Clinical Concepts of Sexual/Erotic Health and Pathology, Paraphilia, and Gender Transpositions in Childhood, Adolescence, and Maturity*. New York: Irvington, 1986.

Eli Coleman

COMSTOCK, ANTHONY; COMSTOCKERY

Comstockery (sometimes Comstockism) refers to an aggressive prudery aimed at eliminating all mention or depiction of sexual matters or erotic stimulation from public expression or commerce, including art and literature. The term comes from the name of an important American reformer, Anthony Comstock (1844–1915).

Comstockery

Comstockery developed from two streams. One was the traditional English common-law suppression of offensively obscene and scandalous material. The other, which gave the phenomenon a special character, was the purity movement as it developed in 19th-century America.

The purity movement in turn grew out of evangelicalism of the early 19th century, in which middle-class Americans used their own aspirations to sexual purity to discredit the lower and upper classes alike, since their sexual standards were at odds with those of the middle-class evangelical Christians.

In Victorian England, evangelicals, along with social conservatives who wished to avoid any discussion of sexual reform (including, in particular, abating prostitution), introduced what was called "the conspiracy of silence" concerning matters sexual. The double standard of morality, in which men were permitted lustful behavior—or at least forgiven it—but women were expected to remain angelically pure, often coexisted with the conspiracy of silence, since men's animality was hidden in private male areas of society. All formally public discussion was, according to the standards that included the conspiracy of silence, to remain purified of anything that might suggest to "a young girl" the existence of sexuality, much less the indulgence of lust or perversity (perversity including anything outside of monogamous marriage). In the United States, this conspiracy of silence was very successful, in part because of the efforts of Comstock.

But in the United States, the purity movement, as Pivar has written, involved not just suppression of the unclean, disorderly, and corrupting but a positive vision of children brought up to be conscientious and pure, with prosocial attitudes and actions undistracted by vice or even by thoughts about impure matters—hence the attempt to remove stimulants to impure thinking. In a society in which industrialism was bringing disorder and great concern about control and discipline, including self-control and self-discipline, emphasizing personal and social purity was an adaptive strategy that could serve both individuals and society well. Only in the 20th century, when new ideas about how to cope with human sexuality became important, did purity begin to appear as a not necessarily positive alternative.

In the 1910s and 1920s, especially, the idea of supersensitive prudishness forced upon the public became an object of ridicule. To some extent, this antipurity criticism was a continuing application of the traditional Victorian dislike of hypocrisy and craving for honesty. In particular, those who believed that sexuality was a strictly private matter therefore satirized such people as Comstock from many points of view. One was the idea that he embodied a harmful repression of healthy sexuality. Another was the idea that public, and especially legal repression, was a violation of privacy and of freedom of expression. And still another was the notion that openness, frankness, and education about matters sexual was the best method of ultimately taming unfortunate human propensities. It was when significant intellectuals began to rebel, especially around the turn of the 20th century, that it became common to refer to public campaigns for sexual prudishness—and particularly censorship of art, literature, and the media—as Comstockery. The term was apparently coined in 1906 when George Bernard Shaw turned Comstock's name into a word for repressiveness.

Anthony Comstock

Comstock earned the eponym by his vigorous public campaigns. His work included unfair entrapment and asserted an extremist stance in the area of public expression. But it was also a distorting caricature of what he attempted to do, as Johnson has shown.

Comstock was born into an initially prosperous and large farm family in New Canaan, Connecticut. Comstock's mother died when he was only age 10, but by then he had already been imprinted with her moral zeal, and he absorbed also the traditional New England community emphasis on duty. Throughout his life, he adhered to the strictest version of a very conventional 19th-century evangelical Protestant religious standard.

Comstock attended the local district school and then the local church academy (secondary school). In 1864, he enlisted in the Union Army and served creditably. In the army, he used his religious devotion to protect himself against the temptations he saw all around him, and in the process he attempted (with, understandably, little success) to reform his comrades in arms. In 1866, after the war, he went to New York City and entered the dry goods business. He lived there the rest of his life as a public figure devoted to cleaning up New York, the nation, and the world.

The young clerk began his reform career in 1868, when he obtained the arrest of a dealer in pornography. In 1872, he came to the attention of wealthy backers of the Young Men's Christian Association (YMCA), and they encouraged and financed his work, which he carried out as part of a committee of the YMCA, the Committee for the Suppression of Vice. In 1873, his activities had become so notorious that the YMCA could no longer sponsor him (some leaders did not want the muck of society raked over but believed that such matters were better left unmentioned). Therefore Comstock's sponsors formed a separate organization, the Society for the Suppression of Vice, and Comstock left the dry goods business and became a full-time crusader as secretary to the Society.

His dress rehearsal for full-time work was his effort early in 1873 in using a display of offensive materials to persuade congressmen in Washington to pass a law forbidding the use of the Post Office to convey any obscene material, including contraceptive information. It became known as the Comstock Law. Comstock also obtained a commission as (unpaid until 1907) special agent of the Post Office, which gave him an additional legal base from which to operate directly to suppress obscenity.

Comstock, in going after sexually stimulating artifacts, classified them with frauds as well as distractions. At the beginning of 1874, Comstock calculated that he had seized and destroyed 134,000 pounds of improper books, 194,000 pictures and photographs of the same kind plus 14,200 pounds of stereotype plates; and 60,300 rubber articles (e.g., dildoes and condoms). But he had also moved against quack remedies (3,150 boxes of pills and powders), and he was very active in attacking gambling, which he viewed also as fraudulent, whether in the form of lotteries or gaming rooms.

Comstock used laws as the expression of social standards that can and should be enforced. But from the beginning, he found that not everyone interpreted those standards as strictly as he did. In 1887, he raided a respected art dealer and confiscated photographs of French classical art. Thereafter, every time he condemned classics in literature or in art, more and more invective and, most damaging, satire was directed against him. As time passed, Comstock accumulated many articulate critics and outright enemies. They exploited two weaknesses of his campaign. One was his penchant to use entrapment and other insensitive and what appeared to be unfair and inhumane tactics, hounding the weak as well as the responsible. The other weakness was the indiscriminate nature of his approach, particularly his assault on those advocating marriage reform—the very restrained "free love" of the day—and medical books and the classics. This reached an extreme when in 1906 he arrested a young female bookkeeper of the Art Students' League in New York because the artists were doing nude drawing in class and had published a pamphlet publicizing their work. By that time the sophisticated press had all joined in condemning and ridiculing him and, by implication, the censorship for which he stood.

In 1913, John S. Sumner appeared as Comstock's de facto successor in the Society for the Suppression of Vice, and while Comstock was never officially dismissed, he was already clearly senile and expired at peace with his God in 1915.

REFERENCES

Boyer, P.S. *Purity in Print: The Vice Society Movement and Book Censorship in America.* New York: Charles Scribner's Sons, 1968.

Bremner, R. Editor's Introduction. In A. Comstock, *Traps for the Young.* Cambridge, Mass.: Belknap Press, 1967.

Broun, H., and M. Leech. *Anthony Comstock: Roundsman of the Lord.* New York: Literary Guild of America, 1927.

Burnham, J.C. The Progressive Era Revolution in American Attitudes Toward Sex. *Journal of American History,* Vol. 59 (1973), pp. 885–908.

Johnson, R.C. Anthony Comstock: Reform, Vice, and the American Way. Doctoral dissertation, Univ. of Wisconsin, 1973.

Pivar, D.J. *Purity Crusade: Sexual Morality and Social Control, 1868–1900.* Westport, Conn.: Greenwood Press, 1973.

Rosenberg, C.E. Sexuality, Class, and Role in 19th-Century America. *American Quarterly,* 25 (1973), pp. 131–153.

John C. Burnham

CONDOM

The condom, or penis sheath, is an ancient contraceptive device, although the first published description of one dates from 1564 in the poem *De Morbo Gallico* by the anatomist Gabriele Fallopio (Latin—Fallopius; 1532–1562). He described a linen sheath. Condoms were also made of animal intestines or skin. Though there are references to condoms made out of the bladders of some air fishes, most historians are suspicious of such references. Since the vulcanization of rubber, most condoms have been made of that material, originally crepe rubber and then liquid latex.

One issue of controversy is the use of the term "condom" itself. The word first appears at the beginning of the 18th century, and some have claimed that the device was named after a Dr. Condom or Conton, a physician at the court of King Charles II (1630–1685) of England. Unfortunately, no such physician has ever been found. Others have argued that the term was derived from the name of a French village, but no historian now accepts this theory. Currently, the origin of the name remains unknown.

REFERENCE

Bullough, V.L. A Brief Note on Rubber Technology: The Diaphragm and the Condom. *Technology and Culture,* Vol. 22 (Jan. 1981), pp. 104–11.

Vern L. Bullough

CONFUCIANISM AND SEX

Confucianism consists of writings attributed to Confucius (Kongzi, or Master Kong, 551–479 B.C.), the first great educator, philosopher, and statesman of China, and his followers, including Mencius (Mengzi, or Master Meng, 372–289 B.C.), a political thinker who believed in democracy. Confucianism dominated Chinese sociopolitical life for most of Chinese history and largely influenced the cultures of Korea, Japan, and Indochina.

There are two components of Confucianism: the earlier Rujia (Confucian school of philosophy) and the later Kongjiao (Confucian religion). The Rujia represents a political-philosophical tradition which was extremely important in imperialist times, and is the element most directly connected with the persons and teachings of Confucius and Mencius—Kong *Meng zhi dao* (the doctrine of Confucius and Mencius). The Kongjiao represents the state's efforts to meet the religious needs of the people within the framework of the Confucian tradition, an unsuccessful attempt which occurred in the late imperial period (960–1911 A.D.).

For some 2,000 years, Confucianism enjoyed almost unassailable prestige as the ideology of the imperial bureaucracy, an essential element of China's political unity. Regardless of how much a particular ruler might prefer Buddhism or Taoism, Confucianism had a practical importance in the affairs of government that could not be denied or neglected. Philosophical Confucianism was very successful as a political ideology, as well as being an impressive system of moral philosophy.

Generally, it has been said that Confucianism is sex-negative. This is not quite true, since Confucius never spoke against sex and felt the whole subject was open to discussion. The Chinese frequently cited some of the sayings from Confucianism's classics as being supportive of people's sexual desires and rights because Confucius said that everyone loved sex. Unfortunately, in most English translations, the Chinese character se has been translated as "beauty," although "sex" is more accurate. Confucius also said, "Food and drink and the sexual relation between men and women compose the major human desires," while his disciple Mencius wrote,

"Eating food and having sex is nature of human beings." The word sex was left out of most English translations until recently.

Mencius's attitude toward sex was both positive and permissive. In fact, some sayings from Mencius concerning marriage are supportive of sexual life. For example: "That male and female should dwell together is the greatest of human relations"; "There are three things which are unfilial, and to have no posterity is the worst of them"; and "When a son is born, what is desired for him is that he may have a wife; when daughter is born, what is desired for her is that she may have a husband."

It was only much later during the Sung dynasty that official or public sexual attitudes began to change, gradually becoming more negative and repressive. The crucial change was initiated by several famous Neo-Confucianists, including Chou Tun-i (1017–73 A.D.), Ch'eng Hao (1032–185 A.D.) and Ch'eng I (1033–1107 A.D.), the founders of Neo-Confucianism; and Chu Hsi (1130–1200 A.D.) who, as the major interpreter and systematizer, was the true father of Neo-Confucianism. Ch'eng I summarized the Neo-Confucian viewpoint in a remark in his *Posthumous Papers*: "Discard human desires to retain the heavenly principles." When asked if a widow was justified in remarrying when pressed by poverty and hunger, he replied, "It is a very small thing to die as a result of starvation, but a very serious evil to lose chastity toward one's dead husband by remarrying."

Chu Hsi repeatedly emphasized his agreement with Ch'eng I. For example, Chu Hsi wrote to a friend urging him not to permit his widowed sister to remarry, justifying his viewpoint by quoting Ch'eng I's opinion, which he described as an unchangeable principle. Chu Hsi's strictly Confucianist interpretation of the classics was more rigorous than any that had gone before. He stressed the inferiority of women and the strict separation of the sexes, and forbade any manifestation of heterosexual love outside of wedlock. This narrow attitude is especially manifest in his commentaries on the love songs of *The Book of Poetry*, the oldest repository of Chinese verse. It was probably first compiled in the early sixth century B.C., collecting 305 poems and folksongs dating from between the 16th and 11th centuries B.C. to the sixth century B.C. Like the *I-Ching* (see "China and Sex"), it is counted among the five Confucianist classics. Chu Hsi reinterpreted the love songs of *The Book of Poetry* as political allegories. The foundations of Neo-Confucianism he laid resulted in it becoming the sole state religion and encouraged a strictly authoritarian form of government, which included the establishment of censorship, thought-control, and repressive policy.

REFERENCES

Legge, J., trans. *The Four Books: The Great Learning, The Doctrine of the Mean, Confucian Analects, and The Works of Mencius, With English Translation and Notes by James Legge, D.D., LL.D.* Reprint. Taipei, Taiwan: Culture Book Co., 1983.

Ruan, F.F. *Sex in China: Studies in Sexology in Chinese Culture.* New York: Plenum Press, 1991.

van Gulik, R.H. *Sexual Life in Ancient China: A Preliminary Survey of Chinese Sex and Society From ca. 1500 BC till 1644* A.D.. Leiden: E.J. Brill, 1961.

Fang-fu Ruan

CONTRACEPTION: BIRTH CONTROL

Theoretically, when a heterosexual couple engages in intercourse without making any attempt to prevent pregnancy, there is a three-percent chance that pregnancy will occur. This means that a pregnancy occurs approximately once in every 33 incidents of coitus. In a healthy population, this could produce a maternity ratio (average number of live births per woman) as high as ten. Since no area has ever had the food supply to sustain such a ratio for long, even with the high infant death rates in the past, people learned to use a variety of methods to control births.

Historical Methods of Birth Control

Celibacy, or abstinence, is one of the surest methods of birth control. Historically, it has been practiced by individual couples, as well as fostered by societies. For example, when large armies went on long campaigns most soldiers were forced by circumstances to be celibate; while it is true that camp followers sold their services as prostitutes during many wars, very often the common foot soldier could not afford the prostitute. The Catholic church maintained celibacy for priests, monks, and nuns. And celibacy has been fostered by raising the marital age, as it was during the potato famines in Ireland during the 19th century when the marriage age went up by almost a decade for both men and women.

Abortions have also been a major method of birth control throughout the ages. (See Abortion.)

The earliest known prescriptions for contraceptives came from Egypt (between 2000 and 1000 B.C.E.). They were written on papyrus scrolls and called for such substances as crocodile dung or honey and gumlike substances to be inserted into the vagina to block the path of the sperm. The ancient Greeks inserted olive oil. The Talmud mentions the use of a sponge soaked in vinegar.

Intrauterine devices were also used. Books attributed to Hippocrates, the great Greek physician, mention their existence in ancient Greece. On a more practical level, Arab camel drivers inserted a round stone into the uterus of the female camel before departing on a long journey to prevent its impregnation during the trip.

Coitus interruptus—the term which describes the withdrawal of the penis from the vagina before ejaculation occurs—is known to have been used in ancient times because it was condemned by Jewish, Christian, and Islamic writers alike. They argued that the male seed was too precious to waste.

The condom was first described by Gabriele Fallopius in the 16th century. (He was also the first to describe the clitoris and the Fallopian tubes which bear his name.) Fallopius probably did not invent the condom but rather described a device that was long in use. He did, however, popularize a linen sheath shaped to fit the erect penis which could be soaked with chemicals and serve as an effective barrier to sperm and to infectious organisms. Condoms of this period were made not only of linen, but also of animal intestines and fish bladders. They were used primarily as a prophylactic device to reduce the possibility of contracting venereal disease rather than as a contraceptive, although their contraceptive properties were known. Because the condoms had to be individually crafted, they were a luxury item used only by well-to-do men. In England, the sheath was named "condom" for reasons that are unknown; stories circulate about a Dr. Condom, supposedly a physician in the king's court, but no actual records of him have been discovered.

The discovery of the process of making liquid latex in 1853 made modern rubber condoms possible and led to the development of diaphragms and cervical caps. Pessaries, which were designed in the 19th century to support a prolapsed uterus, are ring-like structures inserted into the vagina and pushed up to fit around the cervix. Some pessaries blocked the opening in the cervix so they could also be used as a birth control device, although this agenda was often hidden from outsiders. Several of these devices were patented in the 19th century; the precursor to the popular diaphragm used in the 20th century was developed by C. Hasse, a German physician who used the pseudonym Wilhelm P.J.

Mensinga to protect himself from the stigma of dealing with a sexual product. The Mensinga diaphragm was a latex covering for the cervix held in place by a coiled spring that fit behind the pubic bone and over the cervix at the back of the vagina. Arleta Jacobs, a student of Hasse, opened a contraceptive clinic in the Netherlands where she was visited by the American nurse Margaret Sanger, who brought the diaphragm to the United States in 1916. Sanger, a militant socialist, was determined to bring birth control information and technology to American women, particularly poor immigrant women who lived in the big cities. Although the diaphragm had been smuggled in by affluent persons before Sanger set up her clinic on the Lower East Side of New York City, her well-publicized activities offended the authorities and she, her sister Ethyl, and Fania Mindell were arrested for opening the clinic. Sanger went on a hunger strike and was later pardoned by the governor and persisted with single-minded fervor to make family planning services available to women who needed them.

But New York is just one state and contraception was illegal in many states until the U.S. Supreme Court decision in *Griswold v. Connecticut* (1965) made birth control legal in all states, at least for married women. It took several more court cases before all obstacles were removed.

Diaphragms

Diaphragms are a barrier method of contraception. (Barrier methods block sperm from reaching the cervix so they cannot travel to the uterus and the Fallopian tubes where fertilization takes place.)

The diaphragm is a circular spring with a dome of rubber. Contraceptive jelly (about one teaspoon) is smeared inside the dome before the diaphragm is inserted in a position that covers the cervix and the front of the vagina. Because diaphragms are sized to fit the individual woman, a diaphragm must be fit and prescribed by a physician, nurse practitioner, or physician's assistant. The diaphragm should be inserted into the vagina before coitus, where it can safely stay for several hours before the sex act. It should be left in place for at least six hours after intercourse but removed in less than 24 hours to avoid infection.

The failure rate of diaphragms is less than ten per 100 woman-years of use. (This means for every 100 women using the diaphragm with a spermicide for one year, fewer than 10 will become pregnant.) Failures are most likely to occur among new users; more experienced users tend to have failure rates as low as two or three per 100 woman-years.

Since the diaphragm is used only when intercourse is likely to occur, the user who has sex infrequently need not be taking something all the time. Properly fitted and inserted, neither partner is particularly aware of its presence. Negative side effects are rare, and plastic diaphragms are available for the few people who are allergic to rubber. A few women develop cystitis (an inflammation or infection of the bladder) because the diaphragm creates pressure on the bladder.

Cervical Caps

The cervical cap, also a barrier contraceptive, is a small thimble-shaped cup smaller than the diaphragm which fits over the cervix. It was widely used at the beginning of the 20th century in Great Britain, but much less so in the United States. Its limited popularity in the United States may have been because it is more difficult to fit and to learn to insert or because Sanger introduced the diaphragm to American women instead of the cervical cap. The cervical cap was again popularized in the United States in the 1970s, when feminist groups advocated making it available to U.S. consumers. A long testing procedure by the federal Food and Drug Administration (FDA) was required, however, before it could be marketed.

One cap, the Prentif cavity-rim cervical cap, was FDA-approved in 1988; other caps are used in Europe. The Prentif cavity-rim cap, made of soft, pliable latex and about half the size of a diaphragm, is still not widely used—perhaps because of the longer fitting and training time (compared with the diaphragm) required for its prescription and usage.

Vaginal Sponges

As suggested by the fact that they were mentioned in the Talmud, sea sponges soaked in vinegar or lemon juice are a traditional folk method of birth control. Modern commercial contraceptive sponges date only from the mid-1970s, when they were developed by an Arizona research group with a grant from the federal government. Originally, the sponge was designed to be washed and reused, but this tended to wash out the spermicide so the failure rate was high. The sponge currently available with the trademark Today is marketed for one-time use only. It is a mushroom-shaped polyethylene sponge impregnated with the spermicide nonoxynol-9 that the user moistens and inserts

before the sex act occurs. It can be left in place up to 24 hours and used for subsequent acts of intercourse within these 24 hours.

The sponge has a relatively high failure rate (24 per 100 woman-years among older women who have had several pregnancies, and 14 per 100 woman-years among young women). Its major advantage is that it can be purchased in a drugstore without a prescription.

Condoms

The first latex condoms were made in the middle of the 19th century and were designed to fit over only the tip of the penis; that design was soon extended to cover the entire shaft of the penis. Seamless condoms were developed in the early 20th century. Condoms could often be purchased in brothels and barbershops but state laws against contraception prevented them from being sold for that purpose (thus emphasizing their prophylactic use). In the 1920s, Merle Young, a drugstore products salesman, started Young Rubber Company, marketing condoms to drugstores and successfully challenging the laws against the dissemination of condoms. Unfortunately, the quality control of condoms at that time was poor. A survey by the National Committee on Maternal Health in 1938 found that 40 percent of the rubber condoms sold in the United States were defective (usually small holes were found). After the FDA brought condoms under its regulation, the quality of the condoms improved. Today, the quality is high.

Condoms, like other barrier contraceptives, require skill to use. First-time users should read the instructions on the condom package ahead of time and practice putting one on. Most condoms are prerolled. If the condom does not have a reservoir tip, it should be unrolled about one-half inch before placing it on the penis. It is then rolled up the shaft of the penis. Condoms are more effective when a spermicide is inserted into the tip. Oily substances used as lubricants (vaseline, for example) should not be used with condoms because oil weakens the rubber.

For those who use condoms consistently, the failure rates are low, between one and three per 100 couple-years (the term used for male-oriented contraceptives). Inexperienced and occasional users have a higher failure rate, almost 10 percent.

Condoms used with a spermicide prevent the spread of most venereal diseases, including syphilis, gonorrhea, chlamydia, and AIDS, so they are highly recommended at this time because many of the venereal diseases have reached epidemic proportions. Condoms are certainly the contraceptive of choice for anyone who has had or plans to have more than one sex partner in a lifetime. It is also possible to supplement the condom with a second barrier contraceptive, such as a diaphragm or sponge, or to use oral contraceptives along with condoms. These steps increase the effectiveness of contraception, and when a second barrier contraceptive is used, offer further protection against venereal diseases.

Spermicides

Ancient people experimented with various spermicidal preparations long before the invention of the microscope made it possible to visualize sperm. Usually, they mixed a paste, gum, oil, or wax with an acid. Research sponsored by the Rockefeller Foundation in the 1920s helped to develop improved spermicides. In 1937, phenylmercuric acid was produced under the trade name Volpar. It was an effective spermicide but it was removed from the U.S. market because of concerns about the safety of mercury which it included. A breakthrough came in the 1950s with the introduction of the surfactants. These agents act primarily by disrupting the integrity of the sperm membrane. Since they are not strongly acetic they are rarely irritating to the vagina or the penis. Spermicides containing nonoxynol-9, a surfactant spermicide effective as both a contraceptive and a germicide, dominate the market now.

Spermicides, which can be purchased without a prescription, are available as jellies, creams, foaming tablets, or suppositories. The jelly is best for use with diaphragms, cervical caps, or condoms; other preparations can be used alone. The failure rate for spermicide alone is about 15 per 100 woman-years.

Oral Contraceptives

Oral contraceptives are synthetic hormones which prevent pregnancy. First approved by the FDA in 1960—though FDA approval was not then necessary for devices, it was for medications—the pill was the first method of birth control approved by the federal government. The research that finally produced the pill had started three decades earlier as an effort to control menstrual pain. This led to the identification of the hormone progesterone, which prevented ovulation. Ovulation is the process by which the egg ripens and ruptures out of the ovary. If ovulation does not occur there can be no pregnancy, so researchers realized that these hormones could also be used as contraceptives. As research progressed, it was found that a combination of estrogen and progesterone was more effective in preventing ovulation and dysmenorrhea than either hormone alone.

Synthetic progesterone (called progestin) was developed by Carl Djerassi at the Syntex laboratories in Mexico, and this breakthrough led to the development of other synthetic hormones, including estrogen. The experimental trials to test the pill were done in Puerto Rico under the direction of Gregory Pincus. A group of 265 women were given pills containing a combination of synthetic progesterone and estrogen. Before the trial, the pregnancy rate was 63 per 100 woman-years (a very high rate of pregnancy). The results were remarkable. No woman who took the pills faithfully for 20 days of each cycle became pregnant during the two years of the study. However, some women dropped out of the study complaining of nausea, vomiting, dizziness, and pelvic pain. This was also true of those women who took Enovid, the first pill marketed for general use in 1960. However, it was soon realized that the doses of hormone could be reduced markedly, and by 1980 significant side effects had been eliminated for most women.

Oral contraceptives function by interfering with the hormonal control of the female reproductive system. They create a false signaling system so that the brain and the pituitary gland do not send the usual messages to the ovaries and consequently ovulation does not occur. In addition, the oral contraceptives interfere with the work of the Fallopian tubes (which push the egg through the tubes to reach the uterus); they alter the lining of the uterus to make it unfriendly terrain for an egg; and they make the cervical mucous too thick for sperm to penetrate easily.

There are three types of oral contraceptives: combination pills, which include both estrogen and progestin; triphasic pills, which include these same two elements but in different proportions throughout the menstrual cycle; and mini-pills, which are low-dose progestins. The combination pills are the most common. They come in a package that marks off the days of the cycle and are taken from the first day of the cycle until the 21st day. They are then discontinued for seven days while the menstrual period occurs. Some packages include an additional seven pills of some inert substance so the user can take a pill every day. The triphasic pills came on the market in the 1980s and manufacturers claim they have even fewer side effects than the regular pills. Some women report this is true; others see no difference. The minipills made only of progestin may cause heavy menstrual bleeding but eliminate other side effects. They are safe for mothers who are nursing babies because too much estrogen is not good for the baby.

The theoretical effectiveness of the oral contraceptives is 100 percent. In reality, there are between four and ten failures per 100 woman-years because women forget to take their pills or take them off schedule. When a lapse in memory occurs, an alternative form of birth control (such as a condom) should be used in addition to the pills for the remainder of the cycle. Possible side effects of the oral contraceptives include weight gain, edema, nausea, headaches, rash, and sterility for several months after they are discontinued. However, with the current low dosages, most women have no negative side effects after the first couple of months.

Although it is not common, serious cardiovascular problems, including stroke and heart attacks, have been related to oral contraceptive use. Because of this, women with a history of stroke, heart attack, diabetes, or other blood vessel problems should not take the pill. These complications are much more likely to occur in women who smoke because smoking damages blood vessels. For this reason, the pill is ordinarily not given to women over age 30 who smoke. Although it is the smoking that is actually more dangerous, the combination of the pill and smoking may be enough to cause a stroke or related problem.

Oral contraceptives are the most popular form of birth control. They are used by 31 percent of the Americans who use contraceptives. The social impact of the pill is difficult to overestimate. Because of it, for the first time in history, women have the power to control their lives by deciding when and if to become pregnant. The pill is thus clearly an important factor in the revolutionary advances made by women in the last part of the 20th century.

Progestin Implants

Norplant, a progestin implant, which releases small amounts of hormone over three or five years, was approved by the FDA in 1991. The five-year implants come as six hollow capsules made of silicone rubber (silastic); the three-year implants use two solid silastic rods. The capsules or the rods are surgically implanted under the skin on the inside of the upper or lower arm. They gradually release a small amount of progestin which prevents conception. Since women are just starting to use them in the United States, statistics on their effectiveness come from other countries, where a failure rate of less than one

per 100 woman-years is recorded. Norplant may cause irregular menses at first, but the bleeding diminishes over time. If the user decides she wants to become pregnant before the implants have spent their hormones, they can be removed early; otherwise they are removed at the end of the designated time period and new implants can be inserted.

Intrauterine Devices (IUDs)

Because almost any foreign body in the uterus prevents conception, intrauterine devices, of various materials, have been used throughout the ages. But the foreign body can also cause infection, so before antibiotics a pelvic infection was often fatal. The first IUD to be widely used was a ring of gut and silver wire developed in the 1920s by Ernst Graefenberg, a German gynecologist and sex researcher. In 1934, Tenrei Ota of Japan introduced gold-plated silver intrauterine rings. Jack Lippes, a Buffalo, New York, gynecologist in 1962 used the basic design developed by these researchers but changed the material to a plastic loop with an attached thread which fell into the vagina for easy checking or removal. More recent IUD designs use copper, which has some contraceptive properties itself, and some IUDs also contain a reservoir of progestin.

Unfortunately, an IUD called the Dalkon shield was marketed in the 1970s. It was poorly designed, untested, and caused serious infections. By 1976, 17 deaths were linked to its use but the pharmaceutical company that had developed it took no steps to notify the public or health care providers of the danger until 1980. This led to many law suits; the company declared bankruptcy and other IUD companies, fearing similar lawsuits, took their products off the market. Since IUDs are devices, not drugs, they were not controlled by the FDA until after the Dalkon shield incident. The IUDs currently on the market are FDA approved and safe.

IUDs work by stimulating a foreign-body reaction in the uterus, thus damaging the sperm and the egg and making implantation in the uterus impossible. They must be inserted and removed by a health care provider, but once in place, they can stay for several years.

IUDs can cause heavy menstrual periods, so women with bleeding disorders should avoid them. They should also be avoided by women who are likely to contract sexually transmitted diseases because they increase the likelihood of the infection traveling to the pelvis. IUDs work best for women who have had at least one child, so they are seldom used for very young women.

Although current IUDs are among the most effective contraceptives now available (with a failure rate of approximately one per 100 woman-years), they are not very popular because of the fear caused by the Dalkon shield incident.

Abstinence

The only totally effective way to avoid pregnancy is to avoid all heterosexual intercourse. Although homosexuals often do this, and others may abstain for religious reasons, most people using abstinence as a method of birth control abstain during the woman's menstrual midcycle when ovulation occurs. This method, once called the rhythm method, is now called natural family planning, and it is the only form of birth control that is not banned by the Catholic church.

To be successful with natural family planning, the couple must be able to identify or calculate when ovulation occurs and abstain from intercourse for several days before and after the expected date of ovulation. While ovulation in most women occurs 14 days before the next menstrual period, it is not always possible to know exactly when the next menstrual period will start. This is particularly true of women with irregular menses. To improve the calculations, some women take their temperature each day. It usually starts to rise midcycle at the time of ovulation. Two Australian physicians, John and Evelyn Billings, have developed a method of periodic abstinence based on changes in the cervical mucous. (The mucous at the time of ovulation is thin and slippery, while it is thick at other times.)

Natural family planning is without risk to the body but the failure rate is high among people with irregular menstrual cycles and those who are not conscientious about measuring and assessing the clues that signal ovulation. The failure rate is approximately 20 per 100 woman-years, but careful use of the method employing multiple indicators of ovulation can lower this figure to eight per 100 woman-years.

Sterilization

Many couples who do not want children or have finished bearing their desired number of children seek voluntary sterilization. In 1992, female sterilization was the most popular worldwide approach to family planning with an estimated 140 million, or 16 percent of the women of reproductive age being sterilized. The procedure is particularly popular in China, South Korea, Thailand, the Dominican Republic, El Salvador, Mexico, and the United States. In 1988, 23 percent of the women and 13 percent of the men in the United States had been sterilized.

Worldwide, an estimated 40 million couples rely on male sterilization using an operation that cuts the vas deferens, the tube that carries the sperm from the testes. The surgery can be done on an outpatient basis, and the record of safety for the procedure is high. It takes about six weeks to clear all of the sperm from the system, so intercourse should be delayed until then, and the ejaculate should be examined under a microscope to make sure it is clear of sperm before the couple resumes intercourse. Vasectomy is a major family planning method in the United States, New Zealand, Australia, Great Britain, Canada, the Netherlands, China, India, and South Korea.

Women are sterilized by blocking or cutting and tying the Fallopian tubes. Since 1960, two simplified procedures have developed: laparoscopy and minilaparotomy. A laparoscope is a slender stainless steel tube containing a set of lenses and a fiber-optic cable connected to a light source. The surgeon visualizes the Fallopian tubes through the laparoscope and blocks or cuts the tubes with instruments inserted through the laparoscope or inserted through a second abdominal incision.

The minilaparotomy involves making a small incision either just above the pubic hair or below the navel for postpartum procedures. Each tube is pulled up to the incision, where it is blocked or cut. Sterilization is also possible by removing the uterus, or ovaries. One of these later procedures might be chosen if the operation is done at the time of a Cesarean section, or if there is some other problem involving the uterus or ovaries.

Other Birth Control Methods

Coitus interruptus—the withdrawal of the penis from the vagina before ejaculation occurs—has a long history of usage, but is less popular now because there are safer approaches with better failure rates. The failure rate with coitus interruptus is 32 per 100 couple-years.

Coitus reservatus, keeping the penis in the vagina until the erection passed, was used as a ceremony in ancient India and China. It was believed that a loss of *yang* would occur with ejaculation, so many tried to preserve it by practicing coitus reservatus. Actually, the ejaculate oozes out and drains into the bladder (retrograde ejaculation). It is not an effective birth control method because there is seepage of semen even without ejaculation.

Douching with an acidic solution, such as vinegar and water, has a failure rate of 40 per 100 woman-years. It is better than no birth control method at all.

RU–486 is an antiprogesterone developed by the French pharmaceutical firm Roussel-Uclaf. When it is taken four days before the menses, it prevents the fertilized egg from being implanted in the uterus. Dizziness, severe cramps, and heavy bleeding have been reported by some users. It is also used as a "morning after" pill when unprotected intercourse has occurred. It has not yet been approved by the FDA for general use, but it has been approved for testing. It is politically controversial in the United States because it can be used as an abortion pill. However, it shares some of the properties of the oral contraceptives and the IUD since it prevents implantation of the egg in the uterus.

Summary

Birth control methods of some type have been used by most peoples in the past, but most of the effective methods have been developed in this century. The three most effective methods are the oral contraceptives, the IUD, and sterilization. However, many experts are advising the condom or the diaphragm, used with contraceptive jelly, because the barrier contraceptives also cut down the spread of disease.

References

Billings, E., and A. Westmore. *The Billings Method: Controlling Fertility Without Drugs or Devices.* New York: Random House, 1980.

Boston Women's Health Collective. *Our Bodies: Ourselves: A Book by and for Women.* New York: Simon & Schuster, 1979.

Bullough, V.L., and B. Bullough. *Contraception; A Guide to Birth Control Methods.* Buffalo, N.Y.: Prometheus Books, 1990.

Can You Rely on Condoms? *Consumer Reports,* Vol. 54 (Mar. 1989), pp. 136–141.

Hatcher, R.A., *et al. Contraceptive Technology, 1990– 92.* 15th Rev. Ed. New York: Irvington Publishers, Inc. 1990.

Hormonal Contraception: New Long-Acting Methods. *Population Reports,* Series K, No. 3 (Mar.-Apr. 1987), Vol. 16, No. 1, K, pp. 66–68

Mishell, D.R. Medical Progress: Contraception. *New England Journal of Medicine,* Vol. 320 (1989), pp. 777–787.

Sanger, M. *Margaret Sanger; An Autobiography.* Reprinted. New York: Dover Publications, Inc., 1971.

Voluntary Female Sterilization: Number One and Growing. *Population Reports,* Series C, No. 10 (Nov. 1990), pp. 1–23.

Bonnie Bullough

COUNSELING: SEXUALITY COUNSELING

Sexuality counseling is a professional role, a service to clients, and a process of human interaction. What Weinstein and Rosen termed "sexuality counseling" is not sex therapy, although the distinction between counseling and therapy in general never has been resolved. The American Association of Sex Educators, Counselors, and Therapists (AASECT) has as its central mission the certification of sex educators, sex counselors, and sex therapists. The certification program defines the requirements and roles of each specialization, but the certification philosophy acknowledges that the roles overlap. In the end, the distinctions among sex educators, sex counselors, and sex therapists comes down to the commonsense notion that educators educate, counselors counsel, and therapists engage in therapy. In short, these three professional roles describe more professional training and self-identity than articulating what the professionals do when working with clients.

The American Board of Sexology is even less specific in its description of diplomates as sex therapists, sex educators, sex counselors, and sex researchers. Unlike AASECT, the doctorate or appropriate terminal degree for the field of study is specified as a requirement for diplomate status with the American Board of Sexology. Of course, sexuality counseling can be done by persons other than sex counselors and sex therapists. However, sexuality counseling by the general counselor may be an exception rather than the rule. In the past, counseling theorists have tended to shy away from sexual issues. It has only been since the late 1970s that sexual orientation has been given expanded attention in the counseling literature. Even today, students in counseling training programs still are not getting an integration of sexual orientation in their professional development. In fact, the wealth of literature on sexual behaviors and feelings experienced by clients along with sex identity development continues to be neglected in the general training of counselors. The theory and training of the general counselor still tends to avoid sexual issues.

Counseling vs. Psychotherapy

Counseling and psychotherapy are often distinguished from each other. For psychologists, counseling and therapy are contrasted in terms of clinical training of the professional and the severity of the client's distress. However, counselors and therapists often share the same goals and utilize the same theories and allied research data when attempting to help the client. When the counselors or therapists succeed, they tend to do so under the same conditions. In theory, counseling and therapy are different, but in practice the distinction tends to vanish. In part, debates over the similarity and differences between counseling and psychotherapy are associated with the development of the two professional roles of counseling psychology and clinical psychology. Counseling psychology has its roots in the vocational guidance movement. Until recently, the majority of counseling psychologists worked in an educational setting. As the needs of society changed, the roles of counseling psychology changed. Initially clinical psychology emerged under the influence of psychiatric theory and practice. Gradually, clinical psychology broke away from those roots. Today, it is difficult to distinguish between the clinical and counseling psychologists. A survey of college counseling services demonstrated that counseling psychologists provide a variety of services, ranging from counseling for personal problems, short-term counseling during profound emotional crisis, and to a lesser extent, long-term counseling for serious emotional problems. Currently, counseling psychologists are employed in mental health centers. More and more counseling psychologists are engaging in private practice providing services not only to persons who are functioning normally but also to those who are severely disturbed. In private practice, counseling psychologists report doing psychotherapy with the emotionally distressed, vocational counseling, and, to some extent, psycho-diagnostic and preventive services.

Still clinical psychologists to a large extent focus on removing "psychopathological symptoms" while counselors tend to ignore them. Rather than treating a personality problem, the counselor attempts to activate existing resources in order to help the client change his or her circumstances or to cope with them more effectively. In general, counseling psychologists are allied with normality and tend to emphasize developmental phenomena. However, the current curriculum for counseling psychologists puts more emphasis on psychopathology and less on adjustment counseling of the normally functioning individual. More and more counseling psychologists are receiving course instruction on a variety of social issues including child sex abuse, incest, and sexual dysfunctions.

In summary, counseling and psychotherapy (or simply therapy) are distinct but overlapping processes. Counseling, on the other hand, is also associated with professional roles (e.g., the counseling psychologist and the most recent professional identity of the certified clinical mental health counselor). Counseling and therapy are attempts to influence another person in an interpersonal context. Thus, in one sense counseling is not unlike any social relationship. In reality, counseling can be much more than a typical social encounter. Increasingly a counselor is professionally certified or licensed to engage in this influence process. Counselors tend to: (1) have expertise in interpersonal relationships and (2) be motivated to help the client rather than to fulfill some personal need. Regardless of theoretical orientation, the intentions of counselors are to:

- Create an expectation of hope that something will change.
- Encourage talking through problems and feelings.
- Challenge maladaptive thinking and replace it with more rational thought.
- Provide feedback about maladaptive and inappropriate behaviors.
- Enhance personal control of feelings and behaviors.
- Foster acceptance and experience of intense feelings.
- Foster understanding of motivations for thoughts, feelings, behaviors, and attitudes.
- Support the development of new skills.
- Reward adaptive changes in the client.
- Work to overcome obstacles to change.
- Challenge old patterns of thinking, behaving, and feeling.
- Use the counseling relationship as a context for developing effective relationship skills.

Empathy, the ability to assume the role of another person without acting in that person's role, is one of the very important skills that counselors develop. In addition, counselors may serve as a mediator between the client and persons who represent the major social institutions within the society. Throughout the relationship, the emphasis is on growth and enhancement of the decision-making skills of the client.

Theoretical Perspectives and Techniques

Today, counselors and therapists, depending on their training and experience, can draw on a variety of theoretical perspectives in working with the client. These include psychoanalytic therapy, Adlerian therapy, existential therapy, person-centered therapy, Gestalt therapy, transactional analysis, behavior therapy, cognitive-behavioral therapies, and reality therapy. In the end, the therapy the client experiences depends on the counselor's personality and professional decisions. Yet, today it is recognized that some theories and techniques are better than others. When development of the client is the goal, some theories and techniques are more effective than others, which is another way of saying that counseling is more than an ordinary social encounter. The counselor must master certain theories and techniques to be effective in the counseling relationship. Some counseling textbooks essentially leave the theoretical choices up to the counselor. By contrast, Burke attempts to present a specific perspective for counseling, which he calls the self-regulation and maturity two-part model. The self-regulation emphasis is rooted in the theories and techniques of behavior therapy. Identification of specific problems and application of specific ways to change behavior are stressed. The maturity component is based on psychoanalytic and person-centered theories. Thus, the second component makes the counseling relationship central to the therapeutic process. This model is clearly in the counseling tradition with its emphasis on adaptivity and maladaptivity rather than on sickness and health. The counseling goal is not only to gain control over thoughts and behaviors, but also to encourage and support continuing growth toward maturity.

Just as the professional roles of counseling psychologists, clinical psychologists, social workers, marriage and family therapists, and mental health counselors imply unique training and skills, so do sex counselor and sex therapist imply the same. (There is a great wealth of literature written by persons engaged in sex therapy listed in the Reference section. Books on sexuality counseling, however, are rare. Hopefully, that situation will be remedied in the decade of the 1990s.)

Sexual Counseling

The professional backgrounds of sex counselors are diverse. Clients may seek sexuality counseling because of a need to better understand sexuality. More often clients are thrown into sexuality counseling as a result of some traumatic event or crisis (e.g., sexual assault, unexpected pregnancy, or relationship problems with a partner). Sexual counseling is an interactive process involving a client and a professional. In this special relationship, clients are permitted to explore and to seek to understand sexual feelings, values, needs, actions, and responsibilities. The focus in sexuality counseling is on identifying and resolv-

ing sexual problems. Professionals who regard themselves as sex counselors tend to deal with a broad range of sexual issues, whereas sex therapists tend to specialize in treating sexual dysfunctions. In the past, sexuality counseling was largely done by psychiatrists and clinical psychologists. But today clients concerned about family planning, relationship problems, or concerns emerging from some trauma or crisis will find sexual health professionals who are neither psychiatrists nor clinical psychologists.

Kaplan has proposed a triphasic model for human sexuality. From that perspective, a sexual dysfunction is a disturbance of sexual desire, sexual excitement, or the orgasmic response. But clients also have a broad range of sexual concerns that can be called sexual problems, which include partner conflicts of frequency of sexual intercourse, partner disagreements over sexual activities, a feeling of sexual dissatisfaction, and sexual boredom. In this context, distinction between sexuality counseling and sex therapy can become blurred. In some cases, sexual functioning may be enhanced by more adequate sex knowledge and improved communication skills. Yet these very same issues may suggest a dysfunctional marital unit or a set of unresolved attitude and value conflicts. In those cases, marital counseling or individual therapy may be more appropriate than sex therapy or sexuality counseling.

No one simple explanation can account for the growing need for sexuality counseling. A part of the need is driven by an exposure to rigid sexual standards of right and wrong and related sex role socialization. More and more individuals are finding the values, attitudes, and guides for behavior learned in childhood out of step with the social realities of adulthood. Media treatment of sexuality has raised expectations for a more satisfying sexual life. Gays and lesbians have become more visible in society. Drug abuse has contributed to a variety of sexual dysfunctions. There is more public awareness of sexual assault and child sex abuse. Greater sexual freedom has resulted in unexpected and unwanted pregnancies among the teenage population. The elderly, brought up in a more restrictive sexual climate, are learning about sexual rights once denied.

Individuals seek sexuality counseling because of problems in sexual functioning or need for support and information during a particular stage in the life cycle. Sometimes individuals seek counseling following divorce or death of a partner. Because of stigmatization, gays and lesbians frequently seek counseling. Some clients are disabled or parents of the disabled. Family planning counseling and counseling for unplanned and unwanted pregnancies are services provided by some sex counselors. More and more sexuality counseling services are extended to the sexually abused and incest survivors as well as victims of sexual assault. Chemical dependency, alcohol abuse, chronic physical illness, and sexually transmitted diseases often prompt individuals to explore sexual concerns.

The need for sexuality counseling can emerge within the context of personal counseling or therapy. However, sexual concerns are more likely to surface when the professional has a sex counselor identity. When a female client discloses the experience of incest during childhood, the sex counselor will probably ask explicit questions about other possible forms of abuse within the family. Within the sex counseling relationship, the reality of the incest is affirmed and acknowledged. Incest is treated as an important life experience and its possible relationship to present sexual concerns is explored. The counseling goal is to develop the identity of an incest survivor rather than that of the "helpless incest victim." In university women who have repressed incest, the general treatment goal is to offer the experience of emotional catharsis in a safe and accepting counseling context, to gain integration of past experiences with present relationships along with fostering insight in understanding the family dynamics that produced the incest, to promote positive sense of self-worth, and to extend trust to others along with increasing comfort for intimate relationships. In some incest and sex abuse case management, the counseling needs of the individual and family may demand more resources than the individual sex counselor can provide. In such cases, case management teams, often composed of psychologists, psychiatrists, nurses, social workers, and marriage and family counselors, may be able to help where the individual counselor cannot. Clients must be made aware that there are legal mandatory reporting requirements associated with incest and child sex abuse.

An unwanted pregnancy may lead to a need for specialized counseling, which includes information about options and support during the decision process. Sexuality counseling may be needed by some women who had an abortion without the knowledge or support of friends and family. In such cases, complaints of depression may be related to failure to process unresolved grief associated with the abortion. Such women may deny grief, the experience of loss, and the need to talk about the experience.

Non-conformity to a heterosexual orientation was indicative of mental illness until 1973, when the American Psychiatric Association Board essentially reversed that long-standing tradition. Just how and why that decision was reached continue to be controversial. Today, sexual orientation is generally viewed as an identity issue. However, the process of sexual identity formation may not be the same for gays, lesbians, and bisexuals. In addition to sex identity clarification, adolescent homosexuals and bisexuals often need support in coping with the stigmatization associated with the emerging sexual orientation, counsel on minimizing the risk of AIDS, and suicide prevention counseling. Because of the continuing stigmatization associated with homosexuality, parents may need counseling to understand and accept the homosexual or bisexual identity of the adolescent. Sex counselors are more likely to be more consistent in attitudes toward homosexuals than are nonspecialized counselors and therapists. Society continues to be antigay. While counselors and therapists formally no longer regard homosexuality as a mental illness, far too often they hold the contradictory view that being gay or lesbian is a problem. Thus, the gay client may be put at risk when the counselor does not recognize the personal prejudicial bias. The development of a gay identity typically starts with a feeling of being different followed by an awareness of sexual attraction for persons of the same sex, an identity crisis, and finally the acceptance of a gay identity. The general pattern may not hold for a developing lesbian identity and does not recognize the additional stigmatization due to racism that black gays and lesbians experience. While the social community may support the development of racial and ethnic identities, because of the prevalence of negative attitudes toward homosexuality, that same social community may not support the development of a homosexual identity. To the extent that the counselor or therapist lacks sensitivity to multicultural issues, the effectiveness of sexuality counseling with minority gays and lesbians may be compromised.

Healthy individuals may seek sexuality counseling because of fear of acquiring AIDS through social contact with an HIV-infected person. Family members may require support in understanding AIDS and in coping while caring for an AIDS victim. The AIDS victim experiences a variety of situations resulting in emotional distress which can be alleviated through counseling. Circumstances producing emotional distress include abandonment by parents, loss of employment, indifference of public agencies, and feeling trapped in a relationship. In some cases, counseling intervention may be required in response to irresponsible behavior that unnecessarily puts others at risk with human immunodeficiency virus (HIV) infection. In addition to all these problems, the AIDS victim has to cope with and come to terms with death. Given the stigmatization associated with homosexuality, unresolved issues about gayness may emerge as well as feelings of shame and guilt for acting on one's gayness. Finally, those who are in grief over the loss of a person having died with AIDS may seek counseling support as well.

Sexual assault (commonly known as rape) is forced sexual contact without a person's consent. The perpetrator of the sexual aggression may be a stranger or someone well known to the victim. Either form of rape can have immediate consequences and long-term effects. In acquaintance rape, or date rape, a woman may not acknowledge that she has been sexually assaulted. Sexual assault is often unexpected, not the result of a woman's behavior, and almost certainly traumatic. Crisis intervention rather than counseling and therapy is a common support for a woman who understands that she has been sexually assaulted. Crisis intervention focuses on processing the traumatic experience and providing the necessary support in dealing with actions and decisions that the circumstances require. However, it is not unusual for a woman to seek counseling and therapy because of complaints of depression, alcohol and drug dependency, irrational fears, panic attacks, and obsessive-compulsive tendencies. Sometimes these symptoms are related to a history of sexual assault. Not uncommonly women develop problems in sexual functioning. For some, the first sexual intercourse occurs during stranger or acquaintance rape. The counseling process can help a woman deal with her feelings about loss of virginity. Sexually experienced women may develop a pattern of avoiding sex with their partners. The goals for these women in counseling are to deal with the shock, denial, symptoms and anger that follow from the rape experience and to reestablish healthy sexual functioning.

Sexism is a social attitude that devalues, restricts, or discriminates based on one's biological sex, gender role, or sexual orientation. Gender role refers to behaviors and social roles expected by society based on one's sex. Sex counselors are developing an appreciation that men and women have different issues to be resolved and needs to be met during counseling. There is also a growing recognition by counselors that the counsel-

ing process can be influenced by sexism and assumptions about gender roles made by the counselor. Finally, societal rules about gender role behavior are undergoing radical change. Today, clients have a need to understand these societal changes and to integrate these changes in their identities and relationships.

Sex counselors provide diverse sexuality counseling services. Sexuality counseling is, however, not limited to sex counselors. A person having a need for sexuality counseling must decide who among the professionals has the best training and experience to assist with the sexual concern. A sex counselor can help clarify the client's needs and make appropriate referrals when necessary to do so. The American Association of Sex Educators, Counselors, and Therapists identifies professionals who have met the organization's standards for certification as a sex counselor. The American Board of Sexology lists professional counselors who have met their standards for diplomate status as sex counselors.

REFERENCES

American Association of Sex Educators, Counselors and Therapists. *1990–1991 Membership Directory of the American Association of Sex Educators, Counselors and Therapists*. Chicago: American Association of Sex Educators, Counselors, and Therapists, 1990.

American Board of Sexology. *The Register of Diplomates of the American Board of Sexology. 1993 Edition*. Washington, D.C., 1992.

Anderson, W. Services Offered by College Counseling Centers. *Journal of Counseling Psychology*, Vol. 17 (1970), pp. 380–82.

Barret, R.L. Counseling Gay Men with AIDS: Human Dimensions. *Journal of Counseling & Development*, Vol. 67 (1989), pp. 573–75.

Berger, R.M. What Is a Homosexual? A Definitional Model. *Social Work*, Vol. 28 (1983), pp. 132–35.

Bloom, J., et al. Model Legislation for Licensed Professional Counselors. *Journal of Counseling & Development*, Vol. 68 (1990), pp. 511–23.

Bradley, L.J., and M.A. Ostrovsky. The AIDS Family: An Emerging Issue. *Counseling & Human Development*, Vol. 22 (1989), pp. 1–12.

Briskln, K.C., and J.M. Gary. Sexual Assault Programming for College Students. *Journal of Counseling and Development*, Vol. 65 (1986), pp. 207–08.

Brown, R.A., and J.R. Field, eds. *Treatment of Sexual Problems in Individual and Couples Therapy*. PMA Publishing Corp., 1988.

Bruhn, J.G. Counseling Persons with a Fear of AIDS. *Journal of Counseling & Development*, Vol. 67 (1989), pp. 455–57.

Burkel, J.F. *Contemporary Approaches to Psychotherapy and Counseling: The Self-regulation and Maturity Model*. Pacific Grove, Calif.: Brooks/Cole Publishing Co., 1989.

Coleman, E., and G. Remafedi. Gay, Lesbian, and Bisexual Adolescents: A Critical Challenge to Counselors. *Journal of Counseling & Development*, Vol. 68 (1989), pp. 36–40.

Corey, G. *Theory and Practice of Counseling and Psychotherapy*. Fourth ed. Pacific Grove, Calif.: Brooks/Cole Publishing Co., 1991.

Erickson, S.H. Counseling the Irresponsible AIDS Client: Guidelines for Decision Making. *Journal of Counseling & Development*, Vol. 68 (1990), pp. 454–55.

Good, G.E., L.A. Gilbert, and M. Scher. Gender Aware Therapy: A Synthesis of Feminist Therapy and Knowledge about Gender. *Journal of Counseling & Development*, Vol. 68 (1990), pp. 376–80.

Harman, J.I. Relations Among Components of the Empathic Process. *Journal of Counseling Psychology*, Vol. 33 (1986) pp. 371–76.

Heesacker, M., and B.J. Gilbert. E. Joseph Shoben, Jr.: Synthesizer in an Age of Specialization. *Journal of Counseling & Development*, Vol. 66 (1987), pp. 5–11.

Hill, C.E., and K.E. O'Grady. List of Therapist Intentions Illustrated in a Case Study and with Therapists of Varying Theoretical Orientations. *Journal of Counseling Psychology*, Vol. 32 (1985), pp. 3–22.

Hotelling, K., and L. Forrest. Gilligan's Theory of Sex-Role Development: A Perspective for Counseling. *Journal of Counseling & Development*, Vol. 64 (1985), pp. 183–90.

Iasenza, S. Some Challenges of Integrating Sexual Orientations into Counselor Training and Research. *Journal of Counseling & Development*, Vol. 68 (1989), pp. 73–76.

Ivey, A.E., M.B. Ivey, and L. Simek-Downing. *Counseling and Psychotherapy: Integrating Skill, Theory, and Practice*. Second ed. Englewood Cliffs, N.J.: Prentice-Hall, 1987.

Josephson, G.S., and M.L. Fong-Beyette. Factors Assisting Female Clients' Disclosure of Incest During Counseling. *Journal of Counseling & Development*, Vol. 65 (1987), pp. 475–78.

Joy, S.S. Abortion: An Issue to Grieve? *Journal of Counseling & Development*, Vol. 63 (1985), pp. 375–76.

———. Retrospective Presentations of Incest: Treatment Strategies for Use with Adult Women. *Journal of Counseling & Development*, Vol. 65 (1987), pp. 317–19.

Kaplan, H. Singer. *The New Sex Therapy Volume 2. Disorders of Sexual Desire, and Other New Concepts and Techniques in Sex Therapy*. New York: Brunner/Mazel, 1979.

King, P.T., and W.R. Seymour. Education and Training in Counseling Psychology. *Professional Psychology*, Vol. 13 (1982), pp. 834–42.

Kinnier, R.T. The Need for Psychosocial Research on AIDS and Counseling Interventions for AIDS Victims. *Journal of Counseling & Development*, Vol. 64 (1986), pp. 472–74.

Larrabee, M.J., and S.S. McGeorge. Date Rape: Understanding the Acquaintance Assault Phe-

nomenon. *Counseling & Human Development*, Vol. 22 (1989), pp. 1–16.

Leary, M.R., and R.S. Miller. *Social Psychology and Dysfunctional Behavior: Origins, Diagnosis, and Treatment*. New York: Springer-Verlag, 1986.

Leitenberg, H., and L. Slavin. Comparison of Attitudes toward Transsexuality and Homosexuality. *Archives of Sexual Behavior*, Vol. 12 (1983), pp. 337–46.

Leong, F.T., and M.A. Poynter. The Representation of Counseling Versus Clinical Psychology in Introductory Text Books. *Teaching of Psychology*, Vol. 18 (1991), pp. 12–16.

Lewis, L.A. The Coming-Out Process for Lesbians: Integrating a Stable Identity. *Social Work*, Vol. 29 (1984), pp. 464–69.

Loiacano, D.K. Gay Identity Issues Among Black Americans: Racism, Homophobia, and the Need for Validation. *Journal of Counseling & Development*, Vol. 68 (1989), pp. 21–25.

Lowe, C.M. The Need of Counseling for a Social Frame of Reference. *Journal of Counseling Psychology*, Vol. 15 (1968), 485–91.

Martin, D.J. Human Immunodeficiency Virus Infection and the Gay Community: Counseling and Clinical Issues. *Journal of Counseling & Development*, Vol. 68 (1989), pp. 67–72.

Messina, J.J. The National Academy of Certified Clinical Mental Health Counselors: Creating a New Professional Identity. *Journal of Counseling & Development*, Vol. 63 (1985), pp. 607–08.

Mintz, L.B., and J.M. O'Neil. Gender Roles, Sex, and the Process of Psychotherapy: Many Questions and Few Answers. *Journal of Counseling & Development*, Vol. 68 (1990), pp. 381–87.

O'Neil, J.M., and M.R. Carroll. A Gender Role Workshop Focused on Sexism, Gender Role Conflict, and the Gender Role Journey. *Journal of Counseling & Development*, Vol. 67 (1988), pp. 193–97.

Patterson, C.H. What Is Counseling Psychology? *Journal of Counseling Psychology*, Vol. 16 (1969), pp. 23–29.

———. New Light for Counseling Theory. *Journal of Counseling & Development*, Vol. 63 (1985), pp. 349–50.

Rudolph, J. Counselors' Attitudes toward Homosexuality: A Selective Review of the Literature. *Journal of Counseling & Development*, Vol. 67 (1988), pp. 165–68.

Schacht, T.E. DSM-III and the Politics of Truth. *American Psychologist*, Vol. 40 (1985), pp. 513–21.

Sharma, A., and H.E. Cheatham. A Women's Center Support Group for Sexual Assault Victims. *Journal of Counseling & Development*, Vol. 64 (1986), pp. 525–27.

Spitzer, R.L. DSM-III and the Politics-Science Dichotomy Syndrome: A Response to Thomas E. Schacht's "DSM-III and the Politics of Truth." *American Psychologist*, Vol. 40 (1985), pp. 522–26.

Wagner, W.G. Child Sexual Abuse: A Multidisciplinary Approach to Case Management. *Journal of Counseling & Development*, Vol. 65 (1987), pp. 435–39.

Watkins, Jr., *et al.* Contemporary Counseling Psychology: Results of a National Survey. *Journal of Counseling Psychology*, Vol. 33 (1986), pp. 301–09.

Weinstein, E., and E. Rosen. *Sexuality Counseling: Issues and Implications.* Pacific Grove, Calif.: Brooks/Cole Publishing Co., 1988.

Robert A. Embree

COURTESANS

As in other professions, prostitution has its status hierarchies. In contemporary society, the common streetwalker and the high-priced call girl are both available—depending on the thickness of his wallet—to attend the biological urgencies of the male. In former times, prostitution was more stratified. In ancient Greece, there were three kinds of prostitutes: the brothel-based *pornae*, the prettier and more entertaining *auletrides* (roughly corresponding to current streetwalkers and call girls, respectively), and the exulted *hetaerae*. The wealthier and more refined Greeks disdained the first two types in favor of the *hetaerae,* who were high-class courtesans. Thus, courtesans are prostitutes with a courtly, wealthy, or upper-class clientele.

Courtesans in ancient Greece were prized not only for their sexual expertise but also for their intellectual stimulation; the wealthier Greeks liked their lust spiced with literature and philosophy.

In ancient India, too, the *devadasis* (servants of the Gods) provided cultured conversation along with other services as temple prostitutes. Their singing, dancing, and other diverse entertainment skills marked them as courtesans and distinguished them from the common harlots of the street. Although their services were provided for all who could pay, their primary customers were the Brahmans, the highest members of the Hindu caste system.

Perhaps the most famous courtesans of all are the *geisha* (person of artistic performance) of Japan. Unlike the *hetaerae* of Greece, who were women of high birth who had fallen on hard times, the *geisha* usually came from impoverished homes and were apprenticed out by their parents. They were rigorously trained in conversation, singing, dancing, the tea ceremony, as well as in the more esoteric of the erotic arts.

Courtesans were not limited to the Eastern world; they also existed in Europe, particularly in Renaissance Italy. Although no rigorous training in the intellectual and musical arts was required of the Italian courtesans in the manner of the *geisha*, the best of them were almost certainly so versed. Probably the height of the courtesan phenomenon was the 19th century in Europe and America when many women used their ability to please men to rise to roles of power and influence.

REFERENCES

Bullough, V., and B. Bullough. *Women and Prostitution: A Social History.* Buffalo, N.Y.: Prometheus Books, 1987.

Lawner, L. An English Writer Views the Venetian Courtesan. In *Lives of the Courtesans.* New York: Rizzoli, 1987.

Anthony Walsh

COURTSHIP

Courtship refers to everything that passes between two people as they become sexually and emotionally interested in each other, and as they become sexually intimate with each other. Sometimes, people say "courtship" when they mean "making plans to get married," but courtship includes much more than either seduction or becoming engaged to marry. It has psychological, emotional, symbolic, religious, and even body-language aspects that involve each person deeply and fully. What passes between the two people during courtship—in the broad sense just defined—can sometimes lead to serious miscommunication and even serious problems, such as date rape.

Heterosexual courtship that leads to marriage has played a large role historically in many people's lives, and they often think that courtship simply means falling in love. But courtship involves more than love rituals, because to be successful, courtship must create deep mutual understanding and agreement of a kind that almost never occurs in any other sort of relationship. So courtship includes everything that passes between the two people, not merely their holding hands in the rain, glancing across a crowded room, or even deciding to share a bank account. It also involves more than happiness, because the courting pair must make decisions that sometimes are difficult—for example, decisions about giving up the pleasures of single life for a life of committed responsibility with another person.

Because courtship is so complex, and because the emotions of joining together with another person are multicolored, many—perhaps most—people feel that it cannot be studied by scientists and scholars. But that is not true. Courtship has many surprises, and no individual can judge the full range of what passes between two people just on the basis of that individual's own personal experiences. Scholars can bring to understanding courtship a wider range of knowledge and sympathy than the layperson may have and can offer insights based on the lives of many other people, from other places, times, and cultures. The following description addresses primarily adult heterosexual courtship. Similar patterns appear in gay couples, but gay courtship has not been so well researched, nor has courtship among teenagers, such as high school students.

In America, and probably elsewhere, courtship depends on women's active engagement in seeking partners and in communicating their interest to them. In research done in the United States and Canada, Perper and Weis found striking similarities in women's courtship plans and strategies and called women's active communication of interest "proceptivity." They defined proceptivity to mean "any behavior pattern a woman employs to express interest in a man, to arouse him sexually, or to maintain her sociosexual interaction with him." This involves her choice of dress and clothing, invitations by her to private or secluded places, establishment of a romantic mood by music and dancing, talking in sexy and romantic ways, smiling, laughing, making eye contact, and, of course, touching and kissing.

Many people know that women can sometimes be seductive, but the important point of speaking of proceptivity is to stress that such strategies are not recipes for random promiscuity or a checklist of things to do to find the perfect man. Instead, women often thoroughly understand their own and the man's reactions to entering into sexual intimacy, and they can describe not only what the woman does but also how the man responds, as well as what it means emotionally when he responds—or does not respond—in a certain way. By contrast, many men are unable or unwilling to explain such things and focus instead on sexual intimacy itself. It is a kind of romantic division of labor, with women initiating the interaction proceptively, and men responding sexually.

This finding is one of the surprises about courtship because there is a common belief that men, not women, are the sexual initiators and that women are usually sexually reluctant and hesitant. Sometimes, of course, women are reluctant and men are eager. That happens most often if the woman is not sure of her own feelings and does not fully understand or trust the man's motivations: are they purely sexual, or is he offering love and a relationship? Under those circumstances, many women adopt a wait-and-see policy; a woman will date the man but forestall his efforts towards sexual intimacy until she knows

him, and his motivations, much better. If the woman is sure she likes and wants the man, however, she can be quite direct in letting him know, using many of the strategies previously mentioned.

Some women know they want nothing to do with a man who has just introduced himself. Many women are reluctant to be impolite, and they may talk distantly to the man and avoid sending signals to him, while ignoring whatever signals he sends. Other women may forthrightly tell him they are not interested in him and cut the conversation short.

So there is a spectrum of women's behavior and feeling during a courtship interaction. At one end of the spectrum, she knows she likes him and sends direct, sexy signals, such as wearing enticing clothing, touching him, smiling, and talking about how interesting he is. In the middle ground, the same woman may feel uncertain about a man, holding him off sexually while dating him a few times to test the waters. At the other end of the spectrum, the woman may find a man uninteresting and maybe even obnoxious, and try to send clear, if polite, signals that she is not interested at all.

What about the man? For many men, opening what might possibly be a sexual relationship with a woman is emotionally trying and difficult. Men often speak of "getting shot down" by a woman they liked or found interesting, and after a while many men develop defenses against showing exactly how interested they are. If the woman says she is not interested in sex but is willing to date—the middle ground mentioned above—he may decide that she means no sex at all under any foreseeable circumstances and become emotionally distant with her. Then she will probably decide that he does not like her, and the courtship will fail. Other men feel more or less angry at women in general for previous rejections and express hostile contempt for women. They, too, guarantee failure for themselves. Other men will continue to press the woman for sex, even after she has politely declined the offer. Then the two people may become very angry with each other and exchange insults and accusations. Still other men become awkward and shy, finding themselves unable to behave naturally with the woman and creating an unpleasant, artificial ambience for a date. But other men will find the woman's behavior exactly to his liking, and his and her feelings and behavior mesh.

When that happens, many people say "the chemistry was right" or "it was just electric." Popular magazines and books have been written about such "chemistry," but here the scholar can make a useful contribution to understanding what is really going on. Is it just chemistry—"that ole black magic," as the song goes—or are there patterns and sense in an interaction that succeeds?

It turns out that there are patterns, and both men and women would be greatly helped to understand each other if they accepted that courtship involves a sequence of events, emerging from their interaction itself rather than being foreordained by the stars, or by good chemistry, or by other mysterious forces and processes. And here, based on several thousand hours of observation, is an outline of that pattern.

Often, men and women communicate interest for the first time by eye contact. One woman said, "A held glance says, 'Hey, I like you.'" And she is right. Of course, sometimes a held glance becomes a stare, which many women find extremely unpleasant, especially if the man eyes her body up and down. Such looks are often the best way not to start a relationship. But even so, when it occurs, that held glance can be very powerful indeed, because it is forthright on both sides.

Usually, that held glance is followed by an "approach"—which means that one person, often the woman, moves physically closer to the other person. For many people, this easy-sounding step is one of the hardest of all. One man said that walking over to a woman is like climbing Mt. Everest: he meant that all his buddies were watching him and waiting for him to get shot down. The woman being approached is also watching the man, if only out of the corner of her eye. It is very difficult for the man to tell if she is thinking "Who is this bozo and how do I get rid of him" or "Here comes this cute guy." The man's life is made easier if the woman approaches him, and many women do, but then the woman may feel the same shyness and uncertainty that he feels approaching a woman.

The reason for stressing the approach as the first overt stage of courtship is that many people firmly believe that it all starts with the "opening line," usually something the man says that he thinks is clever, interesting, funny, or otherwise attractive to the woman. But by the time he has walked all the way over to her, she has had a while to make an initial judgment about him—usually based on his looks, dress, and how he carries himself. If she has decided that he is a sloppy-looking drunk, it does not matter at all what his opening line is, and his line may make things much worse—she may well tell him she is not interested. However, if she thinks he is prob-

ably all right, she will likely respond pleasantly to him regardless of what his opening line is.

Assuming she does think he is potentially acceptable in looks, manners, and bearing yet she may still be quickly turned off by at least some lines men report using. Sure-fire dead-end lines include insults—"Hey, when did they let you out?"—and efforts to be crude but funny, such as "I bet I can drink you under the table" or "How's your sex life, gorgeous?" The best lines, as described by women, include simple self-introductions, requests by the man to join the woman talking, and comments on the surrounding setting. These are social, friendly, and nonthreatening, and communicate the message that the man is nice and not a foolish buffoon, nerd, or creep.

The approach and the opening of a conversation illustrate an important point. These interactions proceed stepwise, by little increments, not by sudden leaps to sexual intimacy. Each step involves each person testing the other's interests and attractiveness, often in subtle and complex ways. And whenever one person makes an overture that would increase their intimacy, it is the other person who decides to accept or reject that small overture. This last principle is called "escalation." It means that the man who approached the woman escalated their interaction, because she, not he, will determine what happens next. Throughout the entire sequence, the same principle holds: the person who sends the signal does not determine how it is received.

So, imagine that the woman and the man have started talking, each having passed initial muster in the other's eyes. She says something that genuinely interests him, and he smiles and turns a bit to face her as he answers. He has escalated their interaction by turning, whether or not he knows it or intends it. The reason is that now she, not he, determines what happens next. If she likes him, somewhat or a bit, she will find his turning acceptable—it signals his attentive interest in her. So she responds by turning a bit to face him. The escalation has been accepted. But if she is getting bored by him, she might not want to continue talking, and as a result she does not turn toward him. She is rejecting his interest.

The partner whose overture has been rejected has very little recourse but to back down. The man cannot reach out and forcibly turn her body toward him, and if he does, she will be quick to tell him to stop and perhaps even call for help. Many women are extremely sensitive today to men who push their attentions on them, and may express clear dislike and contempt.

But let us assume that she finds his increased interest acceptable and nice. So she turns further to face him, and then he turns more toward her, until, after a while, they are fully facing each other. By this time, they are also probably maintaining eye contact, smiling, talking enthusiastically, gesticulating, and feeling good about each other. As they do so, probably the most crucial step in the entire process may now occur: the first time one of them touches the other.

When women touch men in this manner, they touch lightly, even fleetingly. She might reach out a hand and touch his arm while saying something like "Yes, that's interesting." Such touches are not grabs, caresses, fondles, or even overtly sexual. Nonetheless, they communicate a powerful message.

If the two people are genuinely communicating, the message is one of warmth and continued, growing interest. From there, the interaction is likely to proceed to what is called "body-movement synchronization," not a euphemism for sexual intercourse but a pattern of movement in which each person spontaneously mirrors the movements of the other person. Thus, they each reach for their drinks, lift them, sip, and replace them on the table, as if a mirror had been placed between them. Few people seem to notice synchronization, because emotionally it represents their fascination with each other and not with details of body language.

However, all too often men fail to understand the message the woman intends when she touches him, smiles at him, or even is willing to talk to him in the first place. Many men, if not all, believe—because they want to believe it—that the woman's signals, such as her touching him, mean "I want to have sex with you." Very rarely is that what the woman means. Instead, she is saying, using body language, that "I want to get to know you better." A man who wants sex, and nothing but sex, can ruin whatever chances he might have had by touching the woman too soon, too intimately, and too frequently. She will very possibly be repelled, and not at all attracted, by such a man.

A particularly bad example of such touching occurs when the man, perhaps a bit drunk, suddenly puts his arms around the woman and starts kissing her. In her eyes, she has sent no signals whatsoever that would explain or elicit his sudden sexual attack. So she feels that he is about to rape her—and she is frightened and angry. But, because he has not been paying attention to her signals—perhaps he feels that men make the first move and that all a man has to do is to get the woman alone and then arouse her—he feels that

she has suddenly turned on him and is now falsely "crying rape." He might defend himself, perhaps later to a police officer, by saying that she agreed to be alone with him, and that that "meant" she wanted to have intercourse with him. But that is false—she may have initially felt quite safe with him, until suddenly he attacked her sexually.

In this interaction, what actually went wrong? Society all too easily blames the woman, saying that she should have stopped the man earlier, but that is unfair to the woman. Earlier she may have liked him, and not at all been able to foretell that he was going to attack her. But there is one thing she could have done that might have forestalled such an attack, and that is to explain to him, in simple words, that she does not have sex with men until she knows them well. Then he has no excuse at all if he does attack her.

But, in reality, the man is much more to blame in situations like these. He, not she, was out of control, unable to regulate his own sexual urges according to social principles and good manners, to say nothing of respect for her. Unable to face her rejection—or what seems to him to be a rejection—he is then unable to behave like a grown, mature man, who may smile ruefully, perhaps, but still is able to take no for an answer.

REFERENCES

Perper, T. *Sex Signals: The Biology of Love.* Philadelphia: ISI Press, 1985.
Perper, T., and D. Weis. Proceptive and Rejective Strategies of U.S. and Canadian College Women. *Journal of Sex Research,* Vol. 23 (1987), pp. 455–480.

Timothy Perper

COUVADE

Couvade, or couvade syndrome (CS), when translated literally from French, means "to brood, or to hatch." It is used to describe symptoms of pregnancy in expectant fathers. In recent years, the term has been extended to apply to symptoms manifested by lovers of a pregnant female. CS has been documented in most Western societies; in the United States the reported incidence ranges from 22 percent to 79 percent. In some nontechnological cultures, couvade has been documented as well, with the male ritualistically imitating the pregnancy and delivery of his wife in order to draw evil spirits away from her.

According to Broude, it is important to view the couvade as a set of practices embedded in a larger cultural context rather than as a custom affecting only the behavior of the fathers. There is a tendency for the custom associated with the couvade to apply to other family members as well as to the father. For example, the family's children as well as the father of the Chiriguanoa Indians of Paraguay lie-in and fast at the birth of a new child.

Physical manifestations attributed to CS include a wide spectrum of discomforts, some that are remarkably similar to those experienced by pregnant women. Most are gastrointestinal symptoms (e.g., nausea, vomiting, heartburn, and constipation), abdominal swelling, unintentional weight gain or loss, appetite changes, and general feelings of ill health.

Physiological symptoms often linked to CS include restlessness, irritability, insomnia, generalized anxiety, depression, headache, and difficulty concentrating.

In Clinton's longitudinal study, symptoms of 86 expectant fathers were compared with those of a control group of 66 nonexpectant men. The expectant fathers suffered significantly more bouts of irritability and stomachaches during the first trimester. However, expectant fathers differed most from other men during the early postpartum period, with significantly more frequent and serious episodes of restlessness, insomnia, excessive fatigue, and difficulty concentrating. The most accurate predictors of CS were lower income, poor health status the year prior to the pregnancy, unplanned pregnancy, and high levels of stress during pregnancy.

Until the late 1960s, CS was regarded as primarily a neurotic phenomenon. Recently, it has been associated with developmental crisis theory. In a study, also by Clinton, it was found that previously healthy men developed numerous symptoms during the pregnancy of their wives, suggesting that the transition to fatherhood is a normal development stage accompanied by a certain amount of stress.

REFERENCES

Broude, G.J. Rethinking the Couvade: Cross-Cultural Evidence. *American Anthropologist*, Vol. 90, No. 4(12) (1988), pp. 902–911.

Clinton, J. The Couvade Syndrome. *Medical Aspects of Human Sexuality*, Vol. 21, No. 11 (1987), pp. 115, 132.

Francoeur, R., et al. *A Descriptive Dictionary and Atlas of Sexology.* Conn.: Greenwood Press, 1991.

Hope E. Ashby

CROSS-DRESSING

Cross-dressing is a simple term for a complex phenomenon. It ranges from wearing one or two items of clothing of the opposite sex to a full-scale burlesque, from a comic impersonation to a serious attempt to pass as the opposite gender, from an occasional desire to experiment with gender identity to an attempt to live full time as a member of the opposite sex. Researchers at the turn of the 20th century, most of them physicians or psychiatrists, tended to use a medical model that conceptualized variations from the norms of gender behavior as an illness. Such definitions were emphasized in an effort to uncover the causes of the "disease" or "problem" on the assumption that once they have been determined, steps could be taken to "cure" the patient or client.

One first step in this process was to name and label the phenomenon. The term "transvestism" (Latin for "cross-dressing") was coined by Hirschfeld in 1910. Ellis, his contemporary, felt that the term was much too literal and that it overemphasized the importance of clothing while failing to include the "feminine" identity factors present in male cross-dressers. More or less ignoring the possibility of female cross-dressers, Ellis coined the term "eonism" based on a historical personage, the Chevalier d'Eon de Beaumont (1728–1810), who spent much of his adult life living as a woman. Since that time other terms have been advanced, including "gynemimesis" (literally "woman mime") and its counterpart andromimesis, femme mimic, femmiphile, androphile, female or male impersonator, fetishistic transvestite, transgenderist, preoperative transsexual (to distinguish the person from a postoperative one), gender dysphoric, and many others. Most of these terms imply more than simple cross-dressing and are used to describe different levels or different points of view.

Historical Cross-Dressing

This entry uses the term "cross-dressing" in order to include all aspects of the behavior and to emphasize that gender-crossing has been a ubiquitous phenomenon which has existed since males and females adopted sex-differentiated clothing and symbols.

Mythology of most cultures includes instances of gods or goddesses impersonating the opposite sex and even of some actually changing their sex. Similarly, mortals had their sex changed by the gods or for some reason impersonated the opposite sex. Many societies have institutionalized a supernumerary gender or third sex to allow certain people to live outside the gender norms of the culture. In scholarly literature, this role traditionally has been described as the berdache one, but in recent years the term berdache has been restricted to men crossing the gender boundary and the term "amazon" has been used to describe women who performed as men. Such crossing over not only existed in tribal societies but also in sophisticated religions such as Hinduism, where a special class of males, the *hijras*, live as women. Classical Greek culture, while not institutionalizing a permanent role for cross-dressing, did so on a temporary basis at festivals and ceremonies and some of this continued into Roman society.

Cross-dressing was common among early fertility cults, and it was probably to distinguish their believers from these "pagan" cults that the early Hebrews prohibited men from wearing "that which pertaineth to a woman" and women from "that which pertaineth to men" (Deuteronomy 22:5). Such a prohibition, however, was never entirely enforced and in fact there are records of Jewish soldiers adopting women's dress as a disguise during military operations. The Talmud specifically encourages women who are going on a journey among potentially unfriendly peoples to disguise themselves as men. Similarly, men disguised themselves as women at the feast of Purim and the practice of cross-dressing was sanctioned at wedding feasts and celebrations. Though the Christian Bible included the prohibition against cross-dressing, it continued to exist during such occasions as Halloween and festivals such as Mardi Gras.

Generally, it was more permissible for females to cross-dress and impersonate males than vice versa. This was because being male and masculine implied a much higher status in society than being female and feminine. Women in effect gained status by cross-dressing and impersonating males while men who cross-dressed lost status. One of the more fascinating aspects of the history of cross-dressing is the large number of Christian female saints who were thought to be men when they were alive, for example St. Pelagia (also known as Margarite). In fact, it was their successful denial of what society assumed to be feminine weakness and their ability to live as men that led to their sainthood when their true sex was discovered at their death.

Historically, in Western culture, many women are known to have lived and worked as men, literally thousands of them, while, until the 20th century, only a handful of men are known to have lived the role of women full time. A major motivation for the crossover was the restrictions society imposed on women. Women living and

working as men had greater freedom of action. Moreover, society in general was very understanding of such women when they were unmasked.

Because women's role was so restricted, however, it allowed for female impersonation in areas where women were not permitted. Women, perhaps because the medieval theater developed in the church and around the altar, were excluded from the stage and males played female roles. These men were not stigmatized for acting in these roles. In the West, it was usually the apprentice actors who played the female roles but by the time of Shakespeare some continued to play such roles. In Japan and China, female impersonation on stage became a life-time occupation and in Japan has been kept alive in the Kabuki theater. In England, it was not until the end of the 17th century that women appeared on stage in their own right. Males even sang the female roles in opera and to enable them to do so as adults, many underwent castration. The *castrati* remained dominant in opera almost up to the 19th century.

Some of those who cross-dressed were homosexual or lesbian but many of those for whom detailed information exists were not. The primary interest of many of the female cross-dressers was in the greater opportunity and freedom afforded by the male lifestyle.

One of the most detailed accounts of female impersonation is that of the Abbé de Choisy (1614–1713), whose memoirs of his cross-dressing experiences have survived. His fellow cross-dresser, Philippe d'Orléans, brother of King Louis XIV, was homosexual. In the 18th century in London there were special clubs for male cross-dressers, which were also centers of homosexuality.

It was Hirschfeld who emphasized that cross-dressing was more complicated than had been assumed and that there were men who really wanted to express a feminine side and women to express a masculine side by their cross-dressing, and that the cross-dresser could be homosexual, bisexual, heterosexual, or sex neutral.

Development of the Medical Model to Explain Transvestism

Neither Hirschfeld's nor Ellis's studies were widely accepted by the professional medical community. Instead, the developing field of psychoanalysis adopted a medical model to label certain cross-dressers as transvestites and to explain transvestism as a type of fetishism. The link to fetishism occurred because many of the cross-dressers seen by the doctors seemed to be fixated on items of clothing. The medical community attributed the condition to castration anxiety in men and penis envy in women. Later, in the mid-20th century, the psychoanalytic writers argued that the condition stemmed from an overly protective mother and an absent father. Since these were also the explanations for homosexuality at that time, the two conditions were often linked in both the public and medical mind.

Current Patterns of Cross-Dressing

Starting in the late 19th century the pattern of cross-dressing changed, with fewer women changing their sex roles and more men periodically cross-dressing for erotic pleasure. Presently, there is a disproportionate number of men compared with women involved, a quite different situation from the past. This has led to speculation that for many men the feminine role is much more attractive than it once was, and the masculine role is less attractive to women than it once was.

Several factors served to renew public attention to cross-dressing in the 1950s and 1960s. One was the massive publicity given to the Christine Jorgensen case, the American who in 1953 underwent castration and penectomy in Denmark and officially had his sex altered on his passport from male to female. Though the operating surgeon, C. Hamburger, and his colleagues originally called Jorgensen a transvestite, the case led to widespread discussion and ultimately a distinction between transvestism and transsexualism. Benjamin developed a three-point scale of transvestism, with transsexualism being considered an extreme form of transvestism, although he later came to regard it as a different entity.

Further emphasizing the difference were the activities of Virginia Prince, a Los Angeles transvestite, who beginning in the 1960s published a magazine devoted to the heterosexual transvestite. Prince was disdainful of cross-dressers who allowed themselves to be "mutilated" by surgery. Encouraged by readers of the publication *Transvestia*, Prince established a "sorority" with chapters in various major cities, emphasizing the heterosexuality of transvestism and the importance of allowing the "girl within" to appear. Prince began to live full time as a woman, and decided to devote more or less full time to spreading her ideas of transvestism and establishing a movement. She traveled worldwide, giving interviews, appearing on television, and attracting thousands of followers. One result was a surge in research into the topic, since there were cross-dressers available for research projects who had not come from a psychiatrist's office. As the movement spread and grew, dissident voices also appeared, and Prince, who is still alive at this writing, gradually stepped down from leadership, and a number of different publications and movements emerged. As of 1992, there are cross-dressing groups that emphasize heterosexuality, homosexuality, and bisexuality. Some include transsexuals, others do not, and there is a small industry that fulfills the clothing and other needs of the male transvestite. Some individuals live full time in the opposite gender role, others dress only occasionally and partially; there is also a whole range in between.

Presently, female cross-dressers are less numerous and less noticeable than male cross-dressers, partly because women are generally allowed more deviations in dress before they are noticed and labeled as cross-dressers. The current generation of female cross-dressers is primarily lesbian, although there are a few who focus their erotic attention on their dress rather than on their sex partner, which tends to be the case with male transvestites. The late Lou Sullivan, who edited the newsletter *FTM* for female-to-male cross-dressers and transsexuals, argued that many of his readers were simply women who cross-dressed and did not want surgery. He held that the literature of transvestism was simply biased in not including more about women cross-dressers.

Research About Cross-Dressing

Researchers are not agreed on the factors involved in cross-dressing but increasingly recognize that some of it is normative and that there is a basic curiosity about the opposite gender and the clothes and ornamentation associated with it. In some people, the curiosity goes deeper, and it probably has biological as well as social-psychological causes. While no particular biogenic cause for cross-gender behavior has been isolated, research suggests that this may happen in the future. That factor may be common for other related behaviors, such as homosexuality. (In many societies, men who demonstrate a desire for the feminine and who cross-dress are simply labeled as homosexuals. In many of these societies, the cross-dressing homosexual is the receptor rather than the penetrator in intercourse, and in fact the penetrator himself is not labeled as homosexual.)

There are also social factors involved. The heterosexual cross-dresser as an adolescent is able to display a more masculine side to his companions and to keep his cross-dressing secret from them. Studies have indicated that these young men, at least those who end up in the transvestite clubs, were well integrated into the male society of their age group at least superficially.

Most of heterosexual cross-dressers emphasize that they began cross-dressing early, and certainly by their teens. It was also associated with experiencing an erection and masturbation or a spontaneous ejaculation. Cross-dressing is also exhilarating for many because it is forbidden and the dangers associated with being caught and exposed add to the sexual excitement.

There are, however, many forms of cross-dressing, and any attempt to give a simple explanation is doomed to failure. Some of those who cross-dress were kept in clothes of the opposite sex as children or forced to don such clothes as punishment. Recent research, however, has tended to emphasize that something more than simple conditioning must take place to establish a pattern of cross-dressing.

Various studies on the organized transvestite groups indicate that most transvestites were married at some time in their life and two thirds or more were at the time they were studied. In a detailed study of occupations based on a scale of occupational prestige, the occupational level of the transvestite group was higher than the norms for the total American population. Studies done in the 1970s and early 1980s indicate that the majority of the men considered themselves heterosexual, although later studies have modified this somewhat as the club movement has broadened. Other studies report that many transvestites are heterosexual when they are not cross-dressed but prefer male sex partners when they are dressed as women.

As transvestites age, their reasons for cross-dressing change, and if they had fetishistic urges earlier, they have less of this drive later. One researcher reported that many of the older transvestites in his study cross-dress in order to temporarily escape the pressure of being masculine rather than for any erotic experience. It is only in the feminine role that they are able to give release to emotions that society has labeled as feminine.

Various researchers have developed classification schemes to categorize cross-dressers. Most of the schemes try to account for three variables: (1) the extent of the cross-gender orientation, (2) the degree to which there is erotic arousal with cross-dressing, and (3) sexual orientation toward the same or opposite sex. It is clear that there is significant variation on all of these parameters.

It seems clear that the current understanding of cross-dressing is changing. As cross-dressers come out of the closet and become more vocal, appear on television, or have their stories appear in the local newspapers, the numbers of cross-dressers seem to increase. It might well be that the understanding of the phenomenon is where the study of homosexuality was in the 1960s, when homosexuality was still mainly an underground movement. Once homosexuality was removed from the category of a pathology in the American Psychiatric Association's *Diagnostic and Statistical Manual*, it came to be seen as an alternative form of sexual activity. Though it was recognized that some people had psychological problems because they could not accept their homosexuality, basic homosexuality became one of the potential variants in human sexuality instead of a diagnosis. Similarly, cross-dressing may come to be thought of as a pattern of behavior that does not need a diagnostic label.

In spite of these hopeful assumptions, there are still cross-dressers who want and need professional help. Probably the best thing a therapist can do is to help the client come to terms with himself or herself. If the cross-dresser is a married man, as is often the case, the therapist is often called on to give help and support to the family. Many wives see cross-dressing as a threat to their own feminine image and regard themselves as failures as wives. They are also fearful of exposure and of the effect on children. Certainly cross-dressers who are married and want to remain married have to work out agreements with their spouses on the limits of their cross-dressing activities. Often these are problems that can be worked out only with the help of a neutral third party, such as a therapist.

REFERENCES

American Psychiatric Association. *Diagnostic and Statistical Manual of Mental Disorders.* Third Edition Revised: DSM-III-R. Washington, D.C.: American Psychiatric Association, 1987.

Benjamin, H. *The Transsexual Phenomenon.* New York: Julian Press, 1966.

Buhrich, N., and N. McConaghy. Parental Relationships During Childhood in Homosexuality, Transvestism and Transsexualism. *Australian and New Zealand Journal of Psychiatry,* Vol. 12 (1978), pp. 103–108.

Buhrich, N., and T. Beaumont. Comparison of Transvestism in Australia and America. *Archives of Sexual Behavior,* Vol. 10 (1981), pp. 269–79.

Buhrich, N., and N. McConaghy. Three Clinically Discrete Categories of Fetishistic Transvestism. *Archives of Sexual Behavior,* Vol. 14 (1985), pp. 413–19.

Bullough, V. L., and B. Bullough. *Cross Dressing, Sex, and Gender*. Philadelphia: Pennsylvania Univ. Press, 1992.

Bullough, V. L., B. Bullough, and R. Smith. Childhood and Family of Male Sexual Minority Groups. *Health Values: Achieving High Level Wellness*, Vol. 7 (July/August, 1983), pp. 19–26.

———. A Comparative Study of Male Transvestites, Male to Female Transsexuals and Male Homosexuals. *Journal of Sex Research*, Vol. 19 (August, 1983), pp. 238–57.

———. Masculinity and Femininity in Transvestites, Transsexual, and Gay Males. *Western Journal of Nursing Research*, Vol. 7 (1985), pp. 317–22.

Bullough, V. L., and T. S. Weinberg. Women Married to Transvestites: Problems and Adjustment. *Journal of Psychology and Human Sexuality*, Vol. 1 (1988), pp. 83–104.

Docter, R.F. *Transvestites and Transsexuals*. New York: Plenum Press, 1988.

Ellis, H. *Eonism and Other Supplementary Studies*. Vol. 6 in *Studies in the Psychology of Sex*. Philadelphia: F.A. Davis, 1926.

Hamburger, C., G.K. Sturup, and H.E. Dahl-Iversen. Transvestism: Hormonal, Psychiatric, and Surgical Treatment. *Journal of American Medicine*, Vol. 152 (May 30, 1953), p. 396.

Hirschfeld, M. *The Transvestites: The Erotic Drive to Cross Dress*. M.A. Lombardi-Nash, trans. New York: Prometheus Books, 1991.

Prince, V., and P.M. Bentler. Survey of 504 Cases of Transvestism. *Psychological Reports*, Vol. 31 (1972), pp. 903–17.

Stoller, R.J. *Sex and Gender: On the Development of Masculinity and Femininity*. London: Hogarth Press, 1968.

Weinberg, T.S., and V.L. Bullough. Alienation, Self Image, and the Importance of Support Groups for the Wives of Transvestites. *Journal of Sex Research*, Vol. 24 (1988), pp. 262–68.

Whitam, F.D. A Cross-Cultural Perspective on Homosexuality, Transvestism, and Trans-sexualism. In G.D. Wilson, ed., *Variant Sexuality: Research and Theory*. London: Croom Helm, 1987.

Vern L. Bullough
Bonnie Bullough

d

DANCE AND SEXUALITY

Dance is a body art. The vehicle, instrument, and implicit subject of dance is the body. The body is also where sensual, sexual, and gender distinctions originate. Our embodied identity and that identity's attendant questions are intimately presented and explored in the art of dance.

The prominence of sexuality in dance depends on the form of dance one considers, the point of view one takes as either participant or viewer, and the historical period or the culture one examines. Sexuality may be seen as the wellspring of our creative, life-producing energy eros. The goal of eros is life, creativity, power, nurturing, abundance, and health. The eminent dance historian Curt Sachs said, "Every dance is and gives ecstasy." Ecstasy, from the Greek *ekstasis* (i.e., to stand outside oneself) is associated with the attempt to dance into a trance or a frenzy, to dance into intoxicated abandonment, to dance until one is spent, until one drops. Dance and sexuality may both be seen as metaphors, whether sublimated or overt, for each other as each moves toward culmination or climax in ecstasy. Sexuality, spirituality, sensuality, even rationality are salient features in many forms of dance, but sexuality "can never really be extricated from dance, since the sex act itself may be considered as the ultimate form of dance."

The form of dance and the specific dance type are relevant to the degree of sexual expression. Generally accepted categories of dance include folk, ethnic, social, and theatrical dance. Within these broad delineations, dances exist that feature or embody sexuality to lesser or greater degrees.

Historical Forms of Dance

Dance and the other arts in so-called primitive cultures most often served utilitarian purposes and were directly involved in daily life activities (e.g., hunting, war, entertainment, worship, healing, courtship or mating, and sexuality). Sex is closely correlated with primitive human fertility dances, drawn from two different phases of sexual activity: the meeting and wooing, and the act itself. The sex act is not completed at the place of dancing, although overt sexuality can include focusing on the pelvis or spine, breasts, and hips; portraying in a fantastic manner the act while wearing large phalli; dancing around someone of the opposite sex with the unmistakable positions and gestures of the act itself; disrobing within a dance; swinging grass skirts and lifting the skirt. Other erotic motifs are the group circle dances and dances around a pole or a tree (e.g., the famous Maypole dance). Fertility dances associated with planting, food, or procreation are functional activities in primitive societies, not allegorical portrayals. Primitive dances also accompany rituals of circumcision, puberty, first menstruation, marriage, and mating.

Dance in ancient Egypt, Greece, and Rome used sexual themes and ideas. Dances at various periods in antiquity were used partly as a form of entertainment and display by females (or young males) for the pleasure of males. References and descriptions from the Bible as well as from the epic poems of the *Iliad* and *Odyssey* describe young men and maidens dancing. Fertility rites offered to Dionysus, the Greek god of vitality, fertility, rebirth, ecstasy, and wine, with the mythological satyr companions, were significant parts of the early history of dance and theater. Indeed, the early unrestrained, orgiastic celebrations of Dionysus gradually moderated and evolved into a loosely organized dance ritual known as the Dithrambic Chorus, which further evolved into the formalized Classical Greek Theatre. Over many hundreds of years, the ancient Greeks changed the early ecstatic, orgiastic dance celebration into a more civilized practice within the new conventions of the theater and their interest in the rational and aesthetic nature of mankind which allowed the concept of sexuality and beauty to unfold within an aesthetic perspective. Whereas the Greeks idolized the body as well as the intellect, by the time the Roman Empire was at its zenith, dance had been reduced to mainly bawdy entertainment and spectacle. The artistic, intellectual, and religious sides were neglected while the display of females and young males for the pleasure of males continued to be the most marked feature of performed dance.

The early church fathers approved of dance in religious rituals, but the medieval church eschewed everything Greco-Roman, including the view of the body and human sexuality, and attempted to prohibit dancing altogether. A thousand years later, again propelled by a religious point of view, Calvinism reclaimed an official disapproval of earthly, bodily pleasures and proclaimed dancing as a contradiction to the right way of worship. Peasant dances, which acknowledge and celebrate life and its sexual aspects, lived on.

The physically abundant dances of many ethnic groups in Western cultures were adapted for the court dancing of the Renaissance and eventually formed the movement vocabulary of the art of ballet. European courts, with an emphasis on the semblance of decorum, public image, and an ordered political state, sublimated the erotic domain of the interior muscles of the pelvis and torso and shifted attention in the court dance to peripheral movement of the limbs and the choreography of figured floor patterns. Torso and pelvic movements were constrained, and movement was hidden by the structure, design, and weight of the costumes of the day. Though sexuality was sublimated in the court dances and early ballet, sexual energy and intrigue often provided the substrate for many of the movements and scenarios of the developing ballet arts.

During the latter part of the 18th century, social or ballroom dance (which, like ballet, also emanated from folk or peasant dance) had become a popular recreation for the growing mercantile classes. Motifs of polite courtship were readily accepted, but motions and positions that harkened away from the semblance of aristocratic demeanor toward more primitive expressions of dance sexuality seemed to threaten this social order. These unstately developments in social dance from the preclassical era until recent times have ranged from changing attitudes toward facing, touching, and lifting one's partner to orgiastic spinning, pressing together of torsos, smooth embraces, and the bumping of hips. Sexual attitudes of all eras can be studied through the developments in social and ballroom dance, since movement practices encode cultural knowledge.

Gender has always played an important role in dance. By the end of the 17th century, ballet became a profession. Its earliest stars were women, who shared the stage with men. By the middle of the 19th century, the idolized female of the romantic male imagination became so prevalent in the ballet arts that serious participation of males dwindled significantly. Women became the stars, while men were the directors and choreographers who placed their idealized vision of woman on the pedestal of her pointes where she required a man's support and direction. Whereas ballet had, for three centuries in the cast of the European courts, reflected a patriarchy in which both genders participated, ballet theater became, as in ancient Roman diversions, a place for males to watch female display. Males were the choreographers indulging a romantic mystique through the ballet's scenarios and movements. Public theaters and even the Paris Opera, for example, became havens for the mistresses of wealthy men.

The rising line of female dancers' skirts is a theme that follows the improvement of female technique throughout the romantic era. One aspect regards the need for audiences to see the ballerina's limbs as pointe work and quick movements of the legs became the mode. But there is no doubt that the male audience enthusiastically perceived this art of limbs with a licentious bent. Nineteenth-century America, imitating the European ballet, was a home for "leg" shows, such as the extravaganza "The Black Crook," which featured rather perfunctory movement arrangements and surreptitiously starred women's limbs. In America and England, females often took male roles where tights could disclose a fuller line of the leg for the pleasure of male audiences.

The art dance of the 20th century began with the ideals of such pioneers as Isadora Duncan, who turned toward more feminine, body-oriented, matriarchal sensibilities. These body-oriented philosophies came in part through the work of Françoise Delsarte, who emphasized the intellectual, emotional and spiritual, and physical planes of the body. The lower trunk and legs were the physical plane.

Ted Shawn, noted as the "father of modern dance," credited Delsarte as being the first to reveal that tension and relaxation or contraction and release are the foundation for all movement and, therefore, all dance. Delsartian philosophy rejected the predominantly patriarchal, rational, and idealized animus of the ballet world and encouraged the outward expression of anima and eros as a part of the aesthetic of dance.

The word "dance" may be traced etymologically through the Germanic *tanz* to the original sanskrit *tan*. The tension/release concept is intrinsic in the original Sanskrit, where *tan* means tension or stretching. Dance cannot exist without such muscular activity because muscle fibers have the ability only to either contract or to release from that contraction. One of the most striking aspects of sexual performance is the development of neuromuscular tensions throughout the body. If orgasm is regarded as the consummate release, the concept of tension and its ultimate release is a domain of the dance.

The technique of Martha Graham, stemming from visceral applications of tension and release, best illustrates the concept. Muscular control in the "contractions" of the Graham technique emanates from the pubo-coccygeal muscle, which forms the floor of the pelvis and which is penetrated by the rectum, birth canal, urethra, and ducts leading to the male prostate gland. Pelvic focus and sexuality are implicit for males and females in Graham technique.

Issues of Sexuality in Dance

Gender issues are still relevant in professional dance. The female "Dionysian" sensibilities of modern dance, with an emphasis on the creation of individual, authentic movement born of feel-

ing, contrast with those of the patriarchal, "Apollonian," worlds of ballet and tap dance, where typical "masculine" attributes of form, technique, strength, and the ability to realize complicated rhythmic patterns dominate. Male choreographers have controlled the professional worlds of ballet and entertainment tap dance, but even in the matriarchal-oriented world of modern dance, male choreographers have risen to prominence, particularly since the 1960s. Sexist environments in the top echelons of ballet, modern dance, and tap dance may dominate over biological factors.

Sexism is also at the root of female numerical dominance in the grass-roots dance world. One cause has been the prevalence of dance education within the world of women's physical education in the first two thirds of the 20th century. There is also a disproportionate number of female dance teachers and students at community dance studios and, somewhat less, in college situations. The distribution is more equal in conservatory training in America. The image communicated continually to the lay male world within sexist educational setups is that dance is an approved activity for females but not for males. The concept of dance and women as synonyms is institutionalized.

The proportionally large percentage of homosexuals in dance, particularly among males, raises questions regarding the nature of dance and some dancers' sexual orientation. While there is little doubt that stereotypical attitudes are fed by the numerous homosexual performers in dance (and in theater), it is doubtful that the sexuality inherent in dance causes homosexual expression. The questions surrounding homosexuality in dance and the performing arts deserve greater research.

Issues of sexuality within the male-female, teacher-student roles at all institutional levels in dance or sports include problems of touching, seeming intimacy, use of sexual descriptions, and understanding the boundaries of behavior. In directing dance and rehearsals, poetic statements, often based on sensual or sexual imagery, can elicit the "correct" movements by the dancers. The separation of the sexes as occurs in the learning of sports is neither warranted nor desirable in the learning of dance skills.

Although sexuality and the body must be integrated within the personae of the professional dancer, dancers tend to neutralize and sublimate their awareness of sexual implications involved in the experiences of touching, holding, and stroking others on stage, in class, or in rehearsals. The professional, nearly clinical, way that dancers customarily train to provide a dance experience for the audience demands that the unit of mind and body be an instrument for expression. Dance allows the awareness of sexuality as a form of sensuality. The sexual energy of the dancers is tapped as they move through the planned patterns set by a choreographer or by the dancers themselves through improvisation.

Gender stereotypes are changing in the latter part of the 20th century. Close proximity and levered lifts involving one or more dancers in ballet, contact improvisation, and the repertoire of certain contemporary companies challenge traditional gender roles. The assumptions based on gender—that males lift and support women, who are more flexible than they are and that males do not excel in adagio or precision work—is changing. Choreographers today still recognize common differences in body structure between males and females, but often break the stereotypes. Experiments by groups such as Pilobolus and Harry have extended the realm of accepted movement vocabularies for both male and female dancers.

The natural drive for sexuality might be what causes an audience to enjoy dance, perhaps by stimulating the viewer's subconscious both sensually and sexually. The dancer must also like displaying the body, must like the body (or want to like the body), and must show this delight. Dance that obviously looks as if it moves externally, with little stimulation from the "inside," seems dull, mechanical, and uninteresting save for the most visually stimulating theatrical devices, such as unique costuming or lighting. Though we have lost touch with our carnality, we can still engage in a vicarious thrill by watching the dancer, through physical feats or a clever movement aesthetic, build up to a climax of motion and bring us along. Some spectators can turn to dance to recover vicariously what their own bodies are not capable of doing.

In postmodern dance, the idea of the audience as gazer who looks at, consumes, or otherwise possesses the one being looked at has changed. Postmodern choreographers examined the similarities and differences between formal dance movement and the performance artifice and pedestrian movement presented as dance in venues other than the traditional stage. Dance was sometimes presented more as a shared communal activity in an attempt to subvert the traditional, patriarchal, male gaze, which distances, objectifies, and possesses the narcissistic, subservient performer.

Great works of Western, traditional performing art introduce the audience to a situation and its complexities. In doing so, the tension builds to a satisfactory climax followed by a resolution. This temporal metaphor for the tension and release of orgasm gives such works of art a metaphor for our overall sexuality as well as for our social, sexual, and gender power structures. Introduction, development, complication, and intensification are meant to lead to a resolution that was planned from the beginning by lover or artist. Some choreographers, such as Merce Cunningham, and many 20th century musical composers and playwrights, are either not interested in, or deliberately avoid, this Western historic time arrow of composition. Dance and the other time arts are driven by a dynamic urgency that shapes their temporal structures. One could say that this "telic" structure or flight of time relates to the way a choreographer controls "telos" or consummation, meaning completion of a cycle. Telos, then, can reflect any sexual activity dominated by a drive toward orgasm. In this model of dance and music, the climax results from the actions that lead up to it and that, conversely, give the climax its energy.

The viewpoint of sexuality in dance varies among dancers and dance watchers. For the dancer, it is altered by the level of commitment and the social or cultural context in which the dance is performed. The individual may be a professional trained by years of study or a recreational dancer whose training is derived from informal learning experiences. The dancer may perform on a stage or be part of a communal effort. Dance watchers are affected by their own individual or communal attitudes, which reflect their role or place in their culture, as well as prevailing societal norms regarding sex and sexuality. The way dance is used by performers and audiences reflects a culture's world view and is a barometer of societal attitudes toward sex, gender roles, and the body, as well as theater, education, and religion.

REFERENCES

Daly, A. Unlimited Partnership: Dance and Feminist Analysis. *Dance Research Journal*, Vol. 23, No. 1 (Spring, 1991), pp. 2–5.

Fraleigh, S.H. *Dance and the Lived Body: A Descriptive Aesthetics.* Pittsburgh, Penn.: Univ. of Pittsburgh Press, 1987.

Hanna, J.L. *Dance, Sex and Gender: Signs of Identity: Dominance, Defiance and Desire.* Chicago: Univ. of Chicago Press, 1988.

Kleinman, S., ed. *Sexuality and Dance* [National Association of Health, Physical Education, Recreation, and Dance]. Washington: Dance Publications Unit, 1980.

Kraus, R., and S.A. Chapman. *History of the Dance.* Englewood Cliffs, N.J.: Prentice-Hall, Inc., 1981.

Sachs, C. *World History of the Dance.* B. Shonberg, trans. New York: W.W. Norton & Co., Inc., 1937.

Myron Howard Nadel
Donald Kutschall

DATE RAPE; ACQUAINTANCE RAPE

The term "rape" generally refers to a situation in which a person uses physical force or the threat of such force to engage in some form of sex, usually intercourse. Legal definitions of rape vary from state to state. In addition to the force requirement, several states have broadened their definitions to include situations where the perpetrator gets the unwilling participant drunk or drugged, or where the victim is otherwise mentally unable to consent. Date rape is rape by someone the victim has been or is dating. Acquaintance rape is rape by someone the victim knows. The terms date rape and acquaintance rape technically have different meanings, but they are often used interchangeably. (See also Coercion.)

Although date and acquaintance rape have been common occurrences throughout history, only in the last couple of decades have the media and social scientists focused on issues related to these types of nonconsensual sexual interaction. Since the late 1960s, feminists have argued that rape is a major social problem. In addition to working for better treatment of rape survivors and reform of rape laws, the women's movement has challenged society's traditional views about both the definition and cause of rape.

The commonly accepted view had been that one could be raped only by a stranger and that a rapist typically used a weapon and either threatened to inflict or inflicted extensive physical injuries on a victim. The stereotypic rape involved a woman being surprised and attacked at night and then being forced to engage in sexual acts in a dark alley or behind bushes. Forced sex between acquaintances was usually not regarded as rape. Surveys of high school and college populations have shown that substantial proportions of these students do not define forced sex between acquaintances in a variety of situations as rape. For example, they partially justified a man forcing his date to have sex with him if she got him sexually excited, led him on, said she would have sex with him and then changed her mind, let him spend a lot of money on her, or had dated him a long time. Surveys of general adult popu-

lations indicated that certain categories of women were considered legitimate targets of sexual victimization. For example, if a woman was viewed as a "tease," "economic exploiter," or "loose," she was often considered a legitimate target for sexual exploitation. Women who were thought to be of "high moral character" and had "good reputations" were considered more credible victims of rape.

One goal of feminists and sex educators is to increase people's awareness of the seriousness of the rape problem and correct the many false beliefs about it. Recent studies have shown, for example, that acquaintance rape is far more prevalent than stranger rape and that rape by intimates is more prevalent than rape by nonromantic acquaintances. Studies also indicate that even though younger women are more likely to be victims of acquaintance rape, women of all ages and from all kinds of backgrounds are victims, and the experience is overwhelmingly negative. Most survivors of acquaintance and stranger rape report feelings of terror, humiliation, degradation, and both immediate and long-term behavioral and psychological difficulties.

It has been difficult to obtain accurate statistics on the incidence of date and acquaintance rape (the number of such rapes that occur in a given period) and its prevalence (the number of people who have ever been raped). Experts agree that this type of rape is one of the most underreported of all crimes. Many survivors are embarrassed or afraid to publicly acknowledge that they have been raped. In reporting their experiences to police or in court, survivors often complain they are treated insensitively and made to feel that they rather than their attacker are to blame. Obtaining accurate statistics is also hindered by the failure of some perpetrators and victims to define as rape intercourse between acquaintances resulting from the use of force. However, numerous surveys have shown that date and acquaintance rape are common and indeed a major social problem.

Two of the earliest surveys were conducted in the 1950s—even before the second wave of the feminist movement in the 1960s. From surveys administered in the fall of 1956, Eugene Kanin found that 13 percent of 262 college women reported forceful attempts at sexual intercourse during their senior year in high school, and Kanin and Clifford Kirkpatrick found that 21 percent of 292 college women were offended by forceful attempts at intercourse in the 1954–55 academic year. In these two studies, the majority of the forceful attempts were made by men who were the offended women's regular or steady dates or their fiancés. The other offenders were categorized as a first or occasional date or someone who had given them a ride home.

In the most comprehensive recent study of the incidence and prevalence of sexual aggression and victimization of college students involving over 6,000 men and women at 32 institutions of higher education, Mary Koss and her colleagues found that 27.5 percent of women reported experiencing and 7.7 percent of men reported perpetrating an act that met a legal definition of rape, which included attempted rape. The discrepancy between women who reported and men who admitted being involved in forced sex experiences may be due to (1) women including noncollege men as perpetrators, (2) different perceptions of such experiences by men and women, and (3) a general reluctance by men to admit or to even acknowledge that their forceful sexual strategies could be defined as rape. Eighty-nine percent of the rapes reported in the Koss study were committed by men the women knew and more than half occurred on dates. Only 5 percent of the rapes were reported to police and 73 percent of the women did not define their forced sex experience as rape, possibly because of the general negative societal reaction to rape victims or because of the tendency for rape survivors to blame themselves for their victimization.

A government-funded study involving 4,000 women interviewed by telephone in 1991 supported the view that rape is more common than had been previously estimated. If the results from that study are generalized to all American women, 12.1 million women have been raped at least once in their life. Only 22 percent of victims in that study identified their assailant as a stranger. Most of the victims were uninjured, while 24 percent suffered minor injuries, and 4 percent were seriously hurt. The report did not reveal whether the majority of injuries were associated with nonacquaintance assaults. However, other studies have consistently found that acquaintance assaults are less likely either to involve a weapon or to result in physical injury to the victim than are assaults by strangers.

Social scientists and feminists have devoted considerable attention to the causes of date and acquaintance rape. Most agree that explanations of sexual aggression are complex and involve combinations of psychological and physiological characteristics with sociocultural factors. Feminists emphasize sociocultural factors. They stress that rape occurs in cultures characterized by other forms of violence, that rape results from inequities between the genders, and that rape is used by men to establish or to maintain control and power over women. Others argue that traditional socialization (e.g., women being encouraged to be passive, kind, and submissive and men to be tough, dominant, and aggressive) and the dating system contribute to rape. In this view, men and women have been socialized to pursue opposite goals and roles in dating and courtship and that this aspect of socialization leads to an adversarial situation where date rape is likely to occur.

Studies have also investigated characteristics of men who use forceful strategies with women to have sex. Compared with nonforceful men, these men are more likely to accept the use of physical force in a variety of contexts, hold stereotypic views of gender roles, believe heterosexual relationships are adversarial and that game playing and deception are normal, consider violence manly, have callous or hostile attitudes toward women, and lack a social conscience. One study of admitted date rapists found them to be products of a highly sexually oriented peer group socialization which started early in high school. The peer groups of these men accepted the view that sexual conquest of women enhanced their self-worth. Compared with the nonrapists, the rapists had had more sex partners and were dramatically more sexually active.

It has been difficult for social scientists to come up with a "type" of female who is the victim of date and acquaintance rape. A few studies have found that victims are more sexually experienced than nonvictims in that they reported an earlier age of first intercourse and more sex partners. Women who were not able to stop an offender were also more sexually passive and less likely to use methods of avoidance, such as screaming or running away, than successful resisters.

Aspects of a date that might increase the likelihood of forceful sex acts have also been examined. Such acts were found to occur more often when the man initiated the date, paid the date expenses, and drove; when there was miscommunication about sex; and when both persons were moderately or extremely intoxicated.

To reduce the incidence and prevalence of date and acquaintance rape, experts advocate more widespread and comprehensive sex education for children and adolescents. Sex education courses and rape prevention programs need to teach young people how to communicate their feelings assertively and effectively and to include a variety of topics in their curricula—from sexual socialization and the double standard of sexuality to practical methods to reduce the risk of date and acquaintance rape.

REFERENCES

Burgess, A., ed. *Rape and Sexual Assault.* Vol. 2. New York: Garland Publishing, Inc., 1988.

Craig, M. Coercive Sexuality in Dating Relationships: A Situational Model. *Clinical Psychology Review*, Vol. 10 (1990), pp. 395–423.

Kanin, E. Date Rapists: Differential Sexual Socialization and Relative Deprivation. *Archives of Sexual Behavior*, Vol. 14 (1985), pp. 219–231.

———. Male Aggression in Dating-Courtship Relations. *American Journal of Sociology*, Vol. 63 (1957), pp. 197–204.

Koss, M., C. Gidycz, and N. Wisniewski. The Scope of Rape: Incidence and Prevalence of Sexual Aggression and Victimization in a National Sample of Higher Education Students. *Journal of Consulting and Clinical Psychology*, Vol. 55 (1987), pp. 162–170.

Malamuth, N. Predictors of Naturalistic Sexual Aggression. *Journal of Personality and Social Psychology*, Vol. 50 (1986), pp. 953–962.

Muehlenhard, C., and M. Linton. Date Rape and Sexual Aggression in Dating Situations: Incidence and Risk Factors. *Journal of Counseling Psychology*, Vol. 34 (1987), pp. 186–196.

Ilsa Lottes

DAVIS, KATHARINE BEMENT

Social hygienist, sociologist, prison reformer, and suffragette, Katharine Bement Davis (1860–1935) spent her early career working to ameliorate domestic problems of urban industrial families. She received her Ph.D. in 1900 from the University of Chicago, where she studied political economy and sociology with Thorstein Veblen, among others. As the first superintendent of the model women's reformatory at Bedford Hills, New York, she initiated training for inmates at various trades and domestic work. Her goal was to rehabilitate inmates, many of whom were prostitutes. In 1912, the Laboratory of Social Hygiene was established at Bedford Hills, underwritten by John D. Rockefeller, Jr., to aid in Davis's work in prison reform. From Bedford Hills, Davis progressed to Commissioner of Corrections in New York City, a post she held from 1914 to 1916. She was the first woman to head a New York City department. During that time, she was also a vice president of the National American Woman Suffrage Association. During World War I, she was vice-chairman of a relief organization raising over $2 million for afflicted women and children in Europe.

Davis was general secretary of the Bureau of Social Hygiene from 1918 to 1928. She had been on the original committee that had established the Bureau seven years earlier to eradicate prostitution; later the Bureau's activities expanded to financing and publishing studies of the international white slave trade, public health, and sex education.

In 1929, Davis published a significant social hygiene study entitled *Factors in the Sex Life of Twenty-two Hundred Women.* Previously, information concerning the sex lives of women came from institutionalized women and social deviates. Davis studied normal, middle-class women to determine normal sexual experiences on which to base educational programs. She believed sex education would bring about more satisfactory sexual relationships. The exhaustive study resulted in a publication that produced almost 200 statistical tables and additional correlation tables and charts, and analyzed case studies. Women between the ages of 21 and 83 responded to eight to twelve pages of questions regarding use of contraceptives; happiness of married life and sexual relations; homosexual and auto-erotic practices, and sexual desire of married and unmarried women.

In a poll sponsored by the League of Women Voters, Davis was named one of the 12 greatest living American women.

REFERENCES

Bullough, V.L. Katharine Bement Davis and the Rockefeller Foundation. *Bulletin of the History of Medicine*, Vol. 62 (1988), pp. 74–89.

James, E.T., ed. *Notable American Women 1607–1950.* Vol. 1. Cambridge: Harvard Univ. Press, 1971.

Katharine Davis, Reformer, 75, Dead. *New York Times*, Dec. 11, 1935.

The National Cyclopaedia of American Biography. Current Series Vol. A. New York: James T. White, 1930.

Trattner, W.I. *Biographical Dictionary of Social Welfare in America.* New York: Greenwood, 1986.

Hilary Sternberg

DICKINSON, ROBERT LATOU

Robert Latou Dickinson (1861–1950) was the most significant figure in American sex research before Alfred Kinsey. Dickenson was born on February 21, 1861 in Jersey City, New Jersey, son of Horace and Jeannette Latou Dickinson. He attended Brooklyn Polytechnic Institute and schools in Germany and Switzerland before receiving an M.D. from Long Island College Hospital (later Long Island College of Medicine) in 1882. After a brief internship, he practiced in Brooklyn as a specialist in obstetrics and gynecology until his death.

Almost from the first, Dickinson began collecting sexual histories from his patients. Usually each patient was required to fill out a four-page questionnaire about family and general history as well as particular illnesses and special symptoms. Though the questionnaire contained no questions specifically sexual in orientation, in reviewing it with the patient, Dickinson marked down certain sexual observations. He was strongly convinced many difficulties his patients reported—including insomnia, menstrual irregularities, and certain types of pain—had their roots in sexual problems.

Sketching rapidly and accurately with a crayon, Dickinson also made rough drawings of the anatomy of his patients in order to have on file indicators of problems they might face. The first set of sketches were drawn while the patient was on the examining table and included drawings of their uterus, cervix, and vulva. The patient's first visit was scheduled to last an hour so that he could review the patient's history, do the physical examination, make his sketches (a minimum of five), and talk with his patient about what to expect. Sixty-two sketches were the most he made on a single patient, but this was because of the unusualness of the case. He averaged about 20 sketches per patient drawn over the years he treated them. He took his first sex history as such in 1890. Over the course of his practice, Dickinson gathered case histories on 5,200 women (4000 married and 1200 unmarried), of which only 46 date before 1900.

Dickinson, an early observer of lesbian homoerotic feelings, wrote some 200 research papers—mostly on obstetrics, diseases of women, midwifery, and sex problems—during his years of practice. His books were written late in life. A strong supporter of organized medicine, he also continually urged his fellow physicians to deal with the sexual problems of their patients. He was active in numerous social reform groups and was a founder of the National Committee on Maternal Health in 1923, serving as secretary from that year to 1937, when he became chairman. On becoming secretary of the Committee, Dickinson turned over for its use a large collection of scientific material, including his own library, drawings, card indexes, abstracts, and notes. In 1927, the Committee appointed Lura Beam to review the records for possible publication; two books resulted from this collaboration between Beam and Dickinson on the topics of single women, married women, and sex variants. Dickinson also published a book of his drawings on sexual anatomy which, in addition to his sketches on female anatomy, included chapters on male genital anatomy, the anatomy of coitus, and the anatomy of the control of conception. He also published two books on the techniques of conception control.

Dickinson died on November 29, 1950 in Amherst, Massachusetts. He was married to Sarah Truslow, and was the father of three daughters, one of whom died in infancy.

REFERENCES

Dickinson, R.L. *Human Sex Anatomy*. Baltimore: Williams & Wilkins, 1933. Second ed. rev., 1949.

Dickinson, R.L., and L. Beam. *The Single Woman: A Medical Study in Sex Education*. Baltimore: Williams & Wilkins, 1934.

————. *A Thousand Marriages: A Medical Study of Sex Adjustment*. Baltimore: Williams & Wilkins, 1932.

Vern L. Bullough

DISABILITIES AND SEXUALITY

"The great pleasure in life is doing what people say you cannot do."

Walter Bagehot

There are inherent dangers involved in discussing the sexual needs of individuals on the basis of disability categories or labels. First, individuals with disabilities are much more like "typical" individuals than they are different from them, and there is a risk of promoting stereotypes based on category labels. Also, a number of characteristics are frequently observed across disability categories. This is especially the case as we look at meeting the educational needs of individuals with varying learning difficulties.

People with learning problems include those who traditionally have been labeled deaf or hearing impaired, blind or visually impaired, learning disabled, or mentally retarded, as well as individuals whose emotional or behavioral problems interfere with their ability to learn. Admittedly, the needs of an intelligent blind or deaf person are different from those of a person who is labeled as moderately or severely mentally retarded. However, there are learning limitations for all these individuals, and many of the educational approaches to them are similar. This observation is illustrated, in part, by the following words of Nancy Becker:

> Sex education for deaf people didn't exist. Like every other deaf person, I learned about sex from the gossips and big talkers in school. And, like most deaf people, I learned about it all wrong.

Needs of Individuals with Learning Problems

Certain concerns regarding marriage and parenting are unique to individuals with significant learning problems. These issues have a greater impact on individuals labeled as mentally retarded or severely or multiply handicapped than they do on members of other disability groups. Few people question, for example, whether people who are deaf should marry and have children even though it is known that congenitally deaf parents are more likely to have a deaf child than parents who are not deaf. Similar attitudes prevail with regard to persons with other disabilities, such as blindness, speech and language disorders, and mild physical disabilities. However, in the case of individuals labeled as mentally retarded, severely learning disabled, or multiply handicapped, the questions and concerns are accentuated.

Marriage

No individual, whether he or she has a disability or not, should feel the need to marry to be regarded by others as "normal." However, the right to marry should be available to all. The possibility of marriage for many persons with mental retardation or other disabilities is critical for several reasons:

- Marriage is a fundamental right in American society.
- Marriage creates possibilities for closeness, sharing, intimacy, and bonding with another human being.
- Individuals who may be constrained in their sexual expression due to negative messages from parents or society may be more comfortable expressing their sexuality within marriage.
- Marriage is a means of enhancing a person's self-esteem by creating opportunities for unequivocal acceptance.

The majority of states still have laws that restrict or prohibit marriage by persons with mental retardation. Marafino has pointed out how inappropriate such legislation is due to inconsistent application of the laws; changes in information about the nature of mental retardation; vagueness, imprecision, and archaic language in the laws; and possible violations of fundamental constitutional rights. For states that choose to restrict marriage by people labeled as mentally retarded, she recommends that precisely worded statutes reflect legitimate and clear public policy,

restrictions on the right to marry be no broader than necessary to serve the public policy, and persons affected by the statutory limitations be identified with a high degree of reliability.

Parenting

The issue of parenting by individuals with significant learning disabilities is even more problematic than the issue of marriage. Whitman and Accardo, Haavik and Menninger, and others have pointed out that, as a group, individuals with mental retardation who become parents do not fare as well in their parenting as individuals who are not mentally retarded. However, many people labeled as retarded have proven to be better parents than individuals considered "normal." Additionally, almost no effort has been devoted to developing and implementing educational programs designed to teach these individuals about the responsibilities of parents or specific parenting techniques and behaviors. Marafino argues strongly that persons with mental retardation should be presumed neither more nor less capable of being parents than individuals not so labeled, and that to restrict the possibility of parenting significantly restricts such persons' rights and choices.

It is important to include in curricula for persons with disabilities information and experiences that teach their rights to marriage and childbearing, as well as the advantages and disadvantages of such life choices so they can decide if marriage is best for them. Whether or not they choose to have children, marriage should remain an option for all members of society unless, in individual cases, there are compelling, demonstrable reasons that indicate that this right should be abridged. In a related discussion, Brodeur points out the important need for courts to establish criteria for successful parenting. These criteria would allow for more objectivity and standardization than have existed in the past in decisions on removal of children from the home and termination of parental rights.

Policies and Procedures

A consistent problem in dealing with the sexuality needs of children and adults with disabilities has been the seemingly random ways in which those needs have been addressed. Due to factors such as fear of negative reactions by societal groups, vociferous reactions by one or a few parents, and discomfort with sexuality in general, many schools and agencies adopt a "wait-and-see" stance with regard to the sexuality of students, residents, or clients. What is needed instead is a proactive approach that supports the notion that sexuality is a characteristic that individuals with disabilities share with all humanity. Moreover, to deny the sexuality of such individuals is to compromise their full participation in society and to leave them to the sway of impulse and, consequently, potential abuse.

One way to attempt to meet the sexual needs of people with disabilities is to implement policies and procedures that promote healthy and responsible sexual expression. Haavik and Menninger point out that policies and procedures allow for consistency in staff responses. They suggest that without clear guidelines and consistency of response, an overreaction by a teacher or staff member to a relatively minor infraction of an ambiguous sexual "norm" could have a negative effect on a child's or adult's development of healthy feelings about her or his sexuality. Moreover, policy statements should focus on the positive features of training individuals for responsible sexuality rather than simply identify those procedures undertaken to curb inappropriate sexual behavior. As policies and procedures are developed, it is important to maintain a perspective balanced between the theoretical ideals of normalization and the realities of community living. As Hingsburger emphasizes, we may be doing a disservice to the individuals we are trying to help by teaching them about their right to sexual expression if we are not going to create opportunities for them to express their sexuality. Policy statements should reflect a program's philosophy about sexuality and sexual expression as well as pragmatic aspects of how the program and procedures are to be put into practice.

Principles for Establishing Policies and Procedures

Given that the task of developing appropriate and lasting policies and procedures is often arduous, the following suggestions may prove helpful:

- Have broad-based representation on the committee responsible for the formulation of policies and procedures, including individuals with disabilities, family members, professionals, members of the board of directors of the school or facility, medical personnel, administrators, supervisors, and clergy.
- Build in a system to ensure membership on the policy-planning committee of at least one representative from the administration who has the authority to speak for high-level

officers and members of the board, when applicable.

- Establish an overall philosophical statement, general goals, and subobjectives on which the members of the committee agree. Submit these to administrators and the board of directors and receive feedback and approval before proceeding further.
- Develop policies and procedures that provide:
- Clear definitions of acceptable and unacceptable behaviors;
- Objective means of determining whether a person is capable of consenting to sexual behaviors;
- Procedures for communicating and teaching acceptable behaviors;
- Procedures for interventions to modify unacceptable behaviors;
- Designated individuals who are qualified to provide sexuality education and other interventions; and
- Follow-up procedures to determine whether individuals have achieved identified objectives.

Once the policies and procedures are developed and approved by the board of directors or other official body, they should be communicated and made available in writing to all staff members and adult residents or clients. If in-service training is provided, ensure that all staff members participate.

Implementing Sexuality Education Programs

A number of factors should be considered when planning a sexuality education program. These include:

1. Political climate of the community and the school or agency;
2. Availability of existing curricula and instructional materials;
3. Potential for offering in-service training programs for staff;
4. Resources available for program planning and review and recommendation of instructional materials; and
5. Monetary resources for the purchase of curricula and instructional materials.

In school programs in which quality sexuality education already exists for typical students, the path to programs for students with learning problems and disabilities should be partially paved. When educational or training programs offer no training in human sexuality or are inconsistent in content and quality, parents and family members, professionals, administrators, and board members are challenged to work together to design and implement programs that meet the needs of children or adults. This effort requires a recognition that individuals will express their sexuality in one way or another; it is better to provide education that channels sexuality in considered and responsible ways rather than to deal with behaviors that are random and unpredictable. It also demands a commitment to doing what is necessary to ensure that individuals receive the knowledge and skills they need as fully functioning adults.

Heidi Hudson presents three primary components of sexuality curricula for individuals with learning problems: self-esteem, social skills, and factual information. The amount of energy and time devoted to each of these areas varies with the needs of individuals. Typically, the largest amount of time will be spent on self-esteem, as it is a foundation for other sexuality content.

Gordon presents key concepts that any sexuality program for persons with learning problems, particularly mental retardation, should communicate. The program should convey a view of masturbation as a normal mode of sexual expression, the need for expressing one's sexuality in private, information about the use of birth control by those who do not want children or are not capable of caring for children, the need for protection from sexual exploitation, greater tolerance or acceptance of homosexuality, and the right of consenting adults to sexual expression. He recommends that there be greater acceptance of abortion as a safe, legal, and moral alternative to bringing unwanted children into the world. He also advocates voluntary sterilization as a protection for persons with mental retardation who could function well in a marriage if they did not have children.

The following are suggested as goals of sexuality education for individuals with disabilities:

- To better people's lives by teaching them to express their sexuality in responsible and caring ways;
- To enhance each individual's self-esteem;
- To help learners understand, to the extent they are able, the sexual functioning of human beings, including appropriate facts and terminology;
- To teach decision-making skills so each person will be able to decide:
- With whom to form relationships,
- Whether to be sexually active,
- Whether he or she is capable of becoming a "good" parent or wants to be a parent, and
- Whether marriage is appropriate for him or her;
- To teach individuals who decide they do not want to become parents to practice an effective means of birth control consistently;
- To teach individuals about the nature of sexual abuse, specific ways to avoid abuse, and what to do in the event they are abused;
- To prevent people from contracting sexually transmitted diseases, including AIDS (acquired immune deficiency syndrome);
- To give individuals knowledge, attitudes, and social skills that allow them to relate interpersonally in positive and, if they desire, intimate ways with other people;
- To dispel sexual myths that may have been learned;
- To minimize guilt or other negative feelings about sexual expression when such feelings are not warranted; and
- To help people differentiate between appropriate and inappropriate sexual behavior and to practice appropriate sexual behavior.

Instructional methods depend on both the knowledge of the learner and the curriculum. One cannot determine what methods to use to teach the curriculum until goals and objectives have been specified on the basis of an assessment of the learner's current abilities and predicted needs. The past two decades have brought an empirical base to methodology that previously had not been clear. Although the quest for improved instructional technology continues, considerable knowledge now exists about ways to teach people who have difficulty learning.

The following recommendations are for individuals planning or currently providing sexuality education:

- Do not assume the person has acquired any specific knowledge, attitude, or skill. If unsure, assess what knowledge, skills and attitudes learners do have.
- Do not attempt to eliminate or change people's beliefs or values, but help them to learn new, correct information and to reflect on their beliefs and the beliefs of others.

- Apply similar standards to people with disabilities as to others in society. Do not accept behaviors that are generally unacceptable in society just because the person has learned that he or she can get away with typically unacceptable behavior (e.g., public masturbation) or has not discovered or had an opportunity to learn the standards for ascceptable behavior.

- Assume that all or most individuals express their sexuality in typical, and possibly atypical, ways alone or with others.

- Infuse sexuality content and skills into existing programs. The temptation to bring in outside consultants such as nurses or individuals from family-planning agencies should be replaced by education and training for professionals who work with people with disabilities on an ongoing basis.

- Explore the adoption or adaption of existing curricula and materials before expending time and energy developing materials.

- Do not assume that sexuality is not a concern for individuals with Down's syndrome. Available data indicate that it is unlikely that males with Down's syndrome will father children, but childbearing is quite possible for females. Regardless of childbearing issues, increasing numbers of individuals with Down's syndrome are forming loving relationships and marrying.

- Teach males and females together unless there is some compelling reason to do otherwise.

- Provide many opportunities for making choices and decisions beginning as early in life as is feasible. Provide limits to such choices when the person is young, and reduce the structure as he or she get older.

- Do not refer to anyone over the age of 11 as a "kid."

- Do not be overly concerned about providing too much sexual information to younger students (within reasonable limitations). They grasp what they can at their particular age and developmental level and usually do not process information that is too complex or too emotionally challenging for them at the time.

Strategies for Implementing Lessons and Discussions

- Do not assume that just because the focus is on sex the students will be inherently interested. Provide well-planned and motivating instructional experiences.

- Teach the critical goals and objectives first, using repetition with varied, motivating formats and concrete instructional materials.

- Try to have presenters of both sexes when possible as some learners relate to females and others relate to males.

- Resist the temptation to provide more help and direction than the person needs, and withdraw assistance as soon as the person can act independently.

- Organize the instructional environment to minimize distractions.

- Avoid lectures. Have the learners respond, discuss, and verbally and physically participate in whatever ways they can.

- Use a variety of instructional methodologies and materials.

- Keep lessons moving—a brisk pace helps to sustain attention; a lesson that is overly deliberate may not.

- Facilitate generalization of concepts (i.e., transfer of concepts to real-life settings) by using terminology the person can be expected to use as an adult.

- Begin instruction only after gaining the attention of all learners.

- Design instruction for high rates of success.

- Provide opportunities for individuals to practice the skills being taught.

Instructional Materials

The issue of instructional materials to teach about sexuality to individuals with learning problems and disabilities needs special discussion. Many individuals require concrete, sexually explicit materials and instructional experiences to learn concepts and skills. People with physical disabilities may require photographs that show alternative modes of sexual expression. Individuals with mental retardation may need videotapes, films, three-dimensional models, or other media to understand important concepts and skills. Such items become controversial, and it is important that a distinction be made between materials that are explicit and those that are pornographic, in that the purpose of the materials should be to educate—not to titillate. A hierarchy of instructional materials (e.g., charts, pictures, and films) should be available to the educator that ranges from the abstract to the concrete and explicit. Sexuality instruction should begin with the least explicit materials available and proceed to more explicit levels only when the individuals have been unable to acquire the concepts or skills being taught with less explicit materials. This approach, designed to minimize controversy and questionable practices, is contrary to the usual methodologies for persons with learning problems; these methodologies recommend beginning with the most concrete materials first and then moving to more abstract teaching. Also, it is important that instructors preview all materials before their use and, when appropriate, encourage parents, board members, or other groups to preview them. A final point to keep in mind is that explicit materials may be personally offensive to the persons being instructed and may be counterproductive to the goals and objectives of the program. In such cases, it is important to respect the wishes of the learners.

It is critical to maintain a normalcy perspective in viewing the sexuality of persons with disabilities. It is also now time to start acting on the relevant issues and needs. As James Baldwin wrote, "Not everything that is faced can be changed, but nothing can be changed until it is faced."

References

Brightman, A.J., ed. *Ordinary Moments: The Disabled Experience*. Baltimore: University Park Press, 1984.

Brodeur, D.A. Parents with Mental Retardation and Developmental Disabilities: Ethical Issues in Parenting. In B.Y. Whitman and P.J. Accardo, eds., *When a Parent Is Mentally Retarded*. Baltimore: Paul H. Brookes, 1990.

Gordon, S. Sex Education for Neglected Youth: Retarded, Handicapped, Emotionally Disturbed and Learning Disabled. In *The Sexual Adolescent*. North Scituate, Mass.: Duxbury Press, 1973.

Griffiths, D.M., V.L. Quinsey, and D. Hingsburger. *Changing Inappropriate Sexual Behavior: A Community-Based Approach for Persons with Developmental Disabilities*. Baltimore: Paul H. Brookes, 1989.

Haavik, S.F., and K.A. Menninger, II. *Sexuality, Law, and the Developmentally Disabled Person*. Baltimore: Paul H. Brookes, 1981.

Hingsburger, D. *I Contact: Sexuality and People with Developmental Disabilities*. Mountsville, Pa.: Vida, 1990.

Kempton, W. *Sex Education for Persons with Disabilities That Hinder Learning: A Teacher's Guide*. Santa Monica, Calif.: James Stanfield, 1990.

Marafino, K. The Right to Marry for Persons with Mental Retardation. In B.Y. Whitman and P.J. Accardo, eds., *When a Parent Is Mentally Retarded*. Baltimore: Paul H. Brookes, 1990.

Monat-Haller, R.K. *Understanding and Expressing Sexuality: Responsible Choices for Individuals with Developmental Disabilities*. Baltimore: Paul H. Brookes, 1990.

Shaman, J.M. Persons Who Are Mentally Retarded: Their Right to Marry and Have Children. *Family Law Quarterly*, Vol. 12 (1978), pp. 61–62, 65.

Sobsey, D., S. Gray, D. Wells, D. Pyper, and B. Reimer-Heck. *Disability, Sexuality, and Abuse: An Annotated Bibliography*. Baltimore: Paul H. Brookes, 1991.

Whitman, B.Y., and P.J. Accardo, eds. *When a Parent Is Mentally Retarded*. Baltimore: Paul H. Brookes, 1990.

R. Bruce Baum

THE DOUBLE STANDARD AND SEX

The sexual double standard is the belief or attitude that a specific sexual behavior, or all sexual behavior, is more acceptable for persons of one sex, usually males, than persons of the other sex. More broadly, it may refer to beliefs concerning any differences between males and females in their sexuality, but particularly their basic sexual nature.

Historically, the most common version of the broader concern has been that women are more sexual than men. This view most likely originated in conjunction with the recognition of women's control over fertility. Because of this fundamental power, women came to be both feared and worshipped. Although many ancient societies worshipped a number of gods, often among the most important were the gods of fertility, and the most important of the fertility gods were usually female.

In Hebrew and Christian traditions, the role of Eve as the evil seductress epitomizes the belief in the basic carnal nature of women and their sexual power over men. Similarly, the fundamentally evil nature of witches, persecuted so vigorously during the 15th and 16th centuries, was believed to derive from their sexual power.

Although women were believed to have a strong sexual power, or perhaps *because* they were believed to have such power, it was also believed that they must be controlled. Throughout most of human history, and in nearly all patrilineal societies, women have been accorded a lower status than men. Patriarchies, societies in which men have legal or social dominance over women, are characteristic of Western civilization. In such societies, women have often been viewed as the property of their fathers or husbands, and treated as chattel. The sexual double standard resulting from such a view is well illustrated in ancient Jewish law: a man found guilty of engaging in sexual intercourse with another man's wife was charged only with a violation of property rights, whereas a woman convicted of adultery could be punished by death. Similarly, raping a woman amounted to theft, and a father could legitimately sell the sexual favors of a daughter (technically, prostitution).

Nearly a century after the beginning of the Christian era, debate concerning whether women had souls continued in the Catholic church, and the height of the persecution of women as witches, who were presumed to be possessed by the devil and sexually insatiable, occurred during the 15th and 16th centuries. The widespread use of the chastity belt, also in the 15th century, reflected the fear of women's strong sexual nature and the need to control access to that sexuality by husbands and fathers.

It was not until the 19th century, and the Industrial Revolution, that the beliefs about the sexual nature of women were reversed in Western societies. Victorianism, as the period came to be called, viewed men as the sexual aggressors and women as frail, refined, and asexual beings. Many of the beliefs that characterize 20th-century stereotypes of masculinity and femininity derive from this period. In spite of the change in view of women—from very powerful and dangerous sexual creatures to very weak, asexual ones—some residuals of the earlier history remained. Perhaps the most important among these is the notion that women precipitate sexual assault and rape.

The modern version of the sexual double standard in Western society is founded on the fundamental ideological assumption of gender inequality: that men are superior to women. Sexually, this assumption is linked with the beliefs that men are innately more sexual, having a naturally higher sex drive and, therefore, needing more sexual outlets, or, at the very least, sexual outlet more often, than women. It is the notion, not supported by empirical evidence, that men, innately and probably as a result of hormonal surges, *need* sex, whereas women do not.

Reiss suggested that, at the very simplest level, sexual ideologies could be classified as egalitarian or nonegalitarian. He further identified four parallel tenets of each ideology. Adherents of the nonegalitarian ideology, which is the foundation of and justification for the sexual double standard, believe (1) males are more competent in exercising power and that males should dominate major social institutions, (2) "body-centered sexuality" should be forbidden to women, (3) sexuality is a powerful emotion to be feared by females, and (4) the goal of sexual interaction for females is heterosexual intercourse. Conversely, believers in an egalitarian ideology (1) assume males and females to be equally competent and deserving of equal roles in major institutions, (2) accept body-centered sexuality for both sexes,

(3) consider sexual feelings to be manageable by both sexes, and (4) judge the goals of sexual interaction for both men and women to be pleasure and self-disclosure.

It is abundantly clear that Western society has been dominated by the nonegalitarian ideology during the 19th and 20th centuries. Many researchers and observers of the sexual scene in the United States, for example, have described variations in sexual attitudes and behavior revealing more permissive standards for men than for women and more extensive sexual behavior for men than for women. Among these early researchers of the double standard of premarital sexual intercourse were Ehrmann and Reiss. Both reported that more than 70 percent of men accepted premarital intercourse for their own sex, whereas fewer than 20 percent of women accepted premarital intercourse for women. These data were collected from high school and/or college students, who were undoubtedly more permissive than older persons in the society at that time.

A behavioral double standard paralleled attitudes. Kinsey and his colleagues documented behavior during a period roughly equivalent to the time of Ehrmann's data collection (1947–51). Among men, 71 percent had experienced premarital intercourse by age 25, whereas only 33 percent of women had done so.

The double standards of both attitude and behavior have declined over the years. By the late 1960s, for example, Simon and Gagnon reported that 40 percent of women college students accepted premarital intercourse for women, although no change had occurred for men. By 1973, DeLamater and MacCorquodale reported 95 percent of college-age men and 86 percent of college-age women accepted premarital intercourse for their own sex. Gallup polls conducted during the 1970s also revealed a more widespread acceptance of premarital sex for the society at large.

DeLamater and MacCorquodale offered a subtle but important distinction concerning the double standard. It concerns whether the same individual holds differing standards for men and for women, versus whether both men and women, as groups, hold different standards for men and for women. The latter distinction is illustrated nicely by their own findings. They found no evidence that, on the average, individual men held a more permissive standard for men than for women, or that individual women did either. That is, if a person felt premarital sexual intercourse was acceptable under conditions, say, of a close, intimate relationship, but not in a more casual relationship, that person held the same standard for both men and women. In contrast, Reiss, nearly 15 years earlier, had found some 30 percent of the men and 24 percent of the women had held different standards, a double standard of acceptability for men and women.

DeLamater and MacCorquodale also found, however, that despite the fact that the overwhelming majority of both men and women felt it was acceptable to engage in premarital intercourse under some conditions, the requirements did differ for men and women. The standards held by men (for both men and women) were more permissive than the standards held by women (for both men and women). Specifically, among men, the modal (most common) standard was that it was acceptable for persons (of either sex) to engage in premarital sexual intercourse if "they both wanted to," even though a majority still required some closer relationship. Women, on the other hand, most commonly required that the relationship be one of shared love, and fewer than a third thought sexual intercourse was acceptable if both just wanted to do it. Thus, even if more men and women hold the same standards for men and women, important differences in standards remain.

Reiss introduced the "permissive with affection" notion and developed a scale to measure sexual standards, with the options including abstinence for all, a double standard of acceptability, and permissiveness without affection, as well as permissiveness with affection. Many have used this framework to describe changing standards in American society. Consistently researchers have found that the dominant standard at the end of the 20th century is permissiveness with affection for both men and women. That is, the standard has gradually shifted in two respects: from abstinence until marriage to sexual intercourse being acceptable in a stable relationship involving love between the partners, and from a dramatic difference in what is acceptable for men and women to a smaller difference.

Behaviorally, the double standard has decreased in the United States as well. Kinsey had reported that more than twice as many men than women had experienced premarital intercourse. Researchers during the 1970s revealed a dramatic increase in the percentage of women engaging in premarital coitus. In a series of studies, Zelnik and Kantner reported changes in the percentage of women engaging in premarital intercourse by age 19. That percentage rose from 46 in 1971, to 69 in 1979. The average age of first intercourse also declined. Although more males

were engaging in premarital sexual intercourse too, the women were catching up. In the Zelnik and Kantner 1979 data, 77 percent of the males had engaged in premarital coitus by age 19. Evidence from the 1980s suggests, depending on the study, either that the pattern of rapid increase for women and the closing of the gap between men and women has leveled off at about the same figures as reported a decade earlier by Zelnik and Kantner or that there has been some decline in the percentages, at least for women.

Although the decline in the double standard, defined both in the broadest and narrowest terms, has been substantial, there continue to be many manifestations of its continuance. For example, even though acceptance of women's sexuality has increased, parents are often less accepting of the sexual activities of their daughters than they are of those of their sons. Similarly, teenage women who are as sexually active as their male peers, or who take more assertive and initiating stances, are more likely to be judged negatively.

Also, although both male and female young people are most likely to have their first instance of intercourse with a boyfriend or a girlfriend, more males than females still have that first experience with a casual acquaintance or a stranger. Both Hunt, and Coles and Stokes found more women and men experience ambivalence and negative effects associated with their first experience of intercourse.

Finally, women are still expected to play more traditional roles in sexual interactions than men. For instance, men are still assumed to be the primary initiators of sexual interactions, and women are supposed to set the limits on how far the interaction will go.

Not only does the double standard apply to premarital sexual behavior. Historically, it has been more acceptable for men than women to engage in virtually all heterosexual sexual behaviors except marital intercourse. In particular, such behaviors as oral-genital sexual acts and extramarital sexual relationships have been more acceptable for and more frequently engaged in by men. The one notable exception is homosexuality. Although homosexual behavior is not approved in Western society for either men or women, and more men than women have engaged in homosexual acts, homosexuality is tolerated more for women than for men. Ironically, this difference may be the result of the double standard in that, according to that standard, women's sexuality is less important than men's. Also of note in this context is that the patterns of sexual behavior of gay men and lesbian women often reflect the double standard.

For instance, Bell and Weinberg found that gay men have more partners than lesbian women, on the average, reflecting a permissiveness without a strong commitment standard. Lesbian women, on the other hand, have fewer partners, engage in less cruising behavior, and remain in relationships longer, all evidence of the more conservative standard traditionally dictated for women.

REFERENCES

Bell, A.R., and M.S. Weinberg. *Homosexualities.* New York: Simon & Schuster, 1978.

Bullough, V.L. *Sexual Variance in Society and History.* New York: Wiley, 1976.

Coles, R., and G. Stokes. *Sex and the American Teenager.* New York: Harper & Row, 1985.

DeLamater, J.D., and P. MacCorquodale. *Premarital Sexuality: Attitudes, Relationships, Behavior.* Madison, Wis.: Univ. of Wisconsin Press, 1979.

Ehrmann, W. *Premarital Dating Behavior.* New York: Henry Holt, 1959.

Epstein, L. *Sex, Law, and Customs in Judaism.* New York: KATV, 1967.

Gagnon, J.H. *Human Sexualities.* Glenview, Ill.: Scott, Foresman, 1977.

Gerrard, M. Are Men and Women Really Different? Sex Differences in Emotional and Cognitive Factors Associated With Contraceptive Behavior. In K. Kelley, ed., *Females, Males, and Sexuality: Theories and Research.* Albany, N.Y.: State Univ. of New York Press, 1987.

Hunt, M. *Sexual Behavior in the 1970s.* Chicago: Playboy Press, 1974.

Kinsey, A.C., W.B. Pomeroy, and C.E. Martin. *Sexual Behavior in the Human Male.* Philadelphia: Saunders, 1948.

Kinsey, A.C., W.B. Pomeroy, C.E. Martin, and P.H. Gebhard. *Sexual Behavior in the Human Female.* Philadelphia: Saunders, 1952.

McCormick, N.B., & C.J. Jesser. The Courtship Game: Power in the Sexual Encounter. In E.R. Allgeier and N.B. McCormick, eds., *Changing Boundaries: Gender Roles and Sexual Behavior.* Palo Alto, Calif.: Mayfield, 1983.

Murstein, B. *Love, Sex, and Marriage Through the Ages.* New York: Springer, 1974.

Reiss, I.L. *Journey Into Sexuality: An Exploratory Voyage.* Englewood Cliffs, N.J.: Prentice-Hall, 1986.

————. *Premarital Sexual Standards in America.* New York: Free Press, 1960.

————. *The Social Context of Premarital Sexual Permissiveness.* New York: Holt, Rinehart & Winston, 1967.

Simon, W., and J.H. Gagnon. *Youth Cultures and Aspects of the Socialization Process.* Bloomington, Ind.: Institute for Sex Research, 1968.

Zelnik, M., and J. Kantner. Sexual Activity, Contraceptive Use, and Pregnancy Among Metropolitan-Area Teenagers: 1971–1979. *Family Planning Perspectives,* Vol. 12 (1980), pp. 230–237.

Clive M. Davis
Tara Anthony
Suzanne L. Osman
Sandra L. Davis

e

EDUCATION: SEXUALITY EDUCATION IN THE UNITED STATES

Sexuality education is the lifelong process of acquiring information and forming attitudes, beliefs, and values about identity, relationships, and intimacy. School-based sexuality education is more than teaching anatomy and the physiology of reproduction. It includes an understanding of sexuality from sexual development and reproductive health to interpersonal relationships, and affection and intimacy, to body image and gender roles. Parents, partners, friends, peers, schools, religious institutions, and the media all influence how one learns about sexuality at every stage of life.

Prevalence of Sexuality Education in the United States

As of January, 1993, forty-seven states either recommend or mandate sexuality education. Every state recommends or mandates HIV/AIDS education. Sixty-eight percent of large school districts required some instruction in sexuality education, and 80 percent required some instruction about AIDS. Only two percent discouraged or prohibited teaching about these subjects. However, only a few communities offered comprehensive sexuality education programs at all grade levels. Although between two thirds and three quarters of students said they had received some sexuality education by the time they graduated from high school, few had participated in programs from kindergarten through grade 12. It is estimated that less than ten percent of young people participate in a program from kindergarten through high school. Sexuality topics are most likely first introduced in grade 9 or 10 as part of a discussion of another subject, such as health or physical education. The average amount of time spent on these topics during a year is under 12 hours in grade seven and just 18 hours by grade 12.

A review of state-recommended or state-developed curricula illustrates the limitations of existing programs. Although most of the curricula focus on such important issues as family relationships, dating, gender roles, and parenting responsibilities, few address sexual issues directly. Although 65 percent of the state curricula affirm that sexuality is a natural part of life, only eight percent provide information on sexual behavior. Only half have adequate family planning information. Fewer than one out of six state curricula would provide young people with a complete base of information.

HIV/AIDS curricula are even less likely to deal openly and honestly with sexual topics. HIV/AIDS is generally presented as one more negative consequence of sexual behavior. Although all of the state HIV/AIDS curricula include the important topic of abstinence, only eleven states present a balanced picture of safer sex. Only three states place HIV/AIDS information in a context of positive sexuality. And although thirty-seven states mention condoms, only five states tell young people how to use or obtain them.

Objectives

Sexuality education should be offered as part of an overall comprehensive health education program. Sexuality education can best address the broadest range of issues in the context of health promotion and disease prevention. A comprehensive school-based sexuality education program should have four primary objectives:

1. *Information*: Young people will have accurate information about human sexuality including growth and development, human reproduction, anatomy, physiology, masturbation, family life, pregnancy, childbirth, parenthood, sexual response, sexual orientation, contraception, abortion, sexual abuse, AIDS, and other sexually transmitted diseases.
2. *Attitudes, Values, and Insights*: Young people will question, explore, and assess sexual attitudes and feelings in order to develop their own values, increase their self-esteem, develop their insights concerning relationships with members of both genders, and understand their obligations and responsibilities to others.
3. *Relationships and Interpersonal Skills*: Young people will develop interpersonal skills, including communication, decision-making, assertiveness, peer refusal skills, and the ability to create satisfying relationships. Sexuality education programs should prepare students to understand their sexuality effectively and creatively in adult roles (e.g., as spouse, partner, parent, and community member). This includes helping them to develop their capacities for caring, supportive, noncoercive, and mutually pleasurable intimate sexual relationships in adulthood.
4. *Responsibility*: Young people will exercise responsibility in their sexual relationships by understanding abstinence and how to resist pressures to become prematurely involved in sexual intercourse, as well as encouraging the use of contraception and other sexual health measures. Sexuality education should

be a central component of programs designed to reduce the prevalence of sexually related health problems (e.g., teenage pregnancies, sexually transmitted diseases, including HIV infection, and sexual abuse).

HIV/AIDS education should take place within the context of comprehensive health and sexuality education. It should not be taught as an isolated program, but rather integrated into an approach that includes the objectives listed above. The HIV/AIDS unit should address five primary objectives:

1. *Reducing Misinformation*: Eliminate misinformation about HIV infection and transmission and reduce the panic associated with the disease.
2. *Delaying Premature Sexual Intercourse*: Help young people delay premature sexual intercourse; this includes teaching young people to recognize the implications of their actions and to gain the communication skills with which to confront peer pressure and negotiate resistance.
3. *Supporting Safer Sex*: Help teenagers who are sexually active to use condoms every time they have intercourse or practice only sexual behaviors that do not place them at risk of pregnancy, sexually transmitted diseases, or HIV infection.
4. *Preventing Drug Abuse*: Warn children about the dangers of drug use and teach young people the skills with which to confront peer pressure and negotiate resistance.
5. *Developing Compassion for People With AIDS*: Encourage compassion for people with AIDS and for people who are infected with the HIV virus.

Content of Sexuality Education

Sexuality education programs should address all three learning domains: the cognitive, affective, and behavioral. Sexuality education programs are most effective when young people not only receive information, but have the opportunity to explore their own values and attitudes and develop or strengthen social skills. A wide variety of classroom activities foster learning: lectures, role playing, simulations, individual and group research, field trips, and group exercises.

School-based sexuality education programs must be carefully developed to respect the diversity of values and beliefs represented in each local community. Parents, teachers, administrators, community and religious leaders, and students should all be involved in developing and implementing programs. Local educators need to determine the values, themes, instructional strategies, and classroom activities.

This is not to suggest that there is not a body of information that all young people need to receive. In 1991, the Sex Information and Education Council of the United States (SIECUS), convened a national guidelines task force of health, education, and sexuality professionals to develop national guidelines for sexuality education. Task force members included representatives from the U.S. Centers for Disease Control, the American Medical Association, the National School Boards Association, the National Education Association, the March of Dimes Birth Defects Foundation, and the Planned Parenthood Federation of America, as well as experienced school-based sexuality education teachers.

The task force developed national guidelines for a comprehensive approach to sexuality education for levels from kindergarten through grade 12. Divided into four stages of development—middle childhood, preadolescence, early adolescence, and adolescence—the guidelines are based on the following six key concepts, which represent the highest level of general knowledge of human sexuality and family living.

1. Human development is characterized by the interrelationship between physical, emotional, social, and intellectual growth.
2. Relationships play a central role throughout our lives.
3. Healthy sexuality requires the development and use of specific personal and interpersonal skills.
4. Sexuality is central to being human and individuals express their sexuality in a variety of ways.
5. The promotion of sexual health requires specific information and attitudes to avoid unwanted consequences of sexual behavior.
6. Social and cultural environments shape the way individuals learn about and express their sexuality.

These concepts are further broken down into subconcepts and a topical outline. The National Task Force recommended that 36 topics—each presented with age-appropriate information—be included in a comprehensive program. (See Table I.) Developmental messages are developed for each topic.

Support for Sexuality Education

The vast support for sexuality education—among both the general public and the professional community—has increased over time. A Gallup poll in 1943 found that 70 percent of adults supported sex education; in 1965, 69 percent of adults did, in 1975, 76 percent of adults, and in 1986, 89 percent of adults were in favor of sexuality education. More than 95 percent of adults want HIV/AIDS education taught to their children. Seventy-seven percent think that courses for 12-year-olds should include information about birth control. Almost two thirds say that courses should include information about homosexuality, abortion, sexual intercourse, and premarital sex.

Support for AIDS education is even higher. Ninety-four percent of parents think public schools should have an HIV/AIDS education program, and only four percent think they should not. More than eight out of ten parents want their children to be taught about safe sex as a way of preventing AIDS. Parents of students show their support for sexuality education in another way: given the option of excusing their children from sexuality education classes, less than one to five percent do so.

Moreover, many national professional organizations have adopted policies that support sexuality education. More than 70 national organizations are members of the National Coalition to Support Sexuality Education. These organizations have agreed to work together to ensure that all children and youth receive comprehensive sexuality education by the year 2000. Coalition members include such national organizations as the American Medical Association, the National Education Association, the YWCA of the U.S.A., the American Nurses Association, the Children's Defense Fund, the American School Health Association, the U.S. Conference of Mayors, and the National Urban League.

Resources for More Information

Numerous resources exist for helping school systems develop sexuality and HIV/AIDS education programs. Some states have developed curricula guidelines for school programs and have resource people in the State Department of Education to assist local communities. SIECUS has developed national guidelines for sexuality education programs and a step-by-step guide for implementing programs in a community. ETR Associates, in Santa Cruz, California, has numerous curriculums and teaching materials available. Several organizations, such as the American Association of Sex Educators, Counselors, and Therapists in Chicago; the National Council of Family Relations in Minneapolis; and the

Society for the Scientific Study of Sex in Mount Vernon, Iowa, offer continuing education programs for teachers. Local colleges and universities may also offer training courses.

Table 1

Key Concepts and Topics to Be Covered in a Curriculum for Kindergarten to Grade 12

Key Concept 1: Human development is characterized by the interrelationships among physical, emotional, social, intellectual, and spiritual growth.
Topics:
- Reproductive anatomy and physiology
- Reproduction
- Puberty
- Body image
- Sexual orientation

Key Concept 2: Relationships play a central role throughout our lives.
Topics:
- Families
- Friendships
- Love
- Dating
- Marriage and divorce
- Parenthood

Key Concept 3: Healthy sexuality requires the development and use of specific personal and interpersonal skills.
Topics:
- Values
- Decision making
- Communication
- Assertiveness
- Negotiation
- Finding Help

Key Concept 4: Sexuality is central to being human and individuals express their sexuality in a variety of different ways.
Topics:
- Sexuality through the life cycle
- Masturbation
- Shared sexual behaviors
- Abstinence
- Human sexual response
- Fantasy
- Sexual dysfunction

Key Concept 5: The promotion of sexual health requires that individuals have information, knowledge, and attitudes necessary to avoid unwanted consequences of their sexual behavior.
Topics:
- Contraception
- Abortion
- HIV and STD
- Sexual abuse
- Reproductive health

Key Concept 6: Social and cultural environments shape the way individuals learn about, experience, and express their sexuality.
Topics:
- Gender roles
- Sexuality and the law
- Sexuality and religion
- Sexuality in the arts
- Diversity
- Sexuality and the media

REFERENCES

DeMauro, D. Sexuality 1990: A Review of State Sexuality and AIDS Curricula. In *SIECUS Report,* Vol. 18, No. 2 (Dec. 1989/Jan. 1990), pp. 1–9.

Donovan, P. *Risk and Responsibility.* New York: Alan Guttmacher Institute, 1989.

Gallup, G. *Gallup Pole Public Opinion 1935–1971.* New York: Random House, 1972.

————. Teens Want Right to Obtain Birth Control Devices. Gallup Youth Survey. (News release, Sept. 27, 1980). Princeton, N.J.

Haffner, D. *Sex Education 2000: A Call to Action.* New York: SIECUS, 1989.

————, and D. DeMauro. *Winning the Battle: Developing Support for Sexuality and HIV/AIDS Education.* New York: SIECUS, 1991.

Louis Harris and Associates, Inc. *American Teens Speak.* New York: Planned Parenthood Federation of America, 1986.

National Guidelines Task Force. *Guidelines for Comprehensive Sexuality Education.* New York: SIECUS, 1991.

SIECUS Position Statements. (Dec. 1990). New York.

Debra W. Haffner

EJACULATION

Ejaculation is the expulsion of seminal fluid. Many people assume that ejaculation and orgasm are the same, since most males experience the two simultaneously. Even though this is true for 80 to 90 percent of males, it is not true for all men. For instance, in controlled studies some men have been observed to ejaculate but not have orgasm or have orgasm but are unable to ejaculate. And some men, after prostate surgery, have retrograde ejaculate. (This means the ejaculation goes into the bladder and is expelled during urination.) Retrograde ejaculation is a form of birth control in some cultures, and in certain religious groups men do not ejaculate, believing it debilitates them.

Male Ejaculation

Ejaculation in the male generally occurs with coitus, during masturbation, or during sleep (in what is called a nocturnal emission, or a wet dream). It happens most often when the penis is erect, but can also occur when the penis is flaccid. The ejaculate usually spurts out as the prostate gland and surrounding muscles, as well as those at the base of the penis, contract at orgasm. In young males, the force of the spurt can be strong enough for the ejaculate to hit the upper chest; in older males, it may roll out or go an inch or two up the abdomen.

The ejaculatory content in the male is called semen, and the amount ejaculated varies among men (a healthy male ejaculates about one teaspoonful). The ejaculatory content contains an average of 200 to 400 million sperm. (When the sperm count is low, conception usually does not occur in the normal fashion.) The seminal vesicles release the sperm, which are developed in the testicles, and at ejaculation there is a thick, milky fluid secreted from the prostate gland and added to the mixture, which is yellow, grey, or whitish. Upon reaching puberty, a boy is able to ejaculate the fluid.

Controlling Ejaculation

Ejaculation can be controlled by (1) using the squeeze technique, (2) keeping the testicles from full elevation, and (3) controlling the pubococcygeus (PC) muscle.

In the squeeze technique, strong fingertip pressure is applied to the top and underside of the penis. The pressure must be firm and applied without movement for about 15 seconds, and it must be applied before the point of ejaculatory inevitability. During coitus, either partner may apply the pressure to the base of the penis.

Since ejaculation occurs when the testicles are fully elevated against the perineum, ejaculation can be controlled by applying light pressure to keep the testicles from reaching full elevation.

The PC muscle—the same muscle that starts and stops the flow of urine—can be trained over a two- to three-month period to control ejaculation. Tightening and releasing the muscle 10 to 15 times several times a day will strengthen it. Contracting the muscle and holding the contraction three or four times for 15 seconds will train it to reverse the urge to ejaculate. The 15-second hold must be done before ejaculatory inevitability for ejaculatory control.

Premature Ejaculation

Some men ejaculate as soon as they are aroused, before penetration, or with one or two thrusts in coitus. In addition, because some men never or rarely touch their penis, or allow a partner to touch it, their penis may be so sensitive that any touch is painful or uncomfortable, or produces rapid ejaculation. More touching, stroking, or fondling of the penis in love making often desensitizes the penis enough to enable these men to go longer in intercourse without ejaculating. By masturbating several times a week for 15 or 20 minutes before ejaculating, a man can often reverse the urge to ejaculate rapidly. Erection, ejaculation, or orgasm is not necessary when masturbating for this desensitizing procedure.

Often in premature ejaculation problems, not only is the man reluctant to allow his partner to touch him during foreplay, his partner is also. Both fear he will ejaculate too soon. This reluctance is one of the problems that causes rapid ejaculation in the first place: the penis has not been conditioned to be stimulated for any length of time.

In treatment, the couple do pleasuring nondemand exercises, touching the penis for 15 to 20 minutes. These exercises are performed slowly and with light but total hand pressure over the genitalia without expectations of any kind. If the man comes close to ejaculation, he informs his partner and she can do the squeeze technique for about 15 seconds to reverse his urge to ejaculate. This procedure may occur several times in the 15- to 20-minute period. As the man learns to control the urge to ejaculate, he will be able to go longer without the need to squeeze. But until he learns to identify the point of ejaculatory inevitability, he may need to apply the squeeze as soon as he has an erection. He continues to stimulate the penis further, squeezing every few minutes, until he has gone 15 minutes without ejaculating and trying to come as close as he can to orgasm without having one. Once he has learned to control his climax he can typically go as long as he wishes in intercourse without ejaculating.

The pleasuring nondemand exercises occur only after about an hour of body caressing so that the whole body is relaxed and excited. Although, very often, the man will have an erection during the body caressing stage, stimulation of the genitalia does not proceed until the nondemand pleasuring exercises are over. This allows the man to hold an erection for some time and learn to be comfortable doing so. In this way, both partners can become more secure knowing that the penis can remain erect for a time or realize that if it does subside it will become erect again (since typically erections come and go over a period of time). Men often panic when they begin to lose an erection, not realizing that this is normal and that it will return if they do not become anxious.

Ejaculatory Incompetence

In the research laboratory, men have been observed using unusually heavy pressure on the penis while masturbating, which often results in an inability to ejaculate during intercourse. In therapy, it is suggested that while masturbating they use very light pressure more typical of the pressure they feel in their partner's vagina. However, it may take time for them to develop less need for heavy pressure.

Ejaculatory incompetence can also be a learned behavior. Despite the strong taboos against masturbation or touching the penis, boys often like the feeling it gives them and develop ways to masturbate that are not conducive to ejaculating in intercourse. Some ejaculatory incompetent men pull a sheet, towel, or whatever else they have learned to use between their legs to stimulate themselves to ejaculation. Others may lie on their stomach putting pressure on their penis from the mattress; some cross their legs with the penis between them and rub their legs together. Such masturbatory patterns are not conducive to intercourse even though they may work well in masturbation.

Female Ejaculation

Female ejaculation is the expulsion of fluid, other than urine, from the urethra at orgasm. This topic is debated among experts: some argue that the ejaculate is a mucuous-like secretion coming from the cervical os; others that it is vaginal wall secretions; and others that it is a nonurine expulsion from the urethra.

REFERENCES

Allgeier, E.R., and A.R. Allgeier. *Sexual Interactions.* Lexington, Mass.: D.C. Heath & Co., 1984.

Calderone, M.S., and E.W. Johnson, *The Family Book About Sexuality.* New York: Harper & Row, 1988.

Hartman, W.E., and M. Fithian. *Any Man Can.* New York: St. Martin's Press, 1984.

Ladas, A., B. Whipple, and J.D. Perry. *The G. Spot.* New York: Holt, Rinehart & Winston, 1982.

Masters, W.H., V.E. Johnson, and R.C. Kolodny. *Human Sexuality.* Boston: Little, Brown & Co., 1982.

Zilbergeld, B. *Male Sexuality.* Boston: Little, Brown & Co., 1971.

William E. Hartman
Marilyn A. Fithian

ELLIS, ALBERT

Albert Ellis, born September 27, 1913, is a clinical psychologist who received his Ph.D. from Columbia University in 1947. From 1949 to 1952, he was chief psychologist at the New Jersey Diagnosis Center of the New Jersey Department of Institutions and Agencies; he was also in private practice (for psychotherapy and marriage and family counseling).

Perhaps Ellis's greatest contribution has been his books and articles, which were not only educational but many—such as his works on masturbation and extramarital sex—were innovative and even shocking when they were written. An extremely prolific writer, Ellis authored or edited more than 50 books and monographs, many discussing his theories on sexuality.

In 1959 Albert Ellis founded the Institute for Rational-Emotive Therapy (R.E.T.) in New York City. R.E.T., a unique psychotherapeutic approach to sexual and non-sexual situations, is designed to help people overcome irrational beliefs and unrealistic expectations by blending behavioral therapy with specific strategies for dealing with emotional stressors. As of 1993, Ellis is president of his Institute and continues to conduct individual, couples, and group therapies.

Ellis was a founding member of the Society for the Scientific Study of Sex (SSSS) and its first president (1960–1962). In 1975 SSSS awarded him its Distinguished Scientific Achievement Award. Ellis has also served prominently in other sexology organizations: American Association of Sex Educators (on the board of directors), American Academy of Psychotherapists (vice president), and American Psychological Association (division president).

REFERENCES

Ellis, A. *The American Sexual Tragedy.* New York: Twayne, 1954.

———. *The Art and Science of Love.* New York: Lyle Strauss. Reprinted. New York: Bantam Books, 1969.

———. *The Folklore of Sex.* New York: Bone, 1951.

———. *Humanistic Psychotherapy: The Rational Emotive Approach.* New York: Julian Press, 1973.

———. *If This Be Sexual Heresy.* New York: Lyle Stuart. Reprinted. New York: Tower Publications, 1966.

———. *Reason and Emotion in Psychotherapy.* New York: Lyle Stuart, 1963.

———. *Sex Without Guilt.* New York: Lyle Stuart, 1958.

Ellis, A., and A. Abarbanel, eds. *The Encyclopedia of Sexual Behavior.* New York: Hawthorne, 1961.

Leah Cahan Schaefer

ELLIS, HAVELOCK

Havelock Ellis (1859–1939) was an English physician who challenged Victorian ideas about sexuality by suggesting that sex could and should be enjoyable and that lovemaking should be pleasurable. Although Freud is a better known contemporary, Freud only formulated individual sexual doctrines; Ellis made the more extensive and more representative contribution to sexuality as it is known today. The first six volumes of his great work, *Studies in the Psychology of Sex,* were published between 1897 and 1910, and they established the basic moral categories for nearly all subsequent sexual theorizing.

The first volume of his *Studies—Sexual Inversion*—introduces Ellis's modernist views. In it, he argues that homosexuals are born to their sexual orientation and backs up theories with detailed case histories. The second volume—*Auto-Eroticism*—seeks to dispel the Victorian myth that masturbation leads to serious illness as well as insanity. Ellis even argues that masturbation can be a legitimate source of mental relaxation.

Ellis was concerned with other important questions of his day, and he had many underlying themes with which to address them. For example, the notions of tumescence and detumescence are important themes that recur throughout his work. (Tumescence is defined as the "accumulation" of sexual energy during arousal, and detumescence, the "discharge" of that energy at the moment of climax.) Ellis used these concepts to signify the entire process of sexual arousal and release.

In bringing to light the fact that women have sexual emotions, Ellis was one of the architects of the theory of erogenous zones—the idea that certain parts of the body are more receptive to sexual arousal than others. A pioneer in the field of sexuality in a time when there were many misconceptions, Ellis laid the groundwork for later sexual pioneers to dispel other misconceptions as well as to continue to explain the complexities of human sexuality.

REFERENCES

Francoeur, R.T. "American Sexual Customs." *Becoming a Sexual Person.* New York: Macmillan. 1991:16

Grosskurth, P. *Havelock Ellis: A Biography.* New York: New York University Press, 1985.

Robinson, P. "Havelock Ellis." *The Modernization of Sex.* New York: Cornell, 1989: 1–40.

Hope E. Ashby

EMBRYOLOGY: DEVELOPMENT OF SEXUAL AND GENERATIVE ORGANS

Embryology is the science that describes and explains the development of an organism before its birth. In humans, the main development of the sexual and reproductive organs occurs between the 4th and 18th weeks of pregnancy. This development is closely associated with development of a pair of temporary kidneys, which are replaced in the third month by the permanent kidneys.

Psychosexual development, of which the anatomical development of the sexual and generative organs is an integral and interactive part, has been compared with an analogy to a road map with six prenatal and six postnatal gates. (See Table 1.) The six prenatal gates are the following:

1. Chromosomal (or genetic) sex (established at fertilization);
2. Gonadal sex (established between weeks 6 and 12 of gestation);
3. Hormonal sex (with a critical period extending from the third month to death);
4 and 5. Internal and external sexual anatomy (in the second and third month);
6. Neural template encoding (from the second month to death).

The postnatal gates begin at birth with:
7. Gender assignment.

This is followed by
8. Gender scripting;
9. Gender role;
10. Gender identity (which is finalized age three);
11. Gender orientation (which appears to be finalized somewhere between age five and the onset of puberty); and
12. Adult gender identity-role.

This entry covers only the six prenatal gates of psychosexual development.

The timing and limits on the outcome of development at each of these 12 gates vary. The developmental "gates" that involve anatomical development have narrow, specific temporal "windows" (i.e., times during development when primordial, unspecialized tissues can respond to developmental stimuli). At other "gates," especially those involving behavior, the timing of development is less restricted and may even extend over years. The outcome of development at a specific developmental gate may be one dimensional (i.e., the outcome of that aspect is either-or, male or female). Development at other gates has a two-dimensional outcome that results from two concurrent processes, one process defeminizing a particular aspect of sexual devel- opment by overriding the inherent tendency of some structures to develop in the female path, while a second simultaneous process masculin- izes other related structures.

Table 1. *The 12 "Gates" of Psychosexual Development*

	Prenatal Gate	Temporal Window	Dimensional Character
1.	Genetic sex	When sperm and egg unite	Either XX female or XY male
2.	Gonadal sex	Weeks 6 to 12	Either ovaries or testes
3.	Hormonal sex	Second month of pregnancy through death	Two-dimensional combination of masculinizing and feminizing hormones
4.	Internal sexual anatomy	Second month of pregnancy through death	Two-dimensional: some structures being masculinized while others are feminized
5.	External sexual anatomy	Third month of pregnancy	One-dimensional, either a penis and scrotum or clitoris and labia
6.	Encoding of neural tendency	Second half of pregnancy through death	Two-dimensional com- bination of masculine and feminine tenden- cies and traits; somewhat flexible in some behavioral areas; gender orien- tation tendencies
7.	Gender assignment	Usually occurs at birth; later reassignment possible	One-dimensional: "It's a boy" or "It's a girl."
8.	Gender scripting	From birth onward	Multi-dimensional, culturally flexible combination of masculine or feminine scripts
9.	Gender	From early infancy throughout life	Multidimensional, flexible combination of masculine or feminine roles and behaviors
10.	Gender identity	Believed to be irreversibly set by age 3	One-dimensional, either "I'm a male" or "I'm a female."
11.	Gender orientation	Believed to be irreversibly set by age 5, definitely by late childhood	Oriented to persons of the same gender, other gender, or both genders
12.	Adult gender identity-role	Usually set by the time of puberty, but elaborated on throughout life	Gender identity set as either male or female, with more or less flexibility in gender role behaviors

In the higher animals (mammals), there exists an inherent or default tendency for the sexual and reproductive organs and brain tissues of all embryos to follow the female path through the 12 gates of psychosexual development. This inherent or default tendency does not depend on any genetic and hormonal stimulus or control, except that two X chromosomes are required for development of fertile ovaries. Development of the male organs and male psyche, on the other hand, is said to be additive or cumulative because they depend on two factors, one genetic and the other hormonal. In the second month of pregnancy, the Testes Determining Factor (TDF) gene carried on the Y chromosome directs development of the testes, which then produce three hormones: testosterone, dihydrotestosterone (DHT), and a Müllerian inhibiting hormone (MIH). The critical balance and interaction of these three hormones direct full male development. (See Genetics and Sex.)

Gates 1 and 2: Chromosomal (or Genetic and Gonadal) Sex

Chromosomal (or genetic) sex is determined at fertilization (see Genetics and Sex). Four weeks later, development of the sexual and reproductive system begins with formation of gonadal ridges on the surface of paired intermediate (metanephric) kidneys inside the embryo's thoracic-abdominal cavity and the migration of primordial germ cells from the primitive yolk sac outside the embryo to these ridges. During the sixth week, the sexually undifferentiated gonads may begin developing along a path that will result in testes, which produce a male balance of sex hormones and, after puberty, sperm. If the gonads are not stimulated to become testes in the sixth week, they will wait a few weeks to differentiate into ovaries, capable of producing a female balance of sex hormones and, with puberty, eggs (ova). At this early stage, some cells in the gonads develop to nourish and support development of the eggs and sperm. These are follicular cells in the ovaries and Sertoli cells in the testes.

The either/or development of the undifferentiated gonads into ovaries or testes depends on the fetal genetic constitution established at fertilization. If the cells of the embryo's body contain the TDF gene (usually carried on a Y chromosome), the tissues of the gonadal ridges form seminiferous (sperm-producing) tubules and associated ducts during the sixth week. In week seven, some cells sandwiched between the seminiferous tubules develop into the cells of Leydig and begin producing testosterone, a hormone that will stimulate and direct further differentiation of the reproductive and sexual structures.

If the embryo's body cells do not contain the TDF gene, the undifferentiated gonads do not begin developing until week 12 when, by default, the inherent tendency of the embryo to develop as a female is activated. This inherent tendency has been named the Eve Plan. Development of fertile ovaries requires two X chromosomes in the embryo's body cells. By week 16, the primitive female germ cells are incorporated into millions of primary ovarian follicles. Most of these degenerate during pregnancy, leaving only one million or two million primary oocyte (developing eggs) at birth. These primitive eggs begin the two-stage meiosis, or reduction, cell division that will produce an egg with half the normal number of chromosomes in the body cells. But the cell division stops in what geneticists term "prophase arrest." They remain in this arrested state until cell division resumes sometime after puberty. This phenomenon of arrested egg development increases the risk of abnormalities in the number of chromosomes in the egg and thus in an embryo. (See Genetics and Sex for discussion of Turner and Klinefelter syndromes.)

As the temporary (mesonephric) kidneys degenerate and are replaced functionally by the developing definitive kidneys, the ovaries or testes shift out of the thoracic-abdominal cavity to assume their final position in the pelvic cavity.

Gate 3: Hormonal Sex

In the third month of gestation, the testes begin producing three hormones: (1) testosterone and its derivative, (2) DHT, and (3) MIH. These hormones direct development of the male sexual and generative anatomy and establish behavioral tendencies in the neural pathways of the brain. As these hormones circulate throughout the fetal body, specific transfer enzymes on selective target cells and organs allow these hormones to enter those cells and organs, including the brain. Testosterone and DHT are androgenic (or masculinizing) hormones; MIH has a defeminizing effect on the embryo, blocking the inherent tendency of the embryo to develop as a female. Estrogens, which are produced by both the ovaries and testes, do not appear to be involved in sexual differentiation until puberty. At that time, estrogens stimulate development of secondary sexual characteristics of the female and have some minor effects on the secondary sexual characteristics of males.

Gate 4: Internal Sexual Anatomy

In both male and female embryos, a pair of ducts drain urine from the two temporary kidneys (mesonephros) and carry it to the cloaca for excretion into the amniotic sac. Parallel with these Wolffian (mesonephric) ducts are two Müllerian (or paramesonephric) ducts. The Müllerian ducts move toward the midline as they approach the cloaca, fusing into a single tube which ends at the cloaca without opening into the urogenital sinus.

By the eleventh week, Sertoli cells in the testes are producing MIH. In the male embryo, MIH "defeminizes" by triggering degeneration of the Müllerian ducts. This prevents the Eve Plan from coming into play; in the Eve Plan, the Müllerian ducts would develop into the vagina, uterus, and Fallopian tubes. MIH may also initiate the testes to descend about the time of birth and produce as yet undetected effects of neural pathways late in pregnancy. After birth, MIH has no known function.

In the developing male embryo, during the third month, the cells of Leydig in the testes produce the hormone testosterone, which causes the Wolffian ducts to develop. The portion of these tubes near the testes becomes highly twisted to form the epididymis. The rest becomes the vas deferens, ejaculatory duct, and the seminal vesicles of the male duct system. Tissue surrounding the ejaculatory ducts where they join the urethra forms the prostate gland. The outer urethra and penis develop from the open urogenital sinus as part of the external development described in Gate 5 below. The paired bulbourethral (or Cowper's glands) develop below the prostate from outpocketings of the urethra.

In a fetus that lacks the TDF gene and does not develop threshold levels of masculinizing hormones and MIH in the critical period between weeks 6 and 12, development of internal and external sexual organs—and neural templates—follows the Eve Plan. With no testosterone to stimulate their development into male structures, the Wolffian ducts degenerate and disappear. The absence of MIH allows the Müllerian ducts to develop according to their inherent genetic tendencies in the female path. The portion of the Müllerian ducts near the ovaries become the Fallopian (or uterine) tubes. The remaining caudal portion of the Müllerian ducts fuses in the eighth week, with the medial septum disappearing about week 12. This primordium becomes the uterus, cervix, and vagina. The outer muscles of the uterus and vagina develop from surrounding tissue.

Because the internal sexual system (excluding the gonads) originates from parallel primordial ducts for the male (Wolffian) and the female (Müllerian) systems, anomalous development can result. The internal sexual duct system may, for instance, be masculinized by testosterone, but not defeminized due to a lack of MIH. This would leave the fetus with both internal male and female sexual structures (as discussed below). A second variation, androgen insensitivity (or testicular feminization) syndrome, is caused by a single defective gene (see Genetics and Sex). In this condition, the fetus is defeminized by MIH but not masculinized because none of the body cells can recognize the masculinizing message of the testosterone and DHT. It therefore lacks both male and female internal systems.

Gate 5: External Sexual Anatomy

Differentiation of the external sexual and reproductive organs begins early in week four with appearance of a genital tubercle in the pelvic floor between the legs. A pair of inner urogenital folds and an outer pair of labioscrotal swellings develop behind the genital tubercle. By week eight, in embryos with the TDF gene, testes, and threshold levels of DHT, the genital tubercle, swellings and folds have begun their masculinized development. The tubercle elongates and begins differentiating as a penis. In week 11, the folds form the penile urethral groove and then the penile urethra. The penile urethra becomes surrounded by an erectile tissue, the corpus spongiosum. At the distal end of the penis, the corpus spongiosum enlarges into the penile glans. Within the penile shaft, above the corpus spongiosum, a pair of erectile bodies, the corpora cavernosa, develop.

The foreskin of the penis forms in week 12. It separates from the penile glans before birth or in early infancy. A second invagination in the middle of the glans provides an external opening for the heretofore dead-end penile urethra.

In the male fetus, the paired labioscrotal swellings move together and fuse to form the scrotum. A line of fusion (or median raphe) on the underside of the penis and scrotum mark the line of fusion of the folds and swellings.

Between the fourth month and birth, the testes begin migrating from the upper abdominal region. Paired extensions of the pelvic/abdominal cavity push down into the scrotum to provide a path for this migration. Hormones and a ligament attached to each testis facilitate the descent. The testes usually reach the inguinal canal in the sixth month and the scrotum about the time of birth. However, an estimated one in 50 boys goes into puberty with one or both testes undescended, and one in 500 adult men has one or both testes undescended. After the descent of the testes, the connection with the abdominal cavity closes, isolating the scrotal sac.

In the female fetus, the absence of androgens allows the genital tubercle to elongate and become a clitoris in the fourth month. The urogenital folds remain separate and form the minor (or inner) labia. These labia join in the front of the clitoris to form a clitoral hood. In the perineal region, they become the fourchette (or frenulum). The labioscrotal swellings remain separate and become the major (or outer) labia.

It is commonly acknowledged that the clitoris is homologous to (i.e., from the same embryonic origins as) the male penis and that the clitoral glans is homologous to the penile glans. However, there is considerable confusion about terminology and statements of homologies when anatomists and embryologists discuss the erectile bodies of the penis and their parallels in the clitoris. This confusion can be dealt with by simplifying the traditional overly specific and androcentric labels. This would involve referring to the erectile bodies of the penis as a pair of corpora cavernosa and a single corpus cavernosum urethra. In the female, a simplified labeling would include the clitoral shaft with a pair of corpora cavernosa. Most anatomists refer to the two elongated erectile masses, which run interior to the

labia on either side of the vaginal orifice from the clitoral shaft to the rectum, as the "bulb of the vestibule." Sixty years ago, German anatomists and the American physician and sexologist Robert Latou Dickinson considered this paired erectile structure to be part of the clitoris, referring to them as the "clitoral legs or crurae." In recent years, prompted by some feminist health advocates, this early view has gained acceptance. Renaming the bulb of the vestibule and including it in the clitoral structure are supported by its erectile nature, its direct connection with the clitoral shaft, and its function of narrowing the opening of the vagina and squeezing the male penis during vasocongestion and coitus. (See Table 2.)

The Eve and Adam Plans

The inherent Eve Plan, which allows female development to proceed without hormonal controls, and the Adam Plan, which requires the addition of the TDF gene, androgenic hormones, and MIH to direct male development, raise a question of sexually dimorphic, male versus female, development. Maternal hormones circulate throughout the mother's body and some cross the placental barrier into the developing body of the fetus, be it male or female. Mammalian embryos of both sexes develop in milieu of the mother's uterus. The placenta is also a major source of sex-related hormones, many of which feed back and forth between fetus and mother.

Table 2 *Homologies of the Sexual Organs*

Undifferentiated Structures	Female	Male
Paired gonads	Ovaries	Testes
Wolffian (mesonephric) Ducts	Regress Skene's glands	Vas deferens prostate, seminal vesicles
Müllerian (paramesonephric) Ducts	Vagina, uterus, and Fallopian tubes	Regresses
Genital tubercle	clitoris, clitoral glans, erectile tissue of shaft and clitoral legs (or crurae)	Penis, penile glans, erectile tissue of corpora cavernosa and corpus spongiosum
Genital folds	Minor labia	Penile shaft
Genital swellings	Major labia	Scrotum
Urogenital sinus	Stays open to form vulva	Closes to form penile urethra

How, then, can a fetus successfully negotiate passage through the prenatal gates of psychosexual development along the male path?

Part of the answer is that at least some of the circulating female hormones all fetuses receive across the placental barrier are neutralized by binding them to large molecules. Rendered metabolically inaccessible, these bound estrogens leave the fetus, female or male, free to develop unencumbered by maternal hormones. If the fetus is female, it develops anatomically and neurally as a female because of the inherent tendencies of the Eve Plan. If the fetus is male, the MIH and testosterone produced by the fetal testes can direct sexual development along the male pathway without interference from maternal estrogens.

Gate Six: Sexual Dimorphism in Neural Tendencies

Neutralization of maternal estrogen is most important for sexual dimorphic development of the fetal brain. The limbic system and its hypothalamus have an inherent tendency (or program) for the cyclic production of a hormone that regulates production of follicle-stimulating hormone (FSH) and luteinizing hormone (LH) by the pituitary. (FSH and LH then regulate sperm, egg production, and hormone by the testes and ovaries.) In female fetuses, maternal protein-bound estrogen is too large to enter the fetal brain. Since fetal ovaries do not produce testosterone, no sex steroid reaches the female brain and its inherent cyclic pattern for the limbic system persists. This cyclic pattern results in the monthly cycle of ovulation and menstruation. In male development, the fetal testes produce testosterone, which enters the brain and destroys cyclicity in the limbic system and hypothalamus. However, the testosterone that enters the brain does not function as an androgen. Instead, after entering the brain, testosterone is converted to estrogen. Fetal testosterone is a cryptic way of delivering estrogen to the brain and replacing the cyclic encoding of the hypothalamus with an acyclic pattern of continuous sex hormone production that becomes functional at puberty.

The effects of sex steroids on other seemingly dimorphic neural tendencies in the cerebral cortex and limbic system, and possibly on gender orientations, are hotly debated.

Development of the Mammary Glands

In the fourth week of pregnancy, a parallel pair of primitive mammary ridges appear, extending from the region of the future arm pit to the crotch. These ridges disappear except at the future site of the two midpectoral nipples and breasts. These two primary mammary buds invade underlying tissues and branch to form mammary glands. The branching cords develop canals in the eighth month with milk-carrying ducts that open into a depression in the skin, which is transformed into a nipple after birth. The mammary glands develop during female puberty. However, maternal lactogenic hormones that cross the placenta can cause the secretion of colostrum, known colloquially as "witch's milk," in a male newborn. Female breast development, gynecomastia, can occur in males as part of Klinefelter and other syndromes and in response to exogenous hormones.

Nondevelopment of the nipple and breast is rare. Extra breasts and nipples are inheritable conditions with extra nipples relatively common in males. Inverted nipples are due to a perinatal failure to evert and may cause problems in nursing.

Puberty

Structural and functional maturation of the sexual and generative organs and sexuoerotic maturation occurs during puberty when a complex interaction of somatotropin (growth hormone), estrogens, and androgens regulate (1) development of the primary sexual and generative organs; (2) the onset of ovulation, menstruation, and spermatogenesis; (3) the maturation of the female mammary glands; (4) the onset of libido or sex drive; and (5) the development of secondary sexual characteristics.

Anomalous Developments of the Sexual and Generative Organs

Abnormal sexual developments are to be expected, considering the complex of genetic, hormonal, and environmental factors that affect the sexual development of the fetus.

In hermaphroditism, there is a discrepancy between gonads and external genitalia. True hermaphrodites have a pair of gonads with both ovarian and testicular tissue, or one ovary and one testis, with male, female, or intersex sexual anatomy. In another type of true hermaphrodite, the gonads do not develop or are undifferentiated. In this case, the individual's chromosomal sex conflicts with its external sexual anatomy and gender identity. Most true hermaphrodites have 46 chromosomes, including two X chromosomes, and are well-adapted when raised as females.

The simultaneous hermaphroditism observed in some invertebrates with functional reproductive sexual systems of both sexes does not occur in mammals. The sequential hermaphrodism, observed in some fish and reptiles that can change their sex, usually from female to male, when stimulated by an appropriate change in their environment, is mimiced by the sex change surgery sought by many transsexuals. The sex change operation, however, does not bring reproductive ability in the new sex.

True hermaphroditism is rare in humans. More common is the condition known as pseudohermaphroditism, in which testes occur with female sex organs, or ovaries with male sex organs. In the male pseudohermaphrodite, a mild insufficiency of androgens from testes may result in a small penis, hypospadia (a urethral opening on the under surface of the penis), and a vulva-like scrotum. MIH deficiency allows the Müllerian ducts to form a vagina and uterus with more or less normal external female anatomy. In a female pseudohermaphrodite, the female fetus is virilized (or masculinized) by male hormones from a fetal adrenal tumor, an adrenal malfunction, or from some androgen given to the mother to prevent miscarriage.

The term "intersex" is usually applied in the case of ambiguous external genitals. In such cases, the sex of the gonadal tissue usually determines the gender of assignment.

A rare congenital anomaly, known as retained Müllerian syndrome, occurs in a male with a deficiency of MIH. In such a male, the internal male anatomy develops normally from the Wolffian ducts under the influence of testosterone. At the same time, however, the absence of MIH allows the Müllerian ducts to persist and develop into female structures, the Fallopian tubes, a uterus, and a vagina. The vagina may connect with the rectum or the urethra. In some cases, the uterine tissue may respond to endocrine stimulation, resulting in menstruation through the penile urethra or the rectum.
Note: Related sexual anomalies caused by genetic factors are described under the entry Genetics and Sex.

REFERENCES

Federation of Feminist Women's Health Centers. *A New View of a Woman's Body.* New York: Simon & Schuster, 1981.

Francoeur, R.T. *Becoming a Sexual Person.* 2nd ed. New York: Macmillan, 1991.

Gray, H. *Anatomy: Descriptive and Surgical.* T.P. Pick and R. Howden, eds. New York: Bounty Books, 1977.

Money, J., and A.A. Ehrhardt. *Man & Woman, Boy and Girl: Differentiation and Dimorphism of Gender Identity From Conception to Maturity.* Baltimore: Johns Hopkins Univ. Press, 1972.

Money, J., and P. Tucker. *Sexual Signatures: On Being a Man or a Woman.* Boston: Little, Brown, 1975.

Moore, K.L. *The Developing Human: Clinically Oriented Embryology.* 4th ed. Philadelphia: Saunders, 1988.

Reinish, J.M., L.A. Rosenblum, and S.A. Sanders. *Masculinity/Femininity: Basic Perspectives.* New York: Oxford Univ. Press, 1987.

Tortora, G.J., and N.P. Anagnostakos. *Principles of Anatomy and Physiology.* 6th ed. New York: Harper & Row, 1990.

Robert T. Francoeur

EROTICISM

The *Britannica-Webster Dictionary and Reference Guide* defines anything that relates to, or is marked by, sexual love or desire as erotic. Except for severely repressed persons, most humans are capable of being eroticized by many things, people, or experiences in their daily life. The object of the eroticism may not have particular inherent sexual symbolism; it is also possible that it may not lead to sexual behavior, or be genitally arousing, or even shared with or by anyone else known to the person.

Society has permitted certain erotic symbols, such as movie or rock stars, certain clothing, cars, and explicitly sexual material. But to feel eroticized by smelling and sucking sweaty feet, having sex with someone else's partner, or being tied up (as in bondage) is not as widely accepted. Some feel embarrassed or guilty by the variety of things they find erotic. Others repress any awareness of erotic feeling. Still others keep the objects of their eroticism secret. There is no reason for most people to feel guilty about their erotic potential; in fact, by cutting themselves off from their erotic potential they may become sexually dysfunctional.

Occasionally, what a person finds erotic can be harmful or dangerous. This includes asphyxiophilia (self-strangulation without loss of consciousness to enhance sexual arousal and orgasm), autassassinophilia (staging one's own murder to enhance sexual arousal and orgasm), lust murderism, or in some other type of violent or mutilating behaviors. Therapy, medication, hospitalization, or incarceration are indicated in these cases.

Some people, known as paraphiliacs, are eroticized by only one thing. To experience erotic response, they have to experience the object of their eroticism or at least fantasize it. The difficulty for most paraphilias is that they are limited in their erotic potential to one object, experience, or activity. If the objective of their eroticism is harmful or inappropriate, they may need to be imprisoned, medicated, and/or in long-term therapy. Exploring the varieties of erotic potential in one's life can be rewarding and exciting. For example, one can be eroticized by one's self. Being turned on to one's own sexuality and experiencing that eroticism through masturbation can be both pleasurable and healthful. Self-pleasuring and self-love keeps one's sexual response active. It also helps one know what to tell a sexual partner about how he or she likes to be touched and fondled. Self-eroticism can be self-affirming, relaxing, and a helpful release for tension.

One can also be eroticized by other people. If it were societally acceptable, most people could feel erotic toward either sex. Most sex researchers agree that humans are born with a bisexual potential (see Bisexuality), and research seems to clearly indicate that humans are not by nature monogamous. While monogamy may be the chosen lifestyle in some societies, it is natural for people to fantasize about sexual partners other than one's chosen partner. This does not necessarily mean something is wrong with one's primary relationship. In fact, group sex is a common fantasy, although most people probably never act on it. Humans are born sexual and it is natural and normal to feel erotic feelings for other people. One does not have to act on those erotic feelings if it is against society's or one's own value system.

It is not unusual for humans to also have erotic feelings for a special pet or other animal. While most people do not act on these sexual feelings, some do. Generally, it occurs out of experimentation or when no human partner is available, rather than because a person is eroticized only by animals. Most researchers agree that this type of sexual experimentation is not harmful, unless the person is discovered. Then, it is the reaction of the person who discovers the sexual event that can do the most harm psychologically and emotionally, rather than the experience itself.

Most humans can find eroticism in a myriad of other things: the ocean, art, music, candlelight, intimate conversation, particular clothing, a mountain stream, certain smells or tastes, sweat, a vigorous athletic workout. We are limited only by our imagination. Since everything has erotic potential, there is something for everyone, and there is probably nothing that someone does not feel erotic toward.

Finally, a person can be eroticized by whatever is ultimate or a "Thou" in one's life. This may be science, reason, a deity, or any other ultimate that a person accepts for his or her life. For example, throughout religious history representatives of deity have often been linked to sexuality. In the Bible, the passionate book, *Song of Songs*, is sensual and openly erotic. This is not as evident in Western civilization, with some exceptions. Certainly Teresa of Avila and John of the Cross, two medieval Spanish saints of the Roman Catholic tradition, connected eroticism with spirituality. The testimony of many deeply spiritual people is filled with the transcendent dimension being highly sensual or erotic. More recent examples are the astronomer and poet Carl Sagan, who captures this dimension in his writings, and the New Age poets and musicians, who attest to the erotic and transcendent in life. Eastern cultures and religions also capture the erotic and spiritual dimension of human experience.

Eroticism is built into the very fiber of human existence and can be experienced in all dimensions of human experience.

REFERENCES

Ford, C.S., and F.A. Beach. *Patterns of Sexual Behavior.* New York: Harper Colophon Books, 1951.

Francoeur, R.T. *Becoming a Sexual Person.* 2nd ed. New York: Macmillan, 1991.

Money, J. *Lovemaps: Clinical Concepts of Sexual/Erotic Health and Pathology, Paraphilia, and Gender Transposition in Childhood, Adolescence, and Maturity.* New York: Irvington Publishers, Inc., 1986.

Stayton, W.R. A Theory of Sexual Orientation: The Universe as a Turn On. *Topics in Clinical Nursing.* Vol. 1, No. 4 (Jan. 1980), pp. 1–7.

———. A Theology of Sexual Pleasure. *American Baptist Quarterly,* Vol. 8, No. 2 (June 1989), pp. 94–108.

Weinrich, J.D. *Sexual Landscapes: Why We Are What We Are, Why We Love Whom We Love.* New York: Charles Scribner's Sons, 1987.

William R. Stayton

ETHOLOGY AND SEXOLOGY

Ethology is the branch of biology that addresses individual behavior. Disciplines for higher levels of organization are sociobiology and behavioral ecology and for lower levels neuroethology, neurophysiology, and neurochemistry. The science of ethology evolved from the naturalistic observations of biologists, the most famous of whom were Konrad Lorenz, Niko Tinbergen, and Karl von Frisch. These three men shared the Nobel Prize in physiology and medicine in 1973 for founding ethology and for demonstrating that behavior, like anatomy, evolved by Darwinian natural selection.

Ethologists come from many different formal backgrounds: biology, psychology, anthropology, sociology, history, political science, law, and medicine. All believe that human behavior evolved in the context of natural selection and that an appreciation of this heritage can contribute significantly to an understanding of the behavior of modern humans. As a scientific discipline, ethology is closest to sociobiology. Ethology is an inductive science: it starts by observing the behavior of individuals and from these direct observations arrives at generalizations that may apply to other individuals within the particular species, genus, family, etc. Sociobiology, in contrast, is largely deductive: it starts from evolutionary theory and makes deductive predictions about the behavior of individuals. Sociobiologists are interested in behaviors that are defined more on the basis of their functional outcome than on their structure; ethologists are more interested in the structure of behavior.

"Behavior" means the movement of voluntary muscles over time and space. It has several levels of organization; at the lowest level is the behavior of simple reflexes, such as the knee jerk, which is of interest to neurophysiologists. The next level of behavior is the "coordinated motor pattern," sometimes called "fixed action pattern," which is of interest to ethologists. An example of a coordinated motor pattern is the submissive behaviors one assumes when threatened by an overpowering opponent. Social smiling, crying, flirting, and copulating all contain coordinated motor patterns. These coordinated motor patterns are the units of inheritance first discovered by Lorenz half a century ago. Next is the level of purposeful strategies; these are of interest to both sociobiologists and behavioral ecologists. Examples of such higher level behaviors include living in monogamous versus polygamous unions, waging war on neighbors, and caring for or abandoning an offspring.

Ethological Aspects of Sexual Behavior

Ethology is particularly well suited to sexology because the behaviors involved in finding a mate, courting, and eventually copulating almost certainly were shaped by natural selection. After all, natural selection means differential reproduction of individuals based on the degree to which the outward expression of their genotypes are adapted to survival in the particular environment. Tinbergen stated that to understand a behavior completely, four aspects of the behavior must be addressed: (1) its phylogeny (i.e., history), (2) its ontogeny (i.e., development), (3) its proximate mechanistic causes, and (4) its function or effect. These four aspects can be applied to the understanding of any aspect of human sexual behavior.

Ethology, sociobiology, and behavioral ecology are all aware that there are nonreproductive sexual behaviors (e.g., masturbation, and homosexual and pedosexual behaviors) as well as nonsexual reproductive behaviors (e.g., parturition and parenting). Nevertheless, all sexual and reproductive behaviors evolved in the context of natural selection. One controversial topic in sociobiology is whether variant sexual behaviors, such as homosexual or pedosexual behavior, were ever selected for by natural selection or whether they are simply byproducts of natural selection for adult heterosexuality.

Romantic (erotic) love, an important component of human reproductive and sexual behavior, has its origins in parenting behavior. In reptiles, there is neither parental care nor an affectionate or affiliative bond between the two parents. Parental care evolved separately in birds and mammals and, as first pointed out by Eibl-Eibelsfeldt, "with parental care love came into the world."

Proceptive Behavior

Proceptive behavior is the behavior of one individual toward another individual when there is no sexual commitment by the second individual toward the first. Proceptive behavior can be thought of as "sex with your clothes on," inasmuch as all proceptive sexual behavior occurs in the clothed state and usually in public. Most proceptive behavior takes place without two individuals even touching each other. It is also in proceptive behavior that one finds the most differences between the two biological sexes (male and female) and within each biological sex. There is a rich phylogeny underlying proceptive sexual behavior and no understanding of the sexuality of contemporary humans can be complete without it.

Isogamy means that the germ cells of males and females are of the same size; heterogamy means that the germ cells of males and females are of different sizes. Based on the most general principle that two complementing specialists are potentially more efficient than two identical generalists, once biological variation started generating different size gametes, heterogametic species simply outbred isogametic species. In heterogamy, the female of the species contributes large, nutritious, and rather immobile eggs and the male of the species contributes small, highly mobile sperm.

Heterogamy at the microscopic level has a parallel in sexual dimorphism at the level of the proceptive behavior of individuals. In most mammals, males search and females display. This is very efficient. As a result, proceptive behavior in males involves searching and proceptive behavior in females involves displaying. Displaying has a distinct advantage over other advertisements of sexual receptivity, such as emitting an airborne pheromone. Humans, as a species, exhibit a high degree of "female choice" over which male impregnates them. Because the courtship signals used in human female proceptive displays are largely coded in behavior, a particular female can selectively direct these signals at one male and not at another.

There are two signals, also called "sign stimuli" or "ethological releasing stimuli," that searching adult heterosexual males seek. One is the shape of the nubile female and the second is the movement comprising feminine mannerisms. Interestingly, most feminine mannerisms are derived from submissive motor patterns. Phylogeny provides an explanation for this. In bony fish and reptiles, male courtship is largely dominance display and female courtship is largely submissive display. (Aggressivity is the mood underlying dominance and fear is the mood underlying submission.) In ethology, "mood" means "a *specific* internal readiness to act." Remnants of this relationship between dominance/aggressivity and male sexuality and submission/fear and female sexuality are still very evident in contemporary human sexual behavior, especially when this behavior is not in the context of love. Examples are the paraphilias of sadomasochism (S&M), bondage and discipline (B&D), biastophilia (rape), and kleptomania (eroticized fear from "shoplifting").

Receptive Behavior

Receptive behavior is the behavior between two individuals who are committed to a sexual relationship with each other. It is the behavior of persons obviously in love. Gone are the flirtatious and coy behaviors. In their place are the behaviors of affiliation and tenderness. Tender embraces, holding hands, reassuring glances and smiling at one another are all in their repertoire. Many argue that "romantic love" lasts five to ten years and that after that the love turns into "companionate love." There are probably differences between the behavior and the physiol-

ogy of two persons in romantic versus companionate love, but this has not been studied adequately. There are also very little differences in the receptive sexual behaviors, both between the two biological sexes and within each biological sex.

Conceptive Behavior

Conceptive behavior is behavior that could lead to conception under certain conditions. Most conceptive behavior, however, does not lead to actual conception because if one of the partners is a potentially fertile woman, she probably does not have a fertilizable egg in her Fallopian tube when the behavior occurs. Conceptive behavior is associated with physiological sexual arousal and orgasms, which were first studied and the results published by Masters and Johnson (in 1966). The behaviors in the conceptive phase are very similar in males and females. Most conceptive behavior consists of genital rubbing and pelvic thrusting in a posterior-anterior direction. These pelvic "humping" movements contrast with lateral, *proceptive*-feminine "hip swaying/wiggling" movements, which are more a lateral, "fish-tailing," submissive-fleeing motion. There are some interesting differences in conceptive behaviors between the sexes, however, most of which are physiological. Behaviorally, adult females often emit high-pitched, "yelping" sounds that are almost identical to the sounds that adult women emit during parturition. In addition, the contorted, worrisome, facial effects during conceptive behavior and parturition also are very similar in adult women. Just why natural selection should have configured these sights and sounds of parturition into the human female conceptive repertoire is not known with certainty. Adult females of all mammalian species are most vulnerable during parturition and high-pitched tones are associated with submission more so than lower pitched tones. Parturition-mimicking conceptive behavior in human females may be one more example of the sexual allurement of the *average* male to submissive displays of the *average* female. "Average" is italicized to emphasize that there are yet to be fully understood variations within as well as between the two biological sexes in the relationships involving sex, dominance, aggression, submission, and fear. Ethology is in a unique position to contribute toward this understanding.

REFERENCES

Eibl-Eibesfeldt, I. *Human Ethology*. New York: Aldine de Gruyter, 1989.

Feierman, J., ed. *Pedophilia: Biosocial Dimensions*. New York: Springer-Verlag, 1990.

Lorenz, K. *The Foundations of Ethology*. New York: Springer-Verlag, 1981.

Masters, W.H., and Johnson, V.E. *Human Sexual Response*. Boston: Little, Brown, 1966.

Morris, D. *Manwatching*. New York: Harry N. Abrams, Inc., 1977.

———. *Patterns of Reproductive Behavior*. New York: McGraw Hill, 1970.

Symons, D. *The Evolution of Human Sexuality*. Oxford: Oxford Univ. Press, 1979.

Trevathan, W.R. *Human Birth: An Evolutionary Perspective*. New York: Aldine de Gruyter, 1987.

Wickler, W. *The Sexual Code*. Garden City, N.J.: Anchor Books, 1973.

Wilson, G., ed. *Variant Sexuality: Research and Theory*. Baltimore: Johns Hopkins Univ. Press, 1987.

Jay R. Feierman

EUGENICS

Eugenics derived from Darwin's theory of evolution. It seeks to understand and ultimately to direct the forces that control human inheritance through matings, births, and deaths. Through births, eugenics seeks to improve the average hereditary potential of humans, making it possible for humanity to develop higher intelligence, greater vitality, and more balanced, happier personalities.

According to Osborn, a staunch advocate for eugenics,

[I]t would be a proper national aim to attempt to raise the average level of the nation's people in the direction of its most superior individuals. Eugenics, in asserting the uniqueness of the individual, supplements the American ideal of respect for the individual. Eugenics in a democracy seeks not to breed men to a single type, but to raise the average level of human variations, reducing variations tending toward poor health, low intelligence, and antisocial character, and increasing variations at the highest levels of activity.

Osborn also believed that eugenics and democracy are interrelated. He said:

[T]he eugenics ideal calls for a society so organized that eugenic selection will take place as a natural and largely unconscious process; one in which those persons who make the most effective response to their environment will, in the normal course, have more children than those who respond less effectively. The kind of eugenics would be the only kind possible in a democracy where, except in the case of extreme defect, no one would be given or would assume any right to decide who should or should not have children.

The main idea that runs through the majority of Osborn's works is the fact that with an improvement in the genetic makeup of humans there should be an improvement within the environment in which they live.

The measures envisaged by the eugenist for raising the genetic level are also measures envisaged by the environmentalist for raising the level of the environment in which children are reared. It makes no difference which is the more important, both are taken into account. Each improvement in genetic capacity enables the individual to take better advantage of the improved environment, and the average of developed and measurable intelligence and character is raised accordingly in each generation. (Osborne)

Eugenics was influential in the United States as a social movement between 1890 and 1920. It has been associated with racist political and social programs. The aim of the American Genetic Association was to maintain and improve human populations. The Association had two programs—the positive eugenics program and the negative eugenics program. The positive program provided financial incentives for people to reproduce because they were thought to be in some way superior. The negative program sought to prevent reproduction by parents who were allegedly inferior. For example, in 1907, Indiana introduced negative eugenics into its social policy by adopting a law that required certain people to be sterilized. During World War II, the Nazis also had a negative eugenics program, issuing harsh edicts on sterilization and elimination as well as putting girls to work as breeders. Their ultimate aim was to create a super race. The strong momentum the eugenics movement experienced at the turn of the century was lost after the horrors committed under Hitler became known. Today, eugenics is once again being debated in terms of whether homosexuality is genetic. A 1992 article in *Newsweek* speculated that if a "gay gene" is found to exist, parents who detect that an in utero fetus has this gene may opt to abort or to genetically switch the gene to ensure the child will be heterosexual. If this practice were to become widespread, the gay population could be extinguished.

REFERENCES

Francoeur, R. et al. *A Descriptive Dictionary and Atlas of Sexology*. Westport, Conn.: Greenwood, 1991.

Gelman, D., and D. Foote. Born or Bred? *Newsweek* (Feb. 24, 1992): pp. 46–53.

Osborn, F. *The Future of Human Heredity*. New York: Weybright and Talley, 1968.

Osborn, F. *Preface to Eugenics*. New York: Harper & Brothers, 1951.

Packard, V. *The People Shapers*. Boston: Little, Brown, 1977.

Hope E. Ashby

EXTRAMARITAL SEX

Extramarital sex (EMS) is any sexual activity in which at least one partner is married to someone other than the sexual partner. EMS is a social classification based on marital status (not unique sexual properties), which establishes its social consequences.

Sociobiological Explanations

Evolutionary explanations of the origin of nonmonogamy rely on a reproductive double standard. A female bears relatively few children and is dependent during and after pregnancy. Her inclusive fitness (genetic survival) depends on forming a provisioning bond with her off-springs' father. Since a male's inclusive fitness is increased only by raising his own offspring (and supplemented by seeking promiscuous reproductive opportunities), the female's EMS threatens his inclusive fitness. According to Frayser, females exchange fidelity for provisioning by males; males exchange support for women's confined reproductive potential. In evolutionary terms, so long as provisioning for the mate continues, males' EMS is a peripheral issue.

However, the relationship between coitus and parentage is obscured by the delay between conception and visible pregnancy, coitus with premenarchal and postmenopausal women, difficulty in conceiving, and coitus among sterile partners. If hominids' paternal involvement with their own offspring is motivated by an evolutionary drive, what factor determined which offspring and mates were provided for and which were abandoned? Some factor other than inclusive fitness prioritized their relationships to determine which mates and offspring received continued provisioning.

There is an alternative dynamic. Hominid evolution involved two distinct aspects: at some point hominids' increasing mental capacity supplanted biological with social adaptation. Increasing brain capacity allowed sexual pleasure to become intrinsically desirable, thereby reducing reproductive dependency on estrus. As acceptivity to engage in coitus extended beyond estrus, females could exchange sex for food over sustained periods, creating a pleasure bond with males. Further, obscuring an offspring's paternity by mating with numerous males in the troupe increased the possibility of multiple males providing for a female's offspring or at least being less likely to kill them.

The issue is whether emphasis is placed on individuals' inclusive fitness or on species survival, the true province of evolution. Species survival and individuals' inclusive fitness are maximized by two factors: (1) when each child has different parents, the probability that all a parent's children will inherit identical genetic defects is reduced (e.g., Tay-Sachs); and (2) when males support infants through reciprocal altruism, irrespective of parentage.

Cross-Cultural Research

Cross-cultural research demonstrates that the dependency of pregnant women and infants can be met independent of the biological father's involvement. Among the Tiwi of North Australia conception is believed to be caused by water spirits. Women are married at birth to older men (age 40) and form sequential sexual relationships with several husbands and extramarital partners. Each child might have different biological and social fathers. As with the matrilineal Nayar, on the southwestern or Malabar coast of India, it is the marriage system, not the biological father, that provides for the dependent female and her children. Thus, cultural values determine the importance of biological parentage, monogamy, and EMS.

Cultures vary significantly in their responses to EMS. Frayser estimates that 49 percent of societies strongly prohibit EMS for females, while 23 percent strongly prohibit it for males. In contrast, 26 percent of societies allow EMS for females while 52 percent allow it for males (25 percent of societies weakly prohibit EMS for either females or males). Although 49 percent of societies have consistent sexual standards (26 percent allow and 23 percent prohibit EMS for both sexes), when double standards exist, EMS for females is uniformly restricted more than it is for males.

The pervasive restrictions on females' EMS contradict the evolutionary monogamy argument. At its simplest, the necessity of imposing rules indicates that female monogamy is not biologically established. More persuasive are the associations between a culture's social structures and its acceptance of EMS.

Macrosociology identifies patterns of sexual regulation reflecting a society's stage of cultural evolution. According to Gebhard, up to 60 percent of preliterate societies allow women some form of EMS. Similarly, women's sexual autonomy is greatest in hunting and gathering societies, most restricted in agricultural societies, and according to Sanderson increases again in industrial and postindustrial societies. In agrarian and agricultural societies, property rights ascribe economic status, increasing the importance of inheritance. Patrilineal societies accomplish this by confining women's reproductive potential, whereas matrilineal inheritance minimizes the importance of paternity. Accordingly, Frayser found that 76 percent of patrilineal and nonunilineal versus 14 percent of matrilineal societies strongly restrict females' sexuality. Achieved status typifies hunting and gathering societies as well as industrial and postindustrial ones. The emphasis on personal accomplishment also reduces the importance of paternity, hence the need to confine females' reproductive potential.

Sexually induced pleasure and self-disclosure can lead to intrusions into the marriage and kinship systems that organize social life. Violations of the social boundaries protecting marriage and kinship evoke social concern and personal jealousy. This threat can be addressed through avoidance, segregation, or integration. Avoidance reinforces marital boundaries with sanctions that vary in strength from small fines to death, although it is unclear how consistently sanctions are imposed. One reason for extreme sanctions in avoidance societies is the absence of additional social controls to minimize the effect on kinship systems when extramarital relationships do form.

Segregation establishes social structures to minimize EMS intrusions into the uninvolved partner's life space, just as decentralized polygymous households physically separated cowives to minimize jealousy and conflict. The norms supporting segregation can impose a variety of restrictions on EMS. They may prescribe potential partners (e.g., a Marshallese female's EMS is limited to her sister's husband, or levirate access to an older brother's wife). Restrictions may also give the woman's husband the right to determine her sexual relationships (e.g., wife-lending which the husband may use to establish social and economic ties with other males or communities). Other restrictions may limit location (e.g., not in her own village), time (e.g., only during ceremonial periods), and eligibility (e.g., men but not women).

With integration, additional partners are added to the relationship and sometimes the household. Mahoney distinguishes between EMS and alternative styles of marriage, which incorporate extra members into the marriage. Distinct from polygamy because there is a single marital dyad, integration still brings the external sexual relationship within the marriage structure and therefore technically is not extramarital.

Segregation and integration provide structural mechanisms to minimize the impact of ongoing EMS on marriage and kinship. Avoidance minimizes the complexity external relationships add to marriage, but it allows no ongoing control over relationships that do develop. In contrast, the social norms establishing segregation and integration provide interpersonal and social controls over EMS relationships.

Legacy of EMS in Western Society

Western sexual values reflect two interrelated legacies: Hebrew culture and the Greco-Roman culture. Beginning in the first century A.D., these legacies were combined by the Christian church and early Christianity's heritage continues to dominate sexual values in the United States.

Several feminist scholars have asserted that matrilineal cultures with goddess religions dominated the Middle East until they were overthrown because the sexual autonomy and temple prostitution allowed all women in the goddess religions threatened Hebrew patrilinity and religious authority. Judaism sanctified patrilinity through its doctrine that a male who died without a son to carry his name lost his chance at immortality. Polygyny, concubinage, and the levirate duty helped ensure male offspring, and the confinement of women's reproductive potential ensured legitimacy. Intercourse between a married Hebrew woman and a man not her husband was adultery for which both men and women could be killed. Males' EMS with non-Hebrews or unmarried Hebrew women (e.g., prostitutes) was not considered adultery because it did not affect another Hebrew male's lineage.

The principle of double monopoly on spouses' sexuality did not exist in ancient Greece, where wives belonged to husbands and husbands belonged to themselves. This is made clear in Demosthenes's court oration, "Mistresses we keep for pleasure, concubines for daily attendance upon our persons, and wives to bear us legitimate children and be our housekeepers." Again, women's marital status determined adultery, and an adulterous wife could be divorced or punished by any means short of homicide by citizens if she went out in public.

Under Roman law, adultery became a state matter. The *lex Julia* precluded casual sexual relationships for women eligible to be *matres familias* (matrons of the family). The official penalty for adultery was death, but punishment was the state's prerogative not the father's or husband's, and legal texts identified conditions staying execution. Nor could fathers or husbands conceal women's adultery. If they failed to report it within 60 days, they faced charges of procuring, and a knowledgeable person had four months to report the incident or become an accomplice suffering the same punishment as the adulterers. Adulterers' only escape from judgment was through a general pardon given to criminals at public celebrations, after which husbands had the option to reintroduce charges within 30 days.

Brown concludes that pre-Christian Rome's sexual tone had been set by somber and careful persons. The ease of obtaining divorces eliminated structural impediments that might otherwise lead to adultery. Socially, the EMS double standard was not universally accepted. Husbands' EMS conduct was examined if they sought divorce on grounds of adultery, and the principle of symmetry was used to argue that husbands failed to lead the family when they required chastity from their wives that they did not practice themselves.

The early Christians' sexual legacy was a dramatic revision of sexuality. To second-century theologians, Christ's victory over death could free humans from the "present age" if procreation, which fueled the unidirectional progression to death, was halted. In contrast to the pagans and Jewish, who believed sexuality could be made a positive element in society, early Christian theologians made no distinction between licit and illicit sex: all sex reflected humanity's separation from God. Early Christianity eliminated the Roman and Hebrew double standards by condemning all EMS and blurred the distinction between marital and extramarital sex by identifying as adultery lust toward one's spouse, the marriage of separated persons during their spouses' lifetime, clandestine or illicit marriages, and marriages contracted for wrongful purposes.

In 12th-century southern France, *l'amour courtois* (courtly love) rebelled against marriages contracted for families' economic and political alliances by praising extramarital romantic love. Initially idealized as a spiritual union not possible in marriage, courtly love eventually linked passionate sexuality with romantic love. It was the emerging middle-class, which could not afford

both spouses and lovers, that combined the ideals of romantic love and passionate sex with marriage. The Puritans viewed marital sex as a God-given pleasure, which they supported against adultery by requiring couples to live together peacefully. In challenging the Catholic church, however, other 16th- and 17th-century religious publications recast women's image from licentiousness to purity. Religious and pseudo-medical beliefs desexualized women, denying they had any sexual interests other than reproduction and insisting on protecting them from degeneration stemming from sexual arousal. This ideology restored the traditional double standard rejected by the Catholic church but changed the rationale from restricting women's procreative potential to the moral destructiveness of sex, especially for women.

The Christian rejection of the double standard, courtly love, the romanticization of marriage, and the puritan support of marital sexuality did not eliminate the double standard or sex hostile beliefs. Instead of an evolutionary progression in which new values replaced the old, divergent beliefs introduced competing values which fragmented society.

Contemporary Extramarital Sex

Random samples by different pollsters indicate 40 percent to 47 percent of men and 26 percent to 32 percent of women have experienced EMS at least once. Since 79.3 percent of the population considers EMS to always be wrong, there is reason to suspect that random surveys may underestimate the incidence of EMS. Research showing that initial admissions of EMS by 30 percent of a sample doubled to 60 percent during psychotherapy support for this possibility. Conversely, higher survey results like *Cosmopolitan*'s 69 percent EMS rate for women over age 35 reported by Wolfe, and *Playboy*'s EMS rates for those over age 50 and 70 percent for men and 65 percent for women reported by Peterson, et al., may be biased by readers' self-selection.

Compared with men, women's EMS involvement has increased significantly. The 24-percent rate for EMS involvement by women age 18 to 24 reported by Hunt was three times that reported by Kinsey, results replicated by Tavris and Sadd, and by Blumstein and Schwartz. As this cohort aged, the incidence of EMS among middle-aged women rose to approximate men's. In addition to the cohort effect, by middle-age women often overcome the cultural restrictions on their sexuality; thus, increased EMS might reflect a new, active sexuality directed at fulfilling their own desires.

The impact of EMS varies. In Atwater's sample of urban women, 93 percent reported increased self-esteem, self-confidence, autonomy, and power from their EMS. Gilmartin found similar levels of marital happiness between spouses with secret affairs and a monogamous control group. Nor must EMS always be secret to avoid problems. Cuber and Harroff reported that many people in intrinsic-vital marriages engaged in extramarital sex with their spouses' knowledge or approval. Among the 40 percent of women with EMS experience who were positive their husbands knew, 42 percent stated it caused no problems. Similarly, Hunt found that nearly half of the divorced people with EMS experience did not believe EMS played a role in their divorces. However, Hunt discounted their opinion and the statements of the "many" still married couples who reported no adverse effects from EMS, stressing instead the 50 percent who were affected and pervasive "unseen emotional decay."

Permissive extramarital attitudes are inversely related to female gender, age, religiosity, marital happiness, and marital sexual satisfaction and are directly related to male gender, education, political liberality, gender equality, shared marital power, autonomous heterosexual interaction, premarital sexual permissiveness, sexual pleasure emphasis, and marital sexual experimentation. These variables form three factors: marital satisfaction, sexual permissiveness, and intellectual flexibility, but the factors can obscure important relationships. First, Bell et al. found that 20 percent of wives who described themselves happily married had had EMS. Second, variables like the emphasis on sexuality, increased equality, and autonomy for women identify positive elements in relationships, which coincidentally have nonmonogamous implications. Women's working outside the home alters family dynamics, equalizing wives' and husbands' marital power, gender equality, and autonomous heterosexual interaction. However, there is also an increase in EMS from 27 percent for full-time homemakers to 47 percent for women working part time or full time outside the home.

The causes of EMS can also be classified into push or pull factors which, like a sexually distant partner or a new love, drive or attract spouses away from the marriage. Alternatively, the causes can be classified according to individuals' rationales. Ellis identified healthy and disturbed reasons for EMS with the implication that people might avoid EMS for unhealthy reasons.

Constantine and Constantine further challenged the idealization of monogamy by asking, "What is wrong with *you* and *your* marriage that *drives* you to stay monogamous?"

The term "extramarital sex" emerged in the 1960s and 1970s when research on swinging and open marriage forced the recognition of alternative marital structures. Adams found that clandestine affairs involve second-order changes, wherein one partner covertly disrupts the relationship by unilaterally violating the couple's implicit rules. Such transgression of the rules is likely to produce feelings of guilt and remorse not shared by those who flatly reject them. Even to people involved in traditional affairs, alternative sexual lifestyles threaten the stability imposed by the principle of marriage as a double sexual monopoly. Whereas adultery transgresses individuals' accepted monogamous standards, nonmonogamous alternative lifestyles reject the double sexual monopoly. The challenge experienced by participants is to establish first-order changes and first-order structures in their relationships by establishing explicit, individualized rules governing their behavior. Most EMS research focuses on rejection or transgression by examining the development of alternative marital structures to replace those rejected or the social and individual pathology of transgression.

The structure of EMS is determined by whether the spouses' activity is consensual and independent or joint. The most common form of EMS is nonconsensual and typically involves transgressions where permissive behaviors exceed nonpermissive relationship expectations. In nonconsensual activity, a spouse violates expectations unilaterally and both a husband and wife, acting independently, might create two distinct sets of second-order rules. Whether such EMS is love or pleasure centered, enduring or opportunistic, depends on the second-order rules the EMS partner creates.

Consensual agreements allowed either partner to engage in EMS under specified conditions in 15 percent of marriages. A source of tension in independent consensual EMS is the possibility of being displaced by the outsider, although Rubin and Adams found comparable marital stability in both open and sexually exclusive marriages. Creating first-order structures and rules minimizes this threat through segregation, which regulates the time and resources expended, possible partners, emotional involvement, potential disclosure, the need for spousal approval, and similar concerns. Doing this, however, is a major task in comarital EMS or open marriage. This process negotiates rules similar to the social conventions regulating EMS in nonmonogamous cultures.

In contrast, joint consensual activity creates rules that structure emotional involvement either through segregation or integration. Research suggests two to four percent of the population has engaged in swinging. Swinging activity, in which spouses are sexually exchanged or shared, varies from the emotionally detached "hard core" to emotionally committed forms, such as "interpersonal" or "communal" swinging. Hard-core swinging is strictly physical pleasure centered and minimizes jealousy and the potential for emotional involvements by preventing personal contact except during swinging. The emotional detachment of such swinging is similar to wifelending in which the husband's interest, not the wife's, determines her extramarital partner. In contrast, interpersonal swinging establishes a stable intimate network of emotional ties and occasionally creates a group marriage by extending the definition of family so that extra partners are incorporated.

The assumption of individual pathology among those who engage in EMS is typified by the public's negative perception of swingers. The perception of swingers as deviants misinterprets the rejection of specific sexual values as a general transgression of social norms. In reality, swingers are very conventional in most respects. Compared with nonswingers, swingers have weaker ties to their parents, neighbors, and religion, but are also middle class, politically conservative, more socially active, and better educated. The key factor distinguishing swingers from nonswingers appears to be swingers' low degree of sexual jealousy. Gilmartin identifies the progression from transgression to rejection among women swingers, noting that, "For most women in swinging relationships it took time and considerable difficulty before they were able to undergo this transformation of meaning from their original concept of adultery to their current one." If, however, they make this transition, they tend to enjoy swinging more than men.

Summary

Sexuality is inevitably regulated. When avoidance is used to regulate EMS, there are no social mechanisms to influence the consequences when EMS does occur. The cost of minimizing EMS through avoidance is to maximize the potential for damage when it does occur. Since variables like gender equality, equitable marital power, sexual pleasure, and women's employment are associated with increased EMS, it does not appear that the nonmonogamy reflected in EMS will disappear in the future without dramatic social changes. Reinstating the Roman system of easy divorce combined with strong sanctions against EMS could displace the nonmonogamy of EMS into sequential marital monogamy.

REFERENCES

Adams, B.N. *The Family: A Sociological Interpretation*, 4th ed. New York: Harcourt Brace Jovanovich, 1986.

Atwater, L. *The Extramarital Connection: Sex, Intimacy, and Identity*. New York: Irvington, 1982.

Bell, R.R., S. Turner, and L. Rosen. A Multivariate Analysis of Female Extramarital Coitus. *Journal of Marriage and the Family*, Vol. 37 (1975), pp. 375–384.

Blumstein, P.W., and Schwartz, P. *American Couples*. New York: William Morrow, 1983.

Brown, P. *The Body and Society: Men, Women, and Sexual Renunciation in Early Christianity*. New York: Columbia Univ. Press, 1988.

Brundage, J. Adultery and Fornication: A Study in Legal Theology. In V.L. Bullough and J. Brundage, eds. *Sexual Practices & the Medieval Church*. Buffalo, N.Y.: Prometheus, 1982.

Bullough, V., and B. Bullough. *Sin, Sickness, and Sanity: A History of Sexual Attitudes*. New York: Meridian, 1977.

Buunk, B. Sexually Open Marriages: Ground Rules for Countering Potential Threats to Marriage. *Alternative Lifestyles*, Vol. 3 (1980), pp. 312–328.

Constantine, L.L., and Constantine, J.M. *Group Marriage*. Collier Books, 1973.

Cuber, J.F. How New Ideas about Sex Standards are Changing. In J.S. Delora and J.R. Delora, eds. *Intimate Lifestyles*. Pacific Palisades, Calif.: Goodyear, 1972.

Cuber, J.F., and P.B. Harroff. *The Significant Americans*. New York: Appleton-Century, 1985.

Davis, J.A., and T.W. Smith. *General Social Surveys, 1972–1988: Cumulative Codebook*. Chicago: National Opinion Research Center, 1988.

Eisler, R. *The Chalice and the Blade*. New York: Harper & Row, 1987.

Ellis, A. Healthy and Disturbed Reasons for Having Extramarital Relations. In G. Neubeck, ed. *Extramarital Relations*. Englewood Cliffs, N.J.: Prentice-Hall, 1969.

Fisher, H.E. *The Sex Contract*. New York: Quill, 1982.

Foucault, M. *The Use of Pleasure: The History of Sexuality*, Vol. 2. New York: Vintage, 1986.

Frayser, S.G. *Varieties of Sexual Experience: An Anthropological Perspective on Human Sexuality*. New Haven, Conn.: HRAF Press, 1985.

Gallup, G.G. Unique Features of Human Sexuality in the Context of Evolution. In D. Byrne and K. Kelley, eds. *Alternative Approaches to the Study of Sexual Behavior*. Hillsdale, N.J.: Lawrence Erlbaum Associates, 1986.

Gebhard, P.H. Human Sexual Behavior: A Summary Statement. In D. Marshall and R. Suggs, eds. *Human Sexual Behavior: Variations in the Ethnographic Spectrum*. Englewood Cliffs, N.J.: Prentice-Hall, 1971.

Gilmartin, B.G. Sexual Deviance and Social Networks: A Study of Social, Family, and Marital Interaction Patterns Among Co-marital Sex Participants. In J. Smith and L.C. Smith, eds. *Beyond Monogamy*. Baltimore, Md.: Johns Hopkins Univ. Press, 1974.

————. Swinging: Who Gets Involved and How? In R.W. Libby and R.N. Whitehurst, eds. *Marriage and Alternatives: Exploring Intimate Relationships*. Glenview, Ill.: Scott, Foresman, 1977.

Goodale, J.C. The Tiwi Women of Melville Island, North Australia. Ph.D. dissertation. Philadelphia: Univ. of Pennsylvania, 1959.

Gough, E.K. The Nayars and the Definition of Marriage. In P. Bohannan and J. Middleton, eds. *Marriage, Family, and Residence*. Garden City, N.Y.: Natural History Press, 1968.

Hrdy, S.B. *The Woman That Never Evolved*. Cambridge, Mass.: Harvard Univ. Press, 1981.

Hunt, M.M. *The Natural History of Love*. New York: Minerva, 1959.

————. *Sexual Behavior in the 1970s*. New York: Dell, 1974.

Jenks, R.J. Swinging: A Replication and Test of a Theory. *Journal of Sex Research,* Vol. 21 (1985), pp. 199–205.

Karlsen, C.F. *The Devil in the Shape of a Woman*. New York: W.W. Norton, 1987.

Kenkel, W.F. *The Family in Perspective*. 5th ed. Houston, Tex.: Cap and Gown Press, 1985.

Kinsey, A.C., W.B. Pomeroy, C.E. Martin, and P.H. Gebhard. *Sexual Behavior in the Human Female*. New York: W.B. Sanders, 1953.

Lee, G.R. *Family Structure and Interaction*. 2nd ed. Minneapolis: Univ. of Minnesota Press, 1982.

Mahoney, E.R. *Human Sexuality*. New York: McGraw-Hill, 1983.

Money, J. *The Destroying Angel*. Buffalo, N.Y.: Prometheus, 1985.

————. *Venuses Penuses*. Buffalo, N.Y.: Prometheus, 1986.

Morgan, E.S. The Puritans and Sex. In M. Gordon, ed. *The American Family in Social-Historical Perspective*. 3rd ed. New York: St. Martin's Press, 1983.

Peterson, J., A. Kretchmer, B. Nellis, J. Lever, and R. Hertz. The *Playboy* Readers Sex Survey, Part 2. *Playboy* (March 1983), pp. 90–92, 178–184.

Pietropinto, A., and J. Simenauer. *Beyond the Male Myth*. Philadelphia: Pilgrim, 1977.

Reiss, I.L. *Journey into Sexuality: An Exploratory Voyage*. Englewood Cliffs, N.J.: Prentice-Hall, 1986.

Reiss, I.L., and G.R. Lee. *Family Systems in America*. 4th ed. New York: Holt, Rinehart & Winston, 1988.

Rousselle, A. *Porneia*. Oxford, U.K.: Basil Blackwell, 1988.

Rubin, L. Sex and Sexuality: Women in Midlife. In M. Kirkpatrick, ed. *Women's Sexual Experience: Explorations of the Dark Continent*. New York: Plenum, 1982.

Sanderson, S.K. *Macrosociology*. New York: Harper & Row, 1988.

Stone, M. *When God Was a Woman*. New York: Dorset, 1976.

Tavris, C., and S. Sadd. *The Redbook Report on Female Sexuality*. New York: Dell, 1977.

Van den Berghe, P.L. *Human Family Systems: An Evolutionary View*. New York: Elsevier, 1979.

Vaughan, J., and P. Vaughan. *Beyond Affairs*. Hilton Head Island, S.C.: Dialog, 1980.

Welter, B. The Cult of True Womanhood: 1820–1860. In M. Gordon, ed. *The American Family in Social-Historical Perspective*. 3rd ed. New York: St. Martin's Press, 1983.

Wolfe, L. The Sexual Profile of the Cosmopolitan Girl. *Cosmopolitan* (Sept. 1981), pp. 254–265.

Wyatt, G., S. Peters, and D. Guthrie. Kinsey Revisited, Part I: Comparison of the Sexual Socialization and Sexual Behavior of White Women Over 33 Years. *Archives of Sexual Behavior*, Vol. 17 (1988), pp. 201–239.

Stephen L. Goettsch

f

FANTASIES AND SEX

A fantasy is the mental and/or visual image of some person or persons, object, situation, or thing. Some fantasies are based on past experiences while others are wholly imaginary. It is normal for individuals to fantasize or daydream, and these fantasies may or may not include sexual scenes. The consensus among professionals dealing with sexual fantasies is that they are normal, healthy, safe, useful, personal, private imageries that enhance the quality of life for emotionally stable persons utilizing them.

Fantasies may include dangerous, illegal, and unusual activities, which if acted upon might cause harm to someone, including the fantasizer. Kinsey reported that fantasy accompanied masturbation for the majority (64 percent) of females and almost all males. Fantasy frequency and content vary among persons and at times for the same individual. Further generalizations from the Kinsey data include the following:

1. Masturbatory fantasies typically were consistent with the experience of the subject (i.e., heterosexuals fantasized heterosexual activities). Some subjects reported homosexual, animal, or sadomasochistic fantasies, and some reported several of these types combined. Again, variation occurred at different times in the subject's life. In American culture, with heterosexuality the predominant sexual orientation, heterosexual fantasies predominate in both males and females.

2. Some 2 percent of the female sample reported reaching orgasm by fantasy alone, exclusive of any tactile stimulation of the genitalia.

3. Male nocturnal dreams were closely related to the male subject's overt daytime experiences.

4. Fantasies were more common among the older females.

5. Masturbatory fantasies were usually in accord with the overt experience of the individual. Males often fantasized unfulfilled or repressed desires. Females were less likely to fantasize anything outside their experience. Typically, if kissing had been the limit of the female's petting experience, it was the limit of her fantasies. Only after the petting had included genital manipulations did the fantasies go that far.

More recent studies have reported a higher rate of fantasizing among women. Linda Wolfe reported that in a sample of 15,000 women who were between the ages of 18 and 34, only 2.5 percent said they did not fantasize.

Whipple and her associates have studied orgasm that is triggered by guided imagery without tactile contact. They have speculated as to whether the perception of orgasm is generated directly within the central nervous system or is an expression of a peripheral sympathetic physiological correlate of imagery.

Often, erotic literature, pornography to some, is a stimulation to sexual fantasy. However, because sexual fantasies vary so much among people, the literature that is actually erotic to specific individuals varies widely. Historically in American culture, men have been stereotyped as sexual beings with fantasies and actions to express their eroticism, and early pornographic works were directed towards heterosexual men. In the 1930s and 1940s *True Confessions* and popular romance novels became the reading from which women gathered their fantasy material. Men's sexual fantasy literature was characterized by calendar art, followed in the 1960s by the development of *Playboy* and *Penthouse* as well as more explicit erotic material particularly for the gay and other specialized markets. The 1970s and 1980s saw more erotic fiction aimed at women by women writers such as Nancy Friday. In her book *Women on Top*, Friday argued that women have started a sexual revolution for equality and should complete it with implementation of their sexual fantasies until their erotic nature is fully pursued.

Some experimenters say that when they tried to live out a fantasy, they found that it was a disappointment. One such experiment involved a women's group that viewed a dozen old pornographic films, which included scenes of intercourse with a donkey and a large dog. Several women said they had such fantasies, but after seeing the film they felt that the activity looked much too difficult and would not be fun at all. Fantasies about animal contact are not unusual for either males or females, especially for those from rural areas, and are more apt to be acted on where there are pets and farm animals.

Fantasy can be helpful in therapy. The client can be encouraged to remove blocks to sexual functioning in his or her imagination. For example, where there is fear of penetration on the part of a male or female, guided imagery may be used in fantasy to talk the person through the experience of penetration, orgasm, or ejaculation. Both a male and a female therapist are present for this procedure. It has proven effective for many males and females.

This technique is especially useful when the male fears that he will lose his penis in the vagina or be impaled on a shark-toothed vagina. The male in fantasy proceeds slowly, first placing the penis at the opening of the vagina, inserting it a little way, moving away, then inserting it a little further and moving away again. This process continues until in fantasy the penis is at full penetration. The procedure is reinforced by the therapist, who talks about what the experience will feel like in a positive way until full penetration can be accomplished in fantasy without stress or anxiety, making possible later penetration with a partner in therapy.

REFERENCES

Barbach, L., and L. Levine. *Shared Intimacies*. New York: Anchor Press, 1980.

Fox, S.C. *Joys of Fantasy: The Book for Loving Couples*. New York: Stein & Day, 1977.

Friday, N. *Men in Love*. New York: Dell, 1980.

———. *Women on Top: How Real Life Has Changed Women's Sexual Fantasies*. New York: Simon & Schuster, 1991.

Kinsey, A. *Sexual Behavior in the Human Male*. Philadelphia: Saunders, 1948.

———. *Sexual Behavior in the Human Female*. Philadelphia: Saunders, 1953.

Thorne, E. *Your Erotic Fantasies*. New York: Ballantine Books, 1971.

Whipple, B., G. Ogden, and B.R. Komisaruk. Physiological Correlates of Imagery Induced Orgasm in Women. *Archives of Sexual Behavior* (in press).

Wolfe, L. *The Cosmo Report*. New York: Arbor House, 1981.

William E. Hartman
Marilyn A. Fithian

FASHION, CLOTHING AND SEX

Three aspects of clothing—hierarchy, function, and allure—are intimately involved with sexuality. Once humans adopted clothing, they also made efforts to distinguish one sex from another even though the materials at hand varied from skins to grasses. It was also through clothing that males and females were able to accentuate their interests, tastes, and desires. Deuteronomy (22:5) states that women should not wear men's clothing nor men wear those of women.

With the development of more sophisticated clothing technologies such as weaving, long lengths of textiles could be used to cover the body, and variations related to gender increased. The need for clothing distinction is accentuated or diminished at various times and in different cultures. It is often accentuated when the distinguishing feature of most adult men, the beard, is removed by shaving or plucking. Usually, men have dressed in styles that exaggerate masculine attributes and minimize feminine ones, while women's clothing emphasizes feminine features and minimizes masculine ones. Generally, however, at least in Western culture, women's clothes have been far more confining and limiting of action than those of men, and clothing has been used to make women appear to be weaker and more helpless than they are. Since the medieval period in Western culture, aristocratic men have worn some kind of breeches which were far more suited to horseback riding than the long skirts worn by women. Neither pants nor skirts have to do with anatomical differences, since in China women traditionally wore pants while men wore gowns, as they did in much of the Arabic world. Most societies, however, attempt to draw rigid lines between the sexes in terms of clothing, and women in the west who wore pants, even underpants such as those sported by Amelia Bloomer in the 19th century, were often ridiculed.

Sexual messages are conveyed more directly by clothing or fashion in some periods than in others. In ancient Egypt, men wore a skirted garment that was starched in front to emphasize male virility and constant arousal. In ancient Minoan society, women wore a leather "jacket" that left their breasts completely exposed. Both sexes wore metal waist rings to emphasize their small waists. Generally, any clothing that covers an intimate part of the body can be turned into an eye catcher. The classical example of this axiom is the codpiece: originally a metal case for protecting the male genitals in war, it was adopted by the common man in a leather version during the late medieval period and ended up as a conspicuous piece of apparel, often of color that contrasted with the rest of the costume. Sometimes, to emphasize the penis, the codpiece was stuffed with padding or decorated with ribbons and precious stones. This emphasis on the male genitals has appeared in other societies as well, including among some of the residents of the New Hebrides, where a penis wrapper was the only piece of male clothing for much of the 20th century.

Generally in Western culture, women's genitalia have been covered and not accented by costume accessories, although other parts of the female anatomy have been emphasized, including hips, breasts, buttocks, legs, and feet. One reason might be that men are more attracted to visual stimuli than women are, and for males all of the female body is sexualized and eroticized. Thus exposure of any part of the female body or accentuation of body parts through clothing works more erotically on the male observer than any corresponding exposure of the male body

does on the female observer. Inevitably, this difference has led to considerable misunderstanding between the sexes on what the female means when she dresses in a certain way. Even though a woman might wear a particular form of clothing because it is the fashion, men often read into it a sexual intent that the woman herself has not meant to imply. As a result men tend to accuse women either of being immodest or of inviting sexual advances when this has not been their intention. When accused, some women hold, on the one hand, that they simply have a more "natural" and "healthy" attitude to the body and that men read too much into what women wear. On the other hand, some women respond that they dress to please men and that they are just expressing themselves as females. The fashion industry is very much aware of the eroticization associated with clothing, and one of its unstated aims is to maintain the erotic appeal of clothes by changing areas of emphasis; this has been a fact of Western life since at least the 17th century.

The 17th century saw remarkable changes in the mood of fashion, and clothes became much more flamboyant in contrast to the more modest styles and changes of the past. This was particularly true for men. Some fashion historians have called these changes in men's fashion the "seduction look." Upperclass men wore their hair coiffed in ringlets, known as "love locks," and tied with little bows; they also wore lacy jabots (cravats), ruffles, and wigs. Wigs in fact became extremely fashionable, the period's symbol of aristocracy. Women's costume was marked by elaborate coiffures that towered high above the head and were tiered in the Fontanges manner. The bodice was cut very low and the sleeves at most came to the elbows. Women wore a tight corset, stiffened by a steel busk that formed a straight vertical line from just below the breasts to the end of the trunk. By the end of the 17th century beauty patches had appeared, as had high heels for men.

As the 17th century passed into the 18th costumes became somewhat more practical and easier to wear. Wigs were still the norm but gave way to white ones sprinkled with powder. Necklines were even larger than before, but the waist was only lightly laced; panniers were worn to exaggerate the hips. Hoop skirts also appeared. Madame de Pompadour popularized the negligee.

By the end of the 18th century, however, fashion, particularly for males, underwent a revolution. Flugel called it the "great masculine renunciation," which led men to avoid trying to be beautiful and encouraged them to be useful, strong, and silent instead. Part of this revolution was the adoption of the trousers of the lower class. The leader of male fashion in England and the person who set the new tone of simple elegance for men was George "Beau" Brummel, who had the patronage of the regent of England, later King George IV. Women, however, clung to decoration: ornamentation, concealment, and allurement became the mode in clothing from tight corsets, to hoopskirts, to crinolines, to the bustle, to the gradual raising of the hemline to show the female ankle, which for a time became a focus of male attention.

Fashion magazines aimed at a female audience appeared in 1825 in France and gradually spread elsewhere. The first one in the United States, *Godey's Lady's Book,* appeared shortly before the Civil War. The first haute couturier, the Englishman Charles Frederic Worth, opened a salon in Paris in 1866 and solidified the domination of Paris over women's fashion. There were rebellions against the restrictions that women's clothes imposed on the wearer's activities, and numerous dress reformers appeared, ranging from Dr. Mary Walker, who wore men's clothing, to Amelia Bloomer, who invented the bloomer pant—an immense and very wide-legged garment that tapered at the ankles.

As fashion changed, so did eroticized points of interest. The idea of the bustle, for example, was to have the eye move from the narrow waist to the dome-shaped hoopskirt and finally to the rear—the bustle. This was followed by a new emphasis on the bust and on tighter-fitting clothing instead of the layered garments associated with the bustle. The brassiere was invented by the Parisian couturier Paul Poiret to further emphasize the bosom. For a time the hobble skirt was also popular, a garment which forced the wearer to take small steps to avoid splitting the seams of her skirt. To assist this type of movement a special garter was devised—actually two garters held together by a strip of elastic about three inches long—that when worn under the clothing produced the effect of the woman's taking a bouncing baby step rather than a regular stride. This style was further modified by lampshade-shaped skirts on top of the hobble skirt, which remained fashionable until replaced by the boyish look of the flapper, the new representative of women's emancipation. This flat-chested, close-cropped, page boy look was popularized by Gabrielle "Coco" Chanel, in the process eroticizing the previously hidden legs of women.

During the past 150 years, women in the west have worn brassieres to emphasize their breasts and padding when their natural endowment was not enough, corsets to make themselves wasp-waisted (in the 19th century), bustles to accent their derriere (also in the 19th century), high heels to emphasize their legs and feet, and panniers to emphasize their hips (in the 18th century). They raised their hemlines in the 1920s to emphasize their legs and ultimately wore miniskirts and panty hose to the point where it became difficult to sit or bend. They bound their chests in the 1920s to gain a boyish look and wore heavy shoulder pads during World War II to achieve a more triangular appearance. None of these areas of emphasis are new but instead seem to recycle themselves throughout history. One of the longest lived, and in a sense the most severely handicapping, of the techniques for eroticizing of female body parts was the foot binding practiced in China for centuries. Though men have also used padding on the shoulders and in the crotch and have worn corsets (e.g., the military corset of the 19th century used to restrain the stomach), they have been less prone than women to change their clothing.

Also associated with sexuality in clothing is the tactile impression made by clothes. For some individuals certain kinds of clothing arouse the tactile receptors in the skin. Certain fabrics or tight-fitting garments can cause sexual arousal, such items range from corsets to underclothes made of silk, from clothing made of leather or rubber to clothing of the opposite sex. In some cases the desire is so great that the person is labeled a fetishist and the habit a fetish. Corset fetishes were numerous in the 19th and early 20th centuries and involved members of both sexes. Some fetishes, such as rubber and leather, are common among individuals with an interest in sadomasochism, bondage, or dominance. Some people select one item of clothing for their fetish, while others like to have complete outfits made of leather or rubber. Cross-dressing, or transvestism, involves not only wearing clothing of the opposite sex but sometimes even living the opposite gender role.

With the growth of the fashion industry, no fashion lasted for very long, and change became the order of the day, especially for women. Different parts of the female anatomy, from the bosom to the derriere to the legs, become eroticized by each succeeding wave of fashion. Hemlines were raised and lowered, narrow waists were emphasized and deemphasized, and bosoms and derrieres were accentuated or ignored; but in the process, women's fashions for the most part came to reflect greater comfort and ease of movement, at least for casual wear. The 1960s saw the beginning of unisex clothing, but though the pants may be the same females still manage to look different in them than males.

Some observers have read more into clothing than others, and for a time the psychoanalysts had a field day. Flugel, for example, saw the tight choking collar and the "clogging coat" of the male as symbols of moral restraint to keep men, ever restless, on the narrow path of virtue and destiny. Many a writer has seen the hidden penis as being represented by the male cravat, something that is a less necessary part of the unisex clothing that includes tight-fitting jeans. For females the so-called bra-less look was said to give greater freedom and relief from fashion, but it was accompanied by the mini-skirt which emphasized legs instead.

It is difficult to predict what the new elegant, alluring fashion of the future will be, but it can be taken for granted that it will be designed consciously or unconsciously with sex appeal in mind. Whether women's costumes will be more or less restrictive than they have been in the immediate past probably depends in part on the role that women have in the world and on how much they want to project—or how much they feel the men in their life want them to project—a feeling of helplessness and fragility. Men in their own way seem prisoners of fashion and the business suit and tie still dominate even in areas of the United States where they are not particularly practical. Beards are out and short hair is back in for males, but that too can and will change again.

REFERENCES

Flugel, J.C. *On the Psychology of Clothes*. London: Hogarth Press, 1930.

Frings, G.S. *Fashion: From Concept to Consumer*. Englewood Cliffs, N.J.: Prentice Hall, 1991.

Kybalova, L., O. Herbenova, and M. Lamarova. *The Pictorial Encyclopedia of Fashion*. Translated by Claudia Rosoux. London: Paul Hamlyn, 1968.

Laver, J. *Costume and Fashion: A Concise History*. New York: Thames & Hudson, 1985.

Merriam, E. *Figleaf: The Business of Being in Fashion*. Philadelphia: Lippincott, 1960.

Rudofsky, B. *The Unfashionable Human Body*. Garden City, N.Y.: Doubleday, 1971.

Russell, D.A. *Costume History and Style*. Englewood Cliffs, N.J.: Prentice Hall, 1983.

Michel Hayworth

FEMALE GENITAL MUTILATION

Female genital mutilation is ubiquitous at all levels of society in the greater part of sub-Saharan and central Africa. It also exists, more or less sporadically, on other continents. In Africa alone, along an uninterrupted belt across the center of the continent and along the length of the Nile, an estimated 80 to 100 million female infants, small girls and young women have been genitally mutilated.

Female sexual mutilation is an ancient blood ritual of obscure origins. Among some peoples, partial or complete clitoridectomy is customary. Other groups additionally excise the inner lips of the vulva. The most drastic procedures are found along the Horn of Africa in Somalia, northern and central Sudan, southern Egypt, Djibouti, Mali, parts of Kenya, and Ethiopia. Here the clitoris is excised; the labia minora are removed; and the skin of the labia majora, scraped clean of its fleshy layers, is then sewn together over the wound. When the wound has healed, the labia are fused so as to leave only a small opening, which is most valued by the cultures if it does not exceed the circumference of a match stick. This widely practiced procedure, which virtually obliterates the external genitalia and the introitus, is known as infibulation (or Pharonic circumcision). It is, in effect, an artificially created chastity belt of thick, fibrous scar tissue.

While ethnologists and historians have offered various provocative theories on the origins of female sexual mutilation in general, all such theories rest on speculation and are impossible to substantiate. Infibulation is practiced almost exclusively among Islamic peoples of Africa, but must be regarded as a regional rather than a religious practice, since it is found only sporadically in the rest of the Islamic world. Moreover, it is known to predate Islam by at least 1,200 years. The first reference to the procedure appears in the writings of Herodotus, the Greek historian of the fifth century B.C.E.

The age at which a girl is subjected to the procedure may vary from early infancy to the birth of her first child, depending on the prevailing custom in the area or tribe. Throughout Africa, however, the tendency at the end of the 20th century is to perform the surgery at younger ages because a "small girl is more easily managed."

When a girl has been infibulated, she must thereafter pass her urine and menstrual blood through the remaining tiny opening, until her infibulation is partially torn or cut open when she marries. Extensive cutting and resuturing of the infibulation are done every time she gives birth. The birth process itself becomes progressively more difficult as scar tissues accumulate to hamper it.

The medical and psychic consequences as a result of genital mutilation, most specifically infibulation, can frequently be lifelong and devastating. No definitive statistics are available on the number of deaths resulting from the procedures, but mortality rates are high since most of this ritual surgery is done by medically untrained midwives without anesthesia, and with unsterile razors, scissors, or kitchen knives. Those performing the surgery are most often medically untrained older women, often with defective eyesight, and the operations are performed on the earthen floors of huts with inadequate lighting. Even when the operation is carried out by medically trained midwives or physicians under somewhat more sterile conditions and with the use of local analgesics and antibiotics, it is hazardous surgery.

The most common medical complications are hemorrhaging, shock due to prolonged pain, infection, tetanus, and retention of urine due to occlusion. Long-term complications from infibulation include difficult and painful urination, retention of menstrual blood, renal and reproductive system infections resulting from urinary and menstrual debris accumulating behind the infibulation, inclusion cysts, and fistulae. Because the genital mutilation is usually performed on small children, the causal relationship of the practice to the later health problems is not understood by the populace in general.

The rationale for female circumcision seems to be consistent in most of the societies practicing it and is based for the most part on a combination of myth and ignorance of biological and medical facts. The clitoris is variously perceived as repulsive, filthy, foul smelling, dangerous to the life of the emerging newborn, and hazardous to the health and potency of the husband. Circumcision is also believed, albeit mistakenly, to carry with it a persuasive array of health benefits. For example, it is said to make conception and childbearing easier, to prevent malodorous vaginal discharges, to eliminate vaginal parasites and the contamination of mother's milk, and to prevent various kinds of sickness. Clitoral excision, and more specifically infibulation, is (wrongly) said to reduce the sexual drive, and to protect women not only from aggressive males but from their own rampant sexuality and irresistible inborn drive toward total promiscuity.

In the Sudan and other regions where these ancient blood rituals are practiced, it is believed that the clitoris will grow to the length of a goose's neck, dangling between the legs in rivalry with the male's penis, if it is not cut. Males for their part are so fearful of an uncircumcised woman's growing such a long clitoris that they refuse to consider marrying such "unclean" women. Since marriage and childbearing remain virtually the only options available to most African women (except for prostitution in the urban centers), this leaves women little choice but to submit to the practice and to impose it on their daughters. In fact leaving a daughter uncircumcised leads to social ostracism in many tribes or clans. Radical circumcision, on the other hand, increases the African girl's chances of contracting a favorable marriage and her family's chances of obtaining a high price for the bride.

Throughout history, in fact, infibulation or Pharonic circumcision has distinguished "decent" and respectable women from unprotected prostitutes and slaves, and it carries with it the only honorable and protected status that is possible for a woman in such a society. Without being circumcised, a girl cannot marry and is thereby unable to produce legitimate sons to carry on a husband's patrilineage. An unmarried woman has virtually no rights in most of the African societies where circumcision and infibulation are practiced. Since family honor throughout the Arabic Islamic world is defined, in great measure, by the sexual purity of its women, any behavior on the part of the woman defined as indecent by the culture disgraces the whole family. Only the most stringent measures, including ultimately the death of the woman, can restore it. Infibulation instills security not only in the patrilineal family but also in the girl herself.

Giving birth is complicated by the inelastic infibulation scar, which prevents dilation beyond four of the ten centimeters usually required to pass the fetal head, thereby placing both mother and infant at risk. The infibulation must therefore be cut in an anterior direction, and after birth has taken place it must be resutured.

Sexual pleasure can still exist in even the most mutilated women. In a study conducted by Lightfoot-Klein in the Sudan, close to 90 percent of the 300 excised and infibulated women she interviewed reported having had pleasurable experiences during intercourse, such experiences varying in frequency from every time to almost never and in intensity from mild to extremely strong. She explained this sexual pleasure as in part due to the fact that these women believe their condition is normal. They had generally enjoyed emotionally secure childhoods in strongly supportive, cohesive extended families; possessed a high level of adaptability; and had bonded strongly to their marriage partners. They also had a rigid but clearly defined social role to which they could safely adhere. Though culturally bound to hide sexual interest and pleasure from their husbands, they had access to a number of covert but also clearly defined and easily communicated sex signals and behaviors that they could use without penalty. Similar studies carried out among Egyptian, Nigerian, and Somalian groups all report an equally high incidence of orgasm, an occurrence that seriously calls into question the contention made in some Western feminist and sexological literature that orgasm can be elicited only by clitoral stimulation.

The reports of orgasm among the women are supplemented by secondhand reports of males. The British explorer Sir Richard Burton in the 19th century commented that he observed that rather than dampening sexual desire, genital mutilation tended to intensify it quite possibly because it made orgasm more difficult to achieve. Similar reports have been elicited by investigators who have questioned the women's husbands, and by the observations of Western sex partners.

In virtually all of the societies where genital mutilation is carried out, it is most strongly supported by the mothers and grandmothers who have themselves suffered the mutilation in childhood. In a 1982 Sudanese study, Dareer found that 83 percent of the women and 87 percent of the men supported and defended such practices. Though a law forbidding the mutilations has been passed in Sudan, Kenya, and Egypt in recent decades, it has not been effectively implemented. Early efforts at reform, beginning perhaps with Muhammad in the seventh century and continuing through later missionary efforts and colonial edicts, have all come to naught.

Moreover, there is some evidence that the custom of genital mutilation, in spite of the effort of authorities, is not declining but growing. This is due not only to growth in the population of circumcising people, but also to the migration of merchants and civil servants from circumcising areas into noncircumcising ones. The reasons for the diffusion appear to be largely economic. In the event of intermarriage between circumcising immigrants and noncircumcising indigenous peoples, a far more favorable price for the bride may be obtained by a girl's family if she is circumcised. Consequently, these new, socially less advantaged converts to the custom have come to practice the most extreme and damaging version of the procedure in an effort to make their daughters most desirable and optimally marketable. They refer to such operations as "scraping the girls clean" and justify them as the "modern and hygienic way that educated people do it."

African intellectuals of both sexes have become acutely aware that something is intrinsically very wrong with these ancient blood rituals and wish to see them abandoned. At the same time they resent Western interference in their social and personal affairs, and this means that the only help acceptable in dealing with the problem seems to be material aid to programs directed by Africans themselves.

While many of these same intellectuals declare their intent to begin abolishing the practice by not mutilating their own daughters, few have translated these good intentions into action. There is simply too much family pressure and fear of breaking with tradition. In fact, further complicating the problems of infibulation has been the introduction of *re*infibulation. In this procedure, women are reinfibulated after delivering a baby, with the vaginal opening again being resutured to a pin-hole sized opening. This practice first started among the better educated and higher social classes in Sudan and was usually performed by physicians.

As immigrants adhering to these practices moved to Europe and to the Americas, non-Sudanese physicians have increasingly participated in them. In England, France, and Sweden physicians have been exposed as performing the operation. They have attempted to justify their actions on the basis that without available professional help, untrained laypersons, often female family members, perform the mutilations on the kitchen table. Many such cases end with hemorrhaging girls being rushed to hospitals.

Some African intellectuals have not hesitated to condemn the ritualistic practices. The outspoken pronouncements of Nawal el Saadawi, an Islamic physician from Egypt, for example, have on occasion landed her in prison.

Increasingly, the practice of both female circumcision and infibulation has come under attack by various international organizations and the International Council of Nurses. Still, director of the Foundation for Women's Health, Research and Development, Efua Graham, in Great Britain, views the prospects for change bleakly. Given the poor economic situation facing most African states, many legislators quite simply see female genital mutilation as a nonissue. She adds that "even the African women in the health professions see it as a nonissue."

Outlawing the custom seems simply to drive it underground. Yet forbidding it also creates unequivocal guidelines for the Western medical and nursing establishment and may on occasion even act as a deterrent to the parents, at least while they are residing outside the borders of their own countries. Rituals, particularly blood rituals, have a hold on people that is stronger than reason, stronger than law, and even stronger than religion. Change, if there is to be any change at all, may be expected to come only through painstaking sex education and with the development of economic alternatives to marriage for women.

REFERENCES

Abdalla, R.M.D. *Sisters in Affliction —Circumcision and Infibulation of Women in Africa.* London: Zed Press, 1982.

Assaad, M. *Female Circumcision in Egypt: Current Research and Social Implications.* Cairo: American Univ. Press in Cairo, 1979.

Burton, R. *Love, War and Fancy: Notes to the Arabian Nights.* London: Kimber, 1954.

Cloudsley, A. *Women of Omdurman.* London: Ethnographica, 1983.

Dareer, A. el. *Woman, Why Do You Weep?* London: Zed Press, 1982.

Grassivaro, G.P., and F. Vivianai. Female Circumcision in Somalia. *Mankind Quarterly* (1988), pp. 165–80.

Koso-Thomas, O. *The Circumcision of Women: A Strategy for Eradication.* London: Zed Books, 1987.

Lightfoot-Klein, H. *Prisoners of Ritual: An Odyssey Into Female Genital Circumcision in Africa.* New York: Haworth Press, 1989.

———. Rites of Purification and Their Effects: Some Psychological Aspects of Female Genital Circumcision and Infibulation in an Afro-Arab Islamic Society. *Journal of Psychology and Human Sexuality,* Vol. 2, No. 2 (1989), pp. 79–91.

———. The Sexual Experience and Marital Adjustment of Genitally Circumcised and Infibulated Females in the Sudan. *Journal of Sex Research,* Vol. 16 (Aug. 1989), pp. 375–92.

Lightfoot-Klein, H., and E. Shaw. Special Needs of Ritually Circumcised Women Patients. *Journal of Obstetrical, Gynecological, and Neo-Natal Nursing,* Vol. 20, No. 2 (1991), pp. 102–107.

Saadawi, N. *The Hidden Faces of Eve: Women in the Arab World.* London: Zed Press, 1980.

Hanny Lightfoot-Klein

FEMINISM AND SEXOLOGY

Feminists believe that women's sexuality and men's sexuality must be examined within their social context. Sexual behavior and problems, according to feminists, are socially constructed by cultural institutions that shape the rest of human experience: family, friends, community, the mass media, and various public and private institutions.

Feminists' View of the Social Construction of Sexuality

Sex-role socialization—the process by which individuals learn and relearn what it means to be a girl, boy, woman, or man—is believed to be especially crucial in the social construction of sexuality. That is, feminists assume that intimate interactions are shaped by notions as to which emotions, beliefs, and behaviors are possible or appropriate for women and men and most of all by unequal power relationships. For example, women are expected to be tender and nurturing and therefore are scripted in American society to expect sex to be associated with relatively long-term, loving relationships in which they must make numerous personal sacrifices for a partner. Men, in contrast, are socialized to be aggressive and dominant, a process that encourages them to adopt recreational, predatory scripts for sex or to confuse making love with the demonstration of achievement and power.

Feminists pay particular attention to social inequality, pointing out that women, especially women of color and those from lower socioeconomic status families, have far fewer economic resources and social privileges and considerably less power than men. Acknowledging that male dominance pervades the social system, feminists conclude that sexual interactions and expectations are shaped necessarily by inequality in the nuclear family, schools, workplace, and political arena.

Although feminists disagree vehemently about many aspects of sexual politics, they share these basic assumptions. Men's difficulties with intimacy, sexual dominance, and aggression are seen as the result of male political, social, and economic dominance. Female sexual passivity, dislike of sex, sexual dysfunction, and victimization are viewed as the inevitable result of the political, social, and economic oppression of women. In upholding these assumptions, feminists bring more than a nongendered perspective to the study of sexuality. They believe that science and scholarship cannot be entirely objective (or value free).

Factors Affecting Sexology Research

This is what feminists believe about sexology. Rather than being free of prejudice, the scientific study of sex (like all other aspects of science) reflects the values of the researchers or those who sponsor that research institutionally and financially. Almost always, research is structured around values that predominate in the larger culture. Until the very recent past, sexologists as a group have been unreceptive to feminist work. Texts and scholarly books in the field often neglected feminist contributions to the understanding of human sexuality and frequently were written with a male, heterosexist bias. With the exception of research on rape, childhood sexual abuse, sexual harassment in the workplace, and pornography, little feminist content has been published by the major sexology journals. Although numerous articles have appeared on the subject of women, few truly represent feminist scholarship (the effort to overcome androcentricity or male bias in sexology).

In North American culture and most others, a sexual double standard prevails that allocates more sexual freedom to men than to women. Most sexologists, feminists point out, reinforce the sexual double standard by advocating monogamy for women. A distinction continues to be drawn between "good" women who limit sex to one committed relationship and "bad" women who are promiscuous. Teenage girls who have multiple partners and women who are active in prostitution are studied to understand what went wrong, the research justified with the presupposition that these individuals are at great risk for unwanted pregnancies and sexually transmitted diseases.

In other examples of nonconscious sexism, sexologists often elect not to study women or assume that women are just like men. For example, most studies of homosexuals are based exclusively or predominantly on samples of gay men, even though research indicates that lesbians have considerably different sexual histories and desires. Studies of responsiveness to erotica reflect a similar bias; samples of women and men are exposed to a pornographic film that was typically written by and for men, and women's reactions (subjectively and physiologically) are matched against those of men (the cultural standard-bearers). Decisions such as these reflect the arrogant presupposition that women are worthwhile only insofar as their behavior pleases the dominant group (heterosexual men) or they resemble the culturally ideal group (heterosexual men again).

Feminists believe that values permeate sexology whether or not researchers present themselves as objective scientists and whether or not the audience is in touch with the social and political assumptions that underlie the design of a study and the interpretation of data. According to feminists, even scholars who advocate a society free of sex-role stereotypes (adherents of the so-called nongendered perspective) have values that shape selectively the questions they ask and the conclusions they draw. Masters and Johnson, for example, overlooked several female–male differences to come up with a uniform (nongendered) set of four stages of sexual response. Human beings cannot help but express values in their work. With this in mind, feminist sexologists are not ashamed about being advocates for those they study. Feminist methodology, whether it is quantitative or qualitative, emphasizes an appreciation for the individuality of those who participate in a study. Feminist sexologists define research as a collaborative task with other humans, not as something they do to research "subjects."

Feminists are exquisitely sensitive to possible sexism in their own work (negative stereotypes based on biological sex) as well as heterosexism (prejudice against bisexual persons, lesbians, and gay men). As a result, feminists may pay greater attention than sexologists with other theoretical orientations to both the language they use to describe women's and men's sexual behaviors and feelings and the way that they make inferences (draw conclusions) from their data.

Typically, the values of the dominant culture prevail in sexological research. The interpretation of sexological data has always been shaped by accepted social and political influences. During the early 20th century, pioneering sexologists exaggerated the differences between the sexes to support the culturally prescribed idea that women were innately inferior to men and exhibited a sexuality that was paler and weaker than male sexuality. In contrast, feminists complain that contemporary sexologists have force-fit their data to support the new cultural standard of the equivalence of the sexes, stipulating that women and men are more sexually alike than dissimilar. As a result, there is a tendency to overlook the extent to which sex-role socialization and sexual inequality continue to shape sexual responsiveness and experience. With the requirement that women be men's sexual equals, men's sexual attitudes and behaviors have become the standard; women are expected to imitate men to be sexually normal or fulfilled.

Feminists question traditional definitions of women's sexuality. But there is no party line on how to interpret recent changes in sexual behavior and information on women's lives. According to one group of feminists, sex has become increasingly pleasurable for women because more heterosexual men than ever before know how and why to stimulate their partner's clitoris. Contradicting this, other feminists argue that women's subordination to men has been eroticized, no woman being truly free to refuse sex with a member of the dominant group. Because so many women are the targets of sexual violence, working and sleeping with men are viewed as sleeping with the enemy by this group. A third group of feminists is convinced that Western culture remains sexually oppressive for men and women alike. This liberal group seeks to increase women's opportunities to enjoy multiple female and male sexual partners, masturbation, and a rich variety of sexual experiences.

Recently, sexologists have become increasingly receptive to the ideas of feminists from within their ranks. Nonetheless, the field continues tacitly to support traditional masculine and feminine roles in sexual interactions and a patriarchal model of the ideal family. Why else would researchers think about women's sexuality only insofar as it relates to marriage? The division of sexual attitudes and behaviors into categories—premarital, marital, extramarital, and post-marital—is not arbitrary. Rather, this division reflects the aspects of sex that are considered important for women. Sexologists profess a nonconscious ideology that equates normal, healthy sexuality with monogamous, male-dominated heterosexuality.

Progress in sexology has not always been progress in the service of women's rights. The major justification for sex research and therapy has continued to be the preservation of conventional heterosexual relationships. Nonconsciously, sex researchers and therapists have used their work to defend a male-centered, heterosexual belief system. Instead of allowing women to have unique sexual desires and characteristics, most sexologists judge women as sexually normal or abnormal on the basis of how they compare with sexually active male heterosexuals. In this context, real sex is equated with the hydraulics of sexual intercourse. Implicit in this ideology is the assumption that the best part of sex is when the penis enters the vagina; orgasm is all-important. Everything else is mere foreplay. Exaggerated emphasis on orgasm and sexual frequency is not a woman-affirming model of sex. Many women value physical affection more than sexual intercourse. Sexual pleasure for women is not necessarily linked to frequent genital stimulation.

Sexologists can be criticized for emphasizing the reproductive aspects of women's sexuality over pleasure and autonomy. Although a considerable body of data indicates that masturbation and sexual encounters with other women can be more sexually satisfying for women than

coitus, many sexologists continue to believe that heterosexual intercourse is the best vehicle for mature sexual expression.

The treatment of women's sexual problems has had a sullied history. Mental health professionals define women's psychosexual dysfunctions largely as a failure in the proper performance of heterosexual intercourse. Women's desire for nongenital stimulation and emotional intimacy is overlooked by the experts. A feminist model of sex would put greater emphasis on the emotional aspects of women's intimate relationships; numerous studies indicate that these factors are better predictors of relationship satisfaction than are sexual frequency and orgasm.

Men talk about sex more freely than women because most of the words for sex, including scientific jargon, were invented by men. Feminists argue that it is time for women to rewrite sexual vocabulary in their own terms. Already, lesbians have transformed the word "dyke" from a pejorative term to a description of pride in loving women. Other women in search of a feminist reconstruction of sex have changed the term "foreplay" to "sexual activity" while demoting "sexual intercourse" to the more accurate term "heterosexual afterplay."

Feminists have much to contribute to the future of sex research and therapy. With their inspiration, sexologists could move the study of sex away from sexual bookkeeping, the exhaustive recording of the frequency and variety of genital experiences. From a woman's perspective, sexual bookkeeping distracts sexologists from more important aspects of sexuality: how people think and feel about intimacy. Sexologists, according to feminists, should also stop equating women's sexuality with what they do with their genitals. Reducing sex to a juxtaposition of genitals and orifices denies the magic and breadth of sexual experiences.

Two Camps of Feminists

Feminists agree that male-dominant culture has had a negative impact on women's sexuality. However, they disagree vehemently about both the nature of women's sexual oppression and the best course of action. Two major feminist camps have emerged: radical feminists and liberal feminists. Armed with their own interpretations of sex research and personal observations, radical feminists believe that women are sexual victims who must be protected from men, liberal feminists strive to give women greater access to a variety of sexual pleasures.

Radical Feminists

Seeing eroticized male dominance in all aspects of everyday life, radical feminists believe that the sexual revolution of the 20th century has served mainly to reinforce women's subordinate status. As they explain, girls and women are almost always the victims and boys and men are almost always the perpetrators of rape, sexual harassment, prostitution, domestic violence, and the sexual abuse of children. Radical feminists are strongly opposed to pornography, likening erotic images and literature to an instruction manual by which men are taught how to bind, batter, torture, and humiliate women.

Radical feminists have polarized male and female sexuality—demonizing men and idealizing women in the process. Orthodox radical feminists do not recognize the possibility of consensual heterosexuality or female sexual aggression. For them, there is little difference between conventional sexual intercourse and rape, both acts appearing in their eyes to represent male supremacy. When confronted with the fact that many women appear to enjoy having sex with men and experience orgasm readily, they argue that women have been conditioned to identify with the male aggressor, to be aroused by male dominance.

Most radical feminists agree that women are harmed by pornography and the sex industry. Some are strong advocates of censorship (at least of violent or degrading pornography). In contrast with liberal feminists, who oppose censorship and view prostitution and related work as a legitimate career choice for women, radical feminists believe that women in the sex trades cannot help but be victims, and they do all in their power to end what they describe as the trafficking in women's bodies.

United in their opposition to pornography and prostitution, radical feminists disagree about many other issues. There is considerable controversy within the radical feminist movement as to whether it is possible for women to have a satisfying, nonoppressive, heterosexual relationship and which types of sexual activities are woman-affirming for lesbian and female bisexual couples.

Liberal Feminists

Unlike radical feminists—who have been in the forefront of political activism directed against the pornography and sex-trade industries, rape, child sexual abuse, domestic violence, and sexual deviancy—liberal feminists are less politically active. They have developed their positions more in reaction to the perceived excesses of radical feminism than in response to any particular cause.

Justifying pornography as free speech and invoking women's right to create their own erotic literature and materials, liberal feminists have attacked radical feminists for being hostile to men and denying women their rights to sexual pleasure and autonomy.

Liberal feminists believe that radical feminists' ideas about the reasons for female sexual oppression are misguided. They criticize radical feminists for denying the distinction between representations of forced sex in pornography and actual violence against women.

Liberal feminists complain that the sexual values of radical feminists are no different from those of reactionary political groups (e.g., anti-sex, fundamentalist, religious organizations). These values are seen as reinforcing the virgin/whore dichotomy, the distinction made by the patriarchy between "good" sexually controlled and "bad" sexually active women. The goals of the feminist antipornography movement strike liberal feminists as unrealistic and oppressive. Censorship and legal sanctions, argue liberal feminists, might push pornographers and sex-trade entrepreneurs and workers further into the underground economy. However, such measures would neither eliminate their products and services nor protect sex workers from exploitation.

Liberal feminists criticize radical feminists for advocating politically correct sex. By mistrusting heterosexuality and idealizing monogamous, egalitarian, lesbian sex and celibacy, radical feminists are viewed as reinforcing old prejudices that make anyone who practices a different form of consensual sexuality a social outcast.

Finally, radical feminists are criticized by sex liberals for denying women the possibilities of joyous, empowering sexuality. For instance, a few, extremely sex-negative radical feminists equate all heterosexual sex and even much of lesbian sex with sexual violence and exploitation. In seeking to protect women from sexual harm, this extremist group of radical feminists may unwittingly treat women like children who are really incapable of giving true consent to sex. According to liberal feminists, if women are only sexual victims, they are stripped of their adult autonomy, their potential to secure sexual pleasure on their own behalf.

Feminist Sexology

Feminists have encouraged sexologists to wonder about the meaning and implications of sex. Do women need more sexual freedom or is sex, especially sex with men, so dangerous that they should restrict their sexual activities? Thanks to feminism, sexologists are increasingly able to see how their research, educational work, and treatment of sexual dysfunctions can be biased by assumptions from a male-dominant culture. But what is feminist sexology?

Feminist sexology is the scientific and scholarly study of the relationship between sex-role socialization and sexual behavior. It is the consideration of how sex (being male or female) and beliefs about women and men construct the sexual experiences of lesbian, gay, bisexual, and heterosexual persons. Applied to sex education and therapy, feminist sexology is the advocacy of woman–affirming sexual activities (including equality between partners, open communication, sensuality, an end to all forms of sexual coercion, and the definition of sex as including mutual self-disclosures and warm displays of physical affection). In contrast with their conventional counterparts, feminist sexologists believe that real sex is far more than what people do with their genitals.

Since male sexual aggression and exploitation have taken root and been sustained by institutions that serve a misogynous, patriarchal culture, feminist sexologists seek to use their expertise to understand and eliminate these devastating social problems. A major task of feminist sexology is to increase women's sense of control over their own bodies. The empowerment of women is viewed as a necessary first step to reducing sexual dysfunction and coercion as well as the enhancement of sexual pleasure for women and men of all sexual orientations.

Although they do not always agree on goals, feminist sexologists are committed to positive social change. They hope that their work (be it research, sex education, or therapy) will protect women's freedom to make choices, sexually and reproductively, while increasing sexual equality and physical pleasure in intimate relationships.

REFERENCES

Allgeier, E.R., and N.B. McCormick, eds. *Changing Boundaries: Gender Roles and Sexual Behavior.* Palo Alto, Calif.: Mayfield, 1983.

Ehrenreich, B., E. Hess, and G. Jacobs. *Re-making Love: The Feminization of Sex.* Garden City, N.Y.: Anchor Press/Doubleday, 1987.

Ferguson, A., *et al.* Forum: The Feminist Sexuality Debates. *Signs: Journal of Women in Culture and Society,* Vol. 10 (Autumn 1984), pp. 106–35.

Irvine, J.M. *Disorders of Desire: Sex and Gender in Modern American Sexology.* Philadelphia: Temple Univ. Press, 1990.

Leidholdt, D., and J.G. Raymond, eds. *The Sexual Liberals and the Attack on Feminism.* New York: Pergamon, 1990.

McCormick, N.B. *Sexual Salvation: Affirming Women's Sexual Rights and Pleasures.* New York: Praeger, in preparation.

MacKinnon, C.A. A Feminist/Political Approach: Pleasure Under the Patriarchy. In J.H. Geer and W.T. O'Donohue, eds., *Theories of Human Sexuality.* New York: Plenum Press, 1987.

Pollis, C.A. An Assessment of the Impacts of Feminism on Sexual Science. *Journal of Sex Research,* Vol. 25 (Feb. 1988), pp. 85–105.

Schneider, B.E., and M. Gould. Female Sexuality: Looking Back into the Future. In B.B. Hess and M.M. Ferree, eds., *Analyzing Gender: A Handbook of Social Science Research.* Newbury Park, Calif.: Sage, 1987.

Shulman, A.K. Sex and Power: Sexual Bases of Radical Feminism. In C.R. Stimpson and E.S. Person, eds., *Women, Sex and Sexuality.* Chicago: Univ. of Chicago Press, 1980.

Tiefer, L. Social Constructionism and the Study of Human Sexuality. In P. Shaver and C. Hendrick, eds. *Sex and Gender.* Newbury Park, Calif.: Sage, 1987.

———. A Feminist Critique of the Sexual Dysfunction Nomenclature. In E. Cole and E.D. Rothblum, eds. *Women and Sex Therapy.* New York: Haworth Press, 1988.

Valverde, M. Beyond Gender Dangers and Private Pleasures: Theory and Ethics in the Sex Debates. *Feminist Studies,* Vol. 15 (Summer 1989), pp. 237–53.

Vance, C.S., ed. *Pleasure and Danger: Exploring Female Sexuality.* Boston: Routledge & Kegan Paul, 1984.

Naomi B. McCormick

FESTIVALS AND SEX

Sex has been and continues to be expressed in a myriad of forms in the celebratory activities of humans. These activities may be defined to include ceremonial, festival, and ritual occasions. There is a great deal of crossover in the definitions of these three terms, and they are frequently used interchangeably in socio-cultural literature. For example, a festival may be defined as a periodically recurring social occasion in which, through many forms and a series of coordinated events, all members of a whole community—united by ethnic, linguistic, religious, and historical bonds and sharing a world view—participate directly or indirectly and to various degrees. This overlaps considerably with the anthropological definition of rites of intensification that are regarded as collective rituals in which an entire community participates to celebrate events affecting the group, irrespective of age, sex, or status (e.g., Mardi Gras, Thanksgiving). The definition of "ceremonial" as an event associated with the life cycle or a celebration by the community is virtually interchangeable with many of the definitions of festival and collective ritual found in scholarly publications on the subject. Festivals, collective rituals, and ceremonials are therefore all examples of celebratory events affecting everyone in the community. Rites and rituals may be sacred or secular, and sex may be expressed on such occasions in diverse ways.

Rites of passage are another kind of ritual context in which sexuality may be present. In contrast to the communal aspects of ceremonials, festivals, and rites of intensification, rites of passage focus on the individual and mark a transition to a new status, such as from girl to woman or boy to man.

Human sexuality may be encountered in rituals, ceremonials, and festivals in a variety of ways: symbolically, allegorically, metaphorically, and in simulated or actual sexual behavior. Ritualized sex may include component attributes of sexuality, such as sperm and blood, genital mutilation or manipulation, symbolic or actual intercourse, or a blending of these. Moreover, ritualized homosexuality may be expressed, mythologically as among the Iatmul or behaviorally as among the Sambia and Keraki. Coitus may be used as a metaphor for the metaphysical, as in origin myths where it is embedded in a larger cosmic context—for example, in the mating of the sun and moon or the earth and heavens.

This article presents an overview of several types of ceremonial activities in which sex has an important role. Because discussion is restricted to events in which sexuality is expressed behaviorally, the metaphorical expression of sexuality (e.g., in fertility rituals centering on phallic and vulval symbols) cannot be covered in detail. The following brief description of a Japanese fertility ritual demonstrates the symbology of copulation in the absence of coital behavior. It is provided as an example of the richness and variety of sexual metaphor.

The Japanese festival celebrating the marriage of the god Takeinazuminomikoto with the goddess Arata-hime-nomikoto is an example of a fertility ceremonial in which sex is depicted symbolically. This ceremony features phallic and vulval images at two shrines, one representing the male principle and the other the female. Images of the vulva abound: at the female shrine is a rock in the shape of a vaginal orifice; stalls nearby sell live clams as vulvic symbols, and during a parade a priest carries a banner with a clinical picture of the female genitalia. The male shrine has a large stone phallus at its entrance and houses hundreds of phalli of diverse sizes. The male principle is denoted by a parade of Shinto priests in which a banner of an erect penis is displayed, followed by a litter on which a ten-foot-long carved wooden penis is displayed. This rural ceremony celebrates fertility without the ritualized intercourse or sexual license that accompanies some fertility cult celebrations.

Before an overview of the kinds of sexual behavior associated with ritual events, two caveats are in order. Herdt cautions that the investigation of ritual sexuality should proceed beyond the analysis of symbolic significance to include questions of desire and the pleasure or displeasure of the participants. Unfortunately, this focus is neglected in the majority of the literature on sex and ceremonial. In addition, the ethnographic literature is biased towards descriptions of male sexual behavior.

The Cultural Context of Sex and Celebration

Sex in the celebration must be regarded in the particular cultural and historical context in which it is enveloped. It is related to wider structural elements, including social complexity, technological development, distribution of power and privilege, and level of social organization, as well as economic variables. Sex, both symbolically and behaviorally, may be seen to follow trends associated with population growth, surplus, hierarchy, and centralization of governments. Ceremonial sex may also be a vehicle to ensure that inequality in terms of age, gender, and status is perpetuated in ranked and stratified societies.

Sexual control of populations is a vehicle of more generalized political control. In patriarchal societies in which extramarital sex is restricted (particularly for women), ritual and ceremonial sex may find expression in a "time out" period in which the rules for sexual restraint are lifted and a celebration of unregulated sexuality may occur. This allows for the symbolic expression of conflicts over the regulation and control of individuals' intimate lives by governments.

With the advent of urbanization, ceremonial aspects of sex were transformed. As archaic cities emerged as religious and governmental centers, sacred and ritualized sex became associated with the privileged classes and specialized roles. Consequently, intercourse with priests, priestesses, and temple prostitutes, as well as ceremonialized sex with divine rulers, was practiced in archaic city civilizations. For the urbanized, the fertility cults prevalent among plant cultivators lost their significance over time. According to Greenberg, this change occurred because concepts of "sexual magic" are more harmonious with the polytheistic religions found among farming peoples than with the later monotheistic ones. The increasing regulation associated with centralized authority and urbanization included increasing control over sexuality. This control inhibited many of the expressions of ritualized coitus that may still survive in plant-cultivating societies but remain only as cultural artifacts in more urbanized ones. Finally, ceremonial and ritual sex lost sacred elements as a result of trends toward secularization associated with population increase, state-level political organization, the industrial revolution, and, ultimately, modernity.

Rituals of Reversal and Sexual License

In old Hawaii when a chief died, his constituency engaged in a bacchanalia of excess and lawlessness that included the violation of sexual norms through sexual license. These rituals allowed for variance from the traditional mores of appropriate behavior. Only when the new chief was installed, usually after a few days, was law and order proclaimed. By ritually demonstrating the havoc caused by the breakdown of the social order, this period of sexual normlessness coincidentaly sustained and endorsed the importance of social regulation. Rituals of sexual license such as this function in societies to reduce tension and ventilate pressure where there are strict sexual prohibitions. Mardi Gras and kissing under the mistletoe are modern-day expressions of such practices. As in the Brazilian *carnaval*, elements of reversal are found in these rituals, so that the private act of sex takes on public expression.

Fertility

Rituals to increase human fecundity or generic fecundity may also contain elements of sexual variation from the norm. Fertility rituals abound in plant-cultivating societies in which fecundity is a generic kind of concern. In such societies, an association is made between human fertility and the general abundance of the community and its crops. Davenport has described one of the numerous annual fertility rituals among the Kiwai of coastal Papua-New Guinea. One community-wide fertility ceremony consisted of several nights of erotic singing and sexual abandon. During this period of unrestricted sexuality, the sperm of the men was collected from the women participants and deposited in a container where it was intermixed with other ingredients, illustrating the symbolic importance of fecundity. The collected ejaculate was then shared with the community to dab on whatever object was deemed in need of increased fertility.

The Marind-Anim of New Guinea also participated in a ritual designed to confer fertility. The *otiv-bombari* ceremony was first experienced by a woman after her marriage. Before she was permitted sexual relations with her husband, she was required to have intercourse with all the male members of her husband's clan. This ceremony was known to extend over several nights. It took place on other important occasions as well, such as following the birth of a child. In this case, it symbolically marked the woman's reentry into society. The *otiv-bombari* was also likely to be performed for women who had not conceived in order to enhance their fertility. Apparently, male power and domination, and perhaps concern over infertility, were salient enough to keep women cooperating in this ceremony, despite reports of their dislike of it.

Marriage Ceremonies

Rituals associated with marriage generally incorporate elements celebrating and defining reproductive relations, kinship, and sexual access. In this regard, marriage ceremonies are known for recognizing the importance of fertility, as illustrated by the *otiv-bombari* among the Marind-Anim. These ceremonies may also be demarcated by rituals that demonstrate the virginity of the bride. Such ceremonies occur in patrilineal societies in which certainty regarding paternity is important. These rituals typically center on the bride's blood and not the husband's sperm, since the cultural foci are on the contribution of the bride to the male's consanguineal kin group. Blood from the breaking of the hymen may be publicly exhibited on bed sheets or on the wife's undergarments, as in Morocco; or it may be displayed on barkcloth, as in Fiji, representing a generalized pattern in the southwestern Pacific. Virginity may also be demonstrated prior to intercourse in a defloration ceremony performed by a person of rank or a specialist, as among the Samoans, the Kagaba of South America, or the Seri of Mexico. Concern with various types of displays of virginity has been found among Middle Eastern societies, several Mediterranean peoples, Africans, Pacific Islanders, East Asian populations, and Eastern Europeans. Defloration may occur in less public exhibitions as well: for example, among the Lenge of Africa the practice was a part of the female's initiation ceremony. A special tool made of horn was used for this purpose.

The death of a spouse may require a ritual in which sex is involved. For example, a ceremonial cleansing of widows among the African Twi,

Thonga, and Yao involved decontamination of the wife who had been polluted by her dead husband's spirit. This cleansing was achieved by intercourse with a stranger unaware of her status. The Chaga and Nyakyusa of Africa practiced a form of widow inheritance (in which a son inherited his father's wives with the exception of his mother) that included ritual copulation. Upon inheriting the widows, the son was expected to copulate with all of them (except the pregnant and lactating wives) in one night as a symbolic act of inheritance.

Extramarital sex may also contain ritualized elements, as in the case of the courtly love tradition that flourished between 1000–1300 C.E. Courtly love comprised several phases. It began with a knight adoring a woman from afar, followed by a declaration of his undying love and numerous acts of valor on her behalf. The final phase concluded with admission to the woman's bedchamber. Since the beloved was usually a married woman, if infidelity took place it was engaged in with great discretion.

Rites of Passage

Ritualized homosexuality in New Guinea presents one of the most instructive cases for understanding sexual expression within the cultural context. It is reported to occur in 10 percent to 20 percent of the Melanesian societies. It may be prescribed, preferred, or regarded as acceptable. That it is not a recent innovation is demonstrated by the Sambia, among whom ritualized homosexuality was recorded as early as 1862. Among the Sambia of highland New Guinea, boys participate in a seven-year rite of passage into manhood. In the initial phase, the novice engages in fellatio of older boys. In a later stage of initiation, the boys become the "inseminators" and are subsequently fellated by initiates younger than themselves who have recently entered the rite of passage. This is followed by a bisexual phase in which the boys continue the ritualized homosexuality but are gradually introduced to sex with their newly acquired wives. Their passage into manhood culminates with heterosexuality.

This rite of passage is articulated with the well-known masculine orientation of Melanesian patrilineal societies. Men are made and not born in these societies. The key to growth is through sperm, whose reservoir must be built up in the boy. This is accomplished by ingesting the sperm of the older initiates. From the time the boys reach about 15 years of age until they marry and finally become fathers, they are the inseminators of the younger boys. In the subsequent phases of their rite of passage, they learn the mysteries of renewing their sperm stores in ways other than ingestion. This is necessary because their sperm supply is endangered by ejaculation with their wives.

In these cultures, ritualized homosexuality resonates with male power and prestige, symbolized through the transmission of sperm between men. Historically, highland New Guinea groups such as the Sambia were well known for warfare with neighboring groups. The rite of passage, with its ritualized homosexuality, functioned to consolidate men (crucial for groups who engaged in warfare), fostered a shared identity, and prepared young men through age cohorts to enter a ranked society. Ritualized female homosexuality in Melanesia is virtually unknown, as would be expected from the environmental and cultural milieu. The New Guinea cases of ritualized homosexuality suggest that Western notions of homosexuality cannot describe the experience of boys in these societies and that such clinically derived terms for sexual behavior lose their utility in the cross-cultural context.

Rites of passage may include ritual and ceremonial sexual behaviors that anticipate the novice's new role as an adult, including rights and obligations related to sex and reproduction. For example, among the African Kikuyu peoples, a novitiate boy was required to copulate ritually with an unknown married woman, although this intercourse was performed more usually as a symbolic act. Instead of copulating the young man masturbated in front of the woman and may have ejaculated on her. Completion of this ritual allowed him to take on the status and role of an adult man and to be eligible to marry a Kikuyu woman. Apparently, Kikuyu women also underwent a similar rite of passage for which information is not available. Among the African Ila, a boy's rite of passage encompassed sex education and simulated sexual intercourse with other novices, as well as masturbation. Among several Bantu groups, a girl's first menstruation was followed by a ritualized copulation with her husband, who upon orgasm ejaculated on a cloth. The cloth was subsequently analyzed by a mature woman of the village as to its relative characteristics.

Sex in Temples and Sacred Spaces

Other forms of ritualized sexuality are associated with sacred spaces or places (e.g., temples) and may involve sacred personages in acts of coitus. Ritualized sex may include village headmen in the founding of a building or even a new village. Among the Bemba of Africa, the headman "warms the bush" by copulating ritually with his wife before the huts of a new village are occupied. The Thonga have a similar custom of ritual copulation by the headman and his primary wife on the site of the new village, followed by a community-wide tabu on sex until the new village is completed. Then, after a purification ceremony, each couple in the village copulates in a fixed order of precedence, one every night. Indigenous Polynesian Mangaiian married couples were reported to have engaged in public sex prior to battle while enclosed in special sacred areas denoted for that purpose.

Temple prostitution has captured Westerners' interest, undoubtedly as a result of the exclusion of sex from the religious sector in Western culture. Sacred prostitutes are reported both cross-culturally and historically among the ancient Israelites and in pre-Muslim times in the Middle East. In India, temple priests were known to have copulated with barren women. Temple prostitution operated as both an act of devotion and a means of funding the employees and the temple as an economic enterprise. In addition, evidence exists of homosexual practices among male transvestite temple prostitutes in India. A similar occurrence among the Peruvian Berdache of Puerto Viejo was reported in a description by the Spaniard Cieza de Leon, who stated: "With these [Berdache], almost like a rite and ceremony, on feast and holy days, they have carnal, foul intercourse, especially the chiefs and headman."

During the flourishing of the Greek city-states, sacred prostitutes, the *hierodoules*, were associated with temples and contributed to their economic support. They were thought to have special powers. Other historical examples include a ritualized technique similar to that of modern sensate focus that was practiced in the Ming Dynasty under the Taoist sex ethic. In a special area, young couples would engage in sensual and sexual behavior under the verbal commands of the master teacher. This activity incorporated undressing and touching but not intercourse.

Conclusion

Ritualized sexual behavior is intricately woven into the cultural and historical matrix. Sex, like other human activities, is found in ritual, ceremonial, and festival occasions. This is not surprising given its symbolic and metaphorical parameters that transect both the sacred and the profane. Although ritual, ceremonial, and festival occasions may prohibit the expression of sex, they may also require its expression in culturally specific ways.

References

Abramson, A. Beyond the Samoan Controversy in Anthropology: A History of Sexuality in the Eastern Interior of Fiji. In P. Caplan, ed., *The Cultural Construction of Sexuality*. New York: Tavistock, 1987.

Barrau, J. L'Humide et le Sec: An Essay on Ethnobiological Adaptation to Contrastive Environments in the Indo-Pacific Area. In A.P. Vayda, ed., *Peoples and Cultures of the Pacific*. Garden City, N.Y.: Natural History Press, 1968.

Chapple, E.D., and C.S. Coon. *Principles of Anthropology*. New York: Holt, Rinehart & Winston, 1942.

Combs-Schilling, M.E. Etching Patriarchal Rule: Ritual Dye, Erotic Potency and the Moroccan Monarchy. *Journal of the History of Sexuality*, Vol. 1, No. 4 (1991), pp. 658–681.

Da Matta, R. Carnival in Multiple Planes. In F. Manning and J.-M. Philibert, eds. *Customs in Conflict*. Lewiston, N.Y.: Broadview Press, 1990.

Davenport, W.H. Sex in Cross-Cultural Perspective. In F. Beach, ed., *Human Sexuality in Four Perspectives*. Baltimore: Johns Hopkins Univ. Press, 1976.

Davis, D.L., and R.G. Whitten. The Cross-Cultural Study of Human Sexuality. *Annual Reviews of Anthropology*, Vol. 16 (1987), pp. 69–98.

Falassi, A., ed. *Time out of Time: Essays on Festival*. Albuquerque: Univ. of New Mexico Press, 1987.

Gluckman, M. *Order and Rebellion in Tribal Africa*. New York: The Free Press, 1960.

Greenberg, D.G. *The Construction of Homosexuality*. Chicago: The Univ. of Chicago Press, 1988.

Hendrick, C., and S. Hendrick. *Liking, Loving and Relating*. Monterey, Calif.: Brooks/Cole, 1983.

Herdt, G. *Guardians of the Flutes*. Irvington, N.Y.: Columbia Univ. Press, 1987.

———. Representations of Homosexuality: An Essay on Cultural Ontology and Historical Comparison, Part II. *Journal of the History of Sexuality*, Vol. 1, No. 4 (1991), pp. 603–32.

———. *The Sambia: Ritual and Gender in New Guinea*. New York: Holt, Rinehart & Winston, 1987.

McLeod, J.R. Ritual in Corporate Culture Studies: An Anthropological Approach. *Journal of Ritual Studies*, Vol. 4, No. 1 (1990), pp. 85–97.

Salter, M. An Analysis of the Role of Games in the Fertility Rituals of the Native North American. *Anthropos*, Vol. 69 (1974), pp. 494–504.

Van Gennep, A. *The Rites of Passage*. Translated by M.B. Vizedom and G.L. Caffee. 1909. London: Routledge and Kegan Paul, 1960.

Williams, W. *The Spirit and the Flesh: Sexual Diversity in American Indian Culture*. Boston: Beacon Press, 1986.

Anne Bolin

FLAGELLATION

Flagellation—spanking, caning, whipping, or paddling—has a long history. In the 13th and 15th centuries, flagellation was used as an atonement and to mortify the flesh. It was supported by the church, and sects of flagellants were widespread. However, after it became apparent that the practice was sexually stimulating for some practitioners, the church opposed it.

In the 18th and 19th centuries, private clubs of members who enjoyed whipping and birching could be found in London. Two of these were the Hell Fire Club (whose members were men) and the Order of St. Bridget (a club for women). The erotic appeal of being flogged was clearly presented by George Colman, who published a poem, "The Rodiad," in 1810. Pisanus Fraxi, in *Bibliography of Prohibited Books,* includes works with flagellation themes. *Fanny Hill*, a novel originally published in 1749, includes a description of the whipping of a gentleman by the heroine.

More recently, whipping and other forms of corporal punishment are common within the sadomasochistic subculture, although many masochists do not wish to experience severe discomfort. Spengler, who studied members of sadomasochistic clubs in West Germany, found that 66 percent of his sample preferred being whipped; 60 percent also enjoyed being caned. Whipping was preferred by 47 percent of the males and 39 percent of the females studied by Breslow.

REFERENCES

Breslow, N., L. Evans, and J. Langley. On the Prevalence and Roles of Females in the Sadomasochistic Subculture: Report on an Empirical Study. *Archives of Sexual Behavior,* Vol. 14 (1985), pp. 303–17.

Bullough, V.L. *Sexual Variance in Society and History.* New York: John Wiley & Sons, 1976.

Falk, G., and T.S. Weinberg. Sadomasochism and Popular Western Culture. In T. Weinberg and G.W.L. Kamel, eds., *S and M: Studies in Sadomasochism.* Buffalo, N.Y.: Prometheus Books, 1983.

Fraxi, P. *Bibliography of Prohibited Books.* New York: Jack Brussel, 1960.

Krafft-Ebing, R. von. *Psychopathia Sexualis.* 1881. New York: Stein & Day, 1965.

Spengler, A. Manifest Sadomasochism of Males: Results of an Empirical Study. *Archives of Sexual Behavior,* Vol. 6 (1977), pp. 441–56.

Thomas S. Weinberg

FOREPLAY

Foreplay is a traditional term to describe activities prior to coitus. It is based on an assumption that the sexual activity that will follow is heterosexual intercourse. Inherent in the meaning of the term is the notion that the activities involved are not equivalent to, or the goal of, a fulfilling sexual encounter; nor are they fulfilling in and of themselves. Rather, penile-vaginal intercourse is viewed as the ultimate and legitimate goal. For this reason, some sexologists in recent years have advocated using the term "pleasuring," which encompasses the gamut of sexual behaviors.

Historical religious beliefs influence many beliefs about sexuality. Often, reproduction was to be the only purpose of intercourse. Pleasure, if there was any, was likely to be regarded as sinful, immoral, illegal, or perverted, particularly for women. Even today, some people regard all sexual acts between same-sex people as wrong and potentially perverse, because conception is not the factor motivating their behavior.

The notion that orgasm should occur through a penile-vaginal act of penetration, with the possibility of pregnancy occurring, is inherent in this position. Other forms of sexual expression that are pleasurable in and of themselves become devalued, in spite of the fact that pleasuring activities (e.g., touching, kissing, massaging, manually or orally stimulating, body caressing, or masturbating) can be ends unto themselves, with or without an accompanying orgasm.

The sequence of sexual pleasuring behaviors is unvarying. Heterosexual couples first kiss on the lips, followed by the male's caressing the woman's breasts through her clothing. This is followed by caressing her nipples under her clothing, then feeling her vaginal lips through her underwear. He kisses her breasts. She then moves her hand over his pants and feels his penis. He fingers her unclothed genitals, and she moves her hand under his pants and feels his penis. The male puts his fingers into her vagina, followed by the male's kissing her genitals; she then kisses his penis. Simultaneous kissing of the genitals follows. If the interaction is to proceed to intercourse, she guides his penis into her vagina. The last behavior in the sequence is male entry into the vagina from the rear. This is the order in which these sexual pleasuring behaviors are acquired over time.

Unfortunately, similar sequencing data are not available for homosexually oriented individuals, although sequencing information is available for committed couple relationships. According to noted sexologists Masters and Johnson, in committed lesbian relationships sexual interaction usually begins with full body contact. When breast play is instigated, it is more prolonged than it is in the case of heterosexual couples. Similarly, genital contact is attenuated. In male homosexual couples, full body contact is also the rule, before focus shifts to specific erogenous zones. Kissing and caressing are usually followed by nipple stimulation. This appears to be regarded as more erotic in homosexually oriented rather than heterosexually oriented men. Male couples, in contrast to their heterosexual counterparts, spend more time in nondemanding genital play, which involves more than just the immediate genital area. Teasing, playfulness, and prolonged pleasuring seem to characterize same-sex sexual encounters to a greater degree than is typical of heterosexual episodes. These pairs adopt a slower, less demanding pace. They do not appear as urgently goal oriented, orgasm oriented, as their heterosexual counterparts.

Whether a specific pleasurable sexual act is to be regarded as an end unto itself or as a pathway to orgasmic experience, there is a wide variety of behaviors that couples of all sexual orientations have to choose from. Simple full-body holding and caressing can be a joyful and fully satisfying experience. Sensuous stroking of the skin, the largest erogenous area of the body, affords great comfort and pleasure.

Kissing, both closed and open mouthed, can be an erotic experience. Some people believe that an open-mouthed kiss, or a French kiss, is more intimate than sexual intercourse. Breast stimulation, although pleasurable to both sexes, is most frequently focused on the female in a heterosexual couple, with lesbian couples spending a great deal of time on the breast area. Homosexual male couples also spend some time in this area. Manual stimulation of one's own genitals (self-masturbation), masturbation of the partner, or mutual masturbation are pleasurable in and of themselves, regardless of whether they end in orgasm.

Oral-genital sex is another form of pleasuring. According to Masters and Johnson, the sexual orientation of the stimulator makes little difference in the technique of stimulating the penis, fellatio. There is, however, a difference in tempo and teasing, with heterosexual couples being more performance, and less pleasure, oriented. Oral stimulation of the female vulva, cunnilingus, includes stimulation of the outer lips or labia, the vagina, and the clitoral area. As in the case of male homosexual couples, lesbian couples not only spend more time in pleasuring their partners than do heterosexuals but also show superior and more varied techniques according to

Masters and Johnson. Oral stimulation of the anus, anilingus, is engaged in by some heterosexual couples, but it is more frequently a part of male homosexual encounters.

The variety of sexual toys available for pleasuring is limited only by the individual's imagination. Everyday household objects, such as candles, can cast a romantic mood; feathers can be run sensually across the body to give pleasure. More complex apparatus, such as vibrators or penis-shaped objects, dildos, are made from a variety of materials. They can be used to stimulate the exterior of the body or may be inserted into the vagina or anus.

Some individuals receive pleasure from the controlled use of pain. In sadomasochistic games, control is of primary importance. A clear contract exists between the players as to how much pain is acceptable, and the terms are strictly adhered to.

Environmental manipulation can also be used to heighten enjoyment. The use of different rooms, the enactment of different fantasies, and the wearing or not wearing of special clothing all provide variety that can increase pleasure and delight.

When there is too much emphasis on being goal rather then pleasure oriented, sexual problems can and do arise. All good sex therapy attempts to take the couple back to, or initiate them into, more pleasure. Pressure to achieve erection or orgasm is not only de-emphasized in the early stages of the therapy; in some instances it is forbidden.

In sex therapy, couples are taught how to discover what is pleasurable to themselves and their partners. Key concepts include nondemand contact that is not genitally oriented at first. In a relaxed atmosphere of pleasure and safety, the couple is taught how to communicate verbally and nonverbally. Pleasure can be learned and returned to. Nongenital massage is usually prescribed. A couple experiences relief in just being able to abandon themselves to the pleasure of knowing themselves and their partners at another level of being.

Perhaps some of the old homilies are correct. It is possible to miss the forest for the trees, to miss the wonder of the journey by only focusing on the arrival. Foreplay, or pleasuring, affords individuals a great range of behavioral options to increase their own and their partner's satisfaction.

REFERENCES

Masters, W., and V. Johnson. *Human Sexual Inadequacy*. Boston: Little, Brown, 1966.

————. *Human Sexual Response.* Boston: Little, Brown, 1966.

Susan B. Bond

FRAUD: SEX FRAUD

Fraud associated with sex is ancient, stretching back to love philters sold in the earliest occidental and oriental civilizations. In early modern Europe, with the revival of travel, the resurgence of venereal disease, and the invention of printing, which fostered advertising through handbills and newspapers, quackery of all types expanded, not the least quackery related to sex. Efforts at suppression by law, beginning at this time but largely a product of the 20th century, have curtailed but not eliminated the dangers associated with sex fraud.

The varieties of deception have been numerous. A major strand has promised to reverse impotency and restore the failing powers of aging men. A German immigrant in 18th-century London marketed a "nervous cordial" in a pamphlet dedicated to the king and entitled A *Guide to Old Age or a Cure for the Indiscretions of Youth.* The final phrase regarding the purported cause of lost manhood was destined for two centuries of reiteration.

In the United States, a promoter in 1804 offered "a degree of re-animation" to older men who used his Aromatic Lozenges of Steel. Throughout the 19th century, ads ran rampant in the urban penny press and in cheap magazines offering treatments for "nervous debility" by alleged doctors or patent medicines. A handbill for an institute in Wisconsin promised: "Our wonderful electro medical treatment is saving thousands and will save you." The maker of Turkish Wafers stressed that sultans with harems had successfully used the product. Other proprietors trafficked on the theme of Mormon polygamy, giving their nostrums names like Brigham Young Tablets, Mormon Elders Damiana Wafers, and Mormon Bishop Pills. The last of these came in three colors: red, white, and blue. Other suggestive names included Ponce de León Cream, Red Rooster Pills, and Sporty Days Invigorator. The Von Graef Sexual Troche was recommended for use both "in the Stomach and on the Organ."

Nostrums for impotence were sometimes pitched in traveling medicine shows, for example, Vital Sparks Pills, made from buckshot moistened and rolled in powdered aloe, were claimed to be an extract from a Chinese male turtle. Mail-order marketing, however, was more common. "Sucker lists" of buyers were bartered among sellers: in 1914, when the promoter of Man Medicine was convicted of mail fraud, he was forced to destroy a mailing list of over half a million names. Blackmail sometimes arose from such promotions. An inquiring letter prompted by advertising brought a COD shipment of the product at a very high price. If the recipient refused payment, he might be warned to ante up or his weakness would be made known to his community.

In the 1920s, a Kansas physician, John R. Brinkley, demonstrated the power of radio as an advertising medium by broadcasting his cure for impotence: transplantation of the sliced gonads of goats into the scrotums of inadequate males. Each patient had the privilege of selecting his own goat from the doctor's herd. Brinkley did a thriving business, and the notoriety almost got him elected governor. When the new Federal Radio Commission refused to renew his broadcasting license, he took his powerful station to Mexico.

So-called male-weakness promotions have been a high enforcement priority since the beginning of the century for U.S. postal officials and enforcers of food and drug laws (the U.S. Department of Agriculture's Bureau of Chemistry until 1927, then the Food and Drug Administration, or FDA). Scores of actions have been taken against promotors. Two campaigns of the 1950s illustrate the FDA's zeal. The agency banned from importation and interstate commerce the "Vine That Makes You Virile," pega palo, imported from the Dominican Republic, as an unsafe new drug. The FDA also sought to suppress alleged rejuvenators that contained the male hormone testosterone. Where there truly was a lack of hormone, in some 5 percent of impotency cases, sufficient testosterone might fulfill product claims, but only at the risk of activating dormant prostate cancer cells. In most marketed products, the hormone level was too low to be helpful but still posed risks. Through seizures, injunctions, and criminal prosecutions, the FDA severely shrank the market.

Impotence remains a problem, so the promotion of treat-yourself solutions constantly recurs in the form of devices like plastic penis strengtheners or some type of drug. Impotence, modern scientific medicine maintains, results almost entirely from physical causes that can be treated with some degree of success. The lure of pseudoscience, however, leads to wasted resources and health hazards.

Impotency fraud is related to two other aspects of deception. One is the quest for rejuvenation, for eternal youth. The heyday of this doctrine perhaps came in the 18th century, but it has seen recurrent revivals. Two of history's most celebrated charlatans, Cagliostro and Count de Saint-Germain, worked this field with elixirs of life and talismans of magic characters. Sexual renewal would accompany the overall turning backward of time's clock. Women as well as men were entranced with the prospect of regaining youth; Saint-Germain won the hearts of many women, including Madame de Pompadour, by giving them his rejuvenation water.

Impotency "cures" are also related to aphrodisiacs; indeed, such double duty has not infrequently been claimed in the same nostrum advertisement. In the 19th century, Dr. Hollick's Aphrodisiac Remedy also provided "the only sure and reliable . . . permanent cure of impotence." After World War II, a Flying Fortress gunner who had won the Congressional Medal of Honor promoted Firmo Cream as both an aphrodisiac and a restorer of lost manhood.

Some spurs to sexual performance have relied on ambience, others on ingredients with ancient folkloric reputations. A quack in 17th-century England asserted that, if a wife put the promotor's Sticking Plaster on the pit of her husband's stomach, the husband's "appetite towards family duty" would be so enhanced that he would "love wonderfully and beget a miraculous progeny." In the next century, the flamboyant James Graham rented out a "Grand Celestial" bed in his London Temple of Health, providing also music and fragrances and guaranteeing that beautiful children would be conceived in it. As time went on, aphrodisiacal commerce became simpler. Nostrums were purported to contain the essence of foods (e.g., oysters) or plants (e.g., damiana and mandrake) cherished in tradition as sexual stimulants. Early in the 20th century Damiana Nerve Invigorator was challenged for not containing any damiana; and Nyals' Compound Extract of Damiana, although it had an insignificant amount of that botanical, was cited for containing unlabeled cocaine.

Handbills promoting cures for the French pox appeared in England in the 16th century. As venereal disease spread, so did claims of cures. One charlatan boasted, "I do cure all Persons that have been at *Venus Sports* of the French, Italian, Indian, High Dutch, English or Spanish variety." A 17th-century proprietor pitched his product in rhyme:

> All ye that are of Venus Race
> Apply yourselves to Dr. Case;
> Who, with a box or two of PILLS
> Will soon remove your painful ILLS.

In 1729, the Virginia government council freed a slave and granted him a pension in exchange for his making known his remedy for venereal disease. Franklin's *Pennsylvania Gazette* in 1771 advertised a London nostrum that would cure "the venereal malady." After the 1830s, with the advent of the penny press, venereal disease advertising ran rife, and both nostrum makers and self-styled "specialists" in venereal disease treatments prospered. Some of the latter lured customers with street-level wax museums linked with their offices containing figures that depicted the ultimate ravages of the disease. Treatment could be rugged. One turn-of-the-century New York quack clinic put the naked male patient on a sort of toilet chair, his back against a metal plate, and his scrotum falling into a flowing colored liquid that contained a wire completing an electrical circuit. The patient felt the treatment as soon as he sat down, and its staggering impact, so the quack told him, proved its efficacy.

One American quack of this period appropriated the name of Paul Ehrlich, discoverer of Salvarsan, claiming that his own 914 version of the syphilis remedy far transcended the German scientist's 606 in healing potency. With the population shifts of World War I came an epidemic of venereal disease. Quacks responded to the challenge, offering countless specious cures. With a wary eye on food and drug officials, however, they avoided the terms "venereal disease" and "syphilis" in their promotions, resorting instead to a euphemism recognized by the afflicted, "bad blood." The Bureau of Chemistry stepped up regulatory pressure.

Epidemics always foster health fraud. So, nearly seven decades later, did the epidemic of a new disease, acquired immune deficiency syndome (AIDS), spur a new wave of quackery. With effective therapies for AIDS and its attendant afflictions being very few, promoters offered hundreds of specious treatments to desperate patients. To mention merely substances for injection into the body, the list included amino acids, blood serum, cells from fetal animals, Easter lily bulbs, hydrogen peroxide, ozone, polio vaccine, pond scum, snake venom, vitamins, and the sufferer's own filtered urine. The general public also, frightened and slow to comprehend clearly the routes of AIDS transmission, could be victimized; many bought a plastic shield to cover the mouthpieces of public telephones, a device that allegedly protected a person from the infectious breath and saliva of previous users. Regulatory officials faced a fearful burden.

In some ways, sex frauds have victimized both sexes simultaneously. However, gender distinctions have also been evident, for example in the proliferation of "men's specialists." Cosmetic quackery has been a woman's specialty, and appeals to beauty have often had a sexual implication. In 17th-century London, many creams, powders, and pills were pitched to enhance or restore the complexion, even to eliminate smallpox scars. One product was frankly named Amorous Powder. Two centuries later, American women could purchase Juno Drops and Blush of Youth. Sexual allure became a central theme in 20th-century cosmetic and perfume promotion.

The mid-19th century saw a boom in bust-development advertising, many ads employing before and after illustrations to startling effect. Products bore names like Mammaleon and Mammarial Balm. This field of enterprise continued into the 20th century with mechanical devices offered in addition to creams; both received the attention of regulators. In the 1950s, a plastic surgeon asserted "Today our civilization is in the midst of a 'breast cult' or 'bosom craze,' with men more aroused by breasts than by genitalia." In his practice, he augmented breasts with surgiform sponges. Such "breastplasty" aroused the skepticism of the American Medical Association. Augmentation procedures continue to make alarming headlines.

Problems peculiar to women have prompted promotions over the centuries. The inability to conceive provided a market for a gentlewoman in 17th-century London whose handbill boasted of her "knowledge of the Best, Rarest, and most Wonderful Secrets which Art and Nature can afford for the cure of Barrenness." Two centuries later, an American promoter resorted to verse:

> Lucina Cordial!—Barren wives
> It turns to mothers fair,
> And the fond name of father gives
> To husbands in despair.

(Of course, the problem could have been the husband's infertility, in which case the ad might have recommended the Van Graef Sexual Troche.)

The broad-gauged female tonics pioneered by Lydia E. Pinkham's Vegetable Compound promised to help women not only become pregnant but also avoid miscarriage and lessen the arduousness of labor. Dr. Pierce's Favorite Prescription offered such assurances and more: taking the medicine guaranteed "healthy vigorous offspring, and promote[d] abundant secretion of nourishment on the part of the mother." In time similar claims led to misbranding charges against a nostrum named Mother's Friend.

Mrs. Pinkham first marketed her compound—a brew of several botanicals and 19 percent alcohol—in 1875, and her promotion exploited the obtuseness of orthodox male physicians in treating female complaints. The advertising approach was largely responsible for the product's commercial success. Early labeling for the compound termed it "A Sure Cure for Prolapsus Uteri, or Falling of the Womb and All Female Weakness, [and] . . . Weakness of the Generative Organs." The compound's many competitors made similar claims until eventually restrained by law.

If some women could not become pregnant when they wanted to, other women became pregnant without desiring it. At times, Mrs. Pinkham's Compound was subtly advertised as both a cure for barrenness and abortifacient. Many nostrums promoted as emmenagogues alleged to restore suppressed menstruation were bought in the belief that they would terminate pregnancy. These concoctions dated back to an English patent medicine, Hooper's Female Pills, sold in colonial America and into the 20th century as well. Many nostrums avowedly intended to produce abortions were also advertised in 19th century America. Shady abortionists in various cities had no difficulty placing their ads in the press.

Abortifacient nostrums in due course received the attention of the Bureau of Chemistry, which made known both the ineffectiveness and the hazards of products like Chichester's Diamond Brand Pennyroyal Pills. Later, in the 1930s and 1940s, the Food and Drug Administration carried on a continuous campaign against intrauterine pastes. Women who used them had suffered hemorrhaging and severe injuries, even in some cases death. Two promotors of such pastes were sentenced to short terms in jail.

Sex fraud has exhibited many dire dimensions. Most of the reasons for resorting to it continue to exist, as do credulity and fear on the part of the public and unscrupulous greed on the part of promoters who prey upon the gullible. Therefore, cruel and dangerous deception may be expected to persevere.

REFERENCES

Adams, S.H. *The Great American Fraud*. Chicago: American Medical Association, 1906.

Andrews, C.S. *A Century's Criminal Alliance between Quacks and Some Newspapers*. New York: Stettiner, 1905.

Bush, L.E., Jr. Mormon Elder's Wafers. *Dialogue: A Journal of Mormon Thought,* Vol. 10 (Autumn 1976).

Carson, G. *The Roguish World of Dr. Brinkley*. New York: Rinehart, 1960.

Cramp, A.J. *Nostrums and Quackery*. 3 vols. Chicago: American Medical Association, 1912, 1921, 1936.

Francesco, G. *The Power of the Charlatan*. New Haven: Yale Univ. Press, 1939.

McNeal, V. *Four White Horses and a Brass Band*. Garden City, N.Y.: Doubleday, 1947.

Mohr, J.C. *Abortion in America*. New York: Oxford Univ. Press, 1978.

Stage, S. *Female Complaints: Lydia Pinkham and the Business of Women's Medicine*. New York: W.W. Norton, 1979.

Thompson, C.J.S. *The Quacks of Old London*. London: Brentano's, 1928.

Trimmer, E.J. *Rejuvenation*. London: Robert Hale, 1967.

Young, J.H. *American Health Quackery: Collected Essays*. Princeton, N.J.: Princeton Univ. Press, 1992.

———. *The Medical Messiahs*. Princeton, N.J.: Princeton Univ. Press, 1967.

———. *The Toadstool Millionaires*. Princeton, N.J.: Princeton Univ. Press, 1961.

James Harvey Young

FREUD, SIGMUND

Sigmund Freud, unlike Havelock Ellis and Magnus Hirschfeld, did not focus exclusively on sexuality. Rather he developed a comprehensive theory of human behavior that emphasizes sex as the central aspect of human development. In fact, Freud's most significant contribution to sexuality is his popularization of the importance of sex in human development.

Born at Freiberg in Moravia on May 6, 1846, Freud moved with his family to Vienna, where he lived until he was 82. Then, to escape the Nazis, he fled to London, where he died at the age of 93 on September 23, 1939.

Freud, like Krafft-Ebing, held that sexuality (a natural biological force Freud called the libido) is the most important factor in social existence and that it is important to direct the sex drives, not repress them. His publication of *Three Contributions to the Theory of Sex* in 1905 was greeted with outrage and derision by the establishment intellectuals of the day. Nonetheless, the movement he founded, psychoanalysis, persevered through the torrent of criticism and abuse that marked its emergence to become one of the most influential movements of the 20th century, particularly in the United States.

Unlike other instinctive needs, such as those for food and water, the instinctive need for love and sex, Freud believed, can be repressed by the society or the individual. Even so, its energy source remains, and Freud developed his theory of personality around the fate of the libido. The unfolding of these sexual energies from infancy on is central to Freud's theory of personality development. He taught that early in life, libido is channeled into certain body zones, which then become the center of eroticism. Progressively, individuals pass through psychosexual stages which Freud called oral, anal, phallic, latency, puberty, and genital. Each stage of development involves conflicts to resolve, if they are not, "fixation" occurs in which some libido remains invested in that stage and becomes reflected in adult behavior.

Of particular interest to Freud was the "Oedipal complex." He maintained that children of both sexes develop love and jealous relationships with their parents, first with the mother, then with the father. A boy must shift his identification to his father, although this process is complicated by the young boy's developing sexual desire for his mother, which leads him to fear that his father will cut off his penis. This castration fear leads the boy to repress his desire for his mother and begin to identify with his father. The female Oedipal complex, which some of Freud's students called the Electra complex, results in penis envy because the girl assumes she has been castrated. Blaming her mother for this loss, she shifts her attention to her father; but when she realizes that she cannot compete with her mother for her father's affection, she continues to identify with her mother and develops a feminine identity.

Freud paid comparatively little attention to most forms of variant sexual behavior, but his followers seized on his concepts to emphasize the environmental and accidental causes of variant impulses far more than did Freud, who was much more biologically oriented. Freud, however, also emphasized developmental causes, and though he regarded homoerotic behavior as a normal part of growing up, he held that most individuals move beyond this stage into adult heterosexuality; and so, by implication, adult homosexuality is a distortion of natural development. His explanations for the failure of certain individuals to move beyond the homoerotic phase center around the child-parent relationship, particularly the Oedipal phase. The boy, for example, suppressing his desires for his father, seeks to be like the woman who accepted his father; but unable to reconcile the incestuous sin of a father love, he seeks the father in other males. Such a boy might become effeminate, play the female role in the sex act, and become attracted to other men.

Freud's theories are mainly masculine in orientation, and for him women are essentially inferior to males. This assumption led Freud to conclusions that many feminists have long criticized (for example, his belief that women who have orgasms from stimulation of the clitoris are fixated at an immature phallic stage).

For a time, when psychoanalytic theories dominated American thinking on sexual development, the Freudian explanations seemed to be the only acceptable ones and much of the writing on sex, particularly in the United States, from 1930 to 1960 was dominated by psychoanalysts. Much of sexology since 1960 has focused on undermining many of the psychoanalytic explanations of Freud's followers, who allowed their theoretical assumptions to cloud their research findings. Freud, however, remains a seminal figure in the development of sex research.

REFERENCES

Primary

Freud, S. *Beyond the Pleasure Principle, Group Psychology and Other Works*. Vol. 18 of the *Standard Edition*. London: Hogarth Press, 1955.

————. *Three Essays on the Theory of Sexuality*. Edited and translated by J. Strachey. Reprint. New York: Basic Books, 1963.

Secondary

Jones, E. *The Life and Works of Sigmund Freud*. 3 vols. New York: Basic Books, 1953–57.

Vern L. Bullough

FRIENDSHIP: FEMALE–MALE FRIENDSHIP

Friendship is usually thought of as a close, non-sexual relationship between members of the same sex. Unlike sex, which can be pressured, or love, which can be unrequited, friendship by definition is mutual, equal. Now that more men and women are employed in the same kinds of jobs and meet each other in work-related situations as peers, friendship between them is becoming a viable social option.

Strong cultural pressures are mounted against the development of such friendships, but the advantages to be derived transcend these barriers. These friendships can be the catalyst for breaking down the obstacles of sex-role stereotyping and form a revolutionary way for the sexes to interact. Cross-gender friendship could be the accepted basis of social and business networking for the next generation of men and women.

This entry describes risks and pitfalls to be negotiated before friendship between men and women can be free of the fear and suspicion that now surround it.

Historical Perspective

Aristotle proposed that friendships have three qualities. First is *goodness,* which is manifested in a relationship between two persons having mutual admiration for each other's loyalty or justness. Second, and to a lesser degree, is *utility,* present when two individuals value the benefits their friendship provides. Finally, is *enjoyableness,* exemplified by a friendship that is valued for the sheer pleasure inherent in the presence of the other. Other ancient philosophers cited characteristics men admired (e.g., bravery, loyalty, duty, heroism) as the measures for friends. It was, after all, the friendship of men with which these philosophers were concerned. Women were thought to be incapable of friendship, since they had no masculine attributes and were insufficient in loyalty and sincerity to sustain friendships, even with other women.

Until recently, society cast women in subservient roles, making a friendship of equals between men and women impossible in concept or practice. Although men and women could be colleagues, theirs were apt to be working relationships (e.g., mentor-protege or leader-follower) rather than friendships between equals and peers.

It is not surprising, then, that female-male friendship is an ignored topic in the social science literature. Yet the findings in the scant body of literature dealing with cross-sex friendships support the conclusion that some adults do experience these relationships and consider them a significant part of their lives.

Female-Male Friendship

Because cross-gender friendship is rare, there is no consensus about its nature, dynamics, and meaning. Even language describing this relationship is open to misinterpretation due to the often-maligned phrase of "just a friend."

Wright provides a good working definition for exploring the unique aspects of these relationships: "A voluntary or unconstrained interaction in which the participants respond to one another personally, that is, as unique individuals rather than as packages of discrete attributes or mere role occupants." To this, O'Meara adds other attributes: "Cross-sex friendship is nonromantic, purposefully dissociated from courtship rites, and includes the characteristic of equality." In other words, for a woman and a man to become friends they have to be able to let go of sex-role stereotypes and treat each other as equals and companions, not as potential dates or spouses.

Benefits of Friendship

Male friendships tend to be activity oriented, competitive, and focused on exchange of information about events and interests. In comparison with women's friendships, men's relationships are goal oriented, less personal, less disclosing, and less nurturing. Female friendships tend to be more intimate, confiding, and personally supportive. But despite their differences, both men and women benefit from the trust, acceptance, and enjoyment of friends. In attempting to identify the factors associated with mental health, the sociologist Nan Lin found friendship to be significantly related to good mental health. Moreover, those research subjects with the most positive mental health had a confidant of the opposite sex.

Generally, men experience benefits from their friendships with women that are missing from their friendships with other men, such as nurturance, personal support, and intimacy. According to Rubin, when men said they had a best friend, that person was more likely to be a woman than a man. Women, in contrast, almost always named another woman as a best friend. Rubin reported that "it is common gossip among professional women, for example, that, while their male colleagues—married or single—will exchange professional talk with other men, when they want a sympathetic ear for their problems, whether personal or professional, they'll invite a woman to lunch." Men tend to offer less emotional support to their women friends; consequently, women report an imbalance of emotional rewards in their cross-sex relationships.

Women do benefit from these relationships, albeit in a different way than men. Through their male friends, who act as interpreters of the male psyche, women develop insight into how to relate to men, both personally and professionally. This wisdom not only improves their intimate relationships with men but also gives a boost to their careers. In a study of 50 successful career women, Ruman discovered that virtually all these subjects had experienced close friendships with males early on, during adolescence or childhood, and through these relationships learned how to approach men as people, rather than as mysterious strangers.

Of course, men as well as women gain an "insider's perspective" from their other-sex friends, but the connection to career success is less clear for men than it is for women. However, when researchers at the University of Michigan Business School asked more than 1,000 executives (mostly male) to describe their on-the-job relationships, 22 percent reported sharing close emotional partnerships with other-gender colleagues that did not involve sex, and they said those friendships were a big plus in their careers. "These people shared a self-giving love that had a positive effect on the whole workplace, and in some cases even improved their romantic relationships at home," reported researcher Andrea Warfield.

Barriers to Female-Male Friendship

Despite the obvious advantages of friendship between a man and a woman, it is mostly an ambiguous relationship, one that is regarded in many segments of society as vaguely disturbing or inappropriate. These friendships are suspect and not encouraged for several reasons: (1) society's rigid prohibitions against those relationships, (2) a lack of role definition, and (3) the intensity of internal restrictions, such as sexual jealousy.

Societal Restrictions

A major hurdle for men and women in quest of friendship is the age-old Noah's Ark concept: men and women are naturally destined to walk two by two to the altar and, of course, to multiply. This emphasis on the biological destiny of couples fuels the widely held assumption that all relationships between men and women must include mating to be meaningful. A platonic relationship is automatically regarded with misgivings because of the belief that any adult transaction between men and women has to be linked to seduction and sex.

As a result, male-female friendships have a deviant status because they tend to be regarded as failed romances—not "real" relationships. Couples often feel pressure from relevant social networks that may propel two friends into a dating relationship, when friendship might be more appropriate and desired.

Lack of Role Definition

Because man-woman friendships are ignored or not recognized, society provides no role structure or guidance for their initiation and development. There are no norms, or the norms are unclear, and there is a dearth of role models.

Exacerbating the problem is that the potential for these friendships is sabotaged in the bud. It begins in childhood, when sex separatism is rigorously ingrained. Most parents rear male and female children with very different messages about sex-appropriate behaviors. By school age, the psychologist S.B. Damico says, boys and girls establish separate social systems, have only limited contact with each other, and act as though members of the opposite sex are horrible and to be avoided at all costs. In school, sex enmity is taught by segregating girls and boys into separate lines or pitting them against each other in spelling bees or volleyball. Boys and girls learn quickly that to cross the lines of sex demarcation is to risk the slurs of sissy or tomboy. After years of separation and mutual contempt, adolescents find it difficult, if not threatening, to enter alien territory to initiate a friendship. Future adult relationships are distorted by this early casting of men and women into opposite sex roles and the teaching of the cultural lesson that males and females are incompatible.

Older people, in particular, have had difficulty visualizing the prospect of a man-woman friendship. In Adams's 1985 study of friendships among elderly women, virtually none of the respondents could distinguish between cross-sex friendships and courting relationships. She wrote that "since [the respondents] generally considered cross-sex friendships as romances, they evaluated potential male friends as potential mates and rejected them. . . . Cross-sex friendships had been outside the realm of most of their life histories."

Internal Barriers: Jealousy

The possibility that friendship could lead to physical intimacy, or that it could arouse jealousy, is most frequently cited as the reason why friendship between men and women will not work.

The fragile feeling of being "most important" in the life of the person one loves can be threatened by cross-sex friendship. The fear is that the love relationship could be jeopardized by other emotionally intimate bonds experienced by one's mate or lover. According to this notion, love and intimacy are finite; there is only so much to go around. If love is given to a friend, there will not be enough left for a primary relationship.

A man can be jealous of his lover's intimacy with her female friends, and certainly a woman can be jealous of her male lover's camaraderie with men. But these emotions pale by comparison to the anxiety aroused by a male-female friendship. As Friday observed, "Jealousy is a protective emotion that alerts us to defend what we cherish."

We are taught to guard jealously not only our emotional place in our primary relationships but also the *physical* exclusivity of these relationships as well. Because of the belief that sexual involvement is inevitable, those who are married or in other primary relationships are apt to tread lightly in developing new friendships lest they generate fears or jealousy in their mates.

Such fears tend to seal off most people from the possibility of having a cross-sex friendship. A study by Henri Rix revealed that 80 percent of married people do not have friends of the opposite sex, and about half do not have "best" friends or "good" friends of either sex outside their marriages.

Favorable Conditions for Female-Male Friendship

Despite the obstacles, friendships between men and women are becoming more common where there are places to meet and opportunities to associate with one another. A conducive setting tends to be found most often in the workplace, school, club or association, or athletic organization.

Young, college-educated professionals who work or associate with many people of the opposite sex are most likely to participate in male-female friendships. Moreover, people who have other-sex friends tend to belong to professions or associations in which women have achieved a high degree of equality with men.

Early relationships and associations also play a role in the development of cross-sex friendships. Women with brothers are more comfortable with male friends than are women without brothers. Anyone—man or woman—who had either some type of early, close cross-gender friendship or a sibling of the opposite sex is more likely to develop other-sex friendships in adult life than those who did not. Clearly, these associations remove some of the mystery of the opposite sex and enable both men and women to regard each other simply as human beings.

Sexual Attraction and Female-Male Friendship

Platonic Relationships

What distinguishes platonic friendships from sexual relationships is not so much the absence of sexual attraction as the decision not to become sexually involved. People choose to be friends rather than lovers for countless reasons, including the existence of other romantic attachments or differences of temperament or lifestyle. Alternatively, perhaps the addition of sex would add uncomfortable complications to the relationship or destroy it altogether.

Men are more likely than women to initiate friendships on the basis of sexual attraction. Men also tend to have difficulty distinguishing between platonic and sexual signals from their women friends, especially if the cues are subtle.

Shotland found that men are less likely than women to differentiate among liking, loving, and sexual-interest cues and more likely than women to "perceive people to be interested in sex."

Most men and women friends are able to recognize and appreciate their mutual attraction without feeling compelled to act on it. The sexual chemistry in a friendship may always be strong, but usually the feeling peaks, then subsides or goes into low gear.

Friendships That Include Sex

There is widespread disagreement over whether a friendship between a man and a woman that does include sex should be termed a "friendship." Some observers say that sex has no place in a friendship—that the terms "sexual relationship" and "friendship" are mutually exclusive. Others assert that bona fide friendships can include sex.

"Feelings that arise in a sexual friendship may not be the eternal love sworn by married couples, but these emotions are nonetheless real," says the psychologist Richard Walters. People who have had sexual friendships say that sex is a natural, accepted expression of a loving, caring relationship. But for any number of reasons, it is not a relationship in which the partners view themselves as lovers or potential mates.

The particular problem with sexual friendships is that, at some point, one partner's expectations may change. One might begin to desire a romantic love affair—and the feeling may not be reciprocated.

Conclusion

Male-female friendship can be as difficult as love, perhaps more so, because, unlike love, it often lacks prescribed roles and the support of society. Moreover, it lacks a defined priority among the other relationships men and women experience. A man's female friend is likely also to be someone else's lover or wife. Likewise, a woman's male friend is involved in other roles and relationships. A friendship between a man and a woman has to be cultivated with respect given to the loyalty limitations imposed by primary commitments. It requires coming to terms with sexual tension, should it exist, as well as with the limitations of time and energy and the demands of intimacy itself.

Despite the different friendship styles of men and women, there is, without question, a common meeting ground on which they can become friends. Both have a need for intimate relationships that are not bound by exclusivity, that involve someone who can give insight into a different world, and that are free from the electrically charged atmosphere surrounding spouses or lovers.

As women increasingly enter the labor force, traditional restraints on friendship between the genders are softening. It is becoming more acceptable for a man and a woman to be friends if they work together, are in the same professional field, or are networking; however, there are still restrictions.

Having a discussion at the office, over lunch, or on the way home from work is considered to be appropriate behavior for a male-female friendship. Attending a movie or dining at an upscale restaurant for the evening meal tends to arouse suspicions, particularly if these activities take place during nighttime hours. These observations mean that for friendship between men and women to flourish, there has to be acceptance and support among relevant audiences (i.e., the spouses, friends, and coworkers of the friendship couple). The challenge, then, is for cross-gender friends to develop a shared definition of the bond they experience and to adopt a strategic position in presenting the authenticity of their friendship to others, especially those who would disapprove of it or feel most threatened.

Cross-gender friendship is still uncharted territory, but as men and women begin to know each other as people, the kind of sexism that leads to exploitation and manipulation will diminish. In the comfortable atmosphere of friendship, men and women will develop more empathy for each other as vulnerable and unique individuals.

A provocative aspect of the new alliance formed between men and women lies in the public arena. Undoubtedly, men and women who are unabashedly intimate friends—platonic or erotic—will shake up the segregated sex roles of society's old order by calling for a permanent truce in the battle of the sexes. Female-male friendship is a concept whose time has come.

REFERENCES

Adams, R.G. People Would Talk: Normative Barriers to Cross-Sex Friendships for Elderly Women. *The Gerontologist*, Vol. 25 (1985), pp. 605–11.

Aukett, R., J. Ritchie, and K. Mill. Gender Differences in Friendship Patterns. *Sex Roles*, Vol. 19 (1988), pp. 57–66.

Booth, A., and E. Hess. Cross-Sex Friendship. *Journal of Marriage and the Family*, Vol. 36 (Feb. 1974), pp. 38–47.

Buhrke, R.A., and D.R. Fuque. Sex Differences in Same- and Cross-Sex Supportive Relationships. *Sex Roles*, Vol. 17 (1987), pp. 339–52

Bukowski, W.M., B. Nappi, and B. Hoza. A Test of Aristotle's Model of Friendship for Young Adults' Same-Sex and Opposite-Sex Relationships. *Journal of Social Psychology,* Vol. 127, No. 6 (1987), pp. 595–603.

Burker, E.J., M.W. Goldstein, and G.C. Caputo. Effects of Siblings of the Opposite Sex on Friendships. *Psychological Reports* Vol. 48 (1981), p. 190.

Cassell, C. The Final Frontier: Other-Gender Friendships. *SIECUS Report* (Oct.-Nov. 1989).

Griffin, E., and G.C. Sparks. Friends Forever: A Longitudinal Exploration of Intimacy in Same-Sex Friends and Platonic Pairs. *Journal of Social and Personal Relationships,* Vol. 7 (1990), pp. 29–46.

Lin, N. Friendship Between the Sexes. In L. Pogrebin, *Among Friends.* New York: McGraw-Hill (1987), p. 335.

Metts, S., W.R. Cupach, and R.A. Bejlovec. "I Love You Too Much to Ever Start Liking You": Redefining Romantic Relationships. *Journal of Social and Personal Relationships,* Vol. 6 (1989), pp. 259–74.

O'Meara, J.D. Cross-Sex Friendship: Four Basic Challenges of an Ignored Relationship. *Sex Roles,* Vol. 21 (1989), pp. 525–43.

Pogrebin, L. *Among Friends.* New York: McGraw-Hill, 1987.

Rose, S.M. Same- and Cross-Sex Friendships and the Psychology of Homosociality. *Sex Roles,* Vol. 12 (1985), pp. 63–74.

Rubin, L.B. On Men and Friendship. *Psychoanalytic Review,* Vol. 73, No. 2 (1986), pp. 165–81.

Sapadin, L.A. Friendship and Gender: Perspectives of Professional Men and Women. *Journal of Social and Personal Relationships,* Vol. 5 (1988), pp. 387–403.

Shotland, R.L. Can Men and Women Differentiate Between Friendly and Sexually Interested Behavior? *Social Psychology Quarterly,* Vol. 51, No. 1 (1988), pp. 66–73.

Sigal, J., et al. The Effect of Romantic and Nonromantic Films on Perception of Female Friendly and Seductive Behavior. *Sex Roles,* Vol. 19 (1988), pp. 545–54.

Wright, P.H. Self-Referent Motivation and the Intrinsic Quality of Friendship. *Journal of Social and Personal Relationships,* Vol. 1 (1984), pp. 115–30.

Carol Cassell
Nancy Keith

FROTTEURISM

"Frotteurism" derives from a French word of unknown origin, *frotter,* which means to rub, chafe, stroke, or caress. One who performs the activity is a "froterer" or "frotteur."

The *Diagnostic and Statistical Manual of the American Psychiatric Association* (DSM-III R, 1987), defines frotteurism (also called "touchism") as the continuing sexual arousal and fantasies brought about by rubbing against or touching a fully clothed, nonconsenting person. The touching may be directed toward a particular body part or may be a more general caress. The activity is usually performed by a young male toward a female, and it usually occurs under crowded conditions (e.g., on a bus, in a subway, or on a crowded walkway). Frotteurism is often performed in conjunction with other paraphilias (e.g., voyeurism, exhibitionism, or rape). The froterer may visualize having an affectional relationship with the object of his attention but feels a strong need to get away before his activity is discovered. The person being touched is rarely harmed and usually considers the attention a minor annoyance.

More broadly defined, frotteurism is the rubbing of any part of the body with another part of the body or some other, perhaps inanimate, object. In this context, frotteurism is often incorporated into masturbation, either of oneself or of someone else. It is not uncommon for a woman to rub her clitoris with her finger or to experience sexual feelings when she rubs her thighs together. She may do this while performing household functions, such as sitting at a sewing machine or ironing. Men, women, and children have been observed to rub their genital areas against a cushion, pillow, chair, or other furniture. Crossing the legs to bring thigh pressure to the sexual regions of the body has been used for sexual stimulation, often accompanied by swinging a leg or foot to increase the friction. Particular parts of the body are sometimes requested to be used to stimulate the genitalia: for example, a foot fetishist may request that the froterer use the feet to rub his erect penis before orgasm can occur.

Frotteurism is often used by young people to achieve sexual release without the fear of getting pregnant. A girl will rub the genital area of her boyfriend until he reaches orgasm. He will return the favor. Since this rubbing often takes place through the clothing of the boy or girl, there is no penetration and thus no fear of pregnancy. An individual may also rub the genitals of a member of his or her own sex in a homosexual context. A man may rub his penis against the buttocks of a partner, or two men may rub their penises together through their clothing to achieve orgasm. Because there is no direct exposure of the penis and no anal or oral contact with the penis, some men use this method of homosexual expression to enable each participant to retain the perception of his "masculinity." Homosexual men sometimes stuff a pillow into a pair of jeans or other masculine clothing and achieve orgasm by rubbing their penis on the clothing. In the age of AIDS, some homosexual men are using these methods as a means of assuring safe sex. When two women rub their genital areas together, either through clothing or when naked, the action is called tribadism and lesbians are sometimes called tribades for this reason.

REFERENCES

Allgeier, E.R., and A.R. Allgeier. *Sexual Interactions*. Lexington, Mass.: D.C. Heath, 1991.

Katchadourian, H.A. *Fundamentals of Human Sexuality*. 5th ed. Fort Worth, Tex.: Rinehart & Winston, 1989.

James D. Haynes

g

G SPOT AND FEMALE PLEASURE

The Grafenberg spot, or G spot, is a sensitive area identified through the anterior vaginal wall. It is usually located about halfway between the back of the pubic bone and the cervix, along the course of the urethra and near the neck of the bladder. It swells when it is stimulated, although it is difficult to palpate when in an unstimulated state. It was named by John Perry and Beverly Whipple in 1981 to commemorate the research of Ernst Graefenberg, a German-born obstetrician and gynecologist, who in 1944, along with Robert L. Dickinson, described a zone of erogenous feeling located along the suburethral surface of the anterior vaginal wall. In 1950, Graefenberg wrote that

> an erotic zone could always be demonstrated on the anterior wall of the vagina along the course of the urethra, [which] seems to be surrounded by erectile tissue like the corpora cavernosa [of the penis]. . . . In the course of sexual stimulation the female urethra begins to enlarge and can be easily felt. It swells out greatly at the end of orgasm. The most stimulating part is located at the posterior urethra, where it arises from the neck of the bladder.

Though Graefenberg and others had written about this phenomenon, it was more or less ignored until Perry and Whipple focused renewed attention on it. The two researchers were encouraged to investigate the subject through conversations with women who described what was sexually pleasurable to them. Since the original report the spelling of Grafenberg has been anglicized.

Perry and Whipple reported that they had a physician or nurse examine more than 400 women who had volunteered to be research subjects, and a sensitive area in the vagina was found in each of these women. They cautioned, however, that they could not state with certainty that every woman had such a sensitive area.

Women have reported that it is difficult for them to locate and stimulate the Grafenberg spot in their own bodies (except with a dildo or similar device). A number of women who reported that they were able to locate the Grafenberg spot by themselves say they have done so while seated on a toilet. After emptying the bladder, they explore along the anterior (upper front) wall of the vagina with firm pressure, pushing up toward the navel. Some women have also found it helpful to apply downward pressure on the abdomen with the other hand, just above the pubic bone or top of the pubic hairline. As the Grafenberg spot is stimulated and begins to swell, it can often be felt between the two sets of fingers.

It is easier for women to identify the erotic sensation when the area is stimulated by a partner. The partner inserts one or two fingers (palm up) into the woman's vagina while the woman lies on her back, then applies firm pressure through the upper vaginal wall with a "come here" motion. At the same time, the woman can also apply firm downward pressure on her abdomen just above the pubic hairline. This way the woman and her partner can both feel the swelling: the partner through the vaginal wall and the woman through her abdomen. If a penis is used to stimulate the G spot, the positions most likely to provide effective stimulation are the female sitting on top of the male's penis or the vaginal rear-entry position.

The G spot feels like a small lump or a spongy bean. Stimulation causes it to swell and to increase in diameter from the size of a dime to, in some women, the size of a half-dollar. When the Grafenberg spot is first touched, many women state that it feels as though they have to urinate, even if they have just emptied the bladder. However, within 2–10 seconds of massage, the initial reaction is replaced in some women by a strong and distinctive feeling of sexual pleasure.

Some women report an orgasm from stimulation of this area, and some also report an expulsion of fluid from the urethra when they experience this type of orgasm. Others report the expulsion of fluid following stimulation of the G spot without orgasm, and there have been a few reports of fluid expulsion with stimulation of other genital areas. The fluid looks like watered-down skim milk and does not smell or taste like urine.

Chemical analysis of the fluid and comparison of it to urine have been conducted, and the results have been published in six separate research reports. In three of these studies, the fluid expelled from the urethra was observed by the researchers and subjected to chemical analysis. In two of these studies, the ejaculated fluid was chemically different from urine samples from the same subject, while in the third study no difference was observed. The chemical analysis reported on concentrations of prostatic acid phosphatase, urea, creatinine, glucose, fructose, and pH.

Three additional studies comparing ejaculate and urine have been reported, but in these the expulsion of fluid was apparently not observed by the researchers. Two of these studies demonstrated a statistically significant difference between the ejaculate specimens and urine, while in the third no significant differences were observed. The question of female ejaculate is still being examined and opinions vary, with many arguing that the ejaculate is simply due to the relaxation of muscles, allowing for some urinary incontinence.

Perry and Whipple estimated that perhaps 10 percent of women ejaculate. Subsequent questionnaire responses have yielded higher estimates, from 40 percent to 68 percent. The questionnaire data, however, may be biased because those women who believed that they experienced this phenomenon might have been more likely to complete the questionnaires.

Some women have reported that they had surgery to stop the expulsion of fluid, while other women reported deliberately avoiding orgasm because they thought there was something wrong with them for enjoying vaginal stimulation. Disseminating information about current research findings, even though the issue remains controversial, is important in lessening anxiety and in allowing women both to feel better about sexuality and to find pleasure in their sexual responses.

In a physical examination for vaginal sensitivity, Perry and Whipple found that among 47 subjects, 90 percent reported being highly sensitive in their vaginas at the 12 o'clock position (upper or anterior wall of the vaginal vault), 57 percent at the 11 o'clock position, 47 percent at the 1 o'clock position, 30 percent at the 4 o'clock position, and 37 percent at the 8 o'clock position. The G spot is not normally felt during a gynecological examination, because the area must be sexually stimulated in order for it to swell and be palpable. Physicians do not sexually stimulate their patients and therefore do not find the G spot.

Other researchers have also reported findings of vaginal sensitivity, among them Hoch, Alzate and London, and Alzate and Hoch, but the latter concluded that although there is a zone of tactile erotic sensitivity, evidence remains inconclusive. The Federation of Feminist Women's Health Centers describes this area as the "urethral sponge," a sheath of erectile tissue around the urethra that becomes engorged during sexual excitement and protects the urethra during sexual activity. Zaviacic and colleagues in Czechoslovakia reported a specifically sensitive site with a manually detectable tumescence in 27 women who were palpated. Masters, Johnson, and Kolodny observed that only 10 percent of 100 women had an area of heightened sensitivity in the anterior wall or possessed tissue mass that resembled this sensitive area. Hartman and Fithian reported finding sensitivity in large numbers of women at the 12 o'clock, 4 o'clock, and 8 o'clock positions.

In an anonymous questionnaire distributed to professional women in the United States and Canada, Davidson and colleagues found that 786 (66 percent) of their 1,245 respondents perceived an especially sensitive area in their vagina that, if stimulated, produced pleasurable feelings. Whipple found that of the 800 women who completed a sexual-health questionnaire, 69 percent of the subjects reported 12 o'clock as the most sensitive area.

Perry and Whipple hypothesized that the G spot is probably composed of a complex network of blood vessels, the paraurethral glands and ducts, nerve endings, and the tissue surrounding the bladder neck, but they did not conduct any anatomical studies in this area. Zaviacic and his colleagues have conducted the most extensive immunohistochemical analysis of the paraurethral, or Skene's, glands in women; they found that there was a cross-antigenicity between the male prostate gland and the Skene's gland and that the enzymatic reactions of the male and female prostatic tissues are similar—so similar that Zaviacic held that the term "female prostate" was appropriate. Alzate and Hoch disagreed with such a term, claiming that it is confusing to call the Skene's gland the female prostate.

Despite the evidence that specific anatomical structures correspond to the area defined as the Grafenberg spot, its exact anatomical identity remains inconclusive. All we can say with certainty is that some women report pleasurable vaginal sensitivity and that the anterior wall appears to be the most sensitive area of the vagina. A distinct area identified through the anterior vaginal wall that swells when stimulated has not been found universally by all researchers who have conducted sexological examinations. This seems to imply either that not all women have this distinct area or that perhaps different criteria have been used to identify it. Those women who report having a G spot say the orgasm resulting from stimulation of this sensitive area is different from that resulting from clitoral stimulation, the main difference being that it is "deeper" inside. Some also report a bearing-down feeling during orgasm from G-spot stimulation.

Obviously, women do not have to fit one monolithic model of sexual response, and there might well be individual variations. Women also have been socialized to believe and accept traditional views about their sexuality and female pleasure, and often what they have been taught is different from what they experience. For women, the whole body can be sexual, and women have the potential to experience sexual pleasure from their thoughts, feelings, beliefs, fantasies, and dreams. Each woman has to be aware of what is pleasurable to her, acknowledge it to herself, and then communicate it to her partner. Women should not be encouraged to set up G-spot stimulation or orgasm as a goal, since by setting such goals they miss a lot of pleasure along the way. They should focus on the process rather than the goal of a particular sexual response.

REFERENCES

Addegio, F., and E.G. Belzer, J. Comolli, W. Moger, J.D. Perry, and B. Whipple. Female Ejaculation: A Case Study. *Journal of Sex Research*, Vol. 17 (1981), pp. 13–21.

Alzate, H. Vaginal Eroticism: A Replication Study. *Archives of Sexual Behavior*, Vol. 14 (1985), pp. 529–37.

Alzate, H., and Z. Hoch. The "G spot" and "Female Ejaculation": A Current Appraisal. *Journal of Sex and Marital Therapy*, Vol. 12 (1986), pp. 211–20.

Alzate, H., and M.L. London. Vaginal Erotic Sensitivity. *Journal of Sex and Marital Therapy*, Vol. 10 (1984), pp. 49–56.

Belzer, E.G., B. Whipple, and W. Moger. On Female Ejaculation. *Journal of Sex Research*, Vol. 20 (1984), pp. 403–06.

Bullough, B., M. David, B. Whipple, J. Dixon, E.R. Allgeier, and K.C. Drury. Subjective Reports of Female Orgasmic Expulsion of Fluid. *Nurse Practitioner*, Vol. 9 (1984), pp. 55–59.

Davidson, J.K., C.A. Darling, and C. Conway-Welch. The Role of the Grafenberg Spot and Female Ejaculation in the Female Orgasmic Response: An Empirical Analysis. *Journal of Sex and Marital Therapy*, Vol. 15 (1989), pp. 102–20.

Federation of Feminist Women's Health Centers. *A New View of a Woman's Body*. New York: Simon & Schuster, 1981.

Graefenberg, E. The Role of the Urethra in Female Orgasms. *International Journal of Sexology*, Vol. 3 (1950), pp. 145–48.

Graefenberg, E., and R.L. Dickinson. Conception Control by Plastic Cervix Cap. *Western Journal of Surgery, Obstetrics, and Gynecology*, Vol. 52 (1944), pp. 335–40.

Hoch, Z. The Sensory Arm of the Female Orgasmic Reflex. *Journal of Sex Education and Therapy*, Vol. 6 (1980), pp. 4–7.

Ladas, A., B. Whipple, and J.D. Perry. *The G Spot and Other Recent Discoveries About Human Sexuality*. New York: Holt, Rinehart & Winston, 1982.

Mallon, R.H. Prostatic Tissue in Females. *Journal of Sex Education and Therapy*, Vol. 9 (1983), p. 6.

Pollen, J.J., and A. Dreilinger. Immunohistochemical Identification of Prostatic Acid Phosphatase and Prostate Specific Antigen in Female Periurethral Glands. *Urology*, Vol. 23 (1984), pp. 303–04.

Tepper, S.L., J. Jagirdar, D. Heath, and S.A. Geller. Homology Between the Female Paraurethral (Skene's) Glands and the Prostate. *Archives of*

Pathology and Laboratory Medicine, Vol. 108 (1984), pp. 423–25.

Zaviacic, M. Enzyme Histochemistry of the Adult Human Female Prostate: Acid Phosphatase Distribution. *Cellular and Molecular Biology*, Vol. 30 (1984), pp. 545–51.

———. Enzyme Histochemistry of the Adult Human Female Prostate: Hydrolase and Dehydrogenase Distribution. *Cellular and Molecular Biology*, Vol. 30 (1984) pp. 537–43.

———. The Female Prostate: Nonvestigal Organ of the Female: A Reappraisal. *Journal of Sex and Marital Therapy*, Vol. 13 (1987), pp. 148–52.

Zaviacic, M., S. Dolezalova, I.K. Holoman, A. Zaviacicova, M. Mikulecky, and V. Brazdil. Concentrations of Fructose in Female Ejaculate and Urine: A Comparative Biochemical Study. *Journal of Sex Research*, Vol. 24 (1988), pp. 319–25.

Zaviacic, M., A. Zaviacicova, J. Oberucova, M. Azjickova, and J. Blazekova. Enzyme Histochemical Profile of the Adult Human Female Prostate (Paraurethral Glands). *Histochemistry Journal*, Vol. 17 (1985), pp. 564–66.

Beverly Whipple

GEBHARD, PAUL H.

Paul Gebhard, born July 3, 1917, is a social anthropologist who received his Ph.D. from Harvard University in 1947. He is best known for his work at the Institute for Sex Research, in Bloomington, Indiana.

Until 1946, Gebhard conducted his own experiments in psychiatry and did research in anthropology. In 1947, he became professor of anthropology at Indiana University, where he was subsequently invited to join the famous research team headed by Alfred Kinsey at the university's Institute for Sex Research. From 1947 to 1955, Gebhard was a member of this team, interviewing thousands of people about their sexual experiences.

After Kinsey's death in 1956, Gebhard became director of the Institute for Sex Research. By that time, the Institute's primary efforts were focused on analyzing and publishing its accumulated data. On the basis of this data, Gebhard authored and coauthored many articles and books, including *Pregnancy, Birth and Abortion* (1958), with Wardell Pomeroy, Clyde Martin, and Cornelia Christenson; and *Sex Offenders: An Analysis of Types* (1965), with Pomeroy, Christenson, and William Gagnon.

In the early 1960s Gebhard initiated a course on human sexuality at Indiana University's medical school that he taught to graduate and undergraduate students. In 1982, he retired from his directorship of the Institute and was succeeded by June Reinisch. Gebhard remained at the Institute as Curator of Collections and continued teaching. He retired from teaching as professor emeritus in 1986 and from the curatorship in 1988.

Gebhard has received many prestigious honors, including awards from the Polish Sexological Society and the Czechoslovakian Sexological Society, as well as the Society for the Scientific Study of Sex Award for Distinguished Scientific Achievement (1986).

REFERENCES

Primary

Gebhard, P.H., W. Gagnon, W.B. Pomeroy, and C.V. Christenson. *Sex Offenders: An Analysis of Types.* New York: Harper & Row, 1965.

Gebhard, P.H., C.E. Martin, W.B. Pomeroy, and C.V. Christenson. *Pregnancy, Birth and Abortion.* New York: Harper-Hoeber, 1958.

Kinsey, A.C., P.H. Gebhard, W.B. Pomeroy, and C.E. Martin. *Sexual Behavior in the Human Female.* Philadelphia: Saunders, 1953.

Secondary

Reinisch, J. *The Kinsey Institute New Report on Sex.* New York: St. Martin's Press, 1991.

Leah Cahan Schaefer

GENDER

Sex and Gender

In most dictionaries, "gender" is defined as a class of nouns, varying in size from two to more than 20, that covary with sex or animateness. The familiar languages include two or three classes: for example, masculine and feminine in Spanish and French, with neuter added in Latin and German. As a recent language, English does not mark its nouns directly, but only indirectly by means of pronouns such as "he," "she," or "it."

Within the life and social sciences, "gender" is used carelessly as both a synonym and an antonym of "sex." Yet in 1955, the sexologist John Money adopted the concept of gender from philology and linguistics. Money introduced gender to serve as an umbrella concept, encompassing more than the dimorphic components of biological sex, because he wanted to describe the manliness or womanliness of persons born with sexually indeterminate genitals. In his doctoral dissertation, Money studied hermaphrodites, who would grow up to live as women without female sex organs or as men without a male sex organ. A hermaphrodite living as a man did not literally have a male sex role (sexuoerotic role), since he had no functioning penis for copulation, but he could enact the male sex role (sociosexual role) in attitudes, traits, behaviors, interests, and activities. Money believed that without the term "gender," he would get bogged down in statements like this: "John has a male sex role, except that his sex role with his sex organs is not male and his genetic sex is female." Although Money's contribution was historic, it unfortunately was not uniformly adopted.

Currently, Money says *sex* is one's status as male, female, or intersexed according to the criterion of the external genitalia, and *gender* is one's status as male or female, masculine or feminine—personally, socially, and legally—according to somatic and behavioral criteria more inclusive than the external-genitalia criterion alone. By these definitions, gender is more inclusive than sex; it includes both genital sex and erotic sex, along with other variables (e.g., chromosomes, gonads) used to describe differences between males and females. For Money, there are four grades of male-female sex differences: (1) sex irreducible, (2) sex derivative, (3) sex adjunctive, and (4) sex adventitious. These grades of sex differences are Money's attempt to avoid a simplistic reductionism in which the coding of gender is split into *sex*, belonging to biology, lust, and nature, and *gender,* belonging to social science, romance, and nurture.

In a diecious species—one in which male and female reproductive organs are housed in two distinct individuals—what the individual with male organs does is masculine, what the individual with female organs does is feminine, and what is done by both is sex-shared or ambisexual. Male-only or female-only behavior is rare; statistically, the central tendencies of the sexes as collectivities disperse into overlapping distributions, permitting the relative descriptors "most often" or "more often" to be used when one sex is compared to the other. Given gender ideology, culture-bound dogmas of history still declare, in dichotomous contrast, what males ought to do and what females ought to do. These dogmas of history justify a gender hierarchy of male superiority and female inferiority.

At their scientific best, biologists and social scientists agree that the coding of gender is multivariate, sequential, and developmental, reflecting a complex interaction across the boundaries of disciplines and across so-called biological and social variables. Still, each discipline is tempted to bolster its status by claiming to reduce human complexity to the parameters of its specialty. Such a reductionism to nature or nurture is often strategically employed in the rhetoric of ideological warfare over what men and women *ought* to be and do.

The irreducible sex differences are immutable, by definition, and few, as revealed by nature. They are specifically linked to reproduction. Neither chromosomal nor gonadal sex is irreducible, given a variety of accidents of nature and medical technology. For example, a 46, XY hermaphrodite reared as a woman has had an implanted pregnancy and produced a healthy baby by caesarean section. A demonstration in the male baboon makes it conceivable that a man can support an implanted pregnancy. Genes may be spliced, and hormones reproduced and administered; the science of reproduction advances. But the biological bottom line for sex appears to be the immutable gametes: the male produces sperm for reproduction, and the female produces ova. It is nearly accurate to say that the male irreducibly impregnates, and the female irreducibly menstruates, ovulates, gestates, and lactates. However, it is most accurate to say that fertile male and female gametes combine in the reproduction of humans.

The sex-derivative differences in gender coding originate in the different ratios of steroidal sex hormones in males and females. To call these hormones "male" and "female" overlooks the sequential nature of their synthesis: cholesterol is converted into progestin, which is converted into androgen, which is converted into estrogen. Thus, both sexes have all these hormones, although in males androgen predominates, in females progestin and estrogen.

Scientists agree that these different ratios of sex hormones create differences in body morphology and procreative physiology. A dramatic example of these changes follows from transposing the usual ratios of hormones in transsexuals who are seeking surgery to change their sex. Female-to-male transsexuals grow facial and body hair (even balding later if that is encoded in their genes), lengthen their vocal cords, lessen their body fat, increase their muscle mass (as in the steroid effects sought by some athletes), enlarge their clitoris, and may intensify their orgasms.

Money argued also that sex-shared, but threshold, dimorphic gender coding is a long-term consequence of prenatal and neonatal sex-hormonal effects on the brain. That is, the hormonal effect is to set two thresholds—one higher and one lower—for each sex. The presence or absence of a sex hormone during a critical period of development produces a hormonally coded threshold that is subsequently socially reinforced. A dimorphic (two-formed) threshold (point at which a stimulus has an effect) means that each sex would have different forms of timing in sex-derivative tendencies to respond, for example, to the cries of infants or the pleas of the young. From the Greek word *praxis*, meaning custom or practice, Money selected the word "praxon" to refer to sex-derivative, gender-coded ways of doing things. He said that a praxon is identified by (1) wide distribution across species, particularly primate species; (2) alteration in subhuman species through the experimental administration of sex hormones during a critical period of prenatal or neonatal development; and (3) clinical evidence, usually from studies of anomalous prenatal or neonatal development of sexual and reproductive organs, as well as later behavior, that is consistent with the animal experimentation.

The effects of prenatal hormones on the brain are still in the early stages of scientific investigation; thus, disputes abound. Not all scientists accept that the available evidence supports Money's list of praxons. Still, Money believed that he had identified nine sex-shared but threshold-dimorphic praxons: (1) kinesis or overall muscular energy expenditure; (2) roaming; (3) competitive rivalry, assertiveness, and jockeying for position in the dominance hierarchy of one's peer group; (4) intruder aggression in fighting off marauders and predators; (5) parental aggression in defense of the young; (6) nestling the young and providing a sheltered place not only for their birth but also for their subsequent suckling and nurturance; (7) parentalism; (8) positioning in sexual rehearsal play; and (9) visual sexuoerotic arousal.

Money continued his argument by indicating that sex-derivative gender coding is descended from sex-irreducible coding by way of prenatal sex-hormonal coding, and sex-adjunctive coding is descended from sex-derivative coding by way of social coding that is an adjunct or extension of prenatal coding applied to the sex-divergent division of labor. Money believed that the sex-divergent division of labor had evolutionary roots in the diminished mobility of the female, given gestation and lactation, and that men's labor was compatible with mobility for war, work, or adventure. Recent social changes have swept away the gender-coded division of labor, making the occupational roles of men and women interchangeable. Money held that such changes threaten conservatives, as if social change signaled a biological change of sex or a forfeiture of masculinity or femininity. Still, Money viewed the crossing of occupational gender roles as reflecting a predisposition (biological or social?) to gender-transposed careers.

Sex-adventitious gender coding is the culturally and historically variable ways of distinguishing males and females on the criterion of dress and adornment. Money saw such gender coding as an extension of social coding to the sex-divergent distribution of power. Often, adornment signals that women are dependent showpieces of men's wealth and power. Given cultural rules about concealing the genitals, which are the intrinsic signal of sex, these sex-divergent characteristics are arbitrary and extrinsic signals of male or female sex.

Coalesced into a personal biography, the four grades of sex differences constitute an individual's *gender identity* and *gender role*. Money defined gender identity as "the sameness, unity, and persistence of one's individuality as male, female, or ambivalent as expressed in self-awareness or behavior." Gender role is everything a person says or does to indicate to others or to the self that one is either male, female, or ambivalent. Gender identity is the private experience of gender role, whereas gender role is the public expression of gender identity. Money viewed gender identity/role as two sides of the same coin, introducing the acronym GI/R to unify them as a singular noun. GI/R includes sexual orientation as heterosexual, homosexual, or ambisexual.

Money noted that his reciprocal definition did not take root. Gender identity, in simplistic form, was reduced to *core gender identity*—self-statements that "I am male (or female)." Money said gender role became a social script or social stereotype to which the individual did or did not conform.

By sociologists, sex was defined as an ascribed status, assigned to the person at birth on the basis of dimorphism in the external male and female genitals. Gender was defined as an achieved status, with social, cultural, and psychological components, and as either masculine or feminine as a function of the differential socialization of the sexes. For sociologists, sex is ascribed by one's birth as male or female, whereas gender is acquired as a social role, from a social script. Often, the usage of "sex" is limited to the specifically sexuoerotic; gender is everything else. Money lampooned this as Barbie-doll usage.

The Cultural Anthropology of Gender

Cultural anthropologists study nonliterate cultures. In trying to understand the variations in cultural definitions of gender, they look for underlying patterns in the belief systems that organize gender ideology—a worldview of men, women, and nature. Across cultures, the general features of gender ideologies reveal three important thematic oppositions: (1) males are aligned with culture, females with nature; (2) men control the public domain, women, the domestic; and (3) males are aligned with the social good, females with self-interest or the good of the family. The anthropologists Sherry Ortner and Harriet Whitehead indicated that all three of these oppositions—nature/culture, domestic/public, self-interest/social good—exhibit a central sociological insight: because the sphere of social activity predominantly associated with males encompasses the sphere predominantly associated with females, it is culturally accorded higher value.

Moreover, these anthropologists discussed the general cultural tendency to define men in terms of status and role categories (e.g., warrior, statesman, elder) that have little to do with their relationships with women; in contrast, women are defined almost entirely in relation to men through kinship roles (e.g., sister, wife, mother). Thus, male categories are not drawn just from the public domain but specifically from the sphere of power. To be a warrior or an elder in societies in which these are primary categories of manhood is not just to play a role in the public domain but to be located at the upward end of a hierarchical scheme of culturally ordered prestige. Whenever women are defined as being merely relational dependents of men and the male ranks, they are excluded not only from the structure of masculine prestige but also from other prestige structures in the religious, economic, and political realms. This is so because the gender system not only is a prestige structure but also is meaningfully aligned with all other structures of prestige. The most masculine of men ascend in prestige, whereas entry into the structures of prestige may be denied to the entire female sex.

Furthermore, Ortner and Whitehead noted that women, by contrast, are defined not by roles, such as child-tenders or cooks, derived from their primary activities in the domestic domain but rather by their exclusion from the world of male prestige, except as dependent collaterals to men (wives, daughters) that further foster male prestige. Male honor is often dependent on female behavior; women are often the prize for male prowess. Thus, gender ideology defines man as culture's agent who advances the social good in the public domain and who is to be rewarded by honor and prestige; woman is defined as closer to nature, to domestic nurture, and to particularistic concerns with what is hers in the smaller, private world of family.

In her place—private, domestic, and subordinate—woman is to be protected and warmed by her man's public prestige. Within this ideology of gender, as long as woman's place is encompassed by man's, she remains secondary and he remains primary. Gender ideologies justify this hierarchal arrangement as places (i.e., a ranking of prestige and power) that are given by nature (i.e., separate and unequal natural places).

The concept of gender is situated in a historical context of male dominance. The invidious stratification of the sexes into a hierarchy of gender invests meaning in the concepts of "masculinity" and "femininity." Concepts become meaningful only within a culture. Cultures impart meaning through their forms of language, social processes, and interpersonal transactions. Moreover, the psychologist Jerome Bruner pointed out that the central concept of human psychology is meaning and the processes and transactions involved in the construction of meaning. Thus, like all concepts, "male" and "female" or "masculinity" and "femininity" attain their meanings through interpersonal transactions interpreted within a cultural context.

The historically and socially constructed traditional ideology of gender divided humankind into male and female social categories that justified the power of men as grounded in the superiority of masculine, as compared to feminine, nature. Yet the anthropologist Clifford Geertz said there is no such thing as human nature independent of culture. Given that nature is never independent of culture, the ideological claim that "masculinity equals superiority" serves as a gloss to justify inequality between the sexes. In spite of the democratic value placed on equality in America, the sexist claim remains: "Men's advantages in political, economic, and social power over women are justified by real and biodetermined differences in their essential natures."

Sex Differences

The feminist Ruth Hubbard declared that the interest in differences between the sexes is above all an interest determined by differences in power between them. It is these beliefs about "real" differences that have rationalized gender inequality as following from the natures of the sexes, from masculine superiority and feminine inferiority. Thus, in gender ideology, "is-ness" becomes "ought-ness." The concept of human nature does not describe people; instead, it is a normative concept that incarnates historically based beliefs about what human beings are and how they should behave.

Pioneers in psychology, like James McKeen Cattell and Edward Thorndike, thought that biological differences between the sexes explained the rarity of extremely intelligent women. Francis Galton, in his study of hereditary genius, did not find many women; however, if society says woman's place is private, domestic, and family centered, if women are systematically denied equal educational and occupational opportunity, what else could Galton have found? Present-day psychology offers three possible sex differences in cognitive abilities: (1) verbal ability favors females, (2) mathematical ability favors males, and (3) visual-spatial ability favors males.

Psychologists aggregate data across a number of separate studies by using a meta-analytic method that expresses the difference between males and females, divided by the group standard deviations, as a *d* statistic. Using the *d* metric, 0.20 is small, 0.50 is medium, and 0.80 is a large difference in standard-deviation units.

In verbal ability, the difference favoring women is small, about 0.18 to 0.24. In mathematical ability, the difference favoring men is medium, about 0.45. In visual-spatial ability, the difference favoring men is medium, about 0.45, but varying considerably with the nature of the specific task. For further comparison, the difference in motor ability between men and women, favoring men, is also medium, about 0.49.

All these statistical distributions show great overlap; differences among men and women are far greater than differences between them. Of course, these measures of ability are not pure measures of innate capacity. Estimates of sex differences can be no better than the tests they are based on. Many abilities appear to be multifactorial and thus are more complex than most of their purported measures. Sometimes, multiple strategies can be used to solve the same problem. General ability describes the skill of selecting the best strategy from the repertoire of skills to solve a particular problem; on the spatial-visualization task, the skill most closely aligned with the general-selection skill, the sexes performed no differently, just as tests of general ability have shown no differences in the performance of the sexes.

Moreover, differences in ability or, more accurately, in performance vary with socialization, across cultures, and following special training. For example, assuming women's scores on tests of so-called masculinity (*M*) reflect socialization experiences, women scoring higher on *M* performed better on mathematics and much better on visual-spatial tasks in a meta-analysis of sex differences on cognitive tests. Scores on *M* were about as predictive of performance as sex, improving women's chances of scoring well from 36 percent to 64 percent on mental-rotation tasks

and from 40 percent to 60 percent on spatial-perception tasks. Within Eskimo culture, visual-spatial performance was found not to vary across sex, perhaps because the Arctic environment requires spatial acuteness and because parents give both autonomy and unconditional love to girls. In America, special spatial training of preschool and elementary students reduced or even eliminated sex differences on spatial tasks.

Finally, the size of the sex differences in cognitive abilities has declined over the last 20 years. Has the women's movement had an effect? Even the differences between the sexes in athletic performance, certainly affected by steroidal sex hormones, are narrowing in recent Olympic athletic competition as women become more motivated and highly trained.

In the social realm, traits that are candidates for psychological sex differences include (1) aggression, (2) helping, (3) influenceability, (4) verbal communication, and (5) nonverbal behavior. The best single summary statistic from studies of aggression is a *d* of 0.50, a medium difference favoring boys and men across all types, designs, and measures of aggression. When limited to an analysis of men aggressing against strangers in brief encounters, the *d* was a smaller 0.29. In comparison to women, men accepted the harm their aggression caused, experiencing little fear of retaliation or little guilt.

In brief encounters with strangers that hold some potential danger, men help more than women (*d* = 0.34), particularly if the stranger is a woman and an audience is present. Quantitative reviews of social influence, measured in studies that use group pressure to induce conformity to incorrect group opinion, found men to be more resistant to influence than women, with a relatively small *d* of 0.28.

A narrative review of studies of men's and women's verbal communicative styles concluded that men emphasize hierarchical organization through interactions that are directing and dominating. Women, in contrast, emphasize equality and cooperation through interactions that are expressive, receptive, encouraging, and supportive.

Meta-analytic reviews of sex differences in nonverbal communication favor women's greater skill in decoding emotions from the face (*d* = 0.41), in encoding emotion in their faces (*d* = 1.00), in recognizing a face seen before (*d* = 0.32), and in decoding cues from face, voice, and body (*d* = 0.52).

These studies of verbal and nonverbal communication reported larger differences when the sexes were in same-sex rather than in mixed-sex groups. Such results are compatible with explanations positing gender socialization into different sociolinguistic subcultures. Well-known for her own work on sex differences, the psychologist Eleanor Maccoby argued that all these sex differences might result from segregation into same-sex groups as playmates. Preferences for same-sex play groups emerge by age three and are maintained at a high level between the ages of 6 and 11. Maccoby believed the rough-and-tumble play of boys, their orientation toward competition and dominance, and their resistance to girls' influence led girls to avoid boys. When children move into adolescence, their communicative styles continue, sometimes creating difficulties between the sexes.

The psychologist Donald Mosher continued Maccoby's theme that male concern with dominance and not showing weakness to other men, as well as men's emotionally restrictive style and lack of self-disclosure, was consistent with a macho personality. Mosher theorized that macho men are socialized and acculturated into hypermasculine scripts. Script formation is supported by a normative gender ideology of machismo and instilled by the differential socialization of discrete affects in boys and girls. Macho men magnify the warrior affects of excitement, surprise, anger, disgust, and contempt, whereas women are socialized to magnify the affects of the oppressed—enjoyment, fear, distress, and shame.

REFERENCES

Eagly, A.H. *Sex Differences in Social Behavior: A Social Role Interpretation*. Hillsdale, N.J.: Lawrence Erlbaum, 1987.

Hess, B.B., and M.M. Ferree. *Analyzing Gender: A Handbook of Social Research*. Newbury Park, Calif.: Sage, 1987.

Hyde, J.S. *Psychology of Gender: Advances Through Meta-Analysis*. Baltimore: Johns Hopkins Univ. Press, 1986.

Money, J., and A.A. Ehrhardt. *Man and Woman, Boy and Girl*. Baltimore: Johns Hopkins Univ. Press, 1972.

Ortner, S.B., and H. Whitehead. *Sexual Meanings: The Cultural Construction of Gender and Sexuality*. Cambridge: Cambridge Univ. Press, 1981.

Reinisch, J.M., L.A. Rosenblum, and S.A. Sander. *Masculinity/Femininity: Basic Perspectives*. New York: Oxford Univ. Press, 1987.

Donald L. Mosher

GENDER: PSYCHOLOGICAL MEASUREMENTS OF MASCULINITY AND FEMININITY

The First Generation of Measures

The history of the measurement of individual differences reveals that some proponents have held a normative ideology in which measurement is viewed as discovering and metricizing the real, as quantifying inner essences. Surely, the history of IQ testing amply demonstrates the thesis that some proponents of differences in intelligence have held racist views. Is sexism implicit in traditional measures of masculinity and femininity?

In 1916, the psychologist Lewis Terman introduced the Stanford-Binet intelligence test to America; two decades later, he introduced a measure of masculinity-femininity (*M-F*). The early work on *M-F* was said to reveal an exception to the famous positivist dictum, "If something exists, it exists in some amount and can be measured." In her 1973 review of five measures of *M-F*, the psychologist Ann Constantinople satirically concluded that if something (*M-F*) cannot be measured, it does not exist.

Instead of beginning with a theory of gender or of masculinity and femininity as psychological concepts, psychologists, in their first efforts to measure *M-F*, followed the simplistic strategy of finding empirical differences between the responses of men and women to questionnaire items about their interests and preferences. At its most mindless, such an operational definition equated "masculinity" with men's preferences for taking showers, for work as a business contractor, and for magazines like *Popular Mechanics*, whereas "femininity" was equated with preferences for taking baths, work as a dress designer, and magazines like *Good Housekeeping*—just because these items had empirically discriminated between collectivities of men and women.

Not only did this approach enable them, they believed, to discriminate between men and women on psychological masculinity and femininity, but it was also presumed to permit separation of the heterosexual sheep from the homosexual goats. The logic: males and females are opposites; homosexuals are the inverse of heterosexuals. What's more, healthy men would be masculine, healthy women feminine. Since the congruence of assigned sex and normative sexual role defined psychological health, cross-gendered appearance, personality traits, or household or occupational role behaviors came to define deviance and mental disturbance. Of course, given congruence assumptions, same-sexed sexual activity defined homosexuality as deviant and unhealthy. In fact, all those cross-gendered characteristics aroused suspicions of homosexuality, stigmatizing anyone who manifested gender incongruence, even though Constantinople noted that these measures of M-F failed to discriminate heterosexuals from homosexuals.

The assumption of a healthy congruence of sexuoerotic roles and of masculine and feminine personality stem from a belief that the male and female sex must, should, and do display congruent erotic sex and congruent gender characteristics because their biological or God-given natures make it so. This belief is called *dimorphic sexual essentialism.*

Dimorphic sexual essentialism is defined as a gender-ideological belief that men's and women's natures are two-formed and inherently different, jointly creating a heterosexual and heterosocial complementarity. In such a worldview, men and women necessarily form a complementary whole in heterosexual intercourse and in a heterosocial complementarity of dominance or submission, activity or passivity, and superiority or inferiority. The purpose of intercourse is always to be procreative; all other sex is defined as deviant. Thus, in this patriarchal view, man is head of the household and woman is to serve as his complement.

Although Constantinople recognized that masculinity and femininity were among the muddiest concepts in the psychologist's vocabulary, her critique was more methodological than conceptual. Her review raised two issues: Is *M-F* a single bipolar dimension ranging from extreme masculinity to extreme femininity or two separable dimensions? With the constructs of M, F, or M-F, are we dealing with unitary or multidimensional traits? The second generation of measures of masculinity and femininity responded to these questions. But before telling that part of the story, an understanding of sex stereotypes would be helpful.

Sex Stereotypes

A *sex stereotype* is a widely shared, rigid, simplified, and generalized image or conception that is applied to an individual man or woman simply because of gender assignment and that is invested with ideological affect and meaning. Sex stereotypes are components in a widely shared system of gender-ideological beliefs, both descriptive and prescriptive, that characterize what the sexes as collectivities ultimately are and should be. As a component of traditional gender ideology, sex stereotypes assume dimorphic sexual essential-

ism. Sex stereotypes include both gender traits and gender roles as subtypes, with both being simultaneously *descriptive* and *normative*. When the trait or role is descriptive, it is either *characterizing* (describing one sex but not the other) or *differentiating* (found in both sexes but differentially distributed between them). When the stereotype is *normative,* it prescribes for one sex, in dichotomous contrast to the other, what it should do (roles) or be (traits) and proscribes for one sex, in dichotomous contrast to the other, what it should not do or not be. Descriptions as defining essences are used to justify prescriptions; proscriptions keep everyone in their places.

In sociology, *role* includes the internalized cultural and normative expectations that an individual brings to a particular social location. Sex roles are the normative expectations about the division of labor and the social interactions of men and women existing within an ideology of gender. The sociologist Talcott Parsons described men as fulfilling instrumental roles and women as fulfilling expressive roles in social interactions.

Following World War II, women's lives changed dramatically as they entered the work force in ever-increasing numbers. Yet gender inequalities still remain in earnings, promotion, and prestige. To women's detriment, job-level segregation of the sexes remains, even within similar occupational classifications.

Although women are marrying later, having children later, and divorcing more, they remain principally responsible for household roles and child care. Whether their wife is employed or not, fathers spend far less time with their children. Although the traditional nuclear family is far less common today, many marriages retain a traditional head-complement orientation, with provider and homemaker roles, particularly when the wife is not working. When she works, the senior partner–junior partner model, in which family boundaries are permeable to work for the man and to family demands for the woman, still give the man greater decision-making control. A few marriages employ an egalitarian style, in which all so-called sex roles are up for negotiation.

Psychological research on sex-trait stereotypes used adjectives to characterize the traits that were either "more true" (differentiating) of men or women or "generally true" (characterizing) of men or women. Two clusters of traits similar to Parsons's instrumental and expressive styles emerged from this research on sex stereotypes: men were seen as competent, rational, and assertive, whereas women were seen as warm and expressive.

Pan-cultural similarity in sex stereotypes of the "typical" man or woman emerged from a study of 25 nations. In these 25 countries, men were described in all as adventurous, dominant, and strong, women as sentimental, submissive, and superstitious. Overall, however, the stereotypes of women and men did not differ on an evaluative dimension; men were viewed as strong and active, women as weak and passive.

Both sexes wanted their ideal selves to be more strong and active than their perceived selves. The psychologists John Williams and Deborah Best interpreted this result to mean that both sexes desire, wish, or want to be "relatively more masculine." However, this conclusion conflates the operational definition of a difference score between a perceived self and an ideal self with a befogging idea about desired masculine gender identity. Wanting to be more strong and active, more ambitious and dominant, or more instrumental or agentic is not identical to wanting to be more "masculine" in one's gender identity, just as wanting to be more warm and friendly or more expressive and communal is not the same as wanting to be more "feminine" in gender identity. To want to be the best that any human can be is just to realize the self, to be a fully functioning person, to be an ideal specimen of a human being. It is to discard the dimorphic sexual essentialism of a normative gender ideology in favor of a humanist ideology in which the human being is the measure of all things.

The psychologist Kay Deaux noted that reliance on personality-trait terms to define gender stereotypes has been a persistent but indefensible strategy among social scientists. Gender-linked associations cross a number of realms, permitting a broad range of inferences to be generated from a small amount of information. For better or worse, people use sex assignment as either male or female to organize information. Physical appearance seems to provide cues that strongly weight information about the probability of sexual orientation, occupational roles, role behaviors (e.g., cooking meals), and trait stereotypes. In fact, information about any component of gender influences stereotypic hypotheses about other presumably related components. Although largely ignored in research on sex stereotypes, information about sexuality strongly predicts beliefs about other gender components such as traits or roles. Dichotomous thinking about gender follows from a gender belief in dimorphic sexual essentialism.

Second-Generation Measures of M&F

Two measures of masculinity and femininity introduced in 1974—one by Sandra Bem, the *Bem*

Sex Role Inventory (BSRI), and the other by Janet Spence and Robert Helmreich, the *Personal Attributes Questionnaire* (PAQ)—have generated a plethora of research. They appeared to be a promising innovation, in that they separated masculinity and femininity into two separate dimensions. Moreover, Bem said androgyny promised to capture the best of both the instrumental and expressive worlds.

Unfortunately, neither measure was based on a theory of gender. The BSRI was constructed empirically from a list of 400 adjectives by selecting socially acceptable personality traits said to be more characteristic of either men or women. The PAQ was constructed from positive stereotypic items borrowed from the Sex-Role Stereotype Questionnaire; later, the PAQ became the (expanded) EPAQ when negative stereotypes were added.

Much of the appeal of these measures, given the feminist times, was that Bem's androgyny—as a balance between masculine and feminine traits—appealed to many psychologists as a positive definition of mental health. Women would not have to be limited by role and trait congruence as health-defining but could strive to be both instrumental and expressive. Later on, Bem rejected her own concept of androgyny as placing a double burden on women to be both instrumental and expressive. After some initial confusion about how best to measure androgyny, a meta-analytic pattern of results soon revealed that *M,* but not androgyny or *F* or even congruence, was related to self-esteem and psychological well-being.

At its worst, the measurement of masculinity and femininity by psychologists engendered and strengthened ideological beliefs in the categorical reality of male and female essences. At its best, this mindless body of research may teach the lesson that assuming psychological meaningfulness resides in essences called "masculinity" and "femininity" is a blind positivist faith. Rather than relying on an explicit theory of personality for a psychological theory of gender, the first generation of *M-F* measures trusted in the empirical keying of men's and women's responses to interests, attitudes, and traits to reveal their essences. Learning little, the second-generation measures of *M&F* continued to trust the empirical keying of desirable, stereotypic traits to assess *M*, *F,* and an ill-defined "androgyny." The body of research on *M&F* suggests that *M* might be better called "instrumental-agentic-dominance" and *F* "expressive-friendly-affiliation" when found in individuals of either sex.

Ending Dimorphic Sexual Essentialism

Ideology worked itself deeply into science in the form of dimorphic sexual essentialism. Ideologues seek to justify the traditional hierarchy of gender by discovering biodetermined sex differences that justify men's superior political, economic, and social power and women's inferior status. *Biodeterminism* is a form of reductionism that falsely explains individual behavior and the characteristics of societies in terms of biological functions. It transforms historically created male superiority into "masculinity," as superior to "femininity." It produced a long line of discoveries of biological differences favoring men that failed, upon further research, to achieve replication, much less a scientific consensus. It still produces a bias in the mass media in favor of reporting biological differences believed to be related to gender. It infiltrated work on sex stereotypes by transforming the concepts of masculinity and femininity from rigid images into essences that people strive to attain. It permeated the study of *M-F* and *M&F* by substituting empirical differences in responses for measurement of inner essences and by helping psychologists forget that trait stereotypes are not dimorphic, universal, inner essences of men and women.

In recent years, feminists have urged a new perspective on maleness and femaleness. In their view, gender itself is seen as a principle that organizes social arrangements, cognition, and action. The anthropologist Gayle Rubin argued that it is the system of gender that creates a taboo against the sameness of male and female, a taboo which exacerbates the biological differences between the sexes and thereby creates a belief in gender as encompassing dimorphic sexual essences. Far from being an expression of natural differences, gender identity as cast into dimorphic forms is the suppression of natural similarities for social purposes and by social means.

Within Silvan Tomkins's script theory, gender is defined as a socially inherited ideological script (concerned with the ultimate nature of men and women) that bonds, differentiates, and divides the two sexes into unjustly stratified collectivities. A *gender script* is a set of rules for ordering information in sets of scenes relevant to ideologies of gender; the psychologically magnified rules (often in the absence of conscious awareness) interpret, produce, direct, defend, and evaluate an individual's actions or interpersonal transactions in gender-relevant scenes.

One component of a gender script is a subset of rules ordering information in scenes using a theory about gender—a gender belief system, including causal explanations, that serves as an auxiliary to many scripts. Following Deaux, a *gender belief system* is defined as a set of descriptive beliefs (about what is) and prescriptive opinions (about what should be) concerning males and females and the purported gender qualities of masculine and feminine, including stereotypes of men and women; attitudes toward appropriate roles, relationships, dispositions, and actions of men and women; and attitudes toward individuals who do not fit modal social categories of men and women (e.g., homosexuals, transsexuals).

Gender Dysphoria and Stigmatization

Because gender ideology is a component of normative ideology, it includes the belief that men and women should be rewarded with positive affect only when they live up to gender norms. Traditional gender ideology maintains that failure to embody gender norms is caused by deficits in masculinity or femininity. For adults, these norms of gender include physical appearance, dress and adornment, household and occupational roles, stereotypic traits, and sexual orientation; for children, they include affect display and communication, urination posture, dress and adornment, games and toys, and pastimes and playmates. Any display of cross-gender interests, affect, and behavior—characteristics stereotypically belonging to the sex opposite to that of sexual assignment—activates varying degrees of humiliation from an audience.

Of particular importance as social stimuli are any cues about potential or actual homosexual sexual orientation, as well as physical appearance or adventitious sexual coding that appears cross-gendered. Traditional gender ideology is a variant of a normative ideology that is often characterized as "traditional family ideology." Beneath that rhetorically chosen label lies a cluster of moral and patriarchal beliefs that can be summarized by recalling the teachings of Thomas Aquinas (see *Sexual Values and Moral Development*).

What is and what is not morally acceptable in traditional family ideology? The only morally acceptable sexual motive is procreation. The only morally acceptable sexual object is the spouse. The only morally acceptable sexual activity is coitus in the missionary position for procreation with the spouse. The only morally acceptable sexual affect is shame when fulfilling this prescription; sexual guilt must inhibit or, failing moral restraint, follow all other proscribed sexual linkages or sexual objects. The only morally acceptable context for reproduction is the monogamous marriage. The act of intercourse begins a procreative function that is morally fulfilled only when the offspring reach adulthood. The only morally acceptable climate for raising children is the family; therefore, there can be no divorce. The only morally acceptable division of labor places men at the head of the family; men must make decisions that protect their less capable wives, and women must follow the lead of the men, since they are the men's less competent complement. The foundation of traditional family ideology is the assumption of dimorphic sexual essentialism: that God made man, with woman as his complement, to embody essentially different human natures. Originating in sin, these dimorphic but complementary natures require constant inner vigilance and outward correction if they are to meet moral and gendered norms.

When parents accept traditional gender ideology, they must mold their children to meet these norms rather than enjoy the playfulness and affective spontaneity of their children as ends in themselves. Assigned sex becomes a normative gender ideal that must be met; the son must become a real man, the daughter a real woman. Thus, no so-called cross-gender behavior can be permitted.

Given traditional gender ideology, a failure to manifest stereotypic gender behavior produces censure and stigmatization, a stigma soon to be followed by *gender dysphoria*. Gender dysphoria is defined as dissatisfaction, unhappiness, dejection, and disaffection with one's gender identity/role.

Although homosexuality is no longer a psychiatric diagnosis, the stigmatization of gay and lesbian youths and adults continues. Traditional family and gender ideology stigmatizes homosexual acts and orientations, creating problems in forming a positive gay male or lesbian identity. The sociologist Richard Troiden describes a four-stage model of homosexual identity formation: (1) sensitization, (2) identity confusion, (3) identity assumption, and (4) commitment. The stage of sensitization occurs prior to puberty; it is characterized by feeling marginal, somehow different and set apart from other boys or other girls. Much of this marginality stems from gender-neutral or so-called gender-inappropriate interests or behaviors. Homosexual youths report that they, as boys, felt less "masculine" than other boys and, as girls, felt more "masculine" than other girls. ("Masculinity" sets the standards, given the existing hierarchy of gender.) Gender dysphoria and gender stigmatization walk hand-in-hand.

Given that traditional gender ideology views homosexuality as the inversion of heterosexuality, signs of cross-gender interests and behaviors become a theory of homosexual predisposition because of gender incongruence. The stronger the gender hierarchy in a culture, the stronger is the presumption that homosexuals must be inverts and display inversion. Dichotomous thinking requires that one be either heterosexual or homosexual, just as one must be either male or female and either masculine or feminine. Given such dichotomous thinking, both sexual orientation and gender are dimorphic, with each class homogeneous to its kind and nature. Stereotypes are just such rigid concepts and images of individuals as necessarily sharing the inner essences of their homogeneous group.

This imagery of hyperfemininity in gay men and hypermasculinity in lesbians is a caricature arising from social stereotyping, stigmatization, and the enforced secrecy of many gay and lesbian life-styles. Yet it also creates a self-fulfilling prophecy when gay youths seeking acceptance flaunt cross-gender behaviors, either to announce sexual interest, to try to establish gender identity, or to minstrelize the caricature of gays and lesbians. Cross-gender behavior in gay men is associated cross-culturally with the presence of pronounced gender hierarchy in cultural practices celebrating male superiority and female inferiority.

Gender dysphoria is most pronounced in adult transsexualism or in gender-identity disorders of childhood. Considered a psychiatric diagnosis, this form of gender dysphoria is defined by symptoms of persistent and intense distress and discomfort about one's assigned sex, or even insistence that one belongs to the sex opposite to that assigned. It includes (1) denial or repudiation of one's genitals and secondary sex characteristics and (2) preoccupation with and preference for stereotypic cross-gender adornments, interests, and activities. Many transsexuals prefer the radical solution of surgery to "correct" their anatomical sex and to end their gender dysphoria. Feeling enchained by gender, they cut their chains.

The chain of gender can be loosened by all who identify themselves more as human than male or female; it can be broken by a successful challenge to dimorphic sexual essentialism. As the psychiatrist Harry Stack Sullivan used to say, "All of us are more human than otherwise."

REFERENCES

Bem, S.L. The Measurement of Psychological Androgyny. *Journal of Consulting and Clinical Psychology*, Vol. 42 (1974), pp. 155–62.

Constantinople, A. Masculinity-Femininity: An Exception to a Famous Dictum? *Psychological Bulletin*, Vol. 80 (1973), pp. 389–407.

Mosher, D.L. Sexual Path Preference Inventory. In C. Davis, W. Yarber, and S. Davis, eds., *Sexuality Related Measures: A Compendium*. Lake Mills, Iowa: Stoyles Graphic Services, 1988.

Spence, J.T., and R.L. Helmreich. *Masculinity and Femininity: Their Psychological Dimensions, Correlates and Antecedents*. Austin: Univ. of Texas Press, 1978.

Williams, J.E., and D.L. Best. *Measuring Sex Stereotypes: A Thirty Nation Study*. Beverly Hills, Calif.: Sage, 1982.

————. *Sex and Psyche: Gender and Self Viewed Cross-Culturally*. Beverly Hills, Calif.: Sage, 1990.

Donald L. Mosher

GENDER DYSPHORIA

Gender dysphoria is the term now used by many professionals to describe the psychological state in which an individual does not experience a consistent unity of gender identity and role. Instead, there is confusion or dissatisfaction about self-awareness as male, female, or androgynous. In addition, there may be discomfort with the corresponding socially-defined gender roles or with the body image.

Characteristics

Gender dysphoria can include the following characteristics: discomfort with and a sense of inappropriateness regarding the socially-assigned role as male or female, dissatisfaction with sexual morphology, preoccupation with altering gender characteristics or acquiring the characteristics of the other gender, cross-dressing, and desire to change gender. Gender dysphoria may be associated with heterosexual, bisexual, homosexual, or asexual orientation. The problems and concerns may be chronic, episodic, or transitory.

The characteristics of gender roles vary among different cultures and periods of history. What is apparently not subject to cultural relativity is that all societies have specified two distinct and complementary gender-coded roles. One role is assigned and transmitted specifically for individuals who are born with a penis, and the other role is for individuals who are not. Gender dysphoria is not simply a dissatisfaction with the content of the gender roles of a given society or time, but rather reflects the lack of unity of gender identity and role for an individual.

Gender dysphoria has been described in many different societies and historical periods—from the ancient Greeks to contemporary Asian cultures, from tribal societies to urban subcultures. Societies also have different provisions for individuals who do not fulfill male-female definitions of gender roles—for example, the *hijras* of India or Native American *berdaches*.

Typology

Gender dysphoria may be expressed in a number of characteristically different ways.

Transsexualism refers to the process of seeking sex reassignment after at least two years of persistent discomfort with the socially-assigned sex role. Transsexualism is thus chronic gender dysphoria, which involves dissatisfaction with the complete sex role. Transsexuals have a preoccupation with eliminating the sexual characteristics of their gonadal gender and acquiring the secondary sexual characteristics of the other gender. Sex reassignment procedures include social rehabilitation to enable one to live full-time in the other sex role. Hormonal reassignment involves suppression of the hormonal characteristics of the unwanted gender and administration of the hormones of the other gender. Sex reassignment surgeries and other procedures alter the body to emulate the physical appearance of the other gender. This condition is considered to be rare, with an incidence of less than 1 in 30,000, and the sex ratio of males to females seems to vary among different societies.

Gender identity problems of childhood and adolescence usually involve extremes of nonconformity to the conventional gender role. "Sissy" boys and "tomboy" girls show a lack of interest in the play activities or characteristics stereotypically associated with their socially-assigned gender role. Their interests are more typical of the other gender. They may express a dissatisfaction with their gender and a wish to become the other gender. Rarely, they may express the belief that they are a member of the other gender or will grow up to become that gender. This thought pattern may include a repudiation of their genitalia or a belief that they will develop the sexual characteristics of the other gender when they grow up. One of the major problems these children experience is social teasing and rejection. Boys with these problems are brought in for evaluation much more often than girls.

Sissy boys frequently have homosexual identities in adulthood; this is less consistently reported for tomboyish girls. Few individuals with documented childhood histories of gender identity problems have undergone sex reassignment procedures as adults.

Episodic cross-dressing for social or entertainment purposes (i.e., drag) occurs in some homosexuals and to a much lesser extent in heterosexuals and bisexuals. Cross-dressing by itself does not indicate gender dysphoria. However, some individuals who dress in drag may be uncomfortable with their gender identity or sexual orientation and later seek sex reassignment. Lesbians may dress in masculine styles without defining their presentation as drag. Some of these women may experience gender dysphoria and seek sex reassignment. However, drag is predominantly a male activity.

Transvestic fetishism or *transvestophilia* refers to episodic cross-dressing for sexual excitement (or calming) in heterosexual or bisexual men. Most transvestites are typically comfortable in their masculine gender role and never seek to live more fully in the female role. Others, however, may develop gender dysphoria, although not necessarily ever seek sex reassignment.

Hermaphroditism or physiological intersex conditions include birth defects of the sex organs, hormonal syndromes involving androgen, atypical changes in sexual morphology at puberty, and supernumerary sex-typed chromosomal syndromes. Some individuals with these conditions experience gender dysphoria. However, most affected individuals develop gender identities consistent with their sex of rearing (but not necessarily the chromosomal or gonadal sex), without evident dysphoria. These conditions are rare.

Causes

The causes of gender dysphoria most likely involve an interaction of biochemical or physiological factors, critical periods, and social experience. There is no single determining factor—neither environment nor heredity, neither mind nor body.

The prenatal influence (at critical times in development) of certain hormones and sex-typed genomes may increase the individual's vulnerability to developing gender dysphoria. But there is no known syndrome or pattern of influence that produces gender dysphoria in a majority of affected individuals.

Postnatal experience also plays a role in the development of gender dysphoria. The social labeling of gender roles as they apply to the child, and the content of those roles, is socially transmitted. Serious inconsistencies in the gender typing or labeling of a young child may have a deleterious effect. Initial gender identity is usually developed around the time of the acquisition of language, about 18 months to 2 years of age. Gender constancy is usually developed by age 5 or 6. The period between these two cognitive milestones seems to be the most critical time of risk for developing gender dysphoria of the type that would lead to transsexualism.

In developing a gender identity, the child learns to identify with individuals of one gender and label this gender as applying to the self. The child complements with individuals of the other gender. The learning processes of identification and complementation define gender identity for the child. The mental schemas for both social genders are learned, and they are differentiated as one applying to self and the other not applying to self. In cases of gender dysphoria, both schemas are learned, but they are not differentiated as identification (for self) and complementation (for other). Rather, the content of both genders' characteristics may apply to the self in some ways, which can lead to confusion and gender dysphoria of the type that in adulthood may become transsexualism.

Other types of gender dysphoria are more partial in their content or episodic in their manifestation, and they may have a later onset. Traumatic social sexual experiences, inharmonious pubertal changes, or sexually confusing cognitions may be associated with gender dysphoria of later onset. For transvestism, juvenile social experiences may become imprinted in a way that contributes to gender dysphoria. Pubertal and postpubertal experiences can also precipitate gender dysphoria, such as struggles to understand problems of atypical pubertal development or the content of atypical erotic imagery.

Rehabilitation

Gender dysphoria, like conventional gender identity, is relatively intractable and unlikely to change. Spontaneous changes are rare but may occur. Individuals with gender dysphoria, although experiencing discomfort, may not define themselves as having a problem. Instead, they tend to label themselves according to the type of dysphoria which they consider that they experience. They frequently try to learn from others with similar experiences, and may band together in subcultures or support groups.

The process of rehabilitation for gender dysphoria is designed to help the affected individuals find some satisfactory ways of living their lives. Rehabilitation can involve a wide variety of activities, from self-help groups to medical procedures.

Modern medicine has developed medical and surgical techniques that can assist individuals in altering their bodies to mimic those of the other gender. The availability, and effectiveness, of these procedures was first widely publicized following Christine Jorgensen's sex-change surgery in 1952. It was shortly after this time that the clinical terms "gender dysphoria" and "transsexualism" came into general use. Important in the conceptualization of transsexualism as a clinical disorder amenable to medical treatment were Benjamin's influential book *The Transsexual Phenomenon* (1966) and the research and publications of Money and Green, including *Transsexualism and Sex Reassignment* (1969).

The first gender identity clinic for the evaluation and treatment of transsexualism was established in 1966 at the Johns Hopkins Hospital, where the first sex reassignment operations in the United States were performed that year. At Hopkins, Money developed the two-year, real-life diagnostic test for transsexualism, which set the basic diagnostic and treatment standards for the transsexual rehabilitation of individuals with gender dysphoria.

Treatment of gender-dysphoric individuals involves therapy and often hormonal and surgical sex reassignment. Hormonal and surgical reassignment for transsexual patients who have undergone appropriate evaluation and rehabilitation has a frequency of satisfaction ranging from about 87 percent in male-to-female to 97 percent in female-to-male transsexuals. Sex reassignment is part of the standard approach to treatment around the world. However, it is still subject to some controversy and professional disagreement. Lothstein, for example, believes that intensive psychotherapy is the primary treatment of choice for females, with sex reassignment being necessary only in a minority of cases.

The diagnostic standards for transsexualism, according to the American Psychiatric Association's *Diagnostic and Statistical Manual,* include a "persistent discomfort and sense of inappropriateness about one's assigned sex" and a "persistent preoccupation for at least two years with getting rid of one's primary and secondary sex characteristics and acquiring the sex characteristics of the other sex" in an individual who has completed puberty.

The Harry Benjamin International Gender Dysphoria Association Standards of Care specify the process an individual should undergo to be a candidate for hormonal and surgical sex reassignment. The following are some of the minimum standards: Other preexisting psychiatric or medical problems should be treated. The person must have been seen by qualified clinical behavioral scientists who can document independently the patient's self-report that the patient's gender dysphoria has continuously existed for at least two years. The clinician should have known the patient for at least three months in a therapeutic relationship before making a recommendation for hormonal reassignment and six months before making a recommendation for surgical reassignment. Prior to sex reassignment surgery, the patient should have lived full-time in the social role of the other sex for at least 12 months.

The standards are designed to maximize the likelihood that the individual with gender dysphoria will be successfully rehabilitated in the other gender role. They protect both the patient and the professionals from unfortunate consequences of sex reassignment. Sometimes, individuals who label themselves as transsexuals attempt to speed up the reassignment process or avoid involvement with professionals. This is believed to be associated in some cases with dissatisfaction with the results of sex reassignment.

During the period of the real-life diagnostic test, mental health professionals help individuals in their struggle with confusing and conflicting beliefs about their gender status and in developing realistic expectations about the process of sex reassignment. Other professionals help gender-dysphoric individuals develop more effective cross-gender styles of presentation, including electrolysis for males, speech therapy, and behavioral retraining for all aspects of self-presentation and interpersonal communication.

Many individuals who begin the process of sex reassignment drop out before surgical sex reassignment, although some of them may later return to treatment. Some individuals with gender dysphoria become satisfied with an in-between condition. For example, some may seek social and hormonal reassignment but not genital surgery. For males, some are rehabilitated as "ladies with a penis" and never seek genital sex reassignment. For females, present techniques for surgical construction of a phallus may not produce results they consider satisfactory, and they may forgo or postpone genital surgery while waiting for the development of new procedures. These female-to-male transsexuals may be satisfied with hormonal reassignment and removal of the breasts.

Following sex reassignment, most transsexuals are heterosexual in their orientation, while others are bisexual or homosexual. Sexual orientation is not a criterion in determining suitability for sex reassignment.

In most jurisdictions, after professional treatment transsexuals are able to change their gender legally to correspond to their sex-reassigned status. This includes the right to live, work, and marry according to their reassigned social gender role.

REFERENCES

Benjamin, H. *The Transsexual Phenomenon.* New York: Julian Press, 1966.

Blanchard, R., and B. Steiner, eds. *Clinical Management of Gender Identity Disorders in Children and Adults.* Washington, D.C.: American Psychiatric Press, 1990.

Green, R. *Sexual Identity Conflict in Children and Adults.* New York: Basic Books, 1974.

————. *The "Sissy Boy Syndrome" and the Development of Homosexuality.* New Haven: Yale Univ. Press, 1987.

Green, R., and D.T. Fleming. Transsexual Surgery Follow-up: Status in the 1990s. *Annual Review of Sex Research*, Vol. 1 (1990), pp. 163–74.

Green, R., and J. Money, eds. *Transsexualism and Sex Reassignment.* Baltimore: Johns Hopkins Univ. Press, 1969.

Harry Benjamin International Gender Dysphoria Association. Standards of Care: The Hormonal and Surgical Sex Reassignment of Gender Dysphoric Persons. *Archives of Sexual Behavior*, Vol. 14 (1985), pp. 79–90.

Lothstein, L.M. *Female-to-Male Transsexualism: Historical, Clinical and Theoretical Issues.* Boston: Routledge & Kegan Paul, 1983.

Money, J. *Gay, Straight, and In-between.* New York: Oxford Univ. Press, 1988.

Money, J., and R. Ambinder. "Two-Year, Real-Life Diagnostic Test: Rehabilitation Versus Cure." In H. Brady and J. Brody, eds., *Controversy in Psychiatry*. Philadelphia: Saunders, 1978.

Money, J., and A. Ehrhardt. *Man and Woman, Boy and Girl.* Baltimore: Johns Hopkins Univ. Press, 1972.

Steiner, B., ed. *Gender Dysphoria: Development, Research, and Management.* New York: Plenum Press, 1985.

Walters, W., and M. Ross, eds. *Transsexualism and Sex Reassignment.* New York: Oxford Univ. Press, 1986.

Gregory K. Lehne

GENETICS AND SEX

Genetics, the science of heredity, seeks to explain how characteristics and traits are passed from one generation to the next. Chromosomes, the hereditary material studied by geneticists, are highly structured chains of DNA (deoxyribonucleic acid) with specific sequences of bases and amino acids. Functional units of these DNA chains are known as genes. Chromosomes and genes are the essential foundation of and mechanism for all structural growth and functioning of individual cells and organisms composed of cells. Chromosomes and their genes also allow a male and a female to transmit their characteristics and produce offspring like themselves. When sexually mature male and female individuals produce sperm and ova, the resulting gametes contain half the number of chromosomes in the adult body cells, so that fertilization, or union of the sperm and ovum, gives the resulting new organism the full chromosome complement of the adult parents.

Our sexuality includes all those aspects of our being—the biological, hormonal, neural, psychological, and social—that make us gendered persons, male or female. The relationship between genes and sex is twofold. At fertilization, when a sperm unites with an ovum, the combination of sex chromosomes (in humans, the X and Y chromosomes) determines the essential sexual character of the resulting embryo. Following fertilization, genes on the X and Y chromosomes regulate and direct the production of proteins and enzymes by other genes on the other chromosomes (known as autosomes) to produce the appropriate sexual anatomy, sexual differentiation, and sexual function, along with the other characteristics and functions of our bodies. The expression of the genes is affected by the ever-changing cellular, maternal uterine, hormonal, and outside environments.

The Sex Chromosomes

In genetics, sex chromosomes are distinguished from other chromosomes, the autosomes, because the former are different in males and females and contain genes related to primary sexual differentiation. Many, though not all, organisms possess specialized chromosomes that are associated with being either male or female. These specialized chromosomes segregate during production of the reproductive cells, the egg and sperm, so that at fertilization when the sperm and egg unite, each sex receives its own appropriate complement of sex-determining chromosomes.

In the animal kingdom, several different types of sex chromosomes exist. In the human male, the normal chromosome complement of somatic cells is 44 autosomes, or 22 pairs of body chromosomes, plus an X and a Y chromosome, for a total of 46 chromosomes in each cell nucleus. Having two complete homologous sets of autosomes and two sex chromosomes is referred to as the diploid condition. Human females have 44 autosomes arranged in 22 pairs plus two X chromosomes.

In humans, the X chromosome is much larger than the Y chromosome. The X chromosome contains many genes responsible for the development of the central nervous system, so at least one is essential for embryonic development and a viable organism. Other genes on the X chromosome are associated with clinically significant disorders such as hemophilia, Duchenne muscular dystrophy, and color blindness. Two X chromosomes are essential for the development of ovaries that can produce ova.

The smaller Y chromosome occurs in the human male. The crucial gene on the Y chromosome is known as the Testes Determining Factor gene (TDF). Active in the fifth week of gestation, this gene directs the commitment of the undifferentiated gonads to testicular development in weeks six through nine. If the embryo lacks the TDF gene, its development follows the inherent female path, with ovaries and female sexual anatomy starting to develop in week 12. When the isolated TDF is transplanted into very young mouse embryos, chromosomally female (XX) embryos develop into newborns with normal male anatomy and behavior.

Sperm and Ovum Production

Sexual reproduction, with the offspring developing from the union of a sperm and an egg (ovum), requires that the sperm and egg have exactly half the normal diploid complement of chromosomes that occur in the body cells of the parents. In the male gamete, or sperm, this haploid chromosome number includes 22 autosomes plus either an X or a Y chromosome. The normal egg or ovum has a haploid complement of one set of 22 autosomes and a single X.

To reduce the diploid chromosome number to the haploid status of the sperm or egg, primordial germ cells in the ovaries and testes undergo meiosis, a two-stage process of cell division. During the resting (interphase) stage before meiosis begins, the chromosomes of the primordial germ cell replicate. Homologous pairs of duplicated chromosomes then synapse, or pair up. A bipolar spindle forms as the paired chromosomes arrange themselves on an equatorial plate. The spindle fibers then attach to the homologous chromosomes and separate them. At the end of this first stage, one duplicated chromosome from each homologous pair has migrated to one pole of the spindle, while its mate migrates to the opposing pole. In effect, the chromosome number in these intermediate germ cells is haploid.

During the second stage, two new spindles form at each of the two poles of the original spindle. The twinned chromosomes do not replicate themselves a second time. Instead, they arrange themselves on new equatorial plates, and the duplicated strands of each chromosome are pulled apart by the new spindle fibers. After these DNA strands migrate to opposite poles in each of the two intermediate daughter cells, four daughter cells are produced, each with a haploid chromosome complement.

In production of the egg or ovum, meiosis results in three polar bodies that disintegrate and die producing a single ovum. In sperm production, the result is four functional sperm, from a single spermatogonial cell.

Fertilization, the union of the egg and sperm, restores the diploid chromosome complement and gives the offspring the same chromosomal makeup as its parents.

Sometimes, during production of the egg or sperm, two paired or replicated chromosomes may fail to separate. As a result of this nondisjunction, one germ cell ends up with both chromosomes of a homologous pair, while the other daughter cell is missing that chromosome. Fertilization of a sperm or egg with an extra chromosome can result in Down's syndrome (trisomy 21 or 47, 21+) and Klinefelter's syndrome (47, XXY). Fertilization of a sperm or egg with a missing chromosome can result in Turner's syndrome (45, XO). Nondisjunction of a sex chromosome during cell division in the first few days after fertilization can result in a chromosome mosaic condition that may affect sexual differentiation.

An interesting aspect of the sex chromosomes results from the fact that females have two X chromosomes and males only one X. This gives females a double dose of the X chromosome genes and their products. Female body cells compensate for this phenomenon by partially inactivating one X chromosome in a so-called sex chromatin or Barr body on the nuclear membrane of somatic cells. Thus, in normal female body cells, one X chromosome remains active and functional, and the second X chromosome is partially inactivated. In cells with abnormal chromosome complements, such as 47, XXY and multiple X, the number of Barr bodies is always one fewer than the number of X chromosomes in the cell. The presence or absence of Barr bodies in somatic cells obtained by buccal smear, amniocentesis, or chorionic villi sampling is used in ascertaining chromosomal sex status. Individuals with Turner's syndrome (45, XO) and 46, XY males lack a Barr body; 47, XXY individuals with Klinefelter's syndrome have one Barr body.

Chromosomes and Anomalous Sexual Development

The sexual development of a fetus may deviate from the male or female path either because of an abnormal sex chromosome complement or because of a mutated gene. A missing X chromosome in a Turner's syndrome female and the addition of an X chromosome in a Klinefelter's syndrome male provide the more common examples of sex chromosome variations. The mutation of a single gene can result in conditions known as androgen insensitivity, congenital virilizing adrenal hyperplasia (CVAH), and DHT deficiency syndrome.

A female with Turner's syndrome (or ovarian agenesis) has a normal complement of 22 pairs of autosomes or body-regulating chromosomes, but only one X chromosome instead of the usual XX. Hence the genetic notation 45, XO. These individuals develop a female body type with undeveloped, nonfunctioning ovaries, persistent juvenile genitals, and other symptoms. Although the second X chromosome in a normal 46, XX female is partially inactivated, this second X chromosome is essential for ovarian development. Approximately one in 4,000 newborns has Turner's syndrome. This is lower than expected because many fetuses with this condition miscarry.

Although females with Turner's syndrome lack the second X chromosome, they may appear reasonably normal anatomically until puberty, when a lack of estrogen production in the nonfunctional streak ovaries results in a lack of sexual maturation and secondary sex characteristics. Other symptoms may include webbed skin on the back of the neck, low nape hairline, retarded growth, obesity, spinal deformities, triangular-shaped face, prominent ears, small jaw, hearing defects, and myopia. Swollen tissue and dwarfism are common. Language, motor, and learning deficits are often reported, along with a retarded spatial-nonverbal IQ. Right brain hemisphere impairment may result in low self-esteem, reduced self-confidence, and lack of social adeptness. Reduced spatial and face-interpreting skills may cause adolescent emotional and social problems.

About one in 500 newborn males has Klinefelter's syndrome, characterized by very small, sterile testes. The cells of individuals with this condition have a full set of 22 paired body chromosomes, the usual X and Y chromosomes, and at least one extra X chromosome. Roughly 80 percent are 47, XXY. Much rarer are 48, XXXY and mosaics, with different genotypes in two cell lines and two or more X chromosomes and one or two Y chromosomes. While the condition is often diagnosed in childhood because of the very small testes, diagnosis is more com-

mon in adolescence, since clinical symptoms appear mostly after puberty.

Abnormal development of the testes and sterility with no sperm production result when elastic connective tissue replaces the germinal cells in the testes. An affected male is still capable of erection and coitus, although secondary erectile dysfunction may result from response to lowered libido and gynecomastia, or female breast development. Other symptoms include eunuchoid body with poor male secondary sex characteristics, which give a feminine appearance. In half the cases, the gynecoid impression is accented by gynecomastia. Penile size is usually normal, although pubic hair may be sparse and female in pattern. The axillary and facial hair is also usually sparse. Klinefelter's males are tall and slim, with long arms and legs.

Some experts report that most Klinefelter's individuals are retarded, some severely, while others report that a majority have normal intellectual development. Social adjustment may be poor, in part in response to the tall, eunuchoid body and gynecomastia. Personality and character-trait disturbances, emotional and behavioral troubles, alcoholism, minor criminality, and outright psychosis are common, but their frequencies are not documented.

Individuals can have either Turner's or Klinefelter's syndrome because of a mosaicism in their sex chromosomes, with different combinations of sex chromosomes in two or more cell lines. Also, two embryonic masses, one with 46, XX and the other with 46, XY, may fuse as they move through the Fallopian tube prior to implantation. In these individuals, symptoms vary depending on which cells in the body have the XX and which the XY chromosome complement. Fertilization of one ovum by two sperm and other variations can also result in genetic and sexual mosaicism.

Genetics and Anomalous Sexual Development

Some fetuses have a defective recessive gene on the X chromosome that prevents the normal production of receptors that are necessary for testosterone and its derivatives to enter body cells. Affected individuals have a male chromosome complement (46, XY), testes, and a male balance of hormones. However, the cells of their bodies cannot react to the masculinizing message of testosterone circulating in the blood. This condition is known as testicular feminization or androgen insensitivity syndrome.

Since the circulating testosterone cannot enter its normal target cells, the body is not masculinized but follows the inherent female path. In the androgen insensitivity syndrome, testosterone cannot cause the Wolffian ducts to develop into the internal male system. However, the Mullerian inhibiting hormone prevents female development of the Mullerian ducts. The external genitals differentiate as female, except for a short, blind vagina that is usually not deep enough to allow for coitus unless dilated or surgically lengthened during adolescence. At birth, such individuals appear to be anatomically normal females and are so assigned and raised by their parents. Affected individuals have no menstrual cycle and are infertile. Breast and secondary sex characteristic development is normal for a female because of estrogens from the testes and adrenal glands. However, lactation is not possible.

Another genetic variation that alters the path of sexual development is congenital virilizing adrenal hyperplasia. CVAH can occur in either a male or a female, leading to a pseudohermaphrodite condition. An affected newborn female has virilized, ambiguous genitals. Affected males experience premature puberty.

The immediate result of the genetic mutation behind CVAH is varying degrees of deficiency in the adrenal cortical enzymes—cortisol and aldosterone—needed for synthesis of various steroid sex hormones. The reduced sex hormone output triggers an increase in adrenocorticotropic hormone production, which in turn causes overdevelopment of the adrenal glands and overproduction of androgens. Adrenal malfunction begins before birth and continues unless treated. When left untreated, the severe form is lethal. Treatment can prevent premature death and postnatal virilization, although prenatally virilized females require plastic surgery.

A third genetic mutation that alters sexual development is dihydrotestosterone (DHT) deficiency, or 5-alpha-reductase deficiency. This form of pseudohermaphroditism results from a genetic mutation that creates a deficiency of the enzyme needed to convert testosterone into DHT. DHT is responsible for the masculinization of the external genitals from a bipotential set of primordia.

Affected individuals have 46, XY and testes. The newborn has ambiguous external sexual anatomy with a clitoral-like phallus and more or less fused, scrotal-like labia. Internal duct differentiation is usually male. The affected infant is usually gender-assigned and raised as a female. However, at puberty, the surge of testosterone in such individuals may be sufficient to trigger partial virilization, with the clitoral-like phallus developing into a small penis; weak male secondary sex characteristics also develop.

In the small rural village of Salinas in the Dominican Republic, where most cases have been reported, the "conversion" of a daughter into a son is acceptable because of the strong patriarchal tradition. The affected children are subject to some ridicule, however, being referred to as *quevote* ("penis at 12") or *machihembra* ("first woman, then man"). When the condition occurs in more developed countries, the usual result is much more negative, with severe psychological trauma.

In cases where DHT-deficient children have been clinically and socially raised and conditioned as girls from birth onward with surgical feminization, they become women with a heterosexual orientation as a female, despite chromosomal and gonadal status as male. The extent and success of pubertal psychosexual adjustment, shifting from a female to a male gender identity, is widely disputed and debated.

In summary, the X and Y sex chromosomes and the Testes Determining Factor gene initiate and direct all sexual development, with some latitude of variant developments.

REFERENCES

Money, J., and A.A. Ehrhardt. *Man and Woman, Boy and Girl: Differentiation and Dimorphism of Gender Identity from Conception to Maturity.* Baltimore: Johns Hopkins Univ. Press, 1972.

Moore, K.L. *The Developing Human: Clinical Oriented Embryology.* 4th ed. Philadelphia: Saunders, 1988.

Reinish, J.M., L.A. Rosenblum, and S.A. Sanders. *Masculinity/Femininity: Basic Perspectives.* New York: Oxford Univ. Press, 1987.

Sinclair, A.H., et al. A Gene From the Human Sex-determining Region Encodes a Protein with Homology to a Conserved DNA-binding Motif. *Nature,* Vol. 346 (July 1990), pp. 240–44.

Robert T. Francoeur

GERMAN SEX RESEARCHERS

For a time in the last part of the 19th and first part of the 20th century, German-speaking scholars dominated the field of sex research. Three of these researchers, Richard von Krafft-Ebing, Magnus Hirschfeld, and Sigmund Freud, are the subjects of individual biographies. Freud was from Austria, not Germany, but he wrote in German, while Krafft-Ebing, though German, taught in Vienna. Interestingly, most of the German-speaking researchers were Jewish, although Krafft-Ebing was not. Almost all were physicians.

Several factors, more or less specific to 19th-century Germany, led to the early involvement of German physicians. German physicians had long been interested in the association between physical disorders and sexual problems. They had also attempted to become more specific in their diagnosis of sexual disorders, not only to help their clients but also to refine their testimony before the courts on various sexual matters. A German movement for more effective contraceptives involved a number of specialists in obstetrics and gynecology and led to the invention of the spring-coiled diaphragm. Probably the most important factor, however, was the changing condition of the laws on homosexuality in Prussia (and later united Germany). Much of western Germany had adopted the Napoleonic code, which in effect decriminalized homosexual contacts and relied on such criteria as age of consent and use of force to define illegal conduct. Prussia, however, the dominant German state, under whose aegis a united German Empire evolved in 1870, had not changed its laws and still regarded homosexuality as a criminal act.

Fearful that the movement for German unification might lead to the criminalization of homosexuality in all of Germany, Karl Heinrich Ulrichs (1825–1895), perhaps the world's first "self-proclaimed homosexual," decided in 1862 to devote his life to the defense and explanation of homosexuality. Under both his own name and the pseudonym Numa Numantius, he published some 12 booklets dealing with homosexuality between 1864 and 1879. Ulrichs also appealed to the various German congresses that were considering changes in the law to legalize homosexuality. In his search for allies, Ulrichs aroused the interest of Richard von Krafft-Ebing, and this was a major factor in Krafft-Ebing's subsequent career. Ulrichs was also read by Carl Westphal (1833–1890), the physician usually given credit for putting the study of stigmatized sexual expression on a scientific basis with an article he wrote about two homosexual patients in 1869.

The work of Ulrichs challenged the Hungarian writer Karl Maria Kertbeny (1824–1882) to find a term different from Ulrichs's "urning" and "dioningin" to describe males and females who were attracted to members of their own sex. Kertbeny coined the term "homosexual" which was adopted by Krafft-Ebing. Also heavily influenced by Ulrichs was Albert Moll, a Berlin physician who wrote a book-length study on homosexuality in 1893 and adopted Ulrichs's idea that homosexuality in most cases was in-

born; Moll later changed his mind about this, however.

Encouraged by his fellow physicians' willingness to look at sexual issues, Albert Eulenberg published a series of studies on sadism, masochism, and suicide. Other physician writers on sex included Hans Kurella (1858–1916), Hermann Ploss (1819–1885), Albert von Schrenck-Notzing (1872–1919), Enoch Heinrich Kisch (1841–1918), Max Dessoir (1867–1937), and Max Marcuse (1877–1963). Though none of them achieved the reputation of Krafft-Ebing, Freud, or Hirschfeld, most made significant contributions to the study of sexuality. One of the more important of these figures was the German dermatologist Iwan Bloch (1872–1922), who coined the term *Sexualwissenschaft*, or "sexual science," in 1906 and defined it as including biological, psychological, cultural, social, and other factors. He believed that by studying sexuality in all its manifestations, sexologists could provide answers to physicians to help their patients.

Bloch's concept of *sexualwissenschaft* had considerable influence on certain segments of the German medical community, and at least one of the major medical journals established a section dealing with advances in sexual science. Magnus Hirschfeld also launched a new sexological journal, *Zeitschrift für Sexualwissenschaft*, which solicited articles from Freud, Alfred Adler, Karl Abraham, and Wilhelm Steckel, as well as non-Germans such as Paolo Mantegazza and Cesare Lombroso. Although the high-level scholarly content did not survive beyond the first year, the journal continued to be published under a slightly different title for a more popular audience.

The result was an outpouring of articles and books in German on various aspects of sexuality. Even Havelock Ellis published the first edition of his book on homosexuality in German. However, much of this German dominance was weakened by the outbreak of World War I, and though the German sexological movement revived for a brief period after the war, particularly in the later Weimar Republic, it was effectively destroyed by the rise of Hitler and the Nazis in the early 1930s. One of the first things the Nazis destroyed was Hirschfeld's library and case-study notes in Berlin.

REFERENCES

Bullough, V.L. The Physician and Research into Human Sexual Behavior in Nineteenth-Century Germany. *Bulletin of the History of Medicine*, Vol. 63 (1989), pp. 247–67.

Vern L. Bullough

GONADS

The gonads are those specialized organs—the testes in the male and the ovaries in the female—that produce the sex cells (gametes) called sperm and ova (or eggs). The gonads also produce many hormones, which are usually called the sex hormones. This definition is misleading, however, because although these hormones are necessary for proper sexual functioning in the individual, they are also produced by other organs of the body and stimulate activities that are not sexual. Both "male" and "female" sex hormones are produced in each sex, although they appear in different concentrations.

The gonads are homologous organs that develop from undifferentiated gonadal tissue that appears during the developing embryo's fifth or sixth week of intrauterine life. Although the sex of the gonad is fixed at the time of fertilization by the presence of a single gene (the Testes Determining Factor) on the Y chromosome, determination of the gonad cannot be made until about the seventh week, when if it is not determined to be a testis, it is presumed to be an ovary. More precise definition occurs at about the tenth week, when the forerunners of the follicles become visible if the gonad is going to mature into an ovary.

The ovaries are nodular glands that, after puberty, have an uneven surface, are about one and a half inches long, weigh about 3 grams each, and are located one on either side of the uterus. They are held in place by folds and ligaments and are attached to the posterior surface of the uterus. The ovary contains thousands of microscopic ovarian follicles, which produce the ova. A female is born with all the immature ova she will ever produce (about 2 million, 40,000 of which survive to puberty; 400 mature during her reproductive lifetime, and only a few are ever fertilized). At puberty, the ova appear at differing stages of development.

The ovaries also secrete two important classes of hormones, the estrogens and the progestins. Estradiol is the most important of the estrogens and progesterone of the progestins, but in common usage, estrogen and progesterone represent the "female" sex hormones. These hormones control the production of secondary sex characteristics as well as other maturational changes that occur at puberty, but they do not seem to be crucial for differentiation of the female reproductive system before birth. They regulate the menstrual cycle and are necessary for reproduction. Their effect on female sex drive and behavior is unclear. They are essential for maintaining pregnancy. They are also important for meno-

pausal women who may suffer from vaginal dryness and loss of calcium from the bones (osteoporosis). Many of these symptoms can be alleviated by the use of estrogen replacement therapy.

The word "testis" is the root word for "witness": in ancient times, a man would place his hand on his testes to swear that he was telling the truth—hence the word testify. They are two small ovoid glands about two inches long, weighing about 10 to 15 grams each, and suspended in a sac, the scrotum, beneath the penis. The left one usually hangs a bit lower than the right one. Attachments to the scrotum and the spermatic cords hold them in place. A fibrous capsule encases each testicle, extends into the gland, and divides it into about 200 conical lobes. Each lobe contains one to three tiny coiled seminiferous tubules; the combined length of all the tubules in both testes is about one-quarter mile. Interstitial cells (Leydig cells) are packed between the tubules. The tubules of each testis coalesce to form a tightly coiled tube enclosed in a fibrous casing (the epididymis). The epididymis measures about 20 feet and lies along the top and side of the testis.

The male does not begin to produce sperm (spermatogenesis), a process that occurs in the seminiferous tubules, until he reaches puberty. Sertoli cells are interspersed among the developing sperm within the tubules and provide physical support and nutrition during their development. These cells also help to regulate the secretion of one of the sex hormones. Billions of sperm cells are produced and stored in the seminiferous tubules and eventually are moved into the epididymis by the contractions of the tubules. There they complete their maturation and become motile by the whiplash movement of their tail.

The androgens, of which testosterone is the most important, are the "male" sex hormones that are produced by the interstitial cells. The androgens are responsible for the embryonic development of the male reproductive system. They regulate the secondary sex characteristics that occur in the male at maturity and stimulate protein anabolism that promotes growth of skeletal muscles and bones. They are linked to the male sex drive, and possibly to male aggressive behavior.

The effects of the removal of the testes (castration) have been known for centuries. Eunuchs were created for sexual pleasure and for use as guards for the harem in many ancient cultures. During the 17th century, when women were not allowed to perform on the stage or sing in church, it was not uncommon to castrate young boys to retain their clear, high voices. They became very important in the choirs of the Roman Catholic Church and stars on the grand-opera scene.

REFERENCES

Anthony, C.P., and G.A. Thibodeau. *Textbook of Anatomy and Physiology.* 10th ed. St. Louis: C.V. Mosby, 1979.

Bullough, V.L. *Sexual Variance in Society and History.* New York: John Wiley & Sons, 1976.

Katchadourian, H.A. *Biological Aspects of Human Sexuality.* 4th. ed. Fort Worth: Holt, Rinehart & Winston, 1990.

James D. Haynes

GRAEFENBERG, ERNST

Ernst Graefenberg (1881–1957) is known for his work in the development of the intrauterine device (IUD) and for his studies of the role of the female urethra in orgasm. Graefenberg began practicing as a gynecologist in Berlin in 1910 and by 1920 was one of the most successful in Berlin, with an office on the fashionable Kurfurstendamm. He also served as chief gynecologist of a municipal hospital in Britz, a district of Berlin mainly inhabited by a working-class population.

In 1934, Hans Lehfeldt attempted to persuade Graefenberg to leave Germany, but he refused to do so, believing that since his patients included wives of high Nazi officials, he would be safe. He was wrong, and he was arrested in 1937, allegedly for having smuggled a valuable stamp out of Germany. His release from prison was negotiated by Margaret Sanger, who paid the Nazis a ransom for his release. He finally was allowed to leave Germany in 1940, whereupon he came to the United States and opened a practice in New York City.

Graefenberg had always been interested in sexology and had been active in the German sexological associations. He was also a strong advocate of contraception and promoted the use of both the IUD and the cervical cap. He retained his interest in sexology in the United States, and his own sex history was among those included in the Kinsey Report.

Hans Lehfeldt
Connie Christine Wheeler

GRAFFITI

Of all the forms of human self-expression, perhaps none is more nearly ubiquitous, more provocative, and less admired than the act of producing graffiti. The term (singular, "graffito") is derived from the Italian *graffiare*, meaning "little scratchings," and may be applied to at least three types of inscriptions: public, private, and personal. Public graffiti include names, initials, cryptic symbols, and the like, typically painted, carved, or drawn on walls, fences, trees, trains, buses, or any other places likely to be observed by the masses. Public graffiti may serve as boundary markers for gang territories, as symbols of personal pride or courage, or merely as semipermanent reminders of someone's presence. Private graffiti are inscriptions in more secluded locations, usually on the walls of restrooms and toilet stalls, produced in secrecy and usually of intentionally anonymous authorship. Dundes, an anthropologist and noted authority on folkways, has proposed the more graphic term "latrinalia" as a discriminating label for toilet graffiti. Personal graffiti are tattoos and scars that are intended to beautify, to disfigure, to indicate status, or otherwise to adorn the human body.

Graffiti Categories

Students of graffiti content often attempt to categorize their data further, according to a general theme or to the presumed intent of the graffitist. There is no consistent agreement in the literature on how many or which specific content themes best characterize the varied types of graffiti. However, there are a few categories that appear more frequently than the others and seem deserving both of mention and of example.

Heterosexual—Indicating preference for or solicitation of romantic or erotic relations with persons of the opposite sex. Example: I love to suck cock! (women's restroom).

Homosexual—Indicating preference for or solicitation of romantic or erotic relations with persons of the same sex. Example: Blow jobs here—tap foot for blow jobs (men's restroom).

Political—Indicating concern about political institutions, personal power, and local, regional, or national issues, among other matters. Example: No Nukes! People over Technopoly.

Philosophical—Reflecting on the general nature of humankind or the purpose of life. Example: Live each day as if it were your last, and also as if you had a million more to live. With that balance, you can get through life.

Interpersonal—Indicating the graffitist's desire to better understand or interact with people or to cope with problems of everyday life. Example: I am ugly but human. Can anyone love me?

Ethnocentric/racial—Demonstrating positive or negative attitudes toward any clearly indicated ethnic or racial group. Example: Black may be beautiful and tan may be grand, but white is the color of Americans!

General humor—Attempts to be humorous about any nonsexual or nonscatological topic. Example: What do you call a fish with two knees? A tuny-fish.

Sexual humor—Attempts at humor with clearly sexual themes. Example: A woman without a man may be like a fish without a bicycle, but think of all the fun you can have riding a bicycle! (women's restroom).

Humor of elimination—General scatological humor. Example: Be like brother, not like sis. Lift the lid before you piss (men's restroom).

Graffiti about graffiti—Reference to the reading or writing of graffiti, whether scatological or otherwise. Example:

He who writes on shithouse walls,
Rolls his shit in little balls.
And he who reads these words of wit,
Eats those little balls of shit.

History of Graffiti

Graffiti of all sorts have had a long if not entirely honorable history. Recent archaeological efforts on the coast of France have revealed caves, submerged beneath the encroaching seas for perhaps tens of thousands of years, their walls filled with the arcane products of Paleolithic graffitists. In the Great Basin region of the American West are numerous examples of ancient graffiti, called petroglyphs, presumably recording on the walls of cliffs and canyons the comings and goings of some of the New World's earliest human inhabitants. Best known among the graffiti of antiquity are those from the walls of the city of Pompeii, providing a written account of some of the everyday concerns of Roman subjects. Indeed, the ironic inscription of a Pompeiian graffitist, circa 79 C.E., illustrates how common was the event of graffiti writing:

Oh wall, so many men have come here to scrawl,
I wonder that your burdened sides don't fall.

Among the most thorough and entertaining collections of historical graffiti is the anthology *The Merry-Thought or the Glass-Window Bog-House Miscellany*, published by Hurlo Thrumbo in 1731. Thrumbo transcribed the latrinalia of early 18th-century London inns and taverns to preserve the wisdom and wit that managers of those establishments so callously obliterated with scrub brushes or fresh coats of paint. Despite their quaint turns of phrase, many of Thrumbo's entries demonstrate the same scatological content inscribed frequently in modern toilet stalls:

You are eas'd in your Body,
And pleas'd in your Mind,
That you leave both a Turd and some Verses behind;
But to me, which is worse, I can't tell, on my Word
The reading your Verses, or smelling your Turd.

Interpretations of Graffiti Content

Relatively little empirical research has been conducted regarding the thematic content of graffiti. The psychiatrist Lomas has suggested that the obscene nature of much graffiti has been responsible for this reluctance on the part of most serious students of human behavior to look into the subject. In 1935, Read, an English-language scholar, provided the first rigorous account of American graffiti. Read's interest in graffiti was sparked by a sightseeing trip through western North America, during which he made use of numerous public toilet facilities. Inspired by the varieties of graffiti content and style he observed, Read compiled an extensive glossary that he hoped would contribute to the study of colloquial linguistics.

In 1953, perhaps somewhat in emulation of Read, sexologist Alfred Kinsey and his associates published a study of sex differences in the content of graffiti collected from men's and women's public toilets across the United States. Since Kinsey, a few other social scientists have explored graffiti as unobtrusive, nonreactive indicators of various human attitudes. For example, Sechrest and Flores employed graffiti to measure differences in American and Philippine attitudes toward homosexuality, and Olowu examined similar attitudinal differences in British and Nigerian graffiti. Rudin and Harless explored the sensitivity of graffiti content to current social and political events, and Stocker and his associates provided evidence that graffiti content changes reliably with changes in the political orientations of the population to which graffitists belong.

Sexual Graffiti

Graffiti, especially of the private sort, have the common reputation of dealing overwhelmingly with sexual and scatological topics. Even the graffiti of ancient times seem to be rich in obscenities, sexual insults, and lewd solicitations. Dundes exemplified these recurrent graffiti themes in the very title in his 1966 paper, a play on one of the most familiar of all graffiti verses:

> Here I sit all broken hearted
> Came to shit and only farted.

Not surprisingly, then, a large proportion of graffiti research has been devoted to the analysis of its sexual and scatological content in general, as well as to explications of apparent differences in sexual content between graffiti written by men and those written by women. In his pioneering study of female sexuality, Kinsey reported that men wrote far more graffiti than did women and that most of what was written by women was romantic in content, whereas male-produced graffiti typically had erotic themes. Kinsey attributed these results to basic biosexual differences, such as that women innately have more respect for social conventions than do men. He also noted that three-fourths of all the male graffiti he collected had homosexual content, a fact he attributed not so much to literal preference for homosexuality by the graffitists as to their sublimations of latent homosexual conflicts.

The Freudian perspective reflected in Kinsey's analysis has been a common one with regard to the etiology and characteristics of graffiti. Ernest Jones, a noted Freud biographer, has suggested that public graffiti, such as initials carved on trees, are sublimated forms of the infantile impulse to play with feces. Landy and Steele reached a similar Freudian conclusion in their 1967 study of private-graffiti frequency as a function of college-building utilization. They discovered that women's restrooms contained not only more ashtrays but also many more cigarette butts than were found in men's restrooms, and they suggested that the relative scarcity of graffiti in those same women's restrooms might have been because women are more likely to "smoke out" their unconscious fecal impulses. Dundes provided an even more daring, neo-Freudian analysis of graffiti content. He hypothesized that men inevitably are more likely to write latrinalia than are women because of the psychological process of pregnancy envy. According to Dundes, the act of defecation is the male analogue of childbirth, and the writing of graffiti, especially sexual or scatological, while defecating is a symbolic substitute for the birth of a child.

Other investigators also have noted substantial differences in the frequency and content of men's and women's latrinalia. Stocker and coauthors found that the occurrence of female-produced toilet graffiti on college campuses was very rare, owing, they believed, to different socialization processes that suppressed women's needs for self-expression. Lomas reported that women's restroom graffiti are both "sparse and unimaginative." The preponderance of male-produced graffiti, he argued, is a manifestation of the characteristically male need to have an outlet for potentially destructive fantasies. Presumably because women lack the aggressive hormonal constitution of men, they also have less inherent need to deface property.

The majority of pre-1975 investigations concluded that men write far more graffiti than do women; that male-produced graffiti are much more likely to have erotic sexual content, in general, and homosexual content, in particular; and that these differences may be attributed to fundamental, largely biological differences between men and women. More recent studies in a variety of social contexts, however, have revealed profound changes in the nature of American graffiti that may inform new interpretations.

In 1975, Farr and Gordon collected graffiti from the restrooms on and around a major Eastern university campus. They discovered that women had written 50 percent more graffiti than had men overall, that women had written three times as many graffiti with sexual content, and that more than two-fifths of the women's sexual graffiti were erotic in nature. In their 1976 study of four midwestern public high schools, Wales and Brewer found more than seven times as many graffiti in girls' restrooms as they did in boys' restrooms. Bates and Martin conducted their 1980 research on the campus of a major Eastern state university. Slightly more than half of all the 1,200 graffiti they found in an equal number of men's and women's restrooms had female authorship. Forty percent of the women's graffiti were sexual in content, in contrast to 30 percent of the men's graffiti, and 16 percent of the women's graffiti had homosexual themes, in contrast to 9 percent of the men's graffiti. In 1985, Melhorn and Romig examined the frequencies and themes of male- and female-produced latrinalia found in various taverns and private clubs in the vicinity of a small midwestern university. Slightly more male than female graffiti were collected, but the groups did not differ in percentage of graffiti with sexual content. Moreover, only about one graffito in eight, overall, had a sexual theme, and fewer than one in fifty had homosexual referents.

Who Writes Graffiti?

The most recent research has demonstrated substantial changes from earlier studies, both in the relative frequency of occurrence and the nature of the content of private graffiti. These changes require new interpretations, probably informed by a social-cognitive perspective rather than by a biological or psychosexual perspective. It seems likely that graffiti content varies across time and across cultures, depending on the sorts of issues, values, and conflicts common to the graffitists of a place and time. A remaining question, however, is whether the content of any graffito tells us anything more than what happened to be on the mind of its author at the time of writing. The answer to this question depends on what sort of person it is who is likely to engage in graffiti writing.

Very little is known about the nature of the graffitist. Rhyne and Ullman found in 1972 that as few as one man in 15 may write any graffiti at all and that the presence of graffiti generally may not instigate more graffiti. That is, even when naive subjects are exposed to intentionally provocative graffiti content, very few may choose to respond in kind. Many researchers have found, however, that a number of responses nearly as large as the number of original inscriptions themselves may be observed at a given site. In another vein, Loewenstine and his associates surveyed a large sample of college students in 1982 and found that both men and women judged graffitists to be less mature, although perhaps more humorous, than people in general. Taken together, such results could mean that nearly all graffiti are the products of a small subpopulation whose personality characteristics predispose them to the creating of or the responding to graffiti. Those same predisposing characteristics may make the concerns of the graffitist unrepresentative of the concerns of the larger population.

In contrast to this dismissal of graffiti as the chaotic scratchings of a few social deviants, some communications experts suggest that graffitists represent a kind of psychological and political barometer of a society, much in the same way as legitimate artists. Bates and Martin, for example, hypothesized that current differences in the frequency and content of American male- and female-produced graffiti might be due both to women's increased awareness of their sexual, economic, and political status and to their lack of real power to effect change. Loewenstine similarly concluded that "graffiti may be a manifestation of power differences between the sexes." That women tend to write more issue-oriented and advice-seeking graffiti than do men, whereas men are more likely to write about more superficial aspects of everyday life (e.g., sports, humor, scatology), may be because men have the political and economic power to create the issues, and women, even modern American women, have the power only to write about them.

Graffiti can be entertaining, disturbing, insulting, or annoying to those who read them, and they are outright aggravating to those whose task it is to erase them from view. They may be the products of a sort of comic, arrested adolescence, but they also are the products of a larger social-historical context. In this regard, Dundes has argued that graffiti properly should be considered to be components of a culture's folklore. As such, graffiti may provide eloquent expressions of a society's attitudes and values, as transmitted to and by the otherwise anonymous masses. Given the potential of graffiti as mirrors of ourselves, it would seem prudent for social scientists to continue and to expand investigations of graffiti content.

REFERENCES

Abel, E.L., and B.E. Buckley. *The Handwriting on the Wall*. Westport, Conn.: Greenwood Press, 1977.

Bates, J.A., and M. Martin. The Thematic Content of Graffiti as a Nonreactive Indicator of Male and Female Attitudes. *Journal of Sex Research*, Vol. 16 (1980), pp. 300–15.

Dundes, A. Here I Sit—A Study of American Latrinalia. *Kroeber Anthropological Society Papers*, Vol. 34 (1966), pp. 91–105.

Farr, J.H., and C. Gordon. A Partial Replication of Kinsey's Graffiti Study. *Journal of Sex Research*, Vol. 11 (1975), pp. 158–62.

Kinsey, A., W.B. Pomeroy, C.E. Martin, and P.H. Gebhard. *Sexual Behavior in the Human Female*. Philadelphia: Saunders, 1953.

Landy, E.E., and J.M. Steele. Graffiti as a Function of Building Utilization. *Perceptual and Motor Skills*, Vol. 25 (1967), pp. 711–12.

Loewenstine, H.V., G.D. Ponticos, and M.A. Paludi. Sex Differences in Graffiti as a Communication Style. *Journal of Social Psychology*, Vol. 117 (1982), pp. 307–08.

Lomas, H.D. Graffiti: Some Observations and Speculations. *Psychoanalytic Review*, Vol. 60 (1973), pp. 71–89.

Melhorn, J.J., and R.J. Romig. Rest Room Graffiti: A Descriptive Study. *Emporia State Research Studies*, Vol. 34 (1985), pp. 29–45.

Olowu, A.A. Graffiti Here and There. *Psychological Reports*, Vol. 52 (1983), p. 986.

Read, A.W. *Lexical Evidence from Folk Epigraphy in Western North America*. Privately published. Paris, 1935.

Rhyne, L.D., and L.P. Ullman. Graffiti: A Nonreactive Measure? *Psychological Record*, Vol. 22 (1972), pp. 255–58.

Rudin, L.A., and M.D. Harless. Graffiti and Building Use: The 1968 Election. *Psychological Reports*, Vol. 27 (1970), pp. 517–18.

Sechrest, L., and L. Flores. Homosexuality in the Philippines and the United States: The Handwriting on the Wall. *Journal of Social Psychology*, Vol. 79 (1969), pp. 3–12.

Stocker, T.L., L.W. Dutcher, S.M. Hargrove, and E.A. Cook. Social Analysis of Graffiti. *Journal of American Folklore*, Vol. 85 (1972), pp. 356–66.

Wales, E., and B. Brewer. Graffiti in the 1970's. *Journal of Social Psychology*, Vol. 99 (1976), pp. 115–23.

John A. Bates

GREEKS: SEXUAL CUSTOMS OF THE ANCIENT GREEKS

The ancient Greeks developed a system virtually unique among literate peoples for educating upper-class youth—institutionalized pederasty. There is no evidence for pederasty among the Mycenean Greeks. After the collapse of their civilization during the dark age (1200–800 B.C.E.) and also during the early archaic or renaissance (800–630 B.C.E.), society was enthusiastically if not exclusively heterosexual, as the Homeric and Hesiodic corpuses reveal. But for about a millennium, starting around 600 B.C.E., most upper-class Greek males, forbidden or strongly discouraged from marrying in their 20s, took adolescent boys as their beloveds. In his early 20s, a young aristocrat, the lover (*erastes*), took a boy of 12 the beloved (*eromenos*), to love and train, before going on at about age 30 to matrimony and fatherhood. Then the boy, now grown and having completed compulsory military training himself, in turn took another boy to love and train. Most passed through these homosexual phases, passive and then active, for nearly 20 years (from puberty at 12–14 to age 30). Whatever the amount and kind of physical homosexual intercourse they experienced, if any (and it seems to have varied), they grew up without any special psychological problems. Greek pederasty was believed by the Greeks to have positive benefits, in that it fostered heroism as well as genius.

The writer of this article puts forth the following theses about Greek pederastic practices, some of which are more controversial than others: (1) that the Golden Age of Greek civilization was largely due to pederastic pedagogy and its concomitant institutions, gymnasia (for nude athletics) and symposia (elegant dinner and drinking parties); (2) that this system of institutionalized pederasty began in the late seventh century B.C.E., much later than most have thought; (3) that Cretan lawgivers, or "musicians" (those devoted to the Muses), created the system to control the upper-class population explosion as well as to train and bond warriors, and that it spread rapidly to almost all of the rest of Hellas; (4) that the scantiness of explicit sources, many of which were destroyed by Christian zealots, has helped homophobic historians and classicists to ignore, deny, distort, and condemn Greek pederasty and to exaggerate the criticism of carnal pederasty that a few ancient pagan ascetics, most importantly Plato, made, while downplaying the praise that most others bestowed on it; (5) that homophiles have generally confused Greek pederasty with modern androphilia to justify the latter, while social constructionists now deny that homosexuality (in the sense of more or less exclusive androphilia) even existed in ancient times.

As Friedrich Nietzsche long ago realized, the Greek system of pederastic pedagogy was an indispensable ingredient of the Greeks' unparalleled achievements: "The erotic relations of men with adolescents were, as far as our intelligence can understand, the necessary condition, and the unique one, for all masculine education [in Greece]. Never probably have youths been treated with so much solicitude, affection, and regard to their best qualities as in the sixth and fifth century . . . since mortals in love give the best of themselves."

Some moderns, following Plato, Xenophon, and Plutarch, have theoretized about the usefulness of homoerotic attraction in teaching and in male bonding. In *Eros* (1921), the first work on the subject in the pederastic tradition in both theory and practice, the German educator Gustav Adolph Wyneken even advocated the resurrection of Greek pederasty to improve the educational system of his day. His work is an apologia for pederasty that stresses the aspects of mentoring and character formation. The positive but informal (not sanctioned by the authorities) role of pederasty in public schools and universities in England and in their all-male American equivalents, as well as on the Continent, has often been noted.

The sources of Greek pederasty have been much debated, but it seems clear that pederasty was not institutionalized by illiterates, whether primitive Indo-Europeans, wandering Dorian warriors, or garrisons in dark age castles. Various types of situational homosexuality in Hellas doubtless existed in early times, but on the basis of the surviving evidence, Greek pederasty derived from the Cretans, desirous of controlling the population explosion, who ordained a set of recognized legal and social norms governing the relationship between *erastes* and *eromenos*. Concomitants to institutionalized pederasty were segregation or seclusion of upper-class women, athletic nudity of males, late marriage of males, and men's messes or all-male symposia. Only in Crete were boys abducted by their lovers, and only in Crete and Sparta did "herds" (agelai) of teenage boys live in gangs in the wild. The rigid age-class organization of those militaristic societies was not so strictly followed by the other, more relaxed city-states.

Precariousness of food and other necessities, as was experienced in the Aegean region, where insufficient rainfall often caused crop failure, can render growth dangerous, as it did especially after 600 B.C.E., when the population had expanded exponentially. Anal or oral intercourse with women, abortion, infanticide, lengthy postpartum sex taboos, and even bestiality help limit population to available resources. In overcrowded societies, homosexuality itself, as well as delayed marriage, can also be functional in reducing births as well as in providing helpful uncles or other mentoring males without children of their own. Concern about numbers has often influenced attitudes toward homosexuality, whether or not encouragement, toleration, or prohibition actually affects the birth rate.

Modern scholarship has strikingly confirmed the existence of a demographic explosion in archaic Greece. Some would put the multiple as high as 12 from 800 to 500 B.C.E., a rate very rarely so long sustained in any period in history. Summarizing theories about demography and ecology, Sallares argued that the population explosion, most intense in the eighth century, when population increased sevenfold, as one eminent archeologist concluded from grave sites, tapered off to reach the maximum sustainable in the fourth century. He believed that delayed marriages and the age-class system with its pederasty, which he dated to the second half of the first millennium, helped to keep the population in check. The establishment of colonies after 800 B.C.E. and the deaths from wars and plagues did not sufficiently diminish the pressing need for more resources. The shift from the meat diet of the Homeric heroes to one of cereals in classical times, from expensive animal proteins to cheap grains, is a clear proof of the scarcity of foodstuffs. One tight little Aegean island, Ceos, ordered those who reached 60 to drink hemlock.

Another, Thera, forced some inhabitants to emigrate to the forbidding Libyan shore. The cruel results of overpopulation induced desperate leaders to experiment socially.

A number of ancients, foremost among whom was Aristotle, believed that archaic Cretan sages had institutionalized pederasty to curb the population. These "musicians" evolved a system of interlocking institutions centered on delayed marriage and pedagogical pederasty to hold down the birthrate of "knights" (about 1 percent or 2 percent of the total population) so that their heirs would not overly subdivide their estates, while improving their military training. Each young mounted warrior ritually kidnapped an aristocratic boy of 12 to love and train, dubbed on Crete "the renowned one" to distinguish him from a boy not yet chosen, an "obscure one."

Following the Cretan initiative, it seems probable that other Greeks soon institutionalized pederasty. During or just after the great crisis caused by the revolt of their serfs (helots) in the Second Messenian War (635–615 B.C.E.), Spartans adapted these Cretan institutions designed for cavalry to a wider segment of the population (about 10 percent), the substantial landowners able to afford the expensive heavy armor (cheaper than war horses) and weaponry of the new-style elite infantryman, the hoplite. Because in the phalanx each hoplite's huge shield protected the exposed right of the man on his right, this military reformation, which made knights obsolete on the mainland, required more coordination and male bonding than heroic cavalry charges had. In Crete and Sparta as well as in Elis and Boeotia, which were also agrarian and inward looking, pederastic pedagogy, which concentrated on gymnastics and on instilling courage, inspired heroes, warriors, and athletes rather than scholars and artists.

In Sparta, females, who seemed to have exercised more influence than elsewhere in the Greek world, had more freedom to move about unchaperoned and also received physical training. They married at 18, instead of 15 to 16 as in most other poleis. Spartan husbands, many of whom were apparently accustomed to pederastic relations before marriage, often sodomized their wives, beginning to do so even on the wedding night. The female choruses and other groups of virgins that were most famous in Sparta and on the isle of Lesbos may well have loved one another or their lady leaders, as attested by Sappho's and Alcman's poetry, but we are otherwise hardly informed about this female counterpart of male pederasty. In fact, we scarcely know anything about women's feelings and opinions, because we have no writings of any significance from any Greek woman except Sappho, who, like Homer, may merely have been a name appended to a collection that evolved orally over a long period. Naturally, lower-class women, in contrast to the secluded women of Athens and the Ionian cities, who could go out unchaperoned only very rarely, went out to work regularly.

Greeks believed that pederasty succeeded in diminishing the upper-class population explosion, which is what the rulers worried about. They did not mind if there were more serfs. They worried that their own estates would be overly subdivided by their heirs. Delayed marriage meant that far fewer families were formed by men of 30 than of 20, because many males perished in that interval. Approximately half of the 30-year-old grooms would die by 55, before those of their wives who survived childbirth had their menopause, at about 35. The average Greek marriage would have lasted considerably less than 20 years, and the average wife would have been widowed in her mid-30s. Upper-class widowers tended to remarry, but of upper-class wives only heiresses normally did so. If a child was conceived every two years, as might have happened if wet nurses were employed, this would have produced seven to nine offspring, whereas in fact the average seems to have been only five or six, half of whom might have died before maturity even if not too many were exposed at birth. Unlike famous Romans, famous Greeks after the institutionalization of pederasty rarely had many grown brothers or sisters. Because infanticide or abandonment of females may have been excessive, there may have been approximately as many brides of 15 as bridegrooms of 30. In contrast, Roman aristocrats, who at 17 on average married girls of 12 or 13, had larger families because they married earlier and practiced less infanticide, especially of males.

No polis, not even Sparta—in many ways the most static and conservative after it received its "Lycurgan" constitution, making it a militaristic oligarchy supported by helots, with delayed marriages and institutionalized pederasty—had a permanent, unvarying policy on birth control. Each city-state varied the rules about ages and conditions of marriage, according either to shortages of people during wars, pestilences, or famines, or to surpluses. Given to rational conduct, perhaps more than any other peoples of whom we know, Greeks adjusted sexual customs such as ages at marriage to make population conform to needs. Absentmindedly, Plato prescribed three different ages for males in his *Laws* (24 to 30), and Aristotle recommended age 37.

The Ionian maritime tyrannies and oligarchies of Miletus, Euboea, and Samos, and the neighboring Aeolic port of Mytilene, first adapted for mental instruction the system developed for physical, martial, and character training in militaristic Crete and Sparta, that is, the one-to-one tutorial between an *erastes* and *eromenos*. Beginning around 600 B.C.E., poets and philosophers from Aegean ports, often dominated by tyrants and enriched by overseas trade, became skeptical and sophisticated. Ionian "physicists," who soon originated Greek prose literature, broke through to rationalism, initiating remarkable progress in science, geography, and history. Aeolian poets exuberantly celebrated pederastic loves.

There is no agreement as to what kind of sexual activity prevailed. While the poets were discreet and ambiguous as to what kind of sex occurred, if any, contemporary graffiti crudely described pedication. Using works on public buildings, sculptors idealized the male nude but rarely portrayed sexual activity. Vase painters, however, frequently depicted intercrural sex, foreplay, and gift giving to boys rather than anal intercourse. Oral-genital sexuality, whether pederastic or heterosexual, was apparently rare and much disapproved, wherever mentioned. The only areas that have produced erotic art on the scale and in proportional numbers to the classical world are pre-Columbian Peru, medieval India, 17th- and 18th-century Japan, and Western Europe from the 18th through the 20th centuries. Only beginning in the fourth century B.C.E. did certain pro-Spartan writers declare that Spartan lovers were chaste. Xenophon proclaimed that "in Sparta there is no more physical love between men and boys than there is between parents and children or brother and brother."

Evidence supports speculation that many other forms of homosexuality also flourished, especially among slaves, *metics* (resident foreigners), and commoners, many of whom had no regular access to women and could often not support families. About such acts and customs we have, however, no evidence whatever for the archaic period. The word *kinaidos,* mentioned by Plato, came to mean a much-disparaged adult male, presumed to be extremely effeminate in gait, manner, and dress, who took the passive role. Male adolescent prostitutes (*pornoi*), first attested to in an archaic graffito on Thera, or more datably in Aristophanes, became common by classical times in Athens and other ports such as Marseilles (Massilia). These boy slaves often labored as prostitutes for pimps, but no master is recorded as having had sex with his own male slave before a lone case in Xenophon's *Symposium* of a middle- or lower-class entertainer and his boy. The prohibition of *pornoi* from addressing the Assembly, ascribed to Solon, the Athenian lawgiver of the first half of the sixth century, may be of later provenance. Cross-dressing shamans common to the steppe peoples, as well as hermaphrodites, appeared in myths and perhaps also in fact. Males isolated in castles or camps or on ships must have indulged with one another in classical times as well as during the dark ages. In any case, such situational acts probably did not reorient men's preferences once they were back in the company of females. Consequently, they are of less importance than upper-class institutionalized pederasty.

Entrenched in gymnasia and symposia, which developed along with it, institutionalized pederasty prevailed among upper-class Greeks for a millennium, until the Christians outlawed all forms of what they came to execrate as "sodomitic vice." Providing each boy a devoted tutor, pederastic pedagogy might well have helped make Greeks the most creative of peoples. Historians have often noted that competitiveness was already evident in the Homeric epics, but the introduction of nude gymnastics—with all males of rank discarding their garments, thus underscoring the equality among gym mates—which came in with pederasty, heightened it. Erudite conversations between lovers in symposia and gymnasia, where many of Plato's dialogues are set, encouraged not only scholarship but also creativity in general. Even the Homeric and Hesiodic corpuses, which evolved orally before the institutionalization of pederasty and the seclusion of women, were probably committed to writing only afterwards, when the stories of the love of Zeus for Ganymede, a boy who never grew up, and the great love between Achilles and Patroclus were perhaps interpolated. Although the latter two were actually of the same age, Greeks of classical and later times perceived them as age-asymmetrical lovers, never agreeing as to who was the *erastes* and who the *eromenos*.

The Greeks themselves recognized that what separated them from "barbarians," as they condescendingly called all other people, however civilized, who did not share their language and institutions, was devotion to logic, nude athletics, and their peculiar brand of pederasty designed to instruct noble boys. More than two centuries after most Greeks adapted the Cretan innovations to local needs, Plato distinguished classical Hellenic from despotic "barbarian" civilization: "For the barbarians because of the rule of despots call this [pederasty] ugly, as well as philosophy and nude sports; I suppose it is profitable to their rulers that the subjects should not be great in spirit or make strong friendships and unions, which things love is wont to implant more than anything else" (*Symposium* 182b). Persians and Jews, whose religions apodictically condemned pederasty, were shocked by the Greek practices. While not prohibiting them, Romans did remark about the strangeness of Greek nudity and pederasty, which those devoted to the *mos maiorum* (ancestral customs) considered degenerate.

Greek historians and biographers mentioned numerous pairs of lovers who sacrificed themselves for each other or for their city's welfare, or inspired one another to extreme bravery in battle because each wished to be worthy of the highest praise in the other's eyes. Tyrants, who dominated so many poleis between 650 and 550 B.C.E., came to fear assassination by heroic pederastic couples. Bonding its citizens more than any other state, Sparta, the nemesis of tyrants, which compelled every young warrior to oversee a boy's education before marrying, became invincible in sport and war.

Athens, ruled first by pederastic tyrants and then by other pederasts who introduced democracy, became the greatest Hellenic metropolis by defeating the Persians, who had occupied Ionia. By then, most upper-class Greek boys, except in such "backward" semi-Hellenized regions as Epirus and Macedonia, and perhaps also in mountainous Aetolia and Arcadia, which only adopted the institutions after 400, had a devoted tutor, whom he in turn often loved, to inspire him mentally as well as morally. Pederasty in the service of the intellect climaxed in the late archaic and classical age, in Athens, which had become the "school of Hellas," as its greatest statesman Pericles bragged in 430. *Paiderasteia,* as the Victorian homophile scholar John Addington Symonds observed, "at Athens was closely associated with liberty, manly sports, severe studies, enthusiasm, self-sacrifice, self-control, and deeds of daring, by those who cared for such things." Like most other aspects of life, it was in Athens, as in Ionia, more voluntary and less regimented than in Crete, Sparta, or certain other Dorian societies.

A few Greeks began to criticize pederasty when the institution was still new. Before the end of the sixth century B.C.E., tyrants from time to time closed gymnasia out of fear that they would become centers of conspiracy, and the Persians, after they seized Ionia, began to criticize, suppress, and perhaps outlaw pederasty.

Claiming that man was the measure of all things and that they could make the better seem the worse, fifth-century sophists, whether refugees from such persecutors or merely drawn to Athens by its wealth and freedom, its gymnasia and symposia, and its devotion to and subsidization of culture, increasingly undermined the commitment to character training and morality that previous patriotic pederastic masters had demanded. To restore civic order and personal morality, Socrates and Plato counterattacked, insisting on absolutes. They defended love between males but demanded "tasteful" limitation or, better still, like Xenophon, total sublimation of the sex drive. The older Plato, who in his earlier dialogues tolerated limited physical relationships, in his *Laws* denounced any physical contact between *erastai* and *eromenoi,* as well as sex between females, as contrary to nature.

After the Spartans seized Thebes, pederastic exiles who fled to Athens later reinfiltrated and liberated their city. The plotters organized the Sacred Band of 150 pairs of lovers who, under their leader Epaminondas, inflicted such severe losses on the previously invincible Spartan phalanx in two crucial battles that Sparta never made them good. Many homophile scholars, such as Symonds, have concluded that the great age of Greek pederasty ended at Chaeronea in 338 B.C.E., when the Sacred Band died to the last man fighting heroically against the overwhelming forces of Philip of Macedon, who ended Greek liberty, but actually pederasty continued to be a part of Greek life long afterwards.

The lethal internecine wars of the late fifth and fourth centuries, along with famines and plagues that accompanied them, may have eventually been even more efficacious in checking the population than pederasty and its concomitant institutions. After the great losses due to the wars and colonization of Alexander the Great (d. 323 B.C.E.) and of the Diadochi (his successors) ended, the Greek population on the mainland seems to have continued to decline, especially in Sparta. The greatest historian of the Hellenistic period, Polybius, explained this decline, which was very apparent even in his native Achaea, by the refusal of many men, apparently of all classes, to marry. Many moderns have attributed the Spartiate decline, the most acute, to pederasty, but most ancients blamed it on poverty, which removed Spartiates from full citizenship.

In spite of criticism by philosophers from Socrates on, many Greeks continued to love boys. In the Hellenistic age, when boys were trained more and more for membership in the *oecumene* rather than in the polis, pederasty did indeed lose some of its original civic, social, and educational raison d'être. The Greek romances of imperial times, which have lost Hellenistic prototypes, even began to stress the love of females. But Greek creativity as well as heroism went on. Increased contacts with Egypt and the Near East, which the Greeks now ruled, inspired or underlay extraordinary advances in literature, art, and philosophy as well as in medicine, science, and engineering. The Museum and Library of Alexandria, both sponsored by the Ptolemaic kings of Egypt, descended from Alexander's general and cousin, became a hothouse for philosophers and astronomers. In this "chickencoop," as a contemporary dubbed the Museum, the leading scholars, who often quarreled with each other over the pecking order, penned pederastic verses.

As in classical times, the *eromenos* often succeeded the *erastes* as head of the Athenian philosophical schools, including the Platonic Academy and Aristotelian Lyceum as well as the newer Stoa. Many if not most upper-class Greeks continued to practice pederasty until Christian condemnation combined with an economic decline impoverished gymnasia, left little surplus to finance symposia, and destroyed them after about a millennium. Particularly in the teeming cities of the East, Greeks may have imitated the sexual habits of others, such as loving eunuchs, transvestites, and other effeminates. In the homeland, some middle- and lower-class Greeks may have picked up the pederastic practices formerly restricted to the noble classes.

The collection of verses known as the *Greek* or *Palatine Anthology* attests the persistence of boy love to the reign of the Christian emperor Justinian (527–565 C.E.), whose *Corpus Juris Civilis* prescribed burning for sodomites, and who accused them of causing "earthquakes, famines, and plagues." Its greatest contributor, Strato of Sardis, who lived in the second century C.E., proclaimed:

> I delight in the prime of a boy of twelve, but one of thirteen is much more desirable. He who is fourteen is a still sweeter flower of the Loves, and one who is just beginning his fifteenth year is yet more delightful. The sixteenth year is that of the gods, and as for the seventeenth it is not for me, but for Zeus, to seek it. But if one has a desire for those still older, he no longer plays, but now seeks "And answering him back" [to reciprocate, for the boy to exchange active and passive roles with his lover] (XII, 4).

Christians as far back as Tatian in the second century, as well as Marxists, feminists, and other critics, have pointed out that many aspects of

Greek civilization were indeed detestable: cruelty on the battlefield, slavery and serfdom, misogyny, sexism, seclusion of women, xenophobia bordering on racism, elitism, and class distinctions approaching, in certain states, caste divisions. But what civilization before modern times avoided these vices more than the Greeks did? And how many of these criticisms can be blamed on pederasty? Slavery was widespread in the ancient world with or without pederasty.

Keuls blamed pederasty for Athenian misogyny, but Greek misogyny predated pederasty. Women had their place in Greek society, but it was not a particularly high one. As Demosthenes said: "Mistresses we keep for the sake of pleasure, concubines for the daily care of our persons, but wives to bear us legitimate children and to be faithful guardians of our households" (*Against neaera*, 122). In any case, misogyny among the Greeks predated their institutionalization of pederasty, as shown most strikingly in Hesiod's *Works and Days*. Both may have originated from shortages of goods or of land owing to overpopulation. The difference between Greeks and literate "barbarians" was not that the Greeks had these shortcomings and the others did not, but rather that the Greeks made so many breakthroughs in almost every field of arts, letters, sciences, and politics, while practicing philosophy, nude athletics, and pederasty.

One of the more fascinating historiographical problems is the refusal of so many in the past to report Greek pederasty accurately. Classical literature, which presents the strongest case for a successful form of pederasty among urbanized literates, was bowdlerized. Passages that could not be ignored were reinterpreted to claim that Greek pederasty consisted solely in contemplation of the boy's beauty and entailed no overt sexual contact whatever. In fact, until recently, the majority of those who exalted the so-called Greek miracle denied the existence or at best minimized the role of pederasty.

Increasingly, there is acceptance of a thesis summarized by Dover, who radically changed his opinions between his 1976 book and his 1988 one, that Greek "homosexuality" began late and diffused rapidly by around 600 B.C.E., and that poets and artists then first began to inject homosexual episodes into older myths. Recent scholarship has supported the findings of some of the homophile researchers of the 19th and early 20th centuries, beginning with Heinrich Hoeseli in the 1830s, who described Greek pederasty positively, although few scholars today would accept the analyses on which they and their contemporary critics relied. A host of new reconstructions are being forged out of the crucible into which the old ones were cast when they were discarded. Nagy, for example, has recently argued persuasively that, like Homer, all the other early Greek poets are merely names attached to corpuses that evolved orally: Hesiod, all the other archaic epic writers, and also the early lyricists, including, notably, Terpander ("he who pleases"); Sappho, Alcman, Alcaeus, and Stesichorus ("leader of the chorus"); the early elegists (except Solon), including Callinus, Tyrtaeus, Theognis, and Mimnermus; and the early iambists from Archilochus to Hipponax. Thus, Sappho recedes from history, and a group of males in symposia developed and passed on the lyrics ascribed to her, while a group of females in a chorus, perhaps with female leaders, developed and transmitted the choral odes ascribed to Alcman. One might almost say that Sappho was a group of males and Alcman was a group of females.

Still, no one as yet has succeeded in devising an acceptable conception of the origins or role of pederasty in classical Greece to accord with recent discoveries in archaeology, linguistics, demography, epigraphy, papyrology, biology, and psychiatry. Nevertheless, it is clear that pederasty was deeply imbedded in the Greek culture, although it must be clearly distinguished from later concepts such as sodomy, buggery, sexual inversion, homosexuality, gay, and queer. A proper understanding of Greek history should help to discredit homophobia as such and even the especially virulent hatred of homosexual pederasty, its most persecuted but historically most prevalent variation.

REFERENCES

Bethe, E. Die dorische Knabenliebe: Ihre Ethik und ihre Idee. *Rheinisches Museum für Philologie*, Vol. 62 (1907), pp. 438–75.

Bremmer, J. An Enigmatic Indo-European Rite: Paederasty. *Arethusa*, Vol. 13 (1980), pp. 279–98.

Buffière, F. *Eros aolescent: la pédérasty dans la Grèce antique*. Paris: Les Belles Lettres, 1980.

Bullough, V.L. *Sexual Variance in Society and History*. Chicago: Univ. of Chicago Press, 1976.

Dover, K.J. *Greek Homosexuality*. New York: Oxford Univ. Press, 1978.

———. *The Greeks and Their Legacy*. Oxford: Oxford Univ. Press, 1988.

Foucault, M. *The History of Sexuality*. 3 vols. New York: Pantheon, 1986.

Halperin, D.M. *One Hundred Years of Homosexuality: And Other Essays on Greek Love*. New York: Routledge, 1990.

Keuls, E.E. *The Reign of the Phallus: Sexual Politics in Ancient Athens*. New York: Harper & Row, 1985.

Licht, H. *Sexual Life in Ancient Greece*. London: Routledge & Kegan Paul, 1932.

Marrou, H.I. *A History of Education in Antiquity*. Madison: Univ. of Wisconsin Press, 1956.

Nagy, G. *Pindar's Homer*. Baltimore: Johns Hopkins Univ. Press, 1990.

Pogey-Castries, L.R. *Histoire de l'Amour grec dans l'antiquité*. Paris: Stendhal, 1930.

Sallares, R. *The Ecology of the Ancient Greek World*. Ithaca, N.Y.: Cornell Univ. Press, 1991.

Sergent, B. *Homosexuality in Greek Myth*. Boston: Beacon Press, 1986.

————. *L'homosexualité initiatique dans l'Europe ancienne*. Paris: Payot, 1986.

Symonds, J.A. *A Problem in Greek Ethics*. London: n.p., 1883.

William A. Percy

GUILT: SEX GUILT

Guilt is a reflexive emotional response when the self judges itself as culpable of violating internalized standards of morality. This is an important factor in human sexuality, since traditional standards of morality prohibit many forms of sexual activity, specifying both immoral sexual objects and immoral sexual acts. Within Western culture, these exclusionary sexual standards limit sexual activity to coitus in the missionary position with a monogamous marital partner for procreative purposes, and though commitment should be involved, passionate love or ecstasy should not. Sex is to be neither passionately hedonic nor passionately romantic, since either might interfere with duty to God and God's laws. It is the moral residue from Paul's teaching that it is better to marry than to burn, but it is best to be chaste and celibate.

Thus, in traditional morality, all sexual linkages and all sexual objects except procreative, marital coitus in the missionary position are proscribed. Deviant or immoral sexual acts include childhood sexual play (looking, touching, exploring), sexual fantasy and pornography (imagining, watching, reading), nonmarital heterosexuality (kissing, petting, fornication, and adultery), and sodomy ("unnatural" sexual acts, including touching and fondling breasts, thighs, buttocks, and genitals; women mounted above men or the like in coitus; oral sex; or anal sex) even in marriage. Bans on contraception and abortion highlight that the sexual linkage is to be procreative, and, whether the linkage is marital or non-marital, "innocent" life is to be saved. Immoral sex with deviant objects includes incest; cross-race, -caste, -class, or -kinship sex; sex with demons; adult-child sex; simultaneous or sequential multi-partner sex; prostitution; homosexuality; bestiality; and masturbation.

Traditional morality assumes that such sexual linkages with such sexual objects are sinful and corrupting. At best, they threaten to corrupt the character of the participants, placing them on a slippery slope of sexual sin, where each unnatural act invariably leads to greater debauchery. At worst, they threaten the natural moral order by polluting natural social categories through immoral sexual linkages and by threatening to disintegrate the natural world and its God-given order. These traditional beliefs are the residue of beliefs in demonology as expressed through witchcraft.

Although all Americans do not accept these traditional standards, they remain the point of view, the frame, or the context in which the description, the picture, or the meaning of sexuality is understood. Shifting sexual standards are measured against the traditional moral code. For example, the contemporary marital sexual standard includes many more sexual activities than procreative coitus in the missionary position, and almost any sexual activity may go on between consenting marital partners. However, male preferences may determine what the couple does in a society with a double standard and a hierarchy of gender dominance. Another contemporary community standard is that love justifies the choice of sexual partner and the choice of varied sexual acts. Enjoyment and orgasmic release during any sexual episode have come to be expected, even for women. Contemporary community opinions are divided on the moral acceptability of masturbation, homosexuality, nonmarital heterosexual activity, cross-racial sex, pornography, contraception, and abortion. Still largely taboo are incest, adult-child sex, child-child sexual play, prostitution, and bestiality. Coerced or nonconsenting sexual acts are prohibited by both law and morality.

Sexual guilt is defined as self-mediated control that either prevents one from violating internalized standards of moral sexual behavior or generates remorseful feelings of self-blame after one has violated sexual standards. Psychologists regard sexual guilt as both a personality disposition and an affect. Imagining, participating, or remembering violating a sexual standard triggers both the affect of guilt (the emotion or experiential feeling of guilt itself) and the personality disposition that seeks to avoid, manage, defend, or undo the violation of the sexual standard.

In psychological research, the personality disposition of sex guilt is measured by self-reports on inventories developed by Mosher inquiring about sexual beliefs, standards, actions, and emotions. For example, a participant in such research might choose between two alternatives: (a) sexual relations before marriage are wrong and immoral, or (b) sexual relations before marriage were frequent and fun. Scores summed across a set of items inquiring about childhood sexual experiences, sexual relations before marriage, adultery, and sociosexual guilt are used to define the magnitude of the dispositions to sex guilt within a sample of individuals.

Psychological research demonstrated that individuals disposed to sex guilt have engaged in fewer advanced nonmarital sexual activities (e.g., coitus or oral sex) than their less guilty contemporaries. They had less sex with fewer partners, believing premarital sex to be immoral and reporting that they did or would feel guilty for engaging in sexual activities.

Not only are guilty individuals not to engage in sex; they are not to imagine sex or respond to sexual stimuli. Feelings of guilt were reported by high-sex-guilt individuals following exposure to self-generated sexual fantasies or to presentations of explicit sexual materials. Pornography activated sexual excitement and sexual disgust; many of the sexual acts and sexual objects were regarded as abnormal.

Apparently because of the differential socialization of gender, men scored lower on sex guilt than women. Thus, many sexual activities were more desired and accepted by men than women before marriage. Moreover, men's sexual desire and levels of sex guilt affected the decision to have coitus within dating couples more than did the level of sex guilt in women. The traditional socialization of women places them in a bind: they are to uphold restrictive sexual standards, to submit to men, and to make relationships endure as a gender norm.

Although high-sex-guilt women were more reluctant to engage in premarital sex, use contraception, or seek abortions, they faced these dilemmas relatively unprepared. Because of their traditional sexual standards, having sex was unplanned (since they cannot plan to sin, they must be overcome by love, passion, or persuasion). Less likely to use contraception initially and more likely to delay or avoid using contraception later on than low-sex-guilt women, high-sex-guilt women had more unplanned pregnancies that led to either an unwanted child or an abortion. Were it left up to them, high-sex-guilt subjects would not grant many requests for abortion, particularly following casual sex, because they believe immoral sex should be punished—pre-

sumably an unwanted child fits the sexual crime of casual sex.

Sexually active high-sex-guilt women had difficulty with moral reasoning or with articulating justifications for their traditional law-and-order morality. Their tendency to avoid sex (a taboo) restricted both thought about sexuality and the development of interpersonal skills that come from confronting sexual choices in everyday interactions with peers.

Guilt over masturbation reduced subjective and psychological sexual arousal to sexual materials. Although men masturbated at greater frequencies than women, they remained equally guilty over it, still believing many myths about masturbation and experiencing guilt and disgust over their own masturbation. Women who scored higher on masturbation guilt avoided selecting a diaphragm as a method of contraception, feeling disgusted when they imagined inserting a diaphragm, which—like masturbation—requires touching the genitals. Masturbation guilt apparently produces adverse psychological reactions to having a sexually transmitted disease, including more stress, fear of telling partner, and outbreaks of herpes that are associated with stress. Although masturbation may teach individuals about their own response to sexual pleasure, prepare them for orgasmic response during coitus, and be a safe-sex outlet, it induces guilt in many men and women. Moreover, the more macho men must avoid masturbation as unmanly, increasing the pressure on them to engage in "real" sex, even coercive sex.

A number of studies demonstrated that the disposition to high sex guilt reduced sexual arousal to several forms of explicit sexual material in the laboratory. Such a reduction might follow both from the processes that instigate cognitive concerns about morality (or that avoid sexual fantasy or desire) and from activated shame, guilt, and disgust over explicit sexual material. Believing that they had drunk an alcoholic beverage even when they had not appeared to reduce such cognitive concerns in high-sex-guilt men; they looked at pornography longer; they had fuller penile erections.

Sexologists are concerned about the socialization of sexuality and the moral development of children. Sexual ignorance, myths, and negative affects associated with sexuality do not prepare youths for coping with their sexuality. Sex guilt was associated with lack of sexual information, belief in sexual myths, and traditional moral and gender standards. Sexual dysfunctions are common in marriage, as the inhibiting effects of sexual guilt do not automatically cease with the marital vow; sexual pleasure requires communication and mutual respect. The disposition to sex guilt appears to inhibit sexual arousal; to produce disgust, shame, and guilt; to contribute to sexual ignorance and unwanted pregnancies; and to activate moral condemnation of self and others for moral violations—all without engaging critical ethical reasoning.

Thus, sexual guilt is a rigidly antisexual script that lacks flexibility in judging context and relationship, just as it lacks rationality in moral socialization. The disposition to sexual guilt and the misery of feeling guilty over sexual thoughts, desires, and contacts follow from a punitive socialization of sexuality that seeks to restrict sexuality to narrow channels of moral purity.

Sexual guilt is implicated not only in sexual dysfunctions; it may also play a significant role in the development of paraphilias. More research is needed on this issue. Certainly, we do know that sexual guilt contributes to general depression and to adolescent suicide in reaction to gender dysphoria.

REFERENCES

Kagan, J., and S. Laub. *The Emergence of Morality in Young Children*. Chicago: Univ. of Chicago Press, 1987.

Mosher, D.L. The Development and Multitrait-Multimethod Matrix Analysis of Three Measures of Three Aspects of Guilt. *Journal of Consulting Psychology*, Vol. 30 (1966), pp. 25-29.

———. Sex Differences, Sex Experience, Sex Guilt, and Explicitly Sexual Films. *Journal of Social Issues*, Vol. 29 (1973), pp. 95-112.

Donald L. Mosher

h

HAIRE, NORMAN

Norman Haire (1892–1952), a native Australian, received his degree in medicine at the University of Sydney, moved to London, and opened a practice as a specialist in obstetrics, gynecology, and sexology. He was one of the founders of the first medical birth-control clinics in Great Britain, and in 1922 he served as chairman of the contraceptive section of the International Birth Control Conference in London.

Haire's interest in sex problems started with questions of fertility and sterility but soon covered a much wider field. He visited Magnus Hirschfeld in Berlin and studied briefly with him, and visited many other European countries. He attended the Congress for the International Society for Sexual Research, organized by Albert Moll, but kept in contact with Hirschfeld. Haire was one of the organizers and later an officer of the International Congress of the World League for Sex Reform, whose first officers were Hirschfeld, Havelock Ellis, and August Forel; in 1930, Haire was elected copresident with Magnus Hirschfeld.

After the Nazis came to power, Haire unsuccessfully strove to keep the international sexological movement going. He translated some of Hirschfeld's works and produced his own, including the *Encyclopaedia of Sexual Practice*. He also founded, edited, and financed the *Journal of Sex Education,* which ceased publication after his death in 1952.

REFERENCES

Haire, N., ed. *The Encyclopaedia of Sex Practice*. London: Encyclopaedic Press, 1938.

————. *Sexual Anomalies and Perversion: A Summary of the Works of the Late Magnus Hirschfeld*. London: Encyclopaedic Press, 1938, revised 1952.

Hans Lehfeldt
Connie Christine Wheeler

HERMAPHRODITES

Hermaphroditus, a minor god in the ancient Greek pantheon, was the quintessential androgynous being. According to Greek mythology, Hermaphroditus was the son of the messenger god, Hermes, and Aphrodite, the goddess of love; he became united in one body with a nymph while he was bathing. According to the statue found in Centuripe, Hermaphroditus possessed male genitalia, voluptuously developed female breasts and hips, and soft, feminine facial features. There are many surviving statues and murals from ancient Greece and Rome attesting to the interest shown in this phenomenon by these peoples.

The myth of Hermaphroditus embodies the almost universal belief in the ancient eastern Mediterranean world that sexual attraction is due to the two sexes having originally been one. In his *Symposium*, Plato tells of an ancient time when the world was inhabited by three sexes—males, females, and hermaphrodites. Males had a penis both fore and aft, females had two vaginas, and hermaphrodites had a penis on one side and a vagina on the other. Despite this bounty of organs, reproduction was asexual, being joylessly accomplished by "emission onto the ground, as is the case with grasshoppers." When these proto-humans dared challenge the gods, Zeus had them cut in half lengthwise. Feeling itself an incomplete being, each creature began to yearn for its alter ego. Plato saw in the finding and embracing of one's "better half" the origin of love. Because only the former hermaphrodite creatures had the necessary complement of male and female organs, only they could reproduce; the reuniting of the former male and female spheres resulted in gay and lesbian love.

Hermaphroditism and sex reversal abound among plants and many insects and animals. Earthworms can impregnate or become pregnant—even by themselves—and many narcissistic types apparently prefer self-fertilization. Quahogs (thick-shelled clams) are all born males and remain so during the activity of their youth, after which about half of them metamorphose into the passivity of femaleness. Guppies can switch their sex back and forth within seconds.

Until the present century, the definition of hermaphroditism was quite simple: a hermaphrodite was a person who possessed to varying degrees the sexual genitalia of both sexes. In this age of exploding knowledge in genetics and endocrinology, simple anatomical definitions no longer suffice. The new terminology defines the true hermaphrodite (*hermaphroditus verus*) as an individual who possesses both ovarian and testicular tissue. These may be in the form of one ovary and one testicle, gonads composed of both kinds of tissue (ovotestis), or any combination of the preceding. Individuals with matched gonads (two testes or two ovaries) but whose external sexual appearance is ambiguous are now classified as pseudohermaphrodites, of which there are several varieties.

Humans were all once hermaphrodites of sorts. Our sexual configuration is the product of sex chromosomes passed on by our parents. Because females have only X sex chromosomes, we can receive only an X from our mothers; we can receive an X or a Y from our fathers because males carry both kinds. If we get two Xs, we become XX genotypical females; if we get an X and a Y, we become XY genotypical males. It is the Y chromosome that determines human sex. The "basic" human is female; it is not the presence of two Xs that makes a female, but rather the absence of the Y chromosome. Sometimes children are born with several X chromosomes, such as the XXX, XXY, or even XXXXY patterns. Although the X chromosome carries far more genetic information than the Y, no matter how many X "units" of femaleness the fetus has, the presence of a single Y results in the male pattern of sexual differentiation. The extra Xs, however, do affect development, since it is characterized by hypogonadism. As discussed below, individuals with the extra Xs are classified as having Klinefelter syndrome. The single exception to this male differentiation by possessors of a Y chromosome is the XY genotype with androgen-insensitivity syndrome.

Normal Embryonic and Fetal Development

In the normal course of embryonic and fetal development, certain genetic and hormonal events occur that differentiate us along sexual dimorphic lines compatible with our genotype. At about six to ten weeks, a single gene labeled SRY, for "sex determining region of the Y," causes the rudimentary gonads of the male to change to testes; without the SRY gene, they become ovaries. At about five months, testicular androgens cause the penis and scrotal sacs to develop; without androgens, the vagina, clitoris, and labia develop.

Our brains are also "sexed" dimorphically by the action of fetal testosterone and its by-products, dihydrotestosterone and estrogen, as they interact with the hypothalamus, the limbic system, and the cerebral cortex. These hormonal secretions first sensitize the male brain to the effects of testosterone and later activate the brain to engage in male-typical behavior. Male-female brain differences are particularly striking in areas of the hypothalamus that participate in the regulation of male-typical sexual behavior. There are, however, wide individual variations.

Unlike the external genitals, the internal reproductive structures do not develop from the same anlagen. In this sense, all embryos are hermaphroditic, possessing both male Wolffian and female Müllerian ducts. At about three months, androgens from the male testes cause the Wolffian structures to develop into the male internal sex organs (i.e., vas deferens, seminal vesicles, and ejaculatory duct). The fetal testes also secrete Müllerian inhibiting substance (MIS), which causes the Müllerian structures to atrophy. Without androgens, the Wolffian structures degenerate, and without MIS the Müllerian structures develop into the female internal sex organs (i.e., uterus, Fallopian tubes, and upper portions of the vagina).

Abnormal Genetic Development

With all these (and many other) genetic and hormonal events occurring at the embryonic and fetal stages of life, it is inevitable that nature makes occasional mistakes. The substances (androgens and MIS) secreted by the testes are vital in diverting the fetus from the basic human female form. Without testes and the substances they secrete, a fetus will invariably be a female. Persons with a single X chromosome (XO) are known as Turner's syndrome girls. This condition is typically caused by an X-bearing sperm penetrating a sex chromosome-empty egg. A Turner's syndrome child is unmistakably female (often exaggeratedly so) in her behavioral and intellectual patterns, is very short (about 4' 8"), lacks secondary sex characteristics, and is infertile. Although the Turner's syndrome child usually has a normal verbal IQ, she is significantly below population norms on performance (visual-spatial) IQ, which is reflective of low androgen levels.

The importance of the androgens in masculinization is dramatically manifested in the congenital adrenal hyperplasia (CAH) and the androgen-insensitivity syndromes. CAH is an autosomal recessive trait that, through a number of possible enzymatic defects, causes decreased production of cortisol by the adrenal mesodermal cortex. This allows for an increased secretion of adrenal testosterone and results in precocious sexual development in males and the masculinization of the genitalia in females.

CAH is the most common cause of genital ambiguity among females, with infants showing varying degrees of clitoral enlargement (sometimes to the point of matching the male penis in size) and varying degrees of fusion of the labia. Because the androgen stimulus arrives too late to switch on the Wolffian ducts, virilization involves only the external genitalia. If CAH females are given cortisol treatments and have any defects involving their reproductive organs surgically corrected, they will menstruate, gestate, and lactate. CAH is the only intersex condition in which normal sexual functioning, including fertility, is probable. If CAH is untreated, there may be further masculinization of the external sex organs. CAH females evidence significantly more male-typical behavior than normal females, suggesting that their brains have been masculinized to some extent by excess adrenal testosterone.

The androgen-insensitivity syndrome is an X-linked recessive syndrome that causes an XY genetic male to develop as a phenotypical female. Because MIS has done its job and caused the Müllerian structures to atrophy, there are no internal female organs; but since the androgen cannot do its job developing the Wolffian structures because of cell insensitivity, there are no internal male organs either. Because the external genitalia are unambiguously female, this condition is rarely diagnosed until puberty, when patients become concerned over failure to menstruate. Apart from being about three inches taller than the typical XX female and having both little body hair, which depends on androgens, and a short vagina, the XY androgen-insensitive person is totally female in external appearance. These genetic males, unresponsive to the masculinizing effects of testosterone in the brain, conform to the typical behavioral patterns of normal women.

An interesting variant of the androgen-insensitivity syndrome was discovered among 23 interrelated families in the Dominican Republic by Imperato-McGinley and her colleagues. They studied 38 individuals who appeared at birth to be unambiguous females, and who were raised as such. Actually, these children were XY males who lacked an enzyme important to male sex-hormone synthesis called 5 alpha-reductase. Although these children had normal male levels of testosterone, they almost entirely lacked dihydrotestosterone because of the missing enzyme. At puberty, these children underwent a physical transformation to maleness, including growth of the penis and descent of the testes.

These *guevedoce* ("penis at 12") males were able to make the social and psychological transitions to the male role with relative ease despite 12 years of female socialization. This suggested to Imperato-McGinley that while dihydrotestosterone is necessary for the promotion of the external male sex characteristics at birth, testosterone makes for a relatively normal masculine puberty and has a masculinizing effect on the brain in utero to form the normal male gender identity despite the absence of dihydrotestosterone. A study of five 5 alpha-reductase deficient males raised as females in a much more sex-segregated culture (the Sambia of New Guinea) found these individuals had a more difficult time making the gender switch, sometimes in circumstances of social trauma. Thus, although sociocultural factors are significant in the formation of gender identity, the concept of psycho-sexual neutrality at birth is contrary to the evidence and to the laws of biology.

Klinefelter's Syndrome

Klinefelter's syndrome is when males have two or more X chromosomes and one or more Y chromosomes, the XXY pattern being the most common. They are referred to as genetic hermaphrodites because they have both the female (XX) and male (XY) chromosome patterns. Klinefelter's syndrome boys tend to be born to older mothers, and the syndrome appears to be the result of a fault in the genetic control of cell division in the ova. They are undetectable at birth except by genetic karyotyping; they may have smaller-than-normal testes but a penis that is capable of erection and satisfactory intercourse. As a rule, the ejaculate of these men contains no sperm. They tend to be taller than normal males in adulthood and to develop relatively well-formed breasts at puberty. They have about half the male postpubertal amount of testosterone, which accounts for their low level of sexual activity and the female pattern of hair growth and loss. Klinefelter's males often have sexual identity problems, and they are significantly more likely than XY males to be homosexual, bisexual, transvestites, transsexuals, and inmates in prisons and mental hospitals. The risk of mental retardation is greater than among normal males and becomes more likely the greater the frequency of additional chromosomes.

From the above discussion, it might seem that the anatomical definition of sex may be somewhat anachronistic. Today, there is a relatively simple method of precisely determining sex called nuclear sexing. This method takes advantage of the fact that females have two X chromosomes, which means that they have body cells containing both maternal and paternal chromosomes carrying different genetic information. Geneticists call this phenomenon genetic mosaicism. The female is a natural genetic mosaic; the male is not because he has only one X chromosome.

The genetic instructions on both Xs cannot be activated within the same individual, so the genes on one X are inactivated. Which chromosome is inactivated is randomly determined, with different Xs active in different cells. When a chromosome is inactivated it remains so throughout life. The inactivation of the genes on a chromosome causes a darkly staining material called chromatin to be visible on the cells of females called the Barr body. If staining reveals the Barr body (chromatin), the person is a female; if not, a male.

The anomalous thing about this is that the Turner's syndrome individual is considered a female anatomically and behaviorally, yet she is Barr body negative because of the absence of the second X. The Klinefelter individual—male in appearance and rearing—is Barr body positive because he has two or more Xs. So while some believe that the sex-chromatin method is a helpful criterion for correct sex diagnosis and for revising our concepts of hermaphrodism, it has ambiguities.

True Hermaphroditism

The precise etiology of true hermaphroditism is less well known, although it is known that it is genetic rather than hormonal in nature. One kind of true hermaphroditism for which the etiology is known is XX/XY chimerism. A chimera is an individual organ or part having a diverse genetic constitution; for example, a plant graft union is a compound of incongruous parts. True hermaphroditism is sometimes the result of chimerism—the presence in a single individual of cells derived from different zygotes. Three types of chimerism—blood, transplacental, and whole body—have been identified; whole-body chimerism is the most likely type to result in hermaphroditic sexual development (i.e., the presence of both ovarian and testicular tissue and ambiguous genitalia). Whole-body chimerism results from the fusion of two zygotes that normally would have been separate XX and XY dizygotic twins.

Other mosaic or chimeric complements (e.g., XX/XXY, XX/XXYY, XX/XYY) are known, and there has been one documented case of quadruple mosaicism—XO/XX/XY/XXY. This person has the karyotypes for Turner's syndrome, normal femaleness, normal maleness, and Klinefelter's syndrome. He was raised as a male and phenotypically, except for a very small penis, incomplete labioscrotal fusion, and a femalelike fat pattern, appeared so. It was speculated that this complex mosaicism probably arose from multiple disjunctions involving an XXY zygote during mitosis.

The majority (about 70 percent) of true hermaphrodites have karyotypes indistinguishable from those of the normal male or female. XY hermaphrodites are Barr body negative and XX hermaphrodites are Barr body positive (XX/XY hermaphrodites are Barr body positive, but they have a lower chromatin count than normal). Since both karyotypes have ovarian and testicular tissue, they offer rare proof that ovarian tissue can develop absent a second X chromosome and that testicular tissue can develop absent a Y chromosome.

It is possible that XX and XY hermaphrodites may constitute cases of undetected chimerism, but the great majority of these cases have been traced to genetic accidents. There is a single gene on the Y chromosome that carries the Testes Determining Factor. All females, then, have all the genes necessary to make a male except this crucial one, and all males would be females without its diverting power.

Recent studies of XX males and XY females have verified this. Y-specific DNA has been found in XX males, indicating that Y-linked sequences leading to testis differentiation have been transferred to the X chromosome (translocation). An abnormal gene on the X chromosome homologous to the gene for testis differentiation on the Y chromosome has been discovered among XX hermaphrodites. On the other hand, the loss of these Y-linked sequences in individuals with XY gonadal dysgenesis allows for female differentiation. Thus discordance among karyotype, phenotype, and gonadal histology may be explained in terms of translocation (in the XX case) or deletion (in the XY case) of a critical segment of the Y short arm that carries the Testes Determining Factor. Cases of XX hermaphroditism have been reported that could not be explained by translocation, deletion, or chimerism, however.

Most true hermaphrodites (about 57 percent) are XX, and approximately 80 percent have internal female organs capable of sexual functioning and with some potential for fertility. However, stories of self-fertilization or of true hermaphrodites who have both sired and given birth to infants are fanciful myths. As of 1988, there were only 528 cases of true hermaphroditism documented in the world literature, and pregnancy has been documented in only seven XX true hermaphrodites and in one XX/XY chimera as of 1990. There are no reported cases of male hermaphrodite fertility.

A classification scheme for the external genitalia of true hermaphrodites has been proposed by Luks and his colleagues based on the degree of male or female genital appearance. These classes range from class I (clitoris normal or slightly enlarged) to class VI (penis normal to small) and are distributed in an approximate normal curve with the two extreme classes being the rarest and classes III and IV the most common.

Although it appears that we have come full circle by again using external genital appearance to assign sex of rearing, doing so has practical consequences. The degree of virilization of the genitalia provides an indication of the extent of brain masculinization: the more masculinized the genital features, the more likely the brain has been organized along male lines, the more feminine the genital features, the less brain masculinization has taken place. Although only about 30 percent of true hermaphrodites fall into the "male" classes (V and VI) in the Luks classification scheme, most true hermaphrodites have been reared as males. Physically and psychologically, most hermaphrodites would be better off raised as females. Surgical intervention can correct minor problems of the external female genitalia and even reconstruct a functional genitourinary system, but reconstructing a functioning penis is not possible at this time.

Needless to say, the social and psychological lot of the hermaphrodite is not a happy one. Our sexual and gender identities are fundamental to defining who we are and how others respond to us. Depression, low self-esteem, and suicidal ideation are common among hermaphrodites of all types. Hermaphrodites were usually destroyed at birth in ancient Greece, and at least one female who turned into a male at puberty was burned alive in Rome.

There were some executions of hermaphrodites during the Middle Ages in Europe, although both civil and canon law of the time recognized hermaphroditism and allowed the father or godfather to choose the sex the child would be raised as at the time of baptism. At puberty, hermaphrodites were given the choice to retain the given sex or to change it. Having made the choice, it was imperative, on pain of being charged with sodomy, that they hold to the declared sex for life.

During certain periods in Hindu history, hermaphrodites were considered favorably, probably because of the belief that the Supreme Being possessed both the complete male and female principles. A man was a man only because he had an "excess" of masculinity, and a woman was a woman only because she contained an "excess" of femininity, the ideal being harmony of the male and female principles. Hermaphrodites were also valued in practice as well as in principle as providers of alternative methods of sexual gratification.

REFERENCES

Barbin, H. *Herculine Barbin: Being the Recently Discovered Memoirs of a Nineteenth-Century French Hermaphrodite.* New York: Pantheon, 1980.

Borghi, et al. True Hermaphroditism: A New Case with Complex Mosaicism. *Genetic Counseling*, Vol. 1 (1990), pp. 81–88.

Bullough, V. *Sexual Variance in Society and History*. Chicago: Univ. of Chicago Press, 1976.

Goodman, R. Genetic and Hormonal Factors in Human Sexuality: Evolutionary and Development Perspectives. In G. Wilson, ed., *Variant Sexuality: Research and Theory*. Baltimore: Johns Hopkins Univ. Press, 1987.

Herdt, G., and J. Davidson. The Sambian "turnim man": Sociocultural and Clinical Aspects of Gender Formation in Male Pseudohermaphrodites With 5-alpha-reductase Deficiency in Papua, New Guinea. *Archives of Sexual Behavior*, Vol. 17 (1988), pp. 33–56.

Hoyenga, K.B., and K.T. Hoyenga. *The Question of Sex Differences*. Boston: Little, Brown, 1979.

Imperato-McGinley, J., et al. Androgens and the Evolution of Male Gender Identity Among Male Pseudohermaphrodites With 5 Alfa reductase Deficiency. *New England Journal of Medicine*, Vol. 300 (1979), pp. 1233–37.

LeVay, S. A Difference in Hypothalamic Structure Between Heterosexual and Homosexual Men. *Science*, Vol. 253 (1991), pp. 1034–37.

Luks, F., et al. Early Gender Assignment in True Hermaphroditism. *Journal of Pediatric Surgery*, Vol. 23 (1988), pp. 1122–26.

Money, J. *Love and Lovesickness: The Science of Sex, Gender Difference, and Pair Bonding*. Baltimore: Johns Hopkins Univ. Press, 1980.

Murchie, G. *The Seven Mysteries of Life*. Boston: Houghton Mifflin, 1978.

Page, D., et al. The Sex Determining Region of the Human Y Chromosome Encodes a Finger Protein. *Cell*, Vol. 51 (1987), pp. 1091–1104.

Raine, M. Absence of Y Specific DNA Sequence in Two Siblings With 46XX Hermaphrodism. *Archives of Disease in Childhood*, Vol. 64 (1989), pp. 1185–87.

Simpson, J. *Disorders of Sexual Differentiation: Etiology and Clinical Delineation*. New York: Academic Press, 1976.

Talerman, A., et al. True Hermaphrodite With Bilateral Ovotestes, Bilateral Gonadoblastomas and Dysgerminomas, 46, XX/46, XY Karyotype and a Successful Pregnancy. *Cancer*, Vol. 66 (1990), pp. 2668–72.

Anthony Walsh

HINDUISM

Hinduism, the traditional religion of the Indian subcontinent, teaches that the literature of love and sex is of divine origin, derived from a collection of all knowledge compiled in some 100,000 chapters by Prajāpati, the supreme god, creator of heaven and earth. Included in this was *kāma*, or the pursuit of pleasure, particularly sexual pleasure. The transmission of this knowledge involved a complicated process, but eventually it was put down in the form in which it has survived by the sage Vātsyāna (fl. 450 C.E.) in his *Kāmasūtra* ("love text").

The *Kāmasūtra* covers most aspects of human courtship and mating, including positions in intercourse, and serves as the basic text for later writings on the subject by peoples of the Indian subcontinent. Chronologically next in line are the *Kuttani-mata*, or the *Lessons of a Prostitute*, written by Dāmodaragupta in the eighth century and surviving in fragments; *Samaya-mātrikā*, or *Prostitute's Breviary*, written by Kshemendra (990–1065); the *Rati-rahasya* (*Mysteries of Passion*) by Koka Paṇḍita, dating from the 12th century; *Pañchaśāyala* (*Five Arrows*) written by Jyotirīśa in the 14th century; and the *Anaṅa Raṅga* (*Theater of the Love God*) written by Kalyānamalla in the 15th century. This last, because its author was a Hindu in the employ of a Muslim nobleman, spread throughout the Islamic world. There are many other sex manuals, hundreds of them, many quite crude, found in the various Indian vernaculars as well as Sanskrit; many commentaries on the various love manuals also exist. Though all detail more or less the same themes, some, such as the *Rati-rahasya*, are more detailed in spelling out sexual positions. The *Rati-rahasya* also gives a classification system for a variety of female types.

The number of erotic classics suggests that the peoples of the Indian subcontinent did not hold the fear of sex that some of their Western counterparts did. In fact, unlike the Judaeo-Christian description of the creation of humanity as an asexual affair, Hindus put creation itself in sexual terms. The "Hymn of Creation" in the *Rig Veda* attributes the beginning of creation to sexual desire and calls it the primal germ of the mind. Indian religious documents such as the *Atharva Veda*, the fourth of the Hindu *Vedas*, include many magical formulations and incantations to help or hinder lovemaking, recover virility, or allow one to steal unnoticed into the home of the beloved.

This does not mean that Hinduism was without sex prohibitions. Bestiality was condemned (although not by all), as was incest, rape, and adultery, and there are prohibitions against having sex with a woman during her menses and against having sex with the wrong caste. Although the ancient code of Manu, the mythical Indian lawgiver, has had the effect of law throughout much of the history of Hinduism, interpretations of the law have varied because of the wide range of cultural and doctrinal beliefs combined within Hinduism. This very diversity makes it difficult to single out any view of sexuality as official, since Hinduism lacks a common creed, set of dogmas, or practice and has no universally acceptable canon, no organized church as such, and no uniformity of worship. The religion itself could best be defined as a medley of faiths linked to some degree by the same pantheon of gods. There are hundreds of sects and, within most, numerous splinter groups based on a particular deity, guru, trait, or tenet held sacred. Obviously, within such a multitude of sects, sexual attitudes vary widely, and every generalization has exceptions.

The ultimate ends of men and women—salvation, bliss, knowledge, and pleasure—can be achieved by following any number of different paths, which vary according to the cult, creed, sect, and system. Such a variety is believed necessary because individuals differ in special abilities and competencies. Some adopt the method of good works, others perform the necessary rituals and sacrifices or follow certain ascetic principles, while still others make idols and build and consecrate temples. Usually, no single path is all-sufficient, a blending of two or more being regarded as essential. Faith is balanced with works, devotion with ritual, and so forth. Different sects adopt or encourage different ways, and a number of these emphasize sexuality.

The most celebrated deity of the Hindu pantheon is Krishna, worshiped as an independent god in his own right but also as the eighth incarnation of Vishnu. Krishna is particularly noted for his interest in and devotion to the female sex, having some 16,018 wives according to tradition, each of whom gave him ten sons and a daughter. He is often portrayed in an amorous posture. His favorite sexual partner was Radha, the loveliest of all milk maids, whose love for him was so all consuming that she ignored her family honor and disregarded her husband. Hindu poetry up to the 14th century delighted in describing their stormy, adulterous liaisons, but since that time she has been portrayed as conforming to more conventional mores, and she came to be described as a wife rather than a mistress. One of the more famous poems about the love of the two was *Gita-govinda* ("Song of the Cowherd") by the 12th century Bengali poet Jayadeva. Jayadeva describes their lovemaking in some detail.

With the examples of the gods and the poets before them, the Hindus could give much freer reign to feelings of sensuality and sexuality than the Christians of the West. Sex was not only for procreation but could be engaged in for pleasure, power, and even magical purposes. The sex manuals pay little attention to sex for procreation but emphasize the other purposes. Pleasure, however, is defined primarily from a male rather than a female point of view. Women are portrayed as voluptuous creatures who are fair game for the more predatory male. There are a number of handbooks devoted to S*tritantra,* literally "the female lore," describing different kinds of females and their use as an instrument for man's passion. They also deal with women's physiological functions and other aspects of being female. The handbooks emphasize the need to arouse a woman, and to do so the male must acquire a thorough knowledge of the female erogenous zones—the breasts, nipples, nape of the neck, folds of the buttocks, labia, and clitoris. Different types of women have different sensitive areas or passion pulses to be explored, including the lobe of the ear, the middle of the palm, the navel, the anus, or the arch of the foot.

The chief source of ecstasy in the female is the *yoni* ("holder"), in a narrow sense the vulva; but in a broader sense it includes pubic hair, the opening or cleft of the labia, and the uterus. The *yoni* is considered to have a life of its own, being regarded as a sacred area, a pad of pleasure, an occult region worthy of reverence, and a symbol of the cosmic mysteries. It is described as the abode of pleasure, the source of great bliss, and the delight of delights, and is said to have been created specifically as honey to attract the male organ. It is likened to the second mouth, and it continually sends out a silent command to man to come and sip. It is the chief ruler of the universe, for it brings men in all walks of life under its control and subjection.

The penis is called the *linga,* and like the *yoni* it was also an object of veneration. The center of excitement for the male sexual feelings, the *chakra,* is situated at the root of the penis. The testes disclose the mystery of the *yoni* place, and the semen is called *bindu.* Like women, men have erotic areas, and one especially sensitive place is the *guda* (anus).

In the sexual handbooks, lovemaking is often referred to as a refined form of combat. The man attacks, the woman resists, and, by the subtle interplay of advance and retreat, assault and defense, desires are mutually built up. But love differs from war in that the final result is a delightful victory for both partners. During the various stages of combat, the love partners can bite, scratch, pull each other's hair, or beat or slap each other on the shoulders, back, bosom, and buttocks with the palm of the hand, the back of the hand, the side of the hand, a half-open fist, or even a closed fist. Partners are cautioned, however, to avoid becoming too violent because neither the giving nor the receiving partner is always sensitive to the severity of the blows delivered in passion. Various kinds of love marks (technically *kamanka*), such as the tiger's claw or the broken cloud, are described and placed into two categories, those made with the fingernails and those with the teeth. Lovemaking is also accompanied by vocal sounds, *sitkrita*, varying from a slow expulsion of breath through clenched teeth to sounds like the neighing of a horse, a deep sigh, or the hushing of a baby. There are various sobbing, cooing, moaning, humming, hissing, clucking, bellowing, and roaring sounds, which require the well-matched partners to respond. Occasionally, there are verbal exclamations such as "I can endure no more."

Various postures are described for precoital foreplay and intercourse. There are as many as 16 precoital positions, depending on whether the couple is standing, sitting, or lying down. When the couple engages in intercourse they are faced with choosing from a number of different positions. Vatsyayana describes some 84 postures (if minor variations are included), but one of his commentators lists 729 variations. Not all these variations can be performed by a single couple; some also are highly dependent on the physical peculiarities of the individual or the genitalia. Postures are often named after animals, such as the cow, mule, donkey, cat, dog, tiger, and frog. Movements accompanying the postures are described as being like using the tongs, spinning the top, biting the board, churning the milk, and so forth.

It was a common belief in Hinduism that women enjoy sex much more than men do. One Indian proverb states that woman's power in eating is twice as great as man's, her cunning or bashfulness four times as great, her decisiveness or boldness six times as great, and her impetuosity or delight in love eight times as great.

The sex act is also regarded as a form of psychospiritual communing. The rich, deep fulfillment of love between a man and a woman is a condition of happiness so natural, so simple, yet so real that it is the best of all earthly conditions. Inevitably, it was employed by the mystics as a symbol of divine communication in its transcendent and esoteric meaning. Sex is a way of revealing to man the hidden truth of the universe.

Copulation itself could bring about supernatural power, but only if the practitioner had learned to transcend the carnal state of sexual activity and risen above passion. To realize this state of absoluteness, the man had to conceive of himself as the male deity; then by worship he transfigured his partner until she became a female god and served as a consecrated field for his operation. The pair then united, physically, mentally, and spiritually. Hindu cultism is most active in this aspect of sex, with each sect or cult stipulating different ways of preparing for this union.

Some sects worship the *linga*, or male phallus; others, such as the *Śaktás,* consider the godhead to be essentially feminine and concentrate on Śakti, the wife of Śiva, although both are also known under different names. Her worshipers are broadly divided into two groups: "right-handed" adherents who worship the god in public and "left-handed" ones who worship her in secrecy. The left in Hindu mythology is associated with the female, and this type of worship can be classed as a form of Tantrism, so called because its adherents follow scriptures known as *tantras*. Essentially, tantric cults are antinomian, that is, they teach that men and women are not always bound by moral law but can reach a state that takes them so far beyond its purview that they can cease to obey its precepts. This results in a disregard for societal conventions. Hindu tantrics believe that the goddess Śakti is particularly gratified by prohibited and reprehensible acts that either ignore or transgress the established laws of society, morality, and religion; a key teaching is that spiritual union with the god can best be attained through sexual union in the flesh. One such cult, the Sakhibhava, holds that only the godhead, Krishna, was truly male, while every other creature in the world was female, subject to the pleasure of Krishna. They worship Radha, the favorite consort of Krishna, and the object of their devotion is to become a female attendant upon her. Female followers of the sect grant sexual favors freely to anyone because they believe that all their sexual partners are Krishna himself. Male followers dress like women and affect the behavior, movements, and habits of women, including the imitation of menstruation, during which they abstain from worship. In the past, many of them emasculated themselves, and all were supposed to play the female part during sexual intercourse (allowing themselves to be penetrated) as an act of devotion. The technical term *hijra* is applied to these men, and there are still colonies of them in the India of today.

In the tantric sects, promiscuous intercourse is spoken of as an act of devotion to the deity and regarded as obligatory for all members. Tantrism teaches that there are two kinds of semen, male and female, and that these primordial male and female elements can be united into the nondual state of Absolute Reality through learning the secrets of intercourse. This can be done if the man does not ejaculate but practices coitus reservatus, which, according to tantric belief, allows the semen to be drawn up the spinal column. This technique of not spilling the seed is represented symbolically in Hindu art by the *nīcha meḍhra*, or "down penis." Such a penis is shown on the famous statue of the Jain saint Gomatesvara. Jainism, in fact, teaches that although sex is a gateway to salvation, sexual indulgence itself is a weakness and an evil to overcome because it is the chief manifestation of lust. The most extreme puritanical sect in Jainism is the Digambara, or nude sect, whose members at one time went about nude. Today, only the holy ones observe strict nudity.

All varieties of sexual intercourse were tolerated by Hinduism, although some forms were regarded by some groups with greater hostility than others. Oral-genital contact, for example, was classed by some lawgivers as equivalent to killing a Brahmin, and the sin involved could not be expiated in fewer than 100 incarnations. Nevertheless, the erotic manuals discussed it at length. The anus is regarded as one of the most important centers of psychic energy in the body, and anal intercourse either between males or between males and females is one of the main expedients for using the potential of this erotic center. Some medieval Indian writers regarded the practice as quite common and in no way perverse, but others claimed that men who engaged in it with other men were reborn as men incapable of begetting. Manu said that men who engaged in such activities lost their caste. Nonetheless, it seems clear that sex between males was tolerated if not encouraged at least among some sects of Hinduism. Lesbianism is also mentioned, and the 4th-century writer Kautilya, who looked with some disfavor on such practices, recommended imposing very minimal fines, much less than those for many other sexual activities, when people were discovered in such relationships. Bestiality, though condemned by Manu, was also tolerated under certain conditions, and many of the gods had contacts with animals. Even necrophilia played a part in some of the tantric rituals and in some of the Saivite sects. The practitioner sits in a graveyard or cremation ground with a skull pressed against his genitals. In other cases, he lies prostrate or squats on a cadaver until the flesh decays. In the so-called black ritual, the adept sits astride a recently deceased male and animates the body until the penis becomes erect and ejaculates; the fluid is then collected.

Hinduism embraces a wide variety of cults and sects, and within it can be found a range of adherants from ascetic celibates to necrophiliacs. In all its forms, it recognizes the pleasures inherent in sexuality, and in much of Hinduism this is exalted and praised. Temple statues, particularly those made before the Muslim conquests and the entry of the British into India, often portray sexually symbolic scenes. The gods themselves were very sexual. The Hindu sex manuals have achieved a worldwide reading public and influenced ideas about sex in religious traditions from Buddhism to Islam to Christianity.

REFERENCES

Bullough, V.L. *Sexual Variance in Society and History*. Chicago: Univ. of Chicago, 1956.

Chunder, P.C. *Kautilya on Love and Morals*. Calcutta: Jayanti, 1970.

Devi, K. *The Eastern Way of Love: Tantric Sex and Erotic Mysticism*. New York: Simon & Schaumann, 1977.

Kalyāṇamalla. *Ananga Ranga*. Translated with an introduction and comments by T. Ray. New York: Citadel Press, 1964.

Lal, K. *The Cult of Desire*. New Hyde Park, N.Y.: University Books, 1966.

Meyer, J.J. *Sexual Life in Ancient India*. Reprint. New York: Barnes & Noble, 1953.

Rajneesh, B.S. *The Book of Secrets*. New York: Harper Colophon, 1976.

Thomas, P. *Kama Kalpa or the Hindu Ritual of Love*. Bombay: D.B. Taraporevla, 1959.

Vātsyāna. *Kama Sutra*. Translated by R. Burton. Reprint. New York: Dutton, 1925.

Walker, B. *The Hindu World*. 2 vols. New York: Praeger, 1968.

Vern L. Bullough

HIRSCHFELD, MAGNUS

German sexologist Magnus Hirschfeld (1868–1935) was born in the seaside town of Kolberg, the son of Jewish parents and the seventh of eight children. During his student days, he vacillated between writing and medicine before finally following his father and two older brothers into medicine.

Early in his practice, Hirschfeld received a letter from a patient, an officer who had committed suicide the previous day, on the eve of his wedding. The officer explained that he could no longer pretend to be heterosexual and asked Hirschfeld to make his story public so others could benefit from it. The suicide and Hirschfeld's writing about it strongly influenced him to study sexual variations and to work for the rights of homosexuals.

Hirschfeld probably did more for homosexuals than anyone else of his generation. In 1897, he cofounded the *Wissenschaftlich-Humanitäre Komitee* (Scientific-Humanitarian Committee); its purpose was both to conduct research on homosexuality and other sexual variations and to work toward abolishing Paragraph 175 of the German criminal code, which defined homosexuality as a criminal offense. Himself a homosexual, Hirschfeld viewed homosexuality as a natural, inborn condition, not a sickness, and was deeply committed to eradicating public prejudice against homosexuals through education. After studying 10,000 male and female homosexuals, he used their histories as the basis for his book *Die Homosexualität des Mannes und des Weibes (The Homosexuality of Men and Women),* which convinced many that homosexuality was not a perversion.

In addition to his work on homosexuality, Hirschfeld studied and published on a wide variety of topics, among them love, bisexuality, prostitution, sex crimes, and alcoholism (including the effects of drinking on the unborn fetus and the effects of drugs and alcohol on sexuality). Using direct observation, he was the first to study transvestites and argued that transvestism—a term he coined—is a sexual variation distinct from homosexuality. (Psychoanalysts at the time believed it fell into the category of homosexuality.)

During his long career, Hirschfeld brought to fruition many "firsts" in sexology. In 1899, he edited the first scientific journal on homosexuality, *Jahrbuch für Sexuelle Zwischenstufen (Yearbook for Sexual Intermediaries).* Published for 24 years, it was a valuable recording of the scientific contributions of the time. In 1908, he edited the first scholarly publication dedicated to a wide range of sexual issues, *Zeitschrift für Sexualwissenschaft (Journal of Sexual Science);* it was published for one year before being incorporated into another periodical. And in 1919, he was both consultant and actor for *Anders als die Andern (Different From the Others),* the first film aimed at educating the public about homosexuality.

Also in 1919, Hirschfeld opened the Institute for Sexual Science in Berlin, the first of its kind in the world. Located in a palatial mansion he had purchased, the Institute housed the first marital counseling clinic, a medical department, research laboratories, and a library with more than 20,000 volumes, 35,000 photographs, and 40,000 biographical letters and confessions. The primary aim of the Institute was to conduct research in sexual biology (e.g., the role of the endocrine system in sexual physiology and psychology), sexual pathology (case histories of sexual

minorities or people with psychosexual problems), sexual sociology (e.g., abstinence, marriage, and prostitution) and sexual ethnology (sexuality in other cultures and at other times). Courses were also available to physicians and students interested in sexual science, while question-and-answer sessions were offered to the public. In addition, the Institute provided treatment for problems such as lack of sexual desire, sexually transmitted disease, infertility, and vaginismus, as well as medical and legal expert testimony. In the first year alone, more than 4,000 people, many from other countries, visited the Institute to use its library, learn about ongoing research, and attend lectures. In 1924, Hirschfeld turned the Institute over to the German government; little changed, however, and he continued as director.

Other Hirschfeld "firsts" included cofounding the first sexological society, *Ärztliche Gesellschaft für Sexualwissenschaft und Eugenik* (Medical Society for Sexology and Eugenics), in 1913, and organizing the world's first international congress on sex research, the International Conference for Sexual Reform Based on Sexual Science, in 1921. During the second congress, in 1928, Hirschfeld helped establish the World League for Sexual Reform, whose goal was to organize an international community promoting social progress through science.

With Nazism looming, Hirschfeld left Germany at the end of 1930, beginning what turned out to be a world tour that included the United States, Japan, China, the Philippines, Indonesia, Ceylon, India, Egypt, and Palestine. During the journey, Hirschfeld was enthusiastically received, lecturing to both academics and the public and observing the sexual attitudes and customs of the places he visited.

On May 6, 1933, while Hirschfeld was still abroad, the Nazis dissolved the Institute, destroying the greater part of the library in a public burning. Two months earlier, Karl Giese, Hirschfeld's secretary and collaborator at the Institute, had secretly left Berlin, probably bound for France, taking with him some of the irreplaceable documents and valuables for safekeeping. The fate of these materials is unknown, but some of Hirschfeld's other papers are now in the archives of the Kinsey Institute for Sex Research in Bloomington, Indiana.

Because it was unsafe to return to Germany, Hirschfeld settled in Switzerland and then Paris, where he established the *Institut Français des Sciences Sexologiques.* Although similar to the Berlin Institute, it lacked the staff and wealth of materials of the original and failed to gain much recognition. In 1934, Hirschfeld dissolved the French Institute and moved to Nice, where he died the following year. He was cremated and buried at the Caucade Cemetery in Nice.

REFERENCES

Haeberle, E.J. The Jewish Contribution to the Development of Sexology. *Journal of Sex Research,* Vol. 18 (1982), pp. 305–323.

Hoenig, J. Dramatis Personae: Selected Biographical Sketches of 19th-Century Pioneers in Sexology. In J. Money and H. Musaph, eds., *Handbook of Sexology,* Vol. 1. New York: Elsevier, 1978.

Wolff, C. *Magnus Hirschfeld: A Portrait of a Pioneer in Sexology.* New York: Quartet Books, 1986.

Diane Morrissette

HOMOPHOBIA

George Weinberg is credited with coining and popularizing the term "homophobia" in his landmark book *Society and the Healthy Homosexual.* He used the term to explain the dread felt by heterosexuals when near homosexuals as well as the self-hatred many homosexuals feel in relation to their own sexual orientation. During the 20 years since Weinberg introduced the term, a body of literature has developed that explores and critiques its use. Common usage has expanded the definition to include other negative attitudes about gay and lesbian people. This entry reviews the definitional debates and research findings regarding attitudes about homosexuality and briefly analyzes the role homophobia has played as an emergent concept in the social construction of homosexuality.

Defining Homophobia

In 1967, Churchill used the term "homo-erotophobia" to describe a cultural fear of same-sex eroticism and sexuality. Churchill's contention was that negative attitudes about homosexual behavior and people are a reflection of a sex-negative culture, whereby the sex drive is believed to pose a threat to social organization. Weinberg's later explanation of homophobia emerged from Churchill's theory. Homophobia, according to Weinberg,

> appears as an antagonism directed toward a particular group of people. Inevitably it leads to disdain of these people, and to the mistreatment of them. This phobia in operation is prejudice, which means we can widen our understanding of it by considering the phobia from the point of view of its being a prejudice and uncovering its chief motives.

In this way, Weinberg's use of "homophobia" combines the concepts of both prejudice and discrimination. Defining the term so inclusively, however, has been the basis of some objections to its use. Critics argue that the broad use of "homophobia" to include most negative reactions to homosexuality limits the term's utility. Others object to the suffix "-phobia" because most victims of phobias realize that their fear is disruptive and recognize that their response is irrational. Yet the homophobic person does not ordinarily feel this discomfort. In fact, as Herek has argued, not being homophobic is commonly seen as dysfunctional. He says that to be considered manly in today's society, one must be homophobic, and those who are not are often the ones labeled with suspicion. Within this context, those who are identified as homophobic frequently do not label this condition as dysfunctional or experience it as irrational given their environment.

There seems to be agreement that for some people a phobic response (as traditionally defined) to homosexuality is present but that this fails to account for or accurately describe the complex ways homophobia is experienced by the majority of people. Nonetheless, homophobia is still the commonly accepted term to describe the range of feelings and attitudes that often result in behaviors such as avoidance, joking and derision, violence and homicide, self-hate, and suicide.

Research on Attitudes About Homosexuality

With his explanation of the psychology of positive and negative attitudes toward homosexual people, Herek provides a brief overview of the literature on reactions to lesbian and gay people. He reports that findings are contradictory about the relationship between sex-role conformity and attitudes toward these groups. The consistent patterns that have emerged in the literature are that persons with negative attitudes toward lesbian and gay people are less likely to have had personal contact with them; they are also less likely to report having engaged in homosexual behaviors or to label themselves lesbian or gay. They are more likely, especially if they are males, to perceive their peers as manifesting negative attitudes; more likely to have resided in areas where negative attitudes are the norm; more likely to be older and less well educated; more likely to be religious, to attend church frequently, and to subscribe to a conservative religious ideology; more likely to express traditional and restrictive attitudes about sex roles or to have more guilt and negativity about sexuality; and more likely to express high levels of authoritarianism and related personality characteristics.

With regard to sex differences, the literature is fairly consistent in terms of the direction and intensity of attitudes. Heterosexuals show a tendency for more negative attitudes toward homosexuals of their own sex than of the other sex, and more negative attitudes are reported by males than by females.

Herek provides his own model for explaining attitudes toward homosexuality. Arguing that attitudes serve psychological needs, he suggests that three major needs are likely to be met by one's attitudes toward lesbian and gay people: (1) experiential, (2) defensive, and (3) symbolic. Experiential attitudes are the result of feelings and ideas associated with past contacts with lesbian and gay people, associations which are used to make generalizations about all gay men and lesbians. Defensive attitudes emerge to help an individual deal with an internal, unconscious struggle or anxiety by projecting it onto lesbian and gay people. Attitudes are likely to function defensively when the individual perceives some similarity between his or her own unconscious conflict and homosexual people. A symbolic function occurs when attitudes express abstract ideological concepts that are integral to one's personal and group identities. Symbolic attitudes express values important to one's concept of self, thereby helping individuals to establish their identity and affirm their notion of the sort of person they perceive themselves to be. At the same time, attitudes mediate relations to other important individuals and reference groups. In this way, people who think of themselves as "good Christians" may hold negative views toward homosexuality, if that is consistent with their reference group's Christian interpretation of homosexuality. Likewise, people who conceive of themselves as civil libertarians may hold more positive attitudes as a result.

Whereas Herek's model conceptualizes homophobic attitudes with reference to the psychological needs they serve, Ficarrotto's study was designed to understand the independent roles of sexual conservatism and intergroup prejudice in the development of the homophobic personality. He reports that both sexual conservatism and social prejudice are independent and equal predictors of antihomosexual sentiments. Given that people may hold the same attitudes and beliefs for different reasons, Ficarrotto concludes that for some people homophobia may be a function of a set of rigid beliefs and ingrained feelings

that sexuality is negative. For others, homophobia might be best explained as a general personality trend toward prejudice. Accordingly, someone who is racist and sexist may also be homophobic, but not all people who hold racist and sexist attitudes are necessarily homophobic.

Homophobia has multiple roots and meanings. Any attempts to change antihomosexual attitudes are going to require a range of interventions that individually and collectively address the distinct psychological needs maintained by these various belief systems. Despite this, there is evidence that some educational programs are effective in promoting more positive attitudes toward homosexuality.

Given the apparent relationship between homophobia and the problems of antigay and antilesbian violence, sexism, and teen suicide, combatting homophobia continues to be an important part of the contemporary lesbian, gay, and bisexual political movements' agendas in the United States.

The Social Construction of Homosexuality

It is important to note the role that Weinberg's use of the term "homophobia" plays in shaping the public discourse regarding homosexuality. Weinberg's focus on antihomosexual attitudes, prejudices, and related discriminatory behaviors is significant in relation to ideological shifts in the social construction of the meaning of homosexuality. Although the meanings ascribed to the homosexual person have varied historically, in Western culture over the past few centuries these varied identities have shared the common element of being devalued. The meanings have included sinfulness, criminality, and sickness.

Within the political climate of the civil rights movement and the second wave of the women's movement in the United States, gay liberation emerged publicly in the late 1960s. Part of the political agenda was to combat the medical model that labeled homosexuality as sick or pathological and refocus on the civil liberties of the individual. As a consequence, lesbian, gay, and bisexual people are now often viewed as members of a minority group with the shared experience of oppression due to prejudice and discrimination. This is in contrast to the popular view of lesbian, gay, and bisexual people as sharing a psychiatric diagnosis with other deviates.

Weinberg's use of medical language to talk about the disease of homophobia and the healthy homosexual is symbolic of the shift altering the socially constructed meaning of homosexuality. Given the Stonewall rebellion in 1969, which symbolized the start of the contemporary gay liberation movement in the United States, and the pressure in the early 1970s on the American Psychiatric and American Psychological associations to remove homosexuality from their lists of mental disorders, Weinberg's work can be seen as contributing to and emerging out of a new perspective.

While sinfulness, criminality, and mental illness are seen as historically ascribed meanings of homosexuality, they still persist in various forms today. This analysis is not intended to suggest that the ideas about homosexuality have been altered entirely with the introduction of the concept of homophobia. Rather, the discourse regarding homophobia has been intricately related to this changing ideology by supporting the conceptualization of lesbian, gay and bisexual people as a sexual minority. There is clearly increased acceptance for framing homophobia, and not homosexuality, as a social problem today, and this is in part a function of the discourse on homophobia initiated by Weinberg.

While defining and analyzing the "problem of homophobia" has contributed to creating a more accepting social environment for lesbian, gay, and bisexual people to live in and make meaning out of their lives, there is still significant resistance to this change in frame of reference. Writing for the right-wing watchdog group Concerned Women for America, for example, Lussier says:

> Until recent years, only ethnic groups and the disabled have been considered legal minorities. Members of these groups have no control over the factors that cause them to be a protected class. However, homosexuals who choose to engage in unnatural behavior, are not considered minorities in any legal sense. But if they have their own way, that will change.

As Aguero, Bloch, and Byrne indicate, the greatest dislike for homosexuality is among those whose feelings are negative and believe that homosexuality is a learned "problem." Clearly, Lussier would differ with the assessment of Aguero, Bloch, and Byrne as well as Herek that she is homophobic and that her attitudes probably serve a symbolic need. In fact, she encourages "concerned" citizens to "pray; educate others about this assault on traditional family values; and tell elected officials, the press, and others that we are not 'homophobic.' Rather, we are people who care about the future of the family and our nation and resent immoral people imposing their lifestyle on our children using our tax dollars."

Examining the research on homophobia clearly highlights how personal and emotional dimensions of individual psychology—as well as the complex social psychology of intergroup conflict, prejudice, and changing sexual and political ideologies—interface. While many more lesbian, gay, and bisexual people are living open lives based on self-acceptance, self-definition, and affirmation, there still exists a powerful climate of active violence and oppression. The dialectic between hate and acceptance continues.

REFERENCES

Aguero, J.E., L. Bloch, and D. Byrne. The Relationship Among Sexual Beliefs, Attitudes, Experience and Homophobia. *Journal of Homosexuality,* Vol. 10 (Fall 1984), pp. 95–107.

Churchill, W. *Homosexual Behavior Among Males: A Cross-Cultural and Cross-Species Investigation.* New York: Hawthorn, 1967.

Ficarrotto, T.J. Racism, Sexism, and Erotophobia: Attitudes of Heterosexuals Toward Homosexuals. *Journal of Homosexuality,* Vol. 19 (1990), pp. 111–16.

Friend, R.A. Choices, Not Closets: Heterosexism and Homophobia in Schools. In L. Weis and M. Fine, eds., *Silenced Voices.* Buffalo: State Univ. of New York Press, in preparation.

Herek, G.M. Beyond "Homophobia": Social Psychological Perspective on Attitudes Toward Lesbians and Gay Men. *Journal of Homosexuality,* Vol. 10 (Fall 1984), pp. 39–51.

Lussier, E. Gay. Activists Press Teachers on Sexual Minorities. *Concerned Women for America,* Vol. 13 (Aug. 1981), pp. 1, 11–12.

Weinberg, G.H. *Society and the Healthy Homosexual.* New York: St. Martin's Press, 1972.

Richard A. Friend

HOMOSEXUALITY

In all likelihood, more has been learned about homosexuality in the period since 1970 than at any other time in history. With this explosion of information has come the pleasant problem of interpreting it. But what has been notably lacking in the past 20 years are cogent theories that can make sense of the larger patterns in the data.

In this entry, information about male and female homosexuality is interwoven. Consequently, there is the danger that information about lesbians will be slighted, since there is much more known about male than female homosexuality. Nevertheless, the similarities between the sexes are common enough that much space and effort are saved by such a joint discussion. Readers should keep this caveat in mind.

Definitions

The controversies concerning the definition of sexual orientation are echoed in a similar controversy about the proper definition of homosexuality. The definition we prefer is Money's: "homosexuality" refers to same-sex sexual contact, either (1) as a genital act or (2) as a long-term sexuoerotic status. According to the first aspect of the definition, a homosexual act is any sexual act involving sexual arousal between two members of the same anatomic sex. According to the second aspect, a homosexual person is someone who is able to fall in love only with a person of the same anatomic sex or is able to be sexually aroused only by such a person.

These two aspects of the definition are themselves controversial. Some people believe that only the first aspect is tenable. Kinsey, for example, rejected terms like "a homosexual man" or "homosexuals" and was repeatedly forced to fall back on an unusual construction (i.e., "the homosexual," a noun form, meaning the homosexual as a phenomenon) when he referred to the topic. Even so, he was not able to avoid completely the use of phrases such as "homosexual individuals" or "homosexual males," as is astutely pointed out by Robinson.

Confusion is also generated when the first aspect of the definition is mixed with the second, as happens when it is assumed that people who have had sexual contact with members of their own sex "are" homosexual in orientation. In a free society, but one in which sexual activity is assumed (rightly or wrongly) to reflect a deep intimacy, it is likely that most people who perform consensual homosexual acts are homosexual in orientation. But this is not inevitable, and different segments of society differ in the extent to which acts do indeed reflect intimacy. Homosexual acts by teenage male prostitutes, for example, often do not reflect any underlying homosexual orientation; the same is often true with early adolescent sexual experimentation. In a subculture in which what we now call recreational sex is approved, homosexual acts without homosexual orientation are also more likely. The converse error—for example, after therapy, to assume that the cessation of homosexual acts means a conversion to heterosexuality—is also common.

Social constructionism is a scholarly point of view that asserts, in the case of homosexuality, that homosexuality per se does not exist but is nothing more than a concept constructed by the society in which we live. Social constructionists point out that different societies organize their understanding of homosexual acts in such dizzyingly varied ways that it is futile to try to understand these acts in the light of any assumed essence or underlying "real" phenomenon of homosexuality. For example, other cultures totally lacked our modern construction of homosexuality, as evidenced by the fact that ancient Greece did not have words for "homosexual" and "heterosexual." Although there is important truth in such a point of view, it should not be taken too far. Even in ancient Greece, there was a recognition of our modern categories of heterosexual and homosexual—although it is perfectly true that these categories were not as highly charged emotionally as they are today. Nowadays, we understand that dog lovers tend to have different personality traits than cat lovers; the fact that we do not coin terms for these distinctive tastes ("caniphiles" and "feliphiles," perhaps?) does not mean we deny their existence. Likewise, many writers in ancient Greece clearly understood that there were homosexual and heterosexual persons; it is just that the culture did not attach great emotional or moral significance to these personality types, any more than we do today to dog loving and cat loving. The fact that terms like "caniphile," "feliphile," and even "bipetual" sound bizarre and perhaps stigmatizing underscores the social constructionists' point. Nevertheless, one should not assert that caniphila and feliphilia are nonexistent, nor should one deny the existence of homosexuality and heterosexuality.

The Sexual Aspects of Homosexuality

It used to be a popular stereotype that homosexuals were doomed (a favorite word) to a life of empty one-night stands in a search for that unattainable goal, a long-lasting homosexual partnership. The problem is that if the discussion of homosexuality is allowed to be controlled by the terms "promiscuity" and "monogamy," one will overlook important aspects of the nature of couplehood and relationships in these groups of people.

For example, sexual scientists have often conducted surveys in which homosexual men are asked about the number of sexual partners they have had in their lives. Most of these surveys show that gay men, on average, have more partners, both on a lifetime basis and in the recent past, than demographically comparable heterosexual men. But the distributions that produce these averages are rarely given. In one study, the majority of the sexual partners of a group of gay men were partners of two men in the sample who were male prostitutes. In another study, the majority of the heterosexual encounters in a sample of homosexual and bisexual men were performed by two men.

In the gay community, the most important thing to understand about couplehood and relationships is the extreme diversity of patterns to be seen. There are couples who are just as monogamous as many people's mother and father were, quite possibly more so. There are individuals whose promiscuity would startle a Casanova. And there is everything in between.

The second most important thing to understand is that a desire for a committed partner and a desire for a variety of sexual relationships can coexist in the same person—and that the gay community (especially the gay male community) often openly acknowledges this fact. Couplehood has become very popular in the gay community—a fact that is often attributed to the epidemic of acquired immune deficiency syndrome (AIDS), caused by the human immunodeficiency virus (HIV). However, this trend would probably have occurred anyway, and it has always been strong among homosexual women. Couples form when the members of the couple mature to certain stages of their lives and when social conditions permit the signs of couplehood (e.g., living together or attending events together) to be displayed. Many therapists believe that a long-term gay male couple will eventually split up unless its members find some way to permit occasional "extramarital" flings, whereas a lesbian couple will eventually split up unless its members find some way to prevent such flings. Others disagree. It is common in Europe today to presume that married heterosexual couples need not stay sexually monogamous throughout life. (Although this is not an unknown point of view in America, it is far less often publicly discussed or assumed.) Likewise, at many times in the past, especially where marriages were arranged or severely constrained by social pressures, it was considered normal that married couples would copulate to produce children but seek sexual excitement outside the couple.

Few things irritate modern homosexuals more than to be asked what she or he does in bed. The irritation arises for two reasons: first, the question may presume that homosexuals are a distinct, weird species whose members can be questioned about anything at all (in contrast to "normal" individuals whose privacy is respected); and second, the question may be designed to ascertain whether that individual performs the male or the female role in bed (as if there were only one of each). Putting aside whether these two motives are as salient as they are thought to be,

let us simply note that sexual scientists and readers of encyclopedias are allowed to ask whatever questions they wish in the interests of scholarly inquiry and transmission of knowledge.

The coy answer is that homosexuals do in bed everything that heterosexuals do except penovaginal intercourse. Of course, people who believe that penovaginal intercourse is *the* sexual act are puzzled by this answer, because there seems to be nothing else to do; but surely most educated adults know about oral-genital intercourse, anal intercourse, mutual masturbation, hugging, kissing, stroking, and so on. On those occasions when questioners are indeed so gauche as to inquire about which person plays the man's role and which the woman's, more may well be revealed about the questioners' behavior than the questionees'. A homosexual, asked such a question, might respond with his or her own question: "You mean I have to choose?" or even "You mean that when *you* have sex the man always starts it and he always inserts and he's always on top and he always decides when to stop it? Why do all those things have to be done by the same person?" In comparison with gay men's sexuality, lesbian sexuality has been little studied. Of late, this has undoubtedly been due to the AIDS crisis, since it has been deemed important to know what causes some gay men to strongly prefer anal intercourse, the act most likely to transmit AIDS in this population. In spite of the relative lack of research on female homosexuality, we do know that few lesbians can be characterized as taking only a masculine or only a feminine role in sex—a phenomenon that is called butch-femme.

Some studies indicate that lesbian couples have sex less often than heterosexual or gay male couples. Several studies suggest that lesbian lovemaking is relatively more focused on the entire body (hugging, kissing, stroking) and less directly focused on the genitals (cunnilingus, insertion of dildoes), although there are enthusiastic exceptions to this rule. Explicit erotica written by lesbians for lesbians is becoming increasingly popular. In their labs, Masters and Johnson observed couples of all sexual orientations having sex and noted that lesbians were typically better love makers than heterosexual couples were. One interesting fact: lesbians, when sucking on their partner's breasts, were usually careful to suck equal amounts of time on each breast (as if they had to be "evened out"); this was not true among the heterosexual men or for homosexual men who sucked on their partner's nipples. Apparently, no attempts have been made to discern larger patterns in lesbians' sexual behavior beyond these kinds of statistical or clinical details.

As mentioned previously, the sex lives of gay men have been intensely studied of late due to the AIDS epidemic. Few gay men can be characterized as taking only a masculine or only a feminine role in sex, although men who prefer anal intercourse often indicate a preference either for the "top" (inserting) role by wearing keys or a bandanna handkerchief on the left side, or for the "bottom" (receiving) role by wearing such items on the right.

Although these preferences are real, they should not be taken too seriously; in large cities in the United States, gay men are for the most part expected to be versatile, not only in top versus bottom roles (if any) but also in the choice of particular acts (e.g., oral, anal, masturbatory). This is less true in foreign countries. Let us finally reemphasize the large segment of the gay male community—perhaps a majority of it—that has no interest in such matters. For example, at a typical young-crowd gay disco, one sees few if any exposed key rings or bandanna handkerchiefs.

Investigators are increasingly seeking, and finding, interesting patterns in gay men's sexual behavior that go far beyond the mere statistical summarization of a Kinsey report (or a "Gay Report"). One study found, for example, that gay men's sexual behaviors cluster naturally into three categories (using a technique termed factor analysis). The first category, engaged in by nearly all gay men, consists of oral-genital acts and affectionate behaviors such as hugging and kissing. The second category, engaged in by a large minority or slight majority, consists mostly of acts involving anal sex (mainly insertive and receptive anal intercourse). The third category, engaged in by a small minority, consists of esoteric acts such as sadomasochistic rituals, "fist fucking" (in which a hand, as it happens *not* in the form of a fist, is inserted into the rectum), and so on. Notice that there is no evidence in this clustering of an insertor-insertee dichotomy.

The present author would add a fourth category: imaginary acts, engaged in by no gay men but which have entered the public imagination through the process of urban mythmaking. In this illusory category is "gerbiling," an act apparently invented by a right-wing pseudoscientist with a vividly homophobic imagination for a talk show in Philadelphia. Rumors describing hospital admissions for this practice—which supposedly involves receiving sexual pleasure from the death throes of a gerbil inserted into the rectum—have moved from city to city and involved various local weather forecasters and certain movie stars. As one prominent gay newspaper wrote, in an article debunking this pseudopractice, "Show us the X-rays!" The persistence of such rumors tells us less about the sexual practices of gay men than it does about the latent belief on the part of the rumor mongers that gay men as a class are characterized by doing weird, unbelievable things to their rectums. The fact that fist fucking exists, and would provide perfectly adequate fodder for such a belief, simply makes the success of the gerbiling myth all the more remarkable.

Psychological Adjustment

In the 1950s, it was routinely presumed that homosexuality was an extremely deviant activity and the symptom or even cause of a wide variety of psychopathologies. The path-breaking experiments of Evelyn Hooker disproved this extreme view by demonstrating that trained therapists were unable at better-than-chance levels to differentiate between homosexuals' and heterosexuals' psychological test scores if the therapists were blind to the sexual orientations of the subjects. Now, such a differentiation could probably be made if a score for childhood gender nonconformity were included (see below), but even so there would be many exceptions.

In terms of such mainstream psychological problems as psychosis or schizophrenia, however, Hooker's insights remain as valid as ever. Although there are a few psychological problems that homosexuals may have more often than heterosexuals do, these problems signify reactions to social oppression as opposed to any underlying, causative pathology. Interested readers are referred to Gonsiorek's recent extensive review.

Relationship to Other Phenomena

Homosexuality is often thought to be related to other phenomena such as transvestism, transsexualism, or AIDS. In fact, homosexuality is not equivalent to any of them and for the most part these assumed connections are incorrect stereotypes. For example, transsexualism (i.e., the obsessional insistence that one's innermost feelings of being male or female do not match one's genitalia) can occur in men who are sexually attracted to men, in men attracted to women, in women attracted to men, and in women attracted to women. Of course, when one wishes to change sex, it is not immediately clear whether the terms "homosexual" and "heterosexual" should be used in reference to the original or the desired sex.

In the case of transvestism (in which putting on the clothes of the opposite sex is or has been associated with sexual arousal), we must first face the fact that society's standards for female dress are far more flexible than they are for male attire. A man or boy wearing a dress elicits the strongest possible negative reaction, whereas a woman or girl wearing a coat and tie elicits positive or neutral reactions—or negative reactions only in the case where the act somehow challenges the observer's most basic perceptions of sex difference. According to the late Robert Stoller, there are only three reported cases in the entire world literature of women who became sexually aroused by putting on men's clothing. That all three women had bisexual aspects to their lives is an interesting scientific curio, but it merely underscores the fact that essentially no lesbians or bisexuals are transvestites.

More to the point, although there are adult homosexual men who enjoy wearing women's clothes, there are also adult heterosexuals who enjoy the same. While no good empirical data on the matter are available, the consensus of opinion seems to be that the percentage of male homosexual cross-dressers is no higher than that of male heterosexual cross-dressers. In contrast, a great deal of evidence exists that fetishistic cross-dressing associated with sexual arousal occurs far more often, perhaps exclusively, on the heterosexual side.

An interesting fact concerning cross-dressing (whether erotic or nonerotic) has only recently emerged in research: when cross-dressing occurs early in boyhood (anywhere from the age of three to just before puberty), it is often a harbinger of adult male homosexuality, although the desire to cross-dress typically dies out or dies down soon after puberty. When cross-dressing occurs later in boyhood (beginning around puberty), especially if it is associated with sexual excitement, it is often a harbinger of adult heterosexual transvestism.

Sadomasochism (S&M)—the facilitation or achievement of sexual arousal by giving or receiving pain—is often associated in the popular imagination with male homosexuality, presumably because of the existence of so-called leather bars in the male homosexual subculture. The same can be said of a lighter form of S&M, bondage and discipline, in which pain is absent but dominance and submission themes are prominent. Yet here, too, appearances can be deceiving, and these erotic tastes are found on all sides of the sexual-orientation boundary. For example, the heterosexually directed *Joy of Sex* often gives suggestions for bondage and discipline to be enjoyed by heterosexual men and women alike, and lesbian S&M interests are not unknown. Fetishism (i.e., interest in objects such as hair or shoes) is found in men of every sexual orientation and rarely in women.

The relationship of homosexuality to bisexuality is contentious and complicated—and probably rather different in men and women. When a man declares himself to be bisexual, he is usually disbelieved by most male homosexuals. The presumption is that such a man is deceiving himself: that he is in all likelihood a gay man who has not yet come to terms with his homosexuality. This presumption, right or wrong, is rooted in the fact that every gay man knows many men who used to call themselves bisexual and now call themselves gay. In contrast, when a woman says she is bisexual, the statement is usually taken quite seriously by homosexual women. For example, the possibility that she may permanently leave a homosexual relationship for a heterosexual one is often taken at face value and not regarded as a sham.

It is a common prejudice that homosexual men are particularly prone to pedophilia (i.e., erotic attraction to children) or to ephebephilia (i.e., erotic attraction to pubescents or younger teenagers). But pedophilia and ephebephilia cut across all sexual-orientation boundaries, and thus parents who entrust their children to the care of adults should be just as aware of the possibility of same-sex molestation as of opposite-sex molestation. Even if there were average differences by sexual orientation in rates of pedophilia or ephebephila, such studies would be irrelevant to the social-political controversy—just as would a study demonstrating that one or another racial group was more or less prone to pedophilia. After all, it is clear that the large majority of all sexual (and racial) groups are not pedophiles.

Lesbians are rarely accused of pedophilia or ephebephilia, and when they are it is usually as a result of having been identified with the general concept of homosexuality rather than as lesbians per se (a negative halo effect, if you will). There are, of course, essentially no scientific data on the question, as nearly all pedophiles and ephebephiles are men.

In the popular imagination today, male homosexuality is inevitably associated with AIDS. Of course, there is no denying that gay male culture has been irrevocably affected by the AIDS epidemic, at least in the major cities where AIDS has to date taken so much of its toll, and that coming out as gay also means coming to terms with, and deciding whether to take responsibility for, the necessity for safer sex if one chooses not to remain celibate. This association can also have a pathological tinge, as when a female-to-male transsexual who is sexually attracted to men writes that he considers his AIDS diagnosis to be the quintessential confirmation of his (male) homosexuality, or when a gay man uninfected with HIV insists that symptoms, perhaps of a common cold, are in fact evidence that he has AIDS. Such cases are, of course, rare, but their very extremeness helps to put the more common patterns in perspective.

The negative halo effect applies with special force to the popular image of lesbians and AIDS. Many lesbians are involved in the fight against AIDS and in making sure that lesbians modify their sexual behavior to slow any possible spread of the disease in their community. But this is not the result of elevated levels of the disease in comparison with either heterosexual women or homosexual men. Quite the contrary: lesbians have extremely low rates of AIDS, and a confirmed report of lesbian-to-lesbian sexual transmission would astonish AIDS researchers. Yet many times in popular discourse, people have assumed that lesbians are somehow associated with AIDS in an infectious way. Whether it be a state legislator arguing in favor of a bill denying homosexual women (and men) the right to be foster parents on the basis of AIDS exposure or an estranged husband arguing in court that his wife's lesbianism would expose their children to AIDS, there is scarcely a better documented example of the nonrational genesis of prejudice.

Therapy

Although far more common in the past, it is still not rare for some homosexuals to approach psychotherapists with the request to convert their homosexual orientation into a heterosexual one. In a similar vein, it is apparently still the case that homosexual adolescents are more likely to try to commit suicide than heterosexual adolescents because their homosexual feelings seem socially unacceptable, even shameful. This is not a surprise, given the severely antihomosexual attitudes of society, especially the teenage segment.

Although there is still substantial controversy on this matter, it is now widely regarded as unethical, for a variety of reasons, to offer "therapy" to change a sexual orientation. First and foremost, it does not work. There is a long and shameful list of therapists who have made attempts, only to abandon them, sometimes quietly and sometimes with open discussion. For example, a former president of the Association for the Advancement of Behavior Therapy,

Gerald Davison, not only founded such a therapeutic school ("Playboy therapy") but also repudiated it on many occasions after deciding that it did more harm than good and that it would not have been ethical even if it had worked. Another behavior therapist, Kurt Freund, abandoned his form of aversive therapy for homosexuality after a genital measurement device (called a plethysmograph) showed that the "cured" ex-homosexuals remained sexually aroused by images of naked men.

This unfortunate sequence of events is now being repeated in the claims that homosexuality can be cured by religious conversion or other spiritual methods. "Ex-homosexuals" have been followed by "ex-ex-homosexuals," and there is even a sordid turn of events: on more than one occasion, the men involved in founding and running ex-homosexual ministries have used their followers as sexual partners. Although one cannot, of course, claim that all or even most such ministries are self-deceptive or manipulative, it is chilling to hear managers of such enterprises admitting that homosexuals do not in fact acquire a heterosexual orientation through their programs. It is claimed that the most that can be hoped for is abstinence from homosexual contacts, and perhaps some mild degree of heterosexual arousability—just as an alcoholic cannot be truly cured of the underlying disease of alcoholism. These apologists might pay more attention to Freund's conclusions:

> Almost 20 years ago I started a therapeutic experiment. . . . [t]his was a long-term study, and these marriages [of homosexuals] were followed up for many years. Virtually not one "cure" remained a cure. The patients had become able to enjoy sexual intercourse with females as well [as males], though much less than with males, but there was no true, lasting change in sexual preference. . . . Many patients admitted this only much later than they themselves had clearly noted this fact.

It is indeed depressing that these words, published 15 years ago about therapies conducted 20 years before, remain unappreciated by those who would now hold out false hope to those upset by their faith's rejection of their innermost natures, feelings, and desires.

Conclusion

This is an exciting time for research in homosexuality. Researchers who attended college during the early heyday of campus social groups for gay students acquired the knowledge that gay people are far more ordinary than most of the psychological and psychiatric theories of their professors would have had them believe. Now that they have advanced in their careers and acquired the ability to conduct their own studies, they have begun to address several of the fundamental questions about sexual orientation that earlier generations had deemed unimportant or too controversial. One of these questions concerns biological and hormonal predispositions to particular sexual orientations, but this is far from being the only new avenue of research. Social constructionism, for example, has breathed new life into many controversies relating to homosexuality and challenged its very existence as a definable phenomenon. A great deal of important work on the psychological and social aspects of male homosexuality is being conducted as part of the effort to fight AIDS. Unfortunately, an effect has been the continuing neglect of research on lesbianism. For this and for many other reasons, much work remains to be done.

REFERENCES

Davison, G.C. Constructionism and Morality in Therapy for Homosexuality. In J.C. Gonsiorek and J.D. Weinrich, eds., *Homosexuality: Research Implications for Public Policy.* Newbury Park, Calif.: Sage, 1991.

Freund, K.W. Should Homosexuality Arouse Therapeutic Concern? *Journal of Homosexuality*, Vol. 2, No. 3 (1977), pp. 235–40.

Gonsiorek, J.C. The Empirical Basis for the Demise of the Illness Model of Homosexuality. In J.C. Gonsiorek and J.D. Weinrich, eds., *Homosexuality: Research Implications for Public Policy.* Newbury Park, Calif.: Sage, 1991.

Robinson, P. *The Modernization of Sex: Havelock Ellis, Alfred Kinsey, William Masters and Virginia Johnson.* New York: Harper & Row, 1976.

James D. Weinrich

HOMOSEXUALITY AND LESBIANISM: CROSS-CULTURAL PERSPECTIVES

Homosexuality in some form has always existed. In modern industrial societies, it is estimated that between 5 percent and 10 percent of the population is homosexual. In some societies, such as ancient Greece, male homosexuality was not only practiced but also institutionalized as an integral part of the social structure. In most Western cultures, however, homosexuality was less openly practiced, and much of our information about the phenomenon is derived from legal records. Women rarely appeared in these documents because their relations with other women were seen as friendships and thus encouraged. This is very different from the treatment received by men who were suspected of homosexuality. Historically, European men were expected to avoid close interaction patterns with other men, in contrast to the sometimes ardent interactions of women. Generally, the Judeo-Christian tradition taught that all nonprocreative sexual acts were intolerable but punished sodomy, or anal sex, most severely.

The behavior of male homosexuals was seen as deviant, but what constitutes deviant behavior differs cross-culturally as well as throughout history. Even terms such as "homosexuality" and "homosexual" are modern, originating in the late 19th and early 20th centuries. The sparsely written history of homosexuality is not indicative of the millions of lives lived by homosexuals, but reflects the earlier bias against homosexuality and the fear that studying homosexuality would prove risky in public opinion.

As physicians became interested in homosexuality in the 19th century, they classified homosexuality (as well as prostitution and masturbation) as a disease. Thus, they were inclined to find a cause and a cure for the disease of same-sex love. In 1974, the American Psychological Association removed homosexuality from the category of pathological illness. However, there are still people today who feel that homosexuals can be "treated" and "cured" and turned to a heterosexual life.

In the United States, slow acceptance of homosexual couples is seen not only in the recent view of them as "normal" by psychological standards but also in the prevailing laws, which do not fully sanction same-sex marriages. These marriages, often performed in community churches, are not considered legally binding, so same-sex spouses are denied the tax and insurance benefits granted to heterosexual spouses. Some countries do recognize homosexual marriage and confer on the partners the same rights and obligations that heterosexual couples have. Denmark is one such Western country.

Acceptance is even more common in non-Western societies. In Mombasa, for example, 50 percent of Swahili women live independently of financial support from their husbands and often have lives of their own. There is a strong lesbian subculture that consists of lesbians earning good wages in the business world and living together as couples. This is not seen as problematic because many of them are reasonably wealthy and can support their "wives." There is also a growing number of lesbian salons, or meeting places, where they discuss social issues, the arts, and daily life. These function in much the same way as the salons seen in Paris in the 1930s and 1940s.

These kinds of homosexual arrangements cross-culturally are of great interest to anthropologists, although there has frequently been a reluctance to formally publish information about them. Anthropologists who did write openly about variable sexual lives often found their work censored. For example, in the 1930s and 1940s, the anthropologist E.E. Evans-Pritchard, who worked among the Azande tribe of West Africa, wrote that he found homosexuality practiced by both men and women. His reports, however, were kept from the public by the Anthropological Society until the early 1970s when they were finally published openly.

Writing on homosexuality is generally about men. This is true cross-culturally. The reason may be that men's roles in society have been viewed as more important than women's or that most early anthropological work was done by men.

Problems of Definition

One of the great obstacles in gay and lesbian studies cross-culturally is the absence of a universal word defining male and female homosexuality and the behaviors or attitudes that characterize someone as such. "Lesbian" as a term describing sexuality did not exist until the late 19th century. The term "homosexual" does not exist even today in some parts of the world. Not all people who have engaged in homosexual behavior are homosexuals. Many people all over the world go through a stage of experimentation when they are learning about their sexuality. In most societies, a single, or even several, homosexual encounters do not mean that one is a homosexual. In some cultures, such as New Guinea's, premarital sexual behavior between men is encouraged and considered the normative pattern.

Human identity, including sexual identity, is the product of cultural surroundings and historical situations. One may be willing or desirous of homosexual experimentation, but it may never happen due to these surroundings. This means that one can be a homosexual and never engage in sex with a member of the same sex. Sexual acts do not determine one's sexuality. It is the self-identifying process that brings sexuality to light. It has been said that the way to identify a lesbian or gay man has become a personal matter: "you are one only if you consider yourself one."

Lesbian relationships may have been more difficult to define cross-culturally and histori-

cally because of the state of women's relationships in general. Historically, women have often been encouraged to have intimate relationships with other women. These "romantic friendships" were not seen as a threat to or an acceptable replacement for male-female relations. Cross-culturally, it seems that these friendships were meant to aid women in passing time while men were away, thus reducing demands on men, and in the process these friendships became an economic benefit, providing help with household work and child care. However, not all of these friendships remained platonic.

In the West, for example, many women did not define themselves as lesbians because of the negative connotations of the word. They would freely admit to some that they were in love, physically and emotionally, with another woman but add that they were not lesbians. This is one of the main problems in identifying and studying homosexuality cross-culturally.

If a Western term is applied to a behavior and related beliefs, and this term has no approximate equal in another culture, the process of communicating about the behavior is difficult. An anthropologist may use the term "lesbian" to describe an observed relationship in which two women live together, share a bed and chores, and raise their children together. However, what if the women would not consider their relationship lesbian in nature? Similarly, many women who have had physical love relationships with other women would not define themselves as lesbians.

Historically around the globe, if women did realize that their happiness was to be found only by living romantically with another woman, they had to make life changes to do so. First, they had to find ways of being economically independent from the support of a man. Once a woman could support herself, she could find other women who desired the same life; this led to the beginnings of a lesbian subculture, as seen in Mombasa. There are also many situations in which women who love one another can do so while remaining in culturally acceptable living arrangements.

India

In India, for example, there is a varied population of lesbians. Many are devotees of the various Hindu or Sikh goddesses. The spiritual and physical aspects of their relationships are very important. Here, where homosexual acts between women are not mentioned in the law, homosexual acts between men are illegal. In 1987, however, two policewomen were fired for marrying each other but were not prosecuted.

Most of the writing on lesbians in India is about older, economically independent, educated urban Indian women or foreigners living in India. Many of these women had been sent abroad to a university, and it was in this context that they had their first chance to act on their inner erotic feelings without the direct danger of their families finding out. Many of these Indian women were involved in relationships with other women lasting through their college years. Their desire to return to their homeland, however, eventually took them back to their families and away from their lovers. Some of these relationships, probably, did not involve genital sex, but they were still considered lesbian relationships because of the intense erotic and emotional feelings involved.

When these Indian women who have lesbian relationships abroad return home, they ordinarily marry men their families have chosen for them. Marriage is expected; family structure is often the only hope for social security; a woman living alone is seen as suspect, and it is often difficult to secure housing. Some women will try to find help through women's groups or return to a women's school, but many will work within their culturally acceptable social groups.

Employment opportunities and independent living patterns are not as abundant for women around the world as they are for Western women. That is why it is difficult to find lesbian relationship forms when they exist within common family units. Because Indian culture places a high value on family tradition, these women have intense fears that their behavior would publicly dishonor their families. Their arranged marriages often last a lifetime, and the women describe their husbands as good men with whom they have little in common. The women are available to their children and for occasional intercourse with their husbands. These lesbians, however, are able to skillfully combine monogamous same-sex relationships with their obligations as wives.

In India, mothers-in-law and daughters-in-law are expected to be a great support to one another and to spend time together shopping and cooking. In cases in which a lesbian lives in the same city as her mother-in-law, she may have to explain her close female friend who appears to offer the support that normally a mother-in-law would provide. Many Indian lesbians, however, seem to manage well within the prevailing cultural expectations.

Lovers in India often see each other daily if possible. They may go for a walk or to an exhibition or a women's meeting, and finally spend the rest of the afternoon together in their private quarters separate from their husbands. Female couples whose jobs are controlled by a schedule may meet when convenient at an urban hotel.

Lesbian women in India often report feeling that they embody the qualities of both men and women in their relationships with other women. The butch-femme classification found among Western lesbian couples seems to be much less prevalent. As mentioned earlier, the self-definition of these women differs from Western beliefs. "Lesbian" is not an unfamiliar concept or word, but often these women see themselves as simply women who have and always will love other women. In some conversations, these women may make no distinction between heterosexual and homosexual relations. They may speak of chapti, or lesbianism, but there is no Hindi or Urdu equivalent for the word "lesbian." Often they say that emotions and acts of love are gender free.

Some Western lesbians and feminists might not feel comfortable using "lesbian" to describe these Indian women, since they remain married and continue to live in relationships that are based not on personal choice but cultural expectation. However, it is important to remember the cultural variability of homosexual patterns.

Asia

In China, historically, male homosexuality was tolerated without the threat of severe punishment. A far worse offense was celibacy. Chinese history, fiction, legends, and other written works, as well as oral communication such as jokes and slang, contain a great deal of information on male homosexuality. Many Chinese men from the southeastern provinces went to sea, engaging in fishing expeditions and trades. While they were away, their friendships would often include sexual relations and some loving partnerships. The men would visit young boys when they went into port, and some paid a "bride price" in order to "marry" these young boys.

The women left behind sometimes turned to one another, some taking vows to be lifelong spinsters and never to marry. Others would go through elaborate rituals to "marry" and engaged in sexual pleasures freely. These marriage rituals are not unlike those found around the world. It seems that telling not only one's partner, but also friends and perhaps family, that there is a firm commitment involved in one's relationship is important to most people, whether they are heterosexual or homosexual.

In China, in both men's and women's cases, homosexual relations are often disguised as conventional family relations, such as brothers or sisters. This has been one acceptable way in which lovers could live together and maintain a common household.

Homoerotic fiction has existed in China for centuries. Lesbianism in Asia can be traced back to as early as 520–480 B.C.E., when Buddhist nuns in India wrote lesbian love poetry. Rulers of Chinese states have been the subjects of legendary homoerotic tales of their loves. One emperor, Ai-di, who loved a young man, Tung Xian, cut off his sleeves, upon which the latter was sleeping, so he could arise without awakening his lover. The term duan-xiu ("cut sleeves") thus became another expression for homosexual love.

Many novels came out during the Ming and Qing periods in China that contained elaborate accounts of homoerotic behavior. Because many men were used to portray women in Chinese theater (as in Shakespearean), they were often the objects of male desire. In early Chinese poetry, it is often difficult to determine if the object of a man's love is a woman or another man. Many reviewers of later and more moralistic times rewrote the poems to make clear that the erotic desire was a heterosexual one.

As is the case in many urban areas, first homosexual experiences for Chinese youths often occur at their same-sex boarding school. These schools do not have a higher incidence of homosexuals attending them; they simply provide an environment that makes same-sex loves less traumatic for those who are so inclined. In 1982, the People's Republic of China Criminal Law Code did not expressly prohibit homosexual activities.

Native Americans

The two most popular institutionalized same-sex practices are gender-reversed homosexuality and age-structured homosexuality. In gender-reversed homosexuality, the individual adopts the dress, social roles, gestures, occupation, and sexual behavior of the opposite sex. The Native American *berdache* is the best known of this tradition.

Berdache occurred in at least 113 different tribes. In two-thirds of those cultures, there were only male *berdache*, whereas in the other third there were both male and female *berdache*. Thus, a biologically normal Indian male would take on the *berdache* role, simulate menstruation and pregnancy, and dress as a girl (later as an older woman).

For males, the gender reversal resulted in their feminization and was a lifelong role.

Women who were *berdache* (sometimes called nadles) were respected due to their behavior in their occupation (e.g., skilled hunter or rider), and they were allowed to have marital partners of the same sex, if desired. This type of gender reversal was also found in Brazil, where an explorer encountered many women hunting with the men, each accompanied by another woman she had brought along as her "wife."

New Guinea

Only males have been found to participate in age-structured homosexuality. Males of different ages, never equals, engage in ritualized homosexual practices for years. This activity usually occurs in adolescence and is similar to ancient Greek homosexual practice. The age-structured form has occurred in many places around the world but is best known in New Guinea.

In New Guinea, this type of homosexual behavior co-occurs with warriorhood cults of masculinity, sexual antagonism between boys and girls, and strong restrictive behaviors about sexual practices. Sambia males undergo ritual initiation procedures that fully institutionalize same-sex erotic contact between young boys and unmarried youths. This practice focuses primarily on the beliefs held by their culture concerning the power of semen transmission. Semen is a growth stimulant in the eyes of many tribal cultures. Among the Sambia, ingesting semen is believed actually to secure a boy's maturation. They believe that the male body alone cannot spontaneously produce semen. Thus, males need to take in semen to produce their own for both inseminating their future wives and acting as donors to younger boys.

In Sambia culture, only oral intercourse is permitted for semen transmission, and there has been no record of masturbation to orgasm. Homosexual contacts between females are believed to be absent; however, most of the studies have been done by men, who may have had difficulty uncovering female sexual practices. Approximately 5 percent of Sambia males continue to engage exclusively in homosexual sex after adolescence.

Again, Western vocabulary and criteria make it difficult to define this behavior. The Sambia themselves do not have a noun category for either "homosexual" or "heterosexual." They do not even recognize that someone can be either exclusively homosexual or exclusively heterosexual throughout his or her entire life. The

Sambia see no necessary contradiction in a person's engaging in sex with both females and males as long as this is done at the appropriate stage of life and in an acceptable manner.

A main difference to note in this regard between the United States and Sambia is that the definition of sexual preference in the United States, especially homosexual preference, focuses on the individual and disregards social surroundings and cultural variations. Moreover, the idea of sexuality begins with a conception of sexual orientation as natural attraction to the opposite sex. This notion is quite different from thought patterns in other cultures in which there may be more fluidity in sexual preference from one life stage to the next, as in the case of the Sambia, or more culturally acceptable ways of living beyond one's sex, as with the *berdache*.

Conclusion

The cases presented here are by no means exhaustive and mark only a few examples of homosexuality across cultures. They have been used to illustrate the global and cross-cultural existence of and variability in gay and lesbian lives. Because the gay liberation movement has been based in the West, most critical, in-depth studies have focused on gay and lesbian couples living in Europe or the United States. As more scholars, both homosexual and heterosexual, begin to free up their definitions of homosexuality, a growing number of cross-cultural studies of same-sex partners can be expected. Such an effort is important not only for historical and anthropological studies, but for a generally increased awareness of the variety of successful sexual partnerships found around the world.

REFERENCES

Allen, J. *Lesbian Philosophies and Culture*. New York: State Univ. of New York Press, 1990.

Bullough, V., and B. Bullough. *Sin, Sickness and Sanity*. New York: New American Library, 1977.

Greenberg, D.F. *The Construction of Homosexuality*. Chicago: Univ. of Chicago Press, 1977.

Herdt, G., ed. *Ritualized Homosexuality in Melanesia*. Berkeley: Univ. of California Press, 1984.

Murray, S.G. *Male Homosexuality in Central and South America*. San Francisco: Gai Saber Monograph, 1987.

Pink Book Editing Team. *Second ILGA Pink Book*. Utrecht: Interfacultaire Werkgrouep Homostudies, 1988.

Ross, M.W., ed. *Homosexuality, Masculinity, and Femininity*. New York: Harrington Press, 1983.

Salvatore, L.J., and R.P. Peteren, eds. *Historical Perspectives on Homosexuality*. New York: Haworth Press, 1981.

Xiaomingxiong. *History of Homosexuality in China*. Hong Kong: Samhasha and Pink Triangle Press, 1984.

Liesl L. Gambold

HORMONES: THE ENDOCRINE SYSTEM

From the moment of conception to maturity, sexual development depends on a complex interaction of genetic and dynamic hormonal interrelationships that regulate hypothalamic, pituitary, and gonadal function. The development of neuroendocrine function in relation to growth and sexual maturation of both the female and the male throughout the life cycle is covered here. This discussion focuses on the normal patterns; the various changes, abnormalities, problems, and treatment modalities involving the neuroendocrine system are covered under such topics as castration, compulsion, gender, infertility, impotence, menopause, menstruation, pheromones, physical disabilities, pregnancy, and transsexualism.

Fetal Sexual Development

The sequence of embryonic and physiologic changes that control the sexual differentiation of the fetus begins with fertilization. The sex of the embryo is genetically determined at the instant of fertilization, with the XX karyotype conferring female sex and the XY karyotype conferring male sex.

The embryo has indifferent gonads that can become either testes or ovaries. In the absence of a Y chromosome, the indifferent gonads differentiate into ovaries nine to ten weeks after conception. At about 18 to 20 weeks, the internal and external female genitalia develop, establishing female genital sex. The presence of the Y chromosome causes the indifferent gonads to differentiate into testes at six to eight weeks. Shortly afterwards, testicular Leydig cells begin to secrete testosterone, which stimulates the development of internal and external male genitalia, establishing male genital sex.

In the human fetus of either sex, the fetal gonad is affected by three gonadotropins: placental chorionic gonadotropin (hCG) early in gestation, and later by follicle stimulating hormone (FSH) and luteinizing hormone (LH), both secreted by the fetal pituitary. Fetal serum hCG peaks around the tenth week of gestation and stimulates testosterone secretion by the testes of the male fetus. Unlike the testis, the fetal ovary is only minimally affected by the early appearance of hCG. Growth and function of the fetal ovary is more dependent on the later appearance of the pituitary gonadotropins.

Hormonal Control of Sexual Maturation

The hormonal relationship of the hypothalamic-pituitary-gonadal axis becomes established by two years of age in either sex, functioning quietly until the onset of puberty. In childhood, the negative-feedback response of this axis is extremely sensitive to the small amounts of circulating gonadal steroids, contributing to the low levels of gonadotropins secreted from the pituitary.

Adolescence generally refers to the time between the onset of puberty and the completion of physical maturation. During adolescence, maturation of the gonads is accompanied by accelerated growth, development of secondary sex characteristics, and attainment of reproductive capability manifested by spermatogenesis in the male and ovulation in the female. In anticipation of the onset of puberty, serum concentrations of pituitary FSH rise between the ages of 6 and 8, and at approximately 10 years of age there follows an increase in the secretion of LH by the anterior pituitary. The secretions of LH and FSH are believed to be controlled via the hypothalamus by a single gonadotropin releasing hormone (GnRH). The elevated serum levels of LH and FSH stimulate the growth of the gonads to their adult size, stimulate gametogenesis, and greatly increase the secretion of gonadal steroids. The gonadal-steroid secretion initiates the first physical signs of sexual maturation with development of secondary sexual characteristics. In the female, this includes breast development (thelarche), pubic hair growth (pubarche), axillary hair growth (which usually follows pubarche), somatic growth acceleration, and finally the menarche, or initiation of menses. In the male, a deepening voice; pubic, axillary, and facial hair growth, testicular and phallic enlargement; and somatic growth acceleration indicate sexual maturation. This process generally begins between the ages of 8 and 13 in females, and occurs about two years later in males, with full development over a three-year period. The order of appearance of pubertal features varies greatly among individuals.

In women, release of the gonadotropins occurs on a cyclical basis, creating the reproductive or menstrual cycle. In men, the release is relatively steady, although there are a number of pulses of gonadotropin release in a 24-hour period.

Gonadal Steroids and Sexual Maturation

In females, there are two major reproductive steroids, estradiol (an estrogen) and progesterone (a progestin). The most frequent first sign of female sexual maturation is breast budding, which occurs in response to the increased pubertal levels of estrogen. Both the mammary glands and the adipose tissue of the breast are stimulated to increase in size by estrogen. Increases in body fat and its characteristic deposition, a broader pelvis, and a shorter period of growth of long bones are also effects of estrogen. Progesterone is primarily involved in the menstrual cycle, which is discussed later on.

The major steroid secreted in males is testosterone, although the testes also secrete small amounts of estrogen. Testosterone is responsible for the development of male secondary sexual characteristics. Testosterone helps to initiate the growth spurt of male adolescence and also ultimately ends that growth spurt by stimulating closure of the epiphyses of the long bones. It causes enlargement of the larynx, which deepens the male voice, generally coinciding with the growth spurt. Testicular enlargement occurs, followed by phallic enlargement 12 to 18 months later. Testosterone stimulates growth of muscles and is probably responsible for the higher hematocrit level of men. Gynecomastia, or development of breast tissue, is a normal male response during early puberty, probably due to the higher ratio of estrogen to testosterone secreted by the testes during early and mid-puberty. Testosterone stimulates the growth of facial, body, and pubic hair, and it is a contributing factor in male pattern baldness. It is also required for spermatogenesis and plays an important role in the establishment of sexual interest, or libido.

The adrenal cortex of both sexes also produces small amounts of androgen as a by-product of synthesis of aldosterone and cortisol. The major androgen produced is dehydroepiandrosterone (DHEA). Although a weaker androgen than testosterone, DHEA plays an important role in female sexual development. This adrenal androgen is primarily responsible for the growth of pubic and axillary hair in women and also contributes to the female adolescent growth spurt. DHEA, along with a small amount of androgen secreted by the ovaries, also appears to be responsible for female libido, rather than the "female" sex hormones estrogen and progesterone.

Male Reproductive Function

In the male, the hypothalamus secretes gonadotropin releasing hormone in pulsatile bursts throughout the day. One effect of GnRH is to stimulate the pituitary to increase secretion of the gonadotropins FSH and LH. Pituitary FSH controls spermatogenesis, which occurs in the Sertoli cells. Inhibin is then selected by the Sertoli cells, exerting a negative-feedback control and diminishing the amount of FSH released by the pituitary.

Biosynthesis and secretion of testosterone, the primary male androgen, are carried out by the Leydig (interstitial) cells. Pituitary LH is primarily responsible for stimulating the Leydig cells' secretion of testosterone. Testosterone then acts as an inhibitor of both GnRH secretion from the hypothalamus and LH secretion from the pituitary, another example of a hormonal negative-feedback loop.

Levels of testosterone rise throughout puberty and reach their maximum value by about the age of 20. These relatively high testosterone levels are maintained until the fourth decade, when they begin a gradual decline. The degree of decrease in testosterone levels varies widely from one individual to the next. This decreasing level of testosterone is often compared to the menopausal period of female development.

As testosterone levels decrease, so too does their negative-feedback inhibition on both the hypothalamus and pituitary. This creates a coincidental rise in gonadotropin levels in an effort to stimulate the aging testes to produce more testosterone. In response to diminishing levels of testosterone, target tissues up-regulate their testosterone receptors, cushioning the effects of the lowered levels of androgen. This promotes maintenance of functioning of accessory structures and also helps maintain a level of sexual interest. Spermatogenesis, which is mostly independent of testicular function and levels of testosterone, continues throughout the male life span following puberty.

Female Reproductive Function

The ovaries of the sexually mature female undergo regular cycles, beginning with maturation and ovulation of a follicle. A period of time follows during which hormones secreted by the remnant of the ovulated follicle create a uterine environment receptive to implantation of an embryo. The maturing follicle also functions as an endocrine organ, secreting estradiol, the main source of estrogen in women who are not pregnant. During ovulation, the mature follicle bursts, releasing an ovum into the body cavity, from which it is swept by the fimbriae into a Fallopian tube, where it may be fertilized.

As a follicle matures, it becomes an active endocrine tissue. Just as in the male reproductive system, the hypothalamus secretes GnRH, stimulating the anterior pituitary to secrete both LH and FSH. Both LH and FSH are needed for ovarian cycles. LH stimulates the thecal cells of the mature follicle to supply the granulosa cells of the follicle with androgen, which is converted by the granulosa cells to estradiol and secreted into the blood. Granulosa cells also secrete inhibin, which acts in a negative-feedback relationship as an inhibitor of anterior pituitary release of FSH. LH secretion is not affected by inhibin. Estradiol is responsible for the regulation of LH levels by a negative-feedback loop involving both the hypothalamus and the anterior pituitary. LH secretion does not always behave as if it were regulated by negative feedback, however; the surge of LH that causes ovulation occurs even though estradiol levels are rising. This surge can be explained by the fact that the anterior pituitary responds differently to rising levels of estradiol than it does to moderate, nonfluctuating levels. At moderate, steady levels of estradiol, the anterior pituitary predominantly shuts off its LH secretion by means of negative feedback. When estradiol levels rise rapidly to high levels, as they do during the follicular phase, the pituitary is actually stimulated to secrete a surge of LH.

In the final stage of follicular maturation, the follicle is called a graafian follicle and visibly bulges from the surface of the ovary. Occasionally, more than one graafian follicle is matured and ovulated. If both are fertilized, this multiple ovulation may lead to fraternal twins. Fraternal twins are genetically different and may be of different sexes.

The surge of LH that follows the rise in estrogen level at this time is coupled with a smaller increase in FSH. The rise in FSH level is considerably smaller due to the continued effects of inhibin on the anterior pituitary. The ovum is released from the graafian follicle about 12 to 24 hours after LH has reached its peak concentration. This is called the ovulation phase of the menstrual cycle and occurs 14 days prior to the onset of menstruation.

The ovum is then swept up by fimbriae and carried toward the uterus by the ciliary activity and smooth-muscle contractions of the Fallopian tube. An ovum can be fertilized for only 10 to 12 hours after ovulation. Spermatozoa can survive for up to three days in the female reproductive tract, allowing for a relatively brief span of time in which fertilization can occur during each menstrual cycle.

The female endocrine system relating to pregnancy is a complex interaction of hormones secreted by the corpus luteum, placenta, uterus, and pituitary. The hormones of pregnancy, labor, and lactation include estrogen, progesterone, placental somatomammotropin, oxytocin, relaxin, and prolactin. (Hormones of pregnancy, labor, and lactation are not covered in this entry.)

Following ovulation, the remnant of the follicle becomes a secretory organ called the corpus luteum, which maintains the receptivity of the uterus to a pregnancy by secreting estrogen and progesterone. If pregnancy does not occur, the corpus luteum degenerates approximately 14 days later, and the resultant decrease in levels of estrogen and progesterone causes the uterine endometrium to be shed, initiating menstruation.

The average menstrual cycle lasts 28 days, with a normal range from 21 to 35 days. The first menstrual day is numbered as day 1 and marks the beginning of the follicular phase of the ovarian cycle. Ovulation, which occurs approximately on day 14 of the 28-day cycle, marks the transition from the follicular phase to the luteal phase of the ovarian cycle. During the luteal phase of the cycle, the presence of progesterone secreted by the corpus luteum modifies the responsiveness of the pituitary to the high levels of circulating estrogen, preventing recurrent surges of LH. During the luteal phase, the negative-feedback system again predominates, and LH and FSH remain at relatively low levels. The estrogen and progesterone secreted by the corpus luteum also interact to convert the uterine endometrium into a structure specialized to receive an embryo. The endometrium thickens and becomes a secretory organ, secreting uterine milk, a carbohydrate-rich fluid capable of nourishing the embryo until implantation in the uterine wall occurs.

It is not uncommon for ovulating women to complain of a complex of symptoms during the last week of the menstrual cycle. This symptom complex, known as premenstrual syndrome (PMS), does not occur in children, pregnant women, or anovulatory women. The symptoms may include breast tenderness, bloating, edema of the extremities, and mood swings. Symptoms abate with the onset of menstruation. No specific etiology for PMS has been found, although progesterone secreted by the corpus luteum is strongly suspected to play a significant role.

The cycles of estrogen and progesterone secretion by the ovaries continue throughout the woman's sexually mature years until the menopausal transition, which usually takes place between 45 and 55 years of age. Menopausal transition is characterized by longer cycles and irregular bleeding. These irregular cycles can persist for months or years before complete amenorrhea occurs. During this time, the ovaries undergo an obliterative endarteritis that leads to a reduction in ovarian size and the replacement of the secretory parenchyma with connective tissue. As the ovaries become less able to secrete steroids in response to gonadotropins, the negative-feedback loop disintegrates and gonadotropin levels rise. Thus, as with the testes, the effect of aging is seen at the ovaries rather than the pituitary or hypothalamus. As gonadotropin levels rise and estrogen levels decline, the woman may experience a variety of signs and symptoms of menopause, including sweating, hot flashes, and a reduction in the feminization that occurred at puberty, such as diminishing fat deposits and atrophy of the breast, vulva, and vagina. Prolonged estrogen deficiency is a risk factor for a decrease in bone calcification, leading to the development of osteoporosis. It is increasingly common for women of menopausal years to take estrogen and progesterone supplements to reduce the effects of the failing ovaries.

REFERENCES

Alexander, S.E., S. Aksel, R.R. Yeomon, and J.M. Hozelton. Gonadotropin and Ovarian Hormone Dynamics in Luteal Phase Defects. *American Journal of Obstetrics and Gynecology*, Vol. 166 (Feb. 1992), pp. 652–57.

Bagatell, C.J., R.H. Knopp, W.W. Vale, J.E. Rivier, and W.J. Bremner. Physiologic Testosterone Levels in Normal Men Suppress High-Density Lipoprotein Cholesterol Levels. *Annals of Internal Medicine*, Vol. 116 (1992) pp. 967–73.

Enningham, G.R., W.B. Schill, and E.S.E. Hafex, eds. *Regulation of Male Fertility*. The Hague: Martinus Nijhoff, 1980.

Hershman, J.M. *Endocrine Pathophysiology*, 3d ed. Philadelphia: Lea & Farbiger, 1988.

Schauf, C., D. Moffett, and S. Moffett. *Human Physiology: Foundations and Frontiers*. St. Louis: Mosby, 1990.

Tsatsoulis, A., S.M. Shalet, and W.R. Robertson. Bioactive Gonadotropin Secretion in Man. *Clinical Endocrinology*, Vol. 35 (1991), pp. 193–206.

Uzych, L. Anabolic-Androgenic Steroids and Psychiatric-related Effects: A Review. *Canadian Journal of Psychiatry*, Vol. 37 (1992), pp. 23–28.

Wilson, J.D., et. al. *Harrison's Principles of Internal Medicine*. 12th ed. New York: McGraw-Hill, 1991.

Janice Fulton

HUMOR AND SEX

Throughout the history of world humor, no topic has been more pervasive than sex. Within parameters dictated by each society, humor generally is the most socially acceptable avenue for expressing sex-related fears, confusion, and aggression that cultural constraints otherwise forbid. Sexual humor can be used as an instrument for sublimation, seduction, release, or even education. At a single stroke, it can provide both sexual and comic pleasures.

Folklorist Gershon Legman observes that sexual folklore is almost always humorous, even though it deals with serious fears and problems of life. He likens this type of sexual humor to whistling in the dark. He sees humor as performing the important mental health function of absorbing and controlling anxieties felt in connection with sex-related topics such as venereal disease and castration or with scatological themes such as defecation. It has been suggested that, as societies become more educated and refined, they tend to increase repression of direct sexual expression, and therefore obscene humor becomes more important as a safety valve.

Sexual humor can be a covert way of socializing individuals to the norms of sexual behavior expected within a group and thus maintaining those norms. Some experts feel that this approach is more successful than the use of threats. The resulting sharing of understanding tends to bond individuals in the "in" group together and to differentiate them from outsiders.

In his book *Jokes and Their Relation to the Unconscious,* Sigmund Freud suggests that sex-oriented jokes enable the satisfaction of lustful instincts, even by individuals who are faced with some obstacle such as an inability to deal with open discussion of sex. The kinds of sexual jokes a person tells and enjoys can reflect facets of his or her sexual makeup such as a suppressed tendency toward violent sexual behavior or exhibitionism. They also can serve as a protective mechanism that denies the seriousness of a sexual problem that is troubling the teller.

"Blue" humor can be used by one member of a partnership to seduce the other. The response of the other partner can be taken as a gauge of his or her readiness for further overt sexual activity.

Children begin telling "dirty" jokes at an early age, and sexually suggestive games are common among children in many cultures. According to Legman, a reason for this is that the hardest thing for a child to cope with in his or her environment is the fact of the parents' copulation. On the one hand, children are told to look to their parents as role models, and on the other that the sex act is forbidden to them. They are made to feel uncomfortable discussing their questions and anxieties about their bodies with adults, so they sublimate by whispering sexual innuendos about their teachers and sharing jokes in the school yard.

Sex-related joking relationships usually are confined to members of the same generation. Sharing such a joke with your mother's old college friend, for example, would be considered in poor taste. Joking relationships within a given culture also are circumscribed by its marriage customs and sexual taboos. For example, few cultures consider it appropriate for parents to share sexual humor with their children because of prevailing taboos against incest. When sexual humor is shared by a group, the participants usually are all the same sex. In Sicily, for instance, groups of women commonly entertain themselves in this manner, with the married women imitating men.

Apte has studied joking relationships in many cultures and developed these theoretical propositions comparing the roles of men and women: The two sexes show unequal status, with men generally restricting women's public participation in humor as a means of showing their superiority. Men are intimidated by the idea of sexual equality because of its potential for disrupting this social order. As women age, and especially after they pass menopause, they often gain more freedom to share publicly in sexual humor and obscene language, even to the extent of being allowed to compete with men.

Writing on national styles of humor, Ziv divides American sexual humor into four categories: innocent, where surprise is the key element; innuendo, the most common; hostile; and sex-related humor that reflects cultural attitudes. Widely used on television talk shows, innuendo also is employed on bumper stickers that derive their humor from implied meanings of "it." Ziv observes that innuendo has the advantage that a listener can pretend not to understand. Current examples of humor that reflects cultural attitudes are the books and essays that tell what "real" men and women do and do not do.

Sexually oriented themes occur in the earliest humorous literature. Early Hebrew writings contain parodies on profligacy. In ancient Greece, the epigram was often the vehicle of choice; well-known Greek epigrammatists included Anaxandriades, Aristophon, and Alexis. Sexual innuendos are common throughout Greek literature and often reflect prevailing misogynistic attitudes.

In the Middle Ages, the *fabliaux* of the *jougleurs* were the most common form of comic literature, and dozens of examples survive. Although they were highly sexual in content, they were recited freely in mixed groups and were very popular as after-dinner entertainment. Later, Voltaire's epic poem, *Maid of Orleans,* parodied the life of Joan of Arc and featured a series of sexually oriented jokes.

Almost everyone in contemporary English-speaking society has a favorite obscene joke cast in the form of a limerick:

> The limerick's an art form complex
> Whose contents run chiefly to sex;
> It's famous for virgins
> And masculine urgin's
> And vulgar, erotic effects.

The great Greek comic poet Aristophanes is believed to have written the first limericks around the fourth century B.C.E. Modern limericks also owe something to a 16th-century English verse form called Poulter's measure. The *Oxford English Dictionary* quotes an 1898 reference as stating: "Who applied this name [limerick] to the indecent nonsense verse first it is hard to say." However, it was around that time that the term first came into common usage in England. Except for a few written in French, limericks rarely occur in other languages.

Obscene limericks have been popular for more than a century. Alfred Lord Tennyson is said to have written them as a relief from the stress of more serious writing, but they were destroyed immediately after his death. Algernon Swinburne wrote them and did obscene parodies of some of Edward Lear's most beloved limericks, but they rarely are included in anthologies of his work. Such diverse writers as George Bernard Shaw, Eugene Field, Robert Louis Stevenson, Morris Bishop, and Ogden Nash also were limerick aficionados. The true, "unlaundered" limerick of today is distinguished by its sexual or scatological subject matter, obscene language, close adherence to the prescribed poetic form, and clever word play; it usually has a surprise twist at the end.

Though sexually oriented humor can incite destructive behavior and preserve the dominance of one sex over the other, it also can be used as an instrument for reducing stresses related to sexual function and for informing individuals of the sexual attitudes and behavior that are expected by their society.

REFERENCES

Apte, M.L. *Humor and Laughter: An Anthropological Approach.* Ithaca, N.Y.: Cornell Univ. Press, 1985. (Note: comprehensive bibliography.)

Baring-Gould, W.S. *The Lure of the Limerick.* London: Panther Books, 1970.

Chapman, A.J., and N.J. Gadfield. Is Sexual Humor Sexist? *Journal of Communication,* Vol. 26 (1976), pp. 141–53.

Fine, G.A. Obscene Joking Across Cultures. *Journal of Communication,* Vol. 26 (1976), pp. 134–40.

Freud, S. *Jokes and Their Relation to the Unconscious.* Translated and edited by J. Strachey. New York: W.W. Norton, 1960.

Goldstein, J.H., and P.E. McGhee. *The Psychology of Humor.* New York: Academic Press, 1972.

Highet, G. *The Anatomy of Satire.* Princeton, N.J.: Princeton Univ. Press, 1962.

Janus, S.S., C. Janus, and J. Vincent. The Psychosexuality of Stand-up Comedy. *Journal of Psychohistory,* Vol. 14 (Fall 1986), pp. 133–40.

Legman, G. *The Hornbook: Studies in Erotic Folklore and Bibliography.* New Hyde Park, N.Y.: University Books, 1964.

———. *Rationale of the Dirty Joke, First Series.* New York: Grove Press, 1968.

Levine, J., and F.C. Redlich. *Motivation in Humor.* New York: Atherton, 1969.

Wells, C. *An Outline of Humor.* New York: G.P. Putnam's Sons, 1923.

Ziv, A. *National Styles in Humor.* New York: Greenwood Press, 1988.

Alice P. Stein

HYMEN

The hymen is a membrane, found only in human females, that covers the opening of the vagina at birth. It usually begins to erode shortly after birth and continues to do so throughout childhood and adolescence. Some females are born with a partial or no hymen. At maturity, a young woman may have remnants of hymeneal tissue that form a ring around the vaginal opening. The tissue may also stretch across the opening and vary in size, shape, thickness, and pattern of perforation. The perforations allow for the passage of menstrual fluids and usually permit the insertion of a finger or a tampon. Some females have an imperforate hymen composed of tough fibrous tissue. Such a hymen is not usually detected until menstruation begins; it does not allow for the passage of fluid. The condition can be corrected easily by minor surgery performed in a physician's office.

For a tissue that is not known to function physiologically in any way or to have any evolutionary value, the hymen has been a source of psychological stress in almost all cultures. A common name for the hymen is "maidenhead." Further, a woman who has lost her maidenhead is "deflowered." These terms imply the supposed importance of the presence of the tissue when determining virginity. Because virginity at the time of penetration on the wedding night is prized in so many cultures, the presence of the hymen takes on an importance of its own. In some cultures, the bloody bed sheets are paraded before a waiting audience to prove that the bride was a virgin. If the bride does not have an intact hymen, she may be returned to her parents in disgrace, subjected to public ridicule, starved, tortured, mutilated, or put to death, often by stoning. However, brides and grooms have been known to use the blood of animals or to prick their own fingers to provide the bloody "proof" needed. The deflowering of a virgin sometimes had magical connotations. Certain males and females used special instruments such as horns or stone phalluses to perform ritual deflorations before the wedding night. In some medieval cultures, it was the right of the lord of the manor to deflower the virgins before they were married. Because some men pride themselves on having intercourse with virgins, some prostitutes are quite adept at becoming "virgins" again and again by the use of chicken blood. Indeed, plastic surgeons in some countries (i.e., Italy, Japan) reconstruct hymens for "new virgins" who want to conceal their previous sexual histories from new husbands.

Actually, the presence or absence of a hymen is no indication of the virginity of the female. A physician cannot usually tell if a woman is a virgin, even with a pelvic examination. The hymen may have completely eroded before maturity, or it may have been broken in any number of ways. For example, young girls in rural Egypt, when going to and from the fields, ride astride small donkeys; thus their hymens are often broken. A girl in this situation must then go to the village midwife and get a certificate that explains how her hymen was lost so that when her husband wraps a piece of cloth around his forefinger and inserts it into her vagina on their wedding night, she can use the certificate to prove that she has not had previous intercourse. The hymen may also be broken as a result of vigorous exercise or masturbation. Further, in some women, the hymen is so elastic that it may stretch without breaking during intercourse, and thus a woman may not be a virgin even though she has an intact hymen.

Many women (and men) expect the first intercourse to be painful because they fear the breaking of the hymen (or the taking of the "cherry"). Most such pain, however, results because the female is anxious and unprepared or the attempt at penetration is clumsy or forcible. Thus, first intercourse is traumatic or untraumatic depending on the preparation and understanding of the individuals rather than on the breaking of the hymen.

REFERENCES

Masters, W.H., V.E. Johnson, and R.C. Kolodny. *Human Sexuality*. 3rd ed. Glenview, Ill.: Scott, Foresman, 1988.

Reinisch, J.M. *The Kinsey Institute New Report on Sex*. New York: St. Martin's Press, 1990.

James D. Haynes

i

IMPOTENCE

The term "impotence" refers to a sexual dysfunction in which a man is not able to achieve or maintain an erection sufficient to penetrate the vagina and successfully complete intercourse. Most clinicians use the term "erectile difficulty" or "erectile dysfunction" rather than "impotence" because of the generally negative connotations of the word. All of these terms are used here to describe difficulties in achieving and maintaining erections.

The American Psychiatric Association's *Diagnostic and Statistical Manual* (DSM III-R) describes the criteria for male erectile disorder as either a "persistent or recurrent partial or complete failure in the male to attain or maintain erection until completion of the sexual activity, or [a] persistent or recurrent lack of a submissive sense of sexual excitement and pleasure in a male during sexual activity." The latter criterion refers to problems related to sexual desire. The terms referring to erectile difficulties can be applied to both heterosexual and homosexual relationships and are not limited to attempts at vaginal intercourse.

The occurrence of impotence may be either primary or secondary. In cases of primary impotence, which is rare and usually associated with organic conditions, the male has never been able to successfully achieve an erection for intercourse.

These men are usually able to have erections under other circumstances, such as through masturbation, and may report erections upon awakening from sleep. In secondary impotence, the male has a history of successful intercourse but reports episodes of erectile difficulty during which he is unable to function. Masters and Johnson looked for a failure rate of 25 percent before making the diagnosis of secondary impotence. Secondary impotence is more commonly seen and may have multiple causes as well as significant psychological and relational side effects.

The incidence of impotence is difficult to estimate because of the reluctance of men to report the problem. Kinsey found impotence to be rare in men under 35 years of age but increasingly frequent as they grew older, appearing especially after age 45 and more so after 55. By age 70, 27 percent of the men interviewed reported erectile difficulty; by age 75, the figure was 55 percent. In a more recent study of 100 men of varying ages, Frank found 7 percent of the subjects reporting difficulty obtaining erection and 9 percent reporting an inability to maintain erection.

While figures vary and sex research continues, many clinicians feel that over a lifetime any male may experience an occasional episode of erectile failure, often for one or more of the following reasons: fatigue, anxiety, ignorance of his own sexual functioning or that of his partner (e.g., lacking information about the sexual-response cycle and placing unrealistic expectations on performance), feeling rushed, having too much food or alcohol, not being attracted to his partner, being too goal oriented (e.g., insisting on being able to "give" his partner an orgasm every time), engaging in "spectatoring" (i.e., watching himself perform and trying to "will an erection"), engaging in inappropriate internal self-talk that sets him up for failure, or simply trying to have sex while not at the proper interest or arousal level. Although episodes are common in a given population, they are often the cause of significant concern to a male and his partner if a proper understanding of the causes is not achieved. A single episode of erectile failure, if not properly understood and dealt with appropriately, can set off a cycle of doubt that marks future sexual attempts with anticipatory anxiety, which in itself creates a negative environment and can instigate and perpetuate future failure.

Whatever the incidence of impotence, its causes and effects may be many. It was not too long ago that most cases of impotence, especially secondary impotence, were considered to be of psychological origin. It is true that significant psychological issues (e.g., fear of failure), relationship issues between the sexual partners (e.g., anger), fear of disease, fear of pregnancy, and guilt can lead to erectile failure. Anxiety and guilt about sex itself, often having a basis in religious beliefs, can be a contributing cause of erectile difficulties.

Deeper psychological issues may be important, such as poor self-esteem, traumatic childhood sexual experiences, family-of-origin issues (including negative sexual attitudes), conflicts with women, gender-identity and sexual-orientation conflicts, the presence of a paraphilia or "sexual perversion," significant depression or emotional illness, fear of intimacy, or guilt about pleasure. These are just some of the components that in given cases result in impotence. Erectile difficulties can also be related to external circumstances, such as to a particular partner, where the male is able to function quite adequately with one sexual partner but not with another.

Biological Causes

Many causes of impotence are biologically related. Today, sophisticated techniques are uncovering organic causes of impotence, whereas previously psychological mechanisms were blamed. Some authors suggest that 10–15 percent of cases of impotence are organically based,

while many practitioners feel the percentage is higher, as much as 50–60 percent. The mechanisms of the body—hormonal, vascular, and neural—that cause and maintain erection are vulnerable to the influences of many conditions and agents. Problems that affect these bodily systems as they relate to sexual functioning must be evaluated as part of the diagnosis of impotence.

A partial list of physical conditions that could contribute to erectile difficulties includes any severely debilitating illness associated with the loss of libido (e.g., cardiorespiratory disease). Diabetes, which affects the vascular and neurological system, is another primary illness associated with impotence. Endocrine conditions such as myxedema, thyrotoxicosis, pituitary disease, and Addison's disease have also been associated with impotence. The level of testosterone, the male hormone, may be related more to levels of sexual desire than to sexual performance. Some common physical causes of secondary impotence, according to Kolodny, are the following:

Anatomic: Congenital deformities, hydrocele, testicular fibrosis

Cardiorespiratory: Angina pectoris, coronary insufficiency, myocardial infarction, pulmonary insufficiency, rheumatic fever

Genitourinary: Peyronie's disease, phimosis, priapism, prostatitis, perineal prostatectomy, urethritis

Hematologic: Hodgkin's disease, leukemia, sickle-cell anemia

Infectious: Gonorrhea, mumps, genital tuberculosis

Neurologic: Cerebral palsy, multiple sclerosis, parkinsonism, peripheral neuropathies, cord tumors or transections, sympathectomy

Vascular: Aneurysm, arteritis, sclerosis

Miscellaneous: Chronic renal failure, cirrhosis, obesity, toxicologic agents (e.g., lead, herbicides)

Drugs have become a major concern as contributors to erectile difficulties. At times, prescribed medication may render the patient at risk for experiencing sexual side effects. Alternate medications may be available, but not all patients are able to find substitutes that meet their medical needs while not compromising their sexual functioning. Sometimes it is the interaction of different drugs that affects the sexual system adversely. Some drugs are dose related in their influence on sexual functioning. In certain cases, a drug known to inhibit sexual functioning may actually improve it.

Many commonly prescribed medications have been reported to cause sexual problems: sedatives, hypnotics, anti-anxiety drugs, narcotics, antipsychotic medications, antidepressants, antihypertensives, diuretics, anticancer drugs, and antiandrogens. Some of the drugs are known to contribute to impotence more than others, and physicians can at times make recommendations that do not compromise the health of the patient. Alcohol and many illegal drugs, including cocaine, amphetamines, marijuana, and heroin, have also been found to cause erectile difficulties.

Evaluation

Diagnostic tests are available to assist the physician in diagnosing the presence of organic conditions that cause impotence. These tests involve evaluation of different body systems and include endocrine, neurological, and vascular studies. One of the most recent and helpful diagnostic techniques involves physiological monitoring of erection patterns in men during sleep. These nocturnal penile tumescence (NPT) studies evaluate reflexive erections that all males have during rapid eye movement (REM) sleep. The REM erections, as they are called, occur at regular intervals during sleep and for varying durations, according to the age of the individual. For the most part, men with organic impotence have a disturbance in their REM erections, while men with psychogenic impotence tend to have normal patterns of erections. NPT studies are carried out in sleep laboratories and can be very useful in making accurate diagnoses and planning treatment.

Treatment

Psychogenic impotence has long been the target of various forms of psychotherapy and sex therapy. Traditional forms of psychoanalytic therapy are less used today because more effective forms of treatment have been developed. They include an eclectic intervention that combines behavioral, cognitive, and couples therapy to reduce the anxious, maladaptive behavioral and cognitive patterns leading to the sexual dysfunction. The theory and practice of sex therapy have taken on an international scope, with much research and many innovations in practice and technique emerging each year.

Organically based impotence has also been successfully treated with a variety of interventions, including a medication (Yohimbine) that assists erection as well as injections of papaverine and phentolamine agents directly into the penile musculature to act on the venous system to induce erection. This technique is especially useful in men who have had spinal cord damage resulting in trauma to the nerves in the pelvic area that are needed for erection. A noninvasive technique that is gaining acceptance among sex therapists and urologists involves the use of an external vacuum device. Placed over the penis, the vacuum pump assists in trapping the flow of blood and allows for a temporary erection sufficient for intercourse.

Surgical techniques have also been developed to correct certain vascular problems that cause erectile difficulties. One of the major surgical advances is the use of penile prosthetic implants that allow a male to obtain and maintain an erection at will. The implant allows the male to achieve what looks like a natural erection.

Whatever the form of treatment for impotence, its overall affect on the male must be taken into consideration. During the course of developing erection problems, whether they are organic or psychological, a complicated pattern of behavior and feeling develops between the male and his partner. These patterns can result in much misunderstanding and resentment and need to be attended to as part of the overall recovery from this sensitive male sexual condition.

REFERENCES

American Psychiatric Association. *Diagnostic and Statistical Manual of Mental Disorders.* 3rd ed. rev. Washington, D.C.: American Psychiatric Press, 1987.

Frank, E., et al. Frequency of Sexual Dysfunction in "Normal" Couples. *New England Journal of Medicine,* Vol. 299, No. 3 (1978), pp. 111–15.

Kaplan, H.S. *The New Sex Therapy.* New York: Brunner/Mazel, 1974.

Kinsey, A., W. Pomeroy, and C. Martin. *Sexual Behavior in the Human Male.* Philadelphia: Sanders, 1948.

Kolodny, R., W. Masters, and V. Johnson. *Textbook of Sexual Medicine.* Boston: Little, Brown, 1979.

Masters, W., and V. Johnson. *Human Sexual Inadequacy.* Boston: Little, Brown, 1970

———. *Human Sexual Response.* Boston: Little, Brown, 1966.

Smith, A. Causes and Classification of Impotence. *Urological Clinics of North America.* Vol. 8 (1981), pp. 79–89.

Wagner, G., and R. Green. *Impotence.* New York: Plenum Press, 1981.

Julian W. Slowinski

INCEST

Incest is sexual behavior between people who are too closely related by blood or family ties to be able to marry. Most of the time when we think of incest victims, we think of children. However, according to the definition, two related adults could also be involved in incestuous relationships, such as adult siblings or an adult daughter and her father.

Incest involving children is one form of child sexual abuse. Child sexual abuse is greatly underreported. Authorities receive reports of child sexual abuse in 25 percent of girls and 17 percent of boys under the age of 18. Many more children are undoubtedly abused sexually but do not report it. Not all of these offenses are committed by someone to whom the victim is related. Children are most often sexually abused between the ages of three and eleven. Most children who experience incest have more than one forced sexual encounter.

Behaviors

Children may experience forced sexual contact, such as inappropriate kissing or hugging, oral-genital contact, vaginal or anal penetration, and any discipline (e.g., spanking) that involves the genitals. Noncontact sexual abuse includes exhibitionism, voyeurism, coercion to view or participate in child pornography, obscene sexual language, obscene sexual telephone calls, and any other type of intrusive behavior (e.g., not allowing a child to undress or use the bathroom in privacy).

Most cases of child sexual abuse are incest. In very few incest cases is violence or physical force used. Most of the time, the offender uses bribery, tricks, threats, and manipulation to convince the child that what is occurring is acceptable and should remain a secret.

Incest is never the child's fault. The offender takes advantage of the child's trust and lack of knowledge about sex. A child may become complicit in the abuse, but that is not the same as consent.

Effects

The effects of child sexual abuse are traumatic and can be devastating, especially if the child's report of abuse is not believed. Children rarely lie about sexual abuse. Generally, they do not tell anyone about it.

Incest survivors experience feelings that include anxiety, confusion, betrayal, depression, fear, guilt, helplessness, responsibility, shame, hopelessness, anger, and distrust. These feelings can lead to problems with relationships or intimacy, sexual dysfunctions in adulthood, inability to trust others, low self-esteem or self-image, multiple personalities, social withdrawal, substance abuse, eating disorders, suicidal behaviors, dissociation, self-mutilation, prostitution, promiscuity, or regression to a younger age.

Many survivors of incest and child sexual abuse do not remember the experience. Repression of painful memories is common. However, even those who do not remember may have emotional flashbacks of the event. Memories may be triggered by sights, sounds, events, smells, places, or times that are related to the abuse. Remembering is often a sign of strength and may indicate that the survivor is able to cope with the memory.

If the child of a parent survivor of incest also becomes a victim, the parent may remember his or her own victimization. Recollections are common at three times in a survivor's life: when the first consensual sexual experience occurs, during a first pregnancy or childbirth, or when a child reaches the age when the parent survivor was first abused. Recovery from incest victimization starts after a disclosure, and professional help is usually necessary for maximum recovery.

Controversies surround beliefs about incest. For example, it has been argued that incest between consenting adults is a victimless activity and should not be illegal. Yet sexual relations between an adult daughter and her father still contain an element of power that does not allow the daughter to exercise free choice; there must be an element of coercion or force involved. Regardless of the correctness of this argument, incest is currently illegal and considered immoral by all religions.

REFERENCES

Bass, E., and L. Davis. *The Courage to Heal.* New York: Harper & Row, 1989.

Lew, M. *Victims No Longer.* New York: Harper & Row, 1990.

Sanford, L.T. *The Silent Children.* New York: McGraw-Hill, 1980.

Andrea Parrot

INCUBUS AND SUCCUBUS

These are demons associated with witchcraft that have sexual overtones. An incubus, from the Latin incubare, "to lie upon," was the male form, while a succubus, from the Latin succubare, "to lie under," was the female form. Often, lascivious dreams or "wet dreams" were attributed to the action of an incubus or a succubus. They were often reported to exist in monasteries and convents. Sometimes the devil himself was said to appear as a goat with his penis in the rear to enable him to back up to the female and rub against her.

In some accounts of the incubus and succubus, they are one and the same creature. The succubus receives semen from a man and then turns into an incubus to spend the semen on a woman.

REFERENCES

Bullough, V.L. Sexual Variance in Society and History. Chicago: Univ. of Chicago Press, 1976.

Vern L. Bullough

INDIANS: NATIVE NORTH AMERICANS

It is difficult to generalize about North American Indians. They belonged to many different cultures, spoke dozens of languages, followed different ways of life, and subscribed to disparate religious practices. Likewise, sexual conduct varied widely among tribes. Some Indian cultures tolerated a great variety of sexual expressions and identities; other tribes closely circumscribed sexual behavior. This entry describes the range of sexual behavior found in North America and gives some attention to the impact of European colonization on Indian sexual practices.

On the whole, American Indian societies were more permissive than any of the European Christian nations that began the conquest of Native America in the late 15th century. Among Indians, virginity was not necessarily prized in either sex. Sexual experimentation was regarded as ordinary adolescent behavior, and many tribes permitted—indeed expected—young people to gain sexual experience before marriage. After marriage, some tribes tolerated extramarital sex in both husband and wife, although others prescribed punishments for adultery.

Many tribes accepted polygyny, but this practice was usually reserved to a few powerful men. Most Indians obtained divorce easily by simply declaring that the marriage was over. Serial monogamy was a common marriage pattern throughout North America. A few tribes incorporated ritual sex into their religious life, while other groups regarded sex as a purely private matter. In native society, sexuality was thought to be spiritual as well as an ordinary aspect of worldly life. Spiritual experiences and dreams often revealed gender to individuals, or even to their mothers.

All tribes had sexual divisions of labor and defined gender roles that were often distinct from European norms and which influenced Indian sexual behavior. Indian women were hardworking, productive members of their societies. In some tribes, women farmed, gathered wild plants, prepared food—including the game that their husbands provided—and made clothes, baskets, and pottery utensils. Some societies permitted women to be chiefs and shamans; in other tribes these pursuits were reserved for males. Men hunted, fished, and sometimes farmed. In most tribes, men were the acknowledged political and spiritual leaders. Most Indian tribes provided for an alternate gender, the *berdache*. The *berdache* were biological males who dressed as women and did women's work. Often they married Indian men. The husbands and lovers of the *berdache* were not regarded as homosexuals even though they had sex with males.

As in other cultures, Native American sexual life and identity developed during childhood. The process varied from tribe to tribe in native North America, but most children learned about sexuality from adult behavior and talk. In the Qipi Eskimo society of the eastern Arctic, for example, parents taught about sex through play and example. Mothers and fathers openly touched, kissed, and admired their babies' genitals during infancy. Sexual play among Eskimo children continued well into adolescence. Children talked openly about sexual experiences, and parents took these discussions as a sign of normal child development. Nevertheless, parents discouraged masturbation during childhood. These people did not admire *berdache* behavior and thought that masturbation was a precursor to homosexuality.

Other tribes esteemed sexual variance. The Navajo, for example, placed great value on hermaphrodite (or *nadle*) children. *Nadles* were considered to be lucky and ensured the health of a Navajo family. As the *nadle* child grew older, so did the respect of the community toward the *nadle* until it bordered on reverence. Cross-gender behavior was not limited to men. Although much less is known about female cross-gender behavior, some native women assumed the role of men and participated in every aspect of male life, including, in some tribes, war and tribal councils. These women often took wives and observed, as husbands, taboos at the time of their wives' menstruation; at the same time they denied their own menstruation. The Kaska in Canada not only accepted cross-gender behavior but encouraged it. At the age of five, if her parents chose, a female child was dressed—and taught to act—as a boy. After the girl learned to hunt, her degree of proficiency fostered respect in society. Cross-gender individuals denied having the physical attributes of their biological sex. According to tribal views, these people were not just pretending to be men; they were men, just as *berdache* were women.

While many tribes permitted cross-gender behavior, most Indians adhered to biologically determined sex roles. Puberty marked the onset of adult sexual roles for men and women alike, although marriage might not occur for some time. Many tribes formally recognized the dawn of sexual maturity for young men and women. For men, late adolescence was often a time when older men initiated them into male societies. Young men also had to prove their competence as providers and, in some cases, as warriors before they could marry. Many tribes celebrated the onset of menses in young women. Menarche marked the beginning of a young woman's fertility and was palpable evidence of female power. A woman from the Fox tribe recalled being told to hide herself and that she could drain the power of a man if she looked his way during menstruation. Mountain Wolf Woman of the Winnebago tribe remembered being told to run away into the woods when she first menstruated. She was supposed to remain alone and not to look at anyone, especially men, for a glance from a menstruating woman could contaminate their blood.

While some tribes feared the power of menstruating women, negativism did not characterize Indian attitudes about menstruation and female power. For example, the Lakota Sioux incorporated the buffalo, a sacred symbol of life, birth, and survival, into the ritual celebrating menarche. During the buffalo ceremony, a shaman guided the young woman toward a new stage in her life. During a period of seclusion in which she assumed a sacred state, the shaman joined her, and symbolically they became buffalo man and buffalo woman. They drank a mixture of chokecherries and water that symbolized menstrual blood and the renewal of life. Afterwards, the woman reentered the profane world with a public celebration commemorating her new maturity. The seclusion of the woman at the onset of menarche and during menses reinforced her status as a mature woman with a reproductive role.

Sexual maturity was one of the qualifications for courtship and marriage. Tribal courting styles varied considerably. For example, among the Pima of central Arizona, the young man, accompanied by a married friend, visited the home of his prospective bride. The friend pleaded the

suitor's case to the woman's family while he remained silent. After several nights of this wooing, the suiter became the woman's husband if she accepted him. Among the Hopi, a prospective suitor came to see his beloved while she ground corn in the grinding house. The couple talked through a window, and, if they agreed, they met later that night. Eventually, the woman invited her prospective groom on a picnic where she presented him with *quomi,* a specially prepared loaf of sweetened cornmeal. This was a formal proposal of marriage, and by accepting her gift, he agreed to become her husband. Then they asked for parental approval.

Among the Oglala Sioux, a marriageable woman waited outside her tipi at sunset, while her older kin remained inside and observed her suitors. Prospective suitors approached her, carrying a courting blanket, and—if she was especially popular—formed a line in front of her. Each man placed his arms around her, enveloping her in his blanket, and had a private conversation with her. He had to be brief yet convincing because others waited their turn. The choice of partner then rested with the woman, whose parents generally accepted her decision. The ultimate goal of courtship was marriage. Ordinarily, suitors sought parental approval, but if it was not forthcoming the lovers might elope.

As with other aspects of sexual behavior, marriage rituals differed from tribe to tribe. Marriage formalized a sexual partnership between the couple as well as trading and political alliances between families. Once a young Pima woman accepted a man, he stayed in his bride's home for four days. They then returned to his parents' home. The next morning at dawn, his mother gave the bride a large basket of wheat to grind and make into tortillas by sunrise. His family accepted her upon completion of this task, and the couple was married. The groom presented her with a blanket, and his parents gave her presents.

Marriage among the Oglala was a complicated affair involving a series of gift exchanges between the families. The groom's family gave the young woman many valuable gifts, which she distributed to her parents. Her parents then gave her gifts to distribute to his parents. Afterwards, her family erected a special tipi for the couple, under the direction of her grandmother; the prospective husband furnished it. The women in his family clothed her in a new buckskin dress that his mother made, the family held a huge feast for everyone in the tribe, and the couple were married.

Reproduction was an important part of the marriage relationship, and the absence of children or the birth of deformed or stillborn infants was a matter of grave concern. If an Apache couple did not have children, the community attributed male impotence to bewitchment. Less commonly, Apaches believed that the woman's mother caused her barrenness. Divorce was the common solution for such unhappy problems. Some California tribes killed deformed infants and occasionally the mothers who bore them.

Except in special cases, most Indians believed that the partners in married couples should have sexual relations only with each other. In practice, however, extramarital affairs occurred, and some tribes imposed sanctions on transgressors. Husbands beat, mutilated, and sometimes killed errant wives. In some societies, tribesmen who seduced other men's wives had to pay the wronged husband. As a general rule, husbands who misbehaved were not punished, although historical accounts tell of Indian women who beat their unfaithful husbands.

Adultery was a punishable offense, but many tribes permitted extramarital sexual relations in particular situations. Among the Pueblo Indians and Plains tribes, men commonly gave their wives to visitors for a night. This was a way of demonstrating peaceful intentions and cementing trade relations. On the plains, men who received sexual service were expected to reciprocate with a gift that symbolized a reciprocal relationship between the parties rather than a payment for sex. Among the Mandan and Hidatsa of the upper Missouri River, women copulated with powerful males to physically transfer power to their husbands. Some gamblers wagered sexual access to their wives. It should be noted that women were not free agents in these arrangements. While a husband could give, win, trade, or lose his wife's sex, a woman ordinarily could not do the same for herself without risking the wrath of her husband.

Many tribes incorporated sex in tribal rituals. The Mandan, Hidatsa, Atsina, Blood, and Arapaho tribes had men's societies in which the initiate ceremoniously gave his wife to an older member. In the Black Horn Society of the Blood tribe, an older man who was retiring from the society selected a young man to whom he wished to transfer his membership. The retiree compelled the appointee, regardless of his wishes, to participate in the transfer ceremony. In a public rite, the wife of the retiree painted the new member and his wife, and gave them new clothes and regalia; the appointee and his wife then proceeded to dance with their new insignia. Then there was a private ritual. The new member's wife, wearing only a robe, carried a pipe to the tipi of her ceremonial father, the older man who was transferring his membership. After smoking the pipe, the "father" and the woman left the camp, laid down, and again prayed with the pipe. He then touched his penis to her vagina. If she had led a virtuous life, he bawled like a bison and then copulated. During intercourse, he transferred a piece of prairie turnip to her mouth from his. Then the woman returned to her husband in the Horn tipi; there she remained quietly and fasted for a day. Her "father" concluded the ceremony by painting her, one pattern indicating performance of the first half of the ritual, another pattern signaling completion of the entire ritual and, therefore, honor to the woman and her husband.

The Mandans employed ceremonial intercourse in the Buffalo Dance, which they believed attracted large buffalo herds and brought prosperity to the camp. The tribe thought that intercourse between a well-respected woman and a man of recognized power transferred power from the buffalo to the woman and her husband. The Pueblo Indians also incorporated sexual intercourse in annual ceremonies that were meant to ensure fertility and social harmony.

Pueblo Indian clowns indulged in comic sexual acts and ridiculed any aspect of Indian life; even the sacred was targeted for ridicule. Clowning served an important purpose in Pueblo society. Some religious ceremonies could not begin until everybody had laughed, and the clowns' sexual antics released tension in societies where group harmony and self-control were of prime importance. Thus, a ribald clown copulating with a donkey might precede a carefully choreographed religious ceremony of profound spiritual significance.

The European invasion of America posed a challenge to traditional Indian sexual mores. Indian sexuality reinforced Europeans' negative stereotypes of Indians and helped to justify conquest and colonization. Sexual wantonness—as Europeans saw it—demonstrated that Indians needed Christianity and European civilization. According to European norms, the ideal woman was chaste, submissive, and asexual, while the ideal man was sexual, aggressive, and dominant. Christian marriages were supposed to be lifelong and monogamous bonds absolute. Imbued with Christian sexual values and a desire to convert Indians to the Protestant and Catholic religions, missionaries attempted to persuade Indians that customary sexual practices were violations of divine law. Catholic missionaries for Spain and

France waged unremitting war against Indian sexual practices that contravened Church teachings. Friars gave special attention to polygamy, homosexuality, and extramarital sex but seldom succeeded in eradicating these customs. Instead, many Indians continued to observe customary practices in secret while outwardly observing the forms of Christianity. In the 19th century, Protestant clergy and federal agents carried on the fight for sexual orthodoxy.

European traders who were more interested in commercial advantage than spiritual redemption also transformed Indian sexual behavior. They interpreted the reciprocal exchange of gifts and sex as an act of prostitution. Likewise, the sacred nature of sexual ritual and the transfer of power through coitus were lost on Europeans who interpreted Indian sexuality as lustful while taking advantage of the carnal opportunities that Indian society provided. White traders who entered Indian country without women frequently took Indian wives, at least until white women became available and native women were discarded. Worse, white traders' demand for Indian women led to a trade in captives who were sold to white purchasers. Sacagawea, the Shoshone woman who accompanied the Lewis and Clark expedition across the West, was the most famous of these enslaved women.

Twentieth-century Indian sexual behavior has not been thoroughly described. Many Indians are Christians who observe the sexual requirements of their denominations. The sex lives of other Indians reflect older values and beliefs. The *berdache* tradition, for example, continues in evidence on some reservations, and some urban Indian homosexuals regard themselves as *berdache*. Like everyone else in the United States, Indians have experienced the impact of mass culture, and there can be little doubt that it has affected Indian sexual behavior. Nevertheless, Indian sexuality continues to reflect the variety of native tradition.

REFERENCES

Allen, P.G. *The Sacred Hoop: Recovering the Feminine in American Indian Traditions.* Boston: Beacon Press, 1986.

Blackwood, E. Sexuality and Gender in Certain Native American Tribes: The Case of Cross-Gender Females. *Signs,* Vol. 10 (Autumn 1984), pp. 27–42

Briggs, J.L. Eskimo Women: Makers of Men. In C.J. Matthiason, ed., *Many Sisters: Women in Cross-Cultural Perspective.* New York: The Free Press, 1974.

Coontz, S. The Native American Tradition. In B. Carroll, ed., *The Social Origins of Private Life.* London: Verso, 1988.

Devereaux, G. Institutionalized Homosexuality of the Mohave Indians. *Human Biology,* Vol. 9 (1937), pp. 498–527

Gutiérrez, R. *When Jesus Came the Corn Mothers Went Away: Marriage, Sexuality and Power in New Mexico, 1500–1846.* Stanford, Calif.: Stanford Univ. Press, 1991.

Kehoe, A.B. The Functions of Ceremonial Intercourse Among the Northern Plains Indians. *Plains Anthropologist,* Vol. 48 (1970), pp. 99–103.

Niethammer, C. *Daughters of the Earth: The Lives and Legends of Native American Women.* New York: Collier Books, 1977.

Ronda, J.P. *Lewis and Clark Among the Indians.* Lincoln: Univ. of Nebraska Press, 1984.

Roscoe, W. *The Zuni Man Woman.* Albuquerque: Univ. of New Mexico Press, 1991.

Schlegel, A. Male and Female in Hopi Thought and Action. In A. Schlegel, ed., *Sexual Stratification: A Cross Cultural View.* New York: Columbia Univ. Press, 1977.

Tedlock, D., and B. Tedlock. *Teachings from the American Earth: Indian Religion and Philosophy.* New York: Liveright, 1975.

Terell, J., and D.M. Terell. *Indian Women of the Western Morning: Their Life in Early America.* New York: Dial Press, 1974.

Rebecca Bales
Tina Weil
Charles C. Murdock

INFANT SEXUALITY

For humans in the prenatal stage, the genetic components necessary for sexual development are present at the point of fertilization. Female fetuses have two X chromosomes, and male fetuses have an X and a Y chromosome. If a Y chromosome is present, a testosterone bath occurs in utero to cause sexual differentiation. All fetuses begin to develop in the same way, and if the testosterone bath did not occur early in fetal development, all would become females. Following the testosterone bath (in the case of male fetuses), sometime after the sixth week of gestation, the genitals begin to develop in both males and females.

Sexual Response and Behavior

Human beings are sexual beings even before birth. Ultrasound images of male fetuses indicate penile erections in utero, and some males are born with erect penises. Infant girls are able to have clitoral erections. It is estimated that at least half of all boys experience orgasm by the age of four, although they do not ejaculate in childhood because they lack the hormones necessary to do so at that time. Babies typically begin to masturbate with their hands once they can control their movements, at about eight months of age, and also by rubbing against objects or their cribs.

Circumcision

Today in the United States, approximately half of all male infants are circumcised (i.e., the foreskin covering the glans of the penis is surgically removed). This procedure may be selected for religious or social reasons (e.g., so the boy will look like his father). Many people argue that circumcision is both unnecessary and barbaric. Circumcision is not the norm in most other countries.

If circumcision is chosen for a male, and the penis is injured or severed in the process, parents may decide to raise the child as a girl, using hormones and surgical procedures to change the outward appearance of the genitalia. Such instances are extremely rare, but it is often easier for a child whose penis has been accidentally removed to be raised as a female than to cope with the lack of the symbol of masculinity (i.e., the penis) in this culture.

When adults play the name-the-body-parts game with babies, they tend to bypass the sexual organs and parts. Adults will likely ask the child to name the eyes, nose, mouth, ears, belly button, knees, elbows, feet, and hands; the penis, vulva, and nipples will not be mentioned. This type of omission gives the child important messages about sexual body parts: that they are not to be discussed and perhaps are even something to be ashamed of. This message is also communicated when parents admonish a child for masturbating, rather than telling a child that masturbation is a private behavior to be done in a private place.

Touching and skin contact play an important role in an infant's normal, healthy development. An infant begins to learn sexual messages through the nurturing and bonding process. Being nursed, played with, and cuddled affects a child's development, awareness, and experience of sexuality. Babies who are not touched or nurtured become depressed and antisocial, and they fail to thrive and grow normally. They have trouble developing a sense of well-being and may even become sick and die if they are deprived of skin-to-skin contact.

In infancy, babies learn to receive and express love through the skin. Skin-to-skin contact in infancy and childhood is a precursor to the closeness and intimacy they will derive from such contact in adulthood. The skin is the organ that allows humans to express love, eventually including erotic, sexual love.

Toilet Training

The experiences of diapering, cleaning the genitals, and toilet training can have lasting effects on the view babies develop of their gender, sexuality, and sexual body parts. If the caretaker frowns and says something negative each time a child's genitals are exposed with a dirty diaper, that child may develop negative attitudes about his or her genitals. After all, every time the genitals are exposed, the child is given a negative message. An infant is too young to understand that the unpleasant faces and messages reflect the presence of feces rather than the genitals. Adults may also give messages about gender during potty training, such as saying to a boy that he should stand up, just as daddy does, and to a little girl that she should sit on the seat the way mommy does.

Sexual Socialization

Sexual socialization—learning how males and females are to interact with each other and how to behave in sexual situations—begins at birth. It is a dynamic process, with information being obtained by observation, by being taught, or by experiencing what the culture considers appropriate behaviors for males and females. These expectations vary from culture to culture.

Children learn to respond as sexual beings as early as infancy. Parents tend to treat male and female children differently, reflecting the parents' expectations of how boys and girls, and men and women, should act socially and sexually. During infancy, the child receives cues about gender from adults. Parents dress girls in pink and boys in blue, and say things like "Big boys don't cry" or "Act like a lady." Studies show that parents tend to hold, play with, and touch girl babies differently from the way they handle boy babies. In addition, adults tend to give boys and girls different toys, which prepare them for later interactions with others and the world. Little boys are rarely taught to knit, although that is an activity many girls are taught. Girls are much more likely than boys to be given dolls; boys are more likely to receive trucks. Chromosomes, hormones, and sex organs do not predispose girls to be better at knitting or to enjoy it more than boys do, or boys to want to play with trucks. These differences are established through sexual socialization.

REFERENCES

Calderone, M.S., and E.W. Johnson. *The Family Book About Sexuality*. New York: Bantam Books, 1983.

Halverson, H.M. Genital and Sphincter Behavior of the Male Infant. *Journal of Genetic Psychology,* Vol. 56 (1940), pp. 95–136.

Kinsey, A., W. Pomeroy, and C. Martin. *Sexual Behavior in the Human Male*. Philadelphia: Saunders, 1948.

Andrea Parrot

INFERTILITY

Infertility is currently defined as the lack of ability to conceive a pregnancy or carry a pregnancy to term after having unprotected sexual intercourse for one year. (For couples over age 30, the period to be considered is six months, because older couples have less time for lengthy infertility testing and corrective procedures.) Approximately one in five couples suffers from infertility at some time during their childbearing years. Of those couples with infertility problems, approximately 40 percent have a female problem and approximately 40 percent have a male problem; in the remaining 20 percent of cases, both members of the couple experience some type of infertility.

Each year, an increasing number of persons seek treatment for infertility; however, it is unclear whether the number of infertile persons is increasing or more people are seeking assistance. Currently, 2.4 million U.S. couples who want to have a child must seek medical assistance or turn to other options such as adoption. New infertility cases are estimated at 160,000 per year, with 200,000 to 300,000 patients currently receiving treatment.

Fertility

The chance of achieving a successful pregnancy is slightly more than 30 percent with a perfectly timed menstrual cycle, since some eggs do not become fertilized and some of the fertilized eggs do not grow well in the early developmental stage. For a woman to become pregnant, she must ovulate (i.e., an egg must leave the ovary); the fimbriated (fingerlike) ends of the Fallopian tubes must pick up the egg and move it inside a tube; the sperm must swim through the cervix and uterus and into the Fallopian tube. One sperm must penetrate the egg. The fertilized egg, now an azygote, must move down the tube into the uterus and attach itself to the uterine lining where it is called an embryo. Healthy sperm are believed to live two to three days in a woman, and an ovum is thought to be fertilized 12 to 24 hours after ovulation.

Causes of Infertility

Infertility often results from sexually transmitted diseases (e.g., gonorrhea, syphilis, chlamydia) or other infections (e.g., tuberculosis) that cause scarring and blockage of the Fallopian tubes in women or the vas deferens in men, thereby preventing the passage of ova or sperm. Sometimes an intrauterine device is implicated in the spread of infection to the pelvis, causing pelvic inflammatory disease (PID). Certain viruses, such as herpes simplex, and venereal warts can also lead to problems by damaging the cervical mucus. The rate of infertility following infections increases with age, because the likelihood of contracting a sexually transmitted disease increases with the number of sexual partners.

Men need to produce approximately 60 million sperm per ejaculate to be considered fertile. Most healthy young men produce at least 200 million sperm per ejaculate. However, because sperm count decreases with age, the chances of becoming infertile increase with age. In addition, stress, diet, radiation, excess heat (e.g., saunas), mumps after puberty, a varicocele (i.e., a varicose vein in the scrotum that raises the temperature of the testicles), undescended testicles, drug use, and wearing jockey shorts can interfere with the production of sperm.

Any mechanical problem that interferes with sperm placement can cause infertility. If men are unable to ejaculate because they have erectile dysfunctions, they may be unable to place the sperm in the woman's vagina. Men who seek to reverse a vasectomy may experience low sperm count or infertility if the reversal is unsuccessful or the man has developed antibodies to his own sperm.

Aging women may fail to ovulate, and they are more likely to carry genetic abnormalities. Therefore, the risk of miscarriage increases with age. Other conditions that contribute to infertility in women include endometriosis (i.e., a condition in which part of the endometrial lining of the uterus migrates into the abdominal cavity), vagina acidity (which interferes with sperm motility), thick cervical mucus, cervical polyps, amenorrhea, uterine abnormalities, vaginismus (i.e., the muscles at the entry of the vagina squeeze so tightly that penetration by the penis is impossible), lack of ovulation (sometimes as a result of low levels of the body fat necessary to metabolize sex hormones), smoking, and drug use.

Infertility in Men

The diagnostic workup in a man starts with a complete medical history and physical examination. Attention should be paid to the following factors: significant diseases (e.g., mumps after the age of puberty), undescended testicles, varicocele, or a hernia that has not been repaired. A comprehensive sexual history is done, including level of sexual activity, approximate age of onset of puberty, and incidence of sexually transmitted diseases.

Usually, the first test for infertility in the male is analysis of a semen sample, obtained through masturbation, to determine the presence and quantity of sperm, the ratio of normal to abnormal sperm, and the evidence, if any, of an autoimmune response. The ratio of active sperm cells to the total is extremely important, as is the quality of the cells' movement. Both these indices constitute aspects of motility. Sperm counts as low as 20 million per cubic centimeter can be considered normal provided other parameters are within the normal range. A standard scale is used to evaluate the characteristics of the ejaculate sample (see Table 1).

Table 1: Limits-of-Adequacy Criteria*

Characteristic	Value
Ejaculate volume	1.5–5.0 cc
Sperm density	> 20 million/ml
Motility	> 60%
Forward progression	>2 (scale 1–4)
Morphology	

No significant microscopic sperm clumping
No significant white cells or red cells
No increased thickening of the seminal fluid (hyperviscosity)
* on at least two occasions.

Males can also be tested for the presence of seminal fructose, which can indicate blockage or some failure in development, which can be confirmed through X-ray. Sometimes, a postcoital, or Huhners's, test is done to evaluate sperm survival in cervical mucus just before ovulation. This test also detects possible antisperm antibody formation. Because only preovulatory mucus nourishes sperm and allows it to remain active, scheduling of the activity is required.

Blood testing in the male evaluates levels of testosterone, follicle-stimulating hormone (FSH), and luteinizing hormone (LH). Low FSH and LH levels suggest problems stemming from the hypothalamus or the pituitary gland. High levels suggest a problem in the testicles. A picture of the sperm transport system can be obtained through a procedure called a vasogram, which is usually performed under a short-acting anesthetic. The scrotal sac is opened, dye is inserted into the vas deferens, and an X-ray is taken. A culture of the urethral opening is done to identify any infection.

Immunological factors may play a role in male infertility. An increased incidence of antisperm antibodies has been found in infertile men, and suppression of these antibodies with cortico-steroid treatment has resulted in both improved sperm quality and an increased pregnancy rate.

The investigating practitioner may recommend sperm penetration assays. The ability of the sperm to penetrate an ovum is measured by the hamster test, which uses hamster ova. However, failure to penetrate hamster eggs and failure to penetrate human eggs are not always equivalent.

Infertility in Women

Female infertility may be caused by structural disorders of the Fallopian tubes or uterus, hormonal imbalances, or problems with the cervix. Physical occlusion of the Fallopian tubes, structurally preventing the egg and sperm from meeting, occurs with the scarring and adhesions from PID. Other defects in the tubes can prevent the egg and sperm from passing through them. Structural abnormalities of the uterus may prevent a woman from carrying the fetus to term. A tumor of the uterine wall may be amenable to surgical correction.

Imbalances involving the four major fertility-related hormones—FSH, LH, estrogen, and progesterone—are the source of the problem in 20 percent to 30 percent of infertility patients. These hormonal imbalances can cause ovulatory disturbances and habitual spontaneous abortions usually during the first trimester; they may also result in a failure of the follicle to mature or failure of the embryo to become implanted in the endometrium.

The cervix can be the cause of infertility if there is stenosis (narrowing). Poor mucous production, which inhibits the transport of sperm, is another cervical disorder. Cervicitis, or inflammation of the cervix, may kill sperm or inhibit their movement.

The diagnostic process for women, as for men, involves a number of steps. The reproductive organs can be checked visually and manually by means of a pelvic examination. A history is obtained, including menstrual history, sexual development, previous pregnancies, and sexually transmitted diseases. The basal body temperature (BBT) is plotted each morning before any activity is started. The pattern of the BBT indicates if and when ovulation occurs and provides a data base for scheduling and interpreting hormonal and other tests.

Blood tests, along with the utilization of ultrasound to track follicle growth in the ovary, facilitate charting of the entire menstrual cycle. At the beginning, middle, and end of the cycle, four hormones are tested: FSH, LH, estrogen, and progesterone. Screening tests for prolactin are also done. This hormone should be found only following childbirth, so its presence suggests problems related to the pituitary gland.

Sometimes, an endometrial biopsy is done to further evaluate the menstrual cycle and the quality of the uterine lining for implantation of the embryo. Visualization of the Fallopian tubes for blockage may also be done by means of a hysterosalpingogram (HSG), which takes place in the X-ray department. Contrast dye is slowly injected into the uterine cavity, and the tubes are visualized on a television screen through fluoroscopy. Both of these procedures can be done on an outpatient basis, although cramping may occur.

If further information about the pelvic organs is needed, a laparoscopy may be performed. A general anesthetic is used, and a small incision is made near the navel. A telescopelike instrument is inserted into the pelvic cavity to visualize the area. Since the HSG may miss adhesions and scar tissue and cannot diagnose endometriosis, the laparoscopy may be necessary to detect evidence of scarring from pelvic disease. Direct visualization of the uterine cavity for tumors, adhesions, or congenital anomalies may be done at the time of the laparoscopy.

Treatment of Men

The treatment of male infertility may require surgery or medication or may involve techniques for improving the quality of the sperm. Surgery is directed toward improving the production of sperm or improving its delivery from the site of maturation (testis) and storage (epididymis) to the egg (ovum). Scrotal varicocele is reported in 21 percent to 41 percent of infertile males, three times the rate of occurrence in healthy men. Corrective surgery has been reported to improve semen quality in 67 percent of patients: the average pregnancy rate following varicocele repair is approximately 40 percent with the average pregnancy occurring six to nine months after surgery. Surgery has also been used to reverse vasectomies and the reported pregnancy rate is

now 45 percent to 70 percent with the new microsurgery. Surgical construction of a new link between the epididymis and a distal portion of the vas has resulted in an 11 percent pregnancy rate when the obstruction is at the head of the epididymis and 30 percent when the obstruction is at the tail. Some men have an ejaculatory-duct obstruction, which may be removed in a simple transurethral procedure. New devices based on European prototypes are being developed for cases in which normal sperm pathways are beyond surgical repair. However, success rates are still quite poor.

Medically, male infertility can be treated with hormonal replacement in 5 percent of men and with high-dose cyclic steroid therapy following vasovasotomy procedures. The use of antihistamines and alpha-sympathomimetic drugs has been reported to improve sperm emission in as many as 40 percent of male patients. Forty percent of men presenting with infertility have both normal genitalia and a normal hormone profile, with no apparent reason for their poor semen analysis. Sometimes anti-estrogens (e.g., clomiphene citrate and tamoxifen) increase the levels of LH and FSH. Drug therapy has brought reported improvements in sperm density and motility, with pregnancy rates ranging from 8 percent to 41 percent. Testolactone, which blocks the conversion of testosterone to estradiol, has resulted in reported pregnancy rates of 25 percent to 33 percent. Human chorionic gonadotropin (HCG), a treatment for unexplained low sperm count, has increased sperm count and motility. Some drugs used in the treatment of infertility in the 1950s and 1960s (e.g., arginine, bromocriptine corticosteroids, thyroxin, and oxytocin) are seldom used now.

The testes are heat sensitive and must remain about 4 degrees cooler than the normal body temperature. Scrotal hypothermia is a new treatment being advocated for infertile men. Patients wear a device for 12 to 16 hours daily that cools the scrotum by an evaporation process. However, its efficacy remains speculative.

Treatment of Women

In the case of the woman who is otherwise normal and has a fertile partner, induction of ovulation, or stimulation of ovulation is performed. During monthly ovulation, hormones are released from the hypothalamus and the pituitary. The hypothalamus releases gonadotropin-releasing hormone (Gn RH). This hormone signals the pituitary gland to release FSH and LH, which is responsible for the development of ovarian follicles. Two drugs, Clomidane and

Serophene, have been given if the cause of the problem is in the hypothalamus. Another drug, Pergonal, directly stimulates the ovaries. It has been known to cause multiple gestation in 20 percent of cases, and 5 percent of those result in three or more fetuses. The incidence of birth defects or congenital anomalies has been reported in clinical trials of 287 completed pregnancies as 1.7 percent, which is similar to that reported in the general population.

A drug called Metrodin, which contains FSH, is used for ovulation induction when the LH level is elevated and the FSH level is low to stimulate the ovarian follicle. Ectopic pregnancies have been reported with the use of Metrodin, but again the rate of birth defects did not exceed that found in the untreated population. In clinical trials, 83 percent of cases involved single births and 17 percent multiple births.

Technologies

Technologies may be part of the solution to infertility. These technologies include artificial insemination (AI), in vitro fertilization (IVF), and gamete intrafallopian transfer (GIFT), with all sorts of variations (see the glossary at the end of this entry). AI and IVF are the most common procedures. Another technique, in vitro fertilization and embryo transfer (IVFET), allows the use of sperm from males who have semen of reduced quality and is reputed to be as successful as using embryos fertilized with sperm from men with normal semen. Intrauterine insemination (IUI) involves the placement of large numbers of motile spermatozoa at the approximate time of a female's menstrual cycle. IVF and GIFT have been successful when the male sperm count was the cause of the infertility. Even under the most favorable circumstances, however, these procedures result in less than a 50 percent success rate, so repeated attempts are the norm.

Emotional Impact of Infertility

Infertile couples may experience a "crisis of infertility" characterized by excessive anxiety, damaged self-esteem, grief, uncertainty about the future, and estranged relationships both with each other and with family and friends. The trauma of the diagnosis is also influenced by social and cultural norms. Most people, long before they become sexually active with a partner, assume fertility. They concern themselves with questions of choice: Do I want to have children? When will I have them? With a diagnosis of infertility, choice, in the most fundamental sense of the word, is stripped from the individual or couple.

They become different. People who are childless are often regarded with suspicion or pity. To have children is considered natural. To discover that it is not possible, even temporarily, potentially strips the individual and couple of one of the most important and expected societal roles: that of parent.

Prior to attempting to investigate infertility, the couple must overcome their denial that something is wrong. Societal assumptions and myths are not very useful. Couples are encouraged to relax and let nature take its course, or they are told that if they adopt a baby, they will be able to have their own biological child. They may have to work through these false assumptions and myths before medical intervention can be useful.

After the diagnosis is made, they often experience the same stages of mourning as do people following the death of a loved one. Although both members of the couple may experience the stages of denial, anger, grief, and acceptance, they rarely experience these stages simultaneously. They are mourning the loss of a dream; in the case of miscarriage or stillbirth, they are mourning the loss of a fetus who was tangible to them and whom they may have already felt. These emotional reactions are often dramatic and disruptive to relationships. Some couples split as a result of the strain of infertility or because one member believes he or she might have been a parent already with another partner. In some cases, the infertile partner wants to leave the relationship out of guilt, believing that the fertile partner deserves to become a parent. Although some relationships are strong enough to withstand this emotional trauma, all involuntarily infertile couples who want children are emotionally traumatized.

Furthermore, partners respond to infertility differently. In a qualitative study of married couples' reactions to infertility, wives were found to experience it as a cataclysmic failure and to withdraw from interactions with the fertile world, focusing on the problem of infertility, thinking about it daily, reading about it constantly, and being willing to do whatever was necessary to solve the problem. In contrast, husbands saw infertility as a disconcerting event, something they could accept and put into perspective. This was true regardless of which partner had the reproductive impairment.

Wives were the initiators and leaders in the treatment process, and couples tended to see infertility as a problem for wives. Frustration and lack of communication were consequences of the confrontation between the couple.

Financial Issues

Financial considerations are important to young couples, and most have neither the private resources nor the insurance coverage to pay for diagnosis and treatment. For those with insurance coverage, payment may be based on creative billing and the use of terminology. For example, if the problem causing the infertility is related to a hormonal imbalance, treatment may be covered if the form reads "hormonal insufficiency" rather than "infertility." However, many insurance companies refuse to cover infertility services, claiming that the condition is not an illness. Counterarguments by infertility support groups describe infertility as a body-system malfunction that is as eligible for medical insurance coverage as any other system failure. Some states now require insurance carriers to cover the cost of infertility. Texas limits the coverage of IVF to married women, allowing insemination only with their husband's sperm. This rule eliminates coverage for a woman who has a tubal occlusion and is married to a man with a low or nonexistent sperm count. Massachusetts limits the mandate to private insurance carriers, thus eliminating women who are covered by medical or other governmental programs. Some states limit the coverage for experimental treatments.

Costs are formidable, and a comprehensive diagnostic workup is basic to the treatment plan. According to recent data, the average cost of diagnosis per successful pregnancy is approximately $10,700. Medications to treat infrequent or absent ovulation cost $1,000 to $1,500 per month and require painful injections over a period of 9 to 12 days. IVF can cost $5,000 to $7,000 per attempt.

Legislation

Artificial insemination by donor (AID) has had some unexpected consequences. An unmarried woman obtained sperm from a man who said he had no intention of becoming involved with the resultant child; later, when he sued for visitation rights, the courts ruled that he was entitled to see the child, and he was given the right to be designated the child's father on the birth certificate. When a married woman undergoes AID, the courts have ruled that the man to whom the woman is married is the lawful father of the child. Some states have introduced laws restricting the number of times a particular donor is allowed to father a child.

IVF is unregulated by federal, state, or professional standards and may be potentially dangerous to the consumer. A 1985 survey reported that of 54 IVF clinics responding to a questionnaire, one-half had never sent a woman home with a baby, after having treated more than 600 women. Successes in IVF clinics may be reported as pregnancies per retrieval rate (i.e., the number of eggs fertilized rather than the number of babies born). Other clinics report the percentage of pregnancies per embryo transfer but do not report the number of patients who arrive at that stage. The IVF rate is about 20 percent of achieved egg fertilizations and about 13 percent to 15 percent of actual births.

Glossary

Agglutination of sperm	Sticking together of sperm
Anovulation	Absence of ovulation (menses may occur with anovulation)
Artificial embryonation ("embryo adaption")	Process by which artificial insemination of a woman results in an embryo. The embryo is flushed out five days after conception and implanted in a second woman (typically, the wife of the man who donated the sperm)
Artificial insemination	Introduction of donor semen by donor (AID) into a woman's vagina for the purpose of conception
Artificial insemination by husband	Introduction of the husband's semen into the vagina for the purpose of conception
Azoospermia	Absence of sperm in the ejaculate
Capacitation	Alteration of sperm during their passage through the female reproductive tract that gives them the capacity to penetrate and fertilize the ovum
Cryobank	Site where tissues (i.e., sperm, oocytes, and embryos) are stored in the frozen state
Egg (oocyte) donation	Surgical removal of an egg from one woman for transfer to the Fallopian tubes or uterus of another woman.
Embryo transfer	Introduction of an embryo into a woman's uterus after in vitro or in vivo fertilization
Gamete intrafallopian transfer (GIFT)	Procedure wherein clomiphene citrate, Pergonal, or Metrodin is used to stimulate ovulation, and then the egg is removed by means of

laparoscopy. The egg is immediately mixed with washed sperm, usually from the husband, and is then transferred into the Fallopian tubes, where fertilization may take place

Hamster test (sperm penetration assay)
Test used to determine the ability of a man's sperm to penetrate a hamster egg, with the result considered to be evidence of the sperm's general penetrating ability

Hostility factor
Inability of sperm to survive in the vaginal or cervical environment long enough to swim upward toward the ovum, due to overly acidic secretions or immunological reactions

Human menopausal gonadotropin (hMG) (Pergonal)
Natural product containing both FSH and LH that is extracted from the urine of postmenopausal women and used to treat both male and female infertility by stimulating the development of oocytes in ovulatory patients

Idiopathic (unexplained) infertility
Term used to describe infertility that cannot be explained

Immunological response
Presence of sperm antibodies in the woman or man that tend to destroy sperm action through immobilization or clumping

In vitro fertilization (IVF)
Procedure in which an egg is removed from a ripe follicle and fertilized by sperm cells outside the human body. After the fertilized egg is allowed to divide for about two days, it is inserted back into the uterus, producing the "test tube baby"

In vivo fertilization
Fertilization of an egg by a sperm within the woman's body

Laparoscopy
Direct visualization of the ovaries and the exterior of the Fallopian tubes and uterus by means of a surgical instrument inserted through a small incision below the navel

Necrospermia
Condition in which sperm are produced and found in the semen but are dead and cannot fertilize eggs

Oocyte retrieval
Surgical procedure in which a needle is inserted into the follicles to collect eggs, which are then placed in a medium–filled culture dish

Ovary retention
Failure of the egg to be released even though the follicle has ruptured

Ovulation induction
Use of female hormone therapy to stimulate oocyte development and release

Postcoital test (Huhner test or PK test)
Diagnostic test for infertility in which vaginal and cervical secretions are obtained following intercourse and analyzed under a microscope

Rubin test (tubal insufflation)
Test in which CO_2 gas is blown into the uterus under pressure and allowed to escape out of the Fallopian tubes, if open

Secondary infertility
Inability to conceive or carry a pregnancy after having successfully conceived and carried one or more pregnancies

Sperm bank
Site where sperm is stored in frozen form for future use in artificial insemination

Sperm washing
Technique that separates sperm from the seminal fluid

Spinnbarkheit
Rough measure of how easily sperm cells can enter and penetrate the cervical secretions by the elasticity of the cervical mucus

Surrogate carrier
Woman who gestates an embryo that is not genetically related to her and then gives the child to its genetic parents

Surrogate mother
Woman who becomes pregnant through insemination with the sperm of the husband of an infertile woman and then, following birth, turns the child over for adoption by the couple

Varicocele
Varicose vein of the testicles, which may be the major cause of male infertility

Zygote intrafallopian transfer (ZIFT)
Transfer of a zygote into a Fallopian tube by means of laparoscopy

REFERENCES

Arditti, R., R.D. Klein, and S. Minden, eds. *Test-Tube Women: What Future for Motherhood?* London: Pandora Press, 1984.

Bauman, R. Power and Choice: Sexism and Racism in Reproductive Science and Technology. *Woman of Power,* Vol. 11 (1984), pp. 67–70.

Blank, R.H. Making Babies: The State of the Art. *Futurist Journal,* Vol. 19 (1985), pp. 11–17.

Cook, E.P. Characteristics of the Biopsychosocial Crisis of Infertility. *Journal of Counseling and Development,* Vol. 65 (1987), pp. 465–70.

Cooper, G.S. An Analysis of the Costs of Infertility Treatment. *American Journal of Public Health,* Vol. 76 (1986), pp. 1018–19.

Corea, G., et al. *Man-Made Women: How New Reproductive Technologies Affect Women.* Bloomington: Indiana Univ. Press, 1987.

Garner, C., and G. Patton. *Pathways to Parenthood.* Norwell, Mass.: Serono Symposia, 1989.

Greil, A., T. Leitko, and K. Porter. Infertility: His and Hers. *Gender and Society,* Vol. 2 (June 1988), pp. 172–99.

Harkness, C. *The Infertility Book.* San Francisco: Volcano Press, 1987.

Henifin, M.S. Women's Health and the New Reproductive Technologies. *Women and Health,* Vol. 13 (1987), pp. 1–7.

Hubbard, R. Prenatal Diagnosis and Eugenic Ideology. *Women's Studies International Forum,* Vol. 8 (1985), pp. 567–76.

Lipshultz, L. *Male Infertility.* Norwell, Mass.: Serono Symposia, 1989.

Menning, B.E. *A Guide for the Childless Couple.* Englewood Cliffs, N.J.: Prentice Hall, 1988.

Raymond, C.A. In Vitro Fertilization Faces R&R: (More) Research and Regulation. *Journal of the American Medical Association,* Vol. 260 (1988), pp. 1191–92.

Rhodes, R. Women, Motherhood and Infertility: The Social and Historical Context. *Journal of Social Work and Human Sexuality,* Vol. 6 (1987), pp. 5–20.

Salzer, L. *Infertility: How Couples Can Cope.* New York: G.K. Hall, 1986.

Shapiro, C.H. *Infertility and Pregnancy Loss.* San Francisco: Jossey-Bass, 1988.

Soules, M.R. The in Vitro Fertilization Pregnancy Rate: Let's Be Honest with One Another. *Fertility and Sterility,* Vol. 43 (1985), pp. 511–13.

Spallone, P. *Beyond Conception: The New Politics of Reproduction.* Westport, Conn.: Bergin & Garvey, 1989.

Susan B. Bond
Andrea Parrot
Ann Seidl

INSTITUTE FOR ADVANCED STUDY OF HUMAN SEXUALITY

The Institute for Advanced Study of Human Sexuality was formally incorporated as a private nonsectarian graduate school on June 8, 1976, in San Francisco. On August 13, 1976, the State of California qualified the Institute to grant graduate degrees in the field of human sexuality. The first class of students began work on October 1, 1976. Approximately one year later, following evaluation by a committee on postsecondary educational standards appointed by the State of California, the Institute received approval of the following degrees by the Superintendent of Public Instruction of the State Department of Education under California Education Code Section 94310(b): Master of Human Sexuality (M.H.S), Doctor of Arts in Human Sexuality (D.A.), Doctor of Human Sexuality (D.H.S.), and Doctor of Philosophy in Human Sexuality (Ph.D.). In June 1981, after an on-site visit, the degrees were again approved, but the Doctor of Arts degree was changed to a Doctor of Education in Human Sexuality (Ed.D.) degree.

In 1982, the Institute was granted full accreditation by the National Association of Private Nontraditional Schools and Colleges (NAPNSC). In 1987, the Institute was granted full institutional approval by the State of California, and in February 1989, after careful review, the Institute was reaccredited by the NAPNSC.

What became the Institute had its origin in 1962, when the United Methodist Church, in cooperation with the United Church of Christ, the United Presbyterian Church, the American Baptist Church, and the Southern Presbyterian Church, commissioned a study of the nature and needs of persons in early adulthood. Four cities were chosen for field study, and the Reverend Ted McIlvenna, a United Methodist minister with considerable social-research background, was chosen to direct the San Francisco arm of the project. The issue of sexual identity, especially homosexuality, was a primary area of the project's research. The main conclusion of the study was that one could not understand homosexuality without understanding human sexuality.

Further consultations were held at the Institute for Sex Research, in Bloomington, Indiana (the Kinsey Institute); at the headquarters of the United Methodist Church, in Nashville, Tennessee; at the National Institutes of Mental Health in Washington, D.C.; and in London, England, with representatives from the Dutch Ministry of Culture, the World Council of Churches, and the British Department of Health, as well as a representative from the Vatican, a bishop of the Church of England, a representative of the French Ministry of Health, and five delegates from the United States. One of the conclusions of the London meeting was that persons in the helping professions were woefully lacking in knowledge about human sexuality and that a center specifically designed for training professionals should be established.

In the spring of 1967, a meeting was held at the Institute for Sex Research in Bloomington that included representatives from the original sponsoring church bodies, the National Institutes of Mental Health, the Glide Foundation (an operating foundation), and four other foundations. At the meeting, the Glide Foundation in San Francisco agreed to become the home of the National Sex Forum (NSF), with a mission to study what helping professionals needed to know about human sexuality, the development of effective educational methodologies, and the design of innovative training materials. The NSF began officially in October 1968, as part of the Glide Urban Center.

By the end of the first year, it was obvious that most professionals needed specific training in human sexuality, that there was a lack of educational material, and that the available information had not been organized in any specific way. In October 1969, a team of 12 people committed themselves to the formal study of sexology. Each of these people brought to this study a unique background, and each chose a specialty in addition to general sexological study. The group consisted of two clergy, three physicians, three therapists, one child psychologist, and three sexual educators. Of this group, nine people finished their committed study by 1976, and six of these nine became the core faculty of the Institute. In 1975, the political and economic pressures of the church relationship became so severe that NSF sponsorship was transferred to the Exodus Trust, a California nonprofit trust that has as its sole and exclusive purpose the performance of educational, scientific, and literary functions in relation to sexual, emotional, mental and physical health.

The NSF early became known for developing the Sexual Attitude Restructuring (SAR) process, an innovative method for educating adults about what people do sexually and how they feel about it. Although the SAR process has been misunderstood and misused by untrained imitators, it has proven very effective when used by competent sexologists. The NSF also is the largest supplier of professional educational material dealing specifically with human sexual behavior. The films, slides, audio- and videotapes it developed are used by more than 8,000 professionals and institutions throughout the world.

In the period from 1969 to 1973, the sexological study team worked closely with the University of Minnesota Medical School program in human sexuality, directed by Richard Chilgren, M.D., and the University of California Medical School program in human sexuality, directed by Herbert Vandervoort, M.D. By the beginning of 1974, the NSF staff and sexological study team came to the conclusion that there needed to be an interdisciplinary institute for the education and training of sexologists and that such an institution had to be freestanding, with its own board of directors, and not be beholden to any outside group.

Four tasks were assigned to the sexological study team. McIlvenna was assigned the task of moving the NSF and the future Institute into a new structure. Vandervoort was given the task of organizing the academic work completed by the sexological study team. Laird Sutton was assigned to build the graphic-resource library, and Marguerite Rubenstein, Loretta Haroian, and Phyllis Lyon accepted the challenge of defining the professional training requirements in the emerging field of sexology. As the planning group completed their tasks, a facility was acquired, a library was developed, and additional faculty were included, notably Wardell B. Pomeroy and Erwin Haeberle were added to the resident faculty. The Reverend Lewis Durham, former head of the Glide Foundation and an expert on alternate lifestyles, became the dean of students. The Institute also contracted for part-time services of other leading experts.

The Institute also made a special effort to include other experts. Three times each year, the Institute invited ten experts who had contributed to the emerging field of sexology. These experts were asked to lecture and have their lecture documented on videotapes. These lectures now form the most extensive oral history of contemporary sexology available. In addition, another 20,000 hours of material have been gathered to supplement the basic core curriculum. Finally, it was essential to find a structure and a board that could actively support and protect the objectives of the Institute, withstand changes in the political climate, maintain academic freedom, and preserve standards.

Currently, the Institute for Advanced Study of Human Sexuality offers four graduate degree programs for people wishing academic training in the field of human sexuality. In addition, the activities of the former NSF have been divided into several departments of the Institute, perhaps the most important of which is the adult continuing education program, which provides individual courses for professionals needing training for licensure or relicensure, as well as courses for laypersons who desire to expand their knowledge and experience in human sexuality.

Under the Institute's programs, it is possible for students to continue their professional education without leaving their present employment. A minimum of two or three weeks per trimester is required to be spent on campus, although experience has shown that for the majority of students the more time they spend in residence the better they progress. Reading, viewing videotape courses, writing papers, and similar work required during the trimester may be done in private study at home. Because sexology has emerged as a separate academic and professional field in the United States only in the last 20 years, students admitted to the Institute bring with them backgrounds that vary widely in experience and training. This requires that the process of acceptance into the program and the evaluation of work already completed be as comprehensive as possible, since the Institute tries to adjust the program to the individual and gives a limited amount of credit for previous academic work and professional experience in the field of human sexuality. Whenever a student has special training needs (e.g., statistics, research design, basic counseling skills) that cannot be provided at the Institute, efforts are made to have courses taken at cooperating educational institutions. The Institute restricts its programs to the field of sexology.

Students come from all over the world, as the Institute remains the only school in the world providing graduate degrees exclusively in sexology. The student body is a multilingual, multicultural mix, which in itself is a learning experience. Most students already have had graduate training when they enter the Institute, and many are involved professionally in the field of human sexuality or related helping professions. Current students include teachers, ministers, writers, physicians, social workers, nurses, psychologists, and others, and they range in age from the early 20s to the mid-60s. The Institute has always maintained an almost even number of male and female students. Average enrollment is 85 students.

Graduates of the Institute are located throughout the world. They are teachers in high schools, colleges, and medical schools. Many are in private practice as therapists, while others combine therapy with teaching, writing, and workshops. Some graduates have continued in their previous professions as clergy, social workers, and so forth but now do specialized work in sexology. Others have found a place in the commercial world as writers, publishers, filmmakers, and media specialists.

Because San Francisco is a large metropolitan area containing two large universities and a number of smaller universities and colleges, access to other libraries and academic resources is easy for Institute students. The physical facilities of the Institute include a large classroom with the latest media and environmental accoutrements. The Institute further offers print, film, and videotape libraries, videotape viewing areas, physical therapy facilities, administrative and faculty offices, smaller classrooms, and a common room that serves as a socializing space for students, faculty, and staff. The facility has the latest videotape equipment, comparable to a commercial television studio. There are 11 specialty libraries composed of 85,000 books, 120,000 magazines and pamphlets, 12,000 videotapes, 125,000 films, and more than 500,000 photographs and slides. Together, the Institute's library system and erotological material make up one of the most, if not the most, comprehensive sexological resource in the world. Though students pay tuition, much of the work of the Institute is supported by three special tax-exempt funds that solicit contributions (which are tax-exempt) from the general public: the Exodus Trust General Support Fund, the Scholarship Fund, the Exodus Trust AIDS Project. The Institute is located at 1523 Franklin Street, San Francisco, California 94109.

Ted McIlvenna

INTIMACY

Sexual behavior between couples may be viewed on a continuum from total lack of emotion or feeling, and sex for sex's sake, to a deep emotional bond or commitment. This latter state is intimacy. The essence of intimacy encompasses the biblical concept of two persons becoming "one flesh" through complete pleasurable sharing of the body, personality, and feelings.

Couples in sex therapy often report discovering during an intensive daily treatment program that a shared, mutually enjoyable closeness was the missing ingredient in their relationship. The symptoms of erectile dysfunction or lack of orgasm were resolved—but they were only symptoms.

The importance of intimacy in sex therapy is that where true intimacy exists, there are no sexual problems. There may be some dysfunction, but when a couple is close and intimate, the expectation of performance and the fear of satisfying a partner or oneself ceases. Where there is intimacy, the warm feelings of loving and being loved for who and what you are eradicate fears that so often inhibit good sexual functioning. Differences in desire are often related to a lack of intimacy in a relationship.

Intimacy has only recently emerged as a key concept for consideration by marital and sexual therapists. Schnarch's study summarizes the development of this concept and its therapeutic application.

REFERENCES

Allen, G., and C.G. Martin. *Intimacy: Sensitivity, Sex, and the Art of Love.* Chicago: Cowles, 1971.

Beavers, W.R. *Successful Marriage.* New York: W.W. Norton, 1985.

Clinebell, H.J., and C.H. Clinebell. *The Intimate Marriage.* New York: Harper & Row, 1970.

Malone, T.P., and P.T. Malone. *The Art of Intimacy.* Englewood Cliffs, N.J.: Prentice Hall, 1987.

Schnarch, D.M. *Constructing the Sexual Crucible: An Integration of Sexual and Marital Therapy.* New York: W.W. Norton, 1991.

William E. Hartman
Marilyn A. Fithian

INTRAUTERINE DEVICE: DEVELOPMENT

Intrauterine devices (IUDs) have a long history that dates back to claims that Arab camel drivers put stones in the uterus of camels to prevent conception while on long trips. The IUD's modern history is most closely connected with the name of the German gynecologist Ernst Graefenberg. In 1922, Graefenberg used stars of silkworm gut held in shape by a silver wire as an intrauterine contraceptive. He soon abandoned this method in favor of a silver spiral ring, which gave better results and avoided the possibility of infection that arose from cutting off communication between the vagina and the intrauterine cavity. It was not until 1930 that Graefenberg reported on his experiments with silkworm-gut rings and silver rings, demonstrating that the silver ring was superior to the silkworm-gut device. He held that there was a 3.1 percent failure rate with the silkworm-gut insert and only a 1.6 percent failure rate with the silver ring. Norman Haire, who had contact with Graefenberg, also began using the silver ring in 1929 and at first was enthusiastic, but the danger of infection led

him eventually to drop it, as did Graefenberg. In 1934, Tenrei Ota, of Japan, introduced gold and gold-plated silver rings into the uterus; these intrauterine rings were claimed to be even more effective than Graefenberg's devices. Again, the dangers of infection led Ota temporarily to stop using the device.

With the development of effective antibiotics, particularly in the 1940s, and the reduced dangers of infection, others began experimenting with IUDs. In 1958, Lazar C. Margulies, a member of the obstetrics department at Mount Sinai Hospital in New York City, approached the head of his department, Alan F. Guttmacher, a member of the medical advisory committee of the Council on Population, about the potential of IUDs. Margulies argued that some of the past dangers could be eliminated by making an IUD out of plastic and that infection could be controlled. Guttmacher allowed Margulies to try out the device. Other research on the IUDs serendipitously appeared at the same time, including an article by Willi Oppenheimer, a student of Graefenberg's, who had been using the IUD in Israel. Other Americans, such as Jack Lippes, were also experimenting with IUDs and found difficulties in the removal of both the Graefenberg ring and the Ota ring. Lippes's solution was to attach a filament to the end, which went down through the cervix. He also began to use a polyethylene loop.

These new developments led to an international conference on the IUD in New York in 1952, sponsored by the Population Council. The participants at the conference agreed that there were no serious problems associated with the method, and several devices were discussed, including the ones mentioned above. A Cooperative Statistical Program for the Evaluation of Contraceptive Devices (CSP) was set up, under the direction of Christopher Tietze.

Developments were rapid and a number of IUDs went on the market including the Lippes Loop, the Binberg Bow, and the Margulies Spiral. By 1974, some 20 different IUDs were being produced commercially, and some 15 million women were using them. Among the new devices appearing on the market were copper IUDs like the Tatum-T, the Y-shaped Gravigard, and a progesterone-releasing IUD. The copper devices appeared to be superior. One of the reasons for the use of copper was that in investigating Graefenberg's silver ring, researchers found that it was made not of sterling silver but of an alloy containing a large amount of copper; it was the inclusion of copper that had made it so effective.

In the United States, IUD usage dropped suddenly, not so much because of the growth in popularity of the oral contraceptive as because of the scandal associated with the Dalkon shield. One of the problems with the IUDs was the lack of official testing procedures for them, and not all went through a rigorous period of testing. As the use of IUDs increased, pharmaceutical firms rushed into the market with their own devices, and the A.H. Robbins Company purchased a poorly designed, relatively untested device from Dr. Hugh Davis in 1970. Apparently, most of the reports on testing compiled by Davis for his device were not particularly accurate, and there were also ethical issues involved, since Davis was doing both the testing and the marketing, a violation of professional ethics. Though questions were raised about the Dalkon shield almost as soon as it appeared on the market—insertion was exceptionally painful and there was a high rate of infection—complaints were ignored by Robbins, as were the growing number of deaths associated with use of the device. It was finally withdrawn from the market in 1980. That action was much too late, however, and the company was subjected to a large number of lawsuits, which ultimately led to bankruptcy. In the aftermath of this incident, other companies were also sued, and though the lawsuits were not particularly successful, liability-insurance rates rose so much that companies in the United States ceased to distribute the devices for a period. At the same time, regulation of IUDs came under the jurisdiction of the U.S. Food and Drug Administration, and rigid testing procedures had to be completed before the devices could be sold again in the United States. None of the older IUDs went back on the U.S. market, although the Lippes Loop continued to be used in Canada and in much of the rest of the world. Instead, new devices were allowed onto the market only after rigorous testing, and only two had gained approval by the early 1990s: the TCU–380A IUD, which needs replacing every five years, and the Progestasert IUD, which releases progestin and has to be replaced every year. No such replacement is necessary for the polyethylene devices like the Lippes Loop that have been kept in place as long as ten years without difficulty. Ultimately, however, even these IUDs should be removed periodically.

REFERENCES

Graefenberg, E. An Intrauterine Contraceptive Method. Reprinted in L.L. Langley, ed., *Contraception*. Stroudsburg, Pa.: Dowden, Hutchinson & Ross, 1973.

Ishihama, A. Clinical Studies on Intrauterine Rings. Reprinted in L.L. Langley, ed., *Contraception*. Stroudsburg, Pa.:Dowden, Hutchinson & Ross, 1973.

Lehfeldt, H. Ernst Graefenberg and His Ring. *Mount Sinai Hospital Journal of Medicine*, Vol. 42 (1975), pp. 345–52.

Lippes, J. A Study of Intra-uterine Contraception: Development of a Plastic Loop. In L.L. Langley, ed., *Contraception*. Stroudsburg, Pa.: Dowden, Hutchinson & Ross, 1973.

Lippes, J., T. Malik, and H.J. Tatum. The Post Coital Copper-T Advances. *Planned Parenthood*, Vol. II (1976), pp. 24–29.

Mintz, M. *At Any Cost: Corporate Greed, Women, and the Dalkon Shield*. New York: Pantheon, 1985.

Oppenheimer, W. Prevention of Pregnancy by the Graefenberg Ring Method. Reprinted in L.L. Langley, ed., *Contraception*. Stroudsburg, Pa.: Dowden, Hutchinson & Ross, 1973.

Tietze, C. Intra Uterine Contraceptive Rings: Historical and Statistical Appraisal. In C. Tietze and S. Lewis, eds., *Intra Uterine Contraceptive Devices: Proceedings of the Conference, April 30–May 1, 1962, New York City*. Excerpta Medica, International Congress Series 54. Amsterdam, 1962.

World Health Organization. *Mechanization of Action, Safety and Efficacy of Intrauterine Devices*. Geneva: World Health Organization, 1987.

Hans Lehfeldt
Connie Christine Wheeler
Vern L. Bullough

ISLAM: SEXUAL RELATIONS IN THE MUSLIM WORLD

If delving into sex relations in general is risky and controversial, analyzing them in the Islamic context is like venturing into a mine field. It is not only the dearth of studies that makes it so but also the radical differences between those who believe in greater sexual freedom and those who adhere to traditional values. The inevitable result for the researcher is ostracism by both sides. His or her situation is like that of the man during the Civil War who, wanting to be safe, wore a blue jacket and gray trousers and was shot by both sides. What makes it particularly difficult to report on sexual behaviors and patterns in the Muslim world is that this subject is sensitive and makes many people feel uncomfortable, so much so that public discourse about it is more or less taboo. Privately and separately, both sexes may occasionally discuss it, but even here many areas exist beyond the realm of the permissible. This means that despite its powerful and compelling pressure, sex exists almost in the twilight zone, referred to only rarely and with the utmost caution and embarrassment.

This being true of sex in general, some sexual topics, such as homosexuality, are almost unmentionable. Homosexuality is often referred to casually, superficially, or in a derogatory manner but rarely in an analytical or objective way. This is why the Muslim researcher must be extremely cautious in exploring such sensitive and explosive areas. They involve emotional issues that touch many nerves.

At the same time, Muslims regard sexuality as part of being human, although an individual's behavior and sexuality are determined by basic precepts and concepts and guided by religious beliefs. Humans are created with certain needs and instincts that must be satisfied in order to enjoy a healthy, stable, and balanced life. Within this context, individuals should avoid extremes, which may lead to social and biological dysfunctions.

Islam does not deny or even try to suppress sexual desires. It merely tries to regulate them so they find a proper, healthy outlet within the framework of a sound, rational social system. As a general rule, Islam does not try to impose unrealistic, impractical, and purely idealistic demands, which can neither be met nor withstand the test of time and reality. But if it does not attempt to impose unreasonable prohibitions, it is also leery of permissiveness. Rather, it holds that a healthy balance should exist among one's conflicting desires and that the welfare of society as well as the individual should be considered. Islamic morality is not a mere set of principles, commands, and restrictions but a system that takes into account human nature with all its material and biological, as well as spiritual, imperatives. This is perhaps the centerpiece of sexuality in Islam. If such a delicate balance is shattered—when one desire dominates the others—both the individual and society inevitably suffer anxiety, uncertainty, and insecurity.

It would also be a great error to judge sexual relations in the Muslim world by Western standards and principles. Though no contemporary culture has been totally immune or insulated from the influence of the sexual revolution that has engulfed the West and is spreading to the rest of the globe, no cultural grouping is as concerned, troubled, and even frightened by this phenomenon as the Muslim people. They see it as a deadly threat that, if not checked, contained, and controlled, would eventually destroy their social institutions and perhaps society. They are convinced that neither the family nor the cohesion of society can survive the ruinous impact of Westernism.

For the Muslim believer, sexuality must find its expression within the family, where men and women are the shepherds, responsible for the well-being of the society. It is only within the bounds of the family that the reproductive process should take place. Though sexuality is pleasurable, it must be kept within the bounds of responsibility and morality. Here, one can clearly see the emphasis on collective obligation, as everyone is equally accountable for the stability and cohesion of the family and society. In this context, sexuality is never viewed as an end but merely as a means to achieve certain biological, familial, and societal objectives. At the same time, Islam recognizes the power of seduction, the temptation of the sexual urge, and the human desire for love and companionship. Men and women are naturally attracted to each other, but this affectionate relationship should be conducted within and through the acceptable channel of marriage. For this reason, Muslims are encouraged to marry at the earliest possible opportunity. The Prophet stated that "whoever gets married completes half of his (or her) faith." He also warned that "whoever can afford marriage and refrains from doing so is not one of us." If perchance one lacks the wherewithall to marry, that individual is to remain chaste until God has rewarded him with the ability to get married.

To ensure adherence to God's commands, punishment, in both this world and the next, forms an integral part of Islamic teaching. Muslims are constantly reminded that straying from the straight path effects penalties on the Day of Judgment. God may put off punishment, but He never overlooks the sinful deed. Muslims are particularly cautioned against adultery, which is regarded as ruinous and as a deviant way of releasing sexual energy that has serious repercussions. It may bring venereal diseases, cause destruction of the family, create uncertainty of parental lineage, and result in suspicion, tension, and animosity. It is the duty of the family and society to protect individuals from such actions by giving advice and even scolding. If these methods fail, then punishment is meted out according to strict limitations and considerations. Unless the individuals are caught in the act or for some reason confess to committing adultery, proving adultery in the Islamic world is almost impossible, since it requires four unimpeachable eyewitnesses to testify to the act.

False accusation is viewed with grave concern. The Qur'an report that "those who launch charges against chaste women and produce not four witness, flog them with eighty stripes and reject their testimony ever after, for such people are wicked transgressors." In addition, "Those who slander chaste women are cursed in this life and the hereafter, for them there is a grievous penalty," and on the Day of Judgment their tongues, hands, and feet will bear witness to their deeds (Holy Qur'an, XXIV, No. 4).

Homosexuality

In Islam, homosexuality is believed to be the result of weak character, lack of religious teachings, sexual permissiveness, economic pressure, and circumstances. To most Muslims, it is a serious deviation from nature and an affront to human honor and dignity. The Qur'an, like the Christian and Jewish Scriptures, report the case of Sodom and Gomorrah and make it quite specific that the incident is one of males approaching males, deserting the women who had been specially created for them. Though Lût and his family were saved, He destroyed the rest of the people by showering them with brimstones (Holy Qur'an, XXVI, Nos. 165–173).

Adding to the effect of these verses are others emphasizing that "those men who have intercourse with other men or animals" are cursed. Note that the focus here is on male rather than female homosexuality. Lesbian relationships are seldom, if ever, discussed in Islamic writings, almost as if such relationships did not exist. Hence, if it is unlikely for gays to come out of the closet, it is virtually unthinkable for lesbians to do so.

Although homosexuality exists in the Islamic world, and the literature would indicate that it has always existed, no open, candid, or objective studies have been conducted. Instead it is a subject to which one refers casually or satirically. Some writers have held that Islam is more tolerant of homosexuality than Christianity traditionally has been, but it is extremely difficult to document this. It is true that people are not discriminated against in the job market on the basis of their sexual preference, but this is undoubtedly due to the fact that homosexuality is still practiced in almost complete secrecy and always in fear of exposure. Those publicly identified as homosexuals are often shunned, excluded, or ridiculed at social functions. To practice such unacceptable behavior privately is one thing, but to pronounce it publicly and defiantly would, under present conditions, certainly trigger a violent and perhaps catastrophic reaction.

Equality of the Sexes

Many people, inside and outside the Muslim world, have written extensively about women's equality, or the lack of it, in Islamic life. From its beginning, Islam made it clear that, in the eyes of God, faith, rather than race, color, or sex, would differentiate between people. All humans are viewed and treated with absolute equality, just like the teeth of a comb. Throughout the Qur'an, people are referred to as "men and women" who are endowed with equal, though not identical, rights and obligations, based on their emotional, biological, and functional capabilities. In practice, this means that each has significant rights and responsibilities. To Muslims, it is unnatural for men and women to insist on or believe in performing identical tasks. The Prophet pointedly stated that "cursed are those men who imitate women, and those women who imitate men." This does not mean that either one should be denied equal pay for equal work, nor should they be deprived of equal opportunities in the job market, education, services, and politics. By stating that "seeking knowledge is the duty of every Muslim man and woman," Islam has always urged both men and women to seek education. It allows women to have their own businesses, as exemplified by the Prophet's first wife, and to occupy any position as long as it is within the framework of Islamic principles. Furthermore, not only does Islam establish and define a woman's right to inheritance, but it also prohibits other Muslims from taking a woman against her will or treating her with harshness except when she is guilty of open lewdness. Ideally, a man is supposed to live with women on a footing of kindness and equity (Holy Qur'an, IV, No. 19).

Equality of the sexes in Islam does not, however, entail the denial of natural, biological differences. Women, for example, are exempt from some of the basic rituals and obligations, such as prayer and fasting, during menstrual periods and pregnancy. With biological differences taken into account, it is important not to mix or confuse the functional duties of one sex with those of the other. "Wish not what God endowed the other with" is a standard saying in Islam. Marital relations should be compatible and complementary and not based simply on lust, beauty, wealth, or rivalry. To marry for the latter reasons is to invite humiliation, degradation, and eventual alienation.

In pre-Islamic times, though women were active in business and trade, female infanticide was widely practiced. Modern commentators have held that infanticide was done for economic reasons—for example, because girls were not as productive as boys and too many daughters would lead to the loss of a family's fortune through marriage. Others have argued that it was to prevent tainting the family's name and honor. Still, some think the practice was based on a primitive belief that women were the embodiment of the devil and therefore should be buried alive. It was Islam that put an end to this abhorrent behavior among the Arabs.

Muslims were sternly warned that they would be held accountable on the Day of Judgment for any acts of infanticide. In general, Islam prohibits killing or aborting children of any sex because of poverty or fear of lowering the family's standard of living. It is God who provides for parents as well as children. He is the Creator, Cherisher, and Provider. For this reason, Islam even encourages a good Muslim to marry the poor, for God will enrich the person who does so.

The Muslim Family

Throughout the Muslim world, the family, which is the centerpiece of society, is unmistakably patriarchal, and usually the oldest male is the head of the family. However, tradition, as well as social and financial status, may determine both headship and succession. Because Muslims like to keep their families close and intact, the preferred marriage is between first cousins, especially children of brothers. Although marriage is still generally arranged by parents, this practice has been breaking down because of increased mobility, modernization, and urbanization. Marriage is regarded not merely as a bond between a man and a woman but also as a union between families, clans, and tribes. The focus in Islam is on the family and not on the individual. Couples are matched on the basis of compatibility, family status, and economic position, although the consent of the prospective mates is regarded as essential before the matrimonial agreement is concluded. Still, individuals can be and sometimes are pressured into marriage against their wills, particularly in rural and tribal areas.

Among Muslims, great emphasis is placed on female chastity, purity, modesty, and even (in some areas) complete seclusion and veiling. A matter of constant and permanent concern to Muslim men is the conduct of women, since what they do affects and reflects the family's reputation. The whole family, or in some cases even a village, may be dishonored by the misconduct of a female member. Sometimes, friends assume the role of protectors or guardians of the community's honor. The focus is on the female and not the male because it is widely believed that she is primarily responsible for any relationship with the male. Because consent rather than coercion is the rule, it is her responsibility to ward off any unwanted advances. Men are chastised only for extramarital activities, although women are generally treated more harshly and strictly.

Islam allows men to marry as many as four wives. Whether a woman is in a polygamous or monogamous marriage, her rights and privileges are defined and protected by law and are not dependent on the charity, generosity, or conscience of a man. The allowance of multiple wives was never intended merely to satisfy desires, impulses, or whims. Its justification was to prevent delinquency and the fragmentation and destruction of the family due to immoral or adulterous behavior. Taking a second wife must be done with the full consultation of the first wife. While some believe this means consent, others argue that it entails only informing her of the pending action. Sometimes it is the first wife who urges her husband, due to her sterility or sexual dysfunction, to take a second wife.

There is a prohibitive clause in the Qur'an that sets standards for a husband taking additional wives by insisting that they be treated with equality and fairness although the Qur'an also recognizes also since it states as sort of an afterthought that "none of you will (or can)."

In other words, polygamy cannot be rationalized on the basis of emotions, finances, or social status. It is to be undertaken with great caution, care, and as an absolute necessity. Even then, justice and equality must be taken seriously into consideration. Whether a man has one or more wives, it is incumbent upon him to treat them with great tenderness and kindness before, during, and after sexual intercourse. In fact, men are encouraged to plan an emotional preparation to maximize mutual sexual enjoyment. They are not to behave selfishly or inconsiderately. The Prophet advised them "not to pounce on your wives like animals" and to make certain of mutual sexual gratification.

Islam urges those with marital difficulties to seek professional, medical, or familial assistance, with divorce as the very last resort. Although divorce is relatively easy to obtain, its rate is extremely low, as it is still viewed as a disgrace to both the divorcees and their families. Families and friends intervene, pressure, and arbitrate to solve marital problems. Each party's grievances, particularly the wives', are taken seriously, and reconciliation is tried by every possible means. Furthermore, "divorce, in the eyes of Allah, is the most hated permissible." Hence, for religious, social, familial, and practical reasons, divorce may be considered with great reluctance, for not only is it difficult for divorcees, especially women, to remarry, but also the dissolution of the family casts a permanent shadow over its members' lives. For these reasons, couples are frequently compelled to stay together even when their marriage has become meaningless, worthless, and even hellish. Due to the serious complications and ramifications of divorce, Muslims are urged to approach it with painstaking deliberation and consideration. They are reminded that "you may dislike something (marriage) through which God would effect bountiful good for you" (Holy Qur'an, IV, No. 19).

Women in Islam

In the eyes of Westerners, with feminism and women's liberation firmly established, women in the Muslim world may seem to be oppressed, deprived, and discriminated against. One should, however, be cautious with such a sweeping judgment. First, the concepts of equality and sexuality must be viewed within their cultural context. Second, one must differentiate between Islam's principles and a Muslim's behavior. Third, moral judgments should be rendered with great caution and reservations and in view of the social system. Life is a trade-off, as gains are usually balanced by losses. This means that what is regarded as progress invariably has its price, and as of this writing Muslim women have not challenged traditions in any significant way; where they appeared to do so for a time in Iran and even in Egypt, many of the changes have been overturned. Moreover, contrary to Western stereotypes, there is a case to be made for Islam as a liberating and egalitarian influence in opposition to rigidly sexist tradition. In fact, many of the customs and practices in the Muslim world are cultural and environmental rather than religious. For example, both opponents and proponents of the veil generally agree that no explicit reference to it can be found in Islam. In the Qur'an, men and women are urged to resist temptation, restrain their lust, and be modest. It is incumbent upon adherents "to lower your gaze and guard your modesty." Women should not display their beauty and ornaments, except that which is apparent, and are cautioned to draw their veils over their bosoms (Holy Qur'an, XXIV, Nos. 30–31).

Those who believe in the importance of veiling advance many arguments. Interestingly, none of them come from the scriptures. For example, proponents cite practical considerations by pointing out that the veil provides a degree of equality and peace of mind. Since not all women are endowed with beauty, the less fortunate would often be at a disadvantage. They would be less attractive and perhaps ignored or even mistreated. Yet behind the veil, all women are equal. In addition, the veiling of women existed in pre-Islamic times as a symbol of social status. Later, in the Ottoman Empire, the veil came to symbolize aristocracy and elitism. However, justice and equality are two of the fundamental principles of Islam. Perhaps the strongest point in behalf of the egalitarian interpretation of the Qur'an is the elimination of injustice and the protection of the weak from abuses by the strong. If one accepts this as the overriding message of Islam, even customs once considered to be Muslim might be superseded in the name of this ultimate Islamic principle.

It is advisable, therefore, in defining sex roles and the status of women to differentiate between Islamic and traditional norms that developed with many variations throughout the Muslim world. Undoubtedly, some conservatives tend to be antifeminist and often advocate female subordination. In so doing, they are convinced that they are correctly interpreting and defending Islam. Nevertheless, Muslims in general believe that female unchastity is the most potent threat to family honor and that woman's sexuality threatens the social order. To them, even today, perhaps nothing is more devastating to the family's social status and reputation than a female family member who is sexually promiscuous. Men are vilified, derided, scorned, and perhaps shunned if their women behave outside the bounds of tradition. This naturally affects male protectiveness and guardianship of females' behavior. Fear and concern often lead to confinement as a means of damage control. In many Islamic countries boys and girls are segregated in schools, except at the university level, and even university segregation occurs in some areas. Dating is forbidden and risky, although it is practiced secretly beyond the watchful eyes of families and friends. It is not uncommon for couples to delay courtship until they are actually married and the wife has moved to her new domicile. Premarital pregnancy or loss of chastity is regarded as a calamity with very serious consequences to those involved and their families.

Finally, one must explore briefly the complex areas of Westernization, modernization, feminism, and emancipation. It must be understood that these are not synonyms and are construed differently by various groups and cultures. Muslims, while rejecting Westernization, embrace modernization through education, but only within the framework of their faith and tradition. A few, mainly Westernized women feel that they need Western-style emancipation to achieve independence and equality. But, as has been noted, Islam has allowed women to be active in social and economic affairs as long as such activity does not conflict with or contravene their main responsibilities to the family and society. Most Muslims still hold that the main goal of women is and should continue to be marriage, motherhood, and family. Most Islamic spokesmen regard sexual freedom and permissiveness as the ultimate degradation of womanhood. They couple these practices with materialism and secularism and hold that they have cheapened women, who have become merely sex objects and commodities constantly displayed on the meat block. They resent and detest sex being flaunted and used to commercialize almost everything from toothpaste to cars and liquor. Consequently, to Westernize means to part with traditional values and to blur sex roles. It is significant that in Egypt many of the liberal, Western-oriented laws championed by the wife of the former president have been repealed under pressure, not from men but from educated, veiled women. These and other reversals are the results of social, historical, and political pressures. By rejecting Western modes of life and sexual behavior, Muslims are also protesting and rebelling against Western domination. Does this mean that "East is east and West is west, and the twain will never meet"? The answer depends on the areas of potential cooperation and confrontation. In education, science, and modernization, there are certainly mutual benefits. However, in the area of sexual behavior, it is hard to imagine any reconciliation or common ground. Here the two cultures not only do not but perhaps never should meet. As long as the West is obsessed with sexuality, Muslims would rather live within the confines of their faith and tradition. So, as they object to some aspects of Western culture, Muslims are particularly shocked by what they view as the tasteless, overexposed, public exploitation of women and femininity for hedonistic commercial purposes.

It is clear that Muslims' views and behavior are at variance with those of Westerners. This does not mean, however, that one outlook is better than or superior to the other. It is simply a matter of cultural suitability and compatibility. Every social system has its advantages and disadvantages, but ultimately it is the people who decide what is best suited for their cultural environment. To pass a sound judgment, one must take into consideration freedom and responsibility, enjoyment and consequences, individuals and society, and above all rights and obligations if there is to be a healthy, productive, and meaningful life, with the family always the main focus and concern.

REFERENCES

Anderson, R., and R. Seibert, *Politics and Change in the Middle East*. Englewood Cliffs, N.J.: Prentice Hall, 1990.

Bullough, V.L. *Sexual Variance in Society and History*. Chicago: Univ. of Chicago Press, 1976.

Holy Qur'an. Technically this cannot be officially translated, but there are various Exploration translations in English.

Yaken, F. *Islam and Sex*. Al Rissalah Establishment, 1986.

Mohamed El-Behairy

j

JOHNSON, VIRGINIA E.

Virginia E. Johnson (1925–) is a psychologist, sex researcher, and codirector of the Reproductive Biology Research Foundation, St. Louis, Missouri. She is one-half of the team known as Masters and Johnson, whose research in sexual dysfunction and therapeutic counseling is as familiar to the layperson as it is to the medical community. They have scientifically analyzed the physiological changes that occur in the male and female bodies during sexual stimulation.

In 1959, Masters and Johnson began to apply the knowledge gained from their research by treating couples for sexual inadequacy. Their focus on symptomatic treatment, rather than on underlying psychological problems, was facilitated by a therapeutic team of one male and one female counselor. Johnson developed an exercise to reestablish the physical relationship of the couple through nondemanding touching called "sensate focus." According to Masters and Johnson the success rate among the couples they treat is dramatically high.

Masters and Johnson have established a postgraduate course in their therapeutic techniques at Washington University and have developed workshops for nonmedical professionals on human sexual functioning. Their early books *Human Sexual Response* and *Human Sexual Inadequacy* were written for the medical community; nevertheless, they became best-sellers overnight. Johnson convinced Masters that their research should be made available to the general public, and as a result they have become regular contributors to *Playboy* and *Redbook* magazines.

REFERENCES

Primary

Masters, W.H., and V.E. Johnson. *Human Sexual Inadequacy*. Boston: Little, Brown, 1970.

———. *Human Sexual Response*. Boston: Little, Brown, 1966.

Masters, W.H., and V.E. Johnson, in association with R.J. Levin. *The Pleasure Bond: A New Look at Sexuality and Commitment*. Boston: Little, Brown, 1975.

Masters, W.H., V.E. Johnson, and R.C. Kolodny. *Crisis: Heterosexual Behavior in the Age of AIDS*. New York: Grove Press, 1988.

———. *Masters and Johnson on Sex and Human Loving*. Boston: Little, Brown, 1986.

Secondary

Repairing the Conjugal Bed. *Time*, 25 May 1970, pp. 49–52.

Wilkes, P. Sex and the Married Couple. *Atlantic*, Vol. 226 (Dec. 1970), pp. 82–92.

Hilary Sternberg

JORGENSEN, CHRISTINE

Christine Jorgensen (1926-1989) became a media sensation in December 1952, when information about her change of sex became public. The Hearst press, which contracted for her exclusive autobiography, headlined the story, and Dr. Christian Hamburger, the surgeon in charge of the case, later reported that he was flooded with communications requesting sex change. Jorgensen's trailblazing path of surgical transformation was followed by many others, and there was a growth of organizations and medical specialties to deal with surgical change from male to female and female to male.

Christine Jorgensen's was not the first recorded surgical sex change. One of the earliest such cases was that of Sophia Hedwig in 1882, and later there were others, the most famous of which was probably the case of the Danish artist Einar Wagener, who became Lili Elbe. It was Jorgensen, however, who achieved worldwide notoriety and in a sense popularized the potentialities of what came to be known as transsexualism.

Technically, Jorgensen had not immediately been transformed into a woman by surgical means, since Hamburger only removed the testicles and penis and did not attempt to construct a vagina, a surgical procedure that was perfected later. Hormone therapy was also in its infancy, but such details did not seem to matter to the press or to Jorgensen. A few years after her return to the United States from Denmark, where the original surgery took place, she had a vaginal canal constructed with a skin graft taken from the upper thighs, and with the improvement of hormone therapy, she eventually became a glamorous, curvaceous woman.

Christine Jorgensen was born George William Jorgensen, Jr., on May 30, 1926, in New York City. He served in the U.S. Army from 1945 to 1946, a brief career much publicized at the time of the operation. For a time, he studied photography but left that pursuit to train as a medical technician. Convinced that he should have been born a woman, he began taking the female hormone estradiol while a medical-technician student, and, pleased at the result, he set off for Sweden by way of Denmark (his parents' native country), where he heard sex changes were possible. He never reached Sweden, since he found Hamburger in Denmark, and the end result was to make him, later her, known throughout the world.

On her return to the United States, Christine Jorgensen went on the stage, playing on the notoriety she had achieved and in the process becoming a well-known stage personality by which means she earned her living. In 1967, she wrote her autobiography, and in 1970 a movie was made about her, with John Hansen in the title role.

In spite of her success, she devoted large amounts of her time to helping other transsexuals and served as a role model and inspiration for those who followed her. She died in California on May 4, 1989.

REFERENCES

Bullough, V.L., and B. Bullough. *Cross Dressing, Sex, and Gender*. Philadelphia: Univ. of Pennsylvania Press, 1993.

Hamburger, C. Desire for Change of Sex as Shown by Personal Letters from 465 Men and Women. *Acta Endocrinologica*, Vol. 8 (1954), pp. 231–42.

Jorgensen, C. *Christine Jorgensen: A Personal Autobiography*. New York: Eriksson, 1967.

Vern L. Bullough

JOURNALS: SEXUALITY JOURNALS

Modern sex research dates from the first half of the 19th century. The early research was motivated predominantly by concerns about problems (or at least what were perceived to be problems) related to sexuality, such as contraception, prostitution, homosexuality, and sexually transmitted diseases. It was not until very late in the 19th century that efforts were directed toward understanding what were considered to be the normal expressions of sexuality. As in other fields, the emergence of serious scholarly work eventually led to the establishment of professional journals wherein research results and other scholarly writing about sexuality could be published.

There has been one major difference, however, betwen the field of sexology, the scientific study of sexuality, and most other fields. Until recently, almost all professionals whose work related to sexuality were trained in an established discipline, such as medicine, psychology, history, biology, social work, or education. They were not trained as sexologists; in other words, an independent, multidisciplinary specialty of sexology did not exist. Thus, most writers published their work in the already existing journals of their own field. Although several specialized sexuality journals were established during the first 100 years or so after the initiation of modern sex research, not until 1965 was one published that still survives today.

The first of the specialized sexuality journals was *Jahrbuch für Sexuelle Zwischenstufen*, published in 1899 in Germany and devoted to the topic of homosexuality. A more generalized journal, *Zeitschrift für Sexualwissenschaft*, followed in 1908. Among the well-known writers who published in the early issues of the latter journal are Freud, Adler, Stekel, and Hirschfeld. Another journal, *Sexual Probleme*, was soon integrated with *Zeitschrift für Sexualwissenschaft* and published as *Zeitschrift für Sexualwissenschaft und Sexual Politik*. The *Zeitschrift für Sexualwissenschaft* again emerged in 1914 and was published for nearly two decades before it, and all other sexological work in Germany, was terminated by the Nazi regime.

For a number of years during the mid-20th century, Norman Haire, another of the pioneers in the field, edited a journal called the *Journal of Sex Education* in conjunction with the British Sex Education Society, but the journal ended with Haire's death in 1952. At about the same time, A.P. Pillay, the Indian sex researcher, edited the *International Journal of Sexology* from 1947 to 1955, but that, too, was abandoned following Pillay's death.

Although there are currently many journals whose primary focus is some aspect of sexuality, it remains true that professionals often prefer to publish their work in the disciplinary journals of their field. This is particularly true for scholars who are not doing the majority of their research or scholarly writing in the area of sexuality. A primary reason for this preference is that the disciplinary journals almost always have larger audiences and are frequently judged to be more prestigious by other professionals in that field. Moreover, it remains the case that those who study sexuality are often viewed with suspicion by many of their peers. In contrast, professionals whose work in sexuality is central to their careers are more likely to become committed to the field of sexology, to belong to professional organizations in the field, and to publish in the sexology journals. One consequence of this situation is that anyone wishing to review the literature on a specific topic in sexuality may find it necessary to search journals not only in the sexuality field itself but in several of the disciplinary fields as well.

The Society for the Scientific Study of Sex (SSSS) was formed in 1957, after an earlier effort in 1950 had been unsuccessful. It brought together a diverse group of professionals, including psychologists, psychiatrists, gynecologists, historians, and even lawyers. Among the explicitly stated objectives of the organization was the eventual publication of a scientific journal. By the mid-1960s, the directors of SSSS judged that enough original sexuality research was being generated to warrant the creation of its journal, the *Journal of Sex Research*. Thus, the first scholarly journal in the United States devoted exclusively to sexuality, and now the oldest continuously published journal specializing in sexuality research, began publication in 1965. Today, this interdisciplinary journal publishes mostly research reports, but it also contains theoretical articles, literature reviews, clinical reports, debates, and other forms of scholarly discourse. Book reviews are also published on a regular basis. Although articles may be authored by individuals from any scholarly discipline, the work of social scientists has dominated the publication throughout its history, probably in part because each of its editors has been a psychologist.

The second general sexology journal to emerge was the *Archives of Sexual Behavior*, first published in 1971. Although it is the commercial venture of a publishing firm, it is also the official publication of the International Academy of Sex Research. It, too, is an interdisciplinary journal, with contributions accepted from all academic disciplines. Nevertheless, work in the biological and social sciences has predominated. Of the general sexuality journals, the *Archives* more than any other has published the work of the biological scientists.

In 1990, SSSS launched the *Annual Review of Sex Research*. This development represents a significant milestone for sexology, indicating its growth and maturation to the point that periodic reviews of the literature in the field are warranted.

In the two decades or so following the publication of the *Journal of Sex Research* and the *Archives of Sexual Behavior*, numerous other periodicals, nearly all more narrowly focused, have begun publication. Another general journal has appeared recently, published in Canada and called the *Annals of Sex Research*. Over the years, a number of the more specialized publications have lasted only a short time; however, in some cases work published in extinct journals remains valuable, and issues of these journals can still be found in top-quality university libraries.

Among the specialized journals, the *Journal of Sex & Marital Therapy* focuses on issues relating to sexual functioning and sexual dysfunctions or problems. It often contains reports on the effectiveness of therapeutic or counseling techniques, and it is the leading American journal in its field. It is closely associated with the Society for Sex Therapy and Research. The journal *Sexual and Marital Therapy* is published in England and deals with the same general topics.

The *Journal of Sex Education and Therapy* is the publication of the American Association of Sex Educators, Counselors and Therapists (AASECT). As the name suggests, its contents are directed primarily to practitioners, although empirical studies are also published in this journal if they deal with educational or clinical issues. *SIECUS Report* is the publication of the Sex Information and Education Council of the United States. The focus is sexuality education. It does not publish empirical research; it contains analyses or commentaries by leading people in the field. It also regularly includes book reviews and resources for professionals working with specific populations. A similar publication is *SIECCAN Journal*, a publication of the Sex Information and Education Council of Canada. This journal does include some research articles.

The *Journal of Homosexuality* has been published since 1975. It is an interdisciplinary journal, publishing research results, book reviews, and other scholarly writing pertaining to issues of sexual orientation. An even more narrowly focused journal dealing with sexual orientation issues is the *Journal of Gay and Lesbian Psychotherapy*.

As the field has grown and more professionals from various disciplines have begun to do scholarly work pertaining to sexuality, a number of disciplinary journals addressing sexuality issues have appeared. The oldest of these is *Medical Aspects of Human Sexuality*, published primarily for members of the medical profession. Its content, however, is diverse, including many articles of interest to professionals who are not physicians. Also closely allied with the field of medicine are the journals *Sexuality and Medicine* and *Sexually Transmitted Diseases*.

The *Journal of Psychology and Human Sexuality*, first published in 1988, focuses on psychological variables and their relationship to aspects of human sexuality. A subsequent entry into the field is the *Journal of the History of Sexuality*. *Sexuality and Disability* deals with issues related to the sexuality of disabled persons. The *Journal of Social Work and Human Sexuality* is that field's publication focusing on sexuality.

During the 1980s, acquired immune deficiency syndrome (AIDS) emerged as a major concern among sexuality researchers from nearly all the disciplines. Several journals devoted to AIDS have been founded, and additional AIDS-related journals will probably continue to appear during the remainder of the 20th century. Among the new publications are the *Journal of Acquired Immune Deficiency Syndromes*, *AIDS Education and Prevention*, *Multicultural Inquiry and Research on AIDS*, and the *Annual Review of AIDS Research*. Numerous journals, particularly in the health-related fields, have published a considerable amount of AIDS research, as well as other sexuality research, in the recent past. Among these are the *Journal of Infectious Diseases*, the *American Journal of Public Health*, *Health Education Research*, *Health Education Quarterly*, the *Journal of American College Health*, and *Psychology and Health*.

As suggested earlier, and as the AIDS-related research illustrates, many journals that are not exclusively or primarily sexuality journals publish articles containing sexuality-relevant material sufficiently often that they deserve note. A number of these journals emphasize the family or interpersonal relationships. Among them is *Family Planning Perspectives*, the publication of the Alan Guttmacher Institute, the research arm of the Planned Parenthood Federation. Its focus is on issues related to reproduction and contraception. The *Journal of Marriage and the Family*, published by the National Council on Family Relations, has existed since 1939 (although not originally under that title) and has included many articles involving aspects of sexuality and the family over its history. So, too, has the *Journal of Divorce*. Similarly, *Lifestyles*, originally known as *Alternative Lifestyles*, contains articles about sexuality or articles in which sexuality variables are of major relevance. Other journals of note in closely allied areas are the *Journal of Social and Personal Relationships*, the *Journal of Interpersonal Violence*, and *Sex Roles: A Journal of Research*. The latter regularly contains research relating issues of gender to sexuality.

In medicine, the prestigious *New England Journal of Medicine* and the *Journal of the American Medical Association* often publish work concerning sexuality. So, too, does the British journal *Lancet* and the *Journal of Reproductive Medicine*.

Many psychology journals contain numerous important articles about sexuality. Most notable among these are the *Journal of Personality and Social Psychology*, the *Journal of Applied Social Psychology*, the *Journal of Consulting and Clinical Psychology*, and the *Journal of Social Issues*. Closely related is the journal on aging *Maturitas*. Many journals in the fields of sociology, anthropology, and history also occasionally include sexuality research articles.

A number of journals focusing on sexuality are published outside the English-speaking countries. Included among them are *Zeitschrift für Sexualforschung*, *Nordisk Sexologi*, *Sessualità*, *Revista Latinoamericana de Sexología*, and *Rivista di Sessuologia*.

Judaism and Sexuality

Finally, brief note should be taken of other periodicals devoted to or including substantial content about sexuality. They include popular magazines, such as *Psychology Today* and the exclusively sexually oriented *Forum*. From time to time, newsletters of various organizations also appear. Noteworthy examples are "Sex Over Forty," "Contemporary Sexuality," the newsletter of AASECT, and "Family Life Educator."

REFERENCES

Bullough, V.L. *The Society for the Scientific Study of Sex: A Brief History*. Mt. Vernon, Iowa: SSSS, 1989.

Haeberle, E.J. The Jewish Contributions to the Development of Sexology. *Journal of Sex Research*, Vol. 18 (1982), pp. 305–23.

Clive M. Davis
Sandra L. Davis

JUDAISM AND SEXUALITY

Judaism is the collective name for the religious rites, beliefs, and practices of the Jews. But Judaism is more than a religion; it is a total way of life. For that reason, some consider it to be more like a civilization than like a religion defined mostly by dogma and belief. Further, the Jews have lived among and interacted with more civilizations than almost any other group. The practices of Chinese Jews, Jews of India, and Jews of the American Wild West are very different in important ways.

Even in one place, the variations are great. The Jews of Jerusalem in the year 100 C.E., and the year 1000 C.E., and today represent vastly different life-styles, yet all are considered Jews. The result is that there are many different Judaisms with many different views of sexuality, but certain themes tend to dominate over time. If we emphasize later views and themes nearer in time to the modern period, it is not because they are in some sense more Jewish but only because they are closer to us and to how we live.

In America, for instance, there are now three major Jewish religious communities, the Orthodox, the Conservative, and the Liberal or Reform. The Orthodox, who hold that the Torah or Pentateuch is word for word and letter for letter the work of God, tend to seek detailed and strict observance of the laws based on the Torah. The Reform movement holds the Torah to be a divinely inspired work but a product of human beings, and it reserves the right to evaluate, criticize, and modify the book and to change or even dispense with some of the laws based on it. The Conservatives, while allied with the Reform in their view of the Torah, tend to seek a

somewhat greater degree of conformity to traditional observances.

It is therefore just as arbitrary to take evidence only from the Bible or from the Ashkenazi legal codes, for example, as to cite only modern Western liberal Jewish authorities. Inevitably, any brief survey of Judaism and sexuality will be arbitrary because not every view can be cited, let alone given its proper perspective.

Attitude Toward Sex

At the beginning of the Hebrew Bible, the first recorded divine commandment to humankind was "Be fruitful and multiply." Judaism has generally understood this to indicate that sex, both for procreation and for pleasure, is a blessing and a gift. It is to be used wisely, to be sure, and not for control, debasement, or promiscuity. There are restrictions on it and on its use, but there is little embarrassment traditionally attached to sexual matters.

The book of Leviticus, for example, is filled with references to prohibited sexual relations and activities, and yet it is precisely the section of the Bible traditionally chosen to begin the instruction of little children in biblical Hebrew: "Let the pure little ones begin with the study of the laws of purity." This was a wise pedagogical decision, because such legal material is repetitive, uses a small vocabulary over and over, and offers the sort of text that is excellent for rapid achievement. But the decision also suggests that those who made it had little hesitancy in discussing with children intimate aspects of normal and abnormal sexuality.

In contrast, it was the Jewish community of the Essenes who chose 2,000 years ago to live a celibate life, becoming the forerunners in some ways of the Christian monastic cenobites, the monks and nuns of the Middle Ages, and the celibate priests of today. They may have adopted celibacy only because they felt that they did not have the time to give to conjugal and family relations. But it is also possible that they rejected family life on principle as something in some way physically or spiritually debilitating or demeaning. In any case, monasticism and celibacy—an experiment that was by and large rejected—never became prominent in mainstream Jewish life.

Prohibited and Encouraged Sex

Prohibited sex falls mainly into three categories, based on the prohibitions found in the Hebrew Bible as expanded in the Talmud (i.e., the legal, philosophical, and moral deliberations of the

325

Rabbis from about 150 B.C.E. to 500 C.E.), the legal codes, and the Responsa literature (i.e., published legal opinions and ethical and philosophical guidance of outstanding rabbis up to the present day). First, those relations are prohibited that could never be legally recognized under any circumstances as valid unions (e.g., relations between a mother and her son). This prohibition is based on propinquity of relationship between the principals and cannot be made right after the fact.

An exception to the rule is the biblical law of levirate marriage, under which a childless widow has a claim on the surviving brother to marry her and to try to provide her with a child. That child, the financial and moral responsibility of the surviving brother, is not to carry on the surviving brother's name and house, but the name and house of his dead brother. This law was rendered moot by the Rabbis at a later time.

Prohibited also are sexual relations considered unnatural, or contrary to physical nature, as between a human being and sheep or cattle. Forbidden also, but in a different class, are relations contrary to law, such as adultery. A union might have been possible between the principals involved had there been no marriage to someone else, but once the woman is married to another, sex with her is banned, unless she gets a divorce.

In the Pentateuch as recorded in Leviticus, plural marriage is sanctioned for men but not for women, who can have only one husband at a time. Thus, for a man to have sex with his neighbor's wife is a capital crime both for him and for her, provided she consented and there is no question of force. But for an unmarried woman to have sex with her neighbor's husband may not fall into the same category.

Prohibited also are relations that are psychologically impossible, such as a man marrying two sisters as rivals or a woman together with her daughter. This legislation became moot as well when the Rabbis required that all wives be guaranteed equal rights and privileges, including sexual rights. The woman's sexual rights are spelled out in detail in the legal literature, and a husband's failure to satisfy them is grounds for legal action against him under Jewish law. Among other provisions, Talmudic jurisprudence allows that the wife of a sailor is entitled to demand her sexual rights a minimum of once in six months, while for a scholar the obligation is once a week.

Encouragement to marry and to raise a family is part of the Jewish sex ethic. From Abraham and Moses onwards, religious leaders, both male and female, have commonly been married. When the temple was still standing in Jerusalem, the High Priest was married. Later, when the synagogue/rabbi/Sacrifice-of-prayer system replaced the temple/priest/sacrifice-of-animals system, the rabbis were generally married.

One school holds that a rabbi should necessarily be married, and it is commonly taught that a man without a wife is radically incomplete and is failing to fulfill God's will. There are opinions from time to time suggesting abstention from sex, but these are aberrant to the majority opinion.

Jewish law considers that divine commandments, called *mitzvot,* are precious evidence of God's love and care for God's children. In other words, to fulfill a mitzvah is to fulfill the will of God, and it is seen as a joyous privilege, never as a burden. Not only explicit commands but any truly good deed done with good intentions can qualify as a mitzvah. In that light, it is considered a special mitzvah to have sex on the Sabbath. This is because the Sabbath is called the most precious of days, sanctified by God, and therefore to glorify it and make it something to look forward to is in itself a pious action. Having sex on the Sabbath would make the Sabbath even more delightful, so that it would be a special mitzvah.

Sex is prohibited, however, during menstruation because Jewish law recognizes a powerful taboo against shedding or using blood. Blood even of a properly slaughtered animal, for instance, can never be eaten or allowed to remain in the meat. The contact with catamenial blood is therefore considered a source of temporary ritual impurity, but this is not a judgment on the role of sex or the value of sexual intercourse.

Homosexuality

Homosexual cultic practices were common in biblical times and were associated with abominated pagan religions. The Pentateuch legislation condemns such practices under penalty of stoning. Subsequent Christian concentration on homosexuality has led some scholars to assign it a more prominent position in Jewish law than it really has.

For example, the sin of Sodom, for which that city was destroyed, has often been understood in Christian interpretations to be anal intercourse between males, which is still the legal meaning of "sodomy" in England and America. In the Hebrew commentators, however, the sin of Sodom is commonly held to be violence.

Lesbianism is known in Jewish law and condemned prior to the modern period, but it seldom posed the legal problems that homosexuality did and so was generally ignored. For one thing, whereas homosexual rape is common, lesbian rape is not. For another, if two women in a household enjoy a lesbian relationship, it does not call paternity of offspring into question. Also, intimate, close, loving relations between women were considered normal in many periods. If two or more lesbians, perhaps two wives of one man or two sisters, all shared one household, then who would bring a case before the court? And what would the court be asked to accept as the defining proof of a lesbian action, corresponding to anal penetration of the male by the male? How would credible witnesses ever have been in a position to testify that they had actually seen such an act?

In postbiblical law, homosexuality was still considered a moral failure rather than an illness or an alternate life-style. However, because the mandatory biblical penalty was stoning, an accusation of homosexual practices would automatically become a capital case. As a capital case, it would have to be treated exactly like a murder case. Because of fear of a miscarriage of justice, a capital case was hedged with so many requirements that there is not one case on record in which a homosexual was ever accused and convicted.

Conviction would have been difficult to obtain, since a capital case required the testimony of two disinterested witnesses that they had actually seen the act. Not only did the act have to be witnessed, but the prosecution had to establish the principle of intention. That is, the prosecution had to prove by at least two disinterested and credible witnesses that the accused persons had been warned of the consequences of their action in advance and had indicated full understanding and will. These requirements applied to all capital cases.

In our century, homosexuality and lesbianism have been understood in different ways than in the past. There are today gay and lesbian congregations, often led by gay or lesbian rabbis. Those who belong to them are considered, even by the most Orthodox authorities, no less Jewish than any other Jewish congregants or rabbis. They may run into social rejection, but they are increasingly accepted within the Liberal or Reform Jewish community. While it is possible for Reform theology to consider the question of homosexuality as something other than a moral failure or an illness, that has so far proven impossible for the Orthodox.

Onanism

Masturbation or onanism is not a major problem in Jewish law and practice in biblical times, in the Talmudic period, or in the Responsa literature up to the present day. The reason for this is that Jewish law and practice is on the whole extremely practical. Generally, a case is conceived of as a conflict of interest between two parties who are seeking guidance and justice from a court. Who, then, is bringing the accused masturbator to court, and on what charge? The nature of onanism is such that the presence of credible, disinterested witnesses is not likely.

That is not to say that the practice is favored. There is much uplifting homiletic and instructive literature that ranges from looking on onanism as a corrupting practice to seeing it as a wasteful and diverting substitute for authentic human relations. Sometimes it is seen as an acceptable release of tensions in a situation where other releases are not possible. Some modern Jewish thinkers would incline to the latter view. Some past thinkers dealt with it very little or not at all.

Incidentally, the famous sin of Onan in the Bible was not masturbation at all, as is commonly thought. Although the English and American languages use "onanism" to mean masturbation, the actual sin of Onan, for which he was condemned, was that he refused to give his seed to his dead brother's widow.

Love and Marriage

Romantic love and attraction are a main theme of the Song of Songs in the Bible, but Jewish marriage is based on more than that. Marriage involves a binding, legal relationship between a man and a woman, freely entered into by both sides and witnessed, supported, and underwritten by the authority of God, the community, and the religion. It is at the same time a union of two houses and two families, as well as an act of the community by which it fulfills a divine mitzvah and ensures its own eternity.

That is a lot of weight, and the ceremonies attendant on a Jewish wedding reflect a great deal of solemnity together with boundless, irrepressible joy. It has even been taught that at a wedding, one is permitted to celebrate to excess, which for some may mean to become intoxicated. If such a thing is done to add joy to the wedding feast, it might even be considered a mitzvah. Classically, there are three ways to consecrate a marriage, any one of which has been sufficient. In a modern Jewish marriage, at least in the Orthodox Ashkenazi rites, all three are often included. These are *keseph*, *shetar*, and *bi'ah*.

Keseph, "silver," is the giving of something of value by the groom to the bride, as a way of sealing a legal contract, with the intention of concluding a contract of marriage. Typically, it is a plain gold ring, gold because it has recognizable value, and plain because the value of fancy artwork would be hard to assess in a way that gold itself is not. A coin of great value would do as well, however. All the later interpretations of the meaning of the plain gold ring, such as that its endless circularity points to infinite love, must be considered inspiring and valuable homilies. In many modern Jewish weddings, rings are exchanged, which raises a question of whether there has actually been any giving at all. That question, for those who are troubled by it, can be resolved by the groom's paying for both rings. This gift is a legal transaction and must be witnessed.

Shetar, "contract," is the ritual signing before witnesses of a formal, legal contract, the wedding *ketuvah*. Such *ketuvot* are often decorated with beautiful artwork and displayed prominently in the new home. The traditional text of the *ketuvah* is in Aramaic, a near relative of Hebrew and the onetime colloquial language of the common people of Israel. It guarantees the woman her marital rights, including her sexual rights and her rights to adequate new clothing, cosmetics, and support. It details exactly what she is bringing into the marriage: money, sheets, blankets, all her property, and so on. Her husband is responsible for all of that, and in the event the marriage fails, he is held accountable for it. The document is quite one-sided; it is there as an instrument of the court to protect the woman, not the man. In Orthodox, Conservative, and some Reform weddings, it is read out, affirmed, and signed freely and willingly by both bride and groom in the presence of two disinterested witnesses as part of the wedding ceremony. A number of modern *ketuvot* have substituted more romantic language for the traditional text, and some have tried to make the document more two-sided. In divorce cases, the *ketuvah* has been considered a binding instrument in some civil courts, and its provisions have sometimes been enforced by the civil authorities.

Bi'ah, "intercourse," is a formal part of Orthodox, some Conservative, and (rarely) Reform weddings. The couple is sequestered in a private room for a period, and that sequestering is duly witnessed. This presumptive intercourse must be for the purpose and with the intention of creating a valid marriage. In other words, mere sex without the intention to consummate a marriage does not create a marriage.

Divorce

In a traditional Jewish marriage, the woman's rights are protected by the *ketuvah*. In case of a divorce, the burden of fulfilling the *ketuvah* falls on the husband. Grounds for a divorce are the subject of considerable debate in the Talmud. The House or School of Hillel took the position that, although divorce should be prevented by any means practicable, if it developed that the marriage was hopeless, then any excuse to dissolve the formality was acceptable. This view was embodied in Talmudic idiom by the expression that even if she burned a dish, if it was done with agreement and intention, it could be grounds for divorce. The House of Shammai took the strict view that grounds for divorce should be highly limited. The Sanhedrin majority went with Hillel.

Nonetheless, divorce is looked on as a tragedy and a failure. God is pictured as crying for the pain that a divorce involves, and saving a marriage is considered a great mitzvah. The instrument of religious divorce is called a *get*, "bill of divorcement," and is issued to the wife by the husband or by the court on his behalf. She retains custody of it or of a substitute document that testifies to its existence. This is because biblical law would at one time have allowed a husband to take another wife while still married, but not a woman to take another husband. She, therefore, has a greater need to prove herself free to marry. If the husband does not choose to give the wife a *get,* the court may compel him or act in his behalf, but among the Orthodox the courts often choose to do nothing. This inaction may cause great hardship for the woman and may even make her vulnerable to a kind of blackmail. Further, if a husband abandons a wife and disappears without a trace, there is no provision in Jewish law to presume his death after some years of absence. The wife is regarded as an abandoned married woman, not as a divorced woman, unless someone comes forward to say that the man's death has been witnessed. If she remarries and he reappears, she is ipso facto an unintentional adulteress and her second marriage is invalid. The potential for abuse is obvious, but fortunately it rarely occurs.

The Reform or Liberal Jews have in most cases dispensed with the *get,* partly to avoid the abuses it allows and partly because, in the presence of civil divorce, they feel they can perform a remarriage without requiring evidence of a religious divorce. From an Orthodox point of view, such a remarriage without a prior *get* might be invalid. The Conservatives still use the *get* but do so most effectively as a way of getting the couple into counseling; they avoid abuses by empowering the court to act in behalf of the husband if necessary.

Abortion

The considerations involved in abortion, from a Jewish point of view, in most cases boil down to two: first, what is a person? and second, what is the intention? Under Jewish jurisprudence, the majority opinion inclines to the view that the individual is recognized as a separate human being when he or she is independent of the mother that is, at birth. Prior to that point, the embryo or the fetus is a part of the mother and has no individual and independent human rights as such. In other words, one has to be born to be a person. An alternative view, which is advanced by Roman Catholic theologians, among others, is that the fetus is an individual human being from the moment of conception, and certain individual and independent human rights must be considered from that point on.

These theological and juridical differences have serious implications. If the life of a mother were in jeopardy as a result of a pregnancy, and the physician were only able to save the mother, at the expense of losing the fetus or the fetus at the expense of losing the mother, Jewish law would consider that the mother is a person, with a full right to live, and the fetus is not, and would act to save the mother. The other view might hold that the mother has already been baptized, so that her soul has been saved; the unborn fetus, although unbaptized, is nevertheless possessed of a soul from the time of its conception, and that soul is in far greater jeopardy than the soul of the mother. It may be necessary, therefore, to save the immortal soul of the child even at the cost of the life of the mother.

Practical consequences exist in each case. The Jewish position might leave the mother able to have other children and to minister to her already existing family. The alternative position might provide more effectively for the continuity of future generations, even if that means, in this case, sacrificing the past (the mother) to the future (the child). In the end, the difference between the two positions involves the theological definition of a human being and the time at which one is considered to be a person.

There is an exceptional case, albeit a rare one, in which an unborn child does indeed have rights, and those rights are protected under Jewish law. When parents become aware that a child is on the way, and for reasons of their own wish to disinherit that child or strip him or her of a normal inheritance, the rights of the unborn child are protected by the court.

Such a case involves the principle of intention, the second major consideration here. If the intention of the parents in seeking an abortion is to act on sound medical advice, as for the protection of the life of the mother or for an equally serious purpose, then virtually all Jewish authorities would permit an abortion if not encourage it. An abortion sought for merely casual considerations or convenience would not find acceptance. The acceptable medical consideration might be, and indeed has been, liberally interpreted to include psychiatrically recognizable threats to the mother's mental health and welfare.

Contraception

The view of birth control follows the same pattern of thinking as that regarding abortion, and for the same reasons. The mitzvah is to be "fruitful and multiply." This means reproducing oneself, that is, two parents having two children. There is no obligation to have more children, and if the family cannot provide properly for more children, many authorities would favor contraception. If there is medical opinion that even one child is contraindicated, then most authorities agree that contraception is called for even if there are no children.

Bastardy

A bastard in English and American usage is a child born out of wedlock. There is no concept of bastardy under Jewish law or practice, in biblical jurisprudence, in the Talmud, or in the Responsa literature up to the present day. Perhaps this is partly because the issue of whether someone was born in or out of wedlock has been less important in Judaism than in some other religions. Wedlock, the state of being married, has to do with willing entry into a contractual arrangement and is therefore mainly an action of the two principals, not a benefit or sacrament administered to the principals by a priest or clergy member. The rabbi merely sees that the arrangements are carried out properly; he brings no divine power to the union that the principals do not have themselves. Thus, the Jewish marriage is sanctified, but not by the presence or absence of the rabbi.

In the case of a union that could never have been legitimately possible, such as that between a mother and her son, the issue would be a *mamzer*, "issue of an impossible union." In the same class is the issue of a union between brother and sister or of an adulterous relationship.

Sex for Pleasure

It is possible to dissolve a marriage that has been without issue on the ground of childlessness, but it is not necessary to do so, and in fact such dissolutions historically have been rare. Since a marriage without issue does not fulfill the mitzvah of the first commandment, all such marriages, past and present, presumably are preserved mainly because of the love and pleasure that the partners invest in and derive from them. No guilt attaches to that love or that pleasure in a childless marriage, only some measure of regret that a mitzvah is left unfulfilled.

For the most part, Jewish authorities from classical times to the present find no guilt or prudery attaching to sex for pleasure. There are discussions of oral sex in the rabbinic literature that suggest that whatever pleases both partners, even if it does not conduce to procreation, is permitted and in fact desirable as a way of increasing their delight in one another. The body is, after all, a product of its divine Maker, and although it can be misused and used to hurt, it is not a bad product, and no evil inheres in it by nature.

However, one can find cautions about wicked women in the Bible and warnings about temptation and excess in the Talmud. Among the very pious of our own time, avoidance of any casual contact between the sexes suggests considerable discomfort with the body. On the whole, though, it is fair to say that licit sex for pleasure is accepted, and generally encouraged, as conducive to the proper service of God.

Prostitution

Since the time of the Bible, prostitution has been associated with pagan religions and cults. Most references to the Baals in the Hebrew Bible have to do with fertility gods that were worshiped by Canaanites and Babylonians. The worship of fertility gods and goddesses was seen as a debasing abomination by the Hebrew prophets and teachers, and no doubt the rites attached to that worship were a large part of the reason.

In Babylonia, no woman was considered fit for marriage until she had offered herself by night to a stranger in the temple of the fertility cult. The money paid by the stranger was a donation to the cult of the goddess. In the springtime, sacred prostitutes lay in the furrows of the newly plowed fields awaiting men to perform fertility rituals. That sort of worship pattern was considered an abomination by the Hebrew leaders and was dealt with harshly.

Ordinary prostitutes with no cultic ties did exist, however, and although the practice was considered degrading to both the men and the women, it did not always carry serious penalties. Rahab, the harlot of Jericho, for example, emerges from the Bible story as a kindly and helpful woman, who alone is spared with her family when the city is taken. Furthermore, she was accepted in the community of Israel from then onwards. That does not signify, however, approval of her way of life.

REFERENCES

Ehrman, A. *The Talmud, with English Translation and Commentaries.* Jerusalem: El Am, 1965. See also I. Epstein, *The Babylonian Talmud* (London: Soncino Press, 1933), which is older and more readily available. Both have indexes. A new edition, *The Talmud: The Adin Steinsalz Edition* (New York: Random House, 1989), is incomplete as of this writing.

Felman, D.M. *Marital Relations, Birth Control and Abortion in Jewish Law.* New York: New York Univ. Press, 1968.

Freehof, S. *Reform Jewish Practice and Its Rabbinic Background*, and the various volumes of *Responsa*. Cincinnati: Hebrew Union College Press, 1944–.

Ganzfried, S. *Code of Jewish Law (Kitzur Schulchan Aruch)*. Translated by H.E. Goldin. Rev. ed. New York: Hebrew Publishing, 1961.

Gittelsohn, R.B. *Love, Sex and Marriage.* New York: Union of Hebrew Congregations, 1980.

Jacob, W., ed. *American Reform Responsa: Collected Responsa of the Central American Conference of Rabbis, 1889–1983.* New York: CCAR, 1983.

Roth, C., and G. Wigoder, eds. *Encyclopaedia Judaica.* Jerusalem: Keter, 1972. Readers are advised to compare this encyclopedia with other Jewish works such as I. Singer, ed., *The Jewish Encyclopedia* (New York: Funk & Wagnalls, 1906).

Allen Howard Podet

JUS PRIMUS NOCTIS

Jus primus noctis, literally "right of first night" (also called *droit du seigneur, jambage,* and *jus cunnagii*) is basically an attempt to cloak rape with elements of respectability. It is the claim that nobles had the right of the first night with all women living in their territories (except noble women). Nineteenth- and early-20th-century scholars of sexuality and the family devoted considerable time and energy to ferreting out such a law, and it has often been the subject of popular fiction. Though some have claimed to have found evidence for its existence in ancient Scottish law, it does not exist in Roman law or in any of the European countries that adopted Roman law; neither does it exist in English common law. Canon law also does not mention it.

This lack of evidence does not mean that the practice did not exist, since the powerful male often had near life-and-death authority over many of those under him, and he undoubtedly exercised his prerogative to have sex with young women whom he thought desirable. There was no law allowing this, however, and in the case of women of a certain standing, it was strongly prohibited. What it amounted to was rape of the powerless, which undoubtedly often occurred in the past, still occurs, and may well occur in the future until the disenfranchised and power less have their right to sexual consent recognized.

REFERENCES

Bullough, V.L. *Jus Primae Noctis* or *Droit du Seigneur. Journal of Sex Research*, Vol. 28 (Feb. 1991), pp. 163–66.

Vern L. Bullough

k

KINSEY, ALFRED C.

With his two studies on male and female sexual behavior, Alfred Charles Kinsey (1894–1956) brought sex "out of the closet" and launched the modern era of sex research, influencing our sexual thinking as no one had since Freud. To a public discourse characterized by ignorance and hypocrisy, Kinsey brought straightforward sexual language and facts.

Kinsey's name became a household word overnight with the publication of *Sexual Behavior in the Human Male* in 1948. This volume was followed in 1953 by *Sexual Behavior in the Human Female*. The landmark Kinsey reports, written for the academic and medical communities, quickly became best-sellers. They provided the general public for the first time with broadly based, systematically gathered, detailed descriptive data on American sexual practices.

The Kinsey reports generated a storm of public controversy. A vocal minority reviled the studies as an attack on American values because of their frank discussions of premarital sex, homosexuality, masturbation, and extramarital sex. Kinsey's fight for the right to investigate sexual behavior stands as a milestone in the battle for academic freedom. In papers found after his death, Kinsey had written, "There is hardly another area in human biology or in sociology in which the scientist has had to fight for his right to do research, as he has when he has attempted to acquire a scientific understanding of human sexual behavior."

The man who provoked this furor lived in America's heartland; he was a zoologist by training who specialized in the taxonomic study of gall wasps, a family man, the father of four, and a gardener whose irises were a southern Indiana legend. Born June 12, 1894, in Hoboken, New Jersey, Kinsey developed his love of nature early. An avid Boy Scout, he was one of the first in the United States to attain Eagle rank. In high school, he collected botanical specimens as a hobby, then studied biology at Bowdoin College, graduating magna cum laude in 1916. After receiving his doctorate from Harvard University in 1919, Kinsey accepted a position in zoology at Indiana University, Bloomington, where he remained throughout his career. During the next 20 years, Kinsey established a solid academic reputation for his biology texts and his research in taxonomy and evolution. In 1937, *American Men of Science* listed him as one of their "starred" scientists.

The beginnings of Kinsey's sex research can be traced back to 1938, when the Indiana University Association of Women Students petitioned the university to inaugurate a noncredit course on marriage; Kinsey was asked to coordinate the course and to deliver the lectures on the biological aspects of sex and marriage. The course was an immediate success—enrollment quadrupled during the first two years.

To prepare for his lectures, Kinsey went to the library to search for data. The little he found either was primarily derived from case or small clinical studies or was largely opinion based. Consequently, midway in his academic career, Kinsey turned the energy with which he had amassed a collection of more than five million gall wasps and documented their individual variations toward an area basically unexplored: human sexual behavior in all its individual and group variations.

At first, Kinsey collected data from the students attending the marriage class, then from other students and faculty, and later from almost anyone he could persuade to be interviewed. He developed an interview of 350 questions, the answers to which were encoded to maintain strict confidentiality. Kinsey traveled at his own expense on weekends from Bloomington to other midwestern cities extending his sample to different socioeconomic groups. Without any formal training, he was a master of the face-to-face interview, empathetic and nonjudgmental; approximately 8,000 of the more than 17,000 interviews eventually gathered between 1938 and 1956 were conducted by Kinsey himself.

In 1940, President Herman B Wells of Indiana University, facing pressure from some members of the community and political leaders concerning Kinsey's sex research and his continued teaching of the marriage course, asked Kinsey to choose between the two projects. To the surprise of nearly everyone, Kinsey abandoned the research for which he was renowned and the course that had made him the most popular professor at Indiana University. Kinsey's decision was to dedicate himself to the collection of sexual case histories. He wrote to a colleague that the difficulty of unearthing the facts about human sexual behavior "is one of the things that leads me on."

By the following year, Kinsey's research had attracted the financial support of the National Research Council's Committee for Research in the Problems of Sex, at that time funded by the Rockefeller Foundation. This external funding enabled Kinsey to assemble a multidisciplinary research team and expand his fieldwork. The core of that team was Clyde Martin, Kinsey's student assistant, who became a full-time associate in 1941; Wardell Pomeroy, a clinical psychologist, who joined the group in 1943; and Paul Gebhard, an anthropologist, hired in 1946.

As the number of interviews grew into the thousands, the Institute for Sex Research was established in 1947 as a separate, nonprofit organization, in large part to protect the confidentiality of the sex histories.

In 1948, *Sexual Behavior in the Human Male*, the product of ten years' research, was released by W.B. Saunders, a publisher of medical texts. No one anticipated that Kinsey's dry, academic study would have an audience beyond physicians and scientists. It sold more than 250,000 copies, was translated into a dozen languages, and was distributed worldwide. Only the Communist bloc countries, Ireland, and South Africa banned it.

Five years later, the Institute released its second volume, *Sexual Behavior in the Human Female*. It also sold more than 250,000 copies and was translated widely. Though generally well received by the scientific community, the book caused a furor in the press, among some clergy, and in the U.S. Congress. In the House of Representatives, Congressman Carroll Reece of Tennessee had formed a committee to investigate tax-exempt foundations and their support of un-American activities. The Committee targeted the Rockefeller Foundation for, among other things, its support of the Institute for Sex Research. One member of Congress commented that anyone who studied the sexual behavior of Americans was paving the way for a Communist takeover of the United States. By mid-1954, the Rockefeller Foundation, in an effort to deflect such pressures, withdrew its financial support of the Institute's work as well as other sex-related research. In a move coinciding with this attack, the U.S. Customs Service began seizing shipments of sexual materials to the Institute.

The stress of coping with the press, the conservative backlash, the need to raise funds if the Institute was to continue its work, and Kinsey's normal 13- to 14-hour work days, all took their toll. Although he developed symptoms of cardiovascular disease, Kinsey did not slow down. He died of cardiac failure following pneumonia on August 25, 1956, at age 62.

The Kinsey Reports

Though at this writing it has been more than 40 years since the first Kinsey report was published, Kinsey's studies are still the most widely known and cited works on human sexual behavior. For national estimates on sexual behavior the National Academy of Science's 1986 report on AIDS cited the Kinsey studies and Gagnon and Simon's reanalysis of Kinsey's data.

The studies challenged many widely accepted myths about sexual behavior in American society and thus were highly controversial. Kinsey asked detailed questions about sexual behaviors considered by many to be taboo—extramarital sex, same-sex interactions, bisexual behavior, oral sex, masturbation, and prostitution. Kinsey was not concerned with a cultural-religious or psychoanalytic view of sexual "normality." His primary purpose was to describe the individual and group variations in human sexual behavior from an empirical biological and taxonomic perspective. He did this by looking at the prevalence and frequency of six different "outlets" to orgasm (i.e., masturbation, petting, nocturnal dreams, heterosexual coitus, homosexual responses and contacts, and contacts with animals) and related each outlet to factors of age, educational level, marital status, occupation, decade of birth, and religion.

The most startling of Kinsey's data related to female sexuality, the extent of male homosexuality, and the prevalence of masturbation. At that time, few Americans were prepared for Kinsey's finding that women were interested in sex for more than procreative purposes. To the surprise and shock of many, the data indicated that females are as capable of sexual response and orgasm as males. Half the women interviewed said they had not been virgins when they married, and one-quarter reported they had engaged in extramarital sex.

The view of homosexuality began to change after Kinsey's findings that a third of males and 13 percent of females reported at least one same-sex experience to the point of orgasm by age 45, that approximately 10 percent of male respondents were predominantly homosexual for at least three years between the ages of 16 and 55, and that 4 percent of white males were exclusively homosexual. Kinsey's research challenged the accepted mutually exclusive categories of homosexual and heterosexual, which did not accurately reflect the complexities of the behavior he found. In Kinsey's words, "The living world is a continuum . . . the sooner we learn this concerning human sexual behavior the sooner we shall reach a sound understanding of the realities of sex." He developed a seven-point scale with exclusively heterosexual behavior at one end (0) and exclusively homosexual behavior at the other (6). Throughout a lifetime, a person's pattern of sexual behavior could change. Other data conflicted strongly with traditional views about the rarity and danger of masturbation among normal adults, since more than 90 percent of males and

62 percent of females reported having masturbated.

Kinsey was a pioneer in applying social science techniques to the documentation of sexual behavior. He believed that high refusal rates would result among prospective interviewees if a probability sample was attempted. He developed instead his taxonomic methodology, which involved the collection of a large number of diverse case histories (his original goal was 100,000). This strategy, he believed, would result in a reasonably representative sample. Kinsey attempted to compensate for volunteer bias by obtaining sexual histories from 100 percent of a given organization or group. About one-quarter of the total sample was obtained from these 100 percent groups.

The final male and female samples are most accurately characterized as representing white, middle class, college-educated Americans under 35 years of age. Although Kinsey's sample—gathered when sampling theory was not as developed as it is now and today's sophisticated computers were not available—cannot fairly be compared to current research, no study has yet been conducted that matches the immensity of his effort, either in the size of the sample or in the meticulousness and depth of the interviewing by highly trained personnel.

The Kinsey Institute for Research in Sex, Gender, and Reproduction

The Kinsey Institute's history has mirrored America's changing attitudes toward sexuality and sex research from mid-century through the McCarthy era, the so-called sexual revolution of the 1960s and 1970s, and the AIDS crisis of the 1980s and 1990s. The Institute for Sex Research was established in 1947 at the suggestion of Herman B Wells, then president of Indiana University, as a nonprofit corporation, separate from but closely affiliated with Indiana University. It was President Wells's conviction regarding the need to protect the confidentiality of the sex histories and the ownership of the library and art collections that provided the impetus for the Institute. Kinsey sold the art and library materials he had begun gathering in support of his research to the fledgling Institute for one dollar.

When support from the National Research Council was withdrawn due to pressure from Congress, Kinsey was forced to spend the royalties from the first two reports, funds with which he had planned to establish an endowment for the Institute, to continue the research. After Kinsey's death and the public controversy of the early 1950s, the Institute, under the leadership of Paul Gebhard, sought a lower profile while continuing to maintain a program of research and publication.

The focus turned from data collection to continued analysis of the almost 18,000 interviews gathered. In 1957, the Institute's legal battle with U.S. Customs, led by Harriet Pilpel, a prominent American Civil Liberties Union and First Amendment lawyer, ended with the landmark decision *United States* v. *31 Photographs,* which gave the Institute the right to import erotic materials for scientific research purposes. The Institute's library continued to grow during this period, and the collections were subsequently opened to qualified scholars.

Out of the Institute's unique data base and rich archives came studies by both Institute staff and outside scholars on reproduction, sex offenders, sexual development, erotic art, and Victorian sexual culture. The publications produced under Institute auspices during this period continued to dispel myths about sexual behavior. *Pregnancy, Birth, and Abortion* (1958) reported that 10 percent of women were pregnant before marriage, and three-fourths of those had induced abortions (of which only 6.4 percent were legal therapeutic abortions). *Sex Offenders: An Analysis of Types* (1965) provided evidence that most exhibitionists are not physically dangerous and most voyeurs are not incipient rapists.

In the early 1970s, with grant support from the National Institute of Mental Health (NIMH), the Institute launched major research studies on homosexuality and America's sexual norms. The culminating study from this era was Alan Bell and Martin Weinberg's *Homosexualities: A Study of Diversity Among Men and Women* (1978), which revealed the tremendous range of behaviors, lifestyles, and attitudes evident in gay men and lesbians. One of the more influential findings was that psychological problems were no more prevalent among homosexual men and women than in the population as a whole.

The Institute also assumed during the 1970s a key support role for the field of sexology, publishing a directory of sex research, a thesaurus of sexual nomenclature, catalogs of its social science materials, a sex studies index, and bibliographies from its collections. From 1970 to 1977, funding from NIMH supported the operation of an Information Services desk to handle requests about the research and resources of the Institute.

At Gebhard's retirement, an international search by the Institute's board of trustees led to the appointment in 1982 of June Machover Reinisch, a developmental biopsychologist trained at Columbia University, as director. In accordance with the mandate of the Institute's board and the University's administration, and in consultation with the new Science Advisory Board, the Institute's research program was expanded to include biomedical and psychobiological issues. The Institute was renamed the Kinsey Institute for Research in Sex, Gender, and Reproduction to honor its founder and to reflect its broadened research and educational missions.

Since 1982, research on sexual and psychosexual development has been a major scientific focus, brought to the Institute by Reinisch. Two long-term studies are examining the behavioral consequences for offspring of maternal medical treatment with hormones and drugs during pregnancy. These projects have been funded by grants from the National Institute of Child Health and Human Development and the National Institute on Drug Abuse. The completed data base will represent the largest ever compiled in this area and will serve as a rich resource for many subsequent investigations.

The Institute continues its commitment to sexual behavior research. Because by the mid-1980s most of the research on the behavioral aspects of the AIDS crisis focused on gay men, the Institute began to study the high-risk sexual behavior of women. Two subsequent studies (1988 and 1991) have investigated the sexual behavior patterns of midwestern university students that place them at greatest risk for AIDS and other sexually transmitted diseases (STDs). The results showed that substantial numbers of college-age individuals are having unprotected vaginal and anal intercourse with multiple partners. Nearly one-third of the university women and one-fifth of the men in the 1991 survey had been infected with at least one STD. In 1989, the Institute tested a nationally representative sample of Americans on their knowledge of sexual behavior and health, contraception, and reproductive issues. Questions were designed to reflect the thousands of letters the Institute received each year from the general public. Fifty-five percent of those sampled were unable to answer half the questions. Half the respondents thought that a person can get AIDS by having anal intercourse even if neither partner is infected with the AIDS virus. Only 5 percent knew that there are over-the-counter spermicides containing Nonoxynol-9 that have been shown in laboratory tests to kill the AIDS virus and many other STD organisms. The results demonstrated the persistence in our society of many myths and misconceptions about sexuality and reproduction, as well as the lack of basic sexual knowledge on the part of Americans in all age groups, educational levels, and socioeconomic strata.

The Institute is committed to disseminating its research to the scientific community. To date, more than 228 books, articles, and chapters have been published under Institute auspices. Recently, the Kinsey Institute Series has published *Masculinity/Femininity*, *Adolescence and Puberty*, *Homosexuality/Heterosexuality*, and *AIDS and Sex*, based on interdisciplinary research symposia convened by the Institute since 1983 and attended by experts from both the United States and abroad. *Sex and Morality in the U.S.*, a study of Americans' attitudes and behavior begun in 1970 but whose findings were still valuable in the context of the AIDS crisis, was published in 1989.

Given that most scientific research is supported to a great extent by public funds, the Institute, under the direction of its trustees, has felt a responsibility to seek ways to provide the general public with research-based information. The first step in this direction was the creation of an Information Services Department in the 1970s. Since 1984, the Institute has produced an internationally syndicated newspaper column, "The Kinsey Report," to respond to the public's questions. During its nine years of thrice-weekly publication in newspapers around the world, more than 2,900 questions have been answered about sexual health, sexual behavior, and reproduction, using the most accurate and current research data available from scientists and scholars worldwide. In addition, the Institute produced its first book designed as a resource for the general public. *The Kinsey Institute New Report on Sex: What You Must Know to Be Sexually Literate*, published in 1990, became the Institute's third best-seller. It has been translated into Chinese, French, German, Japanese, Korean, Polish, and Spanish and has also appeared in a British edition.

Underlying and supporting the Institute's research and educational outreach programs is its collection of more than 80,000 print items, 7,800 films and videotapes, 25,000 photographs, 28,500 art objects and artifacts, and various data archives. Institute monies derived from fund-raising projects, book royalties, and private donations, but not targeted for research purposes, support acquisitions. No public funds are ever spent to acquire erotic materials for the collections.

The Institute relies to a great extent on gifts of erotica and other materials related to human sexuality, gender, and reproduction. These gifts come from donors and patrons across the United States and around the world. As in the case of all contacts between the public and the Institute, strict confidentiality of donor names is maintained when requested.

Although various collections address particular aspects of human sexuality, the Institute's archives have the unique aim of making available to scholars the variety of literary, scientific, artistic, and popular-ephemeral materials encompassing all aspects of human sexuality from all times, places, and cultures. The variety of materials and forms testifies to humankind's universal fascination with sex and the diversity and similarity of sexual behavior and attitudes around the world and throughout history. The collections include elegant erotic scrolls from the Far East; ancient Peruvian funerary pottery depicting sexual activity; erotic early-to-mid-20th-century comic books known as 8-pagers; popularized accounts of 18th- and 19th-century adultery trials; nudist magazines; still photographs dating from 1855; one of the largest collections of prints and photographs by George Platt Lynes; a valuable collection of Japanese Shunga wood-block prints, including works by Hokusai (1760–1849) and Kunisada (1786–1865); erotic literary classics and first editions; original biographical materials; art by world-class artists such as Aubrey Beardsley, Henri Matisse, Pavel Tchelitchew, Auguste Renoir, and Leonor Fini, by children, by prisoners, and by psychiatric patients; and films, dating from 1911 that include "blue" movies and footage of mammalian sexual behavior.

Since the mid-1980s steps have been taken to improve the Institute's ability to store, preserve, and make accessible to scholars its unique and valuable collections. By 1988, library staff had increased threefold. Renovations in the latter half of the 1980s added a new art gallery, climate controls for the library stacks, and more than doubled storage space for print materials, the art collections, and visiting patrons. Recently, the Institute's library staff began putting a portion of its catalog on-line. With this project, the Institute's computer data base will become accessible to scholars worldwide through Internet. Use of the collections will continue to be limited, as directed by the 1957 court ruling, to qualified scholars, researchers, professionals, media representatives, and college students with bona fide research projects.

As its focus has expanded and been updated over the nearly four decades since Kinsey's death, the Institute has kept faith with its founder's vision to demythologize sex through research, scholarship, and education, so that individuals can be better equipped to make decisions based on information rather than on ignorance or prejudice.

REFERENCES

Primary

Kinsey, A.F., W.D. Pomeroy, and C.E. Martin. *Sexual Behavior in the Human Male*. Philadelphia: Saunders, 1948.

Kinsey, A.F., W.D. Pomeroy, C.E. Martin, and P.H. Gebhard. *Sexual Behavior in the Human Female*. Philadelphia: Saunders, 1953.

Secondary

Bancroft, J., and J.M. Reinisch, eds. *Adolescence and Puberty*. Kinsey Institute Series. New York: Oxford Univ. Press, 1990.

Bell, A.P., and M.S. Weinberg. *Homosexualities: A Study of Diversity Among Men and Women*. New York: Simon & Schuster, 1978.

Christenson, C.V. *Kinsey: A Biography*. Bloomington: Indiana Univ. Press, 1971.

Cochran, W.G., F. Mosteller, and J.W. Tukey. Statistical Problems of the Kinsey Report. *Journal of the American Statistical Association*, Vol. 48 (1953), pp. 673–716.

Gagnon, J., and W. Simon. *Sexual Conduct: The Social Sources of Human Sexuality*. Chicago: Aldine, 1973.

Gebhard, P.H., and A.B. Johnson. *The Kinsey Data: Marginal Tabulations of the 1938–1963 Interviews Conducted by the Institute for Sex Research*. Philadelphia: Saunders, 1979.

Gebhard, P.H., et al. *Pregnancy, Birth and Abortion*. New York: Harper Brothers, 1958.

———. *Sex Offenders: An Analysis of Types*. New York: Harper & Row, 1965.

Institute of Medicine/National Academy of Sciences. *Confronting AIDS: Directions for Public Health, Health Care, and Research*. Washington, D.C.: National Academy Press, 1986.

Klassen, A.D., C.J. Williams, and E.E. Levitt. *Sex and Morality in the U.S.: An Empirical Enquiry Under the Auspices of the Kinsey Institute*. Middletown, Conn.: Wesleyan Univ. Press, 1989.

McWhirter, D.P., S.A. Sanders, and J.M. Reinisch, eds. *Homosexuality/Heterosexuality: Concepts of Sexual Orientation*. Kinsey Institute Series. New York: Oxford Univ. Press, 1990.

Pomeroy, W.B. *Dr. Kinsey and the Institute for Sex Research*. New York: Harper & Row, 1972.

Reinisch, J.M., with R. Beasley. *The Kinsey Institute New Report on Sex: What You Must Know to Be Sexually Literate*. New York: St. Martin's Press, 1990.

Reinisch, J.M., C.A. Hill, S.A. Sanders, and M. Ziemba-Davis. Sexual Behavior Among Heterosexual College Students. *Focus: A Guide to AIDS Research and Counseling*, Vol. 5, No. 4 (1990), p. 3.

Reinisch, J.M., L.A. Rosenblum, and S.A. Sanders, eds. *Masculinity/Femininity: Basic Perspectives*. Kinsey Institute Series. New York: Oxford Univ. Press, 1990.

Robinson, P. *The Modernization of Sex*. New York: Harper & Row, 1976.

Voeller, B., J.M. Reinisch, and M. Gottlieb, eds. *AIDS: An Integrated Biomedical and Biobehavioral Approach*. Kinsey Institute Series. New York: Oxford Univ. Press, 1990.

Weinberg, M.S., ed. *Sex Research: Studies from the Kinsey Institute*. New York: Oxford Univ. Press, 1976.

June Machover Reinisch
Margaret H. Harter

KIRKENDALL, LESTER A.

Lester Kirkendall (1903–1991) was a pioneer in the field of sexuality education. Born November 15, 1903, Kirkendall received his doctorate from Teacher's College, Columbia University, in 1935. During his early career as an elementary and high school teacher and as a school administrator, Kirkendall often provided informal counseling to his pupils, especially to boys with sexual concerns. This experience was the basis for his first book, *Sex Adjustment in Young Men* (1940), and for his subsequent specialization in sex education, a field in which he became a genuine innovator.

Kirkendall established himself as a sexuality and family life educator and was the first in the United States to teach college-level courses on human sexuality, at Oregon State University in 1960. During this period, he contributed significantly to sex research with his landmark interview study, *Premarital Intercourse and Interpersonal Relations* (1961). Kirkendall retired from teaching in 1969.

With Mary Calderone in 1964, Lester Kirkendall was cofounder of the Sex Information and Education Council of the United States (SIECUS), which was dedicated to promoting sexuality education, supporting the study of human sexuality, and increasing sex education in schools. Kirkendall held many prestigious organizational positions, such as vice president of SIECUS and member of its board of directors, vice president of the American Association of Sex Educators, Counselors and Therapists (AASECT), and charter member of the Society for the Scientific Study of Sex (SSSS).

Kirkendall wrote and edited more than 13 books on sexuality and sex education, outstanding among them *A New Bill of Sexual Rights and Responsibilities* (1976), which was endorsed by approximately 40 authorities in the field of sex education. He wrote more than 300 articles and was associate editor of eight publications, including *Sexology,* the *Journal of Sex Research,* and *Sexual Digest.*

Kirkendall received numerous awards for his unique and humane approach to sex education, including the American Humanist Association's Humanist of the Year award, the World Congress on Sexuality's International Award for Promoting Sexuality Education, and the SSSS 1984 Award for Outstanding Contributions to the Field of Human Sexuality. Lester Kirkendall died in May, 1991 at the age of 87.

REFERENCES

Kirkendall, L.A. Education for Marriage and Family Living. In F. Zeran, ed., *Life Adjustment Education in Action.* New York: Chartwell House, 1953.

———. *A New Bill of Sexual Rights and Responsibilities.* Buffalo: Prometheus Books, 1976.

———. *Premarital Intercourse and Interpersonal Relations.* Stanford, Calif.: Stanford Univ. Press, 1961.

Kirkendall, L.A., and A. Gravatt, eds. *Marriage and the Family in the Year 2020.* Buffalo: Prometheus Books, 1990.

Leah Cahan Schaefer

KRAFFT-EBING, RICHARD VON

Richard von Krafft-Ebing (1840–1902) was one of the founders of modern sexology. His major work in the field was *Psychopathia Sexualis,* originally published in 1886. It went through many editions and there are three translations of the work into English.

Krafft-Ebing was born on August 14, 1840, in Mannheim, Germany, the eldest of four children in an aristocratic family. He inherited the title of *freiherr* ("baron"). His grandfather on his mother's side was a prominent Heidelberg lawyer with whom he lived while attending the University of Heidelberg. This arrangement was probably a factor in his developing interest in medical forensics. After further study in Switzerland, Krafft-Ebing was appointed professor of psychiatry at Strasbourg, and subsequently he occupied similar positions at Graz and Vienna. In addition to his teaching and research, he served as a psychiatric consultant to the German and Austrian courts as well as in other countries.

Though Krafft-Ebing's beliefs and teaching have been called an "unmitigated disaster" for sex research, he, more than anyone else in that period, made sex research respectable. He was, however, very much a man of his own time, and few researchers today would subscribe to his explanations for various forms of sexual behavior. His terminology, such as sadism and masochism, nevertheless, remains part of the modern vocabulary.

Krafft-Ebing married late in life and had two sons and a daughter. He died on December 22, 1902, near Graz, Austria.

REFERENCES

Primary

Krafft-Ebing, R. von. *Psychopathia Sexualis.* Translated from the 7th enlarged edition by C.G. Chaddock. Philadelphia: F.A. Davis, 1894.

Secondary

Brecher, E.M. *The Sex Researchers.* Boston: Little, Brown, 1959.

Vern L. Bullough

1

LANGUAGE AND SEX

Sexual terminology is a rich and fascinating component of language. One should probably refer to "terminologies," however, since many sexual discourses exist and in all languages. This article focuses on English.

Sexual Discourses

Medico-scientific Discourse

At the most formal level, there is medical and technical terminology, the language of physicians, psychologists, and other professionals: "Mr. Smith has an erectile dysfunction, and Mrs. Smith has a desire disorder, but our tests show that she lubricates appropriately when presented with a target stimulus." Or, in typical Masters and Johnson prose:

> Clitoral stimulation during coitus in the female supine position develops indirectly from penile-shaft distention of the minor labia at the vaginal vestibule. . . . [T]his same type of secondary coital stimulation occurs in every coital position when there is a full penetration of the vaginal barrel by the erect penis. (p. 59)

Laypeople undoubtedly wonder about this discourse. The discussion seems to be about sex; however, not only can they barely understand it, but it also sounds terribly dull.

Such language is supposed to sound dull and incomprehensible to the layperson. All sexual discourses are highly specific to particular contexts, which simultaneously implies what these discourses are *not* in other contexts. Thus, medico-scientific discourse about sex is by nature not any of the discourses described in subsequent sections of this article. It is not boasting or complaining about one's sexual experiences, or commenting to a friend about the sexual appeal of a nearby individual, or sharing one's sexual fantasies with a partner. The words used are not those that appear in insults, jokes, limericks, dirty songs, erotica, or love talk.

Medico-scientific language about sex is a highly precise technical discourse, readily understandable to its speakers, that conveys potentially strong emotional content by means of a completely neutral medium. It is no accident that much controversial sex research has been couched in this discourse, since the authors seek to avoid public exposure, sensationalism, emotional reaction, and, probably above all, the slightest hint of sexual stimulation. Terms from medico-scientific sexual discourse are defined in medical and similar dictionaries.

Standard Discourse

Less technical than medico-scientific sex terminology are the standard words and phrases used to discuss sex by educated people in formal contexts, including radio and television broadcasts, newspapers, books by professionals for the public, and instructional settings: "Mr. Smith cannot usually achieve an erection, and Mrs. Smith has trouble becoming aroused." Most people understand this discourse, although not all speak it themselves, and it has become the style of choice for communication among diverse audiences and groups. Terms in this discourse are found in all standard dictionaries, although often in the past definitions tended to be uselessly euphemistic or circular. Like medico-scientific language, the standard discourse of sexuality is also quite precise, with few synonyms.

Informal Discourse and Slang

Slang offers one of the richest lodes of sexual language. Now, Mr. Smith "can't get it up"—or, as Archie Bunker, the television character popular in the 1970s put it, "he's stuck in neutral." Similarly, Mrs. Smith "just can't get turned on" or is "an iceberg" or a "cold fish." In this category as well belong the classic taboo words when used in their literal meanings: "fuck," "cunt," "cock," "tits," "shit," "piss."

All languages have sexual slang, and the journal *Maledicta* has published examples from dozens of languages, from Japanese to Macedonian. In English alone, the imagery is highly varied and colorful, including allusions to war, animals, games, machinery and equipment, and food, among others:

War:	She yielded to him (agreed to a sexual encounter).
	His smile pierced her heart (attracted her romantically or sexually).
Animals:	Stallion (virile man)
	Foxy lady (sexually attractive woman)
	Mount (commence sexual intercourse)
	"An old black ram is tupping your white ewe" (*Othello*, I, i).
Games:	He won her (succeeded in attracting affection or sexual interest).
Machinery and Equipment:	Screw, nail (have sexual intercourse).
Food:	Eat (fellatio, cunnilingus)

Honeypot (vulva, vagina)

Beat your meat (masturbate)

Tube steak (penis, sexual intercourse)

Melons (breasts).

Synonyms and near synonyms abound in sexual slang. Tim Healey in 1980 reported collecting 1,000 terms for penis, 1,200 for vulva, 800 for sexual intercourse, and 2,000 for prostitute. Food in particular is a major source of imagery. Use of sexual slang and sexual language can begin well before adolescence, as early as between five and seven years of age.

Euphemism

Much sexual slang is described as euphemistic, and perhaps some of it is. The major impetus, however, seems to be creativity and language play rather than simply the for avoidance of either taboos or frankness. Still some sexual speech seems influenced largely by a need for avoidance. In euphemistic discourse, our poor Mr. Smith "can't do his husbandly (or marital) duty," while in his wife "that spark of attraction has died."

Bathroom functions have spawned as much euphemism as slang—"widdle," "number one" and "number two," "take care of (do one's) business," "go to the little girl's room," and so on. Most of these expressions are used with children, but they also carry over into adulthood. As invective, "shit" has given birth to "shoot," "shucks," and "sugar."

The key elements of sex—penis, vulva and vagina, and sexual intercourse, together with their slang labels "cock," "cunt," and "fuck"—have likewise generated numerous euphemisms, of which perhaps the most common are "thing" (genitals of either sex), "down there" (vulva, vagina), and "do it" (have sexual intercourse). In this vein, "fuck" has given birth to "frig," "futz" (as in "futz around with"), and "fug," as used both by the musical group the Fugs in the 1960s and by Norman Mailer in his novel *The Naked and the Dead* (1948), written and published at a time when the word "fuck" could not be used in commercially published books. Mailer's use of the term reportedly led Marlene Dietrich to remark when she met Mailer, "So you're the boy who can't spell 'fuck.'"

Particularly striking and amusing are two relatively new slang euphemisms for "in deep shit" (in bad trouble): "in deep yogurt" and "in deep kimchee," both of which were reported to have been used in such "stuffy" situations as corporate board meetings. An interesting reversal of euphemism has occurred with the phrase "give good head" (be skilled at oral sex), since the same construction has been generalized to produce such phrases as "give good meeting" and "give good telephone." The result has been to imbue nonsexual activities with sexual implications as well as to get a laugh for inventive word-play.

Graphically, euphemisms, particularly in cartoons, often appear as dashes, asterisks, or dingbats, such as "F★★★, you dirty @#&%★)!" or simply a stream of symbols that can be glossed only generally as "cursing." Reinhold Aman, the editor of *Maledicta,* proposed, probably tongue in cheek, a systematic approach to coining "genteel profanity" by retaining the initial letter of the offensive word and then adding "ex" (for "expletive"). Thus we might use "shex" for "shit," "fex" for "fuck," and so on.

Intimate Language

The least studied sexual discourse is the language of those who are sexually or socially intimate. Like sexual slang, no two of these languages are alike; they make heavy use of metaphor and allusion, but usually the allusion is to jokes or circumstances known only to the speakers.

Such languages often incorporate private nicknames for the two (or more) individuals: Bunchcrackles, Toadface, Uptown Toots, Angel Buns, Carrot Top, Rubberface, and Balloonbutt have all been reported. Usage also includes special expressions for sexual body parts and acts: "Let's go home and watch TV" means "let's have sex" for one couple and "I want to go back and get a sweater" has been reported to have the same meaning for another couple. "Sucking your thumb" can mean fellatio. William Betcher described one couple who had a numbers game in which each number referred to a sexual act or body part: penis was 7, after James Bond, who was Agent 007, and the convenience store 7-Eleven, which stays open all night; 8 was for manual caressing of the vulva because this was the pattern traced by the fingers.

Particularly fascinating are genital pet names— proper names are given to genitals and other body parts. Among names reportedly paired for the penis and the vulva-vagina are Wilbur/ Wileen, Fred/Freda, Little Willy/Little Joanie, Alice/Wonderland, and Gruesome/Twosome. Breasts have been called Myra/Myrtle and Jackie/ Jill, while testicles are Ping/Pong or John/Henry. A penis has been called an Owl because it stays up all night, or Alexander the Great, or Winston (from the advertising jingle "tastes good like a cigarette should"). In such intimate discourse, Mr. Smith might chuckle ruefully that "Junior" (his penis) "is taking a nap," while Mrs. Smith might say that "Cynthia is bored and cranky" or "the garden is a bit too dry tonight." Intimate sexual language within couples allows the lovers to create something unique and to share it in an enjoyable and playful way. It also facilitates sexual arousal, since many people find talking about sex a powerful sexual stimulant; a private sexual language with a lover makes this process easier and even more enjoyable.

Certainly, "bedroom talk" is a very important part of sexual communication, even when no private slang or special terms are used. Some men and women are aroused by using and hearing common sexual slang, especially taboo words. This use of language is colloquially referred to as "talking dirty" and is sometimes practiced uninhibitedly by those who, out of bed, might say nothing more shocking than "damn." It is the shock value that releases and stimulates.

Although intimate language about sexual body parts and acts is typically individual or couple-specific, sometimes whole families have idiosyncratic terms and phrases for various sexual, bathroom, and related concepts. Farting in particular seems to inspire numerous family slang terms and euphemisms, from "the raccoons were here" to "barking spider," "painting the elevator," and "stepping on a frog."

It is not unknown for whole communities to adopt special jargon. One of the best examples, reported by Charles Adams, involved some 500 people living in the Anderson Valley of Mendocino County, California, between 1881 and 1920. They developed a coined jargon, Boontling, about 15 percent of which was "nonch harpin" or "objectionable talk" used among males, between spouses and lovers, and to insult outsiders without their catching on.

Insults

Better documented than intimate sexual language is the language of sexual insult, which includes at least three types: (1) references to body parts, body functions, sex, or secretions; (2) what might be called blasphemy, since it emphasizes God, saints, or similar references to normative religious beliefs; (3) derogatory sexual references to relatives (e.g., father, mother, siblings). An Italian insult is *testa di cazzo,* or "cock head," while a sample Japanese expression is *asamara no tatanu otoko ni kane kasuna,* literally "never lend money to a man who doesn't have a hard-on in the morning," implying that he must be so sick he is about to die; in the United States, the term "motherfucker" is a typical example. Such imagery is hardly recent: an Egyptian legal document of 950 B.C.E. has the most impressive curse, "May a donkey copulate with you! May a donkey copulate with your wife! May your child copulate with your wife!"

Erotica

Erotica and pornography refer to similiar kinds of discourse. "Erotica" is the term often applied to descriptions or evocations of sexual feelings or behavior that result in sexual arousal and are aesthetically and socially acceptable to the speaker. "Pornography," in contrast, is used for sexual evocations or descriptions that a particular speaker finds unaesthetic, deviant, disgusting, immoral, or harmful. No one particular sexual discourse is common to all erotica. There are, however, two major types of erotic discourse that sometimes occur singly, sometimes overlap, and sometimes do not seem to appear at all in sexually evocative writing.

The first type of discourse is often called soft-core. It is inventive, discursive, metaphoric, and usually indirect. The classic example is *Fanny Hill*, a novel written in 1749, which uses what might be called chaste language to describe erotic scenes. Such language was a standard of the Victorian past, and it is still used effectively in today's romance novels. It has also been a staple of love poetry from the Song of Songs through the work of John Donne and the contemporary poets.

Opposite to this is hard-core: direct, almost brutal, with liberal use of taboo sexual slang. Valerie Kelly distinguished between the two discourses, describing hard-core as using lots of sex words, while soft-core beats around the bush. In hard-core, it cannot be a man at the door; it has to be a hunk who's packing a ten-inch cock in his trousers. "The woman who answers the door is not a housewife who was watching television but a horny wench who has spent her morning jacking herself off for lack of a big prick to tickle her pussy." There is also hard-core poetry, which dates back at least to John Wilmot in the 17th century.

In practice, much material designed to be sexually evocative or arousing tends to fall somewhere between these extremes, sometimes making use of both. These two poles of erotica—the poetic and the taboo—mirror aspects of the talk of real lovers in bed. Poetic erotica attempts to capture the warmth and closeness of a shared intimate language, while the taboo element attempts to capture the urgency and heat of "talking dirty."

Recreational Use of Sexual Language

Sexual slang and insult figure prominently in a number of recreational forms of verbal folklore such as "dirty jokes" and stories, bawdy songs, limericks, and graffiti. Verbal folklore about sex is widespread among all age groups and all periods of history, as evidenced by the sex jokes of children and the graffiti of Pompei. The major collections of dirty jokes and limericks are those of Gershon Legman. Allen Walker Read has collected graffiti. No comprehensive collection of bawdy songs exists although numerous smaller collections have been published.

Pathological Use of Sexual Language

While reading or writing erotica is deemed pathological by some individuals, it is currently neither illegal nor statistically abnormal (with the exception of child pornography). However, two other aspects of sexual language have been deemed pathological by present society—obscene telephone calls and coprolalia in connection with neurological disorders.

Obscene telephone calls, also called telephone scatologia by the *Diagnostic and Statistical Manual of Mental Disorders* and telephone scatophilia by John Money, represent a caricature or perversion of the normal use of sexual talk to facilitate sexual arousal. It involves the act of calling a stranger and attempting either to entice her (most callers are male and victims female) into a sexual conversation or to provoke in her a reaction of anger, shock, or horror. The caller may masturbate during the call or afterwards.

Coprolalia is the abnormal, compulsive, and often inappropriate uttering of socially unacceptable language. It can be a symptom of several central nervous system disorders and also can occur after cerebrovascular accidents. The condition with which it is perhaps most frequently associated is the Gilles de la Tourette syndrome, now called Tourette's disorder.

Tourette's disorder is defined by the presence of highly variable involuntary tics, both physical and vocal. In about a third of the patients, the vocal tics take the form of uttering socially unacceptable words or phrases, with "fuck" and "shit" most frequent but many others used as well. Tourette's disorder patients with coprolalia commonly experience ostracism or punishment on account of their constant and largely uncontrollable obscenities and cursing. Many patients are able to suppress the symptom for a period or to substitute other words, but then they may feel compelled to go somewhere private to release the coprolalia explosively. Symptoms tend to decrease during absorption in a task and cease completely during orgasm.

Researchers have not yet uncovered the cause of Tourette's disorder but postulate the existence of a functional neurological system that stores taboo or socially unacceptable language; somehow abnormal stimulation or short-circuiting of this system may produce coprolalia. At present, some drugs have been found helpful, notably haloperidol.

Male versus Female Use of Sexual Language

Males have long had a reputation as the principal users of sexual language, while it is claimed that women use more "innocent" and euphemistic words and paraphrases. Numerous recent studies affirm this generalization by demonstrating that in public, in private, and on film, men not only use sexual language more frequently than do women but also seem to be more linguistically inventive with sexual discourse, generating more unusual and idiosyncratic terms.

How much of this is due to the stigmatization of women who use inventive language, as compared to the acceptance of such language in men, is unclear. Helen Brown Norden as long ago as 1936 reported that most of her contemporaries described their amorous episodes to each other in the frankest language and with relentless accuracy of detail to the extent that any male who overheard them would have been practically paralyzed into permanent impotence. Norden herself did not write explicitly about sex in her earlier years, but in 1977, writing as Helen Lawrenson, she authored a pointed piece for *Esquire* entitled "How Now, Fellatio! Why Dost Thou Tarry?"

Women may eventually achieve greater parity with men in this respect. In terms of sexual slang women at least occasionally now match men with street insults in working-class neighborhoods and x-rated stand-up comedy. Likewise, some mostly female professions, such as nursing, have had a reputation for verbal directness about sexual matters, particularly in jokes and stories. There is also evidence that lesbians employ sexual terminology differently than females in general, using fewer euphemisms and formal terms and more slang and so-called obscene words.

Today, a growing number of women writers and other professionals have clearly become comfortable with taboo and sexual terminology. Hundreds of popular and scholarly books about sex by women authors have appeared in the last few decades, ranging from Nancy Friday's *My Secret Garden* to Shere Hite's sex surveys, from Helen Singer Kaplan's classics on sex therapy to Betty Dodson's hymns to masturbation. Women writers and consumers of erotica are growing in numbers, and sex periodicals edited or coedited by women range from the polymorphous *Libido* to the genteel *Yellow Silk*, the half-humorous *On Our Backs*, and the underground sex 'zines published for women such as the British *Girl Frenzy*.

Feminists and others have pointed out that patterns of insult directed at males differ from those directed at females—specifically that insults about females attribute (usually indiscriminate) sexuality to the target, whereas insults directed at males do not. There are no male equivalents of "whore" or "slut," for example, and though "lecher" and "skirt chaser" applied to men have insulting connotations, they are used more to refer to specific behavior than to insult the overall person.

Even the genital-based insults are quite different for men and women. "Cunt" does not imply simple sexual looseness but rather a mix of profound sexual and moral stupidity and miserly nastiness. "Prick," on the other hand, implies a milder form of stupid nastiness, with no hint of sexuality. Only "bitch," strictly speaking no more sexual a word than "cow," lacks sexual connotations, conveying only extreme nastiness; however, when it is applied to males, as in "he was feeling bitchy," it implies homosexuality.

Sexual Lexicography

A good summary of what has been taking place in the area of sexual language becomes evident in a brief overview of sexual lexicography, or how words relating to sex have been treated in dictionaries over the centuries. Vernacular dictionaries (i.e., for nonclassical languages) first appeared in the 15th and 16th centuries. A benchmark in sexual lexicography was Florio's Italian-English dictionary, published in 1598, which contains one of the earliest recorded instances of "fuck," used to define the Italian fottere: "to jape, to fucke, to sard, to suive [swive], to occupy." The first English dictionary, Cawdry's *A Table Alphabeticall . . . of Hard Usual English Words*, appeared in 1604, and though "fuck" did not appear, "buggerie" and "sodomitrie" did.

By the 1700s, dictionaries began to cover the common words, and the first English dictionary to include "fuck" was Henshaw's *Etymologicon Linguae Anglicanae* (1671). Few lexicographers followed his lead, since there was a growing hesitation to use certain "indecent" expressions publicly. Shakespeare, for example, does not use so-called four-letter words, although he does joke about the "focative" case, a deliberate mangling of the grammatical term "vocative" case, and uses' numerous bawdy puns and sexual allusions.

Bailey's *Universale Etymological English Dictionary,* published in 1721, did contain "shite" and "fuck," although the latter was defined only in Latin. The landmark dictionary of Samuel Johnson in 1755 deliberately excluded such terms in the interest of decency. When Johnson did include words such as "libidinous," he used circular definitions, that is, he defined "libidinous" as "lewd and lustful," and "lustful" as "libidinous"; similarly, "lecherous" is defined as "lewd and lustful." With only a few exceptions, those of John Ash (1775) and Francis Grose (1785), the British lexicographers followed Johnson's example until well into the 20th century. The early Americans were even more cautious in dealing with sexual language, particularly Noah Webster, whose dictionaries and their successors left out most sexual and scatological terms until 1973.

The major achievement of English lexicography, the *Oxford English Dictionary (OED)*—totaling 15,487 pages, published in fascicles between 1882 and 1928, and largely the work of James A. Murray—excluded most "obscene" sexual words. Only in the "Wh-Wo" section, published in 1926 after Murray's death, did "windfucker" appear, a name for a kestrel hawk but also an insult. However, when the OED did deal with terms such as "fornication," it gave much more complete definitions than had been the custom before, although even here circuitous and euphemistic definitions were often used, as in the case of the term "sexual intercourse," which referred the reader to "copulation" or "a union of the sexes and the act of generation."

Partridge's *A Dictionary of Slang and Unconventional English,* published originally in 1937, was the first 20th century dictionary to include "fuck" and other colloquial sexual words. The *American Heritage Dictionary* published in 1969 was the first general, college-sized dictionary to follow suit. Others followed soon after and with the 1989 edition of the *OED,* the full range of sexual language was covered.

Recent years have seen a small but eclectic surge of work in sexual lexicography, much of it both scholarly and interesting. The journal *Maledicta,* beginning in 1977, has presented a unique mixture of scholarly and popular work on negatively valued words and expressions. Specialist dictionaries have also appeared, as well as general works on sexual language.

Conclusion

Despite these fascinating and varied aspects, sexual language has been relatively little studied, especially by sexuality professionals. Only a handful of language and literature scholars, as well as a few scholars from other disciplines, have attempted to unravel the complexities of sexual words and their usage. Probably the numbers will gradually grow since it has become harder and harder to avoid sex—both in terms of social issues and in linguistic terms. Not only has the American language become more open, but it has also become more explicit, more technical, and more available to all speakers of English. Sex, here to stay, has become an open part of modern spoken and written English.

REFERENCES

The best sources for those wishing to keep up to date on developments in sexual language are such journals as *Maledicta, Journal of American Folklore, Journal of Sex Research,* and *Sex Roles.* For more general works, see the following bibliography.

Adams, C.C. *Boontling: An American Lingo.* Austin: Univ. of Texas Press, 1971.

Betcher, W. *Intimate Play.* New York: Viking, 1987.

Cornog, M. Naming Sexual Body Parts: Preliminary Patterns and Implications. *Journal of Sex Research,* Vol. 22 (1986), pp. 393–98.

Dickson, P. *Family Words.* Reading, Mass.: Addison Wesley, 1988.

Goldman, R., and J. Goldman. *Children's Sexual Thinking.* London: Routledge & Kegan Paul, 1982.

Jay, T. *Cursing in America.* Philadelphia: John Benjamins, 1992.

Jespersen, O. *Language: Its Nature, Development and Origin.* London: Allen & Unwin, 1922.

Kelly, V. *How to Write Erotica.* New York: Harmony, 1986.

Landau, S. *Dictionaries.* Cambridge: Cambridge Univ. Press, 1989.

Lawrenson, H. How Now, Fellatio! Why Dost Thou Tarry? *Esquire,* May 1977, pp. 128, 131.

Legman, G. *The Horn Book.* New Hyde Park, N.Y.: University Books, 1964.

[————]. *The Limerick.* Paris: Les Hautes Études, 1953.

————. *Rationale of the Dirty Joke: An Analysis of Sexual Humor.* 1st series, New York: Grove Press, 1968; 2nd series, New York: Breaking Point, 1975.

Masters, W., and V. Johnson. *Human Sexual Response.* Boston: Little, Brown, 1966.

Read, A.W. *Classic American Graffiti.* 1935. Reprint, Waukesha, Wis.: Maledicta Press, 1977.

Shapiro, A.K., E.S. Shapiro, J.G. Young, and T.E. Feinberg. *Gilles de la Tourette Syndrome.* 2nd ed. New York: Raven Press, 1988.

Martha Cornog

LAWS AND SEX

This article focuses chiefly on the legal situation in the United States pertinent to sexuality during the period December 1941 through November 1991, the half century following the nation's entry into World War II. Priority is given to selective commentary concerning change. Developments abroad (e.g., in the United Kingdom) are not considered here except when they in some clear way had an influence in the United States. Legal changes in two areas contributed most to social change concerning sex: constitutionally protected increases in freedom of expression and in reproductive freedom. Change in the area of freedom of expression has to do with what is treated as obscenity. Legal restrictions on access to technical sex information, erotic works of literature and art, and erotic entertainment in print, pictures, and live performance have been drastically reduced. The second area of change, that of reproductive freedom, concerns contraception and abortion. It also includes the legal licensing of oral contraceptives. The effects of this technological development, which was not blocked by the U.S. legal system, have been truly extraordinary.

The distinctive feature of the U.S. legal system with respect to sexuality in the last 50 years has been the interpretations of the Constitution by the Supreme Court. Constitutional interpretation is taken here to encompass the written Constitution, especially the Bill of Rights (Amendments I through X) and the Fourteenth Amendment; the process of federal judicial review of both state and federal cases; and the activities of a Supreme Court strongly inclined (during much of the period in question) to protect and even significantly enlarge the freedom of individuals from the restrictive actions of government. A result of this system was implementation of the core idea of protection of individuals (in certain instances) against the tyranny of either the legislative majority or elected or appointed officials. It is precisely because of the legitimacy and effect given to the U.S. Constitution's antimajoritarian principles that the Supreme Court has been able to act in ways protective of sexual and reproductive freedoms. At the moment, because of substantial changes in the composition of the federal courts, including the Supreme Court, we may see consider-

able retreat from constitutional protection of sexual and reproductive freedoms during the next decade or more. Constitutional doctrine in the area of sex law has been so important and powerful a tool that it has overshadowed legislative analysis. The changing composition of the Supreme Court may shift the emphasis to state legislatures.

The due-process revolutions in criminal law, juvenile law, and mental hospital commitment law in the 1960s and 1970s had important effects in restraining the wide-ranging use of coercive public power to control sexual behavior of youths and adults. These effects included a more careful, rational reexamination of some laws in these areas. There was also a withdrawal of previously broad grants of power to police, juvenile court judges, and psychiatrists to exercise wide and largely unsupervised discretion. As a result, it was no longer easy to label unpopular sexual behavior as vagrancy, disorderly conduct, delinquency, or psychiatric illness and to freely employ the coercive powers of the state to suppress it through arrest, incarceration, commitment to a juvenile institution, or even commitment to a mental hospital.

Sex and the law offers a very rich area for analysis. There are eight features to keep in mind:

1. *Importance of law.* In part, perhaps, because for 200 years U.S. society has been heterogeneous and rapidly changing, people in the United States rely on laws, courts, and lawyers much more than do those in many other countries. U.S. law touches a great many matters concerning sexuality. There is the written federal Constitution and system of federal law on the national level, 50 systems of state law plus that of the District of Columbia, and the laws of the U.S. territories, among them Puerto Rico and Guam. In the Anglo-American tradition, the rule of law and notions of due process have been historically important, especially in protecting the rights of the individual.

2. *Legal doctrine, or law in the books.* Details about legal rules, principles, and interpretations based on statutes, cases, and the federal Constitution can be found in works in courthouses and some public libraries (see also the References at the end of this article).

3. *Law in action.* In addition to law in the books, we have what actually happens in the legal system. Some sex laws (e.g., those concerning adultery) are not enforced. Other sex laws (e.g., laws concerning homosexuality or prostitution) are only sporadically or selectively enforced, depending on a wide

range of personal and political factors affecting police discretion. Police may use vague and overbroad provisions with regard to vagrancy or disorderly conduct or may even "arrest on suspicion" as a way of harassing persons whom they regard as sexual undesirables (e.g., transvestites). Sex laws may be used merely as one of the weapons in the prosecutor's armory, as when a reputed mobster sought for his organized crime activities is prosecuted for bringing his female companion with him across state lines for sexual purposes. The attorney general's office may let convenience stores that sell magazines know that it takes a dim view of certain men's publications that feature pictures of unclothed women. Bureaucratic regulations concerning fire codes and building inspections may be used to close down the nightclub act of a comedian who is blasphemous and uses foul language. A federal agency can cancel grants to performance artists criticized by a senator for offending middle-class morality.

4. *Law as both cause and effect of change.* The great example of this dual aspect of the law is increased freedom of expression, including liberalization of the law concerning obscenity. Changing social conditions led to liberalization of the law. Greater freedom to disseminate legally information, artistic work, films, and items of popular culture about sexuality in turn facilitated further social change.

5. *Expectation of change in the law itself.* "Law must be stable and yet it cannot stand still." This statement by Roscoe Pound and Benjamin Cardozo, two major figures in American law, probably would be endorsed by most of us. In matters apart from sex law, Americans tend to believe that the law should change with the times, be up to date, and be practical and realistic. In the case of sex law, however, personal and social ambivalence about sex, as well as a strong moralistic streak in American culture even to this day, tends to complicate the usually pragmatic American legal approach.

6. *Organized movements for change.* Since the 1950s the United States has seen a number of powerful movements for social change that have had important legal ramifications, including effects on sex law. These organized efforts have included the civil rights movement for legal and social equality for black Americans; the women's liberation movement, which mounted an unsuccessful campaign to add an Equal Rights Amendment in the U.S. Constitution; and the gay liberation movement on behalf of legal and social acceptance for gay men and lesbians. Since the 1940s and especially in the 1960s, there was a sexual revolution, not so much a single organized movement as a multiplicity of social and legal changes. Finally, in the 1980s, there were organized efforts by many religious groups such as the Moral Majority and Right to Life, to restore what they called traditional family values, expand legal controls on obscenity, and criminalize abortion.

7. *Ambivalence.* Sex law exists amid personal and social ambivalence. By ambivalence is meant both contradictory feelings (of the individual) and contradictory social norms (of the community and society).

8. *Taboo.* Sex laws deal with taboo areas. "Taboo" refers to a forbidden object or forbidden act that calls forth learned feelings of fear, dread, shame, and guilt. Taboos may be part of a religion, but they can be found in secular society as well. Pictures of sexual acts or of genitalia have in the past been taboo. Same-sex sexual intimacy, as in the case of gay men and lesbians, has for many been a taboo. Controversy about what law and social policy should be concerning taboo subjects can produce powerful reactions of rage or shame. We do not unlearn a sexual taboo all at once. Substantial nonrational responses are likely to remain; they feed personal and social ambivalence. Lingering versions of past taboos make truly effective legal and social changes with regard to sexuality more difficult to achieve.

Enforcement-of-Morals Debate and Its Lessons

More than 150 years ago, Jeremy Bentham, the English philosopher and legal critic, spoke against including in the criminal law what he called imaginary offenses and crimes unsuitable for punishment. Using a similar analysis, American critics of the 1960s spoke of victimless crimes. Included in this category were crimes involving consenting adults (e.g., homosexuality, prostitution) and crimes for which legal prohibitions were substantially ineffective (e.g., abortion).

In Britain, the Wolfenden Report made important recommendations concerning the removal from the criminal law of prohibitions against homosexual conduct in private between consenting adults. Similar recommendations were made with regard to decriminalizing prostitution. Criminal law should not punish private adult consensual conduct that does no harm. According to the Wolfenden Report, "There must remain a realm of private morality and immorality which is, in brief and crude terms, not the law's business."

In a debate that had important effects on law-reform discussions in the United States, Lord Devlin argued against the Wolfenden recommendations, saying that the law should protect society's moral code. Offenses against that moral code should be viewed in the same way as treason against one's country. Judge John Parker in the United States in the mid-1950s said that the American Law Institute's Model Penal Code should define homosexual conduct as criminal. He argued that this conduct should be made criminal to show that the law thinks it is wrong, even if such a law cannot be enforced. Hart refuted Lord Devlin's views, and by implication those of Judge Parker, and supported the position taken by the Wolfenden Report. He argued that the proper role of law is different from, and in general much more limited than, the proper role of morality and various private moral systems of belief.

The American Law Institute's Model Penal Code adopted the view argued by Wolfenden and Hart and recommended decriminalization of adult consensual homosexual conduct. Although that recommendation was accepted as part of a statutory revision in Illinois in 1961, it was rejected by the New York legislature in 1965. Recommended decriminalization of adultery was also rejected in New York. Religious pressure groups successfully threatened to block the entire process of criminal-law reform in New York if the criminal law did not condemn what they regarded as immoral behavior. Adultery remains a crime in New York, but except in a very rare case, such as one involving a highly vengeful spouse, there are no prosecutions. What appears to matter most in this instance is the symbolic victory of keeping adultery on the list of officially condemned behaviors. Actual enforcement of the prohibition, impossible under modern conditions, is not the objective.

Consensual homosexual conduct was eventually stricken from the New York criminal law in the 1980s by court decisions under the New York State (not federal) constitution. The contrast between legal efforts in New York in the areas of homosexuality and adultery is instructive. Law reform was successfully achieved for homosexuality by the use of constitutional test cases in court after the legislative route had failed. Law reform was unsuccessful for adultery, for which only the legislative route seemed to be

available. In the legislative process, groups advocating traditional morality can still rather easily manipulate social and political taboos regarding sexual matters and block change.

Some U.S. lawmakers and members of the public, even if they have never heard of Lord Devlin, probably continue to accept the position he espoused that the criminal law should be patterned after traditional moral rules, including rules about sexuality. The penal law, for them, resembles an official code of morality that must be legally defended. According to a different view, "Private morality and immorality . . . [are] . . . not the law's business." So said the Wolfenden Committee, with Hart in agreement. Generally speaking, the movement of American law during the past 50 years has been strongly in the direction of this latter position, but with some important exceptions or even countercurrents.

It may be that to an increasing extent Americans see sexuality as part of life, a part that one should be free to live according to one's own preferences as long as others are not harmed. Nevertheless, one must keep in mind the powerful fact of social ambivalence (self-contradiction) about sex and the role it plays in the behavior of legislators, district attorneys, mayors, and chiefs of police. Too often on the American political scene government officials privately agree that conflicting beliefs about sexual morality are not the law's business, but in public they still righteously proclaim a legal enforcement-of-morals position.

Four Major Areas of Change

There have been at least four major areas of change in sex law during the past 50 years: (1) freedom of expression and liberalization of the law concerning obscenity; (2) reproductive rights, including contraception and abortion; (3) marriage and divorce law; and (4) the law concerning homosexuality.

Freedom of Expression: Obscenity

The U.S. legal system has been outstanding for its protection of freedom of speech and the press, under the First Amendment to the U.S. Constitution as applied to the federal government and under the Due Process Clause of the Fourteenth Amendment, which applies the First Amendment to the states. Nevertheless, sexual material classified as obscene has been placed in a separate legal category, outside the protection ordinarily associated with freedom of expression. A series of legal tests has been articulated by the courts, including the Supreme Court, for deciding what is obscene, and thus not protected from legal prosecution or suppression, and what is not obscene and thus protected under the Constitution. It seems fair to say that changing social views and changing politics, rather than legal logic, probably have caused these shifting decisions. Sexual expression contains ideas, even when courts deny that it does so. Sexual expression has value at least as entertainment, and America surely values entertainment. Finally, as with other forms of expression, the U.S. system says that there should be a free competition of ideas whereby people judge for themselves rather than having to trust to the judgment of others. The fact that the majority of people in a particular community are offended by a particular expression (including pictures) does not ordinarily justify its suppression. Unfortunately, however, under rulings by the Supreme Court, sexual expression continues to be an exception to this principle.

Under the current three-part legal test for obscenity, the trier of facts (the jury) must find that (1) "'the average person, applying contemporary community standards' would find that the work, taken as a whole, appeals to the prurient interest," (2) "the work depicts or describes in a patently offensive way, sexual conduct specifically defined by the applicable state law," and (3) "the work, taken as a whole, lacks serious literary, artistic, political, or scientific value," *Miller* v. *California* [413 U.S. 15 (1973) at 24]. The legal analysis of this test is quite complex. DeGrazia has recently made available an excellent social as well as legal chronicle of obscenity cases and other relevant government actions concerning obscenity.

Perhaps the highest level of emotion anywhere in the field of sex law currently centers on photographic depictions of nude or partially nude minors. Talk of the need for severe measures (e.g., making such photographs contraband and their possession or sale a crime) to protect an unclothed or partially clad child or youth from what is called exploitation is accepted uncritically. In the case of photographs depicting unclothed children or adolescents, the Supreme Court has made an exception to its constitutional protection of private possession of sexually explicit material in one's home.

In 1990, the Contemporary Arts Center in Cincinnati, Ohio, was charged with obscenity and child pornography for displaying the photographic works of Robert Mapplethorpe. The exhibition included homoerotic photographs of adult males, photographs of flowers, and two photographs of children—a naked boy and a little girl wearing a dress but no underpants. The jury acquitted the gallery and its curator of all charges.

Great artists have painted nude children and youths, and both children and adults experience legitimate curiosity as well as delight concerning the unclothed body of the growing human. Nonetheless, photographic depictions of the naked minor have in recent years become highly dangerous from a legal standpoint. Excessive restrictiveness in the name of child protection, directed toward the depiction of child nakedness, constitutes one of the advancing fronts of a resurgent puritanism.

Contraception and Abortion

In no other area of sex law, with the possible exception of freedom of expression, has the role of law been so important in enabling individuals to have the practical freedom to choose their own course of action in sexual matters, free from the intrusions of the state and the strongly held views of other persons in their community. Contraception and abortion, medically safe and legally available, make it possible for people to choose to separate the reproductive functions of sexuality from the enormously important nonreproductive functions of sexual intimacy. The great story here is how the Supreme Court, finding a zone of privacy embedded in the Constitution though not specifically described there, developed a legally rich area of constitutionally protected rights to control one's own reproduction. One branch of this law involves contraception, initially for married couples in the precedent-setting case *Griswold* v. *Connecticut* [381 U.S. 479 (1965)], then for the unmarried, minors, and members of the public purchasing contraceptives in a drug store or supermarket without a doctor's prescription.

The other branch of constitutional doctrine, the right of women to control their own bodies and their own reproduction through abortion, involved the landmark case of *Roe* v. *Wade* [410 U.S. 113 (1973)] and the many cases that followed it. Legal and other commentary is abundant. Some states, including New York, had made abortion legal prior to *Roe* v. *Wade,* by legislative action or judicial decision. With the current Supreme Court inclined to abandon or drastically restrict the effects of the *Roe* decision, some have predicted that the abortion debate will move to state legislatures. Law in action in this area requires attention to the decreasing availability of legal abortion because of economic factors (e.g., exclusion from Medicaid coverage) and other restrictions.

Another source of legal and political controversy has been RU486/PG, a pill (RU486) that when taken in conjunction with the administration of prostaglandin (PG) produces abortion in early pregnancy. In use in France, RU486 was blocked from importation into the United States. The RU486/PG technology could have important practical effects in some cases as an alternative to abortion by more conventional surgical means.

Marriage and Divorce

In *Griswold* v. *Connecticut*, the Supreme Court said that marriage is a relationship "intimate to the degree of being sacred," that the statute barring physicians from prescribing birth control devices for married people is unconstitutional, and that there is a "zone of privacy" within marriage immune to legal regulation. The Court in *Loving* v. *Virginia* [388 U.S. 1 (1967)] called marriage "one of the 'basic civil rights of man,' fundamental to our very existence and survival" and held that a statute prohibiting miscegenation (interracial marriage) was unconstitutional. Yet another leading case in the area of marriage and divorce, *Orr* v. *Orr* [440 U.S. 268 (1979)] resulted in a Supreme Court ruling that alimony statutes must apply equally to women and men and that an Alabama law requiring only husbands to pay alimony upon divorce was unconstitutional.

Historically, the element of fault played a great role in the grounds for divorce. The defendant husband or wife had to be found guilty of wrongful conduct (e.g., adultery), and the plaintiff seeking divorce had to be seen as completely innocent. Divorce grounds were liberalized from the 1930s onward to include, in some states, cruelty and desertion. The role of fault in enabling one to obtain a divorce, and in determining property division and eligibility for alimony upon the dissolution of a marriage, has drastically decreased. Most states, but not all, now have some version of the "no-fault" divorce introduced in California in 1970. This type of divorce bases marital dissolution on a breakdown of the marriage because of irreconcilable differences, with fault irrelevant. Many states also have included living separately and apart for a specified period—for example, under the terms of a separation agreement (a private contract)—as grounds for divorce.

Broad changes in divorce and marital property law have been based on notions of equality between men and women. Such laws have sometimes reflected the idea of marriage as an economic partnership, with the assets of that partnership to be divided either equally (50-50) or equitably (shares apportioned to each depending on need and fairness) when the marriage is dissolved by divorce. Research has shown, however, that as actually administered by the courts, no-fault divorce has too often resulted in an economically poor outcome for women and children, rather than the fairer outcome that the formal terms of the law promised.

Law Concerning Homosexuality

This topic has been discussed previously in connection with the enforcement-of-morals debate and the legislative initiatives (successful in a number of states) to decriminalize same-sex sexual contacts. Likewise, gay male literature has been involved in the battles for freedom of expression concerning obscenity. On another front, coerced psychiatric hospitalization of gay youths is less likely now because of changes in both psychiatric views and mental health law.

Test cases in court as well as attempts at statutory change in the past decade have produced mixed results with respect to a wide range of legal matters involving homosexuals, among them child custody and visitation, guardianship, employment bias, and domestic partnership. In an innovative 1988 decision involving rent-controlled housing, New York's highest court developed a broadened definition of "family" to include a tenant's gay male life partner. The great disappointment for gay rights activists was the Supreme Court's refusal, in a 5-to-4 decision, in 1986, to strike down a Georgia statute criminalizing sodomy (i.e., oral-genital or anal-genital contact) as applied to consenting adult males acting in private. The complexities of legal doctrine relevant to homosexuality, including equal protection of the laws and the scope of a constitutional right to privacy, have received extensive commentary.

Many gay men, and a smaller number of lesbians, were pulled from their separate communities to serve together as draftees or volunteer recruits in the U.S. military forces during World War II, though the military had, and still has, official legal policies against homosexuality. A recent report, commissioned by the U.S. Department of Defense, states that social-science data fail to show any sound basis for excluding homosexuals from the military.

AIDS (acquired immune deficiency syndrome) in the United States has disproportionately affected gay men. The legal ramifications of this epidemic extend to confidentiality of medical records, communicable-disease reporting laws, employment discrimination, and many other issues. From a law-in-action perspective, a centrally important part of the picture has been the slow and reluctant action of government, especially at the federal level, to deal with AIDS as a problem of disease and public health rather than as a moral issue to be handled through condemnation and denial.

Sex Research and Sex Therapy

It is often forgotten today that the famous Kinsey research reports contained strong commentary on unrealistic and unenforceable sex laws. As Kinsey and his coauthors wrote in 1948, "On a specific calculation of our data, it may be stated that at least 85 percent of the younger male population could be convicted as sex offenders if law enforcement officials were as efficient as most people expect them to be." These reports also mentioned the lack of legal confidentiality of research records and said that the authors had decided to go to jail, if necessary, rather than reveal the private information contained in their carefully coded files. They spoke also of a scientist's right to investigate (akin to academic freedom) and the ordinary individual's right to know what it is that the researcher has learned about sex, as well as about any other matter. The Kinsey Reports had enormous consequences with respect to informing Americans about existing patterns and variations in sexual behavior. They showed also that population-based sex research can be a powerful lever not only for increased understanding but also for social change. In the late 1980s, federally sponsored studies of sexuality, which might have updated the Kinsey findings, were blocked on political grounds.

The fact that Masters and Johnson, the other famous American sex researchers, have successfully avoided legal obstacles to their research concerning human sexual response has in important part been a result of their careful cultivation of understanding and support among key individuals in their community. An issue relevant to the work of Masters and Johnson is that the legal status of surrogate partners in sex therapy remains unclear. In some metropolitan areas, sex surrogates have made efforts to educate law-enforcement officials about the difference between their work and activities that may be defined by law as prostitution. Some might say that the thing to do is immediately to seek to make the law clear, whether concerning sexual surrogacy (i.e., employment of a paid sex partner trained to assist in sex therapy) or observational studies of paid research subjects involved in sexual activities. The great problem is the complexity of social and legal ambivalence concerning sex. Key

public officials may tolerate the unpublicized activities of a few sex surrogates whose work they see as connected with therapy and as arguably helpful. Many of those same officials, if required to take a public stance, would feel it politically necessary to view such activities with alarm.

Child Sexual Abuse

In the late 19th century, adult female patients reported to Sigmund Freud childhood sexual interactions with their fathers. Freud, the primary author of the psychoanalytic movement, eventually chose to interpret these reports as fantasies, not as accounts of real events. During the past 25 years, much attention has been paid to the topic of sexual acts with and sexual touching of children and adolescents by adults or older siblings. Part but not all of this problem area centers on incest, that is, sexual acts with children by a close blood relative, especially the father. Nevertheless, a small number of highly publicized cases have involved criminal prosecutions for sexual abuse of children in day-care or preschool facilities.

Legal responses to what has now become defined as an important social problem have included mandatory reporting laws, civil proceedings concerning child abuse or neglect, removal of the child from the home and placement in foster care, and criminal prosecutions. Other responses have included changes in the legal rules of procedure and evidence in both criminal and civil cases, changes aimed at better protecting the interests of the child and at aiding successful prosecution of these cases. In the area of legal arrangements for social services, specialized child-protection investigation units have been set up. Mandatory child-mistreatment reporting laws, which came into existence in the mid-1960s, have been broadened and strengthened. Congress in 1974 passed the Child Abuse Prevention and Treatment Act, which laid down important requirements that state laws and programs would have to meet to preserve eligibility for federal funds.

The subject of sexual exploitation of children enrages many members of the public as few, if any, other current issues do. If success in dealing with a social and legal problem were measured by the intensity of the emotion generated, sexual exploitation of children clearly would involve our society's most successful problem-solving effort. Concern about the well-being of children has led specialists to make broad assertions that "kids don't lie." Reporting laws, resulting in mandatory investigations by public authorities, are aimed at the level of mere suspicion, as in instances of "reasonable cause to suspect" child abuse or maltreatment.

The problem is highly complex. On the one hand, there are the privacy of the family and protection from undue intrusion by the state. These issues encompass respect for the rights of parents, as well as respect for the interest of the child in having his or her relationship with other family members be free from legal disruption. Society's interests in due process of law and the protection of the rights of accused persons, especially in criminal proceedings, are also highly important. On the other hand, there is great concern about protecting children or adolescents who may be helpless to protect themselves against parents or strangers unless public authorities intervene. Moreover, many realize that ordinary criminal and civil rules, generally aimed at protecting individual rights and family privacy, may not be enough to provide protection in what are suspected to be a large number of cases of child sexual abuse. A result is the great tendency to bend the rules and to close one's eyes to the fact that, especially with very young children, there is no truly dependable way to know what if anything has happened by way of sexual mistreatment.

It can be argued that the administration of well-meaning child sexual abuse laws has had important negative consequences. Child witnesses have been repeatedly interviewed, and then examined and cross-examined in court, about events that may or may not have happened months or years previously. Whatever happened before, trauma resulting from the interview process and the legal proceedings seems highly likely. Understandably, many youths are torn by what they see as the disruption of their family. Children removed from their homes have suffered emotional harm and even abuse when placed in foster care or institutional settings. False charges of sexual abuse made by a vindictive spouse are now thought to be a familiar feature of many custody proceedings. The vulnerability of adults to false or mistaken reports about "bad touching" has created a guardedness among many adult relatives and recreation workers that cannot be constructive for children.

We have relatively little dependable knowledge about the lasting effects of the sexual interactions of parents, other adults, or older siblings with children and adolescents, nor do we know much about the multiple effects of legal interventions. It has not been the custom to tolerate or encourage extensive population-based research on sexuality, leaving aside the landmark Kinsey

Reports. The areas of childhood sexuality, intrafamilial sex, and adult-child sexual contact are especially taboo as research subjects. A prominent exception is the publication of wrenching stories of self-identified victims of incest or other sexual mistreatment. These accounts should spur more systematic research. Nevertheless, enough is already known to suggest certain legal changes. For example, statutes requiring that any pedophile or other child abuser who voluntarily seeks treatment must immediately be reported to the authorities probably defeats preventive aims.

Teenage Sexual Behavior and the Law

An extensive background exists of sociological and legal fascination with problems related to the sexually active adolescent girl. A main problem, as socially viewed, was preventing her from getting pregnant. The risk was seen to be her personal waywardness and maladjustment, and the remedy sometimes was confinement in an institution by order of a court such as the juvenile court or a special adolescent court. The legal characterization used was juvenile delinquent, wayward minor, person in need of supervision, and so on. The girl was unable to become pregnant, so the rationale went, while locked up, under court order, often in a facility operated under religious auspices. Over the past 25 years, changes in juvenile law, availability of oral contraceptives, and changing attitudes about sexuality seem to have substantially decreased enthusiasm for legal recourse to imprisonment as a means of birth control.

There have been due-process changes in mental health law, as well as changes in psychiatric thinking, that now make it unlikely that youths will be committed to a mental hospital by their parents because of either homosexuality or overt heterosexuality. Prior to the mid 1970s, psychiatric hospitalization on the basis of parental request was one of the devices available for controlling nonstandard teenage sexual behavior. Contraceptives and (in most states) abortions are now, in theory at least, legally available to teenagers without parental consent.

Transsexuals

Relatively little law exists concerning transsexuals. Sex-reassignment surgery is regarded as being within the practice of medicine. Some laws provide for a change of sex on the birth certificate following a sex reassignment. In 1976, a New Jersey court, in a very well reasoned opinion, upheld the validity of a marriage involving a male-to-female postoperative transsexual.

REFERENCES

Clark, H.H., Jr. *The Law of Domestic Relations in the United States*. 2d ed. St. Paul: West, 1988.

De Grazia, E. *Girls Lean Back Everywhere: The Law of Obscenity and the Assault on Genius*. New York: Random House, 1992.

Developments in the Law—Sexual Orientation and the Law. *Harvard Law Review*, Vol. 102 (May 1989), pp. 1508–1671.

Devlin, P. *The Enforcement of Morals*. Oxford: Oxford Univ. Press, 1959.

Eberle, P., and S. Eberle. *The Politics of Child Abuse*. Secaucus, N.J.: Lyle Stuart, 1986.

Friedman, S.E. *Sex Law: A Legal Sourcebook on Critical Sexual Issues for the Non-Lawyer*. Jefferson, N.C.: McFarland, 1990.

Green, R. *Sexual Science and the Law*. Cambridge: Harvard Univ. Press, 1992.

Hafner, D. 1992 Report Card on the States: Sexual Rights in America. *SIECUS Report*, Vol. 20 (Feb.–Mar. 1992), pp. 1–7.

Hart, H.L.A. *Law, Liberty and Morality*. Stanford, Calif.: Stanford Univ. Press, 1963.

Kinsey, A.C., W.B. Pomeroy, and C.E. Martin. *Sexual Behavior in the Human Male*. Philadelphia: Saunders, 1948.

Kinsey, A.C., W.B. Pomeroy, C.E. Martin, and P.H. Gebhard. *Sexual Behavior in the Human Female*. Philadelphia: Saunders, 1953.

Mohr, R. *Gays/Justice: A Study of Ethics, Society, and Law*. New York: Columbia Univ. Press, 1988.

Money, J. *Venuses Penuses*. Buffalo, N.Y.: Prometheus Books, 1986.

Nowak, J.E., and R.D. Rotunda. *Constitutional Law*. 4th ed. St. Paul: West, 1991.

Posner, R.A. *Sex and Reason*. Cambridge: Harvard Univ. Press, 1992.

Schur, E.M. *Crimes Without Victims*. Englewood Cliffs, N.J.: Prentice-Hall, 1965.

Shilts, R. *And the Band Played On: Politics, People and the AIDS Epidemic*. New York: St. Martin's Press, 1987; Penguin Books, 1988.

Slovenko, R., ed. *Sexual Behavior and the Law*. Springfield, Ill.: Charles C. Thomas, 1965.

Stein, T.J. *Child Welfare and the Law*. New York: Longman, 1991.

Tribe, L.H. *American Constitutional Law*. 2d ed. Mineola, N.Y.: Foundation Press, 1988.

United Kingdom. Home Office. *Report of the Committee on Homosexual Offences and Prostitution*. Cmnd. 247. 1957. (Wolfenden Report)

Weitzman, L.J. *The Divorce Revolution*. New York: The Free Press, 1985.

Louis H. Swartz

LEARNING THEORIES AND SEXUALITY

Learning theorists begin with the fundamental assumption that most human behavior is dramatically influenced by learning processes. Learning may occur directly through classical conditioning and instrumental or operant conditioning. Learning may also occur through observational learning and instruction.

Simply stated, classical conditioning is based on the foundation that certain responses (reflexes) occur naturally, without learning, in reaction to specific stimuli. These are labeled unconditioned responses and unconditioned stimuli, respectively. When another stimulus is paired with or linked to an unconditioned stimulus, it has the potential to become a conditioned stimulus, that is, a stimulus that can evoke the same (or similar) response as the unconditioned stimulus. When the response is elicited by the conditioned stimulus, rather than the unconditioned one, it is called a conditioned response. The classic example of classical conditioning is that provided by Pavlov, who demonstrated that by repeatedly pairing the onset of a buzzer with the onset of feeding, dogs learned to salivate in the presence of the buzzer alone. Food, the unconditioned stimulus, naturally elicits salivation. When food was paired with the buzzer, the buzzer became a conditioned stimulus, capable of eliciting salivation. Thus, salivation to the buzzer alone was the conditioned or learned response. Classical conditioning is based on this type of association.

Instrumental or operant conditioning is based on the principle that behavior is influenced by its consequences. Specifically, an action, or operation, followed by pleasant consequences (positive reinforcement) or the removal of aversive consequences (negative reinforcement) is more likely to reoccur. Conversely, action followed by aversive consequences or punishment is less likely to occur again.

Learning theorists emphasize that it is important to distinguish between learning and performance. That which has been learned may or may not be performed, depending on the expectation of the consequence: reward or punishment. Thus, to a degree, it can be argued that learning itself is largely a matter of associating or linking a stimulus with a response, whereas performance of a learned response is a function of its anticipated consequences.

Learning theorists also assert that learning may occur through instruction and by observing the actions of others, or modeling. Often these forms of learning are called social learning because they involve at least indirect interaction with others, but classical conditioning and operant conditioning may be social learning as well, in that in many instances the stimuli for these types of learning are other humans. Thus, the distinction between social learning and conditioning is not very useful today. People learn directly as a result of their own behavior and more indirectly by observing the behavior of others and by being instructed by others. Either may be social learning.

Historically, the more direct and behavioristic approaches to learning tended to view the learner as relatively passive in the process, more or less a pawn to the habits of conditioning, to be moved about the chessboard of life by the consequences of behavior. In contrast to the behaviorists were the phenomenologists or cognitive theorists, who argued that the learner was an active participant in learning through the processes of perception and cognition. Although some writers still distinguish between the learning and cognitive approaches, today there is widespread integration of the two approaches and nearly universal recognition of the role of social cognition in human behavior. Occasionally, however, the distinction is still made. Usually, it is made either for historical reasons or to emphasize the relevance of principles of learning, on the one hand, or principles of perception and cognition, on the other hand, to the specific behavior under discussion.

The work of Bandura has been particularly significant in this emergent integration. In the 1960s, he acknowledged the importance of classical and instrumental conditioning to social behavior, but he also asserted that the role of observational learning was critical to understanding a wide range of human behaviors. With colleagues, he conducted hundreds of investigations demonstrating the process of observational learning and illuminating the underlying mechanisms of it. Then, by the late 1970s, he began to expand his theory to encompass many more cognitive variables as well. With his concept of reciprocal determinism, he identifies the continuous interaction among personal, situational, and behavioral factors. It is not uncommon today for some theorists to refer to themselves as social-cognitive, developmental theorists. This self-reference reflects their belief that understanding human behavior requires understanding the interactions among the biological, social or situational, and cognitive or personal factors.

In spite of the fact that early scholarly, albeit mostly pseudoscientific, efforts to understand sexuality were dominated by medical–biological models and emphasized the pathological or deviant aspects of sexuality, the role of experience/learning was acknowledged even in these earliest analyses. Writers such as Tissot and Krafft-Ebing,

although assuming the existence of a natural, biologically predetermined "correct" sexuality, recognized that some of what they considered to be sexual deviations and diseases resulted from the experience of the individuals. This realization led to their strong prohibition of behaviors such as masturbation. Havelock Ellis, in his seven volumes about sexuality published at the end of the 19th and beginning of the 20th century, was strongly biological in his thinking about the causes of sexuality, including variations in sexuality, but also clearly recognized the importance of sexual experience in shaping sexuality. Perhaps Freud, as surprising as it may seem, really opened the door to the application of principles of learning to understanding sexuality. Although Freud believed that basic sexual motivation and the stages of psychosexual development were deemed innately determined, an individual's personality, including his or her sexuality, was significantly influenced by the interaction between these innate developmental forces and the socialization experiences of early childhood. Even though the emphasis was on what could go wrong and produce abnormality, as compared to the learning required for development to be normal, the concept represented, nonetheless, an integration of learning into the matrix in a very explicit way.

Few of the early learning theorists devoted attention to sexuality, but Watson, a key figure in early behaviorism, collected data early in the 20th century concerning physiological sexual responses. Although he did not apply learning theory to his analyses of sexual behavior in any systematic way, Kinsey and his colleagues certainly stressed the importance of learning and experience in understanding the many aspects of sexuality he described in the two volumes published in the late 1940s and early 1950s. Also, quite early in his work, Bandura wrote about the relevance of social learning to sexuality topics. Today, nearly all psychologists and sociologists apply principles of learning in their efforts to analyze the variations among individuals in their beliefs about, their attitudes toward, and their experiences of sexuality (i.e., their sexual behavior).

Perhaps the theorists who have made the most concerted effort to link learning theory directly to an explanation of human sexuality are Gagnon and Simon. Applying their script theory to sexuality, they assert that there is no biological sex drive or instinct; instead, even sexual motivation is learned. They argue that the domain of meaning and conduct called sexuality is accumulated through social learning. Although they acknowledge the importance of the biological foundations of sexuality in setting the capacities for and the limits to what is possible sexually, the role of the sociocultural influences is viewed as critical to understanding individual and group variations. A sexual script is a rough plan, or guideline, providing answers to the questions about what to do, with whom to do it, how often, when, where, and even why. They argue that the answers to these questions are learned through a continuous process of learning: learning that is both direct and indirect and includes classical and operant conditioning, observational learning, and instruction. It occurs in a specific cultural context. From this perspective, Simon and Gagnon, and other social-cognitive theorists, explain both the commonalities and the differences in the sexuality of individuals and groups, including issues of sex differences, sexual orientations, sexual variations, and sexual dysfunctions.

Inspection of the empirical literature concerning sexuality published over the past decade or so in the major sexuality journals, such as the *Journal of Sex Research* and *Archives of Sexual Behavior*, reveals that the dominant theoretical foundation for the hypotheses being tested is a social-cognitive, learning foundation. The work of Byrne and Fisher and their colleagues in the area of contraceptive behavior, and the work of Mosher and his colleagues concerning sex guilt and other personality dimensions of sexuality, are good illustrations.

Learning principles also have been widely applied in the treatment of sexual problems or dysfunctions. Although organic factors clearly are important in understanding sexual functioning and are at the root of many forms of sexual dysfunction, most authorities believe that the majority of sexual problems are primarily psychological in nature. Numerous forms of sexual counseling and therapy have evolved since Masters and Johnson first described their program in 1970. The Masters and Johnson program is behavioristic. That is, the focus is on extinguishing old behaviors that have caused or are the problem and learning new, desired, or successful behaviors. The focus is not on extensive or indepth psychotherapy. Others, such as Kaplan, combine more intensive psychotherapy with behavioral methods. Virtually all treatment approaches except those that rely on surgery, hormone therapy, or the use of drugs apply principles of learning in their method of treatment.

REFERENCES

Bandura, A. *Social Foundations of Thought and Action: A Social Cognitive Theory*. Englewood Cliffs, N.J.: Prentice-Hall, 1986.

————. *Social Learning Theory*. Englewood Cliffs, N.J.: Prentice-Hall, 1977.

Bandura, A., and R.H. Walters. *Social Learning and Personality Development*. New York: Holt, Rinehart & Winston, 1963.

Byrne, D., and L. Schulte. Personality Dispositions as Mediators of Sexual Responses. *Annual Review of Sex Research*, Vol. 1 (1990), pp. 93–117.

Byrne, D., and W.A. Fisher, eds. *Adolescents, Sex, and Contraception*. Hillsdale, N.J.: Erlbaum, 1983.

Ellis, H.H. *Studies in the Psychology of Sex*. 7 vols. 1896–1928. Reprint. 2 vols. New York: Random House, 1942.

Gagnon, J.H. *Human Sexualities*. Glenview, Ill.: Scott, Foresman, 1977.

Gagnon, J.H., and W. Simon. *Sexual Conduct: The Social Sources of Human Sexuality*. Chicago: Aldine, 1973.

Kaplan, H.S. *Disorders of Sexual Desire*. New York: Brunner/Mazel, 1979.

Kinsey, A.C., W. Pomeroy, and C. Martin. *Sexual Behavior in the Human Male*. Philadelphia: Saunders, 1948.

Kinsey, A.C., W. Pomeroy, C. Martin, and P. Gebhard. *Sexual Behavior in the Human Female*. Philadelphia: Saunders, 1953.

Krafft-Ebing, R. von. *Psychopathis Sexualis*. 1886. Reprint. London: Staples, 1965.

Magoun, H.W. John Watson and the Study of Human Sexual Behavior. *Journal of Sex Research*, Vol. 17 (1981), pp. 368–78.

Masters, W.H., and V.E. Johnson. *Human Sexual Inadequacy*. Boston: Little, Brown, 1970.

Mosher, D.L. Revised Mosher Guilt Inventory. In C.M. Davis, W.L. Yarber, and S.L. Davis, eds. *Sexuality-Related Measures: A Compendium*. Lake Mills, Iowa: Graphic, 1988.

————. A Three-Dimensional Theory of Depth of Involvement in Human Sexual Response. *Journal of Sex Research*, Vol. 16 (1980), pp. 1–42.

Mosher, D.L., and S.S. Tomkins. Scripting the Macho Man: Hypermasculine Socialization and Enculturation. *Journal of Sex Research*, Vol. 25 (1988), pp. 60–84.

Tissot, S.A. *Onanism, or, A Treatise upon the Disorders Produced by Masturbation*. Translated by A. Hume. London: J. Pridden, 1766.

Clive M. Davis
Sandra L. Davis
Tara Anthony
Suzanne L. Osman

LEHFELDT, HANS

Hans Lehfeldt was a link between the sexological movement in Germany and that in the United States. Born October 28, 1899, in Berlin, he was drafted into the German army shortly after he enrolled as a medical student in Berlin in 1917. Due to abdominal postoperative herniations (caused by a childhood perforated appendix, which had resulted in general peritonitis), he was found fit only for "garrison service" and assigned to a post near the university. This allowed him to gain early admission to the premedical test and enabled him to return to fulltime study as soon as the war ended. After reading about Margaret Sanger and her struggle for birth control, he decided to specialize in obstetrics and gynecology.

This decision posed some problems, since it was difficult for a Jewish physician to enter this specialty, but Lehfeldt was finally accepted into the clinic of Erwin Kehrer, provided he took further training in surgery and pathology. Lehfeldt's training was briefly interrupted when Kehrer became involved in a political controversy with the leftist government of Saxony; Kehrer resigned and his assistants were dispersed. Ultimately, however, the controversy was resolved, and Lehfeldt finished his specialty training at Dresden in 1928. His interest in contraception led him to be introduced to Norman Haire, an Australian gynecologist who practiced in London, and he became a close friend of Haire's. In 1928, Lehfeldt, through his contacts with Haire, presented a paper at the Congress of the World League for Sexual Reform in Copenhagen, where he met the Americans Margaret Sanger, Hannah and Abraham Stone, Harry Benjamin, and William Robinson. The League was formally organized at this conference, with Magnus Hirschfeld, Havelock Ellis, and August Forel as copresidents. Later, when Sanger appeared in Berlin with Ernst Graefenberg, Hans Lehfeldt discussed Graefenberg's paper on the intrauterine device (IUD). One result of this discussion was the founding of a contraceptive clinic by Hans Lehfeldt, Franz Hirsch, and Felix A. Theilhaber in Berlin in 1928.

In 1935, Lehfeldt emigrated to the United States, where he began practicing obstetrics and gynecology. In 1958, he founded and directed the Family Planning Clinic of Bellevue Hospital, the first such clinic at a municipal hospital in the United States. He also began meeting with an informal group in the late 1950s, an activity that in 1960 led to the founding of the Society for the Scientific Study of Sex (SSSS), which he later served as president. He was a strong advocate of the cervical cap as a contraceptive device rather than the Mensinga diaphragm, which became standard in the Planned Parenthood clinics in the United States. He was also important in organizing a conference on the potentialities of IUDs and was an early advocate of abortion rights. Lehfeldt continued to do research and to lecture at New York University on contraception. There is an award established in his name by the SSSS. Lehfelt died June 18, 1993.

Connie Christine Wheeler
(interview with Hans Lehfeldt)

LESBIANISM

A dynamic sexual orientation, lesbianism is a preference a woman has for sex with women and a self-identification that goes beyond sex. The word "lesbian" (*Webster's*: of or relating to Lesbos) derives from the name of the Mediterranean island birthplace of Sappho, a lyrically intense poet of the sixth century B.C.E. Sappho ran a school for girls which included participating in worship of the goddess Aphrodite. From her surviving poetry it appears Sappho had sexuoerotic relationships with women. As a result, "Sapphic" sometimes is understood to refer to an erotic relationship between women. The 19th-century American transcendentalist Margaret Fuller thought Sappho's name had universally "threadbare celebrity." The contemporary lesbian-feminist poet Judy Grahn sees Sappho at the end of an ancient lineage of great female poets. As many poets, including H.D., have drawn inspiration from Sappho, her influence continues. In 1927, the woman's club activist Alice Ames Winter wrote that for many, Sappho symbolized uncontrolled womanhood and that any martyrdom came ex post facto.

At least as far back as the ancient Hebrews, commentators assumed two women together could do nothing sexually. For 2,000 years, jurists and ecclesiastics did not believe they would do anything. Medieval courts seldom had cases involving sex between women, and English common law did not forbid it. Words seemingly failed lawmakers in reference to lesbianism, a result of their presumptions about women's susceptibility to suggestions about lesbian "crimes." Vivien W. Ng found more mercy extended to lesbians than to homosexual men after the Chinese state made consensual sodomy a felony in 1740. Notwithstanding appearances of leniency in 16th-century England, France, and Spain toward "the silent sin," punishment for lesbianism—otherwise reserved for heresy and, later, treason—could be burning at the stake. In the English colonies in America, unchaste conduct between women largely went unobserved but might be inconsistently punished. In Virginia in 1776, Thomas Jefferson unsuccessfully recommended as punishment for sodomy piercing a woman's nasal cartilage instead of executing her.

The Dutch republic, in the period 1792–1798 recorded five court cases in which 12 women were charged with "foul sodomical behavior." The evil of lesbianism was pronounced from France to the United States by late-19th- to mid-20th-century writers.

Lesbian sexuality is a legitimate analytical category, but it defies characterization in relation to heterosexuality as a central referent. Not only does lesbian sexuality relate women to women, but it may also function as a psychologism, that is, tending to rupture heterosexist constructions of reality and open a path to a different understanding of female existence. In his intellectual history of sexuality, Michel Foucault describes growth in 19th-century sexual discourse that created new categories of sexuality but Foucault had no value called "gender"; consequently, his work is of limited utility in reconstructing lesbianism's history. Lacking the category "gender," one might rest content with the description—for example, of certain early-19th-century physicians' notes that treated as abnormal reports by women patients of intense orgasms due to stimulation of what has become known as the Graefenberg spot. Lesbian self-reports of sexual practices prompted contemporary rediscovery of the spot.

To describe the demographics of lesbianism accurately would be difficult, as self-disclosure by a lesbian risks a socially stigmatized identity, and this imposes limits on the coming-out process. Existing research is biased in favor of Western, relatively high-income, educated white constituencies. One self-selected sample of readers of *Out/Look* (1990), offspring of left-wing American parents, suggests that although lesbian women come out later than homosexual men, 50 percent of the respondents recognized by age 14 their sexual feelings toward individuals of the same sex. A survey of 81 lesbians from a midwestern city has demonstrated a relationship between their feminism and their psychological health, as well as differing paths to identity development. A 1987 study found that for most respondents powerful affective or social connections with women elicited awareness of their sexual orientation. It now generally is agreed that unsatisfactory or harmful relationships with men are not a factor in the orientation.

Such findings may reflect on polygamous societies, which have a high incidence of lesbianism because the basis for women's social reality is other women. Women with hearing impairments or developmental disabilities, in segregated institutional settings, have a high probability of same-sex sexual relations, with high rates of precursor intimacy occurring in segregated residences. A holocaust survivor reports that such relationships developed by the hundreds among women in the camps. As a founder of the Lesbian Herstory Archives in New York City, Joan Nestle, has suggested, lesbianism is no accident.

Paula Gunn Allen describes lesbianism among aboriginal American women in a spiritual context, with these relations presenting a principle of right action for primary relationships in the tribe. Paradoxically, Mary Wollstonecraft in *The Rights of Women* (1790) looked disapprovingly on young women's "bad habits" in English boarding schools but approvingly on a celibate homoerotic friendship in *Mary, A Fiction* (1788). Romantic, sensual, virtuous friendships flowered openly among middle-class women in England, France, Germany, and the United States from the 16th to the 18th centuries. Faderman's view is that the early-19th-century feminist movement brought out women's sexual potential with women. A 1990 study shows friendship to be a significant factor in long-term relationships among U.S. lesbians.

Except on its own terms, lesbian behavior cannot be understood adequately. A Buffalo, New York–based study of lesbians in the 1950s found that the butch-femme roles to present the lesbian to the heterosexual community were relatively inflexible. There were other models however. Respondents to a 1960 survey in *The Ladder* emphasized choice, autonomy, and self-development as among the reasons they were lesbians. A 1990 study of 70 U.S. lesbian couples showed that they do not take traditional gender roles but espoused an egalitarian ideal, some 45 percent reported sharing power.

A 1987 lesbian parenting anthology finds that parenthood for women couples is nothing new, but increased visibility and opportunities to define it are. Pregnancy can be stressful for a lesbian couple; possible problems range from the lengthy period it may take to conceive to jealousy. Several observers have described lesbian communities as currently undergoing a baby boom. Some lesbians have turned to in vitro fertilization, others to adoption, but most lesbians who want children rely on artificial insemination. Jokes about turkey basters are in vogue. However, serious issues remain. Legally, the non-birth mother in general seems not to have enforceable claims to the child, although two-mother as well as single-mother households constitute a legitimate family structure. Disputing custody with a heterosexual person, a lesbian parent may prevail 50 percent or more of the time: outcomes are not predicted readily nor are they necessarily rational. Judges have awarded custody to grandparents rather than to a lesbian parent, and have justified denials with homophobic attitudes about AIDS (acquired immune deficiency syndrome). Organizations such as the Lesbian Mothers National Defense Fund seek solutions to the many problems.

Lesbian sex therapist JoAnn Loulan has written that "lesbians are passionate people." Sixty percent or more of San Francisco–based lesbian respondents to a 1976 Institute for Sex Research survey saw themselves as wholly oriented toward lesbianism. Ethnicity made no difference. The women appeared to have fewer problems than men in accepting a homosexual orientation. Loulan's San Francisco–based study (1987) found 35 percent of lesbians having sex two to five times per month, with 12 percent of them never having sex and 14 percent having it eleven or more times. Over four-fifths of the respondents were orgasmic; 52 percent reported themselves fairly well or completely satisfied with their sex life. Lesbian couples apparently are less sexually active than heterosexual or gay male couples, with activity said to decline after two years. These couples may not be egalitarian when it comes to initiating or deciding how frequently they will have sex; however, Davis and Kennedy have argued that 40 years ago, leadership in initiation was "authentically lesbian interaction" and not imitative of heterosexuality.

Conflict emerged in the 1970s over whether to reconceptualize "lesbian" to describe women-identified women. Adrienne Rich found lesbianism to echo an experiential range, not confined to sex, that heterosexually constructed reality had made unspeakable; the array involves a choice of self and could include motivation toward political action. Recent research has validated the psychologically affirming aspects of an openly lesbian identification and the prepolitical implications of structuring lesbian community. Apropos of Rich's argument for the introduction of cross-cultural context across history, impulses toward organization have been present in diverse settings, such as early-20th-century settlement houses and 1950s Buffalo bar culture. Lesbians founded the Daughters of Bilitis in 1955 to create a secure structure for coming out, and women in the Mattachine Society felt compelled to address women's issues. Today there is a Lesbian Mothers Union.

Political action has extended into coalitions, peak associations, and other forums. The late Audre Lorde has characterized black lesbian and gay struggles as including bonds with Africans and people of African descent in America, Eu-

rope, and Asia; in a *Signs* interview in 1981, she spoke of "skills and joint defenses." In 1975, the National Organization for Women's national convention authorized spending 1 percent of a $1 million budget on behalf of lesbians. The National Women's Conference in Houston in 1977 took the problems society imposes on lesbians as fit matter for resolution.

Clearly, a lesbian continuum exists. A slide and tape presentation sponsored by the San Francisco Lesbian and Gay History Project in 1979, "She Even Chewed Tobacco," documented growth in lesbian identity among working-class women in the 20th century. A spring 1991 exhibition, "Keepin' On," based on photographs, assembled by the Lesbian Herstory Archives, of African-American lesbians primarily from Harlem in this century has helped establish continuity in these women's lives. Transhistorical documentation of lesbianism locates lesbians in relationship to lesbians, and establishes lesbians as self-defining people with an ethnography and a potential for developing explicitly pluralistic values.

REFERENCES

Bernard, M. *Sappho: A New Translation.* Berkeley: Univ. of California Press, 1958.

Blackwood, E. Breaking the Mirror: The Construction of "Lesbianism" and Anthropological Discourse on Homosexuality. *Journal of Homosexuality,* Vol. 11 (Summer 1985), pp. 1–17.

Brown, J.C. Lesbian Sexuality in Medieval and Early Modern Europe. In M.B. Duberman, M. Vicinus, and G. Chauncey, Jr., eds. *Hidden from History: Reclaiming the Gay and Lesbian Past.* New York: New American Library, 1989.

Bullough, V.L. *Sexual Variance in Society and History.* New York: John Wiley & Sons, 1976.

Davis, M., and E.L. Kennedy. Oral History and the Study of Sexuality in the Lesbian Community: Buffalo, New York, 1940–1960. In M.B. Duberman, M. Vicinus, and G. Chauncey, Jr., eds. *Hidden from History: Reclaiming the Gay and Lesbian Past.* New York: New American Library, 1989.

Everard, M. Lesbian History: A History of Change and Disparity. *Journal of Homosexuality,* Vol. 12 (May 1986), pp. 123–37.

Faderman L. *Surpassing the Love of Men: Romantic Friendship and Love Between Women from the Renaissance to the Present.* New York: William Morrow, 1981.

Hitchens, D. Social Attitudes, Legal Standards, and Personal Trauma in Child Custody Cases. In D.C. Knutson, ed. *Homosexuality and the Law.* New York: Haworth Press, 1980.

Hoaglund, S.L. *Lesbian Ethics: Towards New Value.* Palo Alto, Calif.: Institute of Lesbian Studies, 1989.

McCandlisch, B.M. Therapeutic Issues with Lesbian Couples. *Journal of Homosexuality*, Vol. 16 (1988), pp. 263–307.

Reilly, M.E., and J.M. Lynch. Power-Sharing in Lesbian Relationships. *Journal of Homosexuality*, Vol. 19 (1990), pp. 1–30.

Rich, A. It is the Lesbian in Us. . . . *On Lies, Secrets, and Silences: Selected Prose, 1966–1978.* New York: W.W. Norton, 1979.

Sarah Slavin

LIEF, HAROLD

Harold Lief, born December 29, 1917, is a psychiatrist and an eminent sex therapist. He received his M.D. from New York University in 1942. From 1948 through 1951, Lief was an assistant physician at Columbia Presbyterian Hospital in New York City and a psychiatrist in private practice. In 1951, Lief started teaching psychiatry at Tulane University. He is currently professor emeritus at the University of Pennsylvania and a physician at the University of Pennsylvania Hospital.

Lief's greatest contribution was the introduction of sexuality education in medical schools. In 1960, only three U.S. medical schools offered formal sex-education programs, while in 1984 ninety percent of medical schools included them in their curriculum. From 1969 to 1981, Lief worked in the Center for Study of Sexuality Education in Medicine, was director of the Division of Family Studies at the University of Pennsylvania, and was director of the Marriage Council of Philadelphia.

During the same period, Lief developed important training programs in sex therapy and in sex education for health professionals, noteworthy among which was Lief's and Reed's 1972 Sex Knowledge and Attitude Test (SKAT), a scale used widely in universities and medical schools for gathering information on students' sexual attitudes, knowledge, and experiences. In 1990, Lief, Fullard, and Devlin expanded SKAT to create SKAT-A, which measures adolescent sexual knowledge, attitudes, and behavior, and SERT-A, which measures sexual risk-taking among adolescents.

Lief has written and edited numerous papers and journals, including his well-known Sexual Medicine Series, the first volume of which (1984) consisted of research papers from the World Congress of Sexology. He was also on the editorial boards of *Medical Aspects of Human Sexuality, Journal of Sex Education and Therapy*, and *Contemporary Sexuality*.

Lief has been a dedicated member and officer of many professional organizations. He was president (1968) of the Sex Information and Education Council of the United States, vice president of the World Association of Sexology, and fellow of the Society for the Scientific Study of Sex (SSSS). He received the SSSS Award for Distinguished Scientific Achievement and the 1982 Award for Outstanding Contributions to the Field of Human Sexuality.

REFERENCES

Lief, H., W. Fullard, and S. Devlin. A New Measure of Adolescent Sexuality: SKAT-A. *Journal of Sex Education and Therapy*, Vol. 16 (1990), pp. 79–91.

Lief, H., and Z. Hoch, eds. *International Research on Sexology.* New York: Praeger, 1984.

Lief, H., and D. Reed. Sexual Knowledge and Attitudes Test. Philadelphia: Univ. of Pennsylvania Press, 1972.

Leah Cahan Schaefer

LIMERENCE

This term, not yet found in most dictionaries, was coined by Tennov to refer to the unique and sometimes unpleasant combination of love, attraction, lust, anxiety, depression, and elation that often accompanies sexual erotic interest in another person. In short, it is what many people refer to as lovesickness. It is not sexual frustration but an all-encompassing emotional state in which one person is completely preoccupied by another person's every act and state and is oblivious to most other concerns.

In much of the Western world, limerence is often considered a normal and perhaps inevitable consequence of sexual attraction, but some individuals never experience it. There may well be individuals who are limerence prone. It is most likely to occur when there is a combination of sexual and erotic attraction plus unclear or paradoxical communication in which the desired partner sends messages that perhaps mean that interest might be reciprocated. It is the uncertainty of the response, not the sexual and erotic attraction itself, that generates limerence. Limerence only rarely cures itself, although time may well help. Many therapists argue that it can and should be treated psychotherapeutically, because a limerent individual can otherwise be crippled emotionally by a pattern of repeated anxiety, preoccupation bordering on obsession, and depression alternating with elation. It sometimes turns out that the individual who has stimulated the limerence is aware of his or her effect and enjoys the power it gives over the other person. Often, the limerent individual may decide to withdraw from the afflicted individual entirely.

Full-scale limerence almost never develops if the two individuals are mutually attracted to each other, but only when the interest is one-sided and communication is opaque. It is not a new phenomenon: Hippocrates spoke of it as a disease of the young, and during the medieval period lovesickness was often defined as a disease. In English, it is often referred to as unrequited love. It may well have a physiological basis, and it certainly is a major component of love poetry and popular songs as well as fiction.

REFERENCES

Money, J. *Love and Love Sickness*. Baltimore: Johns Hopkins Univ. Press, 1980.

Tennov, D. *Love and Limerence: The Experience of Being in Love*. New York: Stein & Day, 1979.

Vern L. Bullough

LITERATURE: EROTIC THEMES

In describing literature historically and cross-culturally, the term is here used broadly to include fiction and nonfiction, essays, short stories, drama, and poetry. In short, addressed is a selection of writings that have stood the test of time and have maintained some distinction among scholars and the reading public.

The Ancient World: Eastern Culture

The novel form is thought by some Eurocentric writers to date to some four or five centuries ago, but it can be traced approximately 1,000 years back to a fictional work written by a Japanese courtesan. There is little doubt that similar works existed then or earlier, but they have not survived. Many different styles and attitudes are reflected in literature across cultures and through time—everything from the delicately subtle but quite candid descriptions of the erotic reflected in classic Chinese novels of the 15th century, to the straightforward yet artful sacred writings of India, notably in Kama Sutra, which represents a high sense of the aesthetic and a worshipful yet worldly view of sexuality. These works, and others across the Eastern world, including Japan, may have served a variety of purposes, but all had in common the educative role they played as sex manuals, or "pillow books" as they were called in Japan. Here we see the enmeshment of the sacred with the earthly noted by historians such as Bullough in his *Sexual Variance in Society and History*.

Lest one overemphasize the basically sex-positive view reflected in the writings of Eastern cultures, Foucault, in *The Uses of Pleasure*, draws attention to the anxiety about coitus occasioned not by prudery but by concern for the consequences of overindulgence both for physical health and for the spirit. This concern was shared by Chinese culture, in which relationships between men and women were viewed as a struggle between opposites. There was a special concern evoked by a perceived threat of depletion of energy, culminating in death without "honorable" descendants. Ancient Chinese and Japanese sexual themes in literature frequently addressed the dangers of unregulated sexual activity and its attendant destruction of potency. At the same time, the literature of these ancient cultures strongly endorsed moderation in sexual activity so that such dangers could be avoided and one's health and youthful vitality could be enhanced. Thus, there was also a strong emphasis on sexual pleasure, often through prolonged sexual activity and the postponement of orgasm.

The Ancient World: Greece and Rome

The Greeks and Romans were agrarian peoples. There was a sharp division between the roles of men and women. In ancient Greece, as in some isolated Greek rural areas of today, the woman's role was as wife, mother, and helpmate. Men, by contrast, were free to seek satisfaction outside the home, including homosexual pleasures. In ancient Greece, romantic love was viewed as interfering with reason and unsuitable as a basis for marriage. Still, sexual pleasure was seen in the context of other worldly satisfactions and as a sufficient goal unto itself. Sex did not necessarily have to be procreative, nor did it have to be heterosexual. Greek citizens were great admirers of beauty as an aesthetic value in all things. It was usual to be aesthetically attracted to those of either sex. Further, men customarily formed a mentor-protégé relationship with pubescent or postpubescent boys. These close associations frequently and normally included homosexual behavior. This practice was not customary among consenting adult males, however, unless there was no access to other sexual outlets. The relative availability of slaves of both sexes resulted in sexual exploitation of that group. Greek males were in essence frequently bisexual. Individuals were not categorized as to sexual preference, though unrestrained passions of whatever kind were discouraged, as were other worldly excesses. The ideal was to lead a self-disciplined life, albeit a sensually full one, within the confines of moderation. An aesthetically beautiful and ethically pleasing life was a commonly agreed-upon goal.

The Greek poet Sappho of Lesbos, born ca. 600 B.C.E., was a well-respected poet among the citizens of her time; she was not singled out as a "lesbian" poet, as so often is the case today. Greeks made no such distinctions. Plutarch and Lucian also speak of the existence of homoeroticism among Greek women of the time. Artistic representations of both male and female genitalia were prevalent; they were not, as is often the case today, a medium for titillation or an occasion for disgust, but were depicted with reverence. Greeks viewed their bodies as a whole, aesthetically diffuse as to beauty and sexuality. Their literature does not mention sadomasochism, and they appear not to have recognized as "perverseness" such practices as bestiality. Greek erotic life was generally uninhibited and free of many of the proscriptions of the later Western world. Themes of incest and homosexuality are represented in Greek mythology, for example in connection with the god Zeus, who is shown as having multiple partners and as bisexual. Representing an incestuous theme, Aphrodite was married to one half-brother while enamored of another; when the pair were discovered, they were a source of amusement for the other gods. It is noteworthy that while Greeks made sport of their gods' sexual antics, in a religious sense the same gods were treated with reverence. The duality of sexuality was reflected in the self-indulgent pleasures of the centaurs, associated with degradation and ultimately death, as contrasted to the playful, harmless satyrs. Ancient Greek literature treated the male sex organ as an object of worship, as part of religious life. Later, in Roman Pompeii, for example, phallic images were used as warnings of dire consequences to thieves or other intruders.

Greek drama is replete with erotic themes. Sophocles' tragedy *Oedipus* illustrates the dangers of incestuous love between parent and child. Reflective of the restraints placed on Greek women, comedies often had as their theme conflict between the sexes, notably in *Lysistrata*, in which the women withhold sex until their men agree to stop fighting.

Unlike the later Christian world, the world of the ancient Greeks did not separate physical from nonphysical love, the body from the spirit. The major prohibitive theme of that time was the admonition against unbridled appetites of all sorts, including sexual passions.

Roman culture, while it began as agrarian, grew to encompass a pluralistic empire spanning vast stretches of the known world and enduring for more than 400 years after Christ's birth. As in Greek culture, phallic symbolism continued to occupy a central role in religion and in other spheres of Roman culture. It was from Greek mythology and from Roman views of sex in opposition to death that Freud later was to refine many of his ideas concerning eros and thanatos and to take the name of King Oedipus to signify the sexual attraction between son and mother. In Roman literature, Ovid's *Art of Love* was a guide to those who wished to evoke the sexual passions of the objects of their desire. Ovid, along with other Roman writers such as Virgil, viewed sex and love with a cynical eye and saw women as seductive and manipulative. Roman literature later influenced the work of English writers, including the comedies of William Shakespeare. In the playful tone reflected in Ovid's *Amores*, one can see parallels to Shakespeare's sexual humor:

> Your husband? Going to the same dinner as
>   us?
> I hope it chokes him.
> So I'm only to gaze at you, darling? Play
>   gooseberry
> while another man enjoys your touch?

As was not the case in Greek custom, Roman women were granted a good bit of independence as history progressed. Though virginity was valued, it was prized not for its own sake but for the practical reason that monogamous behavior was expected of married women. Roman men, by contrast, were accorded considerable sexual freedom. Men did not have to be monogamous, but they were to avoid involvement with other men's wives. Prostitution was accepted among poorer Roman women. The sexual, including homosexuality, appears to have been accepted as natural in Roman life. A number of emperors were homosexual or bisexual in their life-styles. The excesses of Roman sexual life, especially of the later era, were decidedly at odds with the moderation and self-control so central to the values of earlier Greek culture.

The Ancient World: Hebrews and Christians

For the early Israelites, a nomadic people, sexual intercourse was highly valued. Though most forms of sex that could not lead to procreation were discouraged, the frequent Christian obsession equating sex with guilt and sin was absent. After the exile to Babylon, sexual mores reflected that more secular culture, resulting in an elevation of legal codes as an important influence. At the same time, women came to be blamed for leading men astray. The Fall in the Old Testament originally had been attributed to man's hubris. This view now became supplanted by the vision of "woman as temptress," as a potentially dangerous influence who must be confined to the home.

Despite signs of increased suppression in some areas of life, there was a celebration of the erotic, as in the Song of Solomon (Song of Songs) in the Old Testament of the Bible:

> How beautiful are thy feet with shoes,
> O prince's daughter! The joints of thy
>   thighs are like jewels, the work of the
>   hands of a cunning workman.
> Thy navel is like a round goblet, which
>   wanteth not liquor: thy belly is like
>   an heap of wheat set about with lilies.
> Thy two breasts are like two young roses
>   that are twins. (Song of Sol. 7:1–3)

While a number of biblical scholars have insisted that these verses are mere metaphors for the love between humans and God, there seems to be little doubt about the earthy, unbridled celebration of fleshly erotic pleasure they describe. The Song of Songs, in its entirety, seems to culminate in joyous coitus.

Unlike much of Christianity, ancient Judaic writings reflect a society in which a man is obligated to pleasure his wife. It had strict laws describing a husband's conjugal obligation: at least once a month for camel drivers, once a week for donkey drivers, and every day for scholars and men of leisure.

The Qur'an similarly places great importance on sexuality in marriage, prescribing that men should approach their wives "when and how you will." In contrast to Hebrew culture, however, there appears to have been more same-sex coupling, perhaps because of the strict segregation of the sexes. Indeed, homosexuality appears to have been a source of some hilarity, as reflected in a number of Arabic writings.

While Jews had purification rites by law, exemplified by cleansing rituals after menstruation and childbirth, the ancient Hebrews were markedly positive about lawful sexual practices. There has been considerable misinterpretation of their prohibitions against sexual practices that could not lead to reproduction. Today's scholars generally agree that these prohibitions were not established as a response to prudery, but rather because of the vital importance of lawful marriage and reproduction for members of this ancient people.

Following the First Exile, some of the attendant pessimism of that time negatively influenced sexual attitudes among some Hebrews. This tendency was reflected in later Talmudic codes and in the sexual attitudes of early Christian converts from Judaism.

Foucault rejects the commonly held notion of a "Judaic-Christian" morality or of rigorously fixed laws governing sexual behavior. The apostle Paul was a major influence in shaping early Christian attitudes about sexual issues. Until the appearance of the New Testament, around 300 C.E., much of early Christianity was strongly affected by the Old Testament writings of the ancient Hebrews. Judaic law dominated Christianity until Roman law became the norm after Constantine.

Influenced by early Stoic philosophers who stressed asceticism, early Christians took up the concept of sex as sinful and to be tolerated, even in marriage, solely for the needs of procreation. This sex-negative asceticism pervaded much of Christianity for some centuries. Vestiges may still be found among some individuals of the Catholic faith today. Later, St. Augustine was to act as a negative influence on Catholic teachings about sexuality. His prohibitive influence was to extend to some branches of Protestantism as well. Echoing the Stoics, Christians highly prized virginity and abstinence. Contraception and nonreproductive sex were strongly prohibited. It was Augustine who firmly linked sexuality and Original Sin. The only "right" sex came to be married sex, with its goal of reproduction.

The Middle Ages

The Church remained the major force in a medieval Europe of widespread superstition, ignorance, and plague, where penitents roamed an increasingly unstable and unpredictable world. Monasteries were virtually the sole repositories of learned writings in the early Middle Ages, and they were generally unsympathetic to preserving materials of an erotic nature. Despite this, some wits among the monks saw fit to hide sexual imagery in the brilliant illuminations framing the manuscripts they so painstakingly copied.

Among the major secular writers somewhat later in the period were Dante Alighieri (1265–1321) and Boccaccio (1313–1375) in Italy and, in England, Geoffrey Chaucer (ca. 1342–1400). In Dante's work, the sadomasochistic imagery of remote and unattainable love objects is readily apparent. At the same time, by the late Middle Ages the troubadours' worship of the presumably untouchable noblewoman established an ideal of romantic love that has found an audience in Western culture to this day.

Existing side-by-side with the literature of courtly love, Chaucer's *Canterbury Tales* reveals another side of the period, an aspect of playfulness and cynicism not unlike that reflected in the poetry of Ovid and others much earlier. Chaucer gives a lighthearted treatment to cuckoldry in his "Prologue" to "The Miller's Tale." Pondering the question of whether one is a cuckold, the miller says:

> I may myself, for ought I know, be one.
> I'll certainly believe that I am none.
> A husband mustn't be curious for his life,
> About God's secrets or about his wife.
> If she gives him plenty and he's in the clover,
> No need to worry about what's left over.

This passage echoes the common medieval theme of the cuckolded husband, often getting what he deserves.

At the same time, the Church maintained its central role. In his vastly influential 13th-century writings, St. Thomas Aquinas attempted to address virtually all possible forms of proscribed sexual behavior. Given the repressiveness of Church teachings, medieval sexuality not infrequently evoked hysterical imaginings, sometimes thought to be special signs of grace. Some deeply religious females dreamed of Christ's visitation upon them in very worldly images of sexual ecstasy.

The Renaissance, the Reformation, the Restoration, and the 18th-Century Romantics

As the Western world moved from the Medieval world into the modern era, the celebration of the sexual emerged once more. At times, women fell victim to roving bands of young men. In Italy during the late Middle Ages and early modern periods, decadence not seen since later Roman times was not unheard of. One thinks of accounts of the noblemen of Florence and their consorts, or of cloaked and masked Venetian men and women in gondolas, slipping through the canals. The excitement of the era was heightened by the knowledge that rogues risked discovery and possible death at the hand of an outraged husband or father. The Italian lyric poet Petrarch (1304–1374), who lived for a time in Venice, speaks of the raptures of worldly love, as in the following passage from his poem "It Was the Morning":

> I feel a captive, Lady, to the sway
> Of your swift eyes: that seemed no time to
> stay
> The strokes of Love: I stepped into the snare

> Secure, with no suspicion: then and there
> I found my cue in man's most tragic play.
> Love caught me naked to his shaft, his sheaf,
> The entrance for his ambush and surprise
> Against the heart wide open through the eyes.

Typical of Renaissance imagery, Petrarch's references to the physical aspects of passion are not difficult to find.

Somewhat later, in France, the writings of François Rabelais (ca. 1483–1553) reflected an earthier view of sexual acts. Rabelais and others often dealt with comedic scatological references equally applicable to both sexes. An example can be found in Rabelais' account, in *Gargantua and Pantagruel*, of "How Ponacrates gave Gargantua such instruction that not an hour of the day was wasted":

> Gargantua awoke at about four in the morning. While the servants massaged him, he would listen to some page of Holy Scripture, read aloud in clear tones and pronounced with fitting respect for the text. . . .
>
> Next, he would repair to secret places to make excretion of his natural digestions; here his tutor repeated what had been read, expanding on its more obscure and difficult features. (Bk. I, chap. 23)

In as natural a vein, though slightly later, Montaigne (1533–1592), in his *Essays*, would address his own sexual behavior as he did any other day-to-day matter. Pascal later remarked on Montaigne's propensity to speak altogether too much of himself.

In the Renaissance England of Edmund Spenser (1552–1599), we see a relaxing of sexual mores observed earlier in Chaucer. Here, as on the Continent, there was evidence enough of license even among members of the clergy. *The Fairie Queene* is an extensive work, in which sexuality is addressed. We see in this poem sexually assertive and sometimes dangerous women, under whose spell men's strength may be sapped. Describing the "Bower of Bliss," Spenser shows a dialectic view of nature and of women as both seductive and dangerous, as in the following passage from *The Fairie Queene*:

> There, whence that musick seemèd heard to
> bee,
> Was the faire witch her selfe now solacing,
> With a new lover, whom through sorceree
> And witchcraft, she from farre did thither
> bring;
> There she had him now layd a slombering,
> In secret shade, after long wanton joyes.

It is not surprising that at about the time of Spenser, the openness of the Renaissance was giving way to strong censure by the Church and by some of the general public. At this time, by papal order, some of the nude figures in Michelangelo's fresco "The Last Judgment" were painted over with makeshift swathes of cloth covering their genitals.

However, repression was not part of the imagery of the poems and plays created by William Shakespeare (1564–1616). Sex was never again to be censored completely. Derivative of Spenser's imagery of the dangers of unbridled passion, a painstakingly detailed account of a sexual assault on an innocent woman is given in Shakespeare's poem *The Rape of Lucrece:*

> Her breasts like ivory globes circled with blue,
>   a pair of maiden world unconquered.

Elsewhere, for example in his comedies *The Taming of the Shrew* and *The History of Troilus and Cressida,* Shakespeare evokes the ribald, playful aspects of sex. This was an age in which sexuality could still serve as a cause for humor, in a worldly way not expressed since the Middle Ages.

The Reformation saw the advance of Puritanism both in England and in the colonies, particularly in Puritan New England. (Even so, there is some evidence of sexual themes in American Puritan poetry of the time.) No American writer has captured more eloquently the repression of that time than Nathaniel Hawthorne (1804–1864). *The Scarlet Letter*'s Hester Prynne is held up to ridicule in her New England Puritan community because of her adulterous affair with a man who heretofore had been a "pillar" of the community; their liaison results in an illegitimate child. Hester, as much as the elaborately embroidered scarlet "A" on the breast of her garment, becomes the focal point for all the scorn and hysteria of a sexually repressed citizenry.

Puritan Calvinism conveyed a strong sense of sex as dangerous, as a procreative necessity that must not give way to unbridled passion even among married couples. It was not sex alone that received disapproval, but also unrestrained joy or playfulness in any sphere of daily life. Vestiges of this jaundiced view of human pleasure can still be found in pockets of New England and, indeed, in the "Bible Belt" of today's United States.

In the 18th century, the middle class served as the primary exemplar of prudery. This attitude was by no means pervasive among the well educated, however. Reflecting the emphasis on the "rational" at this time, John Dryden (1631–1700) wrote in a "Song" from *Marriage à la Mode:*

> Why should a foolish marriage vow,
> Which long ago was made,
> Oblige us to each other now,
> When passion is decayed?

The growing emphasis on reason is reflected to a degree also by Alexander Pope (1688–1744) in *The Rape of the Lock,* in which he counsels a philosophical view of life between men and women, with an acceptance of its inevitable tensions. In a much lighter vein, John Cleland's *Fanny Hill: Memoirs of a Woman of Pleasure* (1748) is still widely regarded as the quintessence of unbridled, and perhaps coarse, sexuality in the English language. No doubt Cleland's novel served as an influence on later frankly bawdy writings.

All together, no period in the history of the written word seems more multifaceted or more widely diverse than the 18th century. This variety reflects the competing political, philosophical, and religious factions of that time of rapid social change.

The Romantic period was a time of upheaval, with the shift away from agrarian society in England and elsewhere, the independence of the American colonies, and the advent of the French Revolution. The term "Romanticism" is often used simplistically by those who are drawn to the literature of that period. In fact, it was a time of widely diverse views, political and otherwise. Writers of the time did not think of themselves as "Romantic." Political and industrial revolution was an abiding theme, and through it all there seems to have been a sense of high energy and great change.

Romantic literature reflects a new interest in emotion and in the value of personal experience. This differed markedly from the elevation of the rational during the Enlightenment. Natural objects came to be viewed symbolically, especially in the writings of such poets as William Blake (1757–1827) and Percy Bysshe Shelley (1792–1822). Despite the unsettled times, much of their writing and that of their counterparts has a sense of the breaking of boundaries. Some of the mood of the time is captured in William Wordsworth's (1770–1850) poem "The Tables Turned":

> Enough of Science and of Art;
> Close up those barren leaves;
> Come forth, and bring with you a heart
> That watches and receives.

France's Jean-Jacques Rousseau (1712–1778) was to depict nature as gentle, with none of the danger perceived by later French writers such as Sade (1740–1814). Some of Sade's writings were direct refutations of Rousseau's overly optimistic view both of nature and of man's relation to it. Sade's writings undoubtedly influenced Freud and others, but they are conspicuously absent in many university curricula today. It has been postulated that liberals are repulsed by his amorality and feminists by his explicit and violent sexuality.

In this period, another Romantic poet, George Gordon, Lord Byron (1788–1824), presented a quite different approach: he deals rather directly with the sexual, including themes of male feminization and incest, as in the case of the effeminate pageboy Kaled in *Lara*. In *Don Juan* he depicts the seductive protagonist as a "most beauteous boy," with Don Juan entering a harem in the guise of a young woman.

Exotic themes similar to those evoked by Byron are found later in the works of Edgar Allan Poe (1809–1849) in America and, more extremely, in the imagery of Sade. Balzac (1799–1850) too, echoed Byron in his androgynous female character (patterned after George Sand) in *Lost Illusions*. All the writers who drew on themes similar to Byron's paved the way for the fascination with the bizarre found later in the Gothic fiction of Poe, Hawthorne, and Emily Brontë. In Germany, Goethe (1749–1832), wrote of sexual ambiguity in the *Sorrows of Young Werther* (1774): Werther recoils from what he sees as the sordidness of male adulthood, retreating into adolescent emotionality and androgyny.

Victorians and the Late Romantics

While sexual repression and hypocrisy reached new heights at this time, particularly in England and the United States, it would be simplistic and historically incorrect to view all of 19th-century life and literature as falling within this dimension. Some writers, such as Robert Browning (1812–1889), resorted to symbolism to mask sexual themes. Rarely is this more evident than in the second verse of his poem "The Last Ride Together":

> The blood replenished in me again;
> My last thought was at least not in vain:
> I and my mistress, side by side
> Shall be together, breathe and ride
> So, one day more am I deified.
> Who knows but the world may end tonight?

Themes of adultery were also found in 19th-century writings, notably in France, in Flaubert's *Madame Bovary* (1857), and in Russia, in Tolstoy's *Anna Karenina* (1875–77). In the United States, Nathaniel Hawthorne echoed this theme in *The Scarlet Letter* (1850).

During this era, a cult emanating from Oxford flourished, one that involved perhaps not altogether platonic worship of prepubescent and pubescent girls. It was notably represented by Charles Lutwidge Dodgson (1832–1898), who wrote his *Alice* books under the nom de plume Lewis Carroll; and Ernest Dowson (1867–1900), author of the famous lines, "I have been faithful to thee, Cynara! in my fashion."

The majority of Victorian culture was sexually repressed, and repressive, during much of this time, and legal censorship was a growing practice. Even the legs of pianos might be covered with scarves so as not to engender erotic thoughts. There was a concerted effort to protect the "purity" of women and children. In the Victorian period, in contrast to the Middle Ages or the Puritan era, repression was driven not so much by the established church as by the pressures of self-appointed "watchdog" groups. These pressure groups were not unlike the politically motivated censorship movements of the latter part of the 20th century, when fundamentalist reactionaries and factions of the women's movement (perhaps motivated to affect a facade of prudery because of their efforts to de-objectify women) found themselves as strikingly curious political bedfellows.

In the 19th century, a good number of the well-educated ruling classes ignored some of the stricter conventions of the time, as did the lower classes, who had more urgent battles to fight. One gifted upper-class, Irish-born writer of the time did not escape the censorious wrath of the public and the legal system. Oscar Wilde (1854–1900) unwisely brought a libel suit against the Marquis of Queensberry, who had publicly accused him of homosexuality. Despite his high educational and class status, he lost his case in the English courts and was sentenced to a brief but difficult prison term. He wrote the *Ballad of Reading Gaol* and *De Profundis* in response to his prison experience. Later, Wilde lived anonymously in Paris, where he died in poverty. To this day, Wilde's work evokes a homophobic response from some, and his writings are omitted from the curricula of certain universities and colleges with fundamentalist religious ties.

The Norwegian dramatist Henrik Ibsen (1828–1906), much ahead of his time, dealt with themes of women's struggles to break the oppressive bonds of male domination, as in the case of Nora in *The Doll's House*. American writers of the era also reflected the several themes of Victorian culture. Among these was the poet Emily Dickinson (1830–1886), given little notice while she lived and today often treated with sentimentality and oversimplicity. Her "sentimental" inclinations may more accurately be seen from the perspective of another, darker side: Paglia observes that "the brutality of this belle of Amherst would stop a truck."

Modern Literature

Among novelists writing at the beginning of the 20th century, themes of decadence, evoking Byronic Romanticism, reappeared. Turn-of-the-century German art and literature was increasingly inclined toward a view of the world as decadent. This outlook is clearly demonstrated in Thomas Mann's *Death in Venice* (1912), with its images of the longing of a German artist for a lovely Polish boy while languishing in Venice. The artist's passion for the boy, whom he simply wishes to watch from a distance, finally reduces the man to a dyed and rouged caricature. He stays far too long in plague-ridden Venice, a city of ruin that serves as a metaphor for the decadence and decay Mann saw in his time.

Meanwhile in the United States, there existed an increasingly urbanized and depersonalized working class, as in Theodore Dreiser's *An American Tragedy* (1925). Here, a young man of promise is destroyed not by the untouchable and beautiful, but by a shabby fling with a young working woman. Indeed, both are brought down in this overwritten but socially revealing novel. Dreiser's *Sister Carrie* with its central "fallen woman" theme is an even more compelling example and was suppressed by its publisher at the time for "immorality." Around this time and somewhat after, Henry James (1843–1916) and Edith Wharton (1862–1937) wrote of a different America, one of privilege and oppressive custom. Henry James addressed "social suffocation" in *The Bostonians*, in which two strikingly different suitors—one a somewhat older feminist lesbian, the other an attractive but dominant heterosexual young man—vie for the heart (and mind) of a young "lady."

By contrast with James, Wharton's writings are refreshingly free of tentative phrasing. Gore Vidal points out, in his introduction to *The Edith Wharton Omnibus*, that "spades got called spades" in Edith Wharton's novels; as a result, she saw herself as ever at war with "editorial timidity." Like James, she found life abroad more congenial. As an intelligent upper-class woman, she enjoyed a much freer life in Paris, where other intellectuals would not only acknowledge but also admire her gifts and where she had no need to worry about offending "a non-existent clergyman in the Mississippi valley." She writes quite openly, in her short story "New Year's Day," of

a character recalling an adulterous affair in which upper-class lovers used to meet at an upper East Side hotel. An elderly man responds, "They might meet in the middle of *Fifth Avenue* nowadays, for all that anybody cares." Still, the dominant repression of middle-class Victorian England and America persisted well into the 20th century.

The agent provocateur and preeminent rebel against sexual prudery is Henry Miller (1891–1980), who quite deliberately used rawly explicit sexual description to provoke a response from a sexually repressed culture. He, too, left for Paris, an increasingly popular haven for exiles among the "angry young men" (and women) of the earlier 20th century. It was one of a number of European locales to which James Joyce (1882–1941), arguably the greatest writer of his time, was drawn after leaving his native Ireland.

Of English culture of the time after World War I, the French-born editor and publisher Girodias wrote:

> England was so strongly prudish in those post war years. It seems hard to understand how a whole generation of men who had been through the toughest of wars—and won—could be reduced to the level of schoolchildren, and be told what to read and what not to read by a conglomerate of spinsters and bowler-hatted policemen. [My father was] revolted by the near-hysterical conformism of that society which covered with abuse a man like D.H. Lawrence, (author of *Lady Chatterly's Lover*) and let him be tormented and quartered by the hounds of decency. (pp. 13–14)

Despite the times, especially as experienced in England and America, the most outstanding work of literature containing vivid sexual imagery appeared in Paris in 1922: James Joyce's *Ulysses*. Even those who have never read the whole of this work are aware of the soliloquy Molly Bloom delivers as she drifts toward sleep. She reminisces about the men in her life, collectively referred to as "he" (which heightens the centrality of the sexual in this passage). She ends, as does the book, with the following words:

> And I thought well as well him as another and then I asked him with my eyes to ask again yes and then, he asked me would I yes to say yes my mountain flower and first I put my arms around him yes and drew him down to me so he could feel my breasts all perfume yes and his heart was going like mad and yes I said yes I will Yes.

Before the middle of the century, Ernest Hemingway (1899–1961) was to reflect the angst of the relatively privileged professional class. He wrote in a hypermasculine style, which reflected a threatened male identity. His themes were of the stereotypical primal male figure, whose identity and freedom are under siege by sexually aggressive women. His protagonists must struggle repeatedly to prove to themselves and to others that they have not been symbolically (or in one case, literally) emasculated. Hemingway's misogynist "man's world" imagery was to reappear later in the writings of Norman Mailer (1923–), as in *The Deer Park*. A more furtive struggle to meet the "ideal" definition of contemporary manhood is a repetitive theme in the novels of John Updike (1932–). In the final book of the Rabbit series, Harry Angstrom has become an aging male spending much of his later marital life in a Florida condominium. He struggles both to deny a failing body and to "keep up with" his increasingly self-confident and sexually vital wife. The ascendance of female sexuality and independence, albeit painfully purchased, is an increasingly apparent theme in the writings of both contemporary English and American woman authors, such as Margaret Drabble (1939–), Doris Lessing (1919–), and Joyce Carol Oates (1938–).

Echoes of a recurring theme of decadent Romanticism in 20th-century Anglo-American writers are found in the fiction and in the posthumously published journals of John Cheever (1912–1982). They illuminate his struggles to come to terms both with his feelings about his ambivalent sexual identity and with his alcoholism.

The upheaval of the Great War in the early 20th century accelerated changes in Europe and America, and these changes were reflected in the works of a number of writers of the time—for example, in their treatments of the 1920s. This was a period of gains in women's rights and, with the growing accessibility of the automobile, of relaxation of sexual mores both for the educated classes and, to an extent, for the working classes. The sexual availability and exploitation of working-class women were clearly addressed by Dreiser. By contrast, in F. Scott Fitzgerald's *The Great Gatsby* (1925), Daisy Buchanan, the privileged, narcissistic young woman with whom Gatsby is obsessed, is described as having a very "indiscreet" voice, one that is "filled" with the sound of money. While she, too, suffers psychologically, it is the maltreated wife of a gas station owner whose life is lost when she is run over by the careless Daisy. Later, writers such as Norman Mailer were to rail against the male's struggles with mothers or

mother figures who would try to render males impotent.

Among Latino writers, despite the historical constraints posed by Catholicism in Latin-American countries, the literature of the later decades of the 20th century reflects richness and exuberance. This quality is not unlike the sensuality present in the love of color, ritual, and celebration that is so much a part of Latino life in general. The unrestrained approach to the sexual in some of the writings of Gabriel García Marquéz (1928–) and of the Nobel Prize-winning poet Octavio Paz (1914–) attests to the fullness with which the Latino culture embraces the many emotions of life, including sexual passion. Pablo Neruda (1904–1973) captures the moment with a sensuality, passion, and existential appreciation so untypical of the heritage of Anglo-Saxon writers. His poem "Love" (translated by Alastair Reid) contains a clear illustration of appreciation of the moment:

> Of everything I have seen,
> It's you I want to go on seeing;
> Of everything I've touched,
> It's your flesh I want to go on touching.
> I love your orange laughter.
> I am moved by the sight of you sleeping.

A similarly rich culture of frank and open treatment of sexual themes, both homo- and heteroerotic, has long been represented in the work of African-American men and women, among them such diverse writers as James Baldwin (1924–1987), Maya Angelou (1928–), and Alice Walker (1949–). Typical of the sensuality of African-American poetry is a passage from "Harlem Sweeties," by Langston Hughes (1902–1967):

> Brown sugar lassie,
> Caramel treat,
> Honey-gold baby
> Sweet enough to eat.

Conclusion

In recognition of the late-20th-century anxieties over individual, sexual, and political depersonalization, it seems appropriate to note George Orwell's anticipation of increasing political repression and the erosion of sexual and other individual rights as portrayed in his prescient novel *1984*. This discussion of erotic themes in modern literature ends on a troubling note: the advent of the AIDS (acquired immune deficiency syndrome) epidemic, extending to every part of the world, underscores an already reactionary agenda. Reflecting an additional concern, the Canadian writer Margaret Atwood, in *The Handmaid's Tale*, describes a world in which the sexual is subverted to the will of a theocratic police state and its supporters. Procreation is depicted as an obligation on the part of fertile women, who are kept as virtual slaves to couple with men who are their masters in every sense of the word. Sexual behavior once again is shown as a furtive, mechanical business, to be conducted without disrobing and to be experienced without joy. Abortion is strictly forbidden. While far from the major theme of sexual imagery in literature at the current time, it reflects all too well a world in which self-appointed "others" admonish women, with force if necessary, to play out the role of procreative vessels. The welfare of offspring, once born, is of strikingly little interest to late-20th-century watchdogs of public (and where possible, private) morality. It is within this historical moment that Atwood created her not-altogether-futuristic novel.

REFERENCES

Bullough, V.L. The Christian Inheritance. In V.L. Bullough and J. Brundage, eds. *Sexual Practices and the Medieval Church*. Buffalo, N.Y.: Prometheus Books, 1982.

———. *Sexual Variance in Society and History*. New York: John Wiley & Sons, 1976.

Foucault, M. *The Uses of Pleasure*. New York: Random House, 1985.

Girodias, M., ed. *The Olympia Reader*. New York: Grove Press, 1965.

Kingdon, F. Literature and Sex. In A. Ellis and A. Abarbanel, eds. *The Encyclopedia of Sexual Behavior*. New York: Jason Aronson, 1973.

Paglia, C. *Sexual Personae*. New York: Vintage, 1991.

Veronica Diehl Elias

LOVE AND SEX

Love and sex occupy strangely separate but intermingled positions within the Western tradition of values. Following Plato, the early church drew a fine line between sacred love (agape) and profane love (eros), associating the former with the spirit and the latter with the flesh. The church enshrined and blessed agape as the vehicle by which the soul ascended to heaven, but consigned wanton eros to hell, along with the "vile" body that gave it life. The medieval tradition of courtly love considered it more noble if love were not debased by sexual consummation, and more sensible if sex were not complicated by love. The modern *Playboy* philosophy also separates love from sex, but pays more attention to

the shudder of the loins than the flutter of the heart.

Although a happy concomitance is often observed, love and sex for the individual human being are certainly distinct phenomena that can, and often are, pursued independently. But the position taken here is that love is an evolutionary epiphenomenon of sex that evolved to serve the species, a position taken by Schopenhauer ("Love is a snare set by sex to ensure the survival of the species.") However, love is much more than a simple derivative of sex. Love springs from sex, and thus shares with it a certain oneness of essence, but love pursues an independent existence and, in doing so, elevates and ennobles that from which it sprang.

Our sexual appetites are more than sufficient to ensure plentiful pregnancies, but reproduction alone is not sufficient for the survival of a species whose young experience such a long dependency period. As we ascend the phylogenetic tree, offspring dependency periods become longer and longer, and increasing emotional attachment of mother and offspring is observed.

However, a similar increase in emotional attachment between nonhuman mammalian adult males and females is not observed as we go up the phylogenetic tree. No lovelike affinity is observed among stallions, bulls, or dogs for the last mare, cow, or bitch mated with, and the feeling is mutual. For species with short-lived dependency periods, the only necessary male role is the provision of stud service. Thus, the "love as derivative of sex" proposition is not a general biological principle throughout the entire mammalian kingdom.

An emotional attachment between men and women that is qualitatively different from the frenetic mating of lower species had to evolve, not to simply attract them to one another but also to keep them attached to one another sufficiently long to raise the vulnerable fruits of their passion. Human love in its ideal form is attraction *plus* attachment. Anthropological evidence suggests that infant and child mortality rates among Plio-Pleistocene hominids were very high, and would have risen to levels threatening the survival of the species had not some evolutionary mechanisms been selected into the human repertoire of traits to bond male and female together as a child-rearing team.

The evolution of love probably had a lot to do with the importance of intelligence for our species. Humans are a physically puny species with low fecundity. Such a combination of disabilities would have been disastrous for our hominid ancestors had they been as highly adapted to a particular ecological niche as many species are. The more a species is adapted to a particular niche, the more responses to environmental stimuli are fixed and invariable. In essence, this means that the genes of such a species code for brains with neurons that are "hard wired" (directly and permanently connected) to assure that species members will instinctively pay attention and respond appropriately to aspects of the environment that are vital and ubiquitous.

Because of the vulnerability of our hominid ancestors to predators, they had to depend on guile to survive encounters with them and had to migrate frequently to new environments to avoid them. Hard-wired, fixed responses to stimuli would be counterproductive to organisms inhabiting highly variable environments in which new responses were constantly required. This meant that the genes had to surrender much of their behavioral control of proto-humans to a less rigid and fixed system for determining responses to stimuli—the plastic human brain.

Human infants are developmentally about one year behind most other mammalian infants at birth, and their brain weight triples during the first year. If the human infant were as developmentally precocious as nonhuman mammals, its head would be too large to pass through the birth canal. To accommodate natural selection for increasing human brain size, evolution settled on the strategy of human infants being born at earlier and earlier stages of development.

The helpless infant needs someone to administer to its needs unconditionally. The selfless and unconditional care and regard for another human being is called love. It is during this period of maximum dependency that the infant's brain is quite literally being "wired" (the process of synaptogenesis) by its experiences. Whether or not the neuronal pathways to the pleasure centers are sufficiently strong to enable the organism to love (as opposed to simply copulating) as an adult depends to a great extent on this early experience.

Hormonal and neuronal substrates that cement mother-infant love have been identified. For instance, estradiol lowers the threshold for the firing of nerve fibers in the medial preoptic area of the female brain, an area associated with increased nurturing behavior in females. The male preoptic is insensitive to estradiol. It has been shown that progesterone and estradiol administered artificially to virgin rats will evoke maternal behavior and that oxytocin, released in response to suckling, "intensifies" maternal behavior.

A strong propensity to become emotionally attached to mother and to other care givers who provide food, protection, and a secure base from which to explore the environment has obvious survival value for the young of the species. As a child gets older, we may adequately account for its attachment behavior as a function of its history of operant reinforcement (well-loved children are strongly attached, neglected and maltreated children hardly at all, or maladaptively so). But something a lot more basic than a cognitive appreciation of rewards and punishments must provide the foundation for attachment. A biological system of internal rewards and punishments had to evolve.

The endorphin peptides, the brain's natural opiates, probably provide the chemical foundation of attachment. When an infant is snuggled in mother's arms, its endorphins keep it contented. Separate the infant from its mother and its endorphin levels fall, and levels of the stress hormone cortisol rise, triggering anxiety and crying. It has been shown that only the administration of exogenous endorphins will mollify separated infants in the same way that reunion with mother will.

The intimate link between love and sex has its origins in the primary love bond between mother and infant, which is a function of the long human dependency period, which is in turn the result of evolutionary pressures selecting for intelligence. Two other evolutionary processes—the human female's loss of estrus and the species' gradual development of upright bipedalism—probably also contributed. Females have a large investment in parenthood; males contribute a few pelvic thrusts, after which they can be on their way. Nature had to devise a system by which males could be persuaded to remain with females after copulation to provide food and protection for them and their offspring. Let us be aware that it was the male that nature had to capture in love. Strong evolutionary pressures had already awakened general feelings of attachment in the female by virtue of her motherhood role. These same nascent feelings were also present in the male by virtue of his early attachment to his mother, which he now had to transfer to other females, and sex was the vehicle by which this was accomplished.

We know that most nonhuman mammalian species are sexually receptive only during estrus and are of interest to males only at that time. There was certainly a time in the history of our species when our female ancestors also experienced estrus. Some hominid females must have enjoyed longer periods of sexual receptivity than others. Males would have naturally been more solicitous of such females, providing them with extra food and protection (it is often noted that other primate males are far more attentive and generous to females when they are in estrus). Females enjoying long periods of sexual receptivity would be more likely to survive, as would their offspring. Over time, natural selection would spread the genes for longer receptivity throughout the population, eventually leading to the disappearance of human estrus altogether.

Assuming that natural selection for upright bipedalism was taking place coterminously with the gradual loss of estrus, sight would have largely replaced smell as the impetus to mate. Upright posture in hominids, with genitals now moved more toward the front, led to the uniquely human practice of frontal intercourse. Frontal intercourse involves far more skin contact than the old method of seizing the female from behind and staring off into space. Because of the intimate connection between the skin and the brain, formed as they are in utero by the same layer of tissue, humans find tactile stimulation very pleasurable. Under such conditions, sexual intercourse began more and more to recall the pleasures lovers once found in their mother's arms. The sucking of the lover's breasts; the warmth of skin contact, eye gazing, and nose nuzzling; and the feeling that all is right with the world (the endorphins in action) evoke deep unconscious memories of the mother-infant bond. Frontal intercourse mimicked and capitalized on the primary mother-infant bond and thus elevated the sexual drive above simple genital pleasure.

Frontal intercourse involves more of the human senses than were involved in the impersonality of belly-buttocks coupling. The evolution of intelligence and language enabled lovers to "know" the individual by translating their physical and visual pleasures into words and by naming each other. He or she is no longer simply a set of genitals, but a unique individual who captures and holds the imagination. The imagination allowed our ancestors, as it allows us, to replay previous sexual encounters with their lovers, to anticipate future ones, and to come to value sexual intercourse as the ultimate celebration of love.

Just as there is a chemistry of attachment, there is a chemistry of attraction. When we meet someone with whom we are to fall in love, his or her unique characteristics have an anabolic effect on the hypothalamic-pituitary-gonadal axis. It may be his intellect, power, athletic prowess, accent, or any number of things that sets her axis in motion. For the male, more reactive to visual stimuli, it may be her smile, the silkiness of her skin, or the delightful way her buttocks undulate as she walks.

Our intellectual appreciation of the loved one, combined with information relayed from our senses of sight, hearing, and touch, is processed in the limbic system, the brain's emotional center. The pleasure centers of the limbic system process the flood of information and sends it on to the hypothalamus, the part of the limbic system that, among other things, synthesizes hormones and activates sexual behavior. The excited hypothalamus instructs the pituitary gland to release a peptide called adrenocorticotropin releasing hormone (ACTH). ACTH is then transported through the bloodstream to receptors on the adrenal gland, which then releases a stress-related substance called corticosterone. This substance increases the metabolism of glucose, which results in the classic symptoms of love—flushed skin, sweating, heavy breathing, genital lubrication, and a pounding heart. When this intensely exciting state strikes us, we become different people. Our perceptions are drastically altered, the loved one becomes the center of our universe, the whole world seems to be a better place. Nature has emotionally enriched the human reproductive impulses with love, and in doing so she has immensely increased our enjoyment of both.

If this all sounds very much like a drug-induced high, that's because it is. Stimulant drugs such as cocaine and amphetamine have much the same effect as love's natural high. Whether we fall in love or take a stimulant drug, the upshot is increased limbic system activity in the form of increased neurotransmitter activity and neuroreceptor sensitivity. Nature has chemically wired us to feel good when we do things that encourage species survival: the opiates keep us safely attached as youngsters, and the stimulants excite us when we experience sexual attraction as adults.

There are no known neuroreceptors specific to exogenous stimulants such as the amphetamines. The primary action of amphetamine is to prompt the release of the excitatory catecholamine neurotransmitters such as dopamine and norepinephrine and to block their re-uptake at synaptic terminals. There is evidence suggesting that the stimulant substance that probably mediates our experience of romantic love is a naturally occurring amphetamine-like (and also mildly hallucinogenic) substance called phenylethylamine (PEA). Since amphetamine is the prototype drug of PEA, it is not at all surprising that certain people are at risk of becoming "love junkies." In fact, love addiction has been characterized as the most common form of addiction known. Love addicts flit from person to person, falling in love with love (or more correctly, perhaps, with PEA) rather than with the person. They fall for all kinds of people indiscriminately because the reward is not the attributes of the lover, for he or she simply functions as a PEA-releasing mechanism.

The human connection between sex (attraction) and love (attraction plus attachment) is woman. There is a lot of truth in the aphorism that women give sex to get love and men give love to get sex. There is abundant evidence that women are more deeply embedded in the emotional life than are men. A study by Balzs and Walsh found that love was about 2.8 times more important to women than men. Tarvis and Sadd's study of 100,000 American women found that the most important aspect of sexual activity for women was emotional and "other" oriented rather than physical and "me" oriented. When asked what they enjoyed most about sex, most answered "feeling of closeness to my partner"; followed by "satisfying my partner"; "orgasm" was a distant third. Men tend to view sex as an end in itself, the *product* of which is orgasm, while women tend to view it as a *process* by which emotional closeness is achieved.

Male-female love-sex bonds are to a large extent governed by female reproductive behavior, which is governed by female regard for the survival of her offspring. Mother-infant and male-female bonds are biological; the infant-father bond is a purely human cultural concept. The fusion of these basic bonds became a template for the evolution of ever more complex human relationships and bonds—kinship, family, tribe, and so on up to society itself.

The pivotal figure in the extension of basic biological bonds to cultural bonds is woman, for she is the only figure common to both biological bonds. Such a pivotal figure might be expected to possess some special biological features. It has been suggested that the lesser degree of brain lateralization among women allows them greater verbal access to their emotions than men have. Another neural mechanism that may be involved in female emotionality is the prefrontal cortex. According to MacLean, the prefrontal area evolved in close relationship to the part of the limbic system involved in maternal care. Through its connection with the limbic system, it helps us to empathize, to gain insight into the felt life of others, and to understand it as if it were our own. It is the mechanism that leavens our rationality with feeling and guides our emotions through thought. Chauchard calls the prefrontal brain "the brain of the heart, the organ of love."

Given the close relationship between the prefrontal cortex and those areas of the limbic system involved in maternal care, it is reasonable to assume that the emotional messages arriving from the limbic system will retain more of their power after cortical integration in women than they will in men. In fact, it has been shown experimentally that women enjoy a greater capability than men to integrate pleasurable experiences into the neocortex. This capability may well be a function of the female brain's lesser degree of laterality. Pearsall believes so, and sees the tendency of males to be generally more self-oriented as a function, at least in part, of their left-brain tendency. He views the "whole-brain" tendency of females as producing beings more "other" and "us" oriented, and he also claims that the female orientation to the world is more in tune with the principles of healthy living. The implication is that woman's greater capacity for love, rooted within the limbic system and its associated endocrine processes, is augmented and reinforced within her rational brain, and is thus more capable of wide diffusion.

Conclusion

There was certainly a time in our evolutionary history when love, the active concern for the well-being of another, did not exist. The mating of male and female was all that was necessary for species survival when our distant ancestors slithered around in the primordial mud. Proto-humans became increasingly intelligent as environments became more complicated, and the selection for human intelligence necessitated the selection for human love. The first human love bond was between mother and infant, and nature capitalized on this bond and on the sex drive to develop male-female love bonds.

Sex can be seen as an empirical manifestation of a more fundamental principle that points to, but by no mean exhausts, the "essence" of love. The design of this principle is nothing less than the survival of the human species. Viewed in this larger evolutionary context, love and sex are complementary parts of an inclusive whole. We can connect genitals, and enjoy doing so, without connecting our souls, and we can enjoy the connection of souls without connecting our genitals. But when we connect both we experience the ultimate pleasure that nature has designed for us. As far as we know, we are the only creatures in the universe who can grasp the meaning and joy of love: that love is what we give as well as what we get, and that it is the creative medium by which we and our lovers become more than we ever thought possible.

REFERENCES

Chauchard, P. *Our Need for Love*. New York: P.J. Kennedy, 1968.

Kalil, R.E. Synapse Formation in the Developing Brain. *Scientific American*, Dec. 1989, pp. 76–85.

Konnor, M. *The Tangled Wing*. New York: Holt, Rinehart & Winston, 1982.

Liebowitz, M.R. *The Chemistry of Love*. New York: Berkley, 1984.

Long, M. Visions of a New Faith. *Science Digest*, Vol. 89 (1981), pp. 36–42.

MacLean, P. *A Triune Concept of Brain and Behavior*. Toronto: Univ. of Toronto Press, 1980.

McEwen, B.S. Neural Gonadal Steroid Actions. *Science*, Vol. 211 (1981), pp. 1303–11.

McGuinness, D. Away from Unisex Psychology: Individual Differences in Visual, Sensory and Perceptual Processes. *Perception*, Vol. 5 (1976), pp. 279–94.

Mellen, S. *The Evolution of Love*. San Francisco: W.H. Freeman, 1981.

Montagu, A. *Growing Young*. New York: McGraw-Hill, 1981.

Peele, S., and A. Brodsky. *Love and Addiction*. New York: Signet, 1975.

Pearsall, P. *Superimmunity*. New York: Ballantine Books, 1987.

Rossi, A.S. Parenthood in Transition. In J. Lancaster, et al., eds. *Parenting Across the Lifespan*. New York: Aldine De Gruyter, 1986.

Shaver, P., C. Hazan, and D. Bradshaw. Love and Attachment: The Integration of Three Behavioral Systems. In R. Sternberg and M. Barns, eds. *The Psychology of Love*. New Haven: Yale Univ. Press, 1988.

Tarvis, C., and S. Sadd. *The Redbook Report on Female Sexuality*. New York: Delacorte, 1977.

Walsh, A. Neurophysiology, Motherhood, and the Growth of Love. *Human Mosiac*, Vol. 17 (1983), pp. 51–62.

———. *The Science of Love: Understanding Love and its Effects on Mind and Body*. Buffalo: Prometheus Press, 1991.

Walsh, A., and G.J. Balazs. Love, Sex, and Self-Esteem. *Free Inquiry in Creative Sociology*, Vol. 18 (1990), pp. 37–42.

Wilson, P. *Man, the Promising Primate*. New Haven: Yale Univ. Press, 1980.

Anthony Walsh

LOVEMAPS

Lovemaps is a new sexological term initially coined for classroom lectures in the late 1970s. It was first published in 1981 in an abstract for a conference in Sydney, Australia, and appeared more formally in an encyclopedia article titled "Pairbonding and Limerence," by John Money in 1983. The term was introduced as follows: "Children who grow up together manifest remarkable conformity in the way they speak. There is less conformity in the features of their mental lovemaps. The explanation for nonconformity almost certainly lies in the fact that society forbids overt juvenile age–mate sharing of rehearsals of erotosexualism."

In these three sentences, it is predicated of lovemaps that, like native language, they are not inborn as a finished product; that their formation is contingent on social input in childhood; and that individual nonconformities in their formation are related to the sexology of child rearing. As functional entities, lovemaps exist synchronously in the brain and the mind (the brainmind). They are a product of neither nature nor nurture acting alone but of each in conjunction with the other at a critical developmental period. Then, once formed, lovemaps are typically tenacious and long lasting. The formal definition of lovemap is as follows: "A developmental representation or template in the brain or mind in which is depicted the idealized lover, the idealized love affair, and the idealized program of sexuoerotical activity with that lover, projected in imagery and ideation, or in actual performance."

With respect to sexuoerotical orientation toward a partner, a lovemap may develop so as to be ultimately heterosexual, bisexual, or homosexual. Very rarely, partner orientation is omitted from the lovemap, and it is said to be asexual or anerotic. For the majority of the population, the lovemap is heterosexual, for a minority homosexual, and for an unknown proportion bisexual. By definition, a minority in any population is not statistically average, typical, or normal. However, being statistically nonaverage, atypical, or abnormal does not mean that a minority is, therefore, ideologically abnormal in the stigmatized sense of being undesirable or deviant. It was in recognition of this principle that the American Psychiatric Association in the 1980 revision of its *Diagnostic and Statistical Manual* removed the stigma of deviancy and mental illness from the minority of the population with a homosexual lovemap, and reclassified this minority simply as a minority—just as people with a mental map for left-handedness are a minority. People do not choose or prefer to have a homosexual lovemap, or a heterosexual or a bisexual one. Lovemaps are the outcome of their own combined prenatal and postnatal laws of development—laws that are still in the process of being discovered.

Irrespective of sexuoerotical orientation, if a lovemap forms so as to be other than normophilic, then it may be functionally hypophilic (insufficient), hyperphilic (excessive), or paraphilic (altered). Normophilic might be defined as conforming to the statistical norm. In the United States, however, sexological surveys from which to ascertain the statistical norm are interdicted by the federal government. By default, therefore, normophilic means conforming to an ideological norm. What is ideal in sex, and hence ideal in the lovemap, varies historically and transculturally; for the most part it is imposed by those with more power on those with less. Thus, there are no absolute dividing lines between normophilic and hypophilic or hyperphilic sexuoeroticality, or between normophilic and paraphilic.

Paraphilic sexuoeroticality is known on the street as kinky or deviant sex, and in psychoanalysis and the criminal justice system as perverted. Money's formal definition of paraphilia is as follows:

> A condition occurring in men and women of being compulsively and obligatively fixated on an unusual and personally or socially unacceptable stimulus or scene, which may be experienced perceptually or ideationally and imagistically, as in fantasy or dream, and which is prerequisite to initiation and maintenance of sexuoerotical arousal and the facilitation or attainment of orgasm (from Greek, *para-*, altered, + *philia,* love).

Paraphilic lovemaps and their manifestations in imagery, ideation, and behavior do not, of and by themselves alone, qualify as pathological. They may be playful (ludic), in which case they do not have the tenacious hold of fixation or addiction and are not obsessively and compulsively repetitious in defiance of consequences. In addition, they do not intrude on the inviolacy of the partner, and they are not brutally violent, injurious, or murderous toward the self or others. There are 40-odd lovemaps named for the 40-odd paraphilias listed by Money (1993). The exact number depends on how detailed are the criteria of classification.

In paraphilia, and likewise in hypophilia and hyperphilia, there is a cleavage between love and lust in the design of the lovemap. In hypophilia, the cleavage is such that lust is dysfunctional and infrequently activated, whereas love and lovebonding are intact. In hyperphilia, lust and lustbonding displace love and lovebonding, and the genitalia function in the service of lust alone, typically with a plurality of partners and with compulsive frequency. In paraphilia, love and lovebonding are compromised because the genitalia continue to function in the service of lust, but according to the specifications of a metamorphosed lovemap and often with compulsive frequency also. The redesigned lovemap manifests itself in ideation and fantasy, and in the staging of that fantasy in an actual performance with a partner in lust who is not the same as the partner in affectionate lovebonding.

In response to the neglect, suppression, or traumatization of its normophilic formation, a lovemap develops with paraphilic distortions—namely, omissions, displacements, and inclusions—that would otherwise have no place in it. A paraphilia permits sexuoerotical arousal, genital performance, and orgasm to take place, but only under the aegis, in fantasy or live performance, of the special substitute imagery and ideation of the paraphilia.

A paraphilia is a strategy for turning tragedy into triumph according to the flip-flop principle of opponent-process theory, whereby that which was negative flip-flops to positive. This strategy preserves sinful lust in the lovemap by dissociating it from saintly love.

Sexosophy, the philosophy of sex characteristic of each major religion, influences the childhood development of lovemaps and their paraphilias. The definitive characteristic of the sexosophy of Christendom is the doctrine of the split between saintly love and sinful lust. This doctrine is all-pervasive. It penetrates all the institutions of contemporary Christendom. One way or another, usually quite deviously, it penetrates all our child-rearing practices. Inevitably, therefore, it penetrates the formation of lovemaps in the early years of childhood. That is why the pathological lovemaps of the paraphilias are understandable, developmentally, in saint-and-sinner terms.

It has not hitherto been recognized that very ancient teachings or paleodigms, expressed as religious parables, strategies, or formulas, undergo transformation so as to be scarcely recognizable in their new guise, as in a paraphilia, for example. To understand the significance of religious paleodigms is to open a new universe of discourse in the etiology, treatment, and prevention of sexological as well as other disorders. Paleodigms have ready applicability in pastoral counseling and in designing sexual-learning programs for parents intent on rearing their children so as to maximize the developmental healthiness of their lovemaps.

Paraphilias are not generated at random. They belong to one of seven categories: sacrificial/ expiatory; marauding/predatory; mercantile/venal; fetishistic/talismanic; stigmatic/eligibilic; solicitational/allurative, and subrogational/ understudyship. The 40 or so paraphilias distributed among these six categories have not only an individual or ontogenetic history but also a species or phylogenetic history. There are specific phylogenetic components or phylisms, which may become ontogenetically entrained or recruited into the lovemap as a consequence of a sexologically negative childhood. If that happens, then the childhood development of the lovemap changes from normophilic into paraphilic.

The lovemaps of normophilic people are not identical but, like faces and fingerprints, individually variable in their details. Nonetheless, there are ten general principles, or constants, that lovemaps all over the world share in common:

1. *Age:* Lovemaps specify the ideal partner's age or age range, which may or may not be concordant with one's own age.
2. *Physique:* Lovemaps are typically very detailed in specifying the physical characteristics of the ideal partner, ranging from body build and facial features to eye and hair color, and lightness or darkness of the skin.
3. *Gender:* Lovemaps specify whether the ideal partner will be male or female, or either.
4. *Kinship:* Lovemaps specify whether the ideal partner will or will not be a close or distant member of the same kinship group, irrespective of whether kinship is societally defined according to the criterion of genetic or totemic relatedness or of relatedness through marriage.
5. *Caste or class:* From beginnings early in life, lovemaps incorporate ideals of partner eligibility and exclusion on the criteria (in addition to age, physique, and appearance) of tribe, race, nationality, language, religion, caste, social class, education, occupation, wealth, and health, as well as insignia of group membership, such as the right to wear a uniform.
6. *Number:* Lovemaps incorporate criteria as to whether the number of partners in the course of a lifetime will be none, one, or more.
7. *Overlap:* Lovemaps incorporate strategies for the realization of multiple partnerships as being ideally either concurrent or sequential.
8. *Span:* Lovemaps specify whether multiple partnerships, ideally, will be casual and transient, formal and long lasting, or a combination of both.
9. *Privacy:* Lovemaps specify the degree to which social, courtship, and sexuoerotical interaction with a partner will ideally be chaperoned or unrestricted, and whether it will ideally take place concealed and in private or exposed and in public.
10. *Accessories:* Lovemaps specify the degree to which romantic and sexuoerotical interaction will ideally be straitlaced and prudish or hedonic and emancipated both in scope and in the use of erotic or sexual accessories, including contraception.

The male-female difference in lovemaps has become enmeshed in the outmoded shibboleth of nature versus nurture. The dogma of the contemporary school of social constructionists is that the difference is attributable exclusively to nurture. Constructionism defines its adversary as essentialism and equates it with biology and the medical model.

It is indisputable that the formation of lovemaps in childhood is highly responsive to gender stereotypes and to other social input, both negative and positive. Nonetheless, it is similarly indisputable, notably on the basis of experimental animal evidence, that social input is superimposed on a species-derived (phylogenetic) male-female difference. In the human species, as in other primates, male lovemaps are, by phylogenetic design, more visual in their content, whereas female lovemaps are, also by phylogenetic design, more tactile or haptic. This difference is not absolute. There is a great deal of male-female overlap and also of individual difference.

One sign of the predominantly visual nature of male lovemaps is the explicit visual imagery of boys' wet dreams at puberty, for which there are no exact counterparts in girls. The visual imagery of wet dreams is the equivalent of pictorial pornography. In females, the counterpart of visual imagery and pornography is touchy-feely or haptic imagery and pornography. This difference is the source of age-old sexuoerotical misunderstanding between males and females—for example, between mothers and their adolescent sons, and fathers and their adolescent daughters.

Reciprocal matching of the lovemaps of two people brings intense and euphoric mutual satisfaction. Mismatching, the source of love unrequited, brings intense suffering and lovesickness. In a sex-negative society, disclosure of the intimate personal details of one's own lovemap allows one to be vulnerable to the misery of lovemap mismatching and the failure of mutual intimacy. In a budding romance, reciprocal disclosure of lovemaps reduces, but does not eliminate, the risk of mismatching.

It is not possible to borrow or copy another person's lovemap. Moreover, lovemaps are not caught by social contagion from role models, good or bad, nor are they caught by social contagion through contact with pornography, either normophilic or paraphilic. They have their own principles and timetable for growth in childhood. Lovemap biographies indicate, time and again, that the years around age eight are of crucial importance. After that, though finishing touches may be added, lovemaps are for the most part in place, ready to unfold in full, along with the hormones of puberty and adolescence.

REFERENCES

Money, J. *Gay, Straight, and In-Between: The Sexology of Erotic Orientation*. New York: Oxford Univ. Press, 1988.

————. *Lovemaps: Clinical Concepts of Sexual/ Erotic Health and Pathology. Paraphilia, and Gender Transposition in Childhood, Adolescence, and Maturity*. New York: Irvington, 1986; Buffalo, N.Y.: Prometheus Books, 1993.

————. Pairbonding and Limerence. In B.B. Wolman, ed. *International Encyclopedia of Psychiatry, Psychology, Psychoanalysis and Neurology*. Volume I. New York: Macmillan, 1983.

————. Pedophilia: A Specific Instance of New Phylism Theory as Applied to Paraphilic Lovemaps. In J.R. Feierman, ed. *Pedophilia: Biosocial Dimensions*. New York: Springer-Verlag, 1990.

John Money

m

MARTIN, CLYDE E.

Clyde Martin, born January 2, 1918, is a socio-logical researcher best known for his work on the Kinsey Reports, the world-renowned studies on human sexuality. He coauthored *Sexual Behavior in the Human Male* (1948) with Alfred Kinsey and Wardell Pomeroy and *Sexual Behavior in the Human Female* (1953) with Kinsey, Pomeroy, and Paul Gebhard. After Kinsey's death in 1956, Martin continued working at the Institute for Sex Research. He coauthored *Pregnancy, Birth, and Abortion* (1958) with Pomeroy, Gebhard, and Cornelia Christenson.

In 1960, Martin resigned from the Institute for Sex Research to pursue his doctoral degree. He received his Ph.D. (in social relations) from Johns Hopkins University in 1966. From 1966 until 1989, he did research, specializing in gerontology and sociology at the Francis Scott Key Medical Center in Baltimore, Maryland. Martin then published many studies, including "Factors Affecting Sexual Functioning in 60–79 Year Old Married Males" (1981) in the *Archives of Sexual Behavior*. Clyde Martin retired in 1989.

REFERENCES

Gebhard, P.R., W.B. Pomeroy, C.E. Martin, and C.V. Christenson. *Pregnancy, Birth and Abortion*. New York: Harper-Hoeber, 1958.

Kinsey, A.C., W.B. Pomeroy, and C.E. Martin. *Sexual Behavior in the Human Male*. Philadelphia: Saunders, 1948.

Kinsey, A.C., W.B. Pomeroy, C.E. Martin, and P.H. Gebhard. *Sexual Behavior in the Human Female*. Philadelphia: Saunders, 1953.

Martin, C.E. Factors Affecting Sexual Functioning in 60–79 Year Old Married Males. *Archives of Sexual Behavior*, Vol. l0 (1981), pp. 399-400.

Pomeroy, W.B. *Dr. Kinsey and the Institute for Sex Research*. New York: Signet, 1972.

Leah Cahan Schaefer

MASOCHISM

Masochism is the eroticization of submission. The term was first coined by the psychiatrist Richard von Krafft-Ebing, who derived it from the name of the writer Leopold von Sacher-Masoch. Masochism and the related phenomenon, sadism, have traditionally been considered as individual psychopathologies or paraphilias. Krafft-Ebing, for example, defined masochism as "a peculiar perversion of the psychical sexual life in which the individual affected, in sexual feeling and thought, is controlled by the idea of being completely and unconditionally subject to the will of a person of the opposite sex; of being treated by this person as by a master, humiliated and abused." Sigmund Freud also considered masochism to be a perversion and believed it to be "nothing but a continuation of sadism directed at one's own person in which the latter at first takes the place of the sexual object."

Masochism is not easily separable from sadism, since, as Freud pointed out, they are intricately interrelated. In fact, he noted that "the most striking peculiarity of this perversion lies in the fact that its active and passive forms are regularly encounterd together in the same person." Ellis also argued that the distinction made between sadism and masochism is artificial. He saw them as complementary, rather than as opposed, emotional states. These early writers were correct about the relationship between sadism and masochism, although Freud was in error when he stated that masochism is derived from sadism. In fact, there is evidence that the opposite is true; many sadists start out as masochists. Additionally, Spengler found that only a minority of his sample were exclusively sadistic or masochistic. He observed that people alternated between these roles, thereby maintaining flexibility with different partners.

Recent writers have begun to treat sadism and masochism as sociological phenomena, characterized in terms of an organized subculture or subcultures. Most contemporary research focuses on the social organization of sadomasochists and the acquisition of sadomasochistic identities, while other writers have begun to develop new theories on masochism and the self. Baumeister, for instance, utilizing self-awareness and action identification theories, has conceptualized masochism as "essentially an attempt to escape from self, in the sense of achieving a loss of high-level self-awareness." In essence, he sees masochism as temporarily replacing a sense of self as an abstract, symbolically constructed identity with a low-level awareness of self as a physical entity. Such an escape provides a kind of relief from concerns with autonomy, self-esteem needs, and external demands for responsibility, and it is therefore similar to other escapes, such as the use of drugs and alcohol and involvement in risk-taking activities.

Although a number of writers consider masochism to be synonymous with the receiving of pain for sexual gratification, this is an inaccurate understanding of this orientation. While many masochists do require painful stimulation, not all of them wish to feel even mild discomfort. What masochists desire is the feeling that they are completely under the control of another person. Pain is only one way to symbolize their submission. Some masochists wish, instead, to be verbally abused and insulted, walked upon, given enemas, "forced" to ingest urine or feces, or to be controlled in other ways. Kamel has correctly noted that it is fantasy, rather than whips or chains, that "masters" and "mistresses" use to control the behavior of their "slaves." The terms "dominance and submission" (D/S) or "bondage and discipline" (B/D) are generally preferred by participants to "sadism" and "masochism," which are equated with pain and perceived by them as an inaccurate description of both their identities and their behavior. Within the sadomasochistic community, masochists are referred to as "submissives" or "bottoms."

Califia claims that it is "the will to please (that) is a bottom's source of pleasure." Although it may appear that the sadist is controlling the masochist, in actuality sadomasochistic scenes are both consensual and collaboratively produced. Both partners agree on the limits of their interaction, so that both derive pleasure from their participation. Often code words, such as "yellow" (for slow down) or "red" (for stop) are used to indicate to one's partner that one is nearing one's discomfort limit. Frequently, sadomasochistic scenarios are scripted, so that individuals play designated roles during their interaction. Common fantasies include mistress-master and slave, employer and servant-maid, teacher and pupil, owner and horse or dog, and parent and child.

Sadomasochists often wear costumes of black leather or rubber, which symbolize their sadomasochistic role. There are, for example, slave harnesses and other restraints indicating to potential partners the individual's preferred role in the interaction. Among male homosexuals in the "leathersex" subculture, dominance or submission is signaled by wearing key chains or colored handkerchiefs. Usually, wearing keys on the left indicates that the individual is a top, and the right side signals that he is a bottom. The preference for a specific act is symbolized by the color of the handkerchief; color codes are generally agreed upon within the subculture.

While preference for a dominant or submissive role is not gender linked, in the United States males tend to take the passive role and wish to interact with dominant females. In fact, personal contact magazines, with titles such as *Aggressive Gals* and *Amazon,* have advertisements for partners predominantly from submissive men and dominant women, many of whom are prostitutes. Baumeister has noted differences between male and female masochists. In an analysis of letters to a sexually oriented magazine, he found that males desired more severe pain, more frequently wished to be humiliated, and were especially interested in degrading humiliations and those that involved status loss, partner infidelity, transvestism, and the active participation by persons other than their partners. Females, in contrast, wished more frequent pain, saw pain as punishment for actual behavior, were more likely to report or fantasize being displayed in a humiliating way, to describe sexual intercourse as part of the scenario, and to include nonparticipating spectators.

Masochists meet partners in a variety of ways, most commonly through responding to advertisements. Often, they are unable to find willing female partners and interact with prostitutes specializing in domination. Prior to the AIDS (acquired immune deficiency syndrome) epidemic, bars in which sadomasochists could find one another and engage in sadomasochistic scenes existed in the largest cities, such as New York and San Francisco. These places—such as *Paddles* and *The Hellfire Club* for heterosexuals and *The Mineshaft,* which catered to a homosexual clientele—were closed down either by departments of public health or voluntarily; they are essentially defunct. Sadomasochistic organizations, such as the Eulenspiegel and Janus Societies, which serve as informational forums and hold special events, still exist. Additionally, sadomasochists hold private parties, often with several dozen participants.

REFERENCES

Baumeister, R.F. Gender/Differences in Masochistic Scripts. *Journal of Sex Research,* Vol. 25 (Nov. 1988), pp. 478–99.

————. Masochism as Escape from Self. *Journal of Sex Research,* Vol. 25 (Feb. 1988), pp. 28–59.

Califia, P. A Secret Side of Lesbian Sexuality. *The Advocate,* 17 Dec. 1979, pp. 19–23.

Ellis, H. *Studies in the Psychology of Sex.* Vol. 1, pt. 2. New York: Random House, 1942.

Freud, S. *The Basic Writings of Sigmund Freud.* Edited and translated by A.A. Brill. New York: Modern Library, 1938.

Kamel, G.W.L. Leathersex: Meaningful Aspects of Gay Sadomasochism. *Deviant Behavior An Interdisciplinary Journal,* Vol. 1 (1980), pp. 171–91.

Krafft-Ebing, R. von. *Psychopathia Sexualis.* (1886) Translated by F.S. Klaff. New York: Stein & Day, 1965.

Spengler, A. Manifest Sadomasochism of Males: Results of an Empirical Study. *Archives of Sexual Behavior,* Vol. 6 (1977), pp. 441–56.

Weinberg, T.S. Sadomasochism in the United States: A Review of Recent Sociological Literature. *Journal of Sex Research,* Vol. 23 (Feb. 1987), pp. 50–69.

Weinberg, T.S., and G.W.L. Kamel, eds. *S and M: Studies in Sadomasochism.* Buffalo, N.Y.: Prometheus Books, 1983.

Thomas S. Weinberg

MASTERS, WILLIAM HOWELL

William Howell Masters has been second only to Alfred Kinsey in his influence on American sexology in the last half of the 20th century. He and his collaborator, Virginia E. Johnson, became internationally known almost overnight with the publication, in April 1966, of *Human Sexual Response.* The book was the first to describe in detail how the human body responded to erotic stimulation during both masturbation and coitus. Responses of the penis, scrotum, and testes, the breasts, clitoris, labia, vagina, cervix, uterus, and other parts of the body were all presented and explained. Their experiments were made possible by new technical breakthroughs in photographic and recording equipment not available to their predecessors.

Second to *Human Sexual Response* in influence was *Human Sexual Inadequacy,* published in 1970. This work emphasized their difference with Kinsey, since, unlike Kinsey, they had an explicit therapeutic intent. Kinsey portrayed himself as a pure scientist whose sole concern was to establish the facts, while Masters and Johnson were clinicians first and scientists after. Though the Masters and Johnson style is often turgid and sometimes unclear, and, as has been pointed out by their critics, they claimed greater success in treatment than perhaps was warranted, they became the major figures in the exploding field of sex therapy in the 1960s and 1970s, and remain so at this time. They successfully challenged and undermined the predominant psychoanalytic approach to sexual dysfunction and in the process emphasized a behavioral approach.

Masters was born in Cleveland in 1915 to a well-to-do family. He attended Lawrenceville Preparatory School and then went on to receive a bachelor's degree from Hamilton College in 1938. He enrolled in medical school at the University of Rochester, where he came into contact with George Washington Corner, a major figure on the National Research Council's Committee for Research on Sex Problems. It was Corner who was instrumental in getting funding for Kinsey.

Masters worked with Corner on the estrous cycle in the female rabbit, and it was this experience that seemed to be influential in directing Masters into further research into human sexuality. Masters talked to Corner about the possibility and Corner gave him some often quoted advice: namely, that Masters should wait until he was at least 40 before tackling sex research, should first earn a reputation in some other scientific field, and should wait until he could secure the sponsorship of a major medical school or university. This was advice that Masters followed.

He married in 1942, received his M.D. degree in 1943, and from 1943 to 1947 was an intern and then a resident in obstetrics and gynecology at Barnes Hospital and Maternity Hospital, Washington University School of Medicine, in St. Louis. After completing his residency, he became, successively, an instructor, assistant professor, and associate professor; a specialist certified by the American Board of Obstetricians and Gynecologists; and the father of two children. He also published on a variety of obstetrical and gynecological subjects, although much of his research was concentrated on hormone-replacement therapy for aging women.

In 1954, Masters felt ready to begin a comprehensive study of the physiological responses involved in sexual activity, and he initiated a program within the framework of the department of obstetrics and gynecology at Washington University. As a preliminary step, he interviewed at length and in depth 118 female and 27 male prostitutes, and 11 of them, 8 women and 3 men, participated in a preliminary series of laboratory observations. Though he gained many insights from the prostitutes, he ultimately decided that he could not base his study on them, since many of them exhibited various degrees of pelvic pathology; this, coupled with the fact that they were often transient and undependable, led him to seek volunteers. In all, some 694 individuals, including 276 married couples, participated in the laboratory program Masters established. These individuals were not involved in the therapy programs and were a separate and distinct group.

Originally, Masters did much of the work by himself, but he felt a need to have a woman assist in research interviewing. Virginia Eschelman Johnson, who had applied to the Washington University Placement Bureau for a job following her separation from her husband, was chosen by Masters to join the project, and she increasingly took greater responsibility. In 1959, Masters, in conjunction with Virginia Johnson, launched a therapy program designed to help couples suffering from various sexual inadequacies. This area of the clinic grew in importance, and other therapists joined them. In 1964, the programs were placed under the auspices of the Reproductive Biology Research Foundation.

Masters and Johnson later married, although they separated from each other in 1992. As they aged, Virginia Johnson increasingly withdrew from taking an active part in the clinic, while Masters himself continued working. Currently, he still remains active.

Interestingly, as sex therapists Masters and Johnson put more emphasis on the social-psychological factors of anorgasmia and impotence than on the physical. Generally also, Masters and Johnson have approached the study of sexuality from the point of view of a heterosexual couple. In large part, they felt that the struggle for sexual happiness was essentially a struggle for the mind. This presupposition has been a source of major criticism in recent years. Others have criticized the ambiguity inherent in some of their description of the phases of the sexual response cycle. Still others have criticized their claimed success rate. It may well be, however, that the poorer success rate reported by other therapists is due to the fact that the greater availability of information led to a decline in the number of people who sought therapy for relatively simple problems, leaving more complex problems requiring more intensive treatment. Certainly, the optimism that prevailed at the beginning of the Masters and Johnson era has disappeared.

In spite of various criticisms and various emendations to their classification schemes, their basic findings on the physiology of the sexual response remain intact. Some of their therapeutic techniques, such as the squeeze technique, also remain widely practiced, and, in spite of criticism, much of what they said and did is still at the heart of today's sex therapy.

REFERENCES

Primary

Masters, W.H., and V.E. Johnson. *Human Sexual Inadequacy*. Boston: Little, Brown, 1970.

————. *Human Sexual Response*. Boston: Little, Brown, 1966.

Secondary

Brecher, E.M. *The Sex Researchers*. Boston: Little, Brown, 1969.

Kaplan, H.S. *The New Sex Therapy: Active Treatment of Sexual Dysfunctions*. New York: Brunner/Mazel, 1981.

Robinson, P. *The Modernization of Sex*. New York: Harper & Row, 1976.

Vern L. Bullough

MASTURBATION

Masturbation presents some of the same problems as pornography; we cannot define it, but we know what it is when we do it. The derivation of the word is usually given as "to pollute with the hand" or "to arouse the genitals," but many other parts of the body, as well as inanimate objects, can be used to pollute or arouse. In a narrow sense, masturbation is defined as playing with (directly stimulating) one's own genitals for the purpose of sexual self-pleasuring. In a more expanded definition, it may involve parts of the body other than the genitals (e.g., any erogenous area such as the mouth, tongue, anus, breast, or ear) and include participation with people in pairs or groups (which might be called mutual masturbation), although the latter activity may require an additional element of interaction and often involves the pleasuring of others. The word does not predict outcome; that is, it refers only to the pleasuring that may or may not lead to orgasm or ejaculation. The word sometimes used to describe this expanded definition is "autoeroticism," but even here the prefix "auto-" is not always appropriate. It may also involve elements of frotteurism. The practice has also been called, incorrectly, onanism. The "sin of Onan" occurred when Onan withdrew his penis before he ejaculated into the vagina of his sister-in-law, and thus he spilled his "seed" upon the ground. Therefore, onanism actually refers to coitus interruptus, not masturbation. Masturbation is not genital intercourse, although it may enter into the sexual experience during either foreplay or afterglow. Given all the various interpretations, one can agree with Freud when he said that "the subject of masturbation is quite inexhaustible."

Statistics concerning the number of people who engage in the activity are suspect, regardless of how one defines the term. However, there seems to be general agreement that masturbation is the most common type of sexual activity. This is probably because one can do it alone without the stress of having to satisfy someone else's needs, one does not have to be attractive and thus fear rejection, and one can be in complete control of the experience. Some workers have said that everyone masturbates; others have given particular statistics that indicate that 96 percent of men and 63 percent of women have masturbated sometime in their lives. The numbers for women have increased, according to later studies. The truth probably lies somewhere between. It has been said that 97 percent of men masturbate and the other 3 percent are liars. In any event, masturbation is the norm; lack of masturbation is the unusual.

Likewise, the statistics concerning the frequency of masturbation by an individual are also suspect. Infants have been noted to derive pleasure from rubbing their genitals; indeed, in some cultures, infants have been gently masturbated by their mothers or nurses to calm them so that they can sleep. Some workers have reported the activity by infants in utero. Children, as soon as they discover their genitals, often masturbate regularly. The frequency may increase during times of boredom, such as when sitting in the seat of a supermarket cart while their parents are shopping. The child finds that stroking the genitals is a pleasurable way of passing the time, often to the consternation of the parents. Frequency increases greatly when the child reaches puberty, often to several times a day. It is at this time that a male can begin to ejaculate, a process greatly to be desired. It has often been postulated that masturbatory frequency is greatly reduced or stopped when the individual gets married, but that may not be the case. Many members of married couples find that they still wish to masturbate alone, or they often begin to incorporate the practice into their intercourse. The practice continues into old age, the frequency varying with health, religious, and personal considerations such as divorce or the death of a spouse.

Although most males desire to ejaculate as the result of masturbation, they vary in their methods of reaching that goal. Most males focus on the penis but may include the anus, perineum, scrotum, nipples, or other body parts in their activities. A man may prefer a particular method of masturbation because of the pleasure that it affords him. Thus, he may stimulate the head, corona, or shaft of his penis by placing his fingers in specific positions and stroking, rubbing, squeezing, or pinching the organ. He may roll his penis between his palms, rub it against his stomach, or rub it against inanimate objects such as pillows, sheets, washcloths, or clothing. He may flip the erect organ up and down against his belly or to the right and left. He may use only one hand or alternate between his two hands. He may use only the fluid produced by the Cowper's glands (precome) as a lubricant, or he may use oils, lotions, jellies, saliva, soap, and ointments to prevent painful friction.

The man may grasp the entire shaft in his fist and move the outer skin up and down, or he may use only one or two fingers to stimulate certain areas that give him pleasure. He may use a light or a strong grip. The frenulum, an area supplied with a large number of nerve endings, may serve as a focus for stimulation for both circumcised and uncircumcised males. If the penis is uncircumcised, the foreskin may be pulled forward and used in pleasurable stimulation. The man can become so accustomed to one method of masturbation that he will ask a sex partner to use that method when he is being masturbated by the partner.

The male may use a variety of aids during masturbation. The aids may be naturally occurring objects such as the cardboard core of a roll of toilet tissue, milk bottles, cored apples, liver, and cantaloupes into which the penis is inserted, or toys that have been manufactured for that purpose. These include artificial vaginas and inflatable dolls with receptive mouths and anuses. Anal penetration using dildos, sometimes coupled with vibrators on the nipples and other parts of the body, are often part of the masturbatory sequence.

The masturbatory play may be very rapid; some men have reported ejaculation within 30 seconds of start. The usual time is two or three minutes, but some men reach a point just before ejaculation is inevitable and reduce the stimulation to prolong the pleasure for a much longer period. Although the stroking movements may start slowly, they usually speed up as the man approaches ejaculation; most men stop all movements and simply hold their penis during ejaculation. After ejaculation, most men abruptly stop stimulation because the feelings become so intense that they are painful.

Women commonly masturbate by rubbing or applying pressure to the clitoris, mons, lips of the vagina, or some combination of these areas. The methods by which they do this varies greatly. Fingers or other devices may be used to rub the shaft of the clitoris in an up-and-down motion on either or both sides, or the shaft may be rubbed in a circular fashion. The vaginal lips may be gently pulled; this movement of the inner lips causes the loose skin covering the clitoris to move back and forth, creating a pleasurable sensation. Because the glans of the clitoris is highly sensitive, prolonged stimulation usually becomes irritating, and thus it is not often used as the focus of masturbation.

Relatively few women (some workers estimate about 20 percent) insert anything into their vaginas while masturbating. Those who do usually insert just barely into the opening. However, some women completely insert fingers, dildos, vibrators, and other objects, such as bananas and cucumbers, during masturbation. Hairpins and other small objects have had to be surgically removed from the uterus where they have been deposited as the result of spasms caused by orgasm from masturbation in which the items were inserted into the vagina as a masturbatory aid. The practice of inserting small hollow or solid balls into the vagina probably originated in Japan. These objects, called *rin-no-tama* or *ben-wa* balls, are held in place by a tampon and may be used singly or in pairs. One of the hollow balls may contain a small solid ball of mercury that causes it to move with the movement of the woman. The vibrations of the balls cause pleasurable sensations.

All these methods may involve the use of various kinds of lubricants, and many women stimulate their breasts while stimulating their genitals. Some women use washcloths, clothing, pillows, furs, silks, or other such devices to aid their stimulation. Most women prefer lying on their backs, but some prefer standing or sitting.

While standing or sitting, a woman may rub against certain objects, such as doorknobs, dresser drawer pulls, the edge of chairs, or bedposts. The woman may cross her legs and increase the pressure on her genitals by contracting her lower abdominal, gluteal, and thigh muscles. Water massages may be used. Some women derive sexual stimulation while riding a bicycle or a horse, activities that were at one time forbidden to women for that very reason. However, the pumping of a sewing machine treadle, an activity that was not forbidden, can also produce sexual pleasure.

Female sexual response to masturbation is about the same as for males. Some women have reported orgasm 30 seconds from the start of self-stimulation, while the usual time is a little less than four minutes. Because of a woman's ability to have multiple orgasms, she may maintain her threshold of orgasm far longer than a man.

All the above activities can be performed alone, with one partner, or with multiple partners in group situations. They may be performed by homosexuals or heterosexuals; the two orientations' physiological response to the stimulation appears to be the same, although the psychological response is quite different. These practices may also be part of other sexual activities, such as transvestism, fetishism, sado-masochism, and zoophilia. For example, a male transvestite may use an article of women's clothing to stroke his penis while masturbating; a sock fetishist may use a sock for the same purpose.

Fantasy plays a very important role in masturbatory activities. Because of this, it has been said that if masturbation did not exist, we would have to invent it. Even the older literature, often prejudicial against masturbation, recognizes that this solitary "vice" can be credited with preventing crimes, perversions, and serious mental break-downs. Thus, during masturbation an individual can fantasize activities that he or she would never perform in real life. For example, an individual can harmlessly coerce another person into a sexual situation in a masturbatory fantasy and relieve the stress brought on by the desire. If the coercion were actually carried out, a great deal of harm would be inflicted on the people involved. Only if the fantasy becomes so demanding that the individual actually performs it does it become harmful. Masturbatory fantasy enables one to escape socially imposed sex roles and allows individuals to perform sexually in ways they never would in real life. Thus, an individual may imagine sex with people otherwise unavailable: a heterosexual male can have fantasy sex with men whom he admires, and a homosexual male can likewise have sex with women. In their fantasies, people can participate in orgies, incest, and anal stimulation and penetration, as well as relieve unpleasant notions and experiences. It has been shown that some lesbians may feel their clitoris grows to become a penis, enabling them to penetrate their partner; gay men can believe their hand belongs to another person whom they desire. Gay men may focus on the penis during the fantasy, all other considerations becoming irrelevant.

In addition to helping to build a healthy fantasy life, there are many other positive aspects to masturbation. The practice has been used to calm infants. It helps to relieve frustration by allowing an individual to temporarily escape a challenging world and become self-contained. It can allow a person to relieve sexual tension without having to be concerned with responsibility for the feelings of a partner. Among adolescents, it can relieve sexual tensions at a time of great sexual uncertainty and may actually prevent unwanted pregnancies. Since the masturbator is in control of the fantasies and feelings, he or she can perform whether or not illness, physical disability, age, marital status, and feelings of physical unattractiveness intervene. Masturbation can enhance self-awareness and, indeed, has been credited with helping people to learn about their own sexuality and thus improve their sensitivity toward their sexual partners. In this context, it becomes a positive maturing activity. When employed during intercourse, it may greatly enhance sexual response; some women report that they receive more intense pleasure from masturbation either by themselves or by their partner than they do from coitus, especially if their partner is a male

who has only slight potency. This is because the clitoris receives little direct stimulation during pelvic thrusting in the "missionary position."

Religions have sometimes incorporated masturbation into their myths. In one Indian myth, Lord Shiva was masturbated, and when his semen was accidentally dropped into the Ganges, the misogynist war-god Kartikeh was born. In one Egyptian myth, the god Ptah and a group of gods related to him came into being from the semen masturbated from the god Atum. In another account, Atum masturbated and produced a son and a daughter. In some religious sects, ritual masturbation is one means of effecting mystical union with the deity.

Although attitudes toward masturbation varied greatly among ancient peoples, it was generally accepted that the practice was at least sometimes necessary, and, in certain cultures, it was encouraged. Other cultures had proscriptions against it, but the extreme negative view of masturbation probably evolved because the practice by itself is nonprocreative and solitary. This view is especially prevalent in early Judeo-Christian thought, when it was believed that the only reason for sexual intercourse was procreation and anything that interfered with that function was immoral. Jewish tradition said that man must not waste his seed. The practice is also pleasurable, and that was seen as another reason for its condemnation. Religious bigotry found medical support in the work of S.A.D. Tissot (1728–1787), who published his influential *Onania, or a Treatise upon the Disorders Produced by Masturbation* in 1758. Tissot observed that the body became flushed during and after sexual intercourse, a response which we now know is a result of increased peripheral circulation. Given his religious views, he reasoned that all sex was potentially dangerous because it caused the blood to rush to the head and thus starved the nerves, leaving the person vulnerable to insanity. He recognized that some sex was necessary for reproduction but taught that solitary sex was far more dangerous because it would inevitably lead to excessive ejaculation. He also thought the masturbator was in greater danger because the masturbator realized he was committing a sin and thus was placing his nervous system in an even more precarious situation.

Because of his respectability as a physician, Tissot's views were widely accepted, although some physicians at the time pointed out that he was using his medical practice to further his private moral convictions. His views spread throughout Europe and were eventually embraced in the United States by Benjamin Rush, a signer of the Declaration of Independence and an influential figure in medicine. The views of Tissot and Rush initiated what has been called the "age of masturbatory insanity." Because ejaculation in the male produced feelings of relaxation and general lassitude, it became widely accepted in medical circles that semen was a precious fluid that should be used only when there was a chance of conception occurring. Otherwise, there was no disease of the body or mind that could not be attributed to masturbation. Disasters could occur: the brain would dry up and rattle in the masturbator's head like peas in a pod, the penis and testicles would dry up and fall off, and young girls would cause their own death and the death of others by the practice because of the sin involved. Insanity, syphilis, blindness, deafness, cancer, afflictions of the female reproductive organs, nosebleeds, heart murmurs, sterility, acne, undesirable odors of the skin, epilepsy, headaches, infantile paralysis, infantile rheumatism, pederasty, and homosexuality were only a few of the conditions thought to be caused by masturbation.

The list of activities thought to encourage or cause masturbation is almost as long as the list of effects. They include lack of cleanliness, presence of the prepuce and lips of the vagina, nervousness, prolonged sitting or standing, sitting cross-legged, spanking, petting, corsets, straining of the memory, erotic reading or reading of novels, play, pictures, perfumes, solitude, fondling, rocking chairs, pockets, feather beds, horseback riding, and bicycling.

Of course, there had to be a list of symptoms by which the masturbator could be recognized. These included an enormously enlarged penis, a downcast and averted glance, loss of memory and intelligence, a morose and unequal disposition, aversion or indifference to legitimate pleasures and sports, pursuit of solitude, and the acquisition of a dull, silly, listless, embarrassed, sad, and effeminate exterior.

Because of the dire consequences of masturbation, extreme measures were thought necessary to cure it. Indiana and Wyoming passed statutes making it a crime to encourage a person to masturbate. Women were forbidden to ride astride a horse or on a bicycle. Widows and older unmarried women were forbidden to own a dog or a male slave for fear that they would use them during masturbation. Even into the 1950s, bananas served in women's dormitories in colleges were cut up so the women could not use them. In some cultures, males were forbidden to hold their penis when they urinated unless they were married and their wives were available if

they became excited. Other preventions included the wearing of antimasturbatory belts that prevented the wearer from touching his or her genitals. Patents were issued for devices that would enclose the penis in such a way that if an erection occurred, the penis would push against pins or grippers, causing pain. Girls were tied into their beds in ways that would not allow them to touch their genitals or to slide up and down on the linens. More radical methods included castration and cauterization of the spine and the genitals. The prepuce of uncircumcised boys was pulled across the glans penis and sewn into place, leaving only a small hole for the passing of urine. In the United States, some girls had clitoridectomies performed on them, a practice that continued until about 1886, and both sexes were subjected to blistering of the thighs and genitals. One physician regularly prescribed the application of a white-hot iron to the clitoris.

Circumcision was recommended for both the male and female masturbator. In the United States, female circumcision is now rarely done, but it is still routinely performed on male infants. The practice has its origins in the attempt to prevent masturbation among males, although other reasons are sometimes given. The process was certainly not successful, because in the Middle Eastern countries where the operation is commonly performed after the boy begins to walk or later, the frequency of masturbation tends to increase as the boy attempts to assure himself that nothing of importance has been lost. The incidence of the practice has not declined in the United States. A very radical circumcision was sometimes performed in which the entire outer skin of the penis was removed with the prepuce.

Although there is not one shred of evidence that masturbation is harmful, superstitions and prohibitions against the practice still abound. These were reinforced by two new translations of Krafft-Ebing's *Psychopathia Sexualis* that were published in the United States in 1965. Krafft-Ebing indicates that masturbation during the early years contaminates the masturbator and removes the source of all noble and ideal sentiment. It removes feelings toward the opposite sex and induces neuroses of the sexual apparatus. Thus, we still have parents, teachers, physicians, and Sunday school teachers who warn against the harm of "self-abuse," especially if practiced to "excess." No one has ever defined what is meant by "excess," but most modern men would agree that it is "just a little more than I practice." The only harm that can result from masturbation is if the individual is plagued with feelings of guilt that cause him or her to be uncomfortable with the practice.

Not all writers of the 19th century were so narrow in their thinking about masturbation. Mark Twain delivered a short address extolling its virtues at a private club in Paris in 1879:

> Homer in the second book of the Iliad, says with fine enthusiasm, "Give me masturbation or give me death!" Caesar, in his Commentaries, says, "To the lonely it is company; to the forsaken it is a friend; to the aged and to the impotent it is a benefactor; they that are penniless are yet rich, in that they still have this majestic diversion." In another place this experienced observer has said, "There are times when I prefer it to sodomy." Robinson Crusoe says, "I cannot describe what I owe to this gentle art." Queen Elizabeth said, "It is the bulwark of Virginity." Cetewayo, the Zulu hero, remarked, "A jerk in the hand is worth two in the bush." The immortal Franklin has said, "Masturbation is the mother of invention." He also said, "Masturbation is the best policy." Michelangelo and all the other old masters—Old Masters, I will remark, is an abbreviation, a contraction— have used similar language. Michelangelo said to Pope Julius II, "Self-negation is noble, self-culture is beneficial, self-possession is manly, but to the truly grand and inspiring soul they are poor and tame compared to self-abuse."

The world would be a better place if Twain's healthy attitude had prevailed much earlier.

REFERENCES

Allgeier, E.R., and A.R. Allgeier. *Sexual Interactions.* Lexington, Mass.: D.C. Heath, 1991.

Bullough, V.L. *Sexual Variance in Society and History.* New York: John Wiley & Sons, 1976.

Bullough, V.L., and B. Bullough. *Sin, Sickness, and Sanity: A History of Sexual Attitudes.* New York: Garland, 1977.

Katchadourian, H.A. *Fundamentals of Human Sexuality.* 5th ed. Fort Worth: Holt, Rinehart & Winston, 1989.

Masters, R.E.L., ed. *Sexual Self-Stimulation.* Los Angeles: Sherbourne Press, 1967.

Masters, W.H., V.E. Johnson, and R.C. Kolodny. *Human Sexuality.* 3d ed. Glenview, Ill.: Scott, Foresman, 1988.

Reinisch, J.M. *The Kinsey Institute New Report on Sex.* New York: St. Martin's Press, 1990.

Walker, M. *Men Loving Men: A Gay Sex Guide and Consciousness Book.* San Francisco: Gay Sunshine Press, 1977.

James D. Haynes

MASTURBATORY INSANITY

That masturbation caused insanity was a belief based on the writings of the 18th-century Swiss physician S.A.D. Tissot (1728–1797), who taught that physical bodies suffered a continual waste, and unless this wastage was periodically restored, death would result. Though much of this loss could be restored through adequate nutrition, it was also important to attempt to control the wastage itself. The most debilitating form of wastage was human semen and its female equivalent. It was recognized that semen was essential for procreation, but its waste through other forms of nonprocreative sexual activity had to be controlled. Masturbation was a particularly harmful form of waste and could lead to madness, decay of bodily powers, and numerous other ailments.

Tissot wrote before it was recognized that many of the symptoms he attributed to masturbation were actually due to third-stage syphilis. Tissot claimed that the symptoms were due to an action instead of a disease, and others picked up on his argument, especially in the United States. In the 19th century, a host of "reformers"—ranging from Sylvester Graham, an advocate of unbolted wheat, or graham flour, whose name is commemorated in the graham cracker, to John Harvey Kellogg, who developed cornflakes—widely publicized the dangers of nonprocreative sex. Kellogg, in his book dealing with the topic, provided a two-page listing of the ill effects of masturbation in young people, a list that describes almost everything that American adolescents suffered from or did, ranging from acne to the use of profanity.

One result of such agitation was the development of a number of devices to prevent young people from masturbating, including mittens to be worn to bed and various forms of belts and guards to prevent them from touching themselves (some of which are discussed under Chastity Girdles). A major result of the belief in masturbatory insanity was the widespread growth of male circumcision in the United States. Circumcision, it was claimed, prevented males from having to pull back the foreskin of their penis when they urinated. Since it was believed that this touching of the foreskin provided a pleasurable experience, it was this that led so many boys to masturbate.

The hysteria over masturbation began to die down in the 20th century largely through the identification of the sequelae of third-stage syphilis, but the dangers of masturbation were still widely publicized as late as the 1940s.

REFERENCES

Bullough, V.L. *Sexual Variance in Society and History.* Chicago: Univ. of Chicago Press, 1976.

Money, J. *The Destroying Angel.* Buffalo, N.Y.: Prometheus Books, 1985.

Wallerstein, E. *Circumcision: An American Fallacy.* New York: Springer, 1980.

Vern L. Bullough

MATE SELECTION

On what bases, and through what processes, do people select a marriage partner? Historically and across cultures, these have generally been more salient issues for parents than for young men and women. That is, marriages were arranged between kin groups, often to gain status or to form an economic or social alliance with another family, and the opinions of the bride and groom were of relatively little concern. By the time of the Victorian era, rationalism was the primary influence in the marriage market. The reasons for marriage were procreation and the rearing of children within a congenial home. This goal could best be achieved if husband and wife were of the same socioeconomic background and adhered to their respective institutionalized roles of provider and homemaker. Some people may be quite surprised to learn that love and emotional satisfaction are very recent influences in marital choices, particularly by women. In fact, research shows that the vast majority of contemporary Americans may not even consider marrying someone whom they do not love.

In 1967, Kephart asked more than 1,000 college student respondents if they would marry a person who had all the qualities they desired in a potential mate if they were not in love with that person. Although the majority (65 percent) of men said no, thus suggesting that love was a prerequisite for marriage, only 24 percent of the women said no, indicating that for the majority of women at that time, love was not necessary for marriage. Reasoning that these figures may have changed with the increase in women's independence in the decades since Kephart collected his data, Simpson, Campbell, and Bersheid carried out research, in 1976 and in 1984, on the importance of love to men and women in selecting a marital partner. In support of the idea that with women's increasing economic and social independence fewer women would settle for a marital partner whom they did not love, Simpson, et al., found that by 1976, 80 percent of the women in their sample indicated that they would not marry a man whom they did not love, and this figure rose to 85 percent by 1984.

Men's unwillingness to marry someone they did not love also rose, but far less dramatically: 86 percent of the men sampled in both 1976 and 1984 reported that they would not marry someone they did not love. Allgeier and Widerman asked the Kephart question of nearly 1,000 college students in 1990, and 91 percent of the women and 87 percent of the men indicated that they would not marry someone whom they did not love. Among a sample of more mature adults from the general community, 81 percent of both men and women responded that they would not marry someone they did not love. In general, this association between love and marriage appears to be quite pervasive among contemporary Americans.

Beyond love, what criteria are most important in people's selection of spouses? Contrary to the romantic belief that love transcends any barrier, many practical issues seem to influence marriage choices. For example, proximity has consistently been found to relate to mate selection; that is, we are more likely to choose a mate from those within our immediate surroundings. As Buss noted, "Conceptions of romantic love aside, the 'one and only' typically lives within driving distance." Other considerations, such as premarital pregnancy, may result in matrimonial pairings that would not otherwise have taken place. In contemporary Western societies, there is also much room for assortive mating; the non-random pairing of individuals based on similarity with regard to one or more characteristics. Researchers have considered the actual assortiveness of a wide variety of such qualities. In general, studies have demonstrated that basic demographic variables such as age, ethnic background, religion, and education are most highly assortive, whereas spousal similarity in attitudes and opinions are somewhat less associated with marriage.

Many studies have been done asking for people's preferences regarding qualities in a potential mate. Most of these studies have been similar to that conducted by Hill, who constructed a list of 18 characteristics in a potential mate and asked a large sample of college students to rate how important each quality was in their choice of a spouse. In studies employing this methodology, descriptors such as "kind and understanding," "good companion," "mutual attraction," and "dependable character" characterize what both men and women say they prefer most in a mate. Of course, everyone would like to marry someone who possessed the traits of attractiveness, kindness, dependability, intelligence, and so forth, but is it realistic to assume that because most people express a preference for these qualities, they do indeed marry someone who has them? Despite reporting that they look for mates who possess these positive attributes, the majority of people may have to settle for the closest match to their ideal that they encounter during the period when they are most prepared to marry.

A couple of studies have investigated the degree to which people do actually attain their preferences when it comes to a spouse, as well as the degree to which spouses are similar in the relative value placed on particular characteristics. Among nearly 100 married couples, Buss and Barnes found that spouses' ratings of the importance of such qualities as religiousness, liking children, political conservativism, being socially exciting, artisticness and intelligence were moderately correlated (0.36–0.65), suggesting that spouses are similar in the importance they place on some fundamental dispositions. Buss and Barnes also correlated each spouse's preferences for a variety of personality characteristics with their partner's actual score on measures of those characteristics. Most of the correlations were significant but rather small (around 0.25). In a study of more than 6,000 married or cohabiting couples, Howard, Blumstein, and Schwartz also found significant but modest correlations between peoples' preferences regarding a mate and the partners' self-ratings on those dimensions, the average correlations being around 0.20. These latter researchers went a step further by correlating men's and women's preferences for a mate with their ratings of their partners with regard to the desired qualities. These correlations were larger than those between preferences and partners' self-ratings on the various dimensions, but were still quite modest (0.09–0.44). In general, there appears to be some relationship between what we say we are looking for in a mate and the characteristics of the person whom we marry, but the correspondence is far from perfect.

The list of 18 characteristics in a potential mate developed by Hill has been administered to large samples of college students at several points over the last 50 years, allowing for analyses of trends over a span of three generations. Wiederman's and Allgeier's work on the topic has revealed that men and women may now be more similar in the relative value they place on the listed mate characteristics than they were over the past two generations. Compared to past generations, young women now place more emphasis on the physical attractiveness of a potential mate. Also, compared to past generations, men now rate the items good cook-housekeeper, refinement-neatness, and desire for home and children as less important in a potential spouse. It appears that contemporary men may be putting less emphasis on those characteristics in a mate that stereotypically defined a housewife, whereas women are placing more value on the physical attractiveness of a potential husband.

Despite a high degree of similarity in the relative value placed on most characteristics in a potential mate, research has consistently demonstrated that men and women differ in their ratings of particular selection criteria. Specifically, research employing various methodologies with a variety of samples has shown that men place significantly more importance on the physical attractiveness of a potential partner, whereas women place more emphasis on the ability of a mate to provide material support. With regard to actual mate choice, successful career men are more likely to be married to physically attractive women. These gender differences in mate selection criteria have been found to hold cross-culturally. Buss collected data from 37 samples and more than 10,000 people from Africa, Asia, Eastern and Western Europe, Canada, Australia, New Zealand, South America, and the United States and consistently found that men preferred "good looks" in a mate more than did women, whereas women preferred "good financial prospects" in a potential mate more than did men. Evolutionary theory has been used to explain these robust gender differences in mate selection criteria.

Those taking an evolutionary perspective have argued that gender differences in human mate selection criteria exist as a result of natural selection. The anthropologist Donald Symons proposed that individuals using criteria that resulted in the enhancement of their ability to pass on their genes to the next generation, at least for a period lengthy enough for the next generation to reproduce successfully, would be more likely to have their characteristics—including the criteria they use for mate selection—passed on. Note that this is neither a teleological (doing something for the sake of) model nor a deterministic one. That is, Symons did not suggest that humans (during the period when our species was evolving) consciously sought partners who would increase their likelihood of reproductive success. Rather, he suggested that those men and women who happened to use criteria that ultimately resulted in reproductive success were more likely to have their genes passed on than those who did not. On the issue of determinism, the evolutionary approach does not propose that all men and women are inevitably forced at the genetic level to behave in particular ways or, in this instance, to value specific characteristics in a potential mate over others. Instead, this approach argues from a probabilistic standpoint. Specifically, as represented by Symons's hypotheses, during our evolutionary history, those males whose mate selection criteria included physical attractiveness of women (which also happens to correlate with women's physical and reproductive health) were more likely to have the offspring they helped to conceive survive pregnancy, childhood, and adolescence and go on to reproduce than were those men who selected less physically attractive women (i.e., women who were older or less likely to be healthy and strong enough to carry a fetus to term and raise it to reproductive maturity). In contrast, he suggested that women who selected mates on the basis of the potential mate's ability to provide protection and resources to the woman and her offspring would be more likely to have her genes passed on to subsequent generations.

An alternative explanation for the robust gender differences, demonstrated in research on self-reported mate selection criteria, is the structural-powerlessness hypothesis, which suggests that males and females have the same mate selection preferences, but social structural arrangements produce gender differences. It has been hypothesized that men's relative preference for physical attractiveness, and women's relative preference for a mate with economic resources, may be by-products of the culturally determined differential economic status of men versus women. If women are typically excluded from power and are viewed as objects of exchange, then women may seek mates possessing characteristics associated with power and resource-acquisition skills (e.g., earning capacity). According to Buss and Barnes, marriage is, therefore, a means by which women may improve their economic status. Men, in contrast, may place a premium on the quality of the "exchange object" itself, and so value physical beauty (e.g., enhanced value as a sex object). Physical attractiveness then becomes a central means for designating relative value among exchange commodities. Wiederman and Allgeier conducted a study to test this explanation for the described gender differences in mate selection criteria. Contrary to the structural-powerlessness hypothesis, in samples of both college students and community members women's expected personal income was unrelated to the value placed on the earning ability of a potential husband. In general, women appear to place relatively more emphasis on the earning potential of a mate than do men, and this is true even among women who are financially independent.

A number of other models of mate selection processes have been proposed. One of the earliest is based on psychoanalytic theory. Reminiscent of the old song "I Want a Girl Just Like the Girl Who Married Dear Old Dad," proponents of psychoanalytic theory, with its attendant Oedipal and Electra complexes, have proposed that in seeking a mate, young people are influenced by the characteristics of their parent of the other gender. It is generally expected by advocates of this model that there is a positive relationship between the other-gender parent's physical and psychological characteristics and the characteristics of other-gender peers to whom the mate-seeking person is attracted. Attempts have been made to measure the resemblance between the spousal choice and the physical and psychological characteristics of the other-gender parent, but the results have either failed to support psychoanalytic theory or were highly equivocal. A more precise test of psychoanalytic theory would involve investigation of whether the influence of parental characteristics on mate selection is greater for those individuals who have not resolved their Oedipal complex. Unfortunately, resolution of such conflicts has not been operationalized by proponents of psychoanalytic theory, making the model difficult to test.

Another early and influential model was proposed by the sociologist Robert Winch and was based on the notion of complementary needs. Two needs are complementary "when A's need X is gratifying to B's need Y, and B's behavior in acting out B's need Y is gratifying to A's need X." A's and B's needs may be of the same or a different type. If the need is the same, then Winch hypothesized that each member of the couple should differ in the intensity of that need. For example, if A is very high on the dimension of dominance and B is very low, then the needs are complementary. Winch called this Type 1 complementarity. If different needs are gratified in A and B, the relationship between the partners is hypothesized to be positive or negative depending on the particular pair of needs under consideration. For example, if A has a high need for nurturance, A should select a spouse B who has a high need for succorance. Winch referred to this situation involving two different needs as Type 2 complementarity. Although Winch's theory is intuitively appealing, attempts to validate the model with data from actual couples have been generally unsuccessful. A review and critique of the literature on Winch's complementary-needs theory of mate selection is provided by Murstein. Modified versions of complementary-needs theory have been put forth by others, but empirical support for such theories has been lacking.

Filter theories of mate selection take into account the developmental nature of intimate relationships. The first was offered by Kerckhoff and Davis, who hypothesized that after an initial screening for similarity with regard to basic cultural variables, a further screening takes place on the basis of values and, finally, need compatibility. It was proposed that couples who remain together after this successive filtering process end up marrying. Murstein constructed a more elaborate filter theory of the development of relationships, which he called stimulus–value–role (SVR) theory. Murstein hypothesized that the kinds of variables that can influence the course of development of a relationship fit into three categories: stimulus, value comparison, and role. These variables are operative throughout the course of the relationship but are hypothesized to be maximally influential at different stages of the courtship process.

The stimulus stage of courtship refers to the initial meeting and initial exchange between two people, perhaps at a dance or local meeting place for young people. During this period, the stimulus value of each person to the other is most salient in determining whether or not the courtship process will continue. Obviously, physical attractiveness is the one characteristic most readily selected for at this stage. That is not to say that everyone necessarily attempts to meet the most attractive person at any particular social gathering designed for the potential meeting of a mate. It is likely that the more experienced daters are familiar with rejection and temper their choices on the basis of their own self-perceived attractiveness.

If a couple is approximately equal in their stimulus value to each other, they may progress to the second stage of mate selection: value comparison. This period is characterized by verbal interactions and the gathering of information regarding each other. Each partner gleans information regarding the other's religious orientation; attitudes towards parents, friends, and people in general; interests; talents; and so forth. Each partner also evaluates his or her comfort with the other and the effect each partner's disclosure has on the other. If a couple survives these first two stages of courtship, they may evaluate their relationship quite positively and even decide to marry at this point. However, for most people, it is important to determine if the couple is able to function in compatible roles. The role stage, according to Murstein, "is the evaluation of perceived functioning of oneself in a dyadic relationship in comparison with the role one envisages for oneself and the perceived role function-

ing of the partner with respect to the roles one has envisaged for him or her." There has been research supporting the exchange nature of the SVR model of mate selection, but whether or not relationships leading to marriage follow the hypothesized sequence has yet to be tested.

Despite decades of research and the proposal of a number of theories, there are several aspects of mate selection that have been relatively neglected by researchers. For example, ethnic minorities have rarely been the focus of mate selection research, and the same is true of sexual minorities (homosexuals, bisexuals). The limited research on homosexual's mate selection has found few differences from heterosexuals in what is valued in relationships, but research on many aspects of mate selection among homosexuals remains to be done. As divorce and remarriage are fairly common in Western society, the issue of mate selection the second (or third) time around becomes a salient one. Do people choose partners similar to their prior mate? How is the process of mate selection different after having been married before? Unfortunately, these are questions that remain unanswered. Related to the situation of divorce and remarriage is the issue of relationship satisfaction. Does mate selection based on one set of criteria, or accomplished through one type of process, result in a more satisfying union than selection based on other criteria or other processes? Howard, et. al., found that preference for a physically attractive mate was negatively associated with men's and women's satisfaction with their current relationship, whereas preference for an affectionate, romantic, and expressive partner was positively related to relationship satisfaction. These correlations, however, were quite small (0.05–0.17), and, in general, little more is known regarding links between mate selection and subsequent relationship or marital satisfaction.

It is apparent that many of the details of mate selection criteria and processes remain to be discovered, and we have only a rudimentary understanding of the nature of the phenomena involved. Each model that has been proposed to explain mate selection has been criticized by other investigators, and even the best models offered to date have not been very effective in accurately capturing the nature of the process as it applies to large percentages of people. This fact has led some researchers to suggest that no one model of mate selection will be complete enough to explain all, or even most, couplings and that future investigation should focus on variability in the nature of relationship development. The process by which two people end up in a relatively enduring relationship together is probably a complex combination of cognitive, affective, interpersonal, situational, and other factors. For example, some people may arrive at the point in their lives where marriage is appropriate (or expected) and then search their field of eligibles for the "best" available partner based on a rationally generated "shopping list" of criteria. Others may not be seeking a long-term relationship but inexplicably find themselves involved with, and attached to, someone. Still others may start a relationship for reasons other than mate selection and then, after having invested heavily in the relationship, believe that marriage is the "natural" next step. Regardless of the particular process by which any two individuals come together to form a relationship, research on the topic has a long way to go in explaining this phenomenon in which the vast majority of people participate.

REFERENCES

Allgeier, E.R., and M.W. Wiederman. Love and Mate Selection in the 1990s. *Free Inquiry*, Vol. 11 (1991): pp. 25–27.

Buss, D.M. Sex Differences in Human Mate Preference: Evolutionary Hypothesis Tested in 37 Cultures. *Behavioral and Brain Sciences*, Vol. 12 (1989): pp. 1–14

———. Sex Differences in Human Mate Selection Criteria: An Evolutionary Perspective. In C. Crawford, M. Smith, and D. Krebs, eds. *Sociobiology and Psychology: Ideas, Issues, and Applications*. Hillsdale, N.J.: Erlbaum Associates, 1987.

Buss, D.M., and M. Barnes. Preferences in Human Mate Selection. *Journal of Personality and Social Psychology*, Vol. 50 (1986): pp. 559–70.

Cate, R.M., and J.E. Koval. Heterosexual Relationship Development: Is It Really a Sequential Process? *Adolescence*, Vol. 18 (1983), pp. 507–14.

Catton, W.R., and R.J. Smirich. A Comparison of Mathematical Modes for the Effect of Residential Propinquity on Mate Selection. *American Sociological Review*, Vol. 29 (1964), pp. 522–29.

Centers, R. *Sexual Attraction and Love: An Instrumental Theory*. Springfield, Ill.: C.C. Thomas, 1975.

Commins, W.D. Marriage Age of Oldest Son. *Journal of Social Psychology*, Vol. 3 (1932): pp. 487–90.

Daly, M., and M. Wilson. *Sex, Evolution, and Behavior*. 2d ed. Boston: Willard Grant Press, 1983.

Elder, G.H. Jr. Appearance and Education in Marriage Mobility. *American Sociological Review*, Vol. 34 (1969), pp. 519–33.

Hill, R. Campus Values in Mate Selection. *Journal of Home Economics*, Vol. 37 (1945), pp. 554–58.

Howard, J.A., P. Blumstein, and P. Schwartz. Social or Evolutionary Theories? Some Observations on Preferences in Human Mate Selection. *Journal of Personality and Social Psychology*, Vol. 53 (1987), pp. 196–200.

Hudson, J.W., and L.F. Henze. Campus Values in Mate Selection: A Replication. *Journal of Marriage and the Family*, Vol. 31 (1969), pp. 772–75.

Jedlicka, D. A Test of the Psychoanalytic Theory of Mate Selection. *Journal of Social Psychology*, Vol. 112 (1980), pp. 295–99.

Kephart, W.M. Some Correlates of Romantic Love. *Journal of Marriage and the Family*, Vol. 29 (1967), pp. 470–74.

Kerckhoff, A.C., and K.E. Davis. Value Consensus and Need Complementarity in Mate Selection. *American Sociological Review*, Vol. 27 (1962), pp. 295–303.

Kirkpatrick, C. A Statistical Investigation of Psychoanalytic Theory of Mate Selection. *Journal of Abnormal and Social Psychology*, Vol. 32 (1937): pp. 427–30.

Mangus, A.H. Relationships Between Young Women's Conceptions of Their Intimate Male Associates and Their Ideal Husbands. *Journal of Social Psychology*, Vol. 7 (1936).

McGinnis, R. Campus Values in Mate Selection: A Repeat Study. *Social Forces*, Vol. 36 (1959), pp. 368–73.

Murstein, B.I. *Paths to Marriage*. Beverly Hills, Calif.: Sage, 1986.

———. Stimulus-Value-Role: A Theory of Marital Choice. *Journal of Marriage and the Family*, Vol. 32 (1970), pp. 465–81.

———. *Who Will Marry Whom? Theories and Research in Marital Choice*. New York: Springer, 1976.

Peplau, L.A., and S.L. Gordon. The Intimate Relationships of Lesbians and Gay Men. In E.R. Allgeier and N.B. McCormick, eds. *Changing Boundaries: Gender Roles and Sexual Behavior*. Palo Alto, Calif.: Mayfield, 1983.

Simpson, J.A., B. Campbell, and E. Berscheid. The Association Between Romantic Love and Marriage: Kephart (1967) Twice Revisited. *Personality and Social Psychology Bulletin*, Vol. 12 (1986), pp. 363–72.

Strauss, A. The Influence of Parent-images Upon Marital Choice. *American Sociological Review*, Vol. 11 (1946), pp. 554–59.

Taylor, P.A., and N.D. Glenn. The Utility of Education and Attractiveness for Females' Status Attainment Through Marriage. *American Sociological Review*, Vol. 41 (1976), pp. 484–98.

Townsend, J.M., and G.D. Levy. Effects of Potential Partners' Physical Attractiveness and Socioeconomic Status on Sexuality and Partner Selection. *Archives of Sexual Behavior*, Vol. 19 (1990), pp. 149–64.

Wiederman, M.W., and E.R. Allgeier. Gender Differences in Mate Selection Criteria: Socioeconomic or Sociobiological Explanation? *Ethology and Sociobiology*, Vol. 13 (1992), pp. 115–21.

Winch, R.F. *Mate Selection: A Study of Complementary Needs*. New York: Harper, 1958.

Michael W. Wiederman
Elizabeth Rice Allgeier

MENARCHE

Menarche is the time in the life of a female when she begins her menstrual cycles. It is defined as the first time she spots blood as a discharge from her vagina. In the United States, menarche occurs at an average age of 12.8 years for white and 12.5 years for black females, with a range of from 8 to 18 years. Internationally, the age varies from 12.4 years in Cuban females to 18.8 years among females of the Bundi tribes of New Guinea. The average age of menarche among females in industrialized societies has declined about one year in the last century. Much work has been done to assess the effects of nutrition, health care, race, climate, and family size on the onset of menarche. It is also evident that genetic factors are at work, because the closer the kinship between females, the closer they are in age when they arrive at menarche.

Some researchers have proposed that menarche starts only when a minimum amount of body fat is present. Studies of long-distance runners, ballet dancers, gymnasts, and other athletes have shown that menarche has been delayed when they are in intensive training. Some of these women who have reached menarche stop menstruating.

Menarche usually occurs as breast growth reaches completion, and many hormonal changes begin to occur in the body. This is the time in many cultures when the girl becomes a woman. Vaginal secretions may increase, but it may take up to seven years before the menstrual cycles become regular. The woman may not ovulate regularly during this time; therefore, she may be infertile. This is not a predictable condition and should never be viewed as a means of birth control, because some females do ovulate and can become pregnant. It is during this time, however, that she does eventually become fertile.

Menarche can cause anxiety in a girl. She may be greatly concerned that she has not achieved this status at the same time as her friends, and when she does start menstruating, the physiological changes may be worrisome. She may become concerned because she is not regular in her periods. The attitudes of the adults around her can determine the level of anxiety and acceptance that she experiences with her new status. If they interpret menarche as the beginning of the "curse" she will have to endure every month for the next 40 years and as something to be hidden, then her anxiety will be increased and her feelings of self-worth decreased. If, however, menarche is celebrated as the beginning of her womanhood and regarded as a sign of matu-

ration, she will have much more positive attitudes toward the process and toward herself. Interviews with young women have revealed that if their parents have honestly discussed the physiological changes they are experiencing, and if their new status is recognized in some special way such as with a dinner in their honor, the entire process is far less anxiety ridden.

REFERENCES

Katchadourian, H.A. *Biological Aspects of Human Sexuality*. 4th ed. Fort Worth: Holt, Rinehart & Winston, 1990.

Masters, W.H., V.E. Johnson, and R.C. Kolodny. *Human Sexuality*. 3d ed. Glenview, Ill.: Scott, Foresman, 1988.

Reinisch, J.M. *The Kinsey Institute New Report on Sex*. New York: St. Martin's Press, 1990.

James D. Haynes

MENOPAUSE

Menopause, or the "climacteric," is defined as the permanent cessation of menstrual activity. The average age at which a woman has her last menstrual period continues to be 50 years, as it has been, according to some Greek authors, since the fourth century C.E. The perimenopausal period generally refers to the transitional period beginning with menstrual cycle changes (typically between the ages of 35 and 45) and ending with the resolution of menopausal symptoms (typically between 50 and 58). Premature menopause is defined as cessation of menses before the age of 40 and occurs in approximately 8 percent of women, most often as a result of the surgical removal of the uterus and ovaries. In the Western world, perimenopausal and postmenopausal women form the majority of females with 33 percent of the entire female population being over 55 years old and another 25 percent being between 44 and 55 years old.

Physiologically speaking, ovulation, the release of an egg from the ovary, occurs less frequently as women reach their mid-40s. As a result, hormonal output of estrogen and progesterone is more varied and at lower levels, leading to menstrual periods that are either closer together or more irregular in pattern, as well as changes in the amount of bleeding from lighter periods to very heavy menstrual flows.

While it is possible to describe general patterns of menstrual cycle changes in the menopausal phase, individual experiences of this complex transitional period vary greatly. It is recommended that each woman keep a menopause menstrual record, beginning with the first missed period or marked change in the menstrual cycle and continuing throughout the menopausal phase.

Symptom reports vary widely by culture and have been noted to be decreased in countries and cultures where there is great respect for the wisdom of the aged. In the United States, where increased age is frequently associated with frailness, vulnerability, and lack of productivity, menopause, a distinct sign of aging, has been viewed negatively in the past in both medical and lay literature. Psychiatric literature and lay mythology have portrayed women as "wilted roses," pointing to menopause as a time of depression and lack of clear focus in life. However, reports of recent research, which involved asking women themselves about their menopausal experience, have indicated different and more positive menopausal attitudes, that is, women feeling relieved and more free than ever before in their lives.

In the perimenopausal period, it is generally estimated that 10 percent to 20 percent of American women experience no menopausal symptomatology. Women experiencing symptoms report them to varying degrees, from mild to disabling. Hot flashes are the most frequently reported symptom, with 50 percent to 60 percent of women experiencing one or more hot flashes in the perimenopausal period. Other less frequently reported symptoms include night sweats, weight gain, vaginal dryness, depression, and excitability or anxiety. Of these, however, only hot flashes and night sweats are directly related to menopause; despite the listing of numerous symptoms frequently associated with menopause, such as depression and anxiety, research reports have not shown that these symptoms peak at this time or at any specific age in women.

Osteoporosis, or decalcification and "thinning" of the bones, is a medical problem frequently discussed in relation to menopause. The severity of osteoporosis increases concurrently with the drop in estrogen production in postmenopausal women. Approximately 25 percent of women are at risk of incurring bone fractures with age due to osteoporosis. Genetic or medical factors increasing the risk of osteoporosis and fractures include having a female relative with osteoporosis; being thin; being non-black; having had early menopause (before age 40), chronic diarrhea, or kidney disease; and using cortisone, thyroid medication, Dilantin, or aluminum-containing antacids daily. Life-style factors increasing the risk of osteoporosis include high alcohol use; smoking; lack of exercise; a low-calcium diet; lack of vitamin D from sun, diet, or vitamins; a very high protein diet; and high salt use.

While the recommended daily allowance for calcium is 800 milligrams, most nutritionists believe that women should consume 1,000 to 1,500 milligrams daily during their adult life. Since it is difficult to obtain this level of calcium intake from diet alone, calcium supplementation is frequently recommended for women over 35. Calcium tablets are easily found in the form of 500-milligram calcium carbonate or calcium citrate tablets in pharmacies or health food stores. For women over 35, two 500-milligram calcium tablets a day, taken with food, are generally recommended. It has been noted that calcium from bone meal and dolomite has contained lead and other contaminants, and therefore the intake of bone meal and dolomite tablets is not currently advised. Increasing the intake of calcium-rich foods is recommended for all women over age 35. Some foods rich in calcium are skim-milk powder, cooked collard greens, low-fat milk, canned sardines, and calcium-fortified orange juice.

Estrogen replacement therapy (ERT) during menopause remains one of the most controversial issues dealt with currently. In a series of articles in the *New England Journal of Medicine,* the use of estrogen replacement therapy was consistently found to protect postmenopausal women against coronary heart disease, the most common cause of death in women. Additionally, the use of estrogens by postmenopausal women has been found to slow the progress of osteoporosis and reduce or alleviate perimenopausal symptoms such as hot flashes and vaginal dryness. These benefits, however, have been contrasted with the possible development of breast cancer in association with postmenopausal estrogen use and the known four-fold risk of endometrial cancer among postmenopausal women using unopposed estrogen, or estrogen without progestins.

At this time, there is cautious support in the medical community for the broad use of estrogens among postmenopausal women based on the significant (40 to 50 percent) reduction in the risk of developing coronary heart disease. Feminists and some medical researchers, however, caution that the recent findings of significant estrogen benefits need to be more carefully studied among women willing to be randomly assigned to estrogen use in large clinical trials, rather than continuing to study women who may choose estrogen use (perhaps because they are more health conscious) versus women who do not use estrogens (perhaps because they are not an affordable option). Furthermore, feminists have suggested that the interaction between the societal message of the menopause experience as illness (or the "medicalization of menopause") and the potential of the ever-expanding marketplace for estrogen use be carefully analyzed. Until the results of the national randomized clinical trial (the Women's Health Initiative) are known, the decision to undergo estrogen replacement therapy remains a personal one based on individual and family risk profiles and on obtaining information from medical professionals and personal reading.

In the area of sexuality, the cultural atmosphere that represses the notion of middle-aged sex is being challenged now more than ever before. While experts agree that continued sexual activity until late in life depends almost entirely on two factors, health and attitude, the medical view of problems—"atrophic vaginitis," or dry, fragile vaginal tissue; "dyspareunia," or pain with intercourse; and a type of menopausal frigidity—is being replaced with research reports exploring the complexity of women's sexuality during this time in their lives. In 1976, *The Hite Report* drew attention to large numbers of women speaking candidly and in depth about their own sexuality, but only 14 of 438 pages concerned the older woman. Since then, despite continued difficulty for women in talking about the sexual details of their lives, varied themes have emerged regarding menopause and sexuality: for example, the theme of menopause as signaling a time of freedom, including freedom to fantasize, explore, and experiment; freedom from pregnancy; and freedom to choose not to have unsatisfying sex. According to Reitz, the complexity of the older woman's sexuality is only beginning to be explored.

In the development or maintenance of menopausal or postmenopausal "zest," yearly checkups with a medical practitioner who has a positive attitude toward women are important. At this time, a thorough physical examination is performed, questions and concerns are addressed, the self–breast examination is discussed, and a mammogram is ordered as needed. At least as important during this time is attention to diet, exercise, and a healthy life-style. Specifically, a diet high in vegetables, whole grains, fruit, and calcium-rich foods is optimal for the menopausal woman. Minimizing or eliminating caffeine is recommended, as is lowering the intake of meat, fat, sugar, and salt in the diet. The benefits of exercise are particularly significant during this period and include decreased risk of heart disease and osteoporosis, easier weight control, improved appearance, decreased pain, and better sleep. Finally, decreasing noise, increasing the use of relaxation techniques, and utilizing other stress-reducing methods are recommended during the menopausal period. These measures, together with exercise and good nutrition, are all components of the life-style that has been associated with a positive approach to menopause and aging.

REFERENCES

Goldman, L., and A. Tosteson. Uncertainty About Postmenopausal Estrogen. *New England Journal of Medicine,* Vol. 325 (Sept. 1991), pp. 800–02.

Greenwood, S. *Menopause Naturally.* Rev. ed. Volcano, Calif.: Volcano Press, 1989.

Hite, S. *The Hite Report: A Nationwide Study of Female Sexuality.* New York: Macmillan, 1976.

MacPherson, K. Menopause as Disease: The Social Construction of a Metaphor. *Advances in Nursing Science,* Vol. 3 (1981), pp. 95–113.

Martin, K., and M. Freeman. Postmenopausal Hormone-Replacement Therapy. *New England Journal of Medicine,* Vol. 328 (April 1993), pp. 115–17.

Mishell, D.R. Menopause: Physiology and Pharmacology. Chicago: Year Book Medical, 1987.

Nabulsi, A., A. Folsom, A. White, W. Patsch, G. Heiss, K. Wu, and M. Szklo. Association of Hormone-Replacement Therapy with Various Cardiovascular Risk Factors in Postmenopausal Women. *New England Journal of Medicine,* Vol. 328 (April 1993), pp. 1069–75.

Reitz, R. *Menopause: A Positive Approach.* Radner, Pa.: Chilton, 1977.

Lisa Monagle

MENSTRUATION

Menstruation is the periodic sloughing off of two layers of the uterine endometrium. The bits of tissue and the blood produced from the torn blood vessels produce the monthly "bleeding" that constitutes the menstrual flow. The events and time that occur between any two periods compose the menstrual cycle.

The average length of the menstrual cycle in human females is 28 days but may range from 21 to 40 days. Cycles outside of this range are considered irregular. The first day of the cycle is counted from the abrupt appearance of blood. The cycles usually start (menarche) at about age 12 and continue until about age 48, when they stop (menopause). Although an ovarian cycle is characteristic of all mammals, menstruation occurs only in female apes, some monkeys, and women.

After menarche, the cycles finally become regular and usually remain so. The process is continuous, however, with one cycle following another. The process is controlled by complicated interactions of hormones from the hypothalamus, anterior pituitary gland, and ovaries involving the entire reproductive system, but especially the ovaries, uterus, and vagina.

The menstrual cycle can be divided into four continuous phases. The menstrual phase begins with the appearance of blood on day one and continues for four or five days. The woman loses about one-half cup of blood, which is quickly replaced. Estrogens and progestins are reduced in the bloodstream and thus stop inhibiting the production of follicle stimulating hormone (FSH) by the anterior pituitary gland.

The increased amount of FSH stimulates the growth of several ovarian follicles and their enclosed ova in the ovaries. This marks the beginning of the preovulatory phase, which ends when a follicle migrates to the surface of the ovary and discharges its ovum into the body cavity. Usually, only one ovum matures each cycle. Increasing levels of estrogen produced from the cells of the developing follicle cause thickening of the endometrium and changes in the cervix and vagina. The increased levels of estrogen in the bloodstream reduce the sensitivity of the ovary to FSH. The preovulatory phase lasts from 7 to 19 days, and it is this phase that produces the varied lengths of the menstrual cycle in different women.

The high levels of estrogen stimulate the hypothalamus to release gonadotropin releasing hormone (GnRH), which in turn causes the anterior pituitary to release luteinizing hormone (LH). The ovum is released about 12 to 24 hours after LH has reached its highest concentration, thus marking the ovulation phase, which is the shortest phase of the entire cycle and occurs on about the 14th day of a 28-day cycle, but always occurs 14 days before the onset of menstruation regardless of the length of the cycle.

The postovulatory phase begins as the released ovum starts to move through the Fallopian tube. A tissue called the corpus luteum is produced in the old ovarian follicle. This tissue begins to produce large amounts of progesterone and estrogen, leading to increased levels in the bloodstream. Under the influence of these hormones, the uterine wall begins to thicken and produce a nutrient fluid. Thus, the uterus is prepared for the arrival of a fertilized egg should pregnancy occur. The high levels of estrogen and progesterone in the blood cause the hypothalamus to stop the production of GnRH, causing the rapid decline of production of LH and FSH from the anterior pituitary. The reduction of these hormones decreases stimulation of the corpus luteum, which will degenerate in 10 to 15 days after ovulation unless fertilization of the egg occurs. The loss of the corpus luteum and the subsequent abrupt reduction in the production of estrogen and progesterone cause the endometrium to degenerate and slough off, starting the next menstruation.

Attitudes toward menstruation have varied greatly from culture to culture and among people within cultures. Many cultures have viewed women as impure or unclean during their period and have forced them to be secluded from ordinary social functions during their menstruation for fear that they would defile all that they touched. The fear is especially pronounced if religious objects are involved; this is a reason why women are often denied priesthood. The fluid itself may have been regarded as sacred or as having certain mystical powers. The woman had to undergo various cleansing rituals before she could again enter her usual social place.

In other cultures, menstruation has been considered to be a normal bodily function and necessary for procreation. In cultures where the cycle is understood by both women and men, there is far less superstition concerning its effects. However, certain prejudices may remain and exert either positive or negative influences on sexual interactions as well as the way a woman may regard herself during her period. If her period is regarded as a "curse," as having "the monthlies," or as "being on the rag," she may consider her condition to be a physical or emotional handicap. If, however, she considers her period to be part of her natural cycle, many of these types of trauma can be avoided.

Some women experience amenorrhea, a condition in which they may not menstruate over a long time. Amenorrhea can be brought on by stress, weight loss, or regular strenuous exercise, among other factors. Some women suffer from excessive menstrual flow (menorrhagia) that exceeds the usual 3 to 4 ounces.

There may be actual discomfort and pain associated with a woman's period. Although the severity of the symptoms varies from woman to woman, about half of all women suffer from dysmenorrhea, or painful menstruation, in their early adult life. These cramps are caused by chemical substances, called prostaglandins, that produce contractions of the smooth muscles of the uterus. Some women may regularly suffer from Mittelschmertz, or "middle pain." This is pain or cramps in the lower abdomen or back that occurs during the time of ovulation, or about halfway between menstrual periods. It varies greatly in intensity but is not associated with any disorder of the reproductive organs.

A very controversial condition related to menstruation is premenstrual syndrome (PMS). Although the symptoms of this condition are generalized, the timing makes it unique for an estimated 30 percent to 90 percent of women; the symptoms usually appear between 7 and 14 days before menstruation and disappear with the onset of the flow. There is no widely accepted cause. The symptoms vary greatly in presence and intensity. They range from headaches to stuffy noses, fluid retention, fatigue, depression, irritability, changes in eating habits, forgetfulness, and shifts in sexual desire. The symptoms may be so severe that some women (e.g., in Great Britain and France) have used PMS to demonstrate diminished capacity during the commission of violent crimes. PMS has been used in some arguments to indicate that women are incapable of occupying positions of responsibility. This argument, of course, ignores the fact that men also sometimes suffer from diminished capacity for other reasons.

REFERENCES

Bullough, V.L. *Sexual Variance in Society and History.* New York: John Wiley & Sons, 1976.

Katchadourian, H.A. *Biological Aspects of Human Sexuality.* 4th ed. Fort Worth: Holt, Rinehart & Winston, 1990.

Masters, W.H., V.E. Johnson, and R.C. Kolodny. *Human Sexuality.* 3d ed. Glenview, Ill.: Scott, Foresman, 1988.

Reinisch, J.M. *The Kinsey Institute New Report on Sex.* New York: St. Martin's Press, 1990.

James D. Haynes

MISCEGENATION

"Miscegenation" is from the Latin *miscare*, "to mix," + *genus*, "race." The term was used to describe a mixture of races, especially marriage or cohabitation between a white person and a member of another race.

The discourse on miscegenation proceeds from a Western European point of view that can be traced to the prohibition of marriage between Christians and Jews in the fifth century. Interest in cross-societal breeding is also indicated by the many labels used to describe the offspring of Europeans, sub-Saharan Africans, and aboriginal Americans in the Iberian New World. It is questionable whether these concerns can be considered "racial" in any modern sense of that word. When Africans were enslaved in the English colonies, a repugnance toward sexual relationships between "whites" and "blacks" emerged in the context of racist ideology, law, and science.

Concerns with "race mixing" are peripheral to endogamous norms, which are part of all societies and have as their main purpose the preservation of cultural and economic integrity. In the modern world, endogamy (the custom of marrying within some specified group) takes precedence and antimiscegenation occupies center stage, though the economic, cultural, and political concerns still echo through them.

The genetic blending and sexual relationships of diverse peoples were relatively unproblematic prior to the "age of exploration." Though there have recently been problems of "mixed race" children in Korea and Vietnam, historically the issue was both created and defined by Western Europeans—particularly English speakers. This was due to England's preeminence among the colonial powers and to demographic factors both in the colonies and at home. Although Afro-Asian, Afro-Amerindian, and Asian-Amerindian persons are sometimes considered miscegenated, this happened within the context of European colonialism and anti-Black racism. Though extensive miscegenation characterized all colonial situations, the Spanish and the Portugese recognized intermediate "racial" categories (mulattoes and Creoles), while the English-speaking colonies evolved toward a two-category (black–white) system.

The word "miscegenation" was coined in 1863 by the American journalist David Croly, who held that the Emancipation Proclamation was the desirable first step toward full equality among Americans, an equality that would inevitably involve extensive "interracial" marriage. His term "melaleukon" to describe the children of marriages between "whites" and "blacks" did not survive in the language. The survival of "miscegenation" undoubtedly owes much to its harsh sound and to the confusion of the Latin prefixes *miscere* and *mis* (bad).

Considering the enormous difficulty involved in determining if and how the categorization of human beings should occur, as well as the arbitrariness and political motivation of such categorization, miscegenation has more to do with politics than with biology, sex, or love. That two people having coitus should be considered to be engaging in miscegenation in some instances and not in others is nonsense in isolation from the horrendous and complicated history of "race" relations following the European expansion.

Since 1900, the acknowledged miscegenated peoples have increased at more than twice the rate of world population growth, but it is still a very small group (about 300 million persons, or about 5 percent of the world's 6 billion people). Most of these are Portugese- and Spanish-speaking Afro-Americans and Mestizos (persons of mixed European and native American ancestry). These certainly do not include all "race mixing" that has taken place in the last 500 years, or even a small fraction of the mixing of peoples that has occurred over the millennia of human experience.

If mate selection were "color-blind" and determined solely by chance love matches, 25 percent of marriages in the United States would be "interracial" (author's calculations), when, in fact, less than 2 percent are. Of these "chance" marriages, 19 percent would be between "black" and "white" spouses, but we actually observe that only four-tenths of 1 percent of all marriages are of this type. Because such marriages are so rare, those involved in them are confronted with problems of discrimination, misunderstanding, and identity confusion.

Since, as Goodman and Goodman point out, "the most virulent racial stereotypes are traditionally sexual and the most vicious sexual caricatures racially tinged," miscegenation will continue to be a hotly debated topic in the United States. Despite a slight decline in the marriage rate, most people want to marry. Despite a worsening marriage market (especially for "black" women), most people will be able to marry and have some choice of partners. People will continue to apply standards to potential mates—aesthetic, social, economic, and idiosyncratic. These standards will sometimes be violated and they will change. For the foreseeable future, "race" will be one of the standards used. Sometimes this standard will apply so that the cultural integrity of groups can be maintained. Sometimes "race" will tear lovers, families, and societies apart.

REFERENCES

Goodman, L.E., and M.J. Goodman. "Particularly Amongst the Sunburnt Nations . . .". The Persistence of Sexual Stereotypes of Race in Bio-Science, Part I. *International Journal of Group Tensions,* Vol. 19 (1989), p. 221.

A. Robert Corbin

MISOGYNIST, MISOGYNY

A misogynist is a person who hates women. Most misogynists are men. The condition is believed to develop from some childhood experience such as being raised by a brutal mother or other female. It may reflect an Oedipus complex (negative in men) or be associated with a homosexual conflict: women wishing desperately that they were men or men disappointed and bitter that they are. The range of expression of misogyny runs the gamut from mild avoidance behavior and disparaging remarks to serial torture and murder. Some men who are desperate for companionship engage in misogynistic behavior toward their wives in an effort to maintain power over them and discourage abandonment.

Misogyny is more accepted by some cultures than others, and acceptance may change with time within a given culture. Misogynistic attitudes and practices were commonplace among the early Hebrews, as described in Genesis, and the Homeric and post-Homeric Greek societies, for example. At present, abuse of wives is a serious social problem throughout the Americas and in many other cultures.

Misogyny has been explored as a literary theme at least as far back as the time of Aristotle. One of his pupils, Theophrastus, is credited with a treatise, *On Marriage,* which was widely read and inspired misogynistic undercurrents in the work of Chaucer and many others. Another popular treatise, *Malleus Maleficarum* (1485), by Jacob Sprenger and Heinrich Kramer, depicted women as agents of the devil and promoted misogyny. Writers of the 20th century who have dealt with misogyny include D.H. Lawrence, H.L. Mencken, and the playwright Sidney Howard.

REFERENCES

Forward, S., and J. Torres. *Men Who Hate Women and the Women Who Love Them.* New York: Bantam Books, 1986.

Rogers, K.M. *The Troublesome Helpmate: A History of Misogyny in Literature.* Seattle: Univ. of Washington Press, 1966.

Alice P. Stein

MOLL, ALBERT

Albert Moll (1862–1939) was a major rival to Magnus Hirschfeld. A Berlin neurologist, he wrote an influential book on homosexuality entitled *Die Konträre Sexualempfindug* (1891), in which he distinguished between innate and acquired homosexuality. He regarded innate homosexuality as a stepchild of nature and held that the sex drive was an innate psychological function that could be injured or malformed through no fault or choice of the individual.

He further refined his theory in a general treatise on sexuality, *Untersuchungen über die Libido sexualis* (1897), where he emphasized homosexuality as an illness, probably with an "inherited taint." His major work was his *Handbuch der Sexualwissenschaft* (1911), where he developed association therapy, the replacement of same-sex associations with those of the opposite sex, as a curative technique.

Over the years, Moll grew increasingly hostile to Hirschfeld, in part because of Hirschfeld's polemical style and because of what he regarded as the ethically dubious facets of Hirschfeld's activity. As he did so, he also changed his mind about the innate character of homosexuality and went into full opposition to Hirschfeld by organizing a rival international congress. Though never a Nazi (Moll came from a Jewish background), he mistakenly believed he could continue to be active under them, and after the Nazi takeover he was unable to practice and was more or less under house arrest until he died. His autobiography, *Ein Leben als Arzt der Seele* (1936), was his final attack on Hirschfeld's views. Though he still believed that there might be a few homosexuals whose orientation could be called innate, he felt that most homosexuality was acquired through improper sexual experiences and attacked those who argued for social and legal acceptance of homosexuality.

He pioneered the study of childhood sexuality in his *Sexualleben des Kindes,* and his handbook (mentioned above) was the first comprehensive work on sex. His theory of the sex life of the child had a profound effect on Freudian concepts, though Freud did not acknowledge it.

REFERENCES

Sulloway, F. *Freud, Biologist of the Mind: Beyond the Psychoanalytic Myth.* New York: Basic Books, 1979.

Vern L. Bullough

MONEY, JOHN WILLIAM

John William Money (1921–) has exercised major influence on the development of sexology over the last half of the 20th century. He is perhaps best known for his studies in psychoendocrinology, but he has also paid special attention to diagnostic categories and invented terms for specific behaviors (e.g., love maps). He defined more than 40 paraphilias. He also has written on the history of sexology. In describing his own activities, Money wrote that he has always tried to combine research with clinical care, academic teaching, and public edu-

cation. He has lectured widely and managed to lecture on all continents except Antarctica.

Money is a native of New Zealand. He was born in Morrinsville, New Zealand, on July 8, 1921, the son of Frank and Ruth Read Money. He graduated from Victoria University College in New Zealand in 1943 with a teacher's certificate and a double M.A., one in philosophy-psychology and one in education. He briefly taught in New Zealand before coming to the United States to do graduate work, first at the University of Pittsburgh and then at Harvard, where he received a Ph.D. in psychology in 1952. At Harvard, he became interested in the study of hermaphroditism, and it was on this topic that he wrote his dissertation. He joined the faculty of Johns Hopkins University in 1951 as part of a research team established by Lawson Wilkins, who had shown that the hormone cortisol, then newly synthesized, was the substance that could correct the adrenogenital syndrome known as virilizing adrenal hyperplasia. Shortly after his arrival at Hopkins, Money founded the office of psychohormonal research and, with others, the first gender identity clinic in the United States. He also established the research program for psychohormonal treatment of the paraphilias and of sex offenders and became codirector of the clinic.

Money was active in various public groups, including, from 1967 to 1969, the National Institutes of Mental Health task force on homosexuality; study sections of the National Institutes of Health; the Sex Information and Education Council of the United States (SIECUS); and the Society for the Scientific Study of Sex (SSSS), of which he was a charter member and a former president. A large number of his students also became influential in the development of sexology. Some of the stands Money has taken were fairly controversial, and not all his theories have proved to be viable; however, this is the case with most pioneers, and Money has broken new ground in the study of sex and gender. In addition to a large number of refereed articles, he also has written more popular books, including *Man and Woman, Boy and Girl*, on which he collaborated with A.A. Ehrhardt.

A prolific editor and writer, Money has authored more than 10 books and 300 journal articles, as well as coauthored or edited more than 20 books. Many of his articles have been collected together in books, one of which was entitled *Venuses Penuses*. This volume includes a brief autobiographical sketch and a complete bibliography of his works. He also coedited, with H. Musaph, a series of books entitled *Handbook of Sexology*, dealing with various aspects of sex and hormones, as well as other topics.

Money has received many honors and awards. In 1987, he received both the Harry Benjamin Distinguished Scholar Award and, from the National Institute of Child Health and Development, the Outstanding Research Accomplishments Award. In addition, he has been honored by the American Psychological Association, the Royal Society of Medicine, the American Psychiatric Association, and the SSSS.

REFERENCES

Money, J. *Destroying Angel*. Buffalo, N.Y.: Prometheus Books, 1985.

———. *Love and Love Sickness*. Baltimore: Johns Hopkins Univ. Press, 1980.

———. *Lovemaps*. Buffalo, N.Y.: Prometheus Books, 1988.

———. *Sex Errors of the Body*. Baltimore: Johns Hopkins Univ. Press, 1968.

———. *Venuses Penuses*. Buffalo, N.Y.: Prometheus Books, 1986.

Money, J., and A.A. Ehrhardt. *Man and Woman, Boy and Girl*. Baltimore: Johns Hopkins Univ. Press, 1972.

Money, J., and H. Musaph. *Handbook of Sexology*. 6 vols. with supplement. Amsterdam: Elsevier, 1977–91.

Sari Locker

MONOGAMY

Monogamy is a marriage form in which one man is married to one woman. In Murdock's ethnographic atlas of 849 human cultures, 709 (83.5 percent) allowed polygyny (one man with two or more wives), 137 (16.1 percent) were entirely monogamous (one man, one wife), and 4 (0.047 percent) were polyandrous (one wife with two or more husbands). Even though there are more polygamous cultures than cultures requiring monogamy as the only legal marriage form, monogamy is the only marriage form that is accepted in all societies and is by far the predominant form, even in cultures allowing for other forms.

Monogamy as a legal marriage form may be contrasted with monogamy as a behavior limiting one's sexual activity to a single partner. Monogamy in the latter sense is often contrasted with promiscuity (mating with a number of partners) rather than with other legally allowable forms of marriage. An individual in a monogamous culture who is in a monogamous legal relationship can engage in extramarital affairs without serious legal difficulties, but if he or she marries the partner with whom the affair is being conducted while at the same time being married to the original partner, he or she has committed bigamy, for which there are criminal penalties in all cultures allowing only for monogamous marriage.

Size differences between the sexes within the various primate species are related to the degree of monogamy-promiscuity among them. The more promiscuous the species the greater the size difference between the sexes. Baboons are the most promiscuous of the primates, with males being about 22 percent taller and 80 percent heavier than females. Gibbons are the most monogamous of the primates, and males and females are approximately the same height and weight. Humans lie between baboons and gibbons both in terms of size differences, with males being about 7 percent taller and 18 percent heavier than females, and in terms of monogamous-promiscuous behavior.

Gibbons select and stay with a mate throughout life, and this monogamy rule assures that males of all sizes have an equal chance to mate; however, baboons engage in a ferocious scramble to impregnate as many females as they can during mating season. The biggest and strongest males are able to mate more frequently, with the smallest and weakest perhaps enjoying no opportunity to mate at all. This mating scramble led to the evolutionary selection for greater size among male baboons and to a greater and greater divergence in size between the sexes.

A voluminous literature, as well as the ubiquity of prostitution and rape, attests to the fact that men are much more attracted to plural partners than are women. This behavioral sexual dimorphism, according to Naftolin, probably arose out of different reproductive mechanisms. Naftolin reminds us that the female reproductive pattern is periodic; she sheds one or more of a finite number of ova each month. To reproduce, she requires a fertile egg, the proper uterine environment, sexual receptivity, and a healthy partner. If the male reproductive pattern were also periodic, sperm shedding, sexual receptivity, and the aggressive impulses necessary to fend off competitors would have to be synchronized with the female's pattern. Such a synchronicity would be very difficult, and many precious ova would be wasted. The biologically efficient strategy required that males constantly produce fertile sperm and be constantly able and willing to shed them.

Endowed with cheap and plentiful sperm, and relatively free of responsibility for the care of offspring, males were freed by this reproductive pattern to spread their genes as far as their aggressive capabilities and good fortune allowed. Females would be better served reproductively by being more monogamous. Females certainly would have attracted numerous males to fertilize their eggs if they behaved promiscuously, but offspring survival, not simple fertilization, is the goal of the female reproductive strategy. A monogamous sentiment would be more likely to assure reproductive success through the care and protection of a jealous mate. After all, a male could not be expected to remain with a woman and her offspring and provide them with the support they need were he not reasonably sure of his paternity.

The issue of monogamy-promiscuity as sexually differentiated reproductive strategies is summed up by Mayr:

> The male has little to lose by courting numerous females and by attempting to fertilize as many of them as possible. Anything that enhances his success in courtship will be favored by selection. The situation is quite different for the female. Any failure of mating with the right kind of male may mean total reproductive failure and a total loss of her genes from the genotype of the next generation.

If evolutionary pressures favor promiscuity for males and monogamy for females, how can we account for the overwhelming popularity of monogamous marriage in a world in which men make the rules? Certainly, polygyny is much more favorable to the male reproductive strategy. The answer appears to be that the influence of genes and sex hormones is drastically reduced in species with social organization—monogamy is a cultural rather than a biological trait. Intelligent Homo sapiens realize that there are remote as well as immediate consequences attached to behavior and that often we have to sacrifice immediate gratification of our impulses for the long-term good. Freud pointed out that the sublimation of our sexual drives is necessary for cultural development, and, writing in the 19th century, Engels saw that monogamy was to become the dominant marriage form as societies became more complex.

There are many social, psychological, and economic reasons that make monogamous marriage the predominant marriage form in the world today. Quale lists a number of these reasons: (1) almost all members of society have maximal opportunity to marry, with relatively few being left out; (2) a method of sexual gratification is provided for both sexes; (3) intrasex jealousies and quarrels are minimized; (4) emotional needs of both sexes are more easily fulfilled in a monogamous relationship than in other marriage forms; (5) closer emotional bonds can exist between parents and children in a monogamous marriage; and (6) sociolegal issues such as inheritance, property rights, legitimacy, and lineage are less complicated than they are in other marriage forms. Additionally, the compact size of the monogamous nuclear family is best suited to life in industrial and postindustrial societies, in which frequent geographical mobility is often required. So despite all that has been written about "alternate marriage forms" over the past few decades, sociolegal monogamy will probably remain the world's predominant marriage form, even if tempered now and again by adultery.

REFERENCES

Engels, F. *The Origin of the Family, Private Property and the State*. 1884. Reprint. New York: International, 1972.

Eshleman, J.R. *The Family: An Introduction*. 5th ed. Boston: Allyn & Bacon, 1988.

Freud, S. *Civilization and Its Discontents*. Translated and edited by J. Strachey. New York: W.W. Norton, 1961.

Mayr, E. Sexual Selection and Natural Selection. In B. Campbell, ed. *Sexual Selection and the Descent of Man 1871–1971*. London: Heineman, 1972.

Murdock, G.P. *Ethnographic Atlas*. Pittsburgh: Univ. of Pittsburgh Press, 1967.

Naftolin, F. Understanding the Bases of Sex Differences. *Science*, Vol. 211 (1981), pp. 1263–64.

Nicholson, J. *Men and Women: How Different Are They?* New York: Oxford Univ. Press, 1984.

Quale, G.R. *A History of Marriage Forms*. Westport, Conn.: Greenwood Press, 1988.

Walsh, A. *Science and Love: Understanding Love and Its Effects on Mind and Body*. Buffalo, N.Y.: Prometheus, 1991.

Anthony Walsh

MORALITY: SEXUAL MORALITY

On the surface, the topic of sexual morality is not especially popular in the sexual-education materials published today. Only a few of the general textbooks even mention the topic of personal values as they refer to sexual decision making. The one major exception was the 1979 text by Meyners and Wooster, which gave extended treatment to value decisions in choosing one's sexual life-style. Perhaps as Diamond and Karlen acknowledged in their text, some individuals object to discussion of certain topics in sex education on moral grounds.

Can sexual science avoid the question of values? Certainly not in the view of Scruton. This contemporary philosopher includes an entire chapter on sexual morality in his book *Sexual Desire: A Moral Philosophy of the Erotic*. Some sexual scientists would agree that sexology has significant dialogue with value issues. When Money introduced the term "sexosophy" into the literature, he argued that even the so-called hard sciences are not value free. In Money's analysis, sexosophy is about tradition, history, and religion. Sexology, the science of sex, he argues, must not be limited by any particular sexosophy. Sexology, the science of sex, and sexosophy, the philosophy and moral principles of sex, are influenced by and reflect values. Thus, it will be argued here that sexual scientists can study the sexual morality of individuals and cultures; that sexual science is affected by the value assumptions that sex educators, sex researchers, and clinicians make; and that scientific data and theory can in turn affect values.

The "value free" stance on moral issues pragmatically makes good sense when dealing with controversial sexual topics. However, in doing so, the sexual scientist risks the fallacy of mixing up the meanings of relativism. "Descriptive relativism" acknowledges cultural differences and cultural conflicts. "Normative relativism" advocates that what is acceptable in one society may not be in another. "Metaethical relativism" contends that there is no rational way to justify any particular set of moral principles. Thus, according to Rich and DeVitis, to insist that sex education, sex therapy, and sex research must be value free is to assume that there are no universal sexual standards. To assume that there are no universal sexual standards is a moral position, hence not neutral; thus, sexologists are not "value free." They may be "value fair," in that the emphasis is on dialogue and critical thinking about value assumptions and moral traditions.

The sexosophy-sexology tension is not unique to sexual science. Kurtines, Alvarez, and Azmitia argue that the philosophy of science has rejected the legitimacy of the value-free assumption. They go on to identify critical issues for science in general and for those who would study moral phenomena in particular. "Normative assumptions" refer to norms, values, and principles. In general, moral theory is concerned about normative assumptions. Issues and conflicts can arise between scientists and moralists at different levels of inquiry. D'Andrade grouped science into the categories of physical sciences, natural sciences, and semiotic sciences. Psychology, some sociology, and some anthropology are natural sciences. Some psychology, sociology, and anthropology are semiotic sciences. Semiotic sciences study those phenomena that are "imposed" on the individual and society rather than being the consequence of the natural world. To some extent, sexual morality is imposed on the individual. Thus, the scientific study of sexual morality is a semiotic science. The moral assumptions of the sexual scientist, however, are sexosophy rather than sexology.

Kurtines and his colleagues identify three major moral periods in the Western tradition. Classical moral theory (500 B.C.E.–400 C.E.) is described as being "objectivistic, rationalistic, and naturalistic." Objective moral standards were thought to be derivable from the natural world. The moral theory in this period tended to stress justice and happiness. During the medieval moral period (400–1400), naturalism and secular assumptions were rejected. A theistic worldview, which Centore has called "psychosomaticism with belief in immorality," was dominant. Thus, the source of moral theory was spiritual and outside the natural world. Faith rather than reason was stressed. Love, especially the love of God, was emphasized as the major moral concern. By the 17th century, modern moral theory was established within Western culture. Modern moral theory can be described as being once again naturalistic but relativistic. Thus, modern scientific truth is "contingent truth" rather than "objective truth." Scientific conclusions are always subject to change in response to new research findings.

Kurtines and his colleagues also discuss five dimensions or categories of normative assumptions: (1) universal, unchanging standards versus norms and values relative to a given culture, a time in history, a specific situation, or personal judgment; (2) ultimate goals and ultimate values versus obligations and principles of human conduct; (3) primacy of reason, insight-intuition, or sensory experience; (4) emphasis on natural law versus revelations from a supernatural power or supernatural being; and (5) the nature of the values, principles, or standards emphasized, such as justice or the good life.

When the scientist's conclusions are challenged by the moralist, "theoretical discourse" takes place between the scientist and the moralist. When the scientist challenges existing values or norms or the legitimacy of institutions that set the standards for conduct, the communication becomes "practical discourse." When the arguments focus on the theory of truth itself, then the scientist and moralist are engaging in "metatheoretical discourse."

As a sexual scientist, Money has characterized U.S. society as a "sexual dictatorship." His observations, briefly summarized below, illustrate a call for "practical discourse." Sexual taboo in this society has a long tradition and is extremely powerful. The sexual taboo proscribes sexual behavior and what one can think about as well. Anything that falls outside the narrow range of what is doctrinally correct is sexual heresy. In contemporary society, disobedience is punished by secular authorities rather than by church authorities. Secular legislative bodies create laws derived from the authority of the church. Governmental agencies seek out and punish sexual heretics. As a semiotic science, sexology will inevitably challenge some of the normative ethics of religion and government. Some challenges may be welcomed, while others may be bitterly contested, especially if the distinction between sexology and sexosophy is not understood and maintained.

Traditional Roman Catholic ideology, for example, condemned homosexuality. Consistent with this moral tradition, homosexuality was long viewed as a mental-health problem by the mental professionals. Fifty years ago, Fuller noted that many crimes mirror the moral values of the society and went on to assert that the moral issue on homosexuality was clearly settled. But his conclusion was premature. In 1973, by action of the governing board of the American Psychiatric Association, homosexuality was dropped as a diagnostic category. That decision was controversial at the time, although the change reflected a growing scientific sentiment. In like manner, the treatment of homosexuality in sociology and psychology textbooks increasingly reflects accurate scientific data rather than the normative ethics of the society.

While there is controversy over what is meant by moral behavior and moral character, there is ample evidence that morality can be studied scientifically. According to the judgment of Kurtines and Gewirtz, there are four basic approaches to the psychological study of morality, moral behavior, and the development of moral judgment: (1) the "cognitive-developmental structural approach," (2) the "stage-structural constructivist approach," (3) the "learning-behavioral developmental approaches," and (4) the "social-personality theory approaches." Sapp identifies four models also, namely, "structural-developmental theory," "personological and psychodynamic explanations," the "social-learning theory approach," and "cognitive-developmental theory and pragmatic philosophy of science." Rich and DeVitis emphasize the centrality of the work of the French sociologist Emile Durkheim, who noted the conflicting interests of the individual

and society. Rich and DeVitis discuss diverse approaches to moral development, with emphasis on moral development during childhood, adolescence, and while attending a college or university.

It has often been observed that individuals are prone to make moral evaluations. The intent of those moral evaluations often is to influence the future behavior of someone, or to have the hope of doing so. Simon and Gagnon have called the rules that govern sexual behavior "cultural scenarios." Since part of that sexual scripting is moral education, formally and informally, sexual science is a semiotic science when it investigates sexual morality. It has been shown that considerable effort has been expended in the study of various aspects of sexual morality. What is needed is a more systematic and more theoretically guided research. It is clearly evident that sexual scientists make value assumptions and that those value assumptions influence the field. Since this is the case, sexology can, and even has the ethical duty to, engage in "practical discourse" with the defenders of normative sexual ethics.

Potential contributions of the scientific study of sexual morality to society and the individual are summarized as follows: (1) the investigation of individual differences in sexual ethics and the potential consequences of those values for the welfare of others in society; (2) the clarification of the relationship of sexual problems and normative sexual ethics; (3) a challenge to sexual ethics that implies scientific data which is actually nonexistent or that is defended by theory and data which are scientifically flawed; (4) the development of scientific theories of sexual moral development; and (5) the documentation of arbitrary and unfair discrimination based on poorly justified moral evaluation of divergence from normative sexual ethics.

As sexual scientists deal with these and similar issues, it is to be hoped that they will also be more willing to discuss their ethical assumptions.

REFERENCES

Centore, F.F. *Persons: A Comparative Account of the Six Possible Theories*. Westport, Conn.: Greenwood Press, 1979.

D'Andrade, R. Three Scientific World Views and the Covering Law Model. In D.W. Fiske and R.A. Shweder, eds., *Metatheory in Social Sciences*. Chicago: Univ. of Chicago Press, 1986.

Diamond, M., and A. Karlen. *Sexual Decisions*. Boston: Little, Brown, 1980.

Fuller, R.C. Morals and the Criminal Law. *Journal of Criminal Law and Criminology,* Vol. 32 (1942), pp. 624–30.

Habermas, J. *Knowledge and Human Interest.* Boston: Beacon Press, 1971.

Kelley, H.H. Attribution in Social Interaction. In E.E. Jones, D.E. Kanouse, H.H. Kelley, R.E. Nisbett, S. Valins, and B. Weiner, eds. *Attribution: Perceiving the Causes of Behavior.* Morristown N.J.: General Learning Press, 1972.

Kurtines, W.M., and J.L. Gerwitz, eds. *Morality, Moral Behavior, and Moral Development.* New York: John Wiley & Sons, 1984.

Meyners R., and C. Wooster. *Sexual Style: Facing and Making Choices About Sex.* New York: Harcourt Brace Jovanovich, 1979.

Money, J. Sexosophy: A New Concept. *Journal of Sex Research,* Vol. 18 (1982), pp. 364–66.

———. *Venuses Penuses: Sexology, Sexosophy, and Exigency Theory.* Buffalo, N.Y.: Prometheus Books, 1986.

Rich, J.M., and J.L. DeVitis. *Theories of Moral Development.* Springfield, Ill.: Charles C. Thomas, 1985.

Sapp, G.L., ed. *Handbook of Moral Development: Models, Processes Techniques, and Research.* Birmingham, Ala.: Religious Education Press, 1986.

Scruton, R. *Sexual Desire: A Moral Philosophy of the Erotic.* New York: The Free Press, 1986.

Simon, W., and J.H. Gagnon. Sexual Scripts: Permanence and Change. *Archives of Sexual Behavior,* Vol. 15 (1986), pp. 97–120.

Robert A. Embree

MORROW, PRINCE A., AND THE SOCIAL HYGIENE MOVEMENT

Prince A. Morrow (1846–1913), an American physician and reformer and the effective founder of the social hygiene movement, was born in Mt. Vernon, Kentucky. He graduated from Princeton College, a small institution in Kentucky, in 1864, financing his education by teaching school. He took an M.D. from New York University in 1874 and studied extensively in Europe as he established himself as a specialist in dermatology in New York City.

In that day, venereal diseases were a part of the specialty of dermatology, but Morrow made his reputation initially by work on skin diseases in general, especially leprosy. In 1880, he translated a book about the terrible consequences of venereal disease, Jean-Alfred Fournier's *Syphilis and Marriage.* But Morrow showed little special interest in the subject until 1893, when he edited a book on syphilis. In 1899, he attended at his own expense the first of two international conferences in Brussels—largely on the initiative of Fournier—concerning venereal diseases as public health problems (both syphilis and gonorrhea had taken on much graver aspects as a result of medical findings of the late 19th century).

Upon his return, Morrow spoke indignantly in professional groups about the tragedy of syphilis of the innocent, that is, the wives and children who contracted the disease from immoral husbands and fathers but who were themselves entirely innocent of sexual transgressions. Also, in the 1890s, Morrow, unlike others of that time, came to believe that medical inspection of prostitutes was not an effective way of combating venereal diseases.

After the second Brussels conference, in 1902, Morrow was asked to found an American organization to work for venereal disease control, comparable to the French Society of Sanitary and Moral Prophylaxis, founded in 1900 by Fournier. Morrow instead wrote a book, *Social Diseases and Marriage,* and not until 1904 did he attempt to found an organization. He was not encouraged, because the subject was one that could not be discussed openly in the United States.

Finally, in 1905, he assembled 25 people—a mixture of lay and medical personnel, just as in the successful contemporary antituberculosis organizations—at the New York Academy of Medicine. They founded the American Society of Sanitary and Moral Prophylaxis, dedicated to limiting "the spread of diseases which have their origin in the Social Evil," that is, prostitution. The society made slow progress at first because of the startling approach that the otherwise conservative Morrow and his colleagues took.

Morrow first of all urged a vigorous campaign of propaganda to educate the public at large about the dangers of venereal diseases. Then he also urged a powerful movement to abolish prostitution. Both of these approaches breached widespread customs and beliefs in the United States. But eventually the group expanded and gained organizational support throughout the country from both medical professionals and laypersons, with the medical people at first constituting the largest contingent. Within a few years, the purity groups converged with Morrow's group, which in 1910 became the American Federation for Sex Hygiene. That organization formally joined with the purity groups in 1913 to form the American Social Hygiene Association (which much later became the American Social Health Association). To the previous antiprostitution and disease-prevention emphases the purity groups brought particular emphasis on monogamous marriage as a positive alternative to promiscuity and the old double standard.

The social hygiene movement flourished for many decades and had decisive effects on American standards of sexual behavior, particularly on ideals of marriage. The American movement, in fact, lasted far longer and had far more profound social effects than the original French group on which Morrow modeled his efforts. Morrow died in 1913, but he had already assembled a formidable set of successors. They all appealed to reformers in their fund-raising and enjoyed some of their successes because they were an integral part of the Progressive reforms of the opening years of the 20th century. Sometimes the emphasis was on education, including sex education in the schools. Sometimes their efforts were directed primarily to the detection and cure of venereal diseases. Sometimes the emphasis tended to be on fighting prostitution or on encouraging personal purity. But all of the work could be traced back to the impetus of Morrow, who first effectively challenged the conspiracy of silence and the double standard.

REFERENCES

Brandt, A.M. *No Magic Bullet; A Social History of Venereal Disease in the United States Since 1880.* New York: Oxford Univ. Press, 1985.

Burnham, J.C. The Progressive Era Revolution in American Attitudes Toward Sex. *Journal of American History*, Vol. 59 (1973), pp. 885–908.

Clarke, C.W. *Taboo: The Story of the Pioneers of Social Hygiene.* Washington, D.C.: Public Affairs Press, 1961.

John C. Burnham

MOSHER, CLELIA DUEL

A physician and professor of personal hygiene, Clelia Duel Mosher (1863–1940) was a pioneer in the study of women's sexuality. Her unpublished study *Statistical Survey of the Marriages of Forty-Seven Women* is the earliest known survey of American women's sexual behavior and attitudes. Begun prior to 1900 and continued through 1920, Mosher's research involved questionnaires that posed such questions as the reason for intercourse, the ideal and actual frequency of sexual relations, the frequency of orgasm, whether contraception was used, and the number of conceptions by choice and by accident. The majority of participants, raised and married in the 19th century, responded in a manner contrary to the accepted Victorian view of women's sexuality—women desired sexual intercourse and experienced orgasms.

Mosher's 30 years of research on menstruation (1890 to 1920) determined that menstrual difficulties were caused by constrictive corsets, which deformed internal organs and bone structure. Her solution was sensible clothing and deep-

breathing exercises to build up weak abdominal muscles. Mosher also studied fear of menopause. She claimed that the problem was more psychological than physiological and less difficult for professional women involved in their work than for homemakers, whose role in life had changed since their children had grown and left home. For them, she prescribed better health by filling empty hours with volunteer work.

After ten years of private practice as a physician, Mosher chose to return to academia to resume her research. She became a professor of personal hygiene and medical adviser to women at Stanford University, where she remained for nineteen years until her retirement in 1929.

REFERENCES

Primary

Mosher, C.D. *Health and the Woman Movement.* New York: Young Women's Christian Association, 1916.

———. *Personal Hygiene for Women.* Stanford, Calif.: Stanford Univ. Press, 1927.

———*Woman's Physical Freedom.* New York: Woman's Press, 1923.

Secondary

Degler, C.N. What Ought to Be and What Was: Women's Sexuality in the Nineteenth Century. *American Historical Review,* Vol. 79 (Dec. 1974), pp. 1467–90.

Jacob, K.A. The Mosher Report. *American Heritage,* Vol. 32 (June–July 1981), pp. 57–64.

MaHood, J., and K. Wenburg, eds. *The Mosher Survey: Sexual Attitudes of 45 Victorian Women.* New York: Arno, 1980.

Hilary Sternberg

MOVIES: SEXUALITY IN CINEMA

The psychological impact of the cinematic process makes film the most overwhelming purveyor of sexual fantasy ever devised. Cinema, often expressive of sexuality, was, however, tempered by the mores of society and limited by censorship.

A kiss is perhaps the first known example of sex in the cinema. In the 1890s, a kiss between John C. Rice and May Irwin in a Broadway play called *The Widow Jones* routinely caused no stir in the audience. In 1896, when this scene was turned into a brief, episodic film on a large screen, the audience suddenly felt intimately involved. Some were scandalized; others favored the film. Over the decades, the use of large-size screens and the development of technological innovations amplified the psychological impact of film.

Filmmakers quickly learned that sexuality and violence in cinema attracted audiences. Such content also elicited a heated cry to censor films to protect the innocent, as they were societally defined. Rather than risk the boycott of a film, Hollywood succumbed to censorship pressures to ensure that each film would be shown in the greatest number of movie houses. Only by appealing to the broadest possible audience could a maximum profit be achieved.

Censorship

A filmed version of a belly dance, *Fatima* (1897), is credited with the birth of screen censorship. The Dance of the Seven Veils, performed in person by Fatima at the Chicago Columbian Exposition in 1893, caused no great alarm. However, the response of the audience to the dance on film was so emphatic that it prompted one early censor to paint obscuring lines above and below the waist of the dancer.

American film censorship was imposed by means of statute, actions of producers and distributors, or pressure from private groups, including religious authorities. Cities such as Chicago practiced film censorship as early as 1907. In 1915, the U.S. Supreme Court found that prior restraint (precensoring films before public viewing) was not a violation of freedom of speech guaranteed under the First Amendment of the Constitution. After this decision, Maryland, New York, and other states followed the lead set earlier by Pennsylvania in 1911 and appointed official censorship boards, which actually engaged in reediting films before they were publicly shown.

What Hollywood stars did offscreen, and how they were portrayed by journalists such as William Randolph Hearst, affected the public's opinion of them, their careers, and ultimately the course of film history. After a series of scandals, Hollywood became known as home to rapists, bigamists, drug addicts, and murderers. Wilbur Craft, a Protestant clergyman and a major proponent of censorship at that time, advocated the need "to rescue the motion pictures from the hands of the devil and 500 un–Christian Jews." Many joined this call for reform.

Hollywood producers feared the growth of restrictive regulations, including federal censorship. They organized the Motion Picture Producers and Distributors Association of America (MPPDAA) in 1921 to voluntarily practice preproduction self-censorship. Will B. Hays, a former campaign manager for Warren G. Harding and a Presbyterian elder, was appointed to head the MPPDAA, which subsequently became known as the Hays office. Hays first worked mainly as a lobbyist to counter the scandals of the film stars and prevent censorship legislation. Soon, the Hays office proposed adding "morality clauses" to Hollywood contracts, whereby stars who became involved in scandal could be dismissed legally. By 1927, the Hays office had devised a production code of "Don'ts and Be Carefuls" to ensure "good taste."

Power to enforce this policy came in 1934 through the Production Code Administration. Hays appointed Joseph Breen, a journalist with Catholic newspapers, to head the Administration. Films conforming to the "code" were given the Administration's seal of approval. Without the seal, exhibitors commonly did not show a film out of fear that the Legion of Decency, or others, would condemn the film and boycott the theater. When Breen resigned more than a decade later, his duties were assumed by the newly formed Motion Picture Association of America (MPAA).

The Catholic Church's Legion of Decency, established in 1934, urged parishioners, under pain of mortal sin, to avoid films it condemned. The Legion's condemnation was feared for its economic impact.

Sexuality in Early Films

Early in the 20th century, episodic films, two to three minutes in length, were popular in penny arcades. Some provoked Victorian sensibilities. In one arcade film, *How Bridget Served the Salad Undressed*, a maid, who misunderstands instructions, serves the salad wearing little more than her petticoat (Lennig 36). In another, *In a Woman's Boudoir*, a woman disrobes to her petticoat. A popular "plot" showed dancers in various stages of undress.

One-reelers followed, and they retained the same modesty but advanced cinema to simple stories with crime or illicit sex as favorite topics. Films such as *Wages of Sin*, a catalog of delightful transgressions, uniformly ended in moral preachment. This pattern, known as the law of compensating values, became a Hollywood tradition. A film could depict all kinds of human misbehavior, including sexual immorality, as long as in the last reel virtue triumphed and evil received its just punishment.

Early European films featured nudity and were shown alongside puritanical American products. They posed no language problem, as visuals told the story in these silent films. French filmmakers dominated world cinema in the first decade of the 20th century and were inspired by famous paintings of nudes, such as *The Birth of Venus* by Botticelli. Early German filmmakers favored literary adaptations, often suggestive, such as *Salome*, while Italian cinema pioneered the "spectacle," featuring earlier, "barbaric," civilizations, which provided the excuse for nudity as well as scenes of violence such as rape. German, French, and various South American filmmakers made pornography at this early time. Pornography was not produced for public viewing but for viewing privately, sometimes in bordellos.

American producers lured audiences to the theater with the expectation of witnessing depraved behavior. A typical plot might involve a naive country girl coming to the city to improve her life. When unmet by the agent who had promised her a legitimate job, she finds herself abandoned and without resources. A "stranger" convinces her that her only alternative is a life of prostitution. One of many such pictures featuring white slavery was George Loane Tucker's *Traffic in Souls* (1913).

Actresses in early Hollywood films portrayed either seductive manipulators, vamps, or innocents. The film *The Vampire* (1913), with Alice Hollister, popularized the role of the vamp in America, while Theda Bara came to personify the character in *A Fool There Was* (1914). Characteristically, the men in such films abandon their family and become addicted to alcohol or drugs used by the vamp as accessories in her seduction. Mary Pickford and the Gish sisters all portrayed young and wholesome women who maintain their innocence. Such a woman offers a husband her virginity on their wedding night, but only after she successfully rebuffs a villain. In D.W. Griffith's *Birth of a Nation* (1915), Mae Marsh commits suicide after an act that implied rape by a black soldier. In another episode, the Ku Klux Klan saves Lillian Gish, who is pressured by a mulatto (Silas Lynch) to marry him. The film was banned in Europe for decades because of its blatant racism.

There were several notable actresses in early cinema. The Polish exotic actress Pola Negri portrayed an unrepentant and sexy flirt in such German films as *Madame DuBarry* (1919), released as *Passion* in America. Her first American film, *Bella Donna*, featured a Negri so subdued to avoid censorship that the film was a disappointment. Her personal life, including involvements with Charlie Chaplin and Rudolph Valentino, was publicized by the studio to promote an "adventuress" image.

In *Flaming Youth* (1923), Colleen Moore, one of the first flappers, portrays a self-confident woman who enjoys parties, defies convention, is susceptible to redemption, and achieves true happiness at film's end. Casualness and independence personified the flapper, so named for wearing goloshes unhooked (hence, they "casually" flapped). Clara Bow, in *It* (1927), became known as the "It Girl"—the girl with sex appeal. In her films, Bow, the most famous flapper, typically danced, gyrated, and wiggled but was, essentially, a "good girl" in terms of conventional morality.

In the 1920s, Greta Garbo, the great Swedish actress, had been known in Europe as a seductress and frequently played the role of a woman "with a past." In America, her image was that of an intriguing, glamorous, sensual, unpredictable, soft, and vulnerable woman who could be happily in love with the right man. The films' endings were never happy, because she would have made a prior commitment, or even consummated a marriage, with an older man whom she did not love. Her first American film, eminently popular, was *The Torrent* (1926). She also portrayed prostitutes in *Anna Christie* (1930) and *Susan Lenox: Her Fall and Rise* (1931).

Hollywood had two types of leading men. Douglas Fairbanks, the athletic "all-American boy," was rather straitlaced in his approach to sex and was respectful toward women. In contrast, leading men like Adolph Menjou were male "vamps." The most famous of such men was Rudolph Valentino, whose first film was *Four Horsemen of the Apocalypse* (1922). These were the dangerous "Latin lovers." Though Valentino himself was pictured as seduced in some films, in his famous *Son of the Sheik* (1926) he carries a woman off on horseback and then "has her" by force, a literal "rape." Many women publicly responded that they would be willing victims indeed if he were to be the "rapist."

Eric von Stroheim became known as America's "leading villain." In *Foolish Wives* (1922), which he directed, he plays a European gigolo who attracts the neglected wives of American workaholics. Other films he directed depict eccentric sexual fetishes. In *The Wedding March* (1926), a rape takes place in a slaughterhouse. As the couple lies writhing on the floor, blood drips on them from a recently slaughtered cow. In *The Merry Widow* (1925), one character keeps the shoes of each of his "conquests" as a souvenir.

Cecil B. DeMille exploited the law of compensating values. According to DeMille, a brief act of redemption could hardly be shown if the sin had not been well witnessed, as in *The Ten Commandments* (1923).

Visuals compensated for what films lacked in sound. DeMille's films showed lavish bathrooms with comely maidens, such as Gloria Swanson, in discreet poses and elegant bedrooms with double beds inviting sexual activity by implication. Plots featured the sexual pursuit of someone young, attractive, and generally easily available. Starting in 1914, Max Sennett, in his Keystone Cops routines, included "bathing beauties," whose bathing suits revealed bare legs and caused titillation, if not shock.

Early Modern Film

The Great Depression had a severe impact on film receipts. Producers had to adjust their strategy. Films, now with sound, reflected social reality by picturing crimes that plagued the nation, especially bootlegging. Mobsters and their women, "gun molls," shared the same social values, but the molls suffered rough treatment. Some men were blatantly sadistic. James Cagney, in *Public Enemy* (1931), enthusiastically mashes half a grapefruit in his girl's face. In *Taxi* (1932), he gives a woman a black eye, and in *Lady Killer* (1933), he drags a woman around by her hair. Clark Gable also displayed this sadism—for example, roughing up Norma Shearer—in films like *Free Soul* (1931).

Actresses presented an image of brazen hussiness. Marlene Dietrich, in the German film *Blue Angel* (1930), plays a coldhearted vamp who humiliates a school teacher obsessed with her. Yet Dietrich, in her first American film, *Morroco* (1930), portrays a good-hearted "entertainer" who must choose between a rich, older man (Adolph Menjou) and a poor legionnaire (Gary Cooper) with whom she shares a "chaste" friendship.

The "blonde bombshells," Jean Harlow and Mae West, represented sexually aggressive women who enjoyed men. Jean Harlow, in *Hell's Angels* (1930), utters the line still heard, "Would you mind if I slip into something comfortable?" This meant a diaphanous boudoir set that clearly revealed the contours of her body. In this film, Harlow seduces her fiancé's brother, and others, with no hint of bashfulness. Mae West in *She Done Him Wrong* (1932) is equally blatant. West was famous for sexual double entendres and rated her lovers' performances with lyrics to songs such as "I Like a Guy Who Takes His Time" and "I Wonder Where My Easy Rider's Gone."

Censors reacted and imposed new levels of constraint through the Hays Office and the Legion of Decency. Literary works were sanitized for films. William Faulkner's novel *Sanctuary* was released as *The Story of Temple Drake* (1933),

minus its famous references to sexual perversity. *The Barretts of Wimpole Street* (1934), by Sidney Franklin, was dramatized without incest. The strong lesbian element in the play *The Children's Hour* disappeared in the film version released by William Wyler as *These Three* (1936). In 1962, Wyler redid the film, finally entitled *The Children's Hour*, but only gingerly touched on its homosexual content. Tolstoy's *Anna Karenina* (1935), directed by Clarence Brown, presented the central infidelity within a gentler framework.

Stars known for their sexuality had to portray subdued characters. In Jack Conway's *Saratoga* (1937), Jean Harlow's blatant sexual aggression disappears. Joan Crawford, a flapper, found a new screen personality. Bette Davis, a new star, plays in *Of Human Bondage* (1934), directed by John Cromwell, with an implied but never displayed sexual appetite. Child stars who were "innocent" of sex became popular, especially Shirley Temple, Mickey Rooney, and Judy Garland.

Implied sexuality pervaded American films. Ingrid Bergman, in *Intermezzo: A Love Story* (1939), has an illicit affair with a married man, but the sin is not documented and she realizes her "mistake." When the chastened hero and heroine travel together, they occupy separate rooms in a hotel. Censorship of this period allowed married couples to be shown in separate, single beds, clad in conservative nightclothes. At the close of the 1930s, romantic heroes such as Tyrone Power and Errol Flynn portrayed men of action whose sexual rewards were presented innocently.

Foreign films escaped puritanization. Many European countries in the 1920s and 1930s passed laws setting 14 to 18 years of age as the minimum for admission. In the Czechoslovakian film *Ecstasy* (1933), directed by Gustav Machaty, Hedy Lamarr swims in the nude and consummates an illicit affair in the out-of-doors. The Legion of Decency condoned the film's release in this country after cuts and reshooting created a toned-down version. Nevertheless, many states still would not allow the film to be shown.

By the 1940s, there was no overt sexuality in American cinema. Musicals, highly popular at the time, permitted attractive women to appear in scanty costumes for the spectacle of dance and music, not as an enticement for sexual display. Betty Grable, a prominent leading woman in musicals, had a famous rear-view pin-up pose; her head, turned back over her shoulder, highlighted her shapely legs. More than 2 million fans, many of whom were among the 11 million soldiers at that time, requested a copy of her sexually enticing still. Rita Hayworth wore a slip in a revealing pin-up that was also popular with soldiers. The photograph was a still from *Gilda* (1946), directed by Charles Vidor, which features Hayworth dancing provocatively and being accused wrongfully of infidelity. Two other popular pin-ups of the war period were Hedy Lamarr and Veronica Lake.

The American woman of World War II did not express herself sexually while her husband was away in the army. Instead, "Rosie the Riveter" left home to enter the workplace, and motion pictures reflected this. Two romantic rather than sexual films of career-oriented leading women were *His Girl Friday* (1940), directed by Howard Hawks and starring Rosalind Russell, and *Adam's Rib* (1949), directed by George Cukor and starring Katharine Hepburn.

The Outlaw (1946), openly promoted as a sexually explicit film, provoked an active battle with the Hays office. The promotional stills revealed Jane Russell, another popular pin-up of the late war years, lying on her back on a haystack wearing a partially open blouse. Another controversial film was *Forever Amber* (1947), starring the sexually attractive Linda Darnell. Because the novel on which the film was based detailed amorous adventures of the mistress of Charles II, the Legion of Decency wanted no film made of it. The director, Otto Preminger, persevered but had to surrender the integrity of the story by sanitizing the film.

In Europe, normal film production was disrupted by the war. The Nazis produced films glorifying the Aryan race and did not find an interest or use for films involving sexuality. In one film, Veit Harlan's *Jude Süsse* (1940), a Jewish financier rapes an Aryan woman in front of her husband, who has just been savagely beaten on the orders of the "Jew." At the film's end, the "Jew" is executed by slow roasting at the hands of the "masses of people."

Interrupted by World War II, Italian film production quickly resumed as early as 1945. Roberto Rossellini, in *Open City* (1945), depicted drug addiction, prostitution, and out-of-wedlock pregnancy. Another postwar Italian neorealist film was Rossellini's *Paisan* (1946). This episodic film revealed the brutal conditions endured by the Italian populace at the end of the war. In one episode, an American soldier meets a prostitute but does not recognize that she is the "innocent" he had encountered earlier during the war.

Modern Film

The last half of the 20th century brought new freedom to filmmaking. New York City Catholics urged the banning of Rosellini's short film *The Miracle* (1950) on the grounds of sacrilege. On appeal, the U.S. Supreme Court decided, in 1952, that motion pictures enjoyed protection under the First and Fourteenth Amendments to the U.S. Constitution. Films portraying religious dogma were no longer subject to prior restraint. A number of subsequent decisions by the Court reaffirmed protection against infringement on freedom of expression.

The Miracle precipitated the reversal of the 1915 position of the U.S. Supreme Court on prior restraint. In it, Anna Magnani, believing that a passing stranger is St. Joseph, becomes pregnant by him. She is humiliated by her neighbors but has the child and breast-feeds him. Decades later, *Hail Mary* (1985) by Jean-Luc Godard portrays a contemporary Mary engaged to a taxi driver named Joseph, but their involvement is chaste. She tries to convince her fiancé that her pregnancy is an "immaculate" conception. A number of theologians of various Christian denominations found Godard's exploration to be sensitive and motivated by high purpose. Others felt the treatment was sacrilegious and that a nude, pregnant Mary was the final, intolerable insult.

Financial pressures resulting from competition from television forced Hollywood producers in new directions. To survive, producers began to risk boycott by the Legion of Decency. Otto Preminger released *The Moon Is Blue* (1953) without the seal of approval and with a condemned rating from the Legion of Decency for the use of the terms "virgin," "mistress," and "pregnancy." The film drew a better audience than anticipated. By 1968, when Mike Nichols released *Who's Afraid of Virginia Woolf,* few words were considered too obscene to be used freely in film.

Producers pursued the audiences of the "art" theaters which featured adult films pioneered by foreign filmmakers. One of the first American films aimed at the new adult market was Billy Wilder's *Sunset Boulevard* (1950). A young, unemployed screenwriter, William Holden, is the "kept" man of a no-longer-fashionable silent-era film star, Gloria Swanson. Moral retribution is achieved by presenting Holden, the narrator, as already deceased and Swanson, his killer, as having lost her mind. George Stevens's *A Place in the Sun* (1951), based on Theodore Dreiser's novel *An American Tragedy*, brought to the screen illicit sex and abortion, the latter a subject that had been scrupulously avoided.

Films presented their daring subject matter conservatively, without nudity or overt sexual acts. Elia Kazan's *A Streetcar Named Desire* (1950) was based on Tennessee Williams's successful Broadway play. Stanley (Marlon Brando) confronts Blanche (Vivian Leigh) with her too-frequent association with men and then rapes her. Stanley's wife (Kim Hunter) leaves him because he is an uncivilized man, in her view.

Passionate feelings were implied rather than enacted. In Fred Zinneman's *From Here to Eternity* (1953), based on James Jones's acclaimed novel about the pre-World War II army, Burt Lancaster and Deborah Kerr lie on the beach, clad in bathing suits, kissing passionately. Consummation of their passion is conveyed by the rising crescendo of pounding waves breaking on the beach. Other films commonly used cinematic devices such as soft focus or a long fade-out in place of overt sexual activity. In Otto Preminger's *Carmen Jones* (1954), Dorothy Dandridge expresses desire by cleaning Harry Belafonte's pants.

Actresses represented three distinct levels of sexuality. Marilyn Monroe on film was basically submissive, available, and vulnerable, but never acted in the nude. Little flesh is shown beyond a full view of her legs in *The Seven Year Itch* (1955), a film about a middle-aged married man's sexual fantasy. Monroe was both available and appealing in musicals, such as *How to Marry a Millionaire* (1953), which also starred Jane Russell and Betty Grable.

More sexually explicit was a French actress, Brigitte Bardot. She was serene, sexy, compliant, and famous for her pouting expression. In the film *And God Created Woman* (1956), directed by her husband Roger Vadim, she appeared nude. Other similarly appearing Italian actresses were Sophia Loren and Gina Lollabrigida.

The American star Grace Kelly was conservative, sexy, and sophisticated; she personified the third level. In films such as Hitchcock's *To Catch a Thief* (1955) and *Rear Window* (1954), with James Stewart, her own background of wealth and breeding merged with her screen portrayal.

American films, emerging from the confines of prior restraint, were still unsophisticated by European standards of adult content. In Elia Kazan's *Splendor in the Grass* (1961), Warren Beatty unsuccessfully pressures his high-school girl, Natalie Wood, to have a sexual relationship. The popular young singer Elvis Presley, in film, heralded an overt masculinity by his "sexual" gyrations. *Dr. No* (1962) features a promiscuous male character, James Bond, played by Sean Connery, who seduces a string of females in a tale of "free love" and violence. In *Lolita* (1962),

directed by Stanley Kubrick, Sue Lyons plays Shelly Winters's underaged daughter who is courted by her middle-aged stepfather, James Mason.

Sexuality in American films steadily became more daring. Tony Richardson's *Tom Jones* (1963) celebrates life fully, especially the pleasures of eating and sexual lust. *Elmer Gantry* (1960), directed by Richard Brooks and starring Burt Lancaster and Jean Simmons, features the "deflowering" of a female evangelist. Sidney Lumet's *The Group* (1966), based on Mary McCarthy's novel, starred Candice Bergen as a lesbian. Robert Mulligan's *Love with the Proper Stranger* (1963) explores the choices faced by an unmarried, pregnant woman played by Natalie Wood.

Shown in art theaters in America, European films were occasionally graphic but not exploitative of sexually taboo material. The Swedish director Ingmar Bergman, in *Virgin Spring* (1959), horrified audiences by suggestion rather than explicit sexual violence. Based on a Swedish folk tale, the film depicts a Christian family that sends their virginal daughter some distance to a church, but two tramps, accompanied by a young boy, brutally rape and then murder her. The father discovers their guilt and slays the vagabonds, including the young boy. A virgin spring erupts at the site of the girl's murder as her father retrieves her body. He vows to build a church on the spot as atonement.

European films sought new horizons of restrained sexual realism. In the 1960 low-budget, high-profit-earning Greek film by Jules Dassin, *Never on Sunday*, Melina Mercouri plays a joyful and generous prostitute who is absolutely unrepentant and unpunished. Louis Malle, who was to acquire a reputation for his skillful handling of taboo subjects, presented a celebration of love over marriage in *Les Amantes* (1959). Recurrent extramarital "experiences" provoked no guilt in the woman.

European filmmakers viewed the aftermath of World War II from a sexual perspective. The facial response of a mother (Sophia Loren) and a daughter depicts the horror of rape in *Two Women* (1960), by Vittorio DeSica. The treatment was bitterly ironic and even philosophical, as the women are ravaged by Morrocan soldiers who were to have "liberated" them. Federico Fellini's *La Dolce Vita* (1960) features a humanistic Marcello Mastroianni who is too deeply affected by the elite decadence of post-World War II Rome to extricate himself. Alain Resnais, in *Hiroshima, Mon Amour* (1959), shows discreet nudity on the part of a racially mixed couple in bed who are committing adultery. Part of the film is presented in flashbacks, that is, the young French woman is seen humiliated by her fellow villagers after an affair with a member of the occupying German army during World War II; the Japanese man, in flashback, attempts to reconcile his memories of Hiroshima.

Sexually Liberated Modern Film

With Sidney Lumet's *The Pawnbroker* (1965), a polarization in censorship occurred between the Legion of Decency and Hollywood's MPAA. The Legion of Decency condemned the film for nudity, while the MPAA gave it a seal. In the film, a young, naked woman in a concentration camp is forced to be a concubine for various Nazi officers. In response to her fate, her surviving husband anesthetizes himself emotionally, even against a semiclad black woman who offers herself to him.

A new rating system, devised in 1966 and administered by the Classification and Rating Administration, liberated modern film in the presentation of sexuality. There have been few modifications since. On the basis of the premise that not all movies are made for one audience, the Administration classifies a film in terms of sexuality, language, and violence to determine audience suitability.

I Am Curious, Yellow (1967), by Swedish director Vilgot Sjoman, illustrates the freedom allowed films in Europe. The film explores both the sexual and political exploitation of women. In it, a couple kisses each other's genitals as a form of greeting, and coitus is shown in close-up.

American filmmakers explored new directions in sexuality. In Paul Mazursky's *Bob and Carol and Ted and Alice* (1969), a modern couple cannot go through with a mate-swapping session with friends. A young man, Dustin Hoffman, is seduced by an older woman, Anne Bancroft, in Mike Nichols's *The Graduate* (1967). In John Schlesinger's *Midnight Cowboy* (1969), John Voight comes to New York to find his fortune as a male prostitute. Lacking customers, he finds he must expand his potential clientele to include males. Only a street person, Dustin Hoffman, becomes a real friend, but he soon dies. Americans were shocked but intrigued by this unaccustomed view of this segment of society. Sexual expression evolved to the extent that Ralph Bakshi, in *Fritz the Cat* (1972), created an explicit animation feature based on an underground comic strip.

Ultimately, Hollywood confronted the phenomenon of sexual mating across racial barriers. *Guess Who's Coming to Dinner* (1967), directed by Stanley Kramer, brought interracial coupling, with the sanction of marriage, to the screen. The all-star cast—Spencer Tracy, Sidney Poitier, and Katharine Hepburn—lent their prestige, but the only physical involvement shown was a climactic kiss as the film closed. By 1990, Spike Lee's *Jungle Fever* showed interracial coupling in the kind of detail that was in no way foreshadowed by *Guess Who's Coming to Dinner*.

In the 1970s, European directors, such as Louis Malle, used sexuality to explore the human psyche. Incest, a subject almost never seen on the screen, is discreetly featured in *Murmur of the Heart* (1971). The film asserts that the boy seduced by his mother remains undamaged. In *WR: Mysteries of the Organism* (1971), Dusan Makavejev uses the theories of Wilhelm Reich to explore the political consequences of sexual freedom and repression. A film that disturbed some because of its graphic depiction of a sadistic rape was Stanley Kubrick's *A Clockwork Orange* (1972), based on the Anthony Burgess novel. The brutality and immorality of young Alex (Malcolm McDowell) and his hoods are equated with the brutal repression of an overbearing and corrupt government.

Bernardo Bertolucci's *Last Tango in Paris* (1972) features sadomasochism. An older man, Marlon Brando, enters into an intense sexual relationship with a young woman who willingly submits to his every whim, including anal intercourse. The man confesses that his disdain and cruelty are based on past cruelty known to and inflicted on him. At the point where he is able to "accept" her love, she shoots him.

American films explored sexual themes with serious intent. Mike Nichols's *Carnal Knowledge* (1972) frankly examines two men's sexual attitudes as they reminisce over the experiences of their formative years. Sam Peckinpah's *Straw Dogs* (1972) reveals a mild-mannered couple's hidden capacity for violence—she (Susan George) in a masochistic response to rape, he (Dustin Hoffman) in a sadistic series of revenge murders. This film violated all Hollywood mores that the victim never was to enjoy rape.

Alternate life-styles came under realistic scrutiny. William Friedkin's *Cruising* (1980) depicted the seamier side of male homosexuality by starring Al Pacino as an undercover cop who pursues a violent killer of gays. Paul Mazursky's *Willie and Phil* (1980) features two men who turn to each other for emotional and physical solace when both have been spurned by the same woman. The film is an update of Truffaut's long-popular classic, *Jules and Jim* (1961). In *Torch Song Trilogy* (1988), Paul Bogart translated Harvey

Fierstein's Broadway play into a film starring Fierstein as well as Anne Bancroft and Matthew Broderick. The film developed a humorous spoof, which featured classic homosexual self-deprecating wit, into a serious plea for tolerance. *Taxi Zum Klo* (1981), a German film, both explicit and ardent, by Frank Rapploh, is the strongly autobiographical recounting of the filmmaker's homosexuality. The wide reception of Edouard Molinaro's *La Cage aux Folles* (1978) prompted the production of sequels.

Sexuality motivated by adventure or survival was portrayed with greater realism on screen. In Paul Schrader's *American Gigolo* (1980), Richard Gere seeks rich female clients. The self-confident male prostitute, in achieving the American dream, recognizes that at times he needs to be available to other males. Nicholas Roeg's *Bad Timing: A Sensual Obsession* (1980) depicts the extensive sexual activity of a married couple, both together and with other partners. A Dutch film, *Spetters* (1980) by Paul Verhoeven, follows, in an explicit fashion, the sexual adventures of six people. An Australian film by Bruce Beresford, *The Getting of Wisdom* (1985), features implicit lesbianism when a girl from a remote region of Australia seeks acceptance from her peers at school. Orphans growing up in Bombay and turning to drugs, prostitution, and violence in their survival attempts: *Saalom Bombay* (1988) by Mira Nair dramatizes the seamier side of social reality. Peter Greenaway in *The Cook, the Thief, His Wife and Her Lover* (1990) equates the British government with sexual humiliation and cannabalism. The film *Henry and June* (1990), directed by Philip Kaufman, is based on Henry Miller's erotic autobiography and depicts voyeurism, partner swapping, and both hetero- and homosexuality.

In Hollywood, many taboos were progressively stripped away. Moving toward greater realism, producers increasingly became dependent on the star and the subject matter to attract audiences. Lower-cost films with the right star and subject could be highly profitable. European filmmakers, especially the French, indulged in more nudity than did American filmmakers who had incorporated sexuality into serious cinema. There was no turning away from freedom for sexual expression as the 20th century drew to a close.

American films attained a sophistication in featuring psychosexual themes. The low-budget film, *Sex, Lies and Videotape* (1989), by Steven Soderbergh, depicts anxiety over sexual permissiveness. The protagonist, played by James Spader, videotapes various women relating, in great detail, their early sexual experiences. From them, he finds sexual release in masturbation, until the camera is turned on him and he is able to break out of his cocoon.

Although significant progress has been made toward portraying sexuality with candor on screen, some filmmakers prefer to rework old stereotypes. *Fatal Attraction* (1987) perpetuates the sadomasochistic myth of a vamp. Glenn Close portrays an independent, career-minded woman who is in reality sick, lonely, perverted, and obsessed with possessing a married man at the cost of destroying a family. In Garry Marshall's *Pretty Woman* (1990), Julia Roberts portrays a modern "flapper," now a prostitute, whose business arrangement with a mogul develops into a proposal of marriage.

The Future

Contemporary filmmakers enjoy freedom of expression guaranteed by the First Amendment but fall short of portraying social realism. Underrepresented groups (e.g., women and minorities) charge that filmmakers portray sexuality stereotypically. Some accused Steven Spielberg of regressive stereotyping in *The Color Purple* (1985). No similar charge was credibly made against Spike Lee for *Do the Right Thing* (1989).

Freedom from sexual stereotyping may be achieved in films when diverse groups are economically able to produce and direct films based on their own experiences. Given the minimum cost of $4 million per film, economic reality is the new censor. Diversity among producers and directors does not ensure a progressive view of sexuality, but it may foster one.

(The author gratefully acknowledges her debt to the following: Mary K. Delmont, Kevin Filipski, Gerald Wild, and the International Museum of Photography at George Eastman House.)

REFERENCES

Atkins, T.R., ed. *Sexuality in the Movies.* Bloomington: Indiana Univ. Press, 1975.

Baxter, J. Screen Sexuality: Flesh, Feathers, and Fantasies. In T.R. Atkins, ed., *Sexuality in the Movies.* Bloomington: Indiana Univ. Press, 1975.

Bowser, E. *The Transformation of Cinema 1907–1915.* New York: Scribner's, 1990.

Brownlow, K. *Behind the Mask of Innocence.* New York: Knopf, 1990.

———. *Hollywood: The Pioneers.* New York: Knopf, 1979.

Farber, S. *The Movie Rating Game.* Washington, D.C.: Public Affairs Press, 1972.

Gardner, G. *The Censorship Papers: Movie Censorship Letters from the Hays Office 1934 to 1968*. New York: Dodd, Mead, 1987.

Higashi, S. *Virgins, Vamps, and Flappers: The American Silent Movie Heroine*. Montreal: Eden Press Women's Publications, 1978.

Keyser, L. Sexuality in Contemporary European Film. In T.R. Atkins, ed., *Sexuality in the Movies*. Bloomington: Indiana Univ. Press, 1975.

Knight, A. *The Liveliest Art: A Panoramic History of the Movies*. New York: Mentor, 1957.

Knight, A., and H. Alpert. The History of Sex in Cinema —Part Two: Compounding the Sin. *Playboy*, May 1965, pp. 133–82.

———. The History of Sex in Cinema—Part Six: The Thirties—Censorship and the Depression. *Playboy*, Nov. 1965, pp. 150–221.

Koszarski, R. *An Evening's Entertainment: The Age of the Silent Feature Picture 1915–1928*. New York: Scribner's, 1990.

Leff, L.J., and J.L. Simmons. *The Dame in the Kimono: Hollywood, Censorship and the Production Code from the 1920's to the 1960's*. New York: Anchor, 1990.

Lennig, A. A History of Censorship of the American Film. In T.R. Atkins, ed., *Sexuality in the Movies*. Bloomington: Indiana Univ. Press, 1975.

Mast, G. *A Short History of the Movies*. 4th ed. New York: Macmillan, 1986.

Ramsaye, T. *A Million and One Nights: A History of the Motion Picture through 1925*. New York: Simon & Schuster, 1954.

Randall, R.S. *Censorship of the Movies: The Social and Political Control of a Mass Medium*. Madison: Univ. of Wisconsin Press, 1970.

Sadoul, G. *Dictionary of Films*. Translated, edited, and updated by P. Morris. Berkeley: Univ. of California Press, 1972.

Schumach, M. *The Face on the Cutting Room Floor: The Story of Movie and Television Censorship*. New York: DaCapo Press, 1964.

Shipman, D. *Caught in the Act: Sex and Eroticism in the Movies*. London: Elm Tree, 1985.

Stenn, D. *Clara Bow: Runnin' Wild*. New York: Penguin, 1988.

Waters, J. Hail Mary. *American Film,* Vol. 11 (Jan.-Feb. 1986), pp. 27–29.

Geraldine E. Bard

MULTIORGASM

Early-20th-century sex researchers focused on female orgasm as a major topic. Their questioners sought interviews with female subjects concerning their orgasmic response patterns. Small numbers of these respondents reported multiorgasmic patterns. In 1929, for example, G.V. Hamilton reported that five of his 100 female subjects were "repeaters," that is, they had multiple orgasms. He said that they reported any-where from two or three to a score or more orgasms to the man's one. Lewis Terman, in 1938, reported that 96 of his sample of 792 women were typically multiorgasmic. This was 12.6 percent of those responding. Multiorgasm was not closely correlated to the reported marital happiness of respondents.

Next, chronologically, came the studies of Kinsey and his associates in 1948 and 1953. It is not always clear whether the Kinsey data on multiorgasm resulted from interview or direct observation. Kinsey made it clear that "orgasm may occur without the emission of semen" in men, thus clearly differentiating orgasm from ejaculation. He found that 55.5 percent of his preadolescent male sample was multiorgasmic and explained that this capacity was lost rapidly; by age 15, only 20 percent were still multiorgasmic. Less than 10 percent of the males were multiorgasmic between the ages of 25 and 60. Even though Kinsey clearly distinguishes between ejaculation and orgasm, he apparently used the terms synonymously, along with "climax," in describing the high frequency of male sexual outlet.

Kinsey reported that 14 percent of his female sample of 5,940 subjects "regularly responded with multiple orgasm" in human coitus. He made a comparison of multiple orgasm in females and males, reporting about 15 percent of each to be multiorgasmic at ages 15 to 20. From ages 25 to 60, females remained at the 15-percent level, with 5 percent more typical of the males for this 40-year period. Finally, Kinsey emphasized that only small percentages (5 percent–15 percent) of adult males and females regularly experience multiorgasm in the social context of either petting or coitus.

Masters and Johnson further documented the multiorgasmic capacity of both females and males. In their interviews of multiorgasmic females following the laboratory experience, the respondents reported that they found the subsequent orgasms more subjectively pleasurable than the initial one. These continuous orgasmic experiences contrasted with male subjective reports that the discrete orgasms following the initial orgasm and ejaculation were less pleasurable. Masters and Johnson indicated that many women were unsatisfied with one orgasm and desired multiorgasms for full satisfaction.

Since that time, others have continued to report multiorgasms in various studies. Robbins and Jensen studied multiple orgasm in men at the Center for Marital and Sexual Studies, in Long Beach, California. Individuals associated with the laboratory continued to do research on the topic, on the basis of a sample of 751 subjects, 469 females and 282 males, ranging in age from 18 to 70. The study did not rely on verbal reports of orgasm but monitored it with a Beckman R411 dynograph. Measurement of orgasm involved monitoring of capillary blood flow in various parts of the body, as well as heartbeat, heart rate, respiration, galvanic skin response, and pelvic contractions; the latter was monitored in the anus, vagina, and uterus.

Though the parameters of change varied with the subject, all showed change at orgasm, and the pattern of individual function was established for each subject. These patterns could not be differentiated by sex. During orgasm, the heart rate, which had been at a baseline of approximately 70 beats per minute, rises to approximately 120–130 beats per minute at orgasm for females and to 150–160 beats per minute for males. The subject then returns to a normal resting state. This is called a discrete orgasm. Physical condition and drugs are significant factors in wide variations of cardiac data.

In another pattern, the heart rate starts at a baseline of 70 beats per minute and reaches a peak, but rather than returning to the baseline, it remains high, dropping only 10 to 20 beats between orgasms in a series of continuous orgasms. A third pattern is a combination of the first two, usually with one or two discrete orgasms taking place before what Hartman and Fithian call "continuous orgasms" occur. The same multipleorgasm patterns are seen for both males and females.

In a control study by Hartman and Fithian, both orgasmic and multiorgasmic women were asked to rate their orgasmic intensity on a scale of 1 to 10, with 1 being least intense and 10 most intense. These evaluations were then correlated with physiological measurements. Multiply orgasmic women had more ratings in the 8–10 range than did the singly orgasmic women, who reported a less intense orgasm. This corresponded with their physiological response as measured by the parameters listed above.

The time to orgasm was markedly different for the two groups, with singly orgasmic women taking an average of 27 minutes to reach an orgasm, whereas the multiply orgasmic women averaged only 8 minutes. Multiply orgasmic women took only 1 to 2 minutes, on average, to reach a second orgasm. Subsequent orgasms tended to take less time, and 30-second intervals between orgasms were not uncommon; a few instances of 15-second intervals between orgasms

were recorded. The greatest number of multiple orgasms recorded in the laboratory was 134 in an hour for a female and 16 for a male.

Dunn and Trost interviewed 21 multiply orgasmic men. Their primary group included 13 men who were always multiply orgasmic, and secondarily eight men who became multiorgasmic after age 35. The men attributed most of their multiorgasmic experience to genetic or fortuitous circumstances and rarely to deliberately planned learning. Dunn's and Trost's definition of multiple orgasm in males is similar to that at the Center, where orgasm and ejaculation are regarded as two separate phenomena. To be considered multiply orgasmic, a male must have two or more orgasms within an hour. The Dunn and Trost study differed from the Hartman and Fithian studies, which reported that in some instances the men could completely lose their erection and start over. In the Dunn and Trost sample, subjects reported a high state of arousal between orgasms.

Hartman and Fithian reported that several of their subjects had learned how to have multiple orgasms as adults by following up on an experience in which they had orgasm without ejaculation. They have concluded from their own studies and as a result of their teaching that potentially all males who are orgasmic can probably, with training and practice, become multiorgasmic; they hold the same to be true for women. Many may not want to be multiorgasmic, since time itself is always a factor in multiple orgasms. They simply take longer.

REFERENCES

Brauer, A.P., and D., Brauer. *ESO—Extended Sexual Orgasm.* New York: Warner, 1990.

Campbell, B., W. Hartman, M. Fithian, and I. Campbell. Polygraphic Survey of the Human Sexual Response. *The Physiologist,* Vol. 18 (1975), p. 154.

Clifford, R. Subjective Sexual Experience in College Women. *Archives of Sexual Behavior,* Vol. 7 (1978), pp. 183–97.

Dunn, M.E., and J.E. Trost. Male Multiple Orgasms: A Descriptive Study. *Archives of Sexual Behavior,* Vol. 18 (1989), pp. 377–87.

Hartman, W.E., and M.A. Fithian. *Any Man Can.* New York: St. Martin's Press, 1984.

Kothari, P. *Orgasm: New Dimensions.* Bombay: V.R.P., 1989.

Robbins, M.B., and G.A. Jensen. Multiple Orgasm in Males. *Journal of Sex Research,* Vol. 14 (Feb. 1978), pp. 21–28.

William E. Hartman
Marilyn A. Fithian

MUSIC AND SEX

Music has a long association with sex. Many kinds of musical instruments had their origin in sexual symbols or were taken as representative of the genitals. For example, the flute is not only symbolic of the penis, but the penis itself is often called the one-eyed flute. In New Guinea, among some of the tribes in which initiation involves oral-genital sex between boys and older men, oral sex is called playing the flute. Some instruments in the past have in fact been known as love instruments, such as the *viola d'amore,* which was extensively used in the baroque and postbaroque periods, especially by Antonio Vivaldi.

Music itself has sexual or romantic connotations, but for the most part responses vary by culture and individual, and what is romantic or sexual to one person might not be so to another. This, however, is not the case with lyrics, and there is a long tradition of sexually oriented lyrics. Though we lack the melody, erotic lyrics from the Greco-Roman period have survived. In the High Middle Ages, the verses of the wandering singers were often quite bawdy, with overt sexual references not uncommon. The love lyrics of the troubadours brought courtly love to Europe and were a major factor in the development of romantic love. Not all songs dealt with heterosexual love, however. A 14th-century Florentine ordinance, for example, prohibited the singing of "sodomitical songs."

With the development of musical notation and the appearance of the printing press at the end of the medieval period, dissemination of lyrics and music took place at a more rapid pace. Often, music was used to convey a negative message about sexuality, as did an English ballad of the 16th century entitled "Of the Horrible and Woefull Destruction of Sodom and Gomorra," which was sung to the Tune of the Nine Muses.

Sexual enticement was certainly a major theme of opera, especially after Mozart's *The Marriage of Figaro* (1786). Sometimes the sexuality had a double-edged meaning, since female roles were usually sung by males until well into the 19th century. Most of these males had been castrated as youths to preserve their high range, and many castrati, as they were called, achieved great popularity. One of the most famous was Carlo Broschi (1705–1782), best known by his pseudonym, Farinelli, who exercised great influence on Philip V of Spain and for many years sang nightly for that monarch. Perhaps it was the presence of castrati that led to so much role switching in opera; when women appeared in force on the operatic stage, many of them took over the cross-dressing roles, and they dominate such roles in the modern performances of classic operas.

Sex in many operas is rather explicit. Carnal love is a major theme of many of Richard Wagner's operas, especially *Tristan and Isolde,* and it continued to be a tradition in German opera with Richard Strauss *(Don Juan* and *Salome).* Homosexuality and lesbianism have also been portrayed in opera, sometimes discreetly, as in the work of Benjamin Britten, and sometimes more openly, as in Alban Berg's opera *Lulu,* based on a play by Frank Wedekind. The opera portrays a lesbian countess who belongs to an exclusive society of women artists where she dresses in male costume. The opera had a posthumous premier in 1937, but its third act, with the lesbian scene, was suppressed by Berg's widow and not performed until 1979.

The ability of music both to convey and to arouse emotions was probably nowhere better illustrated than in silent movies, which were usually accompanied by an orchestra in the more expensive theaters or by a pianist or organist in the less expensive ones. As the musical accompaniment to the silent films became more or less standardized, some kinds of music came to be regarded as more sexual than others, since they were played during the more intimate scenes. As movies entered the age of sound at the end of the 1920s, music continued to play a particularly strong role in conveying sexuality, especially when actual sexual scenes could not be portrayed on the screen.

It was in the popular songs, however, where sexuality was most evident. Sexually oriented songs were a staple of the English music hall and American vaudeville, but the same kind of standardization that appeared in movie music appeared in popular lyrics, as illustrated by the work of the professional songwriters centered in New York and collectively styled Tin Pan Alley during the development of the recording industry. Cole Porter, in particular, came to be known for sexual themes in his music.

Outside the mainstream of popular songs were numerous bawdy songs, many of which were collected and recorded by Oscar Brand in a series called *Bawdy Songs and Back Room Ballads* (1955) and periodically rereleased. Such folk songs as "Roll Me Over in the Clover" and "The Money Rolls In" are widely known and exist in variant versions, and some of them date from Elizabethan England, where bawdy songs were a standard. Some well-known literary figures are known to have written bawdy songs, which include Rudyard Kipling's "The Bastard King of England" and Mark Twain's "The Contest." One of the earliest of such bawdy writers was the medieval poet François Villon (1431–?), who wrote lyrics describing his girlfriend, the prostitute Margo, who, after satisfying her customers and making her living, turned to Villon and "mounted" him, to "spare love's fruit."

> I groan, squashed beneath her weight—
> This lechery of hers will ruin me,
> In this brothel where we ply our trade.

Prostitution in fact has a long connection with music. This linkage continued in the 20th century with the spread of jazz from the brothels of Storyville, in New Orleans, to mainstream America. Biographies of the early jazz musicians, such as Ferdinand Joseph (Jelly Roll) Morton and Louis Armstrong, often show them getting their start as musicians in a brothel. Often folk songs that once existed only in a rural oral tradition were suppressed and sometimes lost because either the situations depicted or their language were not considered proper by later generations.

Musicians themselves—ranging from concert-hall figures such as Chopin to popular singers such as Frank Sinatra—have often become sex symbols. Sinatra gained his early reputation because of his appeal to hordes of teenage girls. Both overtly sexual lyrics and sexual gestures were limited in the United States and Europe, however, because of problems of censorship, which began to be relaxed in the 1950s. What were once regarded as obscene gestures broke through before more overtly sexual lyrics did. A key figure in the 1950s breakthrough of the portrayal of more overt sexuality was Elvis Presley, nicknamed "the pelvis." He achieved stardom on the Milton Berle show, where he sang a scorching bump-and-grind version of "Hound Dog." Network television censors were horrified. When he appeared on the Ed Sullivan program, the cameras were forbidden to show him below the waist, and when he appeared on the Steve Allen show, he was forced to stand still.

Originally, rock—a fusion of black rhythm and blues, gospel, doowop harmony singing, white rockabilly, and other elements—was an underground music until Presley became well-known, and much of it was less subject to censorship than the more established swing or jazz. Hints of homosexuality even appeared in the lyrics of Richard Penniman (Little Richard), who appeared on stage wearing mascara and a high, effeminate pompadour.

In the 1960s, rock and roll broadened out into rock, incorporating such elements as electrified quasi-folk music, political protest songs, and complex psychedelic constructions. Though the term rock and roll itself is a euphemism for sexual intercourse, it also became a form of social commentary. The decade was dominated by the Beatles and the Rolling Stones, both of which groups included sexual themes in their lyrics. The Beatles', "A Day in the Life" was kept off many radio stations because of the phrase "I'd love to turn you on." When the Rolling Stones appeared on the Ed Sullivan show, they were forced to change the lyrics of their song "Let's Spend the Night Together" to "Let's Spend Some Time Together." Generally, the Rolling Stones were more specific than the Beatles, and their songs included references to homosexual prostitution in "When the Whip Comes Down" and to oral sex in "Honky Tonk Women." Perhaps the height was reached with their "Cocksucker Blues," which Decca refused to release but which became popular through bootleg recordings. Jim Morrison of the Doors opened up another previously taboo subject, anal intercourse, in 1968, when he proclaimed in song, "I'm a Backdoor Man."

Gender blending was an important element of glitter rock, in which performers set the pace. Most notable were the New York Dolls, who appeared in drag and female makeup. Musical styles changed rapidly in the 1980s, and for a time disco music was dominant. Disco was strongly associated with the gay culture in New York, and songs such as "Macho Man" and "YMCA" emphasized a growing relaxation with regard to sexual content in lyrics. Each new wave of popular singers became increasingly explicit. Punk rock, based on the rock and roll of the fifties but with more explicit lyrics, was for a time an underground movement, until it reached Britain in 1976. Groups such as the Sex Pistols and the Buzzcocks emerged, singing ever more explicitly sexual songs.

Increasingly for a time in the 1980s, androgyny was dominant, with Boy George (who appeared in drag) and Culture Club achieving widespread commercial success. This trend continued into the 1990s with the androgynous Michael Jackson. Other groups, such as Salt and Pepper, an all-woman rap group, included sexual themes in their songs, as did 2 Live Crew, which, among other things, had some of its lyrics banned in Florida and became the subject of a discussion by the U.S. vice president.

Dan Quayle was not the only political figure involved in the backlash against some of the lyrics of songs that not only were sexually explicit but also carried subversive messages about war, racism, and drugs. Some were misogynistic and racist. Ice Cube, for example, sang about hating

Koreans. In 1985 President Ronald Reagan charged that record companies glorified drugs, violence, and perversity. President Bush also weighed in with a condemnation. One result was the foundation of the Parents Music Resource Center in the 1980s which attempted, often successfully, to persuade record companies to put warning stickers on albums and singles with sexually explicit lyrics.

As popular music opened up, so did the Broadway stage musical. What had simply been hinted at in Anita Loos's musical "Gentlemen Prefer Blonds" in the 1920s became more overt in musicals about "The Best Little Whore House in Texas" and "La Cage aux Folles," about gay cross-dressers.

An article such as this can do little more than offer an overview. What seems clear, however, is that sex, whether explicit or implicit, has been a dominant theme in music. Often, the forces of censorship have repressed the overtly sexual, but the songs continued to exist through an underground network, to be resurrected for a wider audience later, as Oscar Brand's work shows. Lyrics emphasize the sexual connotation of music and generalize it more effectively than symphonic music can, but this observation simply means that classical music is more individualized and subjective. There is no doubt that music of all types is a sexual stimulant, but what is sexual is both culturally and individually determined.

REFERENCES

Apel, W. *Harvard Dictionary of Music.* Cambridge, Mass.: Harvard Univ. Press, 1969.

Brand, O., ed. *Bawdy Songs and Backroom Ballads.* New York: Grove Press, 1960.

Cray, E., ed. *The Erotic Muse.* 2nd ed. Urbana: Univ. of Illinois Press, 1992.

Lawrence, D.H. Making Love to Music. In H.T. Moore, ed., *Sex, Literature and Censorship.* New York: Twayne, 1953.

Legman, G. *The Horn Book: Studies in Erotic Folklore and Bibliography.* New Hyde Park, N.Y.: University Books, 1964.

Longstreet, S. *The Real Jazz Old and New.* Baton Rouge: Louisiana State Univ. Press, 1956.

Reeves, J., ed. *The Idiom of the People: English Traditional Verse. Edited with an Introduction and Notes from the Manuscripts of Cecil J. Sharp.* New York: W.W. Norton, 1965.

Sachs, C. *The History of Musical Instruments.* New York: Norton, 1937.

Salisbury, J.E. *Sex in the Middle Ages.* New York: Garland, 1991.

Whicher, G.F. *The Goliard Poets.* Cambridge, Mass.: Harvard Univ. Press, 1949.

Vern L. Bullough

n

NAZIS AND SEX

When Adolf Hitler and the Nazis came to power in 1933, Adolf Sellman, a spokesman for the West German Morality League, reported that all filth (i.e., pornography, homosexuality) and trash vanished from the public domain, that prostitution was banished, and that a correct population policy (i.e., racial purity) was established. At first, this was simply an official policy and there was no change in the civil penal code until 1935, when conduct that was contrary to popular sentiment was punished even though there was no specific applicable law. Everything that respectable citizens deemed sexually improper, if not abnormal, and all that conflicted with general average notions of morality could now be punished by a range of penalties, which included imprisonment, internment in a concentration camp, and execution.

The Nazis looked back on the Weimar republic, the Germany immediately preceding the Nazi takeover, as a society that had granted equality of status to women contrary to their natural biology and thus had estranged them from their function as mothers and guardians of the home. The result, the Nazis and their conservative allies had said, was destruction of the family, loss of respect for parents by children, growing assertiveness among women, and vast growth in homosexuality and prostitution, so much so that Berlin, in their eyes, had become the sinful Gomorrah of a degenerate civilization.

Hitler, in his *Mein Kampf,* had remedies for all these ills. He sought to combat prostitution by promoting early marriage, particularly for the man. He advocated the production of more children by racially pure couples, since marriage could not be an end in itself but had to serve the goal of multiplication and preservation of the race. Through sterilization and ruthless segregation, he wanted to prevent the sick or hereditarily disabled from reproducing; in his mind, the right of personal freedom receded before the duty to preserve the race. He felt that youthful urges toward sex could be overcome by physical education and that the "filth" existing in the theater, art, literature, movies, and press had to be eliminated by censorship and outright repression.

Reality often differed from such ideals, and critics have often pointed out that there were two levels of morality, one for the masses and one for the elite; the Nazi hierarchy felt that they were the elite. Individuals such as Joseph Goebbels poked fun at bourgeois virtues and claimed to abominate moral priggishness. Ernst Röhm, the leader of the Storm Troopers, was an avowed and open homosexual, but only when he seemed dangerous to Hitler was he eliminated.

Still, the official ideal was one of sexual restraint. Sex education emphasized self-denial, self-control, will power, and discipline. There was, however, a worry that segregated male and female groups might lead to homosexuality, and so "harmless" contacts between adolescent girls and boys were encouraged.

Conviction for homosexual behavior between adults resulted in six months imprisonment, after which many were then sent to concentration camps. The purpose of the concentration camp was to compel the homosexuals to work methodically and to prevent them from showing any kind of feminine weakness in the belief that they would eventually recover from their homosexuality. It is estimated that up to 50,000—the number of men known to have been convicted of homosexual activity—were sent to such camps, where they had to wear a pink triangle. A decree of 1935 provided for the compulsory sterilization (i.e., castration) of homosexuals (as well as epileptics, schizophrenics, and other "degenerates"), but many of those convicted were not sterilized. After 1942, conviction for a homosexual act could lead to the death penalty, and this penalty was strongly enforced in the armed forces, where offenders were generally shot. It is impossible to know how many homosexuals were killed because of their homosexuality or how many actually were sent to concentration camps, since records have disappeared and many homosexuals were sent to the camps without any legal proceedings. In the camps, it was probably those who seemed "helplessly" homosexual who were executed. A good estimate of the homosexuals who were executed or who died in concentration camps is that the number amounted to tens of thousands. The legal prohibitions against homosexuality were not extended to females, with the result that lesbianism theoretically was not punished, although in reality some lesbians were punished under the general morality clause. Interestingly, the Nazis added a provision to the Code of Criminal Procedure that gave the public prosecutor the discretion not to prosecute an alleged offender who had been the object of blackmail.

Gender discrimination was widespread in Nazi Germany, and the numbers of women in higher education decreased radically. Quotas of approximately 10 percent of the slots were set for females who sought higher education. Even at the elementary levels, girls were encouraged to study domestic science rather than the more demanding arts or sciences. Physical exercise was, however, emphasized. Most of the women's organizations were headed by men or were adjuncts of

men's organizations. For those whom the Nazis regarded as elite women, however, the Women's Academy of Wisdom and Culture was established. It was limited to blue-eyed women who had superior intellectual gifts as well as grace of mind and body. These women were to serve as wives for the elite of the Nazi regime, and they were expected to choose a racially worthy spouse from the leadership corps of the party or government.

With their ideas of "race" mixing, which defined any non-German as belonging to a different race, the Nazis were very much concerned about the children being born to women in conquered areas, particularly in the Slavic areas. Though the German authorities tried to emphasize that intercourse between German soldiers and female foreign workers was both unworthy and destructive of military potential owing to disease, they were unable to enforce their views. Moreover, the shortage of rubber in Germany was such that toward the end of the war the authorities could not give condoms out to German soldiers; though spermicides were recommended and tried, they were not particularly effective without condoms. Heinrich Himmler's elite SS troops, however, were categorically forbidden to have intercourse with women of foreign blood, and after 1941 all such offenses had to be reported to him personally. Even earlier, Himmler had demanded that any incidence of homosexuality in the SS be reported to him. Those who were found to be homosexual were to be stripped of their rank, expelled, and imprisoned, after which they were to be taken to a concentration camp "and there shot while attempting to escape."

The Nazis were particularly virulent in their condemnation of sex with Jews. Every effort was made to make this unacceptable. Syphilis, long known as the French disease, was called the Jewish disease by the Nazis. Intercourse with Jews was regarded as miscegenation and punishable even before mass numbers of Jews were sent to concentration camps. The Nazis also carried out sterilization experiments on Jews in some camps. Various plants, such as *Caladium seguinum,* were given to subjects to see if they caused sterility. Women were examined to see how long they menstruated under the camp diets. Some women were allowed "to volunteer" for brothel services, although non-Germans could serve only other non-Germans.

Pimps who were arrested were sent to concentration camps but prostitutes were not, in spite of the denunciation of them. In fact, Reinhard Heydrich, who was head of the SS

Security Service, had established the Salon Kitty, in Berlin, as a high-class brothel for important officials. Rooms were wired to see if any secrets were given out. By 1939, medically supervised brothels were allowed throughout Nazi-controlled territories, and there was an attempt to register prostitutes. Experiments were also carried out in some brothels, perhaps with Himmler's consent. Prostitutes at a brothel in Stuttgart, for example, were instructed to preserve semen-filled sheaths after each act of intercourse, and these were then collected in an attempt to find a substitute for plasma in blood transfusions. Little else is known about the experiment, however. Most of the prostitutes were volunteers and in theory could resign or move on at any time.

One of the more ironic contradictions of the Nazis is that they claimed on their ascendancy to power to be restoring old-fashioned family virtues. Though they did officially eliminate pornography, the total effect of their administration was to establish one of the most obscene regimes in human history.

REFERENCES

Bleuel, H.P. *Sexual Society in Nazi Germany*. Philadelphia: Lippincott, 1973.

Heger, H. *The Men with the Pink Triangle*. Boston: Alyson, 1980.

Herzer, M. Nazis, Psychiatrists, and Gays. *Cabirion,* Vol. 12 (1985), pp. 1–5.

Lautman, R. The Pink Triangle. *Journal of Homosexuality*, Vol. 6 (1980), pp. 141–60.

Mosse, G.L. *Nazi Culture*. New York: Grosset & Dunlap, 1966.

Plant, R. *The Pink Triangle: The Nazi War Against Homosexuals*. New York: Holt, Rinehart & Winston, 1986.

Vern L. Bullough

NUDISM

Athletic contests in ancient Greece are perhaps the earliest recorded instances of conscious nudism. With emphasis on health and absence of sensuality the Greeks had their young athletes participate nude in various events, typically the forerunners of modern track and field competitions. They marched nude in processions as well as ate and sang as part of their athletic celebrations.

Nudity then more or less disappeared from the pages of history, although medieval Europeans bathed together in the nude for a time and often slept in the nude. There were also nude protesters, such as the legendary Lady Godiva. The first organized modern nudist park was founded in Germany in 1903—the same year as the Wright brothers' first airplane flight in America. The park grew out of an idea by Richard Ungewitter, who early in 1903 had published a 104-page book advocating that people of both sexes associate together totally nude. Paul Zimmermann followed through by opening the world's first nudist park, near Klingberg, Germany, in 1903. It might more accurately have been called a nude health resort, since it had little in common with modern nudist parks except the absence of clothing. Strict health rules prevailed, including prohibitions against meat, alcohol, and smoking. Most notable was the requirement that all guests arise early each morning for two hours of calisthenics under the supervision of a professional instructor.

In spite of the rigid restrictions, once awareness of nudist activities became public legal efforts were made to control the situation both in England and America. Enactment and enforcement of obscenity laws and ordinances preoccupied reformers, legislators, keepers of the morals, and law enforcement officials.

Still, organized nudism in Germany had an estimated active membership of 50,000 by the mid-1920s, and from Germany it spread elsewhere. Its establishment in the United States took place formally in 1929, when a German immigrant, Kurt Barthel, led a group of three experienced, newly arrived German couples on a nudist outing on Labor Day of that year. The outing took place on the Hudson River near New York City, where the property owner approved of such activity taking place.

Nudist parks were established in New Jersey, California, and Indiana in the early 1930s and are still in operation. Isley Boone, a minister in New Jersey; Hobart Grassey in California; and Alois Knapp, an attorney in Chicago provided the leadership in establishing the three parks and in publicizing and spreading the nudist idea. Nudist publications, originating in the 1930s, continue to exist, as does the major national organization established at that time, the American Sunbathing Association.

Nudist parks traditionally have offered meager facilities. Just the freedom to be nude attracts many adherents. In recent years, however, some parks have gone upscale. Some have mobile home facilities, while others have organized condominium associations. Some have all the facilities a popular nonnudist recreational club would provide (e.g., swimming, tennis, volleyball, hiking, basketball, shuffleboard, and table tennis). Some nudists organize themselves into "travel clubs." They neither own nor rent property but visit established nudist facilities regularly, as a group, by prearrangement.

Self-imposed, ultra-conservative rules have been the means by which nudism has survived and thrived. The need to exercise control from within or be closed down by outside authorities seemingly dominated nudist leadership in establishing and enforcing strict rules for much of the movement's history. The rules generally included the following:

1. No alcohol.
2. No body contact—nude dancing is forbidden even between spouses.
3. No photography unless the subject consents.
4. Application for membership is carefully screened, particularly in the case of single men.
5. Married persons are accepted as couples only.
6. Anyone engaging in improper conduct is removed immediately.
7. Members should follow the same general behavioral standards adhered to in nonnudist social or recreational settings.

In recent years, there has been a relaxation of some of these rules in some nudist parks. Beer and wine are sold in a number of facilities, and there is a lessening of the no-touch regulations.

Numerous studies of the social characteristics of practicing nudists have been conducted in the United States since 1932, when Frances and Mason Merrill wrote a book on the subject. Hartman, Fithian, and Johnson summarized the results of these studies first in 1970, and then updated their work in 1992. Some findings:

1. *Religion*—Johnson's research in the late 1940s indicated nudists were 91 percent Christian (77 percent Protestant and 14 percent Roman Catholic), when at the time Protestants made up 55 percent of the population in the United States and Roman Catholics 34 percent. By 1964, the Hartman-Fithian-Johnson study (*n*=1,388) found only 43 percent of nudists holding church membership and 55 percent with no affiliation. Pre-1960 nudist research showed much higher nudist religious affiliation. Still, it is common for nondenominational religious services to be conducted in the parks on Sunday, and many religious professionals are members.
2. *Personality*—Several studies involved asking nudists to complete an in-depth personality test, the Minnesota Multiphasic Personality Inventory (MMPI). Results indicated very little psychopathology among nudists gener-

ally and nudist women in particular. Nudists, if personality tests are any indicator, are normal men and women.
3. *Marital Status*—Typically, 75 percent to 80 percent of nudists were married. The remainder were single, divorced, or widowed.
4. *Education*—Generally, nudists have been found to be above the U.S. average in completing grade school, high school, and college. In 1960, nudists were two to two and a half times more likely to complete high school and college than the U.S. population.
5. *Introduction to nudism*—Nudist literature was by far the most frequent means of introducing interested persons to nudism (over 40 percent). Friends and spouses were the other major sources.
6. *Age*—Analyzing the ages of nudists showed those below age 30 to be underrepresented when compared to the general population (15 percent to 20 percent) and those in their thirties and forties to be overrepresented (55 percent to 60 percent). Some 15 percent are in their fifties, and less than 10 percent were over 60.
7. *Social Class*—The class status of nudists tends more to the upper end of the scale than the lower. When nudists were evaluated on an expanded Hollingshead Index of Social Class Position, there were five times as many nudists in Hollingshead's class 1 than in the population Hollingshead used to construct his scale, twice as many nudists in classes 2 and 3, two-fifths as many in class 4, and one-quarter as many in class 5.

Is Nudism a Sexual Phenomenon?

Nudists do not believe nudism is a sexual phenomenon, although Americans generally think it is. For nudism to have existed in America for as long as it has, nudists' sexual conduct could not have deviated significantly from the norms or it would have suffered more attacks than it has. Still, both male and female nudists report that nudist participation increased their frequency of sexual relations, although they added that it did not increase their desire for participation in extramarital relations. Most nudists reported "rarely" or "never" being asked to participate in "swinging" activities. Most nudists say they were never involved in such activities.

Nudist marriages, in general, appear happy, possibly because of the agreement to practice such a controversial life-style in the first place. Nudist women in particular reported favorably on the benefits of nudist practices for their husbands and children. Divorced nudists typically noted that nudism was practiced before and after their divorce and was not a factor in it. Nonnudist psychiatrists, social workers, and counselors who have been invited to nudist parks to observe the children, generally report that nudist children are happy, well-adjusted youngsters.

The factors reported for becoming a nudist were relaxation, freedom from clothing, freedom from sickness or disease, all-over tan, enjoyment of fresh air, and social congeniality. Rarely was there evidence that negative factors such as hostility, rebellion, and nonconformity were motivations toward nudity. Factors stated for continuing to be a nudist were physical and mental health, relaxation, freedom from clothes, and friends. Curiosity attracted some newcomers, but other interests have to appear if one is to continue to visit nudist parks.

Studies of nudist dropouts suggest that negative feelings about nudism are not the reason they no longer participate. Instead, moving out of the area, lack of spare time, and distance from nudist parks were the main reasons for discontinuing membership. Many former nudist group members continued to practice nudity at home or in the privacy of their backyard. Nudist parks welcome law enforcement personnel as members or guests and only rarely need assistance in dealing with troublemakers.

Legislators increasingly have taken a hands-off approach, so that social nudism continues to exist in America virtually unchanged, from a legal standpoint, as it has for 60 years. Some local ordinances and individuals, however, cause problems for specific parks. Hartman, Fithian, and Johnson, as a result of their research, suggest that there is therapeutic value in nudism and have suggested that individuals violating laws regarding voyeurism and exposure might well be treated in a nudist setting.

Nudists contend that the removal of clothing brings about greater honesty between people, since clothing produces a false mystique about the body. Nudity, they argue, creates greater equality between the sexes and weakens sexual segregation and discrimination. Research by Story, Vingerhoets, and Bunk tends to support such claims.

Though they are nonnudists themselves, Hartman and Fithian felt, following their original studies on nudism, that nudism might be a potential tool in helping people work through some of the problems they had with self-concept and body imagery. As a result, they conducted two nude marathon counseling sessions in conjunction with Bindrim, and held a third session without him. A number of the participants' problems were successfully addressed. For example, one man, who was impotent, reported that "his penis was too small." The group members pointed out that his penis was as large as, and in fact larger than, those of other members of the group. This greatly enhanced his self-concept and feelings about himself and might have been a factor in his later regaining his potency.

Bindrim continued the use of nudity in group psychotherapy with more than 7,000 clients. A number of other therapists have utilized nudist facilities as the ideal setting for group psychotherapy. Wheatley compared nude psychotherapy groups with traditional clothed groups and reported that nude marathon regression therapy facilitates more significant long-term changes than the traditional encounter marathons analyzed. The subject of nudity as a therapeutic catalyst, however, deserves more investigation before any final conclusions are possible.

REFERENCES

Bindrim, P. Aqua-energetics. In R.J. Corsini, ed., *Handbook of Innovative Therapies.* New York: John Wiley & Sons, 1981.

Casler, L. Some Sociopsychological Observations in a Nudist Camp: A Preliminary Study. *Journal of Social Psychology,* Vol. 64 (1964), pp. 307–23.

Goodson, A. *Therapy, Nudity and Joy.* Los Angeles: Elysium Growth Press, 1991.

Hartman, W.E., and M. Fithian. Enhancing Sexuality Through Nudism. In H. Otto, ed., *New Sexuality.* Palo Alto, Calif.: Science and Behavior Books, 1991.

Hartman, W.E., M. Fithian, and D. Johnson. *Nudist Society.* New York: Crown, 1970; revised by I. Bancroft. Los Angeles: Elysium Growth Press, 1992.

Johnson, D. *The Nudists.* New York: Duell, Sloan & Pearce, 1959.

Merrill, F., and M. Merrill. *Nudism Comes to America.* New York: Knopf, 1932.

Story, M. Comparisons of Body Self-Concept Between Social Nudists and Non Nudists. *Journal of Psychology,* Vol. 118 (Sept. 1984), pp. 99–112.

Vingerhoets, A., and B. Bunk. Attitudes Toward Nudist and Public Beaches: Some Evidence of Dissonance Reduction and Gender Differences. *Journal of Leisure Research,* Vol. 23 (May 1987), pp. 11–21.

Wheatley, P. Effect of Nude Marathon Regression Therapy on Interpersonal and Intrapersonal Change in Self-selected Subjects: Psychological Nudism or Psychic Striptease? Ph.D. Diss., California School of Professional Psychology, Los Angeles, 1974.

William E. Hartman
Marilyn A. Fithian

NYMPHOMANIA

The word "nymphomania" is derived from the Greek and literally means "bride madness." The *Oxford English Dictionary* defines it as "a feminine disease characterized by morbid and uncontrollable sexual desire." Setting the disease issue aside, most definitions of nymphomania include the elements of excessive and uncontrollable sexual desire. The equivalent term for men is "satyriasis." Excessive sexual desire in women (as in men) is a rather ethereal concept. To evaluate what excessive sexual desire or behavior is, it is crucial to understand normative sexual desire. Numerous North American studies have revealed a wide range of variability in the frequency of sexual behavior, with no agreed upon norm except a statistical one. Indeed, there is a great deal of variability within any individual's sexual history. It is not unusual for couples to report engaging in various sexual behaviors with Promethean vigor during the beginning of a sexual relationship or during a crisis in a long-standing relationship. Engaging in sexual behaviors three or four times a day is not unusual in these circumstances. Thus, it is difficult to find a numerical equivalent of "excessive." At the biological level, one might use a marker such as "physiologically harmful" or "tissue injury" to delineate excessive.

The concept of "uncontrollable" sexual desire as part of the picture of nymphomania introduces a more clinical aspect that pertains to motivation. For instance, a woman who had ten sexual contacts in a day might be considered a nymphomaniac from a clinical perspective. A prostitute who had the same number of sexual contacts in a day would presumably not be labeled with this term, because the motivation is assumed to be financial and not her own sexual desire and gratification. The depiction of sexual desire as uncontrollable suggests the possibility of an insatiable libido or other factors that impel the person toward frequent sexual contact. A perusal of the clinical literature reveals no cases of insatiable libido. The most frequently cited factors involved in excessive sexual desire are frequent sexual contacts without gratification or orgasm, emotional tension, manic states, obsessive-compulsive disorders, an inordinate need to be accepted by men, and an attempt to deny homosexual feelings. It would appear that Kaplan's observation that excessive sexual desire is so rare as to constitute a clinical curiosity when it is a primary symptom still holds true.

The elusive nature of nymphomania is further reflected in previously published editions of the *Encyclopedia of Sexual Behavior,* which contains only two references to the term. The first reference, which appears unchanged in all three editions, extols the virtue of treating this condition with androgenic compounds. The rationale for this treatment is as follows: (1) nymphomania is the result of many sexual contacts without gratification due to failure to achieve orgasm; (2) treatment with androgens helps achieve orgasm so that "an excessive number of sexual contacts is no longer necessary." Suffice it to say, this is no longer a treatment of choice for women having trouble reaching orgasm, who would not meet the criteria for nymphomania anyway.

The second reference, which also appears unchanged in all but the first edition, is a brief discussion of nymphomania as male wish fulfillment in the context of pornography. Indeed, it seems that the only place where nymphomania appears to thrive is in the fantasies of males or in depictions of those fantasies. X-rated or hardcore magazines, books, and movies that have a story line tend to follow a similar pattern. They almost always involve sexually insatiable women who are incapable of resisting any type of male sexual advance. In reality, the label of nymphomania is most frequently used by men when they encounter a woman whose sexual desire may be more intense than their own. If a woman is more sexual than they are, she must be a nymphomaniac so the reasoning goes. The gender bias in the perception of sexual appetites is further underscored when one considers that a female with a lusty sexual appetite is often described as "promiscuous," while her male counterpart is more likely to be called "horny" or "ardent." In this respect, we might note that the male equivalent of nymphomania, satyriasis, is much less widely known, at least among college students.

In conclusion, it appears that nymphomania is primarily located in male sexual fantasy and wish fulfillment. For most males, this is the safest place to encounter the nymphomaniac. As Symons noted, the sexually insatiable woman is to be found primarily, if not exclusively, in the ideology of feminism, the hopes of boys, and the fears of men.

REFERENCES

Ellis, A., and Abarbanel, A. *The Encyclopedia of Sexual Behavior.* Vol. 1. New York: Hawthorn Books, 1961.

———. *The Encyclopedia of Sexual Behavior.* 2nd ed. New York: Hawthorn Books, 1967.

Kaplan, H.S. *Disorders of Sexual Desire.* New York: Simon & Schuster, 1979.

Symons, D. *The Evolution of Human Sexuality.* New York: Oxford Univ. Press, 1979.

A.R. Allgeier

O

OBSCENE TELEPHONE CALLS

Obscene telephone calls are anonymous telephone calls in which the caller obtains sexual arousal or gratification by making or listening to sexual remarks. The obscene telephone caller is almost always a man who calls women. Most often, the caller randomly chooses phone numbers from the telephone book, primarily looking for women's names.

There are three types of obscene telephone calls. In the most common type, the caller may breathe heavily or describe sexual activities, particularly his masturbatory action, in explicit detail. The second type of obscene call is one in which the caller threatens the listener and instructs her to undress, masturbate, or engage in some form of sexual behavior. One such case involved a Philadelphia-area man who was convicted of making hundreds of threatening obscene calls to women. He told each woman that he was holding her husband hostage, and to guarantee her husband's safety, she must engage in sex with her children so the caller could listen. In the third type of obscene call, the caller tries to convince the listener to reveal intimate details of her sexual behaviors, often stating that he is conducting a survey of sexual practices for an institute or university.

The obscene telephone caller enjoys the startled or frightened response of the listener. It is common for the caller to masturbate during or shortly after the call. Obscene telephone calling may or may not be the individual's primary mode of sexual arousal or gratification. Some callers, particularly adolescents, call only as an occasional or a onetime prank. The pattern of repeated or compulsive obscene telephone calling is termed telephone scatalogia or telephonicophilia. It is often reported that the obscene telephone caller has doubts about his gender identity, and the calls provide him with confirmation of his masculine role.

Recipients of obscene telephone calls may feel revolted, victimized, manipulated, or violated. When someone receives an obscene telephone call, it is best to hang up immediately—not saying anything, not slamming down the receiver. The caller is usually aroused if the recipient expresses fright, shock, or anger. If the caller does not think that the recipient is annoyed, then he may not call again. The recipient should never give her name, address, or any information about herself. Sometimes it is difficult for a person who receives an obscene call for the first time to know to hang up. Often, before using sexual language, the caller may sound friendly or recognizable, manipulating the recipient into responding or carrying on a conversation. If calls persist, the recipient should inform the telephone company and the police.

There are several options that may be helpful in stopping obscene callers. The recipient may change her telephone number and obtain an unlisted number. An unlisted number is inaccessible to callers who chose randomly from the telephone book. Telephone companies can provide Caller ID, a device that attaches to the telephone and instantly displays a local caller's telephone number. This system allows the recipient to screen local calls and report suspect numbers to the police. Call Trace allows the date, time, and phone number of the caller to be recorded by the telephone company. Following the call, the recipient must enter a code into the telephone to activate the trace and notify the phone company to take action with the police. Most state laws provide for a minimum fine of $500 and imprisonment of up to 30 days for obscene telephone calls. Federal law provides fines up to $500 and imprisonment of up to six months for interstate or foreign obscene telephone calls.

The term of "obscene telephone calls" does not encompass sexually explicit phone conversations that are consensual or not anonymous. For example, people who are involved in a sexual relationship may call each other to engage in a sexually arousing conversation over the telephone. Also, in another form of consensual "phone sex," a caller may dial an advertised number to hear sexual talk from someone who is hired to provide that service. The customer pays with a credit card and is usually charged by the minute. This is not an obscene telephone call, since it is completely consensual.

REFERENCES

Masters, W.H., V.E. Johnson, and R.C. Kolodny. *Masters and Johnson on Sex and Human Loving.* Boston: Little, Brown, 1982.

Money, J. *Lovemaps: Clinical Concepts of Sexual/Erotic Health and Pathology, Paraphilia, and Gender Transposition in Childhood, Adolescence, and Maturity.* New York: Irvington, 1986.

Obscene Calls Held the Victims Hostage. *Philadelphia Inquirer,* 2 July 1991.

Sheffield, C.J. The Invisible Intruder: Women's Experience with Obscene Phone Calls. *Gender and Society,* Vol. 3 (Dec. 1989), pp. 483–88.

Warner, P.K. Aural Assault: Obscene Telephone Calls. *Qualitative Sociology,* Vol. 11 (Winter 1988), pp. 302–18.

Sari Locker

ONANISM

Historically, "onanism" has often been used interchangeably with "masturbation" and artificial "birth control." Onanism is taken from the biblical story of Onan. Onan was the son of Judah and an unnamed Canaanite woman. He had an older brother, Er, and a younger brother, Shelah. Judah chose a wife for his firstborn, Er, and her name was Tamar. The story of Onan is as follows:

> For his first son Er, Judah got a wife whose name was Tamar. Er's conduct was evil, and it displeased the Lord, so the Lord killed him. Then Judah said to Er's brother Onan, "Go and sleep with your brother's widow. Fulfill your obligation to her as her husband's brother, so that your brother may have descendants." But Onan knew that the children would not belong to him, so when he had intercourse with his brother's widow, he let the semen spill on the ground, so that there would be no children for his brother. What he did displeased the Lord and the Lord killed him also. (Gen. 38:6–10)

This story has often been proposed as a divine prohibition against masturbation, birth control, and any "wasting" of male sperm. One cannot know the meaning of this story without understanding the concept of the levirate marriage (*levir* = husband's brother) in the Hebrew law. The law was intended to preserve the dead husband's name and his children's right to his inheritance, as well as to ensure the welfare of the widow. The levirate marriage law is as follows:

> If two brothers live on the same property and one of them dies, leaving no son, then his widow is not to be married to someone outside the family; it is the duty of the dead man's brother to marry her. The first son that they have will be considered the son of the dead man, so that his family line will continue in Israel. But if the dead man's brother does not want to marry her, she is to go before the town leaders and say, "My husband's brother will not do his duty; he refuses to give his brother a descendant among the people of Israel." Then the town leaders are to summon him and speak to him. If he still refuses to marry her, his brother's widow is to go up to him in the presence of the town leaders, take off one of his sandals, spit in his face, and say, "This is what happens to the man who refuses to give his brother a descendant." His family will be known in Israel as "the family of the man who had his sandal pulled off." (Deut. 25:5–10)

Thus, the levirate marriage was based primarily on economics, the homogeneity of the family, and justice. By not performing his levirate obligation and willfully preventing his brother's wife, Tamar, from conceiving, Onan intended to get his dead brother's inheritance. He was slain for his selfishness and disobedience to the law. Most biblical scholars today agree that the story of Onan had nothing to do with condemning masturbation, contraception, or any other deliberate "wasting" of sperm.

It was not until 1724, in Boston, that a treatise or sermon by an unknown English author was published called *Onania; or the Heinous Sin of Self-Polution, and all its Frightful Confequences, in both Sexes, Confidered. With Spiritual and Phyfical Advice to Thofe, who have already injur'd themfelves by this Abominable Practice. And Seafonable Admonition to the Youth (of both SEXES) and thofe whofe Tuition they are under, whether Parents, Guardians, Mafters, or Miftreffes. To which is Added, A Letter from a Lady Concerning the Ufe and Abufe of the Marriage-Bed. With the Author's Anfwer thereto.* This treatise linked onanism to masturbation. It also stated that the practice caused many of the major illnesses, such as "palsies, distempers, consumptions, gleets, fluxes, ulcers, fits, madness, childlessness"—all the syndromes of the day were included, even death itself.

Onania caught on and became the basis for hunting down those who practiced masturbation. It was believed that the practice of masturbation would destroy the body itself, unless the sinner stopped the sin. The theory behind the *Onania* doctrine was based on a mythical science that the loss of sperm in the practice of masturbation was debilitating to the body and led to disease and finally death.

A follower of this school of thought was Simon Andre Tissot (1728–1797), a Swiss physician. He took the concepts from *Onania* and wrote them in medical theory. Early editions of his work on masturbation were in Latin and French; the first American translation was published in 1832, under the title *Treatise on the Diseases Produced by Onanism.* This was the beginning of his theory of degeneracy. According to Tissot, the practice of masturbation caused the body to degenerate through "convulsions, paralysis, epilepsy, feeblemindedness, impotence, and bladder disorders." Later, "anti-Onanists" added to Tissot's list of maladies everything from pimples to falling hair, weak eyes, stooped shoulders, gonorrhea, uterine hemorrhage, tuberculosis, schizophrenia, and suicide."

Today, our understanding of sexual anatomy, hormones, and the sexual response cycle completely nullifies all the degeneracy theories that have developed in medicine and religion. Yet onanism is still a concept held by many religious traditions and interpreters of the Bible.

Thus, two great misinterpretations are rooted in one biblical story. First, there is the notion that the sin of Onan had to do with masturbation. No contemporary biblical scholarship would support this assertion. Second, there is the belief that the practice of masturbation and the consequent loss of semen lead to disease and ultimately death, as had happened to Onan, who was killed by the Lord. This view of masturbation is also without any scientific foundation.

Nelson offers three important observations about Onan. First, the story of Onan illustrates the emphasis on procreation. When one is part of a small community of people, it is crucial to see how important procreation is to the survival of the community. That is hardly a problem today, with our increasing population density. Second, there is a profound misunderstanding of biology in the story of Onan. It indicates that the "seed of life" is within the male; thus, when Onan spilled his semen on the ground through the practice of coitus interruptus, he was deliberately destroying human life. There is no concept here that the woman also provides the "seed of life" through eggs and ovulation. This knowledge did not exist in biblical times. Third, the story of Onan has been used to enhance the concept of sexual sin, especially by the male. Throughout Judeo-Christian history, the male, whether in masturbation, homosexuality, or coitus interruptus, has been condemned more vigorously for sexual sin than the female. However, the best biblical scholarship indicates that this story is not about sexual acts, such as masturbation or birth control, but rather is concerned with disobedience to God's commands and greed over inheritance issues. To make this a story of God's view of sex is to misunderstand both the context and the content of the story of Onan.

REFERENCES

Haas, K., and A. Haas. *Understanding Sexuality*. St. Louis: Times Mirror/Mosby, 1987.

Kosnik, A., et al. *Human Sexuality: New Directions in American Catholic Thought*. New York: Paulist Press, 1977.

Lawrence, R.J. *The Poisoning of Eros: Sexual Values in Conflict*. New York: Augustine Moore Press, 1989.

Money, J. *The Destroying Angel*. Buffalo, N.Y.: Prometheus Books, 1985.

Nelson, J.B. *Embodiment: An Approach to Sexuality and Christian Theology*. Minneapolis: Augsburg, 1978.

Strong, B., and C. DeVault. *Understanding Our Sexuality.* 2d ed. St. Paul: West, 1988.

William R. Stayton

ORAL-GENITAL SEX

Oral-genital sex (sometimes called the genital kiss) is the oral stimulation of the genitals of either a female or a male by a partner of either sex. That is, it may be either a homosexual experience or a heterosexual one. The person performing the action may move from other parts of the body (e.g., orally stimulating the breasts of either the male or female) to the genitals, and after reaching them may incorporate other parts of the immediate area (e.g., thighs, perineum) into the experience. Sometimes, oral stimulation of the anus (anilingus) is also practiced at this time. If the activity is being performed on a woman, it is known as cunnilingus ("to lick the vulva"); if performed on a man, it is fellatio ("to suck").

The frequency of oral-genital sex varies greatly. Some researchers report that 80 percent of single men and women between the ages of 25 and 34, and 90 percent of those married and under 25 years of age, have participated during the preceding year. Other workers say that human oral sex is the one family of sexual practices that is truly universal. The practice does seem to be more prevalent among better educated and younger individuals, although many exceptions to these generalizations occur. Although the statistics are unreliable, it may be said that the practice of oral-genital sex is almost as frequent as masturbation. There is an increasing frequency of the practice among adolescents; actually, they are slightly more likely to practice it than coitus, because they recognize it as a means of sex without fear of pregnancy. Heterosexual couples use it for the same reason. Both homosexual and heterosexual partners may use it as a means of expressing deep, intimate feelings. Oral-genital stimulation may be incorporated in foreplay or afterglow when other techniques are used to achieve orgasm, or it can be employed as the only means of reaching orgasm. Oral-genital sex has been used as a method of sexual interaction when a male has difficulty attaining an erection or if intercourse is painful. It has been successfully used by people with disabilities, such as spinal cord injuries. Heterosexual couples have found it useful during late pregnancy or after childbirth when intercourse might be dangerous or painful.

Sexually transmitted diseases (STDs) such as gonorrhea, herpes, warts, yeasts, and syphilis have been shown to be transmitted by oral-genital contact. Opinions vary about the possibility of transmitting HIV (human immunodeficiency virus) by such contact. Some Canadian workers deny that transmission takes place if the mouth and gums are healthy. However, since the virus is transmitted from semen to blood, it is easy to see how it could get into the bloodstream of someone who had a small injury in the mouth. The virus is found in semen, Cowper's fluid, and vaginal secretions. Most workers agree that the risk of transmission is less during oral-genital sex than during anal sex. The use of condoms or dental dams reduces the chance of infection from all STDs.

Attitudes toward oral-genital sex vary greatly. Some people find the idea disgusting because they associate such activity with urine and feces. The view of others is shaped by their attitudes toward the odor, texture, and appearance of the genitals. Still others are concerned with the taste of the genitals or their secretions. All these attitudes may be positive or negative, depending on the individuals involved.

Two major positions are used during oral-genital sex. One is the sixty-nine position (named after the positions of the digits 69), where the participating partners simultaneously stimulate each other's genitals orally. It is thought by some partners that simultaneous orgasm is also desirable. The other position occurs when one partner lies back and is orally stimulated by the other partner. The passive partner may then become the active partner. Consecutive rather than simultaneous orgasms occur when this position is used, and one partner may bring the other to orgasm without obtaining orgasm himself or herself. Some men who identify themselves as heterosexual allow themselves to be fellated by another man in this way because they do not feel as if they are performing a homosexual act. Among homosexual men, this is called "doing trade." The sex of the partners is irrelevant when determining the positions, and the positions may shift often during any particular episode. Masturbation is often also employed.

Cunnilingus is the act of performing oral stimulation on the genitals of a woman by either a man or another woman. The partner gently licks the clitoris or the lips of the vagina and may separate the lips with the hands or tongue. The sides of the clitoris shaft may be massaged with a rapidly flicked tongue. Many women enjoy a slow, steady rhythm, moving backward and forward to the vaginal opening, sometimes with deep insertion of the tongue just before orgasm. Manual stimulation may be employed simultaneously. Gentle biting, sucking, or nibbling actions usually occur. Too much stimulation can be painful. Some women enjoy having their partner blow air into the vagina, but this should be done with great caution because infectious organisms may be introduced into the vagina, uterus, or even the body cavity through the Fallopian tubes.

Men often have mixed feelings when performing cunnilingus. They may become very sexually excited by the view of the genitals and feel that the vagina opens like a flower, with the taste of the secretions being like nectar. Other men like it sometimes but may feel obligated to perform because it is the macho thing to do. Some men will not perform it at all. It is usually conceded that men who perform cunnilingus are more goal oriented and usually do it as a prelude to intercourse and for their own pleasure; they do not prolong the sensations as an end to themselves.

Women who perform cunnilingus (most often lesbians) are usually more effective in giving pleasure to another woman; that is, a woman knows what feels good to another woman. They approach the activity with less haste than men do and prolong it for its own value. Cunnilingus is the preferred method for reaching orgasm for most lesbians.

Fellatio is the oral stimulation of the male genitals by a woman or another man. Attitudes toward the activity vary, ranging from the idea that every man's dream is to be sucked off by a woman to revulsion. Some men express the fear that if they ejaculate in a woman's mouth, they will choke her; others believe that ejaculating into a woman's mouth and having her swallow is something special.

The attitudes of women vary, from the idea that the activity is dirty and perverted to the view that it is normal and pleasurable. Some women prefer it to coitus because there is no fear of unwanted pregnancy. It is the most requested act by the customers of prostitutes and the act that the prostitutes prefer to perform, since they do not have to undress or rent a room, and they can turn more customers in an evening at lower cost.

The glans penis is the primary focus of fellatio, although the shaft, frenulum, perineum, scrotum, testicles, and sometimes the anus receive attention. These areas are usually nibbled, licked, or sucked (the common name "blow job" is inappropriate because there is rarely any "blowing" performed). The penis may be inserted into the mouth to the depth of the glans, or it may be "deep throated" to the base of the shaft.

The gag reflex is usually activated when the penis hits the back of the throat. This problem may be overcome by grasping the base of the penis with the hand and controlling the depth of penetration, or by reconditioning the reflex by practicing slowly taking the penis deeper and deeper into the throat. The gag reflex may also be stimulated by ejaculation into the mouth, either because of aversion to the practice, because of fear of the consequences of swallowing the semen, or because of the taste of the semen. The taste of the semen varies from individual to individual and with the diet of the individual. For example, asparagus gives semen a strong, bitter flavor. Healthy semen is safe to swallow, and it contains only about 5 calories per ejaculation.

Fellatio is probably the most common sexual activity practiced by homosexual men (some workers insist it is anal intercourse). Homosexual men usually approach the activity with less haste than a woman does (although there are many exceptions), and because they know what makes a man feel good, they usually are considered to be able to give more pleasure than a woman who performs fellatio. Most homosexual men swallow the semen; most women do not.

Oral-genital sexual activity has a history dating to antiquity, and its acceptance or rejection varied (and still varies) from culture to culture. The rejection of the practice usually centered around the idea that it was nonprocreative and an "unnatural" act. The ancient Romans practiced a type of fellatio in which the penetrating partner remained relatively motionless and the receptive partner did most of the work; irrumation occurred, with the penetrator engaged in vigorous buccal or laryngeal thrusts.

Some religions tolerated the practice and others actually incorporated oral-genital contact into their rituals. Hinduism regarded oral-genital contact as a sin that could not be expiated in fewer than 100 reincarnations. However, in erotic manuals of the same period, there is an eight-step set of directions to be used by eunuchs when performing the activity. Eunuchs performed cunnilingus in those cultures in which men maintained harems, and, of course, the women participated in the activity with each other.

Ritual fellatio is reported by studies of the Sambia of New Guinea. The Sambia believe that a boy is born with an internal organ that will eventually produce both semen and growth, but it must be supplied with semen from older men before it can do so. Various rules determine who the semen donor will be (e.g., the sister's husband is desirable; the father is not acceptable). The boy, from about the age of ten, tries to accept semen every day by performing fellatio on a proper donor. After six to eight years as an acceptor, he becomes a donor.

The practice of oral-genital sex is well documented in other ancient cultures as well as in modern ones. It is becoming more widely accepted among young and better educated individuals.

REFERENCES

Allgeier, E.R., and A.R. Allgeier. *Sexual Interactions.* Lexington, Mass.: D.C. Heath, 1991.

Bullough, V.L. *Sexual Variance in Society and History.* New York: John Wiley & Sons, 1976.

Katchadourian, H.A. *Fundamentals of Human Sexuality.* 5th ed. Fort Worth: Holt, Rinehart & Winston, 1990.

Marmor, J., ed., *Homosexual Behavior: A Modern Reappraisal.* New York: Basic Books, 1980.

Masters, W.H., V.E. Johnson, and R.C. Kolodny. *Human Sexuality.* 3d ed. Glenview, Ill.: Scott, Foresman, 1988.

Reinisch, J.M. *The Kinsey Institute New Report on Sex.* New York: St. Martin's Press, 1990.

James D. Haynes

ORGANIZATIONS: PROFESSIONAL

Organized sex research began in the last part of the 19th century, and although the researchers from various disciplines knew of the work of others, it was only gradually that they realized there was a need to share information across disciplines. Germany and German-speaking areas served as the focal point for many of these interdisciplinary investigators, and the key organizing figure for much of the early development was Magnus Hirschfeld (1868–1935).

Though Hirschfeld originally became involved in sex research through his studies and political activity on behalf of homosexuals, he became convinced, largely through the effort of Iwan Bloch (1872–1922), that the study of sexuality involved the collaborative efforts of various disciplines and professions. This led to his attempt to found the *Zeitschrift für Sexualwissenschaft* in 1908. Though only published for a year, it included articles by such individuals as Sigmund Freud, Alfred Adler, Paolo Mantgazza, Cesare Lombroso, Wilhelm Stekel, and others. In the next year, the journal was combined with a more popular journal, *Sexual Probleme,* and issued under the title of *Zeitschrift für Sexualwissenschaft und Sexual Politik,* and it was more educational and political than scholarly.

As the number of researchers grew, Hirschfeld joined with Albert Eulenburg in 1913 to establish the Physicians for Sexual Science and Eugenics, the first professional society devoted to sex research. In that same year, Albert Moll established the International Society for Sexual Research. Each organization struggled to consolidate itself by organizing an international congress, efforts which were handicapped by the outbreak of World War I. It was not until 1921 that Hirschfeld and his allies managed to hold the first international sexological congress in Berlin, the International Congress for Sexual Reform on a Sexological Basis. The organizing committee included scientists from Tokyo, Beijing, Moscow, Copenhagen, London, Rome, and San Francisco as well as various cities in Germany. The Congress included 28 papers in four major areas, but the only clear research area was sexual endocrinology. The three other areas—sex and the law, birth control, and sex education—emphasized the political aspects of sex research. This explains why the congress ended with a call for legal and social reform. Though the reforms urged (e.g., dissemination of contraceptives, freedom to divorce, change in marriage laws regarding women, effective sex education) seem modest today, it was the congress's polemical call for action that led to criticism.

One of the major opponents was Albert Moll (1862–1939), who in 1926 organized the International Congress for Sex Research, in Berlin, and to which Hirschfeld was not invited. It was a larger and somewhat more diverse meeting than the first Hirschfeld congress. Hirschfeld countered with a congress in 1928, in Copenhagen, and out of this came the World League for Sexual Reform, with Hirschfeld, August Forel, and Havelock Ellis as copresidents. This organization seemed as much political as sexological and sponsored the next three congresses, in London in 1929, in Vienna in 1930, and in Brno, Czechoslovakia, in 1932.

The League had a rather stormy history, mainly because of disputes among its members over sexual reform in the Soviet Union, with the split centered around the question of whether it was necessary to reform society before sexual reform could take place or whether it was worthwhile to agitate for sexual reform even in an unreformed society. In the 1930s, one of the League's presidents, J.H. Leunbach, insisted that it affiliate with the revolutionary workers' movement, whereas the other president, Norman Haire of England, was determined to keep all revolutionary activity out of the League by emphasizing the need to concentrate on education. It was not the disputes, however, that tolled the death knell of the international organization but the rise of the Nazis and their destruction of the German sexological movement.

Norman Haire attempted, through his writings and organizational skills, to keep his wing of the society alive. Two British organizations emerged, the Sex Education Society and the British Society for the Study of Sexual Psychology. Haire also edited a journal associated with the first group, the *Journal of Sex Education*, but with his death in 1952 the journal ended. Also working to keep some international cooperation going was the Indian sex researcher A.P. Pillay, who edited the *International Journal of Sexology* from 1947 to 1955, a successor to an earlier journal he had started entitled *Marriage Hygiene*. Various birth control organizations, both national and international, continued to exist, as well as a few organizations of homosexuals that tried to disseminate information about homosexuality and lesbianism as well as serve as social organizations.

The next major organizing effort came from the Americans. In one sense, the first organization was the National Council of Family Relations, organized in 1939, which began publishing a journal, *Living*, later known as the *Journal of Marriage and the Family*. Since courtship and sex within marriage were regarded as significant to the study of the family, some aspects of sexual behavior were discussed at society meetings, and studies were published in the journals. Sex research itself had been a major interest of the Rockefeller Foundation, which financed studies by the National Research Council from the 1920s to the 1950s, but most of the scientists involved had preferred to work within their own disciplines and specialties and had discouraged the development of any interdisciplinary group.

The person who took the initial step to organize the disparate groups doing research was Albert Ellis, who formulated the name the Society for the Scientific Study of Sex (SSSS) in 1950, but his efforts to organize a society failed, in part due to the opposition of Alfred Kinsey. Whether Kinsey was fearful that such an organization might compete for funds with his own research institute, as some have said, or whether, having studied the history of the European groups, he was fearful of having sex researchers involved in campaigning for sexual reforms and thus endangering his funds, is not clear. Picking up the effort of Albert Ellis was Hans Lehfeldt, who had been encouraged by his friend Norman Haire, shortly before Haire's death, to contact Albert Ellis and Henry Guze about the establishment of some sort of sexological group

in the United States. In 1957, the three of them joined with Robert Sherwin, a lawyer, and Hugo Beigel, a psychologist, to lay the groundwork for a society. Harry Benjamin lent his support to the group but did not take an active role in planning programs. Ultimately, some 47 professionals were found willing to be listed as charter members, and the society held its first conference on Saturday, November 8, 1958. It was not until 1960, however, that the Society got around to electing officers, with Albert Ellis as first president, and it was not until 1965 that the SSSS was formally incorporated in New York State. Still, the group dates its official organization from 1958. In 1965, the same year it was incorporated, the Society began publishing the *Journal for Sex Research*, which remains the oldest existing publication of any group of organized sexual professionals. It was under the leadership of the SSSS, particularly during the tenure of Jack Lippes in the early 1970s, that the groundwork was laid for the revival of the kind of international sexological conferences held in the 1920s and early 1930s. The World Congress of Sexology met in Paris in 1974, and this was followed by a second meeting, in Montreal, in 1976. Out of this came the World Association of Sexology.

Members of the SSSS were also instrumental in founding the Sex Information and Education Council of the United States in 1964. The organization grew out of informational discussions between Lester Kirkendall and Mary Calderone about the need to disseminate information on sex education more effectively. Both organizations continue to cooperate.

Differing fundamentally from the SSSS in its mission was the American Association of Sex Educators, Counselors, and Therapists (AASECT), organized in 1967, largely through the effort of Pat Schiller. Giving impetus to it was the growing field of sex therapy, growing out of the research of William Masters and Virginia Johnson. Many individuals claimed to be sex therapists, but since there was little state regulation, almost anyone could set himself or herself up in business. AASECT offered certification to those sex therapists who met the standards it set, and it helped raise the level of sex therapy in the country. The SSSS, after considerable debate, had decided not to offer certification, and this meant that for many years AASECT was the only certifying body. Other organizations also emerged, including the American College of Sexologists, which offered certification, and for a time there was considerable rivalry between the groups; SSSS and AASECT often work together, however, as does the American College. AASECT began publishing the *Journal of Sex Education and Therapy* in 1974.

Still another journal appeared in 1971, the *Archives of Sexual Behavior*, published by Plenum Press, and it has become the journal of the International Academy of Sex Research, an interdisciplinary research group founded at about the same time.

There are also separate organizations of sexologists in Canada, Great Britain, Germany, France, Australia, Brazil, Mexico, and many other countries, organizations which are affiliated with the World Congress; many of them publish journals. There are also many specialized sexological organizations, such as Sex Therapy and Research (STAR), as well as subsections of sex researchers within such groups as the Society for the Study of Social Problems and the American Psychological Association. There are also a number of regional organizations which have no affiliation with any national groups.

Many of the groups and organizations have different agendas, and though there is some cooperation between SSSS, SIECUS, AASECT, and STAR, many of the others operate independently. There are also special interest groups, such as those studying AIDS, homosexuality, gender dysphoria, and so forth.

REFERENCES
Bullough, V.L. *The Society for the Scientific Study of Sex: A Brief History*. Mt. Vernon, Iowa: SSSS, 1989.

Vern L. Bullough

ORGASM

Alfred Kinsey and his associates defined sexual climax, or orgasm, as an explosive discharge of neuromuscular tensions at the peak of sexual response. Most authorities attribute it to a reflex, but some focus on the subjective perception of activity in specific genital muscles and organs. After conducting extensive interviews with researchers studying the physiological components of orgasm, Gallager indicated that the consensus focuses on the involuntary response. The stimulus is usually thought to be physical, although recent research demonstrates that imagery is an adequate eliciting stimulus.

On the basis of the results of the research of others as well as their own findings, Komisaruk and Whipple have defined orgasm as the peak intensity of excitation generated by stimulation from visceral and somatic sensory receptors and cognitive processes, followed by a release and resolution of excitation. Under this definition, orgasm is characteristic of, but not restricted to the genital system.

There was little research concerning the physiology of orgasm until the pioneering work of Masters and Johnson, published in the 1960s. They reported that two major alterations in the genital organs—vasocongestion (engorgement with blood) and myotonia (muscle tension)—were the cause of orgasm. The response to these stimuli was specifically focused in the pelvic area, but there was also a total body response.

Orgasm for the male included contractions, beginning with the testes and continuing through the epididymis, vas deferens, seminal vesicles, prostate gland, urethra, penis, and anal sphincter; three or four powerful ejaculatory contractions at 0.8-second intervals, followed by two to four slower contractions; testes at their maximum elevation; sex flush at its peak; heart and respiratory rates at a maximum; general loss of voluntary muscle or motor control; and, in some instances, vocalization. For the female, strong muscle contraction started in the outer third of the vaginal barrel, with the first contraction lasting for two to four seconds and later contractions occurring at 0.8-second intervals; slight expansion of the inner two-thirds of the vagina; contraction of the uterus; peak intensity and distribution of the sex flush; frequently strong muscular contractions in many parts of the body; possible doubling of respiratory rate and heart rate; blood-pressure elevation to as much as a third above normal; and vocalization in some instances.

Masters and Johnson concluded that there were two major differences between the sexual responses of men and women: only men could ejaculate, and only women could have a series of orgasms in a short period. Subsequent findings by Hartman and Fithian have shown that men are capable of multiple orgasms, and research by Beverly Whipple and others has indicated that some women ejaculate a fluid from their urethra at orgasm. However, for the most part, later research has supported and expanded the findings of Masters and Johnson.

According to Mould, the clonic contractions of pelvic and abdominal muscle groups that characterize orgasm are initiated by a spinal reflex. Sherfey has proposed that the orgasmic response is initiated by the firing of stretch receptors in the pelvic muscles. Pelvic engorgement stretches the receptors, which, when reaching a certain point, initiate the spinal reflex.

Hartman and Fithian question the necessity of myotonia (muscle tension). They found that though myotonia was involved in the majority of their subjects, some individuals easily had orgasm without any signs of myotonia.

In a study of the orgasmic response among 751 volunteer research subjects, Hartman and Fithian found that male and female orgasmic patterns are undifferentiated within the orgasmic parameters measured. However, response patterns in individual subjects were individualized. Everyone had their own pattern. In a group of records that included several of the same subject, the records could be pulled out without looking at the name. Of all the parameters studied, the widest variation between people occurred in the cardiovascular functions.

Orgasm in both men and women consists of rhythmic muscular contractions that affect all the sexual organs and the whole body. A few people report spastic contractions of the voluntary muscles of the hands and feet. The respiratory rate may increase to 40 per minute, and pulse rates may increase to 110 to 180 beats per minute. The systolic blood pressure may be elevated 30 to 80 mm Hg. A sex flush, which parallels the intensity of orgasm, is present in about 75 percent of women and 25 percent of men. Extra heart beats and skipped beats are not uncommon in the sexual-response cycle of healthy people during sexual arousal or response. They are much more extensive in those who are not in good physical condition.

The length of an orgasm is variable. Male orgasm usually lasts about 10 to 13 seconds. Bohlen reported muscle contractions during female orgasm lasting between 13 and 51 seconds, although the same women reported their subjective perceptions that orgasm lasted between 7 and 107 seconds.

Ejaculation in men occurs in two stages, both of which involve contraction of the muscles associated with the internal sex organs. During the first stage of emission, sperm and fluid are expelled from the vas deferens, seminal vesicles, and prostate gland into the base of the urethra near the prostate. As the fluid collects, there is a consciousness of imminent ejaculation. During the ejaculation stage, the seminal fluid is propelled by the muscular contractions of orgasm into the portion of the urethra within the penis and then expelled from the urethral opening.

Many people cannot tell if their partner is having orgasm, and both men and women have admitted to faking orgasm. Some women expel fluid at orgasm. This is because lubrication may pool in the back of the vagina and be expelled by the contractions at orgasm, or they may ejaculate from the urethra. In laboratory experiments, some women may need to stimulate themselves for an hour or more before reaching orgasm, but generally, with experience, the time grows shorter. The shortest time for a woman to reach orgasm recorded in the research laboratory is 15 seconds, but this, it should be emphasized, is rare. The average time for most women to reach orgasm in the laboratory is 20 minutes.

Women have reported a variety of orgasmic experiences. Some women have sequential orgasms, a series of orgasms with short breaks in between; others have multiple orgasms with no break in between while stimulation is continued. Women make subjective distinctions between orgasms resulting from stimulation of different areas of their body. A vaginally induced orgasm is described as feeling more internal and deeper than an orgasm resulting from clitoral stimulation. The Singers described three types of female orgasm. They called the orgasm described by Masters and Johnson a vulval orgasm because it was characterized by involuntary rhythmic contractions of the vaginal entrance and was produced by clitoral stimulation. The second kind, the uterine orgasm, results from vaginal stimulation. This type of orgasm appears very similar to the orgasm triggered by stimulation of the Graefenberg spot, a sensitive area felt through the anterior wall of the vagina. The Singers' third type of orgasm, the blended orgasm, is a combination of the vulval and uterine orgasm, usually resulting from stimulation of the clitoris and the vagina.

For most men, orgasm remains concentrated in the genital region. Many men ejaculate rapidly. This is the norm since Kinsey reported that three-quarters of all males reach orgasm within two minutes of the beginning of sexual intercourse. The problem is that this does not give most women enough time to reach orgasm. Men, however, can learn to delay orgasm.

Bohlen found little correlation between perception of orgasm and the physiological parameters measured in the laboratory. The reported intensity of orgasm did not correlate with increases in physiological parameters. This means that pleasure may not be correlated positively with changes in autonomic activity. He monitored women in the laboratory who reported that they experienced orgasms but experienced no contractions. Whipple and colleagues also reported that in their laboratory, some of the women who had orgasm from imagery appeared to be lying still. It may be that these women have isometric skeletal muscular tension during orgasm, or muscle contractions may not be necessary for orgasm to occur.

Similarly, Hartman and Fithian monitored a group of 20 female therapy clients who claimed they were not orgasmic. Three-fourths were found to be undergoing the physiological responses associated with orgasm. Once the women had these changes identified for them as equivalent to an orgasm, all but one were able to identify it for themselves the next time they were monitored. Many had read extensively on orgasm, and they perceived their response to be different from what they believed the literature reported; their preconceived notions about orgasm did not fit the reality.

Orgasm has been reported to occur in response to imagery in the absence of any physical stimulation. Whipple and colleagues compared orgasms from self-induced imagery and from genital self-stimulation. Each generated significant increases over resting control conditions in systolic blood pressure, heart rate, pupil diameter, and pain thresholds. Additionally, the increases in the self-induced-imagery orgasm were comparable in magnitude to those in the genital-self-stimulation-produced orgasm. On the basis of this study, it appears that physical genital stimulation is not necessary to produce a state that is reported to be an orgasm.

Not everyone has an orgasm. It has been estimated that about one-third of women do not have orgasm at all, one-third have orgasm part of the time, and one-third fairly consistently have orgasm. Some men who can have an orgasm through masturbation have difficulty in heterosexual intercourse. One reason might be that they use heavy pressure in masturbating, far stronger than the pressure of vaginal intercourse. Until they learn to have orgasm with lighter pressure, they typically have problems in ejaculating or having orgasm during coitus.

There are other factors related to a lack of orgasm. Some of these are stress, anxiety, anger, fear of loss of control, medication, fatigue, and time pressure. Anger in some individuals can result in such strong emotional feelings against their partners that it inhibits orgasm, while in others it can provide the stimulation that produces arousal. This is why some couples fight and then have sex. For them, the fighting acts as an erotic stimulus. If they seek therapy to end the fighting, they may end their marriage unless they develop other methods of erotic stimuli to replace the fighting they have given up.

Erotic stimulation, in various forms, including overall body stroking, caressing, and fondling, is an important part of lovemaking activity. It produces the engorgement in the vascular tissue of the vagina and the penis. This results in erection in the male and the sweating effect that produces vaginal lubrication in the female. The engorgement also often masks areas that are painful or uncomfortable in the vagina. Where there is insufficient engorgement and lubrication, there may be abrasion from the penile thrusting, pain, or discomfort where the stimulation is of areas that are uncomfortable in an unengorged state.

Large numbers of women who have orgasm do so with manual or oral stimulation or masturbation. Many couples do not have intercourse with sufficient frequency, or do not take enough time, for the women to learn to have orgasm through intercourse.

Orgasm, in a sense, is a learned behavior, and it is learned by trying different activities. Masturbation is the easiest way to learn. Orgasm with intercourse does not feel the same as it does with masturbation, since different areas are usually being stimulated. Actually, orgasm can be elicited from various parts of the body and even by imagery alone. Such orgasms can also produce a pelvic response. The most nerve endings tend to exist in the clitoris in women and the penis in males, although about 10 percent of women have more nerve endings in the labia than in the clitoris. Subjects have been seen to have orgasm in a back caress, as well as through stimulation of other parts of their body. That is why it is suggested that a total body caress be done as a part of erotic stimulation to enhance the probability of response.

There is a hormonal connection between the vagina and breast in the female. Oxytocin (the hormone that triggers the breast milk reflex in women) is released at orgasm. If she is a nursing mother, she may exude milk from her nipples, while even nonnursing mothers may see a drop of fluid on their nipples. Nursing itself has been reported to give genital sensations of pleasure and even orgasm in some women.

When asked to describe an orgasm, most people will smile and say it's like an expulsion, like paradise, like a release, like a volcano, or like a big shiver. People can describe what an orgasm is like, but they cannot say what it is. The scientific explanations for orgasm have clarified the process somewhat, and contemporary researchers are studying the neurophysiology of orgasm and the role of hormones in orgasm, as well as determining the areas of the brain involved in orgasm. Perhaps in future editions we will be able to answer further the question as to what orgasm is.

REFERENCES

Alzate, H., and B. Useche. Heart Rate Change as Evidence for Vaginally Elicited Orgasm and Orgasm Intensity. *Annual Review of Sex Research*, Vol. 2 (1991), pp. 345–57.

Barback, L. *For Yourself: The Fulfillment of Female Sexuality*. New York: Anchor Press/Doubleday, 1976.

Bohlen, J.G. State of the Science of Sexual Physiology Research. In C.M. Davis, ed., *Challenge in Sexual Science*. Philadelphia: SSSS, 1983.

Fisher, S. *The Female Orgasm*. New York: Basic Books, 1973.

Fox, C.A., H.S. Wolff, and J.A. Baker. Measurement of Intra-Vaginal Intra-Uterine Pressure During Human Coitus by Radio Telemetry. *Journal of Reproductive Fertility,* Vol. 22 (1970), pp. 243–51.

Gallager, W. The Etiology of Orgasm. *Discover* (1986), pp. 51–59.

Graber, B. Circumvaginal Musculature and Orgasm: Concluding Remarks. In B. Graber, ed., *Circumvaginal Musculature and Sexual Function*. New York: Karger, 1982.

Heiman, J., L. LoPiccolo, and J. LoPiccolo. *Becoming Orgasmic: A Sexual Program for Women*. Englewood Cliffs, N.J.: Prentice Hall, 1976.

Komisaruk, B.R., and B. Whipple. Physiological Perceptual Correlates of Orgasm Produced by Genital and Non-Genital Stimulation. In P. Kothari, ed., *Proceedings of the First International Conference on Orgasm*. Bombay, India: VRP, 1991.

Ladas, A.K., B. Whipple, and J.D. Perry. *The G Spot and Other Recent Discoveries About Human Sexuality*. New York: Holt, Rinehart & Winston, 1982.

Lowry, T.P., and T.S. Lowry. *The Clitoris*. St. Louis: Green, 1976.

Masters, W.H., and V.E. Johnson. *Human Sexual Response*. Boston: Little, Brown, 1966.

Mould, D. Neuromuscular Aspects of Women's Orgasm. *Journal of Sex Research*, Vol. 16 (1980), pp. 193–201.

Perry, J.D., and B. Whipple. Pelvic Muscle Strength of Female Ejaculators: Evidence in Support of a New Theory of Orgasm. *Journal of Sex Research,* Vol. 17 (1981), pp. 22–39.

Sherfey, M.J. *The Nature and Evolution of Female Sexuality*. New York: Random House, 1972.

Singer, J., and I. Singer. Types of Female Orgasm. In J. LoPiccolo and L. LoPiccolo, eds., *Handbook of Sex Therapy*. New York: Plenum Press, 1978.

Vance, E.B., and N.N. Wagner. Written Descriptions of Orgasm: A Study of Sex Differences. *Archives of Sexual Behavior*, Vol. 5 (1976), pp. 87–98.

Whipple, B., G. Ogden, and B.R. Komisaruk. Physiological Correlates of Imagery Induced Orgasm in Women. *Archives of Sexual Behavior,* Vol. 21 (1992), pp. 121–33.

Beverly Whipple
William E. Hartman
Marilyn A. Fithian

$\mathcal{P}$

PARAPHILIAS

A range of terms has been used in the past to describe variant forms of sexual behavior. Early writings on sex often referred to pathologies, perversions, and deviant or unnatural sex, while others tried to be less judgmental by using terms such as "variant sexual practices" or even "stigmatized sexual practices." Popularly, such behaviors were often called bizarre or kinky. Now they are increasingly called paraphilias, a term derived from the Greek *para*, meaning alongside of, beside, or beyond, and *phile*, literally "other loves."

Paraphilia is defined as an erotosexual and psychological condition characterized by recurrent responsiveness to an obsessive dependence on an unusual or socially unacceptable stimulus. The term has become a legal synonym for perversion or deviant sexual behavior, and it is preferred by many over the other terms because it seems more neutral and descriptive rather than judgmental. The combining form "philia" can be used with various prefixes to describe general categories. Hypophilia, for example, is a term used to describe responses below the normal range, and several sexual dysfunctions belong to this category, such as inhibited sexual desire. Hyperphilia, in contrast, refers to responses above the normal range, such as Don Juanism or nymphomania.

Many of the terms listed below appear in some of the literature, but not all of them are widely used. Sometimes the same phenomenon is described by two or more terms. The most complete listing can be found in the writings of John Money, who coined many of them, although some date from the 19th century and Richard von Krafft-Ebing's attempt to describe sexual pathologies.

Paraphilias	Sexually Attracted to or Aroused by
Acrotomophilia	Amputee partner
Adolescentism	Older person imitating an adolescent
Algophilia	Pain
Amputation fetish	Amputee partner
Androgynophilia	Bisexual orientation
Andromimesis	Impersonating a male
Andromimetophilia	Partner who is a male impersonator or a female-to-male transsexual
Apodysophilia	Exhibitionism
Apotemnophilia	Fantasizing about becoming an amputee
Asphixophilia	Erotic self-strangulation
Autoagonistophilia	Being observed or appearing on stage or in film while engaged in sexual activity

Autoassinatophilia	Staging one's own masochistic death	Homocidophilia	Lust murder, erotophonophilia
Autoerotic death	Near-death or imagined death, and death when miscalculation is involved	Homophilia	Partner of the same sex
		Hybristophilia	Sexual partner who is a criminal
Autoflagellation	Self-inflicted whipping	Hyphephilia	Touching or feeling skin, fur, hair, leather, or fabric
Automasochism	Self-inflicted pain		
Autonecrophilia	Imagining oneself as a corpse	Hypoxyphilia	Erotic self-strangulation
		Infantilism	Impersonating an infant and being treated as a baby; autonepiophilia
Autonepiophilia	Impersonating an infant or being treated as a baby (also called infantilism)		
		Juvenilism	Impersonating a juvenile and being treated as such by a sexual partner
Autopedophilia	Impersonating an infant or being treated as one		
Autophilia	Sexual love of self	Kleptomania	Compulsive stealing
Autoscopophilia	Aroused by looking at one's own body or genitals	Kleptophilia	Compulsive stealing
		Klismophilia	Being given an enema
Bestiality	Sex with animals	Masochism	Receiving punishment, discipline, humiliation; forced servitude
Biastophilia	Surprise and violent attacks on strangers		
		Mixoscopia	Watching others engage in sexual intercourse
Bondage and discipline	Sadomasochistic practices and fantasies		
		Mixoscopia bestialis	Watching someone have sex with an animal
Chrematisophilia	Being charged or forced to pay for sexual services		
		Monopediomania	Partner with one leg
Coprograph	Creating graffiti about excrement	Morphophilia	Partner whose body characteristics are exaggeratedly different or prominent from one's own
Coprolagnia	Thinking about, seeing, smelling, or handling feces		
Coprophagia	Eating feces		
Coprophilia	Smell or taste of feces or seeing someone defecate	Multiphilia	Recurrent short-term limerance (i.e., falling in love with new partners)
Diaperism	Being diapered		
Ecouteurism	Listening to accounts of, or observing, sexual encounters	Mysophilia	Something soiled or filthy (i.e., underwear, menstrual pads)
Eonism	Male cross-dressing		
Ephebophilia	Postpubertal or adolescent partner	Narratophilia	Using or hearing dirty or obscene words or reading or listening to erotic narrative in the presence of a sexual partner
Erotic pyromania	Arson		
Erotic strangulation	Erotic self-strangulation		
Erotolalia	Obscene talk		
Erotomania	Preoccupation with or morbid exaggeration of sexual matters	Necromania	Corpses and death
		Necrophilia	Sexual activity with a corpse
		Nepiophilia	Infants; a pedophile attracted to infants
Erotophonophilia	Lust murder		
Exhibitionism	Publicly exposing one's genitals	Olfactophilia	Smells and odors emanating from parts of the body, especially sexual areas
Fetishism	Any nonsexual inanimate object or a nongenital body part (e.g., the foot)		
		Osmolagnia	Smells and odors emanating from parts of the body, especially sexual areas
Formicophilia	Small creatures, ants, insects, or snails crawling on genitals		
		Pederasty	Adolescent males
Frottage	Rubbing against a stranger in a public place	Pedomania	Girl or boy who is prepubertal or in first stages of puberty
Gerontophilia	Having a much older sexual partner		
		Pedophilia	Girl or boy who is prepubertal or in first stages of puberty
Golden shower	Female urinating on male		
Gynemimesis	Impersonating a woman		
Gynemimetophilia	Having a sexual partner who is a transvestite or male-to-female transsexual	Peeping Tom	Voyeurism

Peodeiktophilia	Exhibitionism; evoking surprise, dismay, or shock, from a stranger by exhibiting the penis
Pictophilia	Viewing erotic pictures, films, or other images alone or with a partner
Polyiterophilia	Repetition of the same activity many times with many partners
Pornographomania	Writing sexually obscene material and graffiti
Pornolagnia	Prostitutes
Rape	Sexual intercourse by force
Rapism	Meeting resistance of a nonconsenting victim to a sexual assault
Raptophilia	Meeting resistance of a nonconsenting victim to a sexual assault
Renifleurism	Particular smells
Retifism	Women's shoes
Sadism	Humiliating, punishing, torturing, inflicting pain on others
Sadomasochism	Reciprocal interaction of sadist with masochist
Saliromania	Filth, ugliness, deformity
Scatophilia	Talking about sexual or obscene matters to an unknown person
Scoptophilia, passive	Having other people view one's genitalia
Scoptophilia, active	Viewing sexual acts or others' genitalia
Somnophilia	Intruding on and fondling a sleeping stranger
Stigmatophilia	A partner who is tatooed or scarified, or having oneself tatooed, particularly in the genital area
Symphorophilia	Stage-managing a disaster and then observing it
Telephone scatophilia	Talking about sexual or obscene matters to an unknown listener over the telephone; recent variant is computer scatophilia
Toucherism	Surreptitiously touching a stranger on an erotic body part (i.e., breasts or genitals)
Transvestism	Cross-dressing
Troilism	Observing one's partner having sex with another
Undism	Urine and urination
Urolagnia	Smell and taste of urine
Urophilia	Being urinated upon or swallowing urine
Voyeurism	Covertly watching another person undressing or engaging in sexual activity
Zoolagnia	Oral contact with animals or smell of animals
Zoophilia	Sex with animals
Zoosadism	Inflicting pain on animals

There are many other paraphilias as well, since new ones are continually being coined.

REFERENCES

Money, J. *Lovemaps*. Buffalo, N.Y.: Prometheus Books, 1986.

Vern L. Bullough

PARTHENOGENESIS

Parthenogenesis is the spontaneous or artificially induced development of an ovum into a fully functional organism without fertilization by a sperm. Literally, the term means "virgin birth." Natural forms of parthenogenesis are limited to the invertebrates, insects, and a few lizards.

Some animal species regularly mix parthenogenetic (asexual) reproduction with sexual reproduction. In such species, both male and female individuals occur. Examples of this include many species of tropical fish, such as mollies and platies, and insects such as the aphids or plant lice. In the latter, seasonal and diet controls determine whether sexual or parthenogenetic reproduction occurs.

Other species are monochoric or monecious, meaning that all members of the species have the same type of gonad, namely ovaries. In monochoric species, the ovum is usually diploid, having two complete sets of chromosomes. Only "females" are produced in such species, and these are genetically identical with the parent. When a whole species is monochoric and reproduces only by parthenogenesis, there are strictly speaking no males or females, only unisexed parthenones.

Among bees, haploid male drones produce haploid sperm and mate with a queen, a fertile female. Such matings produce hundreds of diploid but sterile female workers. If a diploid female larva is fed a special royal jelly, it will become a fertile queen. The queen also produces haploid male drones by parthenogenesis.

The whiptail lizards (*Cnemedophorus uniparens*) are exclusively parthenogenetic. Egg-producing parthenones seek out a nonovulating mate with whom they go through a kind of mating ritual without mating. This activity suggests a bisexual potential in the brain, since an individual whiptail can play either of the sexually dimorphic roles in the mating ritual. The ritual appears to release pituitary hormones that expedite egg formation and increase clutch size. All whiptails are triploid, with no diploid males or females.

Parthenogenesis has been clinically induced in a variety of animal species—frogs, sea urchins, and even mice—by producing sublethal damage to the surface of the ovum by chemical or physical means. Parthenogenesis does not occur in humans.

Parthenogenic origin, being born of a virgin mother impregnated by a god, is commonly claimed for religious prophets such as Jesus and Buddha and legendary leaders such as Genghis Khan and the Roman Emperor Augustus.

REFERENCES

Berrill, N.J. *Sex and the Nature of Things*. New York: Dodd, Mead, 1953.

Crews, D. Functional Associations in Behavioral Endocrinology. In J.M. Reinisch, L.A. Rosenblum, and S.A. Sanders, eds. *Masculinity/Femininity: Basic Perspectives*. New York: Oxford Univ. Press, 1987.

Lawrence, R. The *Poisoning of Eros: Sexual Values in Conflict*. New York: Augustine More Press, 1989.

Ranke-Heinemann, U. *Eunuchs for the Kingdom of Heaven*. New York: Doubleday, 1990.

Robert T. Francoeur

PEDERASTY IN ANCIENT AND EARLY CHRISTIAN HISTORY

Pederasty was a custom valued in ancient Greece and Rome as well as other early societies in Africa, Australia, and New Guinea. It involved a sexual relationship between an adult man and a younger male, usually, but not always, an adolescent male. Reasons for the custom were based on love, education, learning gender roles, and puberty rites. It was not considered a barrier to heterosexual marriage and fatherhood. The concept of exclusive or obligatory homosexuality was not an issue in these cultures. Ambisexuality was normal.

In the fifth century B.C.E., Plato, in the opening of his Protagoras, has a companion talking with Socrates:

> Companion: Where do you come from, Socrates? And yet I need hardly ask the question, for I know that you have been in chase of the fair Alcibiades. I saw him the day before yesterday; and he had got a beard like a man—and he is a man, as I may tell you in your ear. But I thought that he was still very charming.

> Socrates: What of his beard? Are you not of Homer's opinion, who says "Youth is most charming when the beard first appears?" And that is now the charm of Alcibiades.

The issue here was that the companion was chiding Socrates because he thought Socrates' young lover was getting too old. In both ancient Greece and Rome, same-sex relations were considered as normal and acceptable as heterosexual relations are in our day. Some form of pederasty was accepted and valued in both cultures. (See article on Greeks.)

For some readers, it might be interesting to note that Jesus, most probably, had an encounter with a pederast and made no judgment on the practice. One cannot understand the history of the first century C.E. in Palestine without understanding the cultural context. Greek and Roman concepts were widely accepted and promoted by Hellenizers. It is likely that they were not trying to overthrow their ancestral way of life and customs but, like many in the 20th century, were trying to get their people to "keep up with the times" and modernize their approach to life; thus, many Jews were very accepting of common customs and practices of the Romans.

Jesus of Nazareth lived in a cultural context highly influenced by Greek and Roman tradition. There is a story in the gospels of Matthew (8:5–13) and Luke (7:1–10) that most certainly illustrates pederasty as not having a negative value in Jesus's thought. Most versions of the Bible are not accurate in their translation of the story of the centurion and his servant "boy." Most translators just use the term "servant" or "slave," leaving the implication of an adult. However, the Greek word used is the same as a youth in a homosexual relationship with a man (or a pederastic relationship). Biblical scholars believe that Matthew and Luke basically tell the same story taken from a common source, known as the Q source. Matthew's story reads as follows:

> When Jesus arrived in Capernaum, a Roman army captain came and pled with him to come to his home and heal his *servant boy* (italics added) who was in bed paralyzed and racked with pain. [Note: Luke's version adds that the *servant boy* was very dear to him.]
>
> "Yes," Jesus said, "I will come and heal him."
>
> Then the officer said, "Sir, I am not worthy to have you in my home; (and it isn't necessary for you to come). If you will only stand here and say, 'Be healed,' my *servant boy* will get well! I know, because I am under the authority of my superior officers and I have authority over my soldiers, and I say to one, 'Go,' and he goes, and to another, 'Come,' and he comes, and to my *slave boy,* 'Do this or that,' and he does it. And I know you have authority to tell his sickness to go—and it will go!"

Jesus stood there amazed! Turning to the crowd he said, "I haven't seen faith like this in all the land of Israel! And I tell you this, that many Gentiles (like this Roman officer), shall come from all over the world and sit down in the Kingdom of Heaven with Abraham, Isaac, and Jacob. And many an Israelite—those for whom the Kingdom was prepared—shall be cast into outer darkness, in the place of weeping and torment."

Then Jesus said to the Roman officer, "Go on home. What you have believed has happened!" And the *boy* was healed that same hour!

(*The Way: The Living Bible*)

Since pederastic relationships were so common and accepted in the ancient world of Jesus, it is likely that, as the story indicates, Jesus himself had no problem with the practice of pederasty. In fact, Jesus was deeply impressed with the Roman army captain and states, "Nowhere, even in Israel, have I found such faith." From what we know, the relationship of the army captain to his beloved servant boy was probably as a mentor and educator into the world of manhood, as well as sexual. His role would be to introduce the young man to people who would later help him in his advancement, and the captain would teach him how to be a good citizen. It was probably also assumed that when the servant boy got older he would take his place in the world as a heterosexual (or bisexual) man, have a family, and initiate a new boy lover. Increasingly, however, the Romans became uncomfortable with the aristocratic and ruling class having their young men in this relationship and instead assigned young slaves to the pederastic relationship.

This increasing discomfort with pederasty may account for the view of Paul in the New Testament. In his letter to the Romans (1:27), Paul writes, "And the men, instead of having a normal sex relationship with women, burned for lust for each other, men doing shameful things with other men." Many biblical scholars believe that Paul is referring to the practice of pederasty in this passage, in that the Greek phraseology used in this verse is the same used to describe the pederastic relationship. He wanted to make the new religious expression based on Jesus Christ very distinct from Roman and Greek practices, so he would attack those customs and practices he felt to be alien.

Today, we would refer to the practice of pederasty as pedophilia or, in the case of early adolescence, ephebophilia. In the context of our culture, this is considered harmful and damaging to individual development. Indeed, in the context of our culture, this is often true. This illustrates how important cultural context is to understanding any particular sexual behavior. There seems to be nothing inherently harmful or damaging in sexual acts alone, but rather harmfulness and damage must be interpreted within the context of the way each particular behavior is seen in each culture and in terms of its long-range effects on the individual.

REFERENCES

Duberman, M.B., M. Vicinus, and G. Chauncey, Jr. *Hidden from History: Reclaiming the Gay and Lesbian Past.* New York: New American Library, 1989.

Ford, C.S., and F.A. Beach. *Patterns of Sexual Behavior.* New York: Harper Colophon, 1951.

Haeberle, E.J. *The Sex Atlas.* New York: Seabury Press, 1978.

Kloppenborg, J.S., et al. *Q Thomas Reader.* Sonoma, Calif.: Polebridge Press, 1990.

Lawrence, R.J. *The Poisoning of Eros.* New York: Augustine Moore Press, 1989.

Murphy, F.J. *The Religious World of Jesus: An Introduction to Second Temple Palestinian Judaism.* Nashville: Abingdon Press, 1991.

Strong, B., and C. DeVault. *Understanding Our Sexuality.* 2d ed. St. Paul: West, 1988.

William R. Stayton

PETTING

Petting has come to mean noncoital physical touching designed to produce sexual pleasure between human beings in premarital, marital, or extramarital relationships, either homosexual or heterosexual. It may involve passionate kissing (sometimes differentiated from petting as "necking"), manual or oral genital touching, or any other form of tactile or oral stimulation of various body parts short of genital coupling. It is different from foreplay only in the sense that petting is an end in itself, while foreplay is considered a preliminary to sexual intercourse. Of course, a session of erotic touching can only be defined as petting or foreplay after the fact.

Each generation feels that it invented sex (at least, the pleasures it affords us), and each generation might be surprised to discover that all the petting techniques known today have been found in the art and writings of ancient civilizations. Today's generations do seem to be engaging in it at an earlier age, continuing the trend reported by Kinsey from data dating from the 19th century to 1953. A recent Roper poll among youths from 12 to 17 years old found that 73 percent of girls and 50 percent of boys identified social pressure from their peers as the primary reason for engaging in heavy petting. As social pressures against petting diminish, or even become supportive of it, an increasing number of people will engage in it. That petting is quite natural behavior for us can be gauged by the fact that it has been reported that all mammalian species engage in it (e.g., nuzzling, biting, smelling, scratching).

Despite the popularity of petting, the Judeo-Christian tradition has consistently frowned on it, even marital petting if it did not precede sexual intercourse for the purpose of procreation. A Protestant marriage manual by Bovet advises that any and all kinds of sexual excitement toward a young man's fiancée must be assiduously avoided "since it is not good for her"; Stolper gives similar advice in a Jewish Orthodox guide, which even extends the prohibition to holding hands. Catholic instructions, as put forth by Hettlinger, allow for kissing, but only as long as it does not cause a "reaction in the organs of generation." The authors of such proscriptions may as well be King Canute holding back the waves lashing the beach.

People engage in petting precisely because it causes a "reaction in the organs of generation," and because they find that reaction, and all other kinds of sexual touching, to be highly pleasurable. The skin is formed from the same layer of embryonic tissue that forms the brain, so it is no wonder we "light up" so brightly when being touched in intimate ways. Intimate sexual touching recalls the pleasures we once found snuggled in our mother's arms. The warmth of skin-to-skin contact, the sucking of our lover's breasts, the eye gazing all evoke deep and fond subconscious memories of the mother-infant bond—the template of all loving. Thus, we are not likely to respond favorably to exhortations such as, "Pet your dog, not your date."

Given that nature has devised a most agreeable way for humans to perpetuate themselves, the question is not so much why people pet but rather why they limit their sexual activity to petting. Petting without orgasm at an age when hormones are raging for expression echoes the masochism of the anorexic dieter who sniffs the feast without sampling it. Petting without orgasm leads to frustration and discomfort for both males and females, who may have to resort to solitary masturbation to relieve themselves after kissing their dates goodnight.

Why, then, in this day of available contraceptives, is petting still popular? The answer seems to be, despite all the talk about "sexual revolution," that many subcultures still place high value on female virginity. Petting to orgasm allows

young people the sexual release they need while still maintaining "technical virginity." The French have a pejorative name for such a woman—*demivierge* (half a virgin). Petting to orgasm without actual intercourse allows young women to pleasure their dates (and themselves) and still be eligible for a marriage market that insists on female virginity. Parents who are apoplectic about the prospect of their children engaging in premarital intercourse—realizing that it is difficult, if not near impossible, to deny young lovers any kind of sexual outlet—may show an uneasy acceptance of petting. While some people consider petting to be a permissible alternative to sexual intercourse, some heavy petting techniques, such as fellatio and cunnilingus, are still considered criminal activities in some states, even within the bounds of marriage. While it is extremely rare to find such statutes being activated, it is not unknown for men in the United States to be imprisoned for engaging in oral sex, even with willing partners.

A major issue in petting is "how far to go." Crooks and Baur see it as a "contest between the young man and woman, he trying to proceed as far as possible and she attempting to go only as far as respectable." Hunt also views petting as something of a sexual skirmish in the battle between the sexes, with the boy trying to see how much he can get and the girl how little she can decently give in recompense for the attention lavished on her. The better he "made out," the higher was his status among his fellows, while the less she gave in, the more desirable she was considered to be. This male ambivalence (the desire to get, paired with contempt for the giver) appears to be ubiquitous and is probably the origin of the whore/Madonna image of women many men apparently hold. A recent national survey of 815 American males found that 67 percent of them expressed a dislike for women that "gave" on the first date. A survey of students at two universities found that both sexes considered females who had gone no further than petting the most suitable partners for dating or marriage.

All this indicates that a smart strategy for a female to pursue is to begin the dating relationship very slowly, increasing the intensity of her sexual favors as the relationship develops. Collins writes that "males date primarily for sexual conquest, whereas women use sex as a way of attracting men to flatter, entertain, and eventually marry them. . . . Sex is used progressively as bait that gets nibbled up bit by bit, with males paying for increasing sexual favors by increasing commitments." Thus, if a female slowly increases the intensity of her petting over a period, she holds out the tantalizing possibility of what is yet to come. Males in such a relationship may be frustrated, but if they stay in the relationship they will come to know the unique individual for what she is rather than as simply a sex object. Operant psychologists might term this as a "shaping" process, or various incremental stages to falling in love. Ellis shows that these mating tactics are used among many different species. If a female "goes all the way" on the first date, she reinforces the male's perception of her as a sexual object, and he will quickly move on to the next conquest.

Some interesting sex differences were found in a 1986 study of sexual attitudes and behavior. In a dating situation with no particular affection involved, 11 percent of the males and none of the females thought that heavy petting was proper behavior, although 18 percent of the males and 6 percent of the females reported that they had done so. Percentages of males and females who thought oral sex to be proper behavior under the same dating circumstances were 16 and 1, respectively; 10 percent of males and 2 percent of females reported that they had done so, however. In a monogamous dating relationship with love involved, 76 percent of the males and 71 percent of the females approved of heavy petting (81 percent and 82 percent, respectively, reporting that they had done it). In the same kind of relationship, 83 percent of the males and 63 percent of the females thought oral sex to be proper, and 79 percent and 59 percent, respectively, had engaged in oral sex. Thus, petting tends to be tied more closely to love for females than for males, and, except in the case of oral sex, a slightly greater percentage of both sexes have engaged in the behavior than think it proper.

REFERENCES

Arrington, C. A generation of Men Grows Up. *Men's Life,* Vol. 1 (1990), pp. 64–70.

Bovet, T. *A Handbook to Marriage.* New York: Doubleday, 1958.

Collins, R. *Conflict Sociology: Toward and Explanatory Science.* New York: Academic Press, 1974.

Crooks, R., and K. Baur. *Our Sexuality.* Menlo Park, Calif.: Benjamin/Cummings, 1983.

Ellis, L. Evolutionary and Neurochemical Causes of Sex Differences in Victimizing Behavior: Toward a Unified Theory of Criminal Behavior and Social Stratification. *Social Science Information,* Vol. 28 (1989), pp. 605–36.

Harper, R., and W. Stokes. *Levels of Sexual Understanding and Enjoyment.* Englewood Cliffs, N.J.: Prentice Hall, 1971.

Hettlinger, R. *Human Sexuality: A Psychosexual Perspective.* Belmont, Calif.: Wadsworth, 1975.

Hunt, M. *Sexual Behavior in the 1970s.* Chicago: Playboy Press, 1974.

Kinsey, A., W. Pomeroy, C. Martin, and P. Gebhard. *Sexual Behavior in the Human Female.* Philadelphia: Saunders, 1953.

Miller, B., and K. Moore. Adolescent Sexual Behavior, Pregnancy, and Parenting: Research Through the 1980s. *Journal of Marriage and the Family,* Vol. 52 (1990), p. 1029.

Roche, J. Premarital Sex: Attitudes and Behavior by Dating Stage. *Adolescence,* Vol. 31 (1986), pp. 107–21.

Stolper, P. *The Road to Responsible Jewish Adulthood.* New York: Union of Orthodox Jewish Congregations of America, 1967.

Williams, J., and A. Jacoby. The Effects of Premarital Heterosexual and Homosexual Experience on Dating and Marriage Desirability. *Journal of Marriage and the Family,* Vol. 51 (1989), pp. 489–97.

Anthony Walsh

PHEROMONES

Pheromones are chemical substances, produced externally by a species, that cause a response from another member of that same species, usually of the opposite sex. They differ from hormones, which are chemical substances produced by an organism that cause a reaction somewhere else in the body of the organism that produced them.

It has been long known that extremely small amounts of insect pheromones, when produced by the female of a species, can be detected from a great distance by the male of that species and will induce him to seek out the female and mate with her. The males, in turn, produce pheromones that induce the female to copulate. In insects, the response is automatic and irresistible.

Mammals are also known to produce pheromones that incite sexual activity as well as induce other kinds of social interactions. Pheromones in urine and feces attract mates and mark territory. These are usually fast acting and produce immediate effects on the physiology and behavior of the mammal. Other pheromones act more slowly over a longer period. For example, if female mice are housed together, their estrus cycles are interrupted by periods of infertility caused by the lack of a cycle occurring. Exposure to a male mouse, or his urine, will revive the cycles. The odor of male mice will accelerate puberty in young female mice, and the introduction of a foreign male to a colony will suppress the pregnancies of females that have already mated with males from their own colony. Some higher primates (e.g., rhesus monkeys) are known to produce, in their vaginal secretions, volatile fatty acids that induce male behavior such as mounting and ejaculation.

It has long been known that odor has an effect on human sexual interactions. In ancient Greek literature, an older man asks his young lover to return the roses that he has sent to be spread over his bed because they would then contain the fragrance of the lover's body as well as the sweet scent of the roses. Many cultures, certainly in the United States, find body odors and secretions at least mildly repugnant. They may, however, influence behavior, and there is some evidence for the idea that human beings react differently to body odors during times of sexual excitement. For example, depending on their sexual orientation, some men become sexually excited by smelling the soiled undergarments of women or other men.

Although authorities are not in agreement, there is a body of circumstantial evidence that human beings do secrete pheromones. In humans, the reaction is more controlled and less automatic and irresistible. This may be an evolutionary adaptation that produced survival value in the controlling of reproduction.

Women who live together in close quarters such as college dormitories often have their menstrual cycles at roughly the same time. That this synchronization may be brought about by pheromones is illustrated by the fact that when a woman is exposed to a pad that has been worn for 24 hours under the armpit of another woman, the recipient woman's menstrual period shifts closer to that of the donor woman. Men may also secrete pheromones that influence the sexual behavior of women. Women who date men have shorter cycles, and if they sleep with the men, their cycles are likely to be more regular with fewer fertility problems. Evidence that these are reactions to pheromones (or at least to body odors) and not to sexual activity is supplied by the observation that the periods of women become more regular when underarm secretions from men are mixed with alcohol and spread on the women's upper lip. All the studies of human beings have shown correlation but not necessarily cause and effect, although volatile fatty acids similar to those in the rhesus monkey have been found in human vaginal secretions.

The perfume and deodorant industries make use of the powerful effect of odor on sexual activity. They spend billions of dollars in research and development either trying to cover up odors they believe people find offensive or producing odors they believe will incite people into romantic interludes. The idea is not new;

the ancient Egyptians used odor in this way centuries before the common era.

REFERENCES

Hopson, J.L. *Scent Signals: The Silent Language of Sex.* New York: William Morrow, 1979.

Katchadourian, H. *Fundamentals of Human Sexuality.* 5th ed. Fort Worth: Holt, Rinehart & Winston, 1989.

Vandenbergh, J.G., ed. *Pheromones and Reproduction in Mammals.* New York: Academic Press, 1983.

James D. Haynes

PHILOSOPHY AND SEX

What does it mean to say that a certain desire, sensation, or act is "sexual"? Is there such a thing as "plain sex," or is sex always conceptually linked with something else—for example, expressing love, reproduction, or union with some metaphysical entity? What is the difference between sex and love, and is sex that expresses love always superior qua sex to sex for sex's sake? Does it make sense to say that a sexual act could be "perverted," or are there simply sexual variants that can be viewed nonjudgmentally? Does sexual desire solve any ancient philosophical problems? For example, does the intentionality of sexual desire—that sexual desire is ordinarily desire for contact with another person whose desire we want in return—answer the skeptics' claim that we have no proof that there are other persons with minds like our own? (Sartre thought sexual desire did indeed answer the skeptics.) Can one distinguish pornography from erotica? Is adultery always immoral? Are all pedophiles child molesters, or could a child desire sex, consent to it, and receive it from an adult in a nonexploitative way? (This would seem to be an empirical question, but for a philosopher it involves trying to define terms like "child," "adult," "consent," and "power" in a sexual context.) Does sex essentially involve two persons, such that masturbation is only a borderline case of sexual activity? If sex is an appetite like the desire to eat, why do differing sexual tastes generate heated controversies and intolerance that are akin to those found in religion and politics? (Unless a culture makes food into a religion, we do not ordinarily persecute those with bizarre tastes in food.)

Although philosophers have historically not had much to say about such questions (believing, perhaps, that logic and lust don't mix), the second half of the 20th century has seen an explosion of articles and books applying contemporary techniques of philosophical analysis to such conceptual and moral issues. To be sure, someone who claims to be interested only in the empirical aspects of sex may find such discussions tedious. But the philosopher holds that there are no "bare facts" that are not a function—directly or indirectly—of one's conceptual framework. The old view that there can be no lesbians because sex requires a penis is, of course, largely rejected today. Yet presuppositions about what is considered "sexual" can change rapidly. In the 1970s, the prosecutor in the Charles Manson trials denounced one of the defendants for having obtained "orgiastic ecstasy from wallowing in the blood of the victims." Today, he would be roundly denounced for having confused sex with violence. Is this more egalitarian philosophy of sex confirmed by empirical research? Or will it not be true that one's philosophy will determine what the results will be?

The debate among philosophers about what constitutes sex has centered around "reductionist" and "expansionist" accounts. The reductionist rejects traditional utilitarian accounts that sex must justify (purify?) itself by serving some supposedly lofty purpose like reproduction or communication of emotions. Goldman and Vannoy defend this approach, albeit in differing ways. The expansionist account has been updated by new theories defended by Sartre, Nagel, and Solomon. These philosophers view sex as various kinds of intricate patterns of communication between persons, something the reductionists scorn as subjecting sex to another kind of utilitarian requirement.

For Goldman, the essence of sex is nothing more than "a desire for contact with another person's body and for the pleasure which such contact produces." A perversion, for Goldman, would be a desire just to look at someone (voyeurism) or to have contact with something other than another person's body (e.g., a shoe fetish). If, however, the essence of sex is skin rubbing against skin, Goldman's claim that it must be another person's skin leaves masturbation out in the cold. Goldman is willing to admit that masturbation is "borderline" sexual activity if it is accompanied by sexual fantasies of touching someone else. If, however, the essence of sex is epidermal stimulation that yields sexual sensations, there seems to be no reason why it must involve another person's skin rather than one's own skin. For these reasons, Soble rejects Goldman's account because it perversely scorns what is arguably the plainest of plain sex, masturbation.

Another version of the reductionist account, defended by Vannoy, is that sexual desire is the desire for sexual sensations, however they may be produced. This allows masturbation and shoe fetishism to be fully sexual. Vannoy claims that sex intended for reproduction is actually statistically aberrant when one considers the number of children produced as opposed to the number of times a typical couple has sex in their lifetime. Since nature has given sexual desire to the sterile, to those too old or too young to reproduce, and to women who are already pregnant or in a nonfertile cycle, it is clear that what is common to all these desires is a desire for a sexual experience. Indeed, sex as an expression of love presupposes that one has a gift of a sexual experience to give to the beloved, and sex for reproduction presupposes that an enjoyable act makes reproduction much more likely. Thus, Vannoy argues that if nature had not provided us with sexual pleasures, we would not use the term "sexual act" at all. We would speak only of reproductive acts. Even in those cases, such as animals, where sexual desires are present, we do not speak of them in sexual terms when they are ordinarily outside our conceptual framework as to what could cause us sexual pleasure; we merely say that animals breed.

One difficulty with this view is that prostitutes and rape victims are commonly said to have engaged in sexual acts even though a desire for sexual sensations is ordinarily not what they were interested in. Yet, although such acts have the form of sexual acts, those who perform them (or who are forced to do so) would ordinarily view them more as an unpleasant form of calisthenics that one must endure. They are perhaps called "sexual" only in the derivative sense, in that they have the form of a sexual act that in other contexts does provide pleasure or because they provide some degree of sexual pleasure for the rapist or for the prostitute's customer.

Perhaps the most philosophically interesting difficulty with the plain-sex philosophy is trying to define what a sexual experience is. Not all sensations we get from bodily contact are sexual, so what makes some sexual and the others not? Manipulating the genitals in certain contexts ordinarily provides a sexual experience, but what is one to say of the gourmet who claims that, for him, eating roast Peking duck is the ultimate sexual experience? One cannot say that the gourmet's experience is even analogous to genital sensations, except in the broad sense that they both involve "meat," as it were, and both produce an ecstatic experience. Even with one's own body, being whipped in a sadomasochistic encounter is highly sexual for the masochist, even though such an experience does not always correlate with genital arousal and pleasure. Nor can we say that genital pleasures are paradigmatically sexual, whereas the masochist is using the phrase "sexual pleasure" in some unspecified broader sense of the term, for the sexual pleasure in being whipped *is* paradigmatic for the masochist. One might argue that pleasures of the flesh are involved in each of these examples, but this does not explain the sexual experience philosophers sometimes claim to feel while reading (say) Spinoza and contemplating his ideas. The latter experience is doubtlessly rare; yet statistics are irrelevant in deciding what is paradigmatic. The phenomenology of sexual experience is such that, when we are enjoying an intense sexual experience—no matter how common or rare it may actually be—we feel then and there that this sexual experience is utterly unique and irreplicable.

Finally, there is the Freudian view that all sensations obtained from manipulating any part of the body are sexual. Soble, however, writes:

> This answer clearly handles the difficulty we had previously with the pleasurable sensations produced in the wrist without genital arousal. But the cost of this victory is that this view must admit too many pleasurable sensations as the sexual ones. There is some point, after all, in distinguishing the pleasure felt in the mouth when drinking cool water on a warm and dry day, and the pleasure felt in the mouth when performing an oral sex act. And if the position retreats and says, instead, that all parts of the body are (simply) *capable* of producing sexual pleasure (which is undoubtedly true) we are still left with the problem of what makes the manipulation of part x sexual on one occasion but not sexual on another occasion, when on both occasions the physiological components are likely to be the same or at least overlapping.
>
> Perhaps the solution to many of these difficulties is to be a linguistic libertarian and allow each person to decide—although not necessarily achieve—what counts as a paradigmatic sexual experience on a personal basis. (The last sentence in Soble's remarks poses a problem that will be discussed later in this article.)

A final difficulty, at least for those who conceptualize sex as an expression of love, is the reductionists' suspicion of or even rejection of sex as expressing love. Goldman argues that defining sex as an expression of love unduly restricts what counts as sexual, leads to a repressive sexual ethic, and has disastrous consequences when sex is confused with love such that marriage results on that assumption. Yet he grants that sex can express love, and that this may be a fulfilling option in the way that some prefer their coffee with cream and sugar, while others prefer theirs plain to get the full "punch" of the coffee itself undiluted by anything else. What is important for the reductionist is that things like love and reproduction must serve sex rather than the other way around. That is, thoughts about love and reproduction are only *sexually* relevant if they intensify the power of the sexual experience itself.

Vannoy, however, goes even further and argues that sex is best divorced from erotic love entirely. The concept of love, he argues, is beset by numerous contradictions, which bring more torment than joy to the lover. One dilemma is the following:

> Even the most ardent defender of love's unselfishness does not want erotic love to arise out of mere charity or duty. This demand is itself based on self-interest. For one's esteem is damaged if one feels one wasn't chosen for one's merits or appealing qualities and was only worthy of love that is given to just anyone. . . . But if one wants to be chosen for one's appealing qualities, one is committed . . . to the selectivity and exclusiveness that reveal the egoism of one's lover. For he or she will be chosen on the basis of qualities that appeal to the lover's needs and self-interests.

Vannoy's view is diametrically opposed to that of the 18th-century philosopher Immanuel Kant:

> Human love is good will, affection, promoting the happiness of others and finding joy in their happiness. But it is clear that, when a person loves another purely from sexual desire, none of these factors enter into love. . . . Sexual love makes of the loved person an object of appetite; as soon as that appetite has been stilled, the person has been cast aside as one casts away a lemon that has been sucked dry. Sexual love can, of course, be combined with human love and so carry with it the characteristics of the latter, but taken by itself and for itself, it is nothing more than appetite. Taken by itself, it is a degradation of human nature; for as soon as a person becomes an object of appetite for another, all motives of moral relationship cease to function, because as an object of appetite for another a person becomes a thing and can be treated and used as such by everyone.

Kant further argues that only in marriage can two persons treat each other as whole beings. Matrimony, he held, is an agreement between two persons by which they grant to each other reciprocal equal rights, each of them undertaking to surrender the whole of their person to the other with a complete right of disposal over it. This view of marriage, however, seems to lead to a loss of autonomy, but Kant disagrees:

> If I yield myself completely to another and obtain the person of another in return, I win myself back. I have given myself up as the property of another, but in turn I take that other as my property, and so win myself back in winning the person whose property I have become. . . . In this way two persons become a unity of will. Whatever good or ill, joy or sorrow befall either of them, the other will share in it. Thus sexuality leads to a union of human beings.

In trying to overcome the problem of mutual ownership, Kant has made the mystically unified couple into the autonomous individual. This, however, means that the individuals in Kantian love have no independent existence or individuality at all. Furthermore, Kant fails to understand that if sexual desire is inherently exploitative and if love is inherently altruistic, trying to combine the two generates a contradiction rather than a sexual love of persons. Furthermore, it is not penises and vaginas that have sex, but persons; and persons can be generous or selfish with their sexuality irrespective of whether or not they are in love. Even in anonymous sexual encounters, the "you-please-me-and-I'll-please-you" ethic, while doubtlessly of the give-to-get variety, serves the purpose quite nicely, since that is all such persons want.

Indeed, the vulnerability of sexual partners both of whom have, as it were, become their bodies is such that they are hardly in a position to exploit anyone. Only the coolly controlled sadist who refuses to surrender to sexual passion and who insists on essentially remaining a pure consciousness (while turning his body into a torture machine) could succeed in having the absolute control he requires. (Hannibal Lector in the film *The Silence of the Lambs* is an example.) Furthermore, to focus on someone's body in a sexual sense is not the same as objectifying someone in the moralist's sense of the term, that is, treating another person as being of less moral worth than oneself. The latter entails the former, but not vice versa. The contempt for the body that is invariably implicit in the defense of sex with love is also shown by the fact that Kant would surely not be bothered at all if his students fo-

cused solely on his ideas when he lectured on the critique of pure reason. For that is the appropriate thing to do in *that* context. Demands for "wholeness" only seem to arise in those situations when the body is appropriately the primary focus of our attention. Even an eminent philosopher of love such as Irving Singer has attacked Kant's claim that sex requires love, albeit in a nonreductionist way:

> For though sexual interest resembles an appetite in some respects, it differs from hunger or thirst in being an *interpersonal* sensitivity, one that enables us to delight in the mind and character of other persons as well as in their flesh. Though at times people may be used as sexual objects and cast away once their utility has been exhausted, this is no more definitive of sexual desire than its responsiveness to those bodily manifestations without which human beings could not be perceived as just the persons that they are. By awakening us to the living presence of someone else, sexuality can enable us to treat this other being just as the person he or she happens to be. . . . In all areas of life, it can happen that people are treated as means merely, but there is nothing in the nature of sexuality as such that necessarily brings that about or reduces persons to things. On the contrary, sex may be seen as an institutional agency by which persons respond to each other *through* their bodies.

In the case of the expansionists, who would view the reductionists as defending nothing more than a hedonistic pursuit of superficial epidermal stimulation, Sartre, Nagel, and Solomon claim that the sole or primary purpose of sex is a complex form of interpersonal communication. For them, perversion arises when there has been a violation of or a breakdown in the various forms of communication they espouse. None of these theories requires penile-genital intercourse and none is presented by these philosophers as requiring heterosexuality, since homosexuals can have interpersonal communications of desires, attitudes, and feelings as well. Some antigay theorists do, however, use the communication model to try to refute homosexual desire. They argue that sex with a member of one's own sex is like talking to oneself—one's mirror image—whereas "real" communication responds to another who is truly other than oneself. This argument is fallacious, since it assumes that all males or all females are alike. Indeed, the male poet and male boxer who are lovers may be more unalike than many heterosexual partners.

Both Nagel's and Solomon's views are inspired by a Sartrean view of sex, which is part of a complex ontological theory about the nature of human relationship. Sartre argues that personhood is dualistically defined in terms of two radically—even contradictory—types of being: consciousness and freedom ("being for itself") and the body ("being-in-itself"). Although one may not share Sartre's subject-object dualism in a metaphysical sense, there is clearly often an acute phenomenological awareness of such a distinction, (e.g., when a male's penis insists on remaining an inert object when he subjectively wills that it become erect). The question for Sartre is how to unite these two realms into a psychosomatic unity and achieve a feeling of wholeness. He argues that this occurs when two persons sexually desire each other in such a way that each becomes an incarnated consciousness. He writes that being which desires is consciousness *making itself body*: "The revelation of the other's flesh is made through my own flesh; in desire and in the caress which expresses desire. I incarnate myself in order to realize the incarnation of the other. . . . I make her enjoy my flesh through her flesh in order to compel her to feel herself flesh. And so possession truly appears as a double reciprocal incarnation."

However, as soon as sexual desire translates into activity that aims for sexual pleasure, Sartre claims that this fragile psychosomatic unity necessarily self-destructs. If I am overwhelmed by sexual pleasure, then I am transformed into a mere body that masochistically requires only that the other person stare at me so that my feeling of being an object is sustained and enhanced. My partner must then become a pure subject for whom I am an object. If, however, I refuse to become my body and sadistically try to possess my partner in the requisite consciously controlled way, I then become a nonincarnated freedom and my partner becomes an object. My psychosomatic unity and that of my partner (i.e., our completeness as persons) is thus destroyed whichever way we turn.

Personhood in sex is not rescued by love, as it is for Kant. Sartre argues that love is inherently possessive, that is, when I "give" myself to another, it is merely a roundabout way of getting him or her to surrender his or her personhood to me. Since the beloved is doing the same thing, love becomes pure conflict. Kant would also find it remarkable that Sartre would turn to sexual desire in hopes of discovering what he could not find anywhere else—two persons viewing themselves and each other as both subject and object. Indeed, the essence of all human relations, Sartre

argues, is conflict: If I am a subject, the other necessarily becomes an object for me by means of my judgmental, categorizing, Medusa-like stare. If the other is a subject for me, then I similarly become an object for him. Sartrean life thus becomes a struggle to retain one's subjectivity, which can only be accomplished by possessing another's subjectivity. A stolen freedom is, however, no longer free, so even this fails.

All sex, therefore, seems to be a failure in Sartre's system, except—as Oaklander has argued—for the one brief moment when the two partners initially desired each other and each had achieved the mutual mind-body (or subject-object) wholeness they sought. Oaklander holds that Sartre does allow for a momentary success in achieving this goal—something other Sartre scholars have denied. Instead, he states that Sartre held that the moment the communion of desire is realized, each consciousness, by incarnating itself, has realized the incarnation of the other; each one's disturbance has caused disturbance to be born in the other and is thereby so much enriched. By each caress a person experiences his own flesh and is conscious that his flesh which he feels and appropriates through his flesh is flesh-realized-by-the-other.

Oaklander argues that since Sartre's goal of interpersonal communion is on occasion realized but then invariably self-destructs, all sex for Sartre is perverse. This result is remarkable. (Solomon once noted that if one believed Sartre's account, it would be enough to keep one out of the bedroom for a month.) Indeed, Sartre's claim that sexual pleasure causes the true goal of sex (as he sees it) to self-destruct and that ideally sex should not be about sexual pleasure at all would mean that—for the reductionist—Sartre has not given a theory about sex at all. It is merely a curious study of the ontology of human relationships discussed in the language of sex. Feminist philosophers would argue (rightly or wrongly) that Sartre has merely shown that his androcentric conceptualizing of sexual pleasure solely in terms of dominance and submission is incompatible with preserving personhood during the sexual act. Indeed, if the Sartrean caress works, why not remain at that level rather than regard it as merely foreplay? Or is this something men could never do?

Nagel's classic paper "Sexual Perversion," while inspired by Sartre, nevertheless deviated from the latter's pessimistic theory in many ways. Like Sartre, Nagel believes that sex is essentially interpersonal communication and that its ultimate goal is incarnation of consciousness. Unlike Sartre, he believes that sex often does succeed in these goals. The failure to do so constitutes perversion, something he grants may in some cases bring more sexual pleasure than nonperverted sex, which he dubs "complete sex." Thus, as in the theory of Sartre, sexual pleasure does not have the primacy it has for reductionists.

Nagel's most famous idea is that of complete sex, which is also his definition of naturalness. Complete sex requires multiple levels of interpersonal communication of desire, such that sexual desire escalates through feedback into an ultimate mutual incarnation of consciousness. The feedback mechanism operates as follows: I see you and I am aroused; you see me and you are aroused; I then see that you are aroused by me and this arouses me even further; you see that I am aroused by your arousal, and you are aroused even further; this further arousal of yours then arouses me even further, and so on. Nagel writes:

> Let us suppose that Juliet, who is a little slower than Romeo, now senses that he senses her. This puts Romeo in a position to notice, and be aroused by, her arousal at being sensed by him. He senses that she senses that he senses her. This is still another level of arousal, for he becomes conscious of his sexuality through his awareness of its effect on her and of her awareness that this effect is due to him. Once she takes the same step and senses that he senses her sensing him, it becomes difficult to state, let alone imagine, further iterations, though they may be logically distinct. Physical contact and intercourse are perfectly natural extensions of this complicated visual exchange, and mutual touch can involve all the complexities of awareness present in the visual case, but with a far greater range of subtlety and awareness.

For Nagel, sexual perversion results when this feedback mechanism is truncated or incomplete. For example, narcissistic practices and intercourse with animals, infants, and inanimate objects seem to be stuck at some primitive version of the first stage. If the object is not alive, the experience is reduced entirely to an awareness of one's own sexual embodiment. Small children and animals permit awareness of the embodiment of the other, but present obstacles to reciprocity, to the recognition by the sexual object of the subject's desire as the source of the object's sexual self-awareness.

Homosexuality would not be a perversion, since the theory (like Sartre's) is presented as being gender-neutral. Yet while sex-as-communication theories liberate gays and lesbians, who can have Nagel's complete sex just as heterosexuals do, they also view masturbation (Nagel's "narcissistic practices") as perverted. Soble, however, attacks what he calls the binary framework of sexuality as a mere prejudice and defends a unitary theory of sex (the rubbing of flesh against flesh for sexual pleasure), which allows masturbation and intercourse to have equal status.

Nagel's theory also perversely requires that two persons who are already highly aroused by other means (e.g., dildoes) and who meet and instantly have sex are to be considered perverted because they skip the initial multiple levels of arousal of each by the other. Nagel argues that desire is not merely the perception of a preexisting embodiment of the other, but is ideally a contribution to his further embodiment, which in turn enhances the original subject's sense of himself. This, he holds, explains why it is important that the partner be aroused—and not merely aroused, but aroused by the awareness of one's desire.

Elsewhere, however, Nagel claims that sex "involves a desire that one's partner be aroused by the recognition of one's desire that he or she be aroused." He also holds that "physical possession must eventuate in the creation of the sexual object in the image of one's desire, and not merely in the object's recognition of that desire, or in his or her own private arousal." These claims, however, make sexual desire needlessly egocentric.

The third expansionist, Solomon, sharply attacks the notion that sex is primarily for pleasure. Solomon notes that Masters and Johnson have claimed that masturbation provides the most intense orgasm. Why, then, Solomon asks, do people (sometimes risking great personal loss) largely seek out sexual intercourse? Solomon argues that what people really want is to communicate various emotions and attitudes to others, and that sex is a kind of body language for achieving what words alone cannot convey.

As it is for Sartre, sex for Solomon is not essentially about sexual pleasure at all; indeed, it may interfere with communication. Solomon, unlike those who conceptualize sex solely in terms of expressing love (such that sexual violence cannot really be sexual), is quite generous in the range of things he thinks sex can convey: shyness, domination, fear, submissiveness and dependence, love or hatred or indifference, lack of confidence and embarrassment, shame, jealousy, possessiveness.

What of Solomon's claim that we prefer intercourse to masturbation? Does it refute the hedonistic reductionist? Solomon ignores the fact that there are many other reasons besides communication that explain why so many prefer sexual intercourse. With a sexual partner, one may enjoy a variety of sexual techniques, positions, and forms of mutual sensory stimulation and kinesthetic sensations one cannot have alone. Another example Solomon might have used is one Soble evaluates in responding to Solomon: why is it that when I rub my own elbow I feel only a mildly pleasurable sensation, but when someone else rubs it, it may produce an intensely sexually pleasurable sensation? Is it because the other person is bolstering my ego by communicating desire (Nagel)? Is it because the other is communicating a Solomonic message in body language? These psychological phenomena may occur, but they are not essential to my being *sexually* aroused. Although Soble does not solve the elbow puzzle in reductionist terms, the answer is surely that I am aroused because I am being touched by someone I find to be quite sexually attractive and whose body I would like to touch in turn. Desire does not escalate and messages from body language mean nothing sexually unless I first find the flesh of the other to be the embodiment of sensual pleasure. Even when pressure on the wrist is intense enough to communicate dominance, it will still not be sexually arousing unless I have eroticized dominance and the dominant person is seen as embodying dominance in a sexually appealing way—as opposed to another dominant person who is quite unappealing. Thus, the sexual significance of Solomonic messages presupposes what Solomon assigns to peripheral significance—sexual pleasure. Indeed, this is the only way to distinguish a sexual from a nonsexual use of body language.

Moulton criticizes Solomon for failing to recognize that sex is often a less than ideal way to communicate attitudes, since it is not clear that some attitudes are best expressed sexually. Tenderness and trust are often expressed between people who are not sexual partners. The tenderness and trust that exist between an adult and a child is not best expressed sexually. Even if Solomon's claim is taken only to apply to sexual partners, a joint checking account may be a better expression of trust than sexual activity.

For Solomon, a perversion is defined as a misuse of the body language of sexuality (e.g., pretending to communicate love when there is none). He also attacks masturbation because, in his words, masturbation is "self-denial." It represents an inability or refusal to say what one wants to say, and though masturbation is essential as an ultimate retreat, it is empty and without content, the equivalent of a "Cartesian soliloquy."

Solomon, however, fails to recognize that there are ways of communicating with oneself (e.g., keeping a private diary) that are hardly "empty and without content." Soble argues that Solomon's claim that masturbation is an "inability or refusal to say what one wants to say" overlooks the fact that it might be false that one has *something* to say, that there is something *worthy* of being said that is not being said, or that something *ought* to be said. The communication model of sexuality forces people to say things that there might be no compelling reason to say just in order to achieve first-rate sexuality.

Philosophers are contributing important insights about the nature of sexuality, however much they may disagree with each other and however much the philosophy of sex is still in its infancy. To be sure, one may make the old claim that philosophy is futile because philosophers never agree about anything. But is it not also true that sex researchers constantly challenge each other's assumptions (and often even their data)? Indeed, science without controversy would become sterile and much less likely to make progress. So it is with philosophy as well.

REFERENCES

Atkinson, R. *Sexual Morality*. New York: Harcourt, Brace & World, 1965.

Baker, R., and F. Elliston, eds. *Philosophy and Sex*. Rev. ed. Buffalo, N.Y.: Prometheus Books, 1984.

Batchelor, E. *Homosexuality and Ethics*. New York: Pilgrim, 1980.

Bullough, V.L. *Sexual Variance in Society and History*. Chicago: Univ. of Chicago Press, 1976.

Davis, M.S. *Smut, Erotic Reality/Obscene Ideology*. Chicago: Univ. of Chicago Press, 1983.

Goldman, A. Plain Sex. *Philosophy and Public Affairs*, Vol. 6 (Spring 1977), pp. 267–87.

Kant, E. *Lectures on Ethics*. Translated by L. Infield. London: Methuen, 1930.

Moulton, J. Sexual Behavior: Another Position. *Journal of Philosophy*, Vol. 73 (1976), pp. 537–46.

Nagel, T. Sexual Perversion. *Journal of Philosophy*, Vol. 66 (1969), pp. 76–88.

Oaklander, L.N. Sartre on Sex. In A. Soble, ed., *The Philosophy of Sex: Contemporary Readings*. Rev. ed. Totowa, N.J.: Littlefield, Adams, 1991.

Sartre, J-P. *Being and Nothingness*. Translated by H. Barnes. New York: Philosophical Library, 1956.

Singer, I. *The Nature of Love: Courtly and Romantic*. Vol. 2. Chicago: Univ. of Chicago Press, 1984.

Soble, A. Masturbation and Sexual Philosophy. In *The Philosophy of Sex: Contemporary Readings*. Rev. ed. Totowa, N.J.: Littlefield, Adams, 1991.

———. *Pornography: Marxism, Feminism and the Future of Sexuality*. New Haven: Yale Univ. Press, 1986.

————, ed. *The Philosophy of Sex: Contemporary Readings*. Rev. ed. Totowa, N.J.: Littlefield, Adams, 1991.

Solomon, R. Sex and Perversion. In R. Baker and F. Elliston, eds., *Philosophy and Sex*. Rev. ed. Buffalo, N.Y.: Prometheus Books, 1984.

————. Sexual Paradigms. *Journal of Philosophy*, Vol. 71 (1974), pp. 336–45.

Vannoy, R. *Sex Without Love: A Philosophical Exploration*. Buffalo, N.Y.: Prometheus Books, 1980.

Russell C. Vannoy

PHOBIAS

"Phobia" is a technical term describing an anxiety disorder characterized by an obsessive, irrational, intense, and morbid dread or fear of something. It is a term not confined to the sexual behaviors. An Anglophobe, for example, is a person who hates the English. Phobias are manifested in various sex behaviors, although the vocabulary is not as extensive as it is for the paraphilias. Many phobias are a result of sexual fears instilled by parents, teachers, or religious authorities as a means of controlling sexual impulses and behavior, particularly masturbation and premarital sex.

Since the development of psychoanalysis, it has also been widely recognized that phobias not usually associated with sex might well have sexual overtones. Freud, who began writing on the subject at least as early as 1894, argued that phobias were a form of neurotic anxiety and featured a fear all out of proportion to the actual danger of the object. He found the mainspring of the anxiety in the id rather than in the external world, and the object of the phobia represented a temptation to instinctual gratification or was associated in some way with an instinctual object-choice. In other words, behind every such neurotic fear is a primitive wish for the object of which one is afraid. The person wants what he or she fears or wants something that is associated with, or symbolized by, the feared object.

Whether or not one adopts the Freudian view, many forms of phobia directly relate to human sexual performance, and some of these are listed below.

Phobia	Source of Fear
Anal-castration anxiety	Toilets, defecation
Androphobia	Men
Anuptaphobia	Remaining unmarried
Aulophobia	Penislike musical instruments (e.g., the flute)
Automysophobia	Being unclean, dirty; "messy" sex
Bromidrosiphobia	Body smells
Coitophobia	Sexual intercourse
Coprophobia	Defecation and excrement
Cypridophobia	Contacting a sexually transmitted disease
Enosiophobia	Committing a sexual sin
Erotophobia	One's sexuality and responses
Erythrophobia	Color red, and also associated with blushing, sex flush
Eurotophobia	Female genitalia
Gamophobia	Marriage
Genital penetration phobia	Sexual intercourse
Genophobia	Sex
Gymnophobia	Naked body
Gynophobia	Women
Hamartophobia	Committing a sexual sin
Haptephobia	Being touched
Hedenophobia	Experiencing sexual pleasure
Heterophobia	Heterosexual persons
Homophobia	Homosexual persons
Maieusiophobia	Childbirth
Ophidiophobia	Fear of snakes as a symbol of sex
Parthenophobia	Virgins, young girls
Patriphobia	Inherited genetic defect or disease
Peccatophobia	Sexual sins
Penetration phobia	Vaginal, anal, or oral penile penetration
Phallophobia	Penis, especially the erect penis
Proctophobia	Enemas, rectal exams, anal sex
Scataphobia	Defecation and excrement
Scoptophobia	Being looked at or seen naked
Sexophobia	Anything having to do with sex
Snake phobia	Snakes as penis symbols
Spermatophobia	Semen
Teratophobia	Monsters, particularly birth of defective or deformed offspring
Tocophobia	Childbirth

REFERENCES

Money, J. *Lovemaps*. Buffalo, N.Y.: Prometheus Books, 1986.

Freud, S. The Neuro-Psychoses of Defence: (An Attempt at a Psychological Theory of Acquired Hysteria, of Many Phobias and Obsessions and of Certain Hallucinatory Psychoses. In *The Standard Edition of the Complete Psychological Works of Sigmund Freud*. Translated by J. Strachey, et al. 24 vols. London: Hogarth Press, 1953–74, Vol. 3.

———. Obsessions and Phobias: Their Psychical Mechanism and Their Aetiology. In *The Standard Edition of the Complete Psychological Works of Sigmund Freud*. Translated by J. Strachey, et al. 24 vols. London: Hogarth Press, 1953–74, Vol. 3.

Vern L. Bullough

PHYSICAL DISABILITIES AND SEX

Any inquiry into the subject of physical disabilities and sexuality must begin with the basic understanding that every person with the spark of life in them is capable of some sexual functioning. The comprehension of that single fact is essential if one seeks to understand the effects that a physical disability may have on a person's sexuality.

The statement that all people, and therefore all disabled people, are capable of some sexual functioning seems simple enough, but the misunderstanding and denial of it is perhaps the primary reason why the sexual concerns of the physically disabled have been historically dismissed as of no importance by most segments of most societies.

Only recently has society started to deal with the sexuality of previously sexually disenfranchised groups such as the unmarried, the elderly, the young, the incarcerated, and the mentally and physically disabled. Chief among the reasons why so many have for so long dismissed the sexuality of these groups is the connection that sexuality has with procreation. The erroneous belief that the sole purpose and function of human sexuality is or should be procreation leads to the conclusion that many societies have in fact made, that is, the denial of the sexuality of all subgroups that the society has determined cannot or should not bear children. In the collective minds of those societies, that is the thread that connects those six subgroups.

However, over the last several decades there has developed, at least in much of the Western world, a series of advances in thinking about the rights of subgroups that were formerly and systematically ignored. Along with greater recognition of the rights of racial and ethnic minorities and of women, a new sense of the rights of the physically disabled to express and enjoy their individual sexualities is evolving. It is not an accident that a general awareness of and improvements in the sexual rights of the physically disabled followed advances in the other areas.

Before there could be a general acceptance of the sexuality of the physically disabled, two things had to occur first, and in the decades since the mid-1960s both of those prerequisites began to occur. One prerequisite was the development of a genuine concern for the rights and the dignity of subgroups in a society. The other prerequisite was the breaking down of repressively rigid and factually erroneous limits on sexual expression. Along with the onset of changes in both of these areas came an explosion of research in each of them.

Social and biological scientists from a wide range of academic disciplines, as well as other researchers and writers, suddenly discovered in the physically disabled population a virtually unexplored research terrain, which was to yield, and is still yielding, rich returns—rich at least in terms of improving the lives of untold millions of physically disabled people and their loved ones and companions into the indefinite future.

This brief background is vital to an understanding of the sexuality of the physically disabled. It seems almost absurd to state that the physically disabled are people just like everyone else in the community. But that simple concept is, as strange as it may seem, the one that has been traditionally and is still the most commonly misunderstood by the societies of the world. Although much progress has been made in recent decades, there are still some individuals, some groups, and some societies that either ignore or do not grasp the truth of the fact that the physically disabled are no less "people" and as such have sensual and sexual potentials and are capable of the same sexual needs and desires as are others. So even though there has been progress in the recognition of the sexual rights of the physically disabled, that recognition is by no means universal.

People with physical disabilities are as diverse a group as are the able-bodied members of a society. They are found in all age groups. They are of all cultures, all economic and social strata, and both genders. Some are married, single, divorced, widowed, or separated. Some are heterosexual, bisexual, homosexual, or asexual, and some are undetermined as to any sexual orientation. Among the physically disabled there are homosexual, bisexual, and heterosexual transvestites, preoperative and postoperative transsexuals, and some she-males. Likewise, as a group, people with physical disabilities have the same range and diversity of sexual interests and sexual dysfunctions as does the society of which they are a part.

Among the physically disabled there are those who have no offspring and desire to remain childless, those with one or many children, those who desperately wish to have a child but have been unsuccessful in doing so or have not had the opportunity to try, and those who are ambivalent about it. There are people who are actively seeking to practice birth control so as to manage the number and timing of their or their sexual partner's pregnancies or to prevent them entirely.

From that description, it can be seen that all the joys, thrills, and satisfactions that sex can bring to a person are to be found in the global universe of the physically disabled. But it is also true that all the problems and issues about sex that perplex the able-bodied members of a community are also present to be dealt with by the physically disabled portion of that society. In addition, the physically disabled must also face and deal with the unique problems that one or more physical conditions place in the way of sexual functioning and fulfillment.

Some general observations can be made about sexuality and physical disabilities that more or less pertain regardless of the particular disabling condition. One of the most troubling issues that the physically disabled routinely must face regarding their sexuality is that of self-worth (or self-esteem). The issue of self-worth is like a ball in a pinball machine—it trails its way through the maze of barriers in the game of life and bangs up against all of them, setting off bells and whistles and lights as it goes. No aspect of a physically disabled person's sexuality is not in some way affected by his or her perception of his or her self-worth. Of course, that may be said of the able-bodied person as well, and it is true that it is a daunting issue for many of them. But in the case of a physically disabled person, the concept of self-worth takes on a new dimension. In societies such as those in today's developed nations, in which perfection in physical beauty and performance is the ideal, the further away one is from an ideal physical state, the more vulnerable one's ego becomes and the more likely it is that a damaged sense of self-worth will have a negative impact on one's sexual functioning. As is evident from the word "disabled" (or any euphemism for it), the physically disabled, by definition, occupy a distinctly low spot on the totem pole of physical desirability. There are no popular calendars of disabled bathing beauties or male hunks.

For the physically disabled, self-worth may be negatively affected in many different ways—all potentially very important to an individual. Perhaps the most common effect comes from a damaged body image. When one considers that an able-bodied person may feel depressed because of the appearance of a temporary pimple on his or her face, it is understandable that a person who may have both arms and legs missing or has no control over his bowels and bladder and has to use a respirator to breathe has a lot to deal with in terms of self-worth and body image. Self-worth can also be affected by whether or not one sees oneself as a sufficiently productive member of society or of a family unit, or by the extent to which one is physically dependent on others for such things as personal care (e.g., bathing, dressing, eating, elimination), driving a car, opening a door or window, answering a telephone, and so on, or by the amount of control one has over one's life in general.

Self-worth can be particularly affected by how one is able to function sexually. Regardless of the absolute level of sexual functioning, the most important thing to a physically disabled person in this regard is whether he or she can function to a level that is personally satisfying (and that may entail being able to sexually satisfy one's sex partner). That level will be different in each individual case.

Some people, whether physically disabled or not, simply will never be satisfied with any level of sexual functioning that they perceive to be less than the optimum. That type of aspiration is typically destined to be forever denied fulfillment—especially if such a person has a physical disability. The more flexible the disabled person is in terms of the degree of sexual functioning that is felt to be satisfactory and satisfying, the greater is the likelihood that some form of sexual satisfaction may be attained.

The general concept of what sex is also differs from individual to individual. To one person, it might consist solely of intimate touching and holding. Some people find their satisfaction in masturbation, while the sexuality of others may include orgasmic sex with a partner that does not involve genital-to-genital intercourse. Some people consider acceptable sex to be limited to a rare instance of vaginal-penile intercourse with one's spouse in the missionary position for the sole purpose of initiating an intended pregnancy. To such people, the physical ability to carry out the desired act and to have it result as intended may be the extent of his or her concern with sexual functioning. In contrast to such limited sexual desires or goals, some of the physically disabled develop, or at least wish to develop, an extensive sexual and sensual repertoire. It may in fact be said that there are perhaps as many ideas of what constitutes acceptable and desirable sex as there are people. Nevertheless, it is possible to make some sense of such a huge variety of ideas by categorizing them.

Thus, it is useful to say that people value or devalue sex on the basis of such things as the type of relationship that exists between the sex partners, the purpose of the sexual behavior, the particular sex acts involved and how they are conducted, the environment and the circumstances in which the behavior occurs, and the physical and psychological results of the sex activity. Within each of those categories there are many possible variations of circumstances, and the relative importance to a particular person of any of those categories or of any of the variations within the categories may be unique to that person.

To some physically disabled persons, what may be important is the physical positions they may be able to use in sexual activities, or whether or not they are orgasmic, or that their sex partners are usually or sometimes orgasmic. To some males, it may be important whether or not they can ejaculate. To some females, it may be important whether or not sexual activity results in vaginal lubrication. The amount of or lack of sensory feelings over parts of the body, especially in the usually recognized erogenous areas (i.e., genitals, thighs, breasts, buttocks), may be of importance to some physically disabled people. The extent of control over one's bowel and bladder or spastic muscles during sexual activity may be an important factor. The necessity of having to have one's sex partner or a third person prepare and position the disabled person to engage in the anticipated sexual activity may also be of importance.

Consider the case of a person whose physical disability and personal circumstances are such that the realistic prospects are that no sex partner is likely ever to come along, and, in addition, it is physically impossible for him or her to engage in masturbation. Add to that the circumstance that person has a strong sex desire and has no religious, moral, or personal inhibitions about engaging in sex in any possible way with a willing partner. To such a person, the possibility of any of a large variety of sexual circumstances actually occurring to him or her may be most welcome.

Between the extremes of the person who never wants to have a sexual experience with anyone, even with himself or herself, and the person who will willingly do almost anything sexually with almost anyone at almost any time lie all the rest of the disabled population. That brings in the next set of factors that affect the sexuality of the disabled. Just like everyone else, the physically disabled are influenced in various degrees in their personal feelings about sex by such forces as religion, culture, and personal experiences. With regard to what are permissible sex acts, who are legitimate sex partners, and what are the proper purposes of sex, a physically disabled person's opinions and practices may be entirely or only partially controlled by his or her religious beliefs, or they may be formed as a reaction against formerly held religious beliefs or be the product of no such belief system. The cultures (e.g., Hispanic, Polynesian) and the subcultures (e.g., peer groups, socioeconomic class) with which a physically disabled person identifies traditionally have certain customs or beliefs about sex that may be internalized by that person.

The influences of religion and of culture have to do with what is "permissible" sexual behavior, whereas the influences of experience have more to do with what is "possible" and "pleasurable." At times, those influences may be in conflict with each other. Consider, for example, a particular adult male of Mexican heritage, Catholic, who is paralyzed from the chest down from a gunshot wound in a gang cross-fire. His culture and his religion may influence him to have negative feelings about engaging in cunnilingus with his wife. Yet he may have found that all other attempts at pleasuring his wife to orgasm have been unsuccessful. He tries cunnilingus, it works well, and they both enjoy it and will continue doing it. Another individual in a similar circumstance and with a similar heritage and religious background may be opposed to oral sex on religious and cultural grounds and may not choose even to try cunnilingus. A third person in a like circumstance and with a similar background may have tried cunnilingus and found that the prior negative conditioning prevented any enjoyment of it; the one attempt ended unsuccessfully and unpleasantly and will not be repeated.

Each of these three types of influences—culture, religion, and experience—also affect nondisabled people in various ways and degrees. However, the physically disabled are potentially much more susceptible to being affected by them in ways that the nondisabled usually are not. The physically disabled person is much more likely to have physical and practical constraints (from the disability itself) placed on the types of sexual activities in which he or she may engage and to have his or her fertility compromised (biologically, opportunistically, or both) by the disabling conditions. As a result, oftentimes the very methods and purposes that a disabled person's culture, religion, or past experiences dictate as acceptable sexual expressions for that person are, because of the disabling condition, rendered impossible or disturbingly unsatisfactory. When those conflicts exist something has to yield: either the strict adherence to the imperatives of one's background and previous experiences, or the likelihood of attaining some satisfying sex.

The sexuality of many physically disabled people often depends not solely on their personal decisions and wishes and those of any potential sex partners that may be involved, but as much if not more on the personal decisions and wishes of third persons. This most often occurs when the disability is such that the disabled person is by necessity dependent upon a third person for his or her personal care, such as getting in and out of bed, dressing, and being transported. The third person is often in effective control of the disabled person's access to any form of sexual expression. That is particularly true when the third person is a parent or other family member or is a care giver or decision maker in the hospital or other institution in which the disabled person resides. But sexual expression is often just as effectively in the control of a third person when the latter is an employee of the disabled person. In any of these cases, the sexuality of the disabled person may be and often is hostage to the cultural and religious background and personal belief system, or perhaps even the mere whims, of the third person.

In addition to these factors, it is normally the case that the sexual concerns and interests of a particular disabled person will also usually depend on and vary according to that person's age, marital status, sexual orientation, socioeconomic bracket, life experience, age of onset of the disability, strength of sexual desire, amount and quality of adjustment to the disability, and general personal living conditions, general health, and availability and wishes of a sex partner. Therefore, when one contemplates the general subject of the sexuality of the physically disabled, rather than considering the community of the physically disabled as a monolithic entity it is infinitely more appropriate to liken it to a beach strewn with millions upon millions of individual pebbles, each unique.

Disabled people in each age bracket have their own special concerns—concerns that are somewhat similar to those of their able-bodied same-age peers, yet are profoundly different. The differences have to do with the limitations that the disability brings with it in each person's unique case. With the young, concern revolves around acquiring knowledge and experiences; with adolescents and young adults, it usually involves performance anxieties (e.g., how one can func-

tion sexually and socially and compete in the relationship marketplace). With older adults, it may be the same as with the younger adult but is also likely to be concerned with maintaining relationships or getting over those that have ended and moving on. The elderly person often must learn new sensual techniques (e.g., new ways in which to conceptualize sex and engage in it) and become comfortable with an ever-changing physical situation as the disability exacerbates the normal complications of increasing age.

The age at which the disabling condition occurs is an important factor. A person whose disability occurs after many years of an active sex life in which he or she has experienced perhaps a range of sexual feelings, including orgasm from several different methods of stimulation, has a completely different frame of reference from which to begin a sexual rehabilitation process than does a youngster whose disability occurs early in life or perhaps is congenital. The issue of sexual experience prior to disability is particularly a factor in disabilities in which sensory faculties or severe motor functions are impaired.

The earlier in life a disabling condition occurs that seriously affects sensory faculties (e.g., sight, hearing, or touch) or affects motor functions, the greater is the likelihood that the child will need extraordinary assistance throughout childhood, adolescence, and perhaps young adulthood in exploring and learning how his or her body and the bodies of others function sexually and in acquiring the socializing skills that are necessary for the eventual development of intimate relationships.

It is essential, if that socialization process is to work effectively, that disabled children and young adults not be isolated from other disabled and nondisabled peers. But in most instances, much more than that is needed. The type of extraordinary assistance that is required will ordinarily depend on whether a young person is blind or deaf or has severe limb and torso mobility limitations, as well as the age at which the disability occurred. Naturally, any assistance in learning about body characteristics and functions and in gaining socializing skills needs to be age appropriate.

At some point, a particular child, blind at an early age or from birth, may need the assistance of a live model to experience, as opposed to "see," how the body of the other sex is formed. A particular deaf child or blind child may need extensive one-on-one tutoring in the mysterious intricacies of flirting, being seductive, dating, negotiating sensual or sexual engagements, and so forth. A particular youngster whose disability is such (e.g., through paralysis, immobility, or missing limbs and joints) that he or she is rendered incapable of sexually pleasuring himself or herself may need the assistance of another person to experience the sensations their bodies are capable of producing and which their nondisabled peers learn from their own bodies as a matter of course. It is, of course, essential that all disabled children be given age-appropriate sex education that is both accurate and complete—going beyond the merely biological to include the sociosexual knowledge and values that a well-adjusted person must possess.

Physically disabled adults of any age may need some extraordinary assistance in developing or rehabilitating their sexual functioning, depending on their physical and interpersonal situation and expressed desires. That assistance may be explicit instruction in special positions or procedures that are necessary, viewing films or videotapes of others coping in similar circumstances, experimenting and practicing with a sex surrogate, or developing orgasmic responses from stimulation of body areas that still have sensitivity. Physicians, institution administrators, and other care givers have a duty to provide required information or access to privacy, as circumstances require, so as to not unreasonably deny to any physically disabled person, by ignorance or coercion, the right of sexual expression.

There are several methods available for aiding males whose conditions prevent them from attaining an erection or one of a strength or duration sufficient to accomplish the desired sexual activity. He can be taught to self-inject or have someone else inject a substance (commonly prostaglandin E l or a combination of papaverine and phentolamine) into the shaft of his penis, a procedure which produces an erection that may last as long as several hours. Improper use may lead to severe complications. There are also devices that may be surgically inserted into the shaft of the penis; such devices, depending on the type, produce either a permanently rigid or partially rigid erection or an erection that can be produced or released at will. There are also external pumping devices that produce an erection that lasts until a constricting elastic band at the base of the penis is removed, which should normally occur within one-half hour.

There are several somewhat effective methods that are being used to obtain sperm from males who wish to procreate but who are not able to ejaculate in the course of ordinary stimulation or to ejaculate out the end of their penis (the ejaculate going instead into their bladder). The collection procedures are performed by spe-cialized medical personnel. The collected semen is processed and eventually mechanically inseminated into the prospective mother.

It has been demonstrated so often that it is now generally accepted that even severely physically disabled people can function as effective parents. The success of parenting in such cases depends more on the individuals involved than on the disability. Very few physically disabling diseases or conditions render infertile an otherwise fertile female. As a general rule, infertility only occurs in an otherwise fertile female if her disabling condition directly damages her reproductive organs, results in their removal, or sufficiently impairs her body's hormone production or utilization. That is not normally the result of such commonly occurring disabling conditions as spinal cord injury, multiple sclerosis, polio, rheumatoid arthritis, stroke, cerebral palsy, muscular diseases, spina bifida, and most amputations. However, in view of the medical risks of pregnancy that exist in certain cases and the genetic transmissibility of some disabilities, physically disabled women should seek and be provided with medical advice on the subject prior to engaging in any sexual activity that could result in a pregnancy, because counseling for pregnancy prevention may be indicated in some cases.

Although a person's sexuality may be meaningfully expressed as a solo activity, such as by masturbation, most people desire to share their sexuality with another person in some way. Most single able-bodied people from about adolescence onward will admit that the most constant problem they face in developing an intimate relationship, or even a casual onetime sexual relationship, is in finding "the right person."

Multiply that by many orders of magnitude and one can approximate the level of the problem for the typical physically disabled person who would like to have or is actively seeking a new relationship of the intimate or sexual kind. The use of the words "like to have" and "actively seeking" is not a semantic nicety. The range of disabling conditions and personal situations is such that there are large numbers of the physically disabled who would very much "like to have" an intimate partner but, because of their personal situation, are precluded from ever having access to a source of potential partners. For them, even the ability to have some such access would be a breakthrough accomplishment. It is those who do at least have access to potential partners who must learn to penetrate the social veil. It is they who regularly encounter the often immensely frustrating and numbing task of trying to find, if not "the" right one, then "a" right one, and if not for the indefinite future, then for the moment.

It is to the credit of the human species that a "right" one does in fact come along for large numbers of the physically disabled. For the fact is that a large percentage (no one knows accurately how many) of disabled people who do have access to normal socializing situations are successful in finding an intimate partner (or partners). It is rare in nature for animals to mate voluntarily with a disabled candidate, much less pair-bond with one. That it is not so rare among Homo sapiens speaks eloquently of the human spirit and argues mightily for the proposition that each physically disabled person in a civilized society deserves the opportunity to function at the highest level possible. That includes the development, exercise, and enjoyment of their individual sexual potentials.

Some Common Disabling Diseases and Conditions

Following a brief description of some of the more commonly occurring physically disabling diseases and conditions is a table that displays some of their specific ramifications for sexual functioning. In addition to the specific disabling conditions discussed below, there are, of course, many others that are no less serious and no less sure to affect the lives and the sexuality of those who have them. Their omission here is not meant to diminish their importance.

Cerebral Palsy (CP).

CP results when the brain is damaged either before, during, or within a few years after birth. The damage to the brain results in improper signals going to the muscles. As a result, any or all of the following may occur: involuntary or exaggerated voluntary movements, lack of balance, irregular gait, slurred speech, drooling, facial grimacing, or impaired intelligence. The degree of each of the symptoms may range from mild to severe.

Stroke.

A stroke (cerebral vascular accident) occurs when the normal blood supply to the brain is interrupted, as, for example, by a vascular clot, to such an extent that brain cells die due to the lack of their normal oxygen supply. A stroke on one side of the brain of sufficient intensity and duration will result in numbness and paralysis in the face, arms, and legs on the opposite side of the body. In addition, the stroke may affect speech, emotional stability, urinary continence, and sight.

Multiple Sclerosis (MS).

MS is a disease in which, for an unknown reason, the myelin (covering sheath) of the nerves is attacked and destroyed at multiple sites. That results in the interruption of signals passing along those nerves. This disease usually occurs in young adulthood, more often in women than men, and is persistent, with periods of remission and exacerbation. Usually beginning with only mild symptoms, the disease often leads to muscle incoordination, slow and difficult speech, oscillating movements of the eyes, muscular weakness, numbness and paralysis of one or more limbs, and urinary incontinence.

Spinal Cord Injuries (SCI).

Injuries to the spinal cord are most often the result of an impact trauma to the spinal column but may occur as a consequence of a tumor, abscess, or infection or because of a congenital defect. When the causative event results in a partial or complete lesion (discontinuity or loss of function) of the spinal cord, a partial or total interruption of the messages that normally pass through the injured area occurs. If the interruption is in the region of the cervical (neck) vertebrae, quadriplegia (partial or total paralysis in all four limbs) is the usual result. Lesions below that level affect the lower extremities (paraplegia). Sensitivity to touch, pain, and temperature and the use of trunk muscles are partially or totally lost at various levels of the body, depending on the severity and location of the injury. In addition, voluntary control of bowel and bladder is usually lost. Psychogenic responses (triggered by the mind) in the genitals are usually, but may not be, lost as well. Reflexogenic responses (triggered by physical stimulation) in the genitals are usually, but may not be, retained.

Rheumatoid Arthritis (RA).

This disease, which primarily affects women, is a systemic, chronic, and progressive disease that is manifested by inflammation of the joints. Through periods of remission and flare-ups in multiple joints, the disease results in joint swelling and damage accompanied by severe pain. Progressing in stages, this ultimately leads to ankylosis of the joints and to pain and damage to nearby muscles.

Poliomyelitis (Polio).

Polio is an infectious disease that results in damage to the motor nerve cells of the spinal cord. Sensory sensations remain intact. The result of the nerve damage is flaccid paralysis of the affected muscles. The paralysis may range from mild to severe and may affect arms, legs, trunk, or respiratory muscles or any combination of them. Once the virus runs its course, the paralysis is stable and nonprogressive.

Muscular Diseases.

There are several myopathies (muscular diseases) that result in severe physical disabilities. They each result in the gradual and progressive wasting away of voluntary muscles. Depending on the particular myopathy, the onset may be in early childhood, adolescence, or early or advanced adulthood. Different myopathies affect different voluntary muscle systems. Most are genetic in origin. As muscular use is gradually impaired, the consequences of the disability increase.

Amputations.

Amputations may be of part or all of each limb or any combination of them or of part or all of the pelvis or other appendage of the body. An amputation may be the result of a massive accidental trauma to a portion of a body or a disease that renders it imperative that a portion be severed and removed. It occasionally happens that due to a birth defect, a malformed limb that is deemed to be functionally obstructive is removed. Sexual functioning is most directly affected in cases involving the removal of both testicles (orchiectomy) or portions of the penis (penectomy) or the pelvis (hemipelvectomy) or the entire pelvis (hemicorporectomy). Generally, the disabilities that result from an amputation, depending on the body part(s) affected,

involve mobility, dexterity, posture, self-image, and self-sufficiency.

Spina Bifida.

Spina bifida is a developmental anomaly caused by a defect in the spinal column. The spinal column does not close properly at one or more vertebrae. As a result, a sac containing a portion of the spinal cord protrudes through the opening. The defect occurs prenatally. Symptoms are usually apparent at birth but may not appear until the rapid growth period of adolescence. The result is usually that the muscles and nerves of the lower trunk are affected, causing muscle weakness or paralysis, loss of sensation, and partial or total loss of bladder and bowel control.

REFERENCES

Anderson, F., J. Bardach, and J. Goodgold. *Sexuality and Neuromuscular Disease.* Rehabilitation Monograph No. 56. New York: Institute of Rehabilitation Medicine and the Muscular Dystrophy Association, 1979.

Csesko, P.A. Sexuality and Multiple Sclerosis. *Journal of Neuroscience Nursing,* Vol. 20 (1988), pp. 353–55.

Heslinga, K. *Not Made of Stone.* Springfield, Ill.: Thomas, 1974.

Mooney, T.O., T.M. Cole, and R.A. Chilgren. *Sexual Options for Paraplegics and Quadriplegics.* Boston: Little, Brown, 1975.

Phillips, L., M.N. Ozer, P. Axelson, and H. Chizeck. *Spinal Cord Injury.* New York: Raven Press, 1987.

Rabin, B.J. *The Sensuous Wheeler.* San Francisco: Multi Media Resource Center, 1980.

Some Possible Sexual Effects of Disabilities Discussed Above

Effects	Disability
Touch sensation may be impaired	Spina bifida, stroke, RA, MS, SCI
Possible impairment of genital engorgement upon physical stimulation	spina bifida; stroke; SCI: if lesion is complete or is at or below conus medullaris; amputees: only if organs removed; MS
Inability of male to ejaculate	spina bifida: usually; SCI: a few have no trouble, some need electrical or mechanical stimulation, others cannot ejaculate; amputees: only if organs are removed; MS: possibly
Possible difficulties in assuming desired positions	All conditions listed
Dependence on others for physical help with sexual preparations	All conditions listed (except usually not SCI paraplegics or most amputees) when use of limbs or trunk muscles are sufficiently impaired
Certain common sexual positions may be impossible to assume	Usually all conditions listed, except in rare instances of only slight degree of disability
Reproductive capacity likely to be lost	spina bifida: males rarely can reproduce, females likely can; SCI: some males who do not ejaculate by any means; amputees: only if reproductive organs removed

Schuster, C.S. Sex Education of the Visually Impaired Child: The Role of Parents. *Journal of Visual Impairment and Blindness,* Vol. 80 (1986), pp. 675–80

Task Force on Concerns of Physically Disabled Women. *Toward Intimacy: Family Planning and Sexuality Concerns of Physically Disabled Women.* New York: Human Sciences Press, 1978.

Dwight Dixon
Joan K. Dixon

PIMP

A pimp is a man who manages street prostitutes (as opposed to escorts or call girls). Prostitutes support the pimp by giving him a high percentage of their earnings. In turn, the pimp provides food, shelter, sexy clothes, and drugs for the prostitutes. He also arranges bail and helps protect them from police and brutal clients. Pimps may give their prostitutes kindness and love. Many prostitutes have an ongoing sexual relationship with their pimp. Often, prostitutes fall in love with their pimps.

The group of prostitutes working for a pimp is called his "stable." According to Benjamin and Masters, the street prostitute without a pimp is regarded with suspicion and called an "outlaw." Most often the girls or women who enter prostitution seek out the pimp. The pimp does not persuade or coerce women into becoming prostitutes.

In the United States, it has been reported that at least 90 percent of pimps are black. Many pimps feel that they are overcoming a past history of racial oppression, because they have money and power. The pimp spends most of his time drinking or using drugs and leisurely making business arrangements. He rarely goes into the streets, except to collect money from his prostitutes.

The pimp–prostitute relationship may involve physical abuse, but it does not always. In most cases, the abuse is less extreme than husband–wife abuse. As Gray explains, the relationship between a pimp and his prostitutes,

> although it reverses the "financial provider" role of conventional marriage, does show similarities to some kinds of conventional, marital behavior. The pimp serves as the major decision maker and the controller of the funds. The[y] may argue, frequently over money, but as long as the pimp does not administer too severe or brutal a beating the prostitute[s] will accept the occasional use of physical force in their relationship as part of the life.

The prostitutes often become extremely dependent on the pimp, thus leading to his further exploitation of them. Because of its intensity, the relationship is relatively short, lasting less than several years.

Pimping is illegal, with punishment more severe than for prostitution. In some states, punishment includes fines of up to $2,000 and imprisonment for up to 20 years. However, few pimps are arrested, since they are effective at dodging or paying off the police.

REFERENCES

Armstrong, E.G. Pondering Pandering. *Deviant Behavior,* Vol. 1 (1983), pp. 203–17.

Benjamin, H., and R.E.L. Masters. *Prostitution and Morality.* New York: Julian Press, 1964.

Caplan, G.M. The Facts of Life about Teenage Prostitution. *Crime and Delinquency,* Vol. 30 (Jan. 1984), pp. 69–84.

Carmen, A., and H. Moody. *Working Women: The Subterranean World of Street Prostitution.* New York: Harper and Row, 1985.

Gray, D. Turning-Out: A Study of Teenage Prostitution. *Urban Life and Culture,* Vol. 4 (Jan. 1973), pp. 401–25.

Hall, S. *Gentleman of Leisure: A Year in the Life of a Pimp.* New York: New American Library, 1972.

Slim, I. *Pimp: The Story of My Life.* Los Angeles: Holloway House, 1969.

Sari Locker

PLEASURE: SEX AND PLEASURE

People derive many different kinds of pleasure from sex. They may enjoy the physical contact: the kissing, touching, holding, stroking, and warmth of two bodies together. They may enjoy the emotional connection: the affection and the intimacy of shedding clothes and sharing feelings. They may enjoy the childlike abandon of playful sex, the adventure of a new erotic activity, the challenge and anticipation of a new love, the intensely exquisite sensations of skillful lovemaking, the explosive release of orgasm. Under the best of circumstances, they sometimes enjoy a magical, spiritual experience of two bodies and souls merging for a timeless moment in sheer ecstasy.

For certain people, however, sex and pleasure do not necessarily go together. Some think sex is primarily for making babies, and they have no other use for it. Others would like to associate sex with pleasure but have difficulty making that happen. Still others would simply rather read a book or watch television.

This article takes a brief look at the tendency to resist the pleasures of sex and then goes on to explore at greater length the variety of elements that go into the positive experience of sexual pleasure.

Pleasure Resistance

Many people recognize that while they derive pleasure from sex, they could enjoy themselves more intensely and more consistently than they already do. A number of factors, which are not all that uncommon today, may contribute to limiting a person's sexual pleasure.

If, as a child, someone had painful experiences with sex (e.g., being caught at sex play and punished), it is understandable that sex might come to be associated with fear and shame. A surprising number of women and men have been molested as children, and now, as adults, they naturally have mixed feelings and are confused about their sexuality. Some people feel guilty about sex because of religious training. Others, who have learned to be self-critical, are anxious and insecure about their physical desirability to others.

Then, too, there are all those people who grew up with parents who were dissatisfied with their lives, and, fight it though they may, they absorbed attitudes and behaviors consistent with a life of struggle and suffering. Even when their parents' troubles were real and their own lives are more blessed, these people now tend to have a negative, rather than a positive, view of things. One of the most profound ways of resisting pleasure is to devalue it, to associate reality with pain and to see pleasure merely as escape.

But the culture as a whole tends to foster pleasure resistance by undermining pleasure's worth, by valuing sacrifice and pain as character building, and by relegating the taking of pleasure to the realm of selfishness and self-indulgence. Whatever our personal beliefs may be, the larger cultural code of values and ethics still prescribes strict control over pure enjoyment, especially when it comes to sex. All of us learn to resist pleasure in the course of growing up and acquiring self-control. At the very least, there are times when the fulfillment of what is most desired must be postponed. To live in a congenial society naturally requires that we all learn to control our impulses.

But too often, people become overcontrolled and come to fear what they enjoy the most. Instead of acknowledging their desires, they renounce them as weaknesses. They can become critical of themselves for their food preferences, their vocational interests, and the people they are sexually attracted to, as well as whatever it is that piques their sexual appetite. They equate self-control and morality with self-denial. In so doing, they become deprived and undernourished, robbing themselves of their full measure of life's joys.

Wilhelm Reich, the Austrian psychiatrist who was Freud's student and associate, was probably the first major theorist to suggest that because of early sex-negative training, pleasure becomes associated with guilt and shame, and an individual may come to fear and resist pleasure. That means that when such a person is in a situation that generates good feelings, he or she may fear losing control and doing something shameful. To safeguard against that possibility, a person who resists pleasure will often tense rather than relax the body in a potentially pleasurable situation, making sensual and sexual abandonment virtually impossible.

Pleasure resistance can be observed in someone who becomes superstitious every time something good happens, as though any minute the other shoe is going to drop. Feeling obligated to fulfill other people's expectations rather than one's own needs and desires is another typical way to hold back from taking pleasure. Whenever a man, for example, has a tendency to expect the worst to befall him, or a woman, no matter how good she is toward others, finds herself consistently running internal tapes of self-recrimination and guilt, there is a denial of the pleasurable possibilities of that moment. At the very least, each could enjoy a better frame of mind and a lighter heart.

When we look into the physiological effects of pleasure and its linkage with good health, we see how crucial it is to give up this resistance to pleasure that most of us share to some degree because of our earliest sexual experiences—even in these supposedly hedonistic modern times.

Pleasures of Sex

Usually, good sex involves some combination of these basic ingredients: physical arousal, emotional involvement, eroticism, sex play, orgasm, and, at its best, the opportunity to explore one's erotic potential. The physiology of sexual excitement in both men and women depends on the ability of blood to flow into the genital glands and into the supporting tissues and muscles of the pelvis.

It is the full engorgement of blood in the muscles and tissues of the pelvis that eventually triggers orgasm. One reason that women in general may be slower to orgasm than men is because they have a far more complex system of arteries, veins, and capillaries in the pelvic area than men do that must be fully engorged for orgasm to occur.

A person who feels uncomfortable with his or her sexuality will unconsciously tense the muscles in the genitals, thighs, anus, and buttocks, preventing the free flow of blood into the area and thereby limiting the possibility for complete arousal. But a person who can relax and allow energy in the form of blood to flow into the pelvic area and genitals will enjoy the sensations of building excitement.

The sex center of the brain is in the limbic system, an area of the central nervous system that is also involved in emotional reactions, such as anger and fear, and in regulating homeostasis by monitoring such functions as body temperature, blood sugar, blood pressure, and heart rate. The limbic system also contains centers that are specifically associated with pleasure. While research on neural activity and sex is only in its preliminary stages, there is some evidence showing that during sex these pleasure centers are stimulated. It is also likely that sexual activity releases endorphins, the body's own opiates, which trigger feelings of euphoria. These are the same chemicals released during physical exercise and are responsible for what has been called "runner's high."

The Connection Between Pleasure and Health.

New research by medical biologists, neurologists, nurses, psychologists, and sociologists on immunity has provided strong evidence that pleasurable experiences and states of mind can have a highly positive effect on health. This field of study, known as psychoneuroimmunology (PNI), has shown that such diverse events as having faith, listening to music, getting massaged, daydreaming about a loved one, having a view of trees from one's hospital bed rather than a brick wall, caring for a pet, and doing a good deed all have been associated with better resistance to disease, better recovery from illness, and longer life. Sex, as one of life's greatest pleasures, obviously belongs on that list.

However, the connection between sex and health has not been well documented. Ornstein and Sobel suggest that a strong bias exists in the scientific literature against studying any kind of pleasure and that pain and pathology have always dominated medical research. But this bias particularly holds for sex. Thousands upon thousands of studies, articles, and books have been written on sexual dysfunction and on the hazards of sex, but hardly anything has been done to examine the benefits of sexual pleasure.

Nevertheless, Ornstein and Sobel do report on research that shows that pheromones (hormones released in perspiration) given off by a man and inhaled by a woman can help to regulate a woman's menstrual cycle, and that regular sex play in the postmenopausal woman helps in preventing tissue loss in the vagina. Studies reported by Alexander Lowen also show that for both men and woman, emotional satisfaction during sex and coronary health are also related.

Sex is a complex activity and, when broken down into its components, there is plenty of evidence that gratifying sex is healthy. If touch, play, loving feelings, sensual delight, physical exercise, stress reduction, and feeling capable of satisfying one's needs are all associated with an enhanced immune system and greater longevity, as they are, then the same can be said of good sex, which contains all these elements.

Emotional Involvement

Love

The most treasured events in our lives are those that are accompanied by strong positive emotion. Positive feelings are expansive; they impel us forward to reach out for contact and connection. The more love, gratitude, enthusiasm, and joy that is present in a situation, the more meaningful and memorable the event. Many people feel that their most profound pleasures during sex occur when they and their partners feel especially loving toward one another.

Lowen, a student of Reich and founder of bioenergetic analysis, cites research demonstrating that failure to experience emotional satisfaction during sex can adversely affect the heart. In two separate studies of female and male patients hospitalized for heart attacks, nearly two-thirds of each group had significantly more dissatisfaction or problems with sex in the months just prior to the attacks than did a group of controls with no coronary disease. Lowen suggests that when orgasm occurs in combination with a heartfelt emotional response of love, a person's sex life can contribute to a strong and healthy heart.

Intimacy

Intimacy is often considered to be one of the most enjoyable features of positive sexual contact. It is said that a woman needs intimacy to feel sexual, and a man needs sex to feel intimate. Either way, there is no doubt that sexual intimacy, especially when it is fulfilling, forges a strong bond between lovers. It is probably this potential for giving one another great pleasure, as well as the tendency for satisfying sexual contact to encourage self-disclosure, that accounts for the bonding power of a good sexual relationship.

Affectionate Touch

When loving feelings fuel sexual desire, there can be no doubt that a major part of that excitement is being stimulated by the tremendous pleasure people derive from affectionate touch. From the moment of birth, the neonate, the toddler, the child, and the teen, as well as the adult require loving, empathic touch to feel good about themselves and about life in general.

Montague, in his classic book on touching, reports that infants raised in orphanages at the turn of the 19th century who were hardly ever picked up and held died of a disease known as infant marasmus, literally meaning "wasting away." They simply lost interest in living.

Today, prematurely born infants who are handled and stroked three times a day for several weeks can gain as much as 50 percent more weight and leave the hospital as many as six days earlier than their unstroked counterparts. Stroked babies not only were more alert and responsive but also maintained their growth advantage in follow-up studies more than eight months later.

Loving touch is an essential nutrient for healthy living, not just for babies but for adults as well. Ornstein and Sobel report one study where patients with chronic anxiety and muscular tension were treated to ten sessions of deep massage. Physiological measurements taken after each massage often showed a slower heart rate and less muscular tension than before the massage. Many said they felt less distressed and had less need for their medication. Another study showed that patients recovering from heart attacks who live alone but have pets (literally, creatures we enjoy petting) live longer than heart patients without pets.

A person does not have to be in a state of chronic anxiety to benefit from the elixir of empathic touch. Ordinary living, with its everyday stresses, temporary crises, and personal challenges is enough to trigger fear, doubt, and a host of other contracting kinds of feelings. One of the great pleasures of passionate lovemaking is that there is a lot of hugging, kissing, stroking, and squeezing that does not only serve sexual needs but also serves the body's hunger for physical contact. Some people who are touch deprived may have sex when they really only want to be touched. Yet the most pleasurable sexual experiences come when the touching not only expresses caring but also sparks genuine sexual desire.

Angry Passion

However, sometimes it is not love, intimacy, or affection that intensifies sexual passion, but anger. A couple may find that some of their most exciting lovemaking occurs after they have had a screaming match. They may rage furiously at one another, yell at the top of their lungs, chase each other around the house, stomp their feet, flail their arms, and maybe even throw things that perilously whiz by their heads. Then suddenly, someone says something that the other interprets as loving or apologetic, and the fight is resolved. They kiss, perhaps gingerly at first, and make up.

Only the kiss lingers, and more kisses follow as the intensity of the anger becomes transmuted into sexual excitement. It makes sense that this would happen, since the heat of anger, with its rapid heart beat and adrenalized activation level, shares some powerful similarities with the state of sexual arousal. Within seconds, and overcome with desire, the couple, reinterpreting their emotional response, fling themselves down wherever they happen to be and lose themselves in wildly passionate lovemaking.

There is a danger, however, that a couple can become addicted to turmoil to pump up their sexual passion. Naturally, any kind of compulsivity around sex ultimately will cause more pain than pleasure. Eventually, the constant drama grows stale. When people depend on an angry routine to become aroused, they may be able to temporarily enjoy intense sexual passion, but the abuse they suffer together militates against the possibility of having any kind of loving relationship.

Eroticism

The erotic is anything that arouses sexual desire and heightens sexual excitement. This can involve activities that a person does alone or with others; it can be a state of mind or a heightened emotional state; it can be a personal invention or it can involve literature, art, or film. Some of the more popular ways of stimulating the pleasures of the erotic imagination are briefly explored below.

Sensuality

Everything we know of the world comes through our five senses. We either see it, hear it, smell it, taste it, or touch it, and that is known as sensory reception. Sensuality involves those same senses, but instead of merely receiving the data, we take delight in it; we linger over the stimulation and are drawn in by its beauty and the pleasure it gives.

Erotic sensuality involves engaging each sense to augment sexual arousal. Seeing certain body parts, such as firm breasts on a woman or the rounded muscular buttocks of a man, or seeing a person in certain items of clothing like black stockings and a garter belt on a woman or bikini briefs on a man, can be very erotically arousing. Lovers may enjoy the voyeuristic pleasure of watching sexually explicit videotapes or looking at sexy magazines together—typically considered either erotica or pornography, depending on whether one is for or against it. They may enjoy performing before the impersonal "eye" of a video camera for a tape only they will see.

Voyeurism, exhibitionism, even fetishism (investing certain objects with sexual meaning, such as high heeled shoes, and incorporating them into sex play) are problems only when they keep people from having satisfying sex with desirable partners. These can also be ways in which normal, healthy people can playfully heighten their sexual arousal with consenting partners.

Hearing certain sounds during a sexual encounter—such as the raspy sighs and moans of one's lover—certainly can add excitement. Erotic smell can be the most evocative of all the senses, not only in terms of sheer animal arousal but also because pheromones may draw individuals to one another in much the same way as a male dog is drawn to a female dog in heat. Taste is erotic when the mouth drinks in the lover's kisses and body flavors.

Touch has almost become synonymous with eroticism, in the quality of pleasure people experience in the long, slow strokes of a caress and during mutual fondling and embracing. Partners can become proficient at giving each other an erotic massage, where they learn to stimulate each other's bodies with their hands, fingers, or mouths in ways specifically geared to arouse their partner's passions.

Fantasy

To fantasize about sex is to daydream about sexual scenarios, usually because desire has already been aroused but sometimes with the intent of increasing desire. A fantasy can involve imagined activities that a person has never done but may at some time like to try out in reality, such as having oral sex with a new lover. It can be a mental movie of something that would be very unpleasant if it were to happen, such as a rape, but in fantasy, for reasons usually related to one's earliest sexual history, these images trigger sexual arousal. Sometimes people relive in their mind's eye particularly exciting past sexual encounters, and the vivid recall of the details of the past event feeds a present sexual encounter.

Sexual fantasy can be a handy boost to any erotic activity, whether it be masturbation or sex play with a partner. A pleasant sex reverie can even provide a brief, energizing respite from routine with none of the negative side effects of caffeine or candy bars. When people feel troubled that they are spending too much time in fantasy, it is usually because they are dreaming but not acting on their needs, or if they have a partner, they are not expressing to him or her these feelings and desires. But if one's lover is amenable, rather than creating distance a sexual fantasy may be shared in a way that is arousing for both partners and brings them closer together.

Romance

The term "romance" originally comes from the literature written about the adventures of the knights and ladies of the court during the Middle Ages. Modern romance is a kind of commonly held fantasy that flows through our culture and titillates through a variety of fanciful tributaries. The cultural myth etched into our collective unconscious and from which most contemporary scenarios are derived is the medieval saga of the desirable, though unattainable, damsel in distress who is rescued by the powerful male on horseback who can slay dragons.

As a genre, romance novels embellish on this basic story line. They are usually long-drawn-out scenarios of lovers yearning for one another but separated by circumstance, fate, or geography—usually at least until the final few pages of the book. Romantic illusion, on the other hand, seems to have more to do with idealizing a person to whom one is very sexually attracted and then imagining him or her to be perfect in every other way as well. Disillusionment in this case, though painful at first, is typically seen to be a good thing, particularly if the relationship is strong enough to survive the reality check.

Everyday romance, of course, does not have to be quite so dramatic and can add greatly to sexual ardor. Unfortunately for many couples, there seems to be some inherent gender differences in what constitutes romance. When women yearn for their men to be romantic, typically it has to do with being treated as special. Traditionally, women are portrayed as enjoying a gift of flowers or some other token symbolic of sweetness, or being taken to a pretty public place, dimly lit is usually preferable, where the two of them can seclude themselves in a private corner and only have eyes for each other. By most accounts, men do not share the same romantic scenario. For them, boats and mountains and lovemaking in parkas tend to figure more prominently.

Resistance Anticipation

Nothing adds lust to sex better than having to surmount some obstacle to get there. Whatever the impediment, having to work hard to achieve some reward not only provides time for fantasy to operate but also builds in the necessary delay between arousal of interest and attainment of the goal to foment anticipation and appetite.

Tripp has suggested that the highest erotic excitement occurs in those very relationships where it has not all been worked out, and that it is the separateness between lovers that makes for "high" romance. In fact, it appears that a certain amount of resistance and distance are necessary for sexual attraction to occur and to remain. When these factors are not present in a relationship, as when there is too much familiarity and too much taking things for granted, the erotic component of the relationship often suffers.

Pain as an Aphrodisiac

Pain may be emotional, as in guilt, shame, humiliation, and feelings of powerlessness, or pain may be physical, as in being spanked or whipped. Either way, sexually nondisruptive levels of pain can induce a state of physiological excitation that can have an additive effect on sexual arousal—as well as provide juicy plots to intensify emotional involvement.

Morin has suggested that sexual arousal is most intense when there is a strong attraction to a person and one or more barriers stand in the way of attaining that person. The pain of longing for someone hard to get or feeling anxious about the encounter can make for some of the most intense feelings of desire and for highly explosive sex when they do get together.

Sometimes, a more complex linkage between shame and sexual arousal causes intense arousal when two people play out sexual scenarios that involve power games of dominance and submission. The dangers in this kind of behavior lie in making oneself a target for abusive behavior. Masochistic people can get hurt by sadistic partners. They may feel depressed and ashamed of their sadomasochistic encounters, become obsessed with the activity when they are not engaging in it, and feel generally out of control. These conditions do not make for much ongoing pleasure.

Certain people, however, seem capable of gratifying their taste for emotionally complex scenarios in playful, nonabusive ways and with consenting partners. Under carefully controlled conditions, these unique sexual desires need not be disruptive of a person's life and, for such a person, may be considered to be a genuine source of sexual pleasure.

Forbiddenness

Here, the major element of the situation that can arouse intense excitement is the violation of some moral precept or personal pledge. Naturally, some of the aphrodisiac qualities of overcoming obstacles or feeling anxious or ashamed may also apply here. But the main characteristic that builds erotic intensity is that, above all else, it is considered "bad." Violating a taboo may be a part of the appeal when a married person engages in infidelity, especially when sex in the marriage has grown stale and routine.

The association of forbiddenness with intensification of desire is unavoidable in our society as long as childhood sexuality is prohibited and children caught in sexual activity are humiliated and punished. Even though the reproductive system does not mature until puberty, the sexual system begins to function even in utero, and males can get erections and females can lubricate from birth on. Infantile and childhood sexuality is a fact of life, and sex play occurs in children from every culture in the world. Yet adults in our society still tend to respond to a child's sexual interest with discomfort and sexually repressive discipline.

When hiding and defying authority are paired with the intense sexual arousal that often characterizes early sexual exploration in our culture, these qualities become part of the building blocks in our sexual development. Forbidden fruit tastes the sweetest because that is what we cut our teeth on. There is something very exciting about being rebellious and self-assertive that comes with secretive sex. For some people, engaging in forbidden sex is one of the few ways they assert themselves, even if the taboo act remains covert.

Novelty, Adventure, Challenge

There can be no doubt that sexual activity that becomes too familiar and repetitious loses its ability to arouse. The sensory system responds mostly to change, and when stimulation is too constant, we adapt to it and turn off. Again, this is true for all kinds of activity, whether it is mental stimulation we seek or sexual. We are most turned on by new thoughts, new ways of doing things, places to explore we have never been to before, situations that call on us to find and test our personal resources and capabilities and which, ultimately, bring out the best in us.

This makes for enthusiasm at work, in sports, in a relationship, and certainly during sex.

Some situations can always be counted on to produce novelty, adventure, and challenge. New lovers who are also off limits are sure things. Sneaking off for a quickie in a semipublic place, such as in the bathroom of a friend's home during a party, also has a certain romantic and rebellious appeal. No-strings sex, sex that does not lead to long-term commitment, may be erotic, because it is the very absence of emotional entanglement that allows some people to focus on and revel in their own pleasure. But when people become dependent on novelty scenarios to stay interested in sex, eventually this, too, can grow boring. Even novelty can become repetitive and grow stale.

However, if two people can create sexual adventure in a long-term relationship, where they can explore all the variations on a sexual theme of physical arousal, emotional arousal, and eroticism, including a variety of different kinds of sex play and orgasms, this could be the most sexually adventurous opportunity of all. Of course, this is not easy because our cultural bias is that excitement and commitment do not quite go together. But when a committed relationship is not exciting, it is usually because one or both partners is playing it safe and withholding feelings with the other just to keep the peace.

Sometimes, it can be exciting to reveal one's secret likes and dislikes to one's partner. Speaking up about one's unique sexual desires is one way people can take some personal risks with one another. In fact, being self-assertive can itself intensify excitement in any relationship. It feels good to ask for what you want or to give yourself permission to say no to something undesired.

A loving relationship that is pleasure supportive is stimulating because it means people have the courage to say what they want, particularly about sex. In a number of surveys, people who said they felt sexually satisfied in their marriage were also more likely to rate their overall satisfaction in the relationship as high. When two people who love each other are available to travel unexplored sexual terrain and to feel the exhilaration of being sexually free and open with one another, their commitment to sexual fidelity is not likely to feel limiting or restrictive.

Sex Play

Usually, the more intense the arousal prior to orgasm, the more exquisite the pleasure of orgasm. Skillful sex play has an important role in the physical, emotional, and erotic build up of excitement that contributes to generating powerful orgasmic release. Sex play can be solitary, as in masturbation; it can involve pleasurable activity with a partner that does not include penetration—what is often called foreplay; or sex play can include intercourse. The essential features of the contact are not in who does what to whom but in the more important elements of what constitutes play.

Sex play, like any other kind of play, is activity that is intrinsically rewarding. That means it is engaged in for its own sake, because it is pleasurable, and not as a means to some other end. Usually, play involves opportunities to be expressive, energetic, and imaginative. Being absorbed in the events of the moment and experiencing the activity as effortless, even though one may expend a great deal of energy, is a big part of what causes a deep sense of enjoyment.

Sex play during masturbation involves not just rushing through the experience to trigger orgasm but taking time to fully arouse oneself and, in this way, achieve a more gratifying release. Dodson argued that masturbation is a wonderful way for people to discover their own eroticism and to become more proficient at sex with or without a partner. She considers skillful masturbation to be "a meditation on self-love" and recommends that people set up an erotic setting, just for themselves, with soft lights and music, to give themselves greater pleasure.

Sex play with a partner, whether or not it leads to intercourse, involves taking the time to luxuriate in the sensations of the activity. To maximize the pleasures of sex play, it takes two people whose only goal is to enjoy one another. It means not just aiming for orgasm but rather taking delight in, and being fully absorbed by, the events of the moment.

Erotic Potential

There is no reason to assume any automatic ceiling to the amount of sexual pleasure a person is capable of experiencing over a lifetime. Many of us, at different times in our lives, have had sexual experiences that were singularly outstanding and enormously pleasurable. These peak erotic experiences have the right combination of physical, emotional, and erotic elements that make them intensely arousing: the lovers are "hot" for each other, the sex play is inspired, and the orgasms nearly cosmic. But instead of seeing these as rare and fortuitous events, they can also be considered signposts of what is possible in erotic pleasure.

In fact, it is very likely that most people have a potential for erotic enjoyment that they have hardly approached in their lifetime. Schnarch has suggested that probably few people come close to achieving their sexual potential, and those who do are most often in their 50s and even 60s. Aging, rather than inevitably leading to a decline in sexual pleasure, can actually provide the experience and relaxed attitude necessary to reach the heights of erotic ecstasy.

In the same way that Hartman and Fithian's male clients were able to learn how to have multiple orgasms, and women who have never had an orgasm can learn to achieve one, all of us can continually push our sexual limits. There is apparently a whole world of pleasure out there in orgasm that most people have yet to explore (see orgasm and multi-orgasm). Enjoying masturbation and exploring one's erotic potential in solitary pleasuring can be one very effective way of being more sexually experimental. Having a committed relationship can also facilitate this kind of experimentation. Sexual playmates who love and trust one another certainly can provide opportunities for themselves to safely explore their erotic potential together.

What is important is to recognize that pleasurable experiences are essential to health, to the quality of life, and to the quality of our relationships. The more we enjoy ourselves and each other, and the more gratified and fulfilled we feel, the more energy we have not only to realize our own dreams but to nurture and support the dreams of the people we love.

REFERENCES

Calderone, M. Above and Beyond Politics: The Sexual Socialization of Children. In C.S. Vance, ed., *Pleasure and Danger*. London: Pandora Press, 1989.

Cassell, C. *Swept Away*. New York: Fireside, 1989.

Csikszentmihalyi, M. *Flow: The Psychology of Optimal Experience*. New York: Harper & Row, 1990.

Dodson, B. *Sex for One*. New York: Harmony, 1987.

Field, T.M., S.M. Schanberg, R. Scaldi, C.R. Bauer, N. Vega-Lahr, R. Garcia, J. Nystom, and C.M. Kuhn. Tactile/Kinesthetic Stimulation Effects on Preterm Neonates. *Pediatrics*, Vol. 77 (1986), pp. 654–658.

Hartman, W.E., and M.A. Fithian. *Any Man Can*. New York: St. Martin's Press, 1984.

Klein, M. *Your Sexual Secrets*. New York: Dutton, 1988.

Lowen, A. *Love, Sex, and Your Heart*. New York: Macmillan, 1988.

Masters, W.H., and V.E. Johnson. *Human Sexual Response*. Boston: Little, Brown, 1966.

Money, J. *Lovemaps*. Buffalo, N.Y.: Prometheus Books, 1988.

Montagu, A. *Touching: The Human Significance of the Skin*. New York: Harper & Row, 1986.

Morin, J. The Four Cornerstones of Eroticism. In D. Steinberg, ed., *The Erotic Impulse: Honoring the Sexual Self*. Los Angeles: Tarcher, 1992.

Ornstein, R., and D. Sobel. *Healthy Pleasures*. New York: Addison-Wesley, 1989.

Reich, W. *The Function of the Orgasm*. Translated by T.P. Wolfe. New York: Orgone Institute Press, 1942.

Reiss, I.L. *Journey into Sexuality: An Exploratory Voyage*. Englewood Cliffs, N.J.: Prentice Hall, 1986.

Schnarch, D. *Constructing the Sexual Crucible*. New York: W.W. Norton, 1991.

Stubbs, K.R., with L.-A. Saulnier. *Erotic Massage: The Touch of Love*. San Francisco: Secret Garden, 1989.

Tripp, C.A. *The Homosexual Matrix*. New York: Meridian, 1987.

Stella Resnick

—Adapted from the forthcoming book *As Good As It Gets*, to be published by Jeremy P. Tarcher, Inc., a member of the Putnam Berkley Publishing Group.

POLITICAL THEORY: SEX AND POLITICAL THEORY

Sex constitutes a basic need among human beings and a biologically founded category. Historically, political theorists have sought to provide overarching, normatively based explanations for politics that take into account all significant aspects of human existence. From the Book of Genesis in the Bible to contemporary history of ideas, thinkers about politics have included discussions of sex in their treatises defining what politics should be.

Ancient literature is full of sexual symbols, from Plato's cave (representing the womb) to the ever-present sea shells (representing the female genitalia) to the variety of objects representing the phallus. Gender roles and differences are clear. In the epic poems of Homer, the role of the female is housekeeping, motherhood, and faithfulness to the husband. The 19th-century U.S. women's movement theorist Elizabeth Cady Stanton argued in her *Woman's Bible* (1898) that interested parties used the Old and New Testaments alike to prescribe a predestined place in society for females, a place that was far more limited than that for males.

Recent scholarship, in reinterpreting this past, has tended to give new dimensions to the female role. For example, the narratives in Genesis have recently been interpreted as giving women certain social rights, which males in the patriarchy then recognized and to which they consented.

Ancient writers also recognized, at least sometimes, that women would act different if their role in life was different. In the *Ecclesiazusae* (Congress of Women), Aristophanes emphasized that where women had to act as men, they became concerned with private gain, something that a woman was not supposed to do. In Genesis, Sarah, the mother of nations, upholds the law of Mesopotamia in her dealing with the handmaid Hagar. Centuries later (1986), the Canadian author Margaret Atwood, in her *Handmaid's Tale*, projected an unstable, bureaucratically specialized society in which sex role followed function and awareness was ironic and dangerous.

The French theorist Jean-Jacques Rousseau (1712–1778), in *Émile*, explored means by which to obtain the inner tendencies of females and males before their advent in society. He arrived at two conflicting systems of education: the public, which was common to man, and the private or domestic, the female one. "That man is truly free who desires [needs] what he is able to perform, and does what he desires [needs]." Males, Rousseau found, were fitted for consultation on morals and comprehension, the public sphere, while females for consultation on the body and senses, the private sphere. The two differed, though, only in their sex, which was complementary; difficulty lay, Rousseau stated, in determining where sex mattered.

In *The Vindication of the Rights of Women,* Rousseau's contemporary, the English theorist Mary Wollstonecraft (1759–1797), said she differed from Rousseau in that he held that originally everything was all right, while she showed that everything eventually would be all right. Both political theorists emphasized experiential content in the good education; Wollstonecraft, however, also assumed and explicated critical reason in females, assuring her readers that development of this capacity to understand led to the ready assumption of obligation. By comparison, she held, Rousseau sooner would yoke or compel women to do what they needed to do, that is, to become free through the social order and civil liberty.

Wollstonecraft agreed that the environment was not favorable to females but found in its unfavorability compulsion toward civilization's more perfect end. Women would become free when they submitted to reason. Rousseau, by contrast, sought submission to the general will as represented in the social contract. Wollstonecraft lamented the precipitate events of the French Revolution, events that had followed upon otherwise magnanimous conduct, and cast her lot with systematically managed reform.

In *The Origins of the Family, Private Property and the State,* Frederick Engels (1820–1895), the colleague of Karl Marx, did not take as obligatory a relationship between sex and social order. By tracing the evolution from a matrilineal society, or mother right, to primogeniture, or father right, Engels concluded that civilized society's basis in monogamous marriage confined women to private domestic labor. Economics, rather than mutual inclination, determined a woman's choice of a husband, and sexual inequality had emerged during the evolution of a private property–based system. Abolition of contractual relations, including those associated with sex, and women's access to socially productive labor, would be accomplished but only through increasing violence, a manifestation of the contradictions in capitalism's production mode that the state had proven unable to moderate.

The American Charlotte Perkins Gilman (1860–1935) did not adhere to Engels's deterministic view of change, although, along with him, she found in technology an important spur to sexual adaptation. In *Women and Economics: A Study of the Economic Relations Between Women and Men as a Factor in Social Evolution*, Gilman attributed the change in unequal economic relationships between women and men to the development of human social tendencies. Gilman argued that woman first became modified when man acted upon her economic environment; this segregation rendered motherhood pathological. Man also became modified, or at least his destructive force was, by existing in sexual-economic relationships with woman.

Women, nonetheless, moved toward more complex social relations in their recognition of the sexes' specialization and differentiation. "Sweet union of the family group," Gilman contended in *The Home: Its Work and Influence*, required that the mother become engaged actively in work for human progress. This meant that the domestic class had to become socialized, and only self-conscious human beings, living on a plane of separate industry (i.e., in "a personal home") achieved the necessary personality or social evolution associated with collective action.

Despite the institutionalization of technology, science, and law in the 20th century, there was little revolutionary thinking about the social roles of females and males. "The constancy of sex," as Oakley calls it, has remained the source of inquiry about differences between women and men. The study of difference and of inheritance represents one and the same thing, with claims about nature infused with assumptions about normality and deviance. This infusion might well mark an adaptation stimulated by the demands of preindustrial capitalism. Some approaches to this subject, such as sociobiology or biopolitics, tap into a tradition extending back to Plato and treat nature as a conventionally feminine, innate motive.

In *The Second Sex*, Simone de Beauvoir (1908–1986), a French author of the existential school, found women's civil liberties to be imminently theoretical and lacking in economic freedom. In her view, transcendence to reciprocal relations with men gave rise to authenticity in women. She found, however, all too much emphasis on the future and not enough on women's situation in the here and now.

More recently, the French theorist Michel Foucault (1926–1984) found in the subjectivity of modern discourse on rights, among other things, a treacherous form of power called normalization. For Foucault, categorization, grading and monitoring by sex, economics, history, and so on have generated limitations through essentialism. Deconstruction of the subject, an archeological-genealogical task, will reveal that there is no more a "nature" of human beings than there is unlimited freedom. Spurning modernism and transcendence, Foucault spoke to the creation of humanity as a kind of aesthetic, public acting-through-struggle against nonconsensuality. This struggle goes on unendingly in a regulation-oriented society.

A victim of AIDS (acquired immune deficiency syndrome), Foucault left unexplained the possibilities for the collective action he intended; feminist and other theorists also have lamented the failure in Foucault to include gender as a category to clarify issues about differences between the sexes. There remains as well the difficulty inherent in coping with the conflicting needs for constraint and opportunity in order to reconceptualize sex and political life.

Whether in Aristotle's assumption-laden hierarchy and defense of Homer's masculine limitations on women, or in Sabine's *History of Political Theory*, in which a discussion of social class in the Greek city-state never admits to women's existence, mainstream political theory has tended to celebrate manly virtue. In short, males and masculine values have dominated among theorists, even if only by default. Lost in the discussion was the brilliance of Pericles's adviser Aspasia; Mary Wollstonecraft was eclipsed by Tom Paine, and the significance of Charlotte Perkins Gilman, long forgotten. John Locke's relationship with Damaris Cudworth Masham and her influence on his ideas have been the subject of only a few discussions. A major exception is John Stuart Mill's admission of debt to his wife, Harriet Taylor, but current theorists such as Susan Moller Okin have adopted the position that Mill's enrapt perception of Taylor's abilities distorted reality somewhat; and Okin speculates on his discomfort with her advocacy of women's separate, independent existence.

The net result becomes what the feminist theologian Daly has called "the morality of victimization." The U.S. poet and essayist Rich has urged a restructuring of sensibility, to emphasize more feminine concerns such as an ethic of care, which would revolutionize interpretations of relationships between the sexes. MacKinnon, in her examination of the role of power in social relations, has concluded that sexuality and gender are all about power and that the power relationship has traditionally been defined in male terms. She believes that a political transformation is in order. Critics of MacKinnon, such as Wendy Brown, hold that her analysis is harsh and uncompromising and that there needs to be a reconceptualization of the concept of "obligation." For the present, sex and political theory remains dominated by male terminology and theorists.

REFERENCES

Atwood, M. *The Handmaid's Tale.* New York: Fawcett Crest, 1985.

Beauvoir, S. *The Second Sex.* Translated by E.M. Parshley. New York: Knopf, 1953.

Bordo, S. The Cartesian Masculinization of Thought. *Signs,* Vol. 11 (Spring 1986), pp. 450–62.

Bullough, V.L., B. Shelton, and S. Slavin. *The Subordinated Sex.* Athens: Univ. of Georgia Press, 1988.

Butler, M.A. Early Liberal Roots of Feminism: John Locke and the Attack on Patriarchy. *American Political Science Review,* Vol. 72 (March 1978), pp. 135–50.

Daly, M. *Beyond God the Father: Toward a Philosophy of Women's Liberation.* Boston: Beacon Press, 1973.

DiStefano, C. Dilemmas of Difference: Feminism, Modernity, and Postmodernism. *Women and Politics,* Vol. 8 (Summer-Fall 1988), pp. 1–24.

Elshtain, J.B. *Public Man, Private Woman: Women in Social and Political Thought.* Princeton, N.J.: Princeton Univ. Press, 1981.

Engels, F. *The Origins of the Family, Private Property and the State.* 1902. Reprint. New York: International, 1972.

Foucault, M. *The History of Sexuality.* Vol. 1, *An Introduction.* New York: Vintage, 1980.

Gilman, C.P. *The Home: Its Work and Influence.* 1903. Reprint. Urbana: Univ. of Illinois Press, 1972.

———. *Women and Economics: The Economic Factor, Men and Women as a Factor in Social Evolution.* Boston: Maynard, 1898.

MacKinnon, C. *Toward a Feminist Theory of the State.* Cambridge, Mass.: Harvard Univ. Press, 1989.

Oakley, A. *Sex, Gender, and Society.* New York: Harper Colophon, 1972.

————. *Woman's Work: The Housewife, Past and Present.* New York: Harper Colophon, 1972.

Okin, S.M. *Women in Western Political Thought.* Princeton, N.J.: Princeton Univ. Press, 1979.

Rich, A. *Of Woman Born: Motherhood as Experience and Institution.* New York: W.W. Norton, 1976.

Rossi, A. Preface. In A.S. Rossi, ed., *Essays on Sex Equality: John Stuart Mill and Harriet Taylor Mill.* Chicago: Univ. of Chicago Press, 1970.

Rousseau, J.-J. *Émile.* Translated by B. Foxley. 1762. Reprint. New York: Dutton, 1911.

Sabine, G.H. *History of Political Theory.* New York: Holt, Rinehart & Winston, 1961.

Schramm, S.S. *Plow Women Rather Than Reapers: An Intellectual History of Feminism in the United States.* Metuchen, N.J.: Scarecrow, 1979.

Stanton, E. *The Woman's Bible.* 2 vols., New York: European Publishing Co., 1895–98. Reprint. Seattle: Seattle Coalition Task Force on Women and Religion, 1974.

Tronto, J. Beyond Gender Differences to a Theory of Care. *Signs,* Vol. 12 (Fall 1987), pp. 644–63.

Wollstonecraft, M. *A Vindication of the Rights of Woman.* 1792. Reprint. New York: W.W. Norton, 1967.

Sarah Slavin

POLYANDRY

Polyandry ("poly" = "many"; "andry" = "men") is a rare polygamous form of marriage in which a woman is married to two or more men simultaneously. In Murdock's *Ethnographic Atlas* of 849 human cultures, 709 (83.5 percent) were polygynous (one man with two or more wives), 137 (16.1 percent) were monogamous (one man, one wife), and only 4 (0.047 percent) were polyandrous (i.e., Todas, Marquesans, Nayar, and Tibet). Polyandry is overwhelmingly, but not exclusively, fraternal—two or more brothers sharing the same wife. Polyandry is distinguished from the levirate system, the sometimes mandatory marriage of a widow to her dead husband's brother (the rule that so irked Onan who "spilled his seed upon the ground"), in that a woman is married to one or more brothers of her first husband at the same time. Polyandry is associated with extreme poverty and tends to occur in cultures that practice female infanticide, itself a function of extreme poverty. Such a situation leads to a surplus of males, for whom mates must be found.

All polyandrous cultures allow monogamous and polygynous marriages also. Among the Todas of southern India, where fraternal polyandry is practiced by the lower classes, it is not uncommon for the upper classes to practice polygyny, the opposite of polyandry. Other cultures, such as the Yanomama Shirishana of Brazil, have practiced intermittent polyandry during periods in which the sex ratio was severely unbalanced with an abundance of males, and certain native American tribes practiced "circumstantial" fraternal polyandry if an older married brother became disabled. The granting of sexual access to one's wife to siblings among some native American tribes has sometimes been mistaken for polyandry.

Polyandry and polygyny (one man, many women) should not be viewed as sexual mirror images. Sexual variety is undoubtedly a motivator (one among many others) for a man to take extra wives in polygynous cultures, and the choice to take on additional wives is his to make. Wives in cultures practicing fraternal polyandry have little or no say in the matter—if her husband has brothers, she is married to them also. Additionally, and unlike a wife in a polygynous culture, a polyandrously married male can choose to leave the marriage and take his own wife if his resources allow. Although the eldest brother in a polyandrous marriage is the dominant authority figure, each brother is supposed to enjoy equal sexual access to the wife. No sexual favoritism is supposed to occur, but numerous deviations from this ideal have been noted.

Polyandry has an economic rather than a sexual or status-prestige basis. A woman does not take on extra husbands for novel sexual pleasure, nor does the number of husbands she has confer any special status on her. Among the Todas, where there are often two males for every female, a situation further exacerbated by the polygyny of the upper classes, polyandry can be viewed largely as a function of a shortage of women.

However, such a shortage cannot explain the existence of polyandry in Tibet, the most populous polyandrous culture. Goldstein reports that 31 percent of women of childbearing age are unmarried there. Polyandry functions in Tibet in the same way that primogeniture functioned in former times in England, that is, to retain family lands intact. Just as primogeniture maintained family estates over the generations by permitting only one heir, fraternal polyandry accomplishes the same end by keeping brothers tied together with one wife and producing one set of heirs in each generation.

Polyandry has been viewed as a serious challenge to the sociobiological theory of parental investment in that it minimizes the reproductive fitness of its male practitioners (although it maxi-

467

mizes female reproductive fitness). It runs counter to the fundamental principle of evolutionary mating systems of male mammals, a principle which posits that the optimal male reproductive strategy is to maximize matings with as many partners as luck and ability allow. While some common gene transfer is assured in fraternal polyandry, there is certainly some reproductive sacrifice for each brother.

Polyandry is not considered a valued marriage form in the cultures where it is practiced in the same way that, say, monogamy is valued in the United States. It is one born out of harsh economic conditions or female shortages. As economic conditions improve in such cultures, there is a decline in polyandry in favor of monogamy or polygyny. Thus, as survivability becomes less problematic, humans come to conform more to the mating norms of other mammals and become either monogamous or polygynous. Symons views the rarity of polyandry, the harsh economic conditions under which it exists, and its decline when those conditions improve as evidence for panhuman differences in male and female approaches to reproduction and sexuality. We may consider polyandry as an ethnological curiosity destined for extinction.

REFERENCES

Beal, C.M., and M.C. Goldstein. Tibetan Fraternal Polyandry: A Test of Sociobiological Theory. *American Anthropologist,* Vol. 83 (1981), pp. 5–12.

Goldstein, M.C. When Brothers Share a Wife. *Natural History,* Vol. 96 (1987), pp. 38–49.

Murdock, G.P. *Ethnographic Atlas.* Pittsburgh: Univ. of Pittsburgh Press, 1967.

Peters, J.F., and C.H. Hunt. Polyandry Among the Yanomama Shirishana. *Journal of Comparative Family Studies,* Vol. 6 (1975), pp. 197–207.

Quale, G.R. *A History of Marriage Systems.* Westport, Conn.: Greenwood Press, 1988.

Symons, D. *The Evolution of Human Sexuality.* New York: Oxford Univ. Press, 1979.

Anthony Walsh

POLYGAMY

Polygamy is a general term for specific plural marriage forms in which one man is married to two or more women at the same time (polygyny), or one woman is married to two or more men at the same time (polyandry). Bigamy (one man or woman married to just two spouses) is also a form of polygamy. Any form of plural marriage in Western societies is forbidden by law, although polygyny is still practiced by many thousands of fundamentalist Mormons in Utah, Arizona, Ne-

vada, and California despite legal proscriptions and the 1890 ban on the practice by the Mormon Church. By far the most usual form of polygamous marriage is polygyny, so much so that the term "polygamy" is often erroneously used synonymously with polygyny. The prefix "poly-" means "many," and the suffix "-gamy" refers to a union for the purpose of reproduction. (See Polyandry and Polygyny.)

Anthony Walsh

POLYGYNY

Polygyny ("poly"="many"; "gyny"="women") is a polygamous form of marriage in which a man is married to two or more women simultaneously. In Murdock's Ethnographic Atlas of 849 human cultures, 709 (83.5 percent) were polygynous, 137 (16.1 percent) were monogamous (one man, one wife), and 4 (0.047 percent) were polyandrous (one woman married to two or more men). Many people incorrectly use the terms "polygyny" and "polygamy" interchangeably; polygamy is a general term for both polygyny and polyandry. Although most cultures are polygynous, most marriages, even within cultures allowing for polygyny, are monogamous.

Historical and anthropological evidence clearly shows that polygyny occurs mainly in the middle ranges of societal complexity, that is, in the agricultural stage between primitive communism and modern industrialism. Primitive communism was a cultural system in which everything, including sexual partners, was considered common property, or at least in which there was a strong expectation of liberal sharing. Primitive communism died out when cultures settled down in one place and started agricultural economies and when individuals started to think in terms of "this (land, food, woman) is mine." As with life's other amenities, the rich and powerful were able to grab more than their fair share of women.

Why would men dream up the institution of marriage, with all its psychological irritations, obligations, and restrictions? It was not to satisfy their erotic appetites, for marriage, even polygynous marriage, could not compete with earlier sexual communism as a method of gratifying the stirrings in the loins. Perhaps it was animated by the eugenic passion of high-born ancients for transmitting their superior abilities while minimizing the possibility of cuckoldry, by their desire to have cheap slaves, or by their desire to avoid bequeathing their property to progeny not carrying their genes. It may also have been that couples with a propensity to pair-bond (a propensity later formalized by the institution of marriage) increased the survivability of their offspring, thus exerting pressure for the selection of that trait into the human gene pool.

Once the idea of personal property began to take hold (and this would seem to be a very natural idea), men with property desired to protect it from men without it. One way of doing this is to surround the issue of ownership of women with the rites, rules, and regulations of marriage. Islam is the faith most supportive of polygyny, with the Koran permitting a Muslim four legal wives and as many concubines as he can properly support providing he shows all wives equal consideration. Recognizing the difficulties of living up to these provisos, polygyny is not encouraged within Islam as it was, say, among the early Mormons in the United States. Fewer than 10 percent of Muslim marriages are polygynous, and the trend is toward fewer and fewer as those countries develop more along industrial lines. The best estimate of its incidence among the early Mormons is also no more than 10 percent.

Is polygyny the "natural" state of affairs for males? Those of a sociobiological or biosocial persuasion believe that it is. The mammalian animal literature indicates the tendency for female harems to form around a single male in many species, but there is no evidence of the reverse. Sociobiologists see cultural evolution proceeding in concert with biological evolution; that is, culture values the same traits that lead to reproductive success. A corollary of this is that individuals will strive for culturally defined status positions because, ultimately, those positions maximize reproductive success and such behavior is biologically adaptive.

Culture, of course, is a compromise between natural inclinations and cultural proscriptions, but it is always the less privileged who do most of the compromising. One might say that the rich and powerful are freer than the rest of us to indulge their natural inclinations, whatever they may be. In cultures legally allowing for plural marriage, those at the top of the social hierarchy will seek multiple wives, both as a mark of their standing and to increase their reproductive success.

As a subculture with excellent records available, the early Mormons have been the target of many researchers seeking to test the sociobiological theory. These tests have tended to support the sociobiological interpretation, even placing religion in the evolutionary context of reproductive competition. For instance, Brigham Young rivaled King Solomon (reported to have

had 60 wives and 80 concubines) in the number of wives he took (53) and the number of offspring he sired (57), offspring who were called, as their status befits, "bodies of honor." All available evidence shows that polygyny is a perquisite of the privileged, that polyandry is not much more than wife sharing among the destitute, and that monogamy is an uneasy compromise between biological urges and cultural imperatives.

REFERENCES

Anderton, D.L., and R.J. Emigh. Polygynous Fertility: Sexual Competition Versus Progeny. *American Journal of Sociology*, Vol. 94 (1989), p. 839.

Breuer, G. *Sociobiology and the Human Dimension.* Cambridge: Cambridge Univ. Press, 1982.

Faux, F.S., and H.L. Miller. Evolutionary Speculations on the Oligarchic Development of Mormon Polygyny. *Ethology and Sociobiology,* Vol. 5 (1984), p. 21.

Mealey, L. The Relationship between Social Status and Biological Success: A Case Study of the Mormon Religious Hierarchy. *Ethology and Sociobiology*, Vol. 6 (1985), p. 249.

Mellen, S. *The Evolution of Love.* San Francisco: W.H. Freeman, 1983.

Murdock, G.P. *Ethnographic Atlas.* Pittsburgh: Univ. of Pittsburgh Press, 1967.

White, D.R., and M.L. Burton. Causes of Polygyny: Ecology, Economy, Kinship, and Warfare. *American Anthropologist,* Vol. 90 (1988), p. 871.

Anthony Walsh

POMEROY, WARDELL BAXTER

Wardell Baxter Pomeroy (1913–) is best known for his coauthorship of the first two Kinsey reports as well as special studies on sex offenders and on pregnancy, birth, and abortion. He served as director of field research at the Kinsey Institute for Sex Research from 1956 to 1963.

Born in Kalamazoo, Michigan, December 6, 1913, the son of Mary Adelia Baxter and Percy Wardell Pomeroy, he attended Indiana University, where he received a bachelor's degree in 1935 and a master's degree in 1941. He worked as a clinical psychologist at a mental hygiene clinic, then at the Indiana Reformatory, and was working at the Department of Public Welfare in South Bend, Indiana, when he first met Kinsey. He consented to Kinsey's taking his sex history and recruited others to give theirs. He organized an informal group of social workers to help Kinsey get information on sex offenders. In 1942, Pomeroy made a cautious approach to joining the Kinsey team, but the salary was unsatisfactory. He consented to join Kinsey early in 1943 on the condition that he be allowed to continue his studies toward a Ph.D., a degree he eventually received from Columbia University in 1952. At the Kinsey Institute, Pomeroy at first did mainly interviewing, and he estimated that of the 18,000 case histories compiled by Kinsey, about 85 percent were divided equally between Pomeroy and Kinsey.

When Pomeroy left the Institute in 1963, he moved to New York, where he opened an office as a psychotherapist. He remained active in sexology, both in his private practice and in his community activities. Pomeroy was a major force in the development of the Society for the Scientific Study of Sex. In 1976, he moved to San Francisco to become academic dean of the Institute for Advanced Studies in Human Sexuality and remained there until he retired at the end of the 1980s. In this capacity, he was influential in the training of several hundred sex counselors, therapists, and educators.

Pomeroy continued to write on sexual subjects, and in addition to his participation in four books associated with the Kinsey group, he also wrote two popular books dealing with boys and sex and girls and sex. He also wrote an account of his experiences at the Kinsey Institute.

Pomeroy married Catherine Sindlinger on September 4, 1937, and has three children, two sons and a daughter.

REFERENCES

Pomeroy, W.B. *Dr. Kinsey and the Institute for Sex Research.* New York: Harper & Row, 1972.

Vern L. Bullough

PORNOGRAPHY

History

Although pornography is of ancient vintage as a celebration of sex across diverse cultures, within Western culture antisexual ideology has led to a series of moral panics aimed at punishing all who engage in nonprocreative, nonmarital sexuality. In the 15th century, two Dominican monks, Jakob Sprenger and Heinrich Kramer, published *Malleus Mallificarum (The Witches Hammer).* This textbook of the Inquisition abominated witchcraft as a sexual form of heresy. This heresy, they said, not only renounced Christianity but also dedicated the body and soul to evil by acts of coitus with a demon—either a (male) incubus or a (female) succubus—and by sacrificing unbaptized infants to Satan. The demons were collecting souls and semen through sexual acts. According to Thomas Aquinas, these demons secured semen from men as a soul-seducing

succubus, changed form to become an incubus, then seduced and impregnated a woman, creating a monster (birth defects?) through the bad seed. To be possessed by Satan required a sexual act; thus, to save the soul, exorcism must torment the body to drive out Satan.

Witches were stripped naked to search for sexual stigmata (the marks of Satan in erotic zones), tortured to obtain confessions (including sexual torture, e.g., plunging a fiery sword into the vagina), and then punished by burning at the stake, either alive or dead. Deaths of women called witches numbered in the hundreds of thousands. This ideology linked sex, Satan, masturbation, bestiality, sodomy, adultery, incest, and child molesting. Still today, charges of satanism are hurled at lust murderers and child molesters, but the *Malleus Mallificarum* itself was the handbook of sexual torture. The inquisitors were the lust murderers; the witches (variously the insane or mentally disturbed, Jews who had converted to Christianity in Spain to avoid deportation, political enemies, religious heretics, and other misfortunates) were the victims of sexual sadism.

The 16th century created a different heresy for the Catholic Church to contain: the Protestant Reformation. During the Reformation, in 1562, the Council of Trent of the Catholic Church established the *Index of Prohibited Books.* Obscene books were included among the books on theology and witchcraft—each was an instance of sexual, religious, or sexuoreligious heresy—that were prohibited at the directive of Pope Paul IV. Earlier, Paul IV had considered Michelangelo's frescoes in the Sistine Chapel to be obscene and ordered them to be destroyed. A storm of protest forced him to relent; instead, he ordered that clothes be added to the Virgin Mary and the heavenly hosts. And they were. But not by Michelangelo.

By the end of the 17th century, religious influence over sexual mores declined. In that century, one of the dominant figures in European literature was Don Juan, appearing in works in Spanish, French, English, and German and in Mozart's opera *Don Giovanni.* In the standard version, the fictional rake seduced and abandoned a multitude of innocents, resulting in his eventual and presumably inevitable punishment.

In contrast, the *Memoirs* of Casanova (1725–1798) recited a litany of hundreds of seductions of sexually inexperienced girls. After each success, Casanova lost interest but he happily moved on; at the end, he wrote, "I regret nothing."

In the 18th century, the pornographic novel attained a new level of eroticism. *Fanny Hill,* by John Cleland; *Les Liaisons dangereuses,* by Pierre

Laclos; *Bijou indiscrets,* by Denis Diderot; and *Justine* and *Juliette,* by the Marquis de Sade, appeared. *Mary, A Fiction,* by Mary Wollstonecraft, became the first novel to be written about lesbians by a woman.

The 18th century saw also an increase in the social distance between the rich and the powerful and the poor and the helpless in England, accompanied by turmoil between the classes and followed by increased harshness in punishment. Two hundred offenses were punishable by death, many more by flogging. The standard disciplinary practice in schools became whipping. Not unrelated, the first pornographic work on whipping, *A Treatise on the Use of Flogging,* appeared in 1718. (Such works would flourish in the next century, portraying what became known as the English vice—specifically, spanking and whipping but also bondage, discipline, and cross-dressing as punishment.)

In 1709, Edward Ward published *The Secret History of the London Clubs.* It detailed the riotous sexual activities of gentlemen who were above the law because of their power and influence. All were graduates of the flogging of English schools; undisciplined by such discipline, they continued to meet to drink, whore, and play sadistic tricks. Specializing, the Mohocks forcibly exposed women by standing them on their heads, the Blasters preferred exposing their penises to passing women, the Bold Bucks practiced rape, the Hell Fire Club allegedly celebrated black masses with promiscuous sexuality, and the Mollies (a familiar name for Mary) dressed as women to drink and party. The clubs could adjourn to houses of prostitution, including special brothels for flaggelation, and "Molly" houses. Could it be that whipping the masturbating boy did not drive the devil of sex out of him, but traumatized his sexuality, sometimes eroticizing his violence?

But just as religion was losing its power for sexual restraint, gained by portraying sex as sinful and dirty and corrupting, science began to portray sex as dangerous. Fornication became dangerous and onanism (masturbation and all seminal emissions not intended for procreation) more dangerous still. Demon possession was more or less replaced by degeneracy theory. According to the emerging medical-scientific myth of degeneracy, onanism caused degeneracy that caused all manners of physical morbidity, even death. In 1758, S.A.D. Tissot published his work on onanism and the wastage of semen. According to this medical madness, such wastage produced cloudy ideas and madness, coughs and consumption, a numbness and pain, pimples and blisters, impotence and premature ejaculation, priapism and gonorrhea, and constipation and hemorrhoids.

In England, the Industrial Revolution of the 19th century produced a growing middle class that reacted against the immorality of both the lower and the upper classes; it created Victorianism. Victorianism is more than a synonym for prudery; it implies a self-satisfied and self-conscious rectitude, an acceptance of authority because of the superior social evolution of "Great" Britain, the effect of industrialization in creating a private realm of the family to compensate for a difficult world of work, the idealization of home as haven and of woman as homemaker, and the forming of traditional family values, including sexual purity and chastity.

"Masturbation" became medical science's new word for the religious sin against nature; for example, the physician James Foster Scott described masturbation as including coitus interruptus, coitus interfemora, pederasty, bestiality, mutual masturbation, and "self-pollution." For Scott, masturbation led to homosexuality, viewed as a perversion. It was only a baby step from demon-possession to moral-degeneracy theory.

Another English physician, William Acton, taught that sexual activity produced a loss of vital energy, that males must engage in sex infrequently and only briefly, and that God created women to be indifferent to sex to prevent the male's vital energy from being expended. Procreation itself was dangerous, but masturbation compounded the risks, being ten times worse.

In America, Sylvester Graham asserted that the loss of an ounce of semen was equivalent to the loss of several ounces of blood. Married couples should limit their sex to procreation, copulating no more than once a month. Not only orgasms but also sexual imagination posed a threat to the body, according to Graham, as lascivious thoughts excited sexual desire. Everyone knew that pornography—the very writing of whores—excited sexual desire, producing both the social vice (prostitution) and the solitary vice (masturbation). Moreover, sexual desire and insanity were reciprocal causes and effects, each producing the other. Some of his prescriptions were dietary—the Graham cracker.

At the Battle Creek Sanitarium, Graham's disciple John Harvey Kellogg not only was introducing America to new breakfast cereals, flaked to fight against masturbation; he was also alerting America to the suspicious signs of the secret masturbator: round shoulders and a weak back, lassitude and sleeplessness, bashfulness and unnatural boldness, shifty eyes and cold moist hands, epilepsy and bed-wetting, use of tobacco and obscenity, and boys who don't like girls as well as girls who do like boys. New forms of sexual torture were created by physicians for use by parents to prevent masturbation. Kellogg prescribed circumcision in young boys, sewing foreskins closed in older boys, and carbolic acid on the clitoris of girls—all without anesthesia to associate pain with sexual ideas. (Is this a forerunner of aversive conditioning to treat sexual deviants?)

This antisexual "science" employed the idea that stress was increasing with the modern times created by the Industrial Revolution, and it claimed that the more highly educated were more highly evolved (social Darwinism) and thus more susceptible to the dangers of masturbation. The wag calls pornography "the book that is read with one hand"; the literate masturbate. Kellogg even favored acid for the clitoris of girls who mentally masturbated to orgasm through sexual fantasy. It is speculated that Kellogg, a Seventh-Day Adventist, appeared to find coitus repulsive; he may never have consummated his marriage; he may have found sexual satisfaction in klismaphilia, receiving a daily enema from an orderly each morning.

In 1798, Thomas Malthus published *An Essay on the Principle of Population,* proposing that war, vice, and misery resulted from a human sexual urge that increased population at a geometric rate, whereas the supply of food could only increase at an arithmetic rate. Opposed to contraception, Malthus urged men to marry late and to bridle their sexual urges.

Many neo-Malthusians encouraged the use of contraception to control the growth of population. The Massachusetts physician Charles Knowlton proposed the method of douching in 1832; he was fined and jailed, but the attempt at censorship publicized his work. The possible inventor of the cervical cap or diaphragm, Edward Bliss Foote, advocated the right of women to decide when to have children—a radical idea for the time. Using a pseudonym, the Inspector for the Post Office, Anthony Comstock, requested a copy of Foote's pamphlet, then fined Foote for sending obscene material through the mails. Also, Comstock arrested Margaret Sanger, the founder of Planned Parenthood, for sending contraceptive information in the mails. After Comstock attacked one of his plays as obscene, "Comstockery" was coined as an epithet for bluenoses by George Bernard Shaw. Comstockery has come to mean overzealous moral censorship of the fine arts and literature, often mistaking outspoken works for obscenity.

In the 19th century, the Napoleonic Code took the enlightened stance of leaving unpunished any private sexual behavior between consenting adults. Deviant sexual acts were criminal only if they outraged public decency, if they were nonconsenting or violent, or if one party was underage or otherwise unable to give a valid consent. Following William Blackstone, the English (and hence American) law remained harshly punitive about sex. In 1853, the first laws against pornography were passed in England. In 1868, in *Regina* v. *Hicklin,* Lord Alexander Cockburne declared that the test of obscenity was its tendency to deprave and corrupt those whose minds are open to such immoral influences (presumably the lower classes). Pamphlets describing contraceptive methods, including Knowlton's, were swiftly seized as obscene literature. Antisexual attitudes are general, not specific; they are part of a worldview descending from Thomas Aquinas and others in which the only moral sex is coitus in the missionary position within a monogamous marriage for procreation and without too much passion or pleasure.

Each introduction of a new technology of communication appears to have produced new concerns about pornography. From classical painting to the novel, the penny thriller, the photograph, the movie, the magazine, the telephone, the computer bulletin board, the videocassette recorder (VCR), and cable television, each transformation in the means of conveying information has been exploited to convey pornographic images. Just as Lord Cockburne was concerned about those into whose hands such material might fall, opponents of pornography remained concerned about effects on some third party who would be susceptible to corruption or incitement to sexual activity or to sexual violence.

Nonetheless, the most important historical trend, occurring within the last two decades, has been the integration of explicit sexual materials into the mainstream communication media. Sex magazines have entered mainstream bookstores; sex videos are available for rental in general retail outlets. The sexual revolution has changed mores about sexuality, including pornography. Although pornography has remained controversial and antipornography forces continue to claim the moral high ground, contemporary community standards are more accepting of sexual expression, including explicit sexual material.

The Three Commissions

That pornography remains controversial is attested to by three important governmental commissions, two in the United States and one in Britain. In January 1968, President Johnson appointed the President's Commission on Obscenity and Pornography. In July 1977, the British Home Secretary appointed a Committee on Obscenity and Film Censorship, usually referred to as the Williams Committee after its chairman. In May 1985, Attorney General Edwin Meese announced the formation of a Commission on Pornography. These three commissions illustrate contemporary concerns about the effects of pornography on the public: is pornography harmful? Respectively, they answered no, maybe, and yes.

The President's Commission liked neither of the terms, "obscenity" or "pornography," that were used in its title, preferring the neutral phrase "explicit sexual materials." Unlike the other two commissions, it sponsored direct research on pornography and its effects.

The Williams Committee thought the word "obscene" connoted disgust or repulsion and was too exhausted to do more work in the courts. For them, pornography combined two features: (1) a function of or intention to arouse its audience sexually, and (2) a content of explicit sexual representation.

The Meese Commission believed the word "pornography" was used by individuals when sex was depicted in a disapproved way, and "erotica" was used when sex was depicted in a way that the user approved. It approved of the definition of obscenity given in the Supreme Court's 1973 decision *Miller* v. *California;* in fact, it favored more vigorous prosecution under *Miller.* The three prongs of the *Miller* decision that form the current American legal test of obscenity are (1) whether the average person, applying contemporary community standards, finds that the work taken as a whole appeals to prurient interest, (2) whether the work depicts or describes, in a patently offensive way, sexual conduct defined by the applicable state law, and (3) whether the work taken as a whole lacks serious literary, artistic, political, or scientific value.

Most open to social science research, the President's Commission concluded that empirical research found no evidence to support the claim that erotic materials caused sex delinquency or crimes. Beginning with an allegiance to the harm principle (harming others is a good reason for legislative action in a free society), the more agnostic Williams Committee concluded it was not possible to reach conclusions about the influence of pornography on sexual crime. By extending the range of "acceptable" evidence be-

yond social science to include anecdotal evidence from so-called victims who claimed that pornography had incited and corrupted their victimizers and from offenders who admitted being so incited or corrupted, as well as impressions given by criminal-justice and selected clinical professionals that offenders were so incited and corrupted, the Meese Commission reached the conclusion, "unanimously and confidently," that the "available evidence" strongly supports that substantial exposure to sexually violent materials bears a causal relationship to acts of antisocial violence, and possibly to unlawful acts of sexual violence. This conclusion was criticized for including non-cross-examined personal testimonials to harmful effects and for selectively weighting the nonconclusive scientific evidence.

Neither these three commissions, nor social scientists, nor the public can approach the issue of pornography without revealing ideological stances that produce passionate rhetoric in the face of uncertainty about the still largely unknown effects of pornography. Ideology fills the gap of uncertainty; rhetoric becomes the voice of ideology, producing partisan debates about what is true, good, and real.

Three ideological stances are prominent. The first, sexual naturalism, views sexual expression as positive and natural; it defends pornography on First Amendment grounds, turning to scientific evidence to demonstrate the lack of serious and likely harms. The second, traditional morality, views sexual expression as undermining the family by fostering nonprocreative sexual expression and argues that pornography corrupts and depraves, leading to sexual addiction and perversion. The third, women against pornography, views the compulsive heterosexuality of men as violent in nature, arguing that pornography degrades women and promotes violence against them. Although strange bedfellows, the moralist and feminist positions have melded into an antipornography position. (Of course, many feminists include themselves in the sexual naturalist or civil libertarian position, believing that a New Right agenda will curtail many additional freedoms in the name of morality after censoring or prosecuting pornography.) Preferring the labels "anticensorship" and "antipornography," each side accuses the other of selective uses of scientific evidence to suit its ideological ends.

The Evidence

Scientists can agree on one conclusion: exposure to pornography increases sexual arousal, as measured by retrospective reports and by subjective and physiological measures of sexual arousal in the laboratory. Men report more exposure to pornography in everyday life and more subjective sexual arousal than women. In the laboratory, the average heterosexual man reports predominantly positive emotions, usually interest and enjoyment, whereas the average heterosexual woman reports mixed emotions, a combination of interest and disgust. People with less exposure to pornography, less sexual experience, more sexual guilt or erotophobia, and more traditional values report less sexual arousal and more negative affect, rating explicit sexual materials as more pornographic, abnormal, and obscene. Following the viewing of explicit sexual materials, men and women may participate in sexual behavior within established outlets, but there is little evidence consistent with the view that their sexual behaviors become more perverse or violent.

That ideology influences social scientists can be inferred from their positive reaction when studying pornography compared to the negative reaction of social scientists studying violence. Liberal social scientists are more accepting of sexuality than violence. As researchers within the television-violence tradition began to study pornography, their approach was more accepting of the possibility of harms. In the interim between the President's Commission and the Meese Commission, a series of investigations suggested that pornography or violent pornography might have an effect on selected aggressive outcomes, usually the administration of electric shock in the laboratory. At present, the tentative conclusions from such researchers are these: (1) exposure to aggressive pornography may reinforce or strengthen preexisting callous sexual attitudes in men, including rape myths, and (2) exposure to violence, rather than exposure to explicit sexual material, may be linked to aggressive sexual behavior.

Predisposition to sexual aggression, opportunity, and drinking appear to be more plausible contributors to violence than the incitement effect of pornography. The most damaging claim against pornography may be that it might desensitize violence in men or in aggressive men; yet commercial television contains massive amounts of violence. If such violence is as important causally as many psychologists claim, sex does not have to be portrayed explicitly to create a linkage between sex and violence. So an emphasis on containing pornography for its presumed danger of desensitizing, without censoring violence in the mass media, appears to be nonsensical, revealing a hidden view of sex itself as morally corrupting. The violence in the mass media is directed more frequently at other men than at women.

Macho men support male dominance over women and engage in aggressive sexual behavior, but they do not learn this personality script from pornography. The macho personality script (*see* Virility and Machismo) is punitively socialized by preventing boys from crying, from fleeing when afraid, and from hanging their head in shame when significant others threaten, dominate, and humiliate such affective displays of "feminine" emotion. Both parents and sex-segregated male peer groups discourage these so-called "inferior, feminine affects" and encourage the warrior affects of surprise, excitement, anger, disgust, and contempt. Anger, disgust, and contempt are directed toward inferiors—the wimps, faggots, and girls who tremble in fear, weep in distress, and hang their head in shame. It is more plausible that rapists form a toxic script from extensive exposure to scenes in which they are childhood targets of fear, rage, and contempt; sexual violence recasts such victimizing scenes with the now adult rapist as the victimizer. Pornography cannot have much affect unless the affects generated in the imagined scene match the sexual scripts of its consumer, creating a vicarious resonance. Real-life scenes ordinarily generate more dense emotions than vicarious scenes.

The problems of sexual violence and sexism require a more complex analysis than depicting pornography as the root of evils of sexism and violence. Ideologies of sex-as-sinful and sex-as-dangerous permeate the oversimplified claims that pornography is causally linked to sexual perversion and sex crimes.

Pornography Defined

Pornography is a commercial product designed to elicit or enhance sexual arousal by the portrayal of sexually explicit images that produce or activate the consumer's sexual fantasies. Pornography either embodies an intended audience's sexual fantasies as a fictional drama or (if not a narrative) provides an image that serves as a projective stimulus that invites and only partially constrains the sexual fantasies of its audience. Given the intention to stimulate sexual arousal as its exclusive function, pornography presents a cast of supersexual characters whose sexual motivation (and, secondarily, power motivation) is paramount. In pornography, fictional characters experience an erotic reality without the constraints of everyday reality, social norms, and conventional morality. That is, the traditional themes in pornography flaunt the flouting of the social conventions of courtship and monogamy and the moral prohibitions against variety in sexual acts and sexual partners, without producing any unwanted consequences like sexually transmitted diseases, pregnancy, sexual dysfunction, or rejection.

Like sexual fantasy in general, the constraints of everyday reality and the possibility of negative affects are left behind to produce a sexual mood filled with the positive affects of sexual excitement and enjoyment. In pornography, the customary obstacles to sexual contact are more apparent than real, since all the cast is supersexed, uninhibited, and unrestrained regardless of either their role tags as doctor or cleric or their attributes, such as age or gender. Commonly, pornography has been the companion of the solitary masturbating consumer, but, with VCR technology, more couples are using explicitly sexual videotapes to elicit or enhance sexual arousal.

In pornography, unlike more serious art, the protagonist—traditionally male—overcomes apparent obstacles (deviant sexual objects, e.g., nuns or several partners at once; and deviant sexual linkages, e.g., oral or anal sex) with ease, thus failing to undergo the dramatic conflict and transformation in character that distinguishes literature or drama seen as art that illuminates the human condition. If a single image rather than a narrative, the pornographic image is both literally and figuratively naked; it is an explicit image of sexuality rather than an expressive symbol that requires interpretation; the image merely expresses the mundane aspect, not the inexpressible aspects, of sex. It is the conjunction of purpose, exclusively to elicit sexual arousal, and structure, a nonsymbolic image or a lightweight version of fictional drama, that defines a commercial product as pornographic.

Because pornography is a commercial product, it must either fit the sexual scripts of an intended audience or be open to assimilation to the audience's favorite fantasies. An image off a pinup or a split beaver permits easy assimilation into many male masturbation fantasies. Narrative pornography often selects themes that may appeal to men. Market signals include titles like "Bald Beavers," "Oreo Sex," or "Debbie Does Dallas."

Thus, most pornography was developed for heterosexual men by appealing to a range of sexual behaviors and partners that are socially taboo, given the criterion of monogamous marital coitus in the missionary position. The supersexed heterosexual hero finds a wide variety of women, including those of higher or lower social class, who are immediately interested in having hot sex in a variety of linkages, always featuring fellatio with delight.

For pornography to sell, most of the partners and sexual acts must fit the range of sexual fantasies held by heterosexual men. Nonetheless, many of the conventions or stereotypes of stag films include features that do not match the features found in surveys of heterosexual male fantasies.

After the early days of black socks and masks, X-rated film stereotypes included always showing ejaculation outside the vagina, often on the body or face of the woman, who greedily swallowed the ejaculate as she appeared to climax. After Linda Lovelace's starring role, deep throating during fellatio became common. The protagonist usually would have sex with at least three different women, be sexually serviced by two women, have female actors involved in same-sex scenes, and participate in an orgy scene. Absent were expressions of affection, love, or committed relationships. So when women eagerly grasped penises to fellate them, it seemed that foreplay, mutual concern with female pleasure, and cuddling afterplay were unnecessary, at least in the sexual fantasies of men who are masturbating. This illustrates the thesis of supersexed phallic men meeting supersexed receptive women who provide no obstacles to sexual access or to sexual pleasure as the central theme of heterosexual male pornography. Thus, there is no fear of rejection by men, no performance pressure to please the woman, no sexual fear or shame or guilt by either men or women, no distress by women at anal penetration, and no disgust by women at swallowing semen—no negative affect at all is permitted to intrude to break the mood of such lusty heterosexual fantasy.

Recently, in response to VCR technology, women pornographers have begun producing explicit sexual videos "without the raunch." These videos, made by and for women, exclude spurting ejaculate and other stereotypes from stag films; they use sexual fantasies containing more appeal to women. Some evidence suggests that such women-oriented videos may have more appeal to women and perhaps to couples. As yet, no pornography seems to have attained maximum goodness-of-fit to the sexual fantasies of heterosexuals.

Videotapes for gay men include similar sexual acts, excepting penile-vaginal sex. With the onset of AIDS (acquired immune deficiency syndrome), some pornography for gay men has included safer sex as an educational device. The small market for lesbians has more often consisted of magazines rather than videotapes.

A small audience exists for paraphilic pornography. "Paraphilic" means beyond the normal; it includes themes of urination and defecation, sadomasochism and the like. Because these tastes are relatively rare, the appeal for a mass audience is lost. It should be noted that pornography featuring children is not readily available, unless one counts, as the law does, films with female actors like Traci Lords, who were under age 18 but appeared to be fully developed women. Because the theme of younger women appeals to many heterosexual men, female actors often portray teenagers, but the age discrepancy of actress and role is usually noticeable. In America, child pornography remains rare and illegal.

A small amount of material is available with themes of sadomasochism. Such material is designed for an audience of adults who consent to engage in recreational S&M. The encounter is heavily stylized and fetishized to make the scenes dramatic and to match the sexual fantasies of people who participate in S&M. Commercial establishments specializing in S&M usually do not permit sexual contact between the dominant and the submissive, thus staying within the laws against prostitution. In S&M fantasies, the motive of power is even more central than the motive of sex. Recreational participants in S&M are not true sexual sadists or masochists who want to hurt or be hurt, to mutilate or to be mutilated, to kill or to be killed. Instead, they enact dramatic fantasies of dominance and submission. The small commercial market of S&M was not designed for lust murderers, and most lust murderers probably confine their fantasy materials to more readily available horror scenes of violence that include realistic portrayals of blood and gore or violence against nonconsenting victims, not dominance over consenting submissives.

Despite many claims of a large and increasing volume of violent pornography, X-rated videotapes contain little or no violence. R-rated videotapes, in contrast, contain nudity and sexualized but nonexplicit scenes that are linked with violence. Although a sadistic individual or group may have made a personal videotape of a murder, pornography as a commercial product includes few films that portray death, much less recording an actual lust murder—the so-called "snuff" film. Such claims are common in antipornography rhetoric that uses the worst-case scenario to persuade people of its dangers.

Matching Pornography to Fantasy

Sexual-involvement theory posits that deep involvement in the scenes portrayed by pornography requires a goodness of fit between the product and the preferred sexual fantasies of the consumer. Elements that are turnoffs for the consumer either are selectively ignored or disrupt deepening involvement by producing negative affects such as fear, shame, or disgust. Strong attraction to a pornographic product reveals a goodness of fit with the consumer's sexual script. Indifference reveals an absence of fit with a sexual script; the consumer who purchases the wrong product may wonder how anyone can find this explicit material sexually stimulating.

People who hold antipornography positions disregard the commercial motives of producers of pornography, who must satisfy a demand if they are to make money. Selecting worst-case examples of pornography that appeals to few (paraphiles) and offends many (normophiles), they argue that pornography is corrupting and dangerous. Or they argue that the violence in pornography creates violence against women by sloganeering, "Pornography is the theory; rape is the practice." To determine if pornography degrades women, "degrading" must be defined. Certainly, pornography is stereotypic, but it stereotypes everyone it portrays, both men and women, clerics and doctors, gay and straight people, by portraying them as supersexed. If sex degrades, if sexual fantasy degrades, if commercial use of sexual fantasy degrades, then pornography may degrade its cast and its audience. However, if sex is not necessarily degrading of both men and women, and if sexual fantasy is not degrading, then the commercial depiction of explicit sexual activity does not necessarily degrade a consenting cast and audience. If a person believes the only acceptable sexual activity is coitus for procreation in a monogamous married couple using the missionary position, without too much passion or pleasure, then pornography flouts this traditional moral view. Contemporary community standards accept more varied sexual activity between more diverse partners than this traditional more would have it. Contemporary community standards probably do not encompass a full range of deviant linkages and deviant partners. The statistically normative, rather than the moral norm, forms the criterion of a contemporary community standard.

Since the audience for pornography has largely been male, stereotypic male-female relations—male dominance and female submission—are present, given the gender hierarchy in this culture. Whether gender hierarchy and stereotyping are greater or more pernicious in X-rated pornography than in other mass media is debatable. Does anyone take pornography or explicit sexual fantasy seriously as a portrayal of everyday reality? The mass media may be more insidious in its effects. This may be why some civil libertarian feminists argue that what is needed is fewer women against pornography and more women pornographers.

The war over pornography is a war over sexuality as good or evil. For the sexual naturalist, pornography is sexual fluff but not sexual menace. Sex, sexual fantasy, and pornography are accepted expressions of individual and plural sexualities.

For the sexual moralist, pornography is linked to moral evil; to satanism and the moral decay of the family and society; to the corruption of innocence, producing degeneracy through masturbation; to fornication and adultery; to perversion; to rape; and to lust or satanic murders. However, no answer is given as to how to eliminate sexual fantasy and sexual desire, if one were to accept such an impossible mission, out of the minds of either teenagers or adults.

For the antipornography feminist, all pornography degrades women, violating their civil rights. Some antipornography feminists would exclude erotica from the pejorative "pornography," but the line is hard to draw. When balanced on a slippery slope, where does the censor stop—at sexual dissidence, at religious dissidence, at political dissidence? The pornographer's sexual intent is in his or her mind, but disgust is in the mind of the censor. Violent pornography, although hard to find, is condemned as inciting violence. No answer is given as to how to get the violent sexual fantasies out of the minds of rapists. An error of the first feminist revolution was to idealize the sexuality of women as pure, chaste, and moral; an error of the second feminist revolution is to demonize the sexuality of men as objectifying, degrading, and rapacious. Surely, a humanist ethic can argue for freedom of and tolerance for sexual and gender diversity that sets none above the other in power or morality, yet leaves all free to choose so long as they do not harm others.

REFERENCES

Berger, R.J., P. Searles, and C.E. Cottle. *Feminism and Pornography*. New York: Praeger, 1991.

Bullough, V. *Sexual Variance in Society and History*. Chicago: Univ. of Chicago Press, 1976.

Christensen, F.M. *Pornography: The Other Side*. New York: Praeger, 1990.

Copp, D., and S. Wendell. *Pornography and Censorship*. Buffalo, N.Y.: Prometheus Books, 1983.

Donnerstein, E., D. Linz, and S. Penrod. *The Question of Pornography: Research Findings and Policy Implications*. New York: The Free Press, 1987.

Hawkins, G., and F.E. Zimring. *Pornography in a Free Society*. Cambridge: Cambridge Univ. Press, 1988.

Mosher, D.L. Pornography Defined: Involvement Theory, Narrative Context, and Goodness-of-Fit. *Journal of Psychology and Human Sexuality,* Vol. 1 (1988), pp. 67–85.

Weatherford, J.Mc. *Porn Row*. New York: Arbor House, 1986.

Donald L. Mosher

PREGNANCY

Pregnancy is a normal physiological phenomenon, and every healthy young woman is capable of conception, carrying a child, and delivering that child. Pregnancy is possible from the time of puberty to the menopause. At the present time, obstetricians see many teenage pregnancies, with young, basically immature females from ages 9 to 13 becoming pregnant, developing all sorts of complications because of their age and immaturity, and suffering through a very difficult pregnancy. Under normal circumstances, we would prefer not to see a young woman conceive and become pregnant until somewhere around the age of 18. Pregnancy is possible in the older female right up to the menopause. The menopause in the United States today occurs between the ages of 48 and 52, but in reality most spontaneous pregnancies occur before the age of 46. Although there are many complications with the older pregnant woman, they are in general not as severe or as complex as the problems encountered in the young teenager.

The average length of pregnancy is from 270 to 280 days (40 calendar weeks or 9 lunar months). The expected date of delivery of the baby is calculated on the basis of the woman's last menstrual period. Once this date is firmly in hand, we count back three months and add seven days to give us an expected date of delivery. Since the advent of sophisticated ultrasound machines, the expected delivery date can also be calculated if the patient is subjected to abdominal pelvic ultrasound around the 18th week of pregnancy. Pelvic ultrasound after 20 weeks of pregnancy is less accurate.

The normal menstrual cycle averages about 28 days, with the average menstrual period lasting from four to seven days. On a 28-day cycle, the woman is fertile and is capable of conception in midcycle around day 12 to 14. When intercourse occurs, the male sperm from the ejaculate is deposited in the vaginal vault, usually in the posterior fornix, and bathes the cervix. Once the sperm are mixed and bathed with the thin, succulent mucous from the cervix, the sperm then traverse up through the cervix, the endocervical canal, and the endometrium and into the Fallopian tubes. In the vast majority of cases, conception occurs in the outer third of the Fallopian tube, and once conception has occurred, it takes approximately four to five days for the fertilized egg to traverse its way down the Fallopian tube, and implant or imbed itself in the endometrium, which has been prepared by the hormones estrogen and progesterone for the implantation of this fertilized egg.

This sounds like a very simple process, but in reality it is a very delicate and complicated mechanism and is fraught with many complications. For example, spontaneous abortion occurs in at least 10 percent of fertilizations, and some authorities venture to state that the spontaneous abortion rate may be as high as 20 percent. If there are anatomical or structural abnormalities in the uterus or the endometrial cavity, or if there are adhesions in the endometrial cavity, from previous infections, this increases the spontaneous abortion rate.

Pregnancy is still not a totally benign medical procedure, and the maternal death rate in the United States is approximately nine women for every 100,000 pregnancies. How can this maternal mortality rate be kept down? The best and probably only way to do it is by adequate and thorough obstetrical medical preventive management. To achieve this goal, prenatal care should start ten days to two weeks after the first menstrual period is missed. At that time, a complete history is taken, and a complete physical examination should be performed. This should include a complete pelvic examination, with vaginal-cervical cultures to rule out the possibility of early infection that may complicate the pregnancy later on; a Papanicolaou smear is taken to screen for cervical malignancy. Once the patient has been examined and the pregnancy has been confirmed, laboratory work is performed. Certain blood and urine work is mandated by law in many states in the United States.

Instructions must be given covering all facets of the pregnancy. We invariably start with thorough dietary instruction, and it is imperative that the pregnant woman have a high-protein, low-carbohydrate, low-salt, low-fat diet, including about 75 grams of protein daily. One must remember that one quart of skim milk a day provides 35 grams of protein and all the calcium that the pregnant patient requires on a daily basis. One egg a day supplies seven grams of protein and all the iron that the patient needs to meet a daily metabolic requirement for pregnancy. A reduced salt intake is very important, because in pregnancy the high-salt diet combined with the high food intake give the patient an excess of weight gain based on the retention of salt and water. The weight of pregnant women is closely monitored, as is their dietary intake to make sure they receive an adequate nutritional diet sufficient to sustain both the patient and the fetus. During the first three months of pregnancy, we restrict the intake of caffeine because of its effect on the early intrauterine development of the fetus and its stimulating effect and possible developmental effects. Pregnant women should not smoke or use tobacco in any form. Nicotine has a negative impact on the vascular vasomotor system of the woman and on the developing fetal and placental bed. Smoking also decreases the oxygen supply available to the baby, in turn producing a small placenta that does not function well and results in a low-birth-weight infant.

Alcohol is another social problem that confronts the pregnant woman. It is imperative that the patient refrain from the use of alcohol during the entire pregnancy. Excessive use of alcohol affects the growth and development of the child and produces a fetal alcohol syndrome with very definite developmental abnormalities that are grossly identifiable at the time of delivery. Even more dangerous reactions occur with other drugs, such as heroin, and they are summarized at the end of this article. A vitamin supplement is important, and we prescribe any one of a number of good prenatal vitamins that are on the market.

To simplify charting the progress of the pregnancy, it is divided into three periods called trimesters, as the nine months of growth and development. The first trimester is of the utmost importance, because it is during this time that cell division and the development of the nervous system and the circulatory system occur, and noxious elements can contribute to poor growth and development of the fetus, producing an abnormal fetus, which could then be carried on into the second and third trimesters and eventually end up in delivery. The patient may experience nausea and vomiting during the first trimester.

The second trimester is a period when the patient begins to feel better, since the nausea and vomiting are ordinarily gone by the 14th week. Pep and energy, which were diminished during the first 12 weeks, are now back, and the woman is a vigorous individual capable of living a very normal and healthy life.

The third trimester is a period of massive growth in the baby, when the cartilaginous tissue is being transformed, with the deposition of calcium, into the cartilage to create bone structure, and the muscle mass in the infant is also being laid down and developed. An adequate maternal diet is of the utmost importance, because the infant needs extra proteins and calcium. The third trimester is also the time when an infection in the vagina, whether it be preexisting or recently acquired, can cause premature rupture of the membranes and premature labor. This usually occurs around the 32nd or the 34th week and creates serious problems both for the patient and for the obstetrician. This possibility of danger makes it imperative to identify and recognize infections in the genital tract during the third trimester of the pregnancy.

Labor

At the end of the pregnancy, around 270 to 280 days, the patient is beginning to feel very uncomfortable, unwieldy, and bulky. She has great difficulty finding a comfortable place to sit or to lie. Her back is bothering her from the lordosis of pregnancy. Her pelvis feels heavy and has tremendous pressure, because the fetal head is now working its way down into the pelvis prior to the onset of labor. Before the onset of labor, the patient usually has a nesting instinct and is aware of the fact that changes are occurring and that labor is not far away. She will frequently lose two to four pounds in weight, since the hormones that have sustained the pregnancy for 40 weeks are now beginning to subside, and some of the physiological fluid retention of pregnancy is being released through an increased urinary output.

The first sign of labor is the onset of uterine contractions, which the patient is well aware of and can discern very effectively. These contractions, especially if this is a first pregnancy, are usually mild and irregular, occurring every 20 to 30 minutes and lasting for 15 to 45 seconds. The woman is able to move around and has no complaints. As the contractions continue, she frequently notices an increased vaginal discharge that consists of mucous that is clear or slightly blood tinged and nonirritating. As labor progresses, the contractions increase in regularity, and when they are occurring every five minutes by the clock for at least one hour, the patient should go to the hospital. If this is her first pregnancy, she can anticipate a total labor of 18 to 24 hours. If this is the second or a subsequent pregnancy, she can anticipate a total labor time of 6 to 12 hours.

Labor can be divided into three stages. The first stage of labor begins when the patient has established regular uterine contractions with a full cervical dilatation of ten centimeters. The second stage of labor is from the period of full dilatation until the delivery of the child. The third stage of labor is from the delivery of the child until the delivery of the placenta.

One must realize that labor is a mechanism in which the mature fetus at term begins its descent through the maternal pelvis, down through the vagina, passing all the bony anatomical structures in the pelvic girdle and ending up with the presenting part, usually the baby's head, visible at the dilated vaginal introitus. This is a complicated mechanism, and the baby has to rotate from at least 90 to 180 degrees to traverse the pelvis. The true maternal pelvis has basically a 90-degree turn in it in that the baby engages and descends down to what we call the midpelvis; then the baby must do a 90-degree turn to exit from the pelvis.

Labor is categorized as normal or abnormal. Normal labor is characterized by a spontaneous onset with normal progression throughout the three stages of labor and terminating in spontaneous vaginal delivery of an infant. When a problem exists for one of many reasons, the labor is termed abnormal. The patient may purely and simply have what we call a dysfunctional labor, that is, she has a poor uterine contraction pattern and can never establish a normal, effective pattern of contractions that permits the cervix to dilate progressively. A dysfunctional labor can be indicative of cephalopelvic disproportion or an abnormal presentation, such as a persistent occiput posterior, a face presentation where the baby's head is deflexed and the face is presenting instead of the vertex, or a transverse lie where the baby is lying transversely in the mother's abdominal cavity with no presenting part in the pelvis. Last, there are the problems that are associated with a breech (buttocks or foot) presentation.

Management of Labor

In the first stage, which lasts approximately 6 to 12 hours with a prima gravida (first pregnancy), the patient needs constant support and adequate fluid intake either by mouth or intravenously. Strong sedation should be avoided until the patient is dilated approximately five centimeters. If the patient is stressed and is losing control, nonnarcotic medication intramuscularly, such as vistaril, can be used. This medication has the unique ability to calm the patient down, let her resume total control of herself, and permit the labor to continue.

After five centimeters of dilatation, if sedation is required or needed, narcotics such as Demerol, or a newer medication called Stadol, are used. These work very effectively and enable most of the patients to continue their labor in a normal, uninterrupted fashion. Another form of analgesia often used after five centimeters of dilatation is an epidural block. This is a regional anesthetic that gives the patient complete pain relief and permits the labor to progress and continue. There are a few rules that must be followed in the use of the epidural: the patient must be at least five centimeters dilated, the membranes should be ruptured, and the presenting part should be in the midpelvis or below the level of the ischial spines in the midpelvis. If the epidural is given without following these criteria, the labor is prolonged and, in many cases, ends with an operative delivery, such as a low forceps delivery or, in some instances, even cesarean section, all of which would have been unnecessary if the rules for the use of an epidural block were followed.

All labors do not go to fruition uneventfully, and complications do occur. Prolonged labor, due to an ineffectual contraction pattern, can delay descent of the presenting part, necessitating use of medication, such as pitocin, that stimulates effective uterine contractions. This is given intravenously and it is monitored very closely with what is called a Harvard infusion pump. With this technique, it is possible to know exactly how much medication the patient is receiving intravenously on a per-minute basis. Pitocin corrects the ineffectual labor, strengthens contractions, and enables the presenting part to descend into the pelvis. With these complicated labors, however, a spontaneous vaginal delivery is not always possible, and there is very definitely an increased use of forceps with this contraction problem in labor. On occasion, labor has to be terminated by a cesarean section.

The second stage of labor by definition occurs when the cervix has reached full dilatation, and the second stage lasts from the full dilatation of the cervix until the delivery of the presenting part. This time interval is somewhere between 30 minutes and four hours. Once full dilatation occurs and the membranes have been ruptured, either spontaneously or artificially, the presenting part continues to descend through the pelvis. When the presenting part, in most instances the baby's head, reaches the vaginal introitus, it is called crowning, and at this time the fetal scalp and the fetal hair can be seen.

When this occurs, delivery is not far behind. Delivery will either be a spontaneous delivery or it will be an easy outlet forceps delivery. If the woman is a prima gravida, an episiotomy is almost invariably done. This is a surgical incision made in the perineum to facilitate the delivery of the baby's head without a perineum tear. Tears are to be avoided because the tears are jagged and the repair is difficult, involving a prolonged recovery period and pain in the perineum. With a clean episiotomy and a clean surgical repair after the delivery of the placenta, the perineum heals easily and the patient is reasonably comfortable.

When the presenting part, namely the head, is delivered, the obstetrician has an obligation to clean the infant's airway, and we do this by aspirating mucous, blood, and other debris from the nose, throat, and mouth. Once the baby has been completely delivered, the cord is cut and clamped, and the baby is given to the pediatrician in attendance at the delivery. Babies are evaluated immediately after delivery by what is called the apgar score. This is a score that assesses the baby's color, heart rate, muscle tone, and breathing at the time of delivery. Both an immediate and five-minute apgar score are calculated. A normal score will be in the range of 8 to 10, 10 being a perfect score. If the score is below 5, the baby has been subjected to some degree of stress and reduced oxygen supply at the time of delivery. If the score spontaneously reverts to an 8 to 10 rating at the five-minute apgar evaluation, the baby is in good condition and will ordinarily have no significant problems.

The third stage of labor begins with the delivery of the baby and is terminated with the delivery of the placenta. The time frame is usually from 5 to 10 minutes up to one hour. If the placenta has not spontaneously delivered by one hour, removal of the placenta under an anesthetic is advised. Immediately upon delivery of the placenta, the patient is given medication to bring about contraction of the uterus to prevent excessive bleeding. This will be either pitocin administered intramuscularly, an ergot derivative or both. The average blood loss at vaginal delivery is 150 to 200 cubic centimeters. If the blood loss is in excess of 500 cubic centimeters, the patient has had a postpartum hemorrhage.

Cesarean Section

Cesarean section is an operative surgical delivery in which the woman's lower abdomen and uterus are opened and the baby is manually removed from the interior of the uterus. This is done in an operating room under anesthesia. The indications for a cesarean section are twofold: one is maternal, and leading the list for maternal indications for cesarean section is cephalopelvic disproportion. In this instance, the baby is too big for the mother's bony pelvis, and the baby is unable to safely traverse through the bony pelvis because of its size. Another maternal indication for cesarean section is an abnormal presentation. By this is meant a transverse lie where the baby is lying transversely in the uterus with no presenting part in the pelvis. If a woman has a breech presentation, if this is her first baby, and if the baby is in a position called a double footling breech, elective delivery by cesarean section is usually advised. The reason for this is that once the membranes are ruptured, with the double footling breech the incidence of spontaneous prolapse of the umbilical cord is very significant. With spontaneous prolapse of the umbilical cord, the baby is subjected to anoxia and, in many instances, severe and irrevocable changes that are not compatible with a healthy life. Another maternal indication for cesarean section is placenta previa. This means that the placenta, or the afterbirth, is presenting first in front of the baby and totally covers the cervix, so that if and when cervical dilatation occurs, the woman will have severe bleeding, which is life threatening. Another maternal indication for cesarean section is abruptio placenta. The placenta spontaneously separates from the lining of the uterus or the endometrium, creating an acute surgical emergency for both the mother and the infant. This usually occurs with some form of vascular disease. Occasional cesarean sections are done because of preeclampsia, which is a vascular disease, or in the case of twins who share one placenta and one set of membranes.

Fetal Indications for Cesarean Section

The major fetal indication for a cesarean section is acute fetal distress in labor. In modern labor rooms, the fetal heart rate is monitored continuously throughout labor so that attendants are acutely aware of what the fetal heart rate is at any given time. If the infant gets into a situation where there is a compromise in the oxygen supply, the fetal heart rate is drastically reduced. If it stays reduced, this is acute fetal distress, which must be handled by an emergency cesarean section.

Another fetal indication is cord compression, caused by an umbilical cord that is lying close to the fetal head in the pelvis; every time the uterus contracts, the cord is impinged upon and the fetal heart rate drops. Another form of cord compression is when the cord is wrapped tightly around the infant's neck. In this instance, the infant will manifest acute fetal distress on the fetal monitor. Again, if this persists, it is considered a surgical emergency, and the infant must be delivered by cesarean section. Another sig-

nificant fetal indication for a cesarean section is a bowel movement by the fetus into the amniotic fluid during labor, creating a meconium milieu in the amniotic fluid. If this meconium is thick, it is a problem, because the infant may well aspirate a significant amount of this meconium-stained amniotic fluid and develop a meconium aspiration syndrome. This syndrome causes a chemical pneumonitis, and, in many instances, this compromises the infant's life. When the membranes are ruptured and thick meconium is seen, serious consideration is given to effecting delivery by cesarean section.

The Types of Cesarean Section

There are two types of cesarean sections. The classical cesarean section uses an incision in the upper uterine segment, or what is called the fundus of the uterus. This is the original cesarean section done years ago, but it is seldom used now because of problems with increased morbidity and infection in the immediate postpartum period and because of the weakness of the uterine scar and the incidence of spontaneous rupture of this classical incision in future pregnancies. The low cervical transverse incision, which is made transversely in the lower uterine segment below the fundus, is now the surgery of choice. To effect this type of surgical delivery, the vesical peritoneum is opened up and the bladder is reflected down off the lower uterine segment. After the surgery is performed and both infant and placenta are delivered, the uterus is closed with two continuous running sutures and the bladder peritoneum attached in its proper place over the lower uterine segment so that, in essence, this incision is totally exteriorized and does not in any way contaminate the peritoneal cavity. Blood loss with the average cesarean section is between 500 and 700 cubic centimeters, depending on the indications for the cesarean section and the skill of the surgeon.

There is a very definite morbidity attached to cesarean section, and it is not always a benign procedure. The major postoperative problem is infection of either the incision, the lining of the uterus, the endometrium, or the urinary tract and, rarely, a pneumonitis or infection in the lungs.

Pregnancy Complications

The number one complication of pregnancy is spontaneous abortion, the incidence of which runs somewhere between 10 percent and 20 percent. Spontaneous abortions in the first three months of pregnancy are due mainly to the fertilization of a defective egg or the fertilization of an egg by defective sperm, and the products of conception are spontaneously aborted. Once an abortion occurs, approximately 50 percent of the patients with a spontaneous abortion will have to have a D&C (dilatation and curettage) or D&E (dilatation and evacuation) to clean the uterine cavity of the retained products of conception, which, if not removed, will cause continuing bleeding or infection. If it is an early ovular abortion in the first four to six weeks of pregnancy, however, mother nature very effectively cleans out the uterus, and D&C or D&E is rarely indicated.

Another complication of pregnancy occurs around the 20th to the 24th week, and this is spontaneous premature labor or spontaneous dilatation of the cervix due to an incompetent cervix. This means that the cervix is not strong enough and firm enough to keep the products of conception within the uterine cavity for the full 40 weeks of pregnancy. When this is diagnosed, the patient must be put at bed rest, and once the situation is under control, the cervix is sutured with a special suture called a McDonald suture. This suture remains in the cervix until the patient goes into labor at or near term.

Another complication of pregnancy is vaginal and cervical infection. If this is undetected and not diagnosed, and if the patient has a group B-beta hemolytic streptococcus colonizing in the vagina or the cervix, it invariably causes premature rupture of the membranes and premature labor at around the 32nd week of pregnancy. Once this occurs, the membranes rupture and the patient must be delivered quickly because of the danger of infection. Because of the severity of the group beta hemolytic streptococcus on pregnancy, routine culturing of the cervix and the vagina of all patients at the 28th week of pregnancy is now advocated.

Another complication, seen especially in women having their first pregnancy, is the development of preeclampsia. This is a vascular condition characterized by excessive weight gain; fluid retention; swelling of the body, including the legs, hands, and face; elevation of blood pressure; and appearance of protein in the urine, called proteinuria. Once this occurs, the patient and the infant are in a potentially dangerous situation, and the preeclampsia must be treated by hospitalization; bed rest; control of the blood pressure with oral, intramuscular, or intravenous medication; and control of the possible development of convulsions with a drug called magnesium sulfate that is given intravenously. Once the preeclampsia is under control and the blood pressure and urine output are stabilized, the pa-

tient must be delivered. If the cervix is favorable and labor can be induced with pitocin, a vaginal delivery may be possible, but in many of these cases, the pregnancy is terminated by cesarean section.

Cephalopelvic disproportion was alluded to during the discussion of cesarean section. When it does exist, the patient can be given a trial of labor to see if she can possibly deliver her baby vaginally safely before cesarean section is called for.

Medical Problems in Pregnancy

AIDS

AIDS (acquired immune deficiency syndrome) is a serious viral problem today. When a woman is HIV-positive, it usually means that the infant that she delivers will also be HIV-positive. These patients require very intense medical support and care throughout pregnancy. The vast majority of these patients will, however, be able to deliver vaginally if they do not have any serious medical problems that complicate the pregnancy during the nine months.

Drugs

Marijuana, cocaine, crack cocaine, and heroin are all dangerous to the pregnant woman and fetus. Marijuana has a systemic effect on the mother, which in turn is transmitted to the infant. There is also some evidence that marijuana may have a deleterious effect on chromosomes. Cocaine and crack cocaine are absolutely deadly in pregnancy and affect both the mother and the infant. Cocaine, because of its ability to rapidly increase the blood pressure, causes many severe and serious medical complications, such as heart attack, stroke, and premature separation of the placenta, or what is commonly called abruptio placenta. There is no distinction between crack cocaine and cocaine as far as the medical complications are concerned. Heroin has the same devastating effect on both the mother and the infant as cocaine and crack.

Both alcohol and smoking pose dangers. All patients should be warned of the problems with drugs, alcohol, and tobacco and urged to avoid the associated danger.

The Postpartum Period

The postpartum period lasts from the delivery of the infant to six weeks postpartum, and special instructions are required for the patient in this immediate postpartum period. If the patient is breast-feeding, special attention should be paid to the patient's diet. Her protein intake, her calcium intake, and her iron intake may need to be increased to support the patient and also to provide the essential nutrients for the growth of the infant. Patients are advised to continue their prenatal vitamins as long as they are breast-feeding. Breast-feeding lasts from a few months up to a year, depending on the patient's desires. During the breast-feeding period, the patient should abstain from tobacco, drugs, and caffeine. These substances are transmitted to the breast milk, and they all have deleterious effects on the infant.

The episiotomy requires special attention in the immediate postpartum period, and that includes absolute cleanliness and frequent changing of external sanitary pads. Tampons should be avoided during this period. It is important that the patient wash thoroughly after bowel and bladder elimination and wear clean underwear at all times. Cleanliness promotes healthy, rapid healing of the episiotomy. The postdelivery vaginal discharge, called lochia, exists for an average of three weeks. It will manifest itself in many different colors, from bright red bleeding immediately after the delivery to a darker red color to a brown color and then to a yellowish color toward the end of the three-week period. It has a very characteristic odor, and this odor does not mean in any way that there is infection present. It is the odor of the discharge during the healing phase of the lining of the uterus where the placenta was attached.

Sex

Sexual contact should be avoided in the postpartum period until the episiotomy is well healed and the vaginal discharge is completely gone. This usually is somewhere around four weeks. If the patient is going to engage in intercourse, she must give serious consideration to contraception, or she may become pregnant immediately after delivery. Today, women are very healthy, and they resume spontaneous ovulation quite early even though they may be breast-feeding; this is why instructions must be given about contraception and the prevention of pregnancy during the period of breast-feeding.

The Postpartum Examination

All patients should be seen six weeks postpartum for a complete examination, including an examination of all parts of the body and especially the pelvis. On pelvic examination, special attention is paid to the episiotomy and its healing, and the vagina is checked closely. All patients at the postpartum examination get a Papanicolaou smear, probably the first one that they have had since before the pregnancy commenced. After the examination, there is consultation to answer all the patient's questions and to discuss contraception. This is the time to sit down face to face with the patient and discuss all aspects of contraception. There are many methods of contraception available today, and these should be discussed in great detail, one by one, with the patient. Family planning is very important, and a patient, especially a young patient, should not have one pregnancy right on top of the other. If it is possible, at least a two-year interval between pregnancies is advised. In this way, the patient is able to enjoy her new offspring, is able to participate in breast-feeding if that is her desire, has adequate time to enjoy the very interesting years of growth and development, and permits bonding to occur so that there is a very strong connection between mother and child. This is a very significant part of the patient's development and gives the child great emotional and mental stability.

In conclusion, pregnancy is one of the great miracles of life. When one gives sober thought and reflection to the fact that it all starts with conception, when a microscopic egg is released by the ovary and is fertilized by a sperm that has been deposited in the woman's vagina, then growth and development occur and after 40 weeks of gestation a new, healthy infant is delivered into the world, pregnancy is truly remarkable and should be greatly appreciated and respected by all humankind.

W. Robert Penman

PREMARITAL SEXUALITY

The term "premarital sex" refers to a variety of sexual behaviors, including sexual intercourse, oral sex, anal sex, masturbation, and petting before marriage. These behaviors usually occur with a partner. Masturbation is self–genital manipulation, which may be done alone or with a partner. It often occurs long before marriage, even as early as infancy. Therefore, most people engage in premarital sexual activity even if they do not have sexual intercourse before marriage.

Sexual experiences with the same gender is common during adolescence, particularly between the ages of 10 and 16. Some same-sex behaviors, such as mutual touching or masturbation, are considered to be a normal aspect of the transition from childhood to adulthood and not predictive of adult homosexuality.

When research is conducted on premarital sexual behavior, sexual intercourse is usually the focus. Often, when we think of premarital sexual activity, we think of teenagers. However, because many people are postponing first marriage into their 20s or beyond, premarital sexual behavior can be experienced by many people older than adolescence.

Many people still consider sex within marriage the best and only acceptable option for themselves, for either moral or religious reasons. In addition, there seems to have been a slowing in the rate of increase in premarital intercourse and a decrease in the number of partners in the past decade, partly due to the fear of AIDS (acquired immune deficiency syndrome) and other STDs (sexually transmitted diseases). Premarital sex implies that marriage is a norm in this culture and that sex is expected within marriage. In recent decades, sexual behavior has also become the norm, both before and after marriage.

The fear of STDs decreased after the 1940s, when penicillin and other antibiotics became available to cure a number of them. Since the advent of oral contraceptives in the 1960s, there has been an even greater increase in premarital sex, because pregnancy is more easily preventable. When abortion became legal in the United States, there was again an increase in premarital sex rates, because unwanted pregnancies could be safely terminated.

Incidence and Prevalence of Teenage Sexual Activity

Between 1900 and 1960, there was a tenfold increase in the incidence of sexual intercourse among single teenage girls in the United States. More than 70 percent of 19-year-old women and more than 80 percent of 19-year-old men have engaged in sexual intercourse prior to marriage.

Unfortunately, contraceptive usage by teenagers is notably low and sporadic, although it has increased within the last few years. In 1989, more than half of teenage girls and more than three-fourths of teenage boys had engaged in unprotected sexual intercourse at least once.

For each year of age, the proportion of adolescent women reported having premarital intercourse increased at least 55 percent from 1970 to 1988. The largest relative increase occurred among 15-year-olds, while three-quarters of 18- to 19-year-old women reported having had premarital sexual intercourse in 1988. African-American teenage girls consistently report having more premarital sexual activity than white girls, although the gap is closing between the two groups.

Factors That Influence the Initiation of Sexual Activity

The initiation of sexual activity among adolescents is governed by a complex mixture of social, psychological, religious, and physical influences. Girls most frequently mentioned peer pressure, with less frequent mention of being in love, wanting to feel grown up, or having feelings of sexual desire as reasons to have sexual intercourse. Boys also cited social pressure as a reason for having sex, followed by feelings of sexual desire, accomplishment, and curiosity.

For girls, sexual intercourse is usually initiated about four years after menarche. Early-maturing girls are more likely to begin early sexual activity at younger ages than late-maturing girls. Factors that promote the initiation of sexual activity in girls include risk-taking behaviors (e.g., drinking, drug use, not wearing seat belts), low socioeconomic status of the family, a dysfunctional family (with parental drug or alcohol use), poor academic performance, residence in a large inner-city community, low self-esteem, high susceptibility to peer pressure, mother and sister who became pregnant as teenagers, or absence of the father through death or divorce. Several factors that are likely to delay the initiation of sexual activity include the prospect of a college education, career goals, and high religiosity. School-based health clinics seem to decrease the incidence of teenage pregnancy and to delay the onset of the first sexual intercourse.

Contraceptive Use During Premarital Sexual Behavior

Many teenagers who engage in premarital sex do not use birth control for the first six months of intercourse. In the event that the sexual encounter is with a new partner, many young women are reluctant to suggest a condom or indicate that they are on the pill for fear that their "reputation" will be tarnished. The two most common reasons given by teenagers for not using contraceptives are failure to anticipate intercourse and the belief that the risk of pregnancy is small, often due to belief in myths about pregnancy.

Teenage daughters who discuss sex with their parents had attitudes and behavior patterns that lowered their risk of becoming pregnant before marriage and delayed their first sexual intercourse. Since the 1960s, societal attitudes have changed considerably regarding premarital sex. While over 80 percent of parents of college-age students condemned premarital sex for their children in 1967, in 1981 most of the parents interviewed accepted premarital sex for their children who were in love. However, even when premarital sex is considered permissible or acceptable, few parents adequately prepare their children with the information they need about pregnancy and STD prevention.

Providing birth control information to unmarried people was illegal in some States until a 1977 Supreme Court case. Now, young people in the United States have access not only to birth control information before marriage but also to contraceptive devices. Parental consent is not required for unmarried people to obtain birth control or abortion services in most states.

Although premarital sex is common in the United States, and birth control information and services are available, the United States has the highest teenage pregnancy rate in the industrialized world. This is due to the fact that the United States is a sexually repressive culture, which does not provide young people with complete and accurate information about sex or the ability to exercise responsible sexual decision making or behavior.

Risks Associated with Premarital Sexual Activity

The time when adolescents mature physically, psychologically, and cognitively is also the time when many are most likely to become sexually active. Although sexual development and expressions of sexuality are part of the psychosocial maturation of teenagers, they put the ill-prepared teenager at risk for both unwanted pregnancy and infection by sexually transmitted organisms.

Increased sexual activity among adolescents has several common health consequences: gonorrhea, chlamydia, herpes simplex 1 and 2, and pelvic inflammatory disease. Consequences of these diseases are often infertility and ectopic pregnancies. These risks are especially high as a consequence of premarital sexual activity beginning early in adolescence. The earlier teenagers begin sexual activity, the greater is the likelihood of multiple sexual partners. The more sexual partners one has, the greater the risk of contracting an STD.

REFERENCES

Alan Guttmacher Institute. *Teenage Pregnancy: The Problem That Hasn't Gone Away*. New York: Alan Guttmacher Institute, 1981.

American Academy of Pediatrics. *Adolescent Wellness*. Adolescent Sexuality Monographs. Lindenhurst, N.J.: Health Learning Systems, 1989.

———. Committee on Adolescence: Adolescent Pregnancy. *Pediatrics*, Vol. 83 (1989), pp. 132–34.

———. Committee on Adolescence: Care of Adolescent Parents and Their Children. *Pediatrics*, Vol. 72 (1983), pp. 249–50.

Fox, G. The Mother–Adolescent Daughter Relationship as a Sexual Socialization Structure: A Research Review. *Family Relations*, Vol. 29 (1980), pp. 21–28.

Minnesota Clinic. *Population Today*, Vol. 14 (June 1986), p. 4.

Premarital Sexual Experiences Among Adolescent Women: United States, 1970–1988. *Morbidity and Mortality Weekly Report*, Vol. 39 (Jan. 4, 1991), pp. 929–32.

Stoller, R.J., and G.H. Herdt. Theories of Origins of Male Homosexuality: A Cross-cultural Look. *Archives of General Psychiatry*, Vol. 42 (1985), pp. 399–402.

Trussell, J. Teenage Pregnancy in the United States. *Family Planning Perspectives*, Vol. 20 (1988), pp. 262–72.

Andrea Parrot

PREMATURE EJACULATION

The definition of premature ejaculation is imprecise and the subject of disagreement among sex therapists and researchers. Masters and Johnson suggested that ejaculation occurs prematurely if the woman does not reach orgasm during intercourse at least 50 percent of the time. This definition is problematic, as some women reach orgasm very rapidly during intercourse, while for others, orgasm never occurs during intercourse, regardless of duration. Kaplan proposed that a lack of voluntary control over the occurrence of orgasm defined premature ejaculation. However, it is not clear that the ejaculation reflex is truly subject to voluntary control. Rather, the ejaculation reflex, similar to the sneezing reflex, is at best only partially under voluntary control.

The *Diagnostic and Statistical Manual* of the American Psychiatric Association defines premature ejaculation as "ejaculation with minimal sexual stimulation or before, upon, or shortly after penetration and before the person wishes it." This definition acknowledges that there must be a subjective element to the diagnosis of premature ejaculation. As well as considering the duration of intercourse, the nature of the couple's sexual interaction must be evaluated. A couple who engages in 45 minutes of unrestrained manual and oral–genital foreplay, followed by one minute of pleasurable intercourse, would not be considered to be troubled by premature ejaculation. However, ejaculation after ten minutes of intercourse might be premature if this duration can only be achieved by avoiding all foreplay; spraying the penis with a skin anesthetic; wearing three condoms; thinking unpleasant, distracting thoughts; and biting one's tongue so the pain interferes with sexual arousal.

The rates of premature ejaculation found in population studies have varied between 10 percent and 25 percent of men surveyed, probably due to differences in the definition of the problem. In terms of actual duration of intercourse, the 1948 Kinsey Report found that "for perhaps three-quarters of all males, orgasm is reached within two minutes" of intercourse, but Hunt's 1974 study found that the average duration of intercourse had increased dramatically, to 10 to 14 minutes, in the intervening 26 years. This dramatic change in the societal norm for duration of intercourse has increased the distress of men who suffer from premature ejaculation.

Premature ejaculation, according to Bancroft, is typically a younger man's problem, with the majority of cases involving men under the age of 30. Premature ejaculation is typical for young men in their first sexual experiences and might be considered normal at this time. However, as these men have no history of successful sexual relationships as a basis for their sexual self-esteem, self-blame and self-labeling as dysfunctional often occur. With continued sexual experience, most men spontaneously get over their initial premature ejaculation. Along with the effects of experience, as a normal physiological change in aging the time required for a man to reach orgasm increases, but this is a slow change occurring over many years. A young man whose premature ejaculation is not resolved with greater sexual experience would have to wait 20 or 30 years for normal aging processes to solve his problem.

Premature ejaculation does not seem to be caused by any physiological factors or medical conditions. While Kaplan suggested that some local diseases or medications could cause premature ejaculation, Bancroft did not find this to be the case.

Research has also failed to connect premature ejaculation with the complex individual psychodynamic and couple-relationship problems associated with other sexual dysfunctions, such as hypoactive sexual desire. Rather, premature ejaculation seems to be typical of young, sexually inexperienced males who simply have not learned to slow down and modulate their arousal and to prolong the pleasurable process of making love. Men who have sex only infrequently are also prone to ejaculate prematurely. Indeed, Kinsey, Pomeroy, and Martin proposed that the primary cause of premature ejaculation was a

low frequency of sexual activity. Research has indicated that sensory thresholds in the penis are lowered by infrequent sexual activity and that premature ejaculation patients have a low rate of sexual activity. However, it may well be that premature ejaculation makes sex an unpleasant failure experience, which is therefore avoided, rather than that low frequency of sexual activity causes premature ejaculation.

Anxiety and ejaculation both involve activation of the sympathetic nervous system, so anxiety about trying to delay ejaculation can make the problem worse. Masters and Johnson proposed that men learn to be rapid ejaculators during adolescent masturbation, when they often hurry to ejaculate because of fear of being discovered by parents. However, such experiences seem to have been equally common in men who are not premature ejaculators. There has even been some speculation by evolutionary biologists that rapid ejaculation may have been selected for during primate evolution, through a "survival of the fastest" process. A male who could ejaculate rapidly would be more likely to reproduce successfully, as there would be less chance of the female escaping, another male interrupting, or a predator attacking before coitus was completed.

Kaplan proposed that premature ejaculators cannot accurately perceive their own arousal level and therefore cannot engage in self-control. However, one laboratory study comparing premature ejaculators and age-matched normal control subjects actually found that the premature ejaculators were more accurate when their self-ratings were compared to objective measures of physiological arousal. It may be that premature ejaculators, who because of their problem keep their attention focussed on how close they are to ejaculation during sexual activity, have trained themselves to be unusually accurate self-observers of arousal. None of the theories of the cause of premature ejaculation is well supported by research, except that premature ejaculation is typical of younger, less experienced men and men who have sex infrequently.

The treatment of premature ejaculation, using the "pause" and "squeeze" procedures developed by Semans and by Masters and Johnson, has been found to be highly effective. Research has demonstrated that such procedures work well in group as well as in individual treatment, and in self-help programs; they can be practiced in individual masturbation with relatively good transfer of therapeutic gains when sex with a partner is resumed. Success rates of 90 percent to 98 percent are reported.

In the stop-start or pause procedure, the penis is manually stimulated until the man is fairly highly aroused. The couple then pauses until his arousal subsides, at which time the stimulation is resumed. This sequence is repeated several times before stimulation is carried through to ejaculation, so the man ultimately experiences much more total time of stimulation than he ever has before and thus learns to have a higher threshold for ejaculation. The squeeze procedure is much like the stop-start procedure, with the addition that when stimulation stops, the woman firmly squeezes the penis between her thumb and forefinger, at the place where the glans of the penis joins the shaft. This squeeze seems to further reduce arousal. After a few weeks of this training, the necessity of pausing diminishes, with the man able to experience several minutes of continuous penile stimulation without ejaculating. Next, the couple progresses to putting the penis in the vagina but without any thrusting movements. If the man rapidly becomes highly aroused, the penis is withdrawn and the couple waits for arousal to subside, at which point the penis is reinserted. When good tolerance for inactive containment of the penis is achieved, the training procedure is repeated during active thrusting. Generally, two to three months of practice is sufficient for a man to be able to enjoy prolonged intercourse without any need for pauses or squeezes.

We have no real understanding of why the pause and squeeze procedures described by Semans in 1956 and Masters and Johnson in 1970 work. The pause procedure fits Guthrie's theoretical paradigm for counterconditioning by "crowding the threshold." Additionally, the stimulation and pause procedure is typically repeated by the patient several times per week, thus raising the frequency of sex and raising the sensory threshold of the penis. Either or both of these mechanisms may underlie the effectiveness of treatment.

Some variations on the pause and squeeze procedures have been reported, typically as clinical case reports. One variation described by LoPiccolo involves reversing one of the physiological changes that occurs during high arousal. During high arousal, the scrotum contracts and elevates the testes close to the body. As well as having the patient cease stimulation or squeeze on the penis, the patient may also be instructed to stretch out the scrotum and reverse this testicular elevation. However, during high arousal, any additional stimulation of the scrotum and perineum may trigger an ejaculation and thus may make the pause and squeeze procedure in-

effectual. Empirical data on the effectiveness of this technique are lacking.

Another procedure that has been proposed is to have the patient perform a Valsalva maneuver while pausing or squeezing. The Valsalva maneuver involves forced exhalation with the airways closed, as one does to clear the ears when descending in an airplane. The Valsalva maneuver is purported to reduce sympathetic nervous system arousal. Because ejaculation is primarily mediated by sympathetic arousal, the Valsalva should delay ejaculation. However, more recent neurologic evidence by Kedia indicates that there is also some parasympathetic mediation of ejaculation, and parasympathetic arousal is not lowered, and may even increase, during the Valsalva maneuver. Furthermore, performing a Valsalva may simply lower arousal by distracting the patient and may therefore be a type of placebo treatment. Empirical research is lacking in clinical reports on this procedure.

Segraves reported that drugs and medications that block sympathetic arousal often have the effect of delaying ejaculation. Such agents include anti-anxiety, antidepressant, and major tranquilizing medications; sedatives; some medications used to treat high blood pressure; and some antihistamines. However, because of serious side effects, the use of medication in treating premature ejaculation is not recommended, especially when the effectiveness of the behavioral retraining procedure is considered. Many of the recreational or "street" drugs such as alcohol, marijuana, cocaine, "downers" (barbiturates), and heroin also delay ejaculation, and although some men do use such agents to deal with their premature ejaculation, this is even more unwise than the use of prescription medications.

It is somewhat puzzling that although there is little agreement about the definition or cause of premature ejaculation, and no real understanding of how the treatment procedure works, treatment is virtually 100 percent effective. If one has to have a sexual dysfunction, this is the one to have.

REFERENCES

Bancroft, J. *Human Sexuality and Its Problems.* New York: Churchill Livingston, 1989.

Frank, E., C. Anderson, and D. Rubinstein. Frequency of Sexual Dysfunction in "Normal" Couples. *New England Journal of Medicine,* Vol. 299 (1978), pp. 111–15.

Heiman, J.R., B.A. Gladue, C.W. Roberts, and J. LoPiccolo. Historical and Current Factors Discriminating Sexually Functional from Sexually Dysfunctional Married Couples. *Journal of Marital and Family Therapy,* Vol. 12 (1986), pp. 163–74.

Hong, L.K. Survival of the Fastest. *Journal of Sex Research*, Vol. 20 (1984), pp. 109–22.

Hunt, M. *Sexual Behavior in the 1970s*. Chicago: Playboy Press, 1974.

Kaplan, H.S. *The New Sex Therapy*. New York: Brunner/Mazel, 1974.

Kedia, K. Ejaculation and Emission: Normal Physiology, Dysfunction, and Therapy. In R.J. Krane, M.B. Siroky, and I. Goldstein, eds., *Male Sexual Dysfunction*. Boston: Little, Brown, 1983.

Kilmann, P.R., and R. Auerbach. Treatments of Premature Ejaculation and Psychogenic Impotence: A Critical Review of the Literature. *Archives of Sexual Behavior*, Vol. 8 (1979), pp. 81–100.

Kinsey, A.C., W.B. Pomeroy, and C.E. Martin. *Sexual Behavior in the Human Male*. Philadelphia: Saunders, 1948.

LoPiccolo, J. Treatment of Sexual Dysfunction. In A.S. Bellak, M. Hersen, and A.E. Kazdin, eds., *International Handbook of Behavior Modification and Therapy*. 2nd ed. New York: Plenum Press, 1990.

Masters, W.H., and V.E. Johnson. *Human Sexual Inadequacy*. Boston: Little, Brown, 1970.

Sanders, D. *The Woman Book on Sex and Love*. London: Joseph, 1985.

———. *The Woman Report on Men*. London: Sphere, 1987.

Segraves, R.T. Drugs and Desire. In R.C. Rosen and S.R. Leiblum, eds., *Sexual Desire Disorders*. New York: Guilford, 1988.

Semans, J.H. Premature Ejaculation: A New Approach. *Southern Medical Journal*, Vol. 49 (1956), pp. 353–57.

Spiess, W.F., J.H. Geer, and W.T. O'Donohue. Premature Ejaculation: Investigation of Factors in Ejaculatory Latency. *Journal of Abnormal Psychology*, Vol. 93 (1984), pp. 242–45.

Joseph LoPiccolo

PRINCE, VIRGINIA

Virginia Prince (1913–), also known as Virginia Bruce and Charles Prince, all pseudonyms, organized, publicized, and indoctrinated others into her views of cross-dressing. Though biologically male, she has lived as a woman for nearly thirty years and is identified as "she" for this period. She more than any other person, brought male cross-dressing out of the closet by emphasizing the importance of learning to express "the girl within." She established a publishing house that disseminated information about cross-dressing, traveled, made public appearances around the world, organized groups wherever she went, and served as a role model for many transvestites. For some 20 years, from 1960 to 1980, she was the dominant voice of transvestism, and it was only in the 1980s, when she was well past the age of retirement, that others moved into leadership in the transvestite movement.

Born in Los Angeles in 1913 to a middle-class family, Prince began cross-dressing as a teenager, and by age 18 he (I use the male pronoun for this period in Prince's life) was sneaking out of his house in women's clothes. He continued to cross-dress, albeit secretly, after his marriage and while studying for his Ph.D. in biochemistry at the University of California at San Francisco. When he returned to Los Angeles to work as a research chemist, he told his wife about his cross-dressing. She tolerated it but refused to be with him while he did so, and relations between the two deteriorated after the birth of a son. She sued for divorce on the basis of his cross-dressing, and the result was an outburst of lurid newspaper stories that alienated him from many of his friends and acquaintances.

Though he later remarried, this marriage, too, ended in divorce, after which he began to live permanently as a woman. In 1960, she began publishing a magazine, *Transvestia*, and as the number of subscribers grew, she began establishing chapters of what she called a sorority for cross-dressers. She also added a number of other publications on transvestism to her list.

REFERENCE

Prince, V. My Story. *Transvestia*, No. 100 (1977).

Vern L. Bullough

PRISONS: SEX IN PRISONS

When either a male or a female is imprisoned and forcibly denied sexual contact, he or she does not lose libido or sexual energy. Forced abstinence leads naturally to seeking substitute outlets. When prolonged, as in lengthy prison sentences, abstinence may turn into impulsive or compulsive action, such as rape or homosexual involvement. After a period, which differs from individual to individual, he or she must find a way to release the built-up excessive sexual energy. At that point, the individual appears to have three choices: abstinence, masturbation, or homosexual activity.

Abstinence is rarely, if ever, the choice, since sex in prison means more than simply the release of sexual energy. The pressures, fears, anxieties, and frustrations that result from confinement continue to build and need some form of quieting. Sex, then, becomes a tranquilizer, a sleeping pill, an anger release, a way to deal with frustration, a method of providing self-love when feelings of rejection are the greatest, and whatever else the inmate decides to use it for. Abstinence would prevent this solution to so many types of personal problems.

Some prisoners use masturbation as their only sexual outlet for the duration of their sentence, but many others find masturbation unsatisfying, since it does not satisfy the needs for affection, companionship, and security. While initially using masturbation for a sex outlet, this group, after a period, progresses to other forms of human sexuality.

Homosexuality is a simple and easy choice for those prisoners who were homosexually involved or active in the community, but this choice presents a complicated solution for persons who considered themselves exclusively heterosexual before their confinement. Oftentimes, the homosexual activity is not consensual but involves various types of rape.

Rape

By far, the most frequently discussed and reported sexual activity in prisons is homosexual rape. By no means is this problem simple in any way. The dynamics are complicated and are the cause of much conflict among professionals in the field who are studying, speaking, or writing on the subject. Homosexual rape in prison takes several forms. The following example depicts an individual rape: An aggressive heterosexual inmate rapes a young, hairless, slim, passive, frightened young inmate. He uses the victim as his "woman," fantasizing intercourse with his wife or girlfriend in order to perform anal intercourse. The aggressor would never consider reciprocity, and if his "woman" suggests or asks for reciprocation, he could be seriously assaulted or even killed by the aggressor.

This type of homosexual rape could be either a onetime incident, often referred to in prison jargon as a "wolf and punk" rape, or an introduction to a long-term relationship, often referred to in prison jargon as a "daddy and his kid" rape. The relationship develops not because the victim enjoyed the rape but because the aggressor gave him the choice either of being his "kid" in return for protection and other material benefits (e.g., better food, better clothing, better jobs) or of being an open prey for the entire population of inmates.

The gang rapes usually involve a leader of a prison gang who chooses a young, passive, frightened, defenseless, loner-type new inmate to bring into the group. The gangs may use the rape as an initiation or, more often, as proof of their dominance and power. Gang rape could also be a

punishment for an inmate's siding with officers, being a "rat" (informer), or refusing to join the gang or to behave in a manner that they insist on.

There have been a few scholarly studies of sex in prison. Yochelson and Samenow found that sexual release itself is not the objective, but rather the purpose of sex in prison is to establish oneself in a position of dominance. Groth theorizes that when a person feels powerless in regard to controlling his life, he can defend against the discomfort of such an experience by asserting control over someone else. Sexual assault becomes a means of compensating for his sense of helplessness and vulnerability and of retaliating for his feelings of resentment and anger. Accepting this hypothesis explains the large number of these rapes that occur daily in the prison system, both reported and mostly unreported.

The damage that results from male prison rape is incalculable. Formerly adequate male inmates become passive, frightened, submissive individuals who suffer guilt and self-recrimination for being too inadequate to protect themselves from such attack. The results often do not become visible until these rape victims are released and then vent their anger and hatred on society for placing them in prison. They may even inflict their anger on females (mother figures) for not training them to be as manly as their attackers. It is also not uncommon, when their attackers are either released or transferred out of their prison setting, for them to become victimizers of other new and weaker inmates. Thus, the chain is continued.

Rapes are usually not reported. Buffin states that if a person who is the victim of a prison sexual attack has the temerity to complain, the likely result will be (1) retaliation by other prisoners, (2) segregation and attendant loss of privileges within the prison, (3) ridicule and embarrassment, and (4) possible prosecution of the offender, which in fact provides the prisoners with no tangible relief. Reporting also must deal with the problem of "inconsistent enforcement." Due to opposing attitudes of prison staffs, ranging from protective overidentification to moral rejection and punitive anger, the victim of rape in prison never knows what to expect from the prison administration if he or she risks life itself by reporting such attacks. The dilemma is further complicated by the forced allegiance to prison codes. Reporting becomes a two-edged sword in that, if the victim of prison rape reports it, he will be put into protective custody and identified as an informer, and the reporting will soon become common knowledge, placing the victim in additional jeopardy.

Finally, where homosexual rape is concerned, the subject of prevention must be addressed. While a highly controversial issue, conjugal visits appear to be the only means of lessening this difficult problem for young inmates who have made their first serious mistake. While not much research has been done on this in terms of rape, it seems clear that conjugal visits are a means of reducing sexual tension and homosexual rape among prisoners

Consensual Male Homosexual Liaisons

A second common type of sexual activity in prisons is consensual homosexual relationships. Even here, however, there is more than one type. The most straightforward relationship involves two openly homosexual inmates who join together for a mutually supportive, protective, and nurturing relationship that usually only lasts for short periods. If it lasts for the length of the stay for either partner, it rarely continues on the outside. If it does continue on the outside, it rarely lasts, primarily since the common bond and compatibility of being prisoners no longer exists. Even in these relationships, there is usually a dominant and a passive partner who, respectively, plays the male or the female role.

The danger of such a relationship, should it become known, is that the two inmates will be looked down upon both by the prison officials and by the remainder of the prison population, who are threatened by homosexual relationships either due to repressed homosexual feelings of their own or due to strong homophobic rearing. An alternate danger is that other inmates will begin pressuring and even forcing known homosexual inmates to provide them with sexual favors as well.

Homoerotic relationships may also develop between formerly heterosexual males. Money has argued that when a society imposes effective barriers to heterosexual intercourse, there is a likelihood that institutionalized male bisexual practices will result. He stated that under the deprivation of living sex-segregated in prison, a man may discover in himself a bisexual versatility formerly hidden. Then, he may impose a homosexual encounter on a nonconsenting partner, a so-called joy-boy. Thereby, Money demonstrated rather nicely the dependence of a person on his environment to provide him with a partner for an erotic pair-bond.

The homoerotic relationships tend to follow several patterns. A supposedly normal heterosexual individual pair-bonds (Money's phrase)

with an openly passive homosexual. In these cases, secrecy is paramount, and there is usually no reciprocation in the beginning, but there often is at a later time. Bisexual, conscious, or repressed feelings emerge, often due to untreated, unreported early childhood homosexual molestation or abuse, usually willing and long-term. Often, the dominant male never allows emotions or feelings for the younger male to occur, and to prove there are none, he often offers his "kid" to other friends for their pleasure or to solidify a new relationship. This usually occurs when the aggressor begins to feel genuine emotions for the younger male and panics, interpreting these feelings as making him homosexual. Denial is the main factor in these cases.

Homosexual Prostitution

Homosexual prostitution usually is practiced by an admitted young or older homosexual inmate for money, gifts, protection, or friendships. Monogamy is not practiced, and the male prostitute usually has many "clients," who often are jealous of each other and vie for the affection and favors of the prostitute. These are the situations that often result in assaults, stabbings, and other serious situations between the clients and are a major concern of prison administrators and officers. These situations and their dangers account for many prohibitions, as well as for anger on the part of both prison officials and other inmates. In riots, these homosexual prostitutes, if not hidden and protected, often are viciously raped by lines of angry, and damaging, heterosexual inmates. In one such riot, one of these prostitutes was forcibly and violently raped by over 100 inmates, resulting in a damaged anal sphincter that did not close for over a week. The emotional damage made transferring him to another institution necessary.

For a homosexual to escape the usual stigmas attached to his behaviors, Kirkham explains that he must fulfill two criteria: (1) the homosexual act or acts must present only a situational reaction to the deprivation of heterosexual intercourse, and (2) such behavior must involve a complete absence of emotionality and effeminacy—both of which are regarded as signs of "weakness" and "queerness." An inmate who engages in homosexual activity must present a convincing facade of toughness and stereotypical "manliness" to escape being defined as a homosexual.

Female Homosexual Liaisons

There are vast differences in the way that homosexual relationships occur in female prisons and very different motives behind these relationships. While power-dominance relationships do exist in the more dangerous and aggressive female prisons, where the more frightened and passive younger females are forced into lesbian situations, these appear to be the exception rather than the rule and often occur in more of a gang situation than a one-on-one relationship.

A major difference in these homosexual relationships is the "family dynamic" that does not exist in the male prisons to either the degree or the duration that it does in all female institutions. This "family" is composed of a "father," a "mother," and a "child" (or children), all roles assumed by adult female prisoners. The "father" is usually a highly assaultive and aggressive lesbian who is in total control of the "family" and all its members. The "mother" is more passive and compliant and is in charge of the care, nurturance, and protection of the "child(ren)," who remain dependent, close, and loyal to both parents. Knowledge of the family is universal throughout the institution, and the existence of the family is accepted by both inmates and staff.

Research indicates that homosexual liaisons are more frequent in female than in male prisons, but the evidence is rather old and inconclusive. One reason for this is the degree of openness in female prisons concerning these relationships and the secrecy and guardedness that necessarily exists in male institutions.

Another distinction between the two sexes is made by Edelwick and Brodsky, who state that the relationships women formed in prison usually were not sexual in the full sense. Women in prison met their emotional needs by forming little "families"—father, mother, and child, all of them actually grown women.

Homosexual rape does take place in female as well as male prisons. Tollison found that in women's prisons, rape may involve forcing the victim to perform masturbation or cunnilingus on the offender(s), mutual masturbation or cunnilingus, or more violent acts involving vaginal rape with foreign objects.

While power struggles and needs do exist in female prisons, female homosexual rape is far less frequent than it is in male prisons, while consensual homosexual liaisons are more frequent and involve more feelings and human emotions. Relationships that begin in female prisons also carry over into the community more often than do those that begin in male prisons.

Inmate-Staff Sexual Liaisons

Both male and female prisoners who are in need of power and control often try to seduce a staff member. Yochelson and Samenow observed that there is an even greater challenge to establish a sexual liaison with a staff member than a fellow prisoner, since what counts is what the criminal can gain for himself or herself, using sex merely as a means to an end.

Once the staff person becomes involved with the prisoner, the prisoner has the ability to blackmail and to extort whatever he or she pleases from that staff person: food, favors, illegal mail and parcels, even money to be sent to the prisoner's family or friends. Male prostitutes with sociopathic personalities find a great deal of pleasure and satisfaction in "winning" at what they see as a challenge, or big game, and change in personality as soon as they have "hooked a fish." Previously a pleasant, cooperative, friendly inmate, he now takes total control of the frightened and intimidated staff person and uses his sexual prowess to maintain the relationship.

The staff member–victim can be either male or female. Rapists and playboy types choose female officers and staff more often than they choose male staff, often impregnating the staff person and then bragging about how they "got over" (deceived) the system. Female prisoners play the same sex-power game, especially in prisons where there are male officers as well as female officers. This is an increasingly common practice in today's prisons.

In summary, there is a need to understand why sex plays such a great role in the lives of prisoners. Several factors are evident:

1. In cases of forced assaultive homosexual rape in prison, the main motivation on the part of the aggressor does not appear to be sexual but rather a need for power and dominance over another human being, often to deny the aggressor's true feelings of fear of being dominated (reaction-formation).

2. Even in cases of so-called consensual homosexual relationships, there is often a strongly coercive element. Young, passive-inadequate males and females entering prison are often given the "choice" either of being a "kid" to one aggressive protector or of being open prey to anyone and everyone in the prison population.

3. Often, the intense interpersonal and intimate contact with so many members of the same sex and the constant exposure to naked same-sex inmates (showering is often in large, open areas with no privacy, and strip searches are conducted in large rooms with hundreds of naked men in close quarters), coupled with the knowledge that there will

be no heterosexual contact for many years to come, trigger latent, suppressed, or repressed bisexual interests.

4. Guilt and feelings of betrayal of their spouses or partners often result from prison homosexual liaisons in cases of men or women who, prior to prison, considered themselves exclusively heterosexual. Visits with these significant others becomes a problem, and the conflict of confessing their sexual activities or not is an ever-present dynamic.

5. Both men and women prisoners who have been raped and could not or did not report the occurrence to the authorities due to fears or threats against their lives carry an additional burden of guilt, shame, and damaged self-esteem. When the sexual assaults are ongoing and there appears to be no relief in the immediate future, suicidal thoughts begin, and many young prisoners of both sexes have committed suicide as the only solution.

6. For formerly heterosexual male or female prisoners in ongoing consensual and reciprocal homosexual relationships, conflicts over their future identity and life-styles when released are a major problem. This factor is exacerbated when the individual is married and there are children.

7. Upon release, the aggressive, raping types who prey on younger inmates and use them as women or men, maintaining heterosexual fantasies during the sexual behaviors and refusing to consider reciprocation, usually return to heterosexual activity and deny (to themselves) their homosexual relationships and activities in prison. In one such case, when meeting his passive partner on the streets and having the partner suggest a friendship due to their past sexual involvement, the aggressor assaulted the passive individual, who had to be hospitalized for serious injuries.

Heterosexual men who had repressed or suppressed bisexual feelings and interests that became acted upon in prison return to society in a confused state unless the situation has been resolved during the prison sentence through therapeutic intervention. Some of these individuals deny the bisexual feelings and interests to their significant others and continue to masturbate to fantasies of sex with same-sex individuals, even when having intercourse with their heterosexual partners. Without resolution, these former relationships usually end quite soon after the prisoners return to society.

During their incarceration, a surprising number of these inmates find the courage to tell their heterosexual partners (during visits or, more frequently, in letters or telephone calls) about their homosexual partners. Surprisingly, a large percentage of the partners are able to accept the situation, since they feel they cannot compete sexually. Often, a condition of this acceptance is that there is no true "love" involved in the relationship and that it will remain purely physical. It is truly remarkable how many of these relationships survive.

Some people deny the bisexual feelings and behaviors in prison to themselves. These individuals, especially males, often report sexual dysfunctions, ranging from desire-phase dysfunction to impotence.

AIDS

With the increase of prison deaths from AIDS (acquired immune deficiency syndrome), the problem of prison sex exists for all of society. Eventually, many of these infected men and women (from prison unprotected homosexual behavior) return to society and their wives, former partners, or new heterosexual or homosexual partners, not even knowing that they are infected. Prison authorities are still homophobic to the extent that most prison systems will not support the use of condoms or other prophylactic measures. They insist that forbidding the activity and punishing those caught in homosexual behavior will prevent the problem. The facts are that, in most major prisons, the ratio of staff to inmates is at minimum 100:1 and strict surveillance, 24 hours a day, on every prisoner is virtually impossible. The adage "where there's a will, there's a way" wins out.

The problem for the administration, ultimately responsible to society, is that providing condoms or other AIDS-prevention paraphernalia, while motivated by community health, may be (and often is) misinterpreted as condoning homosexual behavior, considered abnormal and perverted by conservative, homophobic community leaders.

Staff overidentification or the need to be liked by the inmates also plays a major role in prison sex. It is not uncommon for certain officers and staff members who themselves may be closeted homosexuals or bisexuals to permit homosexual behavior between inmates. This often occurs on the late-night shift (midnight to 6:00 A.M.) but has also been reported during regular daytime hours as well.

On the opposite side of the scale, the overly homophobic, puritanical, and moralistic officers and staff may go out of their way to set up or catch inmates in covert sexual activity and then demand the harshest possible sanctions. The mixed message given to the prisoners causes further confusion and turmoil.

Conclusion

Most of the research used for this article appeared in the literature between 1971 and 1982. Since that period, interest in this most important topic has waned to a trickle. More research, focusing on solutions rather than explanations, is needed if this all-important and overlooked source of both psychopathology and sexual disease (especially AIDS) is to be eliminated or, at least, lessened.

REFERENCES

Buffum, P.C. *Homosexuality in Prison*. Prepared for the Law Enforcement Assistance Administration. Washington, D.C.: Government Printing Office, 1971.

Edelwick, J., with A. Brodsky. *Sexual Dilemmas for the Helping Professions*. New York: Brunner/Mazel, 1979.

Groth, S.N. *Men Who Rape*. New York: Plenum Press, 1980.

Haberle, E.J. *The Sex Atlas*. New York: Continuum, 1982.

Kirkham, G.L. Homosexuality in Prison. In J.M. Henslin, ed., *Studies in the Sociology of Sex*. New York: Appleton Century Crofts, 1971.

Money, J. *Love and Love Sickness*. Baltimore: Johns Hopkins Univ. Press, 1980.

Prendergast, W.E. *Treating Sex Offenders in Correctional Institutions and Private Practice*. New York: Haworth Press, 1991.

Tollison, C.D., and H.E. Adams. *Sexual Disorders: Treatment, Theory, Research*. New York: Gardner Press, 1979.

Yochelson, S., and S. Samenow. *The Criminal Personality*. Vol. 3, *A Profile for Change*. New York: Jason Aronson, 1976.

William E. Prendergast

PROSTATE

The prostate is a male gland that is located just below the urinary bladder and close enough to the rectum that it can be felt when a finger is inserted. Although the size may vary from man to man, the normal gland is usually about one and one-half to two inches at its widest point, weighs from 15 to 20 grams, and is composed of a glandular and muscular portion. It is usually described as being about the size of a chestnut or walnut. A portion of the urethra (the tube that leads from the urinary bladder) passes through the gland. The ejaculatory ducts, which are produced from the union of the vas deferens and the tubes from the seminal vesicles, run their entire length through the prostate gland and unite with the prostatic urethra. The glandular portion of the prostate produces about 30 percent of the seminal fluid, which is thought to be necessary before sperm can fertilize an egg. Tissue hormones called prostaglandins are produced by the prostate (as well as by many other tissues in the human body) and produce physiological reactions, usually in those tissues adjacent to the location at which they are produced.

Some workers have postulated that women have a "female prostate," which is rudimentary glands (Skene's glands) found around the urethra near the neck of the urinary bladder. These glands are produced from the same embryological tissue that produce the prostate gland. It has been suggested that the "female prostate" is the Grafenberg or G spot, or is at least anatomically related to it. The existence of either the "female prostate" or the G spot has not been adequately demonstrated to the satisfaction of many workers, and certainly not in all women.

The prostate contracts during the various stages of male orgasm. These contractions, along with contractions of other glands and various muscles, cause the semen to spurt from the end of the penis. The prostate is also a source of sexual pleasure for some men who enjoy being recipients of anal sex. The prostate can be stroked by inserting a finger, penis, or some other item into the anus to a depth of about three inches and gently pressing toward the navel. This is actually what a physician does when he or she conducts a digital examination of the prostate. Although these sensations are pleasurable to many men, some find them uncomfortable and, for that reason, are hesitant to submit to a digital examination.

A digital examination of the prostate can reveal changes that are important to the health of the man. The prostate remains about the same size from the time of puberty until about age 50, when it begins to enlarge. This growth can lead to a condition known as benign prostatic hypertrophy (BPH), which affects almost all men after the age of 60. The condition may cause reduction in the size of the prostatic urethra and ejaculatory ducts, thus producing problems of urination and ejaculation. Prostate cancer is the most common cancer of the male sex organs and is the third most common cancer of men. Its cause is unknown. Although it is uncommon in men younger than age 60, some workers believe that virtually all men who reach the age of 80 will have the beginnings of the disease. Because it is such a slow-growing cancer, most men of that age will not show symptoms before they die of some other cause. However, it does cause 17 percent of cancer in men, and, because men are living longer, about 70,000 new cases are reported annually.

Prostatitis (inflammation of the prostate) is an extremely common condition among men. Infectious prostatitis is caused by a bacterium, yeast, or virus and can be sexually transmitted. The condition can be either acute or chronic. Congestive prostatitis is a condition caused by abrupt change in the frequency of sexual activity. Thus, a man who greatly increases his number of ejaculations over a short period of time (this sometimes happens to men who are newly married) or a man who suddenly decreases his number of ejaculations may both develop the condition. This may happen when a spouse becomes ill and sexual contact is no longer possible. Masturbation is sometimes recommended in this case.

The initial symptoms of all of these conditions are general. They are lower-back pain, painful urination, urinary urgency or frequency, pain or discomfort during or after ejaculation, unexpected discharges from the penis, and blood in the urine or semen. Any combination of these symptoms should send the man to his physician, who will palpate the prostate to discover changes in the size, shape, or texture of the gland.

Most problems of the prostate are treated with antibiotics or surgery, especially if the condition is discovered early. Usually, there are no lasting effects from the treatment, although retrograde ejaculation and loss of some erectile ability may be a result of some surgery.

REFERENCES

Greenberger, M.E., and M.E. Siegel. *What Every Man Should Know About His Prostate.* New York: Walker, 1983.

Masters, W.H., V.E. Johnson, and R.C. Kolodny. *Human Sexuality.* 3d ed. Glenview, Ill.: Scott, Foresman, 1988.

Rowan, R.L., and P.J. Gillette. *The Gay Health Guide: A Modern Medicine Book.* Boston: Little, Brown, 1978.

James D. Haynes

PROSTITUTION

Prostitution is one of the most written about topics in the whole field of human sexuality. It has a long history, but it is not clear that everyone is writing about the same thing. This is because what constitutes prostitution is not something that is easy to define. Even in the United States, there is considerable legal ambiguity about definitions. Several state penal codes, for example, define prostitution as the hiring out of one's body for sexual intercourse. Other states fail to stipulate that money has to be exchanged, defining prostitution only as the giving or receiving of the body for indiscriminate sexual intercourse. Sexual intercourse, per se, however, is not always necessary. One dictionary, for example, defines prostitution as the "offering of the body to indicate lewdness for hire," a definition so broad that the girl (or boy) who sells kisses at a church fund-raiser could be labeled a prostitute, since what constitutes lewdness is just as unclear as what constitutes prostitution.

Definition becomes all-important when dealing with sexual workers such as surrogates, used by some sex therapists to help patients overcome impotence or frigidity. These sexual surrogates see their mission as helping patients achieve a more satisfactory sex life. This includes not only offering theoretical analyses of sexual dysfunction but also engaging in intercourse with their clients if it is a necessary part of the teaching-learning process. In other words, they perform sex for hire. Surrogates, however, emphasize the therapeutic aspect of their teaching, but a similar therapeutic function has often been claimed by prostitutes in the past. Does the fact that surrogates work closely with physicians or sex therapists make them paraprofessionals rather than prostitutes?

Traditionally, prostitution has been defined in terms of females, but such a definition excludes the large number of males. For this reason, Havelock Ellis, a pioneer in the scientific investigation of sex, defined a prostitute as "a person who makes it a profession to gratify the lust of various persons of the opposite or the same sex." This definition has the advantage of including both sexes but leaves unanswered a whole host of other issues. Does the person who offers telephone sex to gratify a caller's lust become a prostitute? Does a spouse who is uninterested in having sex at a particular time become a prostitute when she or he engages in sexual intercourse simply to gratify a spouse? Does a person who sells his or her body for lustful purposes a single time become a prostitute, or does he or she need to do so 10 times or 100 times? One canon lawyer argued that a woman had to have had sex with a minimum of 23,000 customers to be called a prostitute.

As far as police records are concerned, a prostitute is a person who has been arrested, charged, and convicted of prostitution, but this ignores some of the more successful prostitutes who have never been arrested. In some European countries where there is state regulation of prostitution, a prostitute is someone who is registered as a prostitute. Parent-Duchâtelet, a 19th-century pioneer in the study of prostitution, restricted the term to those cases where "several mercenary acts of immorality had been legally established, when the person involved was publicly notorious, [and] when she (or he) had been caught in the act by witnesses other than her accuser or the police agent." In short, one had to be arrested to be called a prostitute.

Most definitions of prostitution include phrases about promiscuity, multiplicity of sexual partners, continuous sexual offenses, payment, and an element of notoriety, but no one of these factors is enough to establish a person as a prostitute. Some investigators have argued that the key to determining whether a person is or is not a prostitute is the emotional involvement and the pleasure gained. Probably, most prostitutes are emotionally uninvolved with their clients and most get little pleasure themselves, but this is not always the case, and it is certainly not true for male prostitutes. Moreover, in the past many married women did not obtain sexual satisfaction from intercourse with their husbands and were actually repulsed by the sexual act, but almost no one has suggested that they be called prostitutes.

Is a mistress a prostitute? In most such cases, there is a mercenary relationship, and not infrequently, over time, a woman passes from one love to another, but whether she can be classified as a prostitute ultimately depends not only on the nature of her relationship with her lover but also on her own self-image. But then, not everyone who thinks they are a prostitute might be classed as a prostitute by others. The most comprehensive definition was offered by Iwan Bloch at the beginning of the 20th century; he held that prostitution was a distinct form of extramarital sexual activity characterized by being more or less promiscuous, was seldom without reward, and was a form of professional commercialism for the purpose either of intercourse or of other forms of sexual activities and allurement, resulting in due time in the formation of a special type. This wide-ranging definition allowed Bloch to include the procurer or pimp as well as the prostitute, since he or she engaged in activity associated with the commercialism of sex and its allurement. Bloch, however, wrote before the development of modern advertising, which is in the business of selling products and often does so by hinting at sexual rewards to the buyer. In fact, by Bloch's definition, many professionals in the advertising business could be classified as engaging in prostitution.

However we define prostitution, history is full of examples of it, and we know the names of far more women prostitutes than we do of any other category of women. The Greeks developed a special erotic literature associated with prostitution, telling stories about prostitutes; hence, we get the word "pornography," literally the writings of prostitutes or writings about prostitutes. Though many prostitutes in the Greek world were slaves (both male and female), there was also a special high-class courtesan, the *heterae*, who was trained in the arts of pleasing men. The *heterae* are usually associated with powerful men.

Other societies and ages have also developed highly trained prostitutes, from the *geisha* of Japan to the Western courtesan. The 19th century saw a long list of women who could best be described as courtesans. Courtesans were the high-status prostitutes, and below them, historically, were the brothel prostitutes and below them the streetwalkers. There has always been a hierarchy of prostitutes, and often there are many layers in between. The contemporary call girl is a continuation of the courtesan tradition.

There have also been times of greater and lesser toleration of prostitution, although probably the first great period of repression was associated with the outbreak and spread of syphilis in the 16th century. Prostitution soon rebounded from this setback, and though it was often associated with STDs (sexually transmitted diseases), it was not until the last part of the 19th century that there was a concerted movement to abolish legally tolerated prostitution. The movement gained its greatest influence in the United States, which for the most part abolished brothels in the period following World War I and ran a large-scale campaign to equate prostitution with STDs. Though organized brothel prostitution more or less disappeared, except in some rural areas, new forms of prostitution appeared, from call girls to pickups in bars and hotel lobbies, and many forms of organized prostitution masqueraded under the name of escort services, bar girls, body massagers, taxi dancers, and other occupations, although there were also people in these occupations who were not prostitutes. Often, for a business engaged in prostitution to survive, it was necessary to have the unofficial cooperation of law enforcement officials, and the history of prostitution in the United States cannot be studied independently of political and police graft and corruption.

One of the difficulties with studying prostitution is that, until recently, most of the studies and writing about the topic has been done by males. This means that a masculine bias, conscious or unconscious, has dominated the writing, and very rarely has the topic been looked at from the point of view of the woman, or even from the point of view of the male prostitute. Generally also, the records reflect a class bias, since much of the writing about prostitution has been for or by the upper classes.

Looking at female prostitution from a feminist viewpoint emphasizes that women in most societies were regarded as a form of property. If they were not actually owned by a male, they were under male control, whether by fathers, husbands, sons, or brothers. Any damage to women, including the loss of female chastity or rape, was a violation of male property. Often, a woman so "dishonored" had no alternative except prostitution. In contrast, the male suffered no such disabilities about his sexual promiscuity and was much freer to do as he wanted. The result was a double standard that inevitably led to the establishment of a class of women, prostitutes, free from the restrictions of proper women and with whom other men could have sex. In a way, prostitutes were regarded as different from other women—the proper wife, sister, mother, and daughter—who were acculturated to deny an interest in sex.

One of the reasons for this double standard is that the woman who wanted to engage in sex with the same kind of freedom that men had, in the past faced the ever-present possibility of pregnancy. Though contraceptives have been used throughout history, even the best were not very effective, and the woman who had become pregnant outside of marriage in many societies either had to attempt abortion or suffer through the pregnancy and resulting stigma. The men who got them pregnant were more difficult to identify, and though forced marriages existed in many societies, usually it was the woman who bore the onus of violating societal taboos. Even if an unmarried women did not become pregnant through her sexual activities, her hymen was damaged, and this made her less valuable as a prospective bride.

Moreover, since women in the past have often been confined to the home and limited in the types of occupations they could pursue, prostitution often became the only alternative for those women who were turned down for marriage because they were not virgins, were unable to furnish a dowry, or were for some other reason without homes, husbands, or supporting male relatives. Often, in countries such as China, women were sold into prostitution. Society has tolerated the prostitute rather than face the issues of alternative employment or greater freedom for women. Probably, most women had little to say about prostitution. In a society in which slavery was widespread, many women (and often men as well) were designated as prostitutes. Though women classified as prostitutes were ostracized from the company of proper women, such a woman (or even a man) might achieve status in society if she (or he) became the companion of a powerful man; the position of mistress to a monarch, for example, could give influential position to the family of the woman so chosen. Many well-to-do families were willing to see their daughters become mistresses of kings or powerful princes in order to better the family position or to give them access to the powerful person. They were less willing to have their sons become companions, because this reflected on their own masculinity. This was because in male prostitution, the male who submitted, who was penetrated like a woman, was regarded as a lesser man and stigmatized in many societies. In contrast, the male who penetrated another was and is not today regarded as homosexual at all in many societies. He is simply a machismo male.

Though accurate statistics about prostitution in the past are nonexistent, we do know from the Kinsey and other data that proportionately fewer males in countries like the United States are visiting prostitutes now than in the past and are doing so less frequently. Until the appearance of AIDS (acquired immune deficiency syndrome), however, male homosexual prostitutes were becoming more numerous. Several reasons account for the decline of female prostitution. One factor is the gradual elimination of the double standard, at least in some of the more advanced industrialized countries. This has been made possible by the development of effective contraceptives and by changing attitudes among women themselves. The percentage of young women engaging in premarital coitus is approaching that of men, although the frequency for most women is less. Even among married women, the ability to have some control over their own body through contraceptives has made them less likely to drive their spouse from the marital bed to avoid getting pregnant. Moreover, the growing recognition of women's right to say no to sexual advances has led to somewhat better communication between the two sexes on the question of intercourse. Opportunities for employment are approaching the same level as those for young men, and women can advance up the corporate or institutional ladder to better paying jobs. Divorce is more frequent, and couples who are sexually incompatible no longer need find sexual relief in prostitution or adultery. Publicized findings of researchers on female sexuality have encouraged women to accept the fact that they are sexual beings, although, as a general rule, women are not as aggressive in seeking sexual partners as men, probably due to the fact that aggression itself is associated with testosterone levels. Societal attitudes are at work as well, since the sexually aggressive woman is still not looked upon in the same light as the sexually aggressive man.

There are undoubtedly many other reasons that could be advanced for the decline of prostitution, but the point to emphasize is that it still exists. There is probably no city or town of any size either in the United States or in the world at large that lacks both female and male prostitutes functioning in some way or another, almost entirely to serve male customers.

Since women have a potential for sexual enjoyment that is at least equal to that of men, we have to wonder why there is so little mention of prostitutes to service a female clientele. Occasionally, such prostitutes are mentioned in the fictional literature, but there is still not enough hard data to describe them in the same way we can describe other prostitutes. Although it is a physiological fact that the need for male tumescence creates problems for multiple incidents of intercourse, the refractory period is relatively short in young males and has not proved to be an impossible barrier to the development of male homosexual prostitution. This means that societal factors are a key in this kind of prostitution, as it is in traditional female prostitution. Though there are a number of male gigolos and kept men, the numbers are insignificant compared to their female counterparts. It may well be that men see sex as a physiological function, and women, while viewing it as such, also want more involvement, touching, feeling, and expression, which no prostitute could provide in the comparatively short time that most males spend with prostitutes. Male prostitutes for women are therefore much more expensive than their female counterparts for men.

Still, traditional prostitution emphasizes just how powerful the dominance of men over women has been. One result of this dominance is that female prostitution can be seen as a symptom of the victimization and subordination of women, or, in the case of the male homosexual prostitutes, the victimization of the surrogates who take the role of women. At the same time, prostitution becomes an outstanding example of the perverse resilience of human beings, since women, including prostitutes, have turned their sexual subordination into a weapon that allows them, in turn, to victimize men. This very successful counterplay has been built on the culturally supported myth that men enjoy, want, and need sex more than women, and each generation of girls in most of Western culture has been socialized to believe this myth. This suggests that the two essential conditions for supporting prostitution in the forms in which it traditionally has existed are a belief in the dominance of males and a shortage of willing female sexual partners. These two conditions have also, to a greater or lesser extent, supported the marriage contract. The fewer restrictions that society has placed on sexual activities for women, the less institutionalized prostitution there has been. Having a positive attitude toward sex, however, is not enough, and many societies that recognized female sexuality had a different standard for the sexual conduct of men than they did for women. In the double-standard societies, women were expected to remain virgins until marriage and were punished in various ways for failure to do so. To the extent that such attitudes continue to exist, female prostitution will also continue to exist.

However, other factors are at work as well to maintain prostitution. One is simply the existence of large concentrations of men in areas with few women. Perhaps the best example of this is the traditional military base. Though the integration of women into the armed forces lessens the sexual disparities inherent at such bases, they have not eliminated them, and since most of the males are young and unattached, they turn to available feminine companions, many of whom serve as companions for money. In some sex-segregated institutions, such as prisons, schools, and even restricted military bases, strict sex segregation encourages more male surrogate sexual partners than would be the case in a population where women were available. Not all the homosexual contact in these settings is prostitution, since some of it is collegial, more so in schools than in prisons, but even in the most collegial atmosphere some kind of barter or exchange system often develops. As long as these concentrations of males exist, prostitution will have a market.

Another source of demand for prostitution is a demand for variety in sexual activity. Men satiated with or not aroused by ordinary sexual activities with their traditional partners tend to look for variety. Sometimes, wives, even if they have the desire to do so, cannot satisfy their spouse's sexual desire, as evidenced by the 19th-century taste of many upper-class Englishmen for deflowering young virgins. Brothels specializing in whipping and other sadomasochistic pleasures are well documented, as is the prostitutes' willingness to cater to transvestites and to engage in golden showers and a variety of other sexual activities, such as anal intercourse, which the customer is unwilling to request of his wife or girlfriend. As social clubs that cater to men and women sadomasochists or to organized transvestites spring up, and as such activities come out of the closet, the prostitute alternative becomes less attractive to many. Still, there is a considerable demand for the prostitute who specializes in such customers.

Prostitutes also serve those who are so socially inept that they are unable to communicate effectively with a nonprostitute sexual partner, or who feel so stigmatized that they cannot approach a likely sex partner. Many people have physical disabilities, such as those suffering from multiple sclerosis, quadriplegics, and others with illnesses or handicaps that require assistance in the sex act. Some are developmentally handicapped. Their disabilities do not mean, however, that the sex urge has disappeared, only that it makes having sex more complicated; for such individuals, prostitutes, either female or male, are often an alternative.

Psychological and other factors are involved in seeking out prostitute partners. Stein, for example, who observed the encounters of 1,230 men with call girls, found that the prostitute was completely client centered and that every effort was made to fulfill the needs of the male client. This concern with male performance is satisfying to a number of individuals who do want to engage in reciprocal sex and are fearful of the sexual demands of women who insist on sexual egalitarianism. Edward Glover, an early researcher into the psychology of the male customer, felt that many men were able to enjoy the sex act only with people they did not hold in high esteem, and that these men separated love into sacred and profane; they classified their wives, female friends, mothers, and daughters as worthy only of sacred love, while they equated the prostitute with the profane.

Prostitution, then, is a very complicated topic. It seems clear that laws to outlaw prostitution generally have not been satisfactory, even in extreme totalitarian states. The Soviet Union, for much of its history, denied the existence of prostitution, calling it a capitalist evil, but any visitor to Moscow or Leningrad could find it thriving in spite of harsh penalties. The same was true in Communist China or Communist Cuba.

Pouring more money into law enforcement will not end prostitution, although it will undoubtedly increase the likelihood that the streetwalker will be harassed, and for this reason it might make prostitution less noticeable. Optimistic individuals can hope that the development of a new sex ethic emphasizing mutual enjoyment and emotional as well as physical involvement of male and female partners will lessen the demand for prostitution, but even if this does happen for large numbers of people, there will be those who seek to satisfy their sexual needs through the service of prostitution. Though contemporary societies have come to terms with prostitution in many different ways, each poses different problems.

1. The most extreme procedure has been to try to outlaw prostitution entirely and to throw all the resources into a legal campaign to eliminate prostitution. This policy would take the commitment of an authoritarian state such as the former Soviet Union, and it did not work there. Moreover, such a policy would be much worse than any problem it purports to solve. It would violate privacy, ignore the biological needs or drives of men and women, and try to set aside the economic and social realities of everyday living.

2. Setting up effective governmental control and registration of prostitution, including the requirement of medical inspection, was a favored solution of the 19th century and one still practiced in some areas of Europe. The problem is that medical inspection of prostitution is not particularly effective. Much more effective would be the screening of customers, but no society has ever demanded this. What such governmental control (called reglementation) does is stigmatize the prostitute for life. This occurs even though prostitution is usually a short-term occupation. Most men who go to prostitutes want younger women, and the earning power of prostitutes goes down as they age. Moreover, reglementation implies setting up certain districts in which prostitution is tolerated, and this tends to concentrate crime in those areas and in the long run to drive away customers, who seek partners elsewhere. The result is especially difficult to police. Separated and tolerated districts exist in such areas as rural Nevada where prostitution is legal, and Nevada voters keep it on the books. It is important to emphasize, however, that such officially legal brothel prostitution is not permitted in Las Vegas or Reno, the major cities.

3. A reinterpretation of the laws to concentrate only on certain conducts narrowly defined as prostitution is one approach that many jurisdictions have adopted, often concentrating on solicitation. The real difficulty is determining what constitutes solicitation. Almost every female has been solicited at least sometime in her life, and though female solicitation of males is less blatant and less obvious, most women have to give signals that they would like to know a man better for him to approach her. The whole concept of romantic love is based on the assumption that males and females have some kind of attraction for each other. To get around this problem, courts have sometimes made illegal only overt "solicitation," but what is overt to one person might not be to another. Courts, in wrestling with this problem, have insisted that solicitation specifically be a solicitation to commit a sexual act for money, but this in essence leads to entrapment. Streetwise prostitutes are unwilling to name any fee until the client does so, and most police find trying to use this standard very difficult. If solicitation is regarded as illegal, then should not men who are soliciting a prostitute also be prosecuted? Some jurisdictions have set up police prostitute decoys to arrest men who solicit sex, but this then leads to entrapment. The real difficulty, however, is that only the more obvious prostitutes are arrested, primarily the streetwalkers, and more discreet high-class prostitutes are untouched. The result is a class bias in law enforcement that mocks equal justice under the law.

4. The obvious solution is the decriminalization of sexual activity between consenting adults, whether or not money changes hands. Such a solution would free the vast majority of urban vice squads for other tasks, specifically for crimes involving victims. Prostitutes could be encouraged to be discreet, advertising their services in the so-called underground press, establishing telephone-answering services, recruiting customers in parlors emphasizing erotic massages, soliciting in adult bookstores, being available through special escort services, and encouraging the establishment of erotic clubs to serve individuals with special needs. Those who wanted prostitutes would find them, and those who did not could avoid them. At the same time, the law could protect young girls and boys from being enticed into prostitution, but the laws on statutory rape and age of consent

already deal with this. Strong prohibitions against involuntary prostitution should remain on the books. We believe that prostitution is not going to disappear and that it is important that society deal with prostitution as it exists today in the most positive and least harmful way.

REFERENCES

Bullough, V.L., and B. Bullough. *Women and Prostitution: A Social History.* Buffalo, N.Y.: Prometheus Books, 1987.

Bullough, V.L., B. Elcano, B. Bullough, and M. Deacon. *Bibliography of Prostitution.* New York: Garland, 1977.

Bullough, V.L., and L. Sentz. *Annotated Bibliography of Prostitution: 1970–1992.* New York: Garland, 1992.

Stein, M.L. *Lovers, Friends, Slaves: Nine Male Sexual Types: Their Psycho-Sexual Transactions with Call Girls.* New York: Berkeley, 1974.

Bonnie Bullough
Vern L. Bullough

PSYCHOANALYTIC THEORIES

For much of the 20th century, at least in the United States, psychoanalytic theories were considered almost synonymous with both sex and psychiatry. Although Sigmund Freud (1856–1939), the founder of psychoanalysis, concentrated on nonsexual theories and in fact had a strong metapsychological side in which views and speculations on human destiny and the nature of civilization played a part, in the popular mind Freud and sex were the same.

Freud's ideas about sex changed over time, and, by the 1920s, he had developed what he called a structural approach, in which the instinctual drives, sexual instincts, and aggression were grouped together as the id. Sexuality to Freud encompassed not only the erogenous zones, the mouth, the anus, and the sex organs but also included gratification from tactile sensations, pleasure in looking, and sadomasochism (pleasure in hurting or being hurt), although he later distinguished the latter from the former and considered them as derivatives.

He also held that mature heterosexual genital satisfaction was achieved only through a long process of development, and some people never achieved it at all. Individuals went through several stages in which the focus of the sex drive changed, from oral to anal and finally phallic. For a time, from the sixth year to the development of puberty, the sexual drive went into a phase of relative abeyance that he called the latency period. If periods surrounding a particular phase were especially difficult, the individual may remain essentially fixated in that phase.

Freud wrote from a masculine bias. He argued that during the phallic phase the child's libido is centered on the phallus, something girls do not have, and so girls develop penis envy. The sexual urge that little boys find at this time is normally directed at the mother, and this results in the Oedipus complex, in which the father becomes the rival and is bitterly resented, although the father is also loved and respected for his power. Eventually, to overcome this, the male child redirects his sexuality, although in the process this often leads to castration fears and anxieties.

Development of the girl is different, since her interest during this process must be transferred from the clitoris, the poor female substitute for the penis, to the vagina. She feels somehow that her mother has castrated her, and this leads to penis envy. The process of the girl growing up is to go through a transition from hatred of her mother to an identification with her, called the Electra complex.

Homosexuality for Freud resulted from failure to fully progress through the various phases of development, which he labeled oral, anal, latent phase, and finally the mature genital state (i.e., heterosexuality). At the same time, however, Freud made statements that were remarkably sympathetic to homosexuals as individuals. One of the issues, however, that divided the early psychoanalytic community was whether a homosexual or lesbian might be qualified to be an analyst. Freud answered in the affirmative, although certain conditions had to be met. Ernest Jones (1879–1958), his disciple and translator, disagreed, and in the United States, at least, overt homosexuals were refused training.

To carry his message, Freud organized the Vienna Psychoanalytic Society in 1902 and later, in 1910, the International Psychoanalytic Society, which attempted to impose a kind of orthodoxy on the movement. Freudian psychoanalysis, however, was continually marked by apostasies, and some individuals were influenced to leave because of what they believed was Freud's overemphasis on sex. Alfred Adler (1870–1937) left in part over this in 1911, and his theories downplayed the role of sexuality, although he emphasized what might be called gender issues. For example, though he called women "the weaker sex," he felt that they compensated for this by striving for power over men, using their sex as a device. Carl Gustav Jung (1875–1961) broke a few years later, in part again because he

felt that sexuality was overly stressed in Freud's theory. The libido for him was not essentially sexual but a sort of general life energy taking many forms. Jung also believed that every person essentially encompassed two genders, the masculine and the feminine, within himself or herself. The male frequently repressed the feminine side of his nature, but it survived in the unconscious as the *anima*, a receptive, nurturing trend that normally softens the masculine logical, dominant male form. Just the opposite was true of women, and their masculine side appeared in the *animus*. Homosexuality, he felt, was when the *anima* came to dominate in the male, and lesbianism occurred when the *animus* dominated in the female.

Within the traditional Freudian psychoanalytic school, there were also slight modifications. Anna Freud (1895–1982), Freud's daughter, for example, emphasized how the defense mechanisms of the emergent ego could simulate primary id impulses, and that reality for the child was different than reality for the adult. Erik Erikson (1902–), a Freudian, showed how society influenced the adaptation of the child at each stage. He emphasized, however, that talking about the meanings of life, including one's sexual feelings, is often more important to the adolescent than direct sexual activity.

Somewhat different was Wilhelm Reich (1897–1957), who, in the post–World War I era, set about to incorporate Marxism and Freudian psychoanalysis into a new synthesis. Reich felt there was a crucial interdependence of social and sexual liberation and that any political revolution was doomed to failure unless it was accompanied by abolition of repressive morality. It was this failure that had undermined the Russian Revolution. He also felt that the sexual revolution needed to encompass not only adults but also children and adolescents. The sexual repression of the adolescent in society led to juvenile delinquency, neuroses, perversion, and, of course, political apathy. He devoted numerous pages in his writings to the problem of providing adolescents with the private quarters and contraceptive devices necessary for the fulfillment of their sexual needs. Homosexuality, then, would disappear in the wake of the revolution, as would all other forms of sexual "perversity."

Ultimately, Reich proved a failure in his endeavors to reconcile Marxism and psychoanalysis and was expelled from both the International Psychoanalytic Association and the Communist Party. He ended up, in 1936, in Norway, where he founded the International Institute for Sex-Economy to study the way the human body utilized sexual energy. Motivating this search was his attempt to find the basic physical unit of energy to replace Freud's generalized concept of libido.

In its place, he developed a concept of energy, an actual physical component of humans that could be measured and harnessed, which he spent the rest of his life trying to explain, control, and utilize. In 1939, he came to New York, where he established the Orgone Institute, in Forest Hills; there he attempted to teach others how to use the new kind of energy that could be tapped by body massage, stored in accumulators, and used both to strengthen the body against disease and to increase orgastic potency. The result was the orgone box, a wood and metal enclosure resembling a telephone booth that supposedly collected the orgone energy, transferring it to the patient inside, who could then direct the energy to the genitalia, thereby restoring sexual potency or, in the case of an illness, restoring the individual to a healthy condition. He held that orgastic potency, that is, the capacity of a male or female to achieve orgasm after appropriate sexual stimulation, was the key to psychological health. Orgasm, he held, regulates the emotional energy of the body and relieves sexual tensions that otherwise would be transformed into neurosis.

His claims led not only to his denunciation by the American Medical Association but also to an investigation by the Food and Drug Administration, which enjoined him from distributing orgone accumulators. When Reich defied the ban, he was sentenced to prison, in 1957, where he died of heart disease. Though, obviously, Reich had long since departed from his orthodox psychoanalytic origins and has been regarded by many as being synonymous with "sexual freedom," Reich's great importance to psychoanalytic theory was to emphasize the need to analyze the character structure of the patient. He also opened up the field to include borderline psychotic states, psychopathic personalities, and similar groups of patients early analysts had ignored.

A similar attempt to reconcile psychoanalysis and Marxism was undertaken by Herbert Marcuse (1898–1979), who considered sexual repression one of the most important attributes of the exploitive social order. Under the capitalist order, Marcuse held, sexual love had been stripped of its playfulness and spontaneity and had become a matter of duty and habit carefully circumscribed by the ideology of monogamic fidelity. In fact, the blunting of sensuality was the inevitable by-product of industrial labor, which

had resulted in the atrophy and coarsening of the body's organs. Sex repression contributed significantly to maintaining the general order of repression.

However, sexual repression correlated with the performance principle, a key to capitalism, and this had resulted in the desexualization of the pregenital erotogenic zones and reinforced the genitalizations of sexuality. The libido, in short, became concentrated in one part of the body, the genitals, in order to leave the rest of the body free for use as an instrument of labor. Resexualization of the body was the goal of human fulfillment.

Neither Reich's nor Marcuse's sexual theories were accepted within the mainstream of American psychoanalytic thought, which from the 1920s to the 1950s dominated the field of sex studies. Irving Bieber (1908–1991) and his colleagues, for example, described a triangular system to account for the development of male homosexuality. This study suggested that a homosexual was typically the child of an overly intimate, controlling mother and a detached, hostile, rejecting father causing the young man to be effeminate. Bieber and his colleagues based their system on the differences found between a group of homosexual and a group of heterosexual men. Both groups were in therapy, so that the comparisons involved troubled people, that is, biased samples of both homosexuals and heterosexuals. Even so, 38 percent of the homosexuals did not come from a triangular family system, and 32 percent of the heterosexuals reported such a family background. At most, the Bieber research suggests that many people in therapy, regardless of their sexual orientation, either may be the product of a triangular system or else the psychoanalyst was inclined to view the relationships from a preconceived viewpoint. Subsequent research supports a feminine stage in some homosexual boys but it has not supported the triangular family.

Homosexuality, in fact, was a favored field of investigation and theorizing. Edmund Bergler, for example, held that homosexuality involved a pathological elaboration of an unresolved masochistic attachment to the pre-Oedipal mother, Walter Bromberg held that it was a defense against castration anxiety, and Gustav Bychowski believed the homosexual had an immature ego characterized by fetishistic, narcissistic, and oral-sadistic elements. Frank Caprio, Harry Gershman, René Bozarth and Alfred Gross, and Charles Socarides taught that homosexuality was a sign of an underlying pathology.

By the 1950s, the psychoanalytic dominance of the sex field was under attack by researchers such as Alfred Kinsey, on the one hand, and for its therapeutic lack of success, on the other. In the l950s, H.J. Eysenck produced a statistical study demonstrating that patients treated by psychoanalysts recovered no more quickly, in fact they recovered more slowly, than those who received no therapy at all. Inevitably, many of the physiological assumptions of Freud were undermined by new findings, as in the case of his belief in the importance of the vaginal orgasm. Physiological research by William Masters and Virginia Johnson found that the clitoral and vaginal orgasm were physiologically indistinguishable.

Even within the psychiatric movement, there was a strong attack on psychoanalytic assumptions, as evidenced by the removal of homosexuality, in 1974, from the category of mental illness in the *Diagnostic and Statistical Manual* of the American Psychiatric Association. Not all psychiatrists agreed with this, and the psychoanalyst Irving Bieber, for example, opposed the change, since he said that "all psychoanalytic theories assume that adult homosexuality is psycho-pathologic."

The problem with much of the psychoanalytic theorizing about sex was that the samples were extremely small and almost always were patients of the individual clinician doing the research. Control groups were rarely used, and most of the studies started with a predetermined assumption about what would be found.

As the psychoanalytic theories have come under attack for their lack of objective scientific data, psychoanalysts have fought back, although not so much by offering the scientific data sought by their critics as by arguing, as the neo-Freudian Jacques Lacan has, that psychoanalysis is more a way of viewing life, a poetic or lay philosophy rather than a therapy.

Certainly, it remains strongly entrenched in literary criticism, and Lacan's disciples are closely associated with postmodernism. Within psychiatry, Freudian influence remains important, but increasingly the speculative theories of Freud are being replaced by data-based ones, and psychiatrists such as Judd Marmor, Richard Green, and others operate from many of the same theoretical assumptions as psychologists and others.

Perhaps the greatest importance of psychoanalytic theories is giving sex an important place in the human psyche. Topics, previously ignored, were brought to public attention by psychoanalysts, and, in fact, they dominated much of the nonphysiological research into sex. In the process, they helped to undermine conventional moral certainties about sexuality and to stimulate new thought. Certainly, the challenges of a Wilhelm Reich or a Herbert Marcuse led to a rethinking about the influence of sex in the world at large. Unfortunately, orthodox psychoanalysis did not keep up with the changing research, and, in spite of its valuable insights, many of the assumptions it once operated under are no longer accepted as valid by its critics. Nevertheless, as neo-Freudians such as Lacan demonstrate, its insights remain invaluable.

REFERENCES

Alexander, F.G., and S.T. Selesnick. *The History of Psychiatry*. New York: Harper & Row, 1966.

Bell, A.P., and M.S. Weinberg. *Homosexualities: A Study of Diversity Among Men and Women*. New York: Simon & Schuster, 1978.

Freud, S. *Basic Writings*. New York: Modern Library, 1962.

———. *Collected Papers*. London: Imago, 1924–50.

———. *Three Contributions to Sexual Theory*. New York: Journal of Nervous and Mental Diseases, 1910.

Hall, C.S. *A Primer of Freudian Psychology*. Cleveland: World, 1954.

Reich, W. *The Function of the Orgasm*. Reprint. New York: World, 1971.

Robinson, P.A. *The Freudian Left*. New York: Harper & Row, 1969.

Thompson, C. *Psychoanalysis: Evolution and Development*. New York: Hermitage House, 1950.

Weinberg, M.S., and C.J. Williams. *Male Homosexuals: Their Problems and Adaptations*. New York: Oxford Univ. Press, 1974.

Vern L. Bullough

PSYCHOLOGICAL THEORIES OF SEXUALITY

Psychological theories of sexuality have been few and far between. Outside the psychoanalytic model, there have been few attempts to develop a global theory of sexuality by psychologists. Those theories that have been promulgated to deal specifically with sexuality generally encompass limited topics.

Love and Sexual Arousal

Berscheid and Walster proposed that the experience of love may result from a two-stage process. First, we feel physiological arousal and the responses that accompany it, such as a racing heart and pulse, sweating palms, and heavy breathing. Second, in our desire to understand the source of the arousal, we search for an explanation—a label—for the arousal. They maintain that under some conditions people may experience physiological arousal and conclude that they are feeling love or sexual attraction. If the arousal occurs in the context of sexual intimacy with an appropriate object, this conclusion seems logical. Berscheid and Walster, however, suggested that any source of arousal can, under certain conditions, increase the likelihood that we will label our feelings as love or attraction.

This hypothesis was tested by Dutton and Aron in a somewhat unusual setting—two bridges overlooking the Capilano River in British Columbia, Canada. One of the bridges was 5 feet wide, 450 feet long, and made out of wooden boards attached to wire cables that had a tendency to tilt, sway, and wobble; there was a 230-foot drop to rocks and shallow rapids below the bridge. The "control" bridge was a solid wooden bridge further upriver. This bridge was wider and firmer than the experimental bridge and was only 10 feet above the small, shallow rivulet that ran into the main river.

After walking over either the arousal-inducing bridge or the control bridge, men were approached by either a male or a female interviewer and asked to respond to a short questionnaire, then to write a short story based on a picture of a young woman covering her face with one hand and reaching with the other. Two measures were used to assess the volunteers' sexual arousal. First, the volunteers' stories were examined for sexual content. When the interviewers were female, the stories from the volunteers on the arousing bridge contained significantly more sexual content than those from volunteers on the control bridge. When the interviewer was male, sexual content did not vary according to which bridge the volunteers were on. Second, after the volunteers had completed the questionnaire, they were offered the interviewer's name and telephone number in case they wanted to have the experiment explained in more detail. The researchers hypothesized that volunteers on the arousing bridge would be more likely to call the female interviewer than volunteers on the control bridge. About 50 percent of the males from the arousing bridge did call the female interviewer; this percentage is higher than both the percentage from the control bridge who called the female interviewer and the percentage from either bridge who called the male interviewer.

According to Berscheid and Walster, in general the less able we are to identify the source of our physiological feelings of arousal and the more likely we are to have the chance to interact with the person, the more romantically attracted we will feel toward the person. Strictly speaking,

this finding applies only to the romantic attraction of a man to a woman, because these studies of arousal have used only heterosexual males. Although it may seem reasonable to assume that females and homosexuals respond similarly, research with women and with gay people is needed to determine whether these findings generalize beyond heterosexual men. On the basis of experiments examining the influence of arousal on attraction, Berscheid and Walster concluded that under appropriate circumstances, arousal—regardless of its source—will increase the likelihood that one person will be attracted to another. This analysis may help to explain why someone is attracted to another person when to outside observers there seems to be no logical reason for the attraction. According to this model, people can feel attracted to and aroused by others who apparently provide them with more pain than pleasure.

Limerence

Tennov described infatuation or "love at first sight" as limerence—a love characterized by preoccupation, acute longing, exaggeration of the other's good qualities, seesawing emotion, and aching in the chest. These characteristics can be experienced as either intensely pleasurable or painful, depending on the response of the loved one, or "limerent object." Unlike other forms of love, limerence is an all-or-nothing state that men and women experience in similar ways. On the basis of several hundred descriptions of limerence obtained through personal interviews, Tennov outlined a number of traits that a person in this state may exhibit:

1. *Preoccupation with a limerent object.* You are unable to think about anything else but the object of your affection. Everything you do is calculated in terms of how the limerent object will respond—whether he or she would like or dislike it. You may feel happy or sad, depending on the degree of attention you get from your limerent object.

2. *Intrusive or unintentional thinking about the limerent object.* In addition to spending a great deal of time intentionally fantasizing about the limerent object, you find that thoughts about your beloved intrude and interfere with other mental activity in an apparently involuntary way. You may be working on a paper or performing some task at work when the thoughts and fantasies of a love object come to the fore.

3. *Desire for exclusivity with limerent object.* You crave the limerent object and no one else.

You want commitment to ensure exclusivity even when it is premature or inappropriate. This can lead you to smother the object of your affection with attention and pressure rather than allow the relationship to develop gradually.

Tennov proposed that limerence develops in stages, the first being admiration for another person who possesses valued qualities and for whom one feels a basic liking. This state is followed by an awareness of sexual attraction. Once admiration and sexual attraction are present, the next step is to undergo an experience that raises the probability that these feelings might be reciprocated. This experience could be something as simple as observing a look or gesture or being asked to go to dinner or a party.

At this point in the development of limerence, the first "crystallization" occurs: one begins to focus on the good qualities of the limerent object and to disregard his or her bad qualities. After the first crystallization, if the two people develop a mutual attraction, the intensity of the romantic involvement will be relatively mild. Doubt about the limerent object's commitment, however, can evoke extreme, or "crazy," limerence. The interaction between hopefulness and uncertainty leads to the second crystallization, which results in feeling an intense attraction to the other person. With the individual who is not so infatuated, the developmental process just described stops early, and the intensity of full-fledged limerence is never felt. Nonlimerents are generally more practical about their romantic involvements.

Limerence is a tantalizing state that promises great things that can never be fully realized. In the beginning, it can also be devastating, especially if the limerent object is lost abruptly. Tennov outlined three ways in which limerent attraction can end. The first is through the development of a deeper relationship, which evolves as one is able to withstand the major disappointments and emptiness of fading limerence. The second is through abandonment, owing to a lack of reciprocity on the part of the limerent object. The third is through the transfer of attention to another limerent object—a continuation of the limerent state. Tennov maintains that full-blown limerence cannot develop without an element of uncertainty.

Attachment

Because of the remarkable similarities between human infants and other primate infants, Bowlby theorized that the attachment between infant and care giver forms the basis for later attachments in adulthood. Attachment theory postulates that the original function of this early affectional bonding in humans was to protect infants from predators and other threats to survival. This is accomplished by infants and children constructing mental models of themselves and their caretakers, and these models, as well as behavior patterns influenced by them, affect relationships throughout the life span. There is increasing evidence that supports this theory from infancy through young adulthood. Thus, early attachment between the infant and one or more caretakers appears to play an important part in the development of later affectional relationships.

Forms of Love

Sternberg devised the theoretical framework to account for the various forms that loving can take. He maintained that love could be understood in terms of three components: (1) intimacy, which includes the feelings of closeness and connectedness that one experiences in loving relationships; (2) passion, which refers to the drives that lead to romance, physical attraction, and sexual interaction in a loving relationship; and (3) decision and commitment, which encompass (in the short run) the decision that one loves another and (in the long run) the commitment to maintain the love.

Intimacy, according to Sternberg, is the emotional component of love. It grows steadily in the early phase of a relationship but later tends to level off. It is the major component of most loving relationships that we have with family, friends, and lovers.

Passion is the motivational component of love. Passion develops quickly in relationships but then typically levels off. It involves a high degree of physiological arousal and an intense desire to be united with a loved one. In its most pure form, it may be seen in the "love at first sight" experience.

Decision and commitment are the cognitive components of love. Commitment increases gradually at first and then grows more rapidly as the relationship develops. The love of a parent for a child is often distinguished by a high level of commitment.

Although these three components are all important parts of loving relationships, their strength may differ from one relationship to another and may change over time within the same relationship. The amount of love that one experiences depends on the absolute strengths of these three components, and the kind of love one experiences depends on their relative strengths. When all three components are present in a relationship, there exists what he calls consummate or complete love. According to Sternberg, this is the kind of love that people strive for but find difficult to sustain. It is possible only in very special relationships.

According to Sternberg, friendship occurs when one experiences the intimacy component of love without passion and decision-commitment. It is possible for friendships to evolve into relationships characterized by passion or arousal and long-term commitment, but when this occurs, the friendship goes beyond liking and becomes simply another form of love.

In Sternberg's framework, infatuation involves passion and arousal without the intimacy and decision-commitment components of love. It is essentially the same kind of love that Tennov calls limerence—a love characterized by preoccupation, acute longing, exaggeration of the other's good qualities, and seesawing emotions.

The deeper relationship that may develop out of limerent love or infatuation is characterized by romantic love. Romantic love comprises intimacy as well as passion. It is the "Romeo and Juliet" type of love—liking, with the added excitement of physical attraction and arousal but without commitment.

Sternberg describes empty love as commitment without intimacy or passion. Intimacy and passion have died out and all that remains is commitment. Although North Americans associate this type of love with the final stages of a long-term relationship, in other societies it may be the starting point of a relationship. For example, in cultures in which marriages are arranged, a couple may begin a relationship with little beyond a commitment to try to love each other.

Fatuous love involves passion and commitment but no intimacy. It is the type of love that we associate with whirlwind courtships. This type of love is fatuous or foolish, because commitment is made based on the heady chemistry of passion without the stabilizing effect of intimacy.

Companionate love involves intimacy and commitment but no passion. It is essentially long-term friendship, such as often develops in marriage after a couple's passion has died down.

Psychological Determinants of Sexual Behavior

Byrne and his colleagues have developed a theory concerning the psychological determinants of sexual behavior. The theory proposes that individuals vary in affective responses, informational responses (beliefs and expectancies), and fantasy responses to sexual stimuli. Affective, informational, and fantasy responses to sex are assumed to involve generalized and stable individual differences that function like personality traits. An individual's characteristic feelings, thoughts, and fantasies about sex are thought to determine his or her sexual behavior by mediating the person's response to sexual stimulation. To date, most of the research done on this theory has focused on emotional responses to sexuality. Byrne and his colleagues developed the Sexual Opinion Survey (SOS), where responses can range from primarily negative (erotophobic) to primarily positive (erotophilic). Erotophobic persons' negative feelings about sex appear to mediate avoidance of diverse sexual behaviors, while erotophilic persons' positive feelings about sex seem to mediate approach responses to sex. Erotophobia-erotophilia appears to involve reliable differences and affective responses to sexuality and to determine avoidance or approach responses to a diversity of sexual behaviors.

Sexual Orientation

Storms developed a theory of sexual orientation that used early adolescence as a critical period in the development of a sexual identity as heterosexual, homosexual, or bisexual. His theory takes into account sexual maturation at both the social and the biological levels with the onset of puberty, when masturbation, sexual fantasies, and sexual arousal increase. Most people's sexual fantasies are quite vague at first, gradually becoming more specific and detailed with maturity. Storms maintains that development of sexual identity is closely linked to the development of erotic fantasies. That is, we may use the context of our erotic fantasies to eventually determine our sexual preference.

In this theory, as we begin to mature sexually our environment supplies the material for our erotic fantasies. American children are socially active and form primary friendship bonds with others of the same gender from early childhood through preadolescence. It is during preadolescence that many individuals experience a sharp increase in the desire for interpersonal intimacy, expressed in relationships with "the best friend," gangs, and cliques and in first love. At about age 12 or 13, heterosexual interactions become more common. Early sexual maturation (before the age of 12) occurs among American children in an environment dominated by the same-gender peers and, according to Storms, would be more likely to result in erotic fantasies involving the same gender; the emergence of strong sexual feelings and arousal around 13 years or later occurs in a social world that involves both genders. Sexual maturation at this age, then, would be more likely to lead to heterosexual (and presumably bisexual) fantasies. A major implication of Storms's theory is that homosexual preference develops out of normal, commonplace experiences that happen to nearly everyone during preadolescence. Because of their early sexual maturation, homosexuals tend to eroticize those homosocial experiences, just as heterosexuals do with the heterosocial experiences at a slightly later age, when they begin to develop sexual maturity. Storms's theory is attractive because it attempts to explain sexual orientation, not just homosexuality.

Extramarital Sex

A perceived marital imbalance may lead a husband or wife to feel justified in seeking an extramarital relationship. Walster and colleagues have applied equity theory to try to explain this imbalance. They have distinguished three kinds of imbalance versus balance. First, we may feel overbenefited when our marital rewards are greater than our costs. Second, equity exists when we perceive our rewards as being equal to our investment in the marriage. Third, we may experience deprivation when we perceive our investment as greater than our rewards. It is important to note that rewards and investments can be defined in various ways. People bring diverse contributions to a relationship—financial assets, practical know-how, or physical appeal, for example. Walster, et al., suggested that spouses who perceive themselves to be either overbenefited or in an equitable relationship would be less likely to involve themselves in extramarital affairs than would spouses who saw themselves as deprived. Berscheid, et al., presented evidence from a survey published by *Psychology Today* to support their contention.

Walster, et al., believed that spouses would see the relationship as inequitable if they perceived themselves as more desirable than their mates. Consequently, they assumed that these people would engage in affairs earlier in their relationship and with more partners than would those who perceive themselves to be in an equitable relationship or overbenefited. Their results supported this assumption. Although the frequency of extramarital relationships did not vary according to gender or length of the primary relationship, it did vary according to perceptions of the equity of the primary relationship.

The theories that have been presented here have attempted to explain various aspects of human sexuality from a psychological perspective. One of the most apparent problems that can be observed is a lack of follow-up on the development of these theories through research. This, of course, is not the only area in the study of sexuality that has this problem. In fact, one could argue that one of the great weaknesses for those people trying to develop models or theories of sexuality is the lack of research guided by some coherent framework. This is undoubtedly due to relatively recent scientific interest in sexuality and the hostile social environment encountered by scientific thinking about sexuality. Thus, many able scholars avoid the study of sexuality because of the possible controversy. This situation is changing, however, so increased research can be anticipated in the near future.

REFERENCES

Berscheid, E., and E. Walster. Physical Attractiveness. In L. Berkowitz, ed., *Advances in Experimental Social Psychology.* New York: Academic Press, 1974.

Berscheid, E., E. Walster, and G. Bohrnstedt. The Body Image Report. *Psychology Today,* Vol. 7 (1973), pp. 119–31.

Bowlby, J. *Attachment and Loss.* Vol. 2, *Separation, Anxiety, and Anger.* New York: Basic Books, 1973.

Byrne, D. Social Psychology and the Study of Sexual Behavior. *Personality and Social Psychology Bulletin,* Vol. 1 (1977), pp. 3–30.

Dutton, D.G., and A.P. Aron. Some Evidence for Heightened Sexual Attraction Under Conditions of High Anxiety. *Journal of Personality and Social Psychology,* Vol. 30 (1974), pp. 510–17.

Feeney, J.A., and P. Woller. Attachment Style as a Predictor of Adult Romantic Relationships. *Journal of Personality and Social Psychology,* Vol. 58 (1990), pp. 281–91.

Fisher, W.A., D. Byrne, L.A. White, and K. Kelly. Erotophobia—Erotophilia as a Dimension of Personality. *Journal of Sex Research,* Vol. 25 (1988), pp. 123–51.

Sternberg, R.J. A Triangular Theory of Love. *Psychological Review,* Vol. 19 (1986), pp. 119–35.

Storms, M.D. A Theory of Erotic Orientation Development. *Psychological Review,* Vol. 88 (1981), pp. 340–53.

Tennov, D. *Love and Limerence.* New York: Stein & Day, 1972.

Walster, E., G.W. Walster, and E. Berscheid. *Equity: Theory and Research.* Boston: Allyn & Bacon, 1978.

A.R. Allgeier

V

RACE, SEX, AND MYTHS: IMAGES OF AFRICAN AMERICAN MEN AND WOMEN

A review of the past record of societal beliefs about the sexuality of blacks reveals an attitude that paints the Negro as representing the sexual instinct in its raw state. Moreover, the folk view or the myths surrounding the sexuality of African-Americans is often hard to distinguish from what appears in the scientific literature. To the extent that myths explain why something exists or happens, they may disguise the truth as well as disclose truths. This makes them potentially destructive, particularly when legends become institutionalized. For example, writers such as DeRachewiltz, Jacobus, Purchas, and others have asserted that (1) black men and women are guided by "bestial instinct"; (2) the black man is more animalistic in bed; (3) the black man's penis is larger than the penis of the white man; (4) the black man is a sexual superman whose potency and virility are greater than the white man's; (5) the black man's reproductive capacity is colossal; (6) black men are obsessed with the idea of having sex with white women; (7) all black women want to sleep with anyone who comes along; (8) black women respond instantly and enthusiastically to all sexual advances; and (9) blacks are more permissive in their sexual affairs.

Where do these notions about the sexuality of blacks originate? In part, they derive from 16th-century English accounts of West Africa that, according to Jordan, were replete with images of the lewd, lascivious, bestial black man. The sexual attributes that were embodied by the word "bestial" had a greater impact on the Elizabethan English than they would have today because of the popular belief in demon possession. Demon-possession theory was an all-encompassing concept that could explain all sorts of human tribulations. In particular, the sexual possession of humans by a (male) incubus or a (female) sucubus would lead to "monstrous" birth defects, because incubi and sucubi were not human, hence sexual intercourse with them was likened to bestiality—intercourse with animals. These images of the black man are consistent with what one would expect to find among people who perceived blacks as heathen, savage, beastlike men. This notion is further evidenced by a section in Samuel Purchas's work that describes how these views were interrelated in the minds of Englishmen. He states that

> they [blacks] have no knowledge of God;
> those that traffique and are conversant among

507

strange Countrey people are civiller then the common sort of people, they are very greedie eaters, and no less drinkers, and very lecherous, and theevish, and much addicted to uncleanenesse: one man hath as many wives as hee is able to keepe and maintaine.

In other words, the sexuality of blacks was as to be expected among truculent people. However, the idea of the potent sexuality of the African went far beyond the conceptualization of blacks as savages. Indeed, the notion of blacks as lustful and venerous was well established in European literature long before the first English contact with West Africa.

The medieval writer, Leo Africanus (Al-Hasan ibn Muhammad al-Wazzan al-Zaiyati), in his work *History and Description of Africa*, provided the most influential and authoritative accounts of little-known lands that must have appeared to the European as most exotic and forbidden. Africanus described the African black man as living a "brutish kind of life," devoid of any religion or law and surrounded by swarms of harlots. Another early commentator, Jean Bodin (1530–1596), after reviewing the writings of ancient authorities, concluded that concupiscence was characteristic of the Ethiopian race. Jordan concludes by saying that "depiction of the Negro as a lustful creature was not radically new, therefore, when Englishmen first met Negroes face to face. Seizing upon and reconfirming these long-standing and apparently common notions about Africa, Elizabethan travelers and literati spoke very explicitly of Negroes as being especially sexual."

By the early 1600s, the Englishmen who met the first slaves to arrive at Jamestown had already acquired a viewpoint of blacks that was based on custom and earlier European contacts with Africans. The conception of the libidinous black man was transported to the New World and was well entrenched in the American psyche by the end of the 17th century. These beliefs were carried by plantation owners who used blacks as breeding stock, as well as by prominent thinkers of the period, such as Thomas Jefferson. In his *Notes on the State of Virginia*, Jefferson wrote that "they [black men] are more ardent after their female: but love seems with them to be more eager desire, than a tender delicate mixture of sentiment and sensation." Jefferson also accepted the popular belief that blacks desired sexual relations with whites and even believed in a "beastly copulation" connected with blacks—the copulation of black women with orangutans.

Eighteenth-century science pictured the Negro-ape association as a link in the "chain of being" and argued that male apes are closest to the black race, so it is natural that they be attracted to females of the next evolutionary step. Some of the more striking commentary can be extracted from the work of late 19th-century anthropological writings, in particular the work of the pseudonymous Jacobus. Jacobus was a surgeon in the French army who served in various colonial outposts, particularly North Africa, during the 1880s and 1890s. Because he was a physician, he had the opportunity to examine the organs of many males and females. Thus, Jacobus writes:

In no branch of the human race are the male organs more developed than in the African Negro. I am speaking of the penis only and not of the testicles, which are often smaller than those of the majority of Europeans.

The genital organ of the male is in proper proportion as regards size, to the dimensions of the female organ. In fact, with the exception of the Arab, who runs him very close in this respect, the Sudanese Negro possesses the largest genital organ of all the races of mankind.

The penis is almost as large when flabby as it is in a state of erection. It is among the Muslim Sudanese that I found the most developed phallus, and notable one of the maximum dimensions, being nearly 12 inches in length by a diameter of 2 1/4 inches. This was a terrific machine, and except for a slight difference in length, was more like the penis of a donkey than that of a man. The unfortunate Negro who possessed this "spike" could not find a Negress large enough to receive him with pleasure, and he was an object of terror to all the feminine sex.

Jacobus seems to change his position about this donkey-sized penis. He continues:

The Negro is a real "stallion Man," and nothing can give a better idea (both as to color and size) of the organ of the Negro, when erect, than the tool of a little African donkey. The absence of hair on the pubes, which the Negroes remove, makes the resemblance more complete. Nor is it confined merely to color and size; for the penis of the Negro, even when in complete erection, is still soft like that of the donkey and when pressed by hand feels like a thick India-rubber tube full of liquid. Even when flabby, the Negro's yard still retains a size and consistency that are greater than that of the European, whose organ shrivels up and becomes soft and limp.

Jacobus also made observations about the female vulva. He states that:

> The vulva of the African Negress is black at the entrance, but becomes a bright red in the vagina. It is the same with the lips and the mouth. The pubis is completely hairless. In the adult Negress the vulva is placed very low and descends almost vertically, as does also the vagina, which is much longer but more narrow than in the European woman. The small lips assume, at an early age, an immense development and considerably exceed the great. Is this caused by repeated pulling, or is it a peculiarity of the race? The clitoris of the young Negress is very much developed, often the length of the little finger of a child, for after the nubile age it increases greatly.

Accompanying these organs of such monstrous proportions, it was believed there must also be a sexual appetite that is second to none. Jacobus states that:

> In order to spend [ejaculate] the black requires a very prolonged rubbing and the receptacle is large and well lubricated. A Negro is therefore able to make the act of coition last a long time before he spends and can even, if he likes, keep back the supreme moment by modulating his thrust. He can thus accomplish amorous exploits which would knock up a European. . . .
>
> The Negro takes a much longer time before he spends than the white man does. I should estimate that he is, on an average, quite three times as long in finishing a copulation as the white man is; and I am not exaggerating. The reasons for this are very natural. Firstly, the sensitiveness of the genital apparatus is much less in the black man than in the white, for the same reason that the generative parts of the Negress are endowed with a less acute sensitivity than those of the white woman. It would be abnormal and contrary to the laws of physiology for the black man to accomplish the venereal act as rapidly as a European, while the woman of his race is very slow in coming.
>
> The Negress requires a "man stallion" to make her feel the proper physiological sensations, and she seldom finds him except in the male of her own race. Added to this, her nervous system is not so delicately organized as in the white woman. Her mucous membranes are drier, especially as regards the genital organs. To obtain the sensation of voluptuousness under these conditions, the Negress required a slow copulation which only the black man, with his huge penis, can give her. It is certain that a well-fed, circumcised Negro can perform

on a woman nearly the whole night and only spend five or six times.

As late as 1901, these conceptions were still being expressed. W.H. Thomas wrote:

> Soberly speaking, negro [sic] nature is so craven and sensuous in every fibre of its being that negro manhood with decent respect for chaste womanhood does not exist. . . . Women unresistingly betray their wifely honor to satisfy a bestial instinct. . . . [S]o deeply rooted in immorality are our negro people that they turn in aversion from any sexual relation which does not invite sensuous embraces. . . . Negro social conditions will, however, be but dimly understood, even in their more conspicuous phases, unless we are prepared to realize at every step in our investigation that physical excitation is the chief and foremost craving of the freedman's nature.

Even Havelock Ellis, the noted pioneer in sexology, reported in 1913 that:

> I am informed that the sexual power of Negroes and slower ejaculation are the cause of the favor with which they are viewed by some white women of strong sexual passions in America and by many prostitutes. At one time there was a special house in New York City to which white women resorted for these "buck lovers." The women came heavily veiled and would inspect the penises of the men before making the selection.

The French author Remy de Gourmont stated that "one knows that a cat's tongue is rough; so is the tongue and all other mucous surfaces of Negroes. This roughness of surface notably augments the genital pleasure as men who have known Negro women testify." Shufeldt, in his book *America's Greatest Problem: The Negro*, quotes William Lee Howard as follows:

> Nature has endowed him [the Negro] with several ethnic characteristics which must be recognized as ineffaceable by man . . . especially the large but flexible sex organ which adapts itself to the peculiar sex organs of the female and her demands. . . . These ethnic traits call for a large sexual area in the cortex of the Negro brain which soon after puberty works night and day. . . . The chief, the controlling primal instinct in the African is the sexual.

Neither Ellis's nor Howard's view is supported by scientific evidence of a connection between penis size and the cortex of the brain or pigmentation and sexual passion.

At best, these views describing the sexual nature of blacks were superficial and misleading and at worst supportive of racist ideologies. Genovese noted that "the titillating and violence-provoking theory of the superpotency of [the] superpenis, while whispered about for several centuries, did not become an obsession in the South until after emancipation, when it served the purposes of racial segregationists." That is, the notion of the black's supersexuality became the obverse of the racist belief of black biological inferiority, providing legitimation for racial segregation. Many of these notions are extant in our society today. A contemporary author, Norman Mailer, in *The White Negro,* stated that "the Negro male lives in the present, subsists for the kicks of Saturday night, gives up the pleasures of the mind for the pleasures of the body to the character and quality of his existence in his music." The views espoused by Shufelt and Mailer support and perpetuate the belief that the black man is nothing more than a hypersexual walking phallus of such priapean dimensions that his intellectual abilities are secondary to his lascivious nature.

Griffin, in her study of the relationship of psychosexual security, self-concept, and endorsement of ancient sexual beliefs about black men, on the one hand, and white supremacists' attitudes, on the other, hypothesized that black men would be described as taller than the average man and that the black male's penis would be described as greater in length in erect and nonerect states. Her sample of 197 college-educated white men supported her hypothesis. Griffin chose these particular subjects because they were older than the typical college student, more sophisticated, and presumably had more life experience. She believed they would have developed more stable attitudes and would be likely to engage in the self-examination required to complete the lengthy test battery.

Other investigators, such as Christensen and Johnson, Houston, Reiss, Staples and Roebuck, and McGee, have suggested that blacks are more sexually permissive than whites. However, these studies are difficult to compare because different criteria were used to determine permissiveness. The studies do indicate that blacks as compared to whites engage in coitus at earlier ages and are less likely to masturbate or perform fellatio or cunnilingus. Black males are more likely to experience their first ejaculation during coitus rather than through masturbation, and black females are likely to reach orgasm more frequently in premarital coitus. These findings are usually the basis by which blacks are judged to be more permissive than whites.

The preceding overview clearly demonstrates the depth of the European's, and eventually the Euro-American's, perception of the libidinous nature of blacks in general and the black man in particular. These perceptions represented philosophical positions rather than empirical, sexological evidence; and much of the purported sex research involving blacks today has been a recycling of the cultural beliefs about the sexuality of blacks couched in scientific terminology and interpreted through the veil of white middle-class values. As Noble said, "Philosophical assumptions determine the scientific investigation of psychology. Certainly particular people cannot be meaningfully investigated and understood if their philosophical assumptions are not taken into account." If our theoretical or conceptual starting points are flawed, then our end results will be flawed as well. Indeed, some researchers have suggested that the white researcher, with his "Eurocentric perspective," lacks the sensitivity and ability to understand or to document the black experience. This Eurocentric perspective all too often leads the researcher to look at whites as though they are the control group to which blacks are compared. As described above, it has been reported that black males as compared with white males begin sexual intercourse at an earlier age and have more sexual partners. It would be just as accurate to say that white males as compared with black males begin sexual intercourse at a later age and have fewer sexual partners. Furthermore, the proposition that blacks are more permissive in their sexual affairs as compared to whites can be restated just as accurately that whites are more prohibitive in their sexual affairs. The difference depends on who is doing the interpretation and what philosophical assumptions underpin the analysis.

Examination of the lives of blacks must be principled upon "Afrocentric" philosophical assumptions. For example, the religious traditions of African-Americans reflect African philosophical assumptions, which do not rely on mind-body duality as a guiding principle. Indeed, traditional African cosmology does not separate mind from body. It is the unity of spirit and flesh that provides a sharp contrast between Western and African theological systems of thought, which in turn may account for a different worldview that blacks hold. Without these philosophical assumptions as a theoretical foundation, much of the purported sex research involving blacks, as well as future research, will simply perpetuate myths and stereotypes that both whites and blacks have about black and white sexuality.

Finally, review of the research literature shows such a lack of current material that a Kinsey-like survey needs to be conducted to discover the sexual attitudes and behavior of a broad spectrum of black Americans, using systematic research. This survey should not merely imitate the Kinsey survey methods (e.g., counting frequencies of various sexual acts) but should provide a theoretical framework (Afrocentric) that takes into account the philosophical assumptions of the people under investigation. Then and only then can we know if our historical views regarding blacks are valid or in need of revision. Perhaps instead of images that have been distorted by the figments of the imagination of others that often disguise the truth and are potentially destructive, black Americans will become a people of substance and thus, made whole.

REFERENCES

Africanus, L. *The History and Description of Africa and of the Notable Things Therein Contained.* (1562) London: The Hakluyt Society, 1896.

Belcastro, P.A. Sexual Behavior Differences Between Black and White Students. *The Journal of Sex Research,* Vol. 21 (1985), pp. 56–67.

Bell, A.P. *Black Sexuality: Fact and Fancy.* Paper presented to Focus: Black American Series, Indiana University, Bloomington, Ind., Oct. 1968.

Christensen, H., and L. Johnson. Premarital Coitus and the Southern Black: A Comparative View. *Journal of Marriage and the Family,* Vol. 40 (1978), pp. 721–32.

DeRachewiltz, B. *Black Eros: Sexual Customs of Africa from Prehistory to the Present Day.* New York: Lyle Stuart, 1964.

Edwardes, A., and R.E.L. Masters. *The Cradle of Erotica: A Study of Afro-Asian Sexual Expression and an Analysis of Erotic Freedom in Social Relationships.* New York: Julian Press, 1963.

Ellis, H. *Studies in the Psychology of Sex.* Philadelphia: Davis, 1910–13.

Fanon, F. *Black Skin, White Masks.* New York: Grove Press, 1967.

Genovese, E. *Roll Jordan Roll.* New York: Viking, 1972.

Griffin, A.M. The Relationship of Psychosexual Security, Self-Concept, and Endorsement of Ancient Sexual Beliefs about Black Men to White Supremacist Attitudes. Ph.D. diss., New York Univ., 1979.

Houston, L. Romanticism and Eroticism among Black and White College Students. *Adolescence,* Vol. 16 (1981), pp. 263–72.

Hunt, M. *Sexual Behavior in the Seventies.* New York: Dell, 1975.

Jacobus, X. *Untrodden Fields of Anthropology.* New York: Falstaff Press, 1937.

Jefferson, T. *Notes on the State of Virginia.* Chapel Hill: Univ. of North Carolina Press, 1954.

Jordan, W.D. *White Over Black: American Attitudes Toward the Negro, 1550–1812.* Chapel Hill: Univ. of North Carolina Press, 1968.

Ladner, J.A. *Tomorrow's Tomorrow: The Black Woman.* Garden City, N.Y.: Doubleday, 1971.

Mailer, N. *The White Negro.* San Francisco: City Lights, 1957.

Masters, R.E.L. *Forbidden Sexual Behavior and Morality.* New York: Julian Press, 1962.

Purchas, S. *Haklutus Posthumus, or Purchas His pilgrimes: Contayning a History of the World in Sea Voyages and Lande Travells by Englishmen and Others, by Samuel Purchas.* (1625) Glasgow: Maclehose, 1905.

Reiss, I.L. Premarital Sexual Permissiveness among Negroes and Whites. *American Sociological Review,* Vol. 29 (1964), pp. 688–98.

————. *The Social Context of Premarital Sexual Permissiveness.* New York: Holt, Rinehart & Winston, 1967.

Roebuck, J., and M. McGee. Attitudes Toward Premarital Sex and Sexual Behavior among Black High School Girls. *Journal of Sex Research,* Vol. 13 (1977), pp. 104–14.

Rogers, J.A. *Sex and Race.* 9th ed. New York: Author, 1967.

Shufeldt, R.W. *America's Greatest Problem: The Negro.* Philadelphia: Davis, 1915.

Thomas, W.H. *The American Negro: What He Was, What He Is, and What He May Become.* New York: Macmillan, 1901.

Wilkinson, C.B. The Destructiveness of Myths. *American Journal of Psychiatry,* Vol. 126 (1970), pp. 1087–92.

Zelnik, M., and J.F. Kanter. Sexuality, Contraception and Pregnancy among Young Unwed Females in the United States. In C.F. Westoff and R. Paske, Jr., eds., *Demographic and Social Aspects of Population Growth.* Washington, D.C.: Government Printing Office, 1972.

Herbert Samuels

RAPE

Rape is a violent act that deliberately violates, humiliates, and degrades its victim, usually a woman. Rape is a crime of violence using sex as the weapon. Although sexual in nature, it is not predominantly a sexual act. Issues regarding power, control, helplessness, and degradation of the person being violated have a higher valence in most cases. Use of force, or threat of force, either of a psychological or a physical nature, may be present. Many would argue that psychological threat is always present. Feminists would argue that rape is a political act, a power play, designed to keep women in a frightened, subservient, powerless state.

The chances that a woman will be raped over the course of her lifetime, estimated between 1 in 4 to 1 in 6, exceed her chances of contracting breast cancer, which affects approximately 1 in 10 women. In spite of the fact that women between the ages of 15 and 24 constitute the highest-risk group, no female is safe from rape. Instances of rape have been recorded across the life span, from infancy to old age. Rape is a grossly underreported crime; 90 percent of rapes are never investigated, and only 5 percent of those investigated are successfully prosecuted and result in a jail term. Though males constitute approximately 10 percent of all rape victims, mostly in penal settings, this article addresses rape in relation to women. Many of the same physical, emotional, and psychological issues have to be dealt with by any person who has been raped, regardless of gender.

No other crime places so much blame or responsibility on its victim. Rape victims often feel treated as if they were the criminal. The antecedents for this behavior lie in the past. Throughout recorded history, women have been regarded as possessions. To rape a virgin was to deprive her father of untarnished goods, and reparation had to be made by the rapist. Rape is facilitated by viewing women as objects, properties, and possessions to be bought or sold or stolen: an object to be acted upon rather than self-volitional; an object to be subjugated to men's wills; an object to be taken from another man as a sign of his defeat and humiliation; an object to be shared with other men in a spirit of male bonding and camaraderie. The legacy from the past, then, is a view of the male as the aggressor and of the woman as the more passive object. This perspective still permeates the contemporary socialization of the sexes. From the moment of birth, babies receive differential treatment according to sex. Sex-role stereotyping delineates and defines behaviors as appropriately masculine or feminine. Little boys are socialized to be aggressive, active, physical, nonemotional, tough, rugged, achievement- and outward-oriented. In contrast, little girls are socialized to play the complementary role; that is, to be passive and to be economically and emotionally dependent on men. Little girls are also taught fearfulness and inhibition as core components of femininity. Traditionally, the female role is to project both attractiveness and unavailability.

While the female is instructed in the appropriate feminine ways, her male counterpart is taught his role: to pursue and seduce that which might be attainable if he is persuasive enough. Both sexes are instructed as to the role the other will play. All the potential components for a rape are present: woman as the seductive but passive object to be pursued and attained, man as the aggressor, convincer, and potential owner of the woman. Part of the way in which women and men have been taught to relate to each other is gamelike. The woman is to be passive and reluctant; the man is to be persuasive and coercive. It is an interesting irony that the weaker sex has been and is held responsible for setting the limits for a sexual encounter. The etiology for this seemingly contradictory behavior is found in the myths concerning women and rape. Some of the more popular myths suggest that a woman has a weaker sex drive than a man, so it is easier for her to control the extent of the sexual interaction. Another popular myth suggests that because a woman can enjoy a fantasy of rape in which she has control of the cast of characters and action, she therefore secretly wants to be raped. When this myth is coupled with the belief that a woman cannot be raped against her will, it is easy to see why the onus is on the victim in this crime of violence. Perhaps the most onerous rape myth is that of victim precipitation. Somehow, either as a function of how she is dressed, where she is, her state of sobriety, or her previous relationship with the male, the woman is held responsible for precipitating the crime. It is difficult to know which sex is more maligned by this assumption: the woman, who is represented as an irresponsible agent precipitating a crime of violence against herself, or the male, who is portrayed as unable to think or reason in the grip of his raging hormones.

One of the most dangerous rape myths suggests that the crime is most often committed by a stranger. This is untrue. Only about 20 percent of all rapes are committed by strangers. The majority of rapes fall into the acquaintance-rape category, which subsumes both marital and date rape. Acquaintance rape is usually defined as forced rape between people who already know each other regardless of how casually. Since women have also been raised to believe in the myths of rape, it is not uncommon for a woman in an ongoing relationship to be unclear that a rape has occurred. She is liable to wonder whether she led the man on or had the right to say no after saying yes up to a point, whether the way she was dressed "gave the man the wrong idea," or whether, if she had been drinking, it really was her fault for not being in better control. Men seem similarly confused. They often hold the view that they were only doing what the woman really wanted; that if she had not been interested, she should not have placed herself in compromising circumstances; and that it is the man's role to overcome the token resistance offered by the female.

Women who are the target of acquaintance rape are judged quite harshly by their peers and society. The respectability of the woman and her social role, occupational status, prior sexual history, marital status, perceived careless or provocative behavior, prior knowledge of the rapist, and previous rape experience, as well as the sex of the person making the judgment, all influence the way the rape victim is perceived and judged. Perhaps the only class of women judged more harshly are the victims of marital rape. In most states, definitions of rape specifically exclude the marital relationship. How can one be doing something illegal by taking what is theirs? Beginning with the passage of property from the father of the bride to the groom, the woman in a marital relationship is too often seen as the possession of the male. In the traditional marriage ceremony, the bride is given away by her father or father substitute to the groom. If this does not presume property ownership as well as a need to protect the weaker sex, it is hard to know what would. Access to the wife's body, whether invited or not, is seen as the right of the husband. It is little wonder that these women often have difficulty knowing that they have been assaulted.

During an assault, victims of rape experience extreme fearfulness, followed by numbness and disbelief, disgust, and revulsion. Only 10 percent or less report feeling angry during the attack. Individuals who have been raped experience great emotional and psychological damage, rape trauma syndrome, or posttraumatic stress disorder, which can be long lasting. Generally, immediately following an assault, the individual experiences a state of disorganization characterized by multiple affects. Fear and self-blame are the most frequently expressed emotions, with anger, humiliation, and embarrassment also experienced. Somatic reactions are common during this period. Women routinely experience gastrointestinal distress, insomnia, loss of appetite, or increase in appetite, nightmares, and general tenseness. The woman's overall reaction to the rape may fit the cultural stereotype and be "expressed": the affect is present verbally and nonverbally, or "controlled," where affect was not present or visible. During the syndrome's middle phase, outward adjustment, the victim appears to be returning to normal. She is least amenable to therapy at this time and may incorrectly assume she has worked through the issues surrounding the rape. This is a period of pseudoadjustment in which the emotional issues have been put away rather than worked through. It is important to give a thorough explanation of this to the woman so that when feelings begin to reemerge in the last stage of integration and resolution, the woman will understand what is occurring. Therapeutic work can occur during this stage. The woman can work to incorporate the rape into her life and her view of herself. During this time, she will review and critique her response to the rape. Did she do enough to prevent it? Did she fight hard enough? Is she somehow to blame for what has happened to her? Under conditions of extreme fear, a person becomes concerned with self-preservation and may freeze in response to sudden, unexpected violence. The fright experienced borders on panic, particularly when the individual feels her life may be in danger. This "frozen fear response" seems to offer an intuitively correct explanation for the observation that normal, healthy women who should be able to resist their attackers may offer no resistance at all and even appear friendly and cooperative. A woman who has a frozen-fear response will be especially vulnerable to these questions.

Nightmares, making changes in her life, concern with the reaction of a husband or boyfriend, and working out her feelings toward the rapist are some of the tasks of this stage. It is critical that the woman be helped to develop a sense of autonomy and choice over decisions in her life as soon as possible. Not all women who are raped are able to work through the psychological issues. Some have a "compounded reaction," in which they develop severe depression, psychosomatic disturbances, or psychosis or even attempt suicide. Another group of women develops a "silent reaction." They have usually been assaulted in the past and say nothing to anyone. They may continue to be silent and blunted or have a compound reaction to the present assault.

Rape is neither harder nor easier to claim than any other crime. Societal attitudes toward men and women, along with traditional sex-role stereotyping, would have us believe differently and reflect the depth of misogynist beliefs. The responsibility for a crime rests with the criminal, not the victim. Rape is a crime.

REFERENCES

Bond, S.B., and D.L. Mosher. Guided Imagery of Rape: Fantasy, Reality, and the Willing Victim Myth. *Journal of Sex Research,* Vol. 22 (1986), pp. 162–83.

Brownmiller, S. *Against Our Will: Men, Women and Rape.* New York: Simon & Schuster, 1975.

Burgess, A.W., and L.L. Holmstrom. *Rape: Victims of Crisis.* Bowie, Md.: Brady, 1974.

Estrich, S. *Real Rape.* Cambridge, Mass.: Harvard Univ. Press, 1987.

Finkelhor, D., and K. Yllo. *License to Rape: Sexual Abuse of Wives.* New York: Holt, Rinehart & Winston, 1985.

Growth, A.N. *Men Who Rape: The Psychology of the Offender.* New York: Plenum Press, 1979.

Katz, S., and M. Mazur. *Understanding the Rape Victim: A Synthesis of Research Findings.* New York: John Wiley & Sons, 1979.

Susan B. Bond

RELIGION AND SEXUALITY

In most cultures and societies religion is a primary, or at least among the more powerful, force in establishing and maintaining sexual attitudes and regulating sexual behaviors. Religions draw their strength from a belief system that includes the authority of a divine spiritual being (or beings) who is believed to have created this world, to govern it and to control its destiny. Because this spiritual authority controls the individual destinies of all humans in this life and rewards or punishes them in some kind of life hereafter, religions usually deal with some sort of revelation, contained in a sacred text or passed on through a chosen representative. Such revelations and sacred texts often contain regulations for sexual behaviors, establishing the norms of who can have sex, with whom, under what circumstances, when, how, and for what reasons. These sexual regulations, along with other regulations unrelated to sexual behavior, are interpreted by male priests, rabbis, imams, shamans, or other individuals who claim either direct contact with the divine being or delegation by the supreme being as his representative and interpreter.

Formal or Informal Values

Official public statements by religious authorities, or by official teaching bodies, about the status, roles and relationships of men and women constitute what ethicists and sociologists term a formal value. However, the attitudes and behaviors of individual members of a religious group may deviate from or even contradict such formal values. Individuals whose informal values contravene the formal values may have to deal with guilt or shame for not conforming to the accepted norms. They may also have to deal with the threat of punishment here or hereafter. The Puritans, for instance, formally condemned premarital sex, even though most of them accepted it as a natural outcome of courtship in a rural frontier society where fertility of the bride was

an overriding concern. When enough believers endorse an informal value that counters the formal value, religious leaders may either reinterpret the formal value or create a schism by expelling the deviants. This occurred when the early Protestants rejected the Roman Catholic emphasis on the primacy of celibacy and its denigration of sexual pleasure. Similar shifts have occurred within Protestantism when a variety of social factors led to the acceptance of divorce despite certain apparently clear rejections of divorce by Jesus and, more recently, with the acceptance of homosexuals and their ordination.

Natural or Unnatural Sex

According to early Greek and Roman Stoic philosophers, sexual passion distorted a man's reason. The sole moral justification for sexual relations, in their view, was procreation. This view of the nature of sex was developed and expanded by early Christian thinkers, particularly Augustine of Hippo (c. 300 C.E.). Medieval Christian theologians adopted and extended this early view, classifying sexual acts as either natural or unnatural. Fornication, rape, incest, and adultery were considered illicit indulgences in sexual pleasure because they occurred outside marriage and did not provide for the rearing of offspring. However, because they could result in procreation, they were considered as natural sins. Masturbation, oral sex, and anal sex were much more serious violations of the natural order because they were contraceptive, hence unnatural, as well as illicit. This distinction between natural and unnatural sexual behavior comes up most often in religious debates about homosexuality, contraception, and monogamy.

Control Mechanisms

The mechanisms religions use to control sexual behavior are similar to those used in secular societies. Judaeo-Christian religious beliefs rely on a sense of personal conscience, personal guilt, and on fear of divine punishment. Islam, Hinduism, and Confucianism rely on the sense of shame and responsibility to one's kin to assure conformity to sexual mores.

Two World Views

For well over 2000 years, two quite different world views (weltanschauung) and belief systems about the nature of creation have coexisted and developed in Western thought. Since the time of the Iranian religious philosopher Zoroaster (c. 600 B.C.E.) and the early Greek and Roman philosophers (c. 300 B.C.E. to 200 C.E.),

Western thinkers have chosen to picture our world in one of two ways. Some religious thinkers and doctrines have interpreted the world in terms of a fixed world view with unchangeable laws of nature and the nature of every creature established in the beginning by the creator. Others have pictured a world in the process of evolving with the nature of all things fluid and ever changing as creation continues. The fixed world view, with its unchanging abstract archetypes, and the process world view, with its emphasis on the reality of ever-changing environments and unique developing individuals, represent two ends of a broad spectrum from which have been derived two different and opposing sexual value systems.

The Fixed World View

At one end of this philosophical spectrum, adherents of the fixed world view claim that when God created the first humans he established the unchanging nature of male and female, gender roles, marriage, and heterosexual morality for all time. The biblical story of Genesis describes all humans as fallen from an original state of perfection and grace because of the rebellion of Adam and Eve. This corrupt nature can only be overcome by self-discipline, mortification of the flesh, and by avoiding any indulgence in pleasure, especially sexual pleasure. With Adam and Eve in the Garden of Eden, God established the heterosexual nature of our sexuality, the primacy of the male over the female, and monogamy. The command "increase and multiply" identified the true and only purpose of sexual pleasure and relations (Table 1).

Hasidic and orthodox Jews, orthodox/fundamentalist Muslims, and fundamentalist and evangelical Protestants commonly draw on this world view in articulating their sexual values. In the Roman Catholic tradition, the Vatican adheres with unswerving vigilance to a natural law position as interpreted by the Magisterium, the hierarchical teaching authority. Advocates of the fixed world view commonly condemn contraception, masturbation, oral sex, premarital sex, divorce, consensual extramarital sex, women in positions of authority, and homosexuality, although individuals and some groups may be more tolerant in one or more of these areas.

The Process World View

At the other end of the spectrum is the process view of the world in which human nature is viewed as still evolving, still being created with human cooperation. The basic assumption in this world view is that human nature has never been without flaws. Physical and moral evil are the unavoidable dark side of our struggle to grow as persons to our fuller potential. Good and evil are linked together as we explore and discover new, deeper expressions and meanings of our human potential and sexual nature. Certain general principles of what is right and wrong in human behavior are acknowledged, but specific decisions about what is right and wrong depend on applying those principles to the ever-changing situation and context (Table 1).

A 1987 statement from the Episcopal Diocese of Northern New Jersey highlights the quite different role divine revelation, sacred texts, and traditional teachings play for people who adopt the process view point:

> The Judaeo-Christian tradition is a tradition precisely because, in every historical and social circumstance, the thinking faithful have brought to bear the best interpretation of the current realities in correlation with their interpretation of tradition as they have inherited it. Thus, truth in the Judaeo-Christian tradition is a dynamic process to be discerned and formulated rather than a static structure to be received.

> The Bible is misunderstood and misused when approached as a book of moral prescriptions directly applicable to all moral dilemmas. Rather, the Bible is the record of the response to the word of God addressed to Israel and to the Church throughout centuries of changing social, historical, and cultural conditions. The Faithful responded within the realities of their particular situation, guided by the direction of previous revelation, but not captive to it.

Few religious groups or individuals adhere completely to either one or the other of these two philosophies or world views. Most fall somewhere along the spectrum between the two extremes and shift back and forth along the spectrum, holding to a fixed world view on one issue and maintaining a process world view on another issue. Despite this variation, overall, religious groups and individuals tend to favor one or the other perspective and set their sexual values accordingly.

In the cognitive and moral development models proposed by Jean Piaget and Lawrence Kohlberg, religions based on a fixed or absolutist world view tend to stress specific acts, rules, and commandments while religions that draw on a process world view tend to emphasize the uniqueness of persons, the character of their relationships, and universal ethical principles.

General Comparisons

Several generalizations can be made about the sexual views endorsed by the great religions of the world—Hinduism, Buddhism, Judaism, Christianity, and Islam. These comparisons focus on beliefs about human nature, the origins of evil, the role of sexual pleasure, and the connection between sex, transcendence and the divine.

Cosmologies and religious myths dealing with the origins of the human race are intimately linked with beliefs about human nature and the origins of evil. The Christian interpretation of the Genesis myth talks about an original sin that corrupts and distorts human nature. This belief is quite compatible with the dualistic anthropology of body and soul that entered Christianity from Platonism through Augustine. It is also compatible with the dualistic view that portrays the male as rational and spiritually inclined and the female as dependent, emotional, and a threat because of her connection to sex and reproduction. For the Christian lay person, as well as for many Christian clergy and writers, original sin was (and is) linked with sex. This belief requires a form of redemption in which denial of the body with its emotions and sexual impulses is primary.

Eastern religions do not talk about an original sin, but rather of natural disharmonies or the polarity of two tensions that need to be balanced in every creature. In the East, the female principle is active and the woman the "initiatrix." The male and male principle are passive. Yang and Yin—the principles of masculinity and femininity, active and passive, cold and hot—are complementary polarities found in different balances in both men and women. This view does not try to explain the tensions of life by attributing what is viewed as positive to males and what is seen as negative to females, although the Eastern religions are as patriarchal as those of the West.

In Hinduism and Buddhism, transcendence of human limitations and mortality is achieved by integration and increased awareness of the totality of one's mental, sensual, and erotic experiences. In much of Christian mythology, sex is a barrier to be overcome. Mortality is transcended and salvation achieved by redemption and ascetic denial of the senses, especially one's sexual impulses.

Christian views have generally been very uncomfortable with any form of sensual pleasure, especially erotic and sexual pleasures. In the West, sexual pleasure is disruptive and dangerous to both the individual and society. It is a monster in the groin, which, if unleashed, could drive men to uncontrollable indulgence and destroy society. Work, not play, is redemptive. Sexual pleasure is moral when it leads men and women to undertake the burdens and responsibilities of raising children. In this view, sexual relations are immoral and sinful whenever they are indulged in outside marriage or without an openness to procreation. Thus orthodox Judaism, official Catholicism, and Protestant fundamentalists condemn masturbation and all forms of nonmarital, nonreproductive sex. Also unacceptable are alternate sexual behaviors and relationships—playful/recreational sex, gay unions, pre- and co-marital sex, and intimate friendships.

In contrast, Hinduism celebrates sexual pleasure as a value in its own right, to be enjoyed for what it brings the participants. Kama, "the pursuit of love of pleasure, both sensual and aesthetic," represents one of the four goals of life in the Hindu tradition. In Hindu philosophy, Bhoga (sexual pleasure) is viewed as one of two paths leading to nirvana, the Buddha, and final deliverance. Yoga, spiritual exercise, is the alternate, and more demanding, path to liberation and the merging of the individual with the universal. In the Tantric yoga tradition, a man or woman can even practice channeling his or her sexual energies from the lowest chakra to the highest and achieve cosmic awareness and transcendence in solo sex or masturbation.

Western Sexual Values

The roots of Western sexual values are a tangled jungle of two ancient opposing traditions, the sex-conflicted Hebraic tradition and the dualistic, sex-denying stoicism of syncretistic Greco-Roman philosophy. In much of the Jewish tradition sexuality is simply another, but highly valued piece of human experience, a part of divine creation. This is evident in the erotic love poem, the Song of Solomon. Judaism did not divinize sex as the orgiastic fertility cults did, or turn it into a holy sacrament as Catholicism has. Nor has Judaism demonized sex as it was in Stoicism and much of the Roman Catholic tradition. Judaism has never endorsed sexual asceticism or celibacy. Although coitus is generally approved only within marriage, the Jewish tradition has (consistently and unambiguously) valued sex for the sheer joy and pleasure of it within marriage.

But Judaism is also a very patriarchal Semitic religion. Genesis 19:1-11 and Judges 19 tolerate and accept rape of women as preferable to homosexual rape, and grants men but not women the right to initiate a divorce. The Torah (Deut.

21:15) approved of polygamy and concubinage. The Mishna (200 C.E.) and the Babylonian (300 C.E.) and Jerusalem (400 C.E.) Talmuds provide quite elaborate guidelines for polygamy. The Ashkenazim Jews of Eastern Europe adopted monogamy in the early medieval period, after Rabbi Gershom ben Judah of Worms urged Jews to give up the practice of polygamy to avoid the wrath of the Gregorian campaign against married clergy in the Western church. Only in the mid-20th century did the Chief Rabbinate of the State of Israel extend Gershom's ban on polygamy to the Sephardic Jews of the East.

An ongoing essentialist conflict within Judaism gives it a Jekyl and Hyde contradictory character. This conflict is inherent to Jewish biblical cosmology. It appears first with the contradiction between the mythic statement in Genesis "Let us make Man in our image, after our likeness" and the Jewish belief that God has no body and no sex. Add to this conflict Yahweh's mandate of "increase and multiply" and the Semitic belief that semen is polluting, even when discharged in marital intercourse. Finally, the Jewish tradition contains pervading sex-negative concerns about maintaining ritual or cultic purity, inherited by the rabbis from the early priests who probably adopted these beliefs from neighboring Semites. Contact with menstrual blood and semen renders any man ritually unclean and unfit for cultic service until he undergoes a cleansing rite. Before the exodus from Egypt, Moses required the Jews to abstain from sex for three days (Ex. 19:15). An emission of semen required bathing and rendered whomever it touched unclean until evening (Lev. 15:16ff; 22:4). (This belief is found in Islam also. The Qur'an requires a man or woman who has engaged in sexual intercourse to wash before leaving the house.) Menstruation rendered a woman unclean for seven days and did the same for anyone who had intercourse with her or touched her during that time (Lev. 15:19ff).

The syncretistic civil religions of Greece and Rome that developed alongside Jewish and early Christian belief systems were a mishmash of collected gods, rituals, and philosophies. Despite their diversity, the Greco-Roman religions shared an understanding of personhood that involved an essentially platonic dualism in which an exiled soul, implanted in a body (tomb), awaited liberation. In this anthropology the spark of divinity is the soul and the body its impediment, even its defilement.

"Do nothing for the sake of pleasure" the Roman philosopher Seneca wrote in his letter. For the Stoics, the poisoned breath of sexual passion and emotions were the enemy of man's rational, spiritual nature. The so-called "missionary position" was not the invention of Christian missionaries to Africa or the South Pacific but advocated by the Greek Stoic philosopher Artemidorus (c. 200 C.E.) who taught that the face-to-face male-on-top position for intercourse was the only moral position. He also condemned oral eroticism as "an awful act." The Stoic notion that sex has to be a procreative act, but otherwise has to be looked up under the negative heading of pleasure, not under the heading of love, has left an enduring imprint on Christianity.

During the first three hundred years of Christian history the dualistic philosophy of human nature and the sex-negating tradition of the Stoics were adopted by the Gnostic Christians, who then waged an all-out polemic that led to its triumph over the sex-affirming tradition of the Hebrews and Jesus in orthodox Christianity. Augustine (354-430 C.E.), bishop of Hippo in North Africa, provided the main theological articulation of this sex-negating anthropology that would dominate Christianity until the Protestant Reformation.

In the early Middle Ages as well as before the collapse of the Holy Roman Empire and the start of the Dark Ages, homosexuality appears to have flourished and been widely tolerated among the Catholic clergy. Boswell (1990) concludes from this that social and economic factors may at times be more influential than religious doctrine when believers choose to ignore or selectively enforce biblical strictures against certain sexual practices such as homosexuality.

Although scattered voices affirmed the sensuous and erotic throughout the medieval period, their volume and authority increased in the sixteenth century until the Protestant Reformation shattered Rome's universal and autocratic grip. Sexual laxity in the papal office and among the clergy was widely denounced, even as the Reformers rediscovered Christianity's Jewish roots. In the sixteenth century, Martin Luther almost singlehandedly revived Christianity's interest in the holistic Jewish anthropology. Lawrence claimed that the "Reformation was a defeat for salvation through sublimation or suppression of the sensuous and the sexual, and a victory for the body and sex and for a religion that affirms both."

Subsequent to the Protestant Reformation of the 1500s, the Western world was radically divided between the Roman and Protestant religions. Both camps experienced the cultural and philosophical movements known as the Enlightenment and the Romantic Movement, the privatization of sex, and the rise of secular thought. In the twentieth century the role of religion in formulating sexual values and regulating sexual behavior has been radically altered by the sexual revolutions of the 1920s and the 1960s, a new scientific understanding of sexuality, effective contraceptives, a greater tolerance for pluralistic values and behaviors, a vigorous campaign for civil and gay rights, and since 1981, the crisis of AIDS (acquired immune deficiency syndrome).

The Second Vatican Council (1962–1965) brought serious challenges to the Vatican's condemnation of contraception and its requirement of clerical celibacy. In subsequent decades, the majority of Catholics came to endorse informal values that quietly rejected the Vatican's formal condemnations of contraception, abortion, masturbation, premarital sex, and homosexuality. Reformed and conservative Jewish communities and mainstream Protestant churches were openly challenged by gay and lesbian persons seeking recognition, acceptance in the community of believers, and even ordination.

By the 1990s, every religious community in the Judaeo-Christian tradition was being challenged to reinterpret their biblical traditions and teachings on sexuality and to reject the traditional patriarchal structure of sexual relations that is linked with pornography, sexual violence, and the exploitation and exclusion of heterosexual women, unmarried people, gay men, and lesbians. In the 1990s, debates over the ordination of active gay men and lesbians to the ministry, the acceptability of premarital sex, and recognition of alternates to sexually exclusive monogamy are creating major tensions in many churches, especially the Episcopal, Southern Baptist, United Methodist, Evangelical Lutheran, and Presbyterian churches. Even the conservative Church of the Latter Day Saints (Mormons) has been confronted by fundamentalists seeking to reestablish the church's original practice of polygamy.

These challenges have raised new and perplexing questions about whether certain biblical texts that traditionally have been interpreted as forbidding certain sexual behavior or relations need to be reinterpreted in their historical context and in the light of new medical and psychological understanding of the nature of sexuality and gender orientations. In recent years, several church task forces and special commissions have faced this challenge by urging the appropriateness, even necessity, of such reinterpretations. Such reinterpretations generally concur that the stories of homosexual gang rape in Sodom (Genesis 19:1–11) and heterosexual gang rape in Gibeah (Judges 19) focus on sexual assault and violence and should not be interpreted as condemning homosexual relations as such. Similarly, Leviticus 18:22 and 20:13 are said to speak not to the unnaturalness of same-gender relations but to the issue of cultic purity and the "abomination" of Jews engaging in any activity including sacred prostitution that was associated with the pagan cults. In the New Testament, Romans 1:23-27 and 1 Corinthians 6:9-10 have likewise been subject to careful linguistic and contextual analysis. Instead of focusing on homosexuality, as previous interpretations have done, these recent studies stress that Paul, the author of these texts, was attacking lifestyles of licentiousness and lust common in the Greco-Roman world. These texts, it is claimed, do not speak to the Christian gay and lesbian community today, which values committed and loving relationships based on mutuality and respect for one another. These recent interpretations suggest that Paul condemned men and women we now describe as heterosexual who deliberately and freely gave up "natural" sexual relations for an "unnatural" homosexual depersonalized lust for novelty. Since Paul and the whole of Christian tradition knew nothing of homosexual orientation as a constitution condition, the nature and morality of homosexuality lay outside Christian tradition and theological consideration altogether.

Historically, religions have had much to say about the sexuality, sexual values, and the sexual behaviors and relationships of adults. Religious views and strictures that have been applied to children and adolescents have been derived from doctrines and guidelines articulated for adults. This may be due to the fact that childhood and particularly adolescence as we experience these today are social phenomena that emerged only in the past century or two.

In conclusion, it can be said that all the "great religions of the world," Buddhism, Confucianism, Hinduism, Judaism, Christianity, and Islam, have an essential patriarchal bias that puts women in a subordinate position and role. Eastern religions often portray their gods and goddesses in ritual sexual intercourse (yab-yum) and present women as the sexual experts and initiators. However, as these religious views have been expressed in Eastern cultures, the social role of women is very much inferior to that of the male. Much the same holds for the Islamic tradition, which is still expressed mainly in male-dominated tribal cultures where women have few, if any, rights. Judaism, Protestantism, and Christianity have inherited different contradictions. While Jesus violated important patriarchal values of the Jews and told his disciples that in his kingdom there would be no distinction between male and female, the patriarchal interests of his disciples quickly overpowered this effort towards gender equality. Early Christianity and Catholicism established sexual abstinence as the hallmark of the spiritual life. Both Mary and Joseph, the mother and father of Jesus, were portrayed as virgins; and married couples were urged to have sex only for procreation within otherwise celibate "brother-sister" marriages. Protestants rejected this repression of sex in marriage and in recent years affirmed the equality of men and women by ordaining women to the ministry. Each of the great religions has some sex-positive aspects, but none of them is without conflict on this issue.

However, despite the patriarchal and predominantly antisexual biases of these religions, the history of cultures clearly suggests an important positive outcome of the Judaic and Christian views of sexuality. First, a unique cultural emphasis on and respect for individualism emerged in ancient Greece and Rome. In two thousand years this valuing of the individual, reinforced by Judaic and Christian perspectives, has been a major factor in our recent sexual revolutions and move toward gender equality. Second, Greco-Roman scientific interests combined with the biblical directive for man to "master and rule the earth" to inspire Western cultures to objectify, analyze, and control nature. In recent years, environmentalists have stressed the negative side of this disrespect for nature as promoting a consumerist industrial depersonalized culture and a disastrous exploitation of our environment. At the same time, feminists and others have denounced the patriarchal, anti-sex, and anti-woman biases of Judaism and Christianity. Together, these same secular and religious traditions have combined in Western cultures to create a frontier society unique in human history and unique in the history of human sexuality. The industrial Western cultures increasingly value the individualism and equality of males and females, enable women to move closer to economic independence and equality with men, increasingly recognize and respect the individual man and woman's right to sexual fulfillment, increase our control over the reproductive functions of sexual intercourse, and continue to expand the health, leisure, basic securities of life, and life span of individual citizens. The present and future consequences of these trends for society and for individuals cannot be all on the positive side. However, the balance appears to be more positive than negative as age-old tensions and conflicts between sex and religion lessen.

In analyzing the relationship between religion and sex, it may be well to recall that every religion, like every social system, appears to be built on contradiction and is in some sense at war with itself over the nature, purpose and control of that basic human reality we term sex and sexuality.

REFERENCES

Boswell, J. *Christianity, Social Tolerance and Homosexuality.* Chicago: Univ. of Chicago Press, 1980.

Bullough, V.L. *Sexual Variance in Society and History.* Chicago: Univ. of Chicago Press, 1976.

Bullough, V.L., and J. Brundage. *Sexual Practices and the Medieval Church.* Buffalo: Prometheus Press, 1982.

Bullough, V.L., and B. Bullough. *Sin, Sickness, and Sanity: A History of Sexual Attitudes.* New York: New American Library, 1977.

Eilberg-Schwartz, H. People of the Body: The Problem of the Body for the People of the Book. *Journal of the History of Sexuality,* Vol. 2 (1991), pp. 1–24.

Edwards, G.R. *Gay/Lesbian Liberation: A Biblical Perspective.* New York: Pilgrim Press, 1984.

Francoeur, R.T. Current Religious Doctrines of Sexual and Erotic Development in Childhood. In M. Perry, ed., *The Handbook of Sexology.* Vol. 7. Amsterdam: Elsevier Science Publishers, 1990.

———. Sexual archetypes: Transitions and Insights into the Future. *ICIS (International Center for Integrative Studies) Forum,* Vol. 20 (1990), pp. 19–27.

———. New Dimensions in Human Sexuality. In R.H. Iles, ed., *The Gospel Imperative in the Midst of AIDS: Towards a Prophetic Pastoral Theology.* Wilton, Conn.: Morehouse Publishing, 1989, pp. 79–98.

Gardella, P. *Innocent Ecstasy: How Christianity Gave America an Ethic of Sexual Pleasure.* New York: Oxford Univ. Press, 1985.

General Assembly Special Committee on Human Sexuality, Presbyterian Church (U.S.A.). *Keeping Body and Soul Together: Sexuality, Spirituality, and Social Justice.* Philadelphia: Presbyterian Church (U.S.A.), 1991.

Gupta, B. *Sexual Archetypes, East and West.* New York: Paragon House, 1987.

Kosnick, A., et al. *Human Sexuality: New Directions in American Catholic Thought.* New York: Paulist Press, 1977.

Lawrence, R. *The Poisoning of Eros: Sexual Values in Conflict.* New York and Roanoke, Va.: Augustine More Press, 1989.

Nelson, J.B. *Embodiment: An Approach to Sexuality and Christian Theology.* Minneapolis: Augsburg, 1978.

Paglia, C. *Sexual Personae: Art and Decadence from Nefertiti to Emily Dickinson.* New York: Random House Vintage, 1990.

Ranke-Heinemann, U. *Eunuchs for the Kingdom of Heaven.* New York: Doubleday, 1990.

Thayer, N.S.T., et al. Report of the Task Force on Changing Patterns of Sexuality and Family Life. Newark, N.J.: *The Voice* (Episcopal Diocese of Northern New Jersey), March 1987.

Robert T. Francoeur

RELIGIOUS INFLUENCE ON SEXUAL ATTITUDES AND FUNCTIONING

"Sex is a force that permeates, influences and affects every act of a person's being at every moment of existence. It is not operative in one restricted area of life (that is, simply physical intercourse) but it is at the core and center of our total life response." This statement by an American theologian reflects a truth and a value that, while it is shared by many, calls to attention a view about human sexuality that has taken many centuries to develop.

Western Judeo-Christian society is the inheritor of 2,000 years of tradition about the place and role of sexual experience and expression. Early attitudes were themselves influenced by still earlier pagan and non-Western philosophies. An overview of these historical roots places our modern understanding of human sexuality in better context.

If we use the Bible as a starting place, it is interesting to note that the biblical Hebrew and Greek texts had no word to express the concept of human sexuality that we use today. The Bible was not a code book of sexual ethics, and it regarded sexuality as one aspect of life within the context of the whole community. The ancient Jews saw sex as a natural and good part of living. There was an emphasis on procreation for the good of the community. Sexual practices of pagan cults were strongly reacted against as a way of keeping the Jewish people free of outside influences.

The early Christian attitudes about sexuality also reflected a reaction against pagan influences. But early Christian writers were influenced by popular Greek and Roman philosophy that reflected a distrust of passion and desire. This Stoic philosophy suggested an indifference toward things sensual. A result was seen in a neo-Platonic dualism that viewed a split between the body and the spirit. Self-denial and the taming of sexual passion were seen as virtuous. Sexual desire was eventually seen as sinful, and celibacy, virginity, and chastity were aspired to as virtuous. Sex became a matter of procreation, and, by the Middle Ages, even intercourse within marriage was regulated. Sexual pleasure within marriage was not untainted from some sin. It is not difficult to imagine how such a sex-negative attitude over the centuries resulted in ingrained feelings of guilt and shame about sexual activity. This guilt about sex is part of Western mankind's religious heritage.

Since people in Western culture traditionally have been raised to resist biologically normal responses in the name of religious teachings, many people have difficulty in making the transition to a sexual union that is blessed by church and society. Psychoanalytic writers have repeatedly made the point that anxiety and fear generated from early attitudes and sexual experiences can contribute to adult sexual dysfunctions. Religious orthodoxy was one of the common causative factors for treatment failure cited by Masters and Johnson in their original work on sexual inadequacy. Sin and shame could be seen as interfering with natural biological responses.

Kaplan has described how religious attitudes, particularly those of Orthodox Judaism and Roman Catholicism, with their prohibition of most sexual expressions outside marriage, have contributed to the development of systems of sexual anxiety in her sample of patients. Kaplan also noted the connection between religious beliefs and negative consequences for sexual desire. However, other authors caution us not to oversimplify the relationship between orthodoxy and sexual dysfunction, for there are many devout people who are sexually functional, and there are many sexually dysfunctional people who are not religious.

If we can extrapolate from the findings of these researchers in human sexuality, we can in many cases be sure that there is still in our culture a continuing underlying dualism between body and spirit. There is still an underlying assumption, particularly for those with a religious background, that the body and its natural needs and expressions are somewhat suspect, and matters of the spirit are elevated or better or more pure. Religious and cultural role models still exist that emphasize chastity and abstinence (apart from prudent undertakings to avoid disease and pregnancy) as well as the implied and often stated belief that humankind's spiritual journey would be effected by transcending our bodies and sexual nature. This realization of the erotic nature of human beings has consequences even within sexual unions sanctioned by churches. People report to therapists a sense of guilt and discomfort about sexual feelings, sexual desire, and sexual pleasure that are not related to other emotional problems. These negative feelings are usually related to behaviors that traditional religion has viewed with disapproval but yet are common practices in the human experience. For example, masturbation, artificial contraception, homosexuality and abortion, though not equivalent practices, often cause considerable conflict. A literal understanding of religious teachings is usually at the basis of guilt feelings. A thorough exploration of the particular religious understanding is often helpful in clarifying significant issues.

Clinical Examples

One of the fundamental areas in which sexual difficulties can be attributed to religious experience is that of sexual desire. A primary task of psychological development is becoming aware of one's sexual feelings and understanding them as natural, with the result being acceptance of sexual feelings as a part of the sense of self. While sexual feelings are biologically programmed, it is the socialization and control of them by religious and cultural norms that cause the experience, acceptance, and expression of sexual feelings to be filled with special meaning. It is the meaning, or personal psychological value, given to sexual desire that can prompt so much confusion in people.

If we feel that sexual desire equals sin, then sexual desire can become a natural experience that can lead to anticipatory anxiety rather than to pleasure. What can result is an internal repression of sexual feelings, with the consequent inhibition of sexual desire. In other words, a person can be uncomfortable with internal sexual desire, label it as morally wrong, and feel guilty for what is really a genetically programmed phenomenon. As a result, sexual expression can be repressed or the pleasurable value can be denied. If sexual behavior is engaged in, guilt often accompanies the activity.

In some situations, the conflict over sexual feelings can manifest itself in the development of sexual dysfunctions: inhibited desire, erectile failure, rapid or retarded ejaculation, female anorgasmia, vaginismus, and dyspareunia (painful intercourse). As suggested above, for some people, sexual desire and its consequence, sexual arousal, can be a catalyst for anxiety and guilt rather than pleasure. For example, many women complain of being anorgasmic. Upon evaluation of their complaint, in some cases it is apparent that these women are shutting down their sexual response by interpreting their natural level of sexual arousal with anxiety rather than with pleasure. Not only has their distrust of their own pleasure interfered with their sexual functioning, but their inability to respond often leads to

guilt about not responding to or even satisfying their sexual partner. The experience is not too different in men, but their dysfunction can be more dramatic when erectile or ejaculatory difficulties are involved. The impact of these difficulties on the couple is also more dramatic if the sexual dysfunction is the cause of an inability to conceive. In such cases, the guilt toward the spouse can compound the earlier religious guilt. One can argue from a psychodynamic perspective that a person punishes himself or herself for having forbidden sexual desires by causing the sexual failure and subsequent interpersonal disappointment. As a caution, this interpretation is a speculation and cannot be proven.

The development and maintenance of sexual problems are complicated and subject to many variables, including learned experiences and anxiety that is the result of earlier failures. Some sexual problems become functionally autonomous and many continue even after therapeutic intervention has uncovered an underlying cause that may have been rooted in religious teachings.

Thus far, we have focused on the early stages of the sexual response cycle and how religious influences could negatively affect the phases of desire and arousal. The final phase of the cycle is sexual satisfaction. It is in this final phase of satisfaction that problems are being experienced by people who have no complaints or dysfunctions in their patterns of desire, arousal, or orgasm. Essentially, while no true sexual dysfunction is present, these people complain that their sexual encounters are unsatisfying.

While a dysfunctional relationship is frequently the cause of such a complaint, at other times the problem represents an example of guilt about pleasure and fear of letting go sexually. For some people, the act of letting go sexually involves a focus on the self rather than the partner. This behavior is often labeled as a form of self-centeredness, or even self-love, and can itself inspire guilt, because the person may feel that he or she is using the partner as a means to achieve his or her own sexual satisfaction. This scenario is a good example of the tendency of some religions to emphasize a selfless love over a love that desires fulfillment.

Clinical sex research has shown that sexual difficulties are often more disruptive of relationships than actual sexual dysfunctions. For example, sexual difficulties arise in relationships in the form of disagreements about sexual habits or practices, the amount of foreplay before intercourse, and even an inability to relax during sex. Guilt about pleasure is at times overcome by some people by embracing their particular denomination's teaching about the positive aspects of a blessed marital union. To some extent, this approach sanitizes sex and perpetuates the disembodiment of sexuality from spirituality.

For many believers, the official teachings of their faith stress the existence of certain moral absolutes; beliefs that cannot have exceptions. Therefore, certain actions are forbidden and are seen as morally evil in themselves. Such personal moral beliefs can result in sexual difficulties and can present a barrier to the treatment of some sexual problems or dysfunctions because of the forbidden nature of the acts. For example, treatment that uses masturbation, active sexual fantasies, sexually explicit materials, sexual surrogates, abortion, sterilization, or in vitro fertilization to achieve treatment goals may be excluded from possible use on religious grounds.

There are positive notions today in which some theologians view human sexuality in a more holistic fashion that stresses men and women as equals and views sexual expression as leading toward wholeness. Such views seek to demonstrate that man is a sexual creature as created by God and that a more sex-positive model can replace the traditional dualistic and natural-law approach that placed humankind at odds with its sexual nature. The goals of sexuality as seen holistically are not exclusively procreational but include pleasure, mutuality, and a respect for the other in loving, committed relationships. Such a philosophy of sexuality is inclusive and allows for the development of conscience based on faith, reason, tradition, and experience.

We can see that religious teachings need not lead to guilt and sexual problems. Even within the framework of traditional religious backgrounds, many people are able to incorporate new understandings about their sexuality into their belief system in a positive and growth-producing fashion. At times, only a better understanding of specific church teaching is all that is necessary to gain freedom from old modes of thinking about sexuality. Erroneous beliefs, once corrected, can lead to a new sense of involvement and exploration of one's sexuality.

Finally, whether the person is a committed believer, casually observant, or a nonbeliever, the influence of religion on the attitudes of Western Judeo-Christian culture is significant and cannot be ignored. A close examination of these roots can lead to a clarification and even rediscovery of meaning for many in a secular society where religious mores are constantly evolving.

REFERENCES

Frank, E., et al. Frequency of Sexual Dysfunction in "Normal" Couples. *New England Journal of Medicine*, Vol. 299 (1978), pp. 111–15.

Kaplan, H.S. *Disorders of Sexual Desire*. New York: Brunner/Mazel, 1979.

———. *Sexual Aversion, Sexual Phobias, and Panic Disorder*. New York: Brunner/Mazel, 1987.

Kosnick, A., et al. *Human Sexuality: New Directions in American Catholic Thought*. New York: Paulist Press, 1977.

Leiblum, S., and R. Rosen. *Sexual Desire Disorders*. New York: Guilford, 1988.

Masters, W., and V. Johnson. *Human Sexual Inadequacy*. Boston: Little, Brown, 1970.

Nelson, J. *Embodiment: An Approach to Sexuality and Christian Theology*. Minneapolis: Augsburg, 1978.

———. Religious Dimensions of Sexual Health. In G. Albee, ed., *Promoting Sexual Responsibility and Preventing Sexual Problems*. Hanover, N.H.: Univ. Press of New England, 1983.

Slowinski, J. Sexual Adjustment and Religious Training: A Sex Therapist's Perspective. In R. Green, ed., *Sexuality and Medicine*. Dordrecht, Holland: Reidel/Kluwer, 1991.

Yates, W. The Church and Its Holistic Paradigm of Sexuality. *SIECUS Report,* Vol. 16 (1988), pp. 4–5.

Julian W. Slowinski

RUNDEN, CHARITY EVA

Charity Eva Runden, born October 1, 1910, received her Ph.D. from Indiana University in 1951. Her career spanned the years 1943 to 1985. At the heart of her 40-year career has always been a concern with psychology, sociology, and especially human sexuality. Always, Runden has been an innovator, a pioneer, and a professional who has been completely devoted to the issues that concerned her and the world around her: namely, health care, human sexuality, sex education, women's issues, and issues of aging. Although Runden has partially retired from her positions as college professor and director of the Runden Institute, she continues to lecture and to consult in all the areas of her interest.

Runden is presently professor emerita at Montclair State College, Montclair, New Jersey; was acting dean of the Graduate School at Western Illinois University; and was professor of psychology, sociology, and education at the University of Kentucky and at Indiana University. She was Dean of Women and Associate Dean of the Graduate School at Montclair State College. Runden was founder and executive director of the Educational Foundation for Human Sexuality at Montclair State College (1967–1979), where she was responsible for establishing an M.A. degree program in educational psychology, with a specialization in human sexuality. She has also been a health-education consultant and was a consultant for venereal disease programs during World War II.

Notable among her written work is a study she conducted of "Fifty Happily Married Women." She is currently completing three books on female sexuality and continues to write a series of booklets on family life education, one of which is on sex education for parents of the exceptional child. Runden's reviews appear regularly in *Library Journal* and in *Voice of Youth Advocates*. She is also an accomplished and published poet.

Runden was a board member, secretary, and treasurer of the Society for the Scientific Study of Sex (SSSS). She was a charter member of the American Association of Sex Educators, Counselors and Therapists (AASECT) and of the American College of Sexologists, a fellow of the American Public Health Association and of the Masters and Johnson Institute, and a member of the Sex Information and Education Council of the United States (SIECUS); she is a recipient of the SSSS Award for Distinguished Scientific Achievement.

For the last 45 years, Runden has been married to John P. Runden, professor of English literature at William Paterson College. Given the major interests of this remarkable woman's career, theirs has been an exemplary relationship.

REFERENCES

Runden, C.E. *Selected Readings for Sex Education.* Berkeley, Calif.: McCutchan, 1969.

———. *Sex Education for Parents of Exceptional Children.* Montclair, N.J.: Runden Institute, 1979, 1983.

———. To Be a Woman. In H. Silverman, ed., *Marital Therapy: Moral, Sociological and Psychological Factors.* Springfield, Ill.: Charles C. Thomas, 1971.

———. *Twentieth Century Educators.* New York: Simon & Schuster, 1965.

Leah Cahan Schaefer

S

SACHER-MASOCH, LEOPOLD RITTER VON

Leopold Ritter von Sacher-Masoch (1836–1895) was an Austrian novelist, from whose name the term "masochism" was derived by the psychiatrist Richard von Krafft-Ebing. He was born in Lemberg, Galicia, on January 1, 1836. His father, who had recently been created a chevalier by Emperor Francis I, was chief of police of Lemberg. His mother was a Polish aristocrat. His paternal aunt, who lived with the family during his childhood, was the Countess Zenobia. Sacher-Masoch adored her and was enraptured by the beatings she gave him. It was to these experiences that his later fascination with being dominated by women was attributed.

In 1848, his family moved to Prague. He attended school there, receiving excellent reports and winning a prize for his school leaving essay. Although he was interested in writing and the theater, his father wished him to study law. Sacher-Masoch entered the University of Prague, transferring to the university at Graz and receiving the degree of doctor of law in 1855. He began teaching history at the university the following year. His first published work, which appeared in 1857, was a study of the rebellion in Ghent. It was not well received by historians, being criticized as too novelistic.

In 1861, he became enamored of Anna von Kottowitz, the wife of a physician, who was ten years his senior. She eventually left her husband and children and moved in with him. Their relationship developed into a sadomasochistic one; Anna dominated him, with his encouragement, beating him with her fists and also using whips and birches.

Sacher-Masoch's next significant liaison was with Fanny Pistor. The two of them signed a contract, which stated, in part:

> Herr Leopold von Sacher-Masoch gives his word of honour to Frau Pistor to become her slave and to comply unreservedly, for six months, with every one of her desires and commands. . . . The mistress (Fanny Pistor) has the right to punish her slave (Leopold von Sacher-Masoch) in any way she thinks fit for all errors, carelessness or crimes of *lese-majeste* on his part.

After a long and impassioned courtship with a mysterious woman who called herself "Wanda von Dunayev" after the heroine in his novel *Venus im Pelz,* Sacher-Masoch married her in a private ceremony in 1872. The woman, whose real name was Aurora Rumelin, and he eventually formally married.

During his marriage, Sacher-Masoch's masochistic tendencies continued to develop. His wife beat him with a cat-o'-nine-tails studded with nails. At his urging, she took lovers, while he also occasionally sought out women who might be convinced to dominate him. Eventually, he left her for Hulda Meister, whom he had hired as his chief translator for a magazine he was publishing.

By the time he was in his late 50s, Sacher-Masoch's mental health had begun to deteriorate. By March 1895, his condition had worsened so much that he was becoming violent and suffering delusions. Finally, on March 9, 1895, he was discreetly removed to the asylum for the insane in Mannheim. The public was told that he had died, and flattering obituaries were written about him. These accounts indicated that Sacher-Masoch died in Lindheim, Hesse, on March 3, 1895. Cleugh, however, claims that he actually died in the asylum in Mannheim in 1905.

Sacher-Masoch's novels were realistic and gained a devoted following. Some of his works, such as *Venus im Pelz* (*Venus in Furs*, 1870), depict people deriving sexual pleasure from suffering pain and humiliation. Among his other writings are *Das Vermachtnis Kains* (*The Legacy of Cain*), which appeared in four volumes from 1870 to 1877; *Falscher Hemelion* (*False Ermine*, 1873); *Die Messalinen Wiens* (*The Messalinas of Vienna*, 1874); and *Die Schlange im Paradies* (*The Snake in Paradise*, 1890).

REFERENCES

Cleugh, J. *The Marquis and the Chevalier*. Boston: Little, Brown, 1952.

Krafft-Ebing, R. von. *Psychopathia Sexualis*. Translated by F.S. Klaff. 1886. Reprint. New York: Stein & Day, 1965.

Thomas S. Weinberg

SADE, MARQUIS DE (DONATIEN-ALPHONSE-FRANÇOIS, COMTE DE SADE)

Donatien-Alphonse-François, comte de Sade (1740–1814), born June 2, 1740, was a French nobleman whose name has been linked with acts of sexual cruelty. He was educated at the College Louis le Grand, in Paris, leaving in 1754 to enter the military as a sublieutenant. He achieved the rank of captain and served in the Seven Years' War with Germany. Returning to Paris, he entered into an arranged marriage with the daughter of a family friend.

The notoriety of the Marquis de Sade stems from two well-publicized incidents. The first of these was known as the Keller affair. During Easter week in 1768, he met a young woman, Rosa Keller, who was begging in the streets. On his promise to give her a job, she accompanied him to a house he kept near Paris. After giving her a tour of the place, he took her to the attic, where he forced her to disrobe. De Sade then bound her hands and whipped her until she bled. Applying salve to her wounds, he kept her captive through the night. The next day, finding that her wounds had begun to heal, he reopened them with a knife. Again, he put salve on the woman's injuries. She managed to escape, running nude into the street. De Sade was arrested and jailed. In his defense, he claimed that he was only testing the efficacy of his salve. De Sade was imprisoned for only six weeks and released after paying Rosa Keller for damages.

The second incident occurred during July 1772. The marquis went to a bordello in Marseilles and distributed bonbons to the prostitutes. These chocolates were laced with cantharides, a supposed aphrodisiac popularly known as "Spanish fly." Some reports of the incident claim that one woman killed herself by jumping out a window and that two others died by poisoning. Bloch, however, believes that no deaths occurred. Sade was arrested, and, on September 11, 1772, he was sentenced to death for sodomy and poisoning. Before the sentence could be imposed, Sade fled to Italy. He was arrested there in December; he managed to escape, so the sentence was never carried out. The death decree was finally removed six years later.

Having returned to France in 1777, Sade was imprisoned once again, this time at the fortress at Vincennes. He was able to secure a release briefly in 1778, but he was reincarcerated and later moved to the Bastille in 1784. On July 4, 1789, ten days before the storming of the Bastille, he was sent to the Charenton lunatic asylum for haranguing a crowd from his cell. In 1790, Sade was released from Charenton. He was arrested once more in 1801 for having written a novel, *Zoloe and her Two Acolytes*, which defamed, among others, Josephine de Beauharnais, the wife of Napoleon Bonaparte. Without ever having gone to trial, he was transferred from one institution to another and later returned to Charenton, where he died on December 2, 1814.

In all, the Marquis de Sade spent 27 years in jails, prisons, and asylums. During much of this time he devoted himself to producing novels: *Les 120 Journées de Sodome* (1785), *La Nouvelle Justine* (1791), *Aline et Valcour* (1793), *La Philosophie dans le Boudoir* (1795), and *Juliette* (1797).

REFERENCES

Bloch, I. *Marquis de Sade: His Life and Works.* New York: Castle, 1948.

Cleugh, J. *The Marquis and the Chevalier.* Boston: Little, Brown, 1952.

Saint-Yves, L. *Selected Writings of De Sade.* New York: Castle, 1954.

Thomas S. Weinberg

SADISM

Sadism is the eroticization of dominance and control. The term can be traced to French literature and is linked with the name of Comte Donatien-Alphonse-François, marquis de Sade (1740–1814), whose life and erotic writings were filled with incidents and images of sexual cruelty. Sadism has been dealt with separately from masochism in much of the scientific literature, although this distinction between the two phenomena is artificial. As a number of writers have pointed out, both sadism and masochism can be found in the same individual; many sadomasochists consciously alter their own orientation to adjust to the needs of a potential partner. Additionally, it is very common for people who take the dominant role in sadomasochistic interaction to have started out as submissives.

Krafft-Ebing defined sadism as "the experience of sexual pleasurable sensations (including orgasm) produced by acts of cruelty, bodily punishment afflicted on one's own person or when witnessed in others, be they animals or human beings. It may also," he wrote, "consist of an innate desire to humiliate, hurt, wound or even destroy others in order thereby to create sexual pleasure in oneself." Freud acknowledged that "the roots of . . . sadism can be readily demonstrable in the normal individual." Both he and Krafft-Ebing believed that sadomasochistic-like activities were readily apparent during normal lovemaking. The sadomasochist, however, goes beyond what they saw as acceptable behavior.

Gebhard noted that sadomasochism is embedded in our culture, because our culture is centered on dominance and control in social relationships and that aggression is socially valued. Ellis preferred the term "algolagnia," viewing sadomasochism as a love of pain. He noted that "the sadist desires to inflict pain, but in some cases, if not in most, he desires that it should be felt as love."

Recent writers, starting with the contributions of Gebhard, have begun to study sadomasochism as a sexual subculture, focusing on the organization of the subculture and the norms that serve to regulate social interaction. Both Kamel and Lee, who have studied the leathersex scene among male homosexuals, point out that risk is reduced through agreement on norms and values within the subculture. Kamel, who was particularly interested in how people become sadomasochists, demonstrated that it was part of a learning process, during which the individual becomes aware of role expectations and is socialized into the community.

Sadomasochism has a number of important characteristics. First, central to this phenomenon is control—dominance and submission. Every relationship and interaction explicitly reflects these concerns. Sadomasochistic behavior is highly symbolic; a variety of devices, such as clothing, the use of language, the utilization of restraints, and so forth, serve to indicate a participant's role, either dominant or submissive, in the interaction. Second, fantasy is critical to sadomasochistic interactions. Behavior is frequently scripted, and participants play roles within this interaction. Sadomasochistic scenes are framed by social definitions that give the behavior a specific contextual meaning. This serves to confine the behavior only to that episode, keeping it from spilling over to other aspects of life. It is this fantasy frame that allows people to engage in behaviors or roles that are usually not permitted in everyday life, as, for example, when a man dressed as a maid allows himself to be dominated by a woman. Thus, the framing of interaction enables the participants to enjoy themselves without feeling guilt.

A third characteristic of sadomasochism is that it is consensual. All parties to the interaction must agree to participate. Forced participation is not acceptable within the subculture; it is only the illusion that individuals are coerced that is approved by sadomasochists.

A fourth characteristic, closely intertwined with consensuality, is that sadomasochism is, by its very nature, collaborative. Participants must agree on what will take place during the scene and carefully discuss limits to the interaction. What may appear to the uninitiated observer to be spontaneous behavior is really carefully planned. In this way, the kinds of uncertainties one faces in everyday life do not exist. Participants have a very good idea of what will transpire. Sometimes, however, the dominant partner will test the submissive's limits, going just a bit beyond the agreed on boundaries. This adds a feeling of authenticity to the scene, making the submissive believe that what is happening is "real." Upon receiving any indication that the interaction is becoming too intense, the dominant will back down. This is usually done very subtly, so that the fantasy frame is not broken and interaction can continue on a lower level of intensity.

Fifth, sadomasochistic interaction is explicitly sexual and must be mutually defined in that way by participants. Acts of dominance and submission outside of the sexual arena are simply not perceived by participants as fitting the criteria of sadomasochism. Outside the sadomasochistic scene, dominants are not cruel, nor are submissives necessarily passive. It is only within the sexual context that such behavior is perceived as appropriate.

A sixth characteristic of sadomasochism is that it must be mutually defined in that way. Unless all participants agree on the definition, something other than a sadomasochistic interaction is going on. Finally, sadomasochistic behavior is recreational. It is set aside from other aspects of life, and it is defined as play by participants. They do not see it as "real" in any sense but acknowledge it as a means of temporarily escaping from the everyday world.

Sadomasochistic subcultures are not found universally. According to Gebhard, they appear to be confined to urban-industrial societies. A sociological explanation for the existance of this behavior in some societies but not others is that sadomasochistic interests become institutionalized into a subculture in societies that fill the following criteria: (1) dominance-submission relationships are embedded in the culture and aggression is socially valued; (2) there is a well-developed and unequal distribution of power between social categories, which may make the temporary illusion of its reversal erotically stimulating; (3) there is sufficient affluence enjoyed by at least some segments of the population to enable them to experience leisure-time activities; and (4) imagination and creativity are encouraged and valued assets, as evidenced by the importance of scripts and fantasy in sadomasochism.

REFERENCES

Ellis, H. *Studies in the Psychology of Sex.* Vol. 3, *Analysis of the Sexual Impulse, Love, and Pain; the Sexual Impulse in Women.* 2d. ed. Philadelphia: Davis, 1903, 1926.

Freud, S. *The Basic Writings of Sigmund Freud.* Translated by A.A. Brill. New York: Modern Library, 1938.

Gebhard, P. Fetishism and Sadomasochism. In J.H. Masserman, ed., *Dynamics of Deviant Sexuality.* New York: Grune & Stratton, 1969.

Kamel, G.W.L. Leathersex: Meaningful Aspects of Gay Sadomasochism. *Deviant Behavior,* Vol. 1 (1980), pp. 171–91.

Krafft-Ebing, R. von. *Psychopathia Sexualis.* 1881. New York: Stein & Day, 1965.

Lee, J.A. The Social Organization of Sexual Risk. *Alternative Lifestyles,* Vol. 2 (1979), pp. 69–100.

Weinberg, T.S. Sadomasochism in the United States: A Review of Recent Sociological Literature. *Journal of Sex Research,* Vol. 23 (Feb. 1987), pp. 50–69.

Thomas S. Weinberg

SANGER, MARGARET

A birth control reformer and nurse, Margaret Sanger (1879–1966) helped found and was a leader of the birth control movement in the United States. The traumatic death of one of her patients from a self-induced abortion and the belief that her mother died prematurely from the stress of seven miscarriages and the bearing of 11 children caused Sanger to strive for reproductive autonomy for women.

After completing two years of nursing, Margaret Higgins married William Sanger in 1902. The following year, Sanger began to work as a home care nurse, bore the couple's first child, and became an activist for the International Workers of the World (IWW). The IWW introduced her to the world of socialist and radical politics, where she took as her own the feminist demand for women's reproductive rights. She began publishing articles about female sexuality in the socialist weekly *New York Call* and, later, in her own feminist journal *Woman Rebel,* whose rallying cry was "No Gods, No Masters." In 1914, she was indicted for violation of the postal code under the Comstock Act of 1873, which forbade distribution of contraceptive information through the mail. Before her trial, she fled to Europe, where she studied various methods of birth control and met the physician and sex reformer Havelock Ellis. Later, the government dropped its charges against her.

In October 1916, Sanger and her sister, Ethel Byrne, opened the first American birth control clinic in the Brownsville section of Brooklyn. It was closed by police ten days later. The sisters were imprisoned, and the ensuing trial helped make Sanger a national figure. Convicted, Sanger appealed and won the right of doctors to provide women with contraceptive advice for "the cure and prevention of disease."

In 1921, Sanger established the American Birth Control League, which in 1942 became the Planned Parenthood Federation of America. Two years later, with money from her second husband, millionaire J. Noah Slee, Sanger established the Birth Control Clinical Research Bureau in New York City. Headed by the gynecologist James F. Cooper and the physician Hannah Stone, it was the first American birth control clinic staffed by doctors. The clinic kept records on the safety and effectiveness of various contraceptive methods and served as a teaching facility for physicians. It served as a model for more than 300 birth control clinics established by Sanger in the following 15 years.

Sanger founded the National Committee on Federal Legislation for Birth Control, in Washington, D.C., in 1929 and became its president. In 1936, the committee initiated the case of *United States* v. *One Package*, which challenged the Comstock Act and resulted in the freedom of physicians to receive contraceptives through the mail and import them. From 1952 to 1958, Sanger served as the first president of the International Planned Parenthood Federation, which she helped create.

REFERENCES

Primary

Sanger, M. *The Case for Birth Control*. New York: Modern Art, 1917.

———. *Happiness in Marriage*. New York: Brentano, 1926.

———. *Margaret Sanger: An Autobiography*. New York: W.W. Norton, 1938.

———. *Motherhood in Bondage*. New York: Brentano, 1928.

———. *My Fight for Birth Control*. New York: Farrar, 1931.

———. *The Pivot of Civilization*. New York: Brentano, 1922.

———. *Woman and the New Race*. New York: Brentano, 1920.

Secondary

Gray, M. *Margaret Sanger: A Biography of the Champion of Birth Control*. New York: Marek, 1979.

Lader, L. *The Margaret Sanger Story and the Fight for Birth Control*. Garden City, N.Y.: Doubleday, 1955.

Moore, G., and R. Moore. *Margaret Sanger and the Birth Control Movement: A Bibliography, 1911–1984*. Metuchen, N.J.: Scarecrow, 1986.

Hilary Sternberg

SATYRS, SATYRIASIS; SEXUAL ADDICTION

Satyriasis, also known as the Don Juan syndrome, is excessive, uncontrolled sexual activity by a man with little or no emotional involvement.

The female counterpart to satyriasis is nymphomania.

In satyriasis, the sexual drive is constant, insatiable, impulsive, and uncontrolled, involving many partners and unusual frequency, with no feelings of love for the partner; the partner is merely a vehicle or object rather than an actual participating companion.

A satyr finds sex pleasurable but never achieves a feeling of complete sexual satisfaction. Although orgasm occurs most of the time, he still remains unsatisfied; complete physical and psychological gratification is never achieved. This compels him to continually seek another partner in the hope of finding gratification.

The three major psychiatric theories that attempt to explain the psychodynamics of the compulsively promiscuous male are (1) incestuous desire, (2) memories of infantile eroticism, and (3) the Don Juan syndrome.

1. Incestuous desire. The man has an unconscious desire to sleep with his mother but has an unwillingness to recognize this fact. In an effort to deny these feelings, he seeks out women whom he thinks of as bad (i.e., prostitutes), the exact opposites of the "good" mother he has in his mind, in order to act out his frustrations.

2. Infantile eroticism. The memory of having been eroticized (penis fondled) as a baby or child remains in the mind of the adult male, and he will continually try to recapture those pleasurable feelings he had as a child.

3. Don Juan syndrome. This man dedicates his life to seducing women, particularly married women and virgins. Once the women are successfully seduced, they are immediately discarded. Underlying this complex is a deep-seated hatred of women; the man has a Madonna-whore complex in which the woman is considered to be good until she succumbs to his advances; after intercourse, she is immediately associated, in his mind, with the whore. Thus, the woman hater seeks to prove that even the best, most virtuous woman is basically a whore at heart. He will continually seduce women to reinforce his own worldview.

In the 1990s, the term "sexual addiction" came into use by some to describe such behavior, although there are differing opinions on its validity. The term was introduced in a book entitled *Out of the Shadows: Understanding Sexual Addiction*, by Carnes, a senior fellow at the Golden Valley Institute for Behavioral Medicine, in Minneapolis. Carnes believes that sexual addiction is a loss of control and that the person who engages in this behavior is willing to risk any kind of consequence in order to achieve pleasure; the person is so hooked that he or she cannot stop.

The sexologist Richard K. Sharon believes that until we can define what a "normal" frequency of sexual behavior is, we cannot label people as sex addicts. Another well-known sexologist, John Money, says, "The danger of describing sex as an addiction is that it presupposes that the individual is addicted to all forms of sexual behavior rather than a specific sexual object or set of behaviors." •

Others, including Eli Coleman, argue that a better way of describing and treating the insatiable, impulsive, uncontrolled sex drive is to call it a compulsion. This makes it treatable by drugs as well as psychotherapy.

No matter which theoretical approach is used, the important issue that needs to be raised concerning excessive sexual behavior is one of definition. If satyriasis is defined as "excessive" behavior, what is excessive? One definition of excessive could be completely different from another. I could enjoy having sex once a day, which could be considered excessive to someone else. Consequently, we have to be careful in how we categorize what is normal and what is excessive. The controversy continues as to whether the condition exists and, if it does exist, what terminology should be used to describe it.

REFERENCES

Auerbach, A. Satyriasis and Nyphomania. *Medical Aspects of Human Sexuality,* Vol. 2 (1986), pp. 39–41, 44, 45.

Carnes, P.J. Progress in Sexual Addiction: An Addiction Perspective. *SIECUS Report*, Vol. 7 (1986), pp. 4–10.

Edwards, S.R. A Sex Addict Speaks. *SIECUS Report*, Vol. 24 (1986), pp. 1–3.

Francoeur, R., et al. *A Descriptive Dictionary and Atlas of Sexology.* Westport, Conn.: Greenwood Press, 1991.

Hope E. Ashby

SCIENCE AND SEXOLOGY

The meaning of science has changed dramatically in the last 30 years, and much of the disagreement among sexologists today results from our not having come to terms with the new scientific conceptions. As the status of science rose over the past 400 years, science became increasingly bold in its statements about what should be considered valid knowledge. By the 1920s, logical positivists were affirming that only that which can be verified by sensory experience was to be considered valid knowledge. The certainty and privileged status of scientific knowledge was increasingly emphasized, but it was not to last.

By the 1950s, these logical positivist doctrines came under increasing attack. Popper, in the 1950s and 1960s, attacked positivism by pointing out that events cannot be conclusively verified by sensory experience. In doing so, Popper made science a more vulnerable form of knowledge. Popper proposed that we should accept those theories that cannot be falsified by scientific tests and reject the impossible sensory verification demands of the positivists. This made science only able to say that a particular theory was not, at present, shown to be false. Science could not say that this theory was true, for inductive logic yields only probabilities, and alternate theories are always possible. The significance of Popper for our discussion is his emphasis on the limitations of scientific verification.

Popper's questioning of the verification principle also led others to question the sharp distinction between facts verified by sensory experience and nonverifiable aspects, such as values. Now both facts and values were shown to share this problem of not being fully verifiable. The positivist chasm between empirical observations and nonempirical statements was narrowing. The certainty of our knowledge of the world and the isolation of facts from values were coming under increasing criticism.

After Popper's frontal assault on logical positivism, the barrage intensified. The most lethal blow to positivism came from Kuhn's 1962 book *The Structure of Scientific Revolutions.* Kuhn's important contribution was to demonstrate with great clarity that the empirical data that science gathers represents a selective perspective and is not a precise representation of the "true external reality" of the world.

Kuhn introduced in his book the now widely used notion of the scientific paradigm. He defined a paradigm as a model for problem statements and problem solutions in science. Kuhn argued that scientists in all fields focus on solving the puzzles presented by the particular paradigm that they adopt, and do not typically question that model. Kuhn both rejected the logical positivist's radical separation of empirical and nonempirical worlds and limited the significance of Popper's falsification doctrine. He asserted that the choice of one model of reality, one paradigm, over another cannot be made on empirical evidence alone. The choice of paradigms is based more on what personally appeals to scientists and the problems they wish to solve with that scientific paradigm. Therefore, the paradigm is not chosen solely on the basis of which model holds up best to the falsification tests proposed by Popper.

It follows from Kuhn's perspective that science does not guarantee a "representational" or accurate photographic view of reality. Rather, science, over time, offers many ways of seeing the world, and the one we accept is the one that we believe works best for the problems that confront us inside and outside science. There is, in Kuhn's scientific outlook, no pure vision of the world and no pure sense data about the world like that which most of the logical positivists assumed. We see the world through the lenses of the paradigm that we accept. Science does not have any privileged or insider view of the universe with which to verify the choice of paradigms we make. Accordingly, it is not surprising that the scientific paradigms change over time. Once more, the priority of scientific knowledge over all other knowledge had to be qualified.

Kuhn's point is that there is no way to see the world independently of some paradigm or, if you will, some presuppositions about how the world operates. We need some presuppositional lenses through which to see the world or we are blind. These presuppositions lead into some theory about how the world operates. What we call empirical data or "facts" are shaped by our prior views of reality. Facts are not just there to be discovered. Rather, we begin to observe them after we formulate our presuppositions about how the world operates and begin to view the world through the lenses prescribed by these ideas.

Presuppositions, as the term is used here, are the general assumptions we make about how the world operates, including moral assumptions about how it should operate. An example would be the assumption that humans are rational creatures and that rationality is a good that we can use to benefit each other. With this presupposition, we can then start to observe the "facts" of our rational behavior. Until we make some such set of assumptions about the world, we are unable to think about that world. Once we assume a particular set of presuppositions and theories, we then have a set of lenses that enables us to perceive the world but also limits our vision of other ways of understanding the reality that is out there.

Hanson reported a playing-card experiment that demonstrated how, on a personal level, our presuppositions and theories determine what registers in our minds. A deck of cards was shown to subjects. Inserted in a typical deck were anomalous cards like a black four of hearts or a red six of spades. Those anomalous cards often went unnoticed because the subjects' "lenses" limited their expectations of what could be seen in a deck of cards. In short, they saw the deck of cards through their paradigm or model of what a deck of cards should be like and not as it "really" was.

We do much the same thing in our scientific research. Feminist social scientists remind us of the classic study of the American occupational structure done in 1967 by Blau and Duncan. Twenty thousand individuals involved in different occupations were studied. Not one subject was a woman, and yet the authors called their book *The American Occupational Structure*. Their view of occupations ignored women, much as Hanson's subjects ignored the red six of spades. The more aware we are that we make these assumptions about the world in our scientific work, the more likely we are to choose more wisely what assumptions we make. This increased awareness is one major benefit of the "postpositivist" scientific perspective that we are developing today.

Einstein and Infeld presented a view of science that is compatible with Kuhn's thinking and the ideas developed here. Einstein and Infeld compared science's attempt to understand reality with that of people seeking to understand the mechanism of a closed watch that can never be opened. People see the hands move and hear the ticking, but then they must compose their own theory about what sort of mechanism is inside the watch that could produce such an outcome. There are many possible theories that can explain why the watch works as it does, but there is no way to fully compare these conceptions with "reality."

In today's post-Kuhnian age, science is increasingly seen as much more similar to other forms of knowledge. It—like religion, politics, or philosophy—has its own presuppositions and its own obvious limitations. Science has been dethroned from the position logical positivism assigned to it. Science is not privileged knowledge to be taken as superior to all other ways of knowing the world.

Despite these qualifications of science, it still has great value to any society. No other way of looking at the world is as rigorous and precise and as demanding of relevant evidence. Moreover, scientific rules insist on validity, reliability, peer review, publication of results, disciplined inquiry, careful logic, and reasonable conclusions. In short, science remains a special, well thought out, and valuable way of understanding.

But to employ science fairly, we must also realize the limitations that exist in scientific work.

The scientific presuppositions about what the social and physical world is like, and what the world should be like, are often influenced by our place in society in terms of such characteristics as ethnic group, social class, gender, and religious perspective. No one would deny that our social location is an important determinant of our views on economic, political, or moral thinking. We now realize that this can also be true of our scientific ideas. As will be indicated shortly, this does not lead to relativism or the dismissal of scientific evidence, but it does show scientific knowledge to be an earthly activity engaged in by socialized humans. It also means that if we are to maintain the distinctive norms of good science, we had best become more aware of our presuppositions and in that way prevent them from biasing our research activity.

Feminist and Other Postpositivist Views of Science

One of the clearest and most useful recent perspectives for establishing a new conception of scientific knowledge comes from feminist philosophers such as Longino, Harding, Haraway, and Keller. Longino, for example, discards traditional positivism and recognizes the social context of science, yet she clearly rejects any relativist position and puts forth a pragmatic notion of scientific objectivity.

Longino illustrates in her examination of research on gender differences the importance of scientists' consciously and explicitly choosing their presuppositions. One presupposition relevant to research on gender differences consists of a biological view that stresses the power of hormones to limit the gender roles that men and women play in society. An alternative presupposition stresses the flexibility and power of our thought processes and our socialization in shaping our gender roles.

These presuppositions place limits on the theoretical explanations and on the policy implications that are developed. The biological view sees gender dichotomously as XX or XY and seeks to find evidence regarding how that gender difference is biologically explained. The outcome of such a strong biological presupposition affords little direct support for advocating changes toward gender equality, for it perceives many gender differences as "natural." The biological approach veers toward what some sexologists call an "essentialist" perspective, and it is in part derived from animal studies of rats, monkeys, and apes rather than from an examination of a wide range of human societies. But it is a relevant perspective, because it cannot be denied that human beings are an animal species.

On the other hand, the socialization presupposition concerning gender highlights humans as flexible, thinking individuals in constant interaction with the social environment. This model allows more of a role for human agency and for social change. The socialization perspective on gender differences is based on human models of intentionality, self-consciousness, and societal power differences. Animal models of hormonal forces are minimized.

The choice between these two models cannot simply be made on the basis of which view presents stronger empirical evidence. There is good evidence for the predictability of various outcomes using both models. The two approaches to gender differences involve different presuppositions about how the gender world operates and also may well reflect how various people think the world should operate.

By becoming aware of the major role of presuppositions in our scientific models, scientists can consciously choose that model which is more in line with their own presuppositions about how the world operates. Some may choose to stress the socialization model, in part because they favor change and flexibility and are more interested in understanding how that can be accomplished than in seeing how hormones shape human behavior. The biological model can be formulated to stress the flexibility of biological tendencies, and in that fashion it, too, can be made attractive to researchers who hold presuppositions favoring change.

No scientific model can possibly represent total reality. But the choice of model does have very real effects on the view of the world we as scientists present to others. It is surely one advantage of postpositivistic science that it makes all scientists more aware of the choices of models they are making. That creates a situation where scientists let others know what their presuppositions are, and this aids vigilance that the research process of gathering evidence is not being biased by these presuppositions. This is surely an advantage over the positivistic assumption that only research evidence, and not personal values, enter into the choice of scientific models.

The fact that presuppositions play such an important role in scientific work makes many researchers uneasy. But what is the alternative? Can a human being really have a view about the world that does not reflect some set of basic presuppositions about the world? There is no "view from nowhere." Every scientific project assumes some presuppositions about how the world works, and so we always have a "view from somewhere." Moreover, we can never scientifically say that we have the one correct view of reality.

The very language through which we express our thoughts reflects a particular perspective on the world. Languages vary in what words there are for expressing different colors, different values, different perspectives. The impossibility of having a scientific "view from nowhere"—a view that makes no such assumptions about reality—should be apparent. To say a perspective is unaffected by any assumptions and that it is the one correct view of the world is to play what Haraway calls "the God trick," and that surely is an inappropriate position for a scientist to assert.

But if we grant this reasoning, then how do we avoid becoming relativists and asserting that all viewpoints in science are just subjective meanings and cannot be the basis for any empirical generalizations or any notion of "objective" knowledge? The relativist position is endorsed by many who call themselves "postmodernists." Opposed to them are the postpositivists (among whom this author counts himself). Postpositivists reject a relativistic perspective because relativism eliminates the importance of gathering fair scientific evidence in accordance with the norms of science. In addition, relativism is rejected because it makes any understanding of how to build a better society impossible. Relativism does not permit justifying choices. But what position other than relativism can science take and still support both the objectivity of science and the inevitability of alternative presuppositions?

There is a way to arrive at what we can call "objective knowledge"—knowledge that does not solely depend on our very personal view of the world—and still not deny the fact that we can never be certain about what we agree to call "objective knowledge." One solution is suggested by Longino. She asserts that scientific work is not an individual product, but rather it is the product of a community of scientists negotiating with each other. After all, the norms of science do say to publish your results so they may be evaluated by other scientists, and we do have many journals that perform precisely that service. In this sense, science is a negotiated and somewhat adversarial process.

We can define objectivity in science as those views of the world that come to be agreed on by the scientific community at any one point in time. This is not a view from nowhere about absolute reality, nor is it a privileged insight into reality. Instead, it is a means by which we can put forth our best scientific evidence about what the world is like in the area of our research but still recognize that in time this understanding will likely change. We can accept objective reality without claiming that we possess final knowledge about it.

Change, moreover, is important in science because we can never be certain that we know what the inside of the "closed watch" is like, and thus we can never be certain that we have arrived at the "true" view of the world. There will always be other models that can explain the same set of findings. In science, we have the privilege of criticizing each other's work, and we each strive to show that the scientific quality of our own work will hold up under scrutiny. As that interactive process occurs, certain perspectives gain acceptance and become the "objective" view of that time. In physics, that accepted view was once Newton's mechanistic universe; it is now Einstein's relativistic universe, and a generation or two from now it will likely be modified again. In sexology, our view of the sexual and gender world will grow and change more easily if sexologists accept this more dynamic view of the scientific process.

Preventing Presuppositions from Overwhelming Science

If science is to continue to be one very important way of understanding our world, then we must not permit our presuppositions about our world to become so emotionally charged that they rigidify and overwhelm our scientific enterprise. Though we acknowledge the reality of the influence of our presuppositions on our scientific activity, it is crucial that we not give up our belief in the value of carefully gathered empirical knowledge.

Postpositivism argues for the importance of making explicit the presuppositions we accept and the values incorporated in them so as to put other scientists on guard against our possible biases. No researchers should enter into a project without being aware of the presuppositions they accept, whether they be pro, con, or indifferent to the social issues raised by that research. The point here is that the naive positivist view that says scientists must be "value free" masks the ways in which our presuppositions influence our scientific work. The postpositivist view increases our conscious awareness of potential bias and thereby improves our ability to abide by the norms of fair scientific research. In doing so, it replaces the stress on being value free with an emphasis on being "value aware."

Everyone accepts that our personal preferences may dictate what subject we choose to research, but the postpositivist notion adds that our presuppositions will shape the model we use to understand that subject and the conclusions we are willing to draw from the empirical evidence we gather. In philosophical terms, postpositivism challenges the inviolability of the "context of justification." Our presuppositions will shape the knowledge conclusions we believe are justified by the evidence. If we want more fully to understand the impact of presuppositions on empirical findings, we need to comprehend this idea.

An example from sexological research illustrates this point. In 1989, the author, together with Robert Leik, who is a methodologist and statistician, published a paper evaluating the relative risk of two strategies aimed at lowering an individual's chance of becoming infected with HIV (human immunodeficiency virus). We designed a probability model to estimate the changes in risk of HIV infection when one reduces the number of partners and compared this to the changes in risk that occurred when one used condoms. Of course, reducing partners and also using condoms is the safest strategy, but most people choose one or the other. We compared these two risk-reduction strategies using a probability model that took into account a very wide range of variation in the prevalence of HIV, the infectivity of HIV, the number of partners, and the failure rate of condoms.

This research started with several presuppositions about the sexual world we were examining. Some of the key presuppositions were (1) that sexuality in all its freely chosen forms can be pleasurable and good; (2) that people can and should learn to better avoid for themselves and their partners the unwanted outcomes of sexuality, such as disease, pregnancy, and psychological distress; and (3) that the basis for judging sexual morality should be the amount of honesty, equality, and responsibility in a relationship and not the number of such relationships a person has. Notice that the presuppositions refer to both factual and value assumptions about the world. The tendency is for most of us humans not just to state what the world is like but also to evaluate that aspect of the world.

These presuppositions led me to personally favor condom use as a strategy to avoid HIV infection. Still, I wanted to test that perspective in the most rigorous scientific way to keep my presuppositions from overwhelming the scientific fairness of our model testing. After consulting with the editor of the journal, we decided to add to our probability model a doubling of the prevalence rate every ten months. This would add an epidemic quality to the model and make it more likely that as one added partners over time more of them would be infected and that the risk of condom failure with such partners would be significantly higher. This addition to our probability model helped ensure that my presuppositions about sexuality and condom use would not be allowed to bias our comparison of the two strategies.

The evidence from our probability model showed that even under epidemic conditions, not using condoms and having only one or two partners was far riskier than using condoms and having 20 partners, even when assuming a condom failure rate of 10 percent to 25 percent. This result held under all the many possible combinations of prevalence and infectivity rates that our model contained. We concluded that the evidence supported the greater effectiveness of condom use over partner reduction as a strategy to reduce the risk of HIV infection. It seemed clear to us that this would be good advice to give to people who were deciding between these two strategies. But we soon discovered that people with different presuppositions would interpret our probability findings quite differently.

The great majority of responses to our published study were very supportive, I believe at least partly because my three presuppositions about sexuality are shared by many other sexual scientists. But not all readers were so supportive. One response was from a person working in a disease control clinic. He was primarily interested in the very highest HIV prevalence areas, where even careful condom use contained a risk of HIV infection that he believed was "too high." This person said that although the risk is clearly far lower with condom use, it still was too high in his judgment, and so sex outside very long term relationships should be avoided in these high-risk areas. In areas where HIV prevalence was low, he would still promote having one very long term partner, because he felt that to promote condom use would encourage casual sex, which he believed was not worth even a small increased risk.

Clearly, this critic rejected all three of my presuppositions about sexuality. He did not share my presuppositions about the value of sexuality of various types or the ability to control disease outcomes, and he did seem to believe that having multiple partners was unacceptable. With those different presuppositions, both his interpretation of the evidence and his conclusions about a recommended choice of strategies were radically different. So much for the evidence speaking for itself.

A second type of response we received displayed another questioning of our "clear evidence" for the superiority of the condom-use strategy. This response came from sexologists who counseled young people with sexual problems. They said they did not believe that many people would carefully use condoms, and that if they did use condoms they would likely increase greatly the number of sex partners and be careless with some of them. So they questioned the relevance of our evidence and arrived at different strategy recommendations than we did. The reason once again, I believe, was that they did not accept my three presuppositions—particularly not my second presupposition that asserted that people could learn to control the negative outcomes of sexuality.

One can look at these two types of responses and say that they do not challenge the probability outcome data that our model generated but rather challenge the interpretation of that data. That is true to a degree, but, more important, what all these critics were doing is questioning the worth of the evidence gathered by our particular probability model. Their different presuppositions about sexuality made our model and its evidence useless to them.

These critics did not see any advantage in condom use over partner reduction, primarily because they did not accept my propositions about the disease consequences of sexuality being manageable, nor did they accept my denial of superior moral status to having only one partner. The very design of our model reflected belief in these presuppositions. For example, if I did not believe that condoms could be used effectively, there would be no point in testing a model in which that was one major strategy of avoiding HIV infection. When these critics looked at our findings, they rejected our conclusions about strategy advice regardless of our evidence because they could not accept the assumptions on which our model was based. This example indicates how being explicit about presuppositions can increase understanding concerning how models are chosen and how evidence is interpreted and evaluated in science.

In the case of this HIV strategy project, the scientific community did arrive at a consensus supporting our evaluation of the evidence. But, as indicated, it was not a unanimous decision. Such a negotiated position comprises the objective conclusion of science at any one point in time. Nevertheless, it is important that we listen to scientists with different presuppositions because it broadens our vision of the world and makes us more aware of the type of prescriptive lenses we are wearing. When we choose one set of presuppositions, we at least will be more aware that we are indeed making a choice about what research model is worth examining and what evidence is a sound basis for policy recommendations.

The Scientific Restructuring of Sexology

Awareness of presuppositions in science is vital to the very survival of sexology itself. The future of sexology depends on having a society that shares the presuppositions that legitimate sexological research. The kind of presuppositions that are essential to the continued existence of sexology are the endorsement of a free democratic society, the value of freedom of inquiry, the right to investigate intimate areas of life, and the acceptance of a range of different moral values. There can be no discipline of sexology in a society that lacks fundamental beliefs supporting such values, for sexologists would not be allowed even to undertake sexological research without that type of societal support.

That our society contains powerful political and religious forces that question the values supporting our work was made obvious in the early 1990s, when the federal government took the following actions against sexological research: (1) stopping already funded research into HIV among teenagers by social scientists at the University of North Carolina, and (2) continuing to ban funding of even a pilot test of a national study of sexual behavior related to HIV infection, proposed by the National Opinion Research Center at the University of Chicago. Louis Sullivan, then head of Health and Human Services, stopped the University of North Carolina teenage sexuality study because he thought that being asked questions about sexuality would lead young people to think that Americans approved of casual sex, and this, he felt, would offend many people's values. To think that this position could be taken when more than 140,000 people had already died from HIV infection is proof of how powerful our political value presuppositions can be. Ultimately, Congress acted and directed Health and Human Services, in the future, to fund sex research even into "sensitive" sexual areas. Because sexologists study such sensitive areas, they are especially subject to whatever political presuppositions are operating in a political administration. The continued existence of the scientific study of human sexuality depends on the constant vigilance of sexologists and their willingness to advocate for the presuppositions that make sexological work possible.

Another way in which presuppositions enter into all scientific work on sexuality is in sexology's orientation toward the resolution of our society's sexual problems. The older scientific approaches directed researchers to serve policy makers by giving them information but implied that scientists were to avoid making specific policy recommendations themselves, for that would undermine the belief in their "objectivity." That stance left politicians free to use the research evidence in any way they wished—including ignoring it or misinterpreting it. The postpositivist perspective is aware of how our presuppositions shape our choice of research designs and our judgments about the policy implications of our findings. Therefore, rather than have our findings misused or misinterpreted, it becomes reasonable for scientists to openly affirm what they see as the best ways to utilize their findings toward the reduction of society's many sexual problems.

A science that sees presuppositions about the nature of the world as an inevitable part of scientific activity will place less distance between science and problem solutions. Such a science will be more willing to directly utilize scientific knowledge to help resolve our most threatening sexual problems, such as those involving AIDS (acquired immune deficiency syndrome), teenage pregnancy, rape, and sexual abuse of children. To be sure, all science also needs "pure or basic research" not directly concerned with problem resolution. We need that type of research precisely because it promises to improve our ability to achieve our scientific goals. But the major effort in a postpositivist science will focus on the development of knowledge useful in the control of our society's sexual problems. To effect this change in emphasis, sexology will have to move problem resolution more to its center stage, and sexologists will need to take the risks associated with becoming more directly involved in the resolution of controversial social issues.

If we pretend to be value-free, disinterested scientists, we will be seen by the public and those in power as mere pawns that can be dismissed and manipulated. If sexology is to have a public constituency that will support its research and protect it against future attempts to block the study of "sensitive" areas, then it must convincingly demonstrate to the public that it is useful in resolving America's sexual problems. Sexologists can no longer hide from controversy by pretending to have a scientific "view from nowhere." Whatever stance we take, there will

be controversy, and we can better argue our worth if we are focused on problem resolution rather than "just gathering the facts." Postpositivist science is in part an adversarial science. It is adversarial, as all science is, in the competition of scientists with each other to present their views as best they can. It is adversarial also in the competition with other views about problem resolutions that emanate from politicians and other sources.

It is important to note that the approaches in sexology that stress empathy and understanding of the feelings and thoughts of individuals and the social context in which these develop are fully acceptable in a postpositivist view of science. For example, a "social construction," "contextual," or "interpretive" perspective is well integrated with a postpositivist position that also supports the relevance of personal presuppositions about the world. Still, the supporters of such interpretive perspectives need to be able to accept the legitimacy of the scientific endeavor, since postpositivism seeks to strengthen, broaden, and clarify science, not to eliminate it.

The same integration is possible for the more advocacy-oriented "critical" positions taken by feminists, Marxists, humanists, and others. As noted, the postpositivist position integrates well with a focus on social-problem resolution. This, of course, means that our new sexology will speak directly to some of the major concerns about social equality and acceptance of pluralism on which advocacy groups focus. Once again, however, the advocacy stance would be embedded in a scientific institution that believes in the value of careful scientific research as a basis for deciding and explaining the positions taken in advocacy programs. In all these ways, sexology is well positioned and well motivated to explore the many exciting issues on the frontiers of postpositivistic science.

REFERENCES

Alexander, J.C. *Theoretical Logic in Sociology:* Vol. 1, *Positivism, Presuppositions, and Current Controversies.* Berkeley: Univ. of California Press, 1982.

Blau, P.M., and O.D. Duncan. *The American Occupational Structure.* New York: John Wiley & Sons, 1967.

Braybrooke, D. *Philosophy of Social Science.* Englewood Cliffs, N.J.: Prentice Hall, 1987.

Einstein, A., and L. Infeld. *The Evolution of Physics: The Growth of Ideas from Early Concepts to Relativity and Quanta.* New York: Simon & Schuster, 1950.

Hanson, N.R. *Patterns of Discovery.* Cambridge: Cambridge Univ. Press, 1958.

Haraway, D. Situated Knowledges: The Science Question in Feminism and the Privilege of Partial

Perspective. *Feminist Studies*, Vol. 14 (1988), pp. 575–99.

Harding, S. *Whose Science? Whose Knowledge? Thinking from Women's Lives*. Ithaca, N.Y.: Cornell Univ. Press, 1991.

Keller, E.F. *Reflections on Gender and Science*. New Haven: Yale Univ. Press, 1985.

Kuhn, T. *The Structure of Scientific Revolutions*. 2d ed. Chicago: Univ. of Chicago Press, 1970.

Longino, H. *Science as Social Knowledge: Values and Objectivity in Scientific Inquiry*. Princeton, N.J.: Princeton Univ. Press, 1990.

Popper, K. *Conjectures and Refutations*. London: Routledge & Kegan Paul, 1963.

———. *The Logic of Scientific Discovery*. London: Hutchinson, 1959.

Reiss, I.L. *An End to Shame: Shaping Our Next Sexual Revolution*. Buffalo, N.Y.: Prometheus Books, 1990.

———. *Journey into Sexuality: An Exploratory Voyage*. Englewood Cliffs, N.J.: Prentice Hall, 1986.

Reiss, I.L., and R.K. Leik. Evaluating Strategies to Avoid AIDS: Number of Partners vs. Use of Condoms. *Journal of Sex Research*, Vol. 26 (Nov. 1989), pp. 411–33.

Ira L. Reiss

SEXOLOGICAL EXAMINATION

Undoubtedly, there are various kinds of sexological examinations, but the one described here was created in 1965 as part of a three-year study of nonorgasmic women. Hartman and Fithian developed the procedure, in cooperation with Kenneth Morgan, M.D., who insisted that the senior author have specific training in the female pelvis before beginning the research. At Morgan's suggestion, Hartman spent a year under the tutelage of the late Arnold H. Kegel, M.D., who developed the pelvic exercises that now go by his name. At the time, he was head of the Perineometer Clinic at Los Angeles County General Hospital.

The name "sexological examination" was utilized, since the procedures employed were designed to evaluate and assess various components of human sexuality (e.g., perception, feeling, arousal, and response patterns) present or absent in varying degrees in research and therapy populations. It was created by behavioral scientists for use by behavioral scientists in appropriate research and therapy populations. The examination was in addition to and supplementary to the examination given by a gynecologist or other medical specialist. Hartman and Fithian emphasize that it is important that anyone utilizing the techniques of the sexological examina-

tion receive specific training in its use and that their professional status be unquestionable.

The objectives of the examination include:

1. Providing a learning experience in physiological psychology for a husband and wife, committed partners, or singles.

2. Dealing with the self-concept of men and women who want to know, "Am I normal?" "Is my clitoris too big or too small?" "Are my breasts the right size?" "Are my testicles too long?" "Is my penis too small?"

3. Teaching women four specific vaginal exercises, one of which was developed by Kegel and three of which were developed by Hartman and Fithian. Teaching men pelvic exercises to strengthen the pelvic floor, clear capillaries of fatty buildup, and enable men to last longer in intercourse by use of the pubococcygeus muscle.

4. Giving the therapist a clear picture of the response patterns of the subject through verbal reports of sensations to stimulation in each area of the vagina and/or penis.

5. Identifying, where present, causes of dyspareunia in the female and pain or discomfort found in some males. Some pain or discomfort may be psychological.

6. Giving genitalia their correct anatomical names.

7. Making the individual more at ease with his or her sexuality and sexual functioning.

8. Enhancing communications between couples about genitalia and functioning.

9. Overcoming the reluctance by some individuals to have nonintercourse genital contact, such as touching the penis or putting a finger in the vagina.

10. Intimately exploring each other by having the husband insert a lighted speculum, with the assistance and direction of the therapist, so both husband and wife may see what the inside of the vagina looks like. (This is especially indicated in situations where there is a fear of penile penetration by either partner.)

11. Teaching the use of other techniques to be used later during treatment, in privacy, where they may be carried on to fruition. This, for example, might include the squeeze technique.

12. Explaining other sexual options where, in private, the partner may stimulate the spouse to climax without the use of the penis.

13. Observing psychological conditions and responses to be treated during the therapy.

14. Acquainting the female with her own body to dispel some of the feeling that the genital area is a special place forbidden for all but physicians to see.

15. Checking the clitoris to see that it is free of adhesions. Women typically say their physician has never examined it.

16. Searching for areas where nerve endings come together in a systematic way, suggesting that this may develop positive feelings.

17. Assisting women in determining areas of perception, feeling, and awareness in their vagina. Pointing out areas in the vagina that tend to be more sensitive and responsive for many women (i.e., 12 o'clock, 4 o'clock, and 8 o'clock positions).

18. Determining a woman's response and arousal patterns. Indicating to her whether or not she lubricates well and vasocongests when she does.

19. Locating areas digitally that may be producing pain, discomfort, or problems with sexual arousal or intercourse — such as separation of muscle in the vaginal wall; long labia minora; scarring, which may be tender or fibrous — and to pinpoint the source of "pain" when present.

20. Identifying, where present, reasons for vaginismus, which are not only physiological but psychological.

21. Teaching a male partner how to caress the female's vagina.

Male Sexological Examination

The female is present for the entire male sexological examination. One of the things pointed out is the erection of the male nipples with stimulation.

In the male sexological examination, fetal development is described from a basic female at conception to changes if the fetus is to become male. It is explained that changes occur in the male approximately six to seven weeks after conception, when the major vaginal lip begins to close to form the scrotum; the organ that would be the ovaries in the female comes down into the scrotal sack and becomes testicles in the male. The clitoris, which remains small in the female, elongates and forms the penis in the male, enclosing the urethra as it grows.

On occasion, where indicated, more time is spent with the male who reports little or no sensitivity or feeling in the genitalia. When this occurs, further exploration takes place. After the man has closed his eyes, a wet swab is used to touch various areas of the inner thighs, abdomen, penis, and testicles. Response is rated on a scale of 0 to 5. Reflex action is noted on the scrotum by running the back of the fingernail down the inner thigh toward the genitalia.

Men are taught to contract the pubococcygeus muscle in the pelvis to help counteract the prematurity problem that many have. The male is told to contract the pelvic muscles and hold for a count of three and then to rapidly tighten and relax the muscle. These muscles contract at orgasm, and by exercising them, a male is able to better control ejaculation.

Although referrals to physicians are made when medical problems are identified, the sexological examinations are not medical procedures. They are educational experiences in physiological psychology. The emphasis is on perception, feeling, and response. They are designed, in part, to acquaint a spouse with the nature, location, and function of the genitalia of their partner and themselves. They also include specific instruction in the use of the genitalia for effective sexual function. Just as the medical profession has well documented its rationale for routine checkups, so it is felt to be appropriate in certain specific research and therapy situations that human beings are entitled to be evaluated as sexual beings by dual sex therapy and research teams trained to do so.

Males rarely have an erection occur during the sexological examination, but most of those who do have come as clients because they believed they were impotent, and when this happens, the examination can serve as part of the therapy.

Female Sexological Examination

Direct stimulation of a client toward a high level of arousal is not, and never has been, a part of the sexological examination conducted at the Center. Still, some women do become aroused, and occasionally a sex flush will be observed in the process practice of the vaginal caresses.

The stimulation of the clitoris is not necessary for checking sexual arousal, since the client doing pubococcygeus exercises will develop sufficient vasocongestion in the vagina to check levels of lubrication. Among common reasons for female discomfort during intercourse is that the longer labia minora are being pushed into the vagina during thrusting or penetration, or there is a separation in the muscle wall of the vagina, where a penis may penetrate. Tender surgical scars, such as those from an episiotomy, or fibrous areas in the vaginal wall that are uncomfortable when palpated, are problems for some women. Very frequently, "pain" is perceived with any movement of anything in the vagina. For many dysfunctional women, nothing has ever been in the vagina long enough for them to develop any degree of comfort or response. Most of these conditions are amenable to improvement by pelvic exercises and vaginal caress by the husband or lover. Sometimes, a partner needs to learn how to penetrate the vagina so it is not painful. The vagina, on the average, is only four inches deep, and a partner with a large penis may have to insert under the cervix with less than full penetration to prevent pain or discomfort. Some women suffer discomfort because the uterus is somewhat prolapsed, and the cervix can be hit by penile penetration. Ensuring that the penis goes under the cervix at penetration will eliminate discomfort. Pelvic exercises on the part of the woman often will pull the cervix back up and out of the way. Sometimes, however, they need to be evaluated for surgical correction.

More important than the stimulation of the clitoris in the female sexological examination is the determination of whether or not clitoral adhesions are present. This is a condition where the prepuce is stuck or adhered to the glans clitoris. For preorgasmic women, the inability of the clitoris to withdraw as part of sexual arousal may prevent particular women from full response. Even though some women are orgasmic with clitoral adhesions, freeing them usually results in easier, quicker orgasms and less discomfort due to calcified, trapped smegma.

Another important part of the female sexological examination concerns breasts. In America, the general consensus seems to be that breasts come in two sizes, either too large or too small. In spite of the concern with breasts, some women in treatment are found not to have allowed their breasts to be touched even by themselves and have not developed pleasurable feelings of arousal. Even for those who do have pleasurable sensations, having a female show her partner how she would like to have her breasts touched is important, since, typically, the therapist hears, "He grabs my breasts," or, "He tweaks my nipples," and is too rough. As part of therapy (body caress and nondemand pleasuring), it is essential that her partner touch her breasts in a way that is acceptable and pleasurable to her. A woman needs to make it known what it is she likes rather than have her breasts ignored or hurt by an unthinking or insensitive partner. However, it is important that she does not use suggestions as a means of control in the relationship.

In a female sexological examination at the Center, the husband is not present for the first part of the procedure. This removal of the male partner came about after several instances of the man, after learning of his wife's lack of control of the pubococcygeus muscle or flaccid vagina, blaming her for their sexual problems. While this may have been a factor, it was rarely the underlying problem. The assumption by the man that it was the problem handicapped further therapy. Generally, sexological problems go beyond the realm of the physical, even though they may have first manifested themselves as physiological problems. The psychological overlay is often so great that, even with the resolution of the physical problem, function may not be fully restored unless the psychological aspects are dealt with as well.

Though some physicians, such as Hock, hold that the sexological examination should be done only by a physician, in our experience it is the rare physician who has the time to spend (anywhere from 30 to 90 minutes per client) on such an examination. Thus, for the most part, the examination is given either by other health professionals or by therapists. Those who have studied the sexological examination, such as Barbie Taylor, William Hamilton, and Jeff and Pat Patterson, and those who have used it in their practice, such as Wardell Pomeroy and Mildred Brown, have found it to be a particularly effective way of getting at clients' problems. The major concern that professionals have about the sexological examination is that untrained or unethical therapists might use it unwisely.

References

Hamilton, W.H. The Therapeutic Role of the Sexological Examination. Ph.D. diss., California School of Professional Psychology, 1978.

Hartman, W.E., and M.A. Fithian. *Treatment of Sexual Dysfunction*. Long Beach, Calif.: Center for Marital and Sexual Studies, 1972; New York: Aronson (scheduled 1994).

Hock, Z. A Commentary on the Role of the Female Sexological Examination and the Personnel Who Should Perform It. *Journal of Sex Research*, Vol. 18 (Feb. 1982), pp. 58-63. (See rejoinders by W. Hartman and M. Fithian, and by M. Brown and W. Pomeroy, as well as a reply by Hock, in the same issue.)

Kegel, A. Progressive Resistence Exercise in the Functional Restoration of the Perineal Muscles. *American Journal of Obstetrics and Gynecology*, Vol. 56 (Aug. 1948), pp. 238-48.

William E. Hartman
Marilyn A. Fithian

SEXUAL DYSFUNCTION

Human sexual behavior is a natural phenomenon that has been biologically programmed in the human species. Sexual behavior and response are subject to and influenced by a number of internal and external mechanisms, including environment, health, and emotions. It is the interplay of the biochemical, physiological, and psychological aspects of the human organism that contribute to and influence the natural expression of sexual behavior. As with any bodily system, dysfunctions occur. Few systems are as complicated and sensitive to influence as sexual behavior, and few problems cause such emotional and personal concerns.

Thanks to a more candid approach to sexual issues by the media and a better general awareness about sexual issues in society, more information about sexual functioning and sexual problems is available to the public. Helpful as well as confusing or inaccurate information is available, and, as a result, more and more people have become aware of their sexuality and their sexual likes and dislikes. This has led some people to make efforts to enhance their sexual relationships, while others remain unsure as to what constitutes real sexual problems.

How common are sexual problems in the general population? Masters and Johnson have stated that, at one time or another, 50 percent of marriages have significant sexual problems. Other studies estimate that at any given time, 10 percent of women are completely anorgasmic, 7 percent of men are impotent, 15 percent complain of rapid or premature ejaculation, and 3 percent experience retarded ejaculation. There is also a new term used by sex therapists—inhibited sexual desire—which refers to a complaint of a growing lack of interest in sexual activity. The sex researchers Harold Lief and Helen Kaplan estimate that inhibited desire is a complaint of 20 percent of adult women.

The incidence of sexual difficulties in the general population is not known, but one recent study is suggestive of the extent of the problem. The study involved 100 "happily married" couples, 80 percent of whom felt their sexual relationship was satisfactory. When questioned further, problems surfaced. Forty percent of the men reported erectile or ejaculatory problems, and 63 percent of the women reported arousal and orgasmic dysfunction. When the researchers looked at the area of sexual difficulties, apart from dysfunctions, the numbers were higher: 50 percent of the men and 77 percent of the women complained of a number of difficulties that interfered with satisfaction in sex. What was of interest was that the presence of sexual difficulties had more to do with overall sexual satisfaction in the couple than did the number of dysfunctions.

Sexual Dysfunctions

Sexual dysfunctions are problems that interfere with the natural response of the body to appropriate sexual stimuli and with the satisfactory ability to perform sexually. Dysfunctions can exist in any or several phases of the sexual response cycle and can be caused by a number of biochemical, physiological, psychological, or environmental agents.

The human sexual response cycle consists of several phases that are both reflexive and psychogenic in response. Initial desire and arousal phases lead to greater sexual excitement that eventually culminates in orgasm. Masters and Johnson pioneered in the study of human sexual response and described the phases of sexual response as excitement, plateau, orgasm, and resolution. A more recent conceptualization by Lief uses the acronym DAVOS to describe phases of sexual function: desire, arousal, vasocongestion, orgasm, and satisfaction. These categories are helpful in separating sexual dysfunctions into identifiable phases of the sexual response cycle.

Sexual functioning occurs on a continuum of a wide normal range that extends from inadequacy and inability to function, on one side, to the other side where behavior occurs that society has considered inappropriate or deviant. The focus of this article is on that part of the continuum that reflects an inability to function adequately. Usually, this is divided into two major categories: dysfunctions in desire and arousal, and dysfunctions in orgasm and ejaculation. Many of these dysfunctions can occur as a primary or secondary complaint. A primary sexual complaint is one in which the person has never been able to function adequately, as in the case of a man who has never had an erection sufficient for intercourse. A secondary sexual dysfunction reflects a current difficulty in a person who in the past had no problem functioning, as in a case of situational impotence.

The current psychiatric diagnostic categories recognize sexual dysfunctions as being psychogenic or biogenic in origin. They may be lifelong or acquired (primary or secondary) and can be generalized or situational in their occurrence. The category of sexual desire disorders includes hypoactive sexual desire disorder and sexual aversion disorder. The first diagnosis describes the persistent or recurrently deficient or absent sexual fantasies and desire for sexual activity. Cases of sexual aversion reflect an extreme aversion and avoidance of genital sexual contact with a partner. Desire-disorder problems often reflect complicated psychological issues and can be difficult to treat.

Sexual arousal disorders exist in both males and females. Male erectile disorders, often referred to as impotence or erectile dysfunction, can have a variety of causes and, in cases of psychogenic origin, can be perpetuated by anxiety and relationship problems. The problem consists of an inability to obtain or maintain an erection sufficient for completion of sexual intercourse. Female sexual arousal disorder describes a condition of recurrent partial or complete failure to attain or maintain the lubrication-swelling response of sexual excitement during sexual activity and intercourse. This can also be accompanied by a lack of a subjective sense of sexual excitement and pleasure in the female during sexual activity.

Orgasm disorders also exist in both men and woman. Inhibited female orgasm is often a natural consequence of inhibition in sexual excitement. While there is a normal variation among women in their ability to experience orgasm, this diagnosis refers to a delay or absence of orgasm response in women following an adequate phase of sexual excitement, during which the focus, intensity, and duration of stimulation is considered adequate. There is a range of response in women, and many women who are able to experience orgasm through noncoital clitoral stimulation (e.g., masturbation) are not able to do so through intercourse.

Some women who do not meet the criteria for the diagnosis of an orgasm disorder still may require or request evaluation to explore possible psychological inhibitions or relationship problems. Many women who otherwise function quite well sexually do not experience coital orgasm. Female orgasm has a wide normal variation, and some of the issues surrounding a woman's "right to orgasm" have many political implications aside from the issues of "normal" sexual response.

Orgasm disorders in the male reflect two types of problems in ejaculation: inhibited ejaculation and rapid ejaculation. The diagnosis of inhibited male orgasm describes a condition in which ejaculation is persistently delayed or even absent following a period of sexual excitement and sufficient stimulation. Retarded ejaculation, as the diagnosis is also called, is relatively infrequent in the general population and usually occurs during intercourse, although it can also occur during masturbation. Cases of absolute or primary re-

tarded ejaculation are rarely reported and often involve organic or drug-related components.

Premature or rapid ejaculation is a fairly common experience among men, especially in young men or when initial excitement is high with a new sexual partner. The frequency of sexual activity is also a component, as is the presence of anxiety. It is difficult to diagnosis rapid ejaculation based on duration of intercourse or a partner's orgasmic response (i.e., the male ejaculating before a female partner reaches orgasm during coitus). However, the diagnosis can be made if the male ejaculates before or immediately upon intromission or with minimal stimulation. Sex therapists tend to stress the concept of reasonable ejaculatory control rather than to invoke time parameters for intercourse. Kinsey, a zoologist, found that the average male ejaculated only after one and a half minutes of intromission. He felt rapid ejaculation may have had an adaptive effect from an evolutionary perspective. Uncomplicated cases of premature ejaculation are usually successfully treated with modern sex therapy techniques.

Another category of sexual dysfunctions that is currently recognized is sexual pain disorders. Painful intercourse, or dyspareunia, describes a condition in which either the male or female complains of persistent genital pain during or immediately after intercourse. The condition is rare in the male, but in the female many physical conditions could be responsible, including insufficient vaginal lubrication, vaginal infections, endometriosis, vaginal atrophy, and pelvic adhesions.

Vaginismus refers to persistent involuntary spasm of the musculature of the outer third of the vagina that interferes with intercourse. Vaginal penetration is accompanied by pain because of the tightness of the vaginal entrance caused by the constriction of the perivaginal muscles. While the condition can cause dyspareunia, vaginismus is a separate diagnosis and can be responsible for "unconsummated" marriages. The problem is usually psychogenic and can also exist in nonsexual situations that can interfere with the use of vaginal tampons during menstruation or with gynecologic examinations. After ruling out organic causes or correcting them through proper medical intervention, vaginismus can be successfully treated with sex therapy.

As with many other diagnostic schemes, there are some sexual dysfunctions that are labeled as atypical or not classified by another diagnoses. Examples would be genital anesthesia or a complaint of no erotic sensation despite stimulation and orgasm as well as during masturbation.

Sexual Problems and Difficulties

While sexual dysfunctions reflect diagnosed inadequacies in sexual functioning, the existence of sexual difficulties refers to problems relating to the emotional tone of sexual relationships. They are varied and, as reported above, can sometimes be cause for greater frustration and unhappiness in relationships than the true sexual dysfunctions. These difficulties are not often reported to doctors by patients, and yet they provide many of the complaints seen by sex therapists in their work with individuals and couples, be they heterosexual or homosexual.

Dysfunctions often arise from a combination of educational deficits, physiological problems, inhibitions, and interpersonal conflict. Many of these difficulties refer not to the quality of sexual performance but to the affective tone in the relationship, which in turn affects the perception of the quality of the sexual interactions. Many are situational and are a by-product of a hectic modern life-style. Others reflect sexual misinformation and dysfunctional patterns of communication. Examples are as follows: partners choosing an inconvenient time for sex, inability to relax during sex, disagreement between partners on sexual habits or practices, lack of interest in or indifference toward sex, insufficient foreplay before sex, little tenderness after intercourse, attraction to someone other than one's partner, boredom with sex or with one's partner, being "turned off" by one's partner, unrealistic expectations about sex, lack of trust between partners, illness and fatigue, and power struggles in which sex becomes the battleground.

When the above partial list of issues that contribute to sexual difficulties is examined, it becomes apparent how many potential interferences there are that serve as barriers to satisfactory sexual relationships. It should also be noted that these difficulties can lead to sexual dysfunctions that are consequences of unfulfilling sex. It would be an error to assume that such things will pass with time; they might if the difficulties are situational and temporary, but there is the risk of patterns of dysfunctional behavior forming that can go on undealt with for years.

For some, corrections can be made through simple education, correction of sexual myths, or better and more effective communication with partners about sexual interests and wishes. Unspoken sexual contracts may need to be renegotiated. Many find that they must find for themselves just what are the essential ingredients for good sex. Often, good sex begins with the "four Ts": talk, time, trust, and touch.

REFERENCES

Frank, E., et al. Frequency of Sexual Dysfunction in "Normal" Couples. *New England Journal of Medicine,* Vol. 299 (July 20, 1978), pp. 111–15.

Kinsey, A., et al. *Sexual Behavior in the Human Male.* Philadelphia: Saunders, 1948.

Lief, H. Classification of Sexual Disorders. In H. Lief, ed., *Sexual Problems in Medical Practice.* Washington, D.C.: American Medical Association Press, 1981.

———. *Human Sexual Response.* Boston: Little, Brown, 1966.

Masters, W., and V. Johnson. *Human Sexual Inadequacy.* Boston: Little, Brown, 1970.

Slowinski, J. Sexual Dysfunctions: Common Problems Often Overlooked. *Ob/Gyn Medical Letter,* Vol. 2 (Winter 1989), p. 3.

Julian W. Slowinski

SEXUAL ORIENTATION

Introduction

Although to some people the concept of "sexual orientation" is self-evident, in fact it is usually a poorly defined one, with controversies surrounding each aspect of the definition. There is even controversy about whether the term is itself legitimate, with some scholars preferring "sexual preference" and yet others of the opinion that all such terms are nothing more than social constructions of a particular time and place, of no universal significance.

Those who use the term "sexual orientation" do so to emphasize that what they are talking about is an underlying preference for relationships with a particular sex, a preference which endures despite the circumstances of daily life or the pressures of socialization. For example, men whose spontaneously occurring sexual fantasies only include women can, if imprisoned, make do with males as sex partners. But as soon as they are released, they seek female partners. Likewise, heterosexual female prostitutes are sometimes paid by their male customers to have sexual relationships with other females; the women involved can become aroused under such circumstances, but not because their underlying orientation is homosexual or bisexual. Rather, they are heterosexual women who are engaging in homosexual acts for profit.

This matter is complicated by the fact that most people with persistent homosexual feelings initially deny those feelings (even to themselves), usually for many years or even decades. Sometimes, they succeed in avoiding any homosexual acts that might otherwise have resulted from those feelings, but other times they begin to use what psychologists call the ego defense of splitting. In splitting, one simply decides not to think about or consciously deal with an important aspect of one's personality; one splits it off into its own compartment, so to speak. However, that aspect of the personality continues to be active and will typically have its way sooner or later. The result can be an extremely painful or anxious state of mind in which one feels out of control of one's emotions and (eventually) one's actions. Politicians and other public figures who are embarrassed by being caught in compromising homosexual situations presumably owe their dilemmas to splitting, as do many ordinary people who find themselves engaging in self-destructive behavior patterns pertaining to sexuality.

This acute psychological distress ends when the individual admits his or her homosexual desires to himself or herself, takes responsibility for those feelings, and takes on a homosexual identity. Homosexuals call this process coming out, and it is an essential step forward in the mental health of people with a fundamental homosexual orientation. Coming out can also refer to any subsequent stage of increasing openness in dealing with one's homosexual feelings: for example, coming out to one's family or loved ones means telling them about one's homosexuality, bringing a significant other to family reunions, and so on.

The acutely painful awareness that one's deepest emotions are not in accord with what one has been socialized to expect them to be is the fundamental cause of the awareness most homosexuals have of their sexual orientation. It follows that most heterosexuals may be less fundamentally aware that they have a sexual orientation, because it is in accord with the socialization pressures they experience every day. It also follows that many heterosexuals will conclude, rightly or wrongly, that they became heterosexual as a result of the strong socialization pressures our society provides in that direction, not as a result of any underlying predisposition—and thus that homosexuality probably results from choice or from defects in that socialization process. It finally follows that bisexuals—people who have sexual attractions to both men and women—may have a special perspective on the matter of sexual orientation. On the one hand, pursuit of the heterosexual portion of their feelings may delay their coming to terms with their homosexual aspect. On the other hand, once they do so they may feel separate and distinct from ordinary homosexuals due to the enduring or special nature of their heterosexual attractions. Many

homosexuals go through a stage in which they pretend to themselves that they are bisexual; accordingly, they can be slow to admit the reality of that label when other people take it on.

Assessment of Sexual Orientation

This uncertainty in the definition of sexual orientation is reflected in controversy over the appropriate method of assessing it. Some scientists, especially those who prefer the term "sexual preference," believe that one can only assess sexual orientation by asking the person about it. Others believe that observing a person's behavior is the only accurate method, since people can lie about their behavior and can deny their "true" feelings. Yet others believe that sexual orientation is best assessed by an extensive interview, in which a trained professional arrives at a sexual orientation rating on the basis of a combination of behavior, fantasy, and other aspects of life.

One method of sexual orientation assessment was developed by psychologists trying to assess the effectiveness of treatments to change sexual orientation behavioristically. Behaviorists distrust subjective evaluations of any trait (e.g., "true feelings"), and these workers accordingly developed a penile plethysmograph—a device that is attached to the penis and records penile volume in real time, in response to stimuli (e.g., slides, audiotapes) presented to the subject wearing the device. A man is judged heterosexual or homosexual according to whether it is female or male stimuli that are associated with increases in penile volume. There are also vaginal photoplethysmographs, in which a probe measures the reflectivity of the vaginal wall (which is affected by the blood engorgement of sexual arousal in women). As far as the present author knows, however, vaginal photoplethysmographs have never been used for sexual orientation assessment.

Measures of Sexual Orientation

Many of these confusing matters can be clarified by being precise about what kinds of attractions are under discussion and by taking seriously the notion that there may be more than one kind of sexual attraction. The first such attempt was made by Alfred Kinsey, who developed and used the heterosexuality-homosexuality rating scale (now usually called the Kinsey scale), which rates exclusive heterosexuality as 0, exclusive homosexuality as 6, equal attraction to men and women as 3, and other degrees of bisexuality using the other numbers in between. The rating is assessed on the basis of a face-to-face sex history interview.

The inevitable conflicts between desires and behavior, as well as the wish to encompass other aspects of sexual attractions, led Klein to develop the Klein Sexual Orientation Grid (KSOG), which is usually assessed by self-administered questionnaire. Using the same 0-to-6 numbering scheme as Kinsey, Klein postulated the existence of seven aspects of sexual attractions (i.e., sexual fantasy, sexual behavior, sexual attractions, emotional attractions, social attractions, social behavior, and sexual self-identification) and assessed them at three different periods (past, present, and ideal-future), for a total of 21 different numbers. Statistical analyses of KSOG scores suggest that these 21 different aspects are not entirely independent of each other—that is, fewer than 21 numbers can probably suffice to describe a person's sexual orientation with reasonable scientific completeness—but that a single number is probably insufficient. In particular, these analyses suggest that sexual and social attractions are somewhat independent of each other.

The "Limerent and Lusty" Theory of Sexual Orientation

Insights such as these led the author to develop the limerent-and-lusty theory of sexual orientation, which postulates that there are at least two distinct aspects of sexual attraction and names these aspects "limerent" and "lusty" attractions. It is an important postulate that both of these aspects are sexual and have erotic components. Lusty attractions are those in which the sexual attractiveness of an individual is judged by comparison with a physical standard: for example, "I tend to be attracted to tall, muscular, hairy men with dark eyes," or "I'm attracted to thin blonde women with long legs and small breasts." Lusty attractions can presumably be discovered (in men, at least) through plethysmography. Limerent attractions are those in which the sexual attractiveness of an individual is judged by comparison with an emotional-personality standard: for example, "I'm attracted to women who are smart and independent enough to take care of themselves," or "I tend to be attracted to people who can dominate me but who are always sensitive to my needs and desires." Men are more likely than women to think of their sexuality primarily in lusty terms, although many if not most men are able to be aroused by both aspects of sexiness. Women are more likely than men to think of their sexuality primarily in limerent terms, although many if not most women are able to be aroused by both aspects.

Much of the confusion about sexual orientation can be clarified by being precise about which kind of sexual attraction—limerent or lusty—is being discussed. It is the opinion of the present author that there are very few individuals who have lusty attractions of roughly equal salience to both men and women, thus giving credence to the feeling of many people (especially gay men) that "true" bisexuality is rare or nonexistent. However, it is not difficult, in the opinion of the author, to find people who have limerent attractions to both sexes, even though it is probably the case that most adults have limerent attractions to one sex only. This gives credence to the statements of many bisexuals who believe that homosexuals and heterosexuals reject the notion of bisexuality too quickly, based on their own experience of just lust and not limerence.

What Causes Variability in Sexual Orientation?

Some people criticize attempts to uncover the antecedents, if any, of the various sexual orientations, because they believe that such questions reflect an underlying anti-homosexual bias and will inevitably be misused to prevent homosexuality. These critics claim that it is only because our society stigmatizes homosexuality that people care about such questions. After all, why worry about the causes of differences in height, unless they are the pathological extremes of height, or the causes of different tastes in food? Although this point of view has some validity, scientists are nevertheless interested in more than just abnormal variations. For example, personality psychologists have long been interested in traits like introversion and extroversion, neither of which is typically considered pathological. It is the job of scientists to wonder about the causes of all aspects of human behavior, including personality and sexual behavior.

An important era in research on this question ended with the publication of the Kinsey Institute studies of homosexuality in the late 1970s and early 1980s. These researchers conducted an extensive study of black and white homosexual men and women, examining all the commonly proposed theories of sexual orientation popular at the time with psychologists, sociologists, and other social scientists. In a sophisticated path analysis, the only variable that was consistently shown to be both statistically significant and substantively important with respect to sexual orientation was childhood gender nonconformity. Here, the correlations were so high that the Kinsey workers concluded that childhood gender nonconformity was essentially the same thing as homosexuality—or, more probably, constituted one type of homosexuality seen at an earlier stage of development. The fact that they considered this to be only one type of homosexuality was reflected in the title they chose for their work, *Homosexualities*. Accordingly, these social scientists suggested that biological factors probably play a much larger role in the genesis of the different sexual orientations than they had believed at the time they designed their study. Of course, with one exception (noted below), these researchers had not designed biological variables into their study, so their acceptance of biology was without direct evidence. The exception was that they had asked respondents about their brothers and sisters and, in particular, to report whether those siblings were homosexual or heterosexual. They did not publish these data in their books, but in later unpublished tabulations they did find that their homosexual respondents reported more homosexual brothers and sisters than their heterosexual respondents did. Of course, this does not distinguish between genetic-biological transmission and environmental fostering of the trait, but it is an interesting first step.

The first carefully controlled study of whether sexual orientation tends to run in families was conducted by Pillard and Weinrich, who reported that 22 percent of the homosexual men in their sample reported homosexual brothers, whereas heterosexual men reported only 4 percent homosexual brothers. A corresponding statement held true for homosexual women (unpublished data). This study was the first to confirm the reports of the original subjects by actual inquiries to the brothers and sisters themselves. This finding was confirmed and extended in a recent study by Bailey and Pillard. These workers chose not an ordinary sample of gay men but a sample of homosexual male twins, finding that about half of the co-twins of monozygous ("identical" or single-egg) homosexual twins were also homosexual, whereas only 22 percent of the co-twins of dizygous ("fraternal" or two-egg) homosexual twins were likewise. Further analyses strongly suggested a genetic component to sexual orientation, even in the light of many different parameter values used in their models and no significant evidence that the environments of monozygotic twins were more alike than the environments of dizygotic twins (which otherwise might explain their results). Essentially the same results were obtained in a more recent study of female twins conducted by the same authors.

Note that even in these so-called "biological" studies, substantial amounts of environmental variability were detected. For example, in the Bailey and Pillard twin study, 48 percent of the co-twins of monozygotic homosexual male twins were heterosexual—not a small percentage. Remarkably, very few proponents of the environmental view have shown any interest in examining the environmental contribution to sexual orientation, although it must exist.

Accordingly, any comprehensive theory of the development of the various sexual orientations must take into account genetic, hormonal, early childhood, and later experiences. One such theory is the periodic-table model of the gender transpositions, which assumes that there are not one but at least two underlying dimensions to sexual orientation (as well as other gender transpositions such as transvestism and transsexualism). However, even this theory does not propose a specific mechanism by which sexual orientations are differentiated.

A more recent theory devised by the present author, called the predisposed-imprinting theory, takes its cue from an insight of John Money's: that the true sequence of events in psychosexual development is not just "genetics" followed by "learning," but genetics and hormonal factors followed by sensitive period experiences in early life, followed by ordinary learning. Those sensitive period experiences might be what biologists call imprinting or might merely be sharply constrained and long-lasting learning. The predisposed-imprinting theory proposes that children are strongly predisposed by genetic, hormonal, and perhaps some early life experiences to put themselves into certain situations that, in turn, "imprint" them (or cause certain types of irreversible learning to take place) on sexual objects that will turn out, with the hormones of puberty, to be the sexually attractive objects reflected in their sexual orientations. The most common principle hypothesized for this process is that a mature version of the type of person one is most estranged or separated from in early childhood will become the type of sexually attractive object at puberty and into adulthood.

For example, most typically masculine boys in childhood play with other boys, and not only stay away from girls' play groups but also are excluded (by the girls) from those play groups. Follow-up studies show that the large majority of such boys grow up to be heterosexual men: that is, they are attracted to the mature version (women) of the objects they were excluded from interacting with (girls) when they were boys. In contrast, most so-called "sissy," "effeminate," or feminine boys play with girls in childhood and exclude themselves from boys' play groups (because the boys play "too rough"); also, they are excluded from those groups by the boys in them.

Follow-up studies show that the large majority of such boys grow up to be homosexual men: that is, they are attracted to the mature version (men) of the objects they were excluded from interacting with (boys) when they were young.

As another example, boys who lose their father early in life, or boys who have physically abusive fathers, are excluded from ordinary kinds of psychological contact with this important attachment "object." The predisposed-imprinting theory suggests that this kind of boy is more likely to grow into an adult gay man who seeks older sexual partners who are father figures. Likewise, boys who lose their mother early in life or are otherwise prevented from having ordinary attachments to a mother figure are predicted to grow into adult heterosexual men who are strongly attracted to older women rather than women their age.

Conclusions

Many of the most interesting or controversial questions about sexual orientation cannot be answered without being precise about the aspect of sexual attraction being considered. Accordingly, we have not discussed many of these questions in this essay: for example, can sexual orientation change throughout life? Is there any process (some would say "therapy") by which sexual orientation can be changed? What are the types and subtypes of heterosexual, homosexual, and bisexual, and what (if anything) causes these various subtypes to come into being?

Perhaps the most intriguing question concerns the relationship, if any, between one's sexual orientation and one's preferred erotic role (in or out of bed). In the AIDS (acquired immune deficiency syndrome) era, we need to understand what causes people to prefer particular erotic roles and their associated sexual acts over others, because it is only certain sexual acts that are at high risk for transmitting HIV (human immunodeficiency virus) from an infected to an uninfected partner. Although some first steps have been made in this direction, we need much more detailed descriptions of people's sexual attractions to succeed in this arm of the fight against this terrible disease.

REFERENCES

Bailey, J.M., and R.C. Pillard. A Genetic Study of Male Sexual Orientation. *Archives of General Psychiatry*, Vol. 48 (1991), pp. 1089–96.

Bell, A.P., and M.S. Weinberg. *Homosexualities: A Study of Diversity among Men and Women.* New York: Simon & Schuster, 1978.

Bell, A.P., M.S. Weinberg, and S.K. Hammersmith. *Sexual Preference: Its Development in Men and Women.* Bloomington: Indiana Univ. Press, 1981.

Klein, F., B. Sepekoff, and T.J. Wolf. Sexual Orientation: A Multi-variable Dynamic Process. *Journal of Homosexuality*, Vol. 11 (1985), pp. 35–49.

Pillard, R.C., and J.D. Weinrich. Evidence of Familial Nature of Male Homosexuality. *Archives of General Psychiatry*, Vol. 43 (1986), pp. 808–12.

————. The Periodic-Table Model of the Gender Transpositions: Part I—A Theory Based on Masculinization and Defeminization of the Brain. *Journal of Sex Research,* Vol. 23 (1987), pp. 425–54.

Weinrich, J.D. The Periodic-Table Model of the Gender Transpositions: Part II—Limerent and Lusty Sexual Attractions and the Nature of Bisexuality. *Journal of Sex Research*, Vol. 24 (1988), pp. 113–29.

Weinrich, J.D. Predisposed Imprinting: A New Theory of the Proximate Causes of Sexual Orientation. Submitted for publication.

Weinrich, J.D., I. Grant, D.L. Jacobson, S.R. Robinson, J.A. McCutchan, and the HNRC Group. On the Effects of Childhood Gender Nonconformity on Adult Genitoerotic Role and AIDS Exposure. *Archives of Sexual Behavior*, Vol. 21 (1992), pp. 559–86.

James D. Weinrich

SEXUAL REVOLUTION

The term "sexual revolution" has been applied by historians to change during two separate periods of American history. The first took place in the opening years of the 20th century and is associated with Prince A. Morrrow and the social hygiene movement. The second was much better publicized and took place in the 1960s. Both of these revolutions had some counterparts in other parts of the world—the social hygiene movement for the first, the expanding sexual revolution for the second, but both were, in fact, so important in the United States that they appeared to be peculiar to the American sociocultural setting.

The first sexual revolution grew out of the efforts of social hygienists to fight venereal disease; in so doing, they challenged some fundamental social institutions in an attempt to save the health of many Americans and also the family in the United States. The second sexual revolution was speeded by new technological developments and involved largely replacing middle-class feminine standards with lower-class masculine standards.

In the last part of the 19th century, Americans came closer than other people in the world to observing the traditional ideal of chaste monogamy that was common to all of the West. The ideal was enforced by a strong purity movement that had spread from England as part of an antiprostitution campaign, and many middle-class American mothers (this would include a very large number of northern households) succeeded in inculcating ideals of sexual purity and monogamy in their children—boys as well as girls. Particularly notable was a general public agreement on the so-called conspiracy of silence, by which no public discussion of anything sexual occurred—neither in a printed form nor in decent company. Public discourse was rigorously cleansed of anything that might sully the innocence of "a young girl" and convey any knowledge to her or allude to what she might learn by accident.

In a complex way that seemed to work at the time, there was simultaneously a widely observed double standard. Women were expected to be pure and even asexual, despite the fact that many of the most respectable married women, in private, participated with their husbands in lively or at least satisfying lovemaking.

Men, by contrast, were permitted, and to some extent expected, to indulge their bestial passions whenever they had the opportunity, much as Benjamin Franklin had once advocated venery for the sake of health. The chief focus of men's self-indulgence was a group of women who played the social role of prostitutes, and prostitution was well established in every city, where the existence of the institution was the subject of open discussion (in veiled terms, of course), and in many smaller urban centers. With considerable social support, a whole hierarchy of prostitutes served both unmarried male populations and other men who took advantage of the prevailing customs.

This social arrangement lasted until the terrible results of the STDs (sexually transmitted diseases) led physicians to question whether existing institutions were not better overthrown in favor of new social arrangements. The social hygienists under the leadership of Morrow began, about 1905, to advocate simultaneously educating people about the dangers of venereal disease, about the ways in which monogamous marriage and purity could be made fulfilling for both men and women, and about the necessity for wiping out prostitution and ending the double standard, the chief means by which disease spread at that time. To destroy the institutions of the double standard and prostitution, it was necessary also to end, at least to a substantial extent, the conspiracy of silence, still another well-established institution.

The success of these early-20th-century reformers in their endeavors constituted the first sexual revolution. All over the country, cities established vice commissions to expose prostitution and show ways of curbing it, particularly by getting at the economic base of it by first moving against property owners who owned buildings where prostitutes plied their trade and then agitating against business proprietors who paid women so little that at least part-time prostitution was either attractive or necessary. During World War I, pressure by the federal government against prostitution near armed services facilities carried the reformers very far, so that in the United States prostitution was ended as an institution condoned and supported by much of the middle class and was instead rendered deviant and lower class.

The campaign for education about STDs and the necessity to encourage fulfilling marriages to substitute for prostitution enabled sexual reformers to advocate the equality of women in sexual arrangements and the right of all people, including children, to know the truth about sexual activity. Sex education entered the better school systems, and even entertainment that appeared to be serious moved toward a much more open treatment of subject matter and use of language—what became in the 1920s "the cult of frankness." This postwar cult of frankness was accompanied by what Frederick Lewis Allen characterized as "the revolution in manners and morals"—and, in fact, later surveys suggest that younger women of the 1920s did engage in sexual activity more freely than a previous generation.

This first revolution affected primarily middle-class Americans, and thereafter sexual attitudes tended to differentiate by social class far more than earlier, particularly as non-British ethnics constituted an ever-larger part of the population. With World War II, lower-class standards—usually labeled publicly as libertinism—increasingly came to be imposed on middle-class Americans. At the same time, even lower-class people tended to pick up from the middle-class sexual liberals the desirability of much great variety in sexual activity. It was this combination of much more indulgent quantitative and qualitative standards that came in the 1960s to be named the sexual revolution, and it occurred in a social setting in which traditional urban toleration of "loose" and "deviant" behavior spread and intensified.

This sexual revolution came about particularly because of a number of factors: World War II, penicillin, the Kinsey reports, and the birth control pill.

The leadership of the U.S. armed services in World War II was not moralistic, as was the officer group as a whole during World War I. The atmosphere among troops in the World War II barracks was decidedly not uplifting, and barracks talk shaped many young Americans' attitudes along the lines of exploitive, lower-class male sexual behavior. Frank instructions to the troops likewise failed to distinguish between prostitutes and other women: all "girls" were to be regarded as suitable for casual sexual contact. The coming of penicillin at the end of the war eliminated the strictly institutional motive to discourage contact with casual women, for troops with venereal diseases could now quickly be restored to action rather than being disabled. The ending of the fear of venereal disease as an inhibiting motive to casual coupling also spread rapidly to the rest of the population as "wonder drugs" became generally available in the 1940s and after.

The Kinsey reports (1948 and 1953) suggested that if aggregated together, Americans in fact indulged in a wide variety of sexual behaviors that were neither monogamous nor missionary-position lovemaking. In public discourse, Kinsey's work served to confirm the barracks-room standards to the effect that any sexual activity was not deviant, with an additional motivating belief that a lot of Americans were getting a lot of sexual gratification.

"The Pill," which came in at the end of the 1950s, further helped provide both rationale and means to transform sexual behavior into a nonprocreative activity, undertaken for pleasure or some other personal motive—as opposed to the traditional procreative focus. It was against this background that various figures began to proclaim "the sexual revolution."

In 1961, Boroff explicitly identified "Sex: The Quiet Revolution" in sexual standards and behavior. By 1964, the editors of *Time* and *Newsweek* had discovered the sexual revolution, and that, of course, made the event official. The sexual revolution even had an unofficial organ, *Playboy* magazine, which was founded in 1953 and reached a million circulation even before the 1960s.

Those who argued that a sexual revolution was taking place cited four types of phenomena: much more openness of sexual expression, quantitatively increased sexual activity, growth and tolerance of "deviant" practices, and change in the status and condition of women in sexual arrangements.

The openness of expression about sexual matters was evident for everyone to observe.

Beginning in the mid-1960s, in every city booksellers openly operated so-called adult bookstores (ironically, dedicated to regressive, not adult, material) and explicitly sexual movie arcades. Over many years, literary critics noted how language and description became ever franker, until virtually nothing was proscribed from literature, and journalists followed suit as quickly as they dared. Social scientists charted how much and how often depictions of sexual activity—and what had formerly been offensive expressions—appeared in prime-time television programs as the decades passed. Sexual minorities, so-called, even for a time pedophiles, took advantage of the civil rights movement openly to advocate actions and attitudes that had formerly suffered severe taboos.

Whether other aspects of sexuality, beyond openness of expression, underwent change in American society remains undemonstrated. The question of a quantitative increase illustrates the difficulties in giving a definitive answer as to how much actually changed. Kinsey used the number of orgasms as a basis for quantifying sexuality. People at that time and since questioned that tabulating orgasms or even sexual partners actually provided information about sexuality. For example, they asked, What about intensity? What about just plain quality? Since prescriptive literature made much lovemaking compulsory and compulsive, or ceremonial or merely an adjunct to consumer culture (one book of instructions, *The Joy of Sex*, was obviously patterned after a cookbook, *The Joy of Cooking*), the extent to which such actions were actually sexual came to be questioned. In terms of sexuality as such, a good argument could be made, and some witty essayists did, that it was diluted and displaced, and therefore decreased, in spite of the formal actions that might have been recorded.

Certainly, the many varieties of sexual behavior did gain a great deal more publicity, particularly oral and anal practices and homoerotic partner choice. There was a middle-class movement, with some organization by the 1970s, to further "swinging," that is, multiple-partner orgies. But this movement receded, for reasons that were not clear, and the practice apparently remained restricted to only a tiny minority even before the AIDS (acquired immune deficiency syndrome) scare began in the 1980s.

Gay and lesbian groups that, along with uncensored humorists, did so much to publicize homoerotic partner choice and activity were particularly problematic, because it was not clear that more sexuality of this variety was occurring; many experienced observers believed that it was now being practiced with more openness and dignity rather than more frequency. Certainly, the glimpses that historians had given of the casual occurrence of overtly homosexual practices in earlier periods (e.g., a gay community in Chicago of 10,000 people in 1909) did not support the belief that a sexual revolution had brought more of such behavior.

What the sexual revolution did bring was widespread media publicity about a sexual revolution and so a widely shared belief that something was happening. That actual behavior changed in a revolutionary way, that is, overturning institutions, is extremely dubious. But that the perceived realities of Americans changed was clear, and with these perceptions, as later studies showing generational change suggest, there were changed expectations, particularly about compulsive sexual activity among younger and younger Americans—and, if *Playboy* writers were to be believed, those seeking youth.

The extent to which belief in a sexual revolution affected women was particularly problematic. On the whole, belief in a sexual revolution defined sexuality in terms of a masculine standard, particularly barracks or even old-fashioned pornographic stereotypes. Insofar as the revolution was defined as casual coupling based on singles bar encounters or irresponsible ("uncommitted") living together, the position of women in sexual relationships was severely degraded. As the belief in romantic love and fulfilling marriage had nurtured the custom of dating, in which women retained some control of the setting, by moving sexuality into the public arena and outside of marriage women lost a significant amount of control over male-female relationships. Insofar as women were persuaded to move into the world of pornography (the quest of *Playboy* and more openly pornographic readers for an orgiastic "pornotopia"), as studies of the late 20th century documented from popular literature for women, American women were moved toward a world in which women were often degraded and objectified. It was this move to which many feminists objected vigorously.

On the whole, however, few Americans saw that the sexual revolution they believed in, or wanted to believe in, was essentially based on a partial and compulsive sexuality. Only a few others commented on the conservative nature of the so-called sexual revolution. In addition to possibly moving women's status back to times when they were more subservient to men's sexuality, the sexual revolutionaries served social conservatism very well. No social-class assertiveness

was required. Not even relatively neutral institutions (comparable to the conspiracy of silence or prostitution earlier) had to be overturned. Instead of upsetting the social hierarchy, the sexual revolution distracted people from it. Indeed, some commentators characterized the vaunted sexual liberation as the new, and most effective, opiate of the masses.

REFERENCES

Baldwin, F.D. The Invisible Armor. *American Quarterly*, Vol. 16 (1964), pp. 432–44.

Boroff, D. Sex: The Quiet Revolution. *Esquire*, July 1961, pp. 95–99.

Brandt, A.M. *No Magic Bullet: A Social History of Venereal Disease in the United States Since 1880*. New York: Oxford Univ. Press, 1985.

Burnham, J.C. *Bad Habits: Drinking, Smoking, Taking Drugs, Gambling, Sexual Misbehavior, and Swearing in American History*. New York: New York Univ. Press, 1993.

———. The Progressive Era Revolution in American Attitudes Toward Sex. *Journal of American History*, Vol. 59 (1973), pp. 885–908.

Clark, R.L. Changing Perceptions of Sex and Sexuality in Traditional Women's Magazines, 1900–1980. Ph.D. diss., Arizona State Univ., 1987.

D'Emilio, J., and E.B. Freedman. *Intimate Matters: A History of Sexuality in America*. New York: Harper & Row, 1988.

Ehrenreich, B., E. Hess, and G. Jacobs. *Re-Making Love: The Feminization of Sex*. Garden City, N.Y.: Anchor Press/Doubleday, 1986.

Model, J. *Into One's Own: From Youth to Adulthood in the United States, 1920–1975*. Berkeley: Univ. of California Press, 1989.

Morantz, R.M. The Scientist as Sex Crusader: Alfred C. Kinsey and American Culture. *American Quarterly*, Vol. 29 (1977), pp. 563–89.

Pivar, D.J. Cleansing the Nations: The War on Prostitution, 1917–21. *Prologue*, Vol. 12 (1980), pp. 28–40.

Rosenberg, C.E. Sexuality, Class and Role in 19th-Century America. *American Quarterly*, Vol. 25 (1973), pp. 131–53.

Schur, E.M. *The Americanization of Sex*. Philadelphia: Temple Univ. Press, 1989.

Sherman, A. *The Rape of the A*P*E*; The Official History of the Sex Revolution, 1945–1973; The Obscening of America*. Chicago: Playboy Press, 1973.

Simmons, C. Modern Sexuality and the Myth of Victorian Repression. In K. Peiss and C. Simmons, eds., *Passion and Power: Sexuality in History*. Philadelphia: Temple Univ. Press, 1989.

Thurston, C. *The Romance Revolution: Erotic Novels for Women and the Quest for a New Sexual Identity*. Urbana: Univ. of Illinois Press, 1987

John C. Burnham

SEXUAL VALUES AND MORAL DEVELOPMENT

Sexual Values

The relative worth, merit, or importance of an object is called its value. In sociology, the ideals, customs, institutions, and practices in a society toward which the people have positive or negative affective regard are called values. In ethics, any quality or object that is desirable as a means- or end-in-itself is called a value.

A sexual value reveals an ideological stance about the relative worth, merit, or importance of sexuality in human living. Each society defines sexual ideals for sexual practices; violating these ideals activates negative emotions like shame or guilt—first from responses from others, then from the self.

Sexual Morality

Socially learned normative standards become a society's customary and conventional sexual values or sexual morality. Morality is a social institution concerned with a set of practices defining right or wrong that are pervasively acknowledged within a particular society. Individuals are born into a society, learning its sexual morality. The rules of traditional sexual morality are general and abstract prohibitions rather than specified and particularized action guides initiated by concerns for a specific individual in a given context.

Moral philosophy attempts to justify sexual values as means-in-themselves or ends-in-themselves by a reflective and critical analysis of sexual morality. Moral philosophers attempt to introduce clarity, substance, and precision into moral discourse. They seek to justify an ethical theory of sexual morality by challenging presuppositions, clarifying hidden assumptions, and assessing moral arguments.

Although social moralities are culturally relative, morality itself is not ethically relative. For the philosopher, morality means conformity to the rules of right conduct for morally sound reasons. Ethical action guides for human sexuality are justified by arguments from general moral principles, such as respect for personal autonomy, nonmalevolence, beneficence, and justice.

In common usage, however, both "moral" and "morality" also mean to be sexually virtuous or chaste. Sexual virtue as chastity means the person has not engaged in any unlawful sexual conduct in the eyes of the church. This culturally relative usage of "morality" reflects socially and historically constructed Western traditional sexual values. Within Western culture, traditional sexual morality has positively valued monogamous marital coitus in the missionary position for procreative purposes without the experiencing of excess passion or pleasure. All other sexual motives, sexual linkages, and sexual objects are proscribed as immoral by traditional sexual morality.

Modernity Threatens Traditional Morality

Conventional morality is traditional, but not all traditional morality remains conventional. Modernity threatens the moral status quo. Any change, like acknowledging gay rights or defending free choice in determining the outcome of early pregnancy, is seen as undermining traditional morality; such "threats" produce a backlash against sexual immorality.

Nonetheless, contemporary community standards positively affirm the values of love and pleasure in marriage or committed relationships, as well as a variety of positions for coitus and a variety of sexual activities, including oral sex, within such relationships. Love, self-fulfillment, and pleasure often replace reproduction as motives for sex. Although not traditional, such sexual beliefs and practices have become contemporary community standards for married or committed relationships.

Still, contemporary moral opinion is divided on masturbation, child-child sex, adolescent or adult nonmarital sex, premarital sex, adultery, homosexuality, pornography, prostitution, contraception, and abortion. Even though traditional morality proscribes these behaviors as sinful or wrong conduct, and although many people continue to uphold these proscriptive standards as their stated beliefs, people bypass privately these normative standards. For example, in public, few decry the traditional moral line on adultery, but many Americans secretly cross this line. When it comes to nonmarital sex, the present generation of young Americans engages in coitus at younger ages than their parents did but has no public voice to defend such sexual choices.

In this no-man's-land of sexual moralities at war, sides are chosen and battles rage between the pro-choice position and the right-to-life, between anticensorship and antipornography. In 1973, gay men and lesbians successfully challenged the medicalization of their sexual orientations as a mental disorder, but the characterization of homosexuality by traditional morality as a sexual sin continues. As it challenges tradition or modernity, each side offers moral arguments intended to persuade the majority to accept its view as the conventional one. Some religionists claim that AIDS (acquired immune deficiency syndrome) is God's plague to punish homosexuals. Traditional morality is said to defend traditional family values, values that modernists describe as anachronistic and patriarchal and sometimes as immoral in harming others and unjust in infringing on their personal liberty. At present, most Americans occupy a middle ground in this battle, publicly professing agreement with traditional sexual values but privately acting in accordance with modern sexual values.

Beyond the contemporary pale, still firmly nested within traditional sexual morality, lie the forbidden and taboo lands of incest, adult-child sex, rape, and some paraphilias. But no war is waged here. Ethical theories regard harm to others as placing a necessary limit on sexual freedom. Society should limit coerced sex and sex with children, who lack the competence to understand and authorize sex with adults as an autonomous choice that is not controlled by the more powerful adult. Moral arguments soundly justify such constraints by logical argument from moral principles.

Moral Development

Following the Swiss psychologist Jean Piaget, Lawrence Kohlberg pursued the study of moral reasoning and its developmental progression by asking children to respond to hypothetical moral dilemmas, hoping to discover stages in their moral reasoning. Although this research has played an important historical role, it remains subject to criticism by other experts.

What did Kohlberg do and what did he argue? He developed a system for scoring moral reasoning based on the responses of children in America and around the world to hypothetical moral dilemma. For example, the Heinz story asked children what Heinz should do when his wife might die if she did not receive a certain drug, which Heinz cannot afford; the inventor of the drug refuses to give him the drug for free. Using his scoring manual for moral reasoning, Kohlberg specified six stages of moral development divided into three levels.

In Level I, Preconventional Morality, Stage 1, Heteronomous Morality, what is right is obedience to powerful authorities and avoiding breaking concrete rules supported by punishment. The reasons for doing right are to avoid punishment and the power of authorities. From the perspective of moral realism, goodness or badness is believed to reside in the act; a concrete good or bad act is seen as real, inherent, and unchanging. The child is said to have an egocentric point of view as a social perspective,

not being able to consider the interests of others or to take their point of view.

In Level I, Preconventional Morality, Stage 2, Individualistic, Instrumental Morality, what is right is following rules when it is in your immediate interest; letting others follow their own interests, knowing that interests may conflict; and doing what is fair in an equal exchange. The reason for doing right is to serve one's own interests while recognizing that others have their own interests, too. The social perspective is a concrete individualistic perspective in which everybody has their own interests, which conflict, making what is right relative to the particular situation and the actor's perspective.

In Level II, Conventional Morality, Stage 3, Interpersonal Normative Morality, what is right is living up to what is expected of you by people close to you; being good means having good motives and showing concern for others by honoring mutual relationships of trust, loyalty, respect, and gratitude. The reasons for doing right include the need to be a good person in your own eyes and those of others, the desire to care for others, the belief in the Golden Rule, and the desire to maintain rules and authority supportive of stereotypic good behavior. The social perspective is that of an individual in relationship to other individuals, aware of shared feelings and expectations, acting reciprocally to fulfill an obligation as a debt of gratitude.

In Level II, Conventional Morality, Stage 4, Social System Morality, what is right is fulfilling the actual duties to which you have agreed, upholding the law except in extreme cases of conflict with fixed social duties, and contributing to society. The reasons for doing right include keeping the social institutions going as a whole, avoiding the breakdown of law and order, and meeting one's defined obligations from the imperative of conscience. The social perspective differentiates the societal point of view from interpersonal agreement or motives by taking the point of view of the system that defines the social roles and moral rules and by considering individual relations within the framework of this system.

In Level III, Principled Morality, Stage 5, Human Rights and Social Contract Morality, what is right ordinarily is upholding the social contract of morality—even as one is aware that people hold a variety of values and opinions and that most rules are relative to one's group; what is right always is upholding such nonrelative rights as life and liberty in any society regardless of the majority's opinion. The reasons for doing right include, first, a sense of obligation to law because of the social contract to abide by laws, to promote social welfare, and to protect all people's rights; second, a feeling of freely contracted commitment to family, friendship, and work; and, third, a concern that laws and duties be based on a rational calculation of utility—"the greatest good for the greatest number." The social perspective recognizes that values and rights are prior to society and social attachments; recognizing rights entails a rational decision to embrace the legal and moral point of view of agreements, contracts, impartiality, and due process.

In Level III, Principled Morality, Stage 6, Universal Ethical Principles, what is right is following self-chosen universal ethical principles of justice: the equality of human rights and respect for the dignity of human beings as individual persons. If laws violate these principles, the principles, not the law, have precedence. The reasons for doing right are the belief, as a rational person, in the validity of universal moral principles and a sense of personal commitment to following them. The social perspective is called the perspective of a moral point of view. Social arrangements are seen as derivatives of universal principles of justice or they do not merit respect. Rational individuals recognize the nature of justice and that people must be treated as ends in themselves.

What Kohlberg did was to mass a considerable amount of evidence in support of this perspective while stimulating much research and much criticism. Now, what did he argue?

Kohlberg argued that the last level of moral development is also the most adequate ethically. This breathtaking claim is that he has empirically established the best moral conception, claiming that he has moved from "is" to "ought," and that Kant and Rawls were right, while Aristotle, Hume, Bentham, and Mill were wrong.

Not only that, Kohlberg argues that the transition in moral stages results from individuals seeking to meet moral problems with adaptive mental structures; if present structures cannot assimilate a moral problem to a moral stage, then accommodation takes place by moving to a higher moral stage. Thus, environmental moral dilemmas generate moral conflict, requiring moral reasoning that is adapted to reality; adapting by assimilating to present moral structures when the social environment confirms their adequacy, and accommodating by achieving a new equilibrium within a higher stage when reality requires such rational adaptation. Thus, an empirical "is" leads to an adaptive "ought."

Such sweeping claims beg for informed criticism. Philosophers, such as Owen Flanagan, have responded. His first set of criticisms focused on

the experimental paradigm itself: Kohlberg's use of hypothetical moral dilemmas. The first problem with the hypothetical situation is the presupposition that the subject is putting herself in the role of the protagonist and responding with what she would do in the same situation. Are we assessing the subject's moral reasoning as it occurs in everyday life or only her reflective reasoning about others facing events far from everyday moral concerns? Is talk cheap?

The second problem with the experimental paradigm is the purely verbal nature of the evidence. Whereas Piaget found that his cognitive structures mediate the child's actual behavior when faced with spatial, causal, and logical problems in everyday life, Kohlberg's paradigm describes verbal responses that are not causally linked to everyday moral action or to some convergent criterion of moral action. Moral competence requires not only saying the right things but doing them as well.

The third problem with the paradigm is its lack of comprehensiveness. By selecting dilemmas, there is a small number of options available, usually two. Moreover, the problems are all about justice, only a portion of the domain of morality. Many moral issues remain more open-ended: how can I be a good and loyal friend? Having nothing to say about such actions, how can Kohlberg address the beneficence of the Good Samaritan?

Kohlberg claimed that his six stages are structured wholes that are universal and follow an invariant, irreversible, and increasingly integrative sequence, but Flanagan argued that he has not satisfied these criteria of a stage theory. At best, while awaiting more data, Kohlberg scores a "maybe" on structured wholes and invariant sequence and a "fail" on universality, regression, and integration. All stages do not appear to be found in all cultures and do not appear at specific ages (universality); most people appear lumped into and stuck in the conventional stages. The idealism of stage 5 adolescents may regress to stage 4 concerns with order during adulthood (regression). Integration requires that earlier stages be logically contained within later ones, but it is difficult to see how the principled stages, which deny the meaningfulness of normative moral terms, can integrate the conventional stages, in which normative morality is assumed.

Finally, Flanagan criticizes Kohlberg's thesis that the highest stage is ethically the most adequate. First, Kohlberg has retreated from his claim that stage 6 is more morally adequate than stage 5. Second, there is no constant social or moral world to serve as a ground of convergence in the same way that there was for Piaget to claim a worldwide spatial world that corresponded to his highest stage of spatial development. Third, Kohlberg's highest stage presupposes a technologically advanced social world associated with Western culture. Finally, the most adequate ethical theory must be comprehensive, not limited to a concern with justice.

Caring and Moral Emotion

Gilligan argued that when psychologists traced the origins of morality to the child's discovery of the ideal of justice, they seemed to find that boys were more moral than girls. She countered that women may speak in a different moral voice. She argued that the dynamics of early childhood inequality give rise to a concern with justice and that the dynamics of attachment give rise to a concern with care. Empathy, friendship, and altruism are components of morality, of a caring orientation for which women are well-known. Since everyone is vulnerable both to oppression and to abandonment, two moral orientations develop, both justice and care.

Kagan has pointed out that recent research in psychology has been concerned with three themes in moral development. First, are children biologically prepared to display a moral sense by age two? Emotionality is the obvious feature when a child breaks a toy, dirties a dress, or makes another child cry. By age two, children show distress—about broken or flawed objects, in empathy with another's distress, and over failing to stack blocks high enough

A second theme is the usefulness of the theoretical distinction between conventional and principled moral standards. The mode of establishment of conventions may rest on fear of punishment and a desire to remain attached to important people, whereas a principle of tolerance may be established through identification with parents or by reflectively seeking to make beliefs more consistent and coherent. Also, psychologists believe that violating conventions gives rise to less intense and less moral emotions than violating principled standards. In children, not reason but feelings may lie at the heart of morality.

The third theme considers the relevance of empirical data on moral development to the adequacy of ethical theory. How do we integrate the data of psychologists with the logical analysis of philosophers? The answer may be that each informs the other, that "is" and "ought" mutually illuminate each other.

In such an emotive view, moral development and moral character are closely bound to one another. Perhaps ethical theories that try to re-

duce morality to a single principle restrict its scope to the resolution of difficult problems by the application of reductive theory. Pincoffs so argued, stating that the common life of human beings provides the context for moral talk. If we lived in a more bounteous world, then perseverance and sharing would be less valued. If we lived in a world free of physical and emotional pain, then there could be no cruelty. Benevolence, sympathy, justice, fortitude, and kindness are virtues only in the context of the human condition. Moreover, what is the human condition? Near the beginning of the second millennium, the contemporary pressing ethical issues concern life and death: contraception, abortion, euthanasia, and the ratio of costs to benefits in health care.

Ethical Action Guides for Sexuality

From Piaget to Kohlberg, a practical guide to developing moral reasoning must include open discussions with peers about sexuality, its dilemmas, its emotions, and its outcomes. Practical moral reasoning requires practice in making decisions about moral matters. When you just say no, you do not address the role of sexuality in your life. The reflective saying of either yes or no requires that talking about sex be freed from restraints as immoral in itself. Just as talk about justice does not create it, talk about sex does not release it into inevitable expression. Reflective examination and discussion of sexual choices may improve the adequacy of sexual decision making.

Mosher suggested three questions to serve as guides in making responsible sexual choices. First, is this choice consistent with my sense of who I am and with my plan for life? To answer this question, you must consider what a sexual choice means for you now and in the future. Second, does this choice respect the dignity and worth of my sexual partner? To answer this question, you must consider how this choice affects your partner now and in the future. Third, if everyone made this choice for these reasons, would it create a world that I want to live in? To answer this question, you must ask what are the implications for society of people making this choice for these reasons. Taking the perspectives of self, other, and society requires that you play moral musical chairs. Kohlberg suggested this process of multiple-perspective-taking as a way of finding universalizable or disinterested moral choices.

Everyone is born to be a sexual human being. Not everyone, however, is born to make the same sexual choices. Respect for the autonomy of others to make their own sexual choices, so long as they do not harm others, is tolerance. Tolerance is a virtue; moralistic intolerance remains a vice.

REFERENCES

Gilligan, C. *In a Different Voice: Psychological Theory and Women's Development.* Cambridge, Mass.: Harvard Univ. Press, 1982.

Kagan, J., and S. Lamb. *The Emergence of Morality in Young Children.* Chicago: Univ. of Chicago Press, 1987.

Modgill, S., and C. Modgill. *Lawrence Kohlberg: Consensus and Controversy.* Philadelphia: Falmer Press, 1985.

Mosher, D.L. The Threat to Sexual Freedom: Moralistic Intolerance Instills a Spiral of Silence. *Journal of Sex Research,* Vol. 26 (1989), pp. 492–509.

Pincoffs, E.L. *Quandries and Virtues: Against Reductivism in Ethics.* Lawrence: Univ. of Kansas Press, 1986.

Donald L. Mosher

SEXUALLY TRANSMITTED DISEASES

Like the flu bug, with its constantly changing personality and character, many of the infectious diseases acquired through sexual activity with other people are constantly changing in format and content. As indicated by Holmes, in his printed disclaimer for his textbook, "medicine is an ever changing science so changes are constantly being made in treatment and drug therapy of these some 30 different diseases." Indeed, while this article was being written and rewritten, the Centers for Disease Control and Prevention (CDCP) authorized the use of the new antibiotic Floxin to treat gonorrhea and chlamydia and Zithromycin for the single treatment (eight tablets) of chlamydia during pregnancy. Floxin cannot be used to treat chlamydia during pregnancy.

Curative therapies are still not available for the viral infections (herpes, warts and AIDS). Syphilis, the major threat of the first half of the 20th century, when it caused debilitating illness and death, has been replaced by the new killer, AIDS (acquired immune deficiency syndrome). Abstinence, or no sex at all, is the only 100 percent effective preventive for any STD (sexually transmitted disease), although condoms used along with contraceptive gel or foam are the best protection currently available.

Trichomoniasis

Trichomonas vaginalis was first discovered by a young Frenchman in 1838. Interestingly enough, he thought he had discovered the causative organism for gonorrhea, and the differentiation of the two organisms took another 50 years. Both are caused by organisms, gonorrhea by a gram negative intracellular diplococci, originally called *Neisseria gonorrhea*, and trichomonas by a protozoa.

Before antibiotic therapy developed, trichomoniasis was dramatically different from what it is today; patients sometimes came in with difficulty walking because the genital area was irritated, and the vaginal discharge was so profuse that it literally ran down their legs when they stood up. The discharge, when viewed with the aid of a vaginal speculum, was seen to be thick, frothy, and yellow-green, and it was extremely smelly.

The diagnosis for this particular infection is made by the physician on the spot, who does a microscopic test called a "wet mount," using a slide with either saline or a stained laboratory vehicle for easier microscopic identification. The protozoa can be easily seen moving around on relatively low-power magnification of the microscope. There are occasional false-negative readouts, probably due to overwhelming activity by the body's white blood cells, so that no actual trichomonal organisms can be seen during a test, but are visible at a later examination. This particular test usually gives an instant diagnosis.

The disease is easily treated using metronidazole. This particular drug has been used worldwide for over a quarter of a century. It has an inherent clinical safety record, never having caused death. When a woman who walks into the gynecologist's office has a trichomoniasis diagnosis made and is given the proper medication, that medication is doubled in amount so as to include her sexual partner (or tripled if there is more than one sexual partner). The same procedure is followed for a man at the urologist's office. The urologist writes a prescription not only for the man but also for the woman if she is not being seen by her physician.

Trichomoniasis is not a reportable disease. It is, however, a disease that can be fairly drug resistant, so in the United States the patient is asked to return to the office for a repeat test to make sure that the problem has been solved.

Chlamydia

Another common STD seen in the health care practitioner's office is *chlamydia trachomatis*. Public health experts currently list this particular disease as the most common disease in the United States, with more than five million new cases discovered and treated each year. Until recently, it was not a reportable infection. One of the reasons it was not reportable is that many if not most physicians treat it on the basis of a sexual and social history, combined with the suspicious physical and microscopic findings. They do this because it is extremely difficult to obtain a good culture result (the cultures have a very high percentage of false-negative readouts). The CDCP and the U.S. Public Health Service have now asked that positive serologic tests for chlamydia be reported. Experts on this particular infection indicate such serologic tests are sometimes reported falsely as positive. This can cause legal problems for the patient and the physician.

The real problem with this obligate intracellular parasite is that it causes infertility in women. It is, however, easily treated. The use of tetracycline for seven to ten days by both partners will clear up this infection. If the tetracycline, a most inexpensive drug, causes severe stomach discomfort or other side effects, erythromycin or doxycycline will achieve the same result. However, chlamydia has a strong silent component to its clinical picture; it is often ignored or interpreted by the person who has acquired it as something else. Consequently, no physician is consulted or asked to run a confirmatory culture, and the infected individual unwittingly spreads the disease to others.

Because it is so common, its presence should always be considered, and, of course, the presence or absence of this particular infection is always considered in the many infertility clinics. Women who have the disease and are unaware of its presence may experience significant damage to the interior of the Fallopian tubes. Normal Fallopian tubes are necessary for fertilized-ovum transport. If that reproductive highway has been destroyed, the patient is rendered unable to have a fertilized egg move down her tubes and into her uterine cavity to begin a pregnancy.

Men with chlamydia may see a urethral discharge, so this infection is a common reason for their seeking medical advice. It is not now presently known whether most of the physicians in the United States who treat this problem of chlamydia discharge in men either double the medication and insist that the woman be also treated, or refer her elsewhere.

A variation (there are three variants of this particular infectious disease) is capable of producing blindness, since it causes a disease of the eyes called trachoma. The presence of chlamydia trachomatis is the most common cause of blindness throughout the world. The United States has several well-known research centers working on this disease. One is at the University of California at San Francisco, and the other is at Indiana University–Purdue University Medical Center in Indianapolis, Indiana.

Herpes

Another common sexually transmitted infection in the United States is herpes genitalis. In 1980, when herpes occurred in an epidemic form, its presence made the cover of *Time* magazine and the front page of the *Wall Street Journal.* It is a viral infection transmitted by sexual activity that causes blistering discomfort. Acyclovir is effective in suppressing the circulating activity of the herpes virus, decreasing the discomfort and making the individual less likely to transmit the infection to others.

It is almost uncivilized in the current era, with acyclovir available, to know that one has herpes and yet to deliberately not take the medication and hence infect others. It is an STD that has active states and inactive states, and the level of discomfort varies widely among individuals. Some men have only mild urinary complaints and do not know they have the disease until they accidentally infect a new female sex partner. The infected woman most often experiences flulike symptoms, has pain urinating, and is covered with blisters on her swollen genital area. The resultant discharge is frequently infected with other organisms and can be quite odoriferous.

If the individual is careless in personal habits and touches the areas of the genitals that are involved, then rubs his or her eyes, the disease can be transmitted to the eye, causing a severe form of conjunctivitis that produces blindness. The problem with the eyes can be arrested by using intravenous acyclovir, but it certainly requires the expert attention of an ophthalmologist just to save the eyesight. If one acquires this infection, soap-and-water hand washing and scrupulous attention to all the details of personal cleanliness are extremely important to confine the blisters and the disease activity to the original site.

The disease can produce mental problems or a severe headache, as well as the aforementioned generalized flulike picture. It is also capable of affecting the long nerves of the legs so as to produce sciatica plus a pain with bowel movements.

Herpes is seen in the office involving all ages and all kinds of health complaints and problems. Clinical diagnosis can be made quickly by anyone who has spent several years practicing medicine. Inexperienced nurses and physicians may, however, misdiagnose it as a chronic yeast infection. However, the obverse of this statement is also true: women with chronic yeast vulvar infections will present the clinical picture similar to a chronic deteriorating herpes infection. The test for herpes is a positive vaginal culture. The culture, however, is not 100 percent correct. It is perfectly possible to have herpes and have a negative culture. This can be a serious problem for the pregnant woman, because if the mother has an acute attack of herpes while she is in labor, the infant, who has no immunity to the disease, will acquire the herpes, and before the advent of intravenous acyclovir therapy most would die.

With acyclovir, herpes has come to be an annoying accompaniment to sexual activity, and its only serious problem now is the transmission of an active infection to a newborn infant. Herpes was originally proposed as the infection causing cancer of the cervix, but that has been demonstrated to be scientifically untrue. Herpes is not now believed to cause cancer.

Gardnerella

Another commonly acquired bacterial infection with a reputation for easy diagnosis (i.e., not requiring an expensive laboratory culture test) is *gardnerella vaginalis*. For many years, this infection was known as *hemophilus vaginalis,* but Eldon J. Gardner, a physician who spent his life observing, collecting data, and testing for this infection, was honored posthumously by having his name attached to the genus of bacterium involved. Gardner argued that this was an important reproductive tract organism although often overlooked by many practicing physicians and a real troublemaker for a newborn infant. He felt that it was a major cause of problems in the reproductive system and that it could be very easily diagnosed by well-trained physicians when alerted by the presence of a unique vaginal, fish-like odor.

Prior to the work of Gardner, physicians in positions of authority promoted the infection as a silent infection, or an organism that was thought to be a normal inhabitant of the vaginal vault. Such descriptions still exist and are extremely confusing to laypeople doing library research and to medical students and residents trying to figure out how a troublemaker could be normal. It is not a reportable infection. It is easy to treat using metronidazole (see trichomoniasis, above).

Group B. Beta Hemolytic Streptococcus

A very important infection, which also has the distinction of arising from a bed of disinformation labeled "normal vaginal flora" (and similar confusing clinical designations), is group B. Beta hemolytic streptococcus. The importance of this infection to Americans was worked out by the National Institutes of Health and the U.S. Public Health Service under the influence of Dorland J. Davis, an epidemiologist. In the early 1940s, the disease was observed as a cause of death in newborn infants at Harvard's clinical facilities and at Johns Hopkins Hospital, in Baltimore, with the number of infant deaths attributed to it hovering around 40 a year. As the years went by and constant and progressive observation of the clinical phenomena occurred, it became obvious that the behavior of the organism was that of a sexually transmittable bacteria. Gradually, the number of deaths rose to between 3,000 and 4,000 a year, a number that, unfortunately, still prevails in spite of extensive literature and extensive publicity concerning its damaging effects on newborn children. Apparently, a major reason for the indifference to the presence of such a harmful disease was lack of a requirement to report the infection, a problem now remedied. It is a major cause of mental retardation, cerebral palsy, and deafness. Some of the confusion about the disease is because it is a common inhabitant of the prepuce in the uncircumcised male infant as well as the uncircumcised adult male, in whose foreskin it flourishes. The lack of circumcision frequently predisposes young boys to hospital stays for severe urinary tract and kidney infections.

The acquisition by the woman of unusual forms of group B. Beta hemolytic streptococcus, subdivided into categories by Roman numerals, does not occur until they become sexually active, unless unusual circumstances prevail. Since it can be an STD, both sexual partners, or more if there are other partners, must be treated for this organism simultaneously. The organism remains sensitive to penicillin products, and so far it has not developed the usual picture of antibiotic resistance. If the acquisition of the infection occurs at the end of the pregnancy, or if it has been acquired in a form that absolutely refuses to be cured by means of antibiotics, the woman in labor can be given intravenous ampicillin, and the presence of that medication at the time of labor prevents the child from acquiring the infection. Until very recently, the newborn who acquired the infection died as quickly as the infants who acquired herpes from their infected mothers. Fortunately, it has been recently discovered that attention to the hydration of the infant victim gives a greater chance of survival.

The disease itself can cause a localized vulvar skin infection that looks like psoriasis, cervicitis with an abnormal pap smear, or involvement of the Fallopian tubes, so that the victim will end up with ectopic pregnancies as well as urinary and kidney infections, especially in a pregnant woman. Recent work at Parkland Hospital, in Dallas, suggests that it is a major cause of stillbirths in the United States.

Syphilis

Syphilis first appeared in Europe following the return of Columbus from his voyages. There have been extensive arguments as to whether it was a New World disease that was then carried back to the people of Europe. The answer, of course, lies hidden from our view forever. Suffice it to say that an enormous epidemic of syphilis occurred shortly after Columbus's voyage.

The disease was regarded as revolting because it caused huge bony exostoses that were hideous to look at. In the immediate past, syphilis was the major cause of stillbirth and a variety of congenital malformations. It is so highly infectious that doctors and nurses could get syphilis delivering a newborn baby from an infected mother. The baby itself was highly infectious. Syphilis remained a major medical and social problem until the development of Salvarsan by Paul Ehrlich and S. Hata in 1910. Salvarsan rendered the victim of syphilis noninfectious, but the treatment demanded weekly doses of the drug intramuscularly for at least six to eight weeks. The ability of people to comply with such a laborious regimen was a major problem. The other problem was that the laws of the United States would not allow open discussion of this overwhelming health problem. Finally, in 1936, the surgeon general of the United States, Thomas Parran, was allowed to use the word "syphilis" during a radio broadcast, and the push was on, with federal laws creating clinics and funding for discovery of infected partners.

With the arrival of penicillin 50 years ago and the discovery that it could cure syphilis, public health service interest in this particular disease began to fade. In the 1980s, however, it was realized that individuals who suffer from AIDS are especially susceptible to acquiring syphilis, or vice versa. Syphilis has become a marker for the AIDS infection itself. In addition, the cheapness of crack cocaine and other addictive drugs has increased the number of young women prostitutes who fail to use adequate protection, with the result that syphilis is increasing in urban areas.

Syphilis, a reportable disease, starts out with a hard ulcer, called a chancre, which quickly heals on its own, but the spirochete then spreads throughout the body. In the second stage of the disease, it produces a rash, which can be seen even on the palms of the hands and the soles of the feet, but quite often people are not aware of their rash. The organism then starts to invade the tissues of the central nervous system (including the brain), the heart, and the bones and begins to do its chronic disabling feats of work. Syphilis, in fact, can invade every organ system and imitate almost any disease known to humans. It can, however, be diagnosed inexpensively by a blood test which today is called RPR. This test, approved by the CDCP, has many false-positives so that if the test is positive, another test, the FTA-ABS test, which is both more accurate and more expensive, is given. Sometimes early in the disease, the spirochetes themselves can be lifted out of the hard chancre and placed under the microscope in a visual process called a dark field examination where the spirochete can easily be identified by an expert microscopist, but not by amateurs or the family physician or nurse.

Treatment is by means of antibiotic therapy with very large doses of intramuscular penicillin still being the drug of choice. Treatment schedules and alternative medications are outlined in the guidelines for STDs published approximately every three years by the CDCP.

Gonorrhea

Gonorrhea, acquired in conjunction with syphilis, was also very common in the first part of the 20th century. The Frenchman who discovered the original trichomonad thought he had found the causative organism for gonorrhea. It was not until the German bacteriologist Albert Neisser identified the gonococcus in 1879 that this gram negative diplococcus was precisely defined.

Although gonorrhea can be identified in the doctor's office because of its characteristic yellow discharge and the bacteria easily identified through a gram stain, a culture should always be done to confirm the diagnosis. A reportable disease, it, like chlamydia, is often asymptomatic in women, but it, like chlamydia, can spread into the internal pelvic organs, causing pelvic inflammatory disease. Unrecognized gonorrhea can be spread to newborn infants, causing conjunctivitis and blindness. Because of this, the practice of instilling silver nitrate drops into the eyes of newborns was made mandatory early in the 20th century. In men, gonorrheal urinary tract infections are acutely uncomfortable, so men are likely to seek medical attention. The incidence of gonorrhea fell after the antibiotics became available in the middle of the 20th century and the U.S. Public Health Service mounted a campaign to bring both syphilis and gonorrhea under control. However, success with the campaign brought complacency, and the incidence of both syphilis and gonorrhea has increased. Gonorrhea is as prevalent now as it was 50 years ago.

Venereal Warts

The most commonly discussed but least researched of the worldwide STDs is venereal warts, known since antiquity. Confusion, of course, can reign because there are some 60 different varieties of wart viruses, with each one affecting a specific site on the body. Some of the viruses that create warts in the genital region and around the rectum are not sexually transmitted. As a result, when laypeople set themselves up as experts on the subject of STD and discover that a small child has perirectal warts, guardians, friends, and parents are often falsely accused of childhood sexual abuse because of the widespread ignorance among the general public on the subject. The public is aware of the sexual connotation but totally ignorant of the natural history of the entire spectrum of the disease. We do not consider perirectal warts in little boys and girls sexually transmitted. They are ordinarily due to skin-contact organisms picked up by the child by touching a playmate on the hand or cheek, for example.

The causative organism of genital warts is a papilloma virus; certain strains of this virus are very dangerous and others are not. Although papilloma virus number 6 and papilloma virus number 11 are common causes of genital-area warts, they seldom spread to other parts of the reproductive system, and they cause little lasting damage. The viruses that cause urethral warts in the male are wart virus numbers 53, 54, 55, and 56, and they are *not* transmitted to the female during sexual activity. The wart viruses that produce cervical cell changes and abnormal pap smears are papilloma virus numbers 16 and 18, with a scattering in some of the other numerical categories; however, those two viruses (16 and 18) are the ones currently identified as being the main troublemakers associated with cervical cancer.

There is presently no cure for the virus and no vaccine to prevent acquisition of the virus.

Currently available are various techniques for removing the warts when they grow. Since 50 percent of the people who have the virus do not grow the warts, the transmission of these warts is thoroughly confusing to ordinary people. It seems as though they simply drop out of the sky.

Removal of the obvious wart does not cure the systemic viral disease, so that other new warts can show up as time goes by. This reoccurrence is particularly depressing to the victims. They are extremely upset that the disease will not permanently go away and that repetitive surgical or chemical removal procedures have to be done. Podophyllin is considered to be the first-line office treatment in the nonpregnant female. Interestingly enough, when the warts are removed from the outside of the woman's genital area with the use of laser surgery, that procedure sensitizes the warts to podophyllin treatment—an ancient American Indian remedy—so that, fortunately, in most cases, the subsequent reoccurrence of wart forms can be treated using that particular chemical after laser therapy. There is some evidence that getting rid of a yeast infection, keeping the area clean and dry, and taking vitamin A is also helpful. Podophyllin is now available for home self-treatment by prescription as Condylox.

Molluscum Contagiosum

Another common and frequently seen viral-caused skin involvement is called molluscum contagiosum. This is also a disease of great antiquity, whose early beginnings confuse observers. Quite often, it is mistaken for early new venereal warts when the skin lesions are small, and the white punched-in look in the center of a very red pimple is its common picture. The lesions become raised, and they will not disappear with any antibiotic therapy.

One cannot cure these skin spots (and often there are many) with antibiotics because the cause of the problem is a virus. It will, however, go away by itself. Sometimes, cryotherapy or cutting and lifting out the white plug will speed things up. The small white umbilicated lesions go away principally on their own. They are highly contagious. Cleanliness is important. It is spread by scratching.

Yeasts: Candida Albicans et al.

Candida albicans, one of the yeastlike funguses that reproduce by budding, was formerly called Monilia albicans. Yeast infections are considered by the World Health Organization as well as by the CDCP as an STD, although some women do have a few candida as persistent inhabitants of their vaginas, and they develop infections when they take antibiotics for some other medical reason. The antibiotic kills the normal bacterial flora of the vagina, which has been inhibiting the overgrowth of yeast, and this allows the yeast to take over and run rampant.

The classification of various infectious agents as capable of sexual transmission is not made to encourage people to categorize themselves or others as good or bad people, but to force the treating practitioners to be aware of the fact that the sexual partners of the individual on whom the diagnosis is made must be considered. If the woman has a yeast infection, not only must she be treated, but inquiries must be made as to whether or not the individuals with whom she is having sexual activity are on antibiotics or have candida infections of the mouth or genital organs, which should be treated to avoid a cycle of reinfection.

Yeast infections are diagnosed in the office with a wet mount using potassium hydroxide (KOH). Treatment is ordinarily with suppositories or creams containing one of the fungicides: nystatin, clotromazole, miconazole, or terconazole. New forms are being constantly introduced and some are available without prescription.

Mycoplasma and Ureaplasma Infections

Mycoplasma and ureaplasma organisms acquired with sexual activity can persist for years without their victims being aware of any problem whatsoever until they try to get pregnant and find themselves sterile, due to mycoplasma and ureaplasma. The natural history and clinical importance of these organisms are still a matter of argumentation within the medical profession only because they are organisms that are relatively difficult to identify in the laboratory. Hence, their true incidence is probably currently unknown, although it is believed that they are common and are considered a major cause of infertility. Treatment involves long-term antibiotic therapy. The infection can be silent or it can cause pelvic inflammatory disease or Reiter's disease, as well as postpartum fever, kidney stones, male sterility, habitual abortion, and stillbirth. The diagnosis is made by laboratory tests.

Any individual walking into an infertility clinic is thoroughly checked for the presence of these infections. Their importance lies in the fact that if they are present, generic antibiotic treatment for seven or ten days will not even begin to cure them. The amount of time that must be spent taking the brand-name oral antibiotic Vibramycin is from four to six weeks. Therefore, the identi-

fication of these particular infections can be important to a woman, especially to make sure that she preserves her future fertility. Their presence in the male creates urinary problems. The diagnosis in the woman is made by vaginal culture.

Donovanosis

Donovanosis is a chronic destructive infection of the genitals, also called granuloma inguinale or granuloma venereum. It is sometimes misdiagnosed by untrained people as cancer or syphilis. It is prominent in New Guinea, Australia, India, the Caribbean, and Africa. It is only mildly contagious and apparently repeated sexual exposure is needed for infection. Long-term antibiotic therapy is needed. It seems, at this time, not to be an American problem.

Chancroid

The most common of the STDs worldwide is chancroid, caused by a gram negative bacillus, *Hemophilus ducreyi*. Although it is not a common infection in the United States, occasionally new emigrants from Latin America bring the disease in with them. It is treated with sulfa drugs, although it can be controlled with just about any antibiotic. It produces a soft, destructive ulcer and painful infections of the groin that can grow and rupture. If it goes untreated, it can destroy the genitals of the man but not those of a woman.

Viral Hepatitis

Hepatitis is a viral inflammation of the liver, characterized by jaundice. It is transmitted by contaminated food, needles, or sexual activity or from a mother to infant. Fecal contamination of food or water supplies and rectal or anal intercourse should be considered when the individual is seen in the office. Reports of hepatitis research are constantly updated in a data base at the National Library of Medicine, in Bethesda, Maryland. A vaccine has been developed for the type B form. Immune globulin given promptly after exposure will prevent hepatitis type A. Most hepatitis, however, is non-A, non-B, so prevention by the use of condoms for anal intercourse is important. Fatal fulminant hepatitis can occur. Even though this infection can be acquired in many ways, it is considered a major STD. This only emphasizes that an STD is not always transmitted by sexual activity.

Cytomegalovirus Infections

This infection was uncommon in Northern Europe and North America until the 1980s, when the virus was found in urine, saliva, breast milk, semen, feces, cervical mucous, and blood. Close interpersonal contact is necessary to be infected. It can be transmitted to an unborn child, causing severe problems. It can cause hepatitis, heterophile negative mononucleosis, pneumonitis, and Guilliain-Barre ascending paralysis. Anemia and its effects can be devastating in people who are immunocompromised. It has been related to Kaposi's sarcoma in homosexuals who have AIDS. There is no cure.

Pubic Lice and Scabies

These microscopic insects move from person to person with intimate contact or through the wearing of another person's dirty underwear. They burrow under the skin, causing a rash and intense itching. They can be visualized using an ordinary magnifying glass. Scabies is a great imitator, and its existence can be covered up by corticosteroid creams and lotions. It is cured with topical applications of lindane or Eurax. Over the counter treatments for pubic lice are available.

Enteric Infections

Giardiasis and amebiasis are due to rectal-oral sexual activity. They are diagnosed by special laboratory tests and are cured with the same therapy used for the treatment of trichomoniasis. Camplyobacteria are a major cause of the gay bowel syndromes of diarrhea and dysentery, or gastroenteritis in homosexual men. Identification is by laboratory culture. Antibiotic therapies are available for the cure. The infections can be transmitted to women, and pregnant women can transmit the infection to their newborn child.

AIDS

Finally, the last and currently most publicized STD is AIDS. This virally caused STD was first discovered among the male homosexual communities of the major cities of the United States—Miami, New York, and San Francisco. It was early determined using epidemiological methods that it was an STD. Eventually, because of the death and disease pattern, the male homosexual act, especially rectal intercourse, was held to be responsible for the transference of the infection to the uninfected. However, that pattern is now changing, as more women are being infected by heterosexual contact and newborns are exposed to in utero infection.

AIDS seems to be caused by a retrovirus that is constantly changing its characteristics, making it difficult to create a vaccine against the disease,

because the moment the vaccine is created, the type and variety of virus involved in the epidemic turns out to be totally different from the one utilized in making the vaccine. (The flu vaccine, for example, acts similarly in that it is different every year.)

Treatment is palliative with various drugs, the original one being AZT, which arrests the replication of the virus. All of these drugs are, however, toxic products and, unfortunately, do not make the person who has AIDS incapable of passing the disease on. Therefore, the current treatment not only prolongs the life of the victim of AIDS but also allows him or her a great deal more time in which to spread the disease. The AIDS virus can also contaminate or attach itself to dirty needles that are used by drug addicts. It can be transmitted through blood transfusion as well as by infected semen. The spread of AIDS can be prevented with the use of condoms, especially those with Nonoxyl 9 plus vaginal contraceptive foam (either in tablet form or in pressurized containers). Condoms made of animal membranes do not work in preventing AIDS since microscopic pores exist in the animal membrane that allow the virus to escape.

Death is from one of the several diseases, which attack the body because of the compromised immune system. Such diseases include pneumocystitis carina, Kaposi's sarcoma, tuberculosis, yeast infections, or other opportunistic infections.

Conclusion

It is important that the average American who has some education become aware of various important facts concerning each of the STDs. The profession of medicine, while it is not the Delphic oracle that victims of disease would wish it to be, still has an important place in the treatment of the severe problems that these infections can cause.

The real message is that if you think that you have acquired a sexually transmitted infection, do not just think about it; make an appointment with a gynecologist if you are a woman, a urologist if you are a man, or a venereal disease clinic if you do not have enough funds to pay for your personal medical diagnosis and treatment, and tell the physician that you want to be checked for STDs.

Physicians are not mind readers. If you walk into an STD clinic, you are going to be checked for STDs, but in the private office the physician does not know what your problem is until you start to communicate. Since the infections that occur because of sexual activity are those most people try not to broadcast, the nature of these problems often does not surface right away. Therefore, be honest with the physician and indicate why you are in his or her office. Many young women have been victimized by date rape and hide the fact. Both women and men silently suffer sexual abuse and refuse to tell the physician. Conversely, given the imperfect status of diagnoses, you may find yourself with a diagnosis of an STD where there is none present. Object if that happens to you, but the diagnosis may also be missed. Communication is the key.

The diagnosis of STDs is not a magic act. The technology is still deficient, but, in spite of all sorts of strange legal harassments, most American physicians try very hard to solve health problems. Aware that most Americans like to hide the evidence in these problems, some physicians become very cynical about the human race, and one must deal with that fact.

REFERENCES

CDCP Guidelines on STD—CDCP (USPHS) Atlanta, Georgia, 1990.

Holmes, K.K., P.-A. Mardth, P.F. Sparling, and P.J. Wiesner. *Sexually Transmitted Diseases.* New York: McGraw-Hill, 1983.

Kaminester, L.H. *Sexually Transmitted Diseases: An Illustrated Guide to Differential Diagnosis.* Burroughs Wellcome Company. N.p., n.d.

What You Need to Know about Sexually Transmitted Diseases, HIV Disease and AIDS-STD. Burroughs Wellcome Company. N.p., n.d.

Dorothy I. Lansing

SOCIOBIOLOGY

Sociobiology is the application of principles derived from evolutionary theory to issues in psychology and the social sciences. Wilson advocated a Darwinian approach to psychology and sociology because he thought that existing explanations in these disciplines were fragmentary and piecemeal, since they did not take into account the theory of natural selection. All sociobiological concepts are derived, ultimately, from Darwin's theory of natural selection. This is a process where offspring inherit characteristics from their parents that may be more or less adaptive for the particular environmental conditions in which they live. Reproductive success, then, refers to the extent to which organisms are able to reproduce offspring that survive long enough to pass on their genes to successive generations.

Individuals who produce a relatively large number of children are more likely to have their genes (basic units of heredity) transmitted to future generations. The effect of sheer number of offspring, however, is moderated by the characteristics of those offspring. Some of these characteristics, such as the ability to attract mates, hunting prowess, the ability to forage and store food, and so forth, increase the likelihood that the offspring will go on to produce children of their own. Natural selection can favor us not only through our own reproductive success in the transmitting of our genes but also through the survival of our close relatives with whom we have genes in common. Natural selection, therefore, operates for the maximization of inclusive fitness. Inclusive fitness involves both an individual's reproductive contribution to the gene pool of the next generation and that person's contribution in aiding the survival of kin who pass on their shared genes.

Wilson used the theory of inclusive fitness to suggest a possible evolutionary explanation for the continuing existence of homosexual orientation among some people. At face value, it would seem odd to use a theory associated with natural selection to try to explain why a person would select sexual partners with whom he or she cannot reproduce and thus have their genes passed on to the next generation. Wilson hypothesized that there are genes for homosexual orientation and that these exist in the population because they also exist in the heterosexual relatives of gay people. He theorized that homosexual members of primitive societies, rather than raising families of their own, acted as helpers of their close relatives. The generosity, or altruism, of homosexuals toward their relatives increased the likelihood of the survival and reproductive success of the homosexuals' relatives. Thus, genes for homosexual orientation increased in frequency not because of their beneficial effect on the homosexual but because of the benefits received by the relatives aided by the homosexual person. He held that there was a strong possibility that homosexuality is normal in a biological sense, that it is a distinctive, beneficent behavior that evolved as an important element of early human social organization. Homosexuals, in his words, "may be the genetic carriers of some of mankind's rare altruistic impulses."

The hereditary predisposition suggested by Wilson would not necessarily result in homosexual behavior. The actual expression of homosexual feelings would depend on certain environmental conditions. The adaptiveness of homosexuality as presented by Wilson is particularly interesting in the context of two conditions that threaten human beings: scarcity of resources and overpopulation. If Wilson's hypothesis about the adaptiveness of homosexuality is correct, we may see an increase in overt homosexuality, particularly in those parts of the world most suffering from lack of resources and overpopulation.

It should also be noted that Wilson's analysis assumes that homosexuals do not reproduce. However, a substantial proportion of people who engage in homosexual behavior also enter into heterosexual marriages and have children. If there is a genetic component to homosexuality, we would just as easily argue that those genes are passed on to the next generation through homosexuals who have children. Thus far, however, genes affecting sexual orientation have not been found, and it is not known through what mechanisms erotic orientation toward males or females develops.

Sociobiology suggests that we can ask two kinds of questions about the causes of behavior. Contemporary questions concern how a particular behavior came to exist; that is, they seek the proximate cause of a behavior. These questions involve analysis of the genetic, biological, and psychological causes of a particular behavior.

In contrast, evolutionary questions concern why a behavior exists; that is, they seek the ultimate cause. Answers to questions about ultimate causation will involve some variant of the general rule that a behavior functions in specific ways to maximize the organism's inclusive fitness. Questions about the ultimate causes of behavior are problematic in that they are primarily concerned with the species history. The early environment in which the behavior evolved, however, is gone and cannot be studied. Nonetheless, sociobiologists are primarily concerned with ultimate (evolutionary) questions. They assume that sexual behaviors exist and are maintained because, in the past, they have served the ultimate cause of reproduction. According to this perspective, many of our current sexual activities can be traced back to reproductive behaviors that are believed to have existed in early hunting and gathering groups. Thus, evolutionary thinking involves a way of looking at human behavior that is very different from many of the models widely used in psychology and the social sciences. In the following section, we examine some of the basic principles and models developed to explain sexual behavior.

Parental Investment Theory

Trivers proposed that gender differences in the sexual behavior of a particular species are determined by fathers' versus mothers' amount of investment of resources, time, and energy in their offspring. Darwin's theory of sexual selection described a form of natural selection that depended on differential access to the other sex. Darwin identified its usual forms as intermale competition for access to females and female choice of male sexual partners. These processes lead to male features that aid competition and attract females. Trivers maintained that the reason sexual selection took these forms was because the female initially "invests" more than the male in the offspring. This begins with the relatively greater size of the eggs, or ova, compared with the sperm. The female's ovary releases an egg during her monthly reproductive cycle; this is the human body's largest cell from menstruation to menopause. Sperm are among the smallest cells in the body, and viable sperm can be released by the male from adolescence through old age. According to Trivers, this difference produces different strategies for maximizing fitness in the two sexes. In species where the male is required for parental care, the initial disparity between the sexes will be counterbalanced, or even reversed in some cases. But where the female is able to rear young without the male's assistance, there will be accentuated intermale competition with more risky and costly male strategies, and the evolution of polygyny.

To put this into a more concrete perspective, let us consider the average North American family. Both parents commit various resources to the rearing of the child. In the typical family, the mother probably invests a lot more than does the father. After conception, the mother carries the child for about nine months in her uterus. After giving birth, she feeds the child during the period when it was too helpless to feed itself. This pattern of greater investment in offspring by females than by males is characteristic of humans and, in fact, of most species. This does not mean that human males are lacking in the capability for parental investment. During the evolutionary period in which we evolved, males may have incurred significant risks in hunting for meat and fighting off predators to protect their mates and offspring. But among most humans today, parental investment by females is greater than that by males.

In Trivers's theory, the average parental investment of males versus females in a species influences sexual behavior in at least three ways. Among species such as our own, in which the female invests more, Trivers predicts that (1) male–male competition for female mates will be greater than female–female competition for male mates, (2) there will be greater variation in reproductive success among males than among females, and (3) selective pressure will be greater on males than on females because of the competition among males and because some succeed in mating and some do not. This selective pressure on males would produce larger body size, greater strength, and other attributes that help some males compete successfully for mates against other males who do not have these attributes or who have them to a lesser extent. Selective pressure should also result in greater variation in hair and skin color and more aggressiveness, insofar as those traits help males attract females.

To summarize, among species in which females invest more as parents and thus control reproductive success, males are at a disadvantage. Males, therefore, must try harder to succeed in passing on their genes. Whatever strategies and attributes males have that help them to succeed will be passed on. Characteristics that may render males less successful in competing against other males and attracting females, such as passivity and physical limitations, will tend to drop out of the gene pool. In species in which females have greater parental investment, there is less selective pressure on females because they control reproductive success. This theory would predict that females will be much more cautious and selective in choosing sexual partners than males are because of the female's greater investment if pregnancy ensues as a result of the interaction.

Daly and Wilson used the parent–offspring model derived by Trivers to generate hypotheses about the circumstances under which a child is likely to kill its parents. The parent–offspring model predicts that children would demand more resources from parents than parents would be prepared to give. Siblings would tend to value themselves more highly than they do one another, and parents would value similarly aged siblings to the same extent. Rather than being a conduit of cultural beliefs, socialization is seen, from an evolutionary perspective, as a conflict of interest between two types of individuals. Parents use their position of power to stress the importance of moral values, which serve their own interests by either reducing the time and effort required in parenting or reducing conflicts between siblings. In contrast to the Freudian view, parent–offspring conflict, instead of involving sexual motives, occurs over the allocation of parental resources. There is an imbalance in the fitness interest of parent and child, which changes with age in accordance with their relative reproductive value. Caring for existing offspring becomes a relatively more valuable way of enhancing parents' fitness as parents become older,

whereas parents become less valuable to their offspring with age. Daly and Wilson therefore predicted that parricide would increase with parents' age at the time the child was born. In a review of all reported murders of children by their parents and all murders of parents by their children in Canada between 1974 and 1988, and in Chicago between 1965 and 1981, they found this to be the case.

Mate Selection

The Darwinian principle of sexual selection indicates that there will be sex differences in mating. For males, this principle holds that genetically based characteristics that best attract mates will show up in succeeding generations in spite of the threats they may pose to individual survival. Males compete for mates by acquiring and displaying signs, such as personal and material resources, of their ability to provide for a family. Females accentuate their fertility by trying to appear youthful and attractive. Thus, female mate choices determine which inherited characteristics will persist through the generations as potent sexual attractors. Since females spend more time caring for offspring, they have more incentive to carefully select a partner. This would suggest that men tend to marry women younger than themselves and women would seek out older men who had access to more resources than younger men. Buss attempted to test the veracity of this assumption by studying 33 different societies with more than 10,000 respondents. In all but one of the samples, women placed higher value on the financial prospects of potential partners than men did. In most of the samples, women rated a potential partner's ambition and industriousness more highly than men did, providing moderate support for that expectation. In all but three of the samples, men rated physical attractiveness as more important in selecting a mate than did women. Thus, it appears that men show strong preferences for physical attractiveness when evaluating potential mates, while women pay more attention to a man's social status and material resources.

R and K Selection

A concept used to distinguish between reproductive strategies in the animal kingdom is that of r and K selection. Reproductive strategies are conceptualized as falling on a continuum from r, where organisms produce large numbers of offspring but provide little to no parental care, to K, where organisms produce few offspring and make a large investment in the care and development of offspring. Rushton illustrates the end points of the r-K continuum by placing oysters (thousands of offspring and no parental care) at the r extreme and great apes (few offspring with substantial parental investment) at the K end of the continuum. Rushton proposed that there were racial differences in temperament related to differences in socialization, sexual behavior, impulsivity, and criminality. He maintained that Mongoloids can be found at the K end of the spectrum of reproductive strategies, while Negroids occupy the r end of the spectrum, with Caucasoids occupying an intermediate position with a great deal of interracial variability within each broad grouping. He further claimed that environmental influences account for about 50 percent of the variance on most of the traits that he studied. Rushton's work has been severely criticized as racism in scientific clothing and is an extreme example of the ongoing controversy over the application of evolutionary concepts to human behavior. At its most basic level, this debate focuses on the politically conservative implications of arguing that group differences in behavior are the result of adaptation and are difficult or impossible to alter as a consequence of their genetic basis. Thus, sociobiology has been attacked as a defender of the social status quo by scholars of a liberal persuasion who advocate social change through a more equitable distribution of resources and a restriction of the power that protects the privilege of the elite.

Sociobiology has come under attack for lending ideological support for capitalism, racism, and sexism. It has been argued that sociobiologists pay scant attention to cultural evolution in their attempt to reduce complex social behavior to a genetic drama. This debate is more political than scientific and often involves a great deal of misunderstanding on both sides. Partially in response to the charges of genetic determinism and reductionism, many individuals working in an evolutionary framework now describe themselves as evolutionary psychologists. Evolutionary psychology considers humans to be an evolved species with an evolutionary history, just as sociobiology does. It is more interested, however, in the psychological mechanisms arising from evolution. Regardless of the labels attached to those working within an evolutionary framework, evolutionary theory will continue to play a major role in our understanding of human beings.

REFERENCES

Buss, D.M. Sex Differences in Human Mate Preferences: Evolutionary Hypotheses Tested in 37 Cultures. *Behavioral and Brain Sciences*, Vol. 12 (1989), pp. 1–49.

Daly, M., and M. Wilson. Evolutionary Social Psychology and Family Homicide. *Science*, Vol. 242 (1988), pp. 519–24.

———. *Homicide*. New York: Aldine de Gruyter, 1988.

Fairchild, H.F. Scientific Racism: The Cloak of Objectivity. *Journal of Social Issues*, Vol. 17 (1991), pp. 101–15.

Rushton, J.P. Race Differences in Behavior. A Review and Evolutionary Analysis. *Personality and Individual Differences*, Vol. 9 (1988), pp. 1009–24.

Trivers, R.E. Parent-Offspring Conflict. *American Zoologist*, Vol. 14 (1974), pp. 249–64.

———. Parental Investment and Sexual Selection. In B. Campbell, ed., *Sexual Selection and the Descent of Man*. Chicago: Aldine, 1972.

Wilson, E.O. *Sociobiology: The New Synthesis*. Cambridge, Mass.: Harvard Univ. Press, 1975.

———. *On Human Nature*. Cambridge, Mass.: Harvard Univ. Press, 1978.

Zuckerman, M. Some Dubious Premises in Research and Theory on Racial Differences: Scientific, Social and Ethical Issues. *American Psychologist*, Vol. 45 (1990), pp. 1297–1303.

A.R. Allgeier

SOCIOLOGICAL THEORIES OF SEXUALITY

Sociological explanations of human sexuality cover a wide range of perspectives, from macrosociological theories, such as structural functionalism and conflict theories, which focus on social structures and institutions, to the microsociological theories of symbolic interactionism, ethnomethodology, and phenomenology, which are concerned with the perceptions and behaviors of individual actors. They differ in the kinds of questions they ask as well as in the level of explanations they use. Some of these theories see people as passive role players, acting in terms of role expectations and social definitions they have learned, or as being controlled by external social forces. Others conceptualize humans as active creators of their own interpretations of situations and see norms and expectations as constantly evolving products of interaction. All sociological perspectives, however, make certain common assumptions about people and their sexuality. They all see human sexuality as determined by social, rather than biological, factors. Hormones and other biological forces are seen as potentiating, rather than controlling, sexual responses. Norms, values, and attitudes, which are social products, are viewed as the ultimate elements of sexual response. Sociologists point out that sexual norms, attitudes, and practices vary widely among cultures and that they are consistent with other components of these societies. Structural functionalists, for example, see the particular social expectations a society holds about sexuality as adaptive mechanisms, keeping the family reproductive unit viable and thus having survival value for the social system. The family serves as the primary unit of socialization and, therefore, as the transmitter of social values.

Some sociological theories attempt to account for the role of sexuality in society; others are concerned with sexual development as a social phenomenon; still others attempt to understand the acquisition of sexual identities or the development of particular patterns of sexual behavior. The following discussion gives some idea of the variety of sociological perspectives as they are applied to human sexuality.

Structural-Functional Theories of Sexuality

The structural-functional perspective, most fully developed by the late Talcott Parsons, conceives of society as being in a state of equilibrium. Society is orderly, and there is general consensus among its members about goals, values, and behavior, which are reflected in the social structure and its institutions. The society's norms reflect its values and serve to facilitate the achievement of its goals. The particular norms of a society, its social institutions, and the patterns of behavior regulated by them exist because they serve a social function. Behavior that is no longer functional eventually disappears.

Davis has applied the structural-functional perspective to the study of sexuality. He pointed out that norms regulating sexuality, like other norms, have gone through a long selective process, during which they have proved advantageous for collective survival. The only difference between sexual norms and other kinds of norms is that the former regulate powerful libidinal drives, which have the potential, when unregulated, to disrupt orderly social interaction. By its very nature, sexuality is intertwined with the issues of interpersonal relationships, competition, and reproduction. Thus, sexual norms are linked with a number of social institutions, such as law and religion, and they function to define and regulate a variety of roles and behaviors. Human societies differ, according to Davis, in their sexual norms and patterns of behavior. The sexual norms that exist are generally compatible with other social arrangements and beliefs of a particular society. He noted, for ex-

ample, that the double standard found in Puerto Rico, which allows married men to engage in sexual adventuring but tightly restricts the behavior of their wives, "survives well in an agrarian and highly stratified society. It tends to disintegrate under urban-industrial conditions."

Structural functionalists see the role of sexuality as facilitating, through its connection with affection, trust, and dependence, the formation of interpersonal bonds conducive to the survival of society. Structural functionalists acknowledge the potential of sexual drives to disrupt societal functioning. Incest taboos, for example, which are present in every society, serve to help families avoid sexual conflicts and tension by directing the sexual drive outside of the primary unit. Homosexuality is disapproved of in many societies because it conflicts with the institutionalization of male-female relationships. It does not eventuate in the formation of a family structure within which reproduction can occur.

Conflict theories

Conflict theories, which may be traced back to Karl Marx, view society as composed of opposing forces, differentiated in terms of their economic power. The powerful segments of society, from this perspective, exploit the weaker members. Sexuality, seen from this point of view, involves the exploitation of women by men who are economically more powerful. Women are viewed as mere property, and their sexuality is controlled by men. Women are forced to exchange their sexuality for economic security in a process of sexual bartering.

Heyl used a conflict approach to study prostitution. She observed that economic, status, and power differences exist between males and females in all social systems and that even in the world of prostitution, males dominate females. For example, she identified three male groups, police, pimps, and businessmen, as "differentially powerful" at the different levels of prostitution. "But males dominate at all levels by controlling the conditions under which the prostitute will work in her occupation." Control includes the power to arrest, the ability to take part or all of a woman's earnings, and the capacity to set her up in business, providing apartments, recruiting clients, and so forth. Additionally, clients control her behavior with their consumer power. Calling prostitution "the most sexist of them all," Heyl concluded that "the analysis . . . reveals prostitution as an extreme case of sex stratification—all the males win, and only the women pay the costs."

Symbolic Interactionism

The symbolic interactionist approach sees meaning as central to human experience. Unlike animals, people interpret the actions of themselves and others and act in terms of those meanings. This perspective, along with other microsociological positions such as phenomenology and ethnomethodology, is social constructionist. That is, it is more concerned with social realities than with physical realities. What is important to people, according to symbolic interactionists, is the meanings they place on identities, acts, and situations. Human behavior, including sexual behavior, takes place within a social context, from which people take their cues. They emphasize that sexual situations do not exist apart from their social definitions. Standards of attractiveness, sexually appropriate situations and the like are all socially defined. Sexual activity is activated not by hormones but by social definitions. Gagnon points out that social arrangements create biological responses, not the other way around. Becoming a sexual person, he states, is not a matter of physical maturation; rather, it is a process of acquiring meanings.

In examining the social sources of human sexuality, Gagnon and Simon developed the concept of the sexual script:

> Without the proper elements of a script that defines the situation, names the actors, and plots the behavior, nothing sexual is likely to happen. . . . Scripts are involved in learning the meaning of internal states, organizing the sequences of specifically sexual acts, decoding novel situations, setting the limits on sexual responses, and linking meanings from nonsexual aspects of life to specifically sexual experience.

Given their emphasis on meaning, symbolic interactionists have been particularly interested in the acquisition of sexual identities. For example, Troiden studied how men come to label themselves as homosexual. He noted that what differentiated men who eventually labeled themselves as homosexual from homosexually active men who did not consider themselves to be gay was the meanings they came to attribute to their feelings and behavior. In another study of male homosexuals, Weinberg found that young men engaged in sex with other males without defining either their behavior or themselves as homosexual until they acquired a definition of homosexuality that included sexual behavior. When they defined homosexuals only as men who dressed like women or who kissed each other, they were unable to relate their own sexual behavior to this label. Even when they learned more accurate definitions of homosexuality, they did not consider themselves to be homosexual if their friends persisted in this activity. When the social context changed (i.e., their friends became involved with females), they began to interpret their feelings and behaviors as homosexual.

Ethnomethodology and Phenomenology

Ethnomethodology and phenomenology are closely allied perspectives, which grew out of the work of philosopher Edmund Husserl. Alfred Schutz, building on his ideas, developed them into phenomenological sociology. Harold Garfinkel, a student of Schutz, further refined them, drawing from linguistics, anthropology, and other sociologies. Both frameworks see actors as active rather than passive creators of their social environments. They have in common an interest in how people construct reality and then act on the basis of these social constructions. Phenomenology remains more philosophical than ethnomethodology, which is much more empirical, and it places a greater emphasis on consciousness.

Warren and Johnson, for example, who take a phenomenological approach to understanding homosexual identities, point out that members of the homosexual community see "being gay" as something quite distinct from performing homosexual acts. Thus, they correctly observe that a married man who has sexual relations with his wife can, nonetheless, perceive himself to be "100 percent homosexual," thus "violating the . . . act-definition of bisexuality, and at the same time validating the being significance of homosexuality." They thus emphasize the subjective, rather than the objective, definition of homosexuality. Ethnomethodologists go beyond these philosophically based conceptions by attempting to uncover the actual methods that ordinary people use to construct meaning in their everyday lives, and they have developed a number of concepts to facilitate their studies. They examine how people use language, typifications, and commonsense theories to construct reality. Watson and Weinberg, for instance, studied the ways in which men impute homosexual identities to themselves. One of the techniques they use is what Sacks has called the "consistency rule" in the selection of membership categorizations. The consistency rule says that once people have categorized some population of persons using a particular device, they continue to use that same device to organize their perceptions both retrospectively and in the future. Thus, once a man has labeled himself as homosexual, he looks for confirming evidence, characteristics known as "indexical particulars" (e.g., feminine appearance), which are seen as defining the "underlying pattern" of homosexual. He may now also retrospectively reinterpret previously inconsequential events as "leading up to" and consistent with his new identity.

As can be seen from the brief survey of sociological perspectives, although they vary in the questions they ask and the emphasis they place on social factors, they hold a common view that sexuality is best understood in terms of social, rather than nonsocial, factors.

REFERENCES

Davis, K. Sexual Behavior. In R.K. Merton and R. Nisbet, eds. *Contemporary Social Problems*. 2d ed. New York: Harcourt Brace & World, 1966.

Gagnon, J. *Human Sexualities*. Glenview, Ill.: Scott, Foresman, 1977.

Gagnon, J., and W. Simon. *Sexual Conduct: The Sources of Human Sexuality*. Chicago: Aldine, 1973.

Heyl, B. Prostitution: An Extreme Case of Sex Stratification. In F. Adler and R.J. Simon, eds., *The Criminology of Deviant Women*. Boston: Houghton Mifflin, 1979.

Troiden, R. Becoming Homosexual: A Model of Gay Identity Acquisition. *Psychiatry: Journal for the Study of Interpersonal Processes*, Vol. 42 (Nov. 1979), pp. 362–73.

Warren, C.A.B., and J.M. Johnson. A Critique of Labeling Theory from the Phenomenological Perspective. In R.A. Scott and J.D. Douglas, eds., *Theoretical Perspectives on Deviance*. New York: Basic Books, 1972.

Watson, D.R., and T.S. Weinberg. Interviews and the Interactional Construction of Accounts of Homosexual Identity. *Social Analysis*, Vol. 11 (Oct. 1982), pp. 56–78.

Weinberg, T.S. *Gay Men, Gay Selves: The Social Construction of Homosexual Identities*. New York: Irvington, 1983.

Thomas S. Weinberg

SODOM AND SODOMY

According to Gen. 18:20–21 and 19:24–28, Sodom was a city in ancient Palestine notorious for its inhospitality, wickedness, and corruption. Its destruction by God was held out as the example of the type of punishment that comes to those who neglect or sin against God. Sin was so great and widespread in Sodom that God could not even find ten righteous persons, who could have saved the city from total destruction.

According to the biblical account, after Abram had bargained with the Lord to save the city if ten righteous men could be found, the Lord sent two angels to Sodom, disguised as men. They found Lot sitting at the side of the gate to the city. Lot invited them to his home to be his guests. He would feed them and give them a place to sleep for the night. That evening, all the men of the city, both young and old, came to Lot's house and inquired about the men that they might "know" them. Lot seemed to know that there was no good intent on the part of the men of the city. He begged them not to act so wickedly and offered his two virgin daughters to them for sexual purposes. The men then started to attack Lot, and the angels pulled him back into the house and blinded the men of the city so they could not find the door to the house. The angels then persuaded Lot, his wife, and their two daughters to flee from Sodom. "Then the Lord rained on Sodom and Gomorrah brimstone and fire from the Lord out of heaven; and he overthrew those cities, and all the valley, and all the inhabitants of the cities, and what grew on the ground."

The question that plagues biblical scholars is what was the great sin of Sodom. Christian tradition has held that the destruction of Sodom was a sign of God's disapproval and hatred of homosexuality. There is no agreement among biblical scholars because the text poses a number of questions. First, the homosexual interpretation rests entirely on the verb "to know." It appears 953 times in the Bible; 943 times this verb means "to get acquainted with"; only 10 times is it used to mean sexual intercourse, and each of those times it means heterosexual intercourse. An entirely different Hebrew word was used to describe sexual activity between two men. If for some reason the story is referring to sexual activity, it would seem that the issue was gang rape, presumably by heterosexual men. There is no allegation that there has ever been a city or town just for persons of the same sexual orientation. In fact, sexual orientation was not a concept known to the writers of the Bible. The frightening thing about this passage is that it is not used as an example to describe the treatment of Lot toward his unmarried, virgin daughters. This story does a better job of telling the low place that women held in the society and how easy it was for Lot to offer up his virgin daughters, who were probably quite young, to be sexually abused and raped in order to protect his male guests. There is a parallel story that is even more sexually explicit and violent towards females in Judges, chapter 19.

The second thing about linking this passage with homosexuality is that nowhere in the Scriptures is this linkage made. The first references to the sins of Sodom come from two contemporary prophets, Ezekiel and Jeremiah, many hundreds of years later (c. 600 B.C.E.). Both had basically the same traditional understanding. Ezekiel said it clearly: "Behold, this was the sin of your sister Sodom: she and her daughters lived in pride, plenty, and thoughtless ease; they supported not the poor and needy; they grew haughty, and committed abomination before me; so I swept them away; as you have seen" (Ezek. 16:49–50). Thus, the sin of Sodom was inhospitality, which was a very important issue for the early Hebrew community. There was a high value on hospitality. Jesus also makes reference to Sodom several times in the Gospel stories, always referring to inhospitality as the terrible sin. An example is found in Luke 10:10–13.

The first reference to the sin of Sodom being homosexuality comes from outside the Bible, in the writings of a Hebrew historian, Josephus, who was born in 37/38 C.E. and died sometime after 100. He was a commanding officer of the Galilean Jewish forces in the war against Rome (66–70 C.E.). He hated Rome and wrote history in a way that would question God accepting common Roman practices. One of those practices was homosexual behavior. Josephus went back to the story of Sodom and used the destruction of Sodom as proof that God hated homosexual acts.

Sodomy

Nevertheless, sodomy has come to refer to any number of "unnatural" sexual acts (or "crimes against nature"). From the first century C.E. to the present time, "sodomites" became interchangeable with the term "sodomy" and has been linked at various times to "crimes against nature" like masturbation; oral-genital, oral-anal, anal intercourse; bestiality; some rare and bizarre sexual practices, such as sex with a cadaver (necrophilia); and any other type of sexual activity that did not lead to procreation. "Natural" sex came to mean heterosexual intercourse within the bounds of marriage leading to pregnancy. "Unnatural" was anything that did not enhance the possibility of pregnancy. Therefore, heterosexual or homosexual oral-genital or anal intercourse and any gay or lesbian sexual activity were considered "unnatural" and named sodomy.

Early concepts of sodomy were limited to sexual activity between and among men. Roman emperors who embraced Christianity began to enact laws against sodomy, (i.e., male homosexual behavior). Offenders were often given the death penalty of burning at the stake.

During the Middle Ages sodomy, heresy and disbelief became interchangeable. For example, during the Spanish Inquisition, Jews, heretics, and "sodomites" were burned at the stake. Then, as heterosexuals engaged in the same type of sexual activity, they also became known as "sodomites." Sex was defined by the act, not the orientation of the person, which was an unknown concept before the 19th century.

Sodomy laws in the United States still reflect an intolerant attitude toward noncoital sexual behavior and do not differentiate most of the time between single and married, heterosexual and homosexual, men and women. The penal codes in the majority of our states forbid oral-genital, oral-anal, and anal intercourse, as well as sex with animals, and link them all as "sodomy" or "crimes against nature." While it does not matter whether the persons are heterosexual or homosexual, homosexual persons are prosecuted more often than heterosexuals under the sodomy laws. The penalties are severe and can range up to life imprisonment. Others include being committed to mental institutions as a sexual psychopath.

Some states have repealed their sodomy laws, but the majority have not, Many believe that the final resolution will be through the U.S. Supreme Court. Several years ago, a president of the American Psychiatric Association wrote a letter to the chief justice, pointing out that the vast majority of American heterosexuals and 20 million homosexuals regularly engage in "sodomy," and thus well over 100 million American citizens, without any court record or criminal intent, are "sodomites."

Ironically, those in the field of sex education and therapy often promote or recommend certain behaviors listed as "sodomy" as a way of enhancing the sexual relationship of two consenting partners, regardless of sexual preference.

REFERENCES

Bailey, D.S. *Homosexuality and the Western Christian Tradition*. London: Longman, Green, 1955.

Francoeur, R.T. *Becoming a Sexual Person*. New York: Macmillan, 1991.

Haeberle, E. *The Sex Atlas*. New York: Seabury Press, 1978.

Nelson, J.B. *Embodiment: An Approach to Sexuality and Christian Theology*. Minneapolis: Augsburg, 1979.

Strong, B., and C. Devault. *Understanding Our Sexuality*. 2d ed. St. Paul: West, 1988.

Trible, P. *Texts of Terror*. Philadelphia: Fortress Press, 1984.

William R. Stayton

STERILIZATION

Sterilization is the most effective method of contraception known. At the present time, it is the most widely used method of contraception not only in the United States but in the world. Sterilization, however, has a rather controversial history because of its association with eugenics.

Eugenics grew out of the research of Francis Galton, who published his *Hereditary Genius* in 1869. Galton felt that to improve the human race it was necessary to breed selectively and, in a word, discourage the mating of the unfit. He founded the Eugenics Education Society and established a National Eugenics Laboratory at University College, London. Eugenicists campaigned for effective contraception, at least for certain groups, while at the same time encouraging the intellectually (and materially) endowed to have children. They also encouraged sterilization of the mentally defective, and many states in the United States adopted laws to permit sterilization of certain classes of people. The state of Virginia, for example, adopted a sterilization law in 1924 that permitted sterilization for individuals adjudicated insane, epileptic, or feebleminded by a commission composed of two physicians and a justice of the peace. Before being brought to the commission, the superintendent of one of the state hospitals had to certify that, in his opinion, the patient's condition was caused by heredity and that such a condition could be transmitted to the offspring. Though there were various safeguards, including the appointment of a guardian, to protect the patient, and the ability to appeal in court, the state, over a ten-year period (to 1935), sterilized some 2,000 individuals.

This policy of sterilization eventually came into widespread disrepute with the Nazi adoption of genetic ideas of superior and inferior races and their attempt to exterminate the Jews and sterilize the "morally" unacceptable. As an aftermath, most of the legislation in the United States requiring sterilization for "defectives" was either repealed or declared unconstitutional.

Sterilization today has essentially become a voluntary method of contraception and as such is widespread. Both males and females can be sterilized, although most often it is the woman who is sterilized. Increasingly, however, men also are opting for sterilization, in part because the male operation, until recently, was freer of complications than the female one. The standard method of sterilization in males is the vasectomy. This involves cutting into the vas deferens, the excretory duct of the testis, which transport the sperm from each testicle to the prostatic urethra. It is a simple surgical procedure, usually performed under local anesthesia, and takes from 10 to 15 minutes to complete. The surgeon makes a small opening in the scrotum and severs the vas deferens, either by tying it, blocking it, or cutting out a small piece. He then repeats the operation on the other side, since there are two vas deferens.

The problem with male sterilization seems to be mainly psychological, which is why careful and accurate counseling is essential. Recent research, however, has suggested some immune-system problems related to the development of antibodies to sperm and there is a possible link to prostate cancer. A vasectomy is not suitable for men who desire children at a future date because, in most cases, the procedure is not reversible, and the longer one has a vasectomy, the less reversible it becomes.

Female sterilization is aimed at blocking the Fallopian tubes, which transmit the ova from the ovaries into the uterus. Tying the tubes (tubal ligation) is one of the oldest forms of tubal occlusion. The technique recommended by the International Planned Parenthood Federation's panel of experts involves picking up the tube near the midportion to form a loop, tying (ligating) the base of the loop with an absorbable suture and cutting off (resecting) the top of the loop. The procedure, in recent years, has become greatly simplified with the development of minilaparotomy and laparoscopy. The minilaparotomy can be performed under local anesthesia, and a small insertion of about 2.5 centimeters (approximately one inch) is made. Each Fallopian tube is then pulled up into the incision to be cut and tied.

Laparoscopy involves inserting a laparoscope into the abdomen. The incision is smaller than for a minilaparotomy and can be made close to the umbilicus (navel), where normally no scar is visible. It is easier, however, to make the incision at a spot somewhat lower in the abdomen, since this brings the scope closer to the target organs. It is also possible for the surgeon to enter the abdomen through the vagina (a colpotomy), and this practice is used extensively in India. All these procedures can be carried out on an outpatient basis under local anesthesia and can be completed in about 10 to 20 minutes.

The Chinese have developed a method of female sterilization through chemical occlusion, that is, by occluding the tubes through chemical burning. This method can be done without surgery and is done in China without anesthetic. It involves the insertion of a cannula (a tube) through the cervix and uterus up into the Fallopian tubes, through which an injection of a phenol (carbolic acid) gel is inserted. The procedure is then performed on the other tube. The result is a scarring of the tubes, which ultimately closes the opening. Chemical occlusion is a very low-cost method of sterilization, but it is not reversible.

Except for the chemical-burning method, reversibility is possible in a majority of cases of female sterilization. Some surgeons have achieved restoration to the point at which pregnancy rates of 60 percent have been recorded. As in the case of men, however, the prognosis for reversibility becomes poorer the longer the person has been sterilized. Reversal is considered major surgery, involving microsurgical techniques, and general anesthesia is necessary.

REFERENCE

Bullough, V., and B. Bullough. *Contraception: A Guide to Birth Control Methods.* Buffalo, N.Y.: Prometheus Books, 1990.

Vern L. Bullough

STÖCKER, HELENE

A pioneer for sex reform and birth control, Helene Stöcker (1869–1943) fought all her life to gain equal rights for women. She was devoted to many progressive causes, among them the acceptance of unmarried mothers and their children (Mutterschutz). She was also, with Magnus Hirschfeld, one of the founders of the Scientific Humanitarian Committee, which campaigned for homosexual rights.

Determined to get a Ph.D., something not possible for a woman in Germany, she went to Switzerland, earning a Ph.D. in Bern in 1901, with the highest distinction (summa cum laude). In 1905, she founded the Bunde for Mutterschutz (League for Protection of Motherhood), and a few years later, in 1908, she started a periodical, *New Generation,* which she edited until 1933. She participated in establishing sex advisory clinics in many German cities and continued until Hitler closed them. As early as 1910, Stöcker participated in the International Neo-Malthusian Congress for Birth Control in the Hague, in Holland. One year later, she organized a congress on birth control and sex reform. Actually, two conferences had to be organized, as the two topics were held unfit to be discussed at the same time. She was active in the second international conference for sex reform in Copenhagen, in 1928. Under Hitler, Stöcker was deprived of her German citizenship and her doctorate. She fled in 1933, eventually settling in the United States, where she died from cancer.

She, along with Margaret Sanger, is regarded as one of the world pioneers in campaigning for more effective contraceptives. Like Sanger, she also went on to the larger issues of human sexuality in her campaigns.

REFERENCE

Wickert, C. *Helene Stöcker.* Bonn: Dietz, 1991.

Hans Lehfeldt
Connie Christine Wheeler

STOPES, MARIE CHARLOTTE CARMICHAEL

Marie Charlotte Carmichael Stopes (1880–1958) was a major English sex reformer and popularizer during the first half of the 20th century. Born in Edinburgh on October 15, 1880, she was the daughter of Henry Stopes, a wealthy amateur archaeologist, and Charlotte Carmichael Stopes, a pioneer in women's education who had studied at Edinburgh University.

She had little formal education other than tutoring by her parents until she was 12, when she began attending school in Edinburgh and later a boarding school in London. She graduated from University College, London, in 1902, with honors in botany, geology, and physical geography. She received a doctorate at Munich in botany and joined the science faculty at the University of Manchester, the first woman to do so. In 1911, she married and moved to London, where she was a lecturer on palaeobotany from 1913 to 1920. During this time, she published a textbook on ancient plants and a two-volume catalog of cretaceous flora in the British Museum. During World War I, she engaged in research on coal with R.V. Wheeler.

It was through her work on contraceptives and sex education, however, that she was best known. Her interest in sexuality came from the failure of her 1911 marriage to a Canadian botanist, Reginald Ruggles Gates. In 1916, the marriage was annulled on the basis of nonconsummation, and, in 1918, she married Humphrey Verdon-Roe, an aircraft manufacturer. He was already interested in birth control, and shortly after their marriage they founded the Mothers Clinic for Birth Control, in London, the first of its kind in England. After this, Stopes (who kept her maiden name) relinquished her lectureship at the University of London and devoted herself to family planning and sex education for married people.

Her first book on the subject, *Married Love,* was published in 1918, although she had originally drafted it in 1914 to crystallize her own ideas. It became an immediate success and was translated into numerous languages, causing a sensation at the time of its publication. Though the first edition dealt scarcely at all with birth control, she received so many requests for instruction on the subject that this was followed up by a short book, *Wise Parenthood*. This, too, was an immediate success and within nine years had sold half a million copies in its original English edition. She published a number of other books more or less dealing with the same subject, such as *Radiant Motherhood* and *Enduring Passion*, many of which sounded somewhat overromantic to later generations of readers.

Her great achievement was to move the topic of birth control in much of the English-speaking world from the confines of the physician's office to public discussion. Her husband and, eventually, her son were alienated from her during the last years of her life. Though still interested in sex education and contraceptives, she increasingly spent her later years writing poetry and engaging in literary pursuits. She died at her estate, Norbury Park, on October 2, 1958. Her estate, including her mansion, was bequeathed to the Royal Society of Literature, of which she was a fellow. A portrait of her, painted by Augustus St. John, was bequeathed to the National Portrait Gallery, while one by Gregorio Prieto went to the National Gallery of Edinburgh.

REFERENCES

Briant, K. *Marie Stopes*. London: Hogarth Press, 1962.

Stopes, M.C. *Married Love*. New York: Eugenic, 1918.

Vern L. Bullough

STRESS AND SEXUALITY

Sometimes, sexual dysfunction arises from the stress of a special situation, such as fear of discovery, fear of "not doing well," or even fear of pregnancy. Anxious preoccupation with a situational failure can cause difficulty the next time, starting a vicious cycle of failure involving anticipation, becoming a mental spectator rather than a participant, and further failure. This is one of the commonest causes of secondary impotence and anorgasmia. In such cases, counseling and sex therapy are usually helpful.

There is, however, another kind of stress brought about by such things as unemployment, difficulties on the job, marital and family problems, or any number of factors. Though some stress, like the violin string, is essential to an authentic tone, too much stress produces a questionable tone in both violins and humans, and extreme stress can literally break both violins and humans. The relationship between sexuality and this kind of stress has not been extensively studied, but there are some hints that many individuals seek relief through sexual activity and, in the process, engage in sexual activities that they previously had not done and would not do again, such as exhibitionism.

Some evidence of this came from the experience of Hartman and Fithian with students at California State University at Long Beach. Students in their classes had to keep journals as well as engage in class discussion, and they found an interesting correlation in their sample of some 5,000 students at stress periods such as examination times. Incidence of masturbation increased, as well as incidents of panty raids on female dorms, a common phenomenon for a time on college campuses in the 1950s and 1960s. The health center at the university regularly reported a greater number of women students presenting with vaginal infections during examination times. These observations are congruent with the studies indicating a strong correlation between psychological stress and illness. Hartman and Fithian also found a greater acting out of fantasies among both their students and their clients during times of stress.

If these behaviors violated the law, the danger was that an individual might be arrested and further stigmatized by being labeled "deviant" by himself or herself or by society. Sometimes, the individual was registered as a sex offender if the behavior involved exhibitionism or involved children. Hartman and Fithian emphasize that an individual should not be labeled either by himself or herself or by society as deviant for one or two stress-related incidents but emphasize that the person should seek help and counseling. Early detection and treatment are the best means of prevention.

REFERENCE

Pendergast, W.E. *Treating Sex Offenders in Correctional Institutions and Outpatient Clinics*. New York: Haworth Press, 1991.

William E. Hartman
Marilyn A. Fithian

SURROGATES: SEXUAL SURROGATES

Masters and Johnson reported in 1970 that they had treated 54 single men and three women with what they called "partner surrogates." Though 13 of the men and all three women had provided their own partners, the remaining 41 men were partnered by some 13 different surrogates chosen from 31 volunteers. Masters and Johnson concluded that the use of surrogates could be a wise clinical decision.

In 1970, Hartman and Fithian began training surrogate volunteers, all of whom were licensed professionals. From this group of trained professionals, the training of surrogates spread and led to an organized group, the International Professional Surrogates Association (IPSA), founded in Los Angeles in 1973. One of the first steps IPSA took was to develop a set of professional guidelines, including a code of ethics and standards for surrogate training. Members were carefully screened and agreed to the IPSA code defining 17 specific ethical standards.

Several surrogate therapy programs evolved, with the best known being the Berkeley group that worked with Apfelbaum, a Chicago group working with Dauw, and two groups in southern California, one working with Hartman and Fithian's Center for Marital and Sexual Studies, in Long Beach, and the other with the Center for Social and Sensory Learning, founded by Barbara Roberts, in Los Angeles.

At a May 1976 conference at the University of California at Los Angeles devoted to the professional and legal issues in the use of surrogate partners, Roberts reported findings based on client responses for the past three years. Interestingly, she found that coitus was the least significant aspect of the clients' exploration of emotional intimacy and that becoming comfortable with nudity, touch, and erotic stimulation were far more important.

Similarly, Dauw found that the problem of the sexually dysfunctional male was more social than sexual; that his heterosexual male clients could not effectively relate to a woman either verbally, intellectually, emotionally, or physically; and that the clients needed to learn to love themselves before they could love one another. Over the period from 1970 to 1980, he treated some 501 males (apparently no females), ranging in age from 18 to 78, and his success rate was 98.2 percent for primary impotence to 84.8 for secondary impotence. Similar findings were made by others.

It is in teaching intimacy that sex surrogates have been most effective. One of Dauw's publications is subtitled *A Guide to Emotional Intimacy*, while the book by the former male sexual surrogate, DeHaan, emphasizes the importance of intimacy in dealing with his female clients. Interestingly, where males most often sought out surrogate help in the 1970s and early 1980s, single

females have been far more common since then. Many, but probably not the majority, of both single men and single women have never engaged in coitus before coming to the therapist. The average age of the clients reported by Hartman and Fithian ranged from the mid-to-late-30s, although they also had a 62-year-old woman and a 72-year-old man who worked effectively with surrogates.

Surrogates are selected by the therapists on the basis of the common interests, education, goals, or even occupations with those they work with, and there is an attempt to match couples agewise. Hartman and Fithian, however, reported matching a 70-year-old single male to a much younger woman, since he had always dated younger women. Obviously, the needs and practices of individual clients have to be taken into consideration.

Since the surrogate is considered as a replacement partner for the client, her or his feelings are as important as those of the client. Though different therapists have different rules, Hartman and Fithian insist that the surrogate be regarded as part of the therapy team and impose strict prohibitions against drugs, alcohol, and contact with each other except under therapeutic conditions. Therapists and clients are known to each other only by their first names and do not know each others' telephone number or address. They do allow a client to contact a surrogate after the therapy is over and a waiting period of six months has passed. Several individuals have ultimately married their surrogates, and many become close friends at a later date.

Though surrogates are paid for their interaction with the client, the interaction is not superficial, since the pay is for the surrogate to be honest, express their own feelings, and interact with the partner in a way that can help him or her to overcome problems. It is not only in the United States that surrogate therapy has been established, but it early spread to Canada, where it was started by Frank Sommers, and to Australia, where Derek Richardson utilized it in his practice. The practice, however, remains controversial.

One of the problems is that many view surrogate therapy as a form of prostitution. Defenders of surrogate therapy emphasize that surrogates do not give instant gratification, and sexual intercourse may occur only a few times. Moreover, the quicker a prostitute turns a trick, the more money she makes. This is not true for the surrogate, whose obligation is to overcome the negative feelings about sexuality and intimacy in slow and carefully developed stages. Moreover, a surrogate cannot be provocative in speech, manner, or dress, and the most valued aspect of the therapy is the time spent talking and helping. Surrogates also make far less money than a prostitute. Wardell Pomeroy, one of the early advocates of sexual surrogates, emphasized that the surrogates could not be compared to prostitutes or call girls because the surrogate was a professional whose work was supervised by a therapist, and he or she is carefully brought into the treatment program as well as given homework and instructions for dealing with each case. Most do not earn their living as surrogates but have other jobs, and assumed the surrogate role usually because they had personal or family or close friends who had some kind of sexual problem.

Surrogates have also been criticized for not having a real relationship with their clients. This implies a lack of commitment. Critics also argue that the surrogate is chosen for the client and not by them and that this does not correspond to reality. In contrast, some therapists argue that the use of a surrogate helps resolve sexual problems more easily than working with a married couple, since they do not have the other emotional entanglements which come with a committed relationship.

The American Association of Sex Educators, Counselors and Therapists, an organization that certifies therapists, has no official stand on sex surrogates but emphasizes that if a therapist does use surrogates, they should be used in an ethical way. With the advent of AIDS (acquired immune deficiency syndrome), even though surrogates insist on testing for STDs (sexually transmitted diseases) and all therapists insist on a sex history, the use of surrogates has decreased, and though the teaching of intimacy remains important, sexual intercourse has become even less important. Safe sex itself can become a way to teach intimacy.

Same-sex surrogates have been used in treatment of gay men and lesbians and have been successful here, since they provide a safe and supportive environment for a client who is fearful or apprehensive. Surrogates have also been used in dealing with people with special sexual problems, such as the physically handicapped. They have proven particularly helpful in dealing with some of the emotional problems associated with sex, such as women who have a fear of penetration, or in helping males who have performance anxiety.

In sum, the use of a surrogate is basically a decision that the therapist and the client must themselves agree on. Those therapists who have successfully used surrogates are strong advocates, but there is also much opposition to their use.

REFERENCES

Apfelbaum, B. The Ego-Analytic Approach to Body-Work Sex Therapy. *Journal of Sex Research*, Vol. 20 (1984), pp. 44–70.
———. The Myth of the Surrogate. *Journal of Sex Research*, Vol. 13 (1977), pp. 238–49.
Dauw, D. Evaluating the Effectiveness of the Sex Surrogate Assisted Model. *Journal of Sex Research*, Vol. 24 (1988), pp. 269–75.
———. *The Stranger in Your Bed: A Guide to Emotional Intimacy*. Chicago: Nelson-Hall, 1984.
DeHaan, J. *Reaching Intimacy—A Male Sex Surrogate's Perspective*. New York: St. Martin's Press, 1986.
Hartman, W.E., and M.A. Fithian. *Treatment of Sexual Dysfunction*. Long Beach, Calif.: Center for Marital and Sexual Studies, 1972; New York: Aaronson, 1974.
Kaplan, H.S. *The New Sex Therapy*. New York: Brunner, 1974.
Kaufman, S.A. *Sexual Sabotage*. New York: Macmillan, 1981.
Masters, W.A., and V.E. Johnson. *Human Sexual Inadequacy*. Boston: Little, Brown, 1970.

William E. Hartman
Marilyn A. Fithian

t

TAOISM AND SEX

In China, Taoism has both a philosophical and a religious tradition. Although philosophical Taoism flourished early in the fifth century B.C.E., Taoism as a religion did not develop until the first century C.E. Next to Confucianism, it ranks as the second major belief system in traditional Chinese thought. The philosophy of Taoism is outlined in Lao-tzu's *Tao-te Ching*, offering a practical way of life. Later, its teachings came to be utilized in the popular religion called Tao-chiao. In the Chinese tradition, the two have been separate, but in the West they have often been confused under the one name Taoism.

Lao-tzu's *Tao-te Ching* is so important for China that it has been argued that Chinese civilization and the Chinese character would have been utterly different if the book had never been written. No one can hope to understand Chinese philosophy, religion, government, art, medicine, sexology—or even cooking—without an appreciation of the philosophy taught in this little book. It is said that where Confucianism emphasizes social order and an active life, Taoism concentrates on individual life and tranquility.

Both philosophical Taoism and religious Taoism included in their classics many positive ideas about sex. The historical founder of the Taoist religion was Chang Ling, a popular religious leader and rebel. He urged his followers to read the *Tao-te Ching* and, in 143 C.E., organized them into Tao-chiao, or the Taoist religion. His followers called him Tien Shih, "Heavenly Teacher." After the founding of the Taoist religion, two major schools developed. One, Zheng Yi Pai ("Orthodox Unity School"), that is, Tien Shih Tao, was a highly organized religion. The other Taoist school, Quan Zhen Pai'm ("Perfect Realization School"), sought immortality through meditation, breathing exercises, bathing, gymnastics, sexual arts, medicines, chemistry, and other means. A measure of systemization was brought to this second school of Taoism by Wei Poyang (second century C.E.), who, in his *Chou-i-ts'an-t'ung-chi (Textual Research on the Taoist and Magical Interpretation of the Book of Changes*, or, in short, *Ts'an-tung-chi)*, attempted to synthesize Taoist techniques for achieving immortality and teachings of the occult *I Ching (Book of Change)*.

Later, the Perfect Realization School itself became divided into two major branches: the Northern Branch, which for centuries had its headquarters at Beijing's White Cloud Monastery and recognized Wang Chongyang (1112–1170 C.E.) as its founder; and the Southern Branch, which recognized Zhang Baiduan (Ziyang Zhenren) (984–1082) as its Original Master (hence, it was also called Ziyang Branch).

The difference between the Northern and Southern branches, in a word, is that the Northern Branch denied *fang zhong* (sexual intercourse techniques) and the Southern Branch favored *fang zhong* as the way to achieve longevity and immortality. Zhang Baiduan wrote *Wu Chen Phien* (*Poetical Essay on Realizing the Necessity of Regenerating the Primary Vitalities*) before the division of Northern and Southern branches, and it is the basic book of Taoist sexual regimen.

Taoist sexual techniques were developed on the basis of the *fang shu,* also called *fang zhong,* or *fang zhong shu.* The meaning of these three Chinese words for sexual intercourse techniques are exactly the same, literally "inside the bedchamber" or "the art in bedroom." *Fang-shu* was created by a combination of experts: *fang-shih* (alchemists or prescription writers), *fang-zhong-jia* (experts on sexual techniques or ancient sexologists), and physicians in or before the Han dynasty (206 B.C.E.–220 C.E.); mainly it belonged to the medical field.

For descriptive and analytic purposes, the entire Taoist sexual system may be divided into two categories: (1) beliefs or myths, and (2) methods or techniques.

The major Taoist sexual belief is that longevity or immortality are attainable by sexual activity. One way for men to achieve this is by having intercourse with virgins, particularly young virgins. In Taoist sexual books, the woman sexual partner is called *ding*, originally an ancient cooking vessel with two loop handles and three or four legs, used in the practice of alchemy. The Taoist sexual books, such as the *Hsuan wei Hshin* (*Mental Images of the Mysteries and Subtleties of Sexual Techniques*) and *San Feng Tan Cheueh* (*Zhang Sanfeng's Instructions in the Physiological Alchemy*), written, respectively, by Zhao Liang Pi and Zhang San Feng, state that the most desirable *ding* is a girl about 14, 15, or 16 years old just before or after menarche. *Zhang Sanfeng* went further and divided *ding* into three ranks: the lowest rank, 21- to 25-year-old women; the middle rank, 16- to 20-year-old menstruating virgin girls; and the highest rank, 14-year-old premenarche virgin girls.

There was also a belief in the desirability of multiple sexual partners. For example, Sun Simiao, in his *Prescriptions Worth a Thousand Gold*, wrote that the art of the bedchamber was for a man to copulate on one night with ten different women without emitting semen a single time. Ability to control ejaculation was a key for both men and women. For men, it was called *cai Yin pu Yang* (gathering a woman's yin to nourish a man's yang) and for women *cai Yang pu Yin*

(gathering a man's yang to nourish a woman's yin). The technique was a secret and a learned one, since it was most desirable to have one's partner reach orgasm without having orgasm oneself. This was particularly important for the male, because by practicing coitus reservatus it was believed that the semen found its way to the brain, *huan jing pu lau* (making the seminal essence return to nourish the brain). Thus, at the point of orgasm, the male prevents or interrupts ejaculation by pressing the "point" at the base of the penis. Taoist belief further emphasizes that sexual satisfaction may be derived from coitus without ejaculation.

The major Taoist sexual techniques include teaching how to master the differences of sexual arousal of male and female, harmonizing the sexual will and desire, and liberating and activating the female while relaxing the male.

For example, the Taoist sex handbook *True Manual of the "Perfected Equalization"* states:

> In the Taoist master's sexual "battle" (to give the woman an orgasm while avoiding ejaculation), his enemy is the woman. He should begin by touching her vulva, kissing her lips and tongue, and touching her breasts, making her highly aroused. But he should keep himself under control, his mind as detached as if it were floating in the azure sky, his body sunk into nothingness. He must close his eyes, avoid looking at the woman, and maintain an utter nonchalance so that his own passion is not roused. When she makes sexual movements, the man must remain still rather than take any action. When her hand actively touches the penis, the man avoids her caress. The man can employ stillness and relaxation, to overcome the woman's excitement and movement.

It is important for the male to understand the female sexual responses so he can penetrate her at the appropriate time, use the correct sexual postures, positions and movements that include controlled breathing, preventing ejaculation by stopping and pressing the base of the penis and achieving sexual satisfaction by coitus without ejaculation. Interestingly though, women also had their own techniques that are not discussed in the manuals that were written for men. These techniques remained women's secrets. Still the use of the male technique can be used to prolong the sexual act and contribute to the pleasure of both partners. Many modern sex therapists have adapted the Taoist sexual teachings as a way to treat premature ejaculation and other sexual dysfunctions.

REFERENCES

Bullough, V.L. *Sexual Variance in Society and History.* Chicago: Univ. of Chicago Press, 1976.

Chan, Wing-tsit, translator and compiler. *A Source Book in Chinese Philosophy.* Princeton, N.J.: Princeton Univ. Press, 1963.

Van Gulik, R.H. *Sexual Life in Ancient China: A Preliminary Survey of Chinese Sex and Society from ca. 1500 BC till 1644 AD.* Leiden: E.J. Brill, 1961.

Ruan, F.F. *Sex in China: Studies in Sexology in Chinese Culture.* New York: Plenum Press, 1991.

Zhang Mingcheng. *A History of Traditional Chinese Medicine: Herbs, Acupuncture, and Regimen.* Tokyo: Hisaho, 1974. (In Japanese.)

Zhou Shaoxian. *Daojia yu Shenxian* ("Taoists and Immortals"). 3d ed. Taipei: Chung Hwa, 1982. (In Chinese.)

Fang-fu Ruan

THERAPY: SEX THERAPY

The modern practice of sex therapy is a relatively recent attempt by behavioral and medical scientists to respond to the need for therapeutic intervention in the area of human sexual functioning. The term "sex therapy" refers to a specific focus of treatment rather than to a type of therapeutic technique. The field of sexology as a science has grown to include the understanding of human sexual behavior and functioning from a multidisciplinary perspective that considers the biological, psychological, social, and cultural aspects of sexuality.

From the outset, it is important to stress that a sex therapist should be a fully trained psychotherapist who is familiar with human behavior and psychopathology and is capable of applying a number of therapeutic techniques that are determined by the specific needs of a clinical situation. The sex therapist needs to understand the dynamics of the individual patient as well as the complicated interactions of the patient with his or her sexual partner. The sex therapist is expected to be flexible in the treatment approach lest any "marriage" to one particular theoretical orientation lead to a bias that overlooks appropriate therapeutic intervention.

Ideally, all clinician-therapists would have been trained in sex therapy. Unfortunately, that has not been the case. Training programs in sex therapy are limited throughout the country. At present, there are two certifying bodies, the American Association of Sex Educators, Counselors and Therapists (AASECT) and the American College of Sexology (ACS), which offer certification to those candidates meeting their requirements of training and supervised experi-

ence. There are also well-trained sex therapists who do not seek either AASECT or ACS certification, whether their original license is in medicine, psychology, marriage counseling, or clinical social work. Potential patients should inquire about the credentials of therapists before initiating treatment.

Historical Perspectives

Concern about sexual functioning and the understanding and causes of dysfunctions and their remedies have been evident in literature throughout the centuries. In ancient times, the sexual potency of the king was believed to affect the success of the harvest. Moreover, impotence was often seen as a divine punishment both in pagan and biblical literature. For example, in the Book of Genesis, Abimelech, King of Gerar, was rendered impotent for taking Abraham's wife, Sarah.

In the Middle Ages, witchcraft was believed capable of causing sexual dysfunction. Interestingly, medieval literature on demonology and impotence often bears a close resemblance to the explanations of impotence presented by theologians and the present-day psychodynamic theories. Modern secular literature has also reflected preoccupation with worries about sexual functioning.

Despite reference to sexual concerns over the centuries, myth, superstition, and unfounded scientific speculation generally marked the understanding of sexual function. The modern era of investigating human sexuality was influenced by the publication of *Psychopathia Sexualis*, in 1886, by Richard von Krafft-Ebing. This work stressed a debased nature of sexuality, although it probably conformed to the general assumptions about sex of the time. Following close behind Krafft-Ebing was Sigmund Freud, who also accepted some of the same notions about sexual deviation and disease but added that certain sexual problems are themselves signs of underlying neurosis that have their root in childhood.

It was the writing of Havelock Ellis (1859–1939) that called attention to the normalcy of sexual behavior rather than its deviance. He was able to describe the human sexual experience in positive terms and freed from sexual guilt and repression many notions of sexual behavior. By viewing sexuality as part of the fabric of life, Ellis, in effect, established the foundation for modern sex therapy.

Sex Therapy Today

Historically, the treatment of sexual disorders was regarded as within the domain of psychiatry.

Freudian theory, which viewed symptoms of sexual dysfunction as being surface manifestations of underlying psychological conflicts, was responsible for treating sexual problems chiefly within a psychodynamic framework. It was not unusual for patients to undergo years of psychoanalysis in an attempt to overcome sexual dysfunctions. Treatment was often ineffective and costly. Insight gained in therapy did not always lead to behavioral change. The analytic technique was limited in its ability to make direct therapeutic intervention.

Several other theoretical models developed that seemed better adapted to helping patients with sexual problems. One such model, behavior therapy, provided clinicians with therapeutic techniques that could be directly applied to the treatment of sexual dysfunctions. Arnold Lazarus and Joseph Wolpe were pioneers in the development of behavior therapy in its applications in sex therapy. Basic to their behavior therapy was a learning-theory model, which viewed behavior as a function of its consequences. Maladaptive behavior is maintained by positive and negative reinforcers. Sexual dysfunction could be seen as a learned behavior that is maintained internally by performance anxiety and externally by a nonreinforcing environment. This view of the cause and maintenance of sexual dysfunctions is quite different from the psychodynamic model.

The social-learning-theory model was responsible for the development of a number of sex therapy techniques, including systematic desensitization and relaxation training, that targeted the anxiety response that surrounded inadequate sexual functioning. Patients often achieved adequate sexual functioning by overcoming anxiety about sexual performance. Reeducation of the patient was undertaken with an active role of the patient in treatment being essential. Negative habits were unlearned, new adaptive repertoires of behavior were strengthened, and fear of failure was diminished. The work of Joseph LoPiccolo was important in the development of behavioral sex therapy techniques.

Key to the development of much of modern sex therapy was the research of Masters and Johnson. They not only gave a better physiological understanding of sexual function but also developed new psychosocial approaches to treatment. They introduced the use of conjoint treatment teams into the therapeutic milieu. They also emphasized treating both partners, as the sexual problem was seen as a couple's problem rather than an individual one. Masters and Johnson viewed sex as a natural function, one that cannot be learned, but a person could be helped by removing the obstacles that interfered with normal sexual reflexes and functioning. Masters and Johnson posited that a host of influences, including cultural conditioning, family and childhood attitudes about sex, religious attitudes, poor communication skills, and many other circumstances contributed to the development of sexual dysfunction.

Shortly after the pioneering work of Masters and Johnson, a significant contribution to the treatment of sexual problems was made by Kaplan. Her approach, as developed in her 1974 book *The New Sex Therapy,* provided an integration of behavioral techniques along with a psychodynamic understanding of sexual problems. Kaplan also provided a method of continuing assessment of the levels of the problem that allowed for intervention along both behavioral and psychodynamic lines. Medical aspects of dysfunctions were carefully evaluated, and the use of medication in treatment became an option as ongoing research was conducted into a better understanding of the pharmacology of sexual functioning.

The importance of cognitive aspects in the development and maintenance of sexual problems was stressed by Lazarus. He also introduced the use of imagery techniques in treatment. In conducting a functional analysis of the presenting problem, Lazarus was impressed with the interplay of a number of modalities that are important for treatment that were absent or not emphasized in existing systems. His multimodal therapeutic approach included a variety of assessment areas that spelled the acronym BASIC ID. This useful conceptual and intervention perspective took into account the complexity of the individual's sexual behaviors, affects, sensations, images, and cognitions, as well as the important interpersonal and biological (drug) components of sexual functioning. Lazarus's focus on some of the nonsexual aspects of a couple's relationship, especially communication, has proven helpful in treatment outcome. Such an approach is in line with Lief's statement that "it is impossible to be a competent sex therapist without being a capable marital therapist."

The emphasis on the couple dyad is also the focus of the family-systems-theory approach to treatment, which holds that sexual partners can create a sexually destructive environment through dysfunctional and pathological transactions between them. In this view, sexual functioning is restored by improving the interaction between partners.

Assessment

Adequate treatment cannot be undertaken without a thorough evaluation and assessment of the presenting sexual complaint. This assessment includes a thorough history of the complaint and appropriate diagnostic examinations, including physical examinations by appropriate medical specialists to rule out the presence of organic conditions that frequently are the cause of sexual dysfunction. For example, the sexual complaint could be the result of a disease process, such as diabetes, or could represent the presence of a problem in the nervous or endocrine systems. Medication side effects must be considered. Psychological evaluation should rule out the presence of an emotional condition that could be the basis of the sexual complaint. An evaluation of the relationship, if there is a couple involved, for the presence of other sexual or nonsexual concerns and stresses is important. This is especially important when dealing with dual-career couples who face the stress of the demands of career and family or child-rearing responsibilities. Only when an adequate assessment has been made can treatment planning and appropriate intervention begin.

The taking of a sex history, as pioneered by Alfred Kinsey, Wardell Pomeroy, and Clyde Martin, is one of the most important aspects of evaluation of sexual problems. The initial requirement in coming to an understanding of the presenting sexual problem is a detailed history of the current difficulty: this would include how and when and under what circumstances the problem began, whether there was a sudden situational reaction or a gradual onset of symptoms, the circumstances that contribute to the maintenance of the problem, and whether there is an internal state, such as anxiety or negative cognitions, or external negative reinforcers, such as a dysfunctional relationship or even ignorance about normal sexual functioning. It is also important to find out what the person's understanding of the problem is; what has previously been tried to remedy the situation; under what circumstances the problem occurs and under what circumstances, if any, the problem does not occur; and if there are other sexual dysfunctions present.

Information gained from an evaluation of the chief complaint helps the clinician better understand the presenting problem in terms of its being a sexual concern. This can range from incorrect information about sexuality to a communication problem between sexual partners to a sexual dysfunction such as erectile failure, which may require a specific treatment intervention.

Personal and historical information is also needed to complete the sexual history and to aid in placing the sexual complaint into proper context.

The intention of the personal sex history is to gather facts about the person's background and experiences that influenced how they got to be where they are in terms of sexual experience, sexual attitudes, and values. Therefore, the clinician will review historical and developmental topics, including family background, religious and family attitudes and values about sex, presence or absence of sex discussion at home, and how sexual curiosity was dealt with. The therapist needs to find out if the client experienced any sexual traumas, such as molestation, rape, or incest, the age of first experience of sexual feelings and how they were dealt with; sexual experience during puberty and adolescence; experiences with masturbation and orgasm; and guilt about sexual feelings, thoughts, or activity. Continuing the questioning, the therapist needs to find out what the individual feels about being a male or female, confusion about sexual orientation, content of sexual dreams and fantasies, homosexual or lesbian experiences, early and later dating experiences, marital and extra-marital relationships, personal experience with intercourse from both the emotional and the physical perspective, information about pregnancies and abortions, the existence of variants of sexual behavior or disorders (paraphilias or "perversions"), and use of erotic material or pornography. Though this long listing might seem comprehensive, it is only a partial list of many of the topics contained in a complete sexual history. Often, the clinician may not take a detailed history because of time constraints or a judgment that an intervention can be made from information already available.

Sexual Problems and Therapy

Sexual concerns and difficulties can exist both for individuals and in relationships even when no sexual dysfunctions are present. For example, the person may be having sexual problems because he or she is missing important information about sexual functioning. Sexual ignorance can be eliminated at times by appropriate and accurate sex education or by consulting specialists in the field.

Many sexual concerns are centered around issues of what type of sexual feelings and behavior are "normal," concerns about body image (especially after mastectomy or similar surgery), sexual function after a prostatectomy, fear about aging, rejection by a partner, and religious guilt about sex. Most such concerns are readily diminished by education and counseling.

Sexual difficulties refer to the relational and feeling aspects of sexuality and usually not to sexual functioning. Such difficulties are often the cause for much unhappiness in relationships and are a frequent reason for bringing people to the office of a sex therapist. Examples of sexual difficulties commonly experienced are frequency and type of sexual activity, timing and settings for sex, amount of foreplay preceding intercourse, the extent of a couple's sexual repertoire, coital positions, type and timing of orgasms, afterplay following coitus, and the role of passion and affection in the sexual relationship. These and many other sexual difficulties are often the targets for intervention in sex therapy, and, in the absence of complications, such as serious personality disorders, the therapist can deal with them by giving information or introducing specific sex techniques.

Sexual dysfunctions refer to the occurrence of sexual inability or inadequacy to function within the human sexual response cycle—the usual sequence of internal and emotional feelings that accompany sexual behavior as well as the physical changes that are part of sexual response. These are often summarized by using the acronym DAVOS, standing for sexual desire, arousal, vasocongestion, orgasm, and satisfaction.

Dysfunctions can exist anywhere along the continuum of DAVOS and can represent problems ranging from low levels of desire to inhibition of sexual desire, erection and ejaculation dysfunctions (too early or too late), inhibition of orgasm in women, and painful intercourse (dyspareunia), often caused by inadequate vaginal lubrication or involuntary constriction of musculature surrounding the vagina (vaginismus). The causes of these dysfunctions may be organic (physical or drug related) or psychological (including relational and environmental), and once a proper evaluation has been conducted, sex therapy can address both the causal and the ongoing aspects of the problem.

The practice of sex therapy can follow a number of theoretical and conceptual models and may involve both individual and couple formats. The therapy may be conducted by an individual practitioner or by a co-therapy pair of clinicians, usually a male and a female. The length of treatment varies, but sex therapy is usually conducted in a short-term format that is symptom focused and flexible in its approach. There are times, however, when the therapy uncovers additional material that may require further exploration by the therapist. As in any other therapy, resistance to change is often encountered, and attention will need to be focused on overcoming the resistance in order to move on with treatment.

One of the problems facing all therapists has been determining the extent and depth of therapy necessary to address the problem in order to effect change. Traditional models of treatment, as in the psychoanalytic model, spent much time uncovering material that may or may not have been related to or important to the therapy outcome. With the advent of behavior-therapy techniques, treatment should be both shorter and symptom focused. A combination of techniques, specifically applied, such as in multimodal therapy, should reduce treatment time. Still, a conceptualization of how and when to intervene is needed.

The PLISSIT model developed by Annon provides a way of looking at the presenting problem and suggesting the breadth of treatment initially needed. The model consists of level of intervention; permission giving; providing limited information about the problem or what to do; specific suggestions, which may include specific techniques to overcome the problem; and intensive therapy, required by relatively few cases, which either do not respond to earlier therapeutic attempts or, in the therapist's judgment, require a period of psychotherapy before sex therapy can be undertaken. Most sex therapy tends to use a combination of approaches that fairly approximates the PLISSIT model , even if the therapist is not consciously applying Annon's formula.

Most sex therapy techniques have as their goal a reduction in the level of anxiety that has developed over the course of the problem. In addition to commonly used couple's therapy techniques, such as communication enhancement and clarification and assertiveness training, sex therapy seeks to educate and review negative sexual scripts that have accrued over the years as a result of the person's upbringing and sexual history.

Several specific sex therapy techniques that are frequently used are sensate-focus exercises (touching and massage that concentrate on sensual contact and not performance or arousal demands); masturbation exercises to enhance confidence in obtaining and maintaining erections and gaining control over ejaculation; guided imagery and self-hypnosis exercises to increase confidence in sexual functioning; graduated exercises that move a couple closer to the desired behavior, but avoiding emphasis on performance; vibrators as an aid in achieving orgasm in cases of inhibited female orgasm; exposure to erotic material as a means of enhancing arousal and disinhibiting anxiety about sexual activities; and use of specific medications and surgical implants for the treatment of impotence (penile prosthesis implants).

Sex therapy techniques are not to be randomly applied but are part of the overall treatment plan, in which the patient is informed and guided by the therapist throughout the process. The sex therapist should be a therapist first and should be prepared to change and direct the therapy as determined by the demands and needs of treatment. The field of sex therapy is a young but rapidly growing one, with much research being conducted around the world. The recent availability to the public of accurate sexual information and a greater openness to the discussion of sexual issues has allowed many people to overcome their sexual difficulties on their own initiative. Others, motivated by an acceptance of the naturalness of sex and the right to enjoy one's sexuality, have felt free to consult professional sex therapists for the assistance that they need. Still others, uncomfortable with the perceived stigma of seeking assistance from a mental health professional, continue to suffer their difficulties with no attempt at correction. Finally, there is a large portion of society that has not labeled their sexual functioning and relationships as being problematic but yet are not experiencing the level of sexual satisfaction that could be theirs.

REFERENCES

Annon, J. *The Behavioral Treatment of Sexual Problems.* 2 vols. Honolulu: Enabling Systems, 1975, 1976.

Frank, E., et al. Frequency of Sexual Dysfunction in a "Normal" Couple. *New England Journal of Medicine,* Vol. 299 (1978), pp. 111–15.

Kaplan, H. *The New Sex Therapy.* New York: Brunner/Mazel, 1974.

Lazarus, A. *The Practice of Multimodal Therapy.* New York: McGraw-Hill, 1981.

Lief, H. Foreword. In S. Leiblum and L. Pervin, eds., *Principles and Practice of Sex Therapy.* New York: Guilford, 1980.

Masters, W., and V. Johnson. *Human Sexual Inadequacy.* Boston: Little, Brown, 1970.

———. *Human Sexual Response.* Boston: Little, Brown, 1966.

Pomeroy, W., C. Flax, and C. Wheeler. *Taking a Sex History.* New York: The Free Press, 1982.

Julian W. Slowinski

TOUCH AND SEXUALITY

It has been unusual for the majority of college-level human sexuality texts to discuss the topic of touch, except in the most cursory of descriptions. Most of these texts do not have the word "touch" in their index. Few have more than a page or two on the subject. This is dismaying, for a couple of reasons. The most obvious is that the expression of much of our sexuality occurs through touch and the largest organ of our body, our skin. Also, there is a growing body of writings, theory, and research in the field of touch that is of extreme importance to the studies of human development, health, and sexuality. The contributors to this body of work span the fields of philosophy, medicine, physiology, psychology, sociology, and anthropology. This article is a summary and synthesis of this work, with a special emphasis on the findings related to touch and human sexuality.

Touch and Childhood Development

Arguably, it was not until the appearance of the clinical reports by Spitz (in 1945 and 1947) that the seeds of research in the field of touch were sown. Spitz's reports reflect his anguished quest for a solution to the unexplained deaths and pathologies of infants and toddlers in his care. The diagnosis of that era for these terminal children was marasmus, the withering away and dying of no apparent cause. Spitz finally discovered that medicine, good nutrition, and clean surroundings had not the least impact on the tragic outcome. Only what Harlow was to later call contact comfort turned out to be the "cure" for the excruciating deaths of these children. Touch deprivation is probably most damaging to an infant because, unlike the other four senses, the neonate has an extremely small amount of control over somatosensory self-stimulation due to underdeveloped motor control capacities.

In the arena of social behavior and mother-offspring relationships, Harlow could easily and appropriately be called the "father of touch research." His "deprivation and wire mother" primate research remains one of those classic studies in the evolving history of psychology. However, we are only recently discovering just how important Harlow's work was.

Prior to Harlow's research, Freudian thought dominated, even in the informal field of touch. It was generally believed that touch is a somewhat minor component of the more important feeding process provided by a mother to her child. Mother-child attachment (or bonding) was assumed to occur in humans as a primary result of the mother providing food to the infant.

Harlow's studies done between 1962 and 1979 involved taking newborn monkeys from their mothers and raising them in isolation. The young monkeys were deprived of maternal and social touch (i.e., contact comfort). In every other way, the monkeys were very well cared for. They were well fed, their cages kept clean, and their medical needs attended to. They were "merely" isolated from any physical contact with their mother or other monkeys. Even physical contact with the researchers was severely limited.

In his original classic "wire mother" study, Harlow placed the touch-deprived monkeys in a large cage that contained two crude dummy monkeys constructed of wood and chicken wire. One dummy was bare wire with a full baby bottle attached. The monkeys had been regularly nursed from similar bottles. The other dummy was the same as the first, except that it contained no bottle and the chicken wire was wrapped with terry cloth. Placed in this strange environment, the anxious young monkey very quickly attached itself to the cloth-wrapped dummy and continued to cling to it as the hours passed. The infant monkey could easily see the familiar baby bottle no more than a few feet away on the other dummy. Many hours passed. Although growing increasingly distraught and hungry, the infants in these studies would not release their hold on the soft cloth of the foodless dummy. It was soon apparent that the young monkeys would likely dehydrate and starve before abandoning the terry cloth surrogate mother.

As the isolated monkeys grew older, they were observed to display a highly predictable constellation of behavioral symptoms, even when they were later reunited with their mother and social group. They included highly unusual patterns of self-clasping and self-orality; idiosyncratic patterns of repetitive stereotyped activity; an almost total lack of gregariousness or interest in exploring the environment; timidity and withdrawal from virtually all social situations, with concomitant self-directed stereotyped behaviors; obvious aversion to physical contact with others; hyperaggressivity; gross abnormalities in sexual behaviors; and, later in adulthood, the inability to nurture offspring, with failure to nurse, neglect, and abusive behaviors being highly predictable. In addition, negative physical health consequences and hormonal imbalances were noted in these primate studies.

Additional studies by the Harlow team and others clearly demonstrated that the psychoanalytic "wisdom" of the day was incorrect in its assumptions regarding mother-child attachment. At least with infant and young monkeys, there appeared to be a hunger more powerful than the craving for food. It was science's first view of the pervasiveness and intensity of "touch hunger."

Beginning in the same general era as the Harlow investigations was another direction of research in the area of mother-child attachment. These attachment-theory studies were conducted by the British scientist Bowlby and his American colleague, Ainsworth. As a major extension of the work of Lorenz, their investigations focused directly on the ways human mothers and infants succeeded or failed to bond to one another. In general, Bowlby and Ainsworth discovered that there are highly predictable outcomes to the differing styles of early mother-child attachment patterns. More than two decades of scientific research on human parents and their offspring has generated a wealth of vital information regarding essential requirements for normal human development. Affectionate touch versus neglect or punishing touch is a central theme of attachment theory, and much of this work may be viewed as the human research counterpart to the Harlow studies.

Long before infants develop a useful vocabulary, they employ innate and powerful methods to communicate moods, interests, and needs to their caretakers. This is accomplished with a splendid and increasingly sophisticated variety of sounds, movements, and facial expressions. It is a difficult struggle for any infant to teach its parents about himself or herself. However, we know that babies are universally good "teachers." Sadly though, it has been discovered that most parents and caretakers in the United States are less than adequate "students." As with all good teachers, if you have a poor student the teacher must work harder to help the student learn.

Bowlby and Ainsworth learned that, for healthy parent-child attachments, the parent was a good "student." These parents usually noticed, understood, and responded appropriately to the "lessons" offered by the infant or toddler. Almost all the infants' lessons involved touch. They signal to their parents to "pick me up, hold me, feed me, burp me, soothe me, stimulate me, change me, and make the pain or discomfort go away." Of course, occasionally the signal was, "I'm overstimulated, so please leave me alone for a few minutes." These healthy "parent students" and "child teachers" are synchronized to each other, communicating and learning in a rhythm of increasing complexity.

It was found that, for the "inadequately attached" parent and child, there is a great deal of obvious neglect of the offspring by the parent. The parent "students" usually are uninterested in the lessons offered by their daughter or son and generally ignore the signals of the child. When the infant "teacher" tries even harder to interest these parents, the mother or father usually responds with even more neglect or with verbal or physical abuse. These infants rapidly become impatient teachers and the home "classroom" is filled with the turmoil of rapidly escalating frustration of teacher and student. Within the first year or two, these children eventually give up most efforts to "teach," learn to suppress their signals for attention, and are likely to become sullen, chronically miserable, or ill. Whichever child responses occur, the outcome is commonly devastating on many levels for the child, the parent–child attachment, and subsequent relationships as the child grows to adulthood. Grade schools and high schools are filled with severely withdrawn and troublesome, acting-out children and teens who have given up hope of affectionate pleasure and happiness.

Ainsworth's third category of the "anxiously attached" child is not a median category somewhere between the "adequate" and "inadequate" attachment classifications. The parent of the anxiously attached child may sometimes appear to be a "supermom" or "superdad," in that they tend to hold and give just as much, or more, attention to their child than do the parents of the healthy attachment children. The primary difference is that these, like the inadequate attachment parents, are also very poor parent "students." They and their child are, more often than not, out of synchronization with one another. This frequently "overinvolved" parent is not actually responding to the signals of the child, but instead responds to his or her own personal needs and desires. Because these parents are busily working at trying to care for the child, the toss of the dice says that the parent and child will occasionally be in synch and the child's needs will be met. When this occurs, it confuses the child into believing that the parent is finally "getting it," only to be followed by the majority of situations in which the child's signals are unanswered (or incorrectly answered). The randomly reinforced and anxiously attached child usually does not give up, even though it may be in her or his best interest. In a frustrated and disconsolate manner, the child continues to try to get through to the unreceptive parent and will likely continue these patterns into adulthood with poor choices of enabling relationships.

These studies reveal that the potential for a great deal of psychological human damage occurs at a very early age. Essential aspects of development, including, most importantly, sexual-affectional development, is arrested or severely damaged. In the United States, some researchers estimate that only about 25 percent of children come from a functional home in which adequate attachment occurs.

In the early 1970s, Prescott had been engaged in brain research studying the effects of touch deprivation on laboratory animals. He suspected that neurological deterioration, which had been found to be a predictable sequela to touch deprivation, was also a central and etiological agent in the expression of the violent behavior, as noted by Harlow.

Using the Human Relations Area Files, he examined some 400 societies and concluded that those societies that lavish affectionate touch on their infants and children, and also are tolerant or encouraging of adolescent sexual-affectional behaviors, were the least violent societies on earth, with the converse also being true. His findings, however, remain controversial because the data in the files do not usually give the kind of information he sought, and others who examined them did not classify the data the same way. Still, the fact that American society is often violent as well as one of the least openly physically affectionate societies on this planet might give some support to Prescott's ideas. We do not lavish affectionate touch on our infants and children; we push them aside into high chairs, playpens, car seats, baby beds, their rooms, the backyard, and so forth. We throw toys to them, and we expect television and video games to occupy their time. Moreover, in the United States, we have endless proscriptions against adolescent sexual-affectional behaviors. From very early childhood, the parental admonition, "Don't touch!" has been a powerful one. But just when the pubescent child begins the important physiological changes of puberty and the psychological separation-individuation task, our society warns, "Don't touch anyone, don't let anyone touch you, and don't touch yourself."

Since the normally developing adolescent is increasingly less interested in parental touch and more interested in touch and other forms of interaction with his or her peers, the obedient girl or boy is therefore effectively sentenced to several years of extreme touch deprivation and arrested psychological development. That the majority of teenagers eventually, to some degree, ignore these parental and societal warnings actually results in placing today's teens at higher risk for anxiety, depression, unwanted pregnancy, and sexually transmitted diseases due to "sex guilt." Research by Mosher and his colleagues demonstrates that sex guilt is powerfully related to the avoidance of self-care as well as lower self-esteem. In the United States, we have decided, with no data whatsoever, to support our strongly held beliefs that adolescents are "too immature" to deal with a sexual-affectional relationship. Actual developmental research has largely avoided this topic, although opinions are abundant.

Other researchers have found that the affectional touch climate in the subject's family of origin and parental religiosity are the major psychosocial variables related to a person's current sexual attitudes and behaviors, as well as nongenital affectional behaviors with a partner. Subjects who originated from physically affectionate families were more likely to enjoy more pleasurable, and more frequent, experiences in the sexual-affectional aspects of their adult relationships. These studies clearly demonstrate that adults who experienced rejection and touch deprivation in their childhood tend to treat their adult partners and their own offspring in a similar manner.

The rich findings of the Harlow and Bowlby-Ainsworth research teams, coupled with the reports of Spitz and Prescott, have complemented, and in many ways paralleled, each other. The outcomes of these studies provide clear facts regarding the most central components of human development and relationships. Whether in part or taken as a whole, the results from these findings lead to one inescapable conclusion. That is, the quality of our relationships throughout our lives is massively affected by the quality of our attachments in infancy and early childhood. The quality of these early attachments is primarily influenced by specific aspects of the communication and touch relationship between the child and his or her primary caretakers.

Developmental Neuropsychology of Touch

On the day of our birth, we entered the world with an intense touch hunger. Of all of our neonate senses, neural pathways subserving cutaneous sensation and responses to somasthetic stimulation are the first to develop in the human fetus and infant. Physiological primatologists instruct that the organism's biological systems that are first to develop are those most necessary to survival. A substantial proportion of the central and peripheral nervous systems is dedicated to the reception and processing of somatosensory information and make up what have been labeled "topographic maps" of nervous system utilization. The neonate derives the vast majority of useful information for the first several months of life through his or her skin.

Touch deprivation and somasthetic stress (e.g., pain and "touch trauma") are rapidly followed by dramatic elevations in pituitary-adrenal plasma cortisol levels, while affectionate and soothing touch are associated with low serum plasma cortisol levels. Plasma cortisol levels have been shown to be a reliable physiological indicator of an organism's detection of environmental change or stress. Further, it has been shown that with chronic imbalances of plasma cortisol and other hormones and neurochemicals, there results abnormal brain tissue development as well as the destruction of previously normal brain tissue. In other words, frequent pleasurable touch results in positive changes in brain tissue, and chronic touch deprivation or trauma results in measurably significant brain damage.

Beyond the study of body chemicals and neural tissue, it has been discovered that pleasurable touch is associated with enhanced learning, improved IQ, language acquisition, reading achievement, memory, general neonate development, preterm infant development, reduced self-mutilating behavior in the severely mentally retarded, expanded external awareness in autistic patients, improved geriatric health, decreased childhood clinginess and fears of exploring the environment, elimination of inappropriate self-stimulation and public masturbation behavior in children, and improved visual-spatial problem solving. Hospitalized patients recover more rapidly from injury and physical or psychiatric illness with attention to touch needs. Current thinking defines touch as the primary organizer (or, in the case of neglect and abuse, "disorganizer") of normal human development when viewed at biological, psychological and even social levels. A person's sense of self apparently originates in body awareness, body functions, and body activities that center around the sense of touch

For this reason, the writer often refers his partnerless and isolated psychotherapy clients to a masseuse or massage therapist whenever appropriate. Couples in treatment are usually instructed and assigned touch and massage homework exercises, even for the non–sex therapy clients. Although Masters and Johnson borrowed extensively from researched therapy techniques developed by others when constructing their broad sex therapy treatment regimen, the unique technique they called sensate focus was one of their most important contributions. Perhaps unknowingly borrowing from the treatment methods of physical therapists and speech therapists who deal with their patient's neurological damage, Masters and Johnson devised a method of graduated, lengthy, and redundant touch exercises for their patients.

The neurological damage discussed in this chapter is, by definition, permanent damage since the brain produces no new nerve cells beyond about age five. Fortunately, if the neurological damage is not too severe, the remaining healthy portions of the brain may be "taught" to recover functioning, given the appropriate treatment method. The highly motivated individual or couple can begin to engage in specific graduated and frequent touch exercises to improve receptivity, sensation, and functioning. Masters and Johnson and the large body of subsequent sex therapy research provides potentially important solutions to a large and multiaxial problem for those individuals and societies that seek answers to repairing the damage. Of course, the most obvious solution would be to change the child-rearing practices of those same individuals and societies. To say, "All we need is to be receptive and affectionate with our children," though correct, may miss the greatest obstacle to this major change. That most parents are not neurologically receptive to reciprocal affectionate touch with their child is only one, though important, dilemma.

An Obstacle to Affection

In its most rigid and fundamentalist form, the Judeo-Christian philosophy is staunchly antitouch, anti-body, antipleasure, and antisexual. To our not-so-distant ancestors, the formula touch equals sex equals sin was a bromide to live by. This nonequation is now our cultural heritage in the United States. Some may argue that this is an overstatement of the present-day importance of a dying or changing philosophy. Some may feel a bit smugly insulated because their upbringing did not include a highly fundamentalist or highly orthodox religiosity.

One of the outcomes of prolonged touch deprivation and the resulting neurological deterioration is a hypersensitivity to touch. Some researchers propose that the average person's experience with affectionate touch in the United States and several other countries is so inadequate that it is almost a certainty that the majority of the citizens suffer from some degree of significant neurological impairment. This is especially true if you are male, since males in the United States tend to receive far less affectionate touch from birth than do females. By early adulthood, most of these males have as much or more experience with overstimulating, aversive, painful, and traumatic touch than with soothing and affectionate touch. Even though they move through life with a growing touch hunger, most of these males can tolerate prolonged physical contact with another human only if forced or if they are sexually aroused.

So the cultural philosophy that may have initiated our ancestor's avoidance of touch may not be as important a maintaining factor as some might believe. It is possibly not the direct impact of religious philosophies today that causes a culture to be relatively touch phobic but, rather, a long history of parents who, due to the neurological damage unknowingly inflicted by their parents, were hypersensitive to touch and therefore did not nurture their offspring with the necessary somatosensory stimulation. Highly religious homes tend to provide significantly less affectionate touch (and more punishing touch), beginning in late childhood as the child approaches puberty and more overt sexuality.

For many adults, highly fundamentalist religions probably become an attraction for those who are most touch and sex phobic. The child of the high-religiosity parent or parents will likely experience significantly more difficulty with affectionate touch and sexuality in their adult relationships, even if the offspring no longer subscribe to their parents' beliefs.

We are beginning to understand many more of the developmental issues that impact on our attempts at healthy sexuality and relationships. Touch experiences in childhood appear to be powerful determining influences.

Many people tell of their highly interested and attentive lovers (mostly male) who seem to disappear very soon after orgasm occurs. He or she rolls away, goes to sleep, or gets up, grabs a beer, and goes to the den to watch the ball game—without even saying goodbye. Without the benefit of continuing high levels of sexual arousal, he can no longer tolerate prolonged tactile contact. One report of touch-deprived women revealed that only a tiny percent had ever had an orgasm. A study of touch-deprived men revealed that when given the hypothetical choice between giving up their recreational drugs and alcohol and giving up sex and orgasm, almost all of them said they would give up sex and orgasm. It seems that those who harbor these conflicts between a strong desire for touch and the confusing discomfort with it resolve the conflict by avoiding the difficulties and discomforts associated with touch and finding a replacement in the form of behaviors and chemicals, prescription and nonprescription. Such palliatives ultimately pile brain damage upon brain damage.

Virtually everyone has an intense need to be held and soothed and stimulated, but we find ourselves receptive at relatively brief moments of our lives. If we are not receptive to a given touch, the effect is deleterious rather than ben-

585

eficial. So it is that we do not hold our partners or our infants for very long or very often.

In addition, the United States culture has created handy myths and philosophical constructs that merely serve our touch discomforts. Most parents are too easily convinced that they will "spoil" the child if they run to her "too quickly" when she cries or hold him "too often" or for "too long." We find a substantial percentage of parents who justify their homophobia by withdrawing meager affectionate touch from their toddlers and young children, stating, "Well, I don't want him to turn out homosexual." Some of our incorrect theories of the past are still with us, perhaps doing more damage than ever. Antitouch and antisexual societies have spawned fathers who panic if they happen to experience sexual arousal with their child squirming on their lap, and essentially punish the child severely by withdrawing physical affection from his daughter or son. Worse still is the father who acts on his sexual arousal, using the child as the defenseless object.

REFERENCES

Ainsworth, M.D.S., M.C. Blehar, E. Waters, and S. Wall. *Patterns of Attachment: A Psychological Study of the Strange Situation*. Hillsdale, N.J.: Erlbaum, 1978.

Ainsworth, M.D.S., and B.A. Wittig. Attachment and Exploratory Behavior of One Year Olds in a Strange Situation. In B.M. Foss, ed., *Determinants of Infant Behavior*. Vol. 4. London: Methuen, 1969.

Barnard, K.E., and T.B. Brazelton, eds. *Touch: The Foundation of Experience*. Madison, Conn.: International Universities Press, 1990.

Bowlby, J. *Attachment and Loss*. 3 vols. London: Hogarth Press, 1969, 1973, 1980.

————. Some Pathological Processes Set in Train by Early Mother-Child Separation. *Journal of Mental Science*, Vol. 99 (1953), pp. 265–72.

Brown, C.C., ed. *The Many Facets of Touch*. Skillman, N.J.: Johnson and Johnson, 1984.

Colton, H. *Touch Therapy*. New York: Kensington, 1983.

Diamond, M.C. Cortical Change in Response to Environmental Enrichment and Impoverishment. In C.C. Brown, ed., *The Many Facets of Touch*. Skillman, N.J.: Johnson and Johnson, 1984.

————. Evidence for Tactile Stimulation Improving CNS Function. In K.E. Barnard and T.B. Brazelton, eds., *Touch: The Foundation of Experience*. Madison, Conn.: International Universities Press, 1990.

Diamond, M.C., R.E. Johnson, and C.A. Ingham. Morphological Changes in the Young, Adult, and Aging Rat Cerebral Cortex, Hippocampus, and Diencephalon. *Behavioral Biology*, Vol. 14 (1975), pp. 163–74.

Diamond, M.C., F. Law, B. Lindner, M.R. Rosenzweig, D. Krech, and E.L. Bennett. Increases in Cortical Depth and Glial Numbers. *Journal of Comparative Neurology*, Vol. 128 (1966), pp. 117–26.

Emde, R.N., and R.J. Harmon, eds. *The Development of Attachment and Affiliative Systems*. New York: Plenum Press, 1982.

Fisher, J.D., and S.J. Gallant. Effect of Touch on Hospitalized Patients. In N. Gunzenhauser, ed., *Advances in Touch: New Implications in Human Development*. Skillman, N.J.: Johnson and Johnson, 1990.

Fisher, S., and S.F. Cleveland. *Body Image and Personality*. 2d ed. New York: Dover, 1968.

Freud, S. The Development of the Sexual Function. In *An Outline of Psychoanalysis*. New York: W.W. Norton, 1949.

Gunzenhauser, N., ed. *Advances in Touch: New Implications in Human Development*. Skillman, N.J.: Johnson and Johnson, 1990.

Harlow, H.F. The Heterosexual Affectional System in Monkeys. *American Psychologist*, Vol. 17 (1962), pp. 1–9.

————. Lust, Latency, and Love: Simian Secrets of Successful Sex. *Journal of Sex Research*, Vol. 11 (1975), pp. 79–90.

————. The Nature of Love. *American Psychologist*, Vol. 13 (1958), pp. 673–85.

Harlow, H.F., et al. From Thought to Therapy. *American Scientist*, Vol. 59 (1971), pp. 538–49.

Harlow, H.F., and M.K. Harlow. The Effects of Rearing Conditions on Behavior. *Bulletin of the Menninger Clinic*, Vol. 26 (1962), pp. 213–24.

Harlow, H.F., and C. Mears. *The Human Model: Primate Perspectives*. Washington, D.C.: Winston, 1979.

Harlow, H.F., and M.A. Novak. Psychopathological Perspectives. *Perspectives in Biology and Medicine*, Vol. 16 (1973), pp. 461–78.

Harlow, H.F., and S.J. Suomi. Nature of Love: Simplified. *American Psychologist*, Vol. 25 (1970), pp. 161–68.

Hatfield, R.W. Sexual Intimacies and Affection in Adulthood as Determined by Family Religiousness and Child-rearing Practices. Ph.D. diss., University of Cincinnati, 1986.

Kinsey, A.C., W.B. Pomeroy, C.E. Martin, and P.H. Gebhard. *Sexual Behavior in the Human Female*. Philadelphia: Saunders, 1953.

————. W.B. Pomeroy, and C.E. Martin. *Sexual Behavior in the Human Male*. Philadelphia: Saunders, 1946.

Klaus, M.H., T. Leger, and M.A. Trause, eds. *Maternal Attachment and Mothering Disorders*. Skillman, N.J.: Johnson and Johnson, 1982.

Lorenz, K. *King Solomon's Ring*. London: Methuen, 1952.

Masters, W.H., and V.E. Johnson. *Human Sexual Inadequacy*. Boston: Little, Brown, 1970.

————. *Human Sexual Response*. Boston: Little, Brown, 1966.

Merzinich, M.M., and J.H. Kaas. Principles of Organization of Sensory-Perceptual Systems in Mammals. In J.M. Sprague and A.N. Epstein, eds., *Progress in Psychobiology and Physiological Psychology*, Vol. 9. New York: Academic Press, 1980.

Money, J., and A.A. Ehrhardt. *Man and Woman, Boy and Girl*. Baltimore: Johns Hopkins Univ. Press, 1972.

Montague, A. *Touching: The Human Significance of the Skin*. 2d ed. New York: Harper & Row, 1978.

Mosher, D.L. Measurement of Guilt in Females by Self-Report Inventories. *Journal of Consulting and Clinical Psychology*, Vol. 32 (1968), pp. 690–95.

———. Sex Guilt and Sex Myths in College Men and Women. *Journal of Sex Research*, Vol. 15 (1979), pp. 224–34.

Novak, M.A., and H.F. Harlow. Social Recovery of Monkeys Isolated for the First Year of Life: 1. Rehabilitation and Therapy. *Developmental Psychology*, Vol. 11 (1975), pp. 453–65.

Prescott, J.W. Early Somatosensory Deprivation as an Ontogenic Process in the Abnormal Development of Brain and Behavior. In E. Goldsmith and J. Morr-Jankowski, eds., *Medical Primatology*. Basel: Karger, 1970.

———. Somatosensory Affectional Deprivation (SAD) Theory of Drug and Alcohol Use. National Institute on Drug Abuse Research Monograph Series, no. 30, 1980.

Prescott, J.W., and D.H. Wallace. Body Pleasure and the Origins of Violence. *Bulletin of the Atomic Scientists*, Vol. 11 (1975), pp. 10–20.

Reite, M., and T. Fields, eds. *The Psychobiology of Attachment*. New York: Academic Press, 1987.

Shaver, P., C. Hazan, and D. Bradshaw. Love as Attachment. In R.J. Sternberg and M.L. Barnes, eds., *The Psychology of Love*. New Haven: Yale Univ. Press, 1988.

Spitz, R.A. Hospitalism: A Follow-up Report. In D. Fenichel, P. Greenacre, and A. Freud, eds., *The Psychoanalytic Study of the Child*, Vol. 2. New York: International Universities Press, 1947.

———. *The Psychoanalytic Study of the Child*. 4 vols. New York: International Universities Press, 1945–49.

Suomi, S.J. The Role of Tactile Contact in Rhesus Monkey Social Development. In K.E. Barnard and T.B. Brazelton, eds., *Touch: The Foundation of Experience*. Madison, Conn.: International Universities Press, 1990.

Soumi, S.J., and H.F. Harlow. Abnormal Social Behaviors in Young Monkeys. In J. Hellmuth, ed., *Exceptional Infant: Studies in Abnormality*. Vol. 2. New York: Brunner/Mazel, 1971.

Sternberg, R.J., and M.L. Barnes. *The Psychology of Love*. New Haven: Yale Univ. Press, 1988.

Tribotti, S.J. Effects of Gentle Touch on the Premature Infant. In N. Gunzenhauser, ed., *Advances in Touch: New Implications in Human Development*. Skillman, N.J.: Johnson & Johnson, 1990.

Robert W. Hatfield

TOYS: SEX TOYS

The moniker "sex toys" has been in use less than two decades and even today is not in wide circulation. Broadly defined, it includes any object used to enhance sexual activity, whether or not the item was specifically designed or marketed for that purpose. By that broad definition, if a woman uses a hairbrush handle for vaginal stimulation, or a man masturbates with a silk handkerchief, the hairbrush and the handkerchief are sex toys. However, this discussion will be limited (with one significant exception) to objects designed, marketed, or primarily used for the purpose of sexual stimulation.

When these items are marketed in North America, they are typically called "sex aids" or "marital aids." Both of these terms suggest that potential customers need help with their sexuality, that the sex aids will make up for presumed inadequacy on the part of consumers. Use of the adjective "marital" is surely an attempt to add an air of respectability to use of these objects, the implication being that only married people actually engage in sexual activity. Because these terms were so widely used, it became a requirement of the Food and Drug Administration in the United States that certain sexual or marital aids be labeled "sold as a novelty only," assuring consumers that no therapeutic claims are being made for the use of any product so labeled.

The term "sex toys" was coined in the early 1970s at the same time women were starting to more openly acknowledge their interest in sex and were also becoming much more likely to purchase items previously usually bought for them by their husbands or male lovers. (For many years before that, cylindrical plastic battery-operated vibrators advertised and ostensibly used for facial "massage" had been sold directly to women through advertising in the backs of women's magazines.) The phrase is somewhat problematic, in that the word "toy" still refers in many people's minds exclusively to the playthings of children. Nevertheless, most people exposed to this term for the first time find it pleasing because it reintroduces playfulness into the sometimes all-too-somber sexual ideation of adults.

Dildos

Over time, the most widely recognized sex toy is the dildo, thought of by many as an artificial or substitute penis. Collectors of erotic objets d'art will be familiar with statues of male figures with often exaggerated erect penises, dating from ancient times, and similar objects produced up until the present day by certain indigenous groups in the Third World. It is unlikely that women (or men) use these carved figurines for self stimulation. A variety of cultures have produced dildos, or objects so representational of the penis that it is safe to assume that they were utilized by at least some persons for vaginal or anal stimulation. Female fertility figurines, by contrast, are much less likely to have exaggerated genitals, and there is no indication that carved or molded objects resembling vulvas were historically used as masturbation enhancers by men.

Most dildos available commercially today are mass-produced in Hong Kong (and to a significantly lesser extent in the United States, China, Germany, and Japan), and almost all of them are sold in so-called "adult" stores or by direct mail. Virtually all of them are made of malleable plastic, vinyl or latex stuffed with cotton. Some are very realistic, including a few molded from life, complete with realistic skin colors, bluish veins, and "testicles" that can be manipulated inside the "scrotum."

Some dildos are hollow and are marketed as penile prosthetic aids.

These PPAs—the term used for them in the sex industry—usually have a flimsy elastic strap at the base. The strap is worn around the hips in such a way that a man can, hypothetically, put his flaccid or semierect penis inside the dildo and engage in sexual intercourse. Since men do not readily discuss their sexual functioning with others, particularly if their sexuality is problematic, it is not known how often PPAs are employed in this manner.

Dildos come in many sizes, ranging in length from 4 inches to 12 inches and in diameter from three-quarters of an inch to two inches. Double or double-headed dildos are also available. A few specialty dildos are huge, and one is shaped like a forearm and fist. These extra-large sizes are used almost exclusively by men for anal insertion.

Dildos molded of silicone are also being manufactured in very small quantities by a handful of craftspeople. Designed and manufactured primarily for direct sales to women, these dildos include a wider range of smaller sizes, and relatively few of them resemble penises. Despite the fact they are considerably more costly than mass-produced plastic, vinyl, or latex dildos, they are quite popular because the material they are made of is very smooth, warms quickly to body temperature, and does not have an unpleasant "rubbery" odor. Throughout history, dildos produced in Japan have had fanciful designs; they are often molded to look like people or animals. One

manufacturer of the new silicone dildos includes zucchini and corn cobs, along with dolphins, human figures, and cats, among her many dildo designs.

All the silicone dildos and a few mass-produced dildos flare at the base so that they can be worn in a harness that holds the dildo in place over the pubic bone so the wearer can simulate intercourse. Flimsy vinyl and elastic dildo harnesses have been available for many years at adult stores and through mail-order catalogs that sell adult novelties. People who use dildo harnesses regularly, however, prefer the sturdier all-leather or nylon webbing harnesses. The fact that silicone dildos and leather harnesses are in demand, even though they are considerably more costly than the mass-produced varieties, suggests that many consumers now expect better quality sex toys and are willing to pay higher prices for them.

Vibrators

Today, and presumably since the invention of the hand held massagers/vibrators powered by small electric motors, women have used these devices for clitoral stimulation to generate arousal and orgasm. However, since neither women or men typically discuss their masturbatory practices, both have assumed that a woman wanting to arouse herself would simulate intercourse with an artificial penis of some sort. Only recently have women openly acknowledged that they may use their dildo-shaped vibrators for clitoral stimulation.

The earliest vibrators, and by far the majority of vibrators sold today, are essentially dildos with a small battery-operated vibrating motor inside. The resemblance of most of these hard plastic devices to an erect human penis begins and ends in the fact that they are typically seven or eight inches in length and cylindrical in shape.

A considerable range of styles of battery-operated vibrators is available. In addition to smooth or ribbed hard plastic cylindrical vibrators and softer plain, "realistic" vinyl vibrators, there are egg- and bullet-shaped vibrators and several versions of the "butterfly." The butterfly is a vibrator designed for clitoral stimulation. It is held against a woman's genitals with lightweight elastic straps encircling her hips and thighs, freeing her hands and those of her partner for other activity. Certain vibrators originating in Japan have one "branch" molded to look like a person or animal and designed to be inserted into the vagina, and a shorter "branch," usually looking like an animal, for clitoral stimulation. Like several other vibrators mentioned here, these have a separate battery pack. When they are turned on, the longer branch swivels internally and the shorter one vibrates. Some anal plugs (dildos designed for anal stimulation) are equipped with battery-driven motors as well.

Because of the surreptitious or underground way in which these products are sold in the "adult" market, and because embarrassment usually prevents dissatisfied customers from demanding recourse, little is known about customer satisfaction with these products. But judging from the number of jokes in the culture about battery-powered vibrators malfunctioning "right at the crucial moment," it is safe to assume that for many they are not particularly satisfactory.

With the invention of the electric motor, or perhaps even earlier when exposed by accident or design to other kinds of vibrating equipment or appliances, women have experienced sexual pleasure and even orgasms. For example, the treadle sewing machines, which often involved pelvic movement, were in folklore regarded by some as an erotic stimulus. The historian Maines has recently provided a wealth of information about turn-of-the-century medical treatment of "hysteria" (believed in ancient Egypt and Greece to be the revolt of the uterus against sexual deprivation) using electric vibrators. Maines shows that "the electromechanical vibrator, introduced as a medical appliance in the 1880s and as a household appliance between 1900 and 1905, represented a de-skilling and capital-labor substitution innovation designed to improve the efficiency of medical massage, a task performed since ancient times by physicians, midwives, and their assistants. Medical massage from the time of Hippocrates to that of Freud included the clinical production of orgasm in women and girls."

The object of that medical massage, whether performed with lubricated fingers or an electric vibrator, was the induction of a "hysterical paroxysm," manifested by "rapid respiration and pulse, reddening of the skin, vaginal lubrication and abdominal contractions." Apparently, not all physicians recognized these "paroxysms" as orgasms, but some medical authors through the ages commented on the morally ambiguous character of the treatment, including one physician who observed that genital massage should be reserved to "to those alone who have clean hands and a pure heart."

In 1869 and 1872, George Taylor, an American physician, patented a steam-powered massage and vibratory apparatus for treatment of female disorders, intended for supervised use to prevent overindulgence. By 1909, convenient portable models were available, permitting use on house calls. Until the end of the 1920s, vibrators were advertised in respectable women's magazines as home appliances, primarily as an aid to good health and relaxation. The sexual references in these ads were thinly disguised, since a typical ad reads, "All the pleasures of youth will throb within you."

Within a decade after that, vibrators had disappeared from doctors' offices and magazine advertisements, in part because doctors started to treat hysteria with psychotherapy, and in part because vibrators had started to appear in stag films. Seemingly, as soon as this treatment modality became associated in the popular culture with sexual arousal and pleasure, the embarrassed medical establishment turned away from its use. Since that time, line voltage, brand-name vibrators or massagers have been widely available on the shelves of many drug and department stores. Package inserts do not even hint of possible sexual uses. In fact, one brand's instruction sheet warns ominously, without explanation, "Do not use on genital areas of the body."

Three different types of line-voltage vibrators are currently on the market. One is the wand type, which has a long, cylindrical body or handle and a spherical vibrating head, attached to the body by a flexible "neck." Other vibrators are powered by an electromagnetic coil instead of a small electric motor. This type operates in virtual silence. It is shaped somewhat like a small hair dryer or a hairbrush, with the vibrating head perpendicular to the handle. It is packaged with four to six attachments, designed to massage different parts of the body. One brand-name vibrator of this type is packaged with an attachment ideal for clitoral stimulation, although that is certainly not specified in the packaging.

Vibrators that strap over the back of the hand or Swedish massagers are rarely chosen by women for sexual use, but they are strongly favored by the few men who regularly masturbate with vibrators. Presumably, this is because this is the vibrator most used by barbers for scalp and neck massage and most likely to have been found around the house when men who are now adults were children or adolescents and because the man using this kind of vibrator can do so in a manner very similar to the way he masturbates using his hand alone.

Ben-wa Balls

Ben-wa balls, two solid metal balls about three-quarters of an inch in diameter, are found in virtually every catalog of sex toys and adult stores. Though they are said to give orgasmic satisfaction when they are inserted into the vagina and the body is moved back and forth, many women say they are the most overrated of sex toys. Some report that once the balls are inserted into the vagina, they cannot be felt at all. Curiosity about ben-wa balls, like curiosity about some other sex toys, seems to persist in large measure because information about their ineffectiveness is generally not available to consumers.

Other Sex Toys

Dildos and dildo-vibrators frequently are used for anal stimulation. Safety is an important consideration here, as it is surprisingly easy for a lubricated dildo or vibrator to slip into the rectum. It is advisable to use instead an anal plug (a toy that widens in the middle and has a flared base so that it will neither fall out nor go in too far). Anal beads are a set of five or six small plastic beads strung onto a nylon cord. They are lubricated and fed into the anus one at a time and pulled out all together at the moment of orgasm to heighten the sensation.

Beyond the scope of this entry are the accessories and paraphernalia used by persons who engage in S/M sexual activities such as restraints, whips, nipple clamps, and paddles. They are mentioned here because in the S/M community, they are frequently referred to as toys.

REFERENCES

Blank, J. *Good Vibrations: The Complete Guide to Vibrators.* Burlingame, Calif.: Down There Press, 1982, 1989.

Maines, R. Socially Camouflaged Technologies: The Case of the Electromechanical Vibrator. *EEE Journal of Technology and Society,* 8:2 (June 1989), 3–11, 23.

————. The Vibrator and Its Predecessor Technologies. Paper presented at the Society for the Scientific Study of Sex, Pittsburgh, Oct. 1986.

Joani Blank

TRANSSEXUALISM

Introduction

The syndrome of transsexualism is characterized by a lifelong preference for the opposite gender role, predicated on the conviction of belonging to the opposite sex. This conviction is held and persists despite the painfully obvious fact of normal anatomy and genitalia, before and after puberty, and in the absence of delusional ideation or psychosis. Transsexuals are disgusted with the development of their primary and secondary sexual characteristics; the penis in males and breasts in females are perceived as the offensive organs, and their removal becomes a preoccupa-

tion for transsexual individuals. In addition, these desperately unhappy people seek the anatomical status of the opposite gender, and thus the hallmark of this syndrome is the request for change of sex or sex reassignment surgery (SRS). Feeling they belong to the opposite sex, they feel "unnatural" in a love relationship with someone of the opposite biological sex, considering this to be "homosexual." Perceiving themselves to be members of the opposite sex, they consider it appropriate to have a love relationship with an individual of the same biological sex but of the opposite gender identity. In recent years, we have become aware that some male-to-female transsexuals, after sex reassignment, prefer lesbian relationships with women. Only recently, this homogenderal, albeit biologically heterosexual, relationship has been described in the female-to-male situation. There is some evidence that the sexual activity per se, whether it be considered homosexual or heterogenderal, plays a minor or secondary role. Certainly, the primary goal of the transsexual is to pass successfully in society as a member of the opposite sex. Transsexuals are often sufficiently convincing in their ability to pass that some have lived for many years as members of the opposite sex, even without contrary hormone therapy or SRS. Other transsexuals are not so confident or fortunate, and they present to the physician requesting hormonal and surgical treatment in the hope that this will permit them to realize their lifelong goal of being accepted as members of the opposite sex.

The reader is referred to the original articles listed in the references, which describe in greater detail the adult manifestations of these syndromes in the male-to-female (M-F) and the female-to-male (F-M) situation. Transsexualism as now defined in the American Psychiatric Association's *Diagnostic and Statistical Manual* (*DSM-III-R*) has the following diagnostic criteria:

1. Persistent discomfort and sense of inappropriateness about one's assigned sex (feeling trapped in the wrong body).
2. Persistent preoccupation for at least two years with getting rid of one's primary and secondary sex characteristics and acquiring the sex characteristics of the other sex (a request for hormone treatment and/or SRS).
3. The person has reached puberty (otherwise, the diagnosis of gender identity disorder of childhood would be made).

In addition, the *DSM-III-R* defines a gender identity disorder of adolescence or adulthood, nontranssexual type (GIDAANT). This condition is the same as transsexualism, with persistent cross-dressing (but not for the purpose of sexual excitement) but without the persistent preoccupation with getting rid of one's primary and secondary sex characteristics and acquiring the sex characteristics of the other sex. Finally, the *DSM-III-R* lists the criteria for the diagnosis of childhood gender identity disorder in boys and girls. These include the persistent desire to be a girl (boy) and the insistence that the individual actually is a girl (boy). Also, there is a repudiation of one's anatomical sexual status and strong preference for the role, activities, dress, name, and social status of the opposite sex, all with onset prior to puberty. In *DSM-IV* the term "transsexualism" was removed and replaced by the generic term "gender disorder."

Transsexualism as now defined is clearly more prevalent than previously thought. At least 1 in 50,000 individuals over the age of 15 years is likely to be transsexual. It would appear that the male/female ratio is probably close to 1:1 in most cultures. If a higher male preponderance is present, this could reflect a more negative bias in that culture toward male homosexuality, or it could reflect a lack of availability in that culture for surgical sex reassignment for F-M transsexuals. Whatever the real statistics may turn out to be, this disorder carries more significance than the actual prevalence might indicate. Perhaps there is some gender dysphoria in all of us, no matter how repressed or latent. Certainly, our culture is struggling with issues of women's liberation and equality. Most important, the study of the normative process of gender identification has been well served by our research into the etiology and prevalence of transsexualism.

Historical Perspective

The concept of gender-role reversal has been known since it was first described in the early classic literature from Herodotus to Shakespeare. The first mention of gender dysphoria in the medical literature as an example of a clinical or pathological syndrome was from the German literature. Historical descriptions of various forms of gender dysphoria came from the French and German literature in the 19th century. In the early part of the 20th century, the focus of scientific research on this topic shifted from Europe to the United States. The term "transsexualism" was coined by an American sexologist, D.O. Cauldwell, and was popularized by the pioneering efforts of Harry Benjamin. The publicity surrounding the famous Christine Jorgenson case ushered in what the author has referred to as the modern era of the gender identity movement.

The details of this movement are reported elsewhere, but suffice it to say that currently there is a small cadre of researchers in the gender identity field who report their findings every other year at the Harry Benjamin International Gender Dysphoria Association meeting.

Research in this field was facilitated by the inclusion of transsexualism and gender identity disorders in the American Psychiatric Association's *Diagnostic and Statistical Manual*, third edition, in 1980. To some extent, this inclusion has legitimized these gender identity disorders and defines the criteria for the diagnosis of transsexualism. Further elaboration occurred with the publication of *DSM-III-R,* in 1988, although gender identity disorders are somewhat concealed in the section dealing with conditions that have their onset in childhood or adolescence. Currently, the work group looking at the fourth edition of the *Diagnostic and Statistical Manual* is hoping to find an appropriate and unique section for gender identity disorders. In any event, it is fair to say that these conditions are now well-known in medical and psychiatric circles, even though their prevalence and incidence are quite rare. This gender identity movement has spawned a new medical subspecialty dedicated to furthering understanding and knowledge of the normative process of gender identification and disorders thereof.

Gender Dysphoria and the Spectrum of Gender Identity Disorders

Thus far, this article has emphasized the most extreme manifestation of gender identity misidentification, namely, transsexualism. However, there is clearly a spectrum or continuum along which each and every individual might assume his or her place. The process of gender identification, as a normative development sequence, is only beginning to come under scientific scrutiny. The nature-nurture, genetic-environmental dichotomies are still in contention in attempting to understand this normal developmental process, let alone the problems that arise when normality is not achieved. Certainly, the very early onset (age three to four years) of strong preference for the gender role incongruent with the individual's apparently normal biological sex causes one to consider a biological force, either genetic or hormonal. Unfortunately, the promise of such an early genetic determinant of gender dysphoria, as determined by the H-Y antigen test, appears to have been repudiated. The role of hormone imbalance, probably prenatal, influencing the central nervous system, has been suggested as an important predisposition towards contrary sex-role behavior and gender identity. Money places transsexualism at the extreme end of the cross-gender identity spectrum, with transvestism and homosexuality as less extreme manifestations, all three having their origins in hormonal imbalance during some critical period of development.

In contrast to this hormonal or biological view of the etiology of gender identity disorders are various social or intrafamilial forces that have been postulated to explain this phenomenon. Pauly, Stoller, and Lothstein have underscored the significance of intrafamily dynamics and relationships in the etiology of both M-F and F-M transsexualism. The influence of societal factors, especially the rigidity of society with reference to sex roles, sexual equality, and homosexuality, also has been hypothesized as an etiological factor in the development of transsexualism. In fact, Ross, et al., attempt to prove this hypothesis by comparing the frequency and sex ratio of transsexualism in two different cultures, Sweden and Australia. Although their results suggest significant societal factors bearing on the etiology and development of transsexualism, the authors are quick to point out the limitations of such research. Suffice it to say that hard data in this field are only beginning to emerge. Therefore, the precise cause is far from clear. There may well be multiple factors that operate in sequence, with a biological predisposition being augmented by intrafamily and social forces.

Returning to the issue of variability of behavior among humans, it is sometimes difficult to be sure when gender behavior is sufficiently atypical to warrant evaluation or treatment. Certainly, gender roles are stereotyped and tend to be dimorphic in most Western cultures. In the extreme, there is less uncertainty, and pretranssexual boys and girls behave in a sufficiently cross-genderal fashion that their families have good reason for concern. These effeminate boys, often labeled as "sissies" by their peers, come in for much more abuse than their female counterparts, whose tomboyish behavior is better tolerated. Even so, very young boys are brought to the physician for evaluation of their gender-role behavior. Follow-up studies suggest these young boys with atypical gender-role behavior grow up to demonstrate atypical gender role or atypical sexual preference as adults. Green underscores the fact that effeminate behavior in young boys is a developmental stage in the natural history of male homosexuality. Young girls are less often referred for atypical gender behavior, unless there is an extreme repudiation and denial of their femaleness, in which case the diagnosis of gender identity disorder of childhood is warranted. Suffice it to say, there are a broad range of gender behaviors, which are quite well tolerated by society, unless they become extremely pronounced. Although gender-role behavior is dimorphic, there is some overlap, which makes early detection quite difficult. Also, there appears to be a movement toward less rigidity and stereotyping and more acceptance of atypical gender-role behavior. Whether this unisexed concept will develop to such an extent that individuals will feel less inclined to have to resort to SRS in order to feel comfortable remains to be seen.

As these children grow up into adolescents and adults, they identify themselves as feeling uncomfortable with their biological sex and prefer the opposite gender identity. Often, they try to adjust to the genderal expectations of them by parents and society. However, at one point, the internal pressure to "be myself" intensifies, and the individual makes the disclosure, which results in professional evaluation. Clearly, not everyone who feels that a sex-change operation is the solution to their problems is a good candidate for the procedure. The term "gender dysphoria syndrome" has emerged as the generic name for all those individuals who present with some form of gender discomfort. Under this umbrella term, "gender dysphoria," fall other diagnostic categories, the common denominator of which is displeasure or discomfort with the original genital anatomy and a desire or demand for SRS. Laub and Fisk list the following diagnostic possibilities:

1. Classic Transsexualism of Benjamin—lifelong history of desire to be a member of the gender opposite his or her biological sex.
2. Transvestism—cross-dresser who receives erotic stimulation from wearing female clothing as a prelude to heterosexual activity.
3. Effeminate Homosexuality (Male) or Masculine Lesbianism (Female)—erotically attracted to same biologically sexed individuals and gives history of enjoying the use of their genitalia in homosexual lovemaking.
4. Psychosis—discomfort regarding one's gender identity in the face of a psychotic decompensation only, and does not endure when patient is over the acute episode.
5. Psychopathic or Sociopathic Personality—individuals who wish to achieve notoriety or financial gain from SRS, and who are not

sincere or truthful in their protestations of cross-gender identification.

The primary distinguishing characteristic of the above differential diagnosis is the age of onset and the stability and persistence of the gender dysphoria. This is sometimes difficult to ascertain, since the clinician is at the mercy of the patient's truthfulness and reliability as a historian. Also, most of the intelligent gender dysphoric individuals have become very familiar with literature on this topic and know what the criteria for the genuine article are considered to be. Person and Ovesy make a similar point by distinguishing primary from secondary transsexualism. To confirm the transsexual's history that the gender identity problem originated in early childhood, it is essential to have contact with the parents or other family members. For primary transsexuals, parents do confirm the patient's history that cross-gender identification has persisted since early childhood. However, when either the patient or the family member reports that the individual had developed a comfortable gender identity that was congruent with their biological sex, then one should begin to consider secondary forms of transsexualism or gender dysphoria. Many authors have underscored the multiplicity of diagnostic and personality characteristics of those who request SRS.

Transsexualism and Body Image

The concept of body image has particular relevance to the phenomenon of transsexualism and gender dysphoria. Body image has come to mean not only the way one perceives his or her own body but also the way he or she feels about these perceptions. As such, it is an important part of one's overall self-concept. The transsexual is unable to form a satisfactory body image because of the dissonance between his or her anatomic sex and his or her gender identity. Thus, the reality of the transsexual's body does not conform to the preferred or desired body image. The result is a disturbance in the formation of a complete and consistent self-concept.

The transsexual attempts to reduce this dissonance through a variety of means, the effects of which are to bring the physical form of the body into line with the preferred gender concept. The male transsexual cross-dresses, wears a wig, obtains electrolysis to remove facial hair or covers it up with make-up, uses bra padding, and so forth in an attempt to correct his body image dissatisfaction. In addition to these outward attempts to pass in society as a woman, the male transsexual assumes the preferred body image in fantasies and daydreams. Likewise, the female transsexual dresses in a masculine manner, cuts "his" hair short and in a masculine fashion, flattens "his" breasts, and places padding in "his" crotch to simulate the presence of a penis. Finally, however, the transsexual seeks the alteration of the actual body form, through endocrinological and surgical means, to bring the body into harmony with the preferred body image. This last step is the hallmark of the syndrome of transsexualism, and it is this request for hormone therapy and SRS that brings the transsexual to the physician. Thus, it is only natural that body image becomes one of the conceptual frameworks within which transsexualism can be studied and understood.

In 1975, Lindgren and Pauly introduced a Body Image Scale, which they felt might help in the evaluation and treatment of transsexualism. This 30-item list of body parts asks each respondent to rate his or her feeling about that part of their body on a five-point scale from very satisfied (1) to very dissatisfied (5). Among other things, this research revealed that transsexuals invariably scored certain body parts as (5) or "very dissatisfied," and these body parts were called primary genderal characteristics. For the M-F transsexual, these primary genderal characteristics are the penis, scrotum, testicles, facial hair, body hair, and breasts. For the F-M transsexual, the most hated parts of the anatomy are the breasts, vagina, clitoris, ovaries-uterus, chest, voice, and facial hair (or lack of it). This pattern of dissatisfaction is thought to be quite specific in identifying those gender-dysphoric individuals who are correctly diagnosed as primary transsexuals. Also, the Lindgren-Pauly Body Image Scale has been shown to be useful in following transsexuals from their initial pretreatment phase through hormone therapy and finally SRS. A statistically significant reduction in the overall score indicates that, in well-evaluated cases, this approach is successful in reducing the transsexual's negative body image. The body image scores come down as this sex reassignment treatment continues, so as to closely approximate a normal control group's body image score.

Body image is a useful parameter in the study and evaluation of individuals with a serious gender identity problem, and it allows one to characterize the primary transsexual and distinguish him or her from the secondary transsexual or other gender-dysphoric individuals, who would not be appropriate candidates for sex reassignment. The author has been gratified to find that another researcher, from South Africa, applying the Lindgren-Pauly Body Image Scale, has independently confirmed its usefulness in distinguishing "effectively between pre-operative transsexuals and homosexuals." Dutch workers have also used this instrument to follow transsexuals through hormone treatment and SRS and have confirmed the previous impression that the body image scale is a useful instrument as an objective measure of the individual transsexual's status as he or she progresses through hormone treatment and SRS.

Evaluation

Since transsexualism and gender dysphoria are considered psychiatric disorders, their evaluation requires a fully certified mental health professional, that is, a psychiatrist or psychologist. Individuals requesting SRS do not necessarily agree that their condition is of psychogenic origin, and they usually present to the surgeon or internist. The nonpsychiatric physician is well advised to refer such gender-dysphoric patients to the psychiatrist before recommending any form of treatment. This is not to say that physicians might not wish to perform a medical evaluation (i.e., physical examination, endocrinological studies, including testosterone or estrogen levels, and so forth). Even if the physician is convinced of the patient's sincerity and would like to alleviate his or her suffering, there are good reasons for not responding directly. Not the least of these reasons is the fact that some such patients have changed their minds, after hormone therapy and SRS, and have implicated their treating physicians in malpractice suits. Even if the physician is convinced that transsexualism is not a psychiatric disorder but rather a biological phenomenon, the fact remains that some psychotic individuals do request SRS. The nonpsychiatric physician is skating on thin ice if he or she attempts to make this distinction.

Once the individual comes to the attention of the psychiatrist, the evaluation process is not dissimilar to other clinical evaluations. A very careful past history is required, so that the intensity, duration, and stability of the gender dysphoria can be determined. As has been made clear in the previous section, primary transsexualism is a lifelong identification with the gender role of the opposite biological sex. Since the patient is highly invested in the outcome of the evaluation, he or she may not be entirely candid or truthful. Transsexuals are usually well-read and know what and what not to reveal to their evaluators. However, this dilemma is not unfamiliar to the clinician and need not negate the value of obtaining a careful history. The standards of care recommend that such an evaluation extend over a significant period of time and that an independent source of information about the patient be sought. It would be well to interview the parents or other family members or friends who have known the patient over time. Unfortunately, this is not always possible, since the patient may be estranged from his or her family. In such cases, it is more important to have had even longer contact with the person requesting SRS before a recommendation is made.

A careful mental status examination is required, primarily to rule out the possibility of an underlying psychotic condition, even though the patient may appear quite sane. Thus, it is important to inquire about delusions, auditory hallucinations, and other grandiose or bizarre ideation. Quite apart from the issue of psychosis, the evaluator needs to be alert to the possibility of depression and suicidal ideation. Many gender-dysphoric patients are quite desperate. They have experienced rejection and ridicule, and may regard this attempt at obtaining help as their "last chance." Many investigators have pointed out the prevalence of depression and suicidal ideation in the transsexual prior to the transsexual's undergoing sex reassignment treatment. Obviously, the diagnosis of gender dysphoria or transsexualism need not be the only psychiatric diagnosis. Affective disorders, primarily depression, with or without psychotic features, may also be present. An accurate assessment of IQ is also important, since the evaluator must document that the patient has sufficient capacity and competence to understand the implications and consequences of hormone therapy and SRS.

Trial of Cross-Gender Living— The Real-Life Test

One of the requirements prior to recommending in favor of hormone therapy or SRS is the so-called real-life test. Actually, many primary transsexuals have already passed this test, since they may have lived for some time in the opposite gender role before seeking hormones or SRS. If this is the case, the author would submit that this fact is correlated positively with a favorable outcome from SRS. The fact that the individual had been able to pass successfully without hormone therapy speaks positively to the applicant's confidence in being able to pass in society in the gender role opposite to the sex of birth. This is particularly impressive when the individual was quite young at the time when cross-gender living commenced. Quite often, such individuals have formed close interpersonal relationships during this time and are well accepted by their lovers or partners. The transsexual is perceived by his or her partner as belonging to the gender that the transsexual is portraying. Neither partner sees either the self or the other as homosexual. For these reasons, *DSM-III-R*'s designations of homosexual or heterosexual types are confusing and misleading. The author has suggested the term "hetero-genderal" in lieu of homosexual and "homogenderal" in place of heterosexual as appropriate terms designed to overcome this confusion.

For others, however, cross-gender living is only considered after the recommendation of the evaluation or support of the therapist. Despite the standards of care, which advise cross-gender living of at least three months prior to recommendation for hormone therapy, some transsexuals require the additional help of hormones first. This deviation from the standards of care should not be undertaken by the novice and certainly not without a second opinion. The author has found this trial of cross-gender living not only important to the evaluator, but more so to the individual transsexual. Sometimes, the fantasy of living in the opposite gender role is enjoyed more mentally than in reality. Anxiety over one's ability to pass convincingly must be confronted sooner or later. No matter how strong the opposite gender identification, not all transsexuals are able to pass. Thus, experiencing the long sought after wish to live as a member of the opposite sex may or may not enhance the transsexual's motivation. In some cases, the real-life test is passed quite readily and the individual thrives, feeling much happier that he or she is on the way toward the solution to the gender problem.

For others, however, the real-life test is a painful confrontation that cross-gender living is not really possible, if they are to enjoy any kind of meaningful social interaction. As painful as this confrontation may be, certainly it is better to appreciate this reality before any irreversible physical changes or SRS have occurred. One hopes that the transsexual who is unsuccessful in this trial will have greater motivation to search for a psychotherapeutic approach to his or her gender dysphoria.

It is recommended by some that this real-life test continue for at least two years. In most true transsexuals, this period is often very rewarding, especially if the transsexual finds he or she passes easily and well. Often, the patient is supported through this period with hormone therapy, which helps to reduce negative body image problems and reassures the patient that progress is being made. With or without psychotherapy, with or without hormone therapy, the clinician-evalua-

tor is able to ascertain if the individual is functioning better in the cross-gender role. This assessment should include some substantiation from sources other than the patient alone. In particular, it is important to document the ability to work or be gainfully employed. The ability to relate socially and develop a support system is also important during this period. And finally, it is essential that the patient be able to cope with less anxiety and depression than before cross-gender living. If these hoped-for changes do not occur during this trial of cross-gender living, the evaluator should be quite reluctant to recommend hormone therapy or SRS. Often, the individual will become aware of the inadvisability of proceeding with SRS and, possibly, elect to pursue a nonsurgical approach. Even if he or she is somewhat successful in the role of the opposite gender, perhaps the individual will realize that the reality of the situation is not as exciting as the fantasies about it. Second thoughts may arise that beg the individual to reconsider. It is important for the evaluator-therapist to take a neutral role during this process. By this is meant that the therapist be neither advocate nor detractor. The therapist should offer support and attempt to work through issues but not be prematurely invested in determining in favor of or against proceeding with SRS.

Hormone Therapy

The aim of endocrine treatment in the transsexual patient of either sex is dual: suppression of the existing sexual features (hormonal castration), and development and maintenance of sexual features belonging to the other sex ("paradoxical hormone therapy"). The recommended medications have not changed very much in the last 20 years: Estinyl (ethinyl estradiol) 0.15–0.5 milligrams per day for the M–F transsexual. To this may be added Provera (medroxy-progesterone acetate) 10 milligrams per day. For the F–M transsexual, depo-testosterone 200 milligrams by injection every two weeks is suggested. Hormone therapy reduces the dissonance between the transsexual's actual body configuration and his or her idealized body image.

Hormone therapy is recommended only after careful evaluation and not simply on request or on demand from the self-diagnosed transsexual. Certain irreversible changes, such as testicular atrophy in the male and permanent voice changes and clitoral enlargement in the female, should be explained in detail. A baseline endocrinological evaluation, together with baseline liver function studies, should precede hormone therapy. Administration of hormone therapy in adolescence should be avoided, especially in the female, where testosterone might prematurely close the epiphyses and prevent bone growth and attainment of the optimal height. However, once a careful evaluation has concluded that the individual is a good candidate for SRS and preliminary baseline studies have occurred, hormone therapy becomes the next step in the process of evaluation, after cross-gender living. Most genuine, primary transsexuals "pass" this test, are delighted with the physical changes that improve their body image, feel more self-confident in their ability to pass, and are encouraged with the progress they are making toward their goal. However, some self-select or are selected out of continuing toward SRS by their evaluators, for a variety of reasons.

For an update on hormone therapy for both M-F and F-M transsexuals, the reader is referred to more recent publications by Pauly and Steiner. It should be apparent that this treatment is best provided by an endocrinologist or specialist in the evaluation and treatment of transsexual patients. Suffice it to say that hormone therapy is highly acclaimed by the transsexual, as moving in the correct direction of his or her cherished goal of complete sex reassignment.

Sex Reassignment Surgery for Primary Transsexuals

Those gender-dysphoric individuals who demonstrate a fixed and consistent cross-gender identification, using the above-mentioned criteria, are candidates for SRS. They establish themselves as primary transsexuals and successfully pass the real-life test of cross-gender living and hormone therapy for one to two years. Some are actively engaged in psychotherapy before and during this trial period, but they are all still involved in the evaluation process by a member of the mental health profession. Then, and only then, is it appropriate to recommend the patient to an experienced surgeon for SRS. Again, the specifics of SRS are highly technical and are reviewed elsewhere. Clearly, SRS is more advanced for the M-F transsexual than for the F-M transsexual. Despite this fact, F-M transsexuals report at least as much satisfaction with SRS as do M-F clients.

The genital surgical procedure in the M-F transsexual involves the removal of the penis, scrotum, and testicles and the creation of a functional neovagina. It should be emphasized that a successful outcome is largely dependent on a good functional result. The ability to engage in sexual intercourse without pain or discomfort is highly correlated with postoperative satisfaction

as judged by the transsexual. In addition, the breast enlargement secondary to estrogen therapy is usually not sufficient to preclude breast augmentation mammoplasty. This procedure is not essentially different from that requested by nontranssexual women who wish to enhance the size of their breasts. Other forms of plastic surgery are occasionally requested to improve the feminine appearance, such as facial surgery, rhinoplasty, and thyroid cartilage shave to reduce the size of the Adam's apple. When one compares the pretreatment male transsexual's scores on the Body Image Scale (3.76/5.0) with the postsurgical scores (1.46/5.0), one sees a significant improvement (p = .001).

With reference to the F-M transsexuals, the surgical techniques are not as well developed. Certainly, it is easy enough to remove the breasts by mastectomy. These procedures can be accomplished through a small subareolar, key-hole incision in female transsexuals endowed with small breasts. However, larger inframammary incisions are required for large-breasted female transsexuals. Usually, these postoperative F-M transsexuals are quite pleased with their flat chests and thankful that they no longer have to resort to the use of Ace bandages around their chests to minimize the size of their breasts.

With reference to genital surgery in the F-M situation, total hysterectomy, salpingo-oophorectomy, and vaginectomy are performed initially. The creation of an artificial penis is a very complicated multistage procedure. Emphasis is placed on obtaining surgical results that will (1) allow the patient to stand to void, (2) permit sexual intercourse, (3) provide a presentable male appearance, and (4) be accomplished in a minimum number of operative steps. Although requests for SRS are currently coming equally from male and female patients, most of the attention in the surgical literature has been given to M-F transsexuals. Clearly, the difficulties inherent in the surgical construction of a cosmetically and functionally satisfactory male-appearing perineum have not yet been alleviated to the point where this is readily available. Until this has been accomplished to the same degree as with the M-F transsexual, it will be difficult to achieve a completely favorable outcome from SRS for female transsexuals.

The outcome of SRS is a complicated and difficult subject for review. The author has attempted on several occasions to review these results. The early data were reported in 1965 and 1968. In collaboration with Swedish colleagues, a more recent update was done. Finally, the most recent review of this topic is in collaboration with one of the most prominent and distinguished American surgeons. Nonetheless, SRS is still considered by some to be at least controversial, if not totally contraindicated. There is little question that the vast majority of those evaluated after SRS claim satisfaction with their surgical reorientation and indicate they would pursue such a course if they had it to do again. Satisfaction with SRS is present in 71.4 percent to 87.8 percent of M-F transsexuals, with only 8.1 percent to 10.3 percent expressing dissatisfaction. Likewise, some 80.7 percent to 89.5 percent of F-M transsexuals express satisfaction with SRS, compared with only 6.0 percent to 9.7 percent who do not. This difference between M-F and F-M transsexuals does not reach statistical significance. Blanchard, et al., report a smaller percentage of positive outcomes in heterosexual male transsexuals compared with homosexual male transsexuals, and they recommend caution in referring male transsexuals for SRS who have a history of sexual arousal toward women. More recent studies tend to confirm the transsexuals' satisfaction with SRS.

Conclusion

The study of transsexuals and other gender-dysphoric individuals has resulted in a new subspecialty in medicine. Although only in its infancy, this field is developing into an important basic science helping to define the normative process of gender identification and the disorders thereof. Although considerable attention has been given to the evaluation and treatment of gender identity problems, all would agree that transsexualism and gender dysphoria are better prevented than treated. There is some hope that research in this gender identity field will lead to sufficient understanding of this developmental process so that such gender identity problems can be prevented. Short of this, we must continue to assess what is appropriate for those individuals who are currently dealing with their gender dysphoria and provide the very best treatment available.

REFERENCES

American Psychiatric Association. *Diagnostic and Statistical Manual of Mental Disorders.* 3rd ed. Washington, D.C.: American Psychiatric Association, 1980.

————. *Diagnostic and Statistical Manual of Mental Disorders.* 3rd ed., revised. Washington, D.C.: American Psychiatric Association, 1988.

Barlow, D.H., G.G. Abel, and E.B. Blanchard. Gender Identity Change in Transsexuals: Follow-up and Replications. *Archives of General Psychiatry,* Vol. 36 (1979), pp. 1001–07.

Benjamin, H. Transvestism and Transsexualism. *International Journal of Sexology,* Vol. 7 (1953), pp. 12–14.

————. *The Transsexual Phenomenon.* New York: Julian Press, 1966.

————. For the Practicing Physician: Suggestions and Guidelines for the Management of Transsexuals. In R. Green and J. Money, eds., *Transsexualism and Sex Reassignment.* Baltimore: The Johns Hopkins Press, 1969.

Blanchard, R., S. Legault, and W. Lindsay. Vaginoplasty Outcome in Male-to-Female Transsexuals. *Journal of Sex and Marital Therapy,* Vol. 13 (1987), pp. 265–75.

Blanchard, R., B.W. Steiner, and L.H. Clemmensen. Gender Dysphoria, Gender Reorientation, and the Clinical Management of Transsexualism. *Journal of Consulting and Clinical Psychiatry,* Vol. 53 (1985), pp. 295–304.

Cauldwell, D.O. Psychopathia Transsexualis. *Sexology,* 16 (1949), pp. 274–80.

Eicher, W., M. Spoljar, H. Clere, J. Murken, K. Richter, and S. Stangel-Rutkowski. H-Y Antigen in Transsexuality. *Lancet,* II, No. 8152 (1979), pp. 1137–38.

Fisk, N. Gender Dysphoria Syndrome. In D. Laub and P. Gandy, eds., *Proceedings of the Second Interdisciplinary Symposium on Gender Dysphoria Syndrome.* Ann Arbor: Edwards Brothers, 1974.

Friedreich, J. *Versuch Einer Literargeschichte der Pathologie und Therapie der Psychischen.* Wurzburg: Krankheiten, 1830.

Green, R. Mythological, Historical, and Cross-cultural Aspects of Transsexualism. In H. Benjamin, *The Transsexual Phenomenon.* New York: Julian Press, 1966.

————. *Sexual Identity Conflicts in Children and Adults.* New York: Basic Books, 1974.

————. *The Sissy Boy Syndrome.* New Haven: Yale Univ. Press, 1987.

Green, R., and J. Money, eds. *Transsexualism and Sex Reassignment.* Baltimore: The Johns Hopkins Univ. Press, 1969.

Gorman, W. *Body Image and the Image of the Brain.* St. Louis: Warren H. Green, 1969.

Hamburger, C. Desire for Change of Sex as Shown by Personal Letters from 465 Men and Women. *Acta Endocronologica,* Vol. 14 (1953), pp. 361–75.

————. Endocrine Treatment of Male and Female Transsexualism. In R. Green and J. Money, eds., *Transsexualism and Sex Reassignment.* Baltimore: The Johns Hopkins Univ. Press, 1969, pp. 291–304.

Hamburger, C., G. Sturrup, and E. Dahl-Iverson. Transvestism. *J.A.M.A.,* Vol. 152 (1953), pp. 391–96.

Hoenig, J., and J. Kenna. The Prevalence of Transsexualism in England and Wales. *British Journal of Psychiatry,* Vol. 124 (1974), pp. 181–90.

Hoopes, J. Operative Treatment of the Female Transsexual. In R. Green and J. Money, eds., *Transsexualism and Sex Reassignment.* Baltimore: The Johns Hopkins Univ. Press, 1969.

Kuiper, B., and P. Cohen-Kettenis. Sex Reassignment Surgery: A Study of 141 Dutch Transsexuals. *Archives of Sexual Behavior*, Vol. 17 (1988), pp. 439–58.

Laub, D., and N. Fisk. A Rehabilitation Program for Gender Dysphoria Syndrome by Surgical Sex Change. *Plastic Reconstructive Surgery*, Vol. 53 (1974), pp. 388–403.

Levine, S., and L. Lothstein. Transsexualism or the Gender Dysphoria Syndromes. *Journal of Sexual and Marital Therapy*, Vol. 7 (1981), pp. 85–114.

Lindemalm, G., D. Korlin, and N. Uddenberg. Long Term Follow-up of "Sex Change" in 13 Male-to-Female Transsexuals. *Archives of Sexual Behavior*, Vol. 15 (1986), pp. 187–210.

Lindgren, T., and I. Pauly. A Body Image Scale for Evaluating Transsexuals. *Archives of Sexual Behavior*, Vol. 4 (1975), pp. 639–56.

Lothstein, L. Sex Reassignment Surgery: Historical, Bioethical, and Theoretical Issues. *American Journal of Psychiatry*, Vol. 139 (1982), pp. 417–26.

———. *Female-to-Male Transsexualism*. Boston: Routledge & Kegan Paul, 1983.

Lundstrom, B., I. Pauly, and J. Walinder. Outcome of Sex Reassignment Surgery. *Acta Psychiat. Scand.*, Vol. 70 (1984), pp. 289–94.

Meyer, J. Clinical Variants among Applicants for Sex Reassignment. *Archives of Sexual Behavior*, Vol. 3 (1974), pp. 527–58.

Money, J. *Gay, Straight, and In-Between*. Oxford: Oxford Univ. Press, 1988.

Money, J., and R. Ambinder. Two-year, Real-life Diagnostic Test: Rehabilitation Versus Cure. In H. Brady and J. Brody, eds., *Controversy in Psychiatry*. Philadelphia: Saunders, 1978.

Money, J., and A. Ehrhardt. *Man and Woman: Boy and Girl*. Baltimore: Johns Hopkins Univ. Press, 1972.

Money, J., and A. Russo. Homosexual Outcome of Discordant Gender Identity/Role in Childhood: Longitudinal Follow-up. *Journal of Pediatric Psychology*, Vol. 4 (1979), pp. 29–41.

Pauly, I. Male Psychosexual Inversion: Transsexualism. *Archives of General Psychiatry*, Vol. 13 (1965), pp. 172–81.

———. The Current Status of the Change of Sex Operation. *Journal of Nervous and Mental Diseases*, Vol. 147 (1968), pp. 460–71.

———. Adult Manifestations of Male Transsexualism. In R. Green and J. Money, eds., *Transsexualism and Sex Reassignment*. Baltimore: Johns Hopkins Univ. Press, 1969.

———. Adult Manifestations of Female Transsexualism. In R. Green and J. Money, eds., *Transsexualism and Sex Reassignment*. Baltimore: Johns Hopkins Univ. Press, 1969.

———. Female Transsexualism, Parts I and II. *Archives of Sexual Behavior*, Vol. 3 (1974), pp. 487–525.

———. Sex and the Life Cycle. In H. Kaplan, A. Freedman, and B. Sadock, eds., *Comprehensive Textbook of Psychiatry*, 3rd ed. Baltimore: Williams and Wilkins, 1980.

———. Outcome of Sex Reassignment Surgery for Transsexuals. *Australian and New Zealand Journal of Psychiatry*, Vol. 15 (1981), pp. 45–51.

———. Gender Identity Disorders. In M. Farber, ed., *Textbook of Human Sexuality*. New York: Macmillan, 1985.

———. Terminology and Classification of Gender Identity Disorders. *Journal of Psychology and Human Sexuality*, Vol. 5 (1993), pp. 1–14.

Pauly, I., and M. Edgerton. The Gender Identity Movement: A Growing Surgical-Psychiatric Liaison. *Archives of Sexual Behavior*, Vol. 15 (1986), pp. 315–29.

Pauly, I., and T. Lindgren. Body Image and Gender Identity. *Journal of Homosexuality*, Vol. 2 (1976), pp. 133–42.

Person, E., and L. Ovesey. The Transsexual Syndrome in Males: Parts I and II. *American Journal of Psychotherapy*, Vol. 28 (1974), pp. 4–20, 174–93.

Ross, M.W., J. Walinder, B. Lundstrom, and I. Thuwe. Cross-cultural Approaches to Transsexualism: A Comparison Between Sweden and Australia. *Acta Psychiat. Scand.*, Vol. 63 (1981), pp. 75–82.

Steiner, B., ed. *Gender Dysphoria*. New York: Plenum Press, 1985.

Stoller, R. *Sex and Gender*. New York: Science House, 1968.

———. Near Miss: "Sex Change" Treatment and Its Evaluation. In R. Stoller, *Presentations of Gender*. New Haven: Yale Univ. Press, 1985.

Walinder, J. *Transsexualism*. Akademiforlaget, Goteborg, Sweden: Scandinavian University Books, 1967.

———. Transsexualism: Definition, Prevalence, and Sex Distribution. *Acta Psychiat. Scand.* (Suppl.) Vol. 203 (1968), pp. 255–57.

———. Incidence and Sex Ratios of Transsexualism in Sweden. *British Journal of Psychiatry*, Vol. 119 (1971), pp. 195–96.

Walinder, J., B. Lundstrom, and I. Thuwe. Prognostic Factors in the Assessment of Male Transsexuals for Sex Reassignment. *British Journal of Psychiatry*, Vol. 132 (1978), pp. 16–20.

Walinder, J., and I. Thuwe. *A Social-Psychiatric Follow-up Study of 24 Sex Reassigned Transsexuals*. Goteborg, Sweden: Scandinavian Univ. Books, 1974.

Walker, P., et al. Standards of Care: The Hormonal and Surgical Sex Reassignment of Gender Dysphoric Persons. *Archives of Sexual Behavior*, Vol. 14 (1985), pp. 79–90.

Zucker, K.J. Cross-Gender Identified Children. In B.W. Steiner, ed., *Gender Dysphoria: Development, Research, and Management*. New York: Plenum, 1985.

Zuger, B. Homosexuality in Families of Boys with Early Effeminate Behavior: An Epidemiological Study. *Archives of Sexual Behavior*, Vol. 18 (1989), pp. 155–66.

Ira B. Pauly

U

ULRICHS, KARL HEINRICH

Karl Heinrich Ulrichs (1825–1895) was the founder of homosexual scholarship. Some have called him the "grandfather of gay liberation." Born in Aurich, Hannover, on August 28, 1825, in a German middle-class Lutheran family, he went on to study law at Göttingen and Berlin universities. He then became a civil service attorney in the kingdom of Hannover, but in 1854 he left this position and afterward earned his living by writing and related activities.

After declaring his homosexuality to his family, Ulrichs became concerned that the potential union of the various German states under Prussian hegemony might well lead to the adoption of the restrictive Prussian laws on homosexuality instead of the more liberal Hannoverian ones, which were based on the Napoleonic Code. The Napoleonic Code put restrictions on age and required consent but otherwise allowed a variety of sexual activities. Over the years, he developed a theory of homosexuality that was ultimately published in some 12 booklets, the overall title of which was *Forsungen über das Rätsel der mannmänlichen Liebe,* or *Researches into the Riddle of Love Between Men.* He coined a number of terms to describe same-sex love, such as "urning" for male lovers and "urningin" for female lovers.

The key to his writing was his belief that homosexuals were a third sex and that homosexual love drives were natural and inborn. His writings proved to be extremely influential on writers such as Krafft-Ebing, who adopted many of his ideas, although not his terminology. Ulrichs continued to agitate for rights of homosexuals and went to the Congress of German Jurists to argue his case on August 28, 1867, only to be shouted down. When the harsh Prussian antihomosexual laws were extended to all parts of the country, Ulrichs emigrated to Italy, where he spent his last years, dying there on July 14, 1895.

REFERENCE

Kennedy, H. *Ulrichs: Life and Works of Karl Heinrich Ulrichs, Pioneer of the Modern Gay Movement.* Boston: Alyson, 1987.

Vern L. Bullough

$\mathcal{V}$

VAN DE VELDE, THEODOOR HENDRIK

Theodoor Hendrik van de Velde (1873–1937) was a Dutch gynecologist who was best known for his popular marriage manual, *Ideal Marriage*, published first in German and Dutch in 1926 and widely translated and reprinted. The English edition, published by William Heinemann in 1930, went through 43 printings and sold some 700,000 copies, while the American edition, published by Random House, sold equally well. A revised edition was published in 1965, which also sold well.

Born in 1873, he attended medical school in Leiden and Amsterdam and won recognition as director of the Haarlem Gynecological Clinic. He married his first wife, Henrietta van de Velde-ten Brink, in 1899, but the marriage was not a happy one; after some ten years, van de Velde eloped with one of his patients, a socially prominent married woman, Martha Breitenstein-Hooglandt, eight years his junior. In the ensuing scandal, he was forced to give up his practice, and he and Martha wandered through Europe. He finally received a divorce from Henrietta in 1913 and married Martha soon after, settling down near Locarno. He had no children by either wife.

He himself wrote that he did not begin his book on sex and marriage until he had practiced medicine for more than 25 years and was adjudged suitably old. Some of his data came directly from his patients and their husbands, from observations of his patients, and also from his own experience. He emphasized the importance of love play, including oral-genital contact. He also explored some ten different sexual positions.

He died in 1937 at the age of 64, in Locarno, Switzerland. His book was dedicated to his wife Martha.

REFERENCE

Van de Velde, T. *Ideal Marriage, Its Physiology and Technique*. Translated by S. Browne. New York: Random House, 1930.

Vern L. Bullough

VIRILITY AND MACHISMO

The anthropologist Gilmore defined "machismo" as a masculine display complex involving culturally sanctioned demonstrations of hypermasculinity in the sense of both erotic and physical aggressiveness. Hypermasculine physical and sexual aggressiveness is justified by an ideology of machismo. The psychologists Mosher and Tomkins defined the ideology of machismo as a system of ideas forming a worldview that chauvinistically exalts male dominance by assuming masculinity, virility, and physicality to be the ideal essence of real men, who are adversarial warriors competing for scarce resources (including women as chattel) in a dangerous world.

Machismo is a hypermasculine variant of the traditional gender script that is socially inherited by virtue of being born male within a culture. It permeates the gender belief system, enabling macho men to justify gender inequality: male dominance in the gender hierarchy is a natural function of masculine superiority and feminine inferiority given by the very nature, the inner essence, of men and women.

Machismo stresses norms valuing toughness, aggressiveness, risk taking, and virility, norms reflecting the dominating, coercive, or destructive power over self, other men, nature, and women; it contrasts with norms like achievement and intimacy supporting power to master productive tasks like education and work and integrative tasks like courtship and marriage. As a descendent of the ideology of the warrior, it emphasizes dominance, threat, and violence through hypermasculine physical action. Hypermasculinity is the disposition to engage in exaggerated sex-typed performances by embodying manly action physically, by displaying toughness, daring, virility, and violence in scenes that offer such opportunities or challenges or threats to masculine identity.

Although not necessarily successful by society's standards, the macho man defends his masculine honor and prestige. Honor requires that he command deference from others in interpersonal relations and that he respond to perceived insult with violence. Prestige becomes a matter of reputation, as cool, as tough, as dangerous, as a stud. The informal social structure of all-male groups, whether as gangs, teams, or military units, lacks the social controls of conventional society. A reputation as a man, as a warrior, as macho produces prestige and protection in the form of alliances with other macho men against all others. The personal prestige of a reputation as a macho man within a dangerous world warns that insults and aggression will be met with violence.

Within youth gangs, rape can celebrate machismo and establish a reputation as macho. Feminists have regarded rape as an overconforming acting out of the masculinity mystique: qualities of aggression, power, strength, toughness, dominance, and competitiveness. The anthropologist Sanday found that rape-prone societies were marked by (1) extensive interpersonal violence, (2) the ideology of male toughness or machismo,

and (3) male dominance in political decision making.

When Gilmore reviewed cross-cultural concepts of manhood in the making, he concluded that manhood was a test. Cults of manhood arose wherever men were conditioned to fight for scarce resources, since men were given the dangerous jobs because of their physical strength and expendability. Gilmore believed that male honor became a code of conduct that served as an inducement to dangerous performance in the social struggle for scarce resources and that masculine honor remains evolutionarily or functionally adaptive in the dangerous struggle to protect, provide, and impregnate.

In contrast to an evolutionary or adaptive view, Mosher, using Tomkins's script theory of personality, traced the historical origin of male dominance to adversarial contests over scarce resources. The anthropologist Harris proposed that warfare conserved scarce protein resources by controlling population and spreading out paleolithic ancestors. Among warring stateless groups, female infanticide was frequent, controlling population expansion; the sex ratio of boys to girls under 14 was 128:100, whereas among adults, due to war, it was 101:100. Among warrior groups, boys were trained to be fierce and aggressive; they were rewarded with sexual privileges and deference from women. Gilmore reviewed many cultures where the cult of manhood demanded that men prove their toughness, courage, and virility. Intense ordeals, like the circumcision rites of the Samburu, transformed boys into men. To fail to engage in dangerous missions, to fight or brawl, to drink to excess, or to seek sexual conquests left a man's masculine honor open to ridicule as being effeminate or childlike.

Sanday viewed male dominance, manifested in the exclusion of women from economic and political decision making, as an aggression toward women, as a response to the stresses of endemic warfare, famine, and migration following wars or famine. In cultures where the sexes were equal, there were fewer wars and less food stress than in male-dominant cultures. That men faced death in violent conflicts explained why men have become the dominating sex.

The sociologist Rustow summarized the historical and ethnographic data supporting a thesis of superstratification. Superstratification refers to the multiple historical waves of multiple invasions of planting cultures by nomadic warriors that established hereditary inequality by installing monarchs and ruling classes in high civilizations. First, the war chariot, and later horse cavalry, permitted a massing of mobile force that instilled panic and terror in the infantry of planters. Religious or political ideology justified war, domination, slavery, and stratification into classes.

Thus, it was multiple historical scenes of perceived scarcity that produced warfare, a cult of manhood, ideological justification of warrior violence, harsh socialization of males, and male dominance over women. These repeated changes in a culture's history created by warfare generated dense affect within those victorious and vanquished cultures that scripted both their worldview—myths and narratives, including the ideology of machismo—and their cultural personality (national character). The worldview of the culture was instilled through the socialization of children; given an ideology about the superior nature of men and the inferior nature of women, gender socialization of men as dominant warriors and women as vanquished submissives continued until today.

After citing Rustow and Sanday, Tomkins posited that the superstratification of patriarchal warriors over matriarchal agriculturalists produced a splitting and invidious contrast between the innate discrete affects. The victors in adversarial contests differentially magnified the importance of the warrior affects: surprise, excitement, anger, disgust, and contempt. Only the vanquished, the oppressed, the Other were to tremble in fear, weep in distress, and hang their head in shame; they were weak because they had basked in their dubious, seductive, and relaxed enjoyment of the earth and its bounty. Once the affects were stratified into the victor's "superior" and the vanquished's "inferior," the bifurcated affects were extended to include not only the defeated and the slaves, castes, and lower classes, but also women.

This split in affects was associated with a polarity of ideology: right-wing normative and left-wing humanist. The right identifies with the oppressor and the status quo; the left identifies with the oppressed and change. The normative ideology maintains that human beings are basically evil, they must guard against alien emotions, hierarchies must reward the good and punish the bad, science discovers the true reality, government must maintain law and order, parents must decide what is best for children, and humans deserve love only when they conform to norms. The humanist ideology maintains that human beings are basically good, openness to feelings is enlightening and rewarding, a world of plenitude permits pluralism, creative science fosters self-realization, government must promote human welfare, play and children are fulfilling

and lovable just for themselves, and, above all, humans should be valued as ends in themselves.

Normatives socialize children to conform to gender norms, dividing the affects into so-called superior masculine (e.g., surprise, excitement, anger, disgust, and contempt) and so-called inferior feminine (e.g., fear, distress, shame, and enjoyment). Humanists rewardingly socialize all affects as essentially good and human in both sexes.

Tomkins's theory of affects, ideology, and scripts, as well as his insight into the historical stratification of affects following superstratification, led Mosher to the crucial insight that differential magnification of "superior, masculine" affects over "inferior, feminine" affects powered the socialization of macho men and the enculturation into machismo.

The personality scripts of macho men are created by socialization and acculturation. Seven socialization dynamisms increased the differential magnification of "masculine" over "feminine" affects: (1) unrelieved and unexpressed distress is intensified by the socializer until it is released as anger (boys should not cry; they should get mad); (2) fear expression and fear avoidance are inhibited through parental dominance and contempt until habituation partially reduces them, activating excitement (force a boy to stay with danger until he seeks it out); (3) shame over residual distress and fear reverses polarity through counteraction into exciting manly pride over aggression and daring (shame is left behind as the proud and excited boy fights and flies into the face of danger); (4) pride over aggressive and daring counteraction instigates disgust and contempt for shameful inferiors (the now proud boy lords it over sissies, wimps, faggots, and girls); (5) successful reversal of interpersonal control through angry and daring dominance activates excitement (revenge turns the tables on authorities and bullies who are now excitingly bested in dominance struggles); (6) surprise becomes an interpersonal strategy to achieve dominance by evoking fear and uncertainty (enjoying a reputation as "loco" and wild, the boy keeps others off balance by surprising outbursts of angry and daring action); and (7) excitement becomes differentially magnified as a more acceptable affect than relaxed enjoyment, which becomes acceptable only during victory celebrations (careful not to be seduced into passive, weak, relaxed enjoyment, the excitement-seeking boy limits enjoyment to triumphant celebrations of victory).

Acculturation through participation in male-only groups teaches the boy the ideology of machismo. Three acculturation dynamisms are repeated within such groups as well as the larger culture: (1) celebrations, (2) identification and complementation, and (3) vicarious resonance. Celebrations are male rituals, like finishing military boot camp when macho men get drunk, "get laid," act crazy, and get in a fight. Such macho action celebrates the ideology; the ideology justifies manly action. By identifying with macho men and by receiving deference from other men and women who act as submissive complements, the macho man adds elements to his script and justifications for his belief system. "War stories," myths, and mass-media narratives permit identification with macho heroes, illuminate a worldview, and justify male honor and the cult of manhood. Since vicarious scenes generate less dense affect than lived scenes, vicarious experience informs more than it motivates. Still, when a man has a macho script, that personality script vicariously resonates with the ideology and action of a macho hero in folklore or the mass media.

Mosher and his associates developed a Hypermasculinity Inventory (HMI) to measure (1) violence as necessary, (2) sex as an entitlement, (3) danger as exciting, and (4) toughness as self-control. The subscales measure hypermasculine power over men, women, nature, and self. The HMI serves as a proxy for a macho personality script. A number of psychological studies have demonstrated the construct validity of the HMI as a measure of macho personality.

Macho men reported needs for play, impulsivity, exhibition, aggression, autonomy, and dominance; they do not need to understand, to avoid harm, to structure their thinking, to nurture others, to be orderly, and to do the socially desirable. Macho men described themselves as reckless, tough, aggressive, cruel, adventuresome, courageous, and rigid. They denied being cautious, gentle, sensitive, mild, and softhearted.

Interpersonally, macho men manifested unilateral power strategies of persuading, persisting, demanding, threatening, expressing anger, and angry withdrawal. Their interpersonal style is hostile-dominant. In dating and sexual situations, the HMI was correlated with interpersonal styles described as assured, dominant, competitive, mistrusting, cold, and hostile. Macho men in college samples reported engaging in more minor delinquencies and more serious fights or gang fights. Macho men, whether in college, rock bands, or alcohol rehabilitation, reported a pattern of frequent use of alcohol or drugs. Following alcohol use, they reported more dangerous driving, fighting, and coercive sexual behavior.

Macho men endorsed a double standard, denied the importance of love, and endorsed both sexist attitudes and prejudice against gay men. They prefer Mosher's role enactment path to sexual involvement, which emphasizes "hot" sex by exciting novelty in partners, acts, and settings. Macho men preferred the following sexual fantasies: being a sexual master punishing a slave, overpowering a woman and forcing her to submit to his wishes, delighting many women, being in an orgy, having sex with young girls, doing the sexually taboo or forbidden, having an audience watching sexual performance, making love to more than one woman at a time, and being a male stripper or sexual performer for women.

Macho men hold the woman responsible for contraception, avoiding condoms. They will not interrupt their chance for scoring by inquiring about birth control. They have stereotypic attitudes about birth control as unmanly. Macho men used five styles of coping when jealous: verbal aggression against the rival, physical aggression against the rival, verbal and physical aggression against the partner, acting out, and seeking sexual revenge. Women attracted to macho men showed a similar pattern, whereas, when jealous, most women sought social support and made negative self-comparisons.

Macho personality was associated with self-reports of aggressive sexual behavior across several samples. Although exploitation is most commonly reported by college men, scores on the HMI were also correlated with coercive and assaultive sexual behavior. In the laboratory, macho men report a higher likelihood of using force to gain sex with an attractive and desirable confederate. Macho men reported less disgust, anger, fear, distress, shame, contempt, and guilt while imagining committing the brutal and realistic rape of a stranger. While imagining the rape of an acquaintance, macho men reported less fear, shame, distress, and guilt. Two studies of the guided imagining of marital rape revealed that macho men were even more accepting of marital rape than stranger rape. Marriage created a duty and an entitlement for macho men.

Thus, virility in macho men encompasses a view of women as property who owe sex to men as their duty corresponding to the males' entitlement. Callous sexuality is an integral part of machismo. Seduction is a game played and won by macho men—a seduction that shades into exploitation, that shades into coercion, that shades into assault. Both casual and intimate partners are fair game; after drinking, macho men become even more aggressive. Having a hostile-dominant interpersonal style, using unilateral power strategies, and believing that sex is necessary, their right, and women's duty, the macho man exhibits a callous sexuality that expresses power over women, justified by machismo. Given the ideology of machismo, to be a real man is to be a tough, violent, daring, virile man. Virile manhood requires sexual conquests as a marker of prestige, reputation, and gender superiority.

REFERENCES

Gilmore, D.D. *Manhood in the Making: Cultural Concepts of Masculinity*. New Haven: Yale Univ. Press, 1990.

Mosher, D.L. Macho Men, Machismo, and Sexuality. In J. Bancroft, ed., *Annual Review of Sex Research,* Vol. 2 (1991), pp. 199–247.

Mosher, D.L., and S.S. Tomkins. Scripting the Macho Man: Hypermasculine Socialization and Enculturation. *Journal of Sex Research,* Vol. 25 (1988), pp. 60–84.

Pleck, J.H. *The Myth of Masculinity*. Cambridge, Mass.: MIT Press, 1981.

Donald L. Mosher

Appendix

ADDITIONAL SOURCES OF SEX INFORMATION

How to Do Further Research

There is an axiom among librarians that all information exists—it is merely a matter of knowing how to locate what one needs. "We have ways," mutter librarians to each other and to skeptics.

And for sexuality, vast springs of information—not all of it obvious—may be tapped by the librarian and researcher alike. For this most popular and yet private of topics, the choices among sources are wide: from scholarly to underground, from printed matter to experts, from legal texts to pornography.

How does one find information about sexuality? The following discussion provides a brief introduction to the search process, and then what—in this short space—can be only the sketchiest of maps to sources.

Pathways to Sex Information

Quick Searches

Many questions about sex require relatively brief factual answers: What is the "squeeze technique" for premature ejaculation? How are pornography and erotica defined? Do many people practice oral-genital sex? For these questions, the most helpful sources are the basic reference works listed in the next section. Most can be found in libraries, particularly large public libraries, academic libraries, and medical libraries (usually open to the public, although not with checkout privi-

leges). Also available in libraries and often quite helpful for basic questions are the general encyclopedias, such as the *Encyclopaedia Britannica*, the *Encyclopedia Americana*, and the *Academic American Encyclopedia*. (When using these works, check the index first, not the alphabetic entries.)

For broader information about a particular topic, the classic place to start is a general book on the subject or a key magazine or journal article. But how does one locate this key source?

The fastest way is to visit a nearby library or bookstore, find the shelf with the "sex books," and browse. In libraries, this is likely to be in stack sections marked 306 or HQ, depending on whether that library is arranged by Dewey decimal classification or Library of Congress classification. In bookstores, sex is often included within self-help, psychology, or health.

Getting a Basic Background

For a more thorough review of possibilities, one may begin with the library catalog, together with some of the bibliographies and indexes described below. For recent articles written for the lay audience, try the *New York Times Index*, the *Readers Guide to Periodical Literature*, and the *Alternative Press Index*. For scholarly articles, *Psychological Abstracts* and *Sociological Abstracts* are good pointers to published research.

However, a caution is necessary about what a librarian would call "search terms." We are interested, let us say, in "courtship." We then dutifully go to the library catalog and indexes—and find very little or nothing under that term.

We suspect that the information is there, however, and it probably is—merely a rose by another name. Now one must use a little imagination in finding those "other names." We think, what do we mean by courtship? We mean falling in love, dating, the singles scene, flirtation, even premarital sex. We mean "how to pick up girls," "finding Mr. Right," opening lines, campus parties. We mean how to make friends, how to be popular with the opposite sex, and how to have good sex with a new lover. Many of these phrases can lead to usable search terms, so we keep trying. There are few dead ends in information searching—only false starts; if we find one good article or book under a particular term, we can write that term down and use it to search other catalogs and indexes.

However, even when one finds references on one's exact topic, it is often fruitful to hunt for roses by other names. For teenage pregnancy, related topics include abortion, birth control, and adoption; and for pornography, related topics include erotica, censorship, and adult films. It is always best to start with the narrowest terms and then broaden the search to more inclusive categories if first attempts prove unsatisfactory.

With one or two key books or articles, perhaps the question is answered—but perhaps not. The next step is to use the references in those key sources as pointers to other sources. This has been called "citation pearl growing": the other sources contain bibliographies that provide further references, some highly relevant, and these provide still more references, and so on, and the "pearl" of information grows larger and larger.

Another next step (and sometimes a good first step, depending on the topic) is to go to organizations. As discussed below, it seems that when more than three Americans discover a common interest, they found an association—in sex as well as anything else. There are organized groups of people studying sex, practicing various kinds of sex, and attempting to alleviate various kinds of perceived problems associated with sex. Most have strong interests in promoting their cause and will make available pamphlets, bibliographies, publications, and even experts for consultations and speaking engagements.

In-Depth Investigations

For a no-holds-barred search—for a book, dissertation, major research project, or private obsession—one keeps going. First, one uses the basic books and articles, and then catalogs, bibliographies, and indexes to locate additional basic sources, together with supporting sources. One assiduously uses references in all sources as pointers to still further sources. Simultaneously, one identifies the major organizations and contacts them, perhaps subscribing to their newsletters.

In fact, it is often highly rewarding to make an extra effort to seek out newsletters and "little magazines." Many are listed in the library periodical directories described below. These newsletters usually carry reviews and advertisements and often mention other publications and organizations not listed in any reference works. Furthermore, being on the mailing lists of organizations and newsletters means getting mail from those who buy the lists to sell their publications and organizations, also very likely not mentioned elsewhere.

For example, the *Journal of Gender Studies*, a biannual publication on cross-dressing, transvestism, transgenderism, transsexuality, and androgyny, is not listed in any library periodical directory, nor was its precursor, *Outreach Beacon*. But a free sample copy was sent recently to all members of the Society for the Scientific Study of Sex (SSSS). Similarly, a fascinating list of gay, lesbian, and bisexual underground "'zines"—with titles like *Holy Titclamps* and *Girl Jock*—was included in *Equal Time*, a gay and lesbian newspaper listed both in the Ulrich's and Gale directories (see below).

When one has obtained a good grasp of the topic from reading the literature—scholarly, popular, and underground, as appropriate—the next step is people. Now is the time to correspond with key authors, to attend meetings of the major organizations and "network" with the members (and, at conferences, the exhibitors—another great source of hidden information), and to contact experts of any stripe. What new information is available? What other topics are relevant to the research? Who is doing interesting work in this area? Am I on the right track? Papers presented at scientific meetings are also good indicators of new research not yet appearing in print.

With a fresh and probably widened perspective, one goes back to the literature, bouncing back and forth from indexes to publications, to other publications, to hidden sources, to organizations, to little-known sources, to people and back again until one's project is concluded (or one's obsession is satisfied). The process can take as little as a month or as long as a lifetime, depending on one's needs and interests.

Hiring Help

If one has enough money, one can hire individuals and organizations to assist in the information search or even to take on most of the work. Such assistance is referred to in library circles as either "information on demand" or "fee-based information services." Lists of such help for hire may be found in the *Information Industry Directory* (Gale Research, Detroit; in many libraries—check "information on demand" in the index) and in the *Directory of Fee Based Information Services* (Burwell Enterprises, 3724 FM 1960 West, Suite 214, Houston, TX 77068). Fee-based information services will do manual and computer searches, compile bibliographies, obtain copies of books and articles, verify facts—even act as brokers for translations and contact experts.

However, do not hesitate to ask the librarian for help. Library staff are experts on the collection and can provide much valuable advice free of charge.

Basic Reference Works

Encyclopedias and Dictionaries

The editors and contributors to this encyclopedia hope that it will answer readers' questions about sex as well as refer them to further sources. A recent and more specialized complementary work is the *Encyclopedia of Homosexuality*, edited by Wayne Dynes (Garland, 1990). Earlier and quite comprehensive is the *Encyclopedia of Sexual Behavior*, edited by Albert Ellis and Albert Abarbanel (Hawthorn Books, 1960; reprinted in paperback by Ace).

Dictionaries of sexual terms, happily, have proliferated in recent years. The largest and most current—and both comprehensive and eclectic—is *A Descriptive Dictionary and Atlas of Sexology*, edited by Robert T. Francoeur, Timothy Perper, and Norman A. Scherzer (Greenwood Press, 1991). Another good choice, although much shorter, is *The Language of Sex from A to Z*, by Robert M. Goldenson and Kenneth N. Anderson (World Almanac, 1986). More specialized dictionaries include *The Language of Sadomasochism*, by Thomas E. Murray and Thomas Murrell (Greenwood Press, 1989), *A Feminist Dictionary*, edited by Cheris Kramarae and Paula Treichler (Pandora Press, 1985), and *Signs of Sexual Behavior*, by James Woodward (dictionary of American Sign Language; T.J. Publishers, 1979).

For those interested in Latin and French terms, there are *The Latin Sexual Vocabulary*, by J.N. Adams (Johns Hopkins University Press, 1982) and *Merde! The Real French You Were Never Taught at School*, by Genevieve [Edis] (Atheneum, 1986; also, *Merde Encore,* 1987).

Part encyclopedia, part dictionary, and part how-to book is the famous "Joy of Sex," now *The New Joy of Sex*, edited by Alex Comfort (Crown, 1991), which is nicely written and enjoyable to read, although without references. For gay men, the equivalent is the *New Joy of Gay Sex* by Charles Silverstein and Felice Picano (HarperCollins, 1992); and for lesbians, *Lesbian Sex* (Spinster Books, 1984) and *Lesbian Passion* (Spinster Books, 1987), both by JoAnn Loulan.

Directories and Catalogs

The homosexual community has a well-established and highly useful set of directories: *Gayellow Pages,* covering men's and women's interests (Renaissance House, in national and regional editions), and *Gaia's Guide*, lesbian only (Robin Tyler Productions; Sepulveda, CA). Both are updated regularly and may be ordered from Giovanni's Room (see books, below). Both are segmented geographically and list regional publications, bars and restaurants, religious groups, resorts and accommodations, counseling and networking organizations, hotlines, television and radio shows, bookstores, and other services.

The closest general equivalent (although not regionally oriented) seems to be the out-of-date yet nonetheless fascinating *Catalog of Sexual Consciousness* (Grove Press, 1975), an idiosyncratic grouping of referrals to organizations and publications (with excerpts), arranged by topic: massage, contraception, transvestism, rape, and so forth.

Another very helpful pointer to further sources of gay-related information is the excellent *Gay and Lesbian Library Service*, edited by Cal Gough and Ellen Greenblatt (McFarland, 1990), with many appendixes listing, for example, bibliographies, core materials, publishers, bookstores, special collections, and famous gay people.

Classics

While there have been sex surveys before and after Kinsey (many are listed in Frayser and Whitby, 1987; see below), his companion male and female volumes still constitute the major source of benchmark data on sexual behavior—how many people do what and to whom: *Sexual Behavior in the Human Male*, by Alfred C. Kinsey, Wardell B. Pomeroy, and Clyde E. Martin (Saunders, 1948); and *Sexual Behavior in the Human Female*, by Alfred C. Kinsey, Wardell B. Pomeroy, Clyde E. Martin, and Paul H. Gebhard (Saunders, 1953). Other useful surveys have been done by Shere Hite (*The Hite Report About Female Sexuality*, Macmillan, 1976; *The Hite Report on Male Sexuality*, Knopf, 1981), the editors of *Playboy* magazine ("Playboy Readers Sex Survey," parts 1–5, *Playboy*, January, March, May, July, October 1983), and the editors of *Redbook* magazine (*The Redbook Report on Female Sexuality,* by Carol Tavris and Susan Sadd, Delacorte, 1975). A recent and comprehensive survey is the *Janus Report on Sexual Behavior* by Samuel and Cynthia Janus (Wiley, 1993).

Likewise, benchmarks for the anatomy and physiology of sex—and what can go wrong—are the equally well-known works of Masters and Johnson: *Human Sexual Response,* by William H. Masters and Virginia E. Johnson (Little, Brown, 1966); and *Human Sexual Inadequacy,* by the same authors (Little, Brown, 1970).

Textbooks and Basic Guides

A number of good college-level textbooks on human sexuality are readily available. Most transmit a broadly humanistic set of perspectives about the range of sexual behavior, incorporating biological, psychological, and sociocultural components. As most also provide very basic discussions plus bibliographies and a glossary, they are excellent places for novices to begin a search for sex information. The following list contains some of the most comprehensive and best-known texts:

Sexual Interactions, by Elizabeth R. Allgeier and

Albert R. Allgeier (D.C. Heath, 1990)

Becoming a Sexual Person, by Robert T. Francoeur (Macmillan, 1991)

Fundamentals of Human Sexuality, by Herant A. Katchadourian (Holt, Rinehart & Winston, 1989)

Masters and Johnson on Sex and Human Loving, by William H. Masters, Virginia E. Johnson, and Robert C. Kolodny (Little, Brown, 1988)

Also very good sources of basic physiological and medical information are *The New Our Bodies Ourselves,* by the Boston Women's Health Collective (Simon & Schuster, 1992); and the older but still useful *Men's Bodies, Men's Selves,* by Sam Julty (Dell, 1979); *Woman's Body: An Owner's Manual,* by the Diagram Group (Bantam, 1978); and *Man's Body: An Owner's Manual,* also by the Diagram Group (Bantam, 1977). In addition, the Diagram Group has produced *Sex: A User's Manual* (Putnam, 1981), which—while not up-to-date about such issues as AIDS (acquired immune deficiency syndrome)—is an excellent summary of data about most aspects of human sexuality and incorporates results of many surveys.

Collections

From Dushkin (Guilford, CT) come two regularly updated collections of reprinted articles about sexual issues. *Taking Sides: Clashing Views on Controversial Issues in Human Sexuality,* edited by Robert T. Francoeur, includes "pro" and "con" pieces on each issue, plus short lists of suggested readings. Issues in the 1991 edition include "Can sex be an addiction?" "Should gay people fight for the right to marry?" and "Is rape motivated by aggression instead of sex?" *Human Sexuality,* in the Annual Editions Series, edited by Ollie Pocs, includes reprints from mostly popular magazines, covering a wide range of sexual topics (and opinions) within the broad areas of sexuality and society, sexual biology and health, reproduction, relationships, sexuality through the life cycle, and sexual issues. Unfortunately, only a few of the selections have bibliographies; however, a glossary is included.

Books and Other Monographs

Thousands and thousands of books have been written about sex, and a few thousand more are published each year. Fortunately, the searcher can rely on a variety of bibliographies and other keys to current and retrospective publications.

Library Catalog

The catalog (in card, on-line, or book form) constitutes the subject index to the library's book collection. It is invaluable for library users, but one must be prepared to negotiate unfamiliar webs of index terms and peruse many entries, as the assignment of subject headings to books is likely to have been neither consistent nor comprehensive. Both specific and general terms should be searched—including "sex," which is often used as a catchall. Searchers may want to ask the librarian for the subject heading list in use; it lets one know what one is up against.

Books in Print

Books in Print, Books Out of Print (1983–current), and *Forthcoming Books* (all from Bowker) are the publishers' and librarians' major guides to what books are, have been, and will be available. All have subject indexes, although not finely tuned. Neither are they fully comprehensive, lacking many "little press" and underground publications. All are available on-line (see data bases, below).

Bibliographies

Fortunately, there is a small but valuable number of good bibliographies covering sexuality topics, although keeping up-to-date remains a perpetual problem. These bibliographies include the following:

Studies in Human Sexuality: A Selected Guide, by Suzanne G. Frayser and Thomas J. Whitby (Libraries Unlimited, 1987). Books only, with detailed annotations. A new edition is forthcoming.

Sex Research: Bibliographies from the Institute for Sex Research, by Joan Scherer Brewer and Rod W. Wright (Oryx Press, 1979). Covers both books and periodical articles; complements Frayser and Whitby in covering older materials. No annotations.

Homosexuality: A Research Guide, by Wayne R. Dynes (Garland, 1987). Covers both books and periodical articles. Annotations.

Bibliographies from the Kinsey Institute for Research in Sex, Gender, and Reproduction Information Service (Bloomington, IN). Several hundred topic bibliographies available for purchase; request the complete list. No annotations. All bibliographies are compiled from the Kinsey Institute holdings.

SIECUS bibliographies (Sex Information and Education Council of the U.S.; Mary S. Calderone Library, New York). Fourteen topic bibliographies available, three about HIV (human immunodeficiency virus) and AIDS; request the SIECUS publications catalog. Annotations.

For erotica, a definitive bibliographic work is *The Horn Book*, by Gershon Legman (University Books, 1964). See also his opening chapter in *Libraries, Erotica, and Pornography*, by Martha Cornog (Oryx Press, 1991).

Many more specialized bibliographies are available, some listed in Frayser and Whitby and others in *Gay and Lesbian Library Service* (see above): for example, *Feminists, Pornography, and the Law: An Annotated Bibliography of Conflict, 1970–1986*, by Betty-Carol Sellen and Patricia A. Young (Library Professional Publications, 1987); *Sex Guides: Books and Films about Sexuality for Young Adults*, by Patricia J. Campbell (Garland, 1986); and *AIDS Information Sourcebook*, by H. Robert Malinowsky and Gerald J. Perry (Oryx Press, 1988). *Libraries, Erotica, and Pornography* (see above) also contains a number of bibliographies covering libraries, pornography-erotica, and censorship.

Reviews

Reviews and review articles provide more information than mere bibliography listings. Unfortunately, reviews of materials dealing with sexuality (when they exist at all) are widely scattered, with no central index to make them easily accessible. *Book Review Index* and *Book Review Digest* cover some reviews of only some books, particularly those reviewed in library book selection periodicals—that is, mainstream books by well-established presses.

For sex books in specific, most of the periodicals listed in the next section carry book reviews, particularly the *SIECUS Report* and the *Journal of the History of Sexuality*. Also helpful for women's issues, including lesbian material, is the *Women's Review of Books*. A source for review articles about sex is the *Annual Review of Sex Research* (from SSSS). Topics included in the 1990, inaugural, volume include "Surveys of Heterosexual Behavior," "Physiology and Pathology of Penile Erection," and "Biological Determinants of Sexual Orientation."

Dissertations

Doctoral dissertations are rarely listed in general catalogs, indexes, or bibliographies, but they can be highly valuable in such specialized topic areas as are subsumed within sexuality. The sole access points to dissertations are *Dissertation Abstracts* and *Comprehensive Dissertation Index* (print, on-line, and CD-ROM from University Microfilms).

Since few masters theses and no honors projects are deposited with University Microfilms, it might be worthwhile sometimes to contact the libraries or archives of universities with degree programs in sexuality (see below) to request a search of their research-paper and thesis holdings on a given topic.

Catalog Ordering Sources

A small number of mail-order book distributors specialize in nonfiction sexuality topics. These include:

The Sexuality Library, 1210 Valencia Street, San Francisco, CA 94110. Catalog lists about 200 books, with annotations, on many aspects of sexuality, including some erotica. Also includes some magazines and videos.

C.J. Scheiner Books, 275 Linden Blvd., B2, Brooklyn, NY 11226. Large catalog including much erotica and many out-of-print works. No annotations.

Ivan Stormgart Books, P.O. Box 1232 GMF, Boston, MA 02205. Antiquarian bookseller specializing in interdisciplinary relationships (sexual behavior and sexology). Large catalog, no annotations.

Giovanni's Room, Mail Order Department, 345 South 12th Street, Philadelphia, PA 19107; Lambda Rising, 1625 Connecticut Avenue, N.W., Washington, DC 20009. Both of these offer a good selection of nonfiction and fiction on gay and lesbian topics. Newsletter-format catalogs provide annotations.

Periodicals

In addition to books, periodicals contain much valuable information for those interested in sex, and the information is often more up-to-date than book coverage.

Indexes and Abstracts

Finding out which periodical articles have been published on which topics generally requires consulting abstracting and indexing (A&I) services, many available in print, on-line, and in CD-ROM form. (See next section for more about data bases.) There are hundreds of A&I services that cover both popular and scholarly periodicals (and sometimes books and other monographs, such as dissertations and government reports). Perhaps the most salient for sex information are the following:

Scholarly

ERIC (education-related topics; covers some materials on children and adolescent sexuality)

Index Medicus (on-line: MEDLINE)

Inventory of Marriage and Family Literature (on-line: Family Resource Database)

Psychological Abstracts (on-line: PsycINFO)

Sage Family Studies Abstracts

Social Sciences Index

Sociological Abstracts

Women's Studies Abstracts

Popular

Alternative Press Index

Magazine Index

National Newspaper Index

New York Times Index

Public Affairs Information Service

Many other possibilities exist in specific subject areas; one should ask a librarian or consult a recent directory of data bases (see next section).

Several past indexes have treated sexuality specifically, notably *Sex Studies Index* (G.K. Hall, 1980–81) and *Current Research Updates: Human Sexuality* (CRU Publishing, 1983–1986?). However, to the author's knowledge, neither of these has continued. Neither has there appeared an index to popular sex periodicals, as envisioned, regretfully, by Sanford Berman in his article "If There Were a Sex Index . . ." (1981). Consult *Ulrich's International Periodicals Directory* to find out which indexes cover which periodicals.

Journals and Magazines

One can browse the core sex journals, which—fortunately or unfortunately—make up a relatively short list:

Archives of Sexual Behavior

Journal of Gay and Lesbian Psychotherapy

Journal of Homosexuality

Journal of Psychology and Human Sexuality

Journal of Sex and Marital Therapy

Journal of Sex Education and Therapy

Journal of Sex Research

Journal of Social Work and Human Sexuality

Journal of the History of Sexuality

Maledicta (language)

Medical Aspects of Human Sexuality

Sex Roles

Sexuality and Disability

SIECUS Report

Major popular magazines with sexually oriented nonfiction and sometimes fiction include:

Eidos

Frighten the Horses

Libido

Penthouse

Playboy

Screw

Yellow Silk (entirely literary)

Major popular gay and lesbian periodicals include (there remains considerable turnover with old publications ceasing and new ones appearing):

Advocate (Los Angeles newspaper)

Bad Attitude (erotica for lesbians)

Blade (Washington, D.C. newspaper)

On Our Backs (erotica for lesbians)

Gayellow Pages, Gaia's Guide, and *Gay and Lesbian Library Service* (see above) all include listings of gay newspapers nationwide. Current addresses and descriptive information about these and many other sex-related periodicals may be found in:

Ulrich's International Periodicals Directory (Bowker)

Gale Directory of Publications and Broadcast Media (Gale)

International Directory of Little Magazines and Small Presses (Dustbooks)

The Standard Periodical Directory (Oxbridge)

Newsletters in Print (Gale)

Oxbridge Directory of Newsletters (Oxbridge)

Many of these list homosexuality-oriented publications in a separate section. However, the subject indexing in most ranges from passable to abysmal, making them hard to use for sources of periodical titles on a subject other than homosexuality. To its credit, the *Standard Periodical Directory* index does have a "sex" section that includes many scholarly journals as well as some of the popular magazines; the *International Directory of Little Magazines and Small Presses* has an outstanding section on sex in its index, making it quite usable as a selection tool. However, most other directories, including *Ulrich's,* lump the popular sex magazines under "men's magazines" and scatter the scholarly journals among the various subject disciplines without pulling them together under "sex" in an index or anywhere else. A comprehensive guide to underground "zines" and "little magazines" is the irregular periodical *Factsheet Five,* with "sex" and "queer" [sic] sections.

Data Bases

On-line data bases can provide a fast way of finding information from many periodicals over a long time span. The major abstracting and indexing services mentioned in the previous section are also available on-line or on CD-ROM, and many academic, and some public, libraries will provide searching for a fee (sometimes searches are free).

A few other data bases are ends in themselves for sexuality information:

Comprehensive Core Medical Library (BRS; McLean, VA)—provides complete text of selected medical reference works and textbooks, plus over 80 medical journals.

Data Archive on Adolescent Pregnancy and Pregnancy Prevention (Sociometrics; Los Altos, CA)—original data and text from research studies.

MEDIS (Mead Data Central; Dayton, OH)—complete text of selected journals and textbooks in medicine, plus gateway to other medical data bases.

NEXIS (Mead Data Central; Dayton, OH)—complete text of a large number of popular periodicals.

Research Data Archive of Sexual Behavior (Kinsey Institute for Research in Sex, Gender, and Reproduction—see libraries, below)—full text of sexual behavior case histories.

Human Sexuality (Clinical Communications; Shady, NY; available on CompuServe)—full text of articles and interviews with experts, plus question-and-answer service, bulletin boards, and on-line conferencing. Not all libraries have access to CompuServe, but anyone with access to a PC can get a user account relatively inexpensively.

Sexual Harassment: Employer Policies and Problems (BNA; Washington, DC)—full text of policies, procedures, education and training programs, and experiences of organizations in handling complaints; too expensive for many libraries but has a corresponding print product that might be found in some law libraries.

A number of AIDS information data bases also exist, providing references (indexes and abstracts), full text, or original data.

The best reference work for identifying data bases of all kinds is the *Gale Directory of Computer Databases* (Gale Research). It is large and comprehensive, it has a good index—and, one hopes, it may be found in many libraries.

Conference Papers

Scholars and other professionals working in sexuality, as in other fields, get together at conferences to exchange information about trends and work in progress. Such information, which is presented orally, constitutes the "conference paper." Conference papers can be tedious rehashes of received wisdom or can narrate fascinating breakthroughs in critical areas of interest.

One can get at conference papers in several ways:

1. *Attend the conference.* Pick an organization in one's area (see organizations, below), request a preliminary program for an upcoming conference, register, and attend. This is expensive, but if the organization and the program are of high interest, the information can be invaluable. Professionals nearly invariably employ this route.

2. *Request conference papers from their authors.* Pick an organization, request the preliminary program for an upcoming conference, and select those presentations of interest. Then write or call the presenters to request a printed version. This may be less than effective because (a) there may not be a printed version, or (b) the presenter may not fulfill the request. However, it is worth trying when one does not want to attend a meeting but finds a few presentations of high interest. (Requests can be sent to presenters in care of the organization, or one may call the organization and ask for contact information or a membership directory.)

3. *Purchase tapes.* Some organizations have their conferences taped and then sell the tapes of individual sessions. Call the organization and ask.

Conference papers are listed in very few A&I services; one is *Index to Social Sciences and Humanities Proceedings.* However, sometimes they can be found in bibliographies of articles and books.

Audiovisuals

Films about sexuality include the so-called "adult" films as well as films made for purposes of sex education and professional training. An excellent source of reviews and access information on adult films on videotape is Robert Rimmer's *The X-Rated Videotape Guide* (vol. 1, Harmony Books, 1986; vols. 2 and 3, Prometheus Books, 1991, 1993). For sex education and training audiovisuals, two good sources are "Audio-visuals for Sexuality Professionals: A Selected Bibliography" (with addendum) from the Sex Information and Education Council of the United States (SIECUS), and the catalog of Focus International, a distributor of audiovisuals for sex education, research, and therapy (14 Oregon Drive, Huntington Station, NY 11746-2627). In addition, the Sexuality Library (see address above) sells some erotic tapes and a few for sex education.

Organizations

Many people do not think of going to organizations when they need information, but that would be a serious mistake. The United States has thousands of organizations concerned with every conceivable issue, including sexual issues. Nearly all these organizations provide information: pamphlets, membership lists, bibliographies, library services, hotlines, referrals, meetings, speakers bureaus, lobbying, periodicals, books, and other publications—many services are free or at minimal charge. Organizations are also sources of experts and aficionados of almost any subject.

The guidebook for up-to-date access to many (not all) of these organizations is the *Encyclopedia of Associations* (*EoA*; Gale Research). In three volumes covering 30,000 organizations as of 1991, it may be found in virtually every library. *EoA* has an excellent keyword index; however, although there are cross-references among entries in the text, none appear in the index. Thus the user searching under "rape," say, must remember also to look under "sexual abuse"; for "abortion," also under "family planning" and "right to life." Because the *EoA* has the most up-to-date addresses and telephone numbers for its 30,000 organizations, no contact information is included in this article.

According to the 1991 *EoA,* at least 250 U.S. organizations have as a major focus some aspect of sexuality. Nearly half of these are concerned with gay and lesbian interests; others address just about any other sexual issue one could think of: AIDS; family planning; impotence; nudism; pornography; prostitution; sexual addiction; sexual abuse and rape; sexual freedom for interests other than gays and lesbians, including transvestites, transsexuals, nonmonogamists, and leather fetishists; and sexual health.

These groups fall into several major types:

Professional associations of practitioners or researchers, in sexuality in general or a particular specialty

Advocacy or common-interest organizations promoting or supporting a particular viewpoint or behavior, including the opportunity for members to meet like-minded individuals

Organizations for both professionals and other concerned individuals promoting research, treatment, and public education about a specific disease or social problem

Self-help organizations, for mutual support among those with self-defined problems

Naturally, some groups fall into more than one category, and some sexual issues have produced organizations in every category: there are groups studying homosexuality, groups for gays and lesbians promoting gay interests, groups working against homosexuality, support groups for gay people who want to give up their homosexual behavior, and support groups for spouses and relatives of gays and lesbians.

In addition to these categories, one might add research centers, libraries with noteworthy collections in sexuality, and universities (and other organizations) offering training programs in sexology. These are dealt with separately below.

Professional Associations

Three major professional groups dominate sexology. The Society for the Scientific Study of Sex (SSSS), founded in 1957, is the oldest; its 1,000 members come from all disciplines but focus on research. The American Association of Sex Educators, Counselors and Therapists (AASECT), younger (founded 1967) but larger (3,100 members), focuses on training and accrediting its members and other professionals. Finally, the Sex Information and Education Council of the United States (SIECUS), founded in 1964 and comprising 3,600 members, promotes sex education in all contexts and supports professional training in sex education.

Several dozen other groups are oriented to various types of professionals concerned with sexuality. Some examples include:

Association for the Behavioral Treatment of Sexual Abusers

Association of Nurses in AIDS Care

Association of Lesbian and Gay Psychologists

Society for the Psychological Study of Lesbian and Gay Issues

Society for the Study of Social Problems

Check the *EoA* for others.

Advocacy and Common-Interest Organizations

At least 100 U.S. organizations deal in one way or another with advocacy for gay and lesbian viewpoints or merely provide a vehicle for the gay and lesbian practitioners of a profession or hobby to socialize or work together. These range from the largest and most comprehensive—the National Gay Rights Advocates, the Lambda Legal Defense and Education Fund, and the National Gay and Lesbian Task Force, each with 15,000 or more members-contributors and a

budget in the millions of dollars—to smaller special-interest groups such as these:

Federal Lesbians and Gays (federal government workers)

International Gay Travel Association

Lesbian and Gay Bands of America

Good Gay Poets

Para-Amps (handicapped gays)

Girth and Mirth (overweight gay men)

Gay and Lesbian History on Stamps Club

Similar organizations exist for many sexual viewpoints and behaviors other than homosexuality. An all-too-brief sampling from the *EoA*:

American Sunbathing Association (nudism)

Adult Video Association (pro-pornography/ erotica)

North American Swing Club Association (recreational nonmonogamy)

National Leather Association (leather/S&M aficionados)

National Task Force on Prostitution (pro-prostitution, formerly COYOTE)

Society for the Second Self (transvestites)

Many sexual groups of this type are not listed in the *EoA;* one locates them by reading widely in the particular area, especially newsletters, and cultivating informants. A few of those with addresses are:

Club Latexa (rubber fetishists), Centurian, P.O. Box AE, Westminster, CA 92683

Janus (bisexuals), P.O. Box 6794, San Francisco, CA 94101

SAMOIS (lesbian S&M), P.O. Box 2364, Berkeley, CA 94702

The Kinsey Institute receives many newsletters from these kinds of organizations and can supply addresses.

Organizations Addressing a Specific Disease or Problem

These organizations are the inverse of the ones above: groups working not to promote but to eradicate something. The majority are concerned either with AIDS—perhaps the largest being the Gay Men's Health Crisis—or with right to life, that is, against abortion. Others include:

Impotence Institute of America

Society's League Against Molestation (child sexual abuse)

National Clearinghouse on Marital and Date Rape

Women Against Pornography

A number of what the *EoA* terms "conservative traditionalist" organizations also work against a number of sexual behaviors and issues, typically homosexuality, pornography, and sex education, e.q.:

American Coalition for Traditional Values

Americans for Decency

Christian Voice

Self-Help Organizations

Such organizations also want to eradicate something—but through the particular vehicle of setting up support groups and regular meetings for individuals afflicted with a problem. The granddaddy of this approach is, of course, Alcoholics Anonymous, with thousands of near-clones for other diseases and social problems. Some in the sexual area are:

Homosexuals Anonymous Fellowship Services (gays and lesbians wishing to become heterosexual)

Impotents Anonymous

People with AIDS Coalition

Sexaholics Anonymous

Women Exploited by Abortion

Research Centers

Research centers are not membership organizations but nonprofit concerns, often affiliated with universities. The *Research Centers Directory* (Gale Research) lists, for example, 19 such centers with a focus on birth control, 9 for marriage, 37 for human reproduction, and nearly 70 for various other topics listed under "sex." A few examples:

Center for Population Options

Marriage Council of Philadelphia (affiliated with the University of Pennsylvania School of Medicine)

San Francisco State University Center for Research and Education in Sexuality

Yale University Lesbian and Gay Studies Center

Research centers provide a variety of services, usually including publications reporting research results as well as educational seminars.

Libraries with Collections on Sexual Topics

One might imagine that the best solution to one's need for sexuality information would be to find a library specializing in sex, where the librarians are knowledgeable, completely unflappable, and can spell "Krafft-Ebing" and "limerence" correctly. The largest and best known sexuality libraries are those of the Kinsey Institute for Research in Sex, Gender, and Reproduction; SIECUS; the Planned Parenthood Federation of America (New York City and local affiliates); and the Vern and Bonnie Bullough collection, California State University, Northridge. There are other such places, however, perhaps more than one might expect.

The major reference source for special-topic library holdings is the *Directory of Special Libraries and Information Centers* (Gale Research), available in most libraries. The index to the 1991 edition lists 22 libraries under topics beginning with "sex," 36 under homosexuality-lesbianism, 35 under birth control, 16 under abortion, and 17 under acquired immune deficiency syndrome.

Other sources listing libraries with sex-related collections include:

Alternative Lifestyles: A Guide to Research Collections on Intentional Communities, Nudism, and Sexual Freedom, by Jefferson P. Selth (Greenwood Press, 1985)—lists and describes six collections on nudism and 18 on "sexual freedom."

"Directories of Special Collections on Social Movements Evolving from the Vietnam Era," by Ellen Embardo (*Reference Services Review*, Fall 1990)—includes listing and description of 15 gay and lesbian collections.

Directory of the International Association of Lesbian and Gay Archives and Libraries, compiled by Alan V. Miller (International Association of Lesbian and Gay Archives and Libraries, 1978).

Gay/Lesbian Archives and Libraries in North America (American Library Association Gay and Lesbian Task Force Library Information Clearinghouse, 1989)

Libraries, Erotica, and Pornography, edited by Martha Cornog (Oryx Press, 1991)—see "Erotica Research Collections," by Gwendolyn Pershing, and "Homosexuality Research Collections," by Daniel C. Tsang.

North American gay and lesbian collections are also listed in the *Gayellow Pages, Gaia's Guide,* and *Gay and Lesbian Library Service* (see above).

Universities Granting Degrees in Sexology and Related Programs

One can satisfy one's information needs about sexuality by enlisting in an education program. A list of 24 U.S. and 16 foreign programs in sex education, counseling, and therapy may be obtained on request from SSSS, P.O. Box 208, Mt. Vernon, IA 52314.

People

Finally, we come to people—the ultimate source of all information on any subject. To the individual seeking information about sexuality, people sources come in one or a combination of three types: providers of data, colleagues, and experts.

Many researchers seeking subjects for interviews or for questionnaire studies can use random samples of the general public or (especially) college students near at hand. However, those seeking groups more specialized in terms of sexual interests can often locate subjects through some of the organizations referred to above or by taking out an advertisement in newsletters of these organizations or in other periodicals. (Researchers affiliated with universities or other institutions must take care to follow the appropriate organizational guidelines for studies on human subjects.)

Colleagues and experts in the study of sexuality may be found by joining SSSS or AASECT, as appropriate. (Applicants for these and other professional associations may be asked to provide supporting credentials, such as one's curriculum vitae or résumé and one's research interests.) Both SSSS and AASECT publish directories of members, although research interests are not indicated therein. One directory that does give considerable information about the background and interests of its listees is *Interna-*

tional Who's Who in Sexology, edited by Fernando Bianco, Loretta Haroian, and Gorm Wagner (Specific Press, Institute for Advanced Study of Human Sexuality, 1986). However, it is fast becoming out-of-date and, moreover, has no subject index. A surer and faster route to experts is to seek key books and papers on one's topic and then contact the authors through the publisher of the book or journal, or via the affiliation provided in the "about the author" description.

It is likely that sex information in the near future will only expand, as sexual issues—such as sexual harassment, child sexual abuse, new birth technologies, abortion, and AIDS—continue to occupy the spotlight of media attention and public debate. While a large underground literature will continue to flourish, the mainstream sources will, it is hoped, become more complete and organized to respond to public and professional needs for information. Already, the access tools to AIDS information have expanded to include more than 40 bibliographies and 14 serials (as listed in *Gay and Lesbian Library Service*) all appearing since 1980.

Thus, pathways to sexuality information, while many and devious, are becoming well enough trodden that truly competent maps can be developed. Researchers and librarians may struggle with access currently, but in the next few decades the task is likely to become somewhat easier.

REFERENCES

Ashley, L.R.N. Sexual Slang: Prostitutes, Pedophiles, Flagellators, Transvestites and Necrophiliacs. *Maledicta,* Vol. 9 (1986), pp. 143–98.

Berkman, R.I. *Find It Fast.* New York: Harper & Row, 1990.

Berman, S. 1981. If There Were a Sex Index. . . . In P. Gellatly, ed. *Sex Magazines in the Library Collection.* New York: Haworth Press, 1981.

Kirby, R. No Checks Please, Cash Only: A Critical Glance at Zines. *Equal Time,* Nos. 16–17 (June 7–June 21, 1991).

Martha Cornog

Index

(Bold page numbers are main entry pages.)